BOND EVALUATION, SELECTION, AND MANAGEMENT

To G.B. and Mary Frances Johnson

R. STAFFORD JOHNSON

Xavier University

BOND EVALUATION, SELECTION, AND MANAGEMENT

Blackwell Publishing

350 Main Street, Malden, MA 02148-5020, USA
108 Cowley Road, Oxford OX4 1JF, UK
550 Swanston Street, Carlton, Victoria 3053, Australia

First published 2004 by Blackwell Publishing Ltd

Library of Congress Cataloging-in-Publication Data

Johnson, R. Stafford.
  Bond evaluation, selection, and management / by R. Stafford Johnson.
    p. cm.
Includes bibliographical references and index.
  ISBN 1-4051-0170-9 (hardback only : alk. paper)
1. Bonds. 2. Bonds–Ratings. 3. Bond market. I. Title.

HG4651.B664 2004
332.63′23–dc22

                          2003015468

A catalogue record for this title is available from the British Library.

Set in $9\frac{1}{2}$/11 Ehrhardt
by Newgen Imaging Systems (P) Ltd, Chennai, India
Printed and bound in the United Kingdom
by TJ International, Padstow, Cornwall

For further information on
Blackwell Publishing, visit our website:
http://www.blackwellpublishing.com

BRIEF CONTENTS

CONTENTS

FIGURES

EXHIBITS

TABLES

PREFACE

In 1985, Merrill Lynch introduced the liquid yield option note (LYON). The LYON is a zero-coupon bond, convertible into the issuer's stock, callable (with the call price increasing over time), and putable (with the put price increasing over time). The LYON is a good example of how innovative the investment community can be in structuring debt instruments with option clauses. Probably nowhere has this innovation been more pervasive than in the construction of mortgage-backed securities (MBSs). Faced with the problem of prepayment risk, various types of mortgage securities with different claims (sequential-pay tranches, planned amortorization classes, interest-only MBSs, and principal-only MBSs) were created in the 1980s. The option features embedded in MBSs, LYONs, and many other bonds have made the evaluation of these securities more difficult. A callable 10-year bond issued when interest rates are relatively high may be more like a 3-year bond given that a likely interest rate decrease would lead the issuer to buy the bond back. Determining the value requires taking into account not only the value of the bond's cash flows, but also the value of the call option embedded in the bond.

In addition to the innovations in financial instruments, the investment and management of bonds and debt by financial and non-financial corporations has also experienced significant developments over the last two decades. Today, bond investors use strategies such as cash-flow matching, immunization, cell matching, contingent immunization, and bond selection based on forecasting yield curve shifts or the narrowing or widening of the quality yield spread. Similarly as striking as the growth in bond evaluation and management over the past 20 years is the growth in derivative products. Since the 1970s, the US economy has experienced relatively sharp swings in interest rates. The resulting volatility in rates, in turn, has increased the exposure of many debt positions to market risk. Faced with this risk, many corporate borrowers, money managers, intermediaries, and bond portfolio managers have increased their use of futures and option contracts on debt securities as a hedge against such risk. Today, futures and options contracts on debt securities, as well as such hybrid derivatives as swaps, interest rate options, caps, and floors, are used by banks and financial intermediaries to manage the maturity gaps between loans and deposits, by corporations and financial institutions to fix or cap the rates on future loans, and by fixed-income portfolio managers, money managers, investment bankers, and security dealers in locking in the future purchase or selling price on their fixed-income securities.

Today, understanding the dynamic and innovative fixed-income investment environment requires that finance students and professionals understand the markets for an increasing number of debt securities, the process of securitization and how securitized derivatives are formed and valued, and the fundamental, as well as advanced, bond investment strategies. The purpose of this book is to provide finance students and professionals with a bond and debt management exposition that will take them from the basic bond investment theories and fundamentals that can be found in many investment books to a more detailed understanding of the markets and strategies. It is my hope that this synthesis of fundamental and advanced topics will provide students of finance with a better foundation in understanding the complexities and subtleties involved in the evaluation and selection of bonds and debt positions with detailed structures. The book is written for MBA, MS, and advanced undergraduate finance students, as a training and instructional source for those involved in bond and debt management, and as a reference for CFA preparation for investment professionals. As a text, the book is designed for a one-semester course. Undergraduate students should have had an introductory course in investments, and MBA students should have had an introductory corporate finance course. Some basic statistics and math are used. At the back of the text will be found appendices on exponents and logarithms and statistics to help students who need a review.

CONTENT

All securities can be evaluated in terms of the characteristics common to all assets: value, return, risk, maturity, marketability, liquidity, and taxability. In part I, debt securities are analyzed in terms of these characteristics. Chapter 1 presents an overview of the investment environment, examining the nature of financial assets, the types of securities that exist, the nature and types of markets that securities give rise to, and the general characteristics of assets. With this background, the next three chapters examine bonds in terms of their characteristics: chapter 2 looks at how debt instruments are valued and how their rates of return are measured; chapter 3 examines the level and term structure of interest rates and shows how such factors as market expectations, economic conditions, and risk-return preferences are important in determining the level and structure of rates; chapter 4 describes three types of bond risk – default, call, and market risk – and introduces two measures of bond volatility – duration and convexity.

Part II delineates the different debt securities and their markets in terms of the rules, participants, and forces that govern them. Chapter 5 describes the debt claims of businesses; chapter 6 looks at the types and markets for government securities – Treasury, federal agencies, and municipals; chapter 7 examines intermediary and foreign debt securities. After examining the types, markets, and characteristics of bonds, chapter 8 extends bond analysis from evaluation to investment and management by examining a number of active and passive bond management strategies, including cash matching, bond immunization, indexing, and contingent immunization.

With many bonds having some option clause, the binomial interest rate approach to valuing bonds has become an important pricing model for bonds. In part III, chapter 9 describes how the binomial interest rate tree is used to price bonds with call and put options, sinking fund agreements, and convertible clauses. Chapter 10, in turn, addresses the technical problem of how to construct the tree, examining two models that have been used to estimate the binomial interest rate trees – the arbitrage-free calibration model and the equilibrium model. In chapter 11, asset-backed securities are examined, with particular emphasis on mortgage-backed securities. This chapter explains prepayment risk and its impact on a portfolio of mortgages, how mortgage-backed derivatives are constructed to address the problems of prepayment risk, and how the binomial model is used to value an MBS.

Part IV consists of six chapters covering bond derivatives. Chapters 12 and 14 provide overviews of the markets, uses, and pricing of interest rate futures and options contracts. These chapters provide a foundation for the more detailed analysis of hedging strategies using futures and options contracts that are examined in chapters 13 and 15. In those chapters, futures and options contracts on debt securities are examined in terms of how they are used by banks and financial intermediaries to manage the maturity gaps between loans and deposits, by corporations and financial institutions to fix the rates on floating-rate loans, and by fixed-income portfolio managers, money managers, investment bankers, and security dealers in locking in the future purchase or selling price on their fixed-income securities. In the last two chapters, the construction, use, and markets for interest rate swaps are examined.

The text stresses concepts, model construction, and numerical examples. This is done to empower the reader to understand the tools with which answers can be found rather than just the answers. A number of review questions, problems, and web exercises are provided at the end of each chapter to reinforce concepts; solutions to many of these problems are provided in a separate section at the end of the book. A number of the problems can be done using Excel. The required Excel programs, as well as PowerPoint slides for each chapter and detailed solutions to all end-of-chapter problems, can be accessed by going to www.blackwellpublishing.com/bonds.

ACKNOWLEDGMENTS

Many people have contributed to this text. First, I wish to thank my colleagues at Xavier University and Dr. Thomas O'Brien at the University of Connecticut who have helped me in many different ways. I also wish to thank the following reviewers for their thoughtful critiques:

- Dr. Richard Zuber, University of North Carolina at Charlotte
- Dr. Xiaoquing Eleanor Xu, Seton Hall University
- Dr. Andrew Carverhill, University of Hong Kong.

My appreciation is extended to the staff at Blackwell Publishing, particularly Seth Ditchik and Elizabeth Wald who oversaw the book's development and were a continued source of encouragement. I also wish to thank Al Bruckner for his invaluable help at the beginning of this project. My appreciation is also extended to Shirlee James who helped in the preparation of the manuscript, Juan Lazarde for his assistance on developing the Excel programs, and Paul Stringer for helping me complete the project.

I also wish to thank my wife Jan, and my children, Wendi, Jamey, and Matt, for their support and understanding, and to acknowledge some special people for their inspiration – Jerry Erhart, Dianne Erhart, James McDonald, Irma Johnson, Joan White, Lillian Dansby, Jack Erhart, and JoAnn Erhart. Finally, I wish to recognize the pioneers in the development of fixed-income and debt management theory and strategy: Fisher Black, John Cox, Frank Fabozzi, Lawrence Fisher, John Hull, Robert Kolb, Martin Liebowitz, Frank Macaulay, Robert Merton, Stephen Ross, Mark Rubinstein and others cited in the pages that follow. Without their contributions, this text could not have been written.

I encourage you to send your comments and suggestions to me: johnsons@xu.edu.

R. Stafford Johnson
Xavier University

PART ONE

BOND EVALUATION AND SELECTION

CHAPTER ONE

OVERVIEW OF THE FINANCIAL SYSTEM

1.1 REAL AND FINANCIAL ASSETS

Most new businesses begin when an individual or group of individuals come up with an idea: manufacturing a new type of computer, developing land for a future housing subdivision, or launching a new internet company. To make the idea a commercial reality, though, requires funds that the individual or group generally lacks or personally does not want to commit. Consequently, the fledgling business sells *financial claims* or *instruments* to raise the funds necessary to buy the capital goods (equipment, land, etc.), as well as human capital (architects, engineers, lawyers, etc.) needed to launch the project. Technically, such instruments are claims against the income of the business represented by a certificate, receipt, or other legal document. In this process of initiating and implementing the idea, both real and financial assets are therefore created. The *real assets* consist of both the tangible and intangible capital goods, as well as human capital, which are combined with labor to form the business. The business, in turn, transforms the idea into the production and sale of goods or services that will generate a future stream of earnings. The *financial assets*, on the other hand, consist of the financial claims on the earnings. Those individuals or institutions that provided the initial funds and resources

hold these assets. Furthermore, if the idea is successful, then the new business may find it advantageous to initiate other new projects that it again may finance through the sale of financial claims. Thus, over time, more real and financial assets are created.

The creation of financial claims, of course, is not limited to the business sector. The federal government's expenditures on national defense and the space program and state governments' expenditures on the construction of highways, for example, represent the development of real assets that these units of government often finance through the sale of financial claims on either the revenue generated from a particular public sector project or from future tax revenues. Similarly, the purchase of a house or a car by a household often is financed by a loan from a savings and loan or commercial bank. The loan represents a claim by the financial institution on a portion of the borrower's future income, as well as a claim on the ownership of the real asset (house or car) in the event the household defaults on its promise.

Modern economies expend enormous amounts of money on real assets to maintain their standards of living. Such expenditures usually require funds that are beyond the levels a business, household, or unit of government has or wants to commit at a given point in time. As a result, to raise the requisite amounts, economic entities sell financial claims. Those buying the financial claims therefore supply funds to the economic entity in return for promises that the entity will provide them with a future flow of income. As such, financial claims can be described as financial assets.

All financial assets provide a promise of a future return to the owners. Unlike real assets, though, financial assets do not depreciate (since they are in the form of certificates or information in a computer file), and they are *fungible*, meaning they can be converted into cash or other assets. There are many different types of financial assets. All of them, though, can be divided into two general categories – equity and debt. Common stock is the most popular form of equity claims. It entitles the holder to dividends or shares in the business's residual profit and participation in the management of the firm, usually indirectly through voting rights. The stock market where existing stock shares are traded is the most widely followed market in the world and it receives considerable focus in many investments and security analysis texts. The focus of this book, though, is on the other general type of financial asset – debt. Businesses finance more of their real assets and operations with debt than equity, while governments and households finance their entire real assets and operations with debt. In 2001, the value of outstanding debt claims was $23.8t, which was approximately 50% greater than the $13.6t outstanding value of equity claims. This chapter provides a preliminary overview of the types of debt securities and markets, while chapters 5, 6, and 7 provide a more detailed analysis.

1.2 TYPES OF DEBT CLAIM

Debt claims are loans whereby the borrower agrees to pay a fixed income per period, defined as a coupon or interest, and to repay the borrowed funds, defined as the principal. Within this broad description, debt instruments can take on many different forms. For example, debt can take the form of a loan by a financial institution such as a commercial bank, insurance company, or savings and loan bank. In this case, the terms of the agreement and the contract instrument generally are prepared by the lender/creditor, and the instrument often is

non-negotiable, meaning it cannot be sold to another party. A debt instrument also can take the form of a bond or note, whereby the borrower obtains her loan by selling (also referred to as issuing) contracts or IOUs to pay interest and principal to investors/lenders. Many of these claims, in turn, are negotiable, often being sold to other investors before they mature.

Debt instruments also can differ in terms of the features of the contract: the number of future interest payments, when and how the principal is to be paid (e.g., at maturity (i.e., the end of the contract) or spread out over the life of the contract (amortized)), and the recourse the lender has should the borrower fail to meet her contractual commitments (i.e., collateral or security).

Finally, the type of borrower or issuer – business, government, household, or financial institution – can differentiate the debt instruments. Businesses sell two general types of debt instruments, *corporate bonds* and *commercial paper (CP)*, and borrow from financial institutions, usually with long-term or intermediate-term loans from commercial banks or insurance companies and with short-term *lines of credit* from banks. The corporate bonds they sell usually pay the buyer/lender coupon interest semi-annually and a principal at maturity. For example, a manufacturing company building a $10m processing plant might finance the cost by selling 10,000 bonds at a price of $1,000 per bond, with each bond promising to pay $50 in interest every June 15 and January 15 for the next 10 years and a principal of $1,000 at maturity. In general, corporate bonds are long-term securities (original terms of 10 to 15 years), sometimes secured by specific real assets that bondholders can claim in case the corporation fails to meet its contractual obligation (defaults). Corporate bonds also have a priority of claims over stockholders on the company's earnings and assets in the case of default. Commercial paper, on the other hand, is a short-term claim (less than 1 year) that usually is unsecured. Typically, commercial paper is sold as a zero discount note in which the buyer receives interest equal to the difference between the principal and the purchase price. For example, a company might sell paper promising to pay $1,000 at the end of 270 days for $970, yielding an interest of $30. Term loans to businesses have intermediate- to long-term maturities

(1 to 5 years), often with the principal paid over the life of the loan (amortized). Like all debt instruments, these loans have a priority of claims on income and assets over equity claims, and the financial institution providing the loan often requires collateral. Finally, lines of credit are short-term loans provided by banks and other financial institutions in which the business can borrow up to a maximum amount of funds from a checking account created for it by the institution.

The federal government sells a variety of financial instruments, ranging from short-term *Treasury bills* to intermediate- and long-term claims, such as *Treasury notes* and *Treasury bonds*. These instruments are sold by the Treasury to finance the federal deficit and refinance current debt. In addition to Treasury securities, agencies of the federal government, such as the Tennessee Valley Authority, and government-sponsored corporations, such as the Federal National Mortgage Association and the Federal Farm Credit Banks also issue securities, classified as *Federal Agency Securities*, to finance a variety of government programs ranging from the construction of dams to the purchase of mortgages to provide liquidity to mortgage lenders. Similarly, state and local governments, agencies, and authorities also offer a wide variety of debt instruments, broadly classified as either *general obligation bonds* or *revenue bonds*. The former are bonds financed through general tax revenue, while the latter are instruments financed from the revenue from specific state and local government projects and programs. Finally, there are deposit-type financial institutions such as commercial banks, savings and loans, credit unions, and savings banks that provide debt claims in the form of deposit accounts (demand (checking), time, savings, and transaction accounts) and negotiable and non-negotiable *certificates of deposit (CDs)*.

Web Information
Financial information can be found on many finance websites. To find links to financial websites go to
www.thewebinvestor.com

1.3 FINANCIAL MARKET

Markets are conduits through which buyers and sellers exchange goods, services, and resources. In an economy there are three types of markets: a product market where goods and services are traded, a factor market where labor, capital, and land are exchanged, and a financial market where financial claims are traded. The financial market, in turn, channels the savings of households, businesses, and governments to those economic units needing to borrow.

The financial market can be described as a market for loanable funds. The supply of loanable funds comes from the savings of households, the retained earnings of businesses, and the surpluses of units of government; the demand for loanable funds emanates from businesses who need to raise funds to finance their capital purchases of equipment, plants, and inventories, households who need to purchase houses, cars, and other consumer durables, and the Treasury, federal agencies, and municipal governments who need to finance the construction of public facilities, projects, and operations. The exchange of loanable funds from savers to borrowers is done either directly through the selling of financial claims (stock, bonds, commercial paper, etc.) or indirectly through financial institutions.

The financial market facilitates the transfer of funds from *surplus economic units* to *deficit economic units*. A surplus economic unit is an entity whose income from its current production exceeds its current expenditures; it is a saver or net lender. A deficit unit, on the other hand, is an entity whose current expenditures exceed its income from its current production; it is a net borrower. While businesses, households, and governments fluctuate from being deficit units in one period to surplus units in another period, on average, households tend to be surplus units while businesses and government units tend to be deficit units. A young household usually starts as a deficit unit as it acquires homes and cars financed with mortgages and auto loans. In its mid-life, the household's income usually is higher and its mortgage and other loans are often paid; at that time the household tends to become a surplus unit, purchasing financial claims. Finally, near the end of its life, the household lives off the income from its financial claims. In contrast, businesses tend to invest or acquire assets that cost more than the earnings they retain. As a result, businesses are almost always deficit units, borrowing or selling bonds and stocks; furthermore, they tend to remain that way throughout their entire life. Similarly, the federal government's expenditures on defense, education, and welfare have more often exceeded its revenues from taxes. Thus, the federal government, as well as state and local units, tend to be deficit units.

1.4 TYPES OF FINANCIAL MARKETS

Financial markets can be classified in terms of whether the market is for new or existing claims (primary or secondary market), for short-term or long-term instruments (money or capital market), for direct or indirect trading between deficit and surplus units (direct or intermediary market), for domestic or foreign securities, and for immediate, future, or optional delivery (cash, futures, or options markets).

1.4.1 Primary and Secondary Market

The *primary market* is that market where financial claims are created. It is the market in which new securities are sold for the first time. Thus, the sale of new government securities by the US Treasury to finance a government deficit or a $100m bond issue by Procter & Gamble to finance the construction of a new soap processing plant are examples of security transactions occurring in the primary market. The principal function of the primary market is to raise the funds needed to finance investments in new plants, equipment, inventories, homes, roads, and the like – it is where capital formation begins.

The *secondary market* is the market for the buying and selling of existing assets and financial claims. Its primary function is to provide marketability – ease or speed in trading a security. Given the accumulation of financial claims over time, the volume of trading on the secondary market far exceeds the volume in

the primary market. The buying and selling of existing securities is done primarily through a network of brokers and dealers who operate through organized security exchanges and the over-the-counter market. Brokers and dealers serve the function of bringing buyers and sellers together by finding opposite positions or by taking positions in a security. By definition, *brokers* are agents who bring security buyers and sellers together for a commission. *Dealers*, in turn, provide markets for investors to buy and sell securities by taking a temporary position in a security; they buy from investors who want to sell and sell to those who want to buy. Dealers receive compensation in terms of the spread between the *bid price* at which they buy securities and *asked price* at which they sell securities. Currently, there are over 3,000 brokers and dealers in the US handling billions of dollars' worth of daily security transactions. The major brokerage firms, such as Merrill Lynch and Paine Webber, though, handle 80% of the secondary market security trades.

While both brokers and dealers serve the function of bringing buyers and seller together, exchanges serve the function of linking brokers and dealers together to buy and sell existing securities. In the US, there are two national organized exchanges, the New York Stock Exchange (NYSE) and the American Stock Exchange (AMEX), and several regional organized exchanges. Outside the US, there are major exchanges in such cities as London, Tokyo, Hong Kong, Singapore, Sydney, and Paris. In addition to organized exchanges, existing securities are also traded on the over-the-counter (OTC) market.

New York Stock Exchange: The NYSE was formed in 1792 by a group of merchants who wanted to trade notes and bonds. Since then it has grown to an exchange in which approximately 2,700 stocks and a limited number of bonds and other securities are traded. The NYSE can be described as a corporate association consisting of member brokers. Most brokerage firms with membership (seats) on the NYSE function as commission brokers, executing buy and sell orders on behalf of their clients. The NYSE and the other organized exchanges in the US also provide a continuous market. A continuous market attempts to have constant trading in a security. To have such a feature, time discrepancies caused by different times when investors want to sell and when others want to buy must be eliminated or at least minimized. In a continuous market this is accomplished by having specialists. *Specialists* are dealers who are part of the exchange and who are required by the exchange to take opposite positions in a security if conditions dictate. Under a specialist system, the exchange board assigns a specific security to a specialist to deal. In this role, a specialist acts by buying the stock from sellers at low bid prices and selling to buyers at (they hope!) higher asked prices. Specialists quote a bid price to investors when selling the security and an asked price to investors interested in buying. They hope to profit from the difference between the bid and asked prices; that is, the *bid-asked spread*. In addition to dealing, the NYSE and other exchanges using a specialist system also require that the specialists maintain the *limit order book* (which appears on their computer screens) on the securities they are assigned and that they execute these orders. A *limit order* is an investor's request to his broker to buy or sell a security at a given price or better. On the NYSE, such orders are taken by commission brokers and left with the specialist in that security for execution.[1]

Over-the-Counter Market: The over-the-counter (OTC) market is an informal exchange for the trading of over 70,000 stocks and many corporate and municipal bonds, investment fund shares, mortgage-backed securities, shares in limited partnerships, and Treasury and federal agency securities. There are no membership or listing requirements for trading on the OTC; any security can be traded. It can be described as a market of brokers and dealers linked to each other by a computer, telephone, and telex communications system. To trade, dealers must register with the Securities and Exchange Commission (SEC). As dealers, they can quote their own bid and asked prices on the securities they deal, and as brokers, they can execute a trade with a dealer providing a quote. The securities traded on the OTC market are those in which a dealer decides to take a position. Dealers on the OTC market range from regional brokerage houses making a market in

a local corporation's stock or bond, to large financial companies, such as Salomon Smith Barney, making markets in Treasury securities, to investment bankers dealing in the securities they had previously underwritten, to dealers in federal agency securities and municipal bonds. Like the specialist on the organized exchanges, each dealer maintains an inventory in a security and quotes a bid and an asked price at which she is willing to buy and sell. The *National Association of Security Dealers (NASD)* regulates OTC trading. NASD is a voluntary organization of OTC security dealers who self-regulate the OTC market by overseeing trading practices and by licensing brokers.[2] While no physical exchange exists, communications among brokers and dealers take place through a computer system known as the *National Association of Security Dealers Automatic Quotation System (NASDAQ)*. NASDAQ is an information system in which current bid-asked quotes of dealers are offered, and also a system that sends brokers' quotes to dealers, enabling them to close trades.[3]

Web Information

For information on NYSE stock exchanges go to
    www.nyse.com

For information on the OTC market go to
    www.nasd.com
and
    www.nasdaq.com

Stock and company information can be found at a number of websites:
    www.wsrn.com
    www.quicken.com
and
    www.pinksheets.com

1.4.2 Direct and Intermediary Financial Markets

In addition to dividing the markets for financial instruments into primary and secondary, the markets can also be classified in terms of being either part of the direct financial market or the intermediary financial market.

Direct Financial Market

The *direct financial market* is where surplus units purchase claims issued by the ultimate deficit unit. This market includes the trading of stocks, corporate bonds, Treasury securities, federal agency securities, and municipal bonds. The claims traded in the direct financial market are referred to as *primary securities*.[4]

As is the case with many security markets, the direct financial market can be divided into primary and secondary markets. The secondary market for direct financial claims takes place in both the organized exchanges and the over-the-counter market just discussed. In the primary market, new securities are sold either in a negotiated market or an open market. In a *negotiated market*, the securities are issued to one or just a few economic entities under a private contract. Such sales are referred to as a *private placement*. In an open market transaction, the securities are sold to the public at large. The key participant in *open market trades* is the *investment banker*. The investment banker is a middleman or matchmaker who, for a fee or share in the trading profit, finds surplus units who want to buy the security being offered by a deficit unit (see figure 1.1). The major investment bankers include such firms as Merrill Lynch, Goldman Sachs, First Boston Credit

Suisse, and Salomon Smith Barney. Investment bankers sell a security issue for the issuer for a commission (i.e., for a percentage of the total issue's value) using their *best effort, underwrite* the securities (i.e., buy the securities from the issuer and then sell them at hopefully a higher price), or form an *underwriting syndicate* whereby a group of investment bankers buys and sells the issue. Whatever the arrangements, the primary function of the investment banker is to match the needs of the surplus and deficit units. By performing this function the investment banker reduces the search and information costs to both the investors and the issuer, facilitating the efficient operation of the primary market.

Intermediary Financial Market

The intermediary financial market consists of financial institutions, such as commercial banks, savings and loans, credit unions, insurance companies, pension funds, trust funds, and mutual funds. In this market, the financial institution, as shown in figure 1.2, sells financial claims (checking accounts, savings accounts, certificates of deposit, mutual fund shares, payroll deduction plans, insurance plans, and the like) to surplus units, and uses the proceeds to purchase claims (stocks, bonds, etc.) issued by ultimate

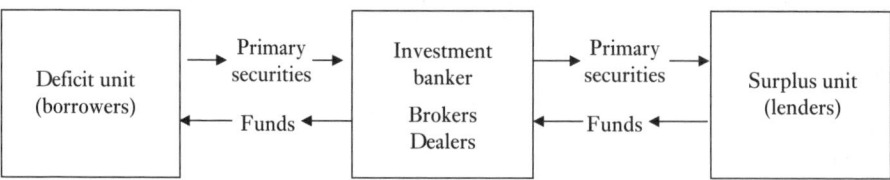

Figure 1.1   Direct financial market

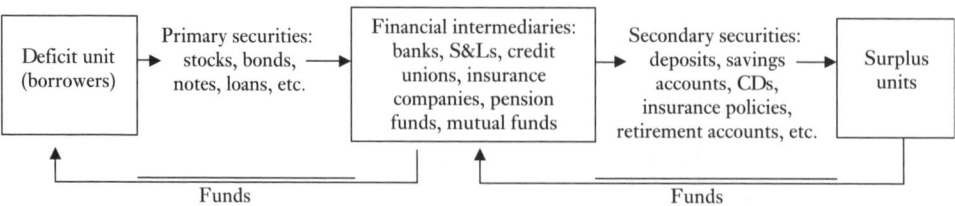

Figure 1.2   Intermediary financial market

deficit units or to create financial claims in the form of term loans, lines of credit, and mortgages. Through their intermediary function, financial institutions in turn create intermediate securities, referred to as *secondary securities*.

Financial institutions can be divided into three categories: *depository institutions*, *contractual institutions*, and *investment companies*. Depository institutions include commercial banks, credit unions, savings and loans, and savings banks. These institutions obtain large amounts of their funds from deposits, which they use primarily to fund commercial and residential loans and to purchase Treasury, federal agency, and municipal securities. Contractual institutions include life insurance companies, property and casualty insurance companies, and pension funds. They obtain their funds from legal contracts to protect businesses and households from risk (premature death, accident, etc.), and from savings plans. Investment companies include mutual funds, money market funds, and real estate investment trusts. These institutions raise funds by selling equity or debt claims, and then use the proceeds to buy debt securities, stocks, real estate, and other assets. The claims they sell entitle the holder/buyer either to a fixed income each period or a pro rata share in the ownership and earnings generated from the asset fund. Also included with investment company securities are *securitized assets*. Banks, insurance companies and other financial intermediaries, as well as federal agencies, sell these financial assets. In creating a securitized asset, an intermediary will put together a package of loans of a certain type (mortgages, auto, credit cards, etc.). The institution then sells claims on the package to investors, with the claim being secured by the package of assets – securitized asset. The package of loans, in turn, generates interest and principal that is passed on to the investors who purchased the securitized asset.[5]

A number of the financial claims created in the intermediary financial market do not have a secondary market; that is, secondary markets where investors sell their bank saving accounts or insurance or pension plans to other investors are rare. However, there are secondary markets for many intermediary securities: negotiable certificates of deposit, mutual fund shares, and securitized assets.

> **Web Information**
> Data on most financial intermediaries is prepared by the Federal Reserve and is published in the *US Flow of Funds* report. The report can be accessed from
> www.federalreserve.gov/releases/Z1/
>
> For additional information on investment funds, see the Investment Company Institute's website:
> www.ici.org

1.4.3 Money and Capital Markets

Financial markets can also be classified in terms of the maturity of the instrument traded. Specifically, the *money market* is defined as the market where short-term instruments (by convention defined as securities with original maturities of 1 year or less) are traded, and the *capital market* is defined as the market where long-term securities (original maturities over 1 year) are traded. The former would include such securities as certificates of deposit, commercial paper, Treasury bills, savings accounts, and shares in money market investment funds, while the latter would include corporate bonds, municipal bonds, securitized assets, Treasury bonds, and investment fund shares, as well as corporate stock. Investors with long-term liabilities or investment horizon periods – including many institutional investors, such as life insurance companies and pensions – buy securities in the capital markets. The issuers of capital market securities include corporations and governments who use the market to finance their long-term capital formation projects. Investors use the money market to earn interest on excess funds that they expect to have only temporarily. They also hold funds in money market securities as a store of value when they are waiting to take advantage of investment opportunities. The sellers of money market securities use the market to raise funds to finance their short-term assets (inventory or accounts receivable), to take care of cash needs resulting from the lack of synchronization between cash inflows and outflows from operations, or in the case of the US Treasury to finance the government's deficit or to refinance its maturing debt. It should be noted that the money market functions primarily as a *wholesale market*, in which many of the transactions are done by large banks and investment firms who buy and sell in large denominations. This feature helped to promote the popularity of money market funds. These funds pool the investments of small investors and invest them in money market securities, providing small investors with an opportunity to obtain higher returns than they could obtain from individual bank savings accounts.

1.4.4 Foreign Security Markets

Over the last three decades there has been a substantial growth in the value of equity and fixed-income securities traded globally. This growth in the size of world equity and debt markets is reflected by the significant increase in international security investments among nonresidents. This popularity of international investments is generally attributed to the growing number of corporations, governments, and financial intermediaries issuing securities in foreign countries, to the emergence of currency futures, options, and swaps markets that have made it possible for investors to better manage exchange-rate risk, and to the potential diversification benefits investors can obtain by adding foreign stocks and bonds to their portfolios.

In general, an investor looking to internationally diversify his bond portfolio has several options. First, he might buy a bond of a foreign government or foreign corporation that is issued in the foreign country or traded on that country's exchange. These bonds are referred to as *domestic bonds*.[6] Secondly, the investor might be able to buy bonds issued in a number of countries through an international syndicate. Such bonds are known as *Eurobonds*. Finally, an investor might be able to buy a bond of a foreign government or corporation being issued or traded in his own country. These bonds are called *foreign bonds*. If the investor were instead looking for short-term foreign investments, his choices would similarly include buying short-term domestic securities such as CP, CDs, and Treasuries issued in those countries, Eurocurrency CDs issued by Eurobanks, and foreign money market securities

issued by foreign corporations and governments in the local country. Similarly, a domestic financial institution or non-financial multinational corporation looking to raise funds may choose to do so by selling debt securities or borrowing in the company's own financial markets, the foreign markets, or the Eurobond or Eurocurrency markets. The markets where domestic, foreign, and Euro securities are issued and traded can be grouped into two categories – the *internal bond market* and the *external bond market*. The internal market, also called the *national market*, consists of the trading of both domestic bonds and foreign bonds; the external market, also called the *offshore market*, is where Eurobonds and Euro-deposits are bought and sold.

For foreign investors, one of the most important factors for them to consider is that their price, interest payments, and principal are denominated in a different currency. This currency component exposes them to *exchange rate risk* and affects their returns and overall risk. Most of the currency trading takes place in the *Interbank Foreign Exchange Market*. This market consists primarily of major banks that act as currency dealers, maintaining inventories of foreign currencies to sell to or buy from their customers (corporations, governments, or regional banks). The price of foreign currency or the exchange rate is defined as the number of units of one currency that can be exchanged for one unit of another. It is determined by supply and demand conditions affecting the foreign currency market.

Web Information

For a more extensive explanation of foreign bonds go to
    www.finpipe.com

Information on historical exchange rates and trade:
    http://research.stlouisfed.org/fred2

Information on current exchange rates and foreign interest rates:
    www.fxstreet.com

Information on foreign stock prices and exchange rates:
    www.stocksmart.com

1.4.5 Spot, Futures, and Options Markets

A *spot market* (also called a *cash market*) is one in which securities are exchanged for cash immediately (usually within one or two business days). When an investor buys a Treasury bill, for example, it is a transaction that takes place in the spot market. Not all security transactions, though, call for immediate delivery. A *futures or forward contract* calls for the delivery and purchase of an asset (either real or financial) at a future date, with the terms (price, amount, etc.) agreed upon in the present. For example, a contract calling for the delivery of a Treasury bill in 70 days at a price equal to 97% of the bill's principal would represent a futures contract on a Treasury bill. This agreement is distinct from buying a Treasury bill from a Treasury dealer in the spot market, where the transfer of cash for the security takes place almost immediately. Similar to a futures contract, an option is a security that gives the holder the right (but not the obligation) either to buy or to sell an asset at a specific price on or possibly before a specific date. Options include calls, puts, warrants, and rights. Both futures and options are traded on organized exchanges and through dealers on the over-the-counter market. In the United States, the major futures exchanges are the Chicago Board of Trade, the Chicago Mercantile Exchange, and the New York Futures Exchange; the major option exchange is the Chicago Board of Option Exchange. Options and futures are referred to as *derivative securities*, since their values are derived from the values of their underlying securities. In contrast, securities sold in the spot market are sometimes referred to as *primitive securities*. Derivative debt securities have become important to both borrowers and investors in managing the risk associated with issuing and buying fixed income securities. Part IV of this book focuses on the markets and uses of debt derivative securities.

In addition to derivative securities, bonds often have *embedded option* features in their contracts. Many bonds, for example, have a call feature giving the issuer the right to buy back the bond from the bondholder before maturity at a specific price. In addition to these so-called callable bonds, there are putable bonds, giving the bondholder the right to sell the bond back to the issuer, sinking fund clauses in which the issuer is required to orderly retire the bond by either buying bonds in the market or by calling them at a specified price, and convertible bonds that give the bondholder the right to convert the bond into a specified number of shares of stock. The inclusion of option features in a bond contract makes the valuation of such bonds difficult. The valuation of bonds with embedded options is the subject of chapters 9 and 10.

1.5 REGULATIONS

Prior to the enactment of federal security laws in 1933 and 1934, the regulations of security trading in the US came under the auspices of state governments who had passed a number of laws to prevent fraud and speculative schemes. The state security laws, known as the *blue-sky laws*, were often hard to enforce since many fraudulent promoters could operate outside a state's jurisdiction. With the passage of the *Securities Act of 1933* and the *Securities Exchange Act (SEA) of 1934*, though, security regulations came more under the providence of the federal government. The 1933 Act, known as the *truth-in-securities law*, requires registration of new issues, disclosure of pertinent information by issuers, and prohibits fraud and misrepresentation. The SEA of 1934 established the *Securities and Exchange Commission (SEC)*, extended the disclosure requirements of the 1933 Act to include traders and participants in the secondary market, and outlawed fraud and misrepresentation in the trading of existing securities. Today, five commissioners appointed by the President and confirmed by the Senate for 5-year terms run the SEC. The SEC is responsible for the administration of both the 1933 and 1934 Acts, as well as the administration of a number of other security laws that have been enacted since then. The 1934 Act gave the SEC authority over organized exchanges. Historically, the SEC has exercised its authority by setting only general guidelines for the bylaws and rules of an exchange, allowing the exchanges to regulate themselves. The SEC does have the power, though, to intervene and change bylaws, as well as close exchanges.

Exhibit 1.1   Security Acts of 1933 and 1934

The **Securities Act of 1933**, also known as the *truth-in-securities law*, required registration of new issues, disclosure of pertinent information by issuers, and prohibited fraud and misrepresentation. To comply with this Act today, a company selling securities across state lines is required to submit a prospectus and audited financial statements on the company's condition to a federal agency or the Securities and Exchange Commission. Once approved, the prospectus is sent to potential investors. Furthermore, any fraud or misrepresentation is subject to legal actions.

The **Securities Exchange Act of 1934** established the *Securities and Exchange Commission*, extended the disclosure requirements of the 1933 Act to include traders and participants in the secondary market, and outlawed fraud and misrepresentation in the trading of existing securities. Today, five commissioners appointed by the President and confirmed by the Senate for 5-year terms run the Securities and Exchange Commission (SEC). The SEC is responsible for the administration of both the 1933 and 1934 Acts, as well as the administration of a number of other security laws that have been enacted since then. The 1934 Act gave the SEC authority over organized exchanges.

Financial Disclosure Requirements: To comply with the disclosure provisions of the Securities Exchange Act (and its 1964 amendments) companies listed on the exchanges and those traded on the OTC market with assets over $13m, are required to file with the SEC *10-K reports*, which are audited financial statement forms, *10-Q reports*, which are quarterly unaudited financial statement forms, and *8-K forms*, which report significant developments by the company.

Fraud and Misrepresentation Provisions: The Securities Exchange Act outlaws price manipulation schemes such as wash sales, pools, churning, and corners. A *wash sale* is a sale and subsequent repurchase of a security or purchase of an identical security. It is done in order to establish a record to show, for example, a capital loss for tax purposes or to deceive investors into thinking there is large activity on the stock. A *pool* is an association of people formed to manipulate the price of a security. *Churning* occurs when a broker manipulates his client to make frequent purchases and sales of a security in order to profit from increased commissions. A *corner* occurs when someone buys up all of the security (or commodity) in order to have the monopolistic power to raise its price and to pressure short sellers to sell at higher prices. An investor or group of investors who try to corner the market could do so by forming pools to manipulate the security's price. In addition to outlawing wash sales and pools, the Securities Exchange Act also requires that all officers, directors, and owners of more than 10% file an *insider* report each month in which they trade their securities. The purpose of this requirement is to eliminate an insider from profiting from inside information.

Exhibit 1.1 summarizes the Security Acts of 1933 and 1934, and exhibit 1.2 describes some of the other important security laws in the US.

The 1933 and 1934 Security Acts are aimed at ensuring that information is disseminated efficiently to all investors and that fraud and misrepresentation are outlawed. There are also laws, regulations, and regulatory agencies that work to ensure the financial system is sound. Of particular note is the Federal Reserve System. Created in 1913, the Federal Reserve (Fed) is the most important central bank in the world. The Fed is responsible for managing the economy's money supply and the general level of interest rates. As we will discuss in more detail in later chapters, the Fed does this by open market operations, changing the reserve requirements banks maintain, and changing the discount rate they charge commercial banks on loans.

Web Information

Information on the laws, regulations, and litigations of the SEC:

www.sec.gov

Information on monetary policy, economic data, and research from the Federal Reserve:

www.federalreserve.gov

Exhibit 1.2   US Federal laws related to security trading

Glass-Steagall Act (enacted in 1933; major provisions repealed in 1999): The Glass-Steagall Act, also known as the Banking Act of 1933, prohibited commercial banks from acting as investment bankers. Enacted after the 1929 stock market crash, the Act also prohibited banks from paying interest on demand deposits (a prohibition that was later eliminated under the Monetary Control Act of 1980), and created the Federal Deposit Insurance Company. As a result of the Glass-Steagall Act, for years most commercial banks in the United States were not allowed to underwrite securities, act as brokers and dealers, or offer investment company shares. The Glass-Steagall Act also served to differentiate US banking activities from those of many countries in which banks were allowed to provide investment banking and security services (merchant banking). Recognizing these differences, the US Congress repealed many of the provisions of the Glass-Steagall Act.

Financial Services Modernization (Gramm-Leach-Bliley) Act (1999): The Act permitted finance companies and banks to form financial holding companies to offer banking, insurance, securities, and other financial services under one controlling corporation.

Federal Reserve Regulations T and U: Regulations T and U give the Board of Governors of the Federal Reserve the authority to set margin requirements for security loans made by banks, brokers, and dealers. Regulation T sets loan limits made by brokers and dealers, and Regulation U sets loan limits made by banks for securities transactions. Since 1934, these requirements have ranged from 40% to 100%. Note: brokerage houses and security exchanges set maintenance margins.

Maloney Act (1936): This Act requires associations such as NASD to register with the SEC and allows them to regulate themselves within general guidelines specified by the SEC.

Trust Indenture Act (1939): This Act gave the SEC the authority to ensure that there are no conflicts of interest between bondholders, trustees, and issuer. The Act was in response to abuses in the 1930s that resulted from the issuer having control over the trustee. Among its provisions, the Act requires that the bond indenture clearly delineate the rights of the bondholders, that periodic financial reports be given to the trustee, and that the trustee act judiciously in bringing legal actions against the issuer when conditions dictate.

Investment Company Act (1940), ICA: This Act extends the provisions of the Security Acts of 1933 and 1934 to investment companies. Like the Security Acts, it requires a prospectus to be approved and issued to investors with full disclosure of financial statements, and it outlaws fraud and misrepresentations. In addition, the Act requires investment companies to state their goals (growth, balance, income, etc.), to have a management firm approved by the investment company's board, and to manage funds for the benefit of the shareholders. The 1940 Act was amended in 1970 (Investment Company Amendment Act of 1970) with provisions calling for certain restrictions on management fees and contracts.

Investment Advisors Act (1940), IAA: This Act requires individuals and firms providing investment advice for a fee to register with the SEC. The Act does not, however, require certification of an advisor's qualifications. The Act also outlaws fraud and misrepresentation.

Employee Retirement Income Security Act (1974), ERISA: This Act requires that managers of pension funds adhere to the *prudent man rule* (a common-law principle) in managing retirement funds. When applied to investment management, this rule requires average portfolio returns and risk levels to be consistent with that of a prudent man. The probable interpretation (which is subject to legal testing) would be that pension managers be adequately diversified to minimize the risk of large losses.

1.6 EFFICIENT FINANCIAL MARKETS

As defined earlier, an asset is any commodity, tangible or intangible good, or financial claim that generates future benefits. The value of an asset is equal to the current value of all of the asset's future expected cash flows (or benefits); that is, the present value of the expected cash flows. Thus, if an investor requires a rate of return (R) of 10% per year on investments in government securities that mature in 1 year, he would value (V_0) a government bond promising to pay $100 interest and $1,000 principal at the end of 1 year as worth $1,000 today:

$$V_0 = \frac{\text{Interest} + \text{Principal}}{1 + R}$$
$$= \frac{\$100 + \$1,000}{1.10} = \$1,000$$

Similarly, an investor who expected ABC stock to pay a dividend of $10 and to sell at a price of $105 1 year later would value the stock at $100 if she required a rate of return of 15% per year on such investments:

$$V_0 = \frac{\text{Dividend} + \text{Expected price}}{1 + R}$$
$$= \frac{\$10 + \$105}{1.15} = \$100$$

In the financial market, if stock investors expecting ABC stock to pay a $10 dividend and be worth $105 1 year later required a 15% rate of return, then the equilibrium price of the stock in the market would be $100. Similarly, if government bond investors required a 10% rate of return, then the equilibrium price of the government bond would be $1,000.

The equilibrium price often is ensured by the activities of *speculators*: those who hope to obtain higher rates of return (greater than 15% in this case of the stock or 10% in the case of the bond) by gambling that security prices will move in certain directions. For example, if ABC stock sold below the $100 equilibrium value, then speculators would try to buy the underpriced stock. As they try to do so, though, they would push the underpriced ABC stock towards its equilibrium price of $100. On the

other hand, if ABC stock were above $100, investors and speculators would be reluctant to buy the stock, lowering its demand and the price. These actions might also be reinforced with some speculators selling the stock short. In a *short sale*, a speculator sells the stock first and buys it later, hoping to profit, as always, by buying at a low price and selling at a high one. For example, if ABC stock is selling at $105, a speculator could borrow a share of ABC stock from one of its owners (i.e., borrow the stock certificate, not money), and then sell the share in the market for $105. The short seller/speculator would now have $105 cash and would owe one share of stock to the share lender. Since the speculator believes the stock is overpriced, she is hoping to profit by the stock decreasing in the near future. If she is right such that ABC stock decreases to its equilibrium value of $100, then the speculator could go into the market and buy the stock for $100 and return the borrowed share, leaving her with a profit of $5. However, if the stock goes up and the share lender wants his stock back, then the short seller would lose when she buys back the stock at a price higher than $100. In general, speculators help to move the market price of a security to its equilibrium value.

Theoretically, a market in which the price of the security is equal to its equilibrium value at all times is known as a *perfect market*. For a market to be perfect requires, among other things, that all the information on which investors and speculators base their estimates of expected cash flows be reflected in the security's price. Such a market is known as an *efficient market*. In a perfect market, speculators, on average, would not earn abnormal returns (above 15% in our stock example). However, if the information the market receives is *asymmetrical* in the sense that some speculators have information that others don't, or some receive information earlier than others, then the market price will not be equal to its equilibrium value at all times. In this inefficient market, there would be opportunities for speculators to earn abnormal returns.

Efficient markets would also preclude arbitrage returns. An *arbitrage* is a risk-free opportunity. Such opportunities come from price discrepancies among different markets.

For example, if the same car sells for $1,000 in Boston but $2,000 in New York, an *arbitrageur* (one who exploits such opportunities) could earn a risk-free profit by buying the car in Boston and selling it in New York (assuming, of course, that the transportation costs are less than $1,000). In the financial markets, arbitrageurs tie markets together. For example, suppose there were two identical government bonds, each paying a guaranteed interest and principal of $1,100 at the end of one year, but with one selling for $1,000 and the other selling for $900. With such price discrepancies, an arbitrageur could sell short the higher priced bond at $1,000 (borrow the bond and sell it for $1,000) and buy the underpriced one for $900. This would generate an initial cash flow for the arbitrageur of $100 with no liabilities. That is, at maturity the arbitrageur would receive $1,100 from the underpriced bond that he could use to pay the lender of the overpriced bond. Arbitrageurs, by exploiting this arbitrage opportunity, though, would push the price of the underpriced bond up and the price of the overpriced one down until they were equally priced and the arbitrage was gone. Thus, arbitrageurs would tie the markets for the two identical bonds together.

Web Information
For more on the efficient market hypothesis:
   www.investorhome.com/emh.htm

1.7 CHARACTERISTICS OF ASSETS

The preceding discussion on the types of financial claims and their markets suggests that there are considerable differences among assets. All assets, though, can be described in terms of a limited number of common characteristics. These common properties make it possible to evaluate, select, and manage assets by defining and comparing them in terms of these properties. In fact, as an academic subject, the study of investments involves the evaluation

and selection of assets. The evaluation of assets consists of describing assets in terms of their common characteristics, while selection involves selecting assets based on the tradeoffs between those characteristics (e.g., higher return for higher risk). The characteristics common to all assets are value, rate of return, risk, maturity, divisibility, marketability, liquidity, and taxability.

Value: As defined earlier, the value of an asset is the present value of all of the asset's expected future benefits. Moreover, if markets were efficient, then, in equilibrium, the value of the asset would be equal to its market price.

Rate of Return: The rate of return on an asset is equal to the total dollar return received from the asset per period of time expressed as a proportion of the price paid for the asset. The total return on the security includes the income payments the security promises (interest on bonds, dividends on stock, etc.), the interest from reinvesting the coupon or dividend income during the life of the security, and any capital gains or losses realized when the investor sells the asset. Thus, if a corporate bond cost $P_0 = \$1,000$ and was expected to pay a coupon interest of $C = \$100$ and a principal of $F = \$1,000$ at the end of the year, then its annual rate of return would be 10% if all the expectations hold true:

$$R = \frac{C + (F - P_0)}{P_0}$$
$$= \frac{\$100 + (\$1,000 - \$1,000)}{\$1,000} = 0.10$$

It should be noted that value (or price) and rate of return are necessarily related. If an investor knows the price she will pay for a security and the security's expected future benefits, then she can determine the security's rate of return. Alternatively, if she knows the rate of return she wants or requires and the security's expected future benefits, then she can determine the security's value or price.

Risk: The third property of an asset is its risk. Risk can be defined as the uncertainty that the rate of return an investor will obtain from holding an asset will be less than expected. Risk can result, for example, out of a concern that a bond issuer might fail to meet his contractual obligations (default risk) or it could result from an expectation that conditions in the market will change, resulting in a lower than expected price of the security when the holder plans to sell the asset (market risk).

Risk, rate of return, and the value of an asset are necessarily related. In choosing between two securities with the same cash flows but with different risks, most investors will require a higher rate of return from the riskier of the two securities. For example, we would expect investors averse to risk to require a higher rate of return on a corporate bond issued by a fledgling company than on a US government bond. If for some reason both securities traded at prices that yielded the same expected rates, then we would expect that investors would want the government bond, but not the corporate. If this were the case, the demand and price of the government bond would increase and its rate of return would decrease, while the demand and price of the corporate bond would fall and its rate of return would increase. Thus, if investors are risk averse, riskier securities must yield higher rates of return in the market or they will languish untraded.

Maturity: The fourth characteristic of an asset is its maturity. Maturity is the length of time from the present until the last contractual payment is made. Maturity can vary anywhere from one day to indefinitely, as in the case of stock or a consul (a bond issued with no maturity). Maturity can be used as a measure of the life of an asset. In defining a bond's life in terms of its maturity, though, one should always be aware of provisions such as a sinking fund or a call feature that modifies the maturity of a bond. For example, a 10-year callable bond issued when interest rates are relatively high may be more like a 5-year bond given that a likely interest rate decrease would lead the issuer to buy the bond back.

Divisibility: The fifth attribute, divisibility, refers to the smallest denomination in which an asset is traded. Thus a bank savings deposit account, in which an investor can deposit as little as a penny, is a perfectly divisible security;

a jumbo certificate of deposit, with a minimum denomination of $10m, is a highly indivisible security. Moreover, one of the economic benefits that investment funds provide investors is divisibility. That is, by offering shares in a portfolio of high denomination money market securities, an investment company makes it possible for small investors to obtain a higher rate of return than they could obtain by investing in a smaller denomination money market security.

Marketability: The sixth characteristic is marketability. It can be defined as the speed in which an asset can be bought and sold. As a rule, for an asset to be highly marketable its price should be independent of the time spent searching for buyers or sellers. Many tangible assets, such as houses, as well as a number of financial assets, require a certain length of time before they can be bought or sold at their fair market values. This does not mean that they can't be sold in a short period of time; but if they must be, they typically fetch a price substantially lower than what the market would yield if adequate time were allowed. In general, highly marketable securities tend to be very standardized items with a wide distribution of ownership. Thus the stock of large corporations listed on the NYSE or Treasury issues are highly marketable securities that can be bought or sold on the exchanges or through a dealer in the OTC market in a matter of minutes. One way to measure the degree of marketability of a security is in terms of the size of the bid and asked spread that dealers in the OTC market or a specialist on the exchanges offer. Dealers who make markets in less marketable securities necessarily set wider spreads than dealers who have securities that are bought and sold by many investors and therefore can be traded more quickly.

Liquidity: The seventh property, liquidity, is related to marketability. Liquidity can be defined as how cash-like a security is. For an instrument to be liquid it must be highly marketable and have little, if any, short-run risk. Thus, a Treasury security that can be sold easily and whose rate of return in the short run is known with a high degree of certainty is said to be liquid. On the other hand, a security such as an NYSE-listed stock is marketable but is not considered liquid given its day-to-day price fluctuations. Technically, the difference between marketability and liquidity is the latter's feature of low or zero risk that makes the security cash-like. It should be noted that while there is a difference between marketability and liquidity, the term liquidity is often used to describe a security's marketability.

Taxability: The eighth characteristic of an asset is taxability. Taxability refers to the claims that the federal, state, and local governments have on the cash flows of an asset. Taxability varies in terms of the type of asset. For example, the coupon interest on a municipal bond is tax exempt while the interest on a corporate bond is not. To the investor, the taxability of a security is important because it affects his after-tax rate of return.

1.8 CONCLUSION

In this chapter, we have given an overview of the financial system by examining the nature of financial assets, the types of markets that they give rise to, and their general characteristics. With this background, we now take up the study of the evaluation and selection of debt claims. In the next three chapters, debt securities are analyzed in terms of their characteristics. Chapter 2 looks at how debt instruments are valued and how their rates of return are measured; chapter 3 examines the term structure of interest rates and shows how such factors as market expectations, economic conditions, taxability, and risk-return preferences are important in determining the structure of rates; chapter 4 describes three types of bond risk – default, call, and market risk – and introduces two measures of bond volatility – duration and convexity.

KEY TERMS

Financial Claims	Limit Order Book	Disintermediation
Real Assets	Limit Order	US Flow of Funds
Financial Assets	Open-Auction or Crieé	Money Market
Fungible	System	Capital Market
Debt Claims	National Association of	Wholesale Market
Corporate Bonds	Security Dealers (NASD)	Domestic Bonds
Commercial Paper (CP)	National Association of	Public Bourse
Lines Of Credit	Security Dealers	Private Bourse
Treasury Bills	Automatic Quotation	Banker Bourse
Treasury Notes	System (NASDAQ)	Eurobonds
Treasury Bonds	Direct Financial Market	Foreign Bonds
Federal Agency Securities	Primary Securities	Internal Bond Market
General Obligation Bonds	Semidirect Market	External Bond Market
Revenue Bonds	Negotiated Market	National Market
Certificates of Deposit (CDs)	Private Placement	Offshore Market
Surplus Economic Units	Open Market Trades	Exchange Rate Risk
Deficit Economic Units	Investment Banker	Interbank Foreign Exchange
Primary Market	Best Effort	Market
Secondary Market	Underwrite	Spot Market
Brokers	Underwriting Syndicate	Cash Market
Dealers	Secondary Securities	Futures
Bid Price	Depository Institutions	Forward Contract
Asked Price	Contractual Institutions	Derivative Securities
Specialists	Investment Companies	Primitive Securities
Bid-Asked Spread	Securitized Assets	Embedded Option

Blue-Sky Laws	Speculators	Rate of Return
Securities Act of 1933	Short Sale	Risk
Securities Exchange	Perfect Market	Maturity
Act (SEA) of 1934	Efficient Market	Divisibility
Truth-In-Securities	Asymmetrical	Marketability
Law	Arbitrage	Liquidity
Securities and Exchange	Arbitrageur	Taxability
Commission	Value	

PROBLEMS AND QUESTIONS

1. Explain how real and financial assets are created through the capital formation process in both the private and public sectors.

2. Comment on what is meant by the statement: "The financial markets are markets for loanable funds."

3. Describe the following markets and their features:

   a. Primary and secondary markets
   b. Direct and intermediary markets
   c. Money and capital markets.

4. Define the following types of primary market sales and participants:

   a. Negotiated market and private placement
   b. Open market sales
   c. Investment banker
   d. Best effort
   e. Underwrite
   f. Underwriting syndicate.

5. Explain the difference between a broker and a dealer.

6. Describe the organizational structure of the New York Stock Exchange.

7. Define and explain the role of the specialist in ensuring a continuous market. Explain how they use the limit book.

8. Describe the following aspects of the over-the-counter market:

   a. How the market trades
   b. Types of securities
   c. Number of securities
   d. National Association of Security Dealers
   e. National Association of Security Dealers Automatic Quotation System.

9. Define the following financial institutions and explain their function in the intermediary financial market:

   a. Depository institutions
   b. Contractual institutions
   c. Investment companies.

10. What are securitized assets? How are they created?

11. Define the following international bonds and markets:

    a. Eurobond market
    b. Foreign bond
    c. Internal market or national market
    d. External market or offshore market
    e. Interbank foreign exchange market.

12. Define a forward contract and an option contract. What is the main difference between the contracts?

13. List some of the major provisions in the Security Acts of 1933 and 1934.

14. What is an efficient market? What is an inefficient market?

15. Define the characteristics of assets.

16. What is the difference between liquidity and marketability?

WEB EXERCISES

1. Learn about the NYSE by going to www.nyse.com and clicking on "About the NYSE" and then "Facts Book." At the site, check on an NYSE-listed stock by going to "Quick Quote" and entering a company's ticker symbol.

2. Find some current prices of OTC securities by going to www.pinksheets.com.

3. Brokerage firms provide a number of services. Identify some of those services by going to the Merrill Lynch site: www.ml.com.

4. Two important security laws are the Securities Act of 1933 and the Securities Exchange Act of 1934. Learn more about these Acts, and others, as well as the activities of the Securities and Exchange Commission by going to www.sec.gov. At the site, click on "Laws and Regulations" and then "Security Act 1933" and "Security Act 1934." As part of these Security Acts, traded companies are required to submit quarterly and annual financial statements. These statements can be found at the SEC site by going to "Search Company filings." Select a company and then look up its reported financial statements.

5. There are a number of websites that provide information on current and historical stock prices of companies, as well as fundamental information.

    a. The NASDAQ site is a good source for stock information. Select a stock and examine its price trends and fundamentals by going to www.nasdaq.com. At the site, enter the company's symbol (you can enter as many as 10 companies). Get printouts of the historical stock price chart, fundamentals, company news, and institutional holdings.
    b. Another good website for stock information is www.hoovers.com. Select a stock and gather the information at that site such as the stock's price charts, company profile and description, fundamentals, earnings estimates, and key ratios and statistics.
    c. A third site to explore is www.quicken.com. Go to that site and obtain information on a company such as its profile, fundamentals, price charts, analyst ratings, and insider trading.

6. Learn more about the financial world by examining some of many websites. To find a number of finance website links go to www.thewebinvestor.com.

NOTES

1. While US exchanges use specialists to ensure continuous trading, the exchanges in some countries trade a security only once or just a few times during a day. These so-called "call" markets use an *open-auction* or *criée system* in which interested traders gather in a designated trading area when the security is called. An exchange clerk then calls out prices until one is determined that clears all trades. In addition to continuous and call markets, there are also exchanges that have elements of both. For example, the Japanese stock exchange has dealers or market makers assigned to actively traded stocks, while thinly traded ones are sold through an open auction.
2. For a security to qualify for the system it must have at least two market makers and its issuer must meet certain financial requirements. For a company to have its stock listed on the NASDAQ system it must satisfy requirements related to its net worth and shares outstanding.
3. Several years ago the NASD merged with the American Stock Exchange.
4. Some scholars refer to direct financial claims as those in which only the ultimate borrowers and lenders trade with each other and a *semidirect market* as one in which brokers and dealers bring borrowers and lenders together. The definition of direct financial market here includes both of these markets.
5. A recent trend in the financial markets is towards disintermediation. *Disintermediation* refers to the shifting from intermediary financing to direct financing. This occurs when a surplus unit withdraws funds from a financial institution and invests the funds by buying primary claims from an ultimate borrower.
6. Security exchanges in different countries can be grouped into one of three categories: public bourse (exchange), private bourse, and banking bourse. A *public bourse* is a government security exchange in which listed securities (usually both bonds and stocks) are bought and sold through brokers who are appointed by the government. A *private bourse* is a security exchange owned by its member brokers and dealers. This is the type of exchange structure that operates in the US. In countries where there are private exchanges a number of the exchanges will usually compete with each other; this is not the case in countries using a public bourse structure. A *banker bourse* is a formal or informal market in which securities are traded through bankers. This type of trading typically occurs in countries where historically commercial and investment banking have not separated.

SELECTED REFERENCES

Livingston, Miles *Money and Capital Markets*, 2nd edn (Miami, FL: Kolb, 1993).

Revell, Jack *The Recent Evolution of the Financial System* (New York: MacMillan, 1997).

Mishkin, Frederic S. and Stanley G. Eakins *Financial Markets and Institutions*, 4th edn (Addison-Wesley, 2003).

CHAPTER TWO

BOND VALUE AND RETURN

2.1 INTRODUCTION

All securities can be evaluated in terms of the characteristics common to all assets: value, return, risk, maturity, marketability, liquidity, and taxability. In this and the next two chapters, we will analyze debt securities in terms of these characteristics. In this chapter we will look at how debt instruments (which we will usually refer to here as bonds) are valued and how their rates of return are measured. It should be noted that this chapter is very technical, entailing a number of definitions. Understanding how bonds are valued and their rates determined, though, is fundamental to being able to evaluate and select bonds.

2.2 BOND VALUATION

2.2.1 Pricing Bonds

An investor who has purchased a bond can expect to earn a possible return from the bond's periodic coupon payments, from capital gains (or losses) when the bond is sold, called, or matures, and from interest earned from reinvesting coupon payments. Given the market price of the bond, the bond's yield is the interest rate that makes the present value of the bond's cash flow equal to the bond's price. This

yield takes into account these three sources of return. In section 2.3 we will discuss how to solve for the bond's yield given its price. Alternatively, if we know the rate we require in order to buy the bond, then we can determine its value.

Like the value of any asset, the value of a bond is equal to the sum of the present values of its future cash flows:

$$V_0^b = \sum_{t=1}^{M} \frac{CF_t}{(1+R)^t} = \frac{CF_1}{(1+R)^1} + \frac{CF_2}{(1+R)^2}$$
$$+ \cdots + \frac{CF_M}{(1+R)^M} \tag{2.1}$$

where: V_0^b is the value or price of the bond, CF_t is the bond's expected cash flow in period t, including both coupon income and repayment of principal, R is the discount rate, and M is the time to maturity on the bond. The discount rate is the required rate, that is, the rate investors require in order to buy the bond. This rate could be estimated by determining the rate on a security with comparable characteristics.

Many bonds pay a fixed coupon interest each period, with the principal repaid at maturity. The coupon payment, C, is often quoted in terms of the bond's coupon rate, C^R. The coupon rate is the contractual rate the issuer agrees to pay on the bond. This rate is often expressed as a proportion of the bond's face value (or par) and is usually stated on an annual basis. Thus, a bond with a face value of $1,000 and a 10% coupon rate would pay an annual coupon of $100 each year for the life of the bond: $C = C^R F = (0.10)(\$1,000) = \$100$. The value of a bond paying a fixed coupon interest each year and the principal at maturity, in turn, would be:

$$V_0^b = \sum_{t=1}^{M} \frac{C}{(1+R)^t} + \frac{F}{(1+R)^M}$$

$$= \frac{C}{(1+R)^1} + \frac{C}{(1+R)^2} + \cdots$$

$$+ \frac{C}{(1+R)^M} + \frac{F}{(1+R)^M} \qquad (2.2)$$

With the coupon payment fixed each period, the C term in equation (2.2) can be factored out and the bond value can be expressed as:

$$V_0^b = C \sum_{t=1}^{M} \frac{1}{(1+R)^t} + \frac{F}{(1+R)^M}$$

The term $\Sigma 1/(1+R)^t$ is the present value of $1 received each year for M years. It is defined as the present value interest factor (PVIF). The PVIF for different terms and discount rates can be found using PVIF tables found in many finance text books. It also can be calculated using the following formula:

$$PVIF(R, M) = \frac{1 - [1/(1+R)^M]}{R}$$

Thus, if investors require a 10% annual rate of return on a 10-year, high-quality corporate bond paying a coupon equal to 9% of par each year and a principal of $1,000 at maturity, then they would price the bond at $938.55. That is:

$$V_0^b = \sum_{t=1}^{M} \frac{C}{(1+R)^t} + \frac{F}{(1+R)^M}$$

$$V_0^b = \sum_{t=1}^{10} \frac{\$90}{(1.10)^t} + \frac{\$1,000}{(1.10)^{10}}$$

$$V_0^b = \$90 \sum_{t=1}^{10} \frac{1}{(1.10)^t} + \frac{\$1,000}{(1.10)^{10}}$$

$$V_0^b = \$90[PVIF(10\%, 10\,\text{yrs})] + \frac{\$1,000}{(1.10)^{10}}$$

$$V_0^b = \$90 \left[\frac{1 - [1/1.10]^{10}}{0.10} \right] + \frac{\$1,000}{(1.10)^{10}}$$

$$V_0^b = \$938.55$$

2.2.2 Bond Price Relations

Relation between Coupon Rate, Required Rate, Value, and Par Value

The value of the bond in the above example is not equal to its par value. This can be explained by the fact that the discount rate and coupon rate are different. Specifically, for investors in the above case to obtain the 10% rate per year from a bond promising to pay an annual rate of $C^R = 9\%$ of par, they would have to buy the bond at a value, or price, below par: the bond would have to be purchased at a discount from its par, $V_0^b < F$. In contrast, if the coupon rate is equal to the discount rate (i.e., $R = 9\%$), then the bond's value would be equal to its par value, $V_0^b = F$. In this case, investors would be willing to pay $1,000 for this bond, with each investor receiving $90 each year in coupons. Finally, if the required rate is lower than the coupon rate, then investors would be willing to pay a premium over par for the bond, $V_0^b > F$. This might occur if bonds with comparable features were trading at rates below 9%. In this case, investors would be willing to pay a price above $1,000 for a bond with a coupon rate of 9%. Thus, the first relationship to note is that a bond's value (or price) will be equal, greater than, or less than its face value depending on whether the coupon rate is equal, less than, or greater than the required rate. That is:

Bond price relation 1:	If $C^R = R \Rightarrow V^b = F$: bond valued at par.
	If $C^R < R \Rightarrow V^b < F$: bond valued at discount.
	If $C^R > R \Rightarrow V^b > F$: bond valued at a premium.

Exhibit 2.1 The value over time of an original 10-year, 9% annual coupon bond selling at par, discount, and premium

Year	Discount bond Price of bond selling to yield 11%	Par bond Price of bond selling to yield 9%	Premium bond Price of bond selling to yield 7%
10	882.22	1,000.00	1,140.47
9	889.26	1,000.00	1,130.30
8	897.08	1,000.00	1,119.43
7	905.76	1,000.00	1,107.49
6	915.39	1,000.00	1,095.33
5	926.08	1,000.00	1,082.00
4	937.95	1,000.00	1,067.74
3	951.13	1,000.00	1,052.49
2	965.75	1,000.00	1,036.16
1	981.98	1,000.00	1,018.69
0	1,000.00	1,000.00	1,000.00

In addition to the above relations, the relation between the coupon rate and required rate also explains how the bond's value changes over time. If the required rate is constant over time, and if the coupon rate is equal to it (i.e., the bond is priced at par), then the value of the bond will always be equal to its face value throughout the life of the bond. This is illustrated in exhibit 2.1 by the horizontal line that shows the value of the 9% coupon bond is always equal to the par value. Here investors would pay $1,000 regardless of the terms to maturity. On the other hand, if the required rate is constant over time and the coupon rate is less (i.e., the bond is priced at a discount), then the value of the bond will increase as it approaches maturity; if the required rate is constant and the coupon rate is

greater (i.e., the bond is priced at a premium), then the value of the bond will decrease as it approaches maturity. These relationships are also illustrated in exhibit 2.1.

Relation between Value and Rate of Return

Given known coupon and principal payments, the only way an investor can obtain a higher rate of return on a bond is for its price (value) to be lower. In contrast, the only way for a bond to yield a lower rate is for its price to be higher. Thus, an inverse relationship exists between the price of a bond and its rate of return. This, of course, is consistent with equation (2.1) in which an increase in R increases the denominator and lowers V^b. Thus, the second bond relationship to note is that there is an inverse relationship between the price and rate of return on a bond. That is:

Bond price relation 2:	If $R\uparrow \Rightarrow V^b\downarrow$ If $R\downarrow \Rightarrow V^b\uparrow$

The inverse relation between a bond's price and rate of return is illustrated by the negatively sloped *price–yield curve* shown in exhibit 2.2. The curve shows the different values of a 10-year, 9% coupon bond given different rates. As shown, the 10-year bond has a value of $938.55 when $R = 10\%$ and $1,000 when

Exhibit 2.2   Price–yield relation (10-year, 9% annual coupon bond)

Required rate	Bond value	Changes in bond value
5%	1,308.87	
6%	1,220.80	−88.07
7%	1,140.47	−80.33
8%	1,067.10	−73.37
9%	1,000.00	−67.10
10%	938.55	−61.45
11%	882.22	−56.33
12%	830.49	−51.73
13%	782.95	−47.54

Bond relation 2:
- Price–yield curve depicts the inverse relation between V and R
- The price–yield curve for the 10-year, 9% coupon bond:

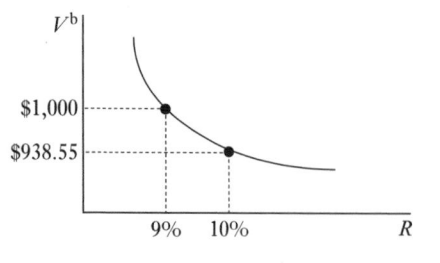

$R = 9\%$. In addition to showing a negative relation between price and yield, the price–yield curve is also convex from below (bowed shape). This convexity implies that for equal increases in yields, the value of the bond decreases at a decreasing rate (for equal decreases in yields, the bond's price increases at increasing rates). Thus, the inverse relationship between bond prices and yields is non-linear.

The Relation between a Bond's Price Sensitivity to Interest Rate Changes and Maturity

The third bond relationship to note is the relation between a bond's price sensitivity to interest rate changes and its maturity. Specifically:

Bond price relation 3:	The greater the bond's maturity, the greater its price sensitivity to a given change in interest rates.

This relationship can be seen by comparing the price sensitivity to interest rate changes of the 10-year, 9% coupon bond in our above example with a 1-year, 9% coupon bond. As shown in exhibit 2.3, if the required rate is 10%, then the 10-year bond would trade at $938.55, while the 1-year bond would trade at $990.91 ($1,090/1.10). If the interest rate decreases to 9% for each bond (a 10% change in rates), both bonds would increase in price to $1,000. For the 10-year bond, the percentage increase in price would be 6.55% (($1,000−$938.55)/$938.55), while the percentage increase for the 1-year bond would be only 0.9%. Thus, the 10-year bond is more price sensitive to the interest rate change than the 1-year bond. In addition, the greater price sensitivity to interest rate changes for longer maturity bonds also implies that their price–yield curves are more convex than the price–yield curves for smaller maturity bonds.

$$V_0^b = \sum_{t=1}^{10} \frac{\$20}{(1.09)^t} + \frac{\$1,000}{(1.09)^{10}} = \$550.76$$

$$\text{Proportional change} = \frac{\$550.76 - \$508.43}{\$508.43}$$

$$= 0.083$$

In this case, the lower coupon bond's price is more responsive to given interest rate changes than the price of the higher coupon bond. Thus:

Bond price relation 4: The lower a bond's coupon rate, the greater its price sensitivity to changes in discount rates.

Exhibit 2.3 Price sensitivity to interest rates and maturity

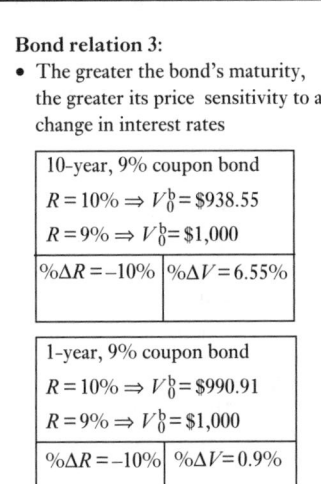

Bond relation 3:
- The greater the bond's maturity, the greater its price sensitivity to a change in interest rates

| 10-year, 9% coupon bond |
| $R = 10\% \Rightarrow V_0^b = \$938.55$ |
| $R = 9\% \Rightarrow V_0^b = \$1,000$ |

| $\%\Delta R = -10\%$ | $\%\Delta V = 6.55\%$ |

| 1-year, 9% coupon bond |
| $R = 10\% \Rightarrow V_0^b = \$990.91$ |
| $R = 9\% \Rightarrow V_0^b = \$1,000$ |

| $\%\Delta R = -10\%$ | $\%\Delta V = 0.9\%$ |

The Relation between a Bond's Price Sensitivity to Interest Rate Changes and Coupon Payments

Consider two 10-year bonds, each priced at a discount rate of 10% and each paying a principal of $1,000 at maturity, but with one bond having a coupon rate of 10% and priced at $1,000, and the other having a coupon rate of 2% and priced at $508.43:

$$V_0^b = \sum_{t=1}^{10} \frac{\$100}{(1.10)^t} + \frac{\$1,000}{(1.10)^{10}} = \$1,000$$

$$V_0^b = \sum_{t=1}^{10} \frac{\$20}{(1.10)^t} + \frac{\$1,000}{(1.10)^{10}} = \$508.43$$

Now suppose that the rate required on each bond decreases to a new level of 9%. The price on the 10% coupon bond, in turn, would increase by 6.4% to equal $1,064.18, while the price on the 2% coupon bond would increase by 8.3% to $550.76.

$$V_0^b = \sum_{t=1}^{10} \frac{\$100}{(1.10)^t} + \frac{\$1,000}{(1.10)^{10}} = \$1,064.18$$

$$\text{Proportional change} = \frac{\$1,064.18 - \$1,000}{\$1,000}$$

$$= 0.064$$

2.2.3 Pricing Bonds with Different Cash Flows and Compounding Frequencies

Equation (2.2) can be used to value bonds that pay coupons on an annual basis and a principal at maturity. Bonds, of course, differ in the frequency in which they pay coupons each year, and many bonds have maturities less than 1 year. Also, when investors buy bonds they often do so at non-coupon dates. Equation (2.2), therefore, needs to be adjusted to take these factors into account.

Semi-Annual Coupon Payments

Many bonds pay coupon interest semi-annually. When bonds make semi-annual payments, three adjustments to equation (2.2) are necessary: (1) the number of periods is doubled; (2) the annual coupon rate is halved; (3) the annual discount rate is halved. Thus, if our illustrative 10-year, 9% coupon bond trading at a quoted annual rate of 10% paid interest semi-annually instead of annually, it would be worth $937.69. That is:

$$V_0^b = \sum_{t=1}^{20} \frac{\$45}{(1.05)^t} + \frac{\$1,000}{(1.05)^{20}} = \$937.69$$

$$V_0^b = \$45 \left[\frac{1 - [1/(1.05)]^{20}}{0.05} \right] + \frac{\$1,000}{(1.05)^{20}}$$

$$= \$937.69$$

Note that the rule for valuing semi-annual bonds is easily extended to valuing bonds paying interest even more frequently. For example, to determine the value of a bond paying interest four times a year, we would quadruple the periods and quarter the annual coupon payment and discount rate. In general, if we let n be equal to the number of payments per year (i.e., the compoundings per year), M be equal to the maturity in years, and, as before, R be the discount rate quoted on an annual basis, then we can express the general formula for valuing a bond as follows:

$$V_0^b = \sum_{t=1}^{Mn} \frac{C^A/n}{(1 + (R^A/n))^t} + \frac{F}{(1 + (R^A/n))^{Mn}}$$

$$(2.3)$$

Compounding Frequency

The 10% annual rate in the above example is a simple annual rate: it is the rate with one annualized compounding. With one annualized compounding, we earn 10% every year and $100 would grow to equal $110 after 1 year: $100(1.10) = \$110$. If the simple annual rate were expressed with semi-annual compounding, then we would earn 5% every 6 months with the interest being reinvested; in this case, $100 would grow to equal $110.25 after one year: $100(1.05)^2 = \$110.25$. If the rate were expressed with monthly compounding, then we would earn 0.8333% (10%/12) every month with the interest being reinvested; in this case, $100 would grow to equal $110.47 after one year: $100(1.008333)^{12} = \$110.47$. If we extend the compounding frequency to daily, then we would earn 0.0274% (10%/365) daily, and with the reinvestment of interest, a $100 investment would grow to equal $110.52 after 1 year: $100(1 + (0.10/365))^{365} = \$110.52$. Note that the rate of 10% is the simple annual rate, while the actual rate earned for the year is $(1 + (R^A/n))^n - 1$. This rate that includes the reinvestment of interest (or compounding) is known as the *effective rate*.

When the compounding becomes large, such as daily compounding, then we are approaching continuous compounding with the n term in equation (2.3) becoming very large. For cases in which there is continuous compounding, the future value (FV) for an investment of A dollars M years from now becomes:

$$FV = Ae^{RM}$$

where e is the natural exponent (equal to the irrational number 2.71828). Thus, if the 10% simple rate were expressed with continuous compounding, then $100 ($A$) would grow to equal $110.52 after 1 year: $100e^{(0.10)(1)} = \$110.52$ (allowing for some slight rounding differences, this is the value obtained with daily compounding). After 2 years, the $100 investment would be worth $122.14: $100e^{(0.10)(2)} = \$122.14$.

Note that from the FV expression, the present value (A) of a future receipt (FV) is

$$A = PV = \frac{FV}{e^{RM}} = FVe^{-RM}$$

If $R = 0.10$, a security paying $100 2 years from now would be worth $81.87, given continuous compounding: $PV = \$100e^{-(0.10)(2)} = \$81.87$. Similarly, a security paying $100 each year for 2 years would be currently worth $172.36:

$$PV = \sum_{t=1}^{2} \$100e^{-(0.10)(t)}$$

$$= \$100e^{-(0.10)(1)} + \$100e^{-(0.10)(2)} = \$172.36$$

Thus, if we assume continuous compounding and a discount rate of 10%, then the value of our 10-year, 9% bond would be $908.82:

$$V_0^b = \sum_{t=1}^{M} C^A e^{-Rt} + Fe^{-RM}$$

$$V_0^b = \sum_{t=1}^{10} \$90e^{-(0.10)(t)} + \$1,000e^{-(0.10)(10)}$$

$$= \$908.82$$

It should be noted that most practitioners use interest rates with annual or semi-annual compounding. Most of our examples in this book, in turn, will follow that convention. However, continuous compounding is often used in mathematical derivations, and we will make some use of it when it is helpful.

Valuing Bonds with Maturities Less than One Year

When a bond has a maturity less than 1 year, its value can be determined by discounting the bond's cash flows by the period rate. Many bonds with maturities less than a year are *zero-coupon bonds* (also called *zeros* and *pure discount bonds*); these bonds pay no coupons and their returns are equal to the differences between their face values and their purchase prices. In valuing bonds with maturities less than 1 year, the convention is to discount by using an annualized rate instead of a period rate, and to express the bond's maturity as a proportion of a year. Thus, on March 1 a zero-coupon bond promising to pay $100 on September 1 (184 days) and trading at an annual discount rate of 8% would be worth $96.19:

$$V_0^b = \frac{\$100}{(1.08)^{184/365}} = \$96.19$$

The $96.19 bond value reflects a maturity using the actual number of days between March 1 and September 1 (184) and 365 days in the year. If we had instead assumed 30-day months and a 360-day year, then maturity expressed as a proportion of year would be 0.5 and the value of the bond would be $96.225 ($= \$100/(1.08)^{0.5}$). The choice of time measurement used in valuing bonds is known as the *day count convention*. The day count convention is defined as the way in which the ratio of the number of days to maturity (or days between dates) to the number of days in the reference period (e.g., year) is calculated. The bond value of $96.19 is based on a day count convention of actual days to maturity to actual days in the year (actual/actual), while the value of $96.225 is based on a day count convention of 180 days to maturity (30 days times six) to 360 days in the year $\left(\frac{30}{360}\right)$. For short-term US Treasury bills and other money market securities, the convention is to use actual number of days based on

a 360-day year. In this book, the day count convention will vary. In many cases, we will follow the actual/actual convention. To simplify our analysis, though, we will occasionally ignore the correct day count convention and use simpler proportions such as 0.5 to evaluate bonds.

Valuing Bonds at Non-Coupon Dates

Equations (2.2) and (2.3) can be used to value bonds at dates in which the coupons are to be paid in exactly one period. However, most bonds purchased in the secondary market are not bought on coupon dates, but rather at dates in between coupon dates. An investor who purchases a bond between coupon payments must compensate the seller for the coupon interest earned from the time of the last coupon payment to the settlement date of the bond.[1] This amount is known as *accrued interest*. The formula for determining accrued interest is:

Accrued interest

$$= \left[\frac{\text{Days from last coupon}}{\text{Days between last coupon and next coupon}}\right]$$
$$\times [\text{Coupon interest}]$$

In calculating the accrued interest, the ratio of days since the last coupon date to the days between coupon dates depends on the day count convention specified in the bond contract. For US Treasury bonds, the convention is to use the actual number of days since the last coupon date and the actual number of days between coupon payments: an actual/actual ratio; for many corporate and municipal bonds, the practice is to use 30-day months and a 360-day year: $\frac{30}{360}$ ratio.

The amount the buyer pays to the seller is the agreed-upon price plus the accrued interest. This amount is often called the *full price* or *dirty price*. The price of a bond without accrued interest is called the *clean price*:

Full price = Clean price + Accrued interest.

As an example, consider a 9% coupon bond with coupon payments made semi-annually and with a principal of $1,000 paid at maturity. Suppose the bond is trading to yield a simple annual rate of $R = 10\%$ (or effective rate of 10.25%) and has a current maturity of 5.25 years. The clean price of the bond is found by first determining the value of the bond at the next coupon date. In this case, the value of the bond at the next coupon date would be $961.39:

$$V_0^b(5 \text{ years}) = \sum_{t=1}^{(5)(2)} \frac{\$90/2}{(1 + (0.10/2))^t}$$
$$+ \frac{\$1,000}{(1 + (0.10/2))^{10}} = \$961.39$$

$$V_0^b(5 \text{ years}) = \$45 \left[\frac{1 - [1/(1.05)]^{10}}{0.05} \right]$$
$$+ \frac{\$1,000}{(1.05)^{10}} = \$961.39$$

Next, we add the $45 coupon payment scheduled to be received at that date to the $961.39 value:

$$\$961.39 + \$45 = \$1,006.39$$

The value of $1,006.39 represents the value of the bond three months from the present. Discounting this value back 3 months and using a day count convention of $\frac{30}{360}$ (3 months/6 months) yields the bond's current value of $982.14:

$$V_0^b(5.25 \text{ years}) = \frac{\$1,006.39}{(1.05)^{3/6}} = \frac{\$1,006.39}{(1.1025)^{3/12}}$$
$$= \$982.14$$

Finally, since the accrued interest of the bond at the next coupon payment goes to the seller, this amount is subtracted from the bond's value to obtain the clean price. Using again a $\frac{30}{360}$ day count convention, the accrued interest is $22.50 and the clean price is $959.64:

$$\text{Accrued interest} = \left[\frac{3 \text{ months}}{6 \text{ months}} \right] (\$45) = \$22.50$$

$$\text{Clean price} = \$982.14 - \$22.50 = \$959.64$$

Thus, the bond's full price (or dirty price) is $982.14, which is equal to its clean price of $959.64 plus the accrued interest of $22.50.

Price Quotes, Fractions, and Basis Points

While many corporate bonds pay principals of $1,000, this is not the case for many non-corporate bonds and other fixed income securities. As a result, many traders quote bond prices as a percentage of their par value. For example, if a bond is selling at par, it would be quoted at 100 (100% of par); thus, a bond with a face value of $10,000 and quoted at $80\frac{1}{8}$ would be selling at $(0.80125)(\$10,000) = \$8,012.50$. When a bond's price is quoted as a percentage of its par, the quote is usually expressed in points and fractions of a point, with each point equal to $1. Thus, a quote of 97 points means that the bond is selling for $97 for each $100 of par. The fractions of points differ among bonds. Fractions are either in thirds, eighths, quarters, halves, or 64ths. On a $100 basis, a $\frac{1}{2}$ point is $0.50 and a $\frac{1}{32}$ point is $0.03125. A price quote of $97\frac{4}{32}$ (97-4) is 97.125 for a bond with a 100 face value. Bonds expressed in 64ths usually are denoted in the financial pages with a plus sign (+); for example, 100.2+ would indicate a price of $100\frac{2}{64}$. It should also be noted that when the yield on a bond or other security changes over a short period, such as a day, the yield and subsequent price changes are usually quite small. As a result, fractions on yields are often quoted in terms of basis points (BPs). A BP is equal to $\frac{1}{100}$ of a percentage point. Thus, 6.5% may be quoted as 6% plus 50 BPs or 650 BPs, and an increase in yield from 6.5% to 6.55% would represent an increase of 5 BPs.

Exhibit 2.4 shows the *Wall Street Journal*'s listings and price quotes of US Treasury bonds and notes, T-bills, and corporate bonds offered for sale or purchase by dealers on March 4, 2003. The first box in the exhibit shows a partial listing of T-bonds and T-notes (the "n" after the maturity month signifies the instrument is a Treasury note, otherwise, the security is a Treasury bond). Bonds and notes both pay semi-annual coupon interest and principal at maturity. They differ in their maturities: Treasury bonds have original maturities greater than 10 years, while notes have original maturities less than 10 years. In the exhibit, the first two columns provide information on the rate and maturity. The rate refers to the coupon

Exhibit 2.4   Financial quotes: Treasury bonds and notes, Treasury bills, and corporate bonds

Treasury Bonds, Notes and Bills

Explanatory Notes

Representative Over-the-Counter quotation based on transactions of $1 million or more. Treasury bond, note and bill quotes are as of mid-afternoon. Colons in bid-and-asked quotes represent 32nds; 101:01 means 101 1/32. Net changes in 32nds. n-Treasury note. i-Inflation-Indexed issue. Treasury bill quotes in hundredths, quoted on terms of a rate of discount. Days to maturity calculated from settlement date. All yields are to maturity and based on the asked quote. Latest 13-week and 26-week bills are boldfaced. For bonds callable prior to maturity, yields are computed to the earliest call date for issues quoted above par and to the maturity date for issues below par. *When issued.
Source: eSpeed/Cantor Fitzgerald

U.S. Treasury strips as of 3 p.m. Eastern time, also based on transactions of $1 million or more. Colons in bid and asked quotes represent 32nds; 99:01 means 99 1/32. Net changes in 32nds. Yields calculated on the asked quotation. ci-stripped coupon interest. bp-Treasury bond, stripped principal. np-Treasury note, stripped principal. For bonds callable prior to maturity, yields are computed to the earliest call date for issues quoted above par and to the maturity date for issues below par.
Source: Bear, Stearns & Co. via Street Software Technology Inc.

Government Bonds & Notes

RATE	MATURITY MO/YR	BID	ASKED	CHG	ASK YLD	RATE	MATURITY MO/YR	BID	ASKED	CHG	ASK YLD
						14.000	Nov 11	141:21	141:22	...	2.19
4.250	Mar 03n	100:06	100:07	-1.	0.95	3.375	Jan 12i	114:05	114:06	5	1.65
5.500	Mar 03n	100:09	100:10	...	0.88	4.875	Feb 12n	110:01	110:02	7	3.55
4.000	Apr 03n	100:13	100:14	...	1.05	3.000	Jul 12i	111:04	111:05	4	1.71
5.750	Apr 03n	100:22	100:23	...	1.07	4.375	Aug 12n	106:01	106:02	7	3.61
10.750	May 03	101:28	101:29	...	0.90	4.000	Nov 12i	103:00	103:00	7	3.63
4.250	May 03n	100:23	100:24	...	1.09	10.375	Nov 12	134:01	134:02	6	2.61
5.500	May 03n	100:23	100:24	...	1.16	3.875	Feb 13n	101:27	101:28	7	3.65
3.875	Jun 03n	100:27	100:28	...	1.10	12.000	Aug 13	146:03	146:04	5	2.81
5.375	Jun 03n	101:10	101:11	-1	1.14	13.250	May 14	157:06	157:07	7	3.04
3.875	Jul 03n	101:02	101:03	-1	1.14	12.500	Aug 14	154:09	154:10	10	3.13
5.250	Aug 03n	101:26	101:27	...	1.13	11.750	Nov 14	151:03	151:04	7	3.20
5.750	Aug 03n	102:01	102:02	...	1.14	11.250	Feb 15	169:04	169:05	11	3.94
11.125	Aug 03	104:14	104:15	-1	1.14	10.625	Aug 15	164:10	164:11	10	4.01
3.625	Aug 03n	101:05	101:06	...	1.17	9.875	Nov 15	157:05	157:06	9	4.06
2.750	Sep 03n	100:28	100:29	...	1.13	9.250	Feb 16	151:07	151:08	12	4.11
2.750	Oct 03n	101:00	101:01	...	1.16	7.250	May 16	130:22	130:23	8	4.19
						7.500	Nov 16	133:19	133:20	8	4.24

Treasury Bills

MATURITY	DAYS TO MAT	BID	ASKED	CHG	ASK YLD
Mar 06 03	1	1.19	1.18	...	1.20
Mar 13 03	8	1.18	1.17	-0.01	1.19
Mar 20 03	15	1.19	1.18	...	1.20
Mar 27 03	22	1.19	1.18	...	1.20
Apr 03 03	29	1.19	1.18	0.02	1.20
Apr 10 03	36	1.16	1.15	-0.01	1.17
Apr 17 03	43	1.17	1.16	...	1.18
Apr 24 03	50	1.17	1.16	...	1.18
May 01 03	57	1.16	1.15	-0.01	1.17
May 08 03	64	1.17	1.16	...	1.18
May 15 03	71	1.17	1.16	...	1.18
May 22 03	78	1.18	1.17	-0.01	1.19
May 29 03	85	1.17	1.16	-0.01	1.18
Jun 05 03	92	1.17	1.16	-0.01	1.18
Jun 12 03	99	1.17	1.16	...	1.18
Jun 19 03	106	1.17	1.16	...	1.18
Jun 26 03	113	1.16	1.15	-0.01	1.17
Jul 03 03	120	1.17	1.16	...	1.18
Jul 10 03	127	1.16	1.15	-0.02	1.17
Jul 17 03	134	1.16	1.15	-0.01	1.18
Jul 24 03	141	1.17	1.16	-0.01	1.18
Jul 31 03	148	1.16	1.15	-0.01	1.17
Aug 07 03	155	1.17	1.16	-0.01	1.18
Aug 14 03	162	1.17	1.16	...	1.18
Aug 21 03	169	1.16	1.15	-0.01	1.17
Aug 28 03	176	1.17	1.16	-0.01	1.18
Sep 04 03	183	1.17	1.16	...	1.18

Source: *Wall Street Journal*, March 5, 2003, p. B12. Republished by permission of Dow Jones, Inc. via Copyright Clearance Center, Inc. @ 2003 Dow Jones and Company, Inc. All Rights Reserve Worldwide.

NEW YORK BONDS

Corporation Bonds

BONDS	CUR YLD	VOL	CLOSE	NET CHG
AES Cp 4½05	cv	172	61.50	-0.50
AES Cp 8s8	11.0	195	72.88	2.88
AMR 9s16	42.6	197	21.13	-0.50
AT&T 6½04	6.5	78	103.50	0.25
AT&T 5⅞04	5.5	403	102	-0.25
AT&T 6⅜04	6.2	80	103	...
AT&T 7½04	7.2	19	103.75	-0.50
AT&T 7s05	6.7	750	104.63	-1.50
AT&T 7½06	7.1	624	106	0.38
ATT 7¾07	7.3	25	105.63	...

BONDS	CUR YLD	VOL	CLOSE	NET CHG
NRurU 5.3s03	5.3	1	100.06	0.31
NETelTel 6¼03	6.3	60	100	...
NYTel 7¼24	7.0	10	103.75	0.13
NYTel 6½05	6.1	5	106.50	-1.38
NYTel 8⅞10	7.4	30	117.25	...
NYTel 6.70s23	6.7	5	100.25	-0.25
NYTel 7s33	6.8	29	103.38	...
Noram 6s12	cv	10	76	...
Nortel 4¼08	cv	8	72	2.00
OcciP 10½09	8.1	40	124.25	1.25
ParkerD 5½04	cv	85	95.75	0.50
Penney 8s10	7.7	25	104	0.50
PhilP 7¼28	6.7	35	106	0.88
ReynTob 8¾07	8.1	10	107.75	0.25
ReynTob 9¼13	8.5	26	109	...
RoyCarib zr2-21	...	17	38	-0.38
Safwy 9.65s04	9.1	68	105.50	0.50

Source: *Wall Street Journal*, March 5, 2003, p. C13. Republished by permission of Dow Jones, Inc. via Copyright Clearance Center, Inc. @ 2003 Dow Jones and Company, Inc. All Rights Reserve Worldwide.

yield, quoted as a percentage of par. Thus, the Treasury bond maturing in November 2012 is paying a coupon of $10\frac{3}{8}\%$ of its face value. Given a face value of $1,000, the annual coupon interest would be $103.75, paid in two semi-annual installments. Columns 3 and 4 show the dealer's bid and asked prices, expressed as a percentage of the face value, or equivalently, as the price of a bond with a $100 par value. The bid price is the price the dealer is willing to pay

for the bond and the asked is what she is willing to sell it for (with the latter, of course, being greater). Note that the numbers to the right of the decimals on the bid and asked prices are in 32nds and not the usual 100s. Thus, the bid price 134:01 means the dealer will pay $134\frac{1}{32}$ (or 134.03125 of par), or $1,340.31 for a face value of $1,000. After the dealer quotes comes the bid change, which is the change in the bid price from the previous day. Finally, the last column shows the T-bond's or T-note's yield to maturity. This is the average annual rate earned on the bond based on the asked price (this concept of yield to maturity is discussed in section 2.3).

The second box in exhibit 2.4 shows the listings for Treasury bills traded on March 4. US T-bills are zero-coupon bonds with maturities less than 1 year. The *Wall Street Journal's* listing includes each bill's maturity date, days to maturity, and the dealer quotes in terms of the bid yield and asked yield. The bid yield is the annualized return expressed as a percent of the par value that the dealer wants if she buys the bill. The asked yield is the rate that the dealer is offering to sell bills. Both yields are calculated as a *discount yield*. The discount yield is the annualized return specified as a proportion of the bill's par value (F):

$$\text{Annual discount yield} = R_D$$

$$= \frac{F - P_0}{F} \frac{360}{\text{Days to maturity}}$$

Given the dealer's discount yield, the bid or asked price can be obtained by solving the yield equation for the bond's price, P_0. Doing this yields:

$$P_0 = F[(1 - R_D(\text{Days to maturity}/360)]$$

Thus, on March 4, 2003, the T-bill that matures on August 7 with 155 days to maturity could have been sold to the dealer at a bid yield of 1.17 or $9,949.62 ($=$10,000 $[1 - (0.0117)$ $(155/360)]$) for a face value of $10,000 or purchased from the dealer at an asked yield of 1.16 or $9,950.05 ($=$10,000 $[1 - (0.0116)(155/360)]$), with the dealer's spread being $0.43. In looking at the bid and asked yields the reader should note that the yields are expressed as a proportion of the par value and not the current price, and that the yields are annualized on a 360-day year, instead of 365 days. The "Chg" column indicates how much the asked yield changed from the previous day. The -0.01 change in the asked discount yield is a decrease of 1 basis point.

The last panel in exhibit 2.4 shows quotations on some of the corporate bonds traded on the New York Stock Exchange. As shown, the information provided includes the bond's coupon rate, maturity, current yield, and price data. For example, the $6\frac{3}{4}$ and 04 information

on the American Telephone and Telegraph (AT&T) bond indicates an annual coupon rate of $6\frac{3}{4}\%$ and maturity year of 2004. The second number, 6.5, is the AT&T bond's current yield. As we will discuss in the next section, the *current yield* of a bond is the ratio of its annual coupon to its closing price. The 78 number shown next refers to the volume of trade on the bond that day; thus, on March 4, 2003, 78 AT&T bonds were exchanged.[2] The next number shown is the closing price of the bond. Here the AT&T bond closed at 103.5% of par ($1,035 given a par of $1,000). Finally, the net change figure number of $+0.25$ indicates AT&T's closing price is 0.25 points above its price of the previous day.

Web Information

There are a number of financial calculators available on the web. Many of these require a fee but do provide a free sample for viewing. See

  www.bondcalc.com

and

  www.derivativesmodels.com

A free calculator that can be used to calculate values and rates is provided by the US Treasury:

  www.publicdebt.treas.gov/sav/
  savcalc.htm

2.3 THE YIELD TO MATURITY AND OTHER RATES OF RETURN MEASURES

The financial markets serve as conduits through which funds are distributed from borrowers to lenders. The allocation of funds is determined by the relative rates paid on bonds, loans, and other financial securities, with the differences in rates among claims being determined by risk, maturity, and other factors that serve to differentiate the claims. There are a number of different measures of the rates of return on bonds and loans. Some measures, for example, determine annual rates based on cash flows received over 365 days, while others use 360 days;

some measures determine rates that include the compounding of cash flows, while some do not; and some measures include capital gains and losses, while others exclude price changes. In this section, we examine some of the measures of rates of return, including the most common measure – the yield to maturity, and in sections 2.4, 2.5, and 2.6 we look at three other important rate measures – the spot rate, the annual realized return, and the geometric mean.

2.3.1 Common Measures of Rates of Return

When the term rate of return is used it can mean a number of different rates, including the interest rate, coupon rate, current yield, or discount yield. The term *interest rate* is sometimes referred to as the price a borrower pays a lender for a loan. Unlike other prices, this price of credit is expressed as the ratio of the cost or fee for borrowing and the amount borrowed. This price is typically expressed as an annual percentage of the loan (even if the loan is for less than 1 year). Today, financial economists often refer to the yield to maturity on a bond as the interest rate. In this book, the term interest rate will mean yield to maturity.

Another measure of rate of return is a bond's *coupon rate*. As noted in the last section, the coupon rate, C^R, is the contractual rate the issuer agrees to pay each period. It is usually expressed as a proportion of the annual coupon payment to the bond's face value:

$$C^R = \frac{\text{Annual coupon}}{F}$$

Unless the bond is purchased at par, the coupon rate is not a good measure of the bond's rate of return, since it fails to take into account the price paid for the bond.

As we just noted in examining corporate bond quotes, the current yield on a bond is computed as the ratio of the bond's annual coupon to its current price. This measure provides a quick estimate of a bond's rate of return, but in many cases not an accurate one since it does not capture price changes. The current yield is a good approximation to the bond's yield, if the bond's price is selling at or

near its face value or if it has a long maturity. That is, we noted earlier that if a bond is selling at par, its coupon rate is equal to the discount rate. In this case, the current yield is equal to the bond's yield to maturity. Thus, the closer the bond's price is to its face value, the closer the current yield is to the bond's yield to maturity. As for maturity, note that a coupon bond with no maturity or repayment of principal, known as a *perpetuity* or *consul*, pays a fixed amount of coupons forever. The value of such a bond is

$$V_0^b = \frac{C}{R}$$

If the bond is priced in the market to equal V_0^b, then the rate on the bond would be equal to the current yield: $R = C/V_0^b$. When a coupon bond has a long-term maturity (e.g., 20 years), then it is similar to a perpetuity and its current yield is a good approximation of its rate of return.

Finally, the discount yield is the bond's return expressed as a proportion of its face value. For example, a 1-year pure discount bond costing \$900 and paying a par value of \$1,000 yields \$100 in interest and a discount yield of 10%:

$$\text{Discount yield} = \frac{F - P_0}{F} = \frac{\$100}{\$1,000} = 0.10$$

The discount yield used to be the rate quoted by financial institutions on their loans (since the discount rate is lower than a rate quoted on the borrowed amount). The difficulty with this rate measure is that it does not capture the conceptual notion of the rate of return being the rate at which the investment grows. In this example, the \$900 bond investment grew at a rate of over 11%, not 10%:

$$\frac{F - P_0}{P_0} = \frac{\$100}{\$900} = 0.111$$

Because of tradition, the rates on Treasury bills are quoted by dealers in terms of the bills' discount yield. Since Treasury bills have maturities of less than 1 year, the discount yields are quoted on an annualized basis. As we noted in the last section, dealers quoting the annualized rates use a day count convention of actual days to maturity but with a 360-day year:

$$\text{Annual discount yield} = \frac{F - P_0}{F} \frac{360}{\text{Days to maturity}}$$

2.3.2 Yield to Maturity

The most widely used measure of a bond's rate of return is the *yield to maturity (YTM)*. As noted earlier, the YTM, or simply the yield, is the rate that equates the purchase price of the bond, P_0^b, with the present value of its future cash flows (CFs). Mathematically, the YTM is found by solving the following equation for y (YTM):

$$P_0^b = \sum_{t=1}^{M} \frac{CF_t}{(1+y)^t} \tag{2.4}$$

The YTM is analogous to the internal rate of return used in capital budgeting. It is a measure of the rate at which the investment grows. From our first example, if the 10-year, 9% annual coupon bond were actually trading in the market for $938.55, then the YTM on the bond would be 10%. Unlike the current yield, the YTM incorporates all of the bond's cash flows. It also assumes the bond is held to maturity and that all CFs from the bond are reinvested to maturity at the calculated YTM.

Estimating YTM: Average Rate to Maturity

If the cash flows on the bond (coupons and principal) are not equal, then equation (2.4) cannot be solved directly for the YTM. Alternatively, one must use an iterative (trial and error) procedure: substituting different y values into equation (2.4), until that y is found that equates the present value of the bond's cash flows to the market price. An estimate of the YTM, however, can be found using the bond's *average rate to maturity, ARTM* (also referred to as the *yield approximation formula*). This measure determines the rate as the average return per year as a proportion of the average price of the bond per year. For a coupon bond with a principal paid at maturity, the average return per year on the bond is its annual coupon

plus its average annual capital gain. For a bond with an M-year maturity, its average gain is calculated as the total capital gain realized at maturity divided by the number of years to maturity: $(F - P_0^b)/M$. The average price of the bond is computed as the average of two known prices, the current price and the price at maturity (F): $(F + P_0^b)/2$. Thus the ARTM is:

$$\text{ARTM} = \frac{C + [(F - P_0^b)/M]}{(F + P_0^b)/2} \tag{2.5}$$

The ARTM for the 9%, 10-year bond trading at $938.55 is 0.0992:

$$\text{ARTM} = \frac{\$90 + [(\$1,000 - \$938.55)/10]}{(\$1,000 + \$938.55)/2}$$

$$= 0.0992$$

2.3.3 Bond-Equivalent Yields

The YTM calculated above represents the yield for the period (in the above example this was an annual rate, given annual coupons). If a bond's CFs were semi-annual, then solving equation (2.4) for y would yield a 6-month rate; if the CFs were monthly, then solving (2.4) for y would yield a monthly rate. To obtain a *simple annualized rate* (with no compounding), y^A, one needs to multiply the periodic rate, y, by the number of periods in the year. Thus, if a 10-year bond paying $45 every 6 months and $1,000 at maturity were selling for $937.69, its 6-month yield would be 0.05 and its simple annualized rate, y^A, would be 10%:

$$\$937.69 = \sum_{t=1}^{20} \frac{\$45}{(1+y)^t} + \frac{\$1,000}{(1+y)^{20}} \Rightarrow y = 0.05$$

$$y^A = \text{Simple annualized rate} = (n)(y)$$
$$= (2)(0.05) = 0.10$$

In this example, the simple annualized rate is obtained by determining the periodic rate on a bond paying coupons semi-annually and then multiplying by two. Since Treasury bonds and many corporate bonds pay coupons semi-annually, the rate obtained by multiplying the semi-annual periodic rate by two is called the *bond-equivalent yield*. Bonds with different payment frequencies often have their rates expressed in terms of their bond-equivalent yield so that their rates can be compared to each other on a common basis. This bond-equivalent yield, though, does not take into account the reinvestment of the bond's cash flows during the year. Therefore, it underestimates the actual rate of return earned. Thus, an investor earning 5% semi-annually would have $1.05 after 6 months from a $1 investment that she can reinvest for the next 6 months. If she reinvests at 5%, then her annual rate would be 10.25% $(= (1.05)(1.05) - 1 = (1.05)^2 - 1)$, not 10%. As noted earlier, the 10.25% annual rate, which takes into account compounding, is known as the effective rate.

2.3.4 Holding Period Yields

The YTM measures the rate of return earned for an investor who holds the security to maturity. For investors who plan to hold the security for a period less than the maturity period, for example holding it for a period of length K (where $K < M$) and then selling the security at a price of P_K, the yield they obtain is referred to as the holding period yield, HPY. The HPY is found by solving the following equation for y:

$$P_0^b = \sum_{t=1}^{K} \frac{CF_t}{(1+y)^t} + \frac{P_K^b}{(1+y)^K} \qquad (2.6)$$

For just one period, the HPY is found by solving for y where:

$$P_0^b = \frac{CF_1 + P_K^b}{(1+y)^1} \qquad (2.7)$$

Here, y can be found algebraically by solving equation (2.7) for y. That is:

$$HPY = y = \frac{CF_1 + (P_K^b - P_0^b)}{P_0^b} = \frac{CF_1 + P_K^b}{P_0^b} - 1$$

$$\qquad (2.8)$$

2.3.5 Yield to Call

Many bonds have a call feature that allows the issuer to buy back the bond at a specific price known as the call price. (Call features and other option features will be discussed in some detail in chapters 4 and 9.) Given a bond with call option, the *yield to call* (*YTC*) is the rate obtained by assuming the bond is called on the first call date. Like the YTM, the YTC is found by solving for the rate that equates the present value of the CFs to the market price:

$$P_0^b = \sum_{t=1}^{CD} \frac{CF_t}{(1+y)^t} + \frac{CP}{(1+y)^{CD}}$$

where CP is the call price and CD is the call date. Thus, a 10-year, 9% coupon bond first callable in 5 years at a call price of $1,100, paying interest semi-annually, and trading at $937.69, would have a YTM of 10% and a YTC of 12.2115%:

$$\$937.69 = \sum_{t=1}^{10} \frac{\$45}{(1+y)^t} + \frac{\$1,100}{(1+y)^{10}} \Rightarrow YTC$$

$$= 0.0610575$$

Simple annualized YTC $= (2)(0.0610575)$

$$= 0.122115$$

Many investors calculate the YTC for each possible call date, as well as the YTM. They then select the lowest of the yields as their yield return measure. The lowest yield is sometimes referred to as the *yield to worst*.

2.3.6 Bond Portfolio Yields

The yield for a portfolio of bonds is found by solving the rate that will make the present value of the portfolio's cash flow equal to the market value of the portfolio. For example, a portfolio consisting of a 2-year, 5% annual coupon bond priced at par (100) and a 3-year, 10% annual coupon bond priced at 107.87 to yield 7% (YTM) would generate a 3-year cash flow of $15, $115, and $110 and would have a portfolio market value of $207.87. The rate that equates this portfolio's cash flow to its portfolio value is 6.2%. That is:

$$\$207.87 = \frac{\$15}{(1+y)^1} + \frac{\$115}{(1+y)^2} + \frac{\$110}{(1+y)^3} \Rightarrow y = 6.2\%$$

Note that this yield is not the weighted average of the YTM of the bonds comprising the portfolio. In this example, the weighted average (R_p) is 6.04%:

$$R_p = w_1(\text{YTM}_1) + w_2(\text{YTM}_2)$$

$$R_p = \left[\frac{\$100}{\$207.87}\right](0.05) + \left[\frac{\$107.87}{\$207.87}\right](0.07)$$

$$= 0.0604$$

Thus, the yield for a portfolio of bonds is not simply the average of the YTMs of the bonds making up the portfolio.

2.4 RATES ON ZERO-COUPON BONDS: SPOT RATES

2.4.1 Formula for the Rate on Pure Discount Bonds

While no algebraic solution for the YTM exists when a bond pays coupons and principal that are not equal, a solution does exist in the case of a zero-coupon bond or pure discount bond, PDBs (we will use both expressions), in which there is only one cash flow (F). That is:

$$P_0^b = \frac{F}{(1 + \text{YTM}_M)^M}$$

$$(1 + \text{YTM}_M)^M = \frac{F}{P_0^b} \qquad (2.9)$$

$$\text{YTM}_M = \left[\frac{F}{P_0^b}\right]^{1/M} - 1$$

where M is the maturity in years. Thus, a pure discount bond with a par value of $1,000, a maturity of 3 years, and trading for $800 would have an annualized YTM of 7.72%:

$$\text{YTM}_3 = \left[\frac{\$1,000}{\$800}\right]^{1/3} - 1 = 0.0772$$

Similarly, a pure discount bond paying $100 at the end of 182 days and trading at $96 would yield an annual rate using a 365-day year of 8.53%:

$$\text{YTM} = \left[\frac{\$100}{\$96}\right]^{365/182} - 1 = 0.0853$$

2.4.2 Rate on Pure Discount Bond with Continuous Compounding

Using the properties of logarithms (see appendix A at the end of the book for a primer on logarithms), the rate on a pure discount bond with continuous compounding is:

$$P_0^b e^{Rt} = F$$

$$e^{Rt} = \frac{F}{P_0^b}$$

$$\ln(e^{Rt}) = \ln\left[\frac{F}{P_0^b}\right]$$

$$Rt = \ln\left[\frac{F}{P_0^b}\right]$$

$$R = \frac{\ln[F/P_0^b]}{t}$$

A pure discount bond selling for $96 and paying $100 at the end of 182 days would yield an annual rate of 8.1868% with continuous compounding:

$$R = \frac{\ln[\$100/\$96]}{182/365} = 0.081868$$

When the rate of return on a security is expressed as the natural log of the ratio of its end of the period value to its current value, the rate is referred to as the *logarithmic return*. Thus, a bond currently priced at $96 and expected to be worth $100 at the end of the period would have an expected logarithmic return of 4.082%: $R = \ln(\$100/\$96) = 0.04082$

It should be noted that the rate on a pure discount bond is called the *spot rate*. As we will see next, spot rates are important in determining a bond's equilibrium price.

2.4.3 Spot Rates and Equilibrium Prices

We previously examined how bonds are valued by discounting their cash flows at a common discount rate. However, given different spot rates on similar bonds with different maturities, the correct approach to valuing a bond is to price it by discounting each of the bond's cash flows, CFs, by the appropriate spot rates for that period (S_t). Theoretically, if the market does not price a bond with spot rates, arbitrageurs would be able to realize a risk-free return by buying the bond and stripping it into a number of pure discount bonds (chapter 6 discusses strip securities), or by buying strip bonds and bundling them into a coupon bond to sell. Thus, in the absence of arbitrage, the *equilibrium price* of a bond is determined by discounting each of its CFs by their appropriate spot rates.

To illustrate this relationship, suppose there are three risk-free pure discount bonds, each with principals of $100 and trading at annualized spot rates of $S_1 = 7\%$, $S_2 = 8\%$, and $S_3 = 9\%$, respectively. If we discount the CF of a 3-year, 8% annual coupon bond paying a principal of $100 at maturity at these spot rates, its equilibrium price, P_0^*, would be $97.73:

$$P_0^* = \frac{C_1}{(1+S_1)^1} + \frac{C_2}{(1+S_2)^2} + \frac{C_3+F}{(1+S_3)^3}$$

$$P_0^* = \frac{\$8}{(1.07)^1} + \frac{\$8}{(1.08)^2} + \frac{\$108}{(1.09)^3} = \$97.73$$

Suppose this coupon bond were trading in the market at a price (P_0^M) of $95 to yield 10%:

$$P_0^M = \sum_{t=1}^{3} \frac{\$8}{(1.10)^t} + \frac{\$100}{(1.10)^3} = \$95$$

At the price of $95, an arbitrageur could buy the bond, then strip it into three risk-free pure discount bonds: a 1-year pure discount bond paying $8 at maturity, a 2-year pure discount bond paying $8 at maturity, and a 3-year pure discount bond paying $108 at maturity. If the arbitrageur could sell the bonds at their appropriate spot rates, she would be able to realize a cash flow from the sale of $97.73 and a risk-free profit of $2.73 (see exhibit 2.5). Given this risk-free opportunity, this arbitrageur, as well as others, would implement this strategy of buying and stripping the bond until the price of the coupon bond was bid up to equal its equilibrium price of $97.73.

On the other hand, if the 8% coupon bond were trading above its equilibrium price of $97.73, then arbitrageurs could profit by reversing the above strategy. For example, if the coupon bond were trading at $100, then arbitrageurs would be able to go into the market and buy proportions (assuming perfect divisibility) of the three risk-free pure discount bonds (8% of bond 1, 8% of bond 2, and 108%

Exhibit 2.5 Equilibrium bond price: arbitrage when bond is underpriced

Market price of 3-year, 8% coupon bond = 95.
Arbitrage:
  Buy the bond for 95.
  Sell three stripped PDBs:
  1-year PDB with $F = 8$: $P_0 = \dfrac{8}{1.07} = 7.47$

  2-year PDB with $F = 8$: $P_0 = \dfrac{8}{(1.08)^2} = 6.86$

  3-year PDB with $F = 108$: $P_0 = \dfrac{108}{(1.09)^3}$

       $= 83.40$
Sale of stripped bonds = $97.73.
$\pi = 97.73 - 95 = 2.73$.

Exhibit 2.6 Equilibrium bond price: arbitrage when bond is overpriced

Market price of 3-year, 8% coupon bond = 100.
Arbitrage:
  Buy 3 PDBs:
  8% of 1-year PDB with $F = 100$: cost =
  $(0.08)\dfrac{100}{1.07} = 7.47$

  8% of 2-year PDB with $F = 100$: cost =
  $(0.08)\dfrac{100}{(1.08)^2} = 6.86$

  108% of 3-year PDB with $F = 100$: cost =
  $(1.08)\dfrac{100}{(1.09)^3} = 83.40$

  Cost $= 7.47 + 6.86 + 83.40 = 97.73$
  Bundle the bonds and sell them as a 3-year, 9% coupon bond for 100.
  $\pi = 100 - 97.73 = 2.27$.

of bond 3) at a cost of $97.73, bundle them into one 3-year, 8% coupon bond to be sold at $100. As shown in exhibit 2.6, this strategy would result in a risk-free profit of $2.27.

2.4.4 Estimating Spot Rates: Bootstrapping

Many investment companies use spot rates to value bonds, and there are a number of securities that have been created by arbitrageurs

Exhibit 2.7   Generating spot rates using bootstrapping

Maturity	Annual coupon	F	P_0^b
1 year	7%	100	100
2 years	8%	100	100
3 years	9%	100	100

S_1
$$100 = \frac{107}{1 + S_1} \Rightarrow S_1 = \left[\frac{107}{100}\right] - 1 = 0.07$$

S_2
$$100 = \frac{8}{1.07} + \frac{108}{(1 + S_2)^2}$$

$$95.52 = \frac{108}{(1 + S_2)^2} \Rightarrow S_2 = \left[\frac{108}{95.52}\right]^{1/2} - 1$$
$$= 0.08042$$

S_3
$$100 = \frac{9}{1.07} + \frac{9}{(1.08042)^2} + \frac{109}{(1 + S_3)^3}$$

$$83.88 = \frac{109}{(1 + S_3)^3} \Rightarrow S_3 = \left[\frac{109}{83.88}\right]^{1/3} - 1$$
$$= 0.0912$$

purchasing bonds valued at rates different than the spot rates, stripping the securities, and then selling them. One problem in valuing bonds with spot rates or in creating stripped securities is that there are not enough longer term pure discount bonds available to determine the spot rates on higher maturities. As a result, long-term spot rates have to be estimated.

One estimating approach that can be used is a sequential process commonly referred to as *bootstrapping*. This approach requires having at least one pure discount bond, such as a Treasury bill. Given this bond's rate, a coupon bond with the next highest maturity is used to obtain an implied spot rate; then another coupon bond with the next highest maturity is used to find the next spot rates, and so on. As an example, consider the three risk-free bonds in exhibit 2.7. Bond 1 is a 1-year pure discount bond selling at $100 and paying $107 at maturity. The 1-year spot rate using this bond is 7%:

$$\$100 = \frac{\$107}{(1 + S_1)^1}$$

$$S_1 = \frac{\$107}{\$100} - 1 = 0.07$$

Bond 2 is an 8% annual coupon bond selling at par to yield 8% (YTM = 8%). The spot rate on a 2-year risk-free bond can be determined by setting this bond's price ($P_0^b = \$100$) equal to the equation for its equilibrium price, P_0^* (price obtained by discounting CFs by spot rates), and then solving the resulting equation for the 2-year spot rate (S_2). Doing this yields a 2-year spot rate of 8.042%:

$$P_0^b = \frac{CF_1}{(1 + S_1)^1} + \frac{CF_2}{(1 + S_2)^2}$$

$$\$100 = \frac{\$8}{(1.07)^1} + \frac{\$108}{(1 + S_2)^2}$$

$$\$100 = \$7.48 + \frac{\$108}{(1 + S_2)^2}$$

$$\$92.52 = \frac{\$108}{(1 + S_2)^2}$$

$$S_2 = \left[\frac{\$108}{\$92.52}\right]^{1/2} - 1 = 0.08042$$

Finally, given 1-year and 2-year spot rates, the 3-year spot rate can be found by setting the price of the 3-year coupon bond equal to its equilibrium price, and then solving the resulting equation for S_3. Doing this yields a 3-year spot rate of 9.12%:

$$P_0^b = \frac{CF_1}{(1 + S_1)^1} + \frac{CF_2}{(1 + S_2)^2} + \frac{CF_3}{(1 + S_3)^3}$$

$$\$100 = \frac{\$9}{(1.07)^1} + \frac{\$9}{(1.08042)^2} + \frac{\$109}{(1 + S_3)^3}$$

$$\$83.88 = \frac{\$109}{(1 + S_3)^3}$$

$$S_3 = \left[\frac{\$109}{\$83.88}\right]^{1/3} - 1 = 0.0912$$

It should be noted that the equilibrium prices of other 1-, 2-, or 3-year bonds can be obtained using these spot rates. For example, the equilibrium price of a risk-free, 3-year, 10% annual coupon would be $102.57:[3]

$$P_0^* = \frac{\$10}{(1.07)^1} + \frac{\$10}{(1.08042)^2} + \frac{\$110}{(1.0912)^3} = \$102.57$$

Exhibit 2.8 Annual realized return (ARR)

Example: You buy a 4-year, 10% annual coupon bond at par ($F = 1,000$). *Assuming* you can reinvest CFs at 10%, your ARR would be 10% given an HD = 3 years:

```
0    1    2    3 = HD                          → Assumption
     100  ────→ 100 (1.10)²  =  121            →Assumption
          100 → 100 (1.10)   =  110
               100 + 1,000   = 1,100
                               1,331
```

$$P_3^b = \frac{1,000 + 100}{(1.10)^1} = 1,000$$

Assumption

$$ARR = \left[\frac{HD\,value}{P_0^b}\right]^{1/HD} - 1 = \left[\frac{1,331}{1,000}\right]^{1/3} - 1 = 0.10$$

2.5 ANNUAL REALIZED RETURN

Equation (2.9) provides the formula for finding the YTM for pure discount bonds. A useful extension of equation (2.9) is the *annual realized return, ARR* (also called the *average realized return* and the *total return*). The ARR is the annual rate earned on a bond for the period from when the bond is bought to when it is converted to cash (which could be either maturity or a date prior to maturity if the bond is sold), with the assumption that all coupons paid on the bond are reinvested to that date. The ARR is computed by first determining the investor's horizon date, HD, defined as the date the investor needs cash; next finding the HD value, defined as the total funds the investor would have at his HD; and third, solving for the ARR using a formula similar to equation (2.9).

To illustrate, suppose an investor buys a 4-year, 10% annual coupon bond selling at its par value of $1,000. Assume the investor needs cash at the end of year 3 (HD = 3), is certain he can reinvest the coupons during the period in securities yielding 10%, and expects to sell the bond at his HD at a rate of 10%. To determine the investor's ARR, we first need to find the HD value. This value is equal to the price the investor obtains from selling the bond and the value of the coupons at the HD. In this case, the investor, at his HD, will be able to sell a 1-year bond paying a $100 coupon and a $1,000 par at maturity for $1,000, given the assumed discount rate of 10%. That is:

$$P_0^b = \frac{\$100 + \$1,000}{(1.10)^1} = \$1,000$$

Also at the HD, the $100 coupon paid at the end of the first year will be worth $121, given the assumption it can be reinvested at 10% for 2 years, $100(1.10)^2 = $121, and the $100 received at the end of year 2 will, in turn, be worth $110 in cash at the HD, $100(1.10) = $110. Finally, at the HD the investor would receive his third coupon of $100. Combined, the investor would have $1,331 in cash at the HD: HD value = $1,331 (see exhibit 2.8). Note that if the rates coupons can be reinvested are the same (as assumed in this example), then the coupon values at the horizon date would be equal to the period coupon times the future value of an annuity of $\$(FVIF_a)$. Coupon value at HD:

$$\text{Value} = \sum_{t=0}^{HD-1} C(1+R)^t$$

$$\text{Value} = C \sum_{t=0}^{HD-1} (1+R)^t$$

$$\text{Value} = C\,FVIF_a$$

$$\text{Value} = C \left[\frac{(1+R)^{HD} - 1}{R} \right]$$

$$\text{Value} = \$100 \left[\frac{(1.10)^3 - 1}{0.10} \right] = \$331$$

Given the HD value of $1,331, the ARR is found in the same way as the YTM for a pure discount bond. In this case, a $1,000 investment in a bond yielding $1,331 at the end of year 3 yields an ARR of 10%:

$$P_0^b = \frac{\text{HD value}}{(1+ARR)^{HD}}$$

$$(1+ARR)^{HD} = \frac{\text{HD value}}{P_0^b}$$

$$ARR = \left[\frac{\text{HD value}}{P_0^b} \right]^{1/HD} - 1 \quad (2.10)$$

$$ARR = \left[\frac{\$1,331}{\$1,000} \right]^{1/3} - 1$$

$$= 0.10$$

Equation (2.10) provides the general formula for computing the ARR. In the above example, the ARR is 10%, which is the same rate at which the bond was purchased (i.e., a 10% coupon bond, selling at par, yields a YTM of 10%). In this case, obtaining an ARR equal to the initial YTM should not be surprising since the coupons are assumed to be reinvested at the same rate as the initial YTM (10%) and the bond is also assumed to be sold at that rate (recall, the YTM measure implicitly assumes that all coupons are reinvested at the calculated YTM). If the coupons were expected to be reinvested at different rates or the bond sold at a different YTM, then an ARR equal to the initial YTM would not have been realized. Such differences, in turn, can be explained in

terms of market risk; this type of bond risk is discussed in more detail in chapter 4. Also note that the ARR can be applied to any period. For example, if the 4-year bond purchased by the investor made semi-annual payments and the 6-month yield were at 5% (a simple annual yield of 10% and an effective annual yield of 10.25% $(=(1.05)^2 - 1)$), then the investor's coupon value, price, and HD value at his HD would respectively be $340.10, $1,000, and $1,340.10:

$$\text{Coupon value} = \sum_{t=0}^{6-1} \$50\,(1.05)^t$$

$$= \$50 \left[\frac{(1.05)^6 - 1}{0.05} \right] = \$340.10$$

$$\text{Price} = \sum_{t=1}^{6} \frac{\$50}{(1.05)^t} + \frac{\$1,000}{(1.05)^6}$$

$$= \$50 \left[\frac{1 - (1/(1.05)^6)}{0.05} \right] + \frac{\$1,000}{(1.05)^6}$$

$$= \$1,000$$

$$\text{HD value} = \$340.10 + \$1,000 = \$1,340.10$$

The investor's semi-annual rate of return would be 5%. Multiplying this rate by two would yield a simple annual rate of 10%:

Semi-annual realized return

$$= \left[\frac{\$1,340.10}{\$1,000} \right]^{1/6} - 1 = 0.05$$

$$ARR = 2\left[\left[\frac{\$1,340.10}{\$1,000} \right]^{1/6} - 1 \right] = 0.10$$

2.6 GEOMETRIC MEAN

Another useful measure of the return on a bond is its *geometric mean*. Conceptually, the geometric mean can be viewed as an average of current and future rates. To see this, consider one of our previous examples in which we computed a YTM of 7.72% for a pure discount bond selling for $800 and paying $1,000 at the end of year 3. The rate of 7.72% represents the annual rate at which $800 must grow to be worth $1,000 at the end of 3 years. If we do not restrict ourselves to the same rate in each year, there are other ways $800 could grow to equal $1,000 at the end of 3 years. For example, suppose 1-year bonds are currently trading at a 10% rate, a 1-year bond purchased 1 year from the present is expected to yield 8% ($R_{Mt} = R_{11} = 8\%$), and a 1-year bond to be purchased 2 years from the present is expected to be 5.219% ($R_{Mt} = R_{12} = 5.219\%$). With these rates, $800 would grow to $1,000 at the end of year 3. Specifically, $800 after the first year would be $880 = $800(1.10), after the second, $950.40 = $800(1.10)(1.08), and after the third, $1,000 = $800(1.10)(1.08)(1.05219). Thus, an investment of $800 that yielded $1,000 at the end of 3 years could be thought of as an investment that yielded 10% the first year, 8% the second, and 5.219% the third. Moreover, 7.72% can be viewed not only as the annual rate in which $800 can grow to equal $1,000, but also as the average of three rates: 1-year bonds today ($R_{Mt} = R_{10}$), 1-year bonds available 1 year from the present ($R_{Mt} = R_{11}$), and 1-year bonds available 2 years from the present ($R_{Mt} = R_{12}$). That is:

$$P_0^b (1 + \text{YTM}_M)^M = F$$
$$= P_0^b [(1 + \text{YTM}_1)(1 + R_{11})(1 + R_{12})$$
$$\times (1 + R_{13}) \dots (1 + R_{1,M-1})]$$

$$(1 + \text{YTM}_M)^M = \frac{F}{P_0^b}$$
$$= [(1 + \text{YTM}_1)(1 + R_{11})(1 + R_{12})$$
$$\times (1 + R_{13}) \dots (1 + R_{1,M-1})] \qquad (2.11)$$

$$(1.0772)^3 = \frac{\$1,000}{\$800} = [(1.10)(1.08)(1.05219)]$$

Mathematically, the expression for the average rate on an M-year bond in terms of today's and future 1-year rates can be found by solving equation (2.11) for YTM_M. This yields:

$$\text{YTM}_M = [(1 + \text{YTM}_1)(1 + R_{11})$$
$$\times (1 + R_{12})(1 + R_{13}) \dots$$
$$\times (1 + R_{1,M-1})]^{1/M} - 1 \qquad (2.12)$$
$$\text{YTM}_3 = [(1.10)(1.08)(1.05219)]^{1/3} - 1$$
$$= 0.0772$$

Equation (2.12) defines the rate of return on an M-year bond in terms of rates that are expected in the future. A more practical rate than an expected rate, though, is the implied forward rate.

2.6.1 Implied Forward Rate

An *implied forward rate*, f_{Mt}, is a future rate of return implied by the present interest rate structure. This rate can be attained by going long and short in current bonds. To see this, suppose the rate on a 1-year, pure discount bond is 10% (i.e., spot rate is $S_1 = 10\%$) and the rate on a similar 2-year pure discount bond is $S_2 = 9\%$. Knowing today's rates we could solve for f_{11} in the equation below to determine the implied forward rate. That is:

$$S_2 = [(1 + S_1)(1 + f_{11})]^{1/2} - 1$$
$$f_{11} = \frac{(1 + S_2)^2}{(1 + S_1)} - 1$$
$$f_{11} = \frac{(1.09)^2}{(1.10)} - 1 = 0.08$$

With 1-year and 2-year pure discount bonds presently trading at 9% and 10%, respectively, the rate implied on 1-year bonds to be bought 1 year from the present is 8%. This 8% rate, though, is simply an algebraic result. This rate actually can be attained, however, by implementing the following locking-in strategy:

1. Sell the 1-year pure discount bond short (or borrow an equivalent amount of funds at the 1-year pure discount bond (spot) rate).
2. Use the cash funds from the short sale (or loan) to buy a multiple of the 2-year pure discount bond.
3. Cover the short sale (or pay the loan principal and interest) at the end of the first year.
4. Collect on the maturing 2-year bond at the end of the second year.

In terms of the above example, the 8% implied forward rate is obtained by:

1. Executing a short sale by borrowing the 1-year bond and selling it at its market price of

$909.09 = \$1,000/1.10$ (or borrowing \$909.09 at 10%).

2. With 2-year bonds trading at $\$841.68 = \$1,000/(1.09)^2$, buy $\$909.09/\$841.68 = 1.08$ issues of the 2-year bond.

3. At the end of the first year cover the short sale by paying the holder of the 1-year bond his principal of \$1,000 (or repay loan).

4. At the end of the second year receive the principal on the maturing 2-year bond issues of $(1.08)(\$1,000) = \$1,080$.

With this locking-in strategy the investor does not make a cash investment until the end of the first year when he covers the short sale; in the present, the investor simply initiates the strategy. Thus, the investment of \$1,000 is made at the end of the first year. In turn, the return on the investment is the principal payment of \$1,080 on the 1.08 holdings of the 2-year bonds that comes 1 year after the investment is made. Moreover, the rate of return on this 1-year investment is 8% $((\$1,080 - \$1,000)/\$1,000)$. Hence, by using a locking-in strategy, an 8% rate of return on a 1-year investment to be made 1 year in the future is attained, with the rate being the same rate obtained by solving algebraically for f_{11}.[4]

Given the concept of implied forward rates, the geometric mean now can be formally defined as the geometric average of the current 1-year spot rate and the implied forward rates. That is:

$$YTM_M = [(1 + YTM_1)(1 + f_{11})(1 + f_{12})$$
$$\times (1 + f_{13}) \ldots (1 + f_{1,M-1})]^{1/M} - 1$$
$$(2.13)$$

Two points regarding the geometric mean should be noted. First, the geometric mean is not limited to 1-year rates. That is, just as 7.72% can be thought of as an average of three 1-year rates of 10%, 8% and 5.219%, an implied rate on a 2-year bond purchased at the end of 1 year, $f_{Mt} = f_{21}$, can be thought of as the average of 1-year implied rates purchased 1 and 2 years, respectively, from now. Accordingly, the geometric mean could incorporate an implied 2-year bond by substituting $(1 + f_{21})^2$ for $(1 + f_{11})(1 + f_{12})$ in equation (2.13). Similarly, to incorporate a 2-year bond purchased in

the present period and yielding YTM_2, one would substitute $(1 + YTM_2)^2$ for $(1 + YTM_1)$ $(1 + f_{11})$. Thus:

$$YTM_3 = [(1 + YTM_1)(1 + f_{11})(1 + f_{12})]^{1/3} - 1$$
$$YTM_3 = [(1 + YTM_1)(1 + f_{21})^2]^{1/3} - 1$$
$$YTM_3 = [(1 + YTM_2)^2(1 + f_{12})]^{1/3} - 1$$

Second, note that for bonds with maturities of less than 1 year, the same general formula for the geometric mean applies. For example, the annualized YTM on a pure discount bond maturing in 182 days (YTM_{182}) is equal to the geometric average of a current 91-day bond's annualized rate (YTM_{91}) and the annualized implied forward rate on a 91-day investment made 91 days from the present, $f_{91,91}$:

$$YTM_{182} = \left[(1 + YTM_{91})^{91/365}\right.$$
$$\left. \times (1 + f_{91,91})^{91/365}\right]^{365/182} - 1$$

Thus, if a 182-day pure discount bond were trading at $P_0^b(182) = \$97$ (assume F of \$100) and a comparable 91-day bond were at $P_0^b(91) = 98.35$, then the implied forward rate on a 91-day bond purchased 91 days later would be 5.7%. That is:

$$YTM_{182} = \left[\frac{100}{97}\right]^{365/182} - 1 = 0.063$$

$$YTM_{91} = \left[\frac{100}{98.35}\right]^{365/91} - 1 = 0.069$$

$$f_{91,912} = \left[\frac{(1 + YTM_{182})^{182/365}}{(1 + YTM_{91})^{91/365}}\right]^{365/91} - 1$$

$$f_{91,912} = \left[\frac{(1.063)^{182/365}}{(1.069)^{91/365}}\right]^{365/91} - 1 = 0.057$$

2.6.2 Usefulness of the Geometric Mean

One of the practical uses of the geometric mean is in comparing investments in bonds with different maturities. For example, if the present interest rate structure for pure discount bonds were such that 2-year bonds were providing an average annual rate of 9% and 1-year bonds were at 10%, then the implied forward rate on a 1-year bond, 1 year from now would be 8%. With these rates, an investor could equate an investment in the 2-year bond at 9% as being equivalent to an investment in a 1-year bond today at 10% and a 1-year investment to be made 1 year later yielding 8% (possibly through a locking-in strategy). Accordingly, if the investor knew with certainty that 1-year bonds at the end of 1 year would be trading at 9% (a rate higher than the implied forward rate), then he would prefer an investment in the series of 1-year bonds over the 2-year bond. That is, by investing in a 1-year bond today and a 1-year bond 1 year from now the investor would obtain 10% and 9%, respectively, for an average annual rate on the 2-year investment of 9.5%; specifically:

Series equivalent YTM$_2$

$$= [(1 + \text{YTM}_1)(1 + \text{Expected spot rate})]^{1/2} - 1$$

Series equivalent YTM$_2$

$$= [(1.10)(1.09)]^{1/2} - 1 = 0.095$$

This, of course, exceeds the 9% average annual rate the investor would obtain if he bought the 2-year bond; thus in this case, the series of 1-year bonds represents the better investment. In contrast, if the investor expected with certainty that, at the end of 1 year, 1-year bonds would be trading at 6% (a rate below the implied forward rate), then a series of 1-year bonds at 10% and 6% would yield a 2-year average annual rate of only 8% (equivalent YTM$_2 = [(1.10)(1.06)]^{1/2} - 1 = 0.08$; a rate below the 9% average annual rate on the 2-year bond. Thus, in this case, the investor would prefer the 2-year bond to the series of 1-year bonds. Finally, if the investor expects the rate in the future to equal the implied rate, then we can argue that he would be indifferent to an

Exhibit 2.9   Geometric mean

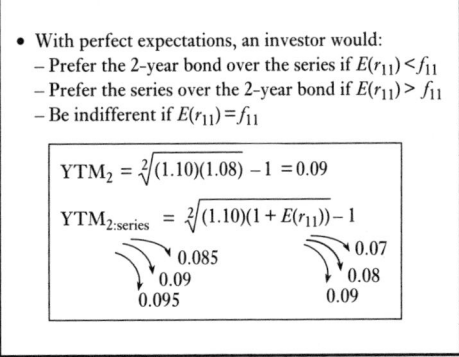

investment in a 2-year bond and a series of 1-year bonds (see exhibit 2.9).

In general, whether the investor decides to invest in an M-year bond or a series of 1-year bonds, or some combination with the equivalent maturity, depends on what the investor expects rates will be in the future relative to the forward rates implied by today's interest rate structure.

2.7   CONCLUSION

For most investors the most important characteristic of an asset is its rate of return. In this chapter we've examined how the rate of return on a bond and its related characteristic, value, can be measured. We are now in a position to take up the question of what determines the rate of return on a bond. Our preceding discussions suggest that the characteristics of bonds – taxability, liquidity, maturity, and risk – ultimately determine the yield on a bond. The two most important of these characteristics are maturity and risk – the subjects for the next two chapters.

KEY TERMS

Price–Yield Curve	Interest Rate	Yield to Worst
Effective Rate	Coupon Rate	Logarithmic Return
Zero-Coupon Bonds	Perpetuity or Consul	Spot Rate
Pure Discount Bonds	Yield to Maturity (YTM)	Equilibrium Price
Day Count Convention	Average Rate to Maturity	Bootstrapping
Accrued Interest	(ARTM)	Annual Realized Return (ARR)
Full Price or Dirty Price	Yield Approximation Formula	Average Realized Return
Clean Price	Simple Annualized Rate	Total Return
Discount Yield	Bond-Equivalent Yield	Geometric Mean
Current Yield	Yield to Call (YTC)	Implied Forward Rate

PROBLEMS AND QUESTIONS

Note on Problems: Many of these problems can be done in Excel by either writing a program or using one of the Excel programs; many also can be done using a financial calculator. For problems requiring a number of calculations, the reader may want to use Excel or a financial calculator.

1. Given a 5-year, 8% coupon bond with a face value of $1,000 and coupon payments made annually, determine its values given it is trading at the following yields: 8%, 6%, and 10%. Comment on the price and yield relation you observe. What are the percentage changes in value when the yield goes from 8% to 6% and when it goes from 8% to 10%?

2. Given a 10-year, 8% coupon bond with a face value of $1,000 and coupon payments made annually, determine its value for the following yields: 8%, 6%, and 10%. What are the percentage changes in value when the yield goes from 8% to 6% and when it goes from 8% to 10%? Comment on the price and interest rate relation you observe for this 10-year bond and the price and interest rate relation you observe for the 5-year bond in question 1.

3. Determine the values of a 5-year, zero-coupon bond with a face value of $1,000 given it is trading at the following yields: 8%, 6%, and 10%. What are the percentage changes in value when the yield goes from 8% to 6% and when it goes from 8% to 10%? Comment on the price and interest rate relation you observe for this zero coupon bond and the price and interest rate relation you observe for the 5-year, 8% coupon bond you observe in question 1.

4. Given a 5-year, 8% coupon bond with a face value of $1,000 and trading at a simple annual rate of 9%, determine the values and effective annualized rates given the bond has the following payment or compounding frequencies:
   a. Semi-annual
   b. Monthly
   c. Weekly

   Comment on the relation you observe.

5. Given a 2-year, zero-coupon bond with a face value of $100 and trading at a simple annual rate of 10%, determine the bond values given the following compounding frequencies:

   a. Monthly
   b. Weekly
   c. Daily
   d. Continuously

   Comment on the relation you observe.

6. Generate the price–yield curve for a zero-coupon bond with a face value of $100 and 260 actual days to maturity using the following annual yields: 4%, 4.25%, 4.5%, 4.75%, 5%, 5.25%, 5.5%, 5.75%, 6%, 6.25%, 6.5%, 6.75%, 7%, 7.25%, 7.5%, 7.75%, and 8%. Use actual/actual day count convention.

7. Given a 10-year, 8% coupon bond with a face value of $100 and semi-annual coupon payments:

   a. Generate the bond's price–yield curve using annual yields ranging from 5% to 10% and differing by 0.5%.
   b. What is the price change when the yield increases from 8% to 8.5%?
   c. What is the price change when the yield decreases from 8% to 7.5%?
   d. Comment on the capital gain and capital loss you observe in (b) and (c).
   e. Comment on the features of the price–yield curve.

8. Suppose an investor bought a 10-year, 10% annual coupon bond at par (face value of $1,000 and paying coupons annually) and then sold it 3.5 years later at a yield of 8%. Determine the full price, clean price, and accrued interest the investor would receive when he sold the bond. Use a $\frac{30}{360}$ day count convention.

9. What would an investor pay for a 4-year, 9% annual coupon bond (face value of $1,000 and paying coupons annually) if the bond were trading to yield 10%? What would the investor receive (full price) if she sold the bond 3.5 years later and bonds with maturities of 0.5 years were trading at 8%? Use a $\frac{30}{360}$ day count convention.

10. Determine the actual prices a dealer would pay (bid) or sell (ask) on the following bonds:

    a. A Treasury bond with $1,000 face value quoted by a dealer at a bid price of 95-4 per $100 face value and fractions in 32nds.
    b. A Treasury bond with $1,000 face value quoted by a dealer at an asked price of 110-4$^+$ per $100 face value with 4$^+$ indicating fractions in 64ths.
    c. A corporate bond with $1,000 face value quoted by a dealer at a bid price of 97$\frac{1}{2}$ per $100 face value with fractions in 100ths.
    d. A zero-coupon bond with $1,000 face value and maturity of 1 year quoted at an asked price to yield 550 basis points.
    e. A T-bill maturing in 52 days and paying $10,000 face value and quoted by a dealer at an asked annual discount yield of 4%.

11. Suppose you have an A-rated bond with an 8% annual coupon, face value of $1,000, and due to mature in 5 years. Presently, the YTM on such bonds is 10%. You expect the Federal Reserve will tighten credit and force yields up by 50 basis points in the near future. Determine today's price and the expected price.

12. Suppose the AIF Company sold a bond with a 10-year maturity, $1,000 principal and an annual 10% coupon paid semi-annually. What would be the price of the bond if 2 years after the bond were issued the promised YTM were 12%? What is the effective YTM?

13. Define the following rates of return measures:

    a. Discount yield
    b. Interest rate
    c. Coupon rate
    d. Current yield
    e. Rate on perpetuity
    f. Yield to maturity
    g. Average rate to maturity (yield approximation formula)
    h. Bond equivalent yield
    i. Yield to call
    j. Bond portfolio yield
    k. Logarithmic return
    l. Spot rate
    m. Annual realized return
    n. Geometric mean.

14. Using the average rate to maturity (yield approximation formula) approach, estimate the YTM on a 20-year, 7% annual coupon bond, with a face value of $1,000, annual coupon payments, and currently priced at $901.82. What is the value of the bond using the ARTM as the discount rate?

15. Suppose the 20-year, 7% annual coupon bond in question 14 had a call option giving the issuer the right to buy the bond back after 5 years at a call price of 1,000. Given the bond is priced at $901.82, estimate its yield to call using the yield approximation formula (average rate to call, ARTC) approach.

16. A zero-coupon Treasury bill maturing in 150 days is trading at $98 per $100 face value. Determine the following rates for the T-bill:

    a. Dealer's annual discount yield
    b. YTM (use an actual/365 day count convention)
    c. Logarithmic return (use actual/365 day count convention).

Explain the differences in the rates.

17. ABC Trust has the following bond portfolio:

Bond	Maturity (years)	Annual coupon	Face value	Price per $100 face value
A	1	0	100	92.59
B	2	8%	100	100.00
C	3	7%	100	97.42
D	4	10%	100	106.62
E	5	9%	100	104.00
				500.63

The coupon bonds in the portfolio all pay coupons annually and all the bond prices are quoted per $100 face value to yield 8%.

    a. Explain how the bond portfolio's YTM is calculated.
    b. Determine the bond portfolio's YTM using a financial calculator, Excel program, or by trial and error (hint: try YTM = 8%).
    c. Does the portfolio's YTM equal the weighted average yield of the bonds? If so, is this always the case?

18. Bond A is a 10-year, 10% coupon bond with a face value of $1,000 and annual coupon payments. The bond is currently priced at $1,064.18 to yield 9%.

   a. Define the bond-equivalent yield.
   b. Explain how bond A's bond-equivalent yield is calculated.
   c. Calculate bond A's bond-equivalent yield using a financial calculator, Excel program, or by trial and error (hint: try YTM $= 9.013\%$).
   d. What is the importance of the bond-equivalent yield?

19. Suppose A-rated bonds were trading in the market at YTM of 10% on all maturities, and you bought an A-rated, 10-year, 9% coupon bond with face value of $1,000 and annual coupon payments. Suppose that immediately after you bought the bond the yield on such bonds dropped to 8% on all maturities and remained there until you sold the bond at your horizon date at the end of 4 years.

   a. What price did you pay for the 10-year, 9% coupon bond?
   b. Show in a flow matrix (similar to exhibit 2.8) the coupons you received on the bond and their values at your horizon date from reinvesting.
   c. What is the price of the original 10-year bond at your horizon date?
   d. What is your horizon date value and ARR?

20. Given a 10-year, 10% coupon bond with semi-annual payments, $1,000 face value, and currently trading at par, calculate the ARR for an investor with a 5-year horizon date, given the following interest rate scenarios:

   a. Yields on such bonds stay at 10% on all maturities until the investor sells the bond at her horizon date.
   b. Immediately after the investor buys the bond, yields on such bonds drop to 8% on all maturities and remain there until the investor sells the bond at her horizon date.
   c. Immediately after the investor buys the bond, yields on such bonds increase to 12% on all maturities and remain there until the investor sells the bond at her horizon date.

   Comment on the relation between ARR and interest rates.

21. Consider the following spot rates on 1-year to 4-year zero-coupon bonds:

Year	Spot rate
1	8.0%
2	8.5%
3	9.0%
4	9.5%

   a. What is the equilibrium price of a 4-year, 9% coupon bond paying a principal of $100 at maturity and coupons annually?
   b. If the market prices the 4-year bond such that it yields 10%, what is the bond's market price?
   c. What would arbitrageurs do given the prices you determined in (a) and (b)? What impact would their actions have on the market price?
   d. What would arbitrageurs do if the market price exceeded the equilibrium price? What impact would their actions have on the market price?

22. Given a 1-year PDB trading at $100 and promising to pay $106 at maturity and a 2-year 6% coupon bond with face value of $100, annual payments, and trading at $96.54:

   a. Determine the 1-year and 2-year spot rates.
   b. What is the equilibrium price of a comparable 2-year 8% annual coupon bond ($F = 100$)?

23. Using the geometric mean show four expressions for the yield to maturity on a 4-year bond, YTM_4.

24. Bond X is a 1-year PDB trading at \$945 and Bond Y is a 2-year PDB trading at \$870.

   a. Determine algebraically the implied forward rate f_{11}.

   b. Explain how the forward rate can be attained by a locking-in strategy.

25. Explain how you would lock in the following implied forward rates: f_{11}, f_{21}, and f_{23}.

26. Given that current 182-day T-bills are trading at a YTM of 4% and 91-day bills are trading at a YTM of 3.75%, what is the implied forward rate on a 91-day T-bill 91 days from now? Explain how you would lock in the implied forward rate.

WEB EXERCISES

1. There are a number of financial calculators that can be found on the web. For one, try www.publicdebt.treas.gov/sav/savcalc.htm and then go to Savings Planner.

2. Rates on Treasury securities and other bonds can be found in www.bloomberg.com. Using Bloomberg, go to "Rates and Bonds" and explain the relation you observe between coupon rates, yields and bonds prices that you find on quoted T-notes.

3. This chapter discussed how the equilibrium price of a bond is based on spot rates and how arbitrageurs could buy or sell strip securities to ensure this condition. Read more about strip securities by going to www.bondsonline.com and then go to zero coupons and strips.

NOTES

1. An exception to this rule would be when a bond is in default. Such a bond is said to be quoted flat: that is, without accrued interest.

2. The volume of 78 is low. As we will discuss in chapter 6, though, a number of corporate bonds are listed on the exchange, but are more actively traded through dealers on the over-the-counter market.

3. It should be noted that, in practice, the rates of stripped securities differ from spot rates generated from bootstrapping. Also note that other techniques, such as regression models, can be used to estimate spot rates.

4. In chapter 13 we will show that there is good reason to expect that the implied forward rate is equal to the rate implied on a futures contract to buy or sell a debt security at some future date.

SELECTED REFERENCES

Fabozzi, Frank J. *Fixed Income Mathematics* (Chicago: Probus Publishing, 1988).

Fabozzi, Frank J. *Bond Markets, Analysis, and Strategies*, 3rd edn (Upper Saddle River, NJ: Prentice Hall, 1996).

Radcliffe, Robert C. *Investment Concepts, Analysis, and Strategy* (Glenview, IL: Scott, Foresman and Company, 1982).

Rose, Peter S. *Money and Capital Markets* (New York: McGraw-Hill/Irwin, 2003).

CHAPTER THREE

THE LEVEL AND STRUCTURE OF INTEREST RATES

3.1 INTRODUCTION

Over the past three decades interest rates have often followed patterns of persistent increases or persistent decreases with fluctuations around these trends. This is illustrated in figure 3.1 where the rates on Treasury bills are shown from 1970 to 2002. As shown, in the 1970s and early 1980s the US's inflation led to increasing interest rates during that period. This period of increasing rates was particularly acute from the late 1970s through the early 1980s when the US Federal Reserve changed the direction of monetary policy by raising discount rates, increasing reserve requirements, and lowering monetary growth. This period of increasing rates was followed by a period of declining rates from the early 1980s to the late 1980s, then a period of gradually increasing rates for most of the 1990s, and finally a period of decreasing rates from 2000 through 2003. The different interest rate levels observed since the 1970s can be explained by such factors as economic growth, monetary and fiscal policy, and inflation.

In addition to the observed fluctuations in interest rate levels, there have also been observed differences or spreads between the interest rates on bonds of different categories and terms to maturity over this same period. The spreads can be seen in figure 3.2 where the YTM on Treasury bonds, high-quality AAA corporate bonds, riskier Baa quality corporate bonds, and mortgage rates are shown from 1970 to 2002. In general, spreads can be explained by differences in each bond's characteristics: risk, liquidity, and taxability. Figure 3.2 also shows the spreads between rates changing. For example, the spread between yields on Baa and AAA bonds is greater in the late 1980s and early 1990s when the US economy was in recession compared to the differences in the mid to late 1990s when the US economy was growing. Finally, interest rate differences can be observed between similar bonds with different maturities. Figure 3.3 shows two plots of the YTM on US government bonds with different maturities for early 2002 and early 1981. The graphs are known as yield curves and they illustrate what is referred to as the term structure of interest rates. The lower graph in figure 3.2 shows a positively sloped yield curve in early 2002 with rates on short-term government securities lower than intermediate-term and long-term ones. In contrast, the upper graph shows a negatively sloped curve in early 1981 with short-term rates higher than intermediate- and long-term ones.

Understanding what determines both the overall level and structure of interest rates is an important subject in financial economics. In this chapter, we examine the factors that

Figure 3.1   Treasury bill rates, 1970–2002

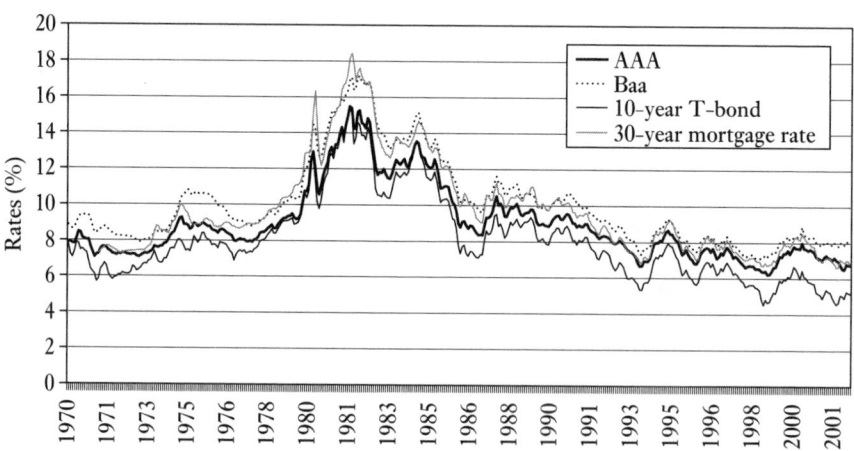

Figure 3.2   Treasury bond, AAA corporate, Baa corporate, and mortage rates, 1970–2002

are important in explaining the level and differences in interest rates. We begin by examining the behavior of overall interest rates using basic supply and demand analysis. With this foundation, we then look at how risk, liquidity, and taxes explain the differences in the rates on bonds of different categories. Finally, we conclude this chapter by looking at four well-known theories that explain the term structure on interest rates.

3.2 BEHAVIOR OF INTEREST RATES: SUPPLY AND DEMAND ANALYSIS

One of the best ways to understand how market forces determine interest rates is to use fundamental supply and demand analysis. In determining the supply and demand for bonds, let us treat different bonds as being alike and

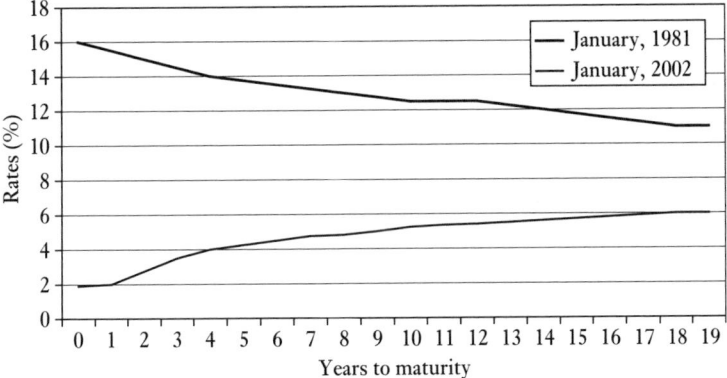

Figure 3.3 Yield curve for US government bonds

simply assume the bond in question is a one-period, zero-coupon bond paying a principal of F equal to 100 at maturity and priced at P_0 to yield a rate i:

$$P_0 = \frac{F}{1+i} = \frac{100}{1+i}$$

$$i = \frac{F - P_0}{P_0} = \frac{F}{P_0} - 1 = \frac{100}{P_0} - 1$$

(Note: the i symbol for the interest rate and the YTM, symbolized as y in the last chapter, are the same.) Given this type of bond, we want to determine the important factors that determine its supply and demand.

3.2.1 Bond Demand

In general, the quantity demanded of a bond, B^D, depends on such factors as its price or interest rate, the overall wealth or economic state of the economy, perhaps as measured by aggregate real output, GDP, the bond's risk relative to other assets, its liquidity relative to other assets, expected future interest rates, $E(i)$, and inflation, and government policies:

$$B^D = f(i \text{ or } P_0, \text{GDP}, E(i), E(\text{Inflation}),$$
$$+ \quad - \quad + \quad - \quad -$$
$$\text{Risk, Liquidity, Government policy})$$
$$- \quad + \quad + \text{ or } -$$

Using traditional supply and demand analysis, the impacts of these variables can be examined by first generating a demand curve for the bond. The curve shows the relationship between B^D and its price, P_0, or interest rate, i, with the assumption that the other factors are constant. Given the demand curve, we can then analyze the impact the other factors have on demand by observing how changes in those variables shift the demand curve.

Exhibit 3.1 shows a bond demand curve $B^D B^D$. To illustrate the relation between bond demand and both its price and interest rate, exhibit 3.1 has two vertical axes. The left axis shows the bond's price, with the price increasing as we go from the bottom up. The right vertical axis shows the associated interest rate, with the interest rate increasing as we move from the top to the bottom. Combined, the two axes capture the inverse relation between a bond's price and interest rate. Thus, at point A on $B^D B^D$, the price of the bond is at 96.1538 and its associated interest rate is 4%; at point B the price is 92.5926 and the associated rate is 8%. The bond demand curve in exhibit 3.1, in turn, is negatively sloped. This reflects the fundamental assumption that investors will demand more bonds the lower the price or equivalently the greater the interest rate. Thus, at point B investors are shown to demand $500B worth of the bond (number of bonds times the face value) when P_0 is 92.5926 and i is 8%, and at point A, bond demand is shown to be only $300B when P_0 is 96.1538 and i is 4%. It should

Exhibit 3.1   Bond demand and supply

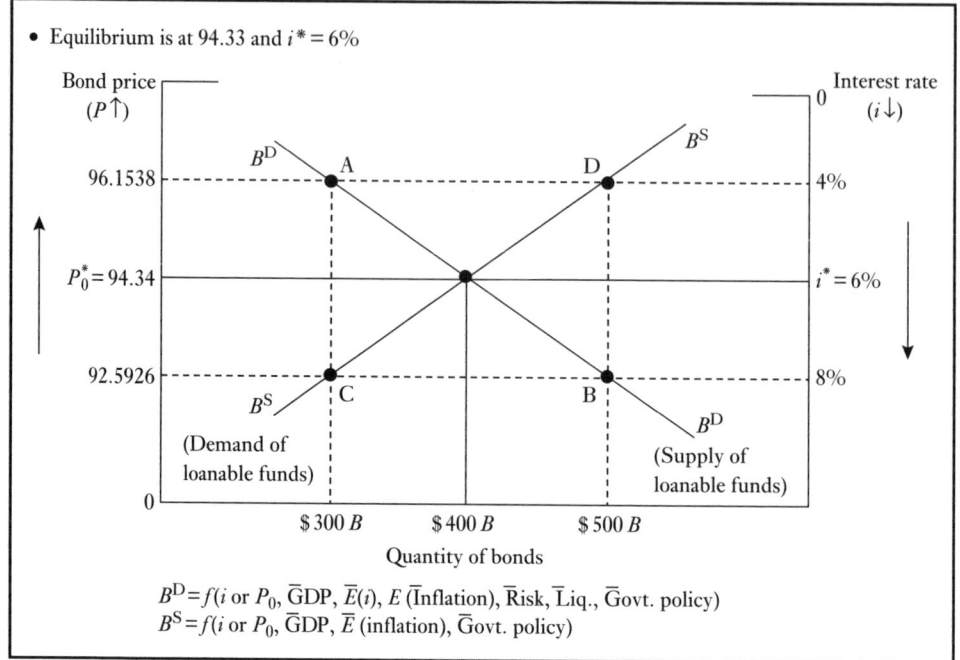

- Equilibrium is at 94.33 and $i^* = 6\%$

$$B^D = f(i \text{ or } P_0, \overline{G}DP, \overline{E}(i), E \text{ (Inflation)}, \overline{R}isk, \overline{L}iq., \overline{G}ovt. \text{ policy})$$
$$B^S = f(i \text{ or } P_0, \overline{G}DP, \overline{E} \text{ (inflation)}, \overline{G}ovt. \text{ policy})$$

be noted that since buying or demanding a bond is equivalent to supplying a loan, the bond demand curve in exhibit 3.1 can also be identified as a *supply of loanable funds* curve.

The impact of changes in the economy, future interest rate expectations, inflation expectations, risk, liquidity, and government policies on bond demand is captured by either rightward or leftward shifts in the demand curve. A priori, we would expect an increase in the demand for the bond at each price or interest rate when the economy is growing and aggregate wealth and output (GDP) are increasing, and a decrease in demand when the economy is in recession. Thus, the bond demand curve will shift to the right in periods of economic growth and to the left in periods of economic decline.

In contrast, we would expect an inverse relation to exist between bond demand and the market's expectation of future interest rates. That is, for those investors who plan to sell their bonds before maturity, an expectation of higher interest rates would mean lower future bond prices and therefore a lower expected rate

of return on our assumed zero–coupon bond. Thus, a market expectation of higher interest rates in the future would lead to lower bond demand and a leftward shift in the demand curve. On the other hand, a market expectation of lower interest rates in the future would mean higher expected rates of return from selling bonds before maturity; this would lead to an increase in demand and a rightward shift. Similarly, an increase in expected inflation would also lower bond demand. If investors expect the prices on goods and services, as well as cars, houses, and other consumer durables, to be higher in the future, they will decrease their current purchases of bonds and other securities and buy more consumption goods and consumer durables. Thus, the bond demand curve will shift to the left if investors expect higher inflation in the future.

A similar inverse relation also exists between bond demand and its relative risk. If bonds become riskier relative to other investments, we would expect a decrease in demand, and if they become less risky relative to other investments, we would expect an increase in demand. For example, if the chance of default on bonds increases or if other investment alternatives such as stock become less risky, then bond demand would fall and the demand curve would shift to the left. On the other hand, if the riskiness of bonds decreases or the risk of another investment alternative increases, then bonds would become more attractive, causing the demand curve to shift to the right. In terms of bond demand and liquidity, if more investors trade the bond, making it more marketable or liquid, then we would expect the demand for the bond to increase at each price or interest rate. An increase in the bond's liquidity would shift the bond demand curve to the right.

Finally, any change in government policy, such as a change in monetary or fiscal policy, that changes bond demand would shift the bond demand curve. For example, two monetary tools used by central banks are changing the discount rate they charge banks for borrowing and changing the amount of reserves banks are required to maintain in order to secure their deposits. These monetary actions, in turn, change the amount of loans banks are willing to offer. In our model, a change in the supply of loanable funds is equivalent to a change in the demand for bonds and would be reflected by a shift in the bond demand curve. Thus, if the central bank were to decrease the amount of reserves banks were required to maintain to back their deposits or if they were to lower the discount rate they charge banks for borrowing, we would expect the supply of loans made by banks to increase. Such actions would be reflected by a rightward shift in the bond demand curve.

3.2.2 Bond Supply

In general, the quantity of bonds supplied by corporations, governments, and intermediaries, B^S, depends on such factors as the bond's price or interest rate, the state of the economy, government policy, and expected future inflation:

$$B^S = f(i \text{ or } P_0, \text{GDP}, \text{Government policy},$$
$$\quad\; - \quad + \quad\; + \qquad\qquad + \text{ or } -$$
$$E(\text{Inflation}))$$
$$\quad +$$

The bond supply curve in exhibit 3.1, $B^S B^S$, is positively sloped. This reflects the fundamental assumption that corporations, governments, and financial intermediaries will sell more bonds the greater the bond's price or equivalently the lower the interest rate. Thus, at point C issuers are shown to supply only $300B$ worth of the bond when P_0 is 92.5926 and i is 8%, while at point D bond supply is shown to be $500B$ when P_0 is 96.1538 and i is 4%. It should be noted that since selling or supplying a bond is equivalent to obtaining or demanding a loan, the bond supply curve in exhibit 3.1 can also be identified as a *demand for loanable funds* curve.

The bond supply curve will shift in response to changes in the state of the economy, government policy, and expected inflation. A priori, we would expect an increase in the supply for the bond at each price or interest rate when the economy is growing, and a decrease in supply when the economy is in recession. When an economy is expanding, business demand for both short-term assets, such as inventories and accounts receivable, and long-term assets, such as plants and equipment, increases. As a result, companies find themselves selling more bonds (demanding more loans) to finance the increases in their short-term and long-term capital formation. In addition to changes in corporate bond supply, aggregate economic growth is also likely to increase both the purchases of cars and homes by household and the number of public projects by municipal government (e.g., roads), augmenting the supply of bonds by financial intermediaries and state and local governments. In contrast, in recessionary periods, there is less capital formation and fewer bonds being sold by corporations, governments, and intermediaries. Thus, we would expect the bond supply curve to shift to the right in periods of economic growth and to the left in periods of economic decline.

The bond supply can also change as a result of the federal government's fiscal and monetary policy. If the federal government has a deficit (government expenditure exceeding tax revenue), then the Treasury will be raising funds in the financial market by selling more Treasury securities. This would increase the supply of bonds at each price, shifting the supply curve to the right. In contrast, if there were a government surplus, the bond supply would decrease if the Treasury decided to use the surplus to buy up existing Treasury securities in order to reduce the government's outstanding debt. In this case, the bond supply curve would shift to the left. In addition to Treasury financing, bond supply and demand is also affected by central bank policies. One important monetary tool central banks employ is an open market operation (OMO). In order to stimulate the economy, the central bank uses an expansionary OMO to lower interest rates. In an expansionary OMO, the central bank buys existing Treasury securities. If we limit the definition of bond supply to those bonds held by the public and not the central bank, then an expansionary OMO leads to a decrease in the supply of bonds and a leftward shift in the supply curve. In contrast, when the central bank is fighting inflation, it may try to slow the economy down by increasing interest rates through a contractionary OMO. Here the bank sells some of its holdings of Treasury securities, increasing the supply of bonds and shifting the supply curve to the right.

Finally, if inflation is expected to be higher in the future, then expected borrowing cost will be higher in the future and more funds (inflated funds) will be needed to finance capital formation. As a result, corporations will find it advantageous to borrow more funds now. This would cause the bond supply to increase and the bond supply curve to shift to the right.

3.2.3 Market Equilibrium

Given the factors determining the supply and demand for bonds, the bond price or interest rate that ultimately prevails in the market is the one at which the quantity demanded of the bond equals the quantity supplied: $B^D = B^S$. The equilibrium rate, i^*, and price, P_0^*, are graphically defined by the intersection of the supply and demand curves. In exhibit 3.1, this occurs at $P_0^* = 94.34$ and $i^* = 6\%$, where the quantity demanded and supplied are both $\$400B$. The equilibrium interest rate of 6% is the market-clearing interest rate and the equilibrium price of 94.34 is the market-clearing price. If the bond price were below this equilibrium price (or equivalently the interest rate

were above the equilibrium rate), then investors would want more bonds than issuers were willing to sell. This excess demand would drive the price of the bonds up, decreasing the demand (movement along the demand curve) and increasing the supply (movement along the supply curve) until the excess was eliminated. On the other hand, if the price on bonds were higher than its equilibrium (or interest rates lower than the equilibrium rate), then bondholders would want fewer bonds, while issuers would want to sell more bonds. This excess supply in the market would lead to lower prices and higher interest rates, increasing bond demand (movement along the bond demand curve) and reducing bond supply (movement along the supply curve) until the excess supply was eliminated. Thus, only at P_0^* and i^*, where bond demand equals bond supply, is there an equilibrium where bondholders and suppliers do not want to change.

3.2.4 Comparative Analysis

The insights that one can gain from supply and demand analysis come from identifying the important factors that affect the positions of the demand and supply curves. Analytically, changes in these factors cause shifts in the demand or supply curves that, in turn, lead to new equilibrium bond price and interest rate levels. In the US and other major industrial countries, some of the most important economic changes that have occurred over the last three decades have been changes in monetary and fiscal policy, energy cost, and technology. The impact these economic events have on interest rates can be analyzed using our supply and demand model.

To illustrate, consider monetary policy. Technically, monetary policy can be defined as central bank actions that alter the composition of asset holdings in the economy. As noted, one of the major monetary tools is an open market operation (OMO) in which the central bank either purchases (expansionary OMO) or sells (contractionary OMO) Treasury securities. Such actions change not only the public's holdings of securities, but also the general level of interest rates in the economy. In addition to open market operations, we also noted that the central bank can affect the level of interest rates

Exhibit 3.2 Comparative equilibrium analysis: impact of a contractionary monetary policy

- Contractionary open market operation: central bank sells bonds, increasing the bond supply and shifting the bond supply curve to the right.
- An increase in the reserve requirement and an increase in the discount rate charged on bank loans by the central bank decreases the supply of loanable funds, shifting the bond demand curve to the left.
- Impact: interest rates increase.

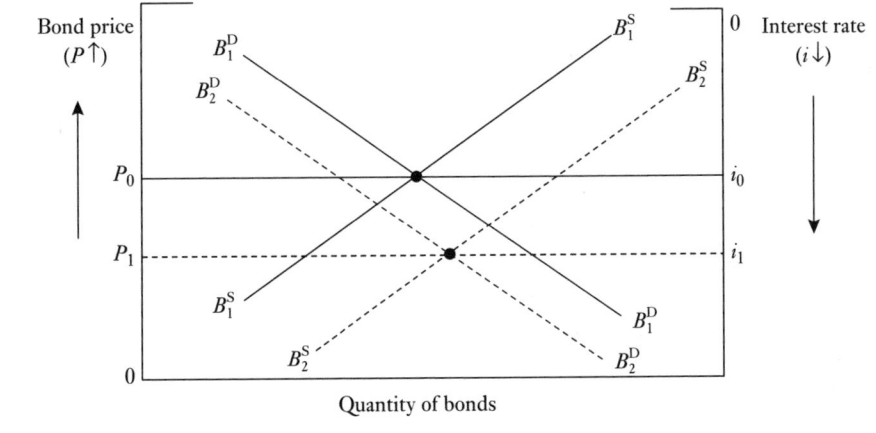

by changing the discount rate it charges banks for borrowing and by reducing the amount of reserves banks are required to maintain to secure their deposits. These actions, in turn, change the amount of loans banks are willing to offer and in our model shift the bond demand curve. For an advanced economy, monetary policy can be an effective tool provided interest rates are not too low or too high. Often contractionary policies are implemented when an economy is experiencing inflationary pressures, while expansionary policies are used when the economy is beset by unemployment, excess capacity, and recessionary pressures.

One of the most dramatic monetary actions was undertaken by the US Federal Reserve (Fed) in the late 1970s and early 1980s. Beginning in October of 1979 and extending through October 1982, the Fed raised the discount rate, increased reserve requirements, and set lower monetary growth targets for its OMOs in an effort to combat the US's high inflation and balance of payments problems. These actions, in turn, represented a directional change in the Fed's policies from the preceding 3-year period in which they maintained lower discount rates

and reserve requirements. While higher energy prices had already contributed to inflation and high interest rates, these contractionary monetary actions served to push up rates even higher. By 1982, rates on Treasury bonds were 10%, mortgage rates were 15%, the prime lending rate charged by banks was 21%, and the Dow Jones Average was at 700! (See figure 3.2.) These empirical observations are consistent with our supply and demand model. In our model, a contractionary OMO causes the bond supply curve to shift to the right as the Fed sells some of its government bonds, and the increase in both reserve requirements and the Fed's discount rate decreases the supply of loanable funds. As noted, the decrease in loanable funds is equivalent to a decrease in bond demand and therefore leads to a leftward shift in the bond demand curve. As shown in exhibit 3.2, at the initial bond price and interest rate level, the monetary actions of shifting the supply curve to the right and the demand curve to the left create an excess supply of bonds in the market. The excess supply, in turn, causes bond prices to decrease and rates to increase until a new equilibrium is attained.

Using supply and demand analysis, we can explain the impact of other exogenous economics forces on the general level of interest rates. Exhibit 3.3 summarizes some of the major economic events occurring in the US over the past three decades and their impact on the general level of interest rates using our model.

3.3 RISK, LIQUIDITY, AND TAXABILITY: THE STRUCTURE OF INTEREST RATES

In the above supply and demand analysis, we treated bonds and loanable funds as alike. This allowed us to focus on the impacts of various factors on the general level of interest rates. We also observe, though, differences in interest rates among different types of bonds. The differences in the interest rate spreads, in turn, can be explained by differences in the fundamental features of bonds: risk, liquidity, taxability, and maturity.

3.3.1 Risk Premium

Investment risk is the uncertainty that the actual rate of return realized from a security will differ from the expected rate. In the case of bonds, there are three types of investment risk: (1) *Default risk*: the uncertainty that the issuer/borrower will fail to meet his contractual obligations to pay interest and principal, as well as other obligations specified in the indenture; (2) *call risk*: the uncertainty that the issuer/borrower will buy back the bond, forcing the investor to reinvest in a market with lower interest rates; (3) *market risk*: the uncertainty that interest rates will change, changing the price of the bond and the return earned from reinvesting coupons. In chapter 4, we will examine in some detail each of these types of bond risk. We can say, though, that in general a riskier bond will trade in the market at a price that yields a greater YTM than a less risky bond. The difference in the YTM of a risky bond and the YTM of a less risky or risk-free bond is referred to as a *risk spread* or *risk premium*. The risk premium, RP, indicates how much additional return investors must

earn in order to induce them to buy the riskier bond:

$$RP = \text{YTM on risky bond}$$
$$- \text{YTM on risk-free bond}$$

Our supply and demand model can be used to explain why normally there is a positive risk premium and why the premium increases, the greater the risk. Exhibit 3.4 shows the demand and supply graphs for a risk-free Treasury bond and a similar corporate bond. If we initially assume that the corporate bond is also risk-free, then both bonds would have identical features. As a result, we would expect the corporate bond to be priced at P_0^C to yield a rate (i_0^C) that would be equal to the rate on the risk-free Treasury (i_0^T). In this case, the risk premium would be zero. Suppose, though, that economic conditions change such that there is now some chance of default on the corporate bond. The increased riskiness of the corporate bond would cause its demand to decrease, shifting its bond demand curve to the left. The corporate bond's riskiness would also make the Treasury security more attractive, augmenting its demand and shifting its demand curve to the right. At the new equilibriums, the corporate bond's price is lower (P_1^C) and its rate (i_1^C) greater than the Treasury's. As shown in exhibit 3.4, the risk associated with the corporate bond leads to a market adjustment in which at the new equilibrium there is a positive risk premium: $RP = i_1^C - i_1^T$. In general, we can conclude that if a bond is risky, it will trade with a positive risk premium and that the premium will increase, the greater the bond's risk.

Risk Premiums and Investors' Return–Risk Preferences

The size of the risk premium depends on investors' attitudes toward risk. To see this relation, suppose there are only two bonds available in the market: a risk-free bond and a risky bond. Suppose the risk-free bond is a zero-coupon bond promising to pay $1,000 at the end of 1 year and that it currently is trading

Exhibit 3.3 The impact of economic events on the level of interest rates

Energy Cost and the Inflation of the 1970s

Nobel Laureate Paul Samuelson described an economic state in which there is both inflation and recession as stagflation. In the 1970s, the US and other industrial economies experienced severe stagflation resulting from increases in energy prices. Specifically, the price of OPEC oil increased from $3 per barrel in 1972 to approximately $35 per barrel in 1980. These energy price increases led to increases in the overall costs of production (which were passed on in the form of higher prices), and lower economic growth rates (in economics, the increase in resource cost is reflected by a leftward shift in the aggregate supply curve). The US suffered recessions in 1973, 1975, and 1978, with each of the recessions accompanied by increases in the inflation rate. For the decade, the annual inflation rate averaged over 10%, while the growth rate in real gross domestic product for the decade was only 5% (by contrast from 1982 to 1995, real aggregate output doubled). During this period, there was also a significant increase in interest rates in the US and other industrial countries (see figure 3.1). The increase can be explained primarily by the high actual and expected inflation. As shown in the figure below, actual and expected inflation increases the real cost of borrowing and the need by corporations and others to borrow more funds, shifting the bond supply curve to the right; inflation also decreases the demand for bonds, shifting the bond demand curve to the left. Combined, the actual and expected inflation cause bond prices to fall (in the graph below, prices go from P_0 to P_1) and interest rates to increase (i_0 to i_1).

The direct impact of expected inflation on interest rates is referred to as the **Fisher effect**, after Irving Fisher, the economist who broached this relation. The Fisher effect is helpful in explaining not just the relatively high interest rates of the late 1970s, when the US inflation rate was relatively high, but also low interest rates when inflation expectations are low. For example, in the late 1990s, Japan experienced very low interest rates and deflation, with Treasury rates actually becoming slightly negative in 1998. Using our model, on the bond supply side, expected deflation (often combined with recession) decreases the bond supply, while on the demand side, the expected deflation increases bond demand. Together the demand and supply response to expected deflation would increase the price of bonds and lower their rate.

Impact of inflation
- An increase in actual and expected inflation increases bond supply, shifting the bond supply curve to the right; an increase in expected inflation decreases bond demand, shifting the bond demand curve to the left.
- Impact: interest rates increase.

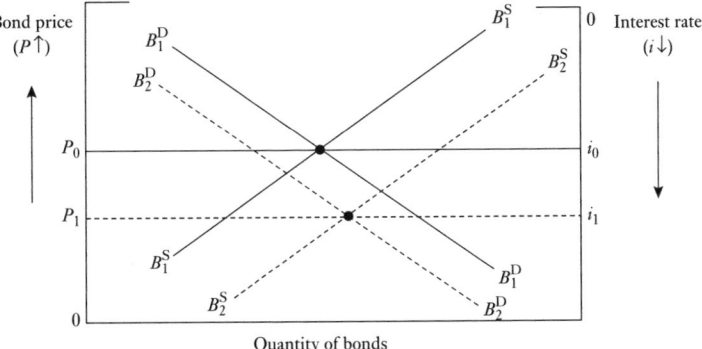

Fiscal Policy Stimulant and the Mid-1980s

Fiscal policy can be defined as government actions that alter the levels of government expenditures and taxes. Expansionary fiscal policy consists of increasing government expenditures or decreasing taxes, while contractionary policy includes decreasing government spending or increasing taxes. An increase in the level of government expenditure or a decrease in taxes augments aggregate output demand through a multiplier, leading to an increase in overall prices and aggregate production. Expansionary fiscal policy may also lead to an increase in interest rates; that is, if the fiscal policy stimulant increases aggregate output, then corporations will issue more bonds to finance their requisite short-term and long-term capital investment needs brought about by the economic expansion. In addition, the fiscal policy stimulant may also lead to an expectation of higher inflation; this expectation could also lead to an increase in bond supply as corporations and others find it more advantageous to borrow when real rates are lower. As shown in the figure below, the increase in aggregate output and expected inflation increases the bond supply, shifting the bond supply curve to the right, pushing bond prices down and interest rates up. On the bond demand side, economic growth would increase bond demand. However, this increase could be offset by a decrease in demand due to higher inflation expectations. In the figure, the increase in bond demand is shown to lead to only a small rightward shift in the bond demand curve. Thus, the net impact of the fiscal policy stimulant is that it increases interest rates by stimulating the economy. By contrast, contractionary fiscal policy lowers aggregate demand, decreasing prices and output, and leading to lower interest rates.

From the late 1960s to the late 1990s, fiscal policy in the US was characterized by deficit spending in which federal government expenditures exceeded tax revenues every year, with the resulting deficits reaching a peak of over \$300b in 1994. Federal government deficits are financed by the Treasury selling securities. The sale of Treasury securities increases the bond supply ($B^S B^S$ curve shifts to the right). All other factors constant, this increase leads to lower bond prices and higher rates. It should be noted that after an initial Treasury security offering, the central bank could subsequently purchase Treasury securities as part of their OMO. (Note: in the US, the Fed is prohibited from purchasing securities from an initial offering.) The analysis of the impact of fiscal policy, therefore, needs to be examined in conjunction with monetary policy. In an expansionary fiscal policy case in which there is a deficit (or an increase in the deficit) and a corresponding expansionary monetary policy, there may be a significant increase in aggregate demand with both the expansionary monetary and fiscal policies increasing overall prices and output. The impact on the interest rate, though, will be ambiguous: the Treasury's financing of the deficit will push rates up ($B^S B^S$ curve shifts to the right), while expansionary monetary policy will push rates down ($B^D B^D$ curve shifts to the right). The Reagan Administration in the 1980s, for example, increased government expenditures and substantially cut taxes. These expansionary fiscal policy actions were accompanied with an accommodating monetary policy by the Fed. The combined expansionary monetary and fiscal policy actions led to the US's economic recovery during the second half of the 1980s and also explained the relatively lower interest rates.

Impact of Expansionary Fiscal Policy

- Expansionary fiscal policy increases aggregate output and actual and expected inflation.
- On the supply side, an increase in aggregate output and actual and expected inflation increases the bond supply, shifting the bond supply curve to the right.
- On the bond demand side, economic growth would increase bond demand. However, this increase could be offset by a decrease in demand due to higher inflation expectations. In this case, the net effect is for a small increase in demand and a rightward shift in the bond demand curve.
- Net impact: interest rates increase.

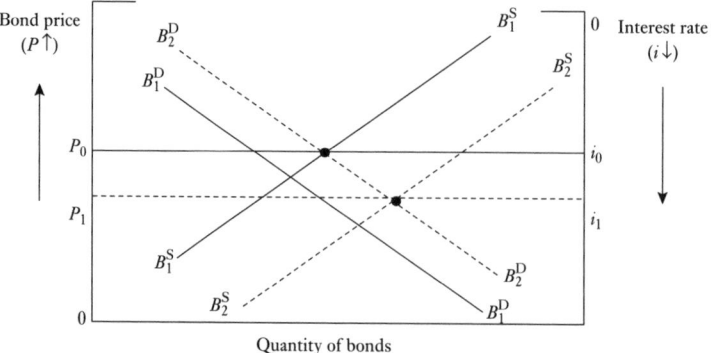

Quantity of bonds

Technological Changes and the 1990s

From 1984 to 1998, America's gross domestic product rose from $3t to over $8t, and the stock market, as measured by the Dow Jones Average, increased over 1,200%, going from 700 in 1984 to over 9,000 in 1998. While some of this extraordinary growth can be explained by the expansionary monetary and fiscal policies of the mid-1980s, the decrease in energy prices, and world economic growth, much can be attributed to the advances in science and technology in such areas as computer technology, genetic engineering, and telecommunications. The advances in technology and science that were realized in the 1990s (though their development was much earlier) increased the productivity of labor and capital. As a result, for much of the 1990s the US and other industrial economies enjoyed not only significant economic growth, but also stable prices (in economics this is reflected by a rightward shift in the aggregate supply curve). During this period, there was a gradual increase in interest rates in the US (see figure 3.1). The increase can be explained primarily by the increase in borrowing (bond supply increase causing a rightward shift in the bond supply curve) needed to finance the capital formation during this period. The reason that interest rate increases were not significant during this extraordinary growth period can be explained in part by the relatively low inflation rate.

for $909.09 to yield a 1-year risk-free rate, R_f, of 10%:

$$P_0 = \frac{\$1,000}{1.10} = \$909.09$$

$$R_f = \frac{\$1,000}{\$909.09} - 1 = 0.10$$

Suppose the risky bond is also a 1-year zero-coupon bond with a principal of $1,000, but there is a chance it could default and pay nothing. In particular, suppose there were a 0.8 probability the bond would pay its principal of $1,000 and a 0.2 probability it would pay nothing. The expected dollar return from the risky bond is therefore $800:

$$E(\text{Return}) = 0.8(\$1,000) + 0.2(0) = \$800$$

Given the choice of two securities, suppose that the market were characterized by investors who were willing to pay $727.27 for the risky bond, in turn yielding them an expected rate of return of 10%:

$$E(R) = \frac{E(\text{Return})}{P_0} - 1$$

$$E(R) = \frac{\$800}{\$727.27} - 1 = 0.10$$

By paying $727.27, investors would have a 0.8 probability of attaining a rate of return of 37.5% ([$1,000/$727.27] − 1) and a 0.2 probability of losing their investment. In this case, investors would be willing to receive an expected return from the risky investment that is equal to the risk-free rate of 10%, and the risk premium, $E(R) - R_f$, would be equal to zero. In finance terminology, such a market is described as *risk neutral*. Thus, in a risk-neutral market, the required return is equal to the risk-free rate and the risk premium is equal to zero.

Instead of paying $727.27, suppose investors like the chance of obtaining returns greater than 10% (even though there is a chance of losing their investment), and as a result are willing to pay $750 for the risky bond. In this case, the expected return on the bond would be 6.67% and the risk premium would be negative:

$$E(R) = \frac{\$800}{\$750} - 1 = 0.0667$$

$$RP = E(R) - R_f = 0.0667 - 0.10 = -0.033$$

By definition, markets in which the risk premium is negative are called *risk loving*. Risk-loving markets can be described as ones in which investors enjoy the excitement of the gamble and are willing to pay for it by accepting an expected return from the risky investment

Exhibit 3.4   Risk premium

Corporate bond market
- The riskiness of the corporate bond decreases its demand, shifting the corporate bond demand curve to the left.
- Impact: a higher interest rate on corporate bonds.

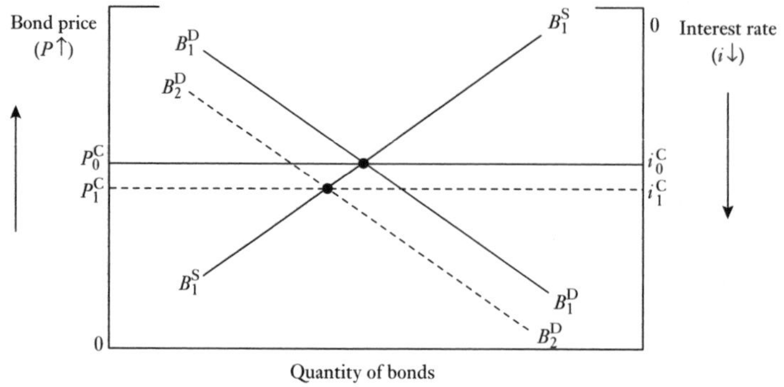

Treasury bond market
- The riskiness of the corporate bond increases the demand for Treasury bonds, shifting the Treasury bond demand curve to the right.
- Impact: a lower interest rate on Treasury bonds.

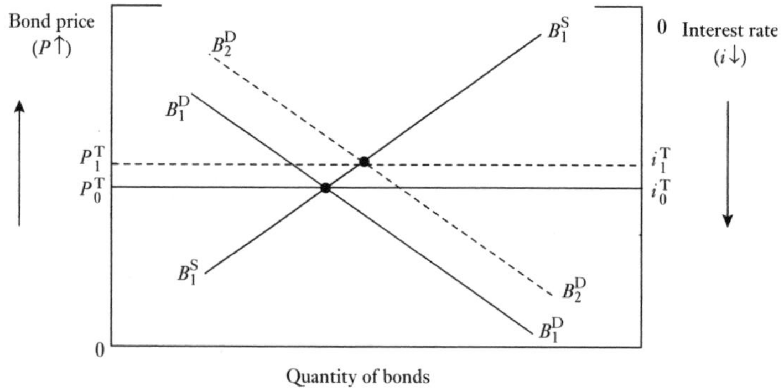

that is less than the risk-free rate. Even though there are some investors who are risk loving, a risk-loving market is an aberration, with the exceptions being casinos, sports gambling markets, lotteries, and racetracks.

While risk-loving and risk-neutral markets are rare, they do serve as a reference for defining the more normal behavior towards risk – *risk aversion*. In a risk-averse market, investors require compensation in the form of a positive risk premium to pay them for the risk they are assuming. Risk-averse investors view risk as a disutility, not a utility as risk-loving

investors do. In terms of our example, suppose most of the investors making up our market were risk averse and as a result were unwilling to pay $727.27 or more for the risky bond. In this case, if the price of the risky bond were $727.27 and the price of the risk-free bond were $909.09, then there would be little demand for the risky bond and a high demand for the risk-free one. Holders of the risky bonds who wanted to sell would therefore have to lower their price, increasing the expected return. On the other hand, the high demand for the risk-free bond would tend to increase its price and lower its rate.[1] For example, suppose the markets cleared when the price of the risky bond dropped to \$701.75 to yield 14%, and the price of the risk-free bond increased to \$917.43 to yield 9%:

$$E(R) = \frac{\$800}{\$701.75} - 1 = 0.14$$

$$R_f = \frac{\$1,000}{\$917.43} - 1 = 0.09$$

In this case, the risk premium would be 5% and the market is defined as being risk averse.

The market for our corporate bond described in exhibit 3.4 can be categorized as a risk-averse market. Historically, security markets such as the stock and corporate bond markets have generated rates of return that, on average, have exceeded the rates on Treasury securities. This would suggest that such markets are risk averse. Since most markets are risk averse, a relevant question is the degree of risk aversion. The degree of risk aversion can be measured in terms of the size of the risk premium. The greater investors' risk aversion, the greater the demand for risk-free securities and the lower the demand for risky ones, and thus the larger the risk premium. As we will examine further in chapter 4, the size of the risk premiums does change as a result of changing economic conditions and interest rates.

3.3.2 Liquidity Premium

Liquid securities are those that can be easily traded and in the short run are absent of risk. Treasury securities, with their wide distribution of ownership, for example, are easy to trade and are therefore more liquid than corporate bonds. In general, we can say that a less liquid bond will trade in the market at a price that yields a greater YTM than a more liquid one. The difference in the YTM of a less liquid bond and the YTM of a more liquid one is defined as the liquidity premium, LP:

LP = YTM on less liquid bond

  − YTM on more liquid bond

The impact of liquidity on interest rates is illustrated in exhibit 3.5, which shows the demand and supply graphs for corporate and Treasury bonds. If we assume that the two bonds have the same features, including liquidity, then they would be equally priced and yield the same rate. In this case, the liquidity premium would be zero. Suppose, though, that the corporate bond becomes less liquid. The decrease in the liquidity of the corporate bond would cause its demand to decrease, shifting its bond demand curve to the left. The decrease in the corporate bond's liquidity would also make the Treasury bond relatively more liquid, increasing its demand and shifting its demand curve to the right. Once the markets adjust to the liquidity difference between the bonds, then as shown in exhibit 3.5, the corporate bond's price is lower (P_1^C) and its rate (i_1^C) greater than the Treasury's. Thus, the difference in liquidity between the corporate and Treasury bonds leads to a market adjustment in which there is a difference between rates explained by the different liquidity features of the bond: $LP = i_1^C - i_1^T$.

Web Information
Historical interest rate data on different bonds can be found at the Federal Reserve site:
  www.federalreserve.gov/releases/h15/data.htm

Also see
  www.research.stlouisfed.org/fred2

For information on Federal Reserve policies go to
  www.federalreserve.gov/policy.htm

For information on the European Central Bank go to
  www.ecb.int.

3.3.3 Taxability

Investors are more concerned with the after-tax yield on a bond than its pre-tax yield. An investor in a 40% income tax bracket who

Exhibit 3.5 Liquidity premium

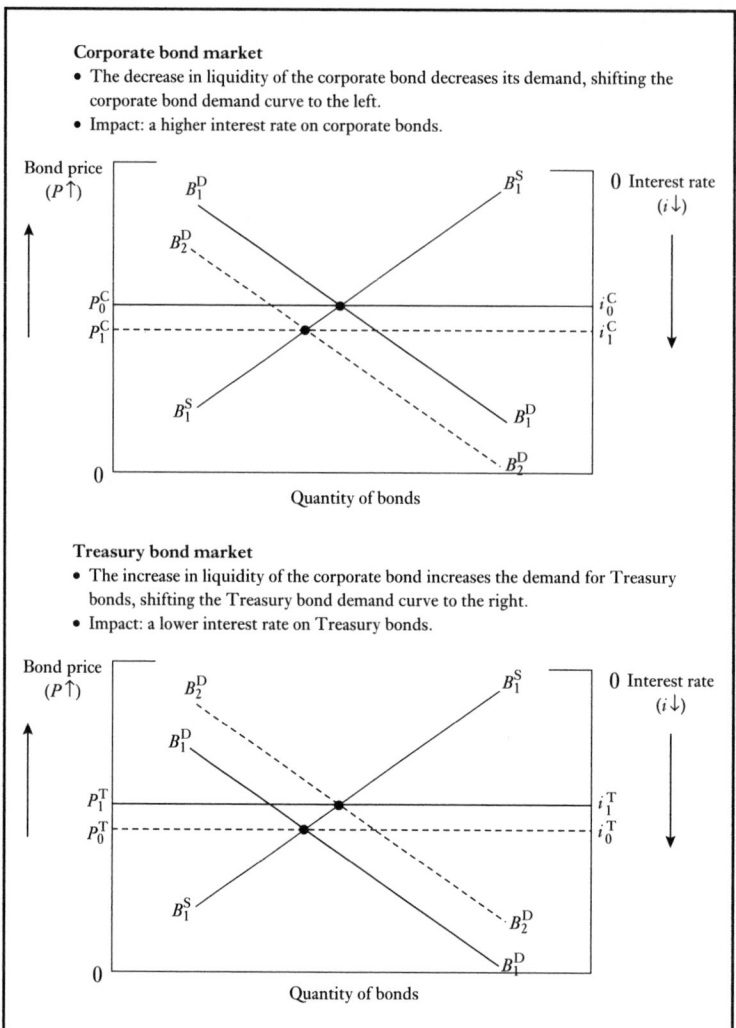

purchased a fully taxable 10% corporate bond at par, would earn an after-tax yield, ATY, of 6%: $ATY = 10\%(1 - 0.4)$. In general, the ATY can be found by solving for that yield, ATY, which equates the bond's price to the present value of its after-tax cash flows:

$$P_0 = \sum_{t=1}^{M} \frac{CF_t(1 - \text{Tax rate})}{(1 + ATY)^t}$$

Bonds that have different tax treatments but otherwise are identical will trade at different pre-tax YTM. That is, the investor in the 40% tax bracket would be indifferent between the 10% fully taxable corporate bond and a 6% tax-exempt municipal bond selling at par, if the two bonds were identical in all other respects. The two bonds would therefore trade at equivalent after-tax yields of 6%, but with a pre-tax yield spread of 4%: $i_0^C - i_0^M = 10\% - 6\% = 4\%$.

As we discussed in chapter 1, taxability refers to the claims the government has on a security's cash flow. In general, bonds whose cash flows are subject to less taxes trade at a lower YTM than bonds that are subject to more taxes. Historically, taxability explains why US municipal bonds whose coupon interest is exempt from federal income taxes have traded at yields below default-free US Treasury securities even though many municipals are subject to default risk.

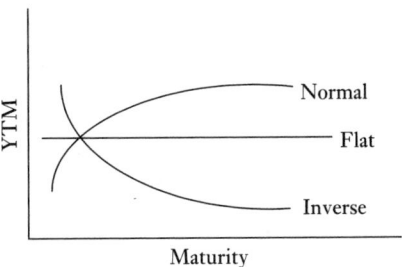

Figure 3.4   Yield curve shapes

3.4 TERM STRUCTURE OF INTEREST RATES

In addition to risk, liquidity, and taxes, the other important factor explaining differences in interest rates is the different terms to maturity on bonds. In the financial literature, the relationship between the yields on financial assets and their maturities is referred to as the *term structure of interest rates*. As noted, term structure is often depicted graphically by a *yield curve*: a plot of YTM against maturities for bonds that are otherwise alike (see figure 3.3). A yield curve can be constructed from current observations. For example, one could take all outstanding corporate bonds from a group in which the bonds are almost identical in all respects except their maturities, then generate the current yield curve by plotting each bond's YTM against its maturity. For investors who are more interested in long-run average yields instead of current ones, the yield curve could be generated by taking the average yields over a sample period (e.g., 5-year averages) and plotting these averages against their maturities. Finally, a widely used approach is to generate a spot yield curve from spot rates (discussed in the previous chapter) using Treasury securities.

Whether they are derived from current rates, averages, or spot rates, empirically generated yield curves have tended to take on one of the three shapes shown in figure 3.4. They can be positively sloped with long-term rates being greater than shorter-term ones. Such yield curves are called *normal* or *upward sloping curves*. They are usually convex from below, with the YTM flattening out at higher maturities. Yield curves can also be negatively sloped, with short-term rates greater than long-term ones. These curves are known as *inverted* or *downward sloping yield curves*. Like normal curves, these curves also tend to be convex,

with the yields flattening out at the higher maturities. Finally, yield curves can be relatively flat, with YTM being invariant to maturity. Occasionally a yield curve can take on a more complicated shape in which it can have both positively-sloped and negatively-sloped portions; these are often referred to as a *humped yield curve.*

The actual shape of the yield curve depends on the types of bonds under consideration (e.g., AAA bond versus B bond), economic conditions (e.g., economic growth or recession, tight monetary conditions, etc.), the maturity preferences of investors and borrowers, and investors' and borrowers' expectations about future rates, inflation, and the state of the economy. Four theories have evolved over the years to try to explain the shapes of yield curves: market segmentation theory (MST), preferred habitat theory (PHT), pure expectations theory (PET), and the liquidity premium theory (LPT). As we will see, each of these theories by itself is usually not sufficient to explain the shape of a yield curve; rather, the full explanation underlying the structure of interest rates depends on elements of all four theories.

3.4.1 Market Segmentation Theory

Market segmentation theory (MST) posits that investors and borrowers have strong maturity preferences that they try to attain when they invest in or issue fixed-income securities. As a result of these preferences, the financial markets, according to MST, are segmented into a number of smaller markets, with

supply and demand forces unique to each segment determining the equilibrium yields for
each segment. Thus according to MST, the
major factors that determine the interest rate
for a maturity segment are supply and demand
conditions unique to the maturity segment. For
example, the yield curve for high-quality corporate bonds could be segmented into three
markets: short-term, intermediate-term, and
long-term. The supply of short-term corporate
bonds, such as commercial paper, would
depend on business demand for short-term
assets such as inventories, accounts receivables,
and the like, while the demand for short-term
corporate bonds would emanate from investors
looking to invest their excess cash for short
periods. The demand for short-term bonds
by investors and the supply of such bonds by
corporations would ultimately determine the
rate on short-term corporate bonds. Similarly,
the supplies of intermediate- and long-term
bonds would come from corporations trying to
finance their intermediate- and long-term assets
(plant expansion, equipment purchases, acquisitions, etc.), while the demand for such bonds
would come from investors, either directly or
indirectly through institutions (e.g., pension
funds, mutual funds, insurance companies,
etc.), who have long-term liabilities. The supply
and demand for intermediate funds would, in
turn, determine the equilibrium rates on such
bonds, while the supply and demand for long-
term bonds would determine the equilibrium
rates on long-term debt securities.

Important to MST is the idea of unique or
independent markets. According to MST, the
short-term bond market is unaffected by rates
determined in the intermediate or long-term
markets, and vice versa. This independence
assumption is based on the premise that
investors and borrowers have a strong need to
match the maturities of their assets and liabilities. For example, an oil company building a
refinery with an estimated life of 20 years would
prefer to finance that asset by selling a 20-year
bond. If the company were to finance with a
10-year note, for example, it would be exposed
to market risk in which it would have to raise
new funds at an uncertain rate at the end of
10 years. Similarly, a life insurance company
with an anticipated liability in 15 years would
prefer to invest its premiums in 15-year bonds;

a money market manager with excess funds for
90 days would prefer to hedge by investing in a
money market security; a corporation financing
its accounts receivable would prefer to finance
the receivables by selling short-term securities.
Moreover, according to MST, the desire by
investors and borrowers to avoid market risk
leads to hedging practices that tend to segment
the markets for bonds of different maturities.

MST in Terms of the Supply and Demand Model

One way to examine how market forces determine the shape of yield curves is to examine
MST using our supply and demand analysis.
Consider a simple world in which there are two
types of corporate bonds – long-term (B_{LT}^C) and
short-term (B_{ST}^C) – and two types of government Treasury bonds – long-term (B_{LT}^T) and
short-term (B_{ST}^T). Exhibit 3.6 shows the markets for each of the sectors and segments and the
resulting yield curves for Treasury and corporate bonds. The supplies and demands for each
sector and segment are based on the following
assumptions:

- The most important factors determining the
demand for short-term bonds (both corporate
and Treasury) are the bond's own price or
interest rate, government policy, liquidity,
and risk. Short-term bond demand, BD_{ST}, is
assumed to be inversely related to its price and
directly related to its own rate (negatively
sloped bond demand curves); government
actions that affect the supply of loanable funds
also can change bond demand (e.g. monetary
policy changing bank reserve requirements).
- The demand for the short-term bond in one
sector is also assumed to be an inverse function of the short-term rate in the other sector,
but not the long-term rate in either its sector
or the other sector given the assumption of
segmented markets. Thus, if the interest rate
on the short-term Treasury security, i_{ST}^T, were
to increase, investors would want more of the
government bond and less of the short-term
corporate bond. The increase in i_{ST}^T would
therefore have an inverse effect on the demand
for the short-term corporate bond, decreasing
its demand and shifting its demand curve
to the left. Conversely, an increase in the

corporate short-term rate, i_{ST}^C, would lower the demand for the short-term Treasury security, shifting its demand curve to the left.

$$BD_{ST}^C = f(i_{ST}^C, i_{ST}^T, \text{Risk}, \text{Liquidity},$$
$$\text{Government policy})$$

$$BD_{ST}^T = f(i_{ST}^T, i_{ST}^C, \text{Risk}, \text{Liquidity},$$
$$\text{Government policy})$$

- The most important factors determining the demand for long-term bonds (both corporate and Treasury), BD_{LT}, are the bond's own price or interest rate, government policy such as monetary actions (e.g., change in bank reserve requirements), liquidity, and risk. Demand is assumed to be inversely related to its price and directly related to its own rate (negatively sloped bond demand curves). In addition, the demand for the long-term bond in one sector, BD_{LT}, is an inverse function of the long-term rate in the other sector, but not a function of the short-term rates given the market segmentation assumption.

$$BD_{LT}^C = f(i_{LT}^C, i_{LT}^T, \text{Risk}, \text{Liquidity},$$
$$\text{Government policy})$$

$$BD_{LT}^T = f(i_{LT}^T, i_{LT}^C, \text{Risk}, \text{Liquidity},$$
$$\text{Government policy})$$

- The supplies of short-term and long-term corporate bonds are directly related to their own price and inversely to their interest rate (positively sloped corporate bond supply curve) and directly related to general economic conditions, increasing in economic expansion and decreasing in recession.

$$BS_{ST}^C = f(i_{ST}^C, \text{GDP})$$

$$BS_{LT}^C = f(i_{LT}^C, \text{GDP})$$

- The supplies of Treasury bonds depend only on government actions (monetary and fiscal policy), and not the economic state or interest rates. This assumption says that the sale or purchase of Treasury securities by the central bank or the Treasury is a policy decision. The assumption that the supply of Treasury securities depends on government actions and

not interest rates means that the bond supply curve is vertical.

$$BS_{ST}^T = f(\text{Government policy})$$

$$BS_{LT}^T = f(\text{Government policy})$$

In exhibit 3.6, the two equilibrium rates for short-term and long-term corporate bonds are plotted against their corresponding maturities (simply denoted as ST and LT) to generate the yield curve for corporate bonds. Similarly, the equilibrium rates for short-term and long-term Treasury bonds are plotted against their corresponding maturities to generate the yield curve for Treasury bonds. These yield curves, in turn, capture an MST world in which interest rates for each segment are determined by the supply and demand for that bond, with the rates on bonds in the other maturity segments having no effect. In general, the positions and the shapes of the yield curves depend on the factors that determine supply and demand for short-term and long-term bonds. In this analysis, the state of the economy determines the positions of the supply curves; the rates on government securities determine the positions of the corporate bond demand curves, while the rates on corporate securities determine the positions of the Treasury bond demand curves; and depending on the type of policy, Treasury and central bank actions affect the Treasury bond supply curves and possibly the bond demand curves. Changes in these factors will cause a change in the structure of interest rates that will be reflected by different shifts in the yield curves. Several cases of yield curve shifts are discussed below.

Case 1: Economic Recession

Suppose the economy moved from a period of economic growth into a recession. As noted, when an economy moves into a recession, business demand for short-term and long-term assets tends to decrease. As a result, many companies find themselves selling fewer short-term bonds, given that they plan to maintain smaller inventories and expect to have fewer accounts receivables. They also find themselves selling fewer long-term bonds, given that they tend to cut planned investments in plants,

Exhibit 3.6   MST model: market equilibrium for short-term and long-term
corporate and Treasury bonds

Corporate Bond Market

- Short-term bonds

  $BD^C_{ST} = f(i^C_{ST}, i^T_{ST}, \text{risk, liquidity, government policy})$

  $BS^C_{ST} = f(i^C_{ST}, GDP)$

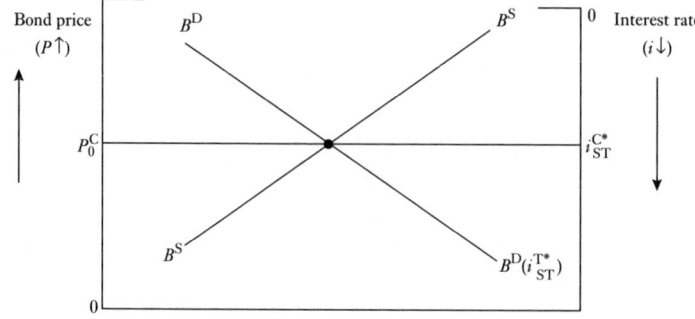

Quantity of short-term corporate bonds

- Long-term bonds

  $BD^C_{LT} = f(i^C_{LT}, i^T_{LT}, \text{risk, liquidity, government policy})$

  $BS^C_{LT} = f(i^C_{LT}, GDP)$

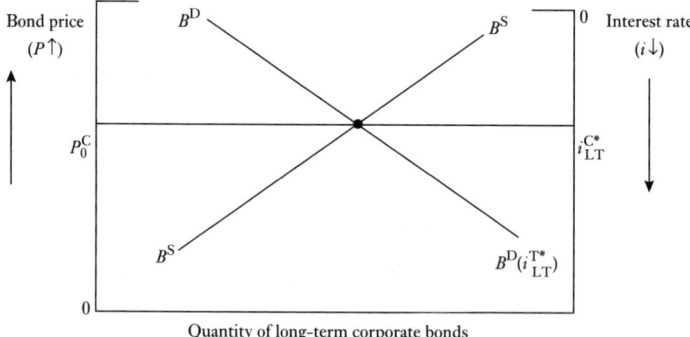

Quantity of long-term corporate bonds

- Yield curve, corporate bond

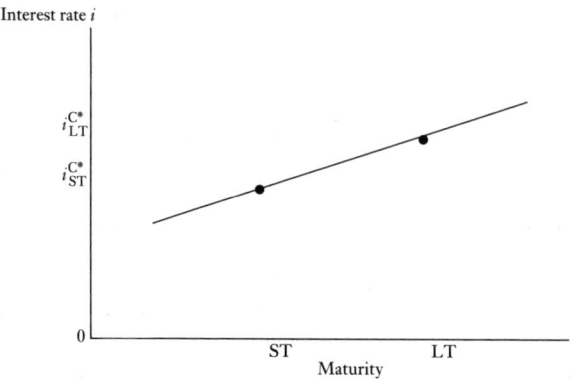

Treasury Bond Market

- Short-term bonds

$BD_{ST}^T = f(i_{ST}^T, i_{ST}^C, \text{risk, liquidity, government policy})$

$BS_{ST}^T = f(\text{government policy})$

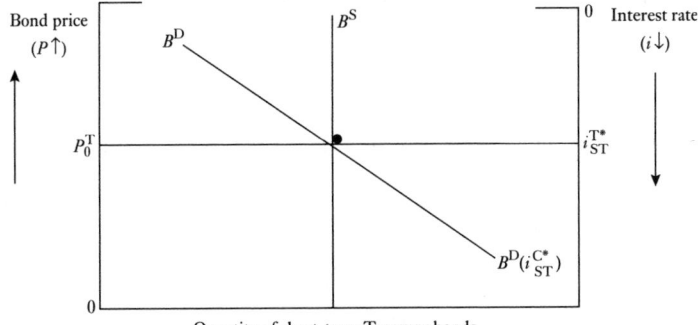

- Long-term bonds

$BD_{LT}^T = f(i_{LT}^T, i_{LT}^C, \text{risk, liquidity, government policy})$

$BS_{LT}^T = f(\text{government policy})$

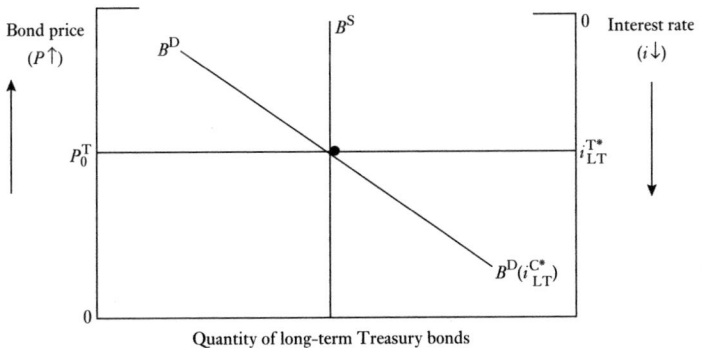

- Yield curve, Treasury bond

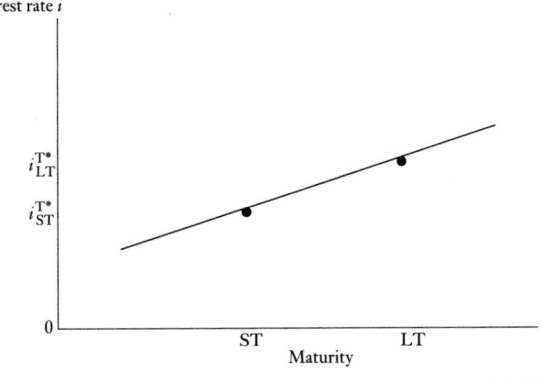

equipment, and other long-term assets. In the bond market, these actions cause the short-term and the long-term supplies of bonds to decrease as the economy moves from growth to recession. At the initial interest rates, the decrease in bonds outstanding creates an excess demand, with bondholders now competing to buy fewer available bonds. This drives bond prices up and the YTM down, decreasing demand until a new equilibrium rate is attained.

Using our supply and demand model (see exhibit 3.7), the recession shifts the corporate short-term and long-term bond supply curves to the left, creating an excess demand for short-term bonds at i_{ST}^{C*} and an excess demand for long-term bonds at i_{LT}^{C*}. The excess demand causes corporate bond prices to rise and rates to fall until a new equilibrium is reached (i_{ST}^{C**} and i_{LT}^{C**}). As the rates on short-term and long-term corporate bonds decrease, short-term and long-term Treasury securities become relatively more attractive. As a result, the demands for short-term and long-term Treasuries increase, shifting the short-term and long-term Treasury bond demand curves to the right and creating an excess demand in both Treasury markets at their initial rates. Like the corporate bond markets, the excess demand in the Treasury security markets will cause their prices to increase and their rates to fall until a new equilibrium is attained. Thus, the supply and demand analysis shows that a recession has a tendency to decrease both short-term and long-term rates for corporate bonds, and by a substitution effect, decrease short-term and long-term Treasury rates. Thus, a recession causes the yield curves for both sectors to shift down as shown in exhibit 3.7.

Note that with this model we cannot explain whether or not the slope of the yield curve also changes. To address that question we need information about the magnitudes of the shifts, as well as their relative slopes. Also, note that the opposite results would occur if the economy moved from recession to economic expansion. This analysis is left to the reader.

Case 2: Treasury Financing

Interest rates on government securities depend, in part, on the size and growth of federal government debt. If federal deficits are increasing over time, then the Treasury will be constantly trying to raise funds in the financial market. As we will discuss in more detail in chapter 6, the Treasury sells a number of short-term, intermediate, and long-term securities. Which securities the Treasury uses to finance a federal deficit affects the yield curve for Treasury securities, and through a substitution effect, the yield curve for corporate bonds. For example, if the Treasury were to finance a deficit by selling short-term Treasury securities, then there would be an increase in the supply of the short-term Treasuries (rightward shift in the BS_{ST}^T curve). The increase in supply would push the price of the short-term government securities down, providing a higher short-term Treasury yield (see exhibit 3.8). In the corporate bond market, the higher rates on short-term government securities would lead to a decrease in the demand for short-term corporate securities (leftward shift in the BD_{ST}^C curve), which, in turn, would lead to an excess supply in that market as short-term corporate bondholders try to sell their corporate bonds in order to buy the higher yielding Treasury securities. As bondholders try to sell their short-term corporate bonds, the prices on such bonds would decrease, causing the rates on short-term corporate bonds to rise until a new equilibrium is reached. Thus, the sale of the short-term Treasury securities increases both short-term government and short-term corporate rates. Since the long-term market is assumed to be independent of short-term rates, the total adjustment to the Treasury's sale of short-term securities would occur through the increase in short-term corporate and Treasury rates. Moreover, given corporate and Treasury yield curves that are initially flat, as shown in exhibit 3.8, the Treasury's action causes the yield curves to become negatively sloped.[2] By contrast, if the Treasury had financed the deficit with long-term securities, the impact would have been felt in the long-term bond market. In this case, the Treasury and corporate bond yield curves would have become positively sloped.

In the case of a budget surplus (such as the brief one that occurred in the US in the late 1990s and early 2000), the yield curve could become negatively sloped if the Treasury used some of the surplus to buy up long-term Treasury securities as a policy to reduce the government's debt. That is, the Treasury's purchase of long-term securities would create an excess demand for long-term Treasury bonds and, by the substitution effect, an excess demand for long-term corporate bonds, leading to higher prices and lower rates on long-term securities.

Case 3: Open Market Operations

The yield curve can also be affected by the direction of monetary policy and how it is implemented. For example, if the central bank were engaged in an expansionary OMO in which it were buying short-term Treasury securities, there would be a tendency for the yield curve to become positively sloped if the central bank were buying short-term securities, and a tendency for the yield curve to become negatively sloped if it were to purchase long-term securities. On the other hand, in a contractionary OMO, there would be a tendency for the Treasury yield curve to become negatively sloped if the central bank were to sell some of its holdings of short-term bills and positively sloped if it were to sell some of its long-term security holdings.

In addition to affecting the Treasury yield curve, open market operations also change the yield curve for corporate securities through a substitution effect. For example, an expansionary OMO in which the Fed purchases short-term Treasury securities would tend to cause the yield curve for corporate securities to become positively sloped. That is, as the rate on short-term Treasury securities decreases as a result of the OMO (short-term Treasury bond supply decreases, see exhibit 3.9), the demand for short-term corporate bonds would increase (short-term corporate bond demand curve shifts right), causing higher prices and lower yields on the short-term corporate securities. Again, since the long-term market is assumed to be independent of short-term rates, the total adjustment to the Fed's purchase of short-term securities would only occur in the short-term corporate and Treasury market and not in the long-term markets. If both the Treasury and corporate yield curves were initially flat, as shown in exhibit 3.9, then the expansionary OMO would result in new positively sloped yield curves.

Summary of MST

The MST provides an economic foundation for explaining the shapes of yield curves in terms of fundamental supply and demand forces. As such, the model can be used to analyze the impacts of a number of economic activities on the term structure of interest rates. While the theory can be used to explain a number of important economic forces, it has two shortcomings. First, by assuming independent markets, the MST does not recognize that it is possible that the rate of return on a bond in a particular maturity segment could increase to a level sufficient to induce investors to move out of their preferred segment and buy the bond with the higher rate in exchange for greater risk exposure. Secondly, MST does not take into account the role of expectations in determining the structure of interest rates. An investor with a 2-year horizon period, for example, might prefer a series of 1-year bonds to a 2-year bond, if she expects relatively high yields on 1-year bonds next year. If there are enough investors with such expectations, they could have an effect on the current demands for 1- and 2-year bonds. These limitations of MST are addressed in the other theories of term structures: the preferred habitat theory, pure expectations theory, and the liquidity premium theory.

Web Information
Current and historical data on US government expenditures and revenues can be found at
  www.gpo.gov/usbudget

3.4.2 Preferred Habitat Theory

MST assumes that investors and borrowers have preferred maturity segments or habitats determined by the maturities of their securities that they want to maintain. The *preferred habitat theory (PHT)* posits that investors and borrowers may stray away from desired maturity segments if there are relatively better rates to compensate them. Furthermore, PHT

Exhibit 3.7   MST model: recession case

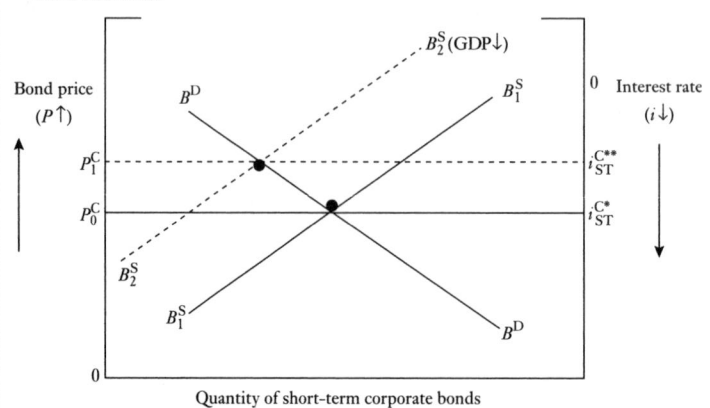

Corporate Bond Market
● Short-term bonds

Bond price $(P\uparrow)$ 0 Interest rate $(i\downarrow)$

$B_2^S(\text{GDP}\downarrow)$

B^D B_1^S

P_1^C i_{ST}^{C**}

P_0^C i_{ST}^{C*}

B_2^S

B_1^S

B^D

0

Quantity of short-term corporate bonds

● Long-term bonds

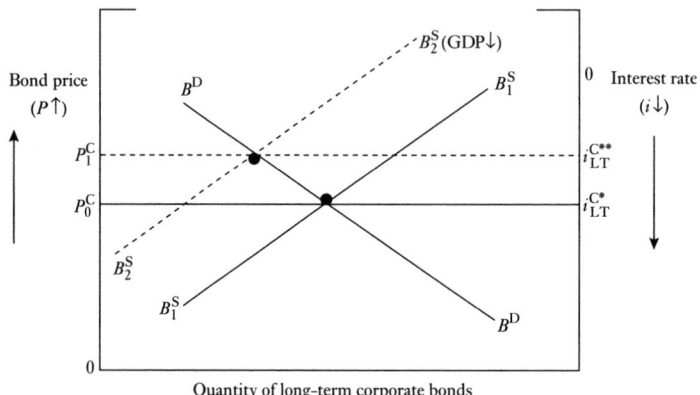

Bond price $(P\uparrow)$ 0 Interest rate $(i\downarrow)$

$B_2^S(\text{GDP}\downarrow)$

B^D B_1^S

P_1^C i_{LT}^{C**}

P_0^C i_{LT}^{C*}

B_2^S

B_1^S

B^D

0

Quantity of long-term corporate bonds

● Yield curve, corporate bond

Interest rate i

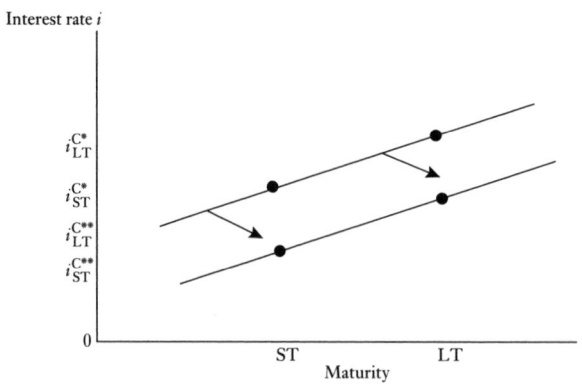

i_{LT}^{C*}

i_{ST}^{C*}

i_{LT}^{C**}

i_{ST}^{C**}

0

ST   LT

Maturity

Treasury Bond Market

- Short-term bonds

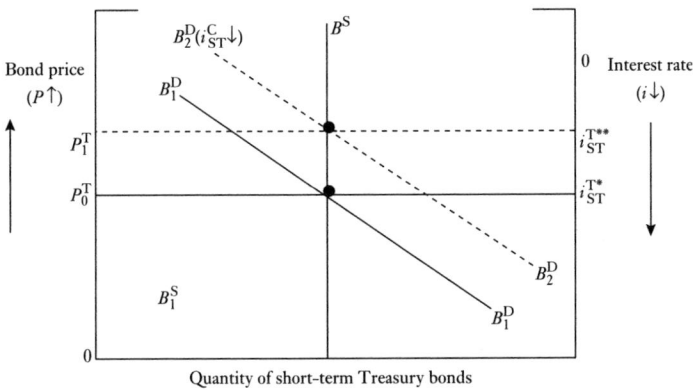

Quantity of short-term Treasury bonds

- Long-term bonds

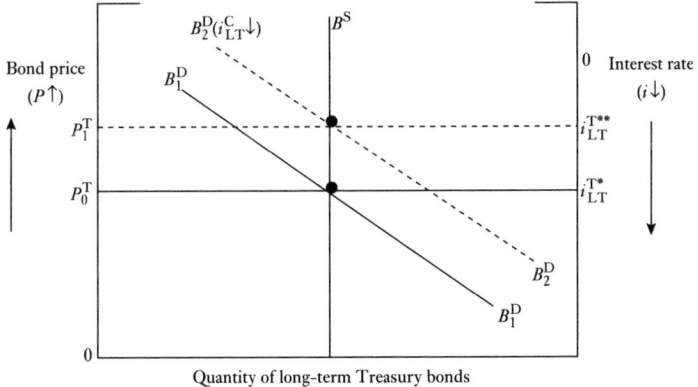

Quantity of long-term Treasury bonds

- Yield curve, Treasury bond

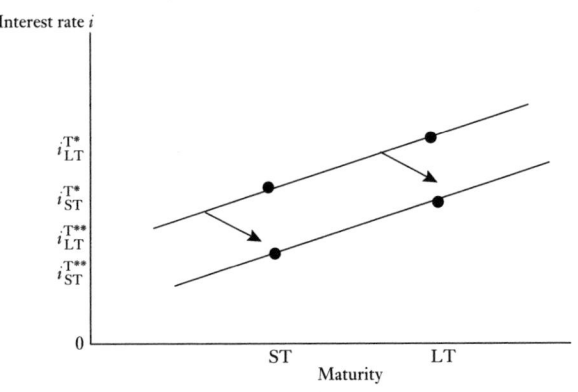

Exhibit 3.8 MST model: Treasury issue of short-term securities

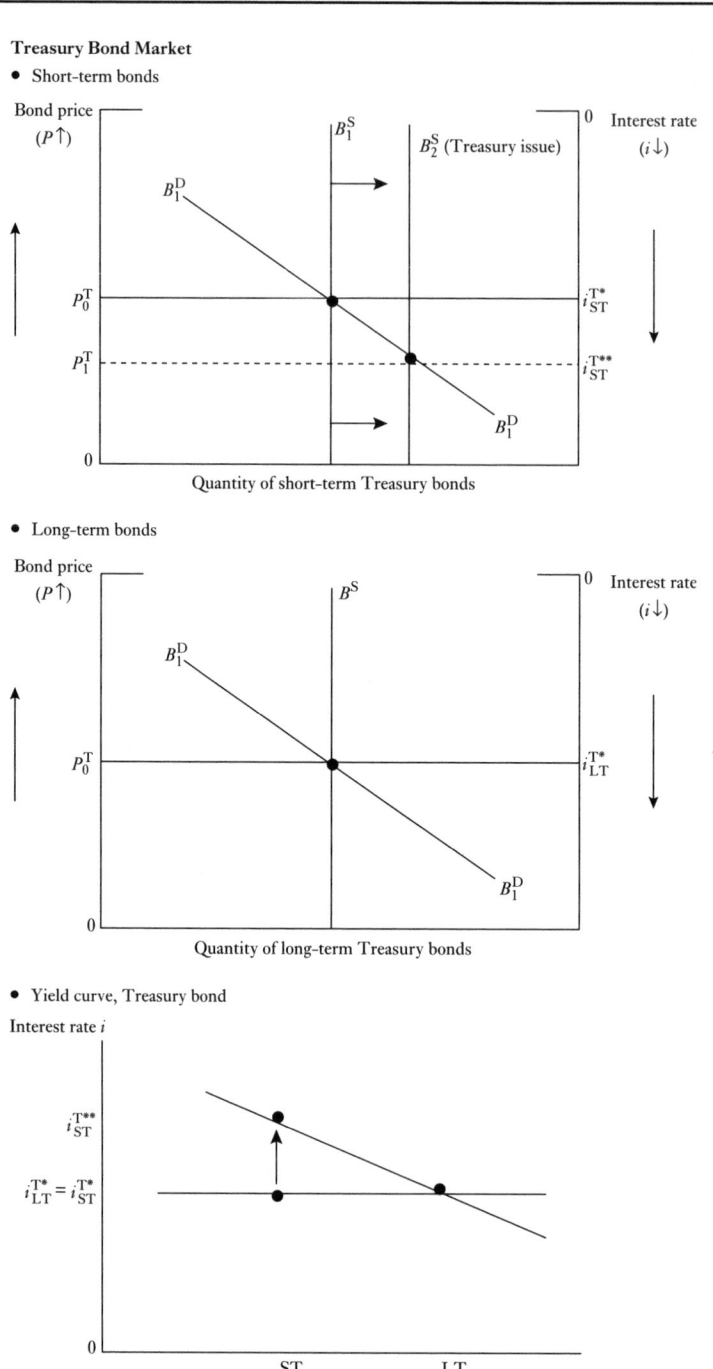

Corporate Bond Market

- Short-term bonds

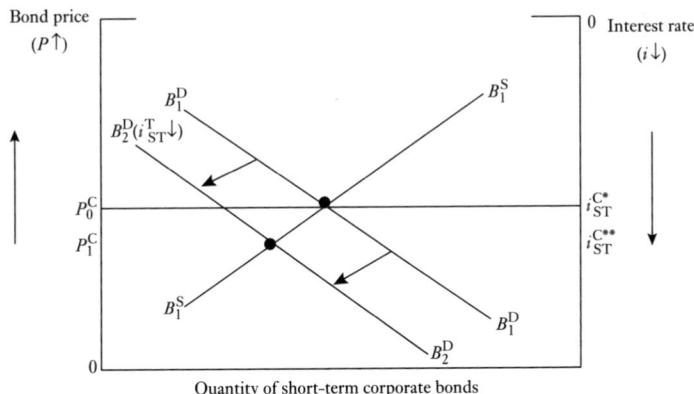

Quantity of short-term corporate bonds

- Long-term bonds

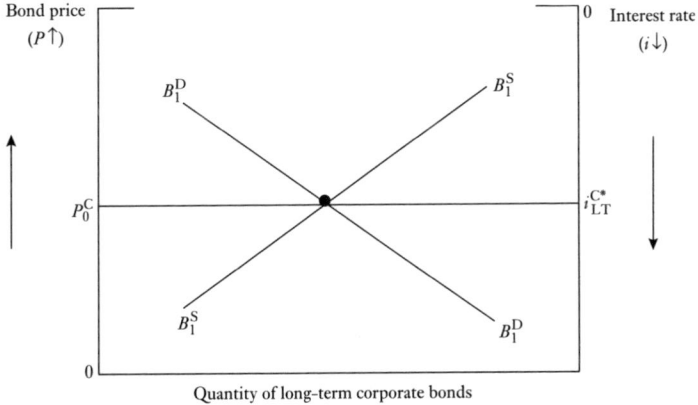

Quantity of long-term corporate bonds

- Yield curve, corporate bond

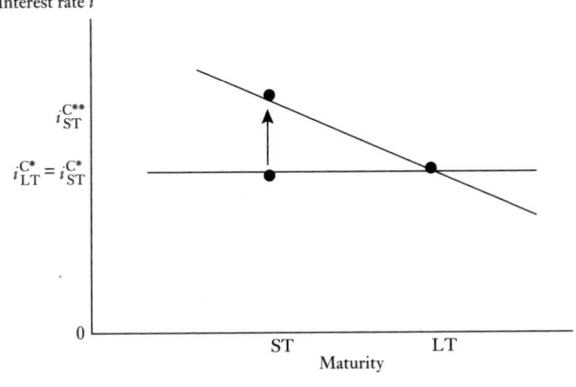

Exhibit 3.9 MST model: central bank purchase of short-term Treasury securities

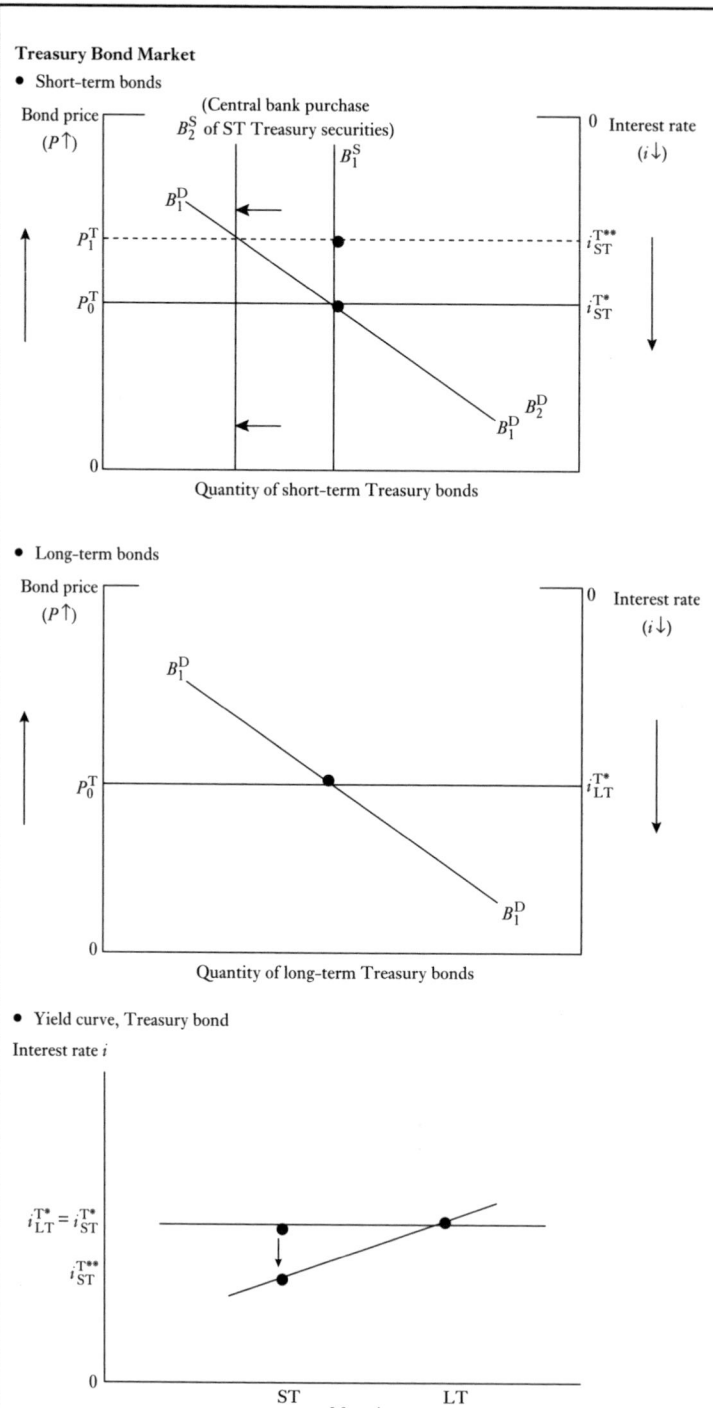

Corporate Bond Market

- Short-term bonds

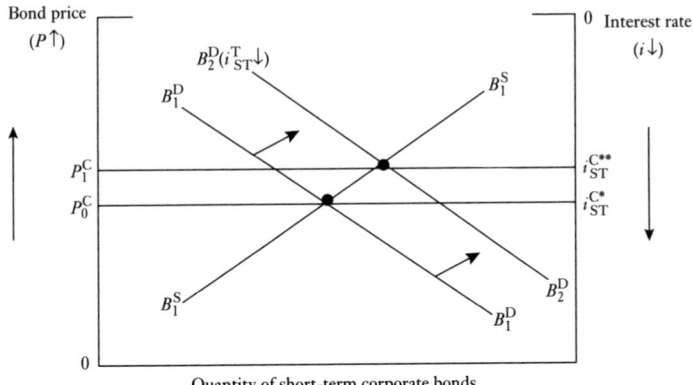

- Long-term bonds

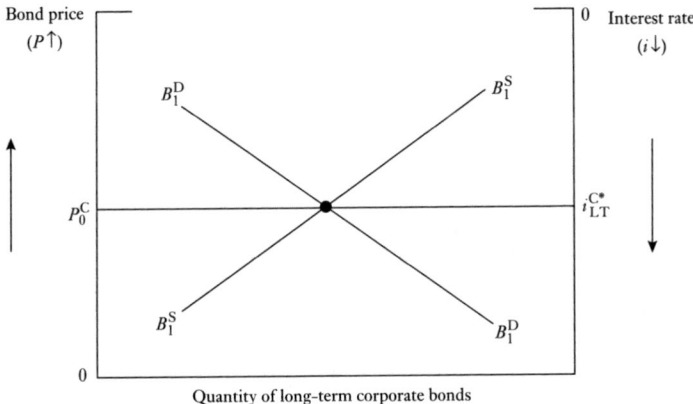

- Yield curve, corporate bond

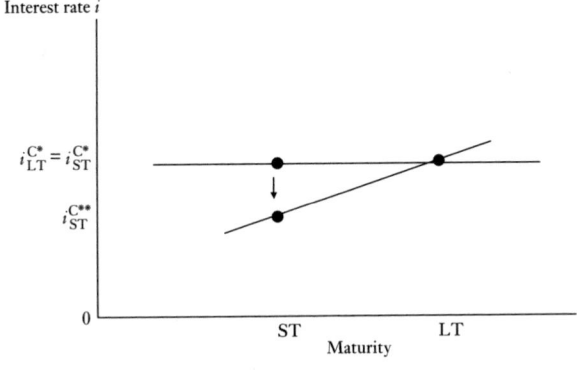

Exhibit 3.10 Preferred habitat theory: market adjustments to poorly hedged economy

- **Poorly hedged economy**: Investors, on average, prefer ST investments; corporate issuers/borrowers, on average, prefer to borrow LT (sell LT corporate bonds):

asserts that investors and borrowers will be induced to forego their perfect hedges and shift out of their preferred maturity segments when supply and demand conditions in different maturity markets do not match.

To illustrate PHT, consider an economic world in which, on the demand side, investors in corporate securities, on average, prefer short-term to long-term instruments, while on the supply side, corporations have a greater need to finance long-term assets than short-term, and therefore prefer to issue more long-term bonds than short-term. Combined, these relative preferences would cause an excess demand for short-term bonds and an excess supply for long-term claims and an equilibrium adjustment would have to occur. As summarized in exhibit 3.10, the excess supply in the long-term market would force issuers to lower their bond prices, thus increasing bond yields and inducing some investors to change their short-term investment demands. In the short-term market, the excess demand would cause bond prices to increase and rates to fall, inducing some corporations to finance their long-term assets by selling short-term claims. Ultimately, equilibriums in both markets would be reached with long-term rates higher than short-term rates, a premium necessary to compensate investors and borrowers/issuers for the risk they've assumed.

As an explanation of term structure, the PHT would suggest that yield curves are positively sloped if investors, on the average, prefer short-term to long-term investments and borrowers/issuers prefer long to short. A priori, such preferences may be the case. That is, investors may prefer short-term investments given that longer maturity bonds tend to be more sensitive to interest rate changes or because there are more investors in the upper middle-age class (with shorter investment horizons) than in the young adult or middle-age class (with longer horizon periods). Borrowers also may have greater long-term than short-term financing needs and thus prefer to borrow long-term. Hence, one could argue that the yield curve is positively sloped because investors' and borrowers' preferences make the economy poorly hedged. Of course, the opposite case in which investors want to invest more in long-term securities than short-term and issuers desire more short-term to long-term debt is possible. Under these conditions the yield curve would tend to be negatively sloped.

3.4.3 Pure Expectations Theory

Expectations theories try to explain the impact of investors' and borrowers' expectations on the term structure of interest rates. A popular

Exhibit 3.11 Pure expectations theory: market expectation of higher interest rate

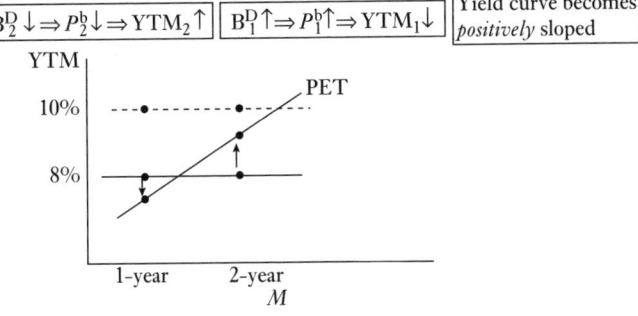

- Expectations of rates increasing from 8% to 10%.
- Investors with HD of 2 years and those with HD of 1 year would prefer 1-year bonds over 2-years bonds.
- Market response:

$$B_2^D \downarrow \Rightarrow P_2^b \downarrow \Rightarrow YTM_2 \uparrow \quad B_1^D \uparrow \Rightarrow P_1^b \uparrow \Rightarrow YTM_1 \downarrow \quad \boxed{\text{Yield curve becomes } \textit{positively} \text{ sloped}}$$

- If the market response to the expectation is only in terms of a change in the 2-year bond, then the equilibrium yield on 2-year bonds will be 9%.

$$B_2^D \downarrow \Rightarrow P_2^b \downarrow \Rightarrow YTM_2 \uparrow$$
$$YTM_2 \uparrow \text{ until } YTM_2 = YTM_{2:series} = 9\% \quad\quad \text{When } YTM_2 = 9\%, YTM_1 = 8\%, \text{ then } f_{11} = E(R_{11}) = 10\%$$

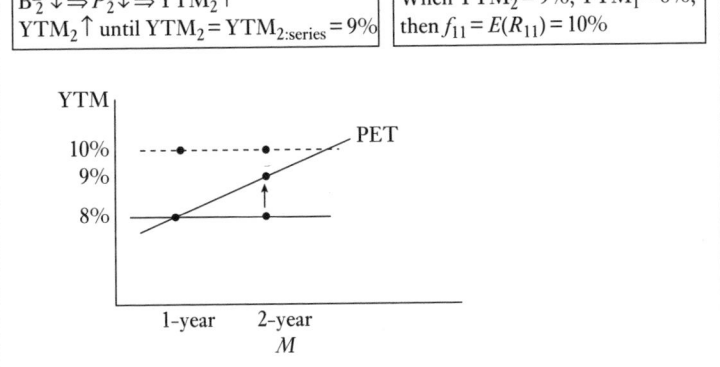

model is the *pure expectations theory (PET)*, also called the *unbiased expectations theory (UET)*. Developed by Fredrick Lutz, PET is based on the premise that the interest rates on bonds of different maturities can be determined in equilibrium where implied forward rates are equal to expected spot rates.

To illustrate PET, consider a market consisting of only two bonds: a risk-free 1-year zero-coupon bond and a risk-free 2-year zero-coupon bond, both with principals of $1,000. Suppose that supply and demand conditions are such that both the 1-year and 2-year bonds

are trading at an 8% YTM. Also suppose that the market expects the yield curve to shift up to 10% next year, but, as yet, has not factored that expectation into its current investment decisions (see exhibit 3.11). Finally, assume the market is risk-neutral, such that investors do not require a risk premium for investing in risky securities (i.e., they will accept an expected rate on a risky investment that is equal to the risk-free rate). To see the impact of market expectations on the current structure of rates, consider the case of investors with horizon dates of 2 years. These investors can buy the 2-year bond with an annual rate of 8%, or they can buy the 1-year bond yielding 8%, then reinvest the principal and interest 1 year later in another 1-year bond expected to yield 10%. Given these alternatives, such investors would prefer the latter investment since it yields a higher expected average annual rate for the 2 years of 9%:

$$E(R) = [(1.08)(1.10)]^{1/2} - 1 = 0.09$$

Similarly, investors with 1-year horizon dates would also find it more advantageous to buy a 1-year bond yielding 8% than a 2-year bond (priced at $857.34 = \$1{,}000/1.08^2$) that they would sell 1 year later to earn an expected rate of only 6%:

$$P_{Mt} = P_{2,0} = \frac{\$1{,}000}{(1.08)^2} = \$857.37$$

$$E(P_{11}) = \frac{\$1{,}000}{(1.10)^1} = \$909.09$$

$$E(R) = \frac{\$909.09 - \$857.34}{\$857.34} = 0.06$$

Thus, in a risk-neutral market with an expectation of higher rates next year, both investors with 1-year horizon dates and investors with 2-year horizon dates would purchase 1-year instead of 2-year bonds.

If enough investors do this, an increase in the demand for 1-year bonds and a decrease in the demand for 2-year bonds would occur until the average annual rate on the 2-year bond is equal to the equivalent annual rate from the series of 1-year investments (or the 1-year bond's rate is equal to the rate expected on the 2-year bond held 1 year). In the example, if the price on a 2-year bond fell such that it traded at a YTM of 9%, and the rate on a 1-year bond stayed at 8%, then investors with 2-year horizon dates would be indifferent between a 2-year bond yielding a certain 9% and a series of 1-year bonds yielding 10% and 8%, for an expected rate of 9%. Investors with 1-year horizon dates would likewise be indifferent between a 1-year bond yielding 8% and a 2-year bond purchased at 9% and sold 1 year later at 10%, for an expected 1-year rate of 8%. Thus in this case, the impact of the market's expectation of higher rates would be to push the longer-term rates up.

Recall that in the last chapter we defined the implied forward rate as a future rate implied by today's rates. In this example, the equilibrium YTM on the 2-year bond is 9% and the equilibrium YTM on the 1-year bond is 8%, yielding an implied forward rate of 10%, the same as the expected rate on a 1-year bond, 1 year from now. That is:

$$YTM_2 = [(1 + YTM_1)(1 + f_{11})]^{1/2} - 1$$

$$f_{11} = \frac{(1 + YTM_2)^2}{(1 + YTM_1)} - 1$$

$$f_{11} = \frac{(1.09)^2}{(1.08)} - 1 = 0.10$$

Thus in equilibrium, the implied forward rate is equal to the expected spot rate.

Yield Curves that Incorporate Investors' Expectations

In the above example, the yield curve is positively sloped, reflecting expectations of higher rates. By contrast, if the yield curve were currently flat at 10% and there was a market expectation that it would shift down to 8% next year, then the expectation of lower rates would cause the yield curve to become negatively sloped (see exhibit 3.12). In this case, an investor with a 2-year horizon date would prefer the 2-year bond at 10% to a series of 1-year bonds yielding an expected rate of only 9% ($E(R) = [(1.10)(1.08)]^{1/2} - 1 = 0.09$); an investor with a 1-year horizon would also prefer buying a 2-year bond that has an expected rate of return of 12% ($P_2 = 100/(1.10)^2 = 82.6446$, $E(P_{11}) = 100/1.08 = 92.5926$, $E(R) = [92.5926 - 82.6446]/82.6446 = 0.12$) to the 1-year bond that yields only 10%. In markets for both 1-year and 2-year bonds, the expectations of lower rates would cause the demand and price of the 2-year bond to increase, lowering its rate, and the demand and price for the 1-year bond to decrease, increasing its rate. These adjustments would continue until the rate on the 2-year bond equaled the average rate from the series of 1-year investments, or until the rate on the 1-year bond equaled the expected rate from holding a 2-year bond 1 year

Exhibit 3.12 Pure expectations theory: market expectation of lower rates

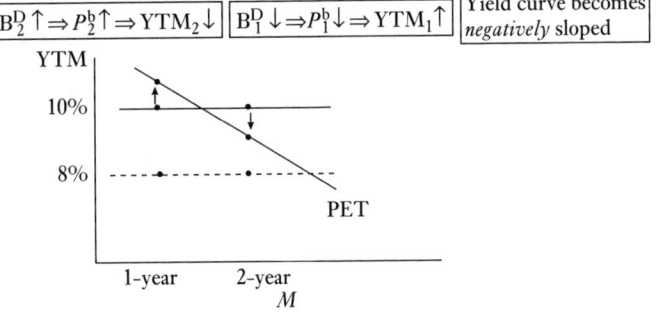

- Expectations of rates decreasing from 10% to 8%.
- Investors with HD of 2 years and those with HD of 1 year would prefer 2-year bonds over 1-year bonds.
- Market response:

$B_2^D \uparrow \Rightarrow P_2^b \uparrow \Rightarrow YTM_2 \downarrow$ $\quad B_1^D \downarrow \Rightarrow P_1^b \downarrow \Rightarrow YTM_1 \uparrow$ $\quad$ Yield curve becomes *negatively* sloped

- If the market response to the expectation is only in terms of a change in the 2-year bond, then the equilibrium yield on the 2-year will be 9%.

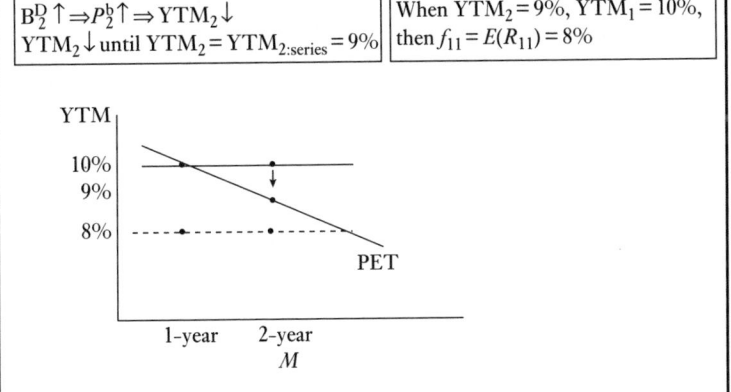

$B_2^D \uparrow \Rightarrow P_2^b \uparrow \Rightarrow YTM_2 \downarrow$ $\quad$ When $YTM_2 = 9\%$, $YTM_1 = 10\%$,
$YTM_2 \downarrow$ until $YTM_2 = YTM_{2:series} = 9\%$ $\quad$ then $f_{11} = E(R_{11}) = 8\%$

(or when the implied forward rate is equal to expected spot rates). In this case, if 1-year rates stayed at 8%, then the demand for the 2-year bond would increase until it was priced to yield 9% – the expected rate from the series: $[(1.10)(1.08)]^{1/2} - 1 = 0.09$ (see exhibit 3.12).

Finally, suppose the yield curve is currently positively sloped, with the rate on the 1-year bond at 8% and the rate on the 2-year bond at 9%. This time, though, suppose that the market expects no change in yields and that this expectation has not yet been reflected in the yield curve. Investors with horizon dates of 2 years would prefer the 2-year bond yielding 9% to a series of 1-year bonds yielding 8% now and 8% expected at the end of 1 year (for a 2-year equivalent of 8%). Similarly, investors with 1-year horizon dates would also prefer the 2-year bond held for 1 year in which the expected rate is 10%, compared to only 8% from the 1-year bond. Given the preference for 2-year bonds, a market response would occur in which demand for the 2-year bond would rise, in turn increasing its price and lowering its yield, and the demand and price for the 1-year bond would decrease, increasing its yield. Thus, the original positively sloped yield curve would become flat, given the expectation of no change in the yield curve.

Features of Pure Expectations Theory

One of the features of the pure expectations theory is that in equilibrium the yield curve reflects current expectations about future rates. From our preceding examples, when the equilibrium yield curve was positively sloped, the market expected higher rates in the future; when the curve was negatively sloped, the market expected lower rates; when it was flat, the market expected no change in rates.

Secondly, PET intuitively captures what should be considered as normal market behavior. That is, whether or not the market is risk neutral, has perfect expectations, or bonds are perfect substitutes, investors, as well as borrowers/issuers do factor in expectations. For example, if long-term rates were expected to be higher in the future (based perhaps on the expectation of greater economic growth), long-term investors (e.g., life insurance company, pension fund, etc.) would not want to purchase long-term bonds now, given that next period they would be expecting higher yields and lower prices on such bonds (they also would be exposed to possible capital losses if they did buy such bonds and were forced to liquidate them next year). Instead, such investors would invest in short-term securities now, reinvesting later at the expected higher long-term rates. In contrast, borrowers/issuers wishing to borrow long-term would want to sell long-term bonds now instead of later at possibly higher rates. Combined, the decrease in demand for long-term bonds by investors and the increase in the supply of long-term bonds by borrowers would serve to lower long-term bond prices and increase yields, leading to a positively sloped yield curve. Thus, a salient feature of PET is that it incorporates expectations as an important variable in explaining the structure of interest rates.

Finally, if PET strictly holds (i.e., we can accept all of the model's assumptions), then the expected future rates would be equal to the implied forward rates. As a result, one could forecast futures rates and future yield curves by simply calculating implied forward rates from current rates (this technique is explained in section 3.4.6).

3.4.4 Liquidity Premium Theory

The *liquidity premium theory (LPT)*, also referred to as the *risk premium theory (RPT)*, posits that there is a liquidity premium for long-term bonds over short-term bonds. Recall that in chapter 2 we examined how long-term bonds were more price sensitive to interest rate changes than short-term bonds. As a result, the prices of long-term securities tend to be more volatile and therefore more risky than short-term securities. According to LPT, if investors were risk averse, then they would require some additional return (liquidity premium) in order to hold long-term bonds instead of short-term ones. Thus, if the yield curve were initially flat, but had no risk premium factored in to compensate investors for the additional volatility they assumed from buying long-term bonds, then the demand for long-term bonds would decrease and their rates increase until risk-averse investors were compensated. In this case, the yield curve would become positively sloped.

3.4.5 Summary of Term Structure Theories

As we noted earlier, the structure of interest rates cannot be explained in terms of any one theory; rather, it is best explained by a combination of theories. Of the four theories, the two major ones are MST and PET. MST is important because it establishes how the fundamental market forces governing the supply and demand for assets determine interest rates. PET, in turn, extends MST to show how expectations impact the structure of interest rates. PHT, by explaining how markets will adjust if the economy is poorly hedged, and LPT, by including a liquidity premium for longer-term bonds, both represent necessary extensions of MST and PET. Together, the four theories help us to understand how supply and demand, economic conditions, government deficits and surpluses, monetary policy, hedging, maturity preferences, and expectations all affect the bond market in general and the structure of rates in particular.

3.4.6 Current and Expected Spot Yield Curves

In the past, many analysts constructed yield curves from yield data on Treasury securities or different corporate bonds. The problem with generating yield curves in this way, though, is finding a sample of bonds that are identical in all respects except maturity (i.e., the same coupon rates, risk, option features, and the like). Today, the convention is to generate a spot yield curve showing the relation between the spot rates and maturity. As noted in chapter 2, a spot Treasury rate is the rate on a zero-coupon Treasury. Since such bonds lack coupons, have no default risk, and, if generated from T-bills, have no risk of call, they are ideal.[3] Once a spot yield curve is generated from Treasury securities, the yield curve for bonds with different coupons and quality can be estimated by including appropriate risk, liquidity, and tax premium as discussed in section 3.3. The obvious problem with generating spot yield curves from Treasury securities is that there are no zero-coupon Treasury securities with maturities greater than 1 year. As noted in the last chapter, though, the theoretical spot yield curve can be determined using a bootstrapping technique.[4]

Forecasting Future Spot Yield Curves

Recall from our earlier discussion of the term structure of interest rates that one of the implications of PET is that the current yield curve is governed by the condition that the implied forward rate is equal to the expected spot rate. Given a spot yield curve, one could therefore use PET to estimate the next period's spot yield curve by determining the implied forward rates.

Exhibit 3.13 shows spot rates on bonds with maturities ranging from 1 year to 5 years (column 2). From these rates, expected spot rates (S_t) are generated for bonds 1 year from the present (column 3) and 2 years from the present (column 4). The expected spot rates shown are equal to their corresponding implied forward rates. For example, the expected rate on a 1-year bond 1 year from now

$(E(S_{Mt}) = E(S_{11}))$ is equal to the implied forward rate of $f_{Mt} = f_{11} = 11\%$. This rate is obtained by using the geometric mean with the current 2-year and 1-year spot rates:

$$S_2 = [(1 + S_1)(1 + f_{11})]^{1/2} - 1$$

$$f_{11} = \frac{(1 + S_2)^2}{(1 + S_1)} - 1$$

$$f_{11} = \frac{(1.105)^2}{(1.10)} - 1 = 0.11.$$

Similarly, the expected 2-year spot rate 1 year from now is equal to the implied forward rate on a 2-year bond purchased 1 year from now of $f_{Mt} = f_{21} = 11.5\%$. This rate is obtained using 3-year and 1-year spot rates. The other expected spot rates for next year are found by repeating this process.

A similar approach also can be used to forecast the yield curve 2 years from the present. The expected 1-year spot rate 2 years from now, $E(S_{12})$, is equal to the implied forward rate f_{12}, which is equal to 12% (see exhibit 3.13). This rate is obtained from 2-year and 3-year spot rates using the geometric mean. The expected 2-year spot rate, 2 years from now, is found by solving for f_{22}. Using 4-year and 2-year spot rates, f_{22} is equal to 12.5%. Finally, f_{32} of 13% is found using 5-year and 2-year bonds. All of these implied forward rates can be found using the following formula:

$$f_{Mt} = \left[\frac{(1 + S_{M+t})^{M+t}}{(1 + S_t)^t} \right]^{1/M} - 1$$

Using Forward Rates as Expected Rates of Return

According to PET, if the market is risk-neutral, then the implied forward rate is equal to the expected spot rate, and in equilibrium, the expected rate of return for holding any bond for 1 year would be equal to the current spot rate on 1-year bonds. Similarly, the rate expected to be earned for 2 years from investing in any bond or combination of bonds (e.g., a series of 1-year bonds) would be equal to the rate on the 2-year bond. This condition can be illustrated using the spot yield curve and expected yield curves (or forward rates) shown in exhibit 3.13. For example, the expected rate of return from

Exhibit 3.13   Forecasting yield curves using implied forward rates

(1) Maturity (years)	(2) Spot rates (%)	(3) Expected spot rates 1 year from present (%)	(4) Expected spot rates 2 years from present (%)
1	10.0	$f_{11} = 11.0$	$f_{12} = 12.0$
2	10.5	$f_{21} = 11.5$	$f_{22} = 12.5$
3	11.0	$f_{31} = 12.0$	$f_{32} = 13.0$
4	11.5	$f_{41} = 12.5$	
5	12.0		

f_{12}

$$S_3 = [(1+S_1)(1+f_{11})(1+f_{12})]^{1/3} - 1$$

$$S_3 = [(1+S_2)^2(1+f_{12})]^{1/3} - 1$$

$$f_{12} = \frac{(1+S_3)^3}{(1+S_2)^2} - 1$$

$$f_{12} = \frac{(1.11)^3}{(1.105)^2} - 1 = 0.12.$$

f_{32}

$$S_5 = [(1+S_1)(1+f_{11})(1+f_{12})(1+f_{13})(1+f_{14})]^{1/5} - 1$$

$$S_5 = [(1+S_2)^2(1+f_{32})^3]^{1/5} - 1$$

$$f_{32} = \sqrt[3]{\frac{(1+S_5)^5}{(1+S_2)^2}} - 1$$

$$f_{32} = \sqrt[3]{\frac{(1.12)^5}{(1.105)^2}} - 1 = 0.13.$$

purchasing a 2-year zero-coupon bond at the spot rate of 10.5% and selling it 1 year later at an expected 1-year spot rate equal to the implied forward rate of $f_{11} = 11\%$ is 10%. This is the same rate obtained from investing in a 1-year bond. That is:

$$E(R) = \frac{90.09 - 81.8984}{81.8984} = 0.10$$

$$E(P_{11}) = \frac{100}{1.11} = 90.09$$

$$P_{20} = \frac{100}{(1.105)^2} = 81.8984$$

Similarly, the expected rate of return from holding a 3-year bond for 1 year, then selling it at the implied forward rate of f_{21} is also 10%. That is:

$$E(R) = \frac{80.43596 - 73.1191}{73.1191} = 0.10$$

$$E(P_{21}) = \frac{100}{(1.115)^2} = 80.43596$$

$$P_{30} = \frac{100}{(1.11)^3} = 73.1191$$

Any of the bonds with spot rates shown in exhibit 3.13 would have expected rates for 1 year

of 10% if the implied forward rate were used as the estimated expected rate. Similar results hold for a 2-year investment period. That is, any bond held for 2 years and sold at its forward rate would earn the 2-year spot rate of 10.5%. For example, a 4-year bond purchased at the spot rate of 11.5% and expected to be sold 2 years later at $f_{22} = 12.5\%$ would trade at an expected rate of 10.5% – the same as the current 2-year spot. Similarly, an investment in a series of 1-year bonds at spot rates of $S_1 = 10.0\%$ and $E(S_{11}) = f_{11} = 11\%$ yields a 2-year rate of 10.5% $(= [(1.10)(1.11)]^{1/2} - 1)$.

Finally, the same conditions also hold for coupon bonds that are valued at spot rates and are expected to be sold at expected spot rates equal to the implied forward rates. For example, a 4-year, 10% coupon bond with a face value of 100 would be worth 95.762 if it is discounted by the spot rates shown in exhibit 4.5–8:

$$V_0 = \frac{10}{1.10} + \frac{10}{(1.105)^2} + \frac{10}{(1.11)^3} + \frac{110}{(1.115)^4}$$

$$= 95.762$$

If that bond were sold 1 year later at the forward rates, its expected price would be 95.3484, yielding a 1-year expected rate of 10% – the same as the 1-year spot rate:

$$E(P) = \frac{10}{1.11} + \frac{10}{(1.115)^2} + \frac{110}{(1.12)^3} = 95.3484$$

$$E(R) = \frac{(95.3484 - 95.762) + 10}{95.762} = 0.10$$

That expected rates from holding any bond (or combination) for M years are equal to the rate on an M-year zero-coupon bond is a direct result of the risk-neutrality assumption of PET. In reality, bond markets are not risk-neutral. Not surprisingly, studies by Fama (1976) and others have shown that forward rates are not good predictors of future interest rates. Analysts often refer to forward rates as *hedgable rates*, and most do not consider forward rates a market consensus on expected future rates. The most practical use of forward rates or expected spot yield curves generated from forward rates is that they provide *cut-off rates*, which are useful in evaluating investment decisions. For example, an investor with a 1-year horizon date should only consider investing in the 2-year bond in our above example if she expected 1-year rates 1 year later to be less than $f_{11} = 11\%$; that is, assuming she is risk-averse and wants an expected rate greater than 10%. Thus, forward rates serve as a good cut-off rate for evaluating investments.

Web Information
Yield curves can be found at number of sites:
www.ratecurve.com
www.bloomberg.com

3.5 CONCLUSION

In this chapter we have examined what determines the level and structure of interest rates. We started our analysis by first developing a supply and demand model for bonds. The model, in turn, helped us to explain how economic factors such as economic growth, monetary and fiscal policy, and inflation determine the general level of interest rates. We next examined how differences in risk, liquidity, and tax features determine the spreads between interest rates on bonds of different categories. Last, we looked at the theories of the term structure of interest rates. The four prominent theories explaining term structure show that such factors as market expectations, economic conditions, and risk–return preferences are all important in determining the term structure of rates.

In our discussion of the structure of interest rates we looked at the general relationship between risk and return. In the next chapter, we turn our attention to the specific types of risk associated with bonds.

KEY TERMS

Supply of Loanable Funds
Demand for Loanable Funds
Default Risk
Call Risk
Market Risk
Risk Spread or Risk Premium
Risk Neutral
Risk Loving
Risk Aversion
Term Structure of Interest
 Rates

Yield Curve
Normal or Upward Sloping
 Yield Curves
Inverted or Downward
 Sloping Yield Curves
Humped Yield Curve
Market Segmentation Theory
 (MST)
Preferred Habitat Theory
 (PHT)

Pure Expectations Theory
 (PET)
Unbiased Expectations
 Theory (UET)
Liquidity Premium Theory
 (LPT)
Risk Premium Theory
 (RPT)
Hedgable Rates
Cut-Off Rates

PROBLEMS AND QUESTIONS

1. Describe the bond demand and supply model presented in this chapter. Include in your description: the definitions of the bond demand and supply curves, the important factors that shift the curves, equilibrium, and proof of equilibrium.

2. Explain how the following events would shift the bond demand curve:
   a. Increase in GDP
   b. Market expectation of inflation
   c. Market expectation of lower interest rates
   d. Increase in the relative risk of bonds
   e. Increase in relative liquidity of bonds
   f. Decrease in reserve requirement by central bank
   g. Increase in central bank discount rate.

3. Explain how the following events would shift the bond supply curve:
   a. Increase in GDP
   b. An expectation of future inflation
   c. Increase in the federal government deficit
   d. Federal government surplus
   e. Expansionary open market operation by the central bank
   f. Contractionary open market operation by the central bank.

4. Using the bond demand and supply model presented in this chapter explain the impacts of the following cases on the level of interest rates:
   a. Expansionary open market operation
   b. Economic recession
   c. Treasury financing of a government deficit
   d. Economic expansion.

5. Given two identical bonds that are priced at the same yields, explain using the supply and demand analysis the adjustments that would take place if events were to occur that would make one of the bonds more risky.

6. Define risk-neutral, risk-averse, and risk-loving markets.

7. Given an economy with two bonds: (1) A 1-year, risk-free zero-coupon bond paying a principal of $1,000 and priced at $952.38 to yield 5%, and (2) a 1-year risky zero-coupon bond with a 0.75 probability of paying $1,000 at the end of the year and a 0.25 probability of defaulting and paying only $100 from liquidation.
   a. What would be the price of the risky bond if the market were risk neutral?
   b. What would be the response of a risk-averse market if the risky bond were priced at its risk-neutral value?
   c. What would be the response of a risk-loving market if the risky bond were priced at its risk-neutral value?

8. Given two identical bonds that are priced at the same yields, explain using the supply and demand analysis the adjustments that would take place if events were to occur that would make one of the bonds less liquid.

9. In question 7, the risk-free bond paid a certain return of $1,000 and was priced to yield a return of 5% and the risky bond had a 0.75 probability of paying $1,000 and 0.25 probability of paying $100, for an expected return of $775. Suppose the probabilities of 0.75 and 0.25 and possible payoffs of $1,000 and $100 are known with absolute certainty (i.e., no one can question the statistics). Explain why the risky bond could still be priced to yield a rate exceeding 5%.

10. Given a 2-year, 8% annual coupon bond selling at par with a face value of $1,000 and with annual coupon payments that is fully taxable and a bond identical except that it is tax free, what would the yield and price on the tax-free bond have to be for an investor in a 35% tax bracket to be indifferent between the two bonds?

11. Using the supply and demand model for a two-sector (government and corporate) and two-segment (short-term and long-term) economy presented in this chapter (see exhibit 3.6), analyze the impacts of the following cases on both the Treasury and corporate yield curves. Assume the initial yield curves are flat.

    a. A period of economic growth
    b. A government surplus in which the Treasury buys existing long-term Treasury bonds
    c. A contractionary open market operation in which the central bank sells some of it short-term Treasury securities to the public.

12. Using the market segmentation theory, outline the impacts on the term structure of interest rates of the following cases:

    a. Economic recession
    b. Economic expansion
    c. Expansionary open market operation in which the central bank buys ST Treasuries
    d. Treasury sale of long-term Treasury bonds
    e. Treasury purchase of long-term Treasury bonds.

13. Explain the equilibrium adjustments that would occur in the short-term and long-term bond markets for the following cases:

    a. Investors in corporate securities, on average, prefer short-term to long-term instruments, while corporations have greater financial requirements to finance long-term assets than short-term, and therefore prefer to issue more long-term bonds than short-term.
    b. Investors in corporate securities, on average, prefer long-term to short-term instruments, while corporations have a greater need to finance short-term assets than long-term, and therefore prefer to issue more short-term bonds than long-term.

    Comment on what the equilibrium adjustments in cases suggests about the market segmentation theory.

14. Explain expectations theory intuitively and with an example. In your example assume a flat yield curve with 1- and 2-year bonds at 6% and an expectation of next year's yield curve being flat with 1- and 2-year bonds at 8%. Explain the theory only in terms of the response to the expectation by investors with 1-year and 2-year horizon dates.

15. Outline the impacts the following market expectations have on the yield curve:

    a. A flat yield curve at 8% with a market expectation of a flat yield curve at 12% 1 year later.
    b. A flat yield curve at 10% with a market expectation of a flat yield curve at 8% 1 year later.
    c. A yield curve with 1-year bonds at 6% and 2-year bonds at 7%, with the expectation of a flat yield curve at 8% 1 year later.

    Explain the impacts only in terms of the response to the expectation by investors with 2-year horizon dates.

16. Explain how borrowers/issuers with 2-year assets to finance would respond to the market expectations cases in question 15. Do the impacts of their actions on the yield curve complement the actions of investors?

17. Assume the following yield curves for zero-coupon bonds with a face value of 100:

Maturity	YTM
1 year	7%
2 years	8%
3 years	8%
4 years	7%
5 years	6%

   a. Using implied forward rates estimate the yield curve 1 year from the present (rates on 1-year, 2-year, 3-year, and 4-year bonds).
   b. Using implied forward rates estimate the yield curve 2 years from the present (rates on 1-year, 2-year, and 3-year bonds).
   c. If you bought the 3-year bond and held it 1 year, what would your expected rate of return be if your expectations were based on implied forward rates?
   d. Without calculating, if you bought a bond of any maturity and held it 1 year, what would your expected rate of return be if your expectations were based on implied forward rates?
   e. If you bought the 4-year bond and held it 2 years, what would your expected rate of return be if your expectations were based on implied forward rates?
   f. Without calculating, if you bought a bond of any maturity and held it 2 years, what would your expected rate of return be if your expectations were based on implied forward rates?

18. Given the following spot yield curve:

Maturity	Spot rate
1 year	6.0%
2 years	6.5%
3 years	7.0%
4 years	7.5%

   a. What is the equilibrium price of a 4-year, 7% annual coupon bond paying a principal of $100 at maturity?
   b. Using implied forward rates estimate the yield curve 1 year from the present (1-year, 2-year, and 3-year spot rates).
   c. What is the expected equilibrium price 1 year from now of a 3-year, 7% annual coupon bond paying a principal of $100 at maturity?
   d. What is the 1-year expected rate of return from investing in the 4-year, 7% coupon bond if your expectations were based on implied forward rates?
   e. Using implied forward rates, estimate the yields for 1-year and 2-year spot rates 2 years from now.
   f. Show that the expected rate from holding the 4-year, 7% coupon bond for 2 years is equal to the 2-year spot rate of 6.5%.

19. Using the theories of term structure of interest rates, identify several scenarios that would have a tendency to cause the yield curve to become negatively sloped.

20. Explain the liquidity premium theory. How could the yield curves in questions 17 and 18 be adjusted to reflect a liquidity premium?

21. Short-answer questions:
    (1) If the yield curve includes investors' expectations, then a positively sloped yield curve would reflect what type of expectation about future interest rates?
    (2) If the yield curve includes investors' expectations, then a negatively sloped yield curve would reflect what type of expectation about future interest rates?
    (3) What impact would an economic expansion have on default risk premiums?
    (4) What would the discount rate on risky bonds be if the market were risk neutral?
    (5) How is an implied forward rate used as a cutoff rate?
    (6) Explain how the YTM on many municipal bonds that are subject to default have historically been less than the YTM on T-bonds that are default free.
    (7) Define the preferred habitat theory.

WEB EXERCISES

1. In this chapter, we examined yield spreads among different types of bonds explained by differences in their features. Go to www.federalreserve.gov/releases/h15/data.htm. The site contains data on a number of different bond yields. Go to historical data and compare the annual historical yields on 10-year Treasury bonds to Moody's Aaa and Baa from 1976 to the most recent period reported. You may want to copy the data to Excel so that the data are easier to compare. Comment on the risk premiums you observe. Do the risk premiums change over time? What explains the risk premium changes?

2. In this chapter, we examined the impact of taxes on yield spreads. Go to www.federalreserve.gov/releases/h15/data.htm and click on historical data. Compare the monthly historical yields on 10-year Treasury bonds to the yields on state and local bonds. You may want to copy the data to Excel so that the data are easier to compare. Comment on the yield difference you observe.

3. Current yield curves can be found by going to www.ratecurve.com. Go to this site and compare the current Treasury yield curve with the yield curve a year ago. Comment on what factors you think contributed to the change in the term structure over the past year. Note: the current yield curve can also be found by going to www.bloomberg.com and clicking on "Market Data" and "Rates and Bonds."

4. Information on the Federal Reserve System can be found by going to the Federal Reserve site: www.federalreserve.gov/policy.htm. The site has useful information on important monetary actions such as open market operations, changes in the discount rate, and reserve requirement changes. Go to the above Federal Reserve site and click on "Monetary Policy" and then go to the "Beige Book." Comment on what you find about the Federal Reserve's outlook for the economy and your Federal Reserve district.

5. Find out information on how the European Central Bank is structured by going to their site: www.ecb.int.

6. Difference in yields can be due to different tax treatments applied to different bonds. Compare tax-free yields with taxable yields by going to www.investinginbonds.com and then clicking on "Tax-free verses US Taxable Yield Comparisons."

NOTES

1. The risk-free bond is risk free because its principal payment is known with certainty; if the bond is sold before maturity, it is subject to market risk.

2. If the corporate yield had been initially positively sloped, then the increase in short-term Treasury rates would have caused the yield curve to become flatter. If the yield curve had been initially negatively sloped, then the rate change would have caused the curve to become even more negatively sloped. In general, we can describe such an impact as "having a tendency to cause the yield curve to become negatively sloped."

3. Note, in the last chapter we argued that the correct way to value bonds is to discount their cash flows by spot rates. If the market does not price bonds this way, then arbitrage opportunities would exist by buying the bond and stripping it, or buying stripped securities and rebundling them.

4. There are techniques other than bootstrapping that are used to estimate spot rates. For a discussion, see Frank J. Fabozzi, *Bond Markets, Analysis, and Strategies*, 3rd edn (Upper Saddle River, NJ: Prentice Hall, 1996): 89–91. Also note that stripped Treasury securities could also be used to determine spot rates. Studies, though, have shown that Treasury stripped securities often sell at rates different than theoretically generated spot rates.

SELECTED REFERENCES

Buser, S. A. and P. J. Hess "Empirical Determinants of the Relative Yields on Taxable and Tax Exempt Securities," *Journal of Financial Economics* 17 (1986): 335–55.

Campbell, J. Y. "A Defense of Traditional Hypotheses about the Term Structure of Interest Rates," *Journal of Finance* 41 (1986): 183–93.

Campbell, T. "On the Extent of Segmentation in the Municipal Securities Market," *Journal of Money, Credit, and Banking* 12 (1980): 71–83.

Cox, J. C., J. Ingersoll, and S. Ross "A Re-examination of Traditional Hypotheses about the Term Structure of Interest Rates," *Journal of Finance* 36 (1981): 769–99.

Cox, J. C., J. Ingersoll, and S. Ross "A Theory of the Term Structure of Interest Rates," *Econometrica* 53 (1985): 385–407.

Culbertson, J. M. "The Term Structure of Interest Rates," *Quarterly Journal of Economics* 71 (1957): 489–504.

Diament, P. "Semi-empirical Smooth Fit to the Treasury Yield Curve," *Journal of Fixed Income* 3(1) (1993): 55–70.

Fabozzi, Frank J. *Bond Markets, Analysis, and Strategies*, 3rd edn (Upper Saddle River, NJ: Prentice Hall, 1996).

Fama, Eugene F. "Forward Rates as Predictors of Future Spot-Rates," *Journal of Financial Economics* 3 (1976): 361–77.

Fama, Eugene F. "The Information in the Term Structure," *Journal of Financial Economics* 13 (December 1984): 509–28.

Fama, Eugene F. "Term Structure Forecasts of Interest Rates, Inflation and Real Returns," *Journal of Monetary Economics* 25 (1990): 59–76.

Froot, R. A. "New Hope for Expectations Hypothesis of the Term Structure of Interest Rates," *Journal of Finance* 44 (1989): 283–305.

Gibbons, M. R. and K. Ramaswamy "The Term Structure of Interest Rates: Empirical Evidence," *Review of Financial Studies* (1994).

Heath, D., R. Jarrow, and A. Morton "Bond Pricing and the Term Structure of Interest Rates: A Discrete Time Approximation," *Journal of Financial and Quantitative Analysis* 25(4) (1990): 419–40.

Ho, T. S. Y. and S. Lee "Term Structure Movements and Pricing of Interest Rate Contingent Claims," *The Journal of Finance* XLI(5) (1986): 1011–29.

Livingston, M. "Bond Taxation and the Shape of the Yield to Maturity Curve," *Journal of Finance* 34 (1979): 189–96.

Lutz, F. A. "The Structure of Interest Rates," *Quarterly Journal of Economics* (November 1940).

Malkiel, B. G. "Expectations, Bond Prices and the Term Structure of Interest Rates," *Quarterly Journal of Economics* (May 1962).

Mishkin, Frederic S. "What Does the Term Structure Tell Us About Future Inflation?" *Journal of Monetary Economics* 25 (1990): 77–95.

Mishkin, Frederic S. and Stanley G. Eakins *Financial Markets and Institutions*, 4th edn (Addison-Wesley, 2003).

Mundell, R. "Inflation and Real Interest," *Journal of Political Economy* 71 (1963): 280–3.

Rose, Peter S. *Money and Capital Markets* (New York: McGraw-Hill/Irwin, 2003).

Sargent, T. J. "Rational Expectations and the Term Structure of Interest Rates," *Journal of Money, Credit and Banking* (February 1972).

Stambaugh, R. "The Information in Forward Rates: Implications for Models of the Term Structure," *Journal of Financial Economics* 21 (1988): 41–70.

Stojanovic, Dusan and Mark D. Vaughn "Yielding Clues and Recessions: The Yield Curve as a Forecasting Tool," *Economic Review, Federal Reserve Bank of Boston* (1997): 10–21.

CHAPTER FOUR

BOND RISK

4.1 INTRODUCTION

Investment risk is the uncertainty that the actual rate of return realized from an investment will differ from the expected rate. As we noted in the last chapter, there are three types of risk associated with bonds and fixed-income securities:

1. *Default risk* (or *credit risk*): the uncertainty that the issuer/borrower will fail to meet the contractual obligations specified in the indenture;
2. *Call risk*: the uncertainty that the issuer/borrower will buy back the bond, forcing the investor to reinvest in a market with lower interest rates;
3. *Market risk*: the uncertainty that interest rates will change, changing the price of the bond and the return earned from reinvesting coupons.

In this chapter, we examine these three types of risk and introduce two measures of bond volatility: duration and convexity.

4.2 DEFAULT RISK

Default risk is the risk that the borrower/issuer will not meet all promises at the agreed-upon times. A failure to meet any of the interest payments, the principal obligation, or other terms specified in the indenture (e.g., sinking-fund arrangements, collateral requirements, or other protective covenants) places the borrower/issuer in default. When issuers default they can file for bankruptcy, their bondholders/creditors can sue for bankruptcy, or both parties can work out an agreement. Many large institutional investors have their own credit analysis departments to evaluate bond issues in order to determine the abilities of companies to meet their contractual obligations. However, individual bond investors, as well as some institutional investors, usually do not make an independent evaluation of a bond's chance of default. Instead, they rely on bond rating companies. Currently, the major rating companies in the United States are Moody's Investment Services, Standard & Poor's, and Fitch Investors Service. These companies evaluate bonds by giving them a quality rating in the form of a letter grade (see exhibit 4.1). The grades start at "A" with three groups: triple A bonds (Aaa for Moody's and AAA for Standard & Poor's) for the highest-grade bonds, double A (Aa or AA) for bonds that are considered prime, and single A for those considered high quality. Grade A bonds are followed by "B" rated bonds, classified as either triple B (Baa or BBB), that have a medium grade, double B (Ba or BB), and single B. Finally,

Exhibit 4.1   Bond ratings

	Very high quality	High quality	Speculative	Very poor
Standard & Poor's	AAA AA	A BBB	BB B	CCC D
Moody's	Aaa Aa	A Baa	Ba B	Caa C

Moody's	S&P	Description
Aaa	AAA	Bonds have the highest rating. Ability to pay interest and principal is very strong.
Aa	AA	Bonds have a very strong capacity to pay interest and repay principal. Together with the highest ratings, this group comprises the high-grade bond class.
A	A	Bonds have a strong capacity to pay interest and repay principal, although they are somewhat susceptible to the adverse effects of changes in economic conditions.
Baa	BBB	Bonds are regarded as having an adequate capacity to pay interest and repay principal. Adverse economic conditions or changing circumstances are more likely to lead to a weakened capacity to pay interest and repay principal for debt in this category than in higher-rated categories. These bonds are medium-grade obligations.
Ba B Caa Ca	BB B CCC CC	Bonds are regarded as predominantly speculative with respect to capacity to pay interest and repay principal in accordance with the terms of the obligation. BB and Ba indicate the lowest degree of speculation, and CC and Ca the highest degree of speculation.
C	C	This rating is reserved for income bonds on which no interest is being paid.
D	D	Bonds rated D are in default, and payment of interest and/or repayment of principal is in arrears.

At times both Moody's and Standard & Poor's have used adjustments to these ratings. S&P uses plus and minus signs: A+ is the strongest A rating and A− the weakest. Moody's uses a 1, 2, or 3 designation – with 1 indicating the strongest.

there are C-grade and lower-grade bonds. Moody's also breaks down bonds by using a 1, 2, and 3 designation, while Standard & Poor's does the same with a plus or minus designation. In interpreting these ratings, triple A bonds are considered to have virtually no default risk, while low B- or C-rated bonds are considered speculative with some chance of default. In general, bonds with a relatively low chance of default are referred to as *investment-grade bonds*, with quality rating of Baa (or BBB) or higher; bonds with a relatively high chance of default are referred to as *speculative-grade* or *junk bonds* and have quality rating below Baa. The term "junk bond" became part of the financial vernacular in the 1980s to refer to low-graded bonds sold by companies with financial problems, often referred to as Fallen Angels.

4.2.1 Historical Default Rates

Since World War II, the percentage of the dollar value of bonds defaulting has been quite low, averaging 0.12% per year. During the 1980s, the default rate became relatively high for junk bonds (3.27%). During that decade, there was a rapid growth in low-rated debt issues. Led by Michael Milken of the investment banking firm of Drexel Burnham Lambert, much of the growth in junk bond financing was due to their use in many hostile takeovers in which many companies sold high-yielding, low-quality bonds to finance their acquisitions of other companies. As a result of this financing, many newly structured companies with high debt-to-equity ratios emerged. Because debt is tax deductible, the potential return to investors was augmented by this increase in leverage, but so also was their exposure to default risk.

Trading at yields 4% to 5% over comparable US government securities, junk bonds were attractive investments to many institutional investors, including many savings and loans (at least until 1989 when Congress passed the *Financial Institutions Reform, Recovery, and Enforcement Act* outlawing the purchase of low-quality bonds by federally sponsored deposit institutions). In the early 1980s, the default experience for such bonds was relatively low. However, slower economic growth in 1990 and the recession in 1991 resulted in a high incidence of defaults by many companies that had issued junk bonds in the 1980s. In 1990, the default rate for junk bonds was 8.74%, and in 1991, it was 9%. Since then the growth of the junk bond market has declined.[1]

4.2.2 Default Risk Premium

Because there is a default risk on corporate, municipal, and other non-US Treasury bonds, they trade with a *default risk premium* (also called a *quality* or *credit spread*). This premium is often measured as the spread between the rates on a non-Treasury security and a US Treasury security that are the same in all respects except for their default risk.

Usually adverse economic conditions result in a greater default risk premium. For corporate issues, such developments could be aggregate economic factors such as a recession; industry factors like declining sales due to competition; or firm factors related to company investment or financing decisions.[2] For municipal issues,

adverse economic developments include declining property values, municipal government deficits, increasing regional unemployment, or increased use of debt reserves. Since World War II, no major industrial country has defaulted on its debt. However, in 2002, Moody's did lower Japan's ratings after its debt level reached nearly 150% of its national output (in contrast, the US debt was 58% of its aggregate output in 2002). While Japan is not likely to default, the lower ratings reflected the possibility that Japan could unilaterally extend the maturity of its maturing debt.

4.2.3 Studies on Default Risk Premiums

A number of empirical studies have examined the factors that determine default risk premiums. Studies by Salomon Brothers and Hutzler looked at the relationship between default risk premiums and the state of the economy; a study by R. E. Johnston examined yield curves for different quality bonds. In both the Salomon Brothers and the Hutzler studies, a moderate widening in the yield spread between moderate (BB) and high-grade bonds was observed during recessions, while the spread narrowed during economic growth. These studies suggest that during recessions investors are more concerned with safety than during expansionary times. As a result, a relatively low demand for lower grade bonds occurs, leading to lower prices for the lower grade bonds and thus a higher interest premium. On the other hand, during periods of economic expansion there seems to be less concern about default. This tends to increase the demand for lower grade bonds relative to higher grade, causing a smaller premium. It should be noted that these studies suggest that speculators could profit from a strategy of investing in low-grade bonds at the trough of a cycle, when demand and prices are low, and selling at the peak of the cycle, when demand and prices are high. In contrast, speculators would find it more profitable to buy high-grade bonds at the peak of the economic cycle, when their demands are relatively low, and then sell at the trough of the cycle. This, of course, assumes that a speculator can reasonably

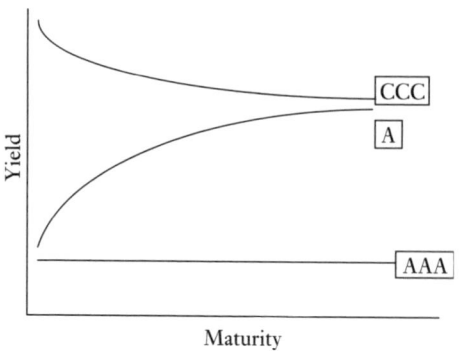

Figure 4.1   Yield curves for different quality bonds

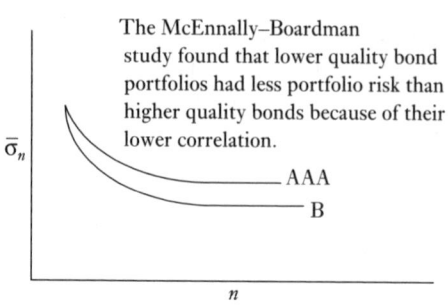

Figure 4.2   Bond diversification

forecast the troughs and peaks of economic cycles.[3]

In the Johnston study, the spread between moderate-grade and high-grade bonds was found to increase as maturity increased, while the spread between low- and moderate- or high-grade bonds was found to decrease as maturity increased. Johnston's results are illustrated in figure 4.1, where a hypothetical flat yield curve for an AAA-grade bond is shown along with a positively sloped yield curve for the A-grade bond (moderate) and a negatively sloped yield curve for the CCC-grade bond (low). The negatively sloped yield curve for low-grade bonds suggests that investors have more concern over the repayment of principal (or the issuer's ability to refinance at favorable rates) than they do about the issuer meeting interest payments. This concern would explain the low demand and higher yields for short-term bonds, in which principal payment is due relatively soon compared to long-term bonds.

4.2.4   Bond Diversification and Quality Ratings

In a 1979 study, McEnnally and Boardman examined the relationship between portfolio risk and size for bonds grouped in terms of their quality ratings. Using the same methodology employed by Evans and Archer in their portfolio risk and size study on stocks, McEnnally and Boardman collected monthly rates of return for over 500 corporate and municipal bonds with quality ratings of Baa or greater. For each quality group (Aaa, Aa, A, and Baa),

they randomly selected portfolios with n bonds ($n = 2$, 3, 4, ... , 40) and calculated the n-bond portfolio's average standard deviation. McEnnally and Boardman's findings are displayed in figure 4.2.

As shown in the figure, McEnnally and Boardman found the same portfolio risk and size relationship for bonds as Evans and Archer had found for stocks. Specifically, as the size of the bond portfolio increased, the portfolio risk decreased asymptotically, with the maximum risk reduction being realized with a portfolio size of 20. More interestingly, though, McEnnally and Boardman also found that the portfolios consisting of the lowest-quality bonds had the lowest portfolio risk when sufficiently diversified.

This seemingly counterintuitive result can be explained in terms of the correlation between bonds in the same quality groups. Specifically, a lower quality bond, while having a greater variance than a higher quality bond, has lower correlations with other lower quality bonds than does a higher quality bond. The relatively lower correlations, in turn, cause the lower quality bond's portfolio variance to be smaller than the higher quality bond's portfolio variance. Intuitively, higher quality bonds have very little, if any, default risk. Consequently, such bonds are affected only by general interest rate changes and, therefore, tend to fluctuate together. With this high correlation, such bonds do not benefit from diversification. By contrast, lower quality bonds are affected by default risk as well as interest rate changes. The rates on these bonds are therefore affected by factors unique to the individual bond's company and industry. As a result, lower quality bonds are not as highly correlated with each other, and therefore their portfolio risk can be reduced with sufficient diversification.

4.3 CALL RISK

Call risk relates to the uncertainty that the issuer will call the bond. A call feature on a bond gives the issuer the right to buy back the bond before maturity at a stated price, known as the call price. The call price usually is set a certain percentage above the bond's par value, say 110 ($1,100, given a par value of $1,000); for some bonds the call price may decrease over time (e.g., a 20-year bond's call price decreasing each year by 5%). Some callable bonds can be called at any time, while for others the call is deferred for a certain period, giving the investor protection during the deferment period. Also, some bonds, as part of their sinking-fund arrangements, are retired over the life of the bond, usually with the issuer having the choice of purchasing the bonds directly at market prices or calling the bonds at a specified call price.

A call provision is advantageous to the issuer. If interest rates in the market decline, an issuer can lower his interest costs by selling a new issue at a lower interest rate, then use the loan proceeds to call the outstanding issue. What is to the advantage of the issuer, though, is to the disadvantage of the investor. When a bond is called, the investor's realized rate of return is affected in two ways. First, since the call price is typically above the bond's face value, the actual rate of return the investor earns for the period from the purchase of the bond to its call generally is greater than the yield on the bond at the time it was purchased. However, if an investor originally bought the bond because its maturity matched her horizon date, then she will be faced with the dis-

advantage of reinvesting the call proceeds at lower market rates. Moreover, this second effect, known as *reinvestment risk*, often dominates the first effect, resulting in a rate of return over the investor's horizon period that is lower than the promised YTM when the bond was bought.

4.3.1 Example of Call Risk

To illustrate the nature of call risk, consider the case of an investor with a 10-year horizon who purchases a 10-year, 10% annual coupon bond at its par value of $1,000 with the bond callable at a call price of 110. In addition, suppose that the yield curve for such bonds is flat at 10% and that it remains that way for the first 3 years the investor holds the bond. At the end of year 3, however, assume the yield curve shifts down to 8% and the issuer calls the bond. The investor's annual realized return (ARR) for the 3-year period would be 12.69%. Specifically, at the end of year 3 the investor's cash value would be $1,431. This would include the $1,100 call price, $300 in coupons, and $31 in interest earned from investing the coupons (see exhibit 4.2), yielding an ARR of 12.69%:

$$ARR_3 = \left[\frac{\$1,431}{\$1,000}\right]^{1/3} - 1 = 0.1269$$

Thus, for the call period, the investor earns a rate of return higher than the initial YTM. However, with a horizon date (HD) of 10 years, the investor must reinvest the $1,431 cash for 7 more years at the lower market rate. If we assume she reinvests all coupons to the horizon date at 8%, then the $1,431 will grow at an 8% annual rate to equal $2,452.48 = $1,431(1.08)^7 at the end of the tenth year, yielding an ARR for the 10-year period of 9.386%. That is:

$$ARR_{10} = \left[\frac{\$2,452.48}{\$1,000}\right]^{1/10} - 1 = 0.09386$$

Note, the 9.386% rate is also equal to the geometric average of the 12.69% annual rate earned for the 3 years and the 8% annual rate earned for 7 years:

$$ARR_{10} = \left[(1.1269)^3(1.08)^7\right]^{1/10} - 1 = 0.09386$$

Exhibit 4.2 Cash flow and ARR for callable bond

1	2	3 = Call date
100	$\xrightarrow{\hspace{2cm}}$	$100(1.10)^2 = 121$
	$100 \quad \longrightarrow$	$100(1.10) = 110$
		$100 + 1,100 = \underline{1,200}$
		$\overline{1,431}$

$$\text{ARR}_\text{C} = \sqrt[c]{\dfrac{\text{Call date value}}{P_0^b}} - 1$$

$$\text{ARR}_\text{C} = \sqrt[3]{\dfrac{\$1,431}{\$1,000}} - 1 = 0.1269$$

$$\text{ARR}_\text{HD} = \sqrt[HD]{\dfrac{\text{HD value}}{P_0^b}} - 1$$

$$\text{ARR}_\text{HD} = \sqrt[10]{\dfrac{\$1,431(1.08)^7}{\$1,000}} - 1 = 0.09386$$

$$\text{ARR}_\text{HD} = \sqrt[10]{(1.1269)^3(1.08)^7} - 1 = 0.09386$$

$$\boxed{\begin{array}{c} \text{ARR}_\text{HD} < \text{YTM} \\ 9.386\% < 10\% \end{array}}$$

With the ARR of 9.386% less than the initial YTM of 10%, the second effect of reinvesting in a market with lower rates dominates the first effect of a call price greater than the bond's face value. This example shows that bonds that are callable are subject to the uncertainty that the actual rate will be less than the investor's expected YTM. Because of this call risk, there is usually a lower market demand and price for callable bonds than non-callable bonds, resulting in a higher rate of return or interest premium on callable over non-callable bonds. The size of this interest premium, in turn, depends on investors' and borrowers' expectations concerning interest rates. When interest rates are high and expected to fall, bonds are more likely to be called; thus, in a period of high interest rates, a relatively low demand and higher rate on callable over non-callable bonds would occur. In contrast, when interest rates are low and expected to rise, we expect the effect of call provisions on interest rates to be negligible. Moreover, several empirical studies tend to support these observations. For example, Jen and Wert examined interest premiums on immediately callable corporate bonds and deferred callable bonds (non-callable were not considered since many corporate bonds are callable) and found the interest premium increased during high interest rate periods and decreased during low interest rate periods.

4.3.2 Price Compression

In addition to reinvestment risk, callable bonds are also subject to *price compression*: limitations on a bond's price. As we discussed in chapter 2, there is an inverse relationship between interest rates and bond prices. For callable bonds, though, the percentage increases in their prices may be limited when interest rates decrease, given that the market expects the bonds to be redeemed at the call price. This limitation is illustrated in figure 4.3. In the figure, the price–yield curve PP is shown for a non-callable bond. This curve is negatively sloped and convex from below. The curve PC

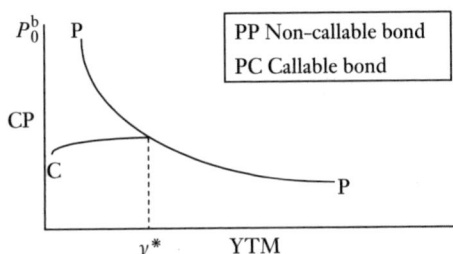

Figure 4.3 Price–yield curve for callable bond

represents the price–yield curve for a comparable callable bond. As shown, this curve flattens out and becomes concave (negative convexity) at rate y^*, where y^* represents a threshold rate that corresponds to a bond price equal, or approximately equal, to the call price. Since the callable bond would likely be called if rates are at y^* or less, we would not expect investors to pay a price for such a bond greater than the call price. Thus, the price–yield curve for the callable bond would tend to flatten out at y^*, as shown in figure 4.3.

4.3.3 Valuation of Callable Bond

When valuing a callable bond, one needs to take into account the possibility that interest rates could decrease, leading to the bond being called. If called, the bond's cash flow patterns would be different than if rates increased and the bond was not called. Given the uncertainty of the bond's cash flows, valuing callable bonds and other bonds with embedded option features is more difficult than valuing option-free bonds. One approach to valuing callable bonds is to incorporate interest rate volatility by using a *binomial interest rate tree*. Another is to determine the value of the call feature. Conceptually, when an investor buys a callable bond, she implicitly sells a call option to the bond issuer, giving the issuer the right to buy the bond from the bondholder at a specified price before maturity. Theoretically, the price of a callable bond should therefore be equal to the price of an identical, but non-callable, bond minus the value of the call feature or call premium. The value of the call feature can be estimated using the option pricing model developed by Black and Scholes. The applications of this

model and the binomial interest rate model for valuing callable bonds and other option features embedded in bonds are described in chapters 9 and 10.

4.4 MARKET RISK

Market risk is the uncertainty that interest rates in the market will change, causing the actual rate of return earned on the bond to differ from the expected return. As noted in our discussion of the ARR in chapter 2, a change in interest rates has two effects on a bond's return. First, interest rate changes affect the price of a bond; this is referred to as *price risk*. If the investor's horizon date, HD, is different from the bond's maturity date, then the investor will be uncertain about the price he will receive from selling the bond (if HD < M), or the price he will have to pay for a new bond (if HD > M). Secondly, interest rate changes affect the return the investor expects from reinvesting the coupon – reinvestment risk. Thus, if an investor buys a coupon bond, he automatically is subject to market risk. One obvious way an investor can eliminate market risk is to purchase a pure discount bond with a maturity that is equal to the investor's horizon date. If such a bond does not exist (or does, but does not yield an adequate rate), a bondholder will be subject (in most cases) to market risk.

4.4.1 Example of Market Risk

To illustrate market risk, consider the case of an investor with a horizon date of 3.5 years who buys a 10-year, 10% annual coupon bond at its par value of $1,000 to yield 10%. If the yield curve were initially flat at 10% and if there were no changes in the yield curve in the ensuing years, then the investor would realize a rate of return (as measured by her ARR) of 10% (see exhibit 4.3a). That is, with no change in the flat yield curve, the investor would be able to reinvest each of her coupons at a rate of 10%, yielding a coupon value of $347.16 at year 3.5. The $347.16 coupon value consists of $300 in coupons and $47.16 in interest earned from reinvesting the coupon; that is, *interest on interest* of $47.16. In addition, with no change in the yield curve, the investor would be able to sell the original 10-year bond (now with a maturity of 6.5 years) for $1,048.81 at the end of 3.5 years. Note, since this bond is being sold at a non-coupon date, its price is determined by discounting the value of the bond at the next coupon date (year 4) when the bond has 6 years left to maturity (P_4) plus the $100 coupon received on that date back 0.5 years to the HD. That is:

$$P_4 = \sum_{t=1}^{6} \frac{\$100}{(1.10)^t} + \frac{\$1,000}{(1.10)^{10}} = \$1,000$$

$$P_{3.5} = \frac{\$1,000 + \$100}{(1.10)^{0.5}} = \$1,048.81$$

Combined, the selling price of $1,048.81 and the coupon value of $347.16 yield an HD value of $1,395.97, which equates to an ARR of 10% for the 3.5 years. This is the same rate as the initial YTM.

As we first discussed in chapter 2, the ARR will equal the initial YTM if the yield curve is flat and remains that way for the horizon period. Suppose that shortly after the investor purchased the bond, though, the flat 10% yield curve shifted up to 12% and remained there for the 3.5 years. As shown in exhibit 4.3b, at her HD the investor would be able to sell the bond for only $961.70, resulting in a capital loss of $38.30. This loss would be partly offset, though, by the gains realized from reinvesting the coupons at 12%. Combined, the investor's HD value would be $1,318.81 – $77.16 less than the HD value of $1,395.97 realized if rates had remained constant at 10%. As shown in exhibit 4.3b, the ARR would be only 8.23%. In contrast, if the yield curve had shifted down from 10% to 8% and remained there, then the investor would have gained on the sale of the bond (selling it at a price of $1,147.44) but would have earned less interest from reinvesting the coupons. In this case, the HD value increases to $1,484.82 to yield an ARR of 11.96% (see exhibit 4.3c).

In these examples, note that interest rate changes have two opposite effects on the ARR. First, there is a direct interest-on-interest effect in which an interest rate increase (decrease) causes the interest earned from reinvesting coupons to be greater (less), augmenting (decreasing) the ARR. Second, there is a

negative price effect, in which an interest rate increase (decrease) lowers (augments) the price of the bond, causing the ARR to decrease (increase). Whether the ARR varies directly or indirectly with interest rate changes depends on which effect dominates. If the price effect dominates, as was the case described above, then the ARR will vary inversely with interest rates. If the interest-on-interest effect dominates, though, the ARR will vary directly with the interest rate changes. For example, suppose our investor had purchased a 4-year, 20% annual coupon bond when the yield curve was flat at 10% (price of $1,317). As shown in exhibit 4.4a, if the yield curve shifted up to 12% shortly after the purchase and remained there, then the investor would have realized an ARR of 10.16%. In this case, the additional interest earned from reinvesting coupons more than offsets the capital loss. But if the yield curve had shifted down to 8%, the investor would have realized a lower ARR of 9.845% (see exhibit 4.4b). With an HD of 3.5 years, the 4-year, 20% bond has an interest-on-interest effect that dominates the price effect, resulting in the direct relationship between the ARR and interest rate changes.

Finally, it is possible to select a bond in which the two effects exactly offset each other. When this occurs, the ARR will not change as rates change, and the investor will not be subject to market risk. For example, suppose our investor had purchased a 4-year, 9% annual coupon for $968.30 to yield 10%. As shown in exhibit 4.5, if the flat yield curve shifted to 12%, 8%, or any other rate, the ARR would remain at 10%. To reiterate, what is occurring in this case is that we have a bond with price and interest-on-interest effects that are of the same magnitude in absolute value; thus, when rates change the two effects cancel each other out.

4.4.2 Duration and Bond Immunization

The last example illustrates how an investor with an HD of 3.5 years can eliminate market risk by buying a 4-year, 9% annual coupon bond. Note, the investor can do this by buying a bond that pays a coupon and has a maturity

Exhibit 4.3 ARR for 10-year, 10% coupon bond: HD 3.5 years, evaluated at rates of 10%, 12%, and 8%

a. If there is no change in the yield curve, then the ARR for 3.5 years is 10%:

$$\text{HD value} = 100(1.10)^{2.5} + 100(1.10)^{1.5} + 100(1.10)^{0.5} + P^b_{3.5} = 1{,}395.97$$

where: $P^b_{3.5} = \dfrac{1{,}000 + 100}{(1.10)^{0.5}} = 1{,}048.81$

$$P^b_4 = \sum_{t=1}^{6} \frac{100}{(1.10)^t} + \frac{1{,}000}{(1.10)^6} = 1{,}000$$

$$\text{ARR}_{3.5} = \left[\frac{1{,}395.97}{1{,}000}\right]^{1/3.5} - 1 = 0.10$$

b. If the yield curve shifts to 12%, then the ARR for 3.5 years is 8.23%:

$$\text{HD value} = 100(1.12)^{2.5} + 100(1.12)^{1.5} + 100(1.12)^{0.5} + P^b_{3.5} = 1{,}318.81$$

where: $P^b_{3.5} = \dfrac{917.77 + 100}{(1.12)^{0.5}} = 961.70$

$$P^b_4 = \sum_{t=1}^{6} \frac{100}{(1.12)^t} + \frac{1{,}000}{(1.12)^6} = 917.77$$

$$\text{ARR}_{3.5} = \left[\frac{1{,}318.81}{1{,}000}\right]^{1/3.5} - 1 = 0.0823$$

c. If the yield curve shifts to 8%, then the ARR for 3.5 years is 11.96%:

$$\text{HD value} = 100(1.08)^{2.5} + 100(1.08)^{1.5} + 100(1.08)^{0.5} + P^b_{3.5} = 1{,}484.82$$

where: $P^b_{3.5} = \dfrac{1{,}092.46 + 100}{(1.08)^{0.5}} = 1{,}147.44$

$$P^b_4 = \sum_{t=1}^{6} \frac{100}{(1.08)^t} + \frac{1{,}000}{(1.08)^6} = 1{,}092.46$$

$$\text{ARR}_{3.5} = \left[\frac{1{,}484.82}{1{,}000}\right]^{1/3.5} - 1 = 0.1196$$

Exhibit 4.4   ARR for 4-year, 20% coupon bond: HD 3.5 years, evaluated at rates of 12% and 8%

a. If the yield curve shifts to 12%, the ARR for 3.5 years is 10.16%:

$$\text{HD value} = 200(1.12)^{2.5} + 200(1.12)^{1.5} + 200(1.12)^{0.5} + P^b_{3.5} = 1,848.12$$

where: $P^b_{3.5} = \dfrac{1,000 + 200}{(1.12)^{0.5}} = 1,133.89$

$$\text{ARR}_{3.5} = \left[\frac{1,848.12}{1,317}\right]^{1/3.5} - 1 = 0.1016$$

Here: $P^b_0 = \displaystyle\sum_{t=1}^{4} \frac{200}{(1.10)^t} + \frac{1,000}{(1.10)^4} = 1,317$

b. If the yield curve shifts to 8%, the ARR for 3.5 years is 9.845%:

$$\text{HD value} = 200(1.08)^{2.5} + 200(1.08)^{1.5} + 200(1.08)^{0.5} + P^b_{3.5} = 1,829.45$$

where: $P^b_{3.5} = \dfrac{1,000 + 200}{(1.08)^{0.5}} = 1,154.70$

$$\text{ARR}_{3.5} = \left[\frac{1,829.45}{1,317}\right]^{1/3.5} - 1 = 0.09845$$

Here: $P^b_0 = \displaystyle\sum_{t=1}^{4} \frac{200}{(1.10)^t} + \frac{1,000}{(1.10)^4} = 1,317$

different than her HD (i.e., it is not a pure discount bond with a maturity equal to her HD). What is distinctive about this 4-year, 9% coupon bond is that it has a duration equal to 3.5 years – the same as the HD. A bond's *duration* (D) can be defined as the weighted average of the bond's time periods, with the weights being each time period's relative present value of its cash flow:

$$D = \sum_{t=1}^{M} t\,\frac{\text{PV}(\text{CF}_t)}{P^b_0} \tag{4.1}$$

In our example, the duration of a 4-year, 9% annual coupon bond is 3.5 years, given a flat yield curve at 10% (see table 4.1). It should be

noted that duration also extends to a portfolio of bonds. The duration of a bond portfolio, D_p, is simply the weighted average of each of the bond's durations (D_i), with the weights being the proportion of investment funds allocated to each bond (w_i):

$$D_p = \sum_{t=1}^{M} w_i D_i \tag{4.2}$$

Thus, instead of selecting a specific bond with a desired duration, an investor could determine the allocations (w_i) for each bond in his portfolio that would yield the desired portfolio duration.

In chapter 8, we will examine bond management strategies; one of them is called **bond**

Exhibit 4.5   ARR for 4-year, 9% coupon bond: HD 3.5 years, evaluated at rates of 12% and 8%

a. If the yield curve shifts to 12%, the ARR for 3.5 years is 10%:

$$\text{HD value} = 90(1.12)^{2.5} + 90(1.12)^{1.5} + 90(1.12)^{0.5} + P^b_{3.5} = 1,351.35$$

where: $P^b_{3.5} = \dfrac{1,000 + 90}{(1.12)^{0.5}} = 1,029.95$

$$\text{ARR}_{3.5} = \left[\frac{1,351.35}{968.30}\right]^{1/3.5} - 1 = 0.10$$

Here: $P^b_0 = \displaystyle\sum_{t=1}^{4} \frac{90}{(1.10)^t} + \frac{1,000}{(1.10)^4} = 968.30$

b. If the yield curve shifts to 8%, the ARR for 3.5 years is 10%:

$$\text{HD value} = 90(1.08)^{2.5} + 90(1.08)^{1.5} + 90(1.08)^{0.5} + P^b_{3.5} = 1,352.49$$

where: $P^b_{3.5} = \dfrac{1,000 + 90}{(1.08)^{0.5}} = 1,048.85$

$$\text{ARR}_{3.5} = \left[\frac{1,352.49}{968.30}\right]^{1/3.5} - 1 = 0.10$$

Here: $P^b_0 = \displaystyle\sum_{t=1}^{4} \frac{90}{(1.10)^t} + \frac{1,000}{(1.10)^4} = 968.30$

Table 4.1   Duration

t	CF_t	$CF_t/(1.10)^t$	$PV(CF_t)/P^b$	$t[PV(CF_t)/P^b]$
1	90	81.818	0.084496	0.084496
2	90	74.380	0.076815	0.153630
3	90	67.618	0.069832	0.209496
4	1,090	744.485	0.768857	3.075428
		$P^b = 968.30$		$D = 3.52$

$$D = \sum_{t=1}^{M} t[(PV(CF_t))/P^b_0]$$

immunization. The objective of bond immunization is to minimize market risk. As our discussion here indicates, one way to achieve this goal is to select a bond or portfolio of bonds with a duration matching the investor's horizon date. Duration, and a related characteristic known as convexity, are also important parameters in describing a bond or bond portfolio's volatility in terms of its price sensitivity to interest rate changes.

4.5 DURATION AND CONVEXITY

4.5.1 Duration Measures

Immunizing a bond against market risk by buying a bond whose duration equals the investor's HD is a relatively new technique in finance. The concept of duration and its applications, though, are not new. Duration was introduced in international economics in the

1800s as a way of reducing exchange-rate risk. Its introduction to finance came later when, in 1938, Frederick Macaulay suggested using the weighted average of a bond's time periods as a better measure of the life of a bond than maturity. J. R. Hicks in 1939, Paul Samuelson in 1945, and F. M. Redington in 1952 also came up with duration measures, each somewhat different, to explain the relationship between price and the life of a bond. In 1971, duration attracted widespread attention when Fisher and Weil published their work on the use of duration as a way of minimizing market risk.

Though duration is defined as the weighted average of a bond's time periods, it is also an important measure of volatility. As a measure of volatility, duration is defined as the percentage change in a bond's price ($\%\Delta P = \Delta P/P_0$) given a small change in yield, dy. Mathematically, duration is obtained by taking the derivative of the equation for the price of a bond with respect to the yield, then dividing by the bond's price (this derivation is presented in exhibit 4.6). This yields:

$$\text{Duration} = \frac{dP/P}{dy} = -\frac{1}{(1+y)} \left(\sum_{t=1}^{M} t \frac{\text{PV}(\text{CF}_t)}{P_0^b} \right)$$

$$(4.3)$$

where: $dP/P_0 =$ percentage change in the bond's price and $dy =$ small change in yield.

The bracketed expression in equation (4.3) is the weighted average of the time periods, defined in the last section as duration. Formally, the weighted average of the time periods is called *Macaulay's duration*, and equation (4.3), which defines the percentage change in the bond's price for a small change in yield, is called the *modified duration*. Thus, the modified duration is equal to the negative of Macaulay's duration divided by $1+y$:

$$\text{Modified duration} = \frac{1}{(1+y)}$$
$$\times [\text{Macaulay's duration}]$$

$$\text{Macaulay's duration} = \left(\sum_{t=1}^{M} t \frac{\text{PV}(\text{CF}_t)}{P_0^b} \right)$$

The 4-year, 9% annual coupon bond (used in the illustrative example in the previous section),

has a Macaulay's duration of 3.5 years, and given the initial yield of 10%, a modified duration of -3.18:[4]

$$\text{Modified duration} = -\frac{1}{(1+y)}$$
$$\times [\text{Macaulay's duration}]$$
$$= -\frac{1}{(1.10)} [3.5] = -3.18$$

Note: for bonds that pay their principal (F) only at maturity and their coupons (C) each period, the modified duration can be found using the following formula:[5]

Modified duration

$$= -\left(\frac{C}{y^2} \left[1 - \frac{1}{(1+y)^M} \right] + \frac{M[F - (C/y)]}{(1+y)^{M+1}} \right) \Big/ P_0^b$$

The above measures of duration are defined in terms of the length of the period between payments. Thus, if the cash flow is distributed annually, as in the above example, duration reflects years; if cash flow is semi-annual, then duration reflects half-years. The convention is to express duration as an annual measure. Annualized duration is obtained by dividing duration by the number of payments per year (n):

Annualized duration

$$= \frac{\text{Duration for bond with } n \text{ payments per year}}{n}$$

Thus, the modified duration measured in half-years for a 10-year, 9% coupon bond selling at par ($F = 100$) with coupon payments made semi-annually is -13 and its annualized duration is -6.5:

Duration in half-years

$$= -\left(\frac{4.5}{0.045^2} \left[1 - \frac{1}{(1.045)^{20}} \right] \right.$$
$$\left. + \frac{20[100 - (4.5/0.045)]}{(1.045)^{21}} \right) \Big/ 100$$

$$= -13$$

$$\text{Annualized duration} = -\frac{13}{2} = -6.5$$

Exhibit 4.6 Derivation of duration and convexity

Duration:

$$P_0^b = \sum_{t=1}^{M} \frac{CF_t}{(1+y)^t} = \sum_{t=1}^{M} CF_t(1+y)^{-t}$$

$$= CF_1(1+y)^{-1} + CF_2(1+y)^{-2} + \cdots + CF_M(1+y)^{-M}$$

Take the derivative with respect to y:

$$\frac{dP^b}{dy} = (-1)CF_1(1+y)^{-2} + (-2)CF_2(1+y)^{-3} + \cdots + (-M)CF_M(1+y)^{-(M+1)}$$

Factor out $-(1+y)^{-1} = -\frac{1}{(1+y)^1}$:

$$\frac{dP^b}{dy} = -\frac{1}{(1+y)}((1)CF_1(1+y)^{-1} + (2)CF_2(1+y)^{-2} + \cdots + (M)CF_M(1+y)^{-M})$$

$$= -\frac{1}{(1+y)}\left((1)\frac{CF_1}{(1+y)^1} + (2)\frac{CF_2}{(1+y)^2} + \cdots + (M)\frac{CF_M}{(1+y)^M}\right)$$

$$= -\frac{1}{(1+y)}((1)PV(CF_1) + (2)PV(CF_2) + \cdots + (M)PV(CF_M))$$

Divide through by P:

$$\frac{dP^b}{dy}\frac{1}{P} = \frac{dP/P}{dy} = -\frac{1}{(1+y)}\left((1)\frac{PV(CF_1)}{P_0^b} + (2)\frac{PV(CF_2)}{P_0^b} + \cdots + (M)\frac{PV(CF_M)}{P_0^b}\right)$$

$$\text{Modified duration} = \frac{dP/P}{dy} = -\frac{1}{(1+y)}\left(\sum_{t=1}^{M} t\frac{PV(CF_t)}{P_0^b}\right)$$

Convexity:
Take the derivative of

$$\frac{dP^b}{dy} = (-1)CF_1(1+y)^{-2} + (-2)CF_2(1+y)^{-3} + \cdots + (-M)CF_M(1+y)^{-(M+1)}$$

$$\frac{d^2P^b}{dy^2} = 2CF_1(1+y)^{-3} + 6CF_2(1+y)^{-4} + \cdots + M(M+1)CF_M(1+y)^{-(M+2)}$$

Divide through by P_0^b and express as a summation:

$$\frac{d^2P^b}{dy^2}\frac{1}{P_0^b} = \frac{d\Delta/P_0^b}{dy} = \text{Convexity} = \frac{\sum_{t=1}^{M}((t(t+1)CF_t)/(1+y)^{t+2})}{P_0^b} = \frac{1}{P_0^b}\left(\frac{\sum_{t=1}^{M} t(t+1)(CF_t)}{(1+y)^{t+2}}\right)$$

4.5.2 Uses of Duration

Recall in chapter 2 we described the relationship between a bond's price sensitivity to interest rate changes and its maturity and coupon rate. Since duration is the percentage change in a bond's price to a small change in yield, these relationships also can be defined in terms of duration. Specifically, the greater a bond's maturity, the greater its duration, and therefore the greater its price sensitivity to interest rates changes; the smaller a bond's coupon rate, the greater its duration, and therefore the greater its price sensitivity to interest rate changes. Thus, in addition to identifying bonds for immunization strategies, duration is also an important descriptive parameter, defining a bond's volatility as measured by its sensitivity to interest rate changes.

Knowing a bond or bond portfolio's duration is important in formulating bond strategies. For example, a bond speculator who is anticipating a decrease in interest rates across all maturities (downward parallel shift in the yield curve) could realize a potentially greater expected return, but also greater risk, by purchasing a bond with a relatively large duration. In contrast, a bond portfolio manager expecting a parallel upward shift in the yield curve could take defensive actions against possible capital losses by reallocating his portfolio such that it had a relatively low portfolio duration. Such strategies are discussed further in chapter 8.

A second application of duration is its use as an estimate of the percentage change in a bond's price for a small change in rates. Consider again the 10-year, 9% coupon bond selling at $100 to yield 9%. If the yield were to increase by 10 annual basis points (from 9% to 9.10%), then using equation (4.3) the bond would decrease by approximately − 0.65%:

$$\%\Delta P^b = \frac{dP^b}{P_0^b} = -[\text{Modified duration}]dy$$

$$\%\Delta P^b = \frac{dP^b}{P_0^b} = -[6.5][0.0910 - 0.09] = -0.0065$$

This is very close to the actual percentage change of − 0.6476%.[6] Note, though, that duration as an estimator is only good for measuring small changes in yields. For example, if the yield had increased by 200 basis points to 11%, instead of only 10 basis points, the approximate percentage change using the duration measure would be −13%:

$$\%\Delta P^b = -[6.5][0.11 - 0.09] = -0.13$$

This contrasts with the actual percentage change of −11.95%.[7] Thus, the greater the change in yields, the less accurate is duration in estimating the approximate percentage change in price.

4.5.3 Convexity

Duration is a measure of the slope of the price–yield curve at a given point (dP/dy). As we noted in chapter 2, the price–yield curve is not linear, but convex from below (bowed shape). While capturing several of the characteristics describing the price–yield curve, duration does not capture this property of the curve. Moreover, the convexity of a bond's price–yield curve is important. Convexity implies that for a given absolute change in yields, the percentage change in price will be greater for the yield increase than for the yield decrease. This is illustrated in exhibit 4.7, where the increase in price (ΔP^+) is greater in absolute value than the decrease in

Exhibit 4.7   Convexity

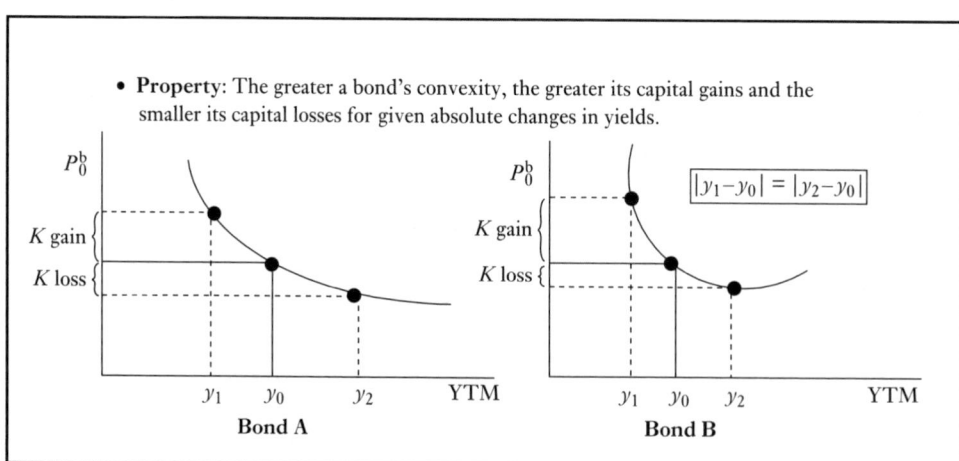

price (ΔP^-), given the same absolute changes in yield. For an investor who is long in a bond, convexity implies that the capital gain resulting from a decrease in rates will be greater than the capital loss resulting from an increase in rates of the same absolute magnitude. Thus, all other things equal, the greater a bond convexity the more valuable the bond.

4.5.4 Convexity Measures

Mathematically, *convexity* is the change in the slope of the price–yield curve for a small change in yield; it is the second-order derivative. It is derived by taking the derivative of equation (4.3) with respect to a change in yield and dividing the resulting equation by the current price. (This derivation is presented in exhibit 4.6.) Doing this yields:

$$\text{Convexity} = \frac{1}{P_0^b}\left[\sum_{t=1}^{M}\frac{t(t+1)(CF_t)}{(1+y)^{t+2}}\right] \quad (4.4)$$

The convexity for a bond that pays fixed coupons each period and the principal at maturity can be measured as:

Convexity

$$= \left(\frac{2C}{y^3}\left[1-\frac{1}{(1+y)^M}\right]-\frac{2CM}{y^2(1+y)^{M+1}}\right.$$
$$\left.+\frac{M(M+1)[F-(C/y)]}{(1+y)^{M+2}}\right)\bigg/P_0^b$$

Like duration, convexity reflects the length of periods between cash flows. The annualized convexity is found by dividing convexity, measured in terms of n payments per year, by n^2:

Annualized convexity

$$= \frac{\text{Convexity for bond with } n \text{ payments per year}}{n^2}$$

Thus, the convexity in half-years for the 10-year, 9% coupon bond with semi-annual payments is 225.43, and its annual convexity is 56.36:

4.5.5 Uses of Convexity

As we discussed earlier, given two bonds that are similar except for their convexity, the one with greater convexity is more valuable since it provides greater capital gains and smaller capital losses for the same absolute changes in yields. This is illustrated in exhibit 4.7 where, for the same changes in rates, bond B with greater convexity than bond A has a greater capital gain and smaller capital loss. Thus, convexity is another distinguishing character-istic of a bond.

In addition to describing an important feature of a bond, convexity also can be used with duration to estimate the percentage change in a bond's price given a change in yield. Unlike duration, which can only provide a good estimate when the yield changes are small, incorporating convexity allows for better estimation of large yield changes. The formula for estimating the percentage change in price for a large change in yields is derived using Taylor expansion. This expansion yields:

$$\%\Delta P^b = [\text{Modified duration}]\Delta y$$
$$+\frac{1}{2}[\text{Convexity}](\Delta y)^2$$

The estimated percentage change in the price of our 10-year, 9% coupon bond given a 200 basis point increase in yields is 11.87%:

$$\%\Delta P^b = [-6.5](0.02)+\frac{1}{2}[56.36](0.02)^2$$
$$= -0.1187$$

The 11.87% decrease is closer to the actual decrease of 11.95% than the estimated 13% decrease obtained using the duration measure. The above formula also results in non-symmetrical percentage increases and decreases. For example, if rates had decreased by 200 basis points, the percentage increase would be

---

Convexity (half-years)

$$= \left(\frac{2(4.5)}{0.045^3}\left[1-\frac{1}{(1.045)^{20}}\right]-\frac{2(4.5)(20)}{(0.045)^2(1.045)^{21}}+\frac{(20)(21)[100-(4.5/0.045)]}{(1.045)^{22}}\right)\bigg/100 = 225.43$$

Annualized convexity $= \dfrac{225.43}{2^2} = 56.36$

14.13%, not the 13% that the duration measure yields. That is:

$$\%\Delta P^b = [-6.5](-0.02) + \frac{1}{2}[56.36](0.02)^2$$

$$= 0.1413$$

4.5.6 Alternative Formulas for Duration and Convexity

Duration and convexity can also be estimated by determining the price of the bond when the yield increases by a small number of basis points (e.g., 2–10 basis points), P_+, and when the yield decreases by the same number of basis points, P_-. These measures are referred to as *approximate duration* and *approximate convexity* and can be estimated using the following formulas:

$$\text{Approximate duration} = \frac{P_- - P_+}{2(P_0)(\Delta y)} \quad (4.5)$$

$$\text{Approximate convexity} = \frac{P_+ + P_- - 2P_0}{P_0(\Delta y)^2}$$

$$(4.6)$$

4.5.7 Caveats

Duration and convexity are important characteristics that can be used to determine a bond's price sensitivity to interest rates and the asymmetry of its capital gains to capital losses for given absolute changes in yields. However, there are two problems with the measures we've defined here for determining a bond's duration and convexity. First, we've assumed a constant YTM. For yield curves that are not flat, one can use appropriate spot rates in determining the present values of the bond's cash flows instead of the same YTM. A second and more serious problem with our measures is that they apply only to option-free bonds. Call, put, and sinking-fund arrangements alter a bond's cash flow patterns and can dramatically change a bond's duration and convexity. Moreover, since many bonds have option features, adjusting their cash flow patterns to account for such features is important in measuring a bond's duration and convexity. In chapters 9 and 10 we will show how bonds with embedded option features can be valued using a binomial interest rate tree. With this valuation model, one can estimate the prices of bonds with call and put option features, then substitute these prices into equations (4.5) and (4.6) to estimate the duration and convexity of bonds with embedded options. The duration and convexity measures using this approach are referred to as *effective duration* and *effective convexity*.

4.6 CONCLUSION

In a world of certainty, bonds with similar features would, in equilibrium, trade at the same rates. If this were not the case, then investors would try to buy bonds with higher rates and sell or short bonds with lower rates, causing their prices and rates to change until they were all equal. We, of course, live in a world of uncertainty. Issuers can default on their obligations, borrowers can redeem their bonds early, and the markets can change. This is why we have differences in the relative demands, prices, and yields on bonds. Thus, an important factor explaining different rates among debt instruments is uncertainty. In this chapter, we've examined the nature and impact of uncertainty by examining default, call, and market risk, and by introducing duration and convexity as volatility measures.

KEY TERMS

Default Risk or Credit Risk	Investment-Grade Bonds	Financial Institutions Reform,
Call Risk	Speculative-Grade or Junk	Recovery, and Enforcement
Market Risk	Bonds	Act

Default Risk Premium or
  Quality or Credit Spread
Reinvestment Risk
Price Compression
Binomial Interest Rate Tree
Price Risk

Interest on Interest
Duration
Bond Immunization
Macaulay's Duration
Modified Duration
Dollar Duration

Convexity
Approximate Duration
Approximate Convexity
Effective Duration
Effective Convexity

PROBLEMS AND QUESTIONS

Note on Problems: Many of these problems can be done in Excel by either writing a program or using one of the Excel programs; many also can be done using a financial calculator. For problems requiring a number of calculations, the reader may want to use Excel or a financial calculator.

1. Explain why default risk premiums widen during recessionary periods and narrow during growth periods.

2. Explain why the yield curve for lower quality bonds could be negatively sloped when the yield curves for other bonds are not.

3. Explain the McEnnally–Boardman study. What were the findings of the study? How do you explain their findings?

4. What impact does the exercising of a call option by an issuer generally have on the investor's rate of return earned for the period from the purchase of the bond to its call and the rate for the investor's horizon period?

5. Explain the relationship between call risk premiums and the level of interest rates in the economy.

6. Explain how interest rate changes affect a bond's return.

7. The AIF Company issued a 10-year bond at par ($F = \$1,000$) that pays a coupon of 11% on an annual basis, and is callable at $1,100. Suppose you bought the bond when it was issued, and at the time of your purchase suppose the yield curve was flat and continued to remain at that level during years 1–4. However, at the start of year 5 (or end of year 4), suppose the yield curve dropped to 8% and AIF called the bond. Assume you reinvest your investment funds in a new 6-year bond at par and the yield curve remains flat at 8%. What is your ARR for the call period? What is your ARR for the 10-year period? How do the ARRs compare to the YTM when you purchased the bond?

8. Suppose you have a horizon date of 10 years and bought an 8-year, 8% coupon bond at par ($F = \$1,000$) that pays coupons semi-annually and is callable at a call price of $1,100. Assume the yield curve is flat at an 8.16% effective yield (or 4% semi-annual yield) and remains constant for 3 years. At the end of year 3, suppose the yield curve drops to an effective yield of 5.0625% (2.5% semi-annual) and the issuer calls the bond. Assume you reinvest your investment funds in a new 7-year bond paying coupons semi-annually, and the yield curve remains flat at 5.0625%. What are your semi-annual rate of return and effective annual rate of return for the call period? What are your semi-annual and effective annual rate for the 10-year period? How do your rates compare to the YTM when you purchased the bond?

9. The yield curve for AA-rated bonds is presently flat at a promised YTM of 9%. You buy a 10-year, 8% coupon bond with face value of $1,000 and annual coupon payments. Suppose your horizon date is at the end of 4 years. What would your ARR be given the following cases:

    a. Immediately after you buy the bond the yield curve drops to 8% and remains there until you sell the bond at your horizon date.

    b. Immediately after you buy the bond the yield curve increases to 10% and remains there until you sell the bond at your horizon date.

    What type of risk is your investment subject to? How could the risk be minimized?

10. Suppose you have a horizon date at the end of 6 years and buy an 8-year, 8.5% coupon bond with face value of $1,000 and annual coupon payments when the applicable yield curve is flat at 10%. What would your ARR be given the following cases:

    a. Immediately after you buy the bond the yield curve drops to 8% and remains there until you sell the bond at your horizon date.

    b. Immediately after you buy the bond the yield curve increases to 12% and remains there until you sell the bond at your horizon date.

    Is there any market risk? If not, why?

11. Calculate both the Macaulay's and modified durations of the 8-year, 8.5% coupon bond given a flat yield curve at 10% in question 10. Given your answers in question 10, comment on duration, horizon date, and bond immunization.

12. Assume the following yield curve for zero-coupon bonds:

Maturity	YTM
1 year	5%
2 years	6%
3 years	7%
4 years	8%
5 years	9%

    a. What is Macaulay's duration of each of the bonds?

    b. Assume your HD is 3 years and you want to buy bonds with 1- and 4-year maturities. What percentage investment should be made in each case to assure a fully immunized portfolio?

13. Calculate Macaulay's duration, the modified duration, and the convexity of the following bonds (annualize the parameters). Assume all of the bonds pay principal at their maturity.

    a. Four-year, 9% coupon bond with a principal of $1,000 and annual coupon payments trading at par.

    b. Four-year, zero-coupon bond with a principal of $1,000 and priced at $708.42 to yield 9%.

    c. Five-year, 9% coupon bond with a principal of $1,000 and annual coupon payments trading at par.

    d. Ten-year, 7% coupon bond with a principal of $1,000 and semi-annual coupon payments (3.5%) and priced at par.

e. Three-year, 7% coupon bond with a principal of $1,000 and semi-annual coupon payments (3.5%) and priced at par.

f. Three-year zero-coupon bond with a principal of $1,000 and priced at $816.30 to yield 7%.

14. Given your duration and convexity calculations in question 13, answer the following:

a. Which bond has the greatest price sensitivity to interest rate changes?

b. For an annualized 1% decrease in rates what would be the approximate percentage change in the prices of bond d and bond e?

c. Which bond has the greatest non-symmetrical capital gain and capital loss feature?

d. If you were a speculator and expected yields to decrease in the near future by the same amount across all maturities (a parallel downward shift in the yield curve), which bond would you select?

e. If you were a bond portfolio manager and expected yields to increase in the near future by the same amount across all maturities (a parallel upward shift in the yield curve), which bond would you select?

f. Comment on the relation between maturity and a bond's price sensitivity to interest rate changes.

g. Comment on the relation between coupon rate and a bond's price sensitivity to interest rate changes.

15. Short-answer questions:

(1) Define market risk.

(2) Define call risk.

(3) Define default risk.

(4) What is a junk bond?

(5) How does price compression apply to callable bonds?

(6) When would there be a direct relation between the ARR and interest rate changes?

(7) When would there be an inverse relation between the ARR and interest rate changes?

(8) When would the ARR be invariant to interest rate changes?

WEB EXERCISES

1. Many bonds were issued in the 1980s to finance corporate takeovers. Examine that period by going to www.encyclopedia.com and searching for "Junk Bonds" and Michael Milken.

2. Examine the creditworthiness of several companies by going to www.moodys.com and then select your company. Note: registration may be required.

3. Get a current description of quality ratings by going to www.standardandpoors.com and clicking on "Credit Ratings Criteria." Note: registration may be required.

NOTES

1. Many targeted companies also sold such bonds to buy up their stock or provide stock dividends in an effort to avoid being acquired. For an excellent account of the history of these deals, as well as the security abuses, see James Stewart's *Den of Thieves*. A good history of Michael Milken can be found in *Fortune*, September 30, 1996, pp. 80–106.

2. In a widely cited study by Lawrence Fisher, yield premiums for corporate securities were found to be directly related to a company's volatility in earnings

and inversely related to the company's equity-to-debt ratio, number of outstanding bonds, and how long the company had been solvent.

3. Hickman found in his study that, for an earlier period (1900–1943), abnormal returns were earned from trading in low- and high-grade bonds during recessions and expansions.

4. The modified duration is the most commonly used measure of duration. Some applications of duration use the *dollar duration*. The dollar duration is the change in the bond price given a small change in yield (dP/dy). The dollar duration is obtained by multiplying both sides of equation (4.3) by P_0:
Dollar duration = (Modified duration) P_0.

5. For a pure discount bond, Macaulay's duration would be equal to the bond's maturity, while the modified duration would be less than the maturity.

6. The actual percentage change is:

$$\%\Delta P^b = \frac{\$99.3524 - \$100}{\$100} = -0.006476$$

where:

$$P = \sum_{t=1}^{20} \frac{\$4.50}{(1.0455)^t} + \frac{\$100}{(1.0455)^{20}} = \$99.3524$$

7. The actual percentage change is:

$$\%\Delta P^b = \frac{\$88.0496 - \$100}{\$100} = -0.1195$$

where:

$$P = \sum_{t=1}^{20} \frac{\$4.50}{(1.055)^t} + \frac{\$100}{(1.055)^{20}} = \$88.0496$$

SELECTED REFERENCES

Bierwag, G. "Immunization, Duration and the Term Structure of Interest Rates," *Journal of Financial and Quantitative Analysis* 12 (1977): 725–43.

Bierwag, G. O., George G. Kaufman, and Alden Toevs "Duration: Its Development and Use in Bond Portfolio Management," *Financial Analysts Journal* (July–August 1983): 15–35.

Campbell, J. Y. "A Defense of Traditional Hypotheses About the Term Structure of Interest Rates," *Journal of Finance* 41 (1986): 183–93.

Chance, D. M. "Default, Risk and the Duration of the Zero Coupon Bonds," *Journal of Finance* 55 (1990): 265–74.

Cox, J., J. Ingersoll, and S. Ross "Duration and the Measurement of Basis Risk," *Journal of Business* 52 (1979): 51–61.

Evans, J. and S. H. Archer "Diversification and the Reduction of Dispersion: An Empirical Analysis," *Journal of Finance* (December 1968).

Fisher, Irving *The Theory of Interest* (New York: Macmillan, 1930).

Fisher, Lawrence "Determinants of Risk Premiums on Corporate Bonds," *Journal of Political Economy* (June 1959): 217–37.

Fisher, L. and R. Weil "Coping with the Risk of Interest Rate Fluctuations: Returns to Bondholders from Naive and Optimal Strategies," *Journal of Business* 44 (1971): 408–31.

Fons, J. "Using Default Rates to Model the Term Structure of Credit Risk," *Financial Analysts Journal* L (1994): 25–32.

Hickman, W. B. *Corporate Bond Quality and Investor Experience* (New York: National Bureau of Economic Research, 1958).

Hicks, J. R. *Value and Capital*, 2nd edn (London: Oxford University Press, 1946).

Johnston, R. E. "Term Structures of Corporate Bond Yields as a Function of Risk of Default," *Journal of Finance* (May 1967).

Macaulay, F. R. *The Movement of Interest Rates, Bond Yields, and Stock Prices in the United States since 1856* (New York: National Bureau of Economic Research, 1938).

Markowitz, H. M. *Portfolio Selection: Efficient Diversification of Investment*, Cowles Foundation Monograph 16 (New Haven, Connecticut: Yale University Press, 1959).

McEnnally, R. "Duration as a Practical Tool in Bond Management," *Journal of Portfolio Management* (Summer 1977).

McEnnally, R. and C. Boardman "Aspects of Corporate Bond Portfolio Diversification," *Journal of Financial Research* (Spring 1979).

Redington, F.M. "Review of the Principles of Life–Office Foundation," *Journal of the Institute of Actuaries* 78 (1952): 286–340.

Stewart, James B. *Den of Thieves* (New York: Simon and Schuster, 1992).

Stigum, M. L. *The Repo and Reverse Markets* (Homewood, IL: Dow Jones-Irwin, 1989).

Stigum, M. L. *The Money Market* (Homewood, IL: Dow Jones-Irwin, 1990).

PART TWO

DEBT MARKETS

CHAPTER FIVE

CORPORATE DEBT SECURITIES

5.1 INTRODUCTION

Today's corporations can be viewed as perpetual investment machines: constantly developing new products and technologies, regularly expanding their markets, and from time to time acquiring other companies. To finance these investments, corporations obtain funds both internally and externally. With *internal financing*, companies retain part of their earnings that otherwise would go to existing shareholders in the form of dividends, while with *external financing* companies generate funds from outside by selling new shares of stock, selling debt instruments, or borrowing from financial institutions. From the corporation's perspective, decisions on internal versus external financing depend on the dividend policy it wants to maintain and the cost of raising funds from the outside. The company's choice of financing with debt or equity, in turn, depends on the return-risk opportunities management wants to provide its shareholders. Since debt instruments have provisions that give creditors legal protection in the case of default, the rate corporations are required to pay creditors for their investments is typically smaller than the rate their shareholders require. As a result, a firm that tends to finance its projects with relatively more debt than equity (i.e., a *leveraged firm*) benefits its shareholders with the

relatively lower rates it pays to creditors. In addition, debt financing also has a major tax advantage to corporations: the interest payments on debt are treated as an expense by the Internal Revenue Service (IRS), and are therefore tax deductible, while the dividends a corporation pays its shareholders are not tax deductible. The relatively lower rates required by creditors and the tax advantage of debt make debt financing cheaper than equity financing for a corporation, all other things being equal. The lower rates on debt, though, are not without costs. Unlike equity financing in which funds are paid to shareholders only if they are earned, the obligations of debt instruments are required to be made. Thus, if a company has a period with poor sales or unexpected high costs, it still has to make payments to the bondholders, leaving fewer earnings available for shareholders. Moreover, very low sales or very high costs could lead to the company being unable to meet its interest and/or principal payments. In this case, the creditors can sue the company, forcing them to sell company assets to meet their obligations.

When a corporation decides to finance its investments with debt, it will do so either by selling corporate bonds or notes or by securing a loan from a financial institution.[1] The larger corporations, whose credit standings are often strong, prefer to finance their long-term and intermediate-term assets by selling corporate bonds and notes, and they often finance their short-term assets by selling commercial paper. These securities, in turn, offer different investment features to investors. In this chapter, we examine these features and the markets for corporate bonds and commercial paper.

5.2 CORPORATE BONDS

A corporate bond is a debt obligation with an original maturity of over 5 years, while a corporate note is an obligation with an original maturity of less than 5 years. Since bonds and notes are similar we will follow the custom of referring to both as corporate bonds.

Corporate bondholders have a legal claim over common and preferred shareholders as to the income and assets of the corporation. Their contractual claim is specified in the bond's *indenture*. An indenture is the contract between the borrower and the lender (all the bondholders). The document is usually very extensive (200 pages or more), detailing all the characteristics of the bond issue, including the time, amounts, manners in which interest and principal are to be paid, the type of collateral, and all restrictive covenants or clauses aimed at protecting the bondholders. In addition to the indenture, a corporation issuing a bond must also file with the Securities and Exchange Commission a *prospectus*. This smaller document is a summary of the main provisions included in the indenture.

By federal law, all corporations offering bonds in excess of $5m and sold interstate must have a *trustee*. A trustee is a third party, often a commercial bank or the trust department of a bank, who is selected to represent the bondholders. The trustee has three major responsibilities: (1) bond certification, which entails ensuring that the bond issue has been drawn up in accordance with all legal requirements; (2) overseeing the issue, which requires assuring the bondholders that the issuer is meeting all of the prescribed functions specified in the indenture; and (3) taking legal action against the corporation if it fails to meet its interest and principal payments or satisfy other terms specified in the indenture.

5.2.1 General Features of Corporate Bonds

The characteristics of many security issues often are determined by the underlying real assets they are financing. For example, to finance the construction of a $100m oil refinery with an estimated economic life of 20 years, an oil company might sell 100,000 corporate bonds priced at par, with each promising to pay $100 each year for 20 years plus a principal of $1,000 at maturity. Given the wide variety of assets and bonds financing them, the differences in corporate bonds can best be explained by examining their general characteristics. These include their interest rates, maturities, principal payments, call features, protective covenants, and collateral.

Interest Rates

Bonds can be classified in terms of how they pay interest. There are three main types: coupon bonds, zero-coupon bonds, and floating-rate or variable-rate bonds.

Coupon Bonds: In the US, most corporate bonds are coupon bonds paying interest semiannually, while outside the US, most coupon bonds pay interest annually. For US bonds, the coupon interest is typically based on a 360-day year and 30-day month ($\frac{30}{360}$ day-count convention). Thus, a $1,000 par value bond with a 9% coupon would pay $90 per year and its interest would accrue at a rate of $7.50 per month ($90/12) and $0.25 per day ($90/360).[2] Technically, a coupon bond is one that has a series of coupons attached to the bond certificate, which the holder cuts out at specified times and sends to a designated party (e.g., trustee) for collection. At one time, most bonds were sold with attached coupons. Such bonds were called *bearer bonds* since their coupon payment was made to whoever had physical possession of the bond. Bearer bonds have been replaced by *registered bonds*. The interest on registered bonds is paid by the issuer or a third party (usually the trustee) to all bondholders who are registered with the issuer or the trustee. If the bond is sold, the issuer or trustee must cancel the name of the old holder and register the new one. In addition, issuers of

US bonds are required by law to report to the IRS all bondholders receiving interest. A variation of registered bonds is bonds sold in *book-entry form*. Such bonds have one master certificate with all bondholder names. A depository holds the certificate and issues ownership receipts to each bondholder.

Zero-Coupon Bonds: As noted in previous chapters, bonds that pay no coupon interest are referred to as zero-discount bonds or as pure discount bonds. In discussing zero-discount bonds or zeros, the difference between the bond's face value and the offering price when the bond is issued is called the *original-issue discount (OID)*. Zero-coupon bonds were first issued in the US corporate market during the high-interest-rate period of the early 1980s. In 1982, for example, Beatrice Foods sold a 10-year, $250m zero-coupon bond priced at $255 per $1,000 face value. In addition to zeros, many firms also issued *deep-discount bonds* that paid low coupon interest. In 1981, DuPont sold a 20-year, 6% bond priced at $468.52 per $1,000 face value. With little or no reinvestment risk, fund managers found zero-coupon and deep-discount bonds attractive investments for matching their future liabilities. In addition, many of these bonds also had call prices equal to their par values, making it unlikely they would be called. Thus, the bonds were characterized by having low market and call risk.[3]

Floating-Rate Notes and Variable-Rate Debt Securities: During the high and often volatile interest-rate period of the late 1970s and early 1980s, a number of companies began selling floating-rate notes (FRNs). Similar to variable-rate loans offered by financial institutions, FRNs pay a coupon rate that can vary in relation to another bond, benchmark rate, or formula. Floating-rate securities originated in Europe and were introduced in the US in 1974 when Citicorp issued a $650m flexible-rate note. Citicorp's note was reset semi-annually to be 1% above the rate on a 3-month Treasury-bill rate. Subsequently, Standard Oil, Georgia Pacific, and other corporations issued FRNs. By 1990, there were approximately 500 variable-rate offerings, with two-thirds being offered by banks and financial service companies.

The term floating-rate note or *floater* is often used to define any bonds with an interest rate that is adjusted periodically. Technically, though, an FRN is defined as a debt instrument with the coupon based on a short-term index (e.g., Treasury-bill rate) and reset more than once a year, while an *adjustable-rate note* or *variable-rate note* is defined as a debt security with its coupon based on long-term rates, with the rate reset no more than once a year. The denominations on floaters range between $1,000 and $100,000, and the coupon rates are based on different benchmarks – Treasury rates, commercial paper rate, prime rate, and the London interbank offer rate, LIBOR (this is the average bank rate paid by London Euro-currency bank, discussed in chapter 7). FRN issues are sometimes sold with sweeteners, such as convertibility to stock, a put option giving the holder the right to sell the bond back, a minimum rate (or floor), a maximum rate (ceiling), or a drop-lock rate (i.e., a rate that will be fixed if it is hit).

Maturity

The maturities of corporate bonds vary from intermediate-term bonds with original maturities of 5 years or less to long-term bonds with maturities of over 5 years. Today, the rapid change in technology has led to more corporate bonds being issued with original maturities averaging 15 years.[4] This contrasts with the 1950s and 1960s when the original maturities on corporate bonds ranged from 20 years to 30 years.

Call and Redemption Features

A call provision in an indenture gives the issuer the right to redeem some or all of the issue for a specific amount before maturity. Such features are quite common on corporate bonds, especially bonds issued when interest rates are relatively high. The provision usually requires that the company redeem the bonds at a price greater than the par value. The additional amount is defined as the *call premium*. Often companies will let the premium be equal to one year's interest for the first year if the bond is called, with the premium declining thereafter. For example, a 10-year, 10%, $1,000 par value bond might be called the first year at a call price of $1,100 ($100 premium $= (0.10)$ ($1,000)), the second year for $1,090 ($90 premium $= (9/10)$ $(0.10)($1,000)$), and so on, with the premium rate declining by $\frac{1}{10}$ each year.

As we discussed in chapter 4, a call option is to the advantage of the issuer. For example, during a period of high interest rates a corporation might sell a 20-year callable bond, with a 12% coupon rate at its par value of $1,000. Suppose 2 years later, though, interest rates on all bonds dropped and bonds similar to this corporation's were selling at a 10% rate. Accordingly, the company might find it advantageous to sell a new 18-year, 10% callable bond with the funds of the new issue used to redeem the 12% issue. If a company decides to call its bond issue, it would send a *notice of redemption* to each holder and then at a specified time a check equaling the call premium.

To the investor, a bond being called provides a benefit to the extent that the call price exceeds the par value. However, if a bond is called, the investor is forced to reinvest her proceeds in a market in which rates are generally lower. Consequently, on balance call provisions tend to work against the investor. As a result, the issuer, in addition to the call premium, might provide the investor with some call protection. For example, while it is often standard for the entire issue to be called, provisions could be included in which only a certain proportion of the bonds issued could be called for a specified period, possibly with those selected to be determined by the trustee by lot. Investor protection might also be provided with a *deferred call* feature that prohibits the issuer from calling the bond before a certain period of time has expired. The investor would therefore have call protection for the period. However, a more common practice is to prohibit the issuer from buying back the bonds during a non-refundable period (e.g., 5 years) from proceeds from a debt issue that ranks senior or par with the bond. Under this type of provision, the issuer has the right to redeem the bonds from excess cash or from the proceeds from the sale of equity, property, or higher interest rate debt. This type of redemption is called *refunding*.

As an example of a callable bond with a redemption provision, consider a 20-year, 10% coupon bond with a par value of $1,000 issued by the ABC Company with the following call provisions:

- The first-year call price is equal to the public offering price plus the coupon; thereafter the call price decreases by equal amounts for 15 years to equal par; thereafter the call price is equal to par.
- During the first 5 years, the issuer can only exercise the call from proceeds coming from cash, equity, or debt inferior to the issue.

Suppose the bonds were issued at 105 ($1,050 per $1,000 par). The first year call price would then be 115 (price $+$ coupon $= 105 + 10$). The call price would then decrease by $1.00 each year ($= (115 - 100)/15$) to equal 100 in year 15; and in years 16–20 the call price would be 100. Finally, for the first 5 years the bond would not be refundable out of any debt issue that ranks senior or par with the bond.

Year	Call price
1	115
2	114
3	113
4	112
5	111
•	•
•	•
15	101
16–20	100

In this example, the refunding provision does not give the bondholders call protection during the first 5 years – they only have protection against certain types of redemptions. Moreover, there have been court cases in which bondholders have challenged bonds that were called under such refunding clauses. For example, in 1983 Archer Daniels Midland issued a 16% bond due in 2011 with a refunding provision similar to the one just described. The bonds were called in 1991, with the source of the refunding being a stock offering. Bondholders subsequently brought legal actions to stop the redemption. The court, though, ruled in favor of Archer Daniels Midland, allowing the redemption. Interestingly, the company later issued new bonds.[5]

Sinking Fund

Most corporations sell their bonds with a principal of $1,000 that is usually paid at maturity. This contrasts with real estate mortgages and consumer loans made by financial institutions. These loans are usually *fully amortized* with the borrower making payments for both interest and principal during the life of the loan such that the loan is gradually repaid by installments before maturity arrives. While most corporate bonds are not amortized, some corporations do sell their bonds as a *serial bond* issue. This type of bond issue consists of a series of bonds with different maturities. While serial bonds reduce a bondholder's concern over the payment of principal, a more common feature to allay such risk is the inclusion of a *sinking-fund* provision in the indenture. A sinking fund used to be simply a provision requiring that the issuer make scheduled payments into a fund often maintained by the trustee, or in some cases to certify to the trustee that the issuer had added value to its property and plant investments. Today, though, many sinking-fund agreements have provisions requiring an orderly retirement of the issue. In recent years, this has been commonly handled by the issuer being required to buy up a certain portion of bonds each year either at a stipulated call price or in the secondary market at its market price. This sinking-fund call option provision benefits the issuer and is a disadvantage to the bondholder. If interest rates are relatively high, then the issuer will be able to buy back the requisite amount at a relatively low market price, and if rates are low and bond prices are high, the issuer will be able to buy back the bonds at the sinking-fund call price. A sinking fund with a call option is therefore valuable to the issuer and should trade at a lower price in the market than an otherwise identical non-sinking-fund bond (the valuation of sinking-fund bonds is discussed in chapter 9).

Sinking funds are usually applied to a particular bond issue. There are, though, non-specific sinking funds (sometimes referred to as *tunnel, funnel,* or *blanket sinking funds*) that are applied to a company's total outstanding bonds. For most bonds, the periodic sinking fund payments are the same each period. Some indentures do allow the sinking fund to increase over time or to be determined by the level of earnings, and some sinking-fund provisions give the issuer the option to double the stipulated amount.

It should be noted that since many sinking-fund provisions require the repayment of the debt in installments, they effectively reduce the life of the bond. As such, a better measure of a sinking-fund bond's life than its maturity is its *average life*. The average life is the average amount of time the debt will be outstanding. It is equal to the weighted average of the time periods, with the weights being relative principal payments:

$$\text{Average life} = \frac{\sum_{t=1}^{M} t(A_t)}{F}$$

where A_t is the sinking fund due at time t. Thus a bond that matures in 10 years and requires equal sinking-fund payments each year would have an average life of 5.5 years (average life $= 0.1(1) + 0.1(2) + \cdots + 0.1(10)$).

Protective Covenants

The Board of Directors hires the managers and officers of a corporation. Since the Board represents the stockholders, this arrangement can create a moral hazard problem in which the managers may engage in activities that could be detrimental to the bondholders. For example, the managers might use the funds provided by creditors to finance projects different and riskier than bondholders were expecting. Since bondholders cannot necessarily seek redress from managers after they've made decisions that could harm them, they need to include rules and restrictions on the company in the bond indenture. Such provisions are known as *protective* or *restrictive covenants*.

The covenants often specify the financial criterion that must be met before borrowers can incur additional debt (debt limitation) or pay dividends (dividend limitations). For example, a debt limitation covenant would be one that prohibits a company from incurring any new long-term debt if it causes the company's interest-coverage ratio (earning before interest and taxes/interest) to fall below a specified level. In addition to limits on debt and dividends, other possible covenants include limitations on liens, borrowing from subsidiaries, asset sales, mergers and acquisitions, and leasing.

Over the last two decades, there has been an increase in the number of mergers, corporate restructurings, and stock and bond repurchases. Often these events benefit the stockholders at the expense of the bondholders, resulting in a downgrade in a bond's quality ratings and a lowering of its price. Bond risk resulting from such actions is known as *event risk*. Certain protective covenants such as poison puts and net worth maintenance clauses have been used to minimize event risk. A *poison put* clause in the indenture gives the bondholders the right to sell the bonds back to the issuer at a specified price under certain conditions arising from a specific event such as a takeover, change in control, or an investment ratings downgrade. A *net worth maintenance clause*, in turn, requires that the issuer redeem all or part of the debt, or give bondholders the right to sell (*offer-to-redeem clause*) their bonds back to the issuer if the company's net worth falls below a stipulated level.

Secured, Unsecured, and Guaranteed Bonds

In most loans, the lender, whether it is a financial institution or a bondholder, has three questions to pose to a borrower: What does she need the money for? How much does she need? What does she plan to do if her idea doesn't work? The latter question usually translates into the type of collateral the borrower intends to pledge in order to pay the lender if she is unable to meet her interest and principal obligations. In the case of corporate bonds, the bonds can be either *secured bonds*, backed by a specific asset, or *unsecured bonds*, backed by a general creditor's claim but not by a specified asset. The latter are called *debentures*. A secured bond is defined as one that has a lien giving the bondholder, via the trustee, the right to sell the pledged asset in order to pay the bondholders if the company defaults. Secured bonds can be differentiated in terms of the types of collateral pledged and the priority of the lien.

Types of collateral

Assets that can be used as security are real, financial, or personal. A mortgage bond and an equipment-trust bond are bonds secured by real assets. A *mortgage bond* has a lien on real property or buildings while an *equipment-trust bond* has a lien on specific equipment, such as airplanes, trucks, or computers. A *collateral-trust bond*, in turn, is secured by a lien on equity shares of a company's subsidiary, holdings of other companies' stocks and bonds, government securities, and other financial claims. Finally, a company might secure its debt with personal property, such as the corporation's cash or liquid assets, accounts receivables, or inventory. Since these assets are short term in nature, they are usually used as collateral for short-term debt obligations.

Mortgage Bonds: In the case of a mortgage bond, if the issuer defaults and the assets are liquidated, then the mortgage bondholders can claim the underlying asset and sell it to pay off their obligation, or if the issuer defaults and the company is reorganized, then the bondholders' mortgage lien will give them a stronger bargaining position relative to other creditors on any new securities created. Often in a mortgage bond, there are provisions in the indenture that allow the mortgaged asset to be sold provided it is replaced with a suitable substitute; some mortgage bonds also have a *release and substitution provision* that allows for the asset to be sold with the proceeds used to retire the bonds. Mortgage bonds are sometimes sold in a series, similar to a serial bond issue, with bonds of each series secured by the same mortgage. Generally, it is more efficient for a company to issue a series of bonds under one mortgage and one indenture than it is to arrange collateral and draw up a new indenture for each new bond issue.

Equipment-Trust Bonds: Usually equipment-trust bonds are secured by one piece of property (e.g., truck) and often are named after the security (e.g., truck bond). Equipment-trust bonds are sometimes formed through a lease-and-buy-back agreement with a third party or trustee. Under this type of agreement, a trustee (e.g., bank, leasing company, or the manufacturer) might purchase the equipment (plane, machine, etc.) and lease it to a company who would agree to take title to the equipment at the termination date of the lease. Alternatively, the company could buy the equipment and sell it to the trustee who would then lease it to them. The trustee would finance the equipment purchase from the company or the manufacturer by selling equipment-trust bonds (sometimes called equipment-trust certificates). Each period the trustee would then collect rent from the company and pay the interest and principal on the certificates. At maturity, the certificates would be paid off, the trustee would transfer the title of the equipment to the company, and the lease would be terminated. This arrangement (sometimes referred to as the *Philadelphia Plan* and *rolling stock*) and other variations work well when the underlying equipment is relatively standard (e.g., plane, railroad car, or computer) and therefore can be easily sold in the event the company defaults on the lease. Airlines and railroad companies are big users of this type of financing.

Collateral-Trust Bonds: A collateral-trust bond is secured by a lien on the company's holdings of other companies' stocks and bonds, other securities and financial claims, or the issuer's subsidiaries. The legal arrangements governing collateral-trust bonds generally require the issuer to deliver to the trustee the pledged securities (if the securities are stock or the stock of a subsidiary, the company still retains its voting rights). The company is usually required to maintain the value of the securities, positing addition collateral (e.g., cash or more securities) if the collateral decreases in value. There are also provisions in the indenture allowing for the withdrawal of the collateral provided there is an acceptable substitute. Finally, some collateral trust bonds are sold as a series like some mortgage bonds, with the same indenture and financial collateral defining each series.

Priority of claims

In designating an asset as collateral, it is possible for a company to have more than one bond issue or debt obligation secured by that asset. When this occurs, bonds and debt obligations must be differentiated in terms of the priorities of their claims. A *senior lien*, or first lien, has priority over a *junior lien* (second or third lien). Thus, if a company defaults and the real property pledged is sold, then the senior bondholders would be paid first, with the second or third lien holders being paid only after the senior holders have been paid in full.[6] It should be noted that such bonds are typically not defined in their title as second or third lien bonds (e.g., second mortgage bond) because of the insinuation of weakness.

Closely associated with priorities in claims are clauses in the indenture that specify the issuer's right to incur additional debt secured by the assets already encumbered. At one extreme, there are *closed-end bonds* (usually mortgage bonds) that prohibit the company from incurring any additional debt secured by a first lien on the assets already being used as security. For example, a company with a processing plant and land valued at $20m might use those assets as security for a $14m bond issue. If the issue were closed-ended, then no other debt obligation with first liens could be obtained. In contrast, an issue silent on this point is an *open-end bond*; it allows for more debt to be secured by the same collateral. Thus in the case of the company with a $14m secured bond, if the company were to later sell a new $6m bond issue, it could secure the new debt with the $20m plant and land assets, provided the earlier issue was open-end. In turn, if the company were to default and the assets were sold for only $14m, then the first bondholders would receive only 70 cents on each dollar of their loan, compared to a dollar on a dollar if their issue had been closed-end.

Because of the adverse effects to investors, most open-end bonds include certain covenants that limit the amount of additional indebtedness the company can incur. A typical case is an open-end bond accompanied with an *after-acquired property clause*. This clause dictates that all property or assets acquired after the issue be added to the property already pledged. Finally, within the extremes of open- and closed-end bonds are bonds with limited open-end clauses that allow the company to incur additional debt secured by assets up to a certain percent of the pledged asset's value.

Debenture

The majority of all corporate bonds are unsecured. As noted, such bonds are defined as debentures. While such instruments lack asset-specific collateral, they still make the holder a general creditor. As such, debenture holders are protected by assets that are not already pledged, and they also have a claim on pledged assets to the extent that those assets have values in excess of the secured debt. For investors, it is important to distinguish between strong companies that sell debentures and have no bonds secured with pledged assets and companies that sell debentures and have bonds secured with pledged assets – the latter need closer scrutiny.

Debentures are often issued with a number of protective covenants. For example, the indenture might include a restriction on additional debt that can be incurred or specifications that new debt can only be incurred if earnings grow at a certain level or if certain financial ratios are met. Debentures can also be classified as either *subordinate* or *unsubordinate*. In the case of liquidation, subordinated debt (junior security) has a claim only after an unsubordinated claim (senior claim) has been met. Accordingly, a debenture can be made subordinate to other claims such as bank loans or accounts payable. Subordination may be the result of the terms agreed to by the firm in its other debt obligations. For example, a bank might require that all future debts of a company be made subordinate to its loans.[7] Since subordinated debenture bondholders are last in line among creditors if the issuer defaults, they are sometimes sold with a sweetener or inducement such as an option to convert to shares of the company's stock, one of its subsidiaries' stock or some other security of the company.

Guaranteed bonds

Bonds issued by one company and guaranteed by another economic entity are defined as *guaranteed bonds*. The guarantee ensures that the bondholders will be paid interest and principal in the event the issuer defaults. With the guarantee, the default risk of the bond shifts from borrower to the financial capacity of the insurer.

The guarantor could be the parent company or another company securing the issue in return for an option on an equity interest in the project the bond is financing. There may also be multiple guarantors. In a joint venture, for example, a limited partnership may be formed with several companies who jointly agree to guarantee the bond issue of the venture. For some corporate issues, a financial institution may provide the guarantee. For example, banks for a fee provide corporations with *credit enhancements* in the form of *letters of credit* that guarantee the interest and principal payment on the corporation's debt obligation. Similarly, insurance companies have expanded their insurance coverage of municipal bonds that they began offering in the 1970s to the coverage of corporate bonds. Finally, municipal governments and governmental agencies offer from time to time guarantees. For example, to promote the gasohol program in the late 1970s, the Farmer's Home Administration provided loan guarantees to companies that developed alcohol-fuels plants.

5.2.2 Corporate Bonds with Special Features

The discussion to this point has focused on the general characteristics of corporate bonds. Many corporate bonds also have special features included in their covenants that make them more identifiable with stocks, options, or other securities.

Income Bonds

Income bonds are instruments that pay interest only if the earnings of the firm are sufficient to meet the interest obligations; principal payments, however, are required. Thus, a failure by the issuer to pay interest does not constitute a default. While income bonds are rare, companies who have been reorganized because of financial distress sometimes issue them. In general, because the interest payments are not required unless earnings hit a certain level, income bonds are similar to preferred stock. In fact, some income bonds have the cumulative dividend feature of preferred stock: if interest is not met, it accumulates. Similarly, some income bonds permit voting or limited voting rights (usually if interest is not paid). Unlike preferred stock, though, income bonds do provide corporations with the tax advantage of interest deductibility. Finally, income bonds often include such features as sinking-fund arrangements and convertibility to the company's stock.

Participating Bonds

Participating bonds provide a guaranteed minimum rate, as well as additional interest up to a certain point if the company achieves a certain earnings level. Like income bonds, participating bonds are similar to preferred stock, except for the interest deductibility benefit. However, for obvious reasons participating bonds are not very popular with shareholders. As a result, such bonds are very rare.

Deferred Coupon Bonds

Some corporations sell bonds with a deferred coupon structure that allows the issuer to defer coupon interest for a specified period. Included in the group of deferred coupon bonds are *deferred-interest bonds, reset bonds*, and *payment-in-kind bonds*. Many of these debt securities with special features were created during the merger period of the 1980s. For example, in 1989, the RJR leveraged buyout created convertible and exchangeable debentures that had both payment-in-kind and reset features.

Deferred-interest bonds (DIBs) have their coupon interest deferred for a specified period. They are often structured so that they do not pay coupons for a specified number of years (e.g., 5 years). At the end of the deferred-interest period, they begin to pay interest, usually semi-annually, until they mature or are called. A reset bond or step coupon bond is similar in structure to a DIB except that it starts with a low coupon interest, which is later increased. A reset bond may have a call option that is likely to be exercised as the coupon level increases. A payment-in-kind (PIK) bond gives the issuer the option on the interest-payment date to pay the coupon interest either in cash or in kind, usually by issuing to the bondholder a new bond. In essence, a PIK bond allows coupons to be paid in units of the security (baby bonds). If the issuer pays in kind, then at maturity the investor would own a number of

bonds and the cash flow from her PIK bond would be similar to that of a zero-coupon bond.

Tax-Exempt Corporate Bonds

To promote investments in projects that are in the public interest, Congress grants tax-exempt status for bonds used for specified purposes. When a project qualifies for tax exemption, the holders of the bond do not have to pay federal income tax on the interest they receive. As a result, investors in tax-exempt bonds will accept a lower interest rate, lowering the interest cost to the issuing corporation. Prior to 1986, a number of activities qualified for tax-exempt status. The Tax Reform Act of 1986, though, significantly reduced the number of eligible activities. Examples of eligible tax-exempt activities would be the construction of solid and hazardous waste disposal facilities.

Bonds with Warrants

A *warrant* is a security or a provision in a security that gives the holder the right to buy a specified number of shares of stock or another designated security at a specified price. It is a call option issued by the corporation. As a sweetener, some corporate bonds, such as a subordinated debenture, are sold with warrants. A warrant that is attached to the bond can only be exercised by the bondholder. Often, the warrant can be detached from the bond as of a particular date and sold separately.

Convertible Bonds

A *convertible bond* is one that has a conversion provision that grants the bondholder the right to exchange the bond for a specified number of shares of the issuer's stock. A convertible bond is similar to a bond with a non-detachable warrant. Like a regular bond, it pays interest and principal, and like a warrant, it can be exchanged for a specified number of shares of stock. Convertible bonds are often sold as a subordinate debenture (convertible debentures). The conversion feature of the bond, in turn, serves as a sweetener to the bond issue. Note: some convertibles can be converted into other securities. For example, a company owning a significant proportion of another company could issue a convertible bond giving the convertible bondholders the right to convert the bond into shares the issuer owns of the other company. Similarly, a gold mining company could issue a bond convertible into gold claims.

To issuers, convertibles tend to lower the interest costs on their debt; the yield on a convertible bond may be 100 basis points lower than the yield on a comparable non-convertible bond. The conversion feature may also make it possible for issuers to reduce the number of protective covenants they normally would include in their debt obligations. In general, convertibles give issuers the opportunity to sell stock at a better price via the convertible than the stock price they currently would receive if the stock were sold directly. This advantage could be negated later if the stock were sold on the convertible at a price below the market. However, most convertibles have a call option that the issuer can use to force the conversion to a price that in some cases would be higher than the price realized in the market. To the investor, convertible bonds provide a floor against a stock price decrease. That is, if the stock price decreases, the value of the convertible will only drop to its value as a straight bond. On the other hand, if the stock price increases, then the convertible bond's price will also increase, providing upside potential. The disadvantage of a convertible to investors is that the yield on the bond is less than the yield on a comparable non-convertible and the issuer can call the convertible, forcing the conversion. The features and valuation of convertible bonds are discussed in more detail in chapter 9.

Putable Bonds

A *putable bond* or *put bond* gives the holder the right to sell the bond back to the issuer at a specified price. In contrast to callable bonds, putable bonds benefit the holder: if interest rates increase and as a result the price of the bond decreases below the specified price, then the bondholder can sell the bond back to the issuer and reinvest in a market with higher rates. As we noted earlier, a bond with a put option may also be used to protect the bondholder

against a decrease in the price of the bond due to a downgrade in its quality rating.

Extendable Bonds

Extendable bonds have an option to extend the maturity of the bond. Typically, the bond issuer holds the option. Some extendable bonds give the holder the right to extend and some give both the issuer and the investor the extension option.

Credit-Sensitive Bonds

Credit-sensitive bonds are bonds with coupons that are tied to the issuer's credit ratings. For example, the coupon rate may be 10% if the bond has a quality rating of A or better, 10.25% if the rating is BBB, 10.5% if the rating is BB, and so on. Such bonds provide bondholders with some protection against management pursuing risky investments or diluting the quality of current bonds by management's increased use of debt financing. However, such clauses also increase the company's interest costs at a time when it may not need higher rates.

Commodity-Linked Bonds

A *commodity-linked bond* is one that has its coupons and possibly principal tied to the price of a particular commodity. The bonds are designed to provide a company with a hedge against adverse changes in the price of a commodity. For example, an oil-producing company might sell an oil-index bond in which the interest is tied to the price of crude oil.

Voting Bonds

As the name indicates, *voting bonds* give voting privileges to the holders. The vote is usually limited to specific corporate decisions under certain conditions.

Assumed Bonds

An *assumed bond* is one whose obligations are taken over or assumed by another company or economic entity. In many cases such bonds are the result of a merger. That is, when one firm takes over or buys a second firm, the second firm usually loses its identity (legally and in name). As a result, the first company takes over the liabilities of the second. Accordingly, the bonds of the second are assumed by the first firm's promise to pay, often with additional security pledged by the first company in order to allay any fears of the creditors.

5.3 BANKRUPTCY

A number of factors can lead to the financial distress and deterioration of a company: poor investments, competition, excessive debt, litigation, and poor management. One of the main risks that an investor assumes when she buys a bond is the chance that the company will become financially distressed and the issuer will default. If a corporation defaults, the amount the investor receives depends, in part, on the security pledged and the priority of the claim; however, equally important is how the bankruptcy is handled.

A company is considered bankrupt if the value of its liabilities exceeds the value of its assets; it is considered in default if it cannot meet its obligations. Technically, default and bankruptcy are dependent. On the one hand, a company with liabilities exceeding assets (bankrupt) will inevitably be in default when the future income from its assets is insufficient to cover future obligations on its liabilities. On the other hand, a company presently unable to meet its current obligations will, if conditions persist, have its asset prices decline. It should be noted that bankruptcy is not limited to size. There have been many large corporations that have declared bankruptcy: Enron, Texaco, Federated Department Stores, Continental Airlines, Penn Central, Eastern Airlines, Southland Corporation, and Pan Am. Also, there are occasions when a company is currently solvent but files for bankruptcy in order to obtain protection against future claimants. This was the motivation for the bankruptcy petition filed by the Manville Corporation in 1982: the company was solvent but had legal claims against it due to asbestos-related diseases.

In the US, when a company defaults on its obligations to bondholders or other creditors, the company can voluntarily file for bankruptcy with the courts; the bondholders (via their trustee) and other creditors can sue for bankruptcy; or both parties can try to work out an agreement. In the first two cases, the court will decide whether the assets should be liquidated or whether the company should be reorganized. In the third case, the parties can settle by extending or changing the composition of the debt with minimum court involvement. In the US, the Bankruptcy Reform Act of 1994 governs bankruptcies. This Act provides the framework under which liquidation and reorganization are considered (see exhibit 5.1 for a summary of the bankruptcy process). In addition, the law also provides stay protection for the distressed company from its creditors.

If the court decides on asset liquidation, creditors with security pledged will receive, to the extent possible, the par value of their debt from the proceeds of the sale of the secured assets. Next, the sale of unsecured assets and any excesses from the secured assets' sale will be used to satisfy priority creditors – uninsured claims, taxes, rents, and labor expenses. Finally, what is left is used to pay unsecured creditors, followed by shareholders.[8]

Alternatively, if a court decides that the value of the company's operation is worth more if it continues as a business than if it is liquidated, then the court may order reorganization. For reorganization to be feasible (or preferable to liquidation) the causes of the firm's insolvency must be rectified and the prospects of a profitable future must be defended. Moreover, to achieve profitability, reorganization often requires a restructuring of the debt. When this occurs, creditors are usually given new claims on the reorganized firm that are at least equal in value to an amount estimated to be received if liquidation had occurred. This could take the form of debenture holders receiving long-term income bonds, stock, or convertible bonds, and short-term creditors receiving long-term claims.

In summary, the amount of funds the bondholder will ultimately receive if the issuer defaults depends on whether the bankruptcy is handled through liquidation, reorganization, or voluntary settlement. Current US law generally

Exhibit 5.1   US bankruptcy process for reorganization

Filing:

(a) A bankruptcy filing by creditors or the debtor (distressed company) is done in the appropriate circuit and district court. Appropriate can mean the court with jurisdiction over the company's headquarters or its principal place of business.

(b) The filing requires the best estimate of the value of the company's assets and liabilities and a listing of its 20 largest creditors.

(c) The company files a petition for protection, creditors are contacted and a meeting is set up.

Debtor-in-Possession:

(a) When a company files for protection it becomes a debtor-in-possession. As a debtor-in-possession, the company continues to operate, but under the supervision of the court.

(b) Court supervision includes the court's approval on major transactions, the appointment of a trustee to oversee, and the possible appointment of an examiner. In certain cases, the court may appoint a trustee to take over control of the business.

(c) The bankruptcy judge issues an automatic stay.

(d) All debt is frozen: creditors are precluded from trying to enforce collection.

(e) Lawsuits are suspended.

Formulation of a Plan:

(a) A committee consisting of officers and representatives for creditors and possibly shareholders is formed to formulate a plan of reorganization.

(b) The debtor must file the plan in 120 days, although the length can be extended.

(c) No other plans can be filed during this period. Thereafter any interested party can submit a plan.

(d) Plans usually consider reorganization, the creation of new financial securities, elimination or changing expensive contracts (e.g., leases or union contracts), and substantial consolidation.

(e) Under substantial consolidation, all assets and liabilities of all of the company's subsidiaries are pooled and used; this can have important ramifications for security holders.

Disclosure Statement:

(a) Once the committee approves the plan for reorganization, the debtor produces and files for approval a disclosure statement.

(b) The disclosure statement summarizes the plan. It also includes pro formas and a liquidation analysis supporting the claim that the creditors will receive more under the reorganization plan than liquidation.

(c) If the court approves the disclosure statement, then it is sent to all impaired parties for approval.

(d) Parties are given 30 days to vote.

(e) To be accepted, at least two-thirds of the impaired parties and half of the claimants must accept the plan.

(f) If approved, the court sets a date for the reorganization.

(g) If the required number of creditors do not approve, the plan may be approved under a cram-down provision. Approval under this provision requires meeting several specified criteria.

Source: Emery and Finnerty, *Corporate Financial Management* pp. 888–93.

---

favors reorganization. Since bankruptcy proceedings can take some time, some speculators specialize in buying defaulted issues. They, in turn, can profit from such investments if the present value of the cash received at liquidation or the value of the new instrument (replacing the defaulted bond) from reorganization exceeds the price they pay for the defaulted bonds. Investments in distressed companies are discussed in chapter 8.

Web Information

For more information on corporate bankruptcy, see "What Every Investor should Know About Corporate Bankruptcy," at

www.sec.gov/investor/pubs/bankrupt.htm

5.4 QUALITY RATINGS

While many institutional investment firms do their own credit analysis, individual bond investors, as well as some institutional investors, usually do not make an independent evaluation of a bond's chance of default. Instead, they rely on bond rating companies. As noted in chapter 4, there are three major rating companies in the United States: Moody's Investment Services, Standard & Poor's, and Fitch Investors Service. Moody's and Standard & Poor's are the two most widely used companies. Both have been rating bonds for almost 100 years. Today, they rate about 2,000 companies in addition to municipals and other debt obligations (a company that wants a rating must apply and is charged a one-time-only fee). The general consensus among bond participants is that the market usually anticipates a ratings change. Standard & Poor's does publish a weekly notice of companies whose credit ratings are under scrutiny for a change that could be either an upgrade or downgrade.

Web Information
Corporate bond spreads and other information can be found by going to
www.bondsonline.com

Moody's rating changes and watch list can be found by going to
www.moodys.com
and clicking on "Watchlist" (registration is required).

Standard & Poor's rating changes and watch list can be found by going to
www.standardandpoors.com
and clicking on "Credit Rating Actions."

Fitch's rating changes can be found by going to
www.fitchratings.com
and clicking on "Corporates" and "Issuer List."

5.5 THE MARKETS FOR CORPORATE BONDS

5.5.1 Primary Market

Billions of dollars of corporate bonds are sold each year in the primary market. The new corporate bonds are sold either in the open market or privately placed to a limited number of investors.

Open Market Sales

Bonds sold in the open market (*open market sales*) are handled through investment bankers. Investment bankers may underwrite the issue themselves or with other investment bankers as a syndicate, or they may use their best effort: selling the bonds on commission at the best prevailing price (see table 5.1 for a listing of the major underwriters and the proportion of their underwriting business).

The way a company chooses to offer an issue to the public depends, in part, on the size of the issue and the risk of a price decrease during the time the issue is being sold. For relatively strong companies, the investment banker often underwrites the issue: buying the issue at an agreed-upon price and then selling it in the market at hopefully a higher price. Such an agreement is referred to as a *firm commitment*. The issuer may choose the investment banker or syndicate, either individually or by a bid process, selecting the underwriting group with the highest price.[9]

Table 5.1 Leading underwriting firms of US debt and equity issues in 2001

Underwriter	Share (%)
1. Citicorp/Salomon Smith Barney	12.0
2. Merrill Lynch	10.6
3. Credit Suisse First Boston	8.5
4. J. P. Morgan Chase	7.7
5. Goldman Sachs	7.4
6. Morgan Stanley	6.8
7. Lehman Brothers	6.4
8. UBS Warburg	6.2
9. Deutsche Bank	5.5
10. Bank of America Securities	4.0

Source: Wall Street Journal, January 1, 2002

With an underwriting arrangement, the selected investment banker will try to profit from the spread between the selling price (retail) and the price paid to the issuer. The spread represents the *floatation cost* to the issuer; it is usually a little less than 1% of the total value of the issue.

When a new issue is underwritten, the investment banker underwriting the issue bears the risk that the price of the issue could decrease during the time the bonds are being sold. A classic example illustrating such risk was the $1b bond issue of IBM in 1979. This issue was underwritten by a syndicate just before the announcement by the Federal Reserve System of a major change in the direction of monetary policy. The Federal Reserve announcement, in turn, led to a substantial increase in interest rates and a decrease in bond prices, causing substantial losses for the underwriters. To avoid such underwriting risk, the investment banker may choose to hedge the issue by taking a position in the futures market (hedging with derivatives is discussed in part IV). Alternatively, the investment banker may elect to sell the issue on a best-effort basis or use a combination of underwriting and best effort by using a *standby underwriting agreement*. In this latter agreement, the investment banker sells the issue on a commission, but agrees to buy all unsold securities at a specified price.

Before the issue is sold to the public, the issuer must file registration statements with the Securities and Exchange Commission (SEC). These statements include the relevant business and financial information of the firm. Once the company has registered, it must then wait while the SEC verifies all the information. Typically the investment banker uses this period to advertise the offering and to distribute to potential buyers a preliminary prospectus called a *red-herring* that details all the pertinent information the official prospectus will have, except the price. Finally, after the SEC confirms the registration statements, the indenture and prospectus become official and the investment banker offers the issue for sale.

In selling the bond issue, the investment banker often forms a selling group. This group consists of the investment banker who, as an underwriter, acts as a wholesaler (or initial distributor if best effort is being used) by selling the issue to a number of dealers who, in turn, sell to their clients. The arrangements between the investment banker and the selling group are specified in a *selling group agreement* (described in the prospectus). The agreement defines the period of time the members of the group have to sell their portion of the issue, commissions that they can charge, and restrictions such as prohibiting members from selling below a certain price.

In summary, the floating of a bond issue can be quite complex, involving the preparation of an indenture, the selection of a trustee, and the formation of a selling group. Since 1983 some corporations have been able to shorten this process, as well as reduce the floatation costs of issuing bonds, by taking advantage of the SEC's *Rule 415*. Rule 415, known as the *shelf registration rule*, allows a firm to register an inventory of securities of a particular type for up to 2 years. The firm can then sell the securities whenever it wishes during that time – the securities remain on the shelf. To minimize costs, a company planning to finance a number of projects over a period of time could register a large issue, and then sell parts of the issue at different times.

Private Placement

An alternative to selling securities to the public is to sell them directly to institutional investors through a private placement. During the 1980s an increasing proportion of new corporate bonds was sold through *private placement*. Because they are sold through direct negotiation with the buyer, privately placed bonds usually have fewer restrictive covenants than publicly issued ones, and they are more tailor-made to both the buyer's and seller's particular needs.[10] Historically, one of the disadvantages of privately placed bonds was their lack of marketability due to the absence of an active secondary market. Under the SEC Act of 1933, firms could only offer securities privately (which did not require SEC registration) to investors deemed sophisticated – insurance companies, pension funds, banks, and endowments. In 1991, the SEC adopted Rule 144A under SEC Act 1933. Under this rule, issuers could sell unregistered securities to one or more investment bankers who could resell the securities to "qualified investment buyers" (QIBs). QIBs could then sell freely with each other in securities that had not been registered. The adoption of *SEC Rule 144A*

Exhibit 5.2   The rise and fall of Drexel Burnham Lambert

Since the US federal tax code allows interest to be tax deductible but not dividends, leveraged companies structured with greater debt-to-equity ratios have more of their earning going to investors (creditors and shareholders) and less to the government, all other factors constant. As the company's debt-to-equity ratio increases, though, its expected bankruptcy costs also increase, augmenting the rate required on the debt and lowering its quality ratings.

In the 1970s, most lower quality bonds were those of fallen angels: companies with investment-grade debt that had been downgraded. In the early 1980s, this changed with the emergence of many leveraged buyout companies (LBOs) formed, in part, to take advantage of the tax law. These LBOs would issue bonds to finance their corporate acquisitions. After the acquisition, the newly structured company would be more highly leveraged, with a greater proportion of the firm's investors now being creditors. With the interest tax deductible, though, the new company would be able to pay less corporate taxes, enabling it to pay a higher interest to its creditors.

With stock prices relatively low and yielding poor returns during the 1970s, Michael Milken of the investment banking firm of Drexel Burnham Lambert was one who saw the potential of selling high yielding corporate bonds created from financing mergers to institutional investors as a substitute for stock. During the 1980s, some 1,800 corporations issued low-quality, high-yielding junk bonds to finance their acquisitions and to change their capital structure. In underwriting a number of these issues, Drexel Burnham Lambert earned fees as high as 2% to 3%. In addition, to facilitate the marketability of these bonds, Milken and Drexel Burnham Lambert also improved the creditworthiness of the bonds by standing ready to renegotiate the debt or to loan funds if the company were in jeopardy of default. The investment company also acted as a market maker, providing a secondary market for junk bonds.

Unfortunately, the economic recession of the late 1980s and early 1990s depressed the earning of many leveraged companies to levels that were not sufficient to pay their high interest obligations. Over 250 companies defaulted between 1989 and 1991, including Drexel Burnham Lambert who filed for bankruptcy in 1990 due to losses on its holdings of junk bonds. The junk bond market did eventually recover from its near collapse in the early 1990s. Today, it is a market used by medium-sized companies to raise funds.

As for Michael Milken, he was convicted of insider trading resulting from feeding information on target companies to Ivan Boesky, a Wall Street hedged fund player, and others. He was sentenced to 3 years in prison; his net worth, though, was reported by *Fortune* to be over $400m in 1993.

eliminated some of the restrictions on the secondary trading of privately placed bonds by institutional investors. As such, it opened up the secondary market for privately placed bonds.

Another reason for the growth in privately placed bonds during the 1980s was their use in financing many of the corporate mergers and takeovers. During this period, many corporations and investment groups sold bonds and borrowed from financial institutions to finance their corporate acquisitions. Because privately placed bonds had less restrictive covenants, they were frequently used to finance these leveraged buyout acquisitions. Moreover, many of these bonds were junk bonds, with relatively low quality ratings. By the late 1980s, junk bonds accounted for approximately one-third of the new corporate bonds offered, with two-thirds of those bonds being used to finance mergers or corporate restructurings aimed at stopping a corporate takeover. Exhibit 5.2 provides a brief history of the growth in this market and the rise and fall of one of its major participants – Drexel Burnham Lambert.

5.5.2 Secondary Market

The long-term maturity and fixed income features of corporate bonds make them a good investment for large institutional investors. Life insurance companies, followed by corporate and private pension funds, dominate the ownership of existing corporate bonds.

Since most corporate bonds are transferable, a secondary market for corporate bonds exists.

Existing corporate bonds are traded on the major organized exchanges (New York Stock Exchange (NYSE), American Stock Exchange (AMEX), and regional exchanges). Much of the trading of existing corporate bonds, though, takes place on the over-the-counter (OTC) market, by brokers and dealers specializing in certain types of issues. In the OTC market, a core of a dozen large dealers dominates the corporate bond market. These dealers buy and sell existing corporate bonds from and to life insurance companies, pension funds, and other institutional investors. They also provide an important wholesale market in which they trade with other dealers and brokers who are executing buy and sell orders from the customers. While a sizable amount of secondary market bond trading occurs on the OTC market, there are still many bonds listed on the NYSE. Dealers on the OTC market who have a large and broad market trade many of these listed bonds. The NYSE promotes the OTC trading by allowing its members to trade listed bonds off the exchange if they can obtain a better price.

It should be noted that, while the amount of corporate bonds outstanding is large, the secondary market activity is somewhat limited compared to the activity in the secondary markets for stocks. The relatively thin secondary market for corporate bonds is due to the passive investment practices of large institutions that tend to buy and hold their corporate bonds to maturity. It is important to remember that the degree of trading activity determines a bond's degree of marketability and the spread between a dealer's bid and asked prices. In the corporate bond markets, the spreads range from a low of $\frac{1}{4}$ to $\frac{1}{2}$ of a point (good marketability) to as high as 2% (poor marketability). For an investor who plans to buy a bond at its initial offering and hold it to its maturity a thin market is not a concern; it is a major concern, though, to a bond speculator or a fund manager who needs marketability or whose profit margins could be negated by a large spread.

5.6 INFORMATION ON CORPORATE BONDS

Information on the trading of existing corporate bonds is reported in the *Wall Street Journal*

(WSJ) and in the financial sections of many newspapers, and information on bond yields and prices for a large number of bonds can be found in *The Daily Bond Buyer* and the *Commercial and Financial Chronicle*. In addition to individual bond information, the WSJ also provides the Dow Jones Bond Average. This is an average of the prices of 20 corporate, 10 utility, and 10 industrial bonds. There also are a number of bond yield indexes formed by pooling several bond issues of similar characteristics and quality ratings. One of the more popular of these is Moody's corporate bond index that is reported in the *Federal Reserve Bulletin*, and the Shearson–Lehman's index. These latter indexes provide monthly averages of interest and capital gains for both corporate and government bonds grouped by maturity class. Finally, detailed information on specific bonds can be found in Moody's *Bond Manual* (summary information in *Moody's Bond Record* and new issues in *Moody's Bond Survey*) and the *S&P Corporation Record* (summary information in *S&P Bond Guide*). The information includes quality rating, use of the bond proceeds, information on the issuer, collateral, guarantees, call and other options, restrictions, and sinking-fund arrangements. For new corporate bond issues, investors also can obtain the prospectus from the SEC, and for distressed companies a good source for information is Dunn & Bradstreet's *Business Failure Record*.

Web Information

For information on Moody's corporate bond yields go to
  www.bondmarkets.com

and click on "Research Statistics." For information on bond market trends click "Research Report."

For information on security laws go to
  www.sec.gov

and click on "Market Regulations" under "SEC Divisions."

For information on current yields go to
  http://bonds.yahoo.com

and click on "Corporate Bond Rates." For identifying bonds that have certain features, click on "Bond Screener."

5.7 COMMERCIAL PAPER

Commercial paper (CP) is a short-term debt obligation usually issued by large, well-known corporations. As a source of corporate funds, CP is a substitute for a bank's line of credit and other short-term loans provided by a financial institution.[11] Some companies use the proceeds from CP sales to finance their cash flow needs between the time when they pay workers, resource suppliers, and the like, and the time when they sell their products. Other companies use CP to provide their customer with financing for the purchase of their products, and some companies use CP as bridge financing for their long-term investments, including corporate takeovers. For example, a company might sell CP to finance the construction of a plant or office building, with the CP paid off with long-term permanent financing from a loan from a financial institution or from a bond sale.

CP investors include pensions, insurance companies, bank trust departments, other corporations, governments, and money market funds. Many of the institutional investors purchase CP as part of their liquidity investments. Other corporation and state and local governments usually buy CP when they have temporary excess cash balances that they want to invest for a short period before they are needed to pay workers, accounts payable, accrued expenses, and other short-term liabilities. Finally, money market funds include CP in their portfolios with other money market securities; it is one of their primary investments.

At any point in time, there are between 600 and 800 companies selling CP, currently worth approximately $1.5t. Of the total, about 40% is direct paper and the balance is dealers' paper.

5.7.1 Direct Paper

As the name suggests, *direct paper* is sold by the issuing company directly to investors, instead of through dealers. The issuing companies include the subsidiaries of large companies, referred to as *captive finance companies*, bank holding companies, independent finance companies, and non-financial corporations. Frequently, these companies employ sales forces to place their CP with large institutional investors. The major

captive finance companies selling direct paper are General Motors Acceptance Corporation (GMAC), Ford Credit Corporation, and GE Credit Corporation. These companies use the proceeds from their CP sales to finance installment loans and other credit loans extended to customers buying the products of their parent companies. Bank holding companies use CP sales to finance equipment purchases they lease to businesses, working capital loans, and installment loans.

5.7.2 Dealer Paper

Dealer paper, also called *industrial paper*, is the CP of corporations sold through CP dealers. Historically, the dealers' market for CP has been dominated by the major investment banking firms. In 1987, though, the Federal Reserve gave the subsidiaries of bank holding companies permission to underwrite CP. This action served to increase the competition among CP dealers. Some of the major CP dealers include Merrill Lynch, Goldman Sachs, Shearson–Lehman, First Boston Credit Suisse, Citicorp, and Banker's Trust. These dealers usually buy the CP from the issuer, mark it up (usually about 1%), and then resell it.

5.7.3 Features of Commercial Paper

Most CP issues are sold on a pure discount basis, although there are some that are sold with coupon interest. CP is quoted on a discount basis like T-bills with a year being 360 days. The yield on CP is higher than the yield on T-bills. This reflects the interest deductibility of T-bills from state and local taxes and the possible default risk associated with CP. CP is assigned quality ratings by the major rating companies (see table 5.2). The original maturities of CP range from 3 days (weekend paper) to 270 days, with the average original maturity being 60 days. The Securities Act of 1933 exempted companies issuing CP from registering with the SEC if the issue were less than 270 days. As a result of this provision, many CP issues have maturities of less than 270 days; this reflects the desire by issuers to avoid the time-consuming SEC registration. Finally, CP issues are usually sold in denominations from

Table 5.2 CP ratings

Moody's	Standard & Poor's	Fitch
Prime-1	A-1	F-1
Prime-1	A-2	F-2
Prime-3	A-3	F-3
Prime-4		

Ratings are from highest quality (1) to lowest (4).

$100,000, although some are sold in $25,000 denominations.

CP is often described as unsecured. The unsecured feature of CP means that there is no specific asset being pledged to secure the issue. Many CP issuers back up their paper with an unused line of credit from a bank. The line of credit is a safeguard in the event the CP issuer cannot pay off the principal or sell new CP to finance the principal payment on the maturing issue.[12] For this commitment, the bank charges a fee of between 0.5% and 1% of the issue. In return, the CP issuer is able to reduce default risk and lower the rate he has to pay by an amount at least equal to the fee. Many smaller, lower quality companies also obtain a letter of credit from a bank or financial institution to secure their issues. As noted earlier, a letter of credit is a certificate in which the bank or institution promises to repay the principal or interest if the issuer defaults. Paper sold with this type of credit enhancement is called *LOC paper*, *documented paper*, or *credit-supported CP*. Credit enhancements can also take the form of a surety bond from an insurance company. Finally, instead of a credit enhancement, some companies collateralize their issue with other assets. Included in this group of asset-based paper is securitized CP, often issued by a bank holding company. In these cases, a bank holding company sells CP to finance a pool of credit card receivables, leases, or other short-term assets, with the assets being used to secure the CP issue.

Web Information

For historical data on CP rates go to
  www.bondmarkets.com

and click on "Statistics" under "Research," and then click on "Money Market Instruments."

5.8 MEDIUM-TERM NOTES

The trend towards shorter maturities on corporate bonds in the 1980s and 1990s is reflected by the growth in *medium-term notes* (*MTNs*) during that period. An MTN is a debt instrument sold on a continuing basis to investors who are allowed to choose from a group of bonds from the same corporation, but with different maturities. MTNs were first introduced in the 1970s when General Motors Acceptance Corporation (GMAC) sold such instruments to finance its automobile loans. However, the market for MTNs did not take off until the early 1980s when Merrill Lynch began acting as an agent in issuing MTNs and also as a dealer by making a secondary market for the notes. The market for MTNs grew from $3.8b in 1982 to $150b in 1998 (this excludes bank MTNs and Euro MTNs discussed in chapter 7). The growth of MTNs can be attributed to the flexibility MTN issues provided corporations in both the types of securities they could offer, and, with the Securities and Exchange Commission Rule 415, the times when they could offer them. As noted earlier, Rule 415 allows issuers to sell several issues over a 2-year period without having to go through costly registration procedures each time.

5.8.1 Issuing Process

A corporation planning to issue an MTN first files a shelf registration form with the SEC. The filing includes a prospectus of the MTN program (different notes, their maturities, par values, and the like). By filing a shelf registration form, the corporation is able to enter the market constantly or intermittently, giving it the flexibility to finance a number of different short-, intermediate-, and long-term projects over a 2-year period. Typically, the MTNs are sold through investment banking firms who act as agents. The agents will often post the maturity range for the possible notes in the program and their offering rates. The rates are often quoted in terms of a spread over a Treasury security with a comparable maturity (see table 5.3). An investor interested in one of the note offerings will notify the agent

Table 5.3   MTN program

MTN	Yield
12 months to 18 months	6.25
18 months to 2 years	6.35
2 years to 3 years	6.45
3 years to 4 years	6.65
4 years to 5 years	6.75
5 years to 6 years	6.85
6 years to 7 years	7.00

Web Information
For information on MTNs go to
   www.federalreserve.gov/releases/
   medterm/about.htm

For information on the
size of the market for
MTNs go to
   www.federalreserve.gov/releases/
   medterm

who, in turn, contacts the issuing corporation for a confirmation. Once an MTN issue is sold, then the company can file a new registration to sell a new MTN issue – an action known as reloading.

In addition to providing issuing corporations with flexibility in their capital budget, an MTN program also gives institutional investors the opportunity to choose notes whose maturities best fit their liabilities, thereby minimizing their market risk. In many instances, the market for MTNs starts with institutional investors indicating to agents the type of maturity they want; this is known as *reverse inquiry*. On a reverse inquiry, the agent will inform the corporation of the investor's request; the corporation could then agree to sell the notes with that maturity from its MTN program, even if they are not posted.

5.8.2 Special Features

Today, MTNs are issued not only by corporations, but also by bank holding companies, government agencies, supranational institutions, and sovereign countries. MTNs vary in terms of their features; some, for example, are offered with fixed rates while others pay a floating rate. There are also MTNs that are combined with other instruments in what is referred to as a *structured MTN*. A corporation, for example, might issue MTNs with floating rates and then take a position in an interest rate swap contract to form a synthetic fixed-rate debt position with the rate lower than a regular fixed-rate debt obligation. Interest rate swaps and their uses are examined in chapter 16.

5.9 CONCLUSION

In the early 1980s, Chrysler Corporation issued a variable-rate subordinated debenture with a maturity of 10 years and exchangable at Chrysler's option into a 10-year, fixed-rate note with the rate to be set at 124% above the 10-year rate on Treasury notes. The variable rate paid on the subordinated security made the note relatively attractive to investors given this period of high interest rates and the option to exchange to a fixed rate note was potentially beneficial to Chrysler given that interest rates were declining at the time of the issue. This security is only one example of the different ways in which corporations structure debt instruments. Given the types of assets being financed and the conditions and risk–return preferences of the financial markets, there are many different types of corporate debt securities extant in the market. The differences that we observe among bonds, in turn, are reflected in different interest rate payments (fixed, floating, or discount), original maturities (CP, medium-term notes, corporate notes, and corporate bonds), option features (callable bonds, redemption features, and putable bonds), sinking fund arrangements, security (collateral, credit enhancements, and guarantees), and protective covenants. In this chapter, we have delineated many of these features that serve to differentiate the numerous types of corporate debt securities offered in the financial markets. In the next chapter, we continue the same analysis for securities issued by the various government bodies: Treasury, federal agencies, and municipalities.

KEY TERMS

Internal Financing
External Financing
Leveraged Firm
Prime Rate
Indenture
Prospectus
Trustee
Bearer Bonds
Registered Bonds
Book-Entry Form
Original-Issue Discount
  (OID)
Deep-Discount Bonds
Floater
Adjustable-Rate Note or
  Variable-Rate Note
Call Premium
Notice of Redemption
Deferred Call
Refunding
Fully Amortized
Serial Bond
Sinking Fund
Tunnel, Funnel, or Blanket
  Sinking Funds
Average Life
Protective or Restrictive
  Covenants
Event Risk
Poison Put
Net Worth Maintenance
  Clause

Offer-to-Redeem Clause
Secured Bonds
Unsecured Bonds
Debentures
Mortgage Bond
Equipment-Trust Bond
Collateral-Trust Bond
Release and Substitution
  Provision
Philadelphia Plan and
  Rolling Stock
Senior Lien
Junior Lien
Closed-End Bonds
Open-End Bond
After-Acquired Property
  Clause
Subordinate Debentures
Unsubordinate
  Debentures
Guaranteed Bonds
Credit Enhancements
Letters of Credit
Income Bonds
Participating Bonds
Deferred-Interest Bonds
  (DIBs)
Reset Bonds
Payment-in-Kind (PIK)
  Bonds
Warrant
Convertible Bond

Putable Bond or
  Put Bond
Extendable Bonds
Commodity-Linked
  Bond
Voting Bonds
Assumed Bond
Open Market Sales
Firm Commitment
Floatation Cost
Standby Underwriting
  Agreement
Red-Herring
Selling Group
  Agreement
Rule 415, Shelf
  Registration Rule
Private Placement
SEC Rule 144a
Commercial Paper (CP)
Direct Paper
Captive Finance
  Companies
Dealer Paper or Industrial
  Paper
LOC Paper
Documented Paper
Credit-Supported CP
Medium-Term Notes
  (MTNs)
Reverse Inquiry
Structured MTN

PROBLEMS AND QUESTIONS

1. What are the major benefits and costs to a corporation of financing its operations with debt instead of equity?

2. Define and briefly explain the following terms:
   a. Amortization
   b. Deep-discount bond
   c. Floater
   d. Protective covenants
   e. Serial bond
   f. Option redemption provision

g. Deferred-call feature
h. Non-refundable clause
i. Debenture
j. Sinking fund requirement
k. Average life
l. Registered bond
m. Bearer bond.

3. Explain some of the common features included in a sinking fund requirement.

4. Comment on the following statement: "By reducing the investor's principal risk, a sinking fund provision benefits the investor."

5. What is the average life of a debt issue with a $100m par value and 10-year maturity that has a sinking fund that makes equal payments in years 7 through 10?

6. What feature of a zero-coupon or deep-discount bond does an institutional investor such as a pension fund find attractive?

7. In the early 1980s, Beatrice Foods issue a 10-year, $250m zero-coupon issue priced at $255 per $1,000 face value. What was the bond's initial YTM?

8. What is the difference between call protection and refunding protection?

9. ABC is issuing a bond with a maturity of 25 year and 10% coupon. The bond is callable with the first year call price equal to the offering price plus the coupon; thereafter the call price decreases by equal amounts to equal par at year 20; thereafter the call price is equal to par. If the bond were sold at $95 ($950 for $F = $1,000), what would be the call prices for each year?

10. Define the major types of secured bonds.

11. What is a release and substitution provision?

12. Explain how an equipment-trust bond is created as part of a lease-and-buy-back arrangement.

13. What are some of the provisions that are included in a collateral-trust bond?

14. Define the following:

a. Priority of claim
b. Closed-end bond
c. Open-end bond
d. After-acquired property clause
e. Subordinate debenture
f. Guaranteed bond
g. Credit enhancement.

15. What are some of the provisions in a debenture that enhance its creditworthiness?

16. Why are guaranteed bonds not considered risk free?

17. G&P is planning to construct a $250m manufacturing and processing plant for the national production of its patented calorie-free chips. G&P's Marketing Research Division has estimated that G&P will gain a significant market share of the US snack-food market and should maintain that share for a period of at least 10 years – a period extending beyond the expiration of its patent. Suppose you work for a large investment-banking firm that advises G&P on its debt issues and who would like to eventually bid on underwriting the issue. To help you in providing advice on the debt issue, identify the pertinent features of the debt issue that need to be considered, the alternatives, and factors that need to be considered in structuring the bond issue.

18. Define each of the following bonds and their features:
    a. Income bond
    b. Participating bond
    c. Deferred-interest bond
    d. Payment-in-kind bond
    e. Tax-exempt bond
    f. Bonds with warrants
    g. Convertible bond
    h. Voting bonds
    i. Assumed bond
    j. Bonds with put options
    k. Credit-sensitive notes
    l. Extendable notes
    m. Commodity-linked bonds.

19. Discuss the nature of protective covenants.

20. Discuss the types of protective covenants that can be found in a bond contract.

21. Define event risk and the protective covenants that can be used to protect bondholders against such risk.

22. Explain the distinction between:
    a. Insolvency and default
    b. Insolvency and illiquidity.

23. Explain the steps in a bankruptcy process that are taken to determine reorganization.

24. List the steps involved in an open market sale of a new bond issue.

25. What is underwriting risk? Provide an example.

26. Define SEC Rule 415. What is the significance of the rule?

27. What is a privately placed bond issue and how does it differ from an open market issue?

28. Define SEC Rule 144A. What is the significance of the rule?

29. List some of the features that characterize the secondary market for corporate bonds.

30. List some of the important features of commercial paper.

31. Explain the typical process a corporation would go through in selling medium-term notes.

32. What is meant by reverse inquiry?

33. What is the main feature contributing to the growth of the MTN market?

WEB EXERCISES

1. Identify companies that have had ratings changes by going to www.moodys.com and clicking on "Corporate Finance" and "Rating Actions." Identify companies on Moody's watch list by clicking on "Watch List." Note: registration may be required.

2. Take a company on Moody's "Watch List" or with a rating change and do an analysis of it with information obtained from www.quicken.com, www.hoovers.com, or www.nasdaq.com.

3. Explore default spreads for different economic periods by comparing CP and T-bill yields and Moody's Aaa and Moody's Baa yields. Data on the yields can be found by going to www.economagic.com and clicking on "Federal Reserve – Interest Rates," and data on GDP (both nominal and real) can be found by clicking "Department of Commerce – BEA National Accounts."

4. Find out what current yields are on corporate bonds given different quality ratings by going to http://bonds.yahoo.com and clicking on "Composite Bond Rates." What is the spread between the different quality corporate bonds with the same maturity?

5. Use the bond selector at http://bonds.yahoo.com to identify several corporate bonds that have certain features you want.

NOTES

1. Small companies, as well as some large ones, obtain their funds primarily from loans from financial institutions. As noted in chapter 1, many companies obtain the financing of their short-term assets by obtaining lines of credit from commercial banks. The rates banks provide on the short-term loans are often quoted in terms of the *prime rate* (also called reference rate). This is the rate banks provide to their most creditworthy clients. Banks and other financial institutions also provide businesses with intermediate- and long-term loans. Many corporations and development companies obtain long-term, permanent financing for the offices, shopping centers, and plants they build with commercial mortgage loans from banks, life insurance companies, and other financial institutions.

2. Interest due on Sundays or holidays is normally paid the next business day with no additional interest paid.

3. Until 1982, issuers also found zeros attractive because the annual interest tax deduction on such bonds was calculated as a proportion of the total discount, making it possible for issuers to deduct interest at a faster rate than it accrued.

4. An exception to this trend was the $150m bond issue of Coca-Cola in 1993 that had a maturity of 100 years.

5. For more discussion of this and some other cases, see Fabozzi, Wilson, and Todd, "Corporate Bonds," in Frank J. Fabozzi (ed.) *The Handbook of Fixed Income Securities*, 6th edn (New York: McGraw-Hill, 2001): 265–71.

6. It should be noted that in terms of priorities it could be the case that a default could lead to the company being acquired by another company. The new company, in turn, may be able to get the

bondholders to agree to subordinate their debt to a new issue; this is quite possible if the bondholders determined that the sale of the pledged assets would be inadequate.

7. Companies often view subordinate debentures as an alternative to preferred stock financing. Preferred stock can be thought of as a limited ownership share. It provides its owners with only limited income potential in the form of a stipulated dividend (preferred dividend) that is usually expressed as a percentage of a stipulated par value. Preferred stock also gives its holders fewer voting privileges and less control over the business than common stock does. To make preferred stock more attractive, companies frequently sell preferred with special rights. Among the most common of these special rights is the priority over common stockholders over earnings and assets upon dissolution and the right to cumulative dividends: if preferred dividends are not paid, then all past dividends must be paid before any common dividends are paid. Subordinated debentures, in turn, are often sold at rates comparable to preferred stock; as a debt instrument, though, subordinated debt's interest is tax deductible while for preferred dividends it is not.

8. In a bankruptcy, holders of zero-coupon bonds can claim the original offering price plus the accrued interest to the date of the bankruptcy filing, but not the principal.

9. When a syndicate bids on an issue, the members must all agree on the correct price. If an agreement cannot be reached, the syndicate may break up and a smaller one put together.

10. Investment banking firms often assist firms in privately placing securities, often using best effort.

11. CP may also be a substitute for the sale of short-term assets, such as the sale of accounts

receivable to a factor (an intermediary who buys receivables).

12. CP issuers often roll CP, selling new issues to pay off maturing ones.

SELECTED REFERENCES

Asquith, P., R. Gertner, and D. Scharfstein "Anatomy of Financial Distress: An Examination of Junk-bond Issues," *Quarterly Journal of Economics* 109(3) (1994): 625–58.

Crabbe, Leland E. "Medium-Term Notes," in Frank Fabozzi (ed.) *The Handbook of Fixed Income Securities* 6th edn (New York: McGraw-Hill, 2001).

Crabbe, L. and J. Helwege *Alternative Tests of Agency Theories of Callable Corporate Bonds* (Washington, DC: Board of Governors of the Federal Reserve System, 1993).

Emery, R. E. and J. Finnerty *Corporate Financial Management* (Upper Saddle River, NJ: Prentice Hall Inc.).

Fabozzi, Frank J., R.S. Wilson, and R. Todd "Corporate Bonds," in Frank J. Fabozzi (ed.) *The Handbook of Fixed Income Securities*, 6th edn (New York: McGraw-Hill, 2001): 265–71.

John, K. "Managing Financial Distress and Valuing Distressed Securities: A Survey and a Research Agenda," *Financial Management* (special issue on financial distress) 22(3) (1993): 60–78.

Kim, I. J., K. Ramaswamy, and S. M. Sundaresar "Valuation of Corporate Fixed-Income Securities," *Financial Management* (special issue on financial distress) 22(3) (1993): 117–31.

Leland, H. "Risky Debt, Bond Covenants and Optimal Capital Structure," *Journal of Finance* 49 (1994): 1213–52.

Moody's Investor Service *Corporate Bond Defaults and Default Rates, 1970–1993* (Moody's Investor Service, Global Credit Research, 1994).

Nayar, N. and M. S. Rozeff "Ratings, Commercial Paper and Equity Returns," *Journal of Finance* 49 (1994): 1431–49.

CHAPTER SIX

GOVERNMENT SECURITIES

6.1 INTRODUCTION

The US Treasury security market began over 225 years ago when Alexander Hamilton, the first Treasury Secretary, sold government securities to finance the new country's debt. The US debt in 1790 consisted of $54m in national debt and $25m in assumed state debt, with most of the debt incurred as a result of the Revolutionary War. Just as it is today, the US debt in 1790 was quite large compared to other sovereign nations. Today, the US Treasury is the largest debt issuer in the world. Its size, as well as its wide distribution of ownership and default risk-free feature, makes the rates on Treasury securities the benchmark for all other securities. In this chapter we extend our analysis of debt securities by examining the markets for US Treasury securities, as well as the debt instruments issued by US federal agencies and municipal government units in the US.

6.2 TREASURY INSTRUMENTS

The US Treasury is responsible for implementing the fiscal policy of the federal government and managing the federal government's enormous debt. As shown in table 6.1, in year 2002 the federal government raised over $1.853 trillion in revenue from income (46%), social

insurance (38%), and corporate (8%) taxes, and it spent over $2.011t on welfare and individual security programs (social security, healthcare, and income security programs (48%)), national defense (19%), interest on the federal government debt (9%), and other expenditures (23%). The government's excess of tax revenues over expenditures in 2002 equated to a deficit of $158b. Since 1930 the US federal government has operated with a deficit in almost every year, with the deficits growing dramatically over the last two decades, averaging $180b per year from the mid-1970s to mid-1990s (see table 6.2). One noticeable exception to annual deficits was the 3-year period from 1999 to 2001 when the US government operated with surpluses of $125b in 1999, $236b in 2000, and $127b in 2001. The accumulation of deficits over the years has, in turn, contributed to a total government indebtedness of over $6.4t as of 2003.

To finance the government's deficit each year and to manage its debt (refinancing maturing issues), the Treasury sells a number of securities. All of the securities sold by the Treasury are backed by the full faith and credit of the US government. As such, they are considered default free.[1] The Treasury's securities can be broken into marketable and non-marketable securities. Of the total government debt of $6.4t in 2003, investors held approximately $3.2737t

Table 6.1   Federal government revenues and expenditures, 2001 and 2002

Item	2001 amount ($ billions)	2002 amount ($ billions)
Revenue:		
Individual income tax	994.3	858.3
Corporate income tax	151.1	148.0
Social insurance taxes and contributions	694.0	700.8
Other revenue sources	151.8	146.1
Total revenue	1,991.2	1,853.2
Expenditures:		
National defense	305.5	384.6
International affairs	16.5	22.4
Healthcare	172.3	196.5
Income security programs	269.6	312.6
Social security and Medicare	432.9	456.4
Net interest on federal debt	206.2	170.9
Other expenditures	460.9	467.8
Total expenditures	1,863.9	2,011.2
Balance	127.3	−158.0

Source: The President's Council of Economic Advisors, *Economic Report of the President.* www.gpo.gov/usbudget

Table 6.2   Federal government revenues, expenditures, and budgets

Year	Total revenue ($ billions)	Total expenditures ($ billions)	Net budget surplus or deficit ($ billions)
1969	186.9	183.6	3.3
1980	517.1	590.9	−73.8
1990	1,031.3	1,251.8	−220.5
1993	1,164.8	1,497.5	−332.7
1997	1,579.3	1,601.2	−21.9
1998	1,657.9	1,667.8	−9.9
1999	1,827.5	1,702.9	+124.6
2000	2,025.2	1,789.0	+236.2
2001	1,991.2	1,863.9	+127.3
2002	1,853.2	2,011.2	−158.0

Source: The President's Council of Economic Advisors, *Economic Report of the President.* www.gpo.gov/usbudget

in marketable securities (see table 6.3). Marketable securities include Treasury bills (T-bills), T-notes, T-bonds, and Treasury inflation-indexed bonds and notes. The Treasury sells these securities using an auction method and there is an active secondary market trading the existing marketable Treasury securities. Non-marketable Treasury debt, in turn, includes the *government account series*, US savings bonds, and non-marketable securities sold to foreign governments. Original investors hold these securities until they mature or are redeemed. The government account series is the largest portion of the non-marketable securities sold. These series include Treasury securities sold to government agencies such as social security and the Tennessee Valley Authority. These agencies use their excess funds to purchase Treasury securities. Currently, the series account for over 40% of the Treasury's total debt holdings.

Table 6.3 Federal debt, 2003

Type	Amount ($ billions)
Marketable debt	
Bills	918.8
Notes	1,616.6
Bonds	585.8
Inflation-indexed notes	107.2
Inflation-indexed bonds	45.3
Total marketable	3,273.7
Non-marketable debt	
Domestic series	30.0
Foreign series	11.6
State and local government series	149.6
US savings securities	196.4
Government account series	2,780.5
Other	3.9
Total non-marketable	3,172.0
Total public debt outstanding	6,445.7

Source: Board of Governors of the Federal Reserve System, www.publicdebt.ustreas.gov/opd/opd.htm

---

Web Information

For information on the US Treasury's debt go to

www.publicdebt.ustreas.gov/opd/opd.htm

For information on government expenditures and revenues go to

www.gpo.gov/usbudget

or go to

www.economagic.com

and click on "Federal Reserve – St. Louis."

6.2.1 Treasury Bills

Treasury bills are short-term instruments sold on a pure discount basis in multiples of $1,000 (par) from the minimum, with the minimum denomination being $1,000. The interest on a T-bill is the difference between the face value and the price paid. This interest, in turn, is subject to federal income taxes, but not state and local taxes. T-bills with original maturities of 26 weeks (91 days) and 52 weeks (182 days) are sold weekly on a regular basis, while bills with a maturity of 1 year are sold monthly on a regular basis. The Treasury also sells special types of T-bills on an irregular basis. Included with this irregular series are *strip bills*. This is a package of T-bills with different maturities in which the buyer agrees to buy bills at their bid price for several weeks. The Treasury also issues additional amounts of an existing security (T-bills, T-bonds, and T-notes). Such offerings are known as *reopenings*. For example, the Treasury may offer 13-week T-bills as a reopening of a previously issued 26-week T-bill. All T-bills are issued and registered in a book-entry form, with the computerized record of ownership maintained by the Federal Reserve at their offices in Washington. At maturity, the Treasury sends a check to the investor of record, unless the holder has requested payment in terms of new T-bills.[2]

As noted in chapter 2, the *Wall Street Journal* and other daily newspapers publish information on existing T-bill issues (see exhibit 2.4 for quotes of T-bills traded on March 4, 2003). Recall, T-bill yields are calculated as an annualized discount yield (R_D) (also called the *banker's discount yield*); this is the annualized return (principal (F) minus price (P_0)) specified as a proportion of the bill's principal:

$$R_D = \frac{F - P_0}{F} \frac{360}{\text{Days to maturity}}$$

Given the dealer's discount yield, the bid or asked price is

$$P_0 = F[1 - (R_D)(\text{Days to maturity}/360)]$$

In order to compare the rate on T-bills with other securities, one can use the annual YTM with a 365-day year ($=(F/P_0)^{365/\text{Days to maturity}} - 1$) or calculate the bond-equivalent yield. The bond-equivalent is obtained by doubling the semi-annual rate that equates the price of the bond to the present value of its cash flows. For T-bills with days to maturity (N) less than 182, the formula for the bond-equivalent (BE) yield given the discount yield is

$$\text{BE yield} = \frac{365\,R_D}{360 - N(R_D)}$$

For maturities greater than 182 days, the formula for the bond-equivalent yield given the price of the T-bill per $1 face value ($p$) is

newspapers. The information includes the dealer's bid and asked prices, expressed as a

$$\text{BE yield} = \frac{-(2N/365) + 2\sqrt{(N/365)^2 - [(2N/365) - 1][1 - (1/p)]}}{(2N/365) - 1}$$

6.2.2 Treasury Bonds and Notes

Treasury bonds and notes are the Treasury's coupon issues. Both are identical except for maturity: T-notes have original maturities up to 10 years (currently, original notes are offered with maturities of 2, 5, and 10 years), while T-bonds have maturities ranging between 10 and 30 years.[3] Both are sold in denominations of $1,000 or more, and both pay semi-annual coupon interest. Like all Treasury securities, interest income from T-bonds and T-notes is subject to federal taxes, but not state and local. Since 1985, the Treasury has not issued callable bonds.

Like T-bills, notes and bonds are issued in a book-entry form with the investor's name and amount maintained in a computerized account. New 2-year T-notes are sold every month, while 5-year and 10-year notes are sold quarterly and T-bonds are sold semi-annually (see table 6.4). Sometimes when bonds or notes are sold in order to refund an earlier issue, they are offered only to the holders of the bond being replaced or called. This special type of issue takes the form of an advanced refunding in which the Treasury sets the maturity of the new issue equal to the remaining life of the bond being replaced to ensure the holder his original maturity.

Information on T-notes and T-bonds can be found in the *Wall Street Journal* and other

percentage of the face value, or equivalently, as the price of a bond with a $100 par value. Recall from chapter 2 that the numbers to the right of the decimals on the bid and ask prices are in 32nds and not the usual 100s.

6.2.3 Treasury Inflation Protection Securities (TIPS)

While Treasury securities are considered default free, they are subject to market risk that we examined in chapter 4 and also to *purchasing-power risk*. Purchasing-power risk is the uncertainty that the rate of return earned from an investment is less than the inflation rate. Equivalently, it is the risk of a negative real interest rate, where the *real interest rate* is the actual or nominal rate minus the inflation rate: real interest = nominal interest − inflation.

To address purchasing-power risk, the Treasury began offering Treasury inflation-indexed bonds in 1997, called *TIPS (Treasury Inflation Protection Securities)*. Inflation-adjusted securities, though, are not new or unique. Many countries have offered such securities for a number of years, and a number of corporations, agencies, and municipalities offer or have offered inflation-adjusted bonds. The US Treasury's TIPS are patterned after the successful inflation-adjusted bonds introduced in Great Britain. They are structured so that each period's coupon payment is equal to a specified fixed rate times an inflation-adjusted principal, and at maturity, the bond pays the larger of the inflation-adjusted principal or the original par value. For example, suppose the Treasury issues 5-year TIPS with a nominal principal of $1,000 and an annual coupon rate of 4%. If there is no inflation in the ensuing 5 years, then the TIPS will pay bondholders $40 each year and $1,000 at maturity. If there is inflation, as measured by the consumer price

Table 6.4 Treasury auction schedule

Issue	Frequency
13-week T-bill	Weekly
26-week T-bill	Weekly
52-week T-bill	Every 4 weeks
2-year T-note	Monthly
5-year T-note	Quarterly
10-year T-note	Quarterly
20-year T-bond	Semi-annual

index, CPI, then the Treasury will adjust the nominal principal. For example, suppose the US experiences an annual inflation rate of 3% during the first year of the bonds. In this case, the inflation-adjusted principal would be $1,030 and a bondholder would receive an annual coupon of $41.20 (= ($1,030)(0.04)). If the 3% inflation continues for each year, then the bondholder would receive coupon interest in each of the next 4 years of $42.44, $43.71, $45.02, and $46.37, and a principal at maturity of $1,159.27:[4]

Year	Inflation	Inflation-adjusted principal	TIPS cash flow
1	3%	$1,030.00	$41.20
2	3%	$1,060.90	$42.44
3	3%	$1,092.73	$43.71
4	3%	$1,125.51	$45.02
5	3%	$1,159.27	$46.37 + $1,159.27

The inflation-adjusted returns from TIPS offset the loss in purchasing power resulting from the inflation. Thus, while the principal and interest fluctuate with the CPI, the purchasing power of each payment and the real rate of return are fixed. Because they fix the real rate of return, Treasury inflation-index bonds are attractive to retirees who have their retirement funds invested in fixed-income securities. Inflation-index bonds also have relatively low correlations with other bonds, and as such provide some diversification benefits when included in a fixed-income portfolio.

6.2.4 Treasury Strips

In the 1980s, one of the more innovative instruments was introduced – the Treasury stripped security or *Treasury strips*. A Treasury strip is formed by a dealer who purchases a T-bond or T-note and then creates two general types of zero-coupon securities to sell to investors: a *principal-only (PO) security* (also called the *corpus*) and *interest-only (IO) securities*. As the name suggests, the PO security is a zero-discount bond that pays the T-bond's principal at its maturity; the IO securities are zero-discount instruments, with each paying a

principal equal to the T-bond's coupon and with a maturity coinciding with the bond's coupon date. For example, to create Treasury strips, a dealer could take a 6-year US Treasury note and strip it into 13 discount bonds, one maturing in 6 years and paying the T-bond's principal, the others paying principals equal to the bond's coupon interest and maturing on the coupon dates.

Merrill Lynch and Salomon Brothers were the first to create and market stripped securities. Both investment banking firms introduced their securities in 1982. Merrill Lynch called its stripped securities *Treasury Income Growth Receipts (TIGRs)*, and Salomon Brothers referred to theirs as *Certificates of Accrual on Treasury Securities (CATS)*. To create these strips, the companies would purchase a Treasury-coupon security and deposit it in a bank custodial account. They would then sell to investors separate IO receipts representing ownership of a coupon and a PO receipt representing ownership of the principal. Following the lead of Merrill Lynch and Salomon Brothers, other investment firms, such as Lehman Brothers, E. F. Hutton, and Dean Witter Reynolds, introduced their own stripped securities, with colorful names such as LIONS, GATORS, COUGARS, and DOGS. Collectively, these receipts were called *trademarks*. One of the problems with trademarks was that dealers only made markets in their own strip securities. In an effort to expand the market, a group of dealers introduced Treasury receipts. Different from trademarks, which represented ownership in a custodial account, Treasury receipts represented ownership in the Treasury security. The US Treasury facilitated the market for these generic stripped securities when in 1985 it initiated the *Separate Trading of Registered Interest and Principal of Securities (STRIPS)* program to aid dealers in stripping Treasury securities.[5] The securities created under the STRIPS program were, in turn, deemed direct obligations of the government, and for clearing and payment purposes, the names of the buyers of these securities were included in the book entries of the Treasury, thus eliminating the need to set up custodial accounts and therefore trademarks.

Stripped securities are attractive investments for institutional investors who buy the strips

Exhibit 6.1   Strip securities

| U.S. Treasury Strips | | | | | ASK |
MATURITY	TYPE	BID	ASKED	CHG	YLD
May 03	ci	99:25	99:25	...	1.07
Jul 03	ci	99:19	99:19	...	1.14
Aug 03	ci	99:16	99:17	...	1.07
Aug 03	np	99:15	99:15	...	1.18
Oct 03	ci	99:12	99:12	...	1.03
Nov 03	ci	99:09	99:09	...	1.04
Nov 03	np	99:05	99:06	...	1.18
Jan 04	ci	99:08	99:08	1	0.86
Feb 04	ci	99:03	99:03	1	0.95
Feb 04	np	98:29	98:30	1	1.15
Apr 04	ci	98:23	98:23	...	1.16
May 04	ci	98:18	98:19	1	1.18
May 04	np	98:18	98:18	1	1.20
Jul 04	ci	98:16	98:17	1	1.09
Aug 04	ci	98:09	98:10	2	1.19
Aug 04	np	98:07	98:08	2	1.23
Nov 04	ci	97:24	97:25	2	1.33
Nov 04	bp	97:24	97:25	2	1.33
Nov 04	np	97:24	97:25	2	1.32
Jan 05	ci	97:30	97:31	2	1.11
Feb 05	ci	97:05	97:07	2	1.46
Feb 05	np	97:07	97:08	2	1.43
Apr 05	ci	96:23	96:24	...	1.57
May 05	ci	96:17	96:18	2	1.60
May 05	bp	96:22	96:23	2	1.52
May 05	np	96:22	96:23	2	1.52
May 05	np	96:20	96:21	2	1.55
Jul 05	ci	96:29	96:31	2	1.31
Aug 05	ci	95:31	96:01	3	1.67
Aug 05	bp	95:30	96:00	3	1.68
Aug 05	np	96:01	96:02	3	1.64
Oct 05	ci	95:22	95:23	...	1.68
Nov 05	ci	95:15	95:16	3	1.72
Nov 05	np	95:11	95:13	3	1.75

Source: Wall Street Journal, March 5, 2003, p. B12.
Republished by permission of Dow Jones, Inc. via
Copyright Clearance Center, Inc. @ 2003 Dow Jones
and Company, Inc. All Rights Reserve Worldwide.

chapter 2, the equilibrium price of a bond is that price obtained by discounting its cash flows by spot rates – the rate on zero-coupon bonds. If the market prices a bond below its equilibrium value, then dealers can earn a risk-free profit by buying the bond and stripping it into IO and PO bonds; if the market prices a bond above its equilibrium value, then dealers can realize a risk-free profit by buying stripped securities and then forming an identical coupon bond to sell. This process is known as *rebundling* or *reconstruction*. Recall, in chapter 2, we examined how spot rates are estimated using the bootstrapping technique. A spot yield curve in which the spot rates are estimated using bootstrapping, in turn, is referred to as a *theoretical spot yield curve*. In practice, the process of stripping and rebundling causes the actual yield curve for Treasury securities to approach the theoretical spot yield curve. As a result, the theoretical spot yield curve estimated by using bootstrapping is often used by practitioners to price financial instruments and by dealers to identify arbitrage opportunities. An example of how to estimate a theoretical spot yield curve and use it to identify arbitrage opportunities is presented in exhibit 6.2. It should be noted that because the liquidity of the stripped market is less than that of Treasury securities, the spot yield curve generated from observed stripped securities is not considered as good an estimate of the Treasury yield curve as the theoretical spot yield curve generated from bootstrapping.

6.2.5   The Markets for Treasury Securities

New issues of Treasury securities are sold through an auction process in which the Treasury announces an issue and dealers and investors submit either a competitive or a non-competitive bid. With a competitive bid, an investor specifies the yield (annualized discount yield for T-bills and annualized YTM for Treasury coupon issues) and the quantity he wants, while with a non-competitive bid an investor specifies only the amount (up to $1m face value for T-bills and $5m for coupon bonds) he wants and accepts the weighted average price. Bidders must file tender forms with one of the Federal Reserve banks or branches or

with maturities that match the maturities of their liabilities, thereby eliminating reinvestment risk. In year 2000, $223b of T-bonds and notes were held as stripped Treasury securities, representing approximately 13 per cent of the $1.7t Treasury coupon securities outstanding. In addition to Treasuries, dealers also strip mortgage-backed securities (examined in chapter 11) and agency and municipal securities. There is also an active secondary market for existing stripped securities. Exhibit 6.1 shows a partial listing of strip securities appearing in the *Wall Street Journal* on March 5, 2003.

For dealers, the creation of strip securities represents an arbitrage. As we examined in

Exhibit 6.2   Theoretical spot yield curve

A theoretical spot yield curve can be constructed from observed yields on T-bills and Treasury coupons defining the Treasury yield curve by using a bootstrapping technique. As described in chapter 2, the bootstrapping technique requires taking at least one pure discount bond and then sequentially generating other spot rates from coupon bonds. To illustrate, consider the Treasury securities shown in the following table.

Security	Type	Maturity (years)	Semi-annual coupon	Annualized YTM (%)	Face value	Current price	Spot rate (%)
1	T-bill	0.5	–	5	100	97.561	5
2	T-bill	1	–	5.25	100	94.9497	5.25
3	T-note	1.5	2.75	5.5	100	100	5.551
4	T-note	2	2.875	5.75	100	100	5.577
5	T-note	2.5	3	6.00	100	100	6.03
6	T-note	3	3.125	6.25	100	100	6.30

There are two T-bills with maturities of 6 months (0.5 years) and 1 year, trading at bond-equivalent yields of 5% and 5.25%. Since T-bills are pure discount bonds, these rates can be used as spot rates (S_t) for maturities of 0.5 years ($S_{0.5}$) and 1 year (S_1). To obtain the spot rates for 1.5 years (18 months) we first take the T-note with a maturity of 1.5 years, annual coupon rate of 5.5% (semi-annual coupons of 2.75), and currently priced at par; next we value that bond by discounting its cash flows at spot rates; finally, we solve for the spot rate for 1.5 years. Doing this yields a spot rate of $S_{1.5} = 5.51\%$. That is:

$$P_{1.5} = \frac{CF_{0.5}}{(1 + (S_{0.5}/2))^1} + \frac{CF_{1.0}}{(1 + (S_1/2))^2} + \frac{CF_{1.5}}{(1 + (S_{1.5}/2))^3}$$

$$100 = \frac{2.75}{(1 + (0.05/2))^1} + \frac{2.75}{(1 + (0.0525/2))^2} + \frac{102.75}{(1 + (S_{1.5}/2))^3}$$

$$94.705956 = \frac{102.75}{(1 + (S_{1.5}/2))^3}$$

$$S_{1.5} = 2\left[\left[\frac{102.75}{94.705956}\right]^{1/3} - 1\right] = 0.0551$$

To obtain the spot rate for a 2-year bond (S_2) we repeat the process using the 2-year bond paying semi-annual coupons of 2.875 and selling at par. This yields a spot rate of $S_2 = 5.577\%$. Continuing the process with the other securities in the table, we obtain spot rates for bonds with maturities of 2.5 years and 3 years: $S_{2.5} = 6.03\%$ and $S_3 = 6.30\%$ (last column of the above table).

Yield curve moving toward theoretical spot yield curve
Consider the arbitrage from buying and stripping the 3-year 6.25% coupon bond. A dealer could buy the issue at par and strip the issue with the expectation of selling the strips at the yields corresponding to their maturities. The proceeds from selling the strips would be 100.1217, yielding the dealer a profit of $0.1217 per $100 face value. In contrast, if the dealer sells at the spot rates defining the theoretical yield curve, the profit is zero and the arbitrage disappears. Thus, the process of stripping will change the supply and demand for bonds, causing their yields to move to their theoretical spot yield curve levels.

Maturity (years)	Semi-annual cash flow	YTM	PV	Spot rates	PV
0.5	3.125	0.0500	3.0488	0.0500	3.0488
1.0	3.125	0.0525	2.9672	0.0525	2.9672
1.5	3.125	0.0550	2.8807	0.0551	2.8804
2.0	3.125	0.0575	2.7900	0.0577	2.7890
2.5	3.125	0.0600	2.6957	0.0603	2.6936
3.0	103.125	0.0625	85.7394	0.0630	85.6210
			100.1217		100.0000

Note: Allow for rounding differences

with the Treasury Bureau of Public Debt. The distribution is determined by first subtracting the non-competitive bids from the total bids; the remainder represents the amount that is awarded to competitive bidders. The distribution to competitive bidders is then determined by arraying the bids from lowest yield (highest price) to highest yield (lowest price). The lowest price at which at least some bills are awarded is called the *stop price* or *stop-out price*. Those bidding above the stop price are awarded the quantity they requested, while those with bids below the stop price do not receive any bills. The bids at the stop price are awarded a proportion of the remaining bids. An example of a T-bill auction is presented in exhibit 6.3.

This auction process used by the Treasury is known as an *English auction* or *first-price sealed-bid auction*. For bidders, an English auction may lead them to either overbid and pay too much for the securities, or underbid and be shut out of the auction. Those shut out, though, can buy them as a secondary market transaction from one of the successful bidders. This English system also may encourage collusion and a cornering of the market. In 1991 Salomon Brothers, for example, was charged with trying to corner the Treasury note market. An alternative to the English auction is the *Dutch auction system* in which securities are ranked, but all are sold at just one price.

The secondary market for Treasury securities is very large. This market is part of the over-the-counter (OTC) market and is handled by Treasury security dealers. It is a 24-hour market with major dealers in New York, London, and Tokyo. The OTC market consists of investors who prefer to buy from dealers instead of through the auctions, investors buying and selling outstanding securities, and the Federal Reserve, which buys T-bills and other Treasury securities as part of their open market operations.[6] In the secondary market, recently issued Treasury securities, called *on-the-run issues*, are the most liquid securities with a very narrow bid–ask spread; approximately 70% of the total secondary market trading involves on-the-run issues. In contrast, Treasury securities issued earlier, referred to as *off-the-run issues*, are not quite as liquid and can have slightly wider spreads.

6.2.6 Government Security Dealers

Because of the difficulty in determining the best price to bid, individual investors, regional banks, fund managers, and corporations often prefer to buy new Treasury securities from dealers who specialize in the Treasury auction market rather than buy them directly at the auction. While any firm can deal in government securities, the Treasury auction is principally carried out with *primary dealers*. Primary dealers are those firms that trade with the Federal Reserve Bank of New York as part of their open market operations. For a firm to be on the primary dealer's list, it must have adequate capital and be willing to trade securities at any time. As of 2002, there were 22 primary dealers participating in the market (see exhibit 6.4 for a list of these dealers). The dealers include many of the major investment banking firms, such as Salomon Smith Barney, Merrill Lynch, and Goldman Sachs, as well as a number of foreign dealers.[7] For new issues, primary dealers distribute new Treasury securities to non-primary dealers and institutional investors. They also maintain large dealer positions in the secondary market.

In addition to the primary and secondary market for Treasury securities, there is also an *interdealer market* in which primary and non-primary dealers trade billions of dollars each day amongst themselves. This interdealer market functions through government security brokers that for a commission match dealers and other investors who want to sell with those wanting to buy.[8] The government brokers include such firms as Cantor Fitzgerald Securities, Garban LLC, Hilliard Farber and Company, Intercapital Government Securities, Liberty Brokerage, and Tullett and Tokyo Securities.

By taking temporary positions, dealers hope to profit from two sources: carry income and position profit. *Carry income* is the difference between the interest dealers earn from holding the securities and the interest they pay on the funds they borrow to purchase the securities. When dealers acquire securities, they often finance the purchase by borrowing from banks, other dealers, and other institutions. One major

Exhibit 6.3   T-bill auction example

Three-month T-bills (13-week or 91-day bills) and 6-month T-bills (26-week or 182-day bills) are auctioned every Monday. Announcements of the auction are made on the Thursday preceding the Monday offering. In the announcement, the Treasury will indicate the size of auction, the proportions of the offering that will be used to replace maturing debt and for new funding, and their estimate of cash needs for the remainder of the quarter. Bidders must file tender forms by Monday. Competitive tenders submit a quantity bid and a yield bid based on a discount yield basis; non-competitive tenders submit only a quantity bid up to $1m face value. Recall, the discount yield is:

$$R_\mathrm{D} = \frac{F - P_0}{F} \frac{360}{\text{Days to maturity}}$$

The price given the discount yield and face value, F, of 100 is:

$$P_0 = 100[1 - R_\mathrm{D}\,(\text{Days to maturity}/360)]$$

The distribution is determined by first subtracting the non-competitive bids from the total bids; the remainder represents the amount that is awarded to competitive bidders. For example, if the volume of bills requested is $12.5b and the amount accepted by the Treasury is $11b with $1.5b being non-competitive, then the issue would be oversubscribed, with $1.5b going to non-competitive bidders and $9.5b going to competitive bidders.

Volume of bills requested	$12.5b
Volume of bills accepted by the Treasury	$11b
Volume of non-competitive offers accepted	$1.5b
Volume of competitive offers	$9.5b

The distribution to competitive bidders is determined by arraying the bids from lowest yield (highest price) to highest yield (lowest price). The discount yield is carried out to three decimal points. In this example, suppose we have the following competitive bids:

Bid discount yield %	Bid price	Quantity bid in billions	Cumulative bids in billions
3.750	99.052	0.20	0.20
3.755	99.051	0.57	0.77
3.760	99.050	0.78	1.55
3.765	99.048	1.25	2.80
3.770	99.047	1.30	4.10
3.775	99.046	1.50	5.60
3.800	99.039	1.70	7.30
3.825	99.033	1.85	9.15
*3.830	99.032	0.75	9.90
3.835	99.031	0.75	10.65
3.840	99.029	0.3	11.00
		11	

* Stop price

The Treasury allocates to competitive bidders until $9.5b is distributed. The lowest price at which at least some bills are awarded is the stop price. In this case, the stop price is 3.83% or 99.032. Those bidders above the stop price of 3.83% are awarded the quantity they requested, while those with bids below the stop price do not receive any bills – shut out. The bids at the stop price are awarded a proportion of the remaining bids. At 3.83%, there are $0.35b left in bids ($9.5b – $9.15b) and $0.75b requested at the stop price. Each of the bidders at 3.83% would therefore receive 46.667% (=0.35/0.75) of his bid. The weighted average bid that the non-competitive bidders receive is 3.786%:

Average bid = ($0.2/$9.5)(3.75%) + ($0.57/9.5)(3.755%) + · · · + (0.35/9.5)(3.83%) = 3.786%

The difference between the stop bid yield and average yield is called the tail; in this case the tail is 0.044% (=3.83% – 3.786%).

Exhibit 6.4   Primary government security dealers, 2002

ABN AMRO Inc.	Goldman Sachs, & Co.
BNP Paribas Securities Corp.	Greenwich Capital Markets, Inc.
Banc One Capital Markets, Inc.	HSBC Securities
Bank of America Securities, LLC	J. P. Morgan Securities, Inc.
Barclays Capital, Inc.	Lehman Brother Inc.
Bear, Stearns & Co. Inc.	Merrill Lynch Government Securities Inc.
CIBC World Markets Corp.	Mizuho Securities USA Inc.
Credit Suisse First Boston Corp.	Morgan Stanley & Co. Incorporated
Daiwa Securities America, Inc.	Nomura Securities International, Inc.
Deutsche Bank Securities In.	Salomon Smith Barney Inc.
Dresdner Kleinwort Wasserstein Securities LLC	UBS Warburg LLC

Federal Reserve Bank of New York: www.newyorkfed.org/markets/pridealers_listing.html

source of funds for them is demand loans from banks. Demand loans are short-term loans to dealers (1 or 2 days), secured by the dealer's securities. These loans are usually renewable and often can be called at any time by the bank. Another important source of dealer funding is repurchase agreements; these are discussed in the next section. When dealers sell their securities, the invoice price is equal to the agreed-upon price plus the accrued interest. Generally, dealers profit with a positive carry income by earning higher accrued interest than the interest they pay on their loans.

The *position profit* of dealers comes from long positions, as well as short positions. In a long position, a dealer purchases the securities and then holds them until a customer comes along. The dealer will realize a position profit if rates decrease and prices increase during the time she holds the securities. In contrast, in a short position, the dealer borrows securities and sells them hoping that rates will subsequently increase and prices will fall by the time he purchases the securities. To minimize their exposure to position risk, dealers do make use of futures and other derivative contracts to hedge against interest rate changes (interest rate futures and other derivatives are discussed in part IV). Some dealers also use forward commitments called *when-issued securities* in which they agree in advance to deliver the securities purchased at the auction date.

Web Information

Information on the Treasury's upcoming and past auctions can be found at
   www.publicdebt.ustreas.gov/of/ ofaucrt.htm

Information on primary security dealers is at
   www.newyorkfed.org/markets/ pridealers_listing.html

Information on requirements to be primary security dealers is at
   www.newyorkfed.org/markets/ pridealers_policies.html

Information on how to buy Treasury securities online is at
   www.publicdebt.ustreas.gov/ols/ olshome.htm

Information on rates can be found at
   www.federalreserve.gov/releases/h15/ data.htm
and
   www.economagic.com

6.3 REPURCHASE AGREEMENTS

As noted above, many dealers finance their temporary holdings of securities with *repurchase agreements*, also called *repos (RPs)*. Under a repurchase agreement, the dealer sells securities to a lender, such as a commercial bank, with an agreement that he will buy the securities back at a later date and price. To the dealer, the RP represents a collateralized loan, with the Treasury securities serving as the collateral. Government security dealers often use overnight repos to finance their positions, agreeing to buy back the securities within the next day or two. To the lender, the RP position, defined as a *reverse repo*, represents a secured short-term investment. Banks, investment banking firms, dealers, corporations, state and local governments, and other institutions find reverse RPs attractive securities for investing their excess cash. The terms repo and reverse repo can be confusing. Some practitioners refer to the party with the repo position (sale/repurchase) as the *collateral seller* and the party with the reverse repo (purchase/resale) as the *collateral buyer*.

As an example, suppose a Treasury dealer plans to buy $20m of T-notes on the Treasury auction day and anticipates holding them for 1 day before selling the securities to her customers for $20m plus a premium. To finance the purchase, the dealer could buy the notes and simultaneously enter a repurchase agreement with an investor. Per the agreement, the dealer would sell the notes for $20m minus the interest paid to the lender. In this market, dealers and lenders state the interest in terms of an annualized *repo rate* based on a 360-day year. If this rate were 6%, then the interest would be $3,333 and the price the dealer would sell the notes for on the repo agreement would be $19,996,667:

Interest

$$= (\text{Principal})(\text{Repo rate})(\text{Length of loan}/360)$$

$$= (\$20,000,000)(0.06)(1/360)$$

$$= \$3,333$$

$$\text{Price sold} = \$20,000,000 - \$3,333$$
$$= \$19,996,667$$

$$\text{Repurchase price} = \$20,000,000$$

One day later, the dealer would buy back the T-notes on the repurchase agreement for $20m and then sell them to her customers for hopefully $20m or more plus the 1 day accrued interest.

6.3.1 Types of Repurchase Agreements

The RP market is not limited to overnight repos or those arranged just with Treasury securities. Repos can have maturities that range from 1 day (overnight) to 1 year. An RP that is not overnight is called a *term repo*.[9] There is also an *open repo* that has no maturity; this is typically an overnight repo that is automatically rolled over into another overnight repo until one of the parties closes (after giving the other party proper notification). For example, the Treasury dealer in the above example might estimate that it could take 1 to 3 days, if not longer, to sell her $20m of T-notes and would therefore find that an open repo was the best way to finance her long position. In addition to Treasury securities, repos are also arranged with federal agency securities, municipals, mortgage-back securities, and money market securities. There are also *dollar repos* that permit the borrower to repurchase with securities similar, but not identical, to the securities initially sold. Finally, there are repos that allow the borrower to replace the collateral. A dealer who foresees the possibility of having to deliver the collateral to a customer during the term of the repo might want such a provision in the repo agreement. With a replacement provision, the dealer could then request a substitution whereby he would agree to deliver another security of equivalent value to the lender who would return the original collateral.

6.3.2 The Market for Repurchase Agreements

The repo market consists of investors with excess cash who find reverse repos to be an attractive investment alternative to other money market securities, and dealers and holders of securities who want to borrow short-term funds and find repurchase agreements to be an efficient and less expensive financing alternative. Many financial and non-financial corporations take both repo and reverse repo positions. A bank, for example, might loan funds to a dealer with an open reverse repo (collateral buyer), while financing part of its short-term loan portfolio with term repos (collateral seller). Similarly, security dealers use repos to set up long positions and reverse repos to form short positions. In the case of a long position, a Treasury security dealer might finance her security acquisition with a repurchase agreement as described above. If interest rates decrease and prices increase, the dealer would then profit from the long position. For short positions, a dealer might sell Treasury securities as part of her normal business with the securities coming from the collateral obtained from taking a reverse repo position. From the combination of a security sale and a reverse repurchase agreement, the dealer would have cash or a liquid position from the security sale and an obligation to deliver the securities on the reverse repo. To profit, the dealer is hoping that rates would increase, causing the price of the underlying Treasury securities to fall.[10] Finally, a dealer might hedge a long position financed with a repurchase agreement with a futures contract, earning just the carry income equal to the difference between the accrued interest earned on the securities held and the rate paid on the repurchase agreement – the repo rate.

Another important use of repurchase agreements is by depository institutions as a way to finance their federal funds position. Federal funds are deposits of banks and deposit institutions with the Federal Reserve (Fed) that are used to maintain the bank's reserve position required to support their deposits. Banks maintain federal funds desks where they manage their federal funds positions: borrowing funds when they are deficient and lending funds when they have an excess amount of reserves. Two common ways in which depository institutions finance a deficient reserve position are through the federal funds market and the repo market. The *federal funds market* is a market in which depository institutions with excess reserves lend to institutions that are deficient. Federal funds market loans are typically overnight to one week, unsecured, and traded directly between the lending bank (usually a small regional bank) and the borrowing bank (often a money center bank). This contrasts with the repo loan that is secured and often offered by dealers making a

market. Because of the security backing the repurchase agreement, their rates tend to be less than the federal funds rate; the spread on overnight federal funds and repurchase agreements is about 25 annual basis points.

On balance, banks and dealers are net collateral sellers (net repo position), while money market funds, bank trust departments, municipalities, and non-financial corporations are net collateral buyers (net reverse repo position). The repo market also includes the Federal Reserve as one of it participants. The Fed uses the repo market as part of its open market operations to influence interest rates; it also uses the market to control seasonal money supply problems. For example, during a holiday time when there is an increase in aggregate spending, the Fed might inject money into the economy for a short period by buying Treasury securities from dealers or banks on a repo agreement requiring the Fed to sell them back to the dealer after a few days.

6.3.3 Risk

Since RPs are secured by Treasury or other high-quality securities they are considered to be high quality. The lender (collateral buyer), though, is subject to some risk. For example, if the borrower (collateral seller) cannot buy back the underlying securities, the lender is left with securities whose price could or may already have decreased. To minimize such risk, a repo agreement may require that the borrower set up an initial margin in the form of cash, pledge additional collateral, or sell securities in excess of the amount of the principal of the trade. In some cases, the agreement may include a maintenance margin provision requiring the borrower to deliver a requisite amount of cash or money market securities if the collateralized securities lose value by a certain amount.

Another risk facing the lender (collateral buyer) is that the borrower may use the collateral fraudulently as security for other repurchase agreements. This could occur when the repurchase agreement allows for the borrower/collateral seller to hold the securities in a separate customers' account maintained by the seller (known as a *hold-in-custody repo* or *letter repo*), instead of actually delivering the securities to the lender/collateral buyer or delivering them to a custodial account set up with a third party. The extent of this type of risk was brought to light in 1985 when it was learned that several government security dealers who had declared bankruptcy (ESM Government Securities and Bevil, Bresler, and Schulman) had used the same securities as collateral on different repurchase agreements. Investors who had purchased these repos included a number of municipalities and state-insured thrifts (many in Ohio); their losses were over $500m. Since that scandal, lenders have tried to avoid such risk by requiring notification of any ownership transfer of the securities if possible (recall, Treasury securities are in book-entry form), and by requiring more detailed accounting. In addition, the scandal led to the passage of the Government Security Act of 1986 that required greater disclosure of repurchase agreements and gave the Treasury the authority to oversee dealers in the repo market.

It should be noted that instead of using a repo agreement, some dealers borrow the securities from financial institutions. The borrowing or short sale of securities is often secured by other securities and either the lender or borrower can usually terminate the security loan. Some financial institutions prefer lending securities to repurchase agreements because the loan appears as a footnote instead of as an asset or liability on their balance sheet.[11]

Web Information
For information on the size of the repo market as a source of dealer financing go to
www.bondmarkets.com
and click on "Research statistics" and "Funding/Repo."

6.4 FEDERAL AGENCY SECURITIES

The US Treasury is responsible for financing and managing the government's debt. In addition to the Treasury, there are also federal agencies and quasi-government corporations that issue securities. Many of these agencies were established to ensure that sufficient credit or liquidity

was provided to certain segments of the economy having difficulties raising funds. Among those entities are farmers, students, homeowners, small businesses, and international businesses. These federal agencies raise funds by issuing short-, intermediate-, and long-term debt securities. They use the proceeds to directly provide loans to farmers, students, and businesses, or to provide loan guarantees and liquidity to private lenders who make loans to those entities.

The federal credit agencies can be divided into two groups: *federally sponsored agencies* and *federal agencies*. Federally sponsored agencies (also referred to as *government-sponsored agencies* and *government-sponsored enterprises*) are privately owned companies with a federal charter. Among these agencies are the Federal National Mortgage Association (FNMA or Fannie Mae), Farm Credit Banks (FCB), Federal Agriculture Mortgage Corporation (FAMC or Farmer Mac), and the Student Loan Marketing Association (SLMA or Sallie Mae) (see exhibit 6.5). These government-sponsored companies sell securities and use the proceeds to provide loans and liquidity to support the housing industry, agriculture sector, and college loan programs. Federal agencies are true federal agencies created by the US government. Included in this group are the Export–Import Bank, Tennessee Valley Authority (TVA), Federal Housing Administration (FHA), Small Business Administration (SBA), and Government National Mortgage Association (GNMA or Ginnie Mae). These agencies obtain financing by borrowing from the Federal Financing Bank, which in turn borrows from the Treasury. Some sell their own securities. TVA, for example, issued over $30b in 1998 ($25b in short-term securities and $6b in long-term) to finance its utility operations and construction projects in the Tennessee River area.

Collectively, the claims sold by federal agencies and government-sponsored companies are referred to as federal agency securities. For investors, these claims are considered virtually default free because of the agency's or company's affiliation with the federal government (some federal agency issues are backed by Treasury bonds and many agencies have lines of credit with the Treasury). Following the bailout of savings and loans institutions and banks

Exhibit 6.5   Federal agencies

Government-sponsored agencies
Farm Credit Banks (FCB)
Federal Home Loan Bank (FHLB)
Federal Home Loan Mortgage Corporation (FHLMC or Freddie Mac)
Federal National Mortgage Association (FNMA or Fannie Mae)
Federal Agriculture Mortgage Corporation (FAMC or Farmer Mac)
Student Loan Marketing Association (SLMA or Sallie Mae)
Financing Corporation (FICO)
Farm Credit Financial Assistance Corporation (FACO)
Resolution Funding Corporation (REFCO)

Federal agencies
Export–Import Bank
Farmer's Home Administration (FMHA)
Federal Housing Administration (FHA)
Government National Mortgage Association (GNMA or Ginnie Mae)
Postal Service
Tennessee Valley Authority (TVA)
Federal Deposit Insurance Corporation (FDIC)
Small Business Administration (SBA)

in the 1980s and early 1990, the General Accounting Office and the Treasury began requiring that all federally sponsored agencies maintain a triple-A credit rating or lose their government support. The yields on federal agency securities are highly correlated with the yields on Treasuries, with the yield spread of federal over Treasury being positive; on occasions some federal agency securities have traded at significantly higher yields than Treasuries (e.g., 200 basis points).

Federal agency issues vary from short to long term in maturity, ranging from overnight issues to bonds with 30-year maturities.[12] Agency money-market securities are sold as zero-discount bonds, while intermediate and long-term notes and bonds are sold as coupon bonds; agencies also sell floating-rate bonds. The denominations on the bonds vary from $1,000 to $50,000 and upwards. FNMA, FHLMC, the FHLB system, and several other agencies also offer *agency benchmark programs* similar to corporate medium-term note issues. These programs provide for the regular issuance of coupon securities covering a range of maturities. Unlike Treasury securities, which are exempt from state and local taxes, and municipal bonds, which are exempt from federal taxes, most federal agency securities are fully taxable. Because of their tax status, as well as their maturities and relatively low risk, federal agency claims are attractive investments for pension and trust funds, state and local governments, banks, and corporations. The Federal Reserve System also trades in some federal agency securities.

Over the last three decades, the debt of federal agencies has grown from $50b (1970) to over $2.3t in 2002 (see table 6.5). The primary market for many federal agency securities is handled through a network of federal security fiscal agents, brokers, and dealers. Depending on the type of security, a new issue can be sold through dealers, by auction, or by direct sales. Short-term securities are sold on a continuous basis, while intermediate issues are sold on a monthly basis, and long-term bonds are offered several times a year. Similar to the primary market for Treasuries, there is also an interdealer market that helps to improve the

Table 6.5 Federal agencies: debt outstanding 1985–2002 ($ billions)

Year	Federal Home Loan Bank	Federal Home Loan Mortgage Corporation	Federal National Mortgage Association	Farm Credit System[1]	Student Loan Marketing Association	Tennessee Valley Authority	Other[2]	Total
1985	74.4	11.9	93.9	68.9	8.4	16.3	20	293.9
1986	88.8	13.6	93.6	62.5	12.2	17.2	19.6	307.4
1987	115.7	17.6	97.1	55.3	16.5	18.1	21.1	341.4
1988	135.8	22.8	105.5	53.8	22.1	18.3	23.2	381.5
1989	136.1	26.1	116.1	55.7	28.7	17.9	31.2	411.8
1990	117.9	30.9	123.4	54.9	34.2	23.4	49.9	434.7
1991	107.5	30.3	133.9	53.5	38.3	22.4	56.9	442.8
1992	114.7	29.6	166.3	53.2	39.7	23.6	56.9	484
1993	139.5	50	201.1	54.4	39.8	29.9	56	570.7
1994	205.8	93.3	257.2	54.4	50.3	27.5	50.3	738.9
1995	243.2	120	299.2	58.6	47.5	29.4	46.7	844.6
1996	263.4	157	331.3	61.3	44.8	27.9	40.2	925.8
1997	313.9	169.2	369.8	64.8	37.7	27.8	39.4	1,022.60
1998	382.1	287.4	460.3	64.7	35.4	26.5	44.2	1,300.60
1999	529	360.7	547.6	70.1	42	26.4	44.2	1,620.00
2000	594.4	426.9	642.7	75.4	45.4	25.7	44.2	1,854.00
2001	623.7	565.1	763.5	77.9	48.4	26.8	44.2	2,149.60
2002	643.1	601	789	82.2	49.6	26.8	44.2	2,235.90

[1]Includes Farm Credit Banks and Farm Credit Financial Assistance Corporation
[2]Includes Defense Department, Export–Import Bank, Federal Housing Administration, GNMA certificates of participation, Postal Service, US Railway Association, Financing Corporation, and the Resolution Funding Corporation

Source: Federal Reserve System: www.federalreserve.gov; also in www.bondmarkets.com

efficiency of the market. Intermediate- and long-term issues are usually sold through a *solicitation method*. Under this method, a fiscal agent puts the selling group together. The selling group then provides potential investors with information on the issues. Given that information, the potential investor indicates the amount of the issue they plan to buy and the price they believe the issue should be. The fiscal agent then sets the price based on the inputs of the potential investors. The secondary market for agency securities is handled through dealers on the over-the-counter market. Information on the trading of existing agency securities in the secondary market is reported in the *Wall Street Journal* and other daily newspapers. As shown in exhibit 6.6, the information reported in the *Journal* includes the coupon rate, maturity, dealer's ask and bid quotes (columns 3 and 4) in which the decimals, like the quotes of Treasury bonds and notes, are in 32nds, and the yields based on the dealer's ask price and a day count convention of $\frac{30}{360}$.

While different federal agency securities have many similar characteristics, the purpose for which each agency and government-sponsored company uses its funds varies considerably. As noted, the major areas of financing for federal agencies are housing, agriculture, savings and loans and bank funding and reorganizing, student loans, and international business. Table 6.6 summarizes the functions of these various federal agencies.

6.4.1 Housing and Real Estate Financing

The Federal National Mortgage Association, the Government National Mortgage Association, the Federal Home Loan Mortgage Corporation (FHLMC or Freddie Mac), and the Federal Agriculture Mortgage Corporation are all agencies involved with providing funding and liquidity for the mortgage industry. Until

Exhibit 6.6 Government agency quotes

Government Agency & Similar Issues

Over-the-Counter mid-afternoon quotations based on large transactions, usually $1 million or more. Colons in bid and asked quotes represent 32nds; 101:01 means 101 1/32.

All yields are calculated to maturity, and based on the asked quote.

*Callable issue, maturity date shown. For issues callable prior to maturity, yields are computed to the earliest call date for issues quoted above par, or 100, and to the maturity date for issues below par.

Source: Bear, Stearns & Co. via Street Software Technology Inc.

Fannie Mae Issues

RATE	MAT	BID	ASKED	YLD
5.13	2-04	103:17	103:19	1.24
4.75	3-04	103:19	103:21	1.14
3.63	4-04	102:18	102:20	1.24
5.63	5-04	105:02	105:04	1.26
3.00	6-04	102:04	102:06	1.27
6.50	8-04	107:09	107:11	1.33
3.50	9-04	103:04	103:06	1.38
1.88	12-04	100:19	100:21	1.50
7.13	2-05	110:17	110:19	1.57
3.88	3-05	104:16	104:18	1.58
5.75	6-05	109:00	109:02	1.67
7.00	7-05	111:31	112:01	1.76
3.13	8-05*	100:22	100:24	1.39
2.88	10-05	102:15	102:17	1.88
2.75	11-05*	100:20	100:22	1.76
6.00	12-05	110:28	110:30	1.93
2.75	12-05*	100:21	100:23	1.83
5.50	2-06	109:25	109:27	2.03
5.50	5-06	109:07	109:09	2.43
5.25	6-06	109:17	109:19	2.20
5.50	7-06*	101:22	101:24	0.69
5.25	8-06*	101:28	101:30	0.79
4.38	10-06	106:31	107:01	2.33
4.50	10-06*	101:29	101:31	1.24
4.00	11-06*	101:19	101:21	1.61
4.75	12-06*	102:22	102:24	1.26
4.75	1-07	107:05	107:07	2.75
5.00	1-07*	109:08	109:10	2.46
5.00	1-07*	103:04	103:06	1.32
7.13	3-07	117:16	117:18	2.51
5.25	3-07*	103:29	103:31	1.41
5.25	4-07	110:11	110:13	2.56
5.00	5-07*	103:28	103:30	1.64
4.25	7-07	106:14	106:16	2.66
6.63	10-07	116:19	116:21	2.75

Freddie Mac

RATE	MAT	BID	ASKED	YLD
3.50	10-07*	101:31	102:01	2.21
3.25	11-07	102:02	102:04	2.76
3.25	1-08	101:27	101:29	2.83
3.50	1-08*	101:05	101:07	2.83
5.75	2-08	113:05	113:07	2.86
6.00	5-08	114:16	114:18	2.95
5.25	1-09	110:29	110:31	3.18
6.38	6-09	117:07	117:09	3.30
6.63	9-09	118:24	118:26	3.39
7.25	1-10	122:26	122:28	3.47
7.13	6-10	122:15	122:17	3.58
6.63	11-10	119:12	119:14	3.70
6.25	2-11	113:28	113:30	4.16
5.50	3-11	111:24	111:26	3.78
6.00	5-11	115:05	115:07	3.82
6.25	7-11*	105:28	105:30	1.83
5.50	10-11*	104:16	104:18	2.60
5.38	11-11	110:23	110:25	3.90
5.00	11-11*	103:02	103:04	3.10
6.00	12-11*	106:14	106:16	2.28
6.00	1-12*	106:17	106:19	2.36
6.13	3-12	116:06	116:08	3.96
6.25	3-12*	107:19	107:21	0.00
5.50	7-12*	105:08	105:10	3.15
5.25	8-12	116:18	116:20	4.38
4.38	9-12	102:13	102:15	4.06
6.25	5-29	114:22	114:26	5.21
7.13	1-30	127:12	127:16	5.21
7.25	5-30	129:10	129:14	5.21
6.63	11-30	120:26	120:30	5.19

RATE	MAT	BID	ASKED	YLD
6.25	7-04	106:19	106:21	1.28
3.00	7-04	102:07	102:09	1.30
4.50	8-04	104:13	104:15	1.35
3.25	11-04	102:30	103:00	1.46
6.88	1-05	109:22	109:24	1.53
1.88	1-05	100:18	100:20	1.54
3.88	2-05	104:10	104:12	1.57
4.50	4-05*	100:13	100:15	0.24
4.25	6-05	105:19	105:21	1.70
3.88	6-05*	101:17	101:19	0.00
7.00	7-05	112:00	112:02	1.76
2.88	9-05*	102:15	102:17	1.84
2.88	9-05*	100:18	100:20	1.73
5.25	1-06	108:29	108:31	2.00
5.50	7-06*	110:14	110:16	2.24
4.88	3-07	108:29	108:31	2.52
4.50	7-07*	102:27	102:29	2.35
3.50	9-07	103:10	103:12	2.70
5.75	4-08	113:14	113:16	2.89
5.13	10-08	110:18	110:20	3.05
5.75	3-09	113:25	113:27	3.20
5.75	4-09*	104:19	104:21	1.64
4.75	8-09*	102:28	102:30	2.66
6.63	9-09	118:28	118:30	3.37
7.00	3-10	121:20	121:22	3.49
6.88	9-10	121:03	121:05	3.63
5.63	3-11	112:25	112:27	3.76
5.88	3-11	111:23	111:25	4.14
6.00	6-11	115:10	115:12	3.81
6.38	8-11*	109:09	109:11	3.44
5.50	9-11	111:25	111:27	3.86
5.75	1-12	113:14	113:16	3.93
6.25	3-12*	110:00	110:02	3.53
6.00	5-12*	104:15	104:17	2.19
5.13	7-12	108:16	108:18	4.02
5.13	8-12*	102:22	102:24	3.16
4.75	10-12*	101:26	101:28	3.99
5.25	11-12*	104:16	104:18	4.16
4.50	1-13	103:05	103:07	4.10
6.75	9-29	122:03	122:07	5.20
6.75	3-31	123:03	123:07	5.17
6.25	7-32	116:02	116:06	5.17

Federal Farm Credit Bank

RATE	MAT	BID	ASKED	YLD
3.88	12-04	104:02	104:04	1.50

RATE	MAT	BID	ASKED	YLD
3.88	2-05	104:07	104:09	1.59
4.88	4-05	105:20	105:22	2.10
2.50	11-05	101:11	101:13	1.96
2.50	3-06	101:08	101:10	2.05

Federal Home Loan Bank

RATE	MAT	BID	ASKED	YLD
5.38	1-04	103:13	103:15	1.18
4.88	4-04	103:31	104:01	1.19
3.63	10-04	103:12	103:14	1.45
4.13	11-04	104:09	104:11	1.50
4.00	2-05	104:16	104:18	1.61
4.38	2-05	105:09	105:11	1.57
6.88	8-05	111:24	111:26	1.90
2.50	12-05	101:09	101:11	2.00
5.13	3-06	108:25	108:27	2.07
2.50	3-06	101:00	101:02	2.13
5.38	5-06	109:21	109:23	2.20
4.88	11-06	108:18	108:20	2.42
4.88	2-07	108:21	108:23	2.54
5.38	2-07	110:08	110:10	2.61
5.80	9-08	113:24	113:26	3.05
6.00	5-11	111:20	111:22	4.29
5.63	11-11	112:04	112:06	3.95
5.75	5-12	113:19	113:21	3.96
4.50	11-12	103:19	103:21	4.04

GNMA Mtge. Issues

RATE	MAT	BID	ASKED	YLD
4.50	30Yr	98:02	98:04	5.00
5.00	30Yr	101:07	101:09	4.77
5.50	30Yr	103:09	103:11	4.68
6.00	30Yr	104:23	104:25	3.64
6.50	30Yr	105:13	105:15	1.94
7.00	30Yr	106:10	106:12	1.15
7.50	30Yr	107:03	107:05	1.71
8.00	30Yr	108:09	108:11	2.32
8.50	30Yr	108:16	108:18	3.15

Tennessee Valley Authority

RATE	MAT	BID	ASKED	YLD
4.75	7-04	104:17	104:19	1.32
6.38	6-05	110:07	110:09	1.74
5.38	11-08	111:19	111:21	3.12
5.63	1-11	112:22	112:24	3.74
6.75	11-25	120:16	120:19	5.19
7.13	5-30	127:16	127:20	5.21

the introduction of mortgage-backed securities (examined in chapter 11), the primary function of FNMA, GNMA, and FHLMC was to provide a secondary market for mortgages. They did this by issuing their own securities and then using the proceeds to buy mortgages from savings and loans, mortgages banks, and commercial banks. (See exhibit 6.7 for a brief history of the secondary mortgage market.) In the 1980s, FHLMC, FNMA, and GNMA began offering *pass-through securities* or *participation certificates (PCs)*. These instruments are securitized assets formed by pooling a group of mortgages and then selling a security representing interest in the pool and entitling

the holder to the income generated from the pool of mortgages. The Federal Agriculture Mortgage Corporation (Farmer Mac) was established in 1988 to provide a secondary market for agriculture real estate. Like FNMA, GNMA, and FHLMC, it buys loans, pools them, and sells claims on the pool.

6.4.2 Agriculture Credit Financing

The Federal Farm Credit Bank System (FFCBS) originally consisted of 12 Federal Land Banks (FLBs), 12 Federal Intermediate

Table 6.6 Federal agencies: functions and securities issued

Agency	Function	Major securities issued
Federal National Mortgage Association (FNMA or Fannie Mae)	Buys mortgages and issues mortgage-backed securities	Sells pass-through securities or participation certificates, which entitle the holder to a cash flow from a pool of mortgage securities
Government National Mortgage Association (GNMA or Ginnie Mae)	Buys mortgages and issues mortgage-backed securities	Sells pass-through securities or participation certificates, which entitle the holder to a cash flow from a pool of mortgage securities
Federal Home Loan Mortgage Corporation (FHLMC or Freddie Mac)	Buys mortgages and issues mortgage-backed securities	Sells pass-through securities or participation certificates, which entitle the holder to a cash flow from a pool of mortgage securities
Federal Home Loan Bank System (FHLBS)	Consists of 12 district Federal Home Loan Banks. Provides loans to qualified S&Ls	Sells bonds separately and jointly for Federal Home Loan Banks
Student Loan Marketing Association (SLMA or Sallie Mae)	Provides funds for lenders participating in the Federally Guaranteed Student Loan Program, and PLUS loan programs (loans to parents of undergraduate students)	Issues discount notes, long-term bonds, and pure discount bonds
Farm Credit Financial Assistance Corporation (FACO)	Provides funds primarily to refinance loans to farmers who defaulted on FCBS loans	Issues FACO bonds that are backed by the Treasury
Financing Corporation (FICO)	Federally sponsored agency established in 1987 to finance defaults of deposits by savings and loans institutions. The 12 Regional Federal Home Loan Banks purchased its stock. By law, FICO is to be dismantled in 2026	Authorized to issue up to $10.805b in bonds
Resolution Trust Corporation (RTC)	Federally sponsored agency responsible for liquidating or restructuring insolvent savings and loans. Stopped operations on December 31, 1995	Authorized to issue up to $40b in long-term bonds
Federal Farm Credit Bank System (FFCBS)	Provides credit to agriculture sector distributed through 11 Farm Credit Banks	Issues bills, notes, and bonds

Credit Banks (FICBs), and 12 Banks for Cooperatives. The Federal Land Banks (created by an Act of Congress in 1916) made mortgage loans and provided financial funds to farmers and ranchers for purchasing or improving their farms and ranches; the Federal Intermediate Credit Banks (created in 1923) provided short-term loans for farmers; the Banks for Cooperatives (created in 1933) provided seasonal loans to farm cooperatives. Prior to 1979, these banks sold their own securities. In 1979, though, they consolidated their financing under the FFCBS and sold separate and joint obligations of the FFCBS. In 1987, the FFCBS

Exhibit 6.7   Brief history of the secondary mortgage market

In the early 1900s, the lack of standardized mortgage contracts and regional differences in real estate inhibited the development of an efficient secondary market for existing mortgage loans. Moreover, the lack of such a market translated into liquidity problems for lenders who were unable to sell their mortgage notes. In 1938, the Federal National Mortgage Association, FNMA, was formed with the initial purpose of acquiring mortgage notes. Combined with the Federal Housing Administration (FHA) and Veterans Administration (VA) default insurance programs, FNMA helped develop the present secondary mortgage market. Specifically, the FHA's program of providing insurance for mortgage lenders against defaults and the VA's program of guaranteeing veterans' mortgages had two major effects on the real estate lending market. Firstly, as intended, it reduced the default risk characteristics of the mortgage, and secondly, FHA and VA by providing such benefits were able to insist on certain provisions governing the maturity, interest, down payments and amortization schedule. This led to a more standardized mortgage contract across the country. Moreover, the combination of uniformity and protection in mortgage notes – qualities that enhanced marketability – facilitated the mortgage purchases made by FNMA and, in turn, accelerated the development of the secondary mortgage market.

In 1968 FNMA was transformed from a federal agency into a privately owned company. FNMA was classified as a government-sponsored company. More precisely, FNMA was defined as a private corporation with a public purpose. As a result, FNMA's charter then stipulated that five of its 15 directors must be appointed by the President, that its debt limit and debt-to-equity ratio be regulated, and that the Treasury hold a certain level of its debts. These actions ensured some limited government control over this once public institution. Operationally, FNMA raised funds through the sale of short-term and intermediate-term securities. From the proceeds they acquired mortgages.

Since FNMA had historically tended to buy from mortgage companies, Congress created the Federal Home Loan Mortgage Company in 1970 to specialize in the purchase of mortgages from Saving and Loans. Operating under the Federal Home Loan Bank Board, FHLMC served not only to help Savings and Loans, but also to extend the secondary market from FHA- and VA-secured mortgages to conventional mortgages (not federally insured). The final participant of note in the secondary market was the Government National Mortgage Association, GNMA. Created after FNMA was converted to a private company, GNMA, under its liquidity management program, initially bought mortgages from Savings and Loans and mortgage bankers and then sold them under a tandem program to FNMA and FHLMC or packaged the mortgages and sold them to large institutional investors.

was, in turn, reorganized under the Agriculture Credit Act. This reorganization led to the merger of the regional FLBs, FICBs, and Banks for Cooperatives into six regional Farm Credit Banks (FCBs) and the Agriculture Credit Bank. These agency banks now make agriculture loans through 32 Federal Credit Bank Associations.

The FFCBS issues three types of securities: short-term money markets securities with maturities ranging from 5 days to 270 days, short-term bonds with maturities from 3 to 9 months, and intermediate bonds with maturities ranging from 1 year to 10. All of the FFCBS obligations are handled by the Federal Farm Credit Bank Funding Corporation, which sells new issues through a selling group of approximately 150 brokers and dealers and sells short-term notes through four dealers. In addition to the FFCBS, Congress in 1987 created the Farm

Credit Financial Assistance Corporation (FACO). This government-sponsored corporation provided capital to the FFCBS when it was facing financing difficulties because of loan defaults by farmers during the early 1980s.

6.4.3   Savings and Loans and Bank Financing

The savings and loans and banking crises of the 1980s led to the passage of the Federal Institutional Reform, Recovery, and Enforcement Act (FIRREA) of 1990. This Act restructured some existing agencies and created several new programs involved in regulating and insuring commercial banks, savings and loans, and savings banks. Prior to the Act, the Federal Home Loan Bank Board (FHLBB) was responsible for regulating federally chartered savings and loans and federally insured state-chartered savings and loans. The passage of the FIRREA significantly curtailed these responsibilities, shifting the FHLBB regulatory authority to the Office of Thrift Supervision and dismantling the Board but keeping the system of 12 regional Federal Home Loan Banks intact. Currently, the Federal Home Loan Bank (FHLB) system's major function is to provide a source of funds for mortgage loans to the approximately 6,500 savings and loans they support. To do this, they raise funds by issuing debt securities.[13]

The FIRREA also took away the FHLB's supervision of the insurance programs for savings and loans. Today, the Federal Deposit Insurance Corporation (FDIC) provides deposit insurance for banks (Bank Insurance Fund: BIF) and savings and loans (Savings & Loan Insurance Fund: SAIF). In this capacity, the FDIC also acts as a receiver for failed banks, acquires the assets of insolvent banks, and sets up bridge banks (new banks set up to manage a failed bank until it is sold). To facilitate the funding of such activities during the savings and loans and bank crises, Congress in 1987 created the Financing Corporation (FICO) to issue debt. FICO, in turn, issued approximately $11b of bonds (the maximum it was authorized to issue) secured by the Treasury.[14] The funding for FICO, though, was not adequate to redress the insolvent savings and loans problems. As a result, a provision in the FIRREA established the Resolution Trust Corporation (RTC) with responsibility for bailing out bankrupt savings and loans. The Resolution Funding Corporation (REFCORP) also was established to issue bonds to finance the RTC, with an initial authorization to issue up to $40b in long-term bonds secured by Treasury bonds. The RTC was responsible for selling over $450b of real estate owned by failed savings and loans. From 1989 to 1995 (when it stopped operations), the RTC seized approximately 750 insolvent savings and loans, selling over 95% of them.

6.4.4 College Student Loans

The Student Loan Marketing Association (Sallie Mae) provides funds and guarantees for lenders who provide loans for college students through the Federal Guaranteed Student Loan Program, and college loans for parents of undergraduates through the PLUS loan program (Parents Loans of Undergraduate Students program). Sallie Mae issues a variety of different debt securities, ranging from zero-coupon bonds to long-term fixed-rate securities.

6.4.5 International Financing

In addition to federal agencies, international organizations such as the International Bank for Reconstruction and Development (World Bank) and various development banks also raise funds through the sale of bonds to finance development and guarantee programs. The World Bank provides loans to private and government sectors in various countries (generally when such loans are not available from private sources) to finance public and quasi-public projects such as educational establishments, power plants, transportation systems, dams, harbors, and other infrastructures. The loans made by the World Bank usually have maturities between 10 and 30 years and often the principal is amortized. Loans are typically made to governments or to firms with guarantees from the government, with an emphasis on building a country's infrastructure. To finance these projects the World Bank borrows directly from the US and other developed countries as well as issuing short-term and intermediate-term World Bank bonds.

Similar in structure to the World Bank are various regional development banks such as the Inter-American Development Bank (IDB), Asian Development Bank (ADB), and the African Development Bank. These institutions provide financing to support private and infrastructure developments in their specific regions.

Web Information

Information on the size of the federal agency debt can be found by going to
www.bondmarkets.com

and clicking on "Research Statistics" and "Federal Agency Debt."

6.5 MUNICIPAL BONDS

In the US, it is estimated that there are as many as 80,000 state, county, and municipal governments and government authorities (agencies created by the government with the authority to float bonds).[15] There has been a substantial increase in the expenditures of these municipal government units over the last 30 years resulting from population growth, shifts from central cities to the subdivisions, and other demographic changes. In 2002, the total expenditure for all state and local governments was approximately $1.38t, three times the level of expenditures for 1980. The major expenditures were allocated to education (33%) and social services (17%), with the remainder (50%) being spread among a variety of state and local government expenditures: transportation, correction facilities, police and fire protection, public safety, environmental clean-up, and interest on debt. The total revenue generated in 2002 by all state and local governments to support these expenditures was approximately $1.28t. The major sources for this revenue came from taxes on sales (20%), property (18%), individual income (12%), and corporations (20%), federal government transfers (20%), and other sources (30%) such as user fees and lotteries.

Like corporations, state and local governments undertake many long-term capital projects such as the construction of school buildings, highways, water treatment facilities, airports, hospitals, inner-city housing, and infrastructures that facilitate economic growth and job creation. To finance these long-term capital investments, they sell two types of notes and bonds: general obligation bonds and revenue bonds. In addition to their long-term investments, state and local governments also have short-term cash flow needs created from differences in their expenditure and revenue patterns and time gaps between when projects begin and when the permanent financing supporting the projects is received. To finance their short-term cash needs, they sell short-term anticipation notes. Security traders collectively refer to short-term anticipation notes, general obligation bonds, and revenue bonds as municipals or munis. Over the last 30 years, there has been a significant increase in borrowing by state and

local government, with the debt being financed primarily through the sale of municipal securities. From 1980 to 2002, the annual issuance of state and local government securities grew from $54b to $430b.

6.5.1 Tax-Exempt Status

While there are a number of different types of municipal debt securities, one feature they all have in common is their tax-exempt status. Specifically, the interest on municipals (but not the capital gain) is exempt from federal income taxes (both personal and corporate). In addition, most states also exempt the coupon interest earned on in-state issues from state income taxes and personal property taxes where it is applicable. This tax-exempt feature makes municipals very attractive to individuals and corporations in the higher income tax brackets and investment funds whose clients are in the higher brackets. An investor in the 35% tax bracket would be indifferent, with all other factors equal, to a fully taxed bond yielding 10% and a tax-exempt bond yielding 6.5%. Alternatively stated, if the yield on a tax-exempt bond is 6.5%, the *investor's equivalent taxable yield* on a fully taxable bond is 10%:

Equivalent taxable yield

$$= \frac{\text{Tax} - \text{Exempt yield}}{(1 - \text{Tax rate})} = \frac{0.065}{1 - 0.35} = 0.10$$

Changes in tax codes affect the demand for municipal securities. If the tax rate increases and the rates on fully taxable bonds and tax-exempt bonds stay constant, then more investors will find tax-exempt bonds relatively attractive; by contrast, if tax rates decrease, tax-exempt bonds become less attractive with other factors constant. The demand for municipals decreased notably after the Tax Reform Act of 1986 lowered rates, reducing the tax-exempt benefits of municipals; the demand, though, increased in 1993 when marginal tax rates were increased. Changes in tax codes can also change the relative preferences among different groups of municipal bond investors. Until the Tax Reform Act of 1986, commercial banks were one of the larger purchasers of municipals. The lowering of the top corporate tax rate from 46% to 35%, though, led to a sizable reduction in their investment in municipal bonds. Today, the leading municipal bonds investors are individual investors and mutual funds, followed by commercial banks and property and casualty insurance companies.

It should be noted that the tax code governing tax-exempt securities is quite complex. For example, consider a municipal bond purchased at a discount from its par at the initial offering, referred to as an *original-issue discount bond (OIB)*. An investor, who buys an OIB and holds it to maturity, can treat the difference between the issued price and the par value as tax-exempt interest. If the bondholder subsequently sells the OIB before maturity, any increase in its price up to its par value is generally considered interest income and is tax exempt, while any increase above the par value is considered a capital gain and is taxable. For an investor who buys an OIB in the secondary market, though, the tax treatment depends on the purchase price relative to what the IRS defines as the market discount cutoff price (the price defining the allowable discount) and the revised issue price (price reflecting the price change over time that must be accreting). Another factor investors need to consider in determining tax liabilities is whether they leveraged the investment. In general, the interest expense on funds borrowed to purchase securities is tax deductible, except when the funds are used to purchase or carry tax-exempt securities. At one point, banks were exempt from this rule and were allowed to deduct all the interest expense; later they were allowed to deduct 85% of the interest expense; finally, in 1986, their interest deductibility for financing tax-exempt bonds was eliminated unless the issue was a bank-qualified issue (generally this is tax-exempt bonds from small issuers and purchased for an investment portfolio). In addition to defining tax-exempt interest and deductibility of interest expenses, there are other tax considerations which individual and institutional investors need to consider, such as the adjustments for specified tax preferences that some taxpayers are allowed or whether personal property taxes are levied on municipal bonds by some state and local governments.

6.5.2 Types of Municipal Securities

Municipal securities can be short-, intermediate- or long-term obligations, and they can be funded either from general tax revenues, the revenues from specific projects, or both. As previously noted, there are three types of municipals: short-term anticipation notes, general obligation bonds, and revenue bonds.

Short-Term Anticipation Notes

To finance short- to intermediate-term cash needs municipal governments issue several types of securities. These securities are sold to obtain funds in lieu of anticipated revenues. They include *tax-anticipation notes (TANs)*, *revenue-anticipation notes (RANs)*, *grant-anticipation notes (GANs)*, *bond-anticipation notes (BANs)*, and *municipal tax-exempt commercial paper*. These obligations are sold primary to local banks and money market funds. They are usually secured by the issuer's taxing power and sell at yield spreads over short-term Treasuries that reflect their tax-exempt status and credit ratings. Most are sold on a pure discount basis, with face values ranging from $5,000 to $1m and maturities ranging from 1 month to 3 years.

TANs and RANs (also referred to as TRANs) are used to cover regular recurring government expenses before taxes and other anticipated revenues are received. BANs are used as temporary financing or construction financing for long-term projects (e.g., roads, correction facilities, university buildings, and libraries), with the principal paid from the proceeds from the sale of a long-term municipal bond. For example, the construction funds needed to build a new College of Business building at the State University could be raised by the state selling a BAN, with the BAN being paid off from the proceeds from a long-term revenue bond. Finally, municipal tax-exempt commercial paper is sold primarily to finance recurring expenses. Like CP sold by corporations, tax-exempt CP has a maturity ranging from 30 days to 270 days and is often secured with a bank letter of credit, line of credit, or a purchase agreement in which the bank agrees to buy the bond if the issuer fails. Some municipal governments also finance their short-term cash needs with a tax-exempt *variable-rate demand obligation* (also called a *floating-rate obligation*). These obligations have a long-term maturity but with a coupon reset frequently (e.g., every day or week) and often with put and call options.

General Obligation Bonds

General obligation (GO) bonds are intermediate- and long-term debt obligations that are secured by the issuing government's general taxing power and can pay interest and principal from any revenue source. The GO bonds issued by states and large municipal governments that have a number of tax revenue sources are referred to as *full faith and credit obligations*. The GO bonds issued by smaller municipalities or authorities whose revenues are limited to only one or two sources (e.g., property tax) are known as *limited-tax GO bonds*. Like corporate bonds, the contract between the issuer and the investor is specified in the GO bonds' trust indenture. With municipals, this document is usually accompanied with an official statement and a legal opinion. The *official statement* is a document, similar to the prospectus for a stock or corporate bond, which details the return, risk, and other characteristics of the issue and provides information on the issuer (see exhibit 6.8). The *legal opinion* is a document that interprets legal issues related to the bond's collateral, priority of claims, and the like. Municipal bond attorneys with Wall Street-based law firms, as well as local firms, prepare legal opinions. In addition, many bank and investment banking firms have their own counsel to review and prepare such documents.

The municipal defaults that have occurred over the last 20 years and the subsequent problems related to legally defining the security, revenue sources, and priorities have made the legal opinion an important information source for assessing a municipal bond's credit risk. In evaluating the creditworthiness of a GO bond, investors need to review the legal opinion to determine the state or local government's unlimited taxing authority. The legal opinion should identify if there are any statutory or constitutional limitations on the jurisdiction's taxing power, as well as any priority of claims on general funds. The legal opinion should also specify what the bondholders' redress is in the case of a default and whether there are any statutory or constitutional questions involved. Municipal defaults are usually handled through a restructuring, which makes the security and priorities as defined in the indenture and explained in the legal opinion important in establishing the types of new debt the municipal bondholders might receive.

Revenue Bonds

Revenue bonds are municipal securities paid by the revenues generated from specific public or quasi-public projects, by the proceeds from a specific tax, or by a special assessment on an existing tax. Occasionally, revenue bonds are issued with some general obligation backing and thus have characteristics of both GO bonds and revenue bonds. For example, some revenue bonds are secured by user charges as well as a GO pledge. Such bonds are referred to as being *double barreled*. Similarly, some revenue bonds are secured by and paid from more than one revenue source. For example, some school districts issue bonds to finance certain capital projects that are paid for by property taxes earmarked for the project and are also secured by special funds of the state such that, in the event of a default, the investors can go to the state. Finally, there are *dedicated tax-backed revenue bonds* that are paid from dedicated revenues such as a tobacco settlement, lottery, or special fee. Some of the more common revenue

Exhibit 6.8 Information in official statement

- Amount of the issue
- Credit rating
- Information on issuer
- Names of the underwriters
- Selling group
- Sources of payments
- Sources and uses of fund statement
- Financial statements
- Debt service required
- Notice of any pending legislation
- Bond insurance (if any)

bonds and their characteristics are summarized in exhibit 6.9.

To the issuer, revenue bonds are an important source of funding for a number of public projects. They are used to finance major capital projects such as roads, bridges, tunnels, airports, hospitals, power-generating facilities, water treatment plants, and municipal and university buildings; they also support educational programs, inner-city housing development, and student loan programs. The revenues used to pay the interest and principal payments on these bonds are usually project specific and include tolls, rents, user charges, earmarked revenues from fees, and specific taxes. It should be noted that many revenue bonds are used to support not just public projects, but also those projects that benefit both public and private interests. In the 1980s, many private-sector companies began to use tax-exempt revenue bonds to finance industrial parks, electricity generating plants, and other capital projects. One popular revenue bond used to support private–public sector projects is the industrial development bond (IDB), also called an industrial revenue bond (IRB). Today, many state and local governments or authorities sell IDBs to finance the expansion of an area's industrial base or to attract new industries. Typically, the government or authority floats a bond issue and then uses the proceeds to build a plant or an industrial facility; it then leases the facility to a company or provides a low interest loan for the company to acquire the asset. Because of the tax-exempt status of municipal bonds, this type of financial arrangement benefits all parties: investors receive a higher after-tax yield, corporations receive lower interest rates on loans or lower rental rates, and the area benefits from a new or expanding industry.[16]

As with GO bonds, revenue bonds have an indenture, legal opinion, and an official statement. Some of the important provisions delineated in the indenture and legal opinion include: (1) whether the issuer can increase the tax or user's fee underlying the revenue source; (2) whether the issuer can incur additional debt secured by the revenue of the project (referred to as minimum revenue clauses) or under what conditions new debt can be incurred; (3) how the revenues of the project are to be directed – if

they are to be paid to bondholders after operating expenses but before other expenses (this is called a net revenue structured revenue bond) or to bondholders first (this is called a gross revenue structured bond); and (4) whether there are any additional collateral or guarantees.

6.5.3 Special Features of Municipals

Two features that are more common among municipal bonds than corporate debt securities are serialization and default insurance. As noted in chapter 5, serialization refers to the breaking up of a bond issue into different maturities. For example, to finance a $20m convention center, a county might sell a serial issue with four types of securities, each with a face value of $5m, but with one maturing in year 5, one in year 10, one in year 15, and one in year 20. Instead of a serial issue, some municipals are sold with a serial maturity structure that requires a portion of the debt to be repaid each year. Like many corporate bonds, a number of municipals are sold with the principal paid at maturity. Many of these term bonds often include sinking-fund arrangements. There are also several GO bonds and revenue bonds sold as zero-discount bonds in which the interest is equal to the difference between purchase price and the face value. Municipal governments and authorities also sell a variation of a zero-coupon bond known as a *municipal multiplier, accretion,* or *compound interest bond*. This bond pays coupon interest, which is not distributed, but rather is reinvested to the bond's maturity, making the bond similar to a zero–coupon bond.

Insured municipal bonds are ones secured by an insurance company. Insurance is provided by single-line or monoline insurance companies whose primary business is providing municipal bond insurance and by large diversified insurance companies. The major monoline insurers include AMBAC Indemnity Corporation (AMBAC), Municipal Bond Investors Assurance Company (MBIA), Capital Guaranty Insurance Company (CGIC), and Financial Guaranty Insurance Company (FGIC). The insurers write insurance policies in

Exhibit 6.9   Types of revenue bonds

Highway Revenue Bonds: These revenue bonds are used to finance highway systems and their related infrastructures (bridges, tunnels, etc.). There are two general types of highway bonds, classified in terms of how the transportation facility or highway is financed. If the highway, bridge, or tunnel is financed by a toll, then the toll revenue pays the bondholder's interest and principal payments. The quality of these bonds depends on the ability of the project to be self-supporting. Financial problems that have arisen from these bonds are often based on poor traffic projections. Alternatively, earmarked revenues from gasoline taxes, driver license fees, or auto registration fees may finance the transportation system. Analysts who evaluate the creditworthiness of bonds often look at such coverage ratios as earmarked revenue to debt service.

Water and Sewer Revenue Bonds: These bonds are issued to finance the building of water treatment plants, pumping stations, and sewers. Local governments or special bond authorities usually issue them. The bonds, in turn, are usually paid for by user charges. Covenants in the indentures may also specify that user charges be a specified proportion of debt services and reserves.

Lease Rental Bonds: These bonds are used to finance the construction of public office buildings, stadiums, university facilities, and the like, and for the purchase of computers and other types of capital equipment. The bonds are paid for by the rents generated from the users: rents, tuitions, earmarked revenues, annual appropriation of a general fund, or stadium receipts. These bonds are sometimes referred to by the facility they are financing: for example, Convention Center Revenue Bond or Sport Stadium Bond.

Hospital Revenue Bonds: These bonds are used to build or expand hospitals, to purchase medical equipment, and so on. The revenues used to finance the bonds are usually established by formulas involving a number of different levels of government and the medical facility's major source of revenue (e.g., Medicare and/or Medicaid).

Airport Revenue Bonds: Airport revenue bonds are used to finance the construction, expansion, or improvements of municipal airports. The bonds are usually secured by leases with the major airlines for the use of the terminals or by the revenues obtained from landing fees or fueling fees paid by the airlines and by the concession fees paid by terminal store users.

Industrial Development Bonds: State and local governments or authorities sell industrial development or revenue bonds (IDBs) to finance the expansion of an area's industrial base or to attract new industries. Typically, the government or authority floats a bond issue and then uses the proceeds to build a plant or an industrial facility; it then leases the facility to a company or provides a low-interest loan for the company to acquire the asset. Because of the tax-exempt status of municipal bonds, this type of financial arrangement benefits all parties: investors receive a higher after-tax yield, corporations receive lower interest rates on loans or lower rental rates, and the area benefits from a new or expanding industry. IDBs have been used to finance industrial parks, electricity-generating plants, and other projects. Because of their use in financing many inherently private-sector capital projects, the Deficit Reduction Act of 1984 placed a limit of $40m on small IDB issues, prohibited certain capital projects from IDB funding, and restricted the total amount of IDBs that could be issued by a state based on its population.

Lottery Bonds: These are secured by expected future lottery revenue. They are often used to finance the construction of new school facilities.

Pollution Control Bonds: These bonds are used to help corporations to purchase pollution control equipment. Often a municipal government will buy the equipment through the sale of the bonds and then lease the equipment to the corporation.

Resource Recovery Revenue Bonds: These bonds finance resource recovery operations that convert solid waste into commercially recoverable products and landfill residue. Revenue from these operations comes from fees for delivering garbage or sales from the products generated.

Public Power Revenue Bonds: These bonds are used to finance construction of electricity generating power plants and distribution systems. The bonds may be issued to finance the construction of one or several power plants with two or more utility companies. In this case, the issue is referred to as joint-power financing.

Sports Complex and Convention Center Bonds: These bonds are issued as permanent financing of sports stadiums and arenas and convention centers. Bonds may be lease-rental bonds paid for by rental income from the facility or they may be paid from revenue generated from outside revenue sources such as local hotel taxes or city or county taxes.

Life-Care Revenue Bonds: These bonds are issued by state and local development agencies to finance the construction of long-term residential care facilities for the elderly managed by non-profit agencies or religious groups. Revenues supporting the bonds are generated from lease rentals or lump-sum payments made by the residents.

Multi-Family Mortgage Revenue Bonds: These bonds are used to finance multi-family structures for low-income families and senior citizens. Some of the facilities are federally secured or provide interest cost subsidies under Section 236 or property tax reductions.

Single-Family Mortgage Revenue Bonds: These bonds are used to secure mortgages on single-family homes insured by FHA, VA, or private mortgage insurance.

Section 8 Bonds: These are municipal bonds issued to finance low- and middle-income rental housing. The bonds are issued under terms specified by the Federal Housing Act. Under Section 8 of the Act, the US Department of Housing and Urban Development (HUD) maintains a cash reserve for each project to protect against the failure of residents to pay rent. In some cases, eligible low-income tenants pay 15% to 30%, with the government subsidizing the remainder. The risk to bondholders comes from the apartment building not maintaining a sufficiently high occupancy rate.

College and University Revenue Bonds: These bonds are used for permanent financing of college buildings (libraries, classroom buildings, dormitories and the like) and other university capital projects (computers and networks). Bondholders' interest and principal is paid from tuition, dormitory rental fees, and special fees. They also fall under the category of lease-rental bonds.

Student-Loan Revenue Bonds: These are bonds issued by state government agencies with the proceeds used to support loans to college students. The proceeds from these bonds are often used for purchasing federally guaranteed student loans made by local banks.

Tax Allocation Bonds: These bonds are issued to finance office and property development in blighted or low-income areas. Bondholders are paid from property taxes that are expected to increase from improved real estate values.

which they agree to pay interest and principal to bondholders in the event the issuer fails to do so. The municipal issuer and not the bond investor usually pay the insurance premium. Once the insurance is issued, the insurance company has a contractual commitment to pay the bondholders if they do not receive interest or principal payments from the issuer. Currently, about 50% of all new municipal bond issues are insured.

In addition to insured bonds, two other types of municipal bonds carrying external protection are letter-of-credit (LOC) bonds and refunded bonds. *Letter-of-credit-backed municipal bonds* are secured by a letter of credit from a commercial bank. In some cases, the government unit must maintain a certain investment quality rating to maintain the guarantee. *Refunded bonds* are municipal bonds secured by an escrow fund consisting of high-quality securities such

as Treasuries and federal agencies. There are also refunded municipals backed by an escrow fund consisting of a mix of Treasuries and non-Treasuries such as municipals. Because of their backing, insured municipal bonds, LOC-backed municipals, and refunded bonds all sell at yields lower than they would without such protection.

In contrast to bonds insured or backed by a bank or collateral, Mello-Roos and moral-obligation bonds are bonds that are not fully backed. *Mello-Roos bonds* are municipal securities issued by local governments in California that are not backed by the full faith and credit of the government. These bonds were the result of Proposition 13. This law, approved in 1978, set maximum property tax rates, prohibited statewide property taxes, and required a two-thirds majority vote of the legislature for approval of any increase in state taxes. With such constraints on revenue, some local governments in California were forced to issue municipal bonds without full backing. *Moral-obligation bonds*, in turn, are bonds issued without the legislature approving appropriation. The bonds are therefore considered backed by the permissive authority of the legislature to raise funds, but not the mandatory authority.

In addition to serial municipal bonds and insured bonds, there are also GO bonds and revenue bonds introduced over the last two decades with elaborate security structures and features. For example, there are municipal put bonds (bonds that can be cashed in at a specific value before maturity), municipals with warrants that allow the holder to buy additional bonds at set prices, municipal floaters (municipal bonds with floating rate tied to a reference rate such as T-bill rates, London interbank offer rate, or municipal bond index), and minibonds (low denomination issues ($100, $500, and $1,000 par) that are sold directly to the public without an investment banker). Like Treasury stripped securities, the municipal bond market has developed interest-only and principal-only stripped municipals and floating-rate and inverse floating-rate stripped securities. Many of these municipal derivatives are created by investment banking firms, such as Goldman Sachs, Lehman Brothers, and Salomon Smith Barney, who buy municipals, place them in a trust, and then create derivative securities.

6.5.4 Default Risk and Quality Ratings

In 1975, the Urban Development Corporation of the state of New York defaulted on a $100m New York City obligation. Three years after that default, Cleveland became the first major US city since the Depression to default on its debt obligations. While both cities were able to work out arrangements with local banks to pay their creditors, these events, nevertheless, raised immediate concern among investors over the quality of municipal bonds – bonds that up until then had been considered second in security to Treasury and federal agency

securities. Unfortunately, these concerns did not abate: in the 1980s, cities such as Washington, Detroit, and Chicago experienced financial crises; approximately 70 municipalities filed for bankruptcy in 1980 (although none of them defaulted). In 1983 the Washington Public Power Supply System (WPPSS) defaulted on a $2b municipal government bond issue, with the courts ruling that bondholders did not have claims to certain revenues identified in the indenture. In the early 1990s, many states, such as California, and a number of cities experienced budget deficit problems resulting from declines in tax revenues and increases in expenditure on welfare and education, crime prevention, and the like; in 1991, 260 municipal governments defaulted. While the aggregate economic growth and prosperity experienced for most of the 1990s served to increase the revenues of many state and local governments, the financial problems faced by many governments in the 1980s and early 1990s pointed to the credit risk associated with municipals and the importance of careful and prudent credit analysis by investors in evaluating municipal bonds. A good indicator of the changes in creditworthiness of municipals during the 1990s was the number of upgrades and downgrades in quality ratings. In 1991, Standard & Poor's had 145 upgrades and 600 downgrades; in 1998, they had 647 upgrades and 128 downgrades.

To assist investors in determining the creditworthiness of municipals, Moody's, Standard & Poor's, and Fitch provide quality ratings on municipal securities similar to the ones they use for corporate bonds. Moody's has nine different categories from Aaa to C, with investment grades being Aaa to Ba. Moody's also includes a numerical modifier to indicate the degree of quality in each category (e.g., Aa1, Aa2, Aa3, A1, A2, and so on). They also use a prefix "con" to indicate when a revenue bond is dependent on the completion of a project or when there is some current limiting condition. Standard & Poor's has ten categories from AAA to D, with AAA to BBB being the investment grades. They use + and − signs to indicate relative strength and a "p" to indicate a bond with "provisional" funds. Moody's and Standard & Poor's also rate notes and tax-exempt commercial paper. Finally, Fitch provides rating categories similar to Standard & Poor's.

Table 6.7 Municipal bond ratings

Moody's ratings	Moody's description	Standard & Poor's ratings	Standard & Poor's description	Fitch ratings	Fitch description
Aaa	Best quality	AAA	Highest rating	AAA	Highest credit
Aa1	High quality	AA	Strong quality	AA	Very high credit
Aa2					
Aa3					
A1	Upper medium grade	A	Strong quality, but susceptible to adverse economic conditions.	A	High credit
A2					
A3					
Baa1					
Baa2	Medium grade	BBB	Moderate quality	BBB	Good
Baa3					
Ba1					
Ba2	Speculative	BB	Low speculation	BB	Speculative
Ba3					
B1	Highly speculative	B	Moderately speculative	B	High speculative
B2					
B3					
Caa	Poor quality				
Ca	Chance of default	CCC	Speculative	CCC	High default
C	In default	CC	Very speculative	CC	High default
		C	Bankruptcy filed	C	High default
		D	In default	DDD	In default
				DD	In default
				D	In default

Moody's: www.moodys.com; Standard & Poor's: www.standardandpoors.com; Fitch: www.fitchratings.com

Table 6.7 summarizes each of these company's ratings categories.

In determining ratings, Moody's, Standard & Poor's, and Fitch consider such factors as the amount of outstanding debt, the economic conditions of the area, the revenue sources backing the issue, the provisions specified in the indenture, and the legal opinion. If the bond is insured, Moody's and Standard & Poor's also look at the credit quality of the insurer. It should be noted that each company can rate an issue differently. When a bond is rated differently, it can reflect a different emphasis that each places on certain parameters or differences in methodologies. Approximately 50% of municipal bonds have an "A" rating, with 10% having a triple-A rating. Included in this group are many of the insured bonds and refunded issues.

6.5.5 Municipal Bond Markets

In the primary market, the sale of GO bonds and some revenue bonds is usually handled through a syndicate of commercial banks and dealers who underwrite the issue and then resell them in the open market. Traditionally, the selection of an underwriter or syndicate was done on a competitive bid basis, with many states requiring GO bonds to be marketed with competing bids. Because of the complexities with municipal bonds, more underwriters are being selected through negotiation. Many revenue bonds and some GO bonds are also sold through private placements with commercial banks, investment funds, insurance companies, and the like, and since 2000, some brokers and dealers have auctioned some municipals over the internet.

Information on upcoming municipal bond sales can be found in the *Bond Buyer*. The *Bond Buyer* is the trade publication of the municipal bond industry. It provides information on future bond sales and the results from recent sales.

In the secondary market, municipal bonds are primarily traded in the OTC market through municipal bond dealers specializing in particular issues. Local banks and regional brokerage firms often handle the issues of smaller municipalities (referred to as *local credits*), while larger investment companies and the municipal bond departments of larger banks handle the issues of larger governments. Many dealers in the secondary market make bid and asked quotes in terms of the yield to maturity or yield to call. With the wide variety of municipal bonds, the spreads on municipals can range from $\frac{1}{4}$ to 1 point. Information on trading and prices can be obtained from the *Blue List*, a daily publication of municipal bond offerings and prices published by Standard & Poor's.

Regulations

From 1930 to 1970, the municipal bond market was relatively free of federal regulations. Municipal securities were exempted from the disclosure and reporting requirements defined under the Security Acts of 1933 and 1934. However, following some of the municipal defaults and state and local government budgetary problems of the 1970s, Congress passed the Security Act Amendment of 1975 that expanded federal regulations to the municipal bond market. While the Act did not require compliance with registration requirements under the 1933 Act, it did put municipal bond dealers, brokers, and bankers under the SEC regulatory system. The amendment also mandated that the SEC establish the *Municipal Securities Rule Board (MSRB)*, a self-regulatory board responsible for establishing rules for brokers, dealers, and banks operating in the municipal bond market. As a result of this board, the Securities and Exchange Commission amended SEC Rule 15c2-12 to prohibit dealers from marketing new municipal issues if issuers did not agree to provide annual financial reports and disclose relevant events such as credit rating changes, property sales, and the like. The SEC also approved a rule limiting

the campaign contributions that municipal security dealers, brokers, and bankers could make to government officials that they did business with who were running for office.

Yield Spreads

The yields on different municipals reflect, in part, the differences in quality ratings. Like corporate bonds, the spreads between municipals with different quality ratings tend to narrow during economic upturns and widen during economic downturns, reflecting a flight to quality. The quality spread also tends to narrow during periods of low interest rates, reflecting a flight to higher yields. In addition to quality spreads, there are also geographical spreads, reflecting differences in state income taxes and perhaps some parochialism. The yields on in-state issues from states with high income taxes tend to be lower than the yields from those states with low or no state income taxes. Finally, the yield curves for municipals tend to be positively sloped and steeper than the Treasury yield curve. In addition, the municipal yield curves tend to be positively sloped even in periods when the Treasury yield curve is flat or negatively sloped.

Web Information

Information on latest events, trades, and prices on a number of the municipal bond trades can be found by accessing
   www.bloomberg.com/markets/
   rates/munievents.html
   www.investinginbonds.com and
   www.bondmarkets.com

For information on specific municipals go to
   http://bonds.yahoo.com
and click on "Bond Screener."

Information on state and local government fiscal conditions is at
   www.bea.gov

For information on municipal ratings go to
   www.moodys.com (registration required)
   www.standardandpoors.com
(registration required) and
   www.fitchratings.com

6.6 CONCLUSION

In this chapter we have examined Treasury, federal agency, and municipal securities. These securities are used to finance a myriad of capital projects, programs, and operations of federal, state, and local governments. The list of issuers of government securities is extensive: US government, government-sponsored agencies, federal agencies, states, state agencies, cities, counties, colleges, school districts, regional economic development authorities, hospitals, public power utilities, toll-road authorities, solid waste authorities, housing authorities, airports, and seaport authorities. For investors, these governments offer many types of instruments, from short-term Treasury bills and municipal anticipation notes to long-term Treasury bonds, federal agencies securities, and municipal GO bonds and revenue bonds. There are also many government securities with special features such as stripped Treasury securities and refunded municipal bonds. In the next chapter we will continue our analysis of securities by examining intermediary and international securities. As we will see, the number and different types of these securities, like corporate and government securities, are also extensive.

KEY TERMS

Government Account Series
Strip Bills
Reopenings
Tax-Anticipation Bills
Banker's Discount Yield
Purchasing-Power Risk
Real Interest Rate
Treasury Inflation Protection
  Securities (TIPS)
Treasury Strips
Principal-Only (PO) Security
Corpus
Interest-Only (IO) Securities
Treasury Income Growth
  Receipts (TIGRs)
Certificates of Accrual on
  Treasury Securities (CATS)
Trademarks
Separate Trading of Regis-
  tered Interest and Principal
  of Securities (STRIPS)
Rebundling or Reconstruction
Theoretical Spot Yield Curve
Stop Price or Stop-Out Price
English Auction or First-Price
  Sealed-Bid Auction
Dutch Auction System
On-the-Run Issues
Off-the-Run Issues
Primary Dealers
Interdealer Market
Carry Income

Position Profit
When-Issued Securities
Repurchase Agreements or
  Repos (RPs)
Reverse Repo
Collateral Seller
Collateral Buyer
Repo Rate
Term Repo
Open Repo
Dollar Repos
Federal Funds Market
Hold-In-Custody Repo or
  Letter Repo
Federally Sponsored Agencies
Federal Agencies
Government-Sponsored
  Agencies
Government-Sponsored
  Enterprises
Agency Benchmark
  Programs
Solicitation Method
Pass-Through Securities
Participation Certificates
  (PCs)
Investor's Equivalent Taxable
  Yield
Original-Issue Discount Bond
  (OIB)
Tax-Anticipation Notes
  (TANs)

Revenue-Anticipation Notes
  (RANs)
Grant-Anticipation Notes
  (GANs)
Bond-Anticipation Notes
  (BANs)
Municipal Tax-Exempt
  Commercial Paper
Variable-Rate Demand
  Obligation or Floating-Rate
  Obligation
General Obligation (GO)
  Bonds
Full Faith and Credit
  Obligations
Limited-Tax GO Bonds
Official Statement
Legal Opinion
Double Barreled
Dedicated Tax-Backed
  Revenue Bonds
Municipal Multiplier,
  Accretion, or Compound
  Interest Bond
Letter-of-Credit-Backed
  Municipal Bonds
Refunded Bonds
Mello-Roos Bonds
Moral-Obligation Bonds
Local Credits
Municipal Securities Rule
  Board (MSRB)

PROBLEMS AND QUESTIONS

1. Define and list the features of the following:

   a. T–bills
   b. T–bonds and T–notes
   c. Non–market series
   d. Treasury Strip Bills
   e. TIPS
   f. Treasury strips.

2. Determine the annual cash flows from an investment in a 4–year, 3% annual TIP bond with an original principal of $1,000, given a 2% inflation rate each year for the next 4 years.

3. Discuss the history of the stripped security market.

4. Given the following Treasury securities and their current prices:

(1) Security	(2) Type	(3) Maturity (years)	(4) Semi-annual coupon	(5) Annualized YTM	(6) Par	(7) Current price
1	T–bill	0.50	0.000	0.0500	100	97.5610
2	T–bill	1.00	0.000	0.0525	100	94.9497
3	T–note	1.50	3.000	0.0600	100	100.0000
4	T–note	2.00	3.250	0.0650	100	100.0000
5	T–note	2.50	3.500	0.0700	100	100.0000
6	T–note	3.00	3.750	0.0750	100	100.0000

   a. Using the bootstrapping approach discussed in chapter 2 generate a theoretical spot yield curve for maturities from 0.5 years to 3 years.
   b. Suppose the yields on the actual spot yield curve were equal to the YTMs on the Treasury securities shown in column 5. Determine the market prices of Treasury strips with maturities from 0.5 years to 3 years created from the 3-year T-note with a semi-annual coupon of 3.75. Determine the values of the strips in terms of semi-annual YTM equal to (Annualized YTM)/2.
   c. Explain the arbitrage that exists from buying the 3-year note, stripping it, and selling the strip securities.
   d. Suppose the actual spot yield curve converges to the theoretical spot yield curve. Determine the market prices of Treasury strips with maturities from 0.5 years to 3 years created from the 3-year T-note with semi-annual coupons of 3.75. Does an arbitrage exist from buying the 3-year note, stripping it, and selling the strip securities?
   e. Comment on the actual yield curve being the theoretical spot yield curve.

5. Outline how the Treasury auction process works.

6. Given the following information on a Treasury auction for a 91–day T-bill issue:

   • Volume of T–bills requested by Treasury = $15b
   • Total volume of T–bills bids submitted = $16.5b
   • Volume of non–competitive T–bill bids submitted = $2b

- Volume of competitive T-bill bids submitted = $14.5b, broken down as follows:

Bid yield	Bid price	Quantity of bid (in billions)
2.750	99.3049	0.4
2.755	99.3036	0.5
2.760	99.3023	0.8
2.765	99.3011	1.3
2.770	99.2998	1.4
2.775	99.2985	1.5
2.800	99.2922	1.6
2.825	99.2859	1.7
2.830	99.2846	1.4
2.835	99.2834	1.3
2.840	99.2821	1.6
2.845	99.2808	0.5
2.850	99.2796	0.5
	Total	14.5

    a. What is the auction's stop price?
    b. How many bids (in dollars) are accepted above the stop price?
    c. What proportion of their request do bids at the stop price receive?
    d. What is the weighted average bid that the non-competitive bidders receive?
    e. What is the tail?

7. What is the difference between the English auction used by the Treasury and a Dutch auction?

8. What are the sources of income for security dealers?

9. What are on-the-run and off-the-run issues?

10. What is the interdealer market?

11. Explain how a repurchase agreement and reverse repurchase agreement are created.

12. A security dealer plans to purchase $100m of T-notes at the next auction. She anticipates holding the securities one day and plans to finance the purchase with an overnight repurchase agreement. Currently overnight repo rates are at 3%.

    a. Explain how the repurchase agreement would work in this case.
    b. Determine the dollar interest, selling price, and repurchase price on the repurchase agreement.
    c. What type of repurchase agreement would the dealer need if she thought there was a possibility that it could take several days to sell her securities?

13. Explain how the following institutions use repurchase agreements:

    a. Commercial banks
    b. Security dealers
    c. Federal Reserve.

14. Explain the default risk associated with a repurchase agreement and how the risk can be reduced.

15. What was the 1985 repo scandal? What factors contributed to the scandal? What were some of the reforms that resulted from the scandal?

16. Explain the role of federal agencies in the capital formation process.

17. Briefly explain the history of the secondary mortgage market.

18. Explain the purposes of the following:

    a. FNMA, GNMA, and FHLMC
    b. The Federal Agriculture Mortgage Corporation
    c. Federal Farm Credit Banks System
    d. Federal Home Loan Bank System
    e. Student Loan Marketing Association, Sallie Mae
    f. World Bank.

19. Describe the solicitation method used by fiscal agents, brokers, and dealers to sell federal agency securities in the primary market.

20. Define the following types of municipal bonds:

    a. General obligations
    b. Full-faith and credit obligations
    c. Limited-tax general obligations
    d. Revenue bonds
    e. Double-barreled revenue bonds.

21. What are some of the important provisions specified in the legal opinion of a municipal general obligation bond that a bond investor should consider in evaluating a municipal bond?

22. Describe some of the different types of municipal anticipation notes that are issued by state and local governments.

23. Explain how changes in tax rates affect the market for municipal securities.

24. How did the Tax Reform Act of 1986 affect commercial bank investments in municipal securities?

25. List some of the capital projects and programs that municipal governments finance with revenue bonds.

26. Explain how municipal governments use industrial revenue bonds. Comment on why they are a popular source of financing for regional economic development.

27. What are some of the important provisions specified in the official statement and the legal opinion of a municipal revenue bond that a bond investor should consider in evaluating a municipal bond?

28. Explain the following special features and types of municipal bonds:

    a. Serial issue
    b. Insured bonds
    c. Letter-of-credit-backed municipal bonds
    d. Mello-Roos bonds
    e. Refunded bonds
    f. Moral-obligation bonds.

29. How are many large municipal bond issues sold in the primary market?

30. Describe the secondary market for municipals.

31. What is the Municipal Securities Rule Board?

WEB EXERCISES

1. Find the yields on T-bills and T-bonds at recent Treasury auctions by going to www.publicdebt.treas.gov and clicking on "Current and Historical Auction." What is the current public debt?

2. Check to see if there have been any changes in the primary security dealers list shown in exhibit 6.4 by going to www.newyorkfed.org/markets/pridealers_listing.html.

3. Treasury-Inflation Index securities were quite popular when they were first introduced. Find the yields on such securities by going to www.economagic.com and clicking on "Interest Rates" and "Treasury-Inflation Index Bonds and Notes."

4. Explore the growth and distribution trends in federal agency securities, municipal securities, and US Treasury securities by going to www.bondmarkets.com. At the site, click on "Research Statistics" and find the following:
   a. The largest issuers of federal agency securities by clicking on "Federal Agency Debt" and "Federal Agency Issuance."
   b. The largest holders of municipal securities by clicking on "Municipal Securities" and "Trends in Holdings." Comment on the historical trend you observe in commercial bank holdings of municipals. What do you attribute this trend to?
   c. The largest holders of Treasury securities by clicking on "U.S. Treasury Ownership."
   d. The growth in repurchase agreements as a source of dealer financing by clicking on "Funding/Repo."

5. Changes in the government debt depend on the federal government expenditures and revenues. Recent and historical information on the US budget can be found at www.gpo.gov/usbudget. At this site, go to "Budget," "List of Spreadsheet," "Historical Tables," and "Summary of Receipts and Outlays." Comment on the number of budget deficits that have occurred over the last 20 years.

6. Determine the growth in the government's debt over the last 20 years by going to www.economagic.com and clicking on "Federal Reserve Bank – Saint Louis" and then going to "Gross Federal Debt held by Public."

7. Find the current yields on municipal bonds given different quality ratings by going to http://bonds.yahoo.com and clicking on "Composite Bond Rates." What is the spread between the AAA 10-year municipal and 10-year T-bond? Comment on why the spread is small or even negative.

8. Use the bond selector at http://bonds.yahoo.com to identify several municipal bonds that have certain features you select.

9. Identify state and local governments that have had ratings changes recently by going to www.moodys.com and clicking on "U.S. Public Finance" and "Ratings Actions." Identify companies on the watch list by clicking on "Watch List." Note: registration required.

10. Take a state and local government on Moody's "Watch List" or with a recent rating change and do an analysis of it with information obtained from the Bureau of Economic Analysis website: www.bea.gov. At the site, go to "Regional" data. You may want to look at personal income, state output, or employment data. State and local government information can also be found by going to www.economagic.com. At the site, click "Browse by Region" or "Bureau of Labor Statistics – State and City Employment."

NOTES

1. There was a threat of default in 1996 due to a political debate over the budget between President Clinton and the US Congress. The debate led to a temporary impasse in which Congress refused to approve a spending program.
2. The Treasury also sells *tax-anticipation bills* to corporations four times a year. The bills mature 1 week after a corporate tax payment is due. They are used to pay corporate taxes.
3. On November 1, 2001, the Treasury announced that they were stopping the issuance of 30-year bonds.
4. Since TIPS pay semi-annual interest, the inflation-indexed principal is based on an interpolation between the two most recent months' CPIs reported prior to the settlement month.
5. At one point, the US Treasury was not a supporter of stripped securities because of their lower tax liability.
6. New Treasuries can also be purchased online. For T-bills, investors can purchase new issues on Thursdays after the Monday auction.
7. Primary dealers are also members of the Treasury Borrowing Advisory Committee. This committee advises the Treasury on the types of securities to sell.
8. Dealers give government security brokers their bid or offer price. The brokers then display the highest bid and lowest offer through a computer network tied to trading desks of dealers.
9. Note that in the case of term repos, the collateral seller still receives any interest paid on the securities.
10. Treasury issues that are in high demand by dealers as a result of their short position are called "specials." Specials can trade 30 BP to 50 BP below other comparable securities.
11. Pensions are prohibited from investing in reverse repos; thus, lending securities gives them the equivalent of a reverse repo.
12. The Resolution Trust Corporation initially issued a 40-year bond. This issue, though, was not successful.
13. The interest on the securities is taxed at the federal level, but not at state and local levels.
14. FICO was created as a provision in the Competitive Equality and Banking Act of 1987.
15. The actual number varies depending on how funding authorities are counted and how long they have existed. Bloomberg, for example, estimates the total number to be closer to 60,000. Whether 60,000 or 80,000, the number is still impressive.
16. The Deficit Reduction Act of 1984 places a limit of $40m on small IDB issues, prohibits certain capital projects from IDB funding, and restricts the total amount of IDBs that can be issued by a state based on its population.

SELECTED REFERENCES

Bikchandani, S. and C. Huang "Auction with Resale Markets: An Exploratory Model of Treasury Bill Markets," *The Review of Financial Studies* 2 (1993): 311–39.

Bollenbacher, G. *The Professional's Guide to the U.S. Government Securities Markets: Treasuries, Agencies, Mortgage-backed Instruments* (New York Institute of Finance, 1988).

Cammack, E. "Evidence of Bidding Strategies and the Information in Treasury Bill Auctions." *Journal of Political Economy* 99 (1991): 100–30.

Dupont, Dominique and Brian Sack "The Treasury Securities Market: Overview and Recent Developments," *Federal Reserve Bulletin* (December 1999): 785–806.

Jegadeesh, N. "Treasury Auction Bids and the Salomon Squeeze," *Journal of Finance* 18 (1993): 1403–19.

Mishkin, Frederic S. and Stanley G. Eakins *Financial Markets and Institutions* 4th edn (Addison-Wesley, 2003).

Rose, Peter S. *Money and Capital Markets* (New York: McGraw-Hill/Irwin, 2003).

Sorensen, Bent E. and Oved Yosha "Is State Fiscal Policy Asymmetric over the Business Cycle?" *Economic Review* (Federal Reserve Bank of Kansas City, Third Quarter 2001): 43–64.

Stigum, M. *The Money Market* (Homewood, IL: Dow-Jones Irwin, 1983).

Sundaresan, S. "An Empirical Analysis of U.S. Treasury Auctions: Implications for Auction and Term Structure Theories," *Journal of Fixed Income* 4 (1994): 35–50.

CHAPTER SEVEN

INTERMEDIARY AND INTERNATIONAL DEBT SECURITIES

7.1 INTRODUCTION

The intermediary financial market consists of commercial banks, savings and loans, insurance companies, investment funds, and other financial intermediaries. These intermediaries sell financial claims to investors, and then use the proceeds to purchase debt and equity claims or to provide direct loans. Commercial banks, for example, obtain funds from investors by providing demand deposits and money market accounts, selling certificates of deposit, and borrowing from other banks. They, in turn, use their funds to satisfy legal reserve requirements, to make loans, and to purchase financial securities. Savings and loans and savings banks function very similarly to commercial banks, except that their use of funds is directed more towards the creation of mortgage loans. Finally, life insurance companies, pensions, trust funds, and investment funds offer financial instruments in the form of insurance policies, retirement plans, and shares in stock or bond portfolios. The proceeds from their premiums, savings plans, and fund shares are used by these institutions to buy stocks, corporate bonds, Treasury securities and other debt instruments, as well as provide corporate, residential, and commercial loans.

In general, financial institutions, by acting as intermediaries, control a large amount of funds and thus have a significant impact on the security markets. For borrowers, intermediaries are an important source of funds; they buy many of the securities issued by corporations and governments and provide many of the direct loans. For investors, intermediaries create a number of securities for them to include in their short-term and long-term portfolios. These include negotiable certificates of deposit, banker's acceptances, mortgage-backed instruments, investment fund shares, annuities, and guaranteed investment contracts. In this chapter, we examine intermediaries and the markets for intermediary securities.

In addition to intermediary securities, the other major group of debt securities we have not yet examined is international. As noted in chapter 1, international investment has been growing throughout the world. Over the last 20 years, many multinational corporations and governments have increased the sales of their securities in external markets to raise funds to finance their global operations, while many investors have found diversification benefits by including international securities in their portfolios. In this chapter, we also examine the characteristics and markets for international debt securities.

7.2 NEGOTIABLE CERTIFICATES OF DEPOSIT

7.2.1 Characteristics

Banks and thrift institutions issue negotiable certificates of deposit (CDs) to finance their loans and investments.[1] They are one of the most popular money market instruments. The maturities on negotiable CDs generally range from 3 to 18 months, although most have maturities of 6 months or less. CDs issued with maturities greater than 1 year are called *term CDs*. CDs are interest-bearing notes, usually sold at their face value, with the principal and interest paid at maturity if the CD is less than 1 year and semi-annually if it is a term CD. The minimum denomination on negotiable CDs is $100,000, with the average denomination being $1m; there are also *jumbo CDs* with face values of $10m or more. Like other bank and savings and loan deposits, the Federal Deposit Insurance Corporation (FDIC) insures CDs up to $100,000 against default. Most negotiable CDs, though, have denominations exceeding $100,000 and are therefore subject to default risk. In the 1980s, it was possible for large investors to avoid such risk by investing in *brokered deposits* that spread the investment across a number of CDs, each with denominations of $100,000 or less.[2] The Federal Deposit Insurance Corporation Improvement Act (FDICIA) of 1991, though, limited the FDIC's insurance on brokered deposits to those established for pension plans at well-capitalized banks. The yields on CDs tend to exceed the rates on Treasury and short-term federal agency instruments. Also, the yields for the CDs of larger (supposedly more secured) banks (called *prime CDs*) tend to be lower than those of smaller banks (called *non-prime CDs*). Finally, the rates that banks pay on CDs are quoted on a 360-day basis, instead of 365 days. Thus, an investor buying a $1m CD, maturing in 180 days and paying 6% interest, would receive $1,030,000 from the bank at maturity ($1,000,000[1 + 0.06(180/360)] = $1,030,000). Quotes of CDs trading in the secondary market, in turn, are made in terms of the bank's discount yield. Thus, if the CD yielding 6% were trading in the secondary market, its rate would be quoted at 5.8% (($1,030,000 − $1,000,000)/ $1,030,000)(360/180) = 0.058).

7.2.2 Markets

Today, approximately 25 dealers and brokers form the core of the primary and secondary markets for CDs, selling new CDs and trading and maintaining inventories in existing ones. Money market funds, banks, bank trust departments, state and local governments, foreign governments and central banks, and corporations are the major investors in CDs.[3] While many of these investors hold their CDs until maturity, there does exist an active secondary market for these instruments. In fact, it was the creation of the secondary market for CDs in 1961 that helped to make CDs popular. (See exhibit 7.1 for a brief history of the secondary market for CDs and its significance.)

There are three types of CDs: domestic, foreign, and Eurodollar. From a US investor's perspective, domestic CDs are those issued by US banks, while foreign CDs are dollar-denominated CDs issued by foreign banks through their US branches; they are often referred to as *Yankee CDs*. Eurodollar CDs, in turn, are dollar-denominated CDs often issued out of London by foreign branches of banks from the US, Europe, and Japan that are incorporated in countries with favorable banking laws. The yields on dollar-denominated Eurodollar CDs are higher than the yields on domestic CDs. This is because foreign subsidiary banks issuing the CDs are incorporated in countries with banking laws that have low or zero reserve requirements.[4]

The growth of the CD market over the last two decades has been accompanied by innovations. In the 1980s, a *floating-rate CD (FRCD)* was introduced. The maturity on an FRCD ranges from 18 months to 5 years, with the coupon rates reset periodically to equal the rate on a comparable CD rate or the London interbank offer rate (this rate is discussed in section 7.8.6). Other CDs with unique features that have been introduced over the years are ones with rates tied to the stock market (*bear and bull CDs*), longer-term CDs with gradually increasing rates (*rising-rates CDs*), and contracts to buy CDs now and in the future (*forward CDs* and *rollover* or *roly-poly CDs*).

Exhibit 7.1   History of the secondary CD market

Prior to 1961, commercial banks lacked an effective instrument to compete for the temporary excess cash funds of corporations and state and local governments. At that time, there was no interest paid on demand deposits, and corporations were reluctant to tie their funds up in non-negotiable CDs. Also, with the rates paid on time deposits fixed by the Federal Reserve's Regulation Q, sometimes at a level below T-bill rates, banks had no security to offer corporations. Consequently, corporations tended to opt for T-bills instead of bank deposits when they invested their excess funds.

The solution to the problem for banks came in 1961 when First Bank of New York (now Citicorp) issued a negotiable CD, accompanied by an announcement by First Boston Corporation and Salomon Brothers that they would stand ready to buy and sell the CDs. Thus, the first secondary market for CDs was born. Moreover, what the secondary market provided was a way for banks to circumvent Regulation Q and offer investors rates competitive with T-bills. To do this, the yield curve needed to be positively sloped and remain that way for the foreseeable future. With Regulation Q setting higher maximum rates on longer-term CDs and the Fed rarely changing the maximum rate, these conditions were met. The existence of a secondary market meant that an investor could earn a rate higher than either the short or longer term CD, by buying the longer term CD and selling it later in the secondary market at a higher price associated with the short-term maturity. For example, if 6-month CDs yielded 5% ($P = 100/(1.05)^{0.5} = 97.59$) and a 1-year CD yielded 6% ($P = 100/1.06 = 94.3396$), then an investor could buy the 1-year CD for 94.3396, hold it for 6 months, and sell it for 97.59 (given the yield curve did not change) to realize an annualized yield of 7% ($= (97.59/94.3396)^{1/0.5} - 1$). Thus, to recapitulate, the significance of the secondary market for CDs was that it provided a way for banks to increase their CD yields to customers without violating Regulation Q.

Following First Bank of New York, Salomon Brothers, and First Boston's lead, other banks, brokers, and dealers quickly entered into the market for negotiable CDs.

7.2.3 Bank Notes

In addition to CDs, commercial banks also issue *bank notes*. Bank notes are similar to medium-term notes. They are sold as a program consisting of a number of notes with different maturities, typically ranging from 1 to 5 years, and offered either continuously or intermittently. Bank notes are usually sold to institutions in high denominations ranging from $5m to $25m, with the total offering ranging from $50m to $1b. Different from corporate MTNs discussed in chapter 5, bank notes are not registered with the SEC, unless it is the bank's holding company, and not the individual bank, issuing the MTN. Banks also sell bank notes and MTNs through international syndicates as part of the Eurocapital market (discussed later in this chapter.)

> **Web Information**
> Yields on CDs and Eurodollar CDs can be found at
>   www.federalreserve.gov/releases

7.3 BANKER'S ACCEPTANCES

Banker's acceptances (BAs) are time drafts (postdated checks) guaranteed by a bank – guaranteed postdated checks. The guarantee of the bank improves the credit quality of the draft, making it marketable. BAs are used to finance the purchase of goods that have to be transferred from a seller to a buyer. They are often created in international business transactions where finished goods or commodities have to be shipped.

To see how BAs originate, consider the case of a US oil refinery that wants to import 80,000 barrels of crude oil at $25 per barrel ($2m) from an oil producer in South America. Suppose the South American oil exporter wants to be paid before shipping, while the US importer wants the crude oil before payment. To facilitate the transaction, suppose they agree to finance the sale with a BA in which the US importer's banks will guarantee a $2m payment 60 days from the shipment date. With this understanding, the US oil importer would obtain a letter of credit (LOC) from his bank. The LOC would say that the bank would pay the exporter $2m if the US importer failed to do so. The LOC would then be sent by the US bank to the South American bank of the exporter. Upon receipt of the LOC, the South American bank would notify the oil exporter who would then ship the 80,000 barrels of crude oil. The oil exporter would then present the shipping documents to the South American bank and receive the present value of $2m in local currency from the bank. The South American bank would then present a time draft to the US bank who would stamp "accepted" on it, thus creating the BA. The US importer would sign the note and receive the shipping documents. At this point, the South American bank is the holder of the BA. The bank can hold the BA as an investment or sell it to the American bank at a price equal to the present value of $2m. If the South American bank opts for the latter, then the US bank holds the BA and can either retain it or sell it to an investor such as a money market fund or a BA dealer. If all goes well, at maturity the oil importer will present the shipping documents to the shipping company to obtain his 80,000 barrels of crude oil, as well as deposit the $2m funds in his bank; whoever is holding the BA on the due date will present it to the US importer's bank to be paid.

The use of BAs to finance transactions is known as *acceptance financing* and banks that create BAs are referred to as *accepting banks*. In the US, the major accepting banks are the money center banks such as Citicorp and Bank of America, as well as some large regional banks. Many of the large Japanese banks have also been active in creating BAs. In the secondary market, BAs are traded as pure discount bonds, with the face value equal to the payment order and with the maturity between 30 and 270 days. With the bank guarantee, they are considered prime-quality instruments with relatively low yields.[5] The secondary market trading of BAs takes place principally among banks and dealers. There are approximately 20 dealers who facilitate trading in the secondary market. The major dealers include the major investment banking firms such as Merrill Lynch (the largest dealer) and Shearson Lehman, as well as a number of money center banks. Money market funds, banks, institutional investors, non-financial corporations, and

municipal governments are the primary purchasers of BAs. The Federal Reserve also buys and sells BAs as part of its open market operations, and commercial banks use BAs as collateral for Federal Reserve loans.

The market for BAs has existed for over 70 years in the US, although its origin dates back to the twelfth century. In the US, this market grew steadily in the 1960s and 1970s. From 1970 to 1985 the market accelerated from $7.6b in 1970 to almost $80b in 1985, reflecting the growth in world trade. Due to alternative financing, though, the BA market has declined marginally since 1985.

Web Information

Historical data on BAs' yields can be found at
    www.federalreserve.gov/releases

For market data on the size of the market for BAs go to
    www.bondmarkets.com

and click on "Research Statistics" and "Money Market Instruments."

7.4 MORTGAGE-BACKED AND ASSET-BACKED SECURITIES

Up until the mid-seventies most home mortgages originated when savings and loans, commercial banks, and other thrift institutions borrowed funds or used their deposits to provide loans to home purchasers, possibly later selling the resulting instruments in the secondary market to the Federal National Mortgage Association (FNMA) or the Government National Mortgage Association (GNMA). To a large degree, individual deposits financed real estate, with little financing coming from corporations or institutions. In an effort to attract institutional funds away from corporate bonds and other capital market securities, as well as to minimize the poor hedge (short-term deposit liabilities and long-term mortgage assets), financial institutions began to sell mortgage-backed securities in the 1970s. These securities provided them with an instrument that could compete more closely with corporate bonds for inclusion in the portfolios of institutional investors, and they provided the mortgage industry with more liquidity.

By definition, mortgage-backed securities (MBSs) are instruments that are backed by a pool of mortgage loans. Typically, a financial institution, agency, or mortgage banker buys a pool of mortgages of a certain type from mortgage originators (e.g., Federal Housing Administration-insured mortgages or mortgages with a certain minimum loan-to-value ratio or a specified payment-to-income ratio). This mortgage portfolio is financed through the sale of the MBS, which has a claim on the portfolio. The mortgage originators usually agree to continue to service the loans, passing the payments on to the mortgage-backed security holders. An MBS investor has a claim on the cash flows from the mortgage portfolio. This includes interest on the mortgages, scheduled payment of principal, and any prepaid principal. Since many mortgages are prepaid early as homeowners sell their homes or refinance their current mortgages, the cash flows from a portfolio of mortgages, and therefore the return on the MBS, can be quite uncertain. To address this type of risk, a number of derivative MBSs were created in the 1980s. For example, in the late 1980s Freddie Mac introduced *collateralized mortgage obligations (CMOs)*. These securities had different maturity claims and different levels of prepayment risk.

An MBS is an asset-backed security created through a method known as *securitization*. Securitization is a process of transforming illiquid financial assets into marketable capital market instruments. Today, it is applied not only to mortgages but also to home equity loans, automobile loans, lines of credit, credit card receivables, and leases. Securitization is one of the most important financial innovations introduced in the last two decades; it is examined in detail in chapter 11.

7.5   INVESTMENT FUNDS

Major brokerage and investment firms and banks offer a wide variety of investment funds. For many investors, shares in these funds are an alternative to directly buying stocks and bonds. Fund investment provides several advantages over directly purchasing securities.

First, investment funds provide divisibility. An investment company offering shares in a portfolio of negotiable, high-denomination CDs, for example, makes it possible for small investors to obtain a higher rate than they could obtain by investing in a lower yielding, small-denomination CD. Second, an investment in a fund consisting of a portfolio of securities often provides an investor with more liquidity than forming his own portfolio; that is, it is easier for an individual investor to buy and sell a share in an investment fund than it is to try to buy and sell a number of securities. Third, the investment companies managing funds provide professional management. They have a team of security analysts and managers who know the markets and the securities available. They buy and sell securities for the fund, reinvest dividends and interest, and maintain records. Finally, since investment companies often buy large blocks of securities, they can obtain lower brokerage fees and commission costs for their investors. In summary, funds provide investors with the benefits of divisibility, diversification, and lower transaction costs.

7.5.1   The Market for Funds

From the end of World War II to the late 1960s, investments in funds grew substantially, boasting as many as 40m investors in the 1960s. Most of the investment funds consisted of stocks, with their popularity attributed primarily to the general rise in stock prices during that period. In the 1970s, investments in funds declined as stock prices fell due to rising energy prices, inflation, and recession. During this period, a number of funds specializing in debt securities were introduced. In the mid-1980s and in the 1990s, though, the popularity of fund investments rebounded. This more recent growth can be attributed to not only the bull market of the 1990s, but also to financial innovations. In addition to the traditional stock funds, investment companies today offer shares in bond funds (municipal bonds, corporate bonds, high-yield bonds, foreign bonds, etc.), *money market funds* (consisting of CDs, CP, Treasury securities, etc.), *index funds* (funds whose values are highly correlated with a stock or bond index), funds with options and futures, *global funds* (funds with stocks and bonds from different countries), and even *vulture funds* (funds consisting of debt securities of companies that are in financial trouble or in Chapter 11 bankruptcy).

A number of investment companies, such as Fidelity and Vanguard, manage a family of mutual funds. From this family (sometimes referred to as a complex) these investment companies are able to offer investors different funds based on the investor's risk–return preferences. Currently there are over 8,000 funds in the US; a number that exceeds the number of stocks listed on the NYSE. Contributing to this large number is the increased percentage of fund investment coming from retirement investments such as individual retirement accounts (IRAs) and 401(k) accounts (discussed in section 7.6). As of year 2000, mutual funds accounted for approximately 21% ($2.5t) of the estimated $12t retirement investment market.

7.5.2 Structure of Funds

There are three types of investment fund structures: open-end funds (also called mutual funds), closed-end funds, and unit investment trusts. The first two can be defined as managed funds, while the third is an unmanaged one.

Open-End Fund

Open-end funds (mutual funds) stand ready to buy back shares of the fund at any time the fund's shareholders want to sell, and they stand ready to sell new shares any time an investor wants to buy into the fund. Technically, a mutual fund is an open-end fund. The term mutual fund, though, is often used to refer to both open- and closed-end funds. With an open-end fund the number of shares can change frequently. The price an investor pays for a share of an open-end fund is equal to the fund's *net asset value (NAV)*. At a given point in time, the NAV of the fund is equal to the difference between the value of the fund's assets (V_t^A) and its liabilities (V_t^L) divided by the number of shares outstanding (N_t): $NAV_t = (V_t^A - V_t^L)/N_t$. For example, suppose a balanced stock and bond fund consists of a stock portfolio with a current market value of

$100m, a corporate bond portfolio with a current market value of $100m, liquid securities of $8m, and liabilities of $8m. The current net worth of this fund would be $200m. If the fund, in turn, has 4 million shares outstanding, its current NAV would be $50 per share: NAV = ($208m − $8m)/4m = $50. This value, though, can change if the number of shares, the asset values, or the liability values change.

Open-end funds can be classified as either *load funds* or *no-load funds*. Load funds are sold through brokers or other intermediates; as such, the shares in load funds sell at their NAV plus a commission. The fees are usually charged up-front when investors buy new shares. Some funds charge a redemption fee (also called an exit fee or back-end load) when investors sell their shares back to the fund at their NAV. No-load funds, on the other hand, are sold directly by the fund and therefore sell at just their NAV. The fund does charge fees for management and for transferring individual investments from one fund to another. Many of these funds are advertised in the financial sections of newspapers, often with a toll-free number that investors can call for information.

Closed-End Fund

A *closed-end fund* has a fixed number of non-redeemable shares sold at its initial offering. Unlike an open-end fund, the closed-end fund does not stand ready to buy existing shares or sell new shares. The number of shares of a closed-end fund is therefore fixed.[6] An investor who wants to buy shares in an existing closed-end fund can do so only by buying them in the secondary market from an existing holder. Shares in existing funds are traded on the over-the-counter market. Interestingly, the prices of many closed-end funds often sell at a discount from their NAVs.

Unit Investment Trust

Although the composition of open- and closed-end fund investments can change as managers buy and sell securities, the funds themselves usually have unlimited lives. In contrast, a *unit investment trust* has a specified number of fixed-income securities that are rarely changed, and the fund usually has a fixed life. A unit investment trust is formed by a sponsor (investment company) who buys a specified number of securities, deposits them with a trustee, and then sells claims on the security, known as *redeemable trust certificates*, at their NAV plus a commission fee. These trust certificates entitle the holder to proportional shares in the income from the deposited securities. For example, an investment company might purchase $20m worth of Treasury bonds, place them in a trust, and then issue 20,000 redeemable trust certificates at $1,025 per share: NAV + commission = ($20m/20,000) + $25 = $1,025. If the investment company can sell all of the shares, it will be able to finance the $20m bond purchase and earn a 2.5% commission of $500,000.

Most unit investment trusts are formed with fixed-income securities: government securities, corporate bonds, municipal bonds, and preferred stock. The trustee pays all the interest and principal generated from the bonds to the certificate holders. Unlike open- and closed-end funds, when the securities in the pool mature, the investment trust ceases. Depending on the types of bonds, the maturity on a unit investment trust can vary from 6 months to 20 years. The holders of the securities, though, usually can sell their shares back to the trustee prior to maturity at their NAV plus a load. To finance the purchase of the certificate, the trustee often sells a requisite amount of securities making up the trust.

7.5.3 Types of Investment Funds

A Board of Directors elected by the fund's shareholders determines the general investment policies of open- and closed-end investment funds. Typically, a management or investment advisory firm, often consisting of those who originally set up the fund, does the actual implementation and management of the policies. Some funds are actively managed, with fund managers aggressively buying stocks and bonds, while others follow a more passive buy and hold investment strategy.

One way of grouping the many types of funds is according to the classifications defined by Weisenberger's *Annual Investment Companies*

Manual for growth funds, income funds, and balanced funds. *Growth funds* are those whose primary goal is in long-term capital gains. Such funds tend to consist primarily of those common stocks offering growth potential. Many of these are diversified stock funds, although there are some that specialize in certain sectors. *Income funds* are those whose primary goal is providing income. These funds are made up mainly of stocks paying relatively high dividends or bonds with high coupon yields. Finally, *balanced funds* are those with goals somewhere between those of growth and income funds. Balanced funds are constructed with bonds, common stocks, and preferred stocks that are expected to generate moderate income with the potential for some capital gains.

A second way of classifying funds is in terms of their specialization. There are four general classifications: equity funds, bond funds, hybrid funds (stocks and bonds), and money market funds. As shown in exhibit 7.2, each of

Exhibit 7.2   Categories of investment funds

Equity funds
Value funds
Growth funds
Sector funds
World equity funds
Emerging market funds
Regional equity funds
Taxable bond funds (short-, intermediate-, and long-term)
Corporate bond funds
High-yield funds
Global bond funds
Government bond funds
Mortgage-backed securities
Tax-free bond funds (short-, intermediate-, and long-term)
State municipal bond funds
National municipal bond funds
Hybrid funds
Asset allocation funds
Balanced funds
Income-mixed funds
Money market funds
Taxable money market funds
Tax-exempt money market funds

these fund types can be broken down further by their specified investment objectives. Bond funds, for example, can be classified as corporate, municipal, government, high-yield, global, mortgage-backed securities, and tax-free. Each category reflects a different investment objective: municipal bond funds, for example, specialize in providing investors with tax-exempt municipal securities; corporate bond funds are constructed to replicate the overall performance of a certain type of corporate bond, with a number of them formed to be highly correlated with a specific index such as the Shearson–Lehman index; money market funds are constructed with money market securities in order to provide investors with liquid investments.

7.5.4 Accumulation Plans

Typically, most fund investors buy shares and receive cash from the fund when it is distributed. For investors looking for different cash flow patterns, investment funds also provide voluntary and contractual accumulation plans with different types of contributions and withdrawal plans. Included here are automatic reinvestment plans in which the net income and capital gains of the fund are reinvested, with the shareholders accumulating additional shares, and fixed contribution plans in which investors contribute (either contractually or voluntarily) a fixed amount on a regular basis for a set period.

7.5.5 Taxes and Regulations

Most mutual funds make two types of payments to their shareholders: a net income payment from dividends and interest and a realized capital gains payment. If an investment fund complies with certain rules, it does not have to pay corporate income taxes. To qualify for this favorable tax treatment, the company must have a diversified portfolio and it must pay out at least 90% of the fund's net income to shareholders. As a result, most investment companies distribute all of the net income from the fund to their shareholders. Investment companies can either distribute or retain their realized capital gains. Most investment companies distribute capital gains. If they retain the gain, they are

required to pay a tax equal to the maximum personal income tax rate; the shareholders, in turn, receive a credit for the taxes paid.[7]

7.5.6 Bond Market Indexes

As noted, bond funds can be classified as corporate, municipal, government, high-yield, global, mortgage-backed securities, and tax-free. Each category reflects a different investment objective. The managers of these various bond funds, as well as the managers of pension, insurance, and other fixed-income funds, often evaluate the performance of their funds by comparing their fund's return with those of an appropriate bond index. In addition, many funds are constructed so that their returns replicate those of a specified index.

A number of bond indexes have been developed in recent years on which bond funds can be constructed or benchmarked. The most well known indexes are those constructed by Dow Jones that are published daily in the *Wall Street Journal*. A number of investment companies also publish a variety of indexes; these include Lehman Brothers, Merrill Lynch, Salomon Smith Barney, First Boston, and J. P. Morgan. The indexes can be grouped into three categories: US investment grade bond indexes (including Treasuries), US high-yield bond indexes, and global government bond indexes. Within each category, subindexes are constructed based on sector, quality ratings, or country. Table 7.1 summarizes some of the indexes.

7.5.7 Other Investment Funds

In addition to open-end and closed-end investment funds and unit investment trusts, two other investment funds of note are real estate investment trusts and hedged funds.

Real Estate Investment Trust (REIT)

A REIT is a fund that specializes in investing in real estate or real estate mortgages. The trust acts as an intermediary, selling stocks and warrants and issuing debt instruments (bonds,

Table 7.1 Bond market indexes

Index	Number of issues	Maturity	Size ($ millions)	Subindexes
US investment grade bond				
Lehman Brothers Aggregate	5,000	Over 1 year	Over 100	Government, corporate, government/corporate mortgage-backed, asset-backed
Merrill Lynch Composite	5,000	Over 1 year	Over 50	Government, corporate, government/corporate mortgage-backed
Salomon Smith Barney Composite	5,000	Over 1 year	Over 50	Bond investment grades, Treasury/agency, corporate, mortgages
US high-yield bond				
First Boston	423	All maturities	Over 75	Composite and by ratings
Lehman Brothers	624	Over 1 year	Over 100	Composite and by ratings
Merrill Lynch	735	Over 1 year	Over 25	Composite and by ratings
Salomon Smith Barney	300	Over 7 years	Over 50	Composite and by ratings
Global government bond				
Lehman Brothers	800	Over 1 year	Over 200	Composite and 13 countries in local currency and US$
Merrill Lynch	9,735	Over 1 year	Over 100	Composite and 9 countries in local currency and US$
J. P. Morgan	445	Over 1 year	Over 200	Composite and 11 countries in local currency and US$
Salomon Smith Barney	525	Over 1 year	Over 250	Composite and 14 countries in local currency and US$

Frank J. Fabozzi (ed.) *The Handbook of Fixed Income Securities*, 6th edn, p. 158.

commercial paper, or loans from banks), then using the funds to invest in commercial and residential mortgage loans and other real estate securities. REITs can take the form of an equity trust that invests directly in real estate, a mortgage trust that invests in mortgage loans or mortgage-backed securities, or a hybrid trust that invests in both. Many REITs are highly leveraged, making them more subject to default risks. REITs are tax-exempt corporations, often formed by banks, insurance companies, and investment companies. To qualify for tax exemptions, the company must receive approximately 75% of its income from real estate, rents, mortgage interest, and property sales, and distribute 95% of its income to its shareholders. The stocks of many existing shares in REITs are listed on the organized exchanges and the OTC market.

Hedged Funds

Hedged funds can be defined as special types of mutual funds. There are estimated to be as many as 4,000 such funds. They are structured so that they can be largely unregulated. To achieve this, they are often set up as limited partnerships. By federal law, as limited partnerships, hedged funds are limited to no more than 99 limited partners each with annual incomes of at least $200,000 or a net worth of at least $1m (excluding home), or to no more than 499 limited partners each with a net worth of at least $5m. Many funds or partners are also domiciled offshore to circumvent regulations. Hedged funds acquire funds from many different individual and institutional sources; the minimum investments range from $100,000 to $20m, with the average investment being $1m.

The funds are used to invest or set up investment strategies reflecting pricing aberrations. Many of these strategies involve bond positions. One of the most famous is that of Long-Term Capital who set up positions in T-bonds and long-term corporate bonds to profit from an expected narrowing of the default spread that instead widened.

7.5.8 Information on Investment Funds

Information on many open- and closed-end funds is provided daily in the *Wall Street Journal*. In addition to daily information from the *Wall Street Journal*, other information on investment companies can be found in Weisenberger's *Survey of Investment Companies*, the *Mutual Fund Fact Book, Vickers Guide to Investment Company Portfolios*, and Morningstar. There are also a number of websites providing information on funds.

Web Information

Information on investment funds:
   www.ici.org

Information on investment funds and ratings:
   www.quicken.com/investments/
   mutualfunds/finder/
   www.morningstar.com

and
   www.lipperweb.com

Information on money market funds:
   www.imoneynet.com

Information on real estate investment trusts:
   www.nareit.com

Information on hedged funds:
   www.thehfa.org
   www.hedgefundcenter.com

and
   www.hedgefund.net

7.6 INSURANCE COMPANIES

Life insurance companies use the premiums paid on various insurance policies and retirement and savings plans to invest in bonds, stocks, mortgages, and other assets. As such, they are important financial intermediaries.

7.6.1 Insurance Products

Insurance companies can be classified as either property and casualty companies or life insurance companies. Property and casualty companies provide property insurance to businesses and households against losses to their properties resulting from fire, accidents, natural disasters, and other calamities, and casualty (or liability) insurance to businesses and households against losses the insurer may cause to others as a result of accidents, product failures, and negligence. Property and casualty insurance policies are short term, often renewed on an annual basis. Since the events being insured by the policies are difficult to predict, insurance companies tend to invest the premiums from property and casualty policies into more liquid assets.[8]

Life insurance companies provide basic life insurance: protection in the form of income to benefactors in the event of the death of the insurer. They also provide disability insurance, health insurance, annuities, and guaranteed investment contracts.

Life Insurance Policies

There are three general types of life insurance policies: term life, whole life, and universal life. A *term life policy* pays a lump sum benefit to the insurer's benefactor if the insurer dies when the policy is in effect. Whole life and universal life policies provide both life insurance benefits and a retirement plan. The premiums paid by the insurer on whole life and universal life policies cover the cost of the life insurance and include a savings program. The interest earned from the savings part of the policy is also tax exempt until it is withdrawn (provided the investment value exceeds the death benefit). In the case of a *whole life policy*, the insurer pays a premium that in the earlier years of the policy exceeds the normal premium on term life. This excess accumulates into a cash value available to insurers or their survivors: if an insurer dies, the survivor receives both the death benefit and the cash value; if the insurer lives past the policy's maturity, then the insurer receives the cash value. In addition, many whole life policies often allow the insurer to borrow against the cash value. Whole life policies began to decline in popularity in the early 1980s because of the low returns they were generating for their policyholders: in the early 1980s, whole life policyholders were significantly better off buying term life and investing the savings themselves. Life insurance companies responded to this decline by offering *universal life policies*. Universal life is similar to whole life, except that the savings portion of the account accumulates at a greater rate. In addition to life insurance, most life insurance companies also offer health insurance, usually through company-sponsored programs. Life insurance companies also negotiate contracts with physician groups through health maintenance organizations (HMOs) and provide disability insurance that pays income to insurers in the event they become ill or suffer from an accident.

Annuities

A life insurance company annuity pays the holder a periodic fixed income for as long as the policyholder lives in return for an initial lump-sum investment (coming for example from a retirement benefit or insurance cash value). Annuities provide policyholders protection against the risk of outliving their retirement income. Thus, in contrast to life insurance policies that provide insurance against dying too soon, annuities provide insurance against living too long. There are three general types of annuities: a *life annuity*, which pays a fixed amount regularly (e.g., monthly) until the investor's death; a *last survivor's annuity*, which pays regular fixed amounts until both the investor and spouse die; a *fixed-period annuity*, which makes regular fixed payments for a specified period (5, 10, 20 years), with payments made to a beneficiary if the investor dies. These

annuities are referred to as fixed annuities. They are constructed based on the rates of return insurance companies can obtain from investing an individual's payment for a period equal to the individual's life expectancy (fixed-life annuity), or for a prespecified period (fixed-period annuity). In addition to fixed annuities, insurance companies also offer a *variable annuity* in which regular payments are not fixed, but rather depend on the returns from the investments made by the insurance company (the insurance company sometimes invests in a mutual fund that they also manage). Finally, insurance companies offer *deferred annuities* (variable or fixed) that allow an investor to make a series of payments instead of a single payment.

Guaranteed Investment Contract

A *guaranteed investment contract (GIC)* is an obligation of an insurance company to pay a guaranteed principal and rate on an invested premium. For a lump-sum payment, an insurance company guarantees that a specified dollar amount will be paid to the policyholder at a specified future date. For example, a life insurance company for a premium of $1m guarantees the holder a 5-year GIC paying 8% interest compounded annually. The GIC, in turn, obligates the insurance company to pay the GIC holder $1,469,328 ($= \$1m(1.08)^5$) in 5 years.

Guaranteed investment contracts, also called guaranteed interest contracts and guaranteed insurance contracts, are similar to zero-coupon debentures issued by corporations. A debenture holder, though, is a general creditor, while a GIC holder is a policyholder who has a senior claim over general creditors of the insurance company. Pension funds are one of the primary investors in GICs. The GICs provide them with not only an investment with a known payment but also an investment that always has a positive value to report; this contrasts with bond investments whose values may decrease if interest rates increase. The growth in GICs started in the 1980s with the increased investment in 401(k) plans. In addition to insurance companies, banks have also become an active participant in this market, offering *bank investment contracts (BICs)*. BICs are deposit obligations with a guaranteed rate and fixed maturity. BICs and GICs are sometimes referred to as *stable value investments.*

The generic GIC, also called a *bullet contract,* is characterized by a lump-sum premium, a specified rate and compounding frequency, and a lump-sum payment at maturity. Maturities can range from 1 year to 20 years, with the short-term GICs often set up like money market securities. There are several variations of the bullet contract. A window GIC, for example, allows for premium deposits to be made over a specified period, such as a year; it is designed to attract the annual cash flow from a pension or 401(k) plan. A GIC may consist of a single type of security, such as a mortgage-backed or other asset-backed security or a portfolio of securities that are managed and immunized to the specified maturity date of the contract; some GICs may also be secured by letters of credit or other credit enhancements. Instead of a specified maturity date, the contract may specify that it will maintain a portfolio with a constant duration. There are also floating-rate GIC contracts in which the rate is tied to a benchmark rate, and there are GIC contracts in which the interest is paid periodically to the policyholder. Finally, a GIC may have a wrapped contract with clauses that give the holders the right to sell the contract and receive the book value or to change the rate under certain conditions.

In managing the funds from GICs, insurance companies may either pool the contracts into a general account (no separate identification of assets for a particular policy) or as a separate account (separate account for the GIC holder or group). The latter GIC is known as a *separate account contract (SAC).* When securities are separated from other liabilities of the insurer and managed separately in a SAC, they are considered legally protected against the liabilities arising from other businesses of the insurance company.

7.6.2 Insurance Companies' Role in the Financial Market

Life insurance companies are a major player in the financial markets, investing into the financial markets billions of dollars of inflows received each year from the premiums from their insurance policies and from their savings and investment products. In 2001, about 41% of the investments of life insurance companies were in corporate bonds, followed by stock (29%), government securities (9.5%), mortgages (7.7%), and direct loans (5.6%).

Web Information

For industry trends:
  www.riskandinsurance.com

For quality ratings and evaluation of insurers:
  www.bestweek.com

7.7 PENSION FUNDS

Pension funds are financial intermediaries that invest the savings of employees in financial assets over their working years, providing them with a large pool of funds at their retirements. Pension funds are one of the fastest growing intermediaries in the United States. The total assets of pension funds (private and state and local government) have grown from $700b in 1980 to approximately $8t in 2000. Part of this growth reflects a workforce of baby boomers making contributions to their pensions. As this generation enters retirement over the next decade and begins to draw from its investments, there is expected to be a marked decline in such growth.

There are two general types of pension plans: a defined-benefit plan and a defined-contribution plan. A *defined-benefit plan* promises the employee a specified benefit when they retire. The benefit is usually determined by a formula. For example, the employee's annual benefit during her retirement might be based on a specified percentage (for example, 2%) times the average salary over her last 5 years ($75,000) times her years of service (30 years): $(0.02)(\$75,000)(30) = \$45,000$. The funding of defined-benefit plans is the responsibility of the employer. Financial problems can arise when pension funds are underfunded and the company goes bankrupt. As a result, over the last two decades most new plans are structured as *defined-contribution plans*. These plans specify what the employee will contribute to the plan, instead of what the plan will pay. At retirement, the benefits are equal to the contributions the employee has made and the returns earned from investing them. The employee's contributions to the fund are usually a percentage of his income, often with the contribution, or a proportion of it, made by the employer. An insurance company, bank trust department, or investment company often acts as the trustee and investment manager of the fund's assets. In many defined-contribution plans, the employee is allowed to determine the general allocation between equity, bonds, and money market securities in his individual accounts. Unfortunately, some companies have pension plans that encourage employees to invest exclusively in their own stock. As the recent collapse of some US corporations painfully showed, this lack of diversification can lead to employees not only losing their jobs but also their pension investments if the company goes bankrupt.

To pension contributors, pension funds represent long-term investments through intermediaries. As of 2000, private funds sponsored by employers, groups, and individuals' private pensions accounted for one of the largest institutional investments in equity, with about 48% of their total investments of $5.129t going to equity and another 18% in mutual fund shares, 9% in government securities, and 6% in corporate and foreign bonds. In 2000, public funds sponsored by state and local governments invested $3.034t with 64% in equity, 12% in federal agency and Treasury securities, and 11% in corporate and foreign bonds.

Pension members are not taxed on their contributions, but they do pay taxes on benefits when they are paid out. Pension funds in the US are governed by the 1974 *Employee Retirement Income Security Act (ERISA)*. ERISA requires prudent management of the fund's investments and requires that all private plans be fully funded; that is, that the assets and income cover all promised benefits. The Act also ensures transferability of plans when employees change jobs, specifies disclosure requirements, and defines the minimum vesting requirements for determining eligibility. In

1974, Congress also created the Pension Benefit Guaranty Corporation (PBGC or Penny Benny) to provide insurance for employee benefits.

In addition to employee and institutional pension plans, retirement plans for US individuals can also be set up through *Keough plans* and *individual retirement accounts (IRAs)*. By tax laws established in 1962, self-employed people can contribute up to 20% of their net earnings to a Keough plan (retirement account) with the contribution being tax deductible from gross income. Since the passage of the Economic Recovery Tax Act, any individual can also contribute up to $2,000 of their earned income to an IRA with no taxes paid on the account until they are withdrawn. In addition to company-sponsored and group-sponsored pensions, bank trust departments, insurance companies, and investment companies offer and manage individual retirement accounts and Keough plans. For small accounts, these institutions often combine the accounts in a *commingled fund*, instead of managing each account separately. A commingled fund is similar to a mutual fund. For accounting purposes, individuals setting up accounts are essentially buying shares in the fund at their NAV and when they withdraw funds they are selling essential shares at their NAV. Like mutual funds, insurance companies and banks offer a number of commingled funds, such as money market funds, stock funds, and bond funds.

Web Information
For information and updates on pension funds:
  www.ifebp.org

7.8 INTERNATIONAL DEBT SECURITIES

Before the 1980s, the US financial markets were larger than the markets outside the US. With the growth of world business and deregulations, this is no longer the case. Today, American corporations, banks, and institutional investors have increasingly tapped the international money and capital markets to raise or invest short-term and long-term funds, just as non-US borrowers and investors have historically tapped the US market to raise and invest funds.

In general, a fixed-income investor looking to internationally diversify his bond portfolio has several options. First, he might buy a bond of a foreign government or foreign corporation that is issued in the foreign country or traded on that country's exchange. These bonds are referred to as *domestic bonds*. Secondly, the investor might be able to buy bonds issued in a number of countries through an international syndicate. Such bonds are known as *Eurobonds*. Finally, the investor might be able to buy a bond of a foreign government or corporation being issued or traded in his own country. These bonds are called *foreign bonds*. If the investor were instead looking for short-term foreign investments, his choices would similarly include buying short-term domestic securities such as CP, CDs, and Treasuries issued in those countries, Eurocurrency CDs issued by Eurobanks, and foreign money market securities issued by foreign corporations and governments in their local countries. Similarly, a domestic financial institution or non-financial multinational corporation looking to raise funds may choose to do so by selling debt securities or by borrowing in his own financial markets, the foreign markets, or the Eurobond or Eurocurrency markets.

The markets where domestic, foreign, and Euro securities are issued and traded can be grouped into two categories – the *internal bond market* and the *external bond market*. The internal market, also called the *national market*, consists of the trading of both domestic bonds and foreign bonds; the external market, also called the *offshore market*, is where Eurobonds and Eurodeposits are bought and sold. There are some bonds that are sold in both the external and internal markets; these bonds are referred to as *global bonds*. The market for just international securities can be divided into the *foreign bond and security markets* (those traded on the national market) and *Eurobonds and Eurocurrency markets* (those traded on the external market). The international debt market can be further classified in terms of the international capital market for intermediate-term and long-term funds and an international money market for short-term funds.

7.8.1 The Foreign Bond Market

A foreign bond market refers to that market in which the bonds of issuers not domiciled in that country are sold and traded. For example, the bonds of a German company issued in the US or traded in the US secondary markets would be part of the US foreign bond market. Foreign bonds are sold in the currency of the local economy. They are also subject to the regulations governing all securities traded in the national market and sometimes to special regulations and disclosure requirements governing foreign borrowers.

Foreign bonds have been issued and traded on national markets for centuries. For example, US bonds sold in London in the nineteenth century financed a large proportion of the US railroad system. In the US, foreign bonds are referred to as *Yankee bonds*; in Japan, they are called *Samurai bonds*; in Spain they are called *Matador bonds*; in the United Kingdom, they are nicknamed *Bulldog bonds*; and in the Netherlands they are called *Rembrandt bonds*. In the US, Yankee bonds are registered with the SEC, and like other US bonds, they typically pay interest semi-annually. The Yankee market tends to be dominated by sovereign government issues or issues guaranteed by sovereign governments. With the growth in the Eurobond market, the Yankee market did experience declines in the 1980s, but has since rebounded, going from a $60b market in 1989 to a $260b one in 2000. However, like a number of other foreign bonds, the size of the Yankee bonds relative to domestic issues is small.

7.8.2 The Eurobond Market

A Eurobond is a bond issued outside the country in whose currency it is denominated. For example, a US company might sell a bond denominated in US dollars throughout Europe. Eurobonds are a very popular debt instrument. Guinness, Volvo, Nestlé, and other multinational corporations finance many of their global operations by selling Eurobonds. Eurobonds are also a source of intermediate- and long-term financing of sovereign governments and supranationals (e.g., the World Bank and the European Investment Bank). Russia, for example, raised $4b in 1997 through the sale of Eurobonds. Currently, about 80% of new issues in the international bond market are Eurobonds. In fact, the Eurobond market currently exceeds in size the US bond market as a source of new funds.

Origin

In the 1950s and early 1960s, New York was the most accessible market for corporations to raise capital. As a result, many foreign companies issued dollar-denominated bonds in the US. The popularity of the Yankee bond market began to decline starting in 1963 when the US government imposed the interest equalization tax (IET) on foreign securities purchased by US investors. The tax was aimed at reducing the interest-rate difference between higher yielding foreign bonds and lower yielding US bonds. Predictably, it led to a decline in the Yankee bond market. It also contributed, though, to the development of the Eurobond market as more foreign borrowers began selling dollar-denominated bonds outside the US. The IET was repealed in 1974.

The Eurobond market also benefited in the 1970s from a US foreign withholding tax that imposed a 30% tax on interest payments made by US firms to foreign investors. There was a tax treaty, though, that exempted the withholding tax on interest payments from any Netherlands Antilles subsidiary of a US-incorporated company to non-US investors. This tax treaty led to many US firms issuing dollar-denominated bonds in the Eurobond market through financial subsidiaries in the Netherlands Antilles. During this time, Germany also imposed a withholding tax on German DM-denominated bonds held by non-residents. Even though the US and other countries with withholding taxes granted tax credits to their residents when they paid foreign taxes on the incomes from foreign security holdings, the tax treatments were not always equivalent. In addition, many tax-free investors, such as pension funds, could not take advantage of the credit (or could, but only after complying with costly filing regulations). As a result, during the 1970s and early 1980s, Eurobonds were often more attractive to foreign investors and borrowers than foreign bonds. The growth of the Eurobond market was also aided in the late 1970s by the investments of oil-exporting countries that had large dollar surpluses. From 1963 to 1984, the Eurobond market grew from a $75m market with a total of seven Eurobond issues to an $80b market with issuers that included major corporations, supranationals, and governments. In 1984, the US and Germany rescinded their withholding tax laws on foreign investments and a number of other countries followed their lead by eliminating or relaxing their tax codes. Even with this trend, though, the Eurobond market had already been established and would continue to remain a very active market, growing from an $80b market in new issues in 1984 to a $525b market by 1990 and to a $1.4t market by 1998.

Underwriting Process

The Eurobond market is handled through a multinational syndicate consisting of international banks, brokers, and dealers. A corporation or government wanting to issue a Eurobond will usually contact a multinational bank that will form a syndicate of other banks, dealers, and brokers from different countries. The members of the syndicate usually agree to underwrite a portion of the issue, which they normally sell to other banks, brokers, and dealers. The multinational make-up of the syndicate allows the issue to be sold in many countries.[9] Approximately one-third of the issues are for more than $300m and one-fourth are for $100m or less. The major investors in the market are institutional investors and corporations.

Market makers handle the secondary market for Eurobonds. Many of them are the same dealers that are part of syndicates that helped underwrite the issue, and many belong to the *Association of International Bond Dealers (AIBD)*. This association oversees an international OTC market consisting of Eurobond dealers; it is similar to the National Association of Securities Dealers, except that there is less government involvement. An investor who wants to buy or sell an existing Eurobond can usually contact several market makers in the international OTC market to get several bid–asked quotes before selecting the best one. While most secondary trading of Eurobonds occurs in the OTC market, many Eurobonds are listed on organized exchanges in Luxembourg, London, and Zurich. These listings are done primarily to accommodate investors from countries that prohibit (or at one time did prohibit) institutional investors from acquiring securities that are not listed. In the early years of the Eurobond market, clearing was done by physical delivery of the securities and payment was by check. In the late 1960s, two clearing firms were established: Euroclear and Cedel. These firms consisted of international banks and investment companies and they were linked to other clearing systems.

Characteristics

Currency Denomination: The generic Eurobond is a straight bond paying an annual fixed interest and having an intermediate- or long-term maturity. There are several different currencies in which Eurobonds are sold, with the major currency denominations being the US dollar, yen, and the euro.[10] Companies tend to denominate their bonds in those currencies they receive from operations. Dollar-denominated Eurobonds are the largest currency segment, currently comprising about 50% of the market. In the future, euro-dominated Eurobonds are expected to gain in popularity. Some Eurobonds are also valued in terms of a portfolio of currencies, sometimes referred to as a currency cocktail.

Credit Risk: Compared to US corporate bonds, Eurobonds have fewer protective covenants, making them an attractive financing instrument to corporations, but riskier to bond investors. Eurobonds differ in term of their default risk and are rated in terms of quality ratings.

Maturities: The maturities on Eurobonds vary. Many have intermediate terms (2–10 years), referred to as Euronotes, and long terms (10–30 years), called Eurobonds. There is also short-term Europaper or Euro CP. Like some CP issues, Europaper issues, as well as some Euronotes, are often secured by lines of credit. The credit lines are sometimes set up through *note issuance facilities (NIFs)* of international banks, also called *revolving underwriting facilities (RUFs)*. These facilities provide credit lines in which borrowers can obtain funds up to a maximum amount by issuing short-term and intermediate-term paper over the term of the line.

Euro Medium-Term Notes: There is a growing market for *Euro medium-term notes,* Euro-MTNs. Like regular MTNs, they are offered to investors as a series of notes with different maturities. In addition, Euro-MTN programs also offer different currencies and are not subject to national regulations. They are sold though international syndicates and also through offshore trusts (offshore centers are discussed later) set up by banks, investment banks, and banking groups.

Non-Registered: One feature of Eurobonds that has served to differentiate them from US bonds is that many of them are issued as bearer bonds.[11] While this feature of Eurobonds provides confidentiality, it has created some problems in countries such as the US, where regulations require that security owners be registered on the books of the issuers. However, to accommodate US investors, the SEC allows US investors to purchase these bonds after they are "seasoned" (sold for a period of time, currently 40 days). Thus, US investors are locked out of initial offerings of Eurobonds, but are active in acquiring them in the secondary market. The fact that US investors are locked out of the primary market does not prevent US borrowers from issuing Eurobonds. In 1984, US corporations were allowed to issue bearer bonds directly to non-US investors; another factor that contributed to the growth of this market.

Other Features: Like many securities issued today, Eurobonds often are sold with many innovative features. There are *dual-currency Eurobonds,* for example, that pay coupon interest in one currency and principal in another, and *option-currency Eurobonds* that offer investors a choice of currency. A sterling/ Canadian dollar bond, for instance, gives the holder the right to receive interest and principal in either currency. A number of Eurobonds have special conversion features or warrants attached to them. One type of convertible is a dual-currency bond that allows the holder to convert the bond into stock or another bond that is denominated in another currency. For example, in the 1980s, the Toshiba Corporation sold a bond denominated in Swiss francs that could be converted into shares of Toshiba stock at a set yen/SF exchange rate. Some of the warrants sold with Eurobonds include those giving the holder the right to buy stock, additional bonds, currency, or gold. There are also floating-rate Eurobonds with rates often tied to the LIBOR and floaters with the rate capped. The Eurobond market has also issued zero discount bonds, and at one time, the market offered perpetual Eurobonds with no maturities; they, however, were not very popular and were discontinued in 1988.

7.8.3 Global Bonds

A global bond is both a foreign bond and a Eurobond. Specifically, it is issued and traded as a foreign bond (being registered in a country) and also it is sold through a Eurobond syndicate as a Eurobond. The first global bond issued was a 10-year, $1.5b bond sold by the World Bank in 1989. This bond was registered and sold in the US (Yankee bond) and also in the Eurobond market. Currently, US borrowers dominate the global bond market, with an increasing number of these borrowers being US federal agencies. The market has grown from a $30b market in the early 1990s to a $100b one in the late 1990s.

7.8.4 Non-US Domestic Bonds

Bonds sold in a national market by companies, agencies, or intermediaries domiciled in that country are referred to as domestic bonds. In the preceding chapters many of the domestic bonds traded in the US were examined. There are, of course, many countries whose corporations, governments, and financial institutions offer bonds that are attractive to US and other foreign investors. For foreign investors, usually the most important factor for them to consider is that their price, interest payments, and principal are denominated in a different currency. This currency component exposes them to exchange-rate risk and affects their returns and overall risk.

Foreign investors who buy domestic bonds also will find differences from country to country in how the bonds are issued and regulated. In a number of countries, banks, instead of investment bankers, underwrite new bonds. In Germany, for example, there has been a long history of no separation between commercial and investment banking. Many banks in Germany have acted as security underwriters and as brokers and dealers in the secondary market, trading existing bonds and stocks through an interbank market. In Europe, though, the *Single European Act* did permit banks and financial institutions in the European Economic Community (EEC), as well as those entering the EEC, to offer a wide variety of the same banking and security services. This Act has led to standardization in the EEC. Japan, like the US until 2000, has had a history of separating its commercial and investment banking activities. In Japan, brokerage houses such as Nikko, Nomura, and Yamaichi broker and underwrite bonds and other securities. In the secondary market, some countries trade bonds exclusively on exchanges, while others, such as the US, Japan, and the United Kingdom, trade bonds on both the exchanges and through market makers on an OTC market.

Bonds sold in different countries also differ in terms of whether they are sold as either registered bonds or bearer bonds. A foreign investor buying a domestic bond may also be subject to special restrictions. These can include special registrations, exchange controls, and foreign withholding taxes. Finally, domestic bonds in other countries differ in their innovations. For example, the British government issues a bond, also referred to as a *gilt*, that has a short-term maturity that can be converted to a bond with a longer maturity. They also issue a gilt that does not mature, although it can be redeemed after a specified date.

7.8.5 Emerging Market Debt

Over the last two decades, *emerging market debt* has become a popular addition to global bond portfolios. Emerging markets include

Latin America, Eastern Europe, Russia, and a number of Asian countries, and their sovereign debt includes Eurobonds, bonds they offer and trade domestically, performing loans that are tradable, and Brady bonds (sovereign bonds issued in exchange for rescheduled bank loans). The opening of markets and the privatization of companies in Russia and Eastern Europe along with the economic reforms in Latin America have enhanced the profit potential of many emerging economies and with that the expected rates of return on their securities. At the same time, such debt is subject to considerable risk. Much of the risk germane to emerging market securities comes from concerns over changes in political, social, and economic conditions (referred to as *cross-border risk*) and *sovereign risk* in which the government is unable, or in some cases unwilling, to service its debt. Some of the more recent sovereign debt crises of note occurred in Latin America in the 1980s, Venezuela in 1994, East Asia in 1994, Mexico in 1995, and Russia in 1998.

One of the more popular emerging debt securities is the **Brady bond**. Named after US Treasury Secretary Nicholas Brady, these bonds were issued by a number of emerging countries in exchange for rescheduled bank loans. The bonds were part of a US government program started in 1989 to address the Latin American debt crisis of the 1980s. The plan allowed debtor countries to exchange their defaulted bank debt for Brady bonds or restructured loans at lower rates. In return for this debt relief, the countries agreed to accept economic reforms proposed by the International Monetary Fund. While there are some variations between plans, the basic Brady plan offered creditor banks two choices for the non-performing loans of emerging countries that they were carrying: (1) a discount bond issued below par (e.g., 50% or 65% of par) in exchange for the original loan or a discount bond paying a floating rate tied to the LIBOR plus $\frac{13}{16}$ in exchange for fewer bonds than the original loan; (2) a bond issued at par and paying a below-market coupon in exchange for the original face value of the loan. The principal on a Brady bond was secured by US Treasury securities (initial bonds were secured by special zero-coupon Treasuries and later ones by Treasury strips), and the interest was backed

by investment grade bonds, with the guarantee rolled forward from one interest payment to the next if the collateral was not used (this is known as a rolling interest guarantee). All Brady bonds were callable and some gave bondholders a "value recovery" option giving them the right to recover some of the debt if certain events occurred such as an increase in gross domestic product or energy prices.

The first country to accept a Brady plan was Mexico, which used it in 1989 to restructure its approximate $50b in foreign debt to commercial banks.[12] Seventeen countries with significant debt repayment problems have taken advantage of the Brady plan. As of 1999, the total Brady debt was approximately $114 billion, with Brazil, Mexico, Venezuela, and Argentina accounting for approximately 73% of the debt (see table 7.2). When they were introduced, the

Table 7.2   Brady debt, 1999

	Brady debt (billions of $)
Latin America	
Argentina	16.69
Brazil	36.27
Costa Rica	0.59
Dominican Republic	0.51
Ecuador	6.05
Mexico	18.63
Panama	2.00
Peru	4.46
Uruguay	0.73
Venezuela	10.96
Non-Latin America	
Bulgaria	4.83
Ivory Coast	1.31
Jordan	0.72
Nigeria	2.05
Philippines	2.49
Poland	5.33
Vietnam	0.55
Russia*	26.22
Total	$113.87

* Russia restructured its debt in 1998. The restructure package is sometimes included as Brady debt, even though it is not officially considered as following under the Brady plan.

Source: Merrill Lynch. Reprinted in Frank J. Fabozzi (ed.) *The Handbook of Fixed Income Securities*, 6th edn, p. 389.

initial holders of Brady bonds were the creditor banks. With the principal and interest guarantees and the potentially high returns, the bonds were attractive investments to hedged funds, global bond funds, growth funds, and emerging market funds. As a result, many banks sold their Brady bonds to non-bank institutional investors who, in turn, became one of the primary holders.[13]

7.8.6 Eurocurrency Market

The Eurocurrency market is the money market equivalent of the Eurobond market. It is a market in which funds are intermediated (deposited or loaned) outside the country of the currency in which the funds are denominated. For example, a certificate of deposit denominated in dollars offered by a subsidiary of a US bank incorporated in the Bahamas is a Eurodollar CD. Similarly, a loan made in yens from a bank located in the US would be an American-yen loan. In both cases, the Eurodollar deposit and the American-yen loan represent intermediation occurring in the Eurocurrency market. Even though the intermediation occurs in many cases outside Europe, the Euro prefix usually remains. An exception is the Asiandollar market, which includes banks in Asia that accept deposits and make loans in foreign currency.

Today the total amount of Eurocurrency deposits is estimated to be in excess of $2t. The actual size of the market, though, is difficult to determine because of the lack of regulation and disclosure. By most accounts, though, it is one of the largest financial markets. The underlying reason for this is that Eurocurrency loan and deposit rates are often better than the rates on similar domestic loans and deposits because of the differences that exist in banking and security laws among countries. Foreign lending or borrowing, regardless of what currency it is denominated in and what country the lender or borrower is from, is subject to the rules, laws, and customs of the foreign country where the deposits or loans are made. Thus, a US bank offering a CD through its foreign subsidiary located in the Bahamas (maybe in the form of a PO box) would be subject to the Bahamian laws with respect to reserve requirements, taxes on deposits,

anonymity of the depositor, and the like. Accordingly, if a country's banking laws are less restrictive, then it is possible for a foreign bank or a foreign subsidiary of a bank to offer more favorable rates on its loans and deposits than it could in its own country by simply intermediating the deposits and loans in that country.[14] Thus, the absence of reserve requirements or regulations on rates paid on deposits in the Bahamas, for example, makes it possible for the rates on Bahamian Eurodollar loans to be lower than US bank loans and the rates on their deposits to be higher.

Brief History of the Eurocurrency Market

The origin of the Eurocurrency market is more political than economic. It started in the 1950s when the Soviet Union maintained large dollar deposits in banks in the US in order to participate in world trade. However, poor political relations, as well as US claims on the Soviet Union originating from the lend-lease policy, led to fears by the Soviet Union that the US government could expropriate their deposits. As a result, the USSR, with the aid of some US banks, transferred their dollar deposits to banks in Paris and London, thus creating the first modern-day Eurodollar deposit. Subsequently, the increase in international trade, the rise of multinationals, the emergence of the dollar as an international reserve currency under the old Bretton Woods exchange rate system, and the policy of some governments to maintain dollar deposits led to a substantial increase in the amount of Eurodollar deposits abroad during the 1960s.

During the early 1960s, most of the Eurodollar deposits were in foreign banks that, in turn, used the deposits to make dollar loans to many US companies, directly competing with US banks. In 1963 there were only a few US banks with foreign operations in Europe, and these banks were there principally to facilitate their corporate customers' international business. In the mid-1960s, though, US banks began to go after Eurodollar deposits and loans by establishing foreign subsidiaries. What brought the American banks to Europe en masse was probably not so much the loss of business to

European banks as it was the opportunity to get around Federal Reserve regulations. Specifically, with lower or no reserve requirements and no regulations governing the maximum rates payable on time deposits, US banks, by offering Eurodollar deposits and loans, now had a way of offering their customers better rates on loans and higher rates on time deposits. By 1969 there were an estimated 40 American banks with branches abroad, lending approximately $14b in Eurodollars. This market, in turn, grew, despite a crisis in 1973, to a $270b market in 1974.

In the late 1970s, many oil-exporting countries used the Eurodollar market, depositing large dollar deposits. Some of these petrodollars were used to make loans to oil-importing countries, leading the dollar deposits from oil revenues to be recycled. By the 1980s, the Eurodollar market had become the second largest market in the world, extending beyond Europe and intermediating in currencies other than the dollar. Accordingly, the market gave rise to the offshore banking centers in such areas as Nassau, Singapore, Luxembourg, and Kuwait. These areas had less restrictive banking laws and thus became a place for intermediation between both foreign lenders and foreign borrowers.

Current Market

Currently, the Eurocurrency market consists of a number of large banks, referred to as Eurobanks, corporations, and governments. The Eurobanks are the foundation of the market, offering various types of loans and deposits. Governments and companies use the market to deposit currencies, as well as to obtain loans to finance assets, infrastructures, and even balance of payment deficits. Eurocurrency market transactions are large deposits and loans, usually $1m or more.

For large investors, the market offers two types of instruments: Eurocurrency CDs and primary deposits. As noted earlier in this chapter, because of favorable regulations in the offshore centers, the rates on the CDs are usually higher than comparable domestic CDs. The maturities on Eurocurrency CDs range from one day to several years, with the most common maturities being 1, 3, 6, and 12

months. For longer-term CDs, the rates can be either fixed or variable. Eurocurrency CDs can also take the form of *tap CDs*; these are CDs issued in single amounts to finance a specific Eurodollar loan. Also there exist *tranche CDs*, which are of a smaller denomination ($10,000), often offered to the public through a broker or an underwriter.

Primary deposits are time deposits with negotiated rates and short-term maturities. Once deposited, these deposits, in turn, are often sold and bought as part of the Eurocurrency's interbank deposit network. In the interbank market, many deposits are bought by large Eurobanks who use the proceeds to make large short-term loans. For example, suppose the ABC Company of Cincinnati wanted to invest $2m excess cash from its operations for 30 days in the Nassau branch of the Midwest Bank of Cincinnati. To initiate this, the treasurer of ABC would call Midwest Bank's Eurocurrency trader in Cincinnati to get a quote on its Nassau bank's 30-day deposit rate. (Note, the Nassau branch of Midwest Bank is likely to be staffed in Cincinnati, with its physical presence in Nassau being nothing more than the Nassau incorporation papers and other documents in a lawyer's office.) The treasurer would give ABC a quote based on similar Eurocurrency rates. If acceptable, a 30-day Eurocurrency deposit would be created with ABC transferring its cash account to Midwest Bank who would set up the Nassau account by recording it in its Nassau books in Cincinnati. Now unless the bank has an immediate need for the $2m, the trader would invest the funds through the interbank market. This might involve selling the deposit to a London Eurobank who might be arranging a 30-day, $10m loan to a Japanese company to finance its inventory of computer equipment purchased in New York.[15] If Midwest and the Eurobank agree, then Midwest would transfer the $2m Eurodollar deposit to the London Eurobank.

The rate paid on funds purchased by large London Eurobanks in the interbank market is called the **London interbank bid rate (LIBID)**, while the rate on funds offered for sale by London Eurobanks is the London interbank offer rate (LIBOR); on average, the spread between them is 0.125%. As pointed out earlier, the average LIBOR among London Eurobanks is a rate commonly used to set the rate on bank loans, deposits, and floating-rate notes and loans. The LIBOR can vary from overnight rates to 30-day ones. There are also similar rates for other currencies (e.g., sterling LIBOR) and areas (e.g., the Paris inter-bank offer rate, PIBOR, or the Singapore interbank offer rate, SIBOR).

In addition to being an important source of funds for banks, the Eurocurrency market is also an important funding source for cor-porations and governments. The loans to corporations and governments can be either short- or intermediate-term, ranging in maturity from overnight to 10 years. The loans with maturities of over 1 year are sometimes called Eurocredits or Eurocredit loans. Since Euro deposits are short-term, Eurobanks often offer Eurocredits with a floating rate tied to the LIBOR. Eurocurrency loans also vary in terms of some of their other features: many take the form of lines of credit; some require a LOC, instead of detailed covenants; loans can be either fixed or floating; loans can be in different cur-rencies and have different currency clauses; and many of the larger loans are provided by a syndicate of Eurobanks.

7.8.7 The Foreign Currency Market and Exchange-Rate Risk

When investors buy securities in the external market, they are subject to the same risk that is incurred when they buy domestically. They are also exposed to two additional risk factors – political risk and exchange-rate risk. *Political risk* is the uncertainty of converting international securing holdings on unfavorable economic terms because of an unexpected change in laws or customs. For investors, political risk can result from a government placing restrictions on cur-rency conversion, freezing assets, or imposing taxes. Such risk is greater in developing countries with unstable political regimes. *Exchange-rate risk* is the uncertainty over changes in the exchange rate. When an investor purchases a foreign security, she usually has to buy foreign currency, and when she receives income and principal from the security, or sells it, she usually has to convert the proceeds back to

her own currency. Such investments are subject to the uncertainty that the exchange rates can change in the foreign currency market. Similarly, when a corporation sells a security or borrows funds in a currency that must be converted to finance operations in a different country, the company is subject to exchange-rate risk.

The Foreign Currency Market

The international buying and selling of goods, services, and assets creates a market in which individuals, businesses, and governments trade currencies. Most of the currency trading takes place in the *interbank foreign exchange market*. This market consists primarily of major banks that act as currency dealers, maintaining inventories of foreign currencies to sell to or buy from their customers (corporations, govern-ments, or regional banks). The banks are linked by a sophisticated telecommunication system and operate by maintaining accounts with each other, enabling them to trade currency simply by changing computerized book entries in each other's accounts.

Transactions occurring in the interbank for-eign currency market can include both spot and forward trades. In the spot market, currencies are delivered immediately (book entries chan-ged); in the forward market, the price for trading or exchanging the currencies (*forward rate*) is agreed upon in the present, with the actual delivery or exchange taking place at a specified future date. The price of foreign cur-rency or the exchange rate is defined as the number of units of one currency that can be exchanged for one unit of another. In exhibit 7.3, the spot and forward exchange rates are shown as they appeared in the *Wall Street Journal* on February 5, 2003. The rates are quoted both in terms of the US dollar price per unit of foreign currency (FC) and the FC price per US dollar. The exchange rates represent the closing quotes made by one bank to another. For example, on February 4, 2003 the spot exchange rate (E_0) for the British pound (BP) was \$1.6485/BP and the 3-month and 6-month forward exchange rates (E_0^f) were \$1.6382/BP and \$1.6283/BP. The FC price of a dollar is the reciprocal of E_0; thus, the spot BP price of a dollar is $1/E_0 = 1/(\$1.6485/BP) = 0.6066BP/\$$.

Exhibit 7.3   Exchange rate quotes

Key Currency Cross Rates
Late New York Trading Tuesday, February 4, 2003

	Dollar	Euro	Pound	SFranc	Peso	Yen	CdnDlr
Canada	1.5147	1.6484	2.4970	1.1245	13835	.01265	...
Japan	119.72	130.29	197.35	88.878	10.935	...	79.037
Mexico	10.9481	11.9148	18.048	8.1279	...	.09145	7.2279
Switzerland	1.347	1.4659	2.2205	...	.12303	.01125	.8893
U.K.	.60660	.6602	...	.4503	.05541	.00507	.40049
Euro	.91890	...	1.5147	.68216	.08393	.00768	.60663
U.S.	...	1.0883	1.6485	.74240	.09134	.00835	.66020

Source: Reuters

Exchange Rates

The foreign exchange mid-range rates below apply to trading among banks in amounts of $1 million and more, as quoted at 4 p.m. Eastern time by Reuters and other sources. Retail transactions provide fewer units of foreign currency per dollar.

Country	U.S. $ EQUIVALENT		CURRENCY PER U.S. $	
	Tue	Mon	Tue	Mon
Argentina (Peso)-y	.3160	.3140	3.1646	3.1847
Australia (Dollar)	.5915	.5846	1.6906	1.7106
Bahrain (Dinar)	2.6523	2.6522	.3770	.3770
Brazil (Real)	.2798	.2845	3.5740	3.5149
Canada (Dollar)	.6602	.6592	1.5147	1.5170
1-month forward	.6595	.6585	1.5163	1.5186
3-months forward	.6576	.6566	1.5207	1.5230
6-months forward	.6544	.6534	1.5281	1.5305
Chile (Peso)	.001346	.001363	742.94	733.68
China (Renminbi)	.1208	.1208	8.2781	8.2781
Colombia (Peso)	.0003378	.0003374	2960.33	2963.84
Czech. Rep. (Koruna)				
Commercial rate	.03438	.03413	29.087	29.300
Denmark (Krone)	.1463	.1449	6.8353	6.9013
Ecuador (US Dollar)	1.0000	1.0000	1.0000	1.0000
Hong Kong (Dollar)	.1282	.1282	7.8003	7.8003
Hungary (Forint)	.004454	.004423	224.52	226.09
India (Rupee)	.02094	.02092	47.756	47.801
Indonesia (Rupiah)	.0001127	.0001127	8873	8873
Israel (Shekel)	.2049	.2066	4.8804	4.8403
Japan (Yen)	.008353	.008316	119.72	120.25
1-month forward	.008362	.008324	119.59	120.13
3-months forward	.008381	.008344	119.32	119.85
6-months forward	.008408	.008371	118.93	119.46
Jordan (Dinar)	1.4085	1.4092	.7100	.7096
Kuwait (Dinar)	3.3523	3.3484	.2983	.2987
Lebanon (Pound)	.0006634	.0006667	1507.39	1499.93
Malaysia (Ringgit)-b	.2632	.2632	3.7994	3.7994
Malta (Lira)	2.5861	2.5668	.3867	.3896

Country	U.S. $ EQUIVALENT		CURRENCY PER U.S. $	
	Tue	Mon	Tue	Mon
Mexico (Peso)				
Floating rate	.0913	.0917	10.9481	10.9016
New Zealand (Dollar)	.5496	.5438	1.8195	1.8389
Norway (Krone)	.1448	.1440	6.9061	6.9444
Pakistan (Rupee)	.01723	.01718	58.038	58.207
Peru (new Sol)	.2863	.2868	3.4928	3.4868
Philippines (Peso)	.01853	.01854	53.967	53.937
Poland (Zloty)	.2622	.2605	3.8139	3.8388
Russia (Ruble)-a	.03142	.03141	31.827	31.837
Saudi Arabia (Riyal)	.2667	.2667	3.7495	3.7495
Singapore (Dollar)	.5755	.5738	1.7376	1.7428
Slovak Rep. (Koruna)	.02607	.02581	38.358	38.745
South Africa (Rand)	.1202	.1173	8.3195	8.5251
South Korea (Won)	.0008529	.0008467	1172.47	1181.06
Sweden (Krona)	.1177	.1167	8.4962	8.5690
Switzerland (Franc)	.7424	.7346	1.3470	1.3613
1-month forward	.7428	.7350	1.3463	1.3605
3-months forward	.7437	.7359	1.3446	1.3589
6-months forward	.7451	.7373	1.3421	1.3563
Taiwan (Dollar)	.02881	.02879	34.710	34.734
Thailand (Baht)	.02342	.02338	42.699	42.772
Turkey (Lira)	.00000061	.00000061	1639344	1639344
U.K. (Pound)	1.6485	1.6435	.6066	.6085
1-month forward	1.6452	1.6401	.6078	.6097
3-months forward	1.6382	1.6330	.6104	.6124
6-months forward	1.6283	1.6231	.6141	.6161
United Arab (Dirham)	.2723	.2723	3.6724	3.6724
Uruguay (Peso)				
Financial	.03550	.03560	28.169	28.090
Venezuela (Bolivar)	.000520	.000520	1923.08	1923.08
SDR	1.3697	1.3765	.7301	.7265
Euro	1.0883	1.0779	.9189	.9277

Special Drawing Rights (SDR) are based on exchange rates for the U.S., British, and Japanese currencies. Source: International Monetary Fund.
a-Russian Central Bank rate. b-Government rate. y-Floating rate.

Exchange-Rate Risk

Investors buying foreign securities in national or offshore markets denominated in foreign currency are subject to changes in exchange rates that, in turn, can affect the rates of return they can obtain from their investments. For example, suppose a US investor bought a French corporation's zero-coupon bond paying 1,000 euros at the end of 1 year for 900 euros when both the $/euro spot and 1-year

forward exchange rates were $0.8915/euro (or 1.1217 euros/$). The US investor's total dollar investment would, therefore, be $802.35.

Dollar investment = ($0.8915/euro)(900 euros)
= $802.35

One year later, the US investor receives 1,000 principal on the maturing French bonds for an 11.11% rate of return in euros (= (1,000 − 900)/ 900). The rate the investor earns on his dollar investment, though, depends on the spot $/euro exchange rate. For example, if the $/euro spot exchange rate decreased (a dollar appreciation) by 15% from $0.8915/euro to $0.757775/euro, the investor would lose 5.5% in dollars:

$$\text{Rate} = \frac{(\$0.757775/\text{euro})(1,000 \text{ euros})}{\$802.35} - 1$$

$$= -0.055$$

The example illustrates that when investors purchase foreign securities they must take into account not only the risk germane to the security, but also the risk that exchange rates will move to an unfavorable level. A similar admonishment applies to borrowers who sell securities or procure loans in currencies that are converted to finance operations in other currencies.

It should be noted that the forward exchange market makes it possible for investors to hedge their investments and loans against exchange-rate risk. In the above case, for example, suppose that when she purchased the French bond, the US investor had entered into a forward contract to sell 1,000 euros 1 year later at the forward rate of $0.8915/euros. At the end of the year, the investor would be sure of converting 1,000 euros into $891.50. Thus, even if the $/euro spot rate fell by 15%, the investor would still be able to earn 11.11% ($= (\$891.50/\$802.35) - 1$) from her dollar investment. Thus by entering a forward contract to sell foreign currency the investor is able to profit from her bond investment.

As we will examine in part IV, there are other ways investors, as well as borrowers, can hedge against exchange risk (futures, options, and swaps). Using these tools, in turn, allows investors and borrowers to focus on the choice of securities and type of funding.

Web Information
Information on Eurobonds, LIBOR, spot and forward exchange rates:
www.fxstreet.com

Information on emerging markets:
www.securities.com

Information on country statistics:
www.worldbank.org/data

Information on world indexes, exchange rates, and other international data:
www.bloomberg.com

Information on historical foreign exchange rates and balance of payments:
www.research.stlouisfed.org/fred2

Information on the European Central Bank and European Monetary Union:
www.euro.gov.uk/
www.ecb.int

and
www.cepr.org

Information on the International Monetary Fund:
www.imf.org

Information on the Bank for International Settlement:
www.bis.org

Information on Brady debt and bonds:
www.bradynet.com

7.9 CONCLUSION

Just like the markets for corporate and government securities, the intermediary financial and international debt security markets offer borrowers and investors a wide array of instruments for financing and investing: from short-term securities, such as CDs, BAs, and shares in money market funds, to intermediate- and long-term instruments, such as mortgage-backed securities, mutual fund shares, pension plans, annuities, GICs, Eurobonds, and foreign bonds. These debt securities, along with the many different types of corporate and government securities, characterize a debt market of both depth and breadth. In examining these debt markets over the last three chapters, our analysis has focused, to some extent, on how corporate, government, and intermediate issuers/borrowers create debt securities to finance their capital formation. In the next chapter we focus more on investors – individual and institutional – and the investment strategies they can use to select and manage bonds and bond portfolios.

KEY TERMS

Term CDs
Jumbo CDs
Brokered Deposits
Prime CDs
Non-prime CDs
Yankee CDs
Floating-Rate CD (FRCD)
Bear and Bull CDs
Rising-Rates CDs
Forward CDs
Rollover or Roly-Poly CDs
Bank Notes
Banker's Acceptances (BAs)
Acceptance Financing
Accepting Banks
Collateralized Mortgage
  Obligations (CMOs)
Securitization
Money Market Funds
Index Funds
Global Funds
Vulture Funds
Open-End Funds (Mutual
  Funds)
Net Asset Value (NAV)
Load Funds
No-Load Funds
Closed-End Fund
Unit Investment Trust
Redeemable Trust Certificates
Growth Funds
Income Funds
Balanced Funds
Real Estate Investment Trust
  (REIT)

Hedged Funds
Term Life Policy
Whole Life Policy
Universal Life Policies
Life Annuity
Last Survivor's Annuity
Fixed-Period Annuity
Variable Annuity
Deferred Annuities
Guaranteed Investment
  Contract (GIC)
Bank Investment Contract
  (BIC)
Stable Value Investments
Bullet Contract
Separate Account Contract
  (SAC)
Defined-Benefit Plan
Defined-Contribution Plans
Employee Retirement Income
  Security Act (ERISA)
Keough Plans
Individual Retirement
  Accounts (IRAs)
Commingled Fund
Domestic Bonds
Eurobonds
Foreign Bonds
Internal Bond Market
External Bond Market
National Market
Offshore Market
Global Bonds
Foreign Bond and Security
  Markets

Eurobonds
Eurocurrency Market
Yankee Bonds
Samurai Bonds
Matador Bonds
Bulldog Bonds
Rembrandt Bonds
Association of International
  Bond Dealers (AIBD)
Note Issuance Facilities
  (NIFs) or Revolving Under-
  writing Facilities (RUFs)
Euro Medium-Term Notes
Dual-Currency Eurobonds
Option-Currency Eurobonds
Single European Act
Gilt
Emerging Market Debt
Cross-Border Risk
Sovereign Risk
Brady Bond
Aztec Bonds
Tap CDs
Tranche CDs
London Interbank Bid Rate
  (LIBID)
Political Risk
Exchange-Rate Risk
Interbank Foreign Exchange
  Market
Forward Rate

PROBLEMS AND QUESTIONS

1. Define the following:
   a. Prime CDs
   b. Non-prime banks
   c. Yankee CDs
   d. Eurodollar CDs

    e. Floating-rate CDs
    f. Bear and bull CDs
    g. Rising-rates CDs
    h. Forward CDs.

2. Describe the primary market for CDs. Who are the some of the major investors in CDs?

3. Explain the history of the secondary CD market. In your explanation bring out the significance of a positively sloped yield curve that is not expected to change.

4. What are bank notes? How do they differ from medium-term notes issued by corporations?

5. Define a banker's acceptance, acceptance financing, and accepting banks.

6. A US oil exploration company drilling in the Gulf of Mexico wants to purchase $20m of drilling equipment from a German tool manufacturing company. Once the transaction agreement is complete, the drilling equipment will be shipped to the US company's drilling assembly operation facility in Houston. Shipping time is expected to take 30 days. Both companies agree to finance the transaction with a banker's acceptance in which the US company's bank will guarantee the US company's payment of $20m with a letter of credit to be sent to the German company's bank. Upon notification of the receipt of the letter of credit, the German company will ship the equipment and take payment from its bank. Explain how the rest of the transactions between the US and German companies would take place and how the banker's acceptance would be created.

7. Describe banker's acceptances as a security, the secondary market for such securities, and some of the principal participants in the market.

8. Define mortgage-backed securities and explain how they are constructed. What is the primary risk that investors in MBSs are subject to?

9. Define and explain the distinguishing features of the following funds:
    a. Open-end fund
    b. Closed-end fund
    c. Real estate investment trust.

10. Define a unit investment trust. Explain how a financial institution would set up a unit investment trust with 10-year T-bonds with $100m par value selling at par as the underlying securities and with 100,000 certificates created.

11. Explain how hedged funds are structured. What types of investments do they make?

12. List the principal classifications of bond funds.

13. What are the primary investment objectives of the following: municipal bond fund, corporate bonds index fund, and money market fund?

14. Define:
    a. Annuities
    b. Life annuity
    c. Last survivor's annuity
    d. Fixed-period annuity
    e. Variable annuity
    f. Deferred annuities.

15. Define a guaranteed investment contract, GIC. List some features of the generic GIC.

16. What would an investor/policyholder receive from investing $1m in a 6-year guaranteed investment contract, GIC, paying 6% interest compounded semi-annually?

17. How does a guaranteed investment contract differ from an investment in a zero–coupon debenture?

18. What makes guaranteed investment contracts an attractive investment for pensions and other institutional investors?

19. What is a separate account guaranteed investment contract?

20. Define the following terms:
    a. Bank investment contracts
    b. Stable value investment
    c. Bullet contract
    d. Window GIC
    e. Floating-rate GIC.

21. What is the difference between a defined-benefit pension plan and a defined-contribution plan?

22. Comment on how well the investments of pension plans are diversified.

23. Define the following:
    a. Employee Retirement Income Security Act (ERISA)
    b. Pension Benefit Guaranty Corporation (PBGC or Penny Benny)
    c. Individual Retirement Accounts (IRAs).

24. Explain how financial institutions manage small IRA accounts as commingled funds.

25. Define the following markets:
    a. Eurobond
    b. Foreign bond
    c. Internal market or national market
    d. External or offshore market
    e. Global bond.

26. List some of the popular foreign bonds and their names.

27. Explain the significance of the interest equalization tax and foreign withholding tax in contributing to the growth of the Eurobond market.

28. Explain how Eurobonds are issued in the primary market through a syndicate.

29. Describe the secondary market for Eurobonds.

30. Explain the following features associated with Eurobonds:
    a. Currency denomination
    b. Non-registered (implication for US investors and issuers)
    c. Credit risk
    d. Maturities
    e. Dual currency clauses
    f. Option–currency clause.

31. How does the US security law requiring the registration of bond investors apply to the issuing of non-registered Eurobonds by corporations? How does the law apply to US investors?

32. What are some of the differences that foreign investors would find when they buy domestic bonds?

33. Define the following:
    a. Emerging market debt
    b. Cross-border risk
    c. Sovereign risk.

34. Explain the following:
    a. Brady bonds
    b. Brady plan
    c. Countries with Brady bonds
    d. Brady bond investors.

35. Define the Eurocurrency market. What is the fundamental factor contributing to the growth of this market?

36. Comment on how the following events impacted the historical development of the Euro–currency market:
    a. USSR
    b. Fixed exchange rate system
    c. US banks circumventing US bank laws
    d. Petrodollars
    e. Offshore centers.

37. What is the interbank Eurocurrency market?

38. Define the London interbank bid rate (LIBID) and London interbank offer rate (LIBOR).

39. List some of the features that characterize Eurocurrency loans.

40. Describe the interbank foreign exchange market.

WEB EXERCISES

1. Examine the trends in banker's acceptances over the last 10 years by going to www. bondmarkets.com and clicking "Research Statistics" and then "Money Market Instruments."

2. Find the current average yields on money market funds and identify some of the money market funds by going to www.imoneynet.com.

3. Learn more about real estate investment trusts by going to www.nareit.com. At the site, click on "Investing in REITs" and "Research and Statistics."

4. Information on exchanges rates, yields on Eurobonds, and interest rate actions by central banks can be found at www.fxstreet.com. At the site, examine the following:
    a. Spot exchange rates by clicking on "Quotes" and "Real Time Tables."
    b. Forward and LIBOR rates by clicking on "Forwards and LIBOR" in "Quotes."
    c. Graph of exchange rate movements by going to "Charts" and clicking on "Real Time."
    d. Eurobond yields by going to "Charts" and clicking on "Bond Yields."
    e. Foreign interest rate trends by clicking on "Interest Rates."

5. The London interbank offer rate, LIBOR, is an important benchmark rate. It is used to determine the rates on many floating-rate bonds and loans, and as we will discuss in chapter 16, it is used to determine the payments on interest rate swap contracts. Find out more about the LIBOR by going to www.bba.org.uk. At the site, click on the "Official Definition." Determine current and past LIBORs by going to "Historical BBA LIBOR" and then to "Archives." How do the most recent US dollar LIBORs compare to earlier LIBORs?

6. Information on investment funds can be found at www.ici.org. Learn more about funds by clicking on "Learn About Investing."

7. Learn more about mutual fund ratings by going to the website of Morningstar and Lipper Analytical Services: www.morningstar.com, www.lipperweb.com, and www.ibcdata.com.

8. Go to www.quicken.com/investments/mutualfunds/finder and find the top 25 funds for the following categories: high-yield bond, emerging markets bond, long government, and Muni National.

NOTES

1. Banks and other deposit institutions also offer non-negotiable CDs to investors. These are deposits that must be held to maturity, often with a penalty for early withdrawal.

2. For example, a large investor with $1m would go to a broker who would break the $1m into ten units of $100,000 each and then buy ten $100,000 CDs at ten different banks. Since each of the deposits was $100,000, they each would qualify for insurance by the FDIC. In 1984, the FDIC passed regulations banning brokered deposits. The ban was challenged in federal court and overturned.

3. Banks, savings and loans, and other deposit-type institutions also offer a number of non-negotiable CDs sold to individuals.

4. Investment in a Eurodollar CD can be fully invested by the foreign subsidiary bank, while a similar investment in a domestic CD cannot because part of the CD proceeds must be used to satisfy reserve requirements.

5. In the US, no investor has lost the principal on a BA in over 60 years.

6. While it is generally true that the number of shares of a closed-end fund is fixed, such funds occasionally issue new shares either through a public offering or through a share dividend, which is sometimes offered to shareholders who are given an option of receiving either cash or new shares based on the NAV of the fund if the dividend or interest income is reinvested. Also, some funds occasionally go into the market and purchase their own shares.

7. Investment funds are regulated under a number of federal laws: the Security Acts of 1933 and 1934 require disclosure of funds and specify anti-fraud rules; the Security Act of 1940 requires that all funds be registered; the Investment Advisors Act of 1940 regulates fund advisors. In addition, SEC rules require that funds publish detailed information on directors and that there be independence of the directors.

8. Approximately 10% of property and casualty insurance policies are reinsured. Reinsurance refers to the allocation of the policy to other insurers.

9. The underwriting of Eurobonds is subject to some underwriting risk. Often the lead or managing underwriter has to handle any issues not sold by second-tier and third-tier underwriters. The underwriting agreement specifies the terms of the issue, including price, before the issue is sold; this is referred to as a bought deal. The increased underwriting risk is often reflected by a bigger spread.

10. The central bank of a country can protect its currency from being used. Japan, for example, prohibited the yen from being used for Eurobond issues of its corporations until 1984.

11. Some Eurobonds, such as those issued by sovereign countries, are sold as registered bonds.

12. *Aztec bonds* preceded the Mexican Brady bonds. These bonds were created in 1988 to redress J. P. Morgan's non-performing loans to Mexico. J. P. Morgan accepted a 30% reduction in the face value of its loan in return for a floating rate tied to LIBOR + 1.625%. The bonds were paid off 8 years after they were issued.

13. Moody's generally rates an emerging country's Brady bonds with the country's sovereign foreign debt.

14. For example, if the US's reserve requirement were 5% on time deposits for a certain size bank, while no requirements existed in the Bahamas, then a US bank, by accepting a domestic deposit, could only loan out 95% of the deposit, earning 95% of the loan rate, in contrast to a Bahamian deposit in which 100% of the deposit could be loaned out to earn the full amount of the loan rate. In a competitive market for deposits and loans, the rates on the Bahamian loans and deposits would have to be made more favorable, since a depositor or borrower would prefer his own country.

15. Midwest might also call an international money broker in New York or London. The broker, in turn, would provide information and make arrangements. The information could be in the form of bid and offer quotes on other Euro-currency deposits.

SELECTED REFERENCES

Ambachtsbeer, Keith P. "How Should Pension Funds Manage Risk?" *Journal of Applied Corporate Finance* 11(2) (Summer 1998): 122–7.

Brauer, Jane Sachar and Douglas Chen "Brady Bonds," in Frank Fabozzi (ed.) *The Handbook of Fixed Income Securities*, 6th edn (New York: McGraw-Hill, 2001).

Dynan, Karen E., Kathleen W. Johnson, and Samuel M. Slowinski "Survey of Finance Companies," *Federal Reserve Bulletin* (January 2002): 1–14.

Fabozzi, Frank J. *The Handbook of Fixed Income Securities*, 6th edn (New York: McGraw-Hill, 2001).

Farinella, J. A. and T. W. Koch "Who Took the Slope out of the Municipal Yield Curve?" *Journal of Fixed-Income* 4(2) (1990): 59–65.

Friedberg, Leora and Michael T. Owyang "Not Your Father's Pension Plan: The Rise of 401(k) and Other Defined Contribution Plans," *Review* (Federal Reserve Bank of St Louis, January–February 2002): 23–34.

Madura, Jeff *International Financial Management*, 6th edn (Cincinnati, OH: South-Western College Publishing, 2000): 57–79.

Mishkin, Frederic S. and Stanley G. Eakins *Financial Markets and Institutions*, 4th edn (Addison-Wesley, 2003).

Rose, Peter S. *Money and Capital Markets* (New York: McGraw-Hill/Irwin, 2003).

Zirky, E. A. and R. M. Mackey "Pension Plan Funding Strategies: Defining Terms," *Pension World* (August, 1993): 40–1.

CHAPTER EIGHT

BOND INVESTMENT STRATEGIES

8.1 INTRODUCTION

The volatile interest rate environment characterizing the last three decades led to the introduction of many different types of fixed-income securities. As we saw in the last three chapters, there are myriad corporate, government, intermediary, and international debt securities, with different collateral and security arrangements, embedded option features, and rate-payment terms. Concomitant with this increase in the number of securities over this time period has been the development of bond investment management strategies. Prior to the 1960s, bond investment strategies could be classified as either active or passive, with active being primarily limited to speculative strategies and passive being simple buy-and-hold strategies. Today, strategies include active and passive, as well as hybrid strategies that combine elements of both, and the number of strategies under these groupings is extensive.

Active strategies involve taking speculative positions in which the primary objective is to obtain an abnormal return. This might include taking a long position in longer duration bonds in anticipation of a decrease in long-term rates, investing in Treasury securities based on the expectation of the Fed implementing an expansionary monetary policy, or investing in lower quality bonds in hopes of future economic growth. Active strategies also include defensive strategies in which the objective is to protect the value of a bond investment. For example, to minimize the potential decrease in a bond fund's value from an expected increase in interest rates, a fund manager might reallocate more of the fund's holdings toward lower duration bonds and away from higher duration ones. Institutional investors, hedged funds, and individual investors all use active strategies. In the case of a hedged fund, the fund itself might be defined by the strategy. For example, Long-Term Capital Management was a hedged fund that could be defined by one of its active strategies of trying to profit from a narrowing of a yield spread. On the other hand, an institutional investor such as a pension or a life insurance company might use an active approach only in the initial investment of its funds, and then afterwards follow a passive or hybrid approach to investment. Finally, institutional fund managers might use an active approach to change the allocation of their existing funds from one bond group to another in order to increase the expected return or as a defensive strategy to protect the value of the fund. This latter active strategy involves liquidating one bond group and simultaneously purchasing another. Such strategies are referred to as *bond swaps*.

A *passive strategy* is one in which no change of position is necessary once the bonds are selected, or in the case of investing in new funds, the investment strategy is not changed once it is set up. Prudence and practicality, though, usually dictate at least minimal monitoring and change. Life insurance companies, deposit institutions, and pensions that have a primary objective of ensuring that there are sufficient funds to meet future liabilities typically use passive strategies. Some investment companies that manage bond portfolios and some mutual funds try to construct bond portfolios whose returns over time replicate those of some specified bond index. Such a strategy is known as *indexing*. This is a passive strategy which, once the fund is constructed or the investment strategy is defined, it is usually not changed.

Hybrid strategies consist primarily of immunization positions. Recall that in chapter 4 we defined immunization as a strategy of minimizing market risk by selecting a bond or bond portfolio with a duration that matched the investor's horizon date. Fund managers of pensions and insurance companies that have future liabilities whose amounts and times of payments are known, or have been estimated, often employ immunization. The discussion of bond immunization in chapter 4 suggested that such a strategy is a passive one of simply matching duration to the horizon date. In practice, though, immunization requires frequent changing or rebalancing of the bond portfolio, and as such can be characterized as having both passive and active management styles. In addition to immunization, other hybrid strategies are contingent immunization and combination matching, both of which also have active and passive elements.

In this chapter we extend our analysis from the evaluation of bond securities to the selection of bonds by examining the various active, passive, and hybrid investment strategies. We begin by first examining some of the popular active selection strategies, including trading strategies based on anticipated interest rate changes, credit strategies, and valuation approaches. This is followed by an analysis of two passive strategies: cash flow matching and indexing. Finally, we conclude the chapter by examining bond immunization strategies.

8.2 ACTIVE INVESTMENT STRATEGIES

In our evaluation of bond characteristics in part I, we identified a number of fundamental relationships. For example, in our discussion of bond price relationships in chapter 2, we noted that the greater a bond's maturity or the lower its coupon rate, the greater its price sensitivity to interest rate changes (or equivalently the greater its duration). In chapter 4, we discussed several empirical studies that presented evidence showing a positive relationship between quality yield spreads and the state of the economy; specifically, the studies showed that the spread between the yields on low- and high-quality bonds widens in periods of economic downturn and narrows in periods of economic growth. We also noted in chapter 4 that the spread between yields on callable and non-callable bonds tended to widen in high interest rate periods and narrow in low-rate periods. Many active bond strategies are, in turn, predicated on these fundamental bond relations. Some of the more popular ones are interest rate expectations strategies based on anticipated changes in interest rates or yield curve shifts, credit strategies based on credit analysis and economic forecast, and valuation strategies based on determining the fundamental values of bonds in order to identify mispriced ones. Each of these strategies can be applied as an approach for investing initial funds or as a bond swap in which two or more bond positions are simultaneously changed in order to change the allocation of a bond portfolio

8.2.1 Interest Rate-Anticipation Strategies

If a bond investor expected interest rates to decrease across all maturities by the same number of basis points (i.e., a parallel shift in the yield curve), she could attain greater expected returns by purchasing bonds with larger durations or, if she is managing a bond fund, by reallocating her portfolio by selling shorter duration bonds and buying longer duration ones. In contrast, if a bond manager expected the yield curve to shift up, she could minimize her exposure to market risk by changing her investments or portfolio to include more bonds with shorter durations. Active strategies of selecting bonds or bond portfolios with specific durations based on interest rate expectations are referred to as *rate-anticipation strategies* and when they involve simultaneously selling and buying bonds with different durations they are referred to as a *rate-anticipation swap*.[1]

Rate-Anticipation Swaps

When interest rates are expected to decrease across all maturities, a bond fund manager, as just noted, could increase the value of his fund by lengthening the portfolio's duration. This could be done with a rate-anticipation swap in which the manager sells her lower duration bonds and buys higher duration ones. By doing this, the portfolio's value would be more sensitive to interest rate changes and as a result would subject the manager to a higher return–risk position, providing greater upside gains in value if rates decrease but also greater losses in value if rates increase.

In contrast, when interest rates are expected to increase, a bond fund manager could use a rate-anticipation swap to try to preserve the value of the fund. In this case, the objective would be to shorten the portfolio's duration by selling longer duration bonds and buying shorter ones. One way to shorten the fund's duration is for the manager to buy *cushion bonds*. A cushion bond is a callable bond with a coupon that is significantly above the current market rate. The bond has the features of a high coupon yield and with its embedded call option a market price that is lower than a comparable non-callable bond. For example, suppose a bond manager had a fund consisting of 10-year, 10% option-free bonds valued at 113.42 per $100 par to yield 8% and there were comparable 10-year, 12% coupon bonds callable at 110 that were trading in the market at a price close to their call price (note that callable bonds cannot trade at prices higher than their call prices). If the manager expected rates to increase, he could cushion the negative price impact on the fund's value by selling some of his option-free bonds and buying the higher-coupon, callable bonds – the cushion bonds. The swap of his existing

bonds for the cushion bonds would in turn provide him with an immediate gain in income plus higher-coupon income in the future. Thus, the interest rate swap of option-free bonds for cushion bonds provides some value preservation. Note: a callable bond has a lower duration than a non-callable one with the same maturity (how to estimate the duration of bonds with embedded options is discussed in chapter 10). The 10-year cushion bond with its call feature and higher coupon rate has a relatively lower duration than the 10-year option-free bond; thus, the swap of cushion bonds for option-free bonds in this example represents a switch of longer duration bonds for shorter ones.

Yield Curve Shifts and Strategies

Interest rate-anticipation strategies require not only forecasting general interest rate movements, but also changes in the term structure of rates. Some rate-anticipation strategies are based on estimating the type of yield curve shift. Three types of yield curve shift occur with some regularity: parallel shifts, shifts with twists, and shifts with humpedness.[2] In a *parallel shift*, yields on all maturities change by the same magnitude (see figure 8.1a). A *twist*, on the other hand, is a non-parallel shift. It implies either a flattening or steepening of the yield curve. As shown in figure 8.1b, if there is a flattening, the spread between long-term and short-term rates decreases; if there is a steepening, the spread increases. A shift with *humpedness* is also a non-parallel shift in which short-term and long-term rates change by greater magnitudes than intermediate rates. An increase in both short- and long-term rates relative to intermediate rates is referred to as a *positive butterfly*, and a decrease is known as a *negative butterfly* (see figure 8.1c).

Given the different types of yield curve shifts, investors actively managing bond portfolios will pursue different strategies based on their yield curve forecast. There are three general types of yield curve strategies used by active bond investors: bullet, barbell, and ladder. The *bullet strategy* is implemented by constructing a portfolio concentrated in one maturity area. For example, a bullet strategy

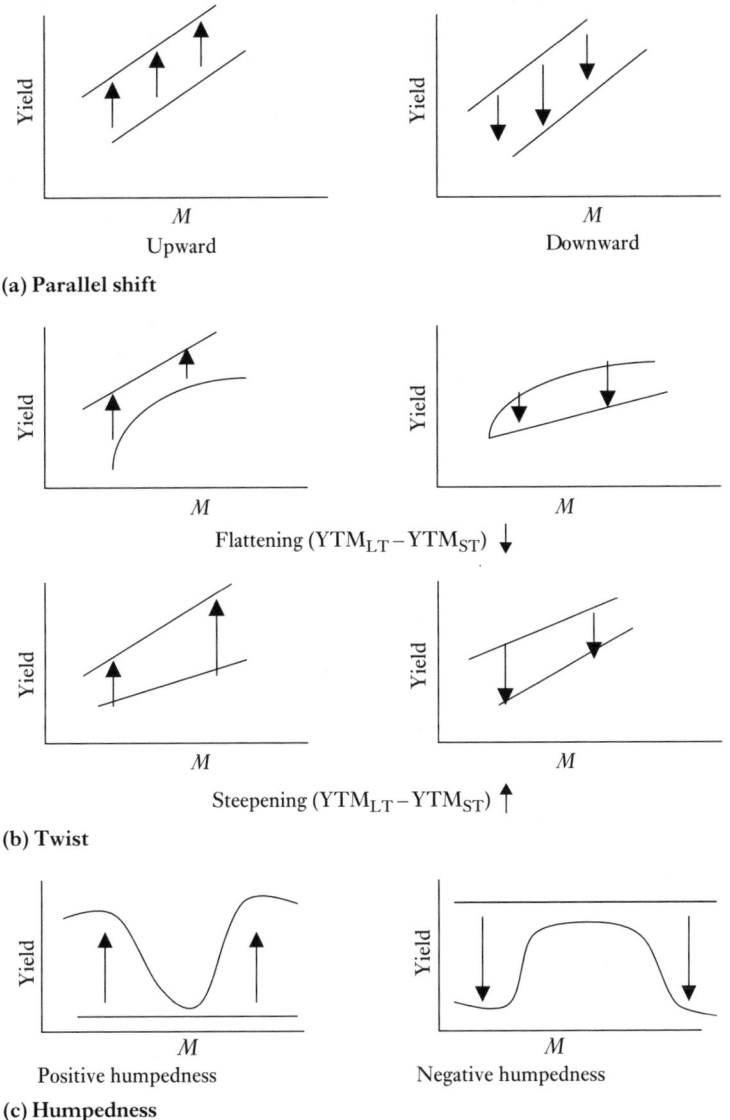

Figure 8.1   Yield curve shifts

consisting of a portfolio of long-term bonds could be formed if there were an expectation of a downward shift in the yield curve with a twist such that long-term rates were expected to decrease more than short-term.[3] Similarly, if investors expected a simple downward parallel shift in the yield curve, a bullet strategy with longer duration bonds would also yield greater returns than an investment strategy in inter-mediate- or short-term bonds if the expectation

turns out to be correct. The *barbell strategy* is one in which investments are concentrated in both the short-term and long-term bonds. This strategy could be profitable for an investor who is forecasting a negative butterfly yield curve shift. Finally, the *ladder strategy* is constructed with equal allocations in each maturity group.

In implementing an active strategy based on a forecasted shift in the yield curve, there is always the question of how to determine the correct yield curve strategy. One method for identifying the appropriate strategy is to use a *total return analysis*. In this approach, potential returns from several yield curve strategies are evaluated for a number of possible interest rate changes over different horizon periods to identify the best strategy. A problem using this type of analysis is included as one of the end-of-the-chapter questions.

8.2.2 Credit Strategies

Active credit investment strategies consist of quality swaps and credit analysis strategies. A quality swap is a strategy of moving from one quality group to another in anticipation of a change in economic conditions. A credit analysis strategy, in turn, involves a credit analysis of corporate, municipal, or foreign bonds in order to identify potential changes in default risk. This information is then used to identify bonds to include or exclude in a bond portfolio or bond investment strategy.

Quality Swap

In a *quality swap*, investors try to profit from expected changes in yield spreads between different quality sectors. Quality swaps often involve a *sector rotation* in which more funds are allocated to a specific quality sector in anticipation of a price change. For example, suppose a bond fund manager expected a recession accompanied by a flight to safety in which the demand for higher quality bonds would increase and the demand for lower quality ones would decrease. To profit from this expectation, the manager could change the allocation of her bond fund by selling some of her low-quality ones and buying more high-quality bonds. On the other hand, suppose the economy were in a recession, but the bond manager believed that it was near its trough and that economic growth would follow. To capitalize from this expectation, the manager could tilt her bond portfolio toward lower quality bonds by selling some of her higher quality bonds and buying lower quality ones.

In addition to sector rotations, quality swaps can also be constructed to profit from anticipated changes in yield spreads between quality sectors. Recall the study of default risk by Salomon Brothers (chapter 4) that showed how quality yield spreads have tended to widen during periods of economic recession and narrow during periods of economic expansion. If the economy were at the trough of a recession and was expected to grow in the future, speculators or a hedged fund might anticipate a narrowing in the spread between lower and higher quality bonds. To exploit this, they could form a quality swap by taking a long position in lower quality bonds and a short position in higher quality bonds with similar durations. Whether rates increase or decrease, speculators would still profit from these positions, provided the quality spread narrows. For example, if rates increase but the quality spread narrows because of economic growth, then the percentage decrease in the price of lower quality bonds would be less than the percentage decrease in the price of higher quality bonds. As a result, the capital gain from the short position in the higher quality bonds would dominate the capital loss from the long position in the lower quality bonds. Similarly, if rates decrease but the quality spread narrows, then the percentage increase in price for the lower quality bonds would be greater than the percentage increase for the higher quality bonds. In this case, the capital gain from the long position in lower quality bonds would dominate the capital loss from the short position in the higher quality bonds.[4]

Credit Analysis

The objective of a credit analysis strategy is to determine expected changes in default risk. If changes in quality ratings of a bond can be projected prior to an upgrade or downgrade announcement by Moody's, Standard & Poor's, or Fitch (if the market is efficient, it may be necessary to project the change before the announcement), bond investors can realize gains by buying bonds they project will be upgraded, and they can avoid losses by selling or not buying bonds they project will be downgraded. The potential gains from effective credit analysis can be realized more from high-yield, low investment-grade bonds (bonds rated

Table 8.1 Financial ratios by ratings classification

Ratings	Interest coverage: EBIT/interest	Leverage ratio: LT debt/total assets	Cash flow: operating CF/LT debt
AAA	21.4	9.7	53.8
AA	10.2	18.9	27.9
A	5.67	28.8	19.6
BBB	2.9	40.7	3.9
BB	2.25	50.2	0.7
B	0.74	62.2	(1.7)

Source: Standard & Poor's, *Global Sector Review*, 1995

below BB) than investment-grade bonds. Over the last two decades, the spread between low investment-grade bonds and Treasuries has ranged from 150 basis points (BP) to over 1,000 BP. At the same time, though, the default risk on such bonds has been relatively high. In a study on cumulative default rates of corporate bonds, Douglass and Lucas found the 5-year cumulative default rate for B-rated bonds was approximately 24% and the 10-year cumulative default rate was approximately 36%; for CCC-rated bonds they found the cumulative default rates to be approximately 46% and 57% for 5 years and 10 years, respectively. In contrast, Douglass and Lucas found the 5-year and 10-year cumulative default rates for A-rated bonds were only 0.53% and 0.98% and for BBB-rated, the rates were 2.4% and 3.67%. The Douglass and Lucas study, as well as several other studies on cumulative default rates, show there is a high degree of default risk associated with low-quality bonds.[5] The study also suggests, though, that with astute credit analysis there are significant gains possible by being able to forecast upgrades and significant losses that can be avoided by projecting downgrades. In fact, the strategy of many managers of high-yield bond funds or funds that have some of their investments allocated to high-yield bonds is to develop effective credit analysis models so that they can identify bonds with high yields and high probabilities of upgrades to include in their portfolios, as well as identify bonds with high probabilities of downgrades to exclude from their fund. Credit analysis can be done through fundamental analysis of the bond issuer and the indenture and with statistical-based models, such as a multiple discriminant model.

Fundamental Credit Analysis: Many large institutional investors and banks have their own credit analysis departments to evaluate bond issues in order to determine the abilities of companies, municipalities, and foreign issuers to meet their contractual obligations, as well as to determine the possibility of changes in a bond's quality ratings and therefore a change in its price.

Corporate Issues: The credit analysis for corporate bonds often includes the following types of examination:

- *Industrial Analysis* Assessment of the growth rate of the industry, stage of industrial development, cyclicality of the industry, degree of competition, industry and company trends, government regulations, and labor costs and issues.
- *Fundamental Analysis* Comparison of the company's financial ratios with other firms in the industry and with the averages for bonds based on their quality ratings. Ratios often used for analysis include: (1) interest coverage (EBIT/interest), (2) leverage (long-term debt/total assets), (3) cash flow (net income + depreciation + amortization + depletion + deferred taxes) as a proportion of total debt (cash flow/debt), and (4) return on equity. The averages for some of these ratios by quality ratings are shown in table 8.1.
- *Asset and Liability Analysis* Determination of the market values of assets and liabilities, age and condition of plants, working capital (current assets minus current liabilities), intangible assets and liabilities (e.g., unfunded pension liabilities), and foreign currency exposure.

- *Indenture Analysis* Analysis of protective covenants, including a comparison of covenants with the industry norms.

Municipal Analysis: In analyzing the creditworthiness of municipals (general obligations, GOs, and revenue bonds), the two most important areas of examination are indenture analysis and economic and credit analysis. Some of the key questions related to indenture analysis were examined chapter 6. The important areas of inquiry in credit and economic analysis relate to debt burden, fiscal soundness, overall economic climate, and red flags.[6]

- *Debt burden* This analysis involves assessing the total debt burden of the municipal issuer. For GOs, debt burden should include determining the total debt outstanding, including moral obligation bonds, leases, and unfunded pension liabilities. The assessment of the debt burden should include ratios based on debt per capita, historical averages, and debt per capita ratios relative to other areas. For revenue bonds, debt burden should also focus on relevant coverage ratios relating the debt on the revenue bond to user charges, earmarked revenue, lease rental, and the like.
- *Fiscal Soundness* The objective of this analysis is to determine the issuer's ability to meet obligations. For GOs, the areas of inquiry can include: what are the primary sources of revenue? Is the issuer dependent on any one particular source of revenue? How well has the budget been managed over the last several years? Are there any large liabilities or contracts? Is there a dependence on short-term debt? For revenue bonds, relevant questions relate to the soundness of the project or operation being financed (e.g., power plant) or the source of income (e.g., rents, student fees, and the like), and the quality of the guarantee.
- *Overall Economic Climate* General economic analysis includes examining fundamentals such as growth rates for income, population, and property values. It also should determine the status of the largest property values and employers.
- *Red Flags* Some of the negative indicators suggesting greater credit risk are decreases in population, unemployment increases, decreases in the number of building permits,

actual revenue levels consistently falling below projections, declines in property values, loss of large employers, use of debt reserves, and declines in debt coverage ratios. For revenue bonds, additional red flags could include cost overruns on projects, schedule delays, and frequent rate or rental increases.

International Debt: The credit analysis of international bonds issued by corporations needs to take into account the same issues of any corporate bond (fundamental ratio analysis, financial soundness, industry analysis, and indentures examination). In addition, the analysis needs to consider *cross-border risk*: risk due to changes in political, social, and economic conditions in countries where the bonds are issued or where the company is incorporated. In the case of sovereign foreign debt, especially the debt of emerging markets, analysis needs to include an examination of sovereign risk: the risk that the government is unable or unwilling (due to political changes) to service its debt.[7] Some of the key areas of inquiry in a credit analysis of a sovereign or private debt issuers of debt from an emerging market country relate to the following fundamental issues:

- Size and diversification of the country's exports. Countries that specialize in exporting only a few products may be more susceptible to recessions.
- Political stability: strength of the legal system, amount of unemployment, and distribution of wealth.
- History of meeting debt obligations.
- Balance of payments ratios: country's total debt to export ratio.
- Economic factors: inflation, growth in gross domestic product, interest rates, and unemployment.
- Susceptibility of country's economy and exports to changes in economic conditions in industrialized countries.[8]

Multiple Discriminant Analysis: Multiple discriminant analysis is a statistical technique that can be used to forecast default or changes in credit ratings. When applied to credit analysis, the model estimates a bond's credit score or index, S_i, to determine its overall credit quality. The score is based on a set of explanatory variables, X_i, and estimated weights or coefficients, c_i, measuring the variables' relative impact on the bond's overall credit quality:

$$S_i = c_0 + c_1X_1 + c_2X_2 + \cdots + c_nX_n$$

For corporate bonds, possible explanatory variables include the financial ratios shown in table 8.1 (interest coverage, leverage, and cash flows), as well as the corporation's capitalization level, profitability (earnings before interest and taxes to total assets), and variability (variance of profitability ratio).[9]

One way to apply multiple discriminant analysis is to compute and then rank the credit quality scores of a number of bonds. This entails estimating the coefficient c_i (possibly using a cross-sectional regression technique) and then determining the current ratios for the companies to be analyzed. Given the c_i and X_i values, each company's current credit quality score S_i can be computed using the above equation. Once the scores are estimated, then the bonds can be ranked in the order of their scores to assess each bond's relative default risk. Discriminant analysis can also be used to forecast a change in default risk. In this case, the expected future financial ratios of each company are estimated and then used in the above equation to determine the company's future score or expected change in score.

High-Yield Bond Funds

As noted earlier, credit analysis is an important tool for managing high-yield funds. Successful funds have fund managers that are able to identify those low-quality bonds that have the potential for being upgraded and therefore should be included in the fund and those bonds that are in jeopardy of being downgraded and therefore should be excluded. It should be noted that today the management of high-yield bond funds has become quite challenging given the many types of high-yield bonds. In the 1980s, many high-yield funds consisted only of privately placed junk bonds of corporations who issued them to finance their mergers. Today many lower quality corporate bonds are sold with special provisions. As we discussed in chapter 5, these bonds include income bonds, reset notes, payment-in-kind bonds, convertibles, putable notes, extendable bonds,

bonds with warrants, and credit-sensitive bonds. In addition, as we saw in chapters 6 and 7, there are also many lower quality municipals and foreign bonds with different features. The successful performance of today's high-yield funds therefore requires not only effective credit analysis of the company, government, or country issuer, but also a careful analysis of the bond's indenture and its special security provisions.

Chapter 11 Funds

A special type of high-yield fund is the *Chapter 11 fund*: a fund consisting of the bonds of bankrupt or distressed companies. Such bonds consist of issues of corporations who are going through a bankruptcy process or those that are in distress, but have not yet filed. The general strategy is to buy bonds whose prices have plummeted as a result of a filing (or on information that indicates a filing is imminent) but where there is a good expectation that there will be a successful reorganization or possible asset sale that will lead in the future to an increase in the debt's value or to the replacement of the debt with a more valuable claim. Chapter 11 funds are sometimes set up as a hedged fund in which large investors buy, through the fund, a significant block of debt of a specific bankrupt company, giving them some control in the reorganization plan (see exhibit 5.1 for a description of the bankruptcy process). The funds are also set up as so-called *vulture funds* that invest in the securities of a number of bankrupt firms. Just like any high-yield fund, the success of Chapter 11 funds depends on the ability of the fund managers to conduct an effective credit-type analysis. In this case, though, the analysis often involves studying the feasibility of the reorganization plan submitted out of the bankruptcy process or trying to project the type of plan that will be submitted.[10]

8.2.3 Fundamental Valuation Strategies

A common approach to stock selection is fundamental analysis. The objective of fundamental stock analysis is to determine a stock's equilibrium price or intrinsic value. By doing this, fundamentalists hope to profit by purchasing stocks they estimate to be underpriced (a stock whose market price is below its intrinsic value) and selling or shorting stocks they determine to be overpriced. The objective of fundamental bond analysis is the same as that of fundamental stock analysis. It involves determining a bond's intrinsic value and then comparing that value with the bond's market price. The active management of a bond portfolio using a fundamental strategy, in turn, involves buying bonds that are determined to be underpriced and selling or avoiding those determined to be overpriced.

A bond fundamentalist often tries to determine a bond's intrinsic value by estimating the required rate for discounting the bond's cash flows. This rate, R, depends on the current level of interest rates as measured by the risk-free rate on a Treasury with the same maturity as the bond in question, R_f, and the bond's characteristics (maturity, option features, and quality risk) and the risk premiums or yield spreads associated with those characteristics: default risk premium (DRP), liquidity premium (LP), and option-adjusted spread (OAS):

$$R = R_f + DRP + LP + OAS$$

Fundamentalists use various models, such as regressions, multiple discriminant analysis, and the option pricing models (discussed in chapter 10), to estimate the various spreads. They also use the binomial interest rate trees (discussed in chapters 9 and 10) to estimate the values of bonds with embedded option features.

A variation of fundamental bond strategies is a *yield pick-up swap*. In a yield pick-up swap, investors or arbitrageurs try to find bonds that are identical, but for some reason are temporarily mispriced, trading at different yields. When two identical bonds trade at different yields, abnormal return can be realized by going long in the underpriced (higher yield) bond and short in the overpriced (lower yield) bond, then closing the positions once the prices of the two bonds converge. It is important to note that to profit from a yield pick-up swap, the bonds must be identical. It could be the case that two bonds appear to be identical, but are not. For example, two bonds with the same durations, default ratings, and call features may appear to

be identical, when in fact they have different marketability characteristics that explain the observed differences in their yields.

The strategy underlying a yield pick-up swap can be extended from comparing different bonds to a portfolio of bonds constructed to have the same features. For example, suppose a portfolio consisting of an AAA quality, 10-year, 10% coupon bond and an A quality, 5-year, 5% coupon bond is constructed such that it has the same cash flows and features as say an AA quality, 7.5-year, 7.5% coupon bond. If an AA quality, 7.5-year, 7.5% coupon bond and the portfolio do not provide the same yield, then an arbitrageur or speculator could form a yield pick-up swap by taking opposite positions in the portfolio and the bond. A fundamentalist could also use this methodology for identifying underpriced bonds: buying all AA quality, 7.5-year, 7.5% coupon bonds with yields exceeding the portfolio formed with those features.

The yield pick-up strategy also can be applied to comparing a bond and a portfolio of strip securities with identical features. In fact, the dealer strategies we discussed in chapter 6 of purchasing a T-note or federal agency security, stripping it, and selling the stripped securities or purchasing a portfolio of stripped securities, bundling them, and selling them as a coupon bond, can be considered yield pick-up strategies of going long and short in two identical positions that are not equally priced.

8.2.4   Other Active Strategies

In the above discussion of active strategies we identified three bond swaps: rate-anticipation swaps, quality swaps, and yield pick-up swaps. In addition to these swaps, two other swaps that should be noted are tax swaps and swaps of callable and non-callable bonds.

Tax Swap

In a *tax swap*, an investor sells one bond and purchases another in order to take advantage of the tax laws. For example, suppose a bond investor purchased $10,000-worth of a particular bond and then sold it after rates decreased for $15,000, realizing a capital gain of $5,000 and also a capital gains tax liability. One way for the investor to negate the tax liability would be to offset the capital gain with a capital loss. If the investor were holding bonds with current capital losses of say $5,000, he could sell those to incur a capital loss to offset his gain. Except for the offset feature, though, the investor may not otherwise want to sell the bond; for example, he might want to hold the bond because he expects an upgrade in the bond's quality rating. If this were the case, then the investor could execute a bond swap in which he sells the bond needed for creating a capital loss and then uses the proceeds to purchase a similar, though not identical, bond. Thus, the tax swap allows the investor to effectively hold the bond he wants, while still reducing his tax liability. Note: for the capital loss to be tax-deductible, the bond purchased in the tax swap cannot be identical to the bond sold; if it was, then the swap would represent a wash sale that would result in the IRS disallowing the deduction.[11] In contrast to the IRS's wash sales criterion on stocks, though, the wash sale criterion used for bonds does permit the purchase of comparable bonds that have only minor differences.

Callable/Non-callable Bond Swaps

During periods of high interest rates, the spread between the yields on callable and non-callable bonds is greater than during periods of relatively low interest rates. Accordingly, if investors expect rates to decrease in the future, causing the spread between callable and non-callable bonds to narrow, they could capitalize by forming a *callable/non-callable bond swap*: short in the callable bond and long in the non-callable one. To effectively apply this bond swap requires investors to not only forecast interest rate changes, but to also forecast changes in the spread. Similar swaps can also be extended to bonds with and without other option features, such as putable and non-putable bonds.

8.3 PASSIVE BOND MANAGEMENT STRATEGIES

The objectives underlying passive management strategies vary from a simple buy-and-hold approach of investing in bonds with specific maturities, coupons, and quality ratings with the intent of holding the bonds to maturity, to forming portfolios with returns that mirror the returns on a bond index, to constructing portfolios that ensure there are sufficient funds to meet future liabilities. Here we look at two passive strategies: indexing and cash flow matching.[12] Indexing strategies involve constructing bond portfolios that are highly correlated with a specified bond index. These strategies are applicable for investment funds whose performances are evaluated on a period-by-period basis. Cash-flow matching strategies involve constructing bond portfolios with cash flows that will meet future liabilities. They are liability management strategies applicable to insurance companies, deposit institutions, and pension funds that have cash outlays which must be made at specific times.

8.3.1 Indexing

Bond indexing involves constructing a bond portfolio whose returns over time replicate the returns of a bond index. Indexing is a passive strategy, often used by investment fund managers who believe that actively managed bond strategies do not outperform bond market indexes.

The first step in constructing a bond index fund is to select the appropriate index. Bond indexes can be either general, such as the Shearson–Lehman Aggregate or the Merrill-Lynch Composite, or specialized, such as Salomon Smith Barney's Global Government Bond Index (see table 7.1). Also, some investment companies offer their own customized index specifically designed to meet certain investment objectives. After selecting the index, the next step is to determine how to replicate the index's performance. One approach is to simply purchase all of the bonds comprising the index in the same proportion that they appear in the index. This is known as *pure bond indexing* or the *full-replication approach*. This approach would result in a perfect correlation between the bond fund and the index. However, with some indexes consisting of as many as 5,000 bonds, the transaction cost involved in acquiring all of the bonds is very high. An alternative to selecting all bonds is to use only a sample.[13] By using a smaller size portfolio, the transaction costs incurred in constructing the index fund would be smaller. However with fewer bonds, there may be less than perfection positive correlation between the index and the index fund. The differences between the returns on the index and the index fund are referred to as *tracking errors*. Using a sample is subject to tracking errors.

When a sample approach is used, the index fund can be set up using an optimization approach to determine the allocation of each bond in the fund such that it minimizes the tracking error. Another approach is to use a *cell-matching strategy*. With this approach, the index is decomposed into cells, with each cell defining a different mix of features of the index (duration, credit rating, sector, etc.). For example, a bond index might be described as having two durations ($D > 5$ years and $D < 5$ years), two sectors (Corporate and Municipal), and two quality ratings (AAA, AA). These features can be broken into eight unique types of cells, C_i ($2 \times 2 \times 2 = 8$):

$$C_1 = D < 5, \text{AAA}, \text{Corp}$$
$$C_2 = D < 5, \text{AAA}, \text{Muni}$$
$$C_3 = D < 5, \text{AA}, \text{Corp}$$
$$C_4 = D < 5, \text{AA}, \text{Muni}$$
$$C_5 = D > 5, \text{AAA}, \text{Corp}$$
$$C_6 = D > 5, \text{AAA}, \text{Muni}$$
$$C_7 = D > 5, \text{AA}, \text{Corp}$$
$$C_8 = D > 5, \text{AA}, \text{Muni}$$

Given the cells, the index fund is constructed by selecting bonds to match each cell and then allocating funds to each type of bond based on each cell's allocation.

Given the number of possible attributes describing an index, cell matching can be quite complex. For example, three duration classes, three sectors, and three quality ratings give rise to 27 cells. To minimize the number of constraints, one approach is to base the cell identification on just two features such as the durations and sectors or the durations and quality ratings. A duration/sector index is formed by matching the amounts of the index's durations that make up each of the various sectors. This requires estimating the duration for each sector comprising the index (e.g., Treasury, federal agency, corporate industry, corporate utility, corporate foreign, sovereign, asset-backed) and determining each sector's

Table 8.2 Duration/sector and duration/quality cell matching

	Percentage of value	Duration
Sector		
Treasury	20	4.50
Federal agency	10	3.25
Municipals	15	5.25
Corporate industry	15	6.00
Corporate utility	10	6.25
Corporate foreign	10	5.55
Sovereign	10	5.75
Asset-backed	10	6.25
	100	Weighted average = 5.29
Quality sector		
AAA	60	5.25
AA	15	5.35
A	10	5.25
BBB	5	5.65
BB	5	5.25
B	5	5.30
	100	Weighted average = 5.29

percentage of value to the index. If 20% of an index's value consists of Treasury securities with the Treasuries having an estimated portfolio duration of 4.5, then the index portfolio being constructed would consist of 20% of Treasuries with an average duration of 4.5 (see top of table 8.2). Instead of sectors, duration matching could be done instead with quality sectors. This would require determining the percentages of value and average durations of each quality-rating group making up the index (see bottom of table 8.2).

It should be noted that an important feature of any bond portfolio or index is its call option exposure. In constructing an index portfolio, an index's call exposure can be difficult to replicate. One approach is to decompose each cell further into callable and non-callable sectors; another is to form duration/sector or duration/maturity cells as just described with the duration estimated using an option-adjusted technique (described in chapter 10).

Whether the index fund is formed with the population of all bonds encompassing the specified index or a sample, the objective of indexing is still to replicate the performance of the index. A variation of straight indexing is *enhanced bond indexing*. This approach allows for minor deviations of certain features and some active management in order to try to attain a return better than the index. Usually the deviations are in quality ratings or sectors, and not in durations, and they are based on some active management strategy. For example, a fund indexed primarily to the Merrill-Lynch composite but with more weight given to lower quality bonds based on an expectation of an improving economy would be an enhanced index fund combining indexing and sector rotation.

8.3.2 Cash-Flow Matching: Dedicated Portfolios

Liabilities of financial institutions can vary. Some liability amounts and timings are known with certainty (for example, a CD obligation of a bank); for others the amount is predictable, but not the timing (e.g., life insurance policy); and in others both the amount and the time are unknown (e.g., property insurance or pension obligations). In the latter two cases, the law of large numbers makes it possible for actuaries to make reasonably accurate forecasts of the future cash outlays. Given projected cash outlays, the objective of the investment manager is to obtain a sufficient return from investing the premiums, deposits, or pension contributions, while still meeting the projected liabilities. Among the most popular approaches used in liability management strategies are cash-flow matching and bond immunization (discussed in section 8.4).

A *cash-flow matching strategy*, also referred to as a *dedicated portfolio strategy*, involves constructing a bond portfolio with cash flows that match the outlays of the liabilities. For example, a pension fund forming a cash-flow matching strategy to meet projected liabilities of $1m, $3m, and $4m for each of the next 3 years would need to construct a bond portfolio with the same, or approximately the same, cash flows.

One method that can be used for cash-flow matching is to start with the final liability for time T and work backwards. For the last period, one would select a bond with a principal (F_T) and coupon (C_T) that matches the amount of that final liability (L_T):

$$L_T = F_T + C_T$$
$$L_T = F_T(1 + C^{R0})$$

where C^{R0} is the coupon rate (C_T/F_T). To meet this liability, one could buy $L_T/(1 + C^{R0})$ of par value of bonds maturing in T periods. Since these bonds' coupons will also be paid in earlier periods, they can be used to reduce the liabilities in each of the earlier periods. Thus, to match the liability in period $T-1$, one would need to select bonds with a principal of F_{T-1} and coupon C_{T-1} (or coupon rate of $C^{R1} = C_{T-1}/F_{T-1}$) that is equal to the projected liability in period $T-1$ (L_{T-1}) less the coupon amount of C_T from the T-period bonds selected:

$$L_{T-1} - C_T = F_{T-1} + C_{T-1}$$
$$L_{T-1} - C_T = F_{T-1}(1 + C^{R1})$$

To meet this liability, one could buy $(L_{T-1} - C_T)/(1 + C^{R1})$-worth of par value of bonds maturing in $T-1$ periods. The C_{T-1} coupons paid on these bonds, as well as the first bonds (C_T), would likewise be used to reduce liabilities in all earlier periods. Thus, to meet the liability in period $T-2$, the next bonds to be selected would have a principal and coupon in which:

$$L_{T-2} - C_T - C_{T-1} = F_{T-2} + C_{T-2}$$
$$L_{T-2} - C_T - C_{T-1} = F_{T-2}(1 + C^{R2})$$

For this liability, one could buy $(L_{T-2} - C_T - C_{T-1})/(1 + C^{R2})$-worth of par value of bonds maturing in $T-2$ periods.

A simple cash-flow matching case is presented in exhibit 8.1. The exhibit shows the matching of liabilities of $4m, $3m, and $1m in years 3, 2, and 1 with 3-year, 2-year, and 1-year bonds each paying 5% annual coupons and selling at par. The $4m liability at the end of year 3 is matched by buying $3,809,524-worth of 3-year, 5% annual coupon bonds trading at par: $3,809,524 = L_3/(1 + C^{R0}) = $4,000,000/1.05. At the end of year 3, the bonds will pay a principal of $3,809,524 and interest of $190,476 ((0.05)($3,809,524)) that match the $4m liability. The $3m liability at the end of year 2 is matched by buying

Exhibit 8.1   Cash-flow matching case

Bonds	Coupon rate	Par	Yield	Market value	Liability	Year
3-year	5%	100	5%	100	$4,000,000	3
2-year	5%	100	5%	100	$3,000,000	2
1-year	5%	100	5%	100	$1,000,000	1

Match strategy:

The $4m liability at the end of year 3 is matched by buying $3,809,524 of 3-year bonds: $3,809,524 = $4,000,000/1.05.

The $3m liability at the end of year 2 is matched by buying $2,675,737 of 2-year bonds: $2,675,737 = ($3,000,000 − (0.05)($3,809,524))/1.05.

The $1m liability at the end of year 1 is matched by buying $643,559 of 1-year bonds: $643,559 = ($1,000,000 − (0.05)($3,809,524) − (0.05)($2,675,737))/1.05.

(1) Year	(2) Total bond values	(3) Coupon income	(4) Maturing principal	(5) Liability	(6) Ending balance (3) + (4) − (5)
1	$7,128,820	$356,441	$643,559	$1,000,000	0
2	$6,485,261	$324,263	$2,675,737	$3,000,000	0
3	$3,809,524	$190,476	$3,809,524	$4,000,000	0

$2,675,737 of 2-year, 5% annual coupon bonds trading at par: $2,675,737 = (L_2 − C_3)/(1 + C^{R1}) = ($3,000,000 − $190,476)/1.05$. At the end of year 2, these 2-year bonds will pay a principal of $2,675,737 and coupon interest of $133,787; this amount combined with the interest of $190,476 from the original 3-year bond will meet the $3m liability of year 2. Finally, the $1m liability at the end of year 1 is matched by buying $643,559 of a 1-year, 5% annual coupon bond trading at par: $643,559 = (L_1 − C_3 − C_2)/(1 + C^{R2}) = ($1,000,000 − $190,476 − $133,787)/1.05$. At the end of year 1, these 1-year bonds will pay a principal of $643,559 and coupon interest of $32,178; this principal and interest plus the interest of $190,476 and $133,787 from the original 3-year and 2-year bonds will meet the $1m liability of year 2.

With cash-flow matching the basic goal is to simply build a portfolio that will provide a stream of payments from coupons, sinking funds, and maturing principals that will match the liability payments. A dedicated portfolio strategy is subject to some minor market risk given that some cash flows may need to be reinvested forward. It also can be subject to default risk if lower quality bonds are purchased. The biggest risk with cash-flow matching strategies, though, is that the bonds selected to match forecasted liabilities may be called, forcing the investment manager to purchase new bonds yielding lower rates. To minimize such risk, one can look for non-callable bonds, deep discount bonds, or zero-coupon stripped securities. There are also option and hedging strategies that can be implemented to hedge the risk of embedded call options.

8.4 BOND IMMUNIZATION STRATEGIES

8.4.1 Classical Immunization

An alternative to cash-flow matching strategies for pensions, insurance companies, and thrifts is to apply immunization strategies to liability management. In chapter 4, we defined immunization as a strategy of minimizing market risk by selecting a bond or bond portfolio with a duration equal to the horizon date. For liability management cases, the liability payment date is the liability's duration. Thus, immunization can be described as a duration-matching strategy of equating the duration of the bond or asset to the duration of the liability. As we examined in chapter 4, when a bond's duration is equal to the liability's duration, the direct interest-on-interest effect (or reinvestment effect), in which the interest earned from reinvesting the bond's coupons changes directly with interest rate changes, and the inverse price effect, in which the bond's price changes inversely to interest rate changes, exactly offset each other. As a result, the rate from the investment (ARR) or the value of the investment at the horizon or liability date does not change because of an interest rate change.

The foundation for bond immunization strategies comes from a 1952 article by F. M. Redington.[14] He argued that a bond investment position could be immunized against interest rate changes by matching durations of the bond and the liability. To illustrate, consider a pension fund with a single liability of $1,352 due in 3.5 years. Assuming a flat yield curve at 10%, the pension fund could immunize its investment against market risk by purchasing a bond with a duration of 3.5 years (using Macaulay's measure), priced at $968.50 ($1,352/(1.10)^{3.5}$). This could be done by buying a 4-year, 9% annual coupon bond with a principal of $1,000.[15] This bond has both a duration of 3.5 years and is worth $968.50, given a yield curve at 10%. If the pension fund buys this bond, then any parallel shift in the yield curve in the very near future would have price and interest rate effects that exactly offset each other. As a result, the cash flow or ending wealth at year 3.5, referred to as the

accumulation value or target value, would be exactly $1,352 (see exhibit 8.2).

Note that in addition to matching duration, immunization also requires the initial investment or current market value of the assets purchased to be equal to or greater than the present value of the liability using the current YTM as a discount factor. In this example, the present value of the $1,352 liability is $968.50 ($= $1,352/(1.10)^{3.5}$), which equals the current value of the bond and implies a 10% rate of return.

Redington's duration-matching strategy is sometimes referred to as *classical immunization*. Again, it works by having offsetting price and reinvestment effects. In contrast, a maturity-matching strategy where a bond is selected with a maturity equal to the horizon date has no price effect and therefore no way to offset the reinvestment effect. This can be seen in exhibit 8.2 where unlike the duration-matched bond, a 10% annual coupon bond with maturity of 3.5 years has different ending values given different interest rates.

8.4.2 Rebalancing

In a 1971 study, Fisher and Weil compared duration-matched immunization positions with maturity-matched ones under a number of interest rate scenarios. They found that while the duration-matched positions were closer to their initial YTM than the maturity-matched strategies, they were not absent of market risk. Two reasons they offered for the presence of market risk with classical immunization were that the shifts in yield curves were not parallel and that immunization only works when the duration of assets and liabilities are matched at all times. To achieve immunization, Fisher and Weil argued that the duration of the bond or portfolio must be equal to the remaining time in the horizon period.

Fisher and Weil's latter point can be illustrated by looking at what happens to the growth path of an investment when there is an interest rate change.[16] Consider a $1,000 investment in a 10% annual coupon bond over a horizon period of 10 years. As shown in figure 8.2a, if the yield curve is flat at 10% and does not change, then the investment will grow at an annual rate of 10% to equal $2,594 at the

Exhibit 8.2 Duration matching and maturity matching

Ending values at 3.5 years given different interest rates for 4-year, 9% annual coupon bond with duration of 3.5 and 10% annual coupon bond with maturity of 3.5 years

Duration = 3.5 Time (years)	9%	10%	11%
1	$90(1.09)^{2.5} =$ $111.64	$90(1.10)^{2.5} =$ $114.21	$90(1.11)^{2.5} =$ $116.83
2	$90(1.09)^{1.5} =$ $102.42	$90(1.10)^{1.5} =$ $103.83	$90(1.11)^{1.5} =$ $105.25
3	$90(1.09)^{0.5} =$ $93.96	$90(1.10)^{0.5} =$ $94.39	$90(1.11)^{0.5} =$ $94.82
3.5	$1,090/(1.09)^{0.5} = \underline{\$1,044.03}$	$1,090/(1.10)^{0.5} = \underline{\$1,039.27}$	$1,090/(1.11)^{0.5} = \underline{\$1,034.58}$
Target value	$1,352	$1,352	$1,352

Maturity = 3.5 years Time (years)	9%	10%	11%
1	$100(1.09)^{2.5} =$ $124.04	$100(1.10)^{2.5} =$ $126.91	$100(1.11)^{2.5} =$ $129.81
2	$100(1.09)^{1.5} =$ $113.80	$100(1.10)^{1.5} =$ $115.37	$100(1.11)^{1.5} =$ $116.95
3	$100(1.09)^{0.5} =$ $104.40	$100(1.10)^{0.5} =$ $104.88	$100(1.11)^{0.5} =$ $105.36
3.5	$1,050 = \underline{\$1,050}$	$1,050 = \underline{\$1,050}$	$1,050 = \underline{\$1,050}$
	$1,392	$1,397	$1,402

end of 10 years ($= \$1,000(1.10)^{10}$). However, suppose after 2 years, the flat yield curve shifted down from 10% to 6% and stayed there. If the original investment had been placed in a 2-year, 10% coupon bond, the investment would be worth $1,210 at the end of year 2, and at the 6% rate, it would grow over the next 8 years to equal only $1,929. If the original investment, though, had been in a 15-year, 10% coupon bond with a modified duration of 7.6 (ignore the negative sign for modified duration), then at the end of year 2 this bond would be worth $1,354 given the 6% rate and would have a modified duration of 8 (Macaulay's duration of 8.6). Given the coupon value of $210 from the first two coupons and the interest earned from reinvesting, the total investment value would be $1,564. At 6%, $1,564 would grow over the next 8 years to equal $2,493. This ending value is, of course, much closer to the original end-of-the period value of $2,594 than the $1,929 (it will not be identical because of convexity). This is because the price increase is on a bond with a duration matching the

remaining horizon period of 8 years. As a result, the price increase offsets the lower reinvestment rate. Note, if the interest rate had instead increased from 10% to 12%, then the $1,210 from the original 2-year bond would grow at 12% over the next 8 years to equal $2,996 (see figure 8.2b). In contrast, if the investment were in an original 27-year, 10% bond (duration of 9.24), then at the end of year 2, the bond would have a modified duration of 8 (Macaulay's duration of 9) and would be worth only $843 given the 12% rate. Given the coupon value of $210, the total investment value would be $1,053 at the end of year 2. This lower value offsets the gain from reinvesting at the higher 12% rates. At 12%, $1,053 would grow over the next 8 years to equal $2,607. This ending value again is much closer to the original end-of-the period value of $2,594, and while it is significantly less than $2,996, it does achieve the objective of minimizing market risk.

The example shows that the price and reinvestment effects will approximately offset each

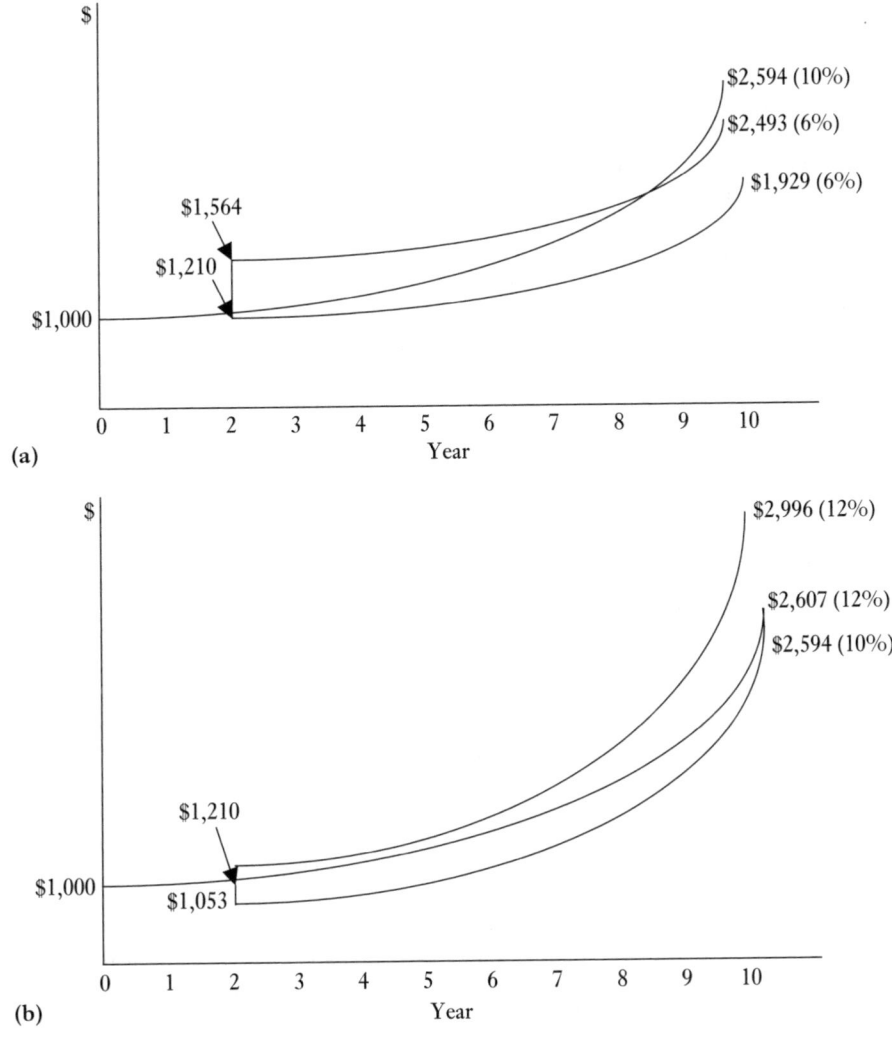

Figure 8.2 Growth path and immunization

other to attain an expected ending wealth value reflecting the initial rate if the investment's duration is approximately equal to the *remaining* horizon; that is, immunization requires that the investment has the correct duration match when the interest rate changes. Immunization strategies should therefore not be considered as passive. Since the durations of assets and liabilities change with both time and yield changes, immunized positions require active management, called *rebalancing*, to ensure that the duration of the portfolio is always equal

to the remaining time to horizon. Thus, a bond and liability that currently have the same durations will not necessarily be equal as time passes and rates change. For one, the duration of a coupon bond declines more slowly than the terms to maturity. In our earlier example, our 4-year, 9% bond with Macaulay's duration of 3.5 years (modified duration of 3.2) when rates were 10%, 1 year later would have duration of 2.77 years (modified of 2.5) with no change in rates. Secondly, duration changes with interest rate changes. Specifically, there is an inverse relation between interest rates and duration: duration increasing as rates decrease and decreasing with interest rate increases.

Maintaining an immunized position when the bond's duration is no longer equal to the duration of the liability or remaining horizon period requires resetting the bond position such that the durations are again matched. This rebalancing could be done by selling the bond and buying a new one with the correct match, adding a bond to form a portfolio that will have the correct portfolio duration, investing the bond's cash flows differently, or perhaps taking a futures, options, or swap position (this is discussed in part IV). In practice, an important consideration for a bond manager immunizing a position is how frequently the position must be rebalanced. Greater transaction costs incurred from frequent rebalancing must be weighed against having a position exposed to less market risk.

In addition to rebalancing the asset position over time and in response to interest rate changes, bond managers also have to decide whether to immunize with a bond or a portfolio of bonds. For a single liability, immunization can be attained with a focus strategy or a barbell strategy. In a *focus strategy*, a bond is selected with a duration that matches the duration of the liability, or a bullet approach is applied where a portfolio of bonds is selected with all the bonds close to the desired duration. For example, if the duration of the liability is 4 years, one could select a bond with a 4-year duration or form a portfolio of bonds with durations of 4 and 5 years. In a barbell strategy, the duration of the liability is matched with a bond portfolio with durations more at the extremes. Thus, for a duration liability of 4 years, an investor might invest half of his funds in a bond with a 2-year duration and half in a bond with a 6-year duration. The problem with the barbell strategy is that it may not immunize the position if the shift in the yield curve is not parallel.

8.4.3 Immunizing Multiple-Period Liabilities

For multiple-period liabilities, bond immunization strategies can be done either by matching the duration of each liability with the appropriate bond or bullet bond portfolio or by

constructing a portfolio with a duration equal to the weighted average of the durations of the liabilities (D_L^P). For example, if a pension fund had multiple liabilities of $1m each in years 4, 5, and 6, it could either invest in three bonds, each with respective durations of 4 years, 5 years, and 6 years, or it could invest in a bond portfolio with duration equal to 5 years:

$$D_L^P = \frac{\$1m}{\$3m}4 \text{ yrs} + \frac{\$1m}{\$3m}5 \text{ yrs} + \frac{\$1m}{\$3m}6 \text{ yrs} = 5 \text{ yrs}$$

The latter approach is relatively simple to construct, as well as to manage. However, studies have shown that matching the portfolio's duration of assets with the duration of the liabilities does not always immunize the positions.[17] Thus, for multiple-period liabilities, the best approach is generally considered to be one of immunizing each liability. As with single liabilities, this also requires rebalancing each immunized position.

The costs of setting up and managing a matching immunization strategy with rebalancing applied to multiple liabilities must be weighed against having a position exposed to market risk. In some cases, a bond manager may find that a cash-flow matching strategy with little or no rebalancing is preferable to an immunization strategy that requires frequent rebalancing.[18] In fact, some managers combine cash-flow matching and immunization strategies. Known as *combination matching* or *horizon matching*, these strategies consist of using cash-flow matching strategies for early liabilities (e.g., 5 years) and an immunization strategy for longer-term liabilities.

8.4.4 Surplus Management and Duration Gap Analysis

The major users of immunization strategies are pensions, insurance companies, and commercial banks and thrifts. Pensions and life insurance companies use multiple-period immunization to determine the investments that will match a schedule of forecasted payouts. Insurance companies, banks and thrifts, and other financial corporations also use immunization concepts for *surplus management*. Surplus management refers to managing the surplus value of assets over liabilities. This surplus can be measured as *economic surplus*, defined as the difference between the market value of the assets and the present value of the liabilities. Thus, a pension with a bond portfolio currently valued at $200m and liabilities with a present value of $180m would have an economic surplus of $20m. Whether the $20m surplus is adequate depends, in part, on the **duration gap**: the difference in the duration of assets and the duration of the liabilities. If the duration of the assets exceeds the duration of the liabilities, then the economic surplus will vary inversely with interest rates: increasing if rates fall and decreasing if rates rise. For example, if the duration of the bond portfolio is 7 years and the duration of the liabilities is 5 years, a decrease in rates by 100 BP would augment the value of the bond portfolio from $200m to approximately $214m (= $200m (1.07)) and increase the present value of the liabilities from $180m to approximately $189m (= $180m (1.05)), causing the economic surplus to increase from $20m to $25m. However, if rates were to increase by 100 BP, then the surplus would decrease from $20m to approximately $15m: economic surplus = $200m (1 − 0.07) − $180m (1 − 0.05) = $15m. On the other hand, if the duration of the bond portfolio is less than the duration of the liabilities, then the surplus value will vary directly with interest rates. Finally, if the durations of assets and liabilities are equal (an immunized position), then the surplus will be invariant to rate changes.

In addition to its use by pensions and insurance companies, duration gap analysis is also used by banks to determine changes in the market value of the institution's net worth to changes in interest rates.[19] With gap analysis, a bank's asset sensitivity and liability sensitivity to interest rate changes is found by estimating Macaulay's duration for the assets and liabilities and then using the formula for modified duration to determine the percentage change in value to a percentage change in interest rates:

$$\%\Delta P = -(\text{Macaulay's duration})(\Delta R/(1+R))$$

As an example, table 8.3 shows the amounts and durations of a small commercial bank's assets and liabilities. The bank has assets and liabilities each equal to $150m with a weighted Macaulay's duration of 2.88 years on its assets and a weighted duration of 1.467 on its liabilities given an interest rate level of 10%. The bank's positive duration gap of 1.413 suggests an inverse relation between changes in rates and net worth. For example, if interest rate were to increase from 10% to 11%, the bank's asset value would decrease by 2.62% and its liabilities by 1.33%, resulting in a decrease in the bank's net worth of $1.93m:

$$\%\Delta P = -(\text{Macaulay's duration})(\Delta R/(1+R))$$

$$\text{Assets}: \%\Delta P = -(2.88)(0.01/1.10) = -0.0262$$

$$\text{Liabilities}: \%\Delta P = -(1.467)(0.01/1.10)$$
$$= -0.0133$$

$$\text{Change in net worth} = (-0.0262)(\$150\,\text{m})$$
$$- (-0.0133)(\$150\,\text{m})$$
$$= -\$1.93\,\text{m}$$

On the other hand, if rates were to decrease from 10% to 9%, then the bank's net worth would increase by $1.93m. Thus, with a positive duration gap an increase in rates would result in a loss in the bank's capital and a decrease in rates would cause the bank's capital to increase. If the bank's duration gap had been negative, then a direct relation would exist between the bank's net worth and interest rates, and if the gap were zero, then its net worth would be invariant to interest rate changes. As a tool, duration gap analysis helps the bank's management ascertain the degree of exposure that its net worth has to interest rate changes.

8.4.5 Contingent Immunization

Developed by Liebowitz and Weinberger, *contingent immunization* is an enhanced immunization strategy that combines active management to achieve higher returns and immunization strategies to ensure a floor.[20] In a contingent immunization strategy, a client of an investment management fund agrees to accept a potential return below an immunized market return. The lower potential return is referred to as the **target rate** and the difference

Table 8.3 Duration gap analysis of a bank

Assets	Amount in millions of $	Macaulay's duration	Weighted duration	Liabilities	Amount in millions of $	Macaulay's duration	Weighted duration
Reserves	10	0.0	0.000	Demand deposits	15	1.0	0.100
Short-term securities	15	0.5	0.050	Non-negotiable deposits	15	0.5	0.050
Intermediate securities	20	1.5	0.200	Certificates of deposit	35	0.5	0.117
Long-term securities	20	5.0	0.667	Fed funds	5	0.0	0.000
Variable-rate mortgages	10	0.5	0.033	Short-term borrowing	40	0.5	0.133
Fixed-rate mortgages	25	6.0	1.000	Intermediate-term borrowing	40	4.0	1.067
Short-term loans	20	1.0	0.133		150		1.467
Intermediate loans	30	4.0	0.800				
	150		2.883				

between the immunized market rate and the target rate is called the *cushion spread*. The acceptance of a lower target rate means that the client is willing to take an end-of-the-period investment value, known as the *minimum target value*, which is lower than the fully immunized value. This acceptance, in turn, gives the management fund some flexibility to pursue an active strategy.

As an example, suppose an investment management fund sets up a contingent immunization position for a client who has just placed $1m with them and who has an investment horizon of 3.5 years. Furthermore, suppose that the yield curve is currently flat at 10% and that while the investment fund can obtain an immunized rate of 10% (for example, it could buy a 4-year, 9% coupon bond trading at 10%), the client agrees to a lower immunization rate of 8% in return for allowing the fund to try to attain a higher rate using some active strategy. By accepting a target rate of 8%, the client is willing to accept a minimum target value of $1,309,131 at the 3.5-year horizon date:

$$\text{Minimum target value} = \$1\,\text{m}(1.08)^{3.5}$$
$$= \$1,309,131$$

The difference between the client's investment value (currently $1m) and the present value of the minimum target value is the management fund's *safety margin* or cushion. The initial safety margin in this example is $62,203:

Safety margin = Investment value

$$\qquad\qquad - \text{PV(Minimum target value)}$$

Safety margin

$$= \$1,000,000 - (\$1,309,131/(1.10)^{3.5})$$
$$= \$62,203$$

As long as the safety margin is positive, the management fund will have a cushion and can therefore pursue an active strategy. For example, suppose the fund expected long-term rates to decrease in the future and invested the client's funds in 10-year, 10% annual coupon bonds trading at par (YTM = 10%). If rates in the future decrease as expected, then the value of the investment and the safety margin would increase; if rates increase, though, the value of the investment and safety margin would

decrease. Moreover, if rates increase to the point that the investment value is equal to the present value of the minimum target value (that is, where the safety margin is zero), then the management fund would be required to immunize the investment position. For example, suppose 1 year later the yield curve shifted down to 8%, as the management fund was hoping (continue to assume a flat yield curve). The value of the investment (value of the original 10-year bonds plus coupons) would now be $1,224,938:

$$\text{Bond value} = \sum_{t=1}^{9} \frac{10}{(1.08)^t} + \frac{100}{(1.08)^9} = 112.4938$$

$$\text{Investment value} = \frac{112.4938}{100}(\$1,000,000)$$
$$+ (0.10)(\$1,000,000)$$
$$= \$1,224,938$$

The present value of the minimum target value would be $1.08m:

PV(Minimum target value)

$$= \frac{\$1,309,131}{(1.08)^{2.5}} = \$1,080,000$$

and the safety margin would be $144,938:

Safety margin = $1,224,938 − $1,080,000
$$= \$144,938$$

Thus, the downward shift in the yield curve has led to an increase in the safety margin from $62,203 to $144,938. At this point, the investment management fund could maintain its position in the original 10-year bond or take some other active position. Note that if the management fund immunized the client's position when rates were at 8% and the safety margin was positive, it would be able to provide the client with a rate of return for the 3.5-year period that exceeded the initial immunization rate of 10%. For example, if the fund sold the bonds and reinvested the proceeds and coupons in bonds with durations of 2.5 years and a yield of 8%, it would be able to lock in a rate of 11.96% for the 3.5-year period:

$$\text{ARR}_{3.5} = \left[\frac{\$1,224,938(1.08)^{2.5}}{\$1,000,000} \right]^{1/3.5} - 1$$
$$= 0.1196$$

Exhibit 8.3 Contingent immunization: investment value, present value of the minimum target value, and safety margin after 1 year given different rates

Interest rate	Investment value ($)	PV(minimum target value) ($)	Safety margin ($)	ARR
0.0800	1,224,937.76	1,079,999.91	144,937.85	0.1196
0.0850	1,191,785.94	1,067,600.48	124,185.46	0.1145
0.0900	1,159,952.47	1,055,399.45	104,553.02	0.1095
0.0950	1,129,376.42	1,043,392.74	85,983.68	0.1047
0.1000	1,100,000.00	1,031,576.39	68,423.61	0.1000
0.1050	1,071,768.38	1,019,946.55	51,821.83	0.0954
0.1100	1,044,629.52	1,008,499.44	36,130.09	0.0909
0.1150	1,018,534.03	997,231.39	21,302.65	0.0865
0.1150	1,018,534.03	997,231.39	21,302.65	0.0865
0.1200	993,435.00	986,138.81	7,296.20	0.0823
0.1225	981,245.15	980,657.23	587.93	0.0802
0.1250	969,287.88	975,218.21	− 5,930.32	0.0781
0.1275	957,557.98	969,821.33	− 12,263.35	0.0761
0.1300	946,050.35	964,466.17	− 18,415.82	0.0741
0.1350	923,682.17	953,879.36	− 30,197.19	0.0701
0.1400	902,145.13	943,454.54	− 41,309.41	0.0663

Investment value = value of 9-year, 10% bond with face value of $1m plus $100,000 coupon interest
PV(minumum target value) = $1,309,131/(1 + rate)^{2.5}
Safety margin = investment value − PV(minimum target value)
Trigger rate = 12.25%
ARR = (investment value$(1 + rate)^{2.5}$)/$1,000,000^{(1/3.5)}$

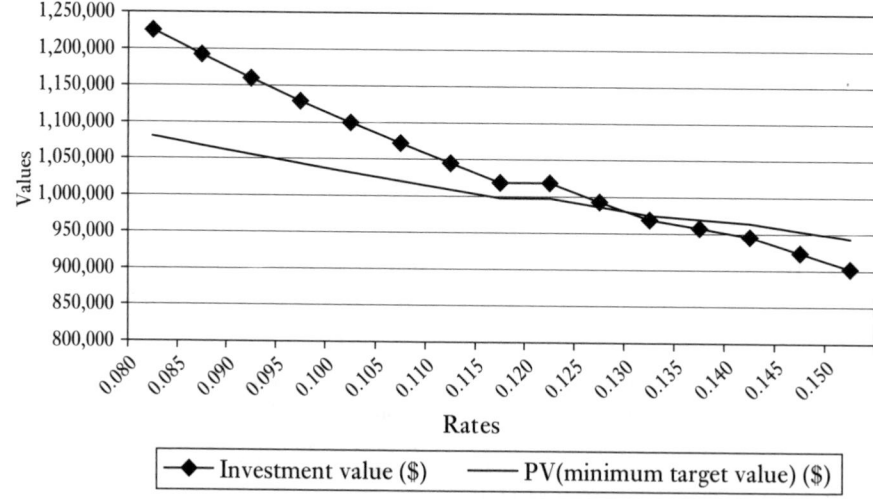

Suppose after 1 year, though, the yield curve shifted up to 12.25% instead of down to 8%. At 12.25%, the value of investment would be only $981,245 and the present value of the minimum target value would be $980,657, leaving the fund with a safety margin that is close to zero ($588):

$$\text{Bond value} = \sum_{t=1}^{9} \frac{10}{(1.1225)^t} + \frac{100}{(1.1225)^9} = 88.1245$$

Investment value

$$= \frac{88.1245}{100}(\$1,000,000) + (0.10)(\$1,000,000)$$

$$= \$981,245$$

PV(Minimum target value)

$$= \frac{\$1,309,131}{(1.1225)^{2.5}} = \$980,657$$

Safety margin $= \$981,245 - \$980,657 = \$588$

The investment management fund now would be required to immunize the portfolio. This could be done by selling the bond and reinvesting the proceeds plus the coupon (total investment of $981,245) in bonds with durations of 2.5 years and yielding the current rate of 12.25%. Doing this would yield a value of $1,309,916, which is approximately equal to the minimum target value of $1,309,131 at the end of the period, and the target rate of 8%:

$$\text{ARR}_{3.5} = \left[\frac{\$981,245(1.1225)^{2.5}}{\$1,000,000} \right]^{1/3.5} - 1 = 0.08$$

Exhibit 8.3 summarizes the investment values, present values of the minimum target value, safety margins, and ARRs for various interest rates. As shown in the table, for rates below 12.25%, safety margins are positive and the ARRs for the 3.5-year period are above the 8% target rate if the position were immunized; for rates above 12.25%, though, safety margins are negative and the ARRs are less than 8%. Thus, 12.25% is the trigger rate for immunizing the position when there are 2.5 years left. The relation between the investment values and the present values of the minimum

target value given different rates is also shown graphically in the figure in exhibit 8.3. The difference between the two lines in the figure shows the safety margins, and the point of intersection of the graphs defines the trigger rate at 12.25%.

In general, the contingent immunization strategy provides investors with a return–risk opportunity that is somewhere between those provided by active and fully-immunized strategies. In practice, setting up and managing contingent immunization strategies are more complex than this example suggests. Safety margin positions must be constantly monitored to ensure that if the investment value decreases to the trigger point it will be detected and the immunization position implemented. In addition, active positions are more detailed, non-parallel shifts in the yield curve need to be accounted for, and if the immunization position is implemented, it will need to be rebalanced.

8.5 CONCLUSION

In this chapter we've extended our analysis of bonds from evaluation to selection and management. As with all investment strategies, the method of selecting bonds or portfolios depends on the objective of the investor. Active strategies can be pursued to obtain abnormal returns. These include trying to profit from forecasting yield curve shifts, taking positions in different quality bonds in anticipation of a narrowing or a widening of the quality yield spread, identifying mispriced bonds, or taking positions in identical bonds that are not equally priced. Active strategies can also be used to set up defensive positions in order to protect the value of a portfolio; for example, moving to lower duration bonds, such as a cushion bond, when rates are expected to increase, or tilting a bond portfolio toward higher quality bonds when economic slowdowns are anticipated. For investors who must meet future liability requirements or obtain maximum returns subject to risk constraints, passive strategies such as cash-flow matching or indexing, or hybrid strategies such as immunization or contingent immunization strategies can be used.

Web Information

For information on bond funds go to
  www.quicken.com/investments/
  mutualfunds/finder

For information on bond funds for emerging economies go to
  www.bradynet.com

Information on state and local economic conditions and industries:
  www.bea.gov

For information on industry trends go to
  www.bigcharts.com

and click on "Industries."

For bonds on the watch list or subject to ratings changes go to the websites of Moody's, Standard & Poor's, and Fitch:
  www.moodys.com
  www.standardandpoors.com
and
  www.fitchratings.com

For information on specific bonds go to
  www.nasd.com

and click on "Market System" and "Bond Information."

For information on bond strategies and trends go to
  www.ryanlabs.com

KEY TERMS

Active Strategies
Bond Swaps
Passive Strategy
Indexing
Rate-Anticipation Strategies
Rate-Anticipation Swap
Cushion Bonds
Parallel Shift
Twist
Humpedness
Positive Butterfly
Negative Butterfly
Bullet Strategy
Barbell Strategy
Ladder Strategy
Total Return Analysis
Quality Swap
Sector Rotation
Industrial Analysis
Fundamental Analysis

Asset and Liability Analysis
Indenture Analysis
Municipal Analysis
Debt Burden
Fiscal Soundness
Overall Economic Climate
Red Flags
International Debt
Cross-Border Risk
Multiple Discriminant
  Analysis
Chapter 11 Fund
Vulture Funds
Yield Pick-Up Swap
Tax Swap
Callable/Non-Callable Bond
  Swap
Pure Bond Indexing
Full-Replication Approach
Tracking Errors

Cell-Matching Strategy
Enhanced Bond Indexing
Cash-Flow Matching Strategy
Dedicated Portfolio Strategy
Accumulation Value or Target
  Value
Classical Immunization
Rebalancing
Focus Strategy
Combination Matching or
  Horizon Matching
Surplus Management
Economic Surplus
Duration Gap
Contingent Immunization
Target Rate
Cushion Spread
Minimum Target Value
Safety Margin

PROBLEMS AND QUESTIONS

1. The yield curve for A-rated bonds is presently flat at a promised YTM of 10%. You own an A-rated, 5-year, 10% coupon bond with annual coupon payments. You expect rates to decrease over the next 2 years and would like to take advantage of your expectation with a rate-anticipation swap. The bond you are considering substituting is an A-rated, 10-year, 10% coupon with annual coupon payments.

   a. Using the table below for guidance, evaluate your rate-anticipation swap by comparing your current bond with the substitute candidate given the following scenario: the yield curve will shift down 1 year from now from 10% to 9%. Assume the coupon date is 1 year from now.

	Current bond: 5 yr, 10% coupon bond	Substitute bond: 10 yr, 10% coupon bond
Current value		
Current Macaulay's duration		
Coupons		
Interest on interest		
Bond price 1 year later		
Dollar return 1 year later		
One-year ARR		

   b. Using the table below for guidance, evaluate your rate-anticipation swap given the following scenario: the yield curve will shift up 1 year from now from 10% to 11%. Assume the coupon date is 1 year from now.

	Current bond: 5 yr, 10% coupon bond	Substitute bond: 10 yr, 10% coupon bond
Current value		
Current Macaulay's duration		
Coupons		
Interest on interest		
Bond price 1 year later		
Dollar return 1 year later		
One-year ARR		

   c. Comment on your rate-anticipation swap.

2. The yield curve for AA-rated bonds is presently flat at 6%. You manage a fund in which you currently have $5m invested in AA-rated, 15-year, 7% coupon bonds with semi-annual coupon payments and currently priced to yield 6%. Interest rates have been decreasing over the last several years and you believe that they are near a trough and will increase over the next year. Given your expectation, you are considering a rate-anticipation swap. The bond you are considering substituting is an AA-rated, 3-year, 10% callable bond with semi-annual coupon payments and priced at its call price of 110.

a. Using the table below for guidance, evaluate your rate-anticipation swap by comparing your current bond with the substitute candidate given the following scenario: the yield curve will shift up 1 year from now from 6% to 7%. Assume the coupon date is 1 year from now.

	Current bond: 15 yr, 7% coupon bond	Substitute bond: 3 yr, 10% coupon bond
Current value per 100 face value		110
Coupons		
Interest on interest		
Bond price 1 year later		
Dollar return 1 year later		
One-year ARR		

b. Comment on your rate-anticipation swap. What term is used to describe the 3-year, 10% bond?

3. Given a current flat yield curve for AAA bonds at 6% and the following bonds:

Bond	Quality	Maturity	Annual coupon (coupons paid annually)	Current price	YTM	Macaulay's duration
A	AAA	5 years	6%	100	6%	4.46
B	AAA	11 years	6%	100	6%	8.36
C	AAA	20 years	6%	100	6%	12.16

a. What is the portfolio duration of a barbell portfolio formed with an equal allocation in Bonds A and C? How does the barbell portfolio's duration compare with a bullet portfolio consisting of Bond B?

b. Using the table below for guidance, calculate (Excel recommended) each bond's and the barbell portfolio's values and dollar returns 1 year later given the parallel shifts in the yield curve shown in the table. What differences do you observe between the barbell portfolio and the bullet portfolio formed with Bond B? What bond or portfolio would you select if you expected a significant downward shift in the yield curve? What bond or portfolio would give you the greatest protection in value if you expected a significant upward shift in the yield curve? Comment on your findings.

Yield curve change in BP	Value			Return			Return		
	A	B	C	A	B	C	Barbell	Bullet	Difference
200									
150									
100									
59									
25									
0									
− 25									
− 50									
− 100									
− 150									
− 200									

c. Suppose yield curve shifts are characterized by a flattening where for each change in Bond B (intermediate bond), Bond A increases by 25 BP and Bond C decreases by 25 BP:

$$\Delta y_A = \Delta y_B + 25\,\text{BP}$$

$$\Delta y_C = \Delta y_B - 25\,\text{BP}$$

Following the table below for guidance, calculate (Excel recommended) each bond's and the barbell portfolio's values and dollar returns 1 year later given the yield changes in Bond B shown in the table. What differences do you observe between the barbell portfolio and bullet portfolio formed with Bond B? How do the differences with the twist compare to the differences with the parallel shifts?

| Yield change for B in BP | Value | | | Return | | | Return | | |
	A	B	C	A	B	C	Barbell	Bullet	Difference
200									
150									
100									
59									
25									
0									
−25									
−50									
−100									
−150									
−200									

4. Suppose you're a strategist for a hedged fund. Your research indicates that the quality spread for BBB bonds and AAA bonds is 150 basis points in periods of economic slowdown and only 100 BP in periods of economic expansion. Currently, the economy is in a recession, and 1- and 2-year zero-coupon bonds for AAA and BBB bonds are trading at 6% and 7.5%. Leading economic indicators, though, strongly point to the economy hitting its trough relatively soon and then expanding over the next year.

   a. Given the economic growth forecast, construct a quality spread for your hedged fund formed by going short in one of the bonds with the proceeds used to purchase the other. Assume perfect divisibility.

   b. Show what your hedged fund's profit or loss could be if you closed your position a year later and the economy were growing and yields on the AAA bond had increased to 7% and the quality yield spread narrowed to 100 BP as you predicted. Assume a flat yield curve.

   c. Show what your hedged fund's position would be if yields on the AAA bond had instead decreased to 5%, but the quality yield spread was still 100 BP as you predicted.

   d. What would happen to your profit or loss if the yield spread widened instead of narrowed?

5. Suppose an arbitrageur for a hedged fund finds two identical bonds trading at different YTMs: Bond A, an AA-rated, 10-year, option-free, 10% annual coupon bond trading at par, and Bond B, an AA-rated, 10-year, option-free, 10% annual coupon bond trading to yield 10.25%. What are the prices of each bond? What swap strategy would you recommend to the arbitrageur? What is the risk in this strategy?

6. Comment on the objective of many strategies based on credit analysis.

7. List the factors that should be considered in conducting a credit analysis of a general obligation bond, and explain some of the ways of measuring them.

8. List the factors that should be considered in conducting a credit analysis of a municipal revenue bond, and explain some of the ways of measuring them.

9. List some of the important factors that should be considered in conducting a credit analysis of a corporate bond.

10. Briefly explain the following types of funds and their strategies:

    a. High-yield bond fund
    b. Chapter 11 fund.

11. Explain the objective of fundamental bond analysis.

12. Explain how a tax swap is used to take advantage of the tax laws.

13. Explain the differences in bond indexing using the full-replication approach and a sample approach.

14. Suppose a bond index consists of municipal and corporate bonds, has durations ranging from 1 to 10, and has quality ratings ranging from B to AAA. Decompose the index into cells based on three durations ranges ($D < 4$; $4 \leq D \leq 7$; $D > 7$), two quality ratings (investment grade and speculative grade), and the two sectors. Explain how you would construct a bond index portfolio using the cells.

15. Given the information on the composition of a bond index in the table below:

Sector	Percentage of value (%)	Duration
Treasury	30	4.50
Federal agency	5	3.25
Municipals	10	5.25
Corporate	35	6.25
Sovereign	10	5.75
Asset-backed	10	6.25
	100	

Quality sector	Percentage of value (%)	Duration
AAA	40	5.25
AA	25	5.35
A	20	5.25
BBB	5	5.65
BB	5	5.25
B	5	5.30
	100	

    a. Explain how you would construct a bond index portfolio using a duration/sector and duration/quality sector approaches.
    b. Define enhanced bond indexing.
    c. How would you apply enhanced bond indexing to your bond index portfolio if you expected a slow economy to improve and grow in the near future?

16. How are call features handled in constructing a bond index portfolio?

17. Suppose an investment management fund has the following liabilities for the next 4 years:

Year	Liability
1	$2m
2	$12m
3	$7m
4	$10m

   a. Construct a dedicated portfolio from 6% coupon bonds with different maturities that will match the liabilities. Assume the applicable yield curve is flat at 6% and coupon payments are annual.
   b. Show, using the outline table below for guidance, that the coupon income and maturing principal each year match the liabilities.

(1) Year	(2) Total bond value outstanding	(3) Coupon income	(4) Maturing principal	(5) Liability	(6) Ending balance (3) + (4) − (5)
1					
2					
3					
4					

18. What is the major risk associated with a cash-flow matching strategy? How can the risk be minimized?

19. A 10-year, 5% coupon bond making annual payments has Macaulay's duration of 8 years if the bond is priced at 92.64 per 100 face value to yield 6%. Show how classical immunization works by showing that the target value and ARR for an 8-year horizon date from an investment in the 10-year, 5% bond are approximately the same given interest rate changes. Specifically, assume there is a one-time shift in the yield curve to 4% and to 8% just after the investment is made (and the duration of the bond still matches the duration of the liabilities). Assume the yield curve is flat.

20. Suppose your horizon date is 6 years and you're considering the following investments:

   (i) AAA-rated, 6% coupon bond with annual coupon payment, maturity of 6 years, and Macaulay's duration of 5.21.
   (ii) AAA-rated, 5% coupon bond with annual coupon payment, maturity of 7 years, priced at 94.42 to yield 6%, and Macaulay's duration of 6.04.

   Suppose the applicable yield curve is flat at 6%.

   a. Determine the target value at your horizon date and the ARR for a classical duration-matching strategy and for a maturity-matching strategy given the following interest rate scenarios:

      • The yield curve shifts down to 4% just after you buy the bond and stays there until you reach your horizon date.
      • The yield curve stays at 6%.
      • The yield curve shifts up to 8% just after you buy the bond and stays there until you reach your horizon date.

   b. Comment on the difference between a classical duration-matching strategy and a maturity-matching strategy.

   c. Determine the target value at your horizon date and the ARR for the duration-matching strategy given the yield curve shifts after 2 years to 4% and 8%, instead of immediately after you buy the bond. What is the duration of your bond after 2 years at 4% and 8%? Does it match your remaining horizon? Comment on your findings.

21. In a 1971 study, Fisher and Weil demonstrated that while duration-matched positions were closer to their initial YTM than maturity-matched strategies, they were not absent of market risk. What reasons did they offer for the presence of market risk with classical immunization and what did they recommend as a method for achieving immunization?

22. Explain how initially immunized positions lose their immunization and how they can be rebalanced.

23. Explain the alternative ways in which multiple-period liabilities can be immunized.

24. What is a combination matching strategy? When is it used?

25. ABC Trust manages a pension fund. The assets of the fund are in a bond portfolio currently worth $500m and with an average duration of 6. The present value of the pension's liabilities is $450m and the average duration of the liabilities is 10.

   a. What is the pension's economic surplus?

   b. What would happen to the economic surplus if interest rates were to increase by 100 BP?

   c. What would happen to the economic surplus if interest rates were to decrease by 100 BP?

   d. How could the fund minimize the impact the interest rate changes have on its economic surplus?

26. Suppose you set up a contingent immunization strategy for a $50m fund you are managing. Suppose the horizon date for the fund is 4 years, the immunization rate is 10%, the minimum target rate is 8%, the yield curve is flat at 10%, and all investment cash flows are annual.

   a. What is the current minimum target value and safety margin?

   b. Suppose you invest in a 15-year, 10% annual coupon bond selling at par. What would be the value of your fund and your safety margin if a year later rates were at 8% on all maturities? What would your contingent immunization strategy be in this case? What would your ARR be if you immunized?

   c. Suppose you invest in a 15-year, 10% annual coupon bond selling at par. What would be the value of your fund and your safety margin if a year later rates were at 11.97% on all maturities? What would your contingent immunization strategy be in this case? What would your ARR be if you immunized?

27. What are some of the practical considerations that are required to effectively manage a contingent immunization position?

WEB EXERCISES

1. Go to www.federalreserve.gov/releases/h15/data.htm. The site contains data on a number of different bond yields. Go to historical data and compare the annual historical yields on 10-year Treasury bonds to Moody's Aaa and Baa bonds from 1976 to the present. Copy the data to Excel and make a chart so that the data are easier to analyze.

   a. Identify points when Treasury yields are at a trough and when they are at a peak. Comment on interest rate-anticipation strategies that bond investors in hindsight could have implemented either to earn higher returns or to protect their bond positions.
   b. Examine the risk premiums on Aaa and Baa bonds to determine if they widen during periods of economic slowdown (such as in the late 1970s and early 1980s and in the late 1980s and early 1990s) and narrow during periods of economic growth (mid-1980s and 1990s). Comment on how sector rotation and quality swap strategies could have been used during these periods.

2. Corporate bonds on Moody's watch list or those undergoing changes can be found by going to www.moodys.com and clicking on "Corporate Finance" and then "Ratings Actions" and "Watchlist" (registration required). Take one of the companies on Moody's watch list or with a recent ratings change and do an analysis of it with information obtained from www.quicken.com or www.hoovers.com.

3. Municipal issues on Moody's watch list or those undergoing changes can be found by going to www.moodys.com and clicking on "US Public Finance," "Ratings Actions," and "Watchlist." Take a state or local government on Moody's watch list or with a recent ratings change and do an analysis of it with information obtained from the Bureau of Economic Analysis website: www.bea.gov. At the site, go to State and Local government data. You may want to look at personal income, state output, or employment data. State and local government information can also be found by going to the www.economagic.com site. At the site, click "Browse by Region" or click "Bureau of Labor Statistics – State and City Employment."

NOTES

1. In chapter 13 we will describe how rate-anticipation swaps can be implemented using futures contracts.
2. For a good discussion on types of yield curve shifts, see Frank Fabozzi's *Bond Markets, Analysis, and Strategies*, 3rd edn (Upper Saddle River, NJ: Prentice Hall, 1996): 393–6.
3. Note that concentrating in one maturity group does not mean constructing a portfolio with a portfolio duration corresponding to that maturity. For example, if an investor expected 5-year bond rates to decrease, but not short-term or long-term rates, she could profit by investing in a bond with a duration of 5 years, but she could incur losses from a portfolio of short- and long-term bonds with a portfolio duration of 5 years.

4. Note that instead of taking positions in different quality bonds, speculators can form a quality swap by taking positions in futures contracts on bonds with different quality ratings (e.g., opposite positions in a Treasury bond futures contract and a municipal bond index contract). Constructing bond swaps with futures is examined in chapter 13.
5. For studies on cumulative defaults see Asquith, Mullins, and Wolff, *Journal of Finance* (September 1989); Altman, *Journal of Applied Corporate Finance* (Summer 1990); Douglass and Lucas, *Moody's Investor's Service* (July 1989).
6. For a more detailed analysis covering the guidelines in the credit analysis of municipals, see Feldstein, "Guidelines in the Credit Analysis of General Obligation and Revenue Municipal Bonds," in Frank Fabozzi (ed.) *The Handbook of*

Fixed Income Securities, 6th edn (New York: McGraw-Hill, 2001): 491–517.

7. For a more detailed discussion of the credit analysis of emerging market debt, see Allen Vine, "High-Yield Analysis of Emerging Markets Debt," in Frank Fabozzi (ed.) *The Handbook of Fixed Income Securities*, 6th edn (New York: McGraw-Hill, 2001): 519–45. Discussions of country analysis can also be found in many international financial texts: for example, see Jeff Madura's *International Financial Management*, 6th edn (Cincinnati, OH: South-Western College Publishing, 2000): 363–80.

8. Several investment companies and bond-rating firms evaluate high-yield bonds. These companies and the publications reporting their analysis include: Merrill Lynch, *High-Yield* and *This Week in High-Yield*; First Boston, *Monthly Market Review* and *High-Yield Handbook*; Lehman Brothers, *High-Yield Portfolio Advisor* and *High-Yield Bond Market Report*; Salomon Smith Barney, *High-Yield Market Update*; Standard & Poor's, *Speculative Grade Debt Credit Review*; Duff and Phelps, *Recommendations and Profiles*.

9. For additional discussion of credit analysis models, see Altman and Nammacher, *Investing in Junk Bonds*, and Reilly and Brown, *Investment Analysis and Portfolio Management*, pp. 629–31.

10. For more discussion on investing in the debt securities of bankrupt firms, see Jane Howe, "Investing in Chapter 11 and Other Distressed Companies," in Frank Fabozzi (ed.) *The Handbook of Fixed Income Securities*, 6th edn (New York: McGraw-Hill, 2001): 469–89.

11. Another type of tax swap involves switching between high- and low-coupon bonds to take advantage of different tax treatments applied to capital gains and income. This swap can be used if the tax rate on capital gains differs from the tax rate on income. If it does, then an investor might find it advantageous to swap a low-coupon bond for a high-coupon bond with the same duration.

12. One of the most well-known approaches to portfolio construction is the use of the Markowitz portfolio model. While most of the applications of the Markowitz model are to stocks, it can be used for constructing bond portfolios. For a discussion of the use of the Markowitz model for bond portfolios, see Edwin Elton, Martin Gruber, Stephen Brown, and William Goetzmann, *Modern Portfolio Theory and Investment Analysis* (New York: John Wiley & Sons, Inc., 2000): 543–6.

13. The study by McEnnally and Boardman discussed in chapter 4 suggests that the maximum diversification benefits from a bond portfolio are realized with a portfolio consisting of approximately 20 bonds.

14. F. M. Redington, "Review of the Principles of Life – Office Foundation," *Journal of the Institute of Actuaries* 78 (1952): 286–340.

15. This example is similar to the one presented in section 4.4.

16. This illustration is based on a similar one presented by Reilly and Brown, *Investment Analysis and Portfolio Management*, pp. 644–5.

17. See Bierwag, Kaufman, and Toevs (1983).

18. For an analysis of the costs and benefits of cash-flow matching and immunization, see Fong and Vasicek (1984).

19. In addition to gap analysis, banks also conduct income gap analysis in which they look at the impact of interest rate changes on the income received and paid on their rate-sensitive assets and liabilities.

20. Martin Leibowitz and Alfred Weinberger, "Contingent Immunization – Part I: Risk Control Procedures," *Financial Analyst Journal* 38 (November–December 1982): 17–32; Martin Leibowitz and Alfred Weinberger, "Contingent Immunization – Part II: Problem Areas," *Financial Analyst Journal* 39 (January–February 1983): 35–50.

SELECTED REFERENCES

Altman, Edward I. "Measuring Corporate Bond Mortality and Performance," *Journal of Finance* 44(4) (September 1989): 909–22.

Altman, Edward I. "Setting the Record Straight on Junk Bonds: A Review of the Research on Default Rates and Returns," *Journal of Applied Corporate Finance* 3(2) (Summer 1990): 82–95.

Altman, Edward I. "Revisiting the High-Yield Bond Market," *Financial Management* 21(2) (1992): 78–92.

Altman, Edward I. *Corporate Financial Distress and Bankruptcy* 2nd edn (New York: John Wiley & Sons, 1993).

Altman, Edward I. and Scott A. Nammacher *Investing in Junk Bonds: Inside the High Yield Debt Market* (New York: John Wiley & Sons, 1987).

Barr, P. G. "Strong Market Boosts Immunized Portfolios," *Pensions & Investments* (May 16, 1994): 16, 96.

Beidleman, Carl (ed.) *The Handbook of International Investing* (Chicago: Probus Publishing, 1987).

Bierwag, G. O. "Immunization, Duration and the Term Structure of Interest Rates," *Journal of Financial and Quantitative Analysis* 12 (1977): 725–43.

Bierwag, G. O., George G. Kaufman, and Alden Toevs (eds) *Innovations in Bond Portfolio Management: Duration Analysis and Immunization* (Greenwich, CT: JAI Press, 1983).

Choie, Kenneth S. "A Simplified Approach to Bond Portfolio Management: DDS," *Journal of Portfolio Management* 16(3) (Spring 1990).

Cox, J., J. E. Ingersoll, and S. Ross "Duration and the Measurement of Basis Risk," *Journal of Business* (January 1979).

Dattatreya, Ravi E. and Frank J. Fabozzi *Active Total Return Management of Fixed Income Portfolios* rev. edn (Burr Ridge, IL: Irwin Professional Publishing, 1995).

Douglass, K. Scott and Douglas J. Lucas *Historical Default Rates of Corporate Bond Issuers, 1970–1988* (New York: Moody's Investors Services, July 1989).

Elton, Edwin, Martin Gruber, Stephen Brown, and William Goetzmann *Modern Portfolio Theory and Investment Analysis* (New York: John Wiley & Sons, Inc., 2000).

Fabozzi, Frank J. *Bond Markets, Analysis, and Strategies*, 3rd edn (Upper Saddle River, NJ: Prentice Hall, 1996).

Fabozzi, Frank J. and Peter F. Christensen "Bond Immunization: An Asset/Liability Optimization Strategy," in Frank J. Fabozzi (ed.) *The Handbook of Fixed Income Securities*, 6th edn (New York: McGraw-Hill, 2001).

Fabozzi, Frank J. and Peter F. Christensen "Dedicated Bond Portfolios," in Frank J. Fabozzi (ed.) *The Handbook of Fixed Income Securities*, 6th edn (New York: McGraw-Hill, 2001).

Feldstein, Sylvan G. "Guidelines in the Credit Analysis of General Obligation and Revenue Municipal Bonds," in Frank J. Fabozzi (ed.) *The Handbook of Fixed Income Securities*, 6th edn (New York: McGraw-Hill, 2001).

Feldstein, Sylvan G., Frank J. Fabozzi, and Patrick M. Kennedy "Municipal Bonds," in Frank J. Fabozzi (ed.) *The Handbook of Fixed Income Securities*, 6th edn (New York: McGraw-Hill, 2001).

Fisher, L. and R. Weil "Coping with the Risk of Interest Rate Fluctuations: Returns to Bondholders from Naive and Optimal Strategies," *Journal of Business* 44 (1971): 408–31.

Fong, H. Gifford "Active Strategies for Managing Bond Portfolios," in Donald Tuttle (ed.) *The Revolution in Techniques for Managing Bond Portfolios* (Charlottesville, VA: The Institute of Chartered Financial Analysts, 1983): 21–38.

Fong, G. and Oldrich Vasicek "A Risk Minimization Strategy for Multiple Liability Immunization," *Journal of Finance* 39(5) (1984): 1541–6.

Garbade, K. "Dedicated Bond Portfolios: Construction, Rebalancing, and Swapping," *Topics in Money and Securities Markets* (New York: Bankers Trust Company, 1985).

Granito, M. "The Problem with Bond Index Funds," *Journal of Portfolio Management* 13(4) (1987): 41–8.

Homer, Sidney and Martin L. Leibowitz *Inside the Yield Book* (Englewood Cliffs, NJ: Prentice Hall, 1972): chapter 5.

Howe, Jane Tri "Credit Analysis for Corporate Bonds," in Frank J. Fabozzi (ed.) *The Handbook of Fixed Income Securities*, 6th edn (New York: McGraw-Hill, 2001).

Howe, Jane Tri "Credit Considerations in Evaluating High-Yield Bonds," in Frank J. Fabozzi (ed.) *The Handbook of Fixed Income Securities*, 6th edn (New York: McGraw-Hill, 2001).

Howe, Jane Tri "Investing in Chapter 11 and Other Distressed Companies," in Frank J. Fabozzi (ed.) *The Handbook of Fixed Income Securities*, 6th edn (New York: McGraw-Hill, 2001).

Ingersoll, J. E. "Is Immunization Feasible? Evidence from CRSP Data," in G. Kaufman, C. Bierwag, and A. Toevs (eds) *Innovations in Bond Portfolio Management: Duration Analysis and Immunization* (Greenwich, CT: JAI Press, 1983).

Ingersoll, J. E., J. Skelton, and R. L. Weil "Duration Forty Years Later," *Journal of Financial and Quantitative Analysis* 13 (1978): 627–50.

Liebowitz, Martin L. "The Dedicated Bond Portfolio in Pension Funds – Part I: Motivations and Basics," *Financial Analysts Journal* 42(1) (January–February 1986): 68–75.

Liebowitz, Martin L. "The Dedicated Bond Portfolio in Pension Funds – Part II: Immunization, Horizon Matching, and Contingent Procedures," *Financial Analysts Journal* 42(2) (March–April 1986): 47–57.

Liebowitz, Martin L. *Matched-Funding Techniques: The Dedicated Bond Portfolio in Pension Funds*. (New York: Salomon Brothers Inc., Mortgage Research, 1987).

Madura, Jeff *International Financial Management*, 6th edn (Cincinnati, OH: South-Western College Publishing, 2000): 363–80.

Merton, R. C. "On the Pricing of Corporate Debt: The Risk Structure of Interest Rates," *Journal of Finance* 29 (1974): 449–70.

Reilly, Frank K. and Keith Brown *Investment Analysis and Portfolio Management*, 6th edn (Fort Worth, TX: The Dryden Press, 1997).

Reilly, F. and R. Sidhu "The Many Uses of Bond Duration," *Financial Analysts Journal* (July–August 1980).

Reilly, Frank K. and David J. Wright "Bond Market Indexes," in Frank J. Fabozzi (ed.) *The Handbook of Fixed Income Securities*, 6th edn (New York: McGraw-Hill, 2001).

Reilly, Frank K., David J. Wright, and Edward I. Altman "Including Defaulted Bonds in the Capital

Markets Spectrum," *Journal of Fixed Income* 8(3) (December 1998): 33–48.

Seix, C. and R. Akhoury "Bond Indexation: The Optimal Quantitative Approach," *Journal of Portfolio Management* 12(3) (1986): 50–3.

Ward, David J. and Gary L. Griepentrog "Risk and Return in Defaulted Bonds," *Financial Analysts Journal* 49(3) (May–June 1993): 61–5.

Weil, R. L. "Macaulay's Duration: An Appreciation," *Journal of Business* (October 1973).

PART THREE

EVALUATION OF BONDS WITH EMBEDDED OPTIONS

CHAPTER NINE

BINOMIAL INTEREST RATE TREES AND THE VALUATION OF BONDS WITH EMBEDDED OPTIONS

9.1 INTRODUCTION

An option is a right to buy or sell a security at a specific price on or possibly before a specified date. As we noted in chapter 4, many bonds have a call feature giving the issuer the right to buy back the bond from the bondholder. In addition to callable bonds, there are also putable bonds, giving the bondholder the right to sell the bond back to the issuer, sinking-fund bonds in which the issuer has the right to call the bond or buy it back in the market, and convertible bonds that give the bondholder the right to convert the bond into a specified number of shares of stock.

The inclusion of option features in a bond contract makes the evaluation of such bonds more difficult. A 10-year, 10% callable bond issued when interest rate are relatively high may be more like a 3-year bond given that a likely interest rate decrease would lead the issuer to buy the bond back. Determining the value of such a bond requires taking into account not only the value of the bond's cash flow, but also the value of the call option embedded in the bond. One way to capture the impact of a bond's option feature on its value is to construct a model that incorporates the random paths that interest rates follow over time. Such a model allows one to value a bond's option at different interest rate levels. One such model is the binomial interest rate tree. Patterned after the binomial option pricing model, this model assumes that interest rates follow a binomial process in which in each period the rate is either higher or lower. In this chapter, we examine how to evaluate bonds with option features using a binomial interest rate tree approach. We begin by defining a binomial tree for one-period spot rates and then showing how the tree can be used to value a callable bond. After examining the valuation of a callable bond, we then show how the binomial tree can be extended to the valuation of putable bonds, bonds with sinking funds, and convertible bonds. In this chapter, we focus on defining the binomial tree and explaining how it can be used to value bonds with embedded options; in the next chapter, we take up the more technical subject of how the tree can be estimated.

9.2 BINOMIAL INTEREST RATE MODEL

A binomial model of interest rates assumes a spot rate of a given maturity follows a binomial process where in each period it has either a higher or lower rate. For example, assume that a one-period, riskless spot rate (S) follows a process in which in each period the rate is equal to a proportion u times its beginning-of-the-period value or a proportion d times its initial value, where u is greater than d. After one period, there would be two possible one-period spot rates: $S_u = uS_0$ and $S_d = dS_0$. If the proportions u and d were constant over different periods, then after two periods there would be three possible rates. That is, as shown in exhibit 9.1, after two periods the one-period spot rate can either equal $S_{uu} = u^2S_0$, $S_{ud} = udS_0$, or

$S_{dd} = d^2S_0$. Similarly, after three periods, the spot rate could take on four possible values: $S_{uuu} = u^3S_0$, $S_{uud} = u^2dS_0$, $S_{udd} = ud^2S_0$, and $S_{ddd} = d^3S_0$.

To illustrate, suppose the current one-period spot rate is 10%, the upward parameter u is 1.1, and the downward parameter d is 0.95. As shown in exhibit 9.2, the two possible one-period rates after one period are 11% and 9.5%,

Exhibit 9.1   Binomial tree of one-period spot rates

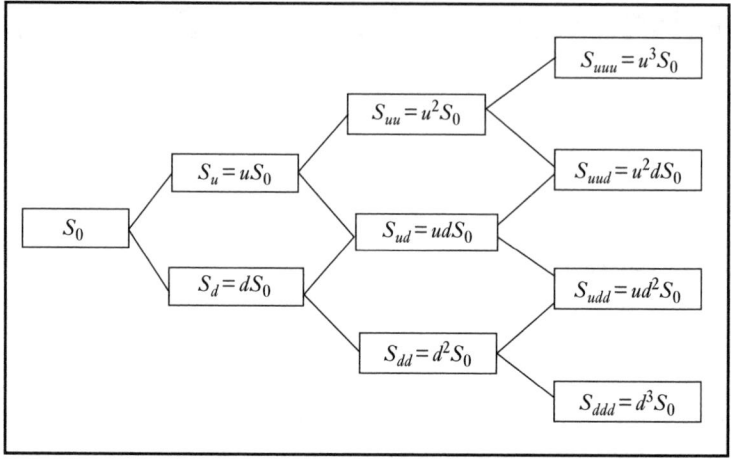

Exhibit 9.2   Binomial tree ($u = 1.1$, $d = 0.95$, $S_0 = 0.10$)

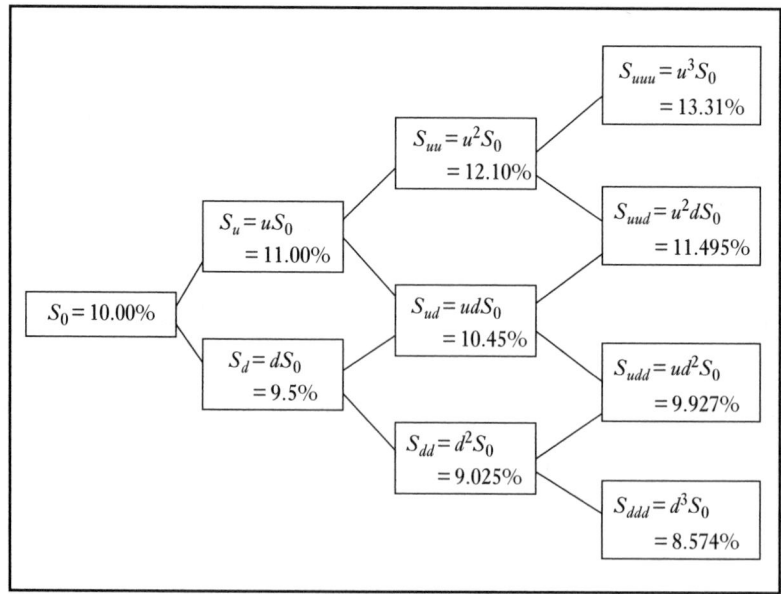

the three possible one-period rates after two periods are 12.1%, 10.45%, and 9.025%, and the four possible rates after three periods are 13.31%, 11.495%, 9.927%, and 8.574%.

9.2.1 Valuing a Two-Period Bond

Given the possible one-period spot rates, suppose we wanted to value a bond that matures in two periods. Assume that the bond has no default risk or embedded option features and that it pays an 8% coupon each period and a $100 principal at maturity. Since there is no default or call risk, the only risk an investor assumes in buying this bond is market risk. This risk occurs at time period one. At that time, the original two-period bond will have one period to maturity where there is a certain payoff of $108. We don't know, though, whether the one-period rate will be 11% or 9.5%. If the rate is 11%, then the bond would be worth $B_u = 108/1.11 = 97.297$; if the rate is 9.5%, the bond would be worth $B_d = 108/1.095 = 98.630$. Given these two possible values in period 1, the

current value of the two-period bond can be found by calculating the present value of the bond's expected cash flows in period 1. If we assume that there is an equal probability (q) of the one-period spot rate being higher ($q = 0.5$) or lower ($1 - q = 0.5$), then the current value of the two-period bond (B_0) would be 96.330 (see exhibit 9.3):

$$B_0 = \frac{q[B_u + C] + (1 - q)[B_d + C]}{1 + S_0}$$

$$B_0 = \frac{0.5[97.297 + 8] + 0.5[98.630 + 8]}{1.10}$$

$$= 96.330$$

Now suppose that the two-period, 8% bond has a call feature that allows the issuer to buy back the bond at a call price (CP) of 98. Using the binomial tree approach, this call option can be incorporated into the valuation of the bond by determining at each node in period 1 whether or not the issuer would exercise his right to call. The issuer will find it profitable to exercise whenever the bond price is above the call price

Exhibit 9.3 Value of two-period option-free bond

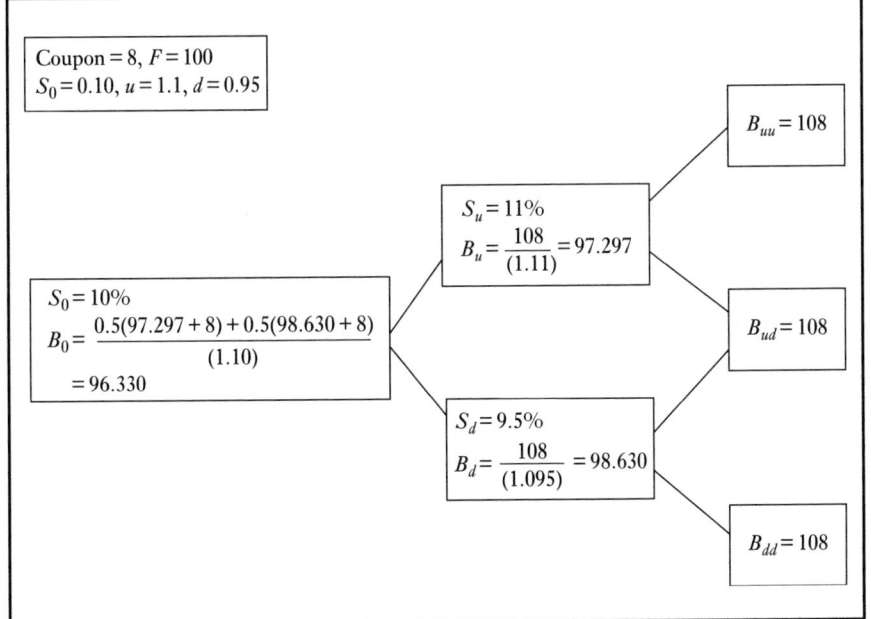

(assuming no transaction or holding costs). This is the case when the one-period spot rate is 9.5% in period 1 and the bond is priced at 98.630. The price of the bond in this case would be the call price of 98. It is not profitable, however, for the issuer to exercise the call at the spot rate of 11% when the bond is worth 97.297; the value of the bond in this case remains at 97.297.[1] In general, since the bond is only exercised when the call price is less than the bond value, the value of the callable bond in period 1 is therefore the *minimum* of its call price or its binomial value:

$$B_t^C = \text{Min}[B_t, \text{CP}]$$

Rolling the two callable bond values in period 1 of 97.297 and 98 to the present, we obtain a current price of 96.044:

$$B_t^C = \frac{0.5[97.297 + 8] + 0.5[98 + 8]}{1.10} = 96.044$$

As we should expect, the bond's embedded call option lowers the value of the bond from 96.330 to 96.044. The value of the callable bond in terms of the binomial tree is shown in exhibit 9.4a. Note, at each of the nodes in period 1, the value of the callable bond is determined by selecting the minimum of the binomial bond value or the call price, and then rolling the callable bond value to the current period.

Instead of using a price constraint at each node, the price of the callable bond can alternatively be found by determining the value of the call option at each node, V_t^C, and then subtracting that value from the non-callable bond value ($B_t^C = B_t^{NC} - V_t^C$). In this two-period case, the values of the call option are equal to their intrinsic values, IVs (or exercise values). The intrinsic value is the maximum of $B_t^{NC} - \text{CP}$ or zero:

$$V_t^C = \text{Max}[B_t^{NC} - \text{CP}, 0]$$

As shown in exhibit 9.4b, the two possible call values in period 1 are zero and 0.63 and the corresponding callable bond values are 97.297 and 98 – the same values we obtained using the

minimum price constraint approach. The value of the call option in the current period is equal to the present value of the expected call value in period 1. In this case, the current value is 0.2864:

$$V_0^C = \frac{0.5[0] + 0.5[0.630]}{1.10} = 0.2864$$

Subtracting the call value of 0.2864 from the non-callable bond value of 96.330, we obtain a callable bond value of 96.044 (see exhibit 9.4b) – the same value we obtained using the constraint approach.

9.2.2 Valuing a Three-Period Bond

The binomial approach to valuing a two-period bond requires only a one-period binomial tree of one-period spot rates. If we want to value a three-period bond, we in turn need a two-period interest rate tree. For example, suppose we wanted to value a three-period, 9% coupon bond with no default risk or option features. In this case, market risk exists in two periods: period 3, where there are three possible spot rates, and period 2, where there are two possible rates. To value the bond, we first determine the three possible values of the bond in period 2 given the three possible spot rates and the bond's certain cash flow next period (maturity). As shown in exhibit 9.5, the three possible values in period 2 are $B_{uu} = 109/1.121 = 97.2346$, $B_{ud} = 109/1.1045 = 98.6872$, and $B_{dd} = 109/1.09025 = 99.9771$. Given these values, we next roll the tree to the first period and determine the two possible values there. Note, in this period the values are equal to the present values of the expected cash flows in period 2; that is:

$$B_u = \frac{0.5[97.2346 + 9] + 0.5[98.6872 + 9]}{1.11}$$
$$= 96.3612$$

$$B_d = \frac{0.5[98.6872 + 9] + 0.5[99.9771 + 9]}{1.095}$$
$$= 98.9335$$

Finally, using the bond values in period 1, we roll the tree to the current period where

Exhibit 9.4 Value of two-period callable bond

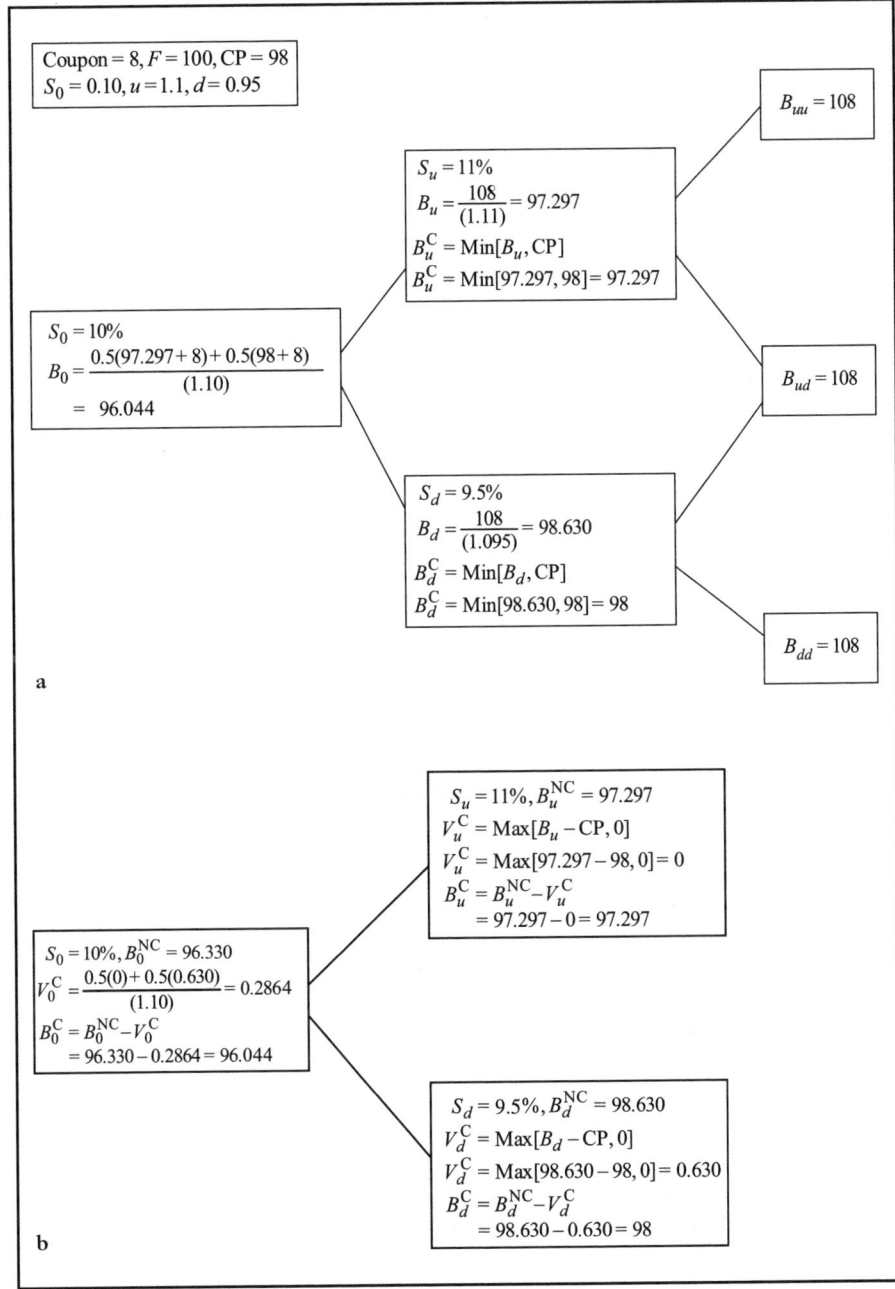

Coupon $= 8, F = 100, CP = 98$
$S_0 = 0.10, u = 1.1, d = 0.95$

$B_{uu} = 108$

$S_u = 11\%$
$B_u = \dfrac{108}{(1.11)} = 97.297$
$B_u^C = \text{Min}[B_u, CP]$
$B_u^C = \text{Min}[97.297, 98] = 97.297$

$S_0 = 10\%$
$B_0 = \dfrac{0.5(97.297 + 8) + 0.5(98 + 8)}{(1.10)}$
$= 96.044$

$B_{ud} = 108$

$S_d = 9.5\%$
$B_d = \dfrac{108}{(1.095)} = 98.630$
$B_d^C = \text{Min}[B_d, CP]$
$B_d^C = \text{Min}[98.630, 98] = 98$

$B_{dd} = 108$

a

$S_u = 11\%, B_u^{NC} = 97.297$
$V_u^C = \text{Max}[B_u - CP, 0]$
$V_u^C = \text{Max}[97.297 - 98, 0] = 0$
$B_u^C = B_u^{NC} - V_u^C$
$= 97.297 - 0 = 97.297$

$S_0 = 10\%, B_0^{NC} = 96.330$
$V_0^C = \dfrac{0.5(0) + 0.5(0.630)}{(1.10)} = 0.2864$
$B_0^C = B_0^{NC} - V_0^C$
$= 96.330 - 0.2864 = 96.044$

$S_d = 9.5\%, B_d^{NC} = 98.630$
$V_d^C = \text{Max}[B_d - CP, 0]$
$V_d^C = \text{Max}[98.630 - 98, 0] = 0.630$
$B_d^C = B_d^{NC} - V_d^C$
$= 98.630 - 0.630 = 98$

b

Exhibit 9.5 Value of three-period option-free bond

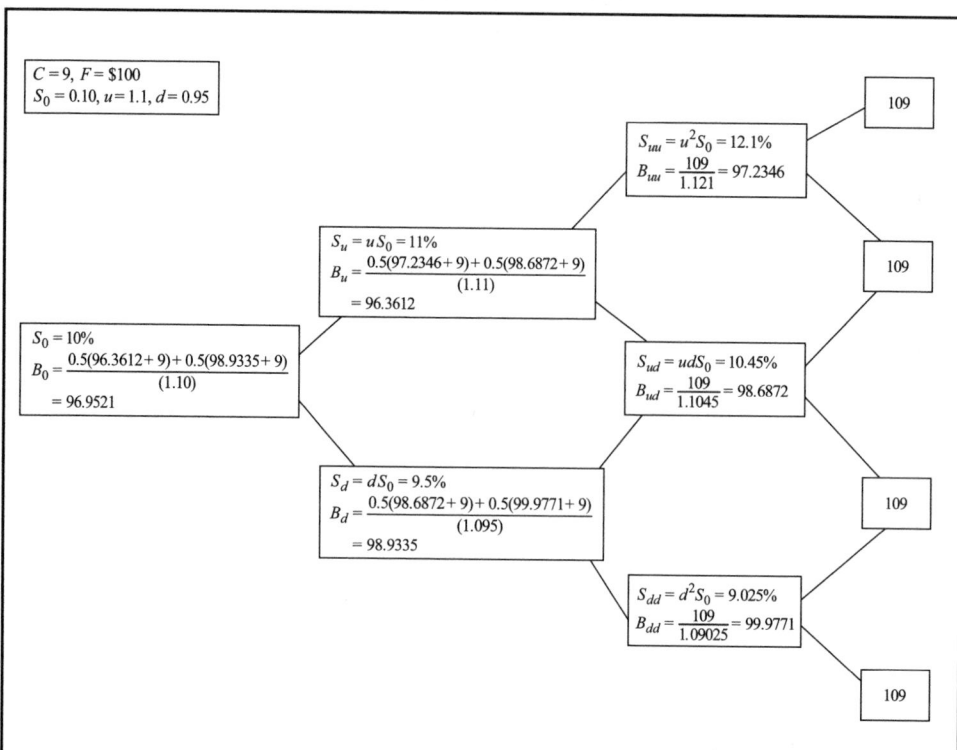

Period	Path 1	Geometric mean	CF	PV
1	0.100000	0.1000000	9	8.18182
2	0.095000	0.0974972	9	7.47198
3	0.090250	0.0950761	109	83.00296
				98.65676

Period	Path 2	Geometric mean	CF	PV
1	0.100000	0.1000000	9	8.18182
2	0.095000	0.0974972	9	7.47198
3	0.104500	0.0998265	109	81.93208
				97.58588

Period	Path 3	Geometric mean	CF	PV
1	0.100000	0.1000000	9	8.18182
2	0.110000	0.1049887	9	7.37101
3	0.104500	0.1048258	109	80.82489
				96.37771

Period	Path 4	Geometric mean	CF	PV
1	0.100000	0.1000000	9	8.18182
2	0.110000	0.1049887	9	7.37101
3	0.121000	0.1103002	109	79.63523
				95.18806

Weighted average value $= (98.65676 + 97.58588 + 96.37771 + 95.18806)/4 = 96.9521$

we determine the value of the bond to be 96.9521:

$$B_0 = \frac{0.5[96.3612 + 9] + 0.5[98.9335 + 9]}{1.10}$$

$$= 96.9521$$

If the bond is callable, we can determine its value by first comparing each of the non-callable bond values with the call price in period 2 (one period from maturity) and taking the minimum of the two as the callable bond value. We next roll the callable bond values from period 2 to period 1 where we determine the two bond values at each node as the present value of the expected cash flows, and then for each case we select the minimum of the value we calculated or the call price. Finally, we roll those two callable bond values to the current period and determine the callable bond's price as the present value of period 1's expected cash flows.

Exhibit 9.6a shows the binomial tree value of the three-period, 9% bond given a call feature with a CP = 98. Note, at the two lower nodes in period 2, the bond would be called at 98 and therefore the callable bond price would be 98; at the top node, the bond price of 97.2346 would prevail. Rolling these prices to period 1, the present values of the expected cash flows are 96.0516 at the 11% spot rate and 97.7169 at the 9.5% rate. Since neither of these values are less than the CP of 98, each represents the callable bond value at that node. Rolling these two values to the current period, we obtain a value of 96.2584 for the three-period callable bond.

The alternative approach to valuing the callable bond is to determine the value of the call option at each node and then subtract that value from the non-callable value to obtain callable bond's price. However, different from

option or she can hold it for another period. The exercising value, IV, is:

$$IV = \text{Max}[B_t^{NC} - CP, 0]$$

while the value of holding, V_H, is the present value of the expected call value next period:

$$V_H = \frac{qV_u^C + (1-q)V_d^C}{1+S}$$

If V_H exceeds IV, the issuer will hold the option another period and the value of the call in this case will be the holding value. In contrast, if IV is greater than V_H, then the issuer will exercise the call immediately and the value of the option will be IV. Thus, the value of the call option is equal to the maximum of IV or V_H:

$$V^C = \text{Max}[IV, V_H]$$

Exhibit 9.6b shows this valuation approach applied to the three-period callable bond. Note, in period 2 the value of holding is zero at all three nodes since next period is maturity where it is too late to call. The issuer, though, would find it profitable to exercise in two of the three cases where the call price is lower than the bond values. The three possible callable bond values in period 2 are:

$$B_{uu}^C = B_{uu}^{NC} - V_{uu}^C = 97.2346$$
$$- \text{Max}[97.2346 - 98, 0] = 97.2346$$

$$B_{ud}^C = B_{ud}^{NC} - V_{ud}^C = 98.6872$$
$$- \text{Max}[98.6872 - 98, 0] = 98$$

$$B_{dd}^C = B_{dd}^{NC} - V_{dd}^C = 99.9771$$
$$- \text{Max}[99.9771 - 98, 0] = 98$$

In period 1, the non-callable bond price is greater than the call price at the lower node. In this case, the IV is 98.9335 − 98 = 0.9335. The value of holding the call, though, is 1.2166:

$$V_H = \frac{0.5[\text{Max}[98.6872 - 98, 0]] + 0.5[\text{Max}[99.9771 - 98, 0]]}{1.095} = 1.2166$$

our previous two-period case, when there are three periods or more, we need to take into account that prior to maturity the bond issuer has two choices: she can either exercise the

Thus, the issuer would find it more valuable to defer the exercise by one period. As a result, the value of the call option is Max[IV, V_H] = Max[0.8394, 1.2166] = 1.2166

Exhibit 9.6   Value of three-period callable bond

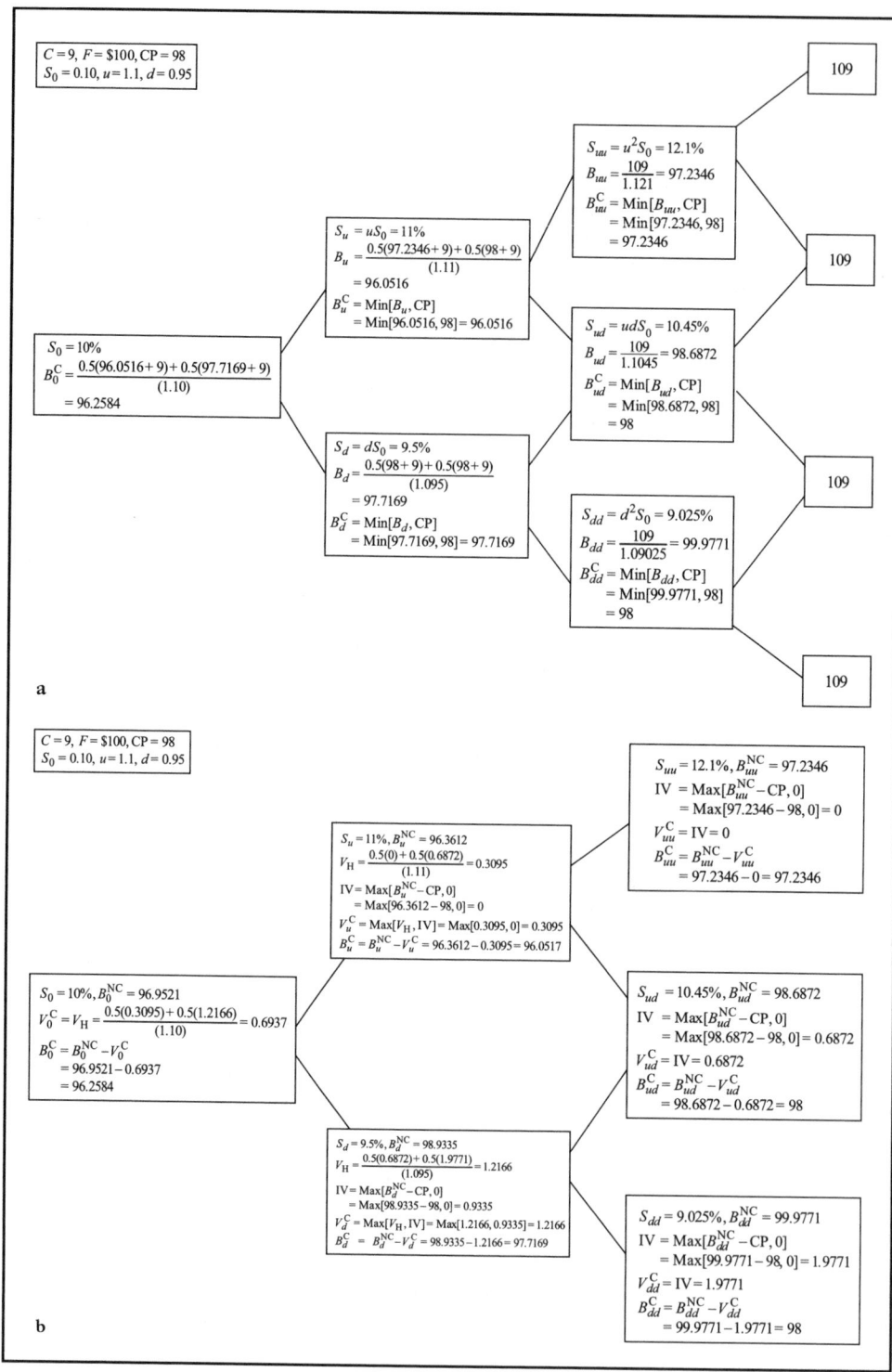

and the value of the callable bond is 97.7169 (the same value we obtained using the price constraint approach):

$$B_d^C = B_d^{NC} - V_d^C = 98.9335 - 1.2166$$
$$= 97.7169$$

At the upper node in period 1 where the price of the non-callable bond is 96.3612, the exercise value is zero. The value of the call option in this case is equal to its holding value of 0.3095:

$$V_H = \frac{0.5[\text{Max}[97.2346 - 98, 0]] + 0.5[\text{Max}[98.6872 - 98, 0]]}{1.11} = 0.3095$$

and the value of the callable bond is 96.0517 (the same value as the constraint one with some slight rounding):

$$B_u^C = B_u^{NC} - V_u^C = 96.3612 - 0.3095$$
$$= 96.0517$$

Finally, rolling the two possible option values of 0.3095 and 1.2166 in period 1 to the current period, we obtain the current value of the option of 0.6937 and the same callable bond value of 96.2584 that we obtained using the first approach:

$$V_0^C = \frac{0.5[0.3095] + 0.5[1.2166]}{1.10} = 0.6937$$

$$B_0^C = B_0^{NC} - V_0^C = 96.9521 - 0.6937$$
$$= 96.2584$$

9.2.3 Alternative Binomial Valuation Approach

In valuing an option-free bond with the binomial approach, we started at the bond's maturity and rolled the tree to the current period. An alternative but equivalent approach is to calculate the weighted average value of each possible path defined by the binomial process. This value is referred to as the *theoretical value*.

To see this approach, consider again the three-period, 9% option-free bond valued with a two-period interest rate tree (exhibit 9.5). For a two-period interest rate tree, there are four possible interest rate paths. That is, to get to the second-period spot rate of 9.025%,

there is one path (spot rate decreasing two consecutive periods); to get to 10.45%, there are two paths (decrease in the first period and increase in the second and increase in the first and decrease in the second); to get to 12.1% there is one path (increase two consecutive periods). Given the three-period bond's cash flows of 9, 9, and 109, the value or equilibrium price of each path is obtained by discounting each of the cash flows by their appropriate one-, two-, and three-period spot rates:

$$B_0^{\text{Path } i} = \frac{CF_1}{(1 + S_1^{\text{Path } i})} + \frac{CF_2}{(1 + S_2^{\text{Path } i})^2}$$
$$+ \frac{CF_3}{(1 + S_3^{\text{Path } i})^3}$$

The t-period spot rate is equal to the geometric average of the current and expected one-period spot rates. For example, for path 1 (path with two consecutive decreases in rates), its one-period rate is $S_t = S_1 = 10\%$, its two-period rate is $S_2 = 9.74972\%$ (geometric average of $S_0 = 10\%$ and $S_d = 9.5\%$), and its three-period rate is $S_3 = 9.50761\%$ (geometric average of $S_0 = 10\%$, $S_d = 9.5\%$, and $S_{dd} = 9.025\%$).

$$S_1^{\text{Path } 1} = S_0 = 0.10$$
$$S_2^{\text{Path } 1} = [(1 + S_0)(1 + S_d)]^{1/2} - 1$$
$$= [(1.10)(1.095)]^{1/2} - 1$$
$$= 0.0974972$$
$$S_3^{\text{Path } 1} = [(1 + S_0)(1 + S_d)(1 + S_{dd})]^{1/3} - 1$$
$$= [(1.10)(1.095)(1.09025)]^{1/3} - 1$$
$$= 0.0950761$$

Discounting the three-period bond's cash flows by these rates yields a value for path 1 of 98.65676:

$$B_0^{\text{Path } 1} = \frac{9}{(1.10)} + \frac{9}{(1.0974972)^2} + \frac{109}{(1.0950761)^3}$$
$$= 98.65676$$

The periodic spot rates and bond values for each of the four paths are shown at the bottom of exhibit 9.5. Given the path values, the bond's weighted average value is obtained by summing the weighted values of each path with the weights being the probability of attaining that path. For a two-period interest rate tree with a probability of the rate increasing in one period being $q = 0.5$, the probability of attaining each path is 0.25. Using these probabilities, the three-period bond's weighted average value or theoretical value is equal to 96.9521 – the same value we obtained earlier by rolling the bond's value from maturity to the current period.

9.3 VALUING BONDS WITH OTHER OPTION FEATURES

In addition to call features, bonds can have other embedded options such as a put option, a stock convertibility clause, or a sinking-fund arrangement in which the issuer has the option to buy some of the bonds back either at their market price or at a call price. The binomial tree can be easily extended to the valuation of bonds with these embedded option features.

9.3.1 Putable Bond

A putable bond, or put bond, gives the holder the right to sell the bond back to the issuer at a specified exercise price (or put price), PP. In contrast to callable bonds, putable bonds benefit the holder: if the price of the bond decreases below the exercise price, then the bondholder can sell the bond back to the issuer at the exercise price. From the bondholder's perspective, a put option provides a hedge against a decrease in the bond price. If rates decrease in the market, then the bondholder benefits from the resulting higher bond prices, and if rates increase, then the bondholder can exercise, giving her downside protection. Given that the bondholder has the right to exercise, the price of a putable bond will be equal to the price of an otherwise identical non-putable bond plus the value of the put option (V_0^P):

$$B_0^P = B_0^{NP} + V_0^P$$

Since the bondholder will find it profitable to exercise whenever the put price exceeds the bond price, the value of a putable bond can be found using the binomial approach by comparing bond

prices at each node with the put price and selecting the *maximum* of the two, $\text{Max}[B_t, \text{PP}]$. The same binomial value can also be found by determining the value of the put option at each node and then pricing the putable bond as the value of an otherwise identical non-putable bond plus the value of the put option. In using the second approach, the value of the put option will be the maximum of either its intrinsic value (or exercising value), $\text{IV} = \text{Max}[\text{PP} - B_t, 0]$, or its holding value (the present value of the expected put value next period). In most cases, though, the put's intrinsic value will be greater than its holding value.

To illustrate, suppose the three-period, 9% option-free bond in our previous example had a put option giving the bondholder the right to sell the bond back to the issuer at an exercise price of $\text{PP} = 97$ in periods 1 or 2. Using the two-period tree of one-period spot rates and the corresponding bond values for the option-free bond (exhibit 9.5), we start, as we did with the callable bond, at period 2 and investigate each of the nodes to determine if there is an advantage for the holder to exercise. In all three of the cases in period 2, the bond price exceeds the exercise price (see exhibit 9.7a); thus, there are no exercise advantages in this period and each of the possible prices of the putable bond are equal to their non-putable values and the values of each of the put options are zero. In period 1, though, it is profitable for the holder to exercise when the spot rate is 11%. At that node, the value of the non-putable bond is 96.3612, compared to $\text{PP} = 97$; thus the value of the putable bond is its exercise price of 97:

$$B_u^P = \text{Max}[96.3612, 97] = 0.97$$

The putable bond price of 97 can also be found by subtracting the value of the put option from the price of the non-putable bond (see exhibit 9.7b). The value of the put option at this node is 0.6388:

$$V_u^P = \text{Max}[\text{IV}, V_H]$$
$$= \text{Max}[97 - 96.3612, 0] = 0.6388$$

Thus, the value of the putable bond is

$$B_u^P = B_u^{NP} + V_u^P$$
$$B_u^P = 96.3612 + 0.6388 = 97$$

Exhibit 9.7   Value of putable bond

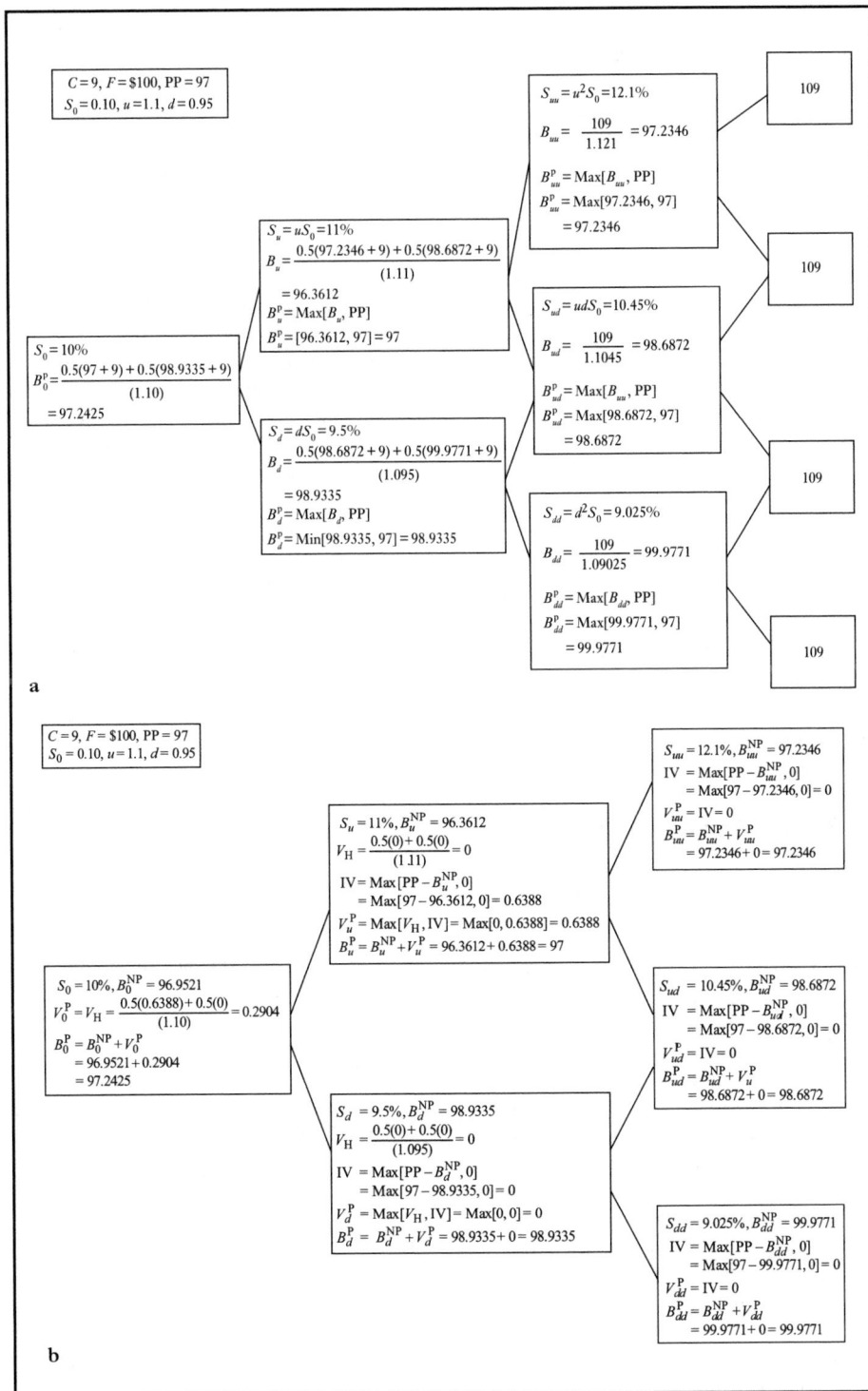

At the lower node in period 1, it is not profitable to exercise nor is there any holding value of the put option since there is no exercise advantage in period 2. Thus at the lower node, the non-putable bond price prevails. Rolling the two putable bond values in period 1 to the present, we obtain a current value of the putable bond of 97.2425:

$$B_0^P = \frac{0.5[97 + 9] + 0.5[98.9335 + 9]}{1.10} = 97.2425$$

This value also can be obtained using the alternative approach by computing the present value of the expected put option value in period 1 and then adding that to the current value of the non-putable bond. With possible exercise values of 0.6388 and 0 in period 1, the current put option value is 0.2904:

$$V_0^P = \frac{0.5[0.6388] + 0.5[0]}{1.10} = 0.2904$$

Thus:

$$B_0^P = B_0^{NP} + V_0^P = 96.9521 + 0.2904$$
$$= 97.2425$$

The inclusion of the put option in this example causes the bond price to increase from 96.9521 to 97.2425, reflecting the value the put option has to the bondholder.

9.3.2 Sinking-Fund Bonds

Many bonds have sinking-fund clauses specified in their indenture requiring that the issuer make scheduled payments into a fund or buy up a certain proportion of the bond issue each period. Often when the sinking-fund agreement specifies an orderly retirement of the issue, the issuer is given an option of either purchasing the bonds in the market or calling the bonds at a specified call price. This option makes the sinking fund valuable to the issuer. If interest rates are relatively high, then the issuer will be able to buy back the requisite amount of bonds at a relatively low market price; if rates are low and the bond price high, though, then the issuer will be able to buy back the bonds on the call option at the call price. Thus, a sinking-fund bond with this type of call provision should trade at a lower price than an otherwise identical non-sinking-fund bond.

Similar to callable bonds, a sinking-fund bond can be valued using the binomial tree approach. To illustrate, suppose a company issues a $15m, three-period bond with a sinking-fund obligation requiring that the issuer sink $5m of face value after the first period and $5m after the second, with the issuer having an option of either buying the bonds in the market or calling them at a call price of 98. Assume the same interest rate tree and bond values characterizing the three-period, 9% non-callable described in exhibit 9.5 apply to this bond without its sinking-fund agreement. With the sinking fund, the issuer has two options: at the end of period 1, the issuer can buy $5m-worth of the bond either at 98 or at the bond's market price, and at the end of period 2, the issuer has another option to buy $5m-worth of the bond either at 98 or the market price. As shown in exhibit 9.8, the value of the period 1 option (in terms of $100 face value) is $V_0^{SF(1)} = 0.4243$ and the value of the period 2 call option is $V_0^{SF(2)} = 0.6937$. Note, since the sinking-fund arrangement requires an immediate exercise or bond purchase at the specified sinking-fund dates, the possible values of the sinking fund's call features at those dates are equal to the intrinsic values. This differs from the valuation of a standard callable bond where a holding value is also considered in determining the value of the call option.

Since each option represents 1/3 of the issue, the value of the bond's sinking-fund option is:

$$V_0^{SF} = (1/3)(0.4243) + (1/3)(0.6937)$$
$$= 0.3727$$

and the value of the sinking-fund bond is 96.5794 per $100 face value:

$$B_0^{SF} = B_0^{NSF} - V_0^{SF}$$
$$B_0^{SF} = 96.9521 - 0.3727 = 96.5794$$

Thus, the total value of the $15m face value issue is $14.48691m:

$$\text{Issue value} = \frac{96.5794}{100}\$15m = \$14.48691m$$

or:

$$\text{Issue value} = \left(\frac{96.9521}{100}\right)\$15m$$
$$- \left(\frac{0.3727}{100}\right)\$15m = \$14.48691m$$

Exhibit 9.8   Value of sinking-fund call

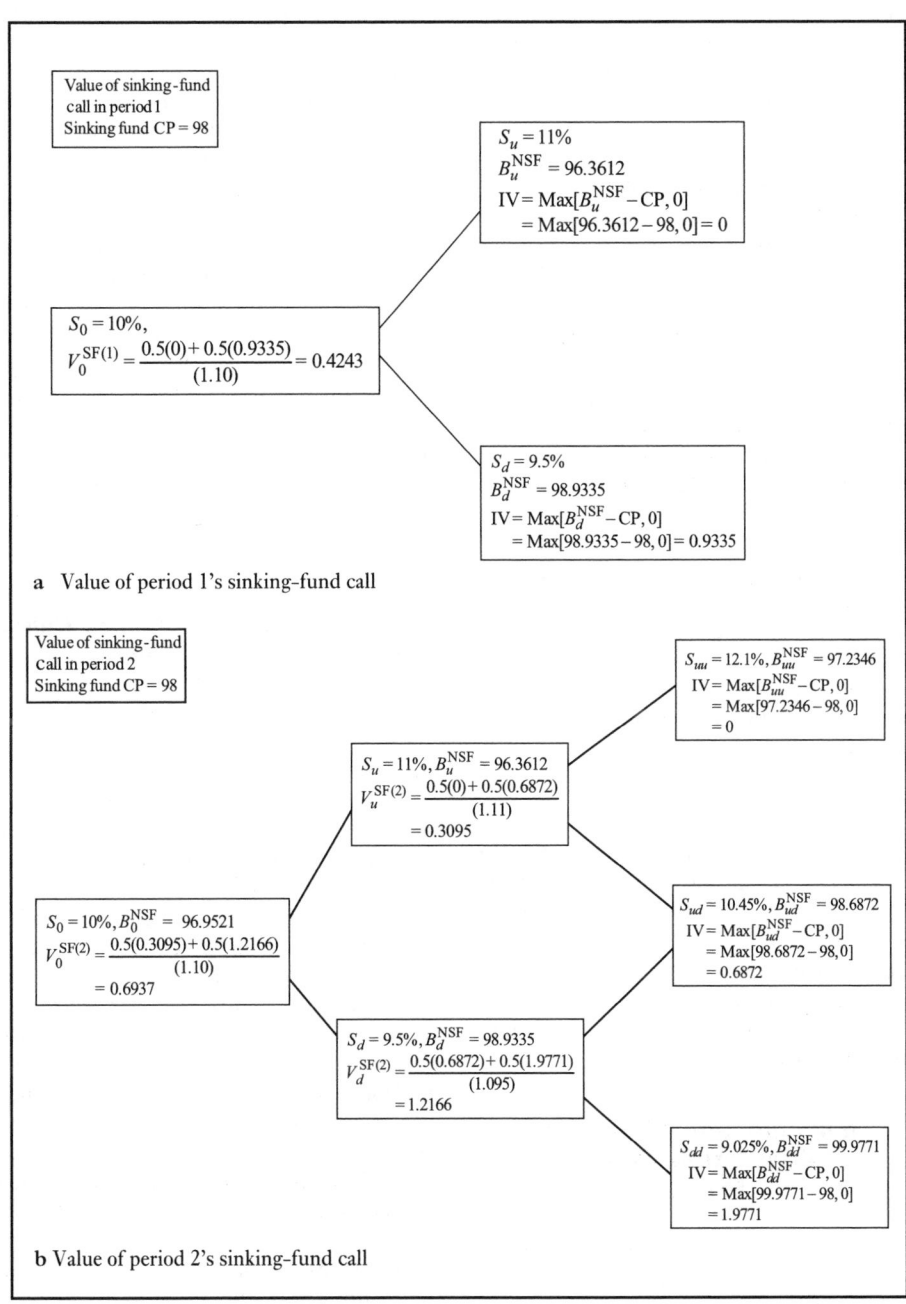

a   Value of period 1's sinking-fund call

b Value of period 2's sinking-fund call

Like a standard callable bond, a sinking-fund provision with a call feature lowers the value of an otherwise identical non-sinking-fund bond.

9.3.3   Convertible Bond

A convertible bond gives the holder the right to convert the bond into a specified number of shares of stock. Convertibles are often sold as a subordinate issue, with the conversion feature serving as a bond sweetener. To the investor, convertible bonds offer the potential for a high rate of return if the company does well and its stock price increases, while providing some downside protection as a bond if the stock declines. Convertibles are usually callable, with the convertible bondholder usually having the right to convert the bond to stock if the issuer does call.

Convertible Bond Terms

Suppose our illustrative three-period, 9% bond were convertible into four shares of the underlying company's stock. The conversion features of this bond include its conversion ratio, conversion value, and straight debt value. The *conversion ratio (CR)* is the number of shares of stock that can be converted when the bond is tendered for conversion. The conversion ratio for this bond is four. The *conversion value (CV)* is the convertible bond's value as a stock. At a given point in time, the conversion value is equal to the conversion ratio times the market price of the stock (P_t^S):

$$CV_t = (CR)P_t^S$$

If the current price of the stock were 92, then the bond's conversion value would be $CV = (4)(\$92) = \$368.$[2] Finally, the *straight debt value (SDV)* is the convertible bond's value as a non-convertible bond. This value is obtained by discounting the convertible's cash flows by the discount rate on a comparable non-convertible bond.

Minimum and Maximum Convertible Bond Prices

Arbitrage ensures that the minimum price of a convertible bond is the greater of either its straight debt value or its conversion value:

$$\text{Min } B_t^{CB} = \text{Max}[CV_t, \ SDV_t]$$

If a convertible bond is priced below its conversion value, arbitrageurs could buy it, convert it to stock, and then sell the stock in the market

to earn a riskless profit. Arbitrageurs seeking such opportunities would push the price of the convertible up until it is at least equal to its CV. Similarly, if a convertible is selling below its SDV, then arbitrageurs could profit by buying the convertible and selling it as a regular bond.

In addition to a minimum price, if the convertible is callable, the call price at which the issuer can redeem the bond places a maximum limit on the convertible. That is, the issuer will find it profitable to buy back the convertible bond once its price is equal to the call price. Buying back the bond, in turn, frees the company to sell new stock or bonds at prices higher than the stock or straight debt values associated with the convertible. Thus, the maximum price of a convertible is the call price. The actual price that a convertible will trade for will be at a premium above its minimum value but below its maximum.

Valuation of Convertibles Using Binomial Trees

The valuation of a convertible bond with an embedded call is more difficult than the valuation of a bond with just one option feature. In the case of a callable convertible bond, one has to consider not only the uncertainty of future interest rates, but also the uncertainty of stock prices. A rate decrease, for example, may not only increase the convertible's SDV and the chance the bond could be called, but if the rate decrease is also associated with an increase in the stock price, it may also increase the conversion value of the convertible and the chance of conversion. The valuation of convertibles therefore needs to take into account the random patterns of interest rates, stock prices, and the correlation between them.

To illustrate the valuation of convertibles, consider a three-period, 10% convertible bond with face value of 1,000 that can be converted to ten shares of the underlying company's stock ($CR = 10$). To simplify the analysis, assume the bond has no call option and no default risk, that the current yield curve is flat at 5%, and that the yield curve will stay at 5% for the duration of the three periods (i.e., no market risk). In this simplified world, the only uncertainty is the future stock price. Like interest rates, suppose the convertible bond's underlying stock price follows a binomial process where in each period it has an equal chance that it either increases to equal u times its initial value or decreases to equal d times the initial value, where $u = 1.1$ and $d = 1/1.1 = 0.9091$, and the current stock price is 92. The possible stock prices resulting from this binomial process are shown in exhibit 9.9, along with the convertible bond's conversion values.

Since spot rates are assumed constant, the value of the convertible bond will only depend on the stock price. To value the convertible bond, we start at the maturity date of the bond. At that date, the bondholder will have a coupon worth 100 and will either convert the bond to stock or receive the principal of 1,000. At the top stock price of 122.45, the convertible bondholder would exercise her option, converting the bond to ten shares of stock. The value of the convertible bond, B^{CB}, at the top node in period 3 would therefore be equal to its conversion value of 1,224.50 plus the $100 coupon:

$$B^{CB}_{uuu} = Max[CV_t, F] + C$$

$$= Max[1,224.50, 1,000] + 100$$

$$= 1,324.50$$

Similarly, at the next stock price of 101.20, the bondholder would also find it profitable to convert; thus, the value of the convertible in this case would be its conversion value of 1,012 plus the $100 coupon. At the lower two stock prices in period 3 of 83.64 and 69.12, conversion is worthless; thus, the value of the convertible bond is equal to the principal plus the coupon: 1,100.

In period 2, at each node the value of the convertible bond is equal to the maximum of either the present value of the bond's expected value at maturity or its conversion value. At all three stock prices, the present values of the bond's expected values next period are greater than the bond's conversion values, including at the highest stock price; that is, at $P^S_{uu} = 111.32$, the CV is 1,113.20 compared to the convertible bond value of 1,160.24; thus the value of convertible bond is 1,160.24:

$$B_{uu} = \frac{0.5[1,324.50] + 0.5[1,112]}{1.05} = 1,160.24$$

$$B^{CB}_{uu} = Max[B_{uu}, CV] = [1,160.24, 1,113.20]$$
$$= 1,160.24$$

Thus, in all three cases, the values of holding the convertible bond option are greater than the conversion values. Similarly, the two possible bond values in period 1 (generated by rolling the three convertible bond values in period 2 to period 1) also exceed their conversion values. Rolling the tree to the current period, we obtain a convertible bond value of 1,164.29. As we would expect, this value exceeds both the convertible bond's current conversion value of 920 and its SDV of 1,136.16 (assuming a 5% discount rate):

$$SDV = \frac{100}{(1.05)} + \frac{100}{(1.05)^2} + \frac{1,100}{(1.05)^3} = 1,136.16$$

As noted, the valuation of a convertible becomes more complex when the bond is callable. With callable convertible bonds, the issuer will find it profitable to call the convertible prior to maturity whenever the price of the convertible is greater than the call price. However, when the convertible bondholder is faced with a call, she usually has the choice of either tendering the bond at the call price or converting it to stock. Since the issuer will call whenever the call price exceeds the convertible bond price, he is in effect forcing the holder to convert. By doing this, the issuer takes away the bondholder's value of holding the convertible, forcing the convertible bond price to equal its conversion value.

To see this, suppose the convertible bond is callable in periods 1 and 2 at a CP of 1,100. At the top stock price of 111.32 in period 2, the conversion value is 1,113.20 (see exhibit 9.10). In this case, the issuer can force the bondholder to convert by calling the bond. The call option therefore reduces the value of the convertible from 1,160.24 to 1,113.20. At the other nodes in period 2, neither conversion by the bondholders nor calling by the issuer is economical; thus the bond values prevail. In period 1, the call price of 1,100 is below the bond value (1,126.92), but above the conversion value (1,012). In this case, the issuer would call the bond and the holder would take the call instead of converting. The value of the callable convertible bond in this case would be the call price of 1,100. At the

Exhibit 9.9   Value of convertible bond

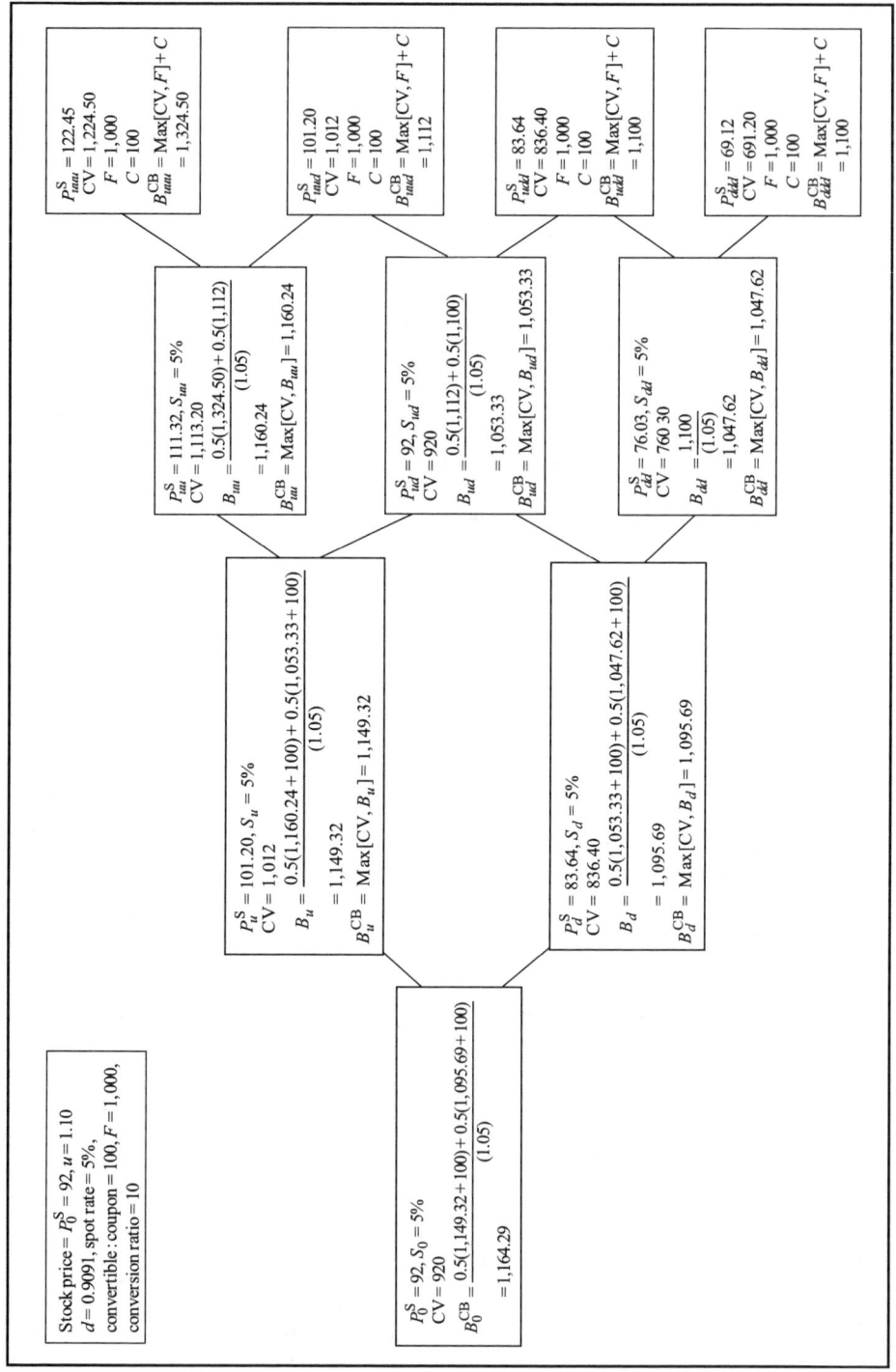

Exhibit 9.10 Value of convertible bond with call

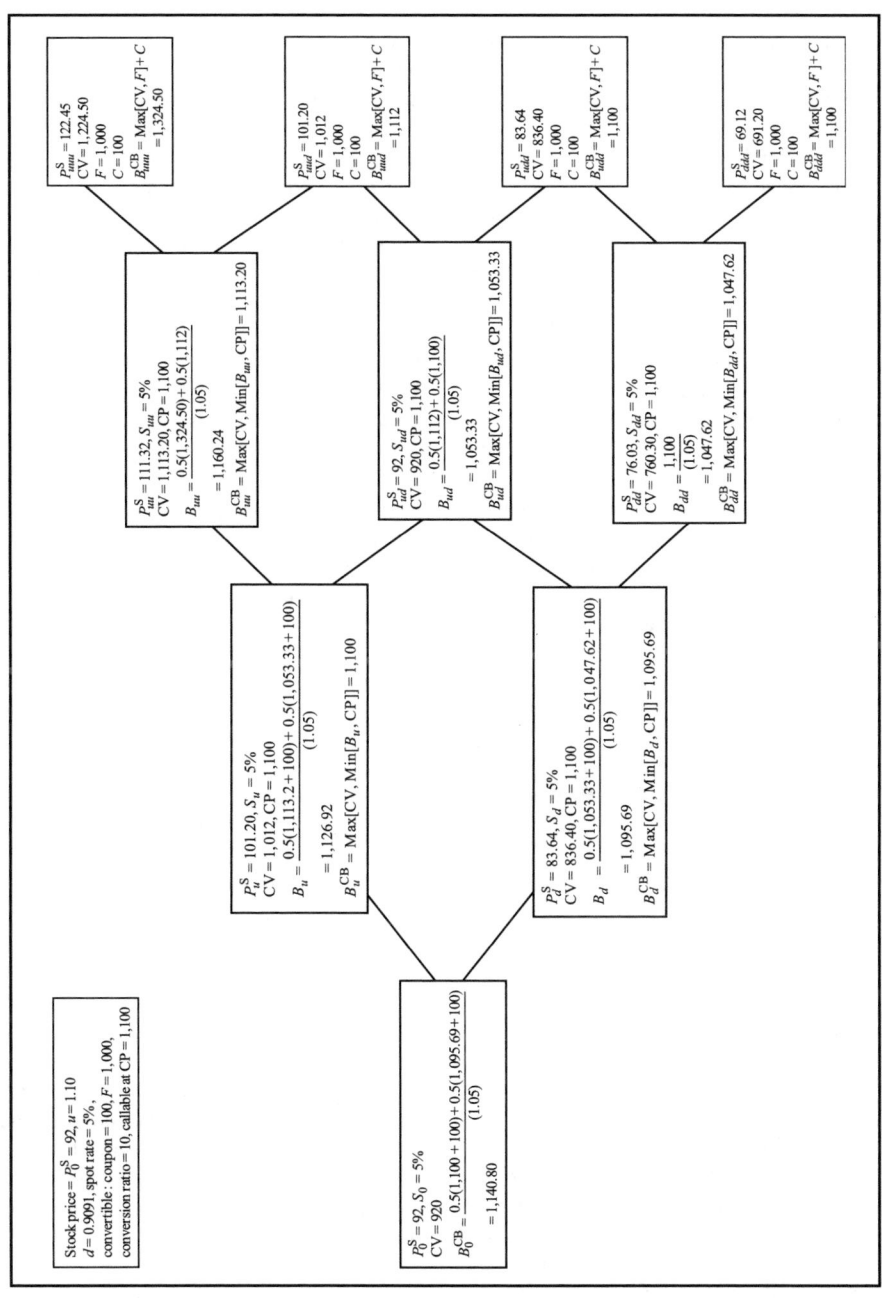

lower node, calling and converting are not economical and thus the bond value of 1,095.69 prevails. Rolling period 1's upper and lower convertible bond values to the current period, we obtain a value for the callable convertible bond of 1,140.80, which is less than the non-callable convertible bond value of 1,164.29 and greater than the straight debt value of a non-callable bond of 1,136.16.

In the above two cases, we assumed for simplicity that the yield curve remained constant at 5% for the period. As noted, the complexity of valuing convertibles is taking into account the uncertainty of two variables – stock prices and interest rates.[3] A simple way to model such behavior is to use correlation or regression analysis to first estimate the relationship between a stock's price and the spot rate, and then either with a binomial model of spot rates identify the corresponding stock prices or with a binomial model of stock prices identify the corresponding spot rates. For example, suppose using regression analysis, we estimated the following relationship between the stock in our above example and the one-period spot rate:

$$S_t = 0.16 - 0.001 P_t^S$$

Using this equation, the corresponding spot rates associated with the stock prices from the three-period tree would be

P_t^S	S_t
111.32	4.87%
101.20	5.90%
92.00	6.80%
83.64	7.64%
76.03	8.40%

Exhibit 9.11 shows the binomial tree of stock prices along with their corresponding spot rates. Given the rates and stock prices, the methodology for valuing the convertible bond is identical to our previous analysis. Again, we start at maturity where we value the bond at each node as the maximum of either its conversion value or face value. Given these values, we then move to period 2, where we first determine the present values of period 3's

expected bond values and coupons using the spot rates we've estimated. We then compare each of those values with the call price and the conversion value. As we noted in the previous case, if the call price exceeds the convertible bond value, then the issuer will call the bond, and the convertible bond's price will reflect what is more profitable for the bondholder: accept the call and receive the call price or convert to stock. As in our previous case, at the top node in period 2, the call price of 1,100 is below the convertible bond value of 1,161.68. In this case, the issuer will call the bond and the holder will find it more profitable to convert; that is, the conversion value of 1,113.20 exceeds the call price of 1,100. Thus, the convertible bond would be equal to the conversion value. The other two convertible bond prices in period 2 are less than the call price, implying the issuer would not exercise; the prices also are greater than the conversion value, implying the holder would not convert. Thus, the values of the convertibles in these two cases are equal to the present values of their expected cash flows for the next period. In period 1, the call price is less than the bond value (1,108.96) and greater than the conversion value (1,012) at the top node. In this case the issuer would call and the bondholder would find it better to accept the call instead of converting; thus, the convertible bond price at this node would be the call price of 1,100. Rolling the tree to the current period with this value and the lower node value, we obtain a convertible bond value of 1,097.99. This value is lower than the previous case in which we assumed a constant yield curve at 5%.

It should be noted that modeling a bond with multiple option features and influenced by random patterns of more than one factor is more complex in practice than the simple model described above. The above model is intended only to provide some insight into the dynamics involved in valuing a bond with embedded convertible and call options given different interest rate and stock price scenarios.

9.4 CONCLUSION

In 1985, Merrill Lynch introduced the liquid yield option note (LYON). The LYON is a

Exhibit 9.11   Value of convertible bond with call and different spot rates

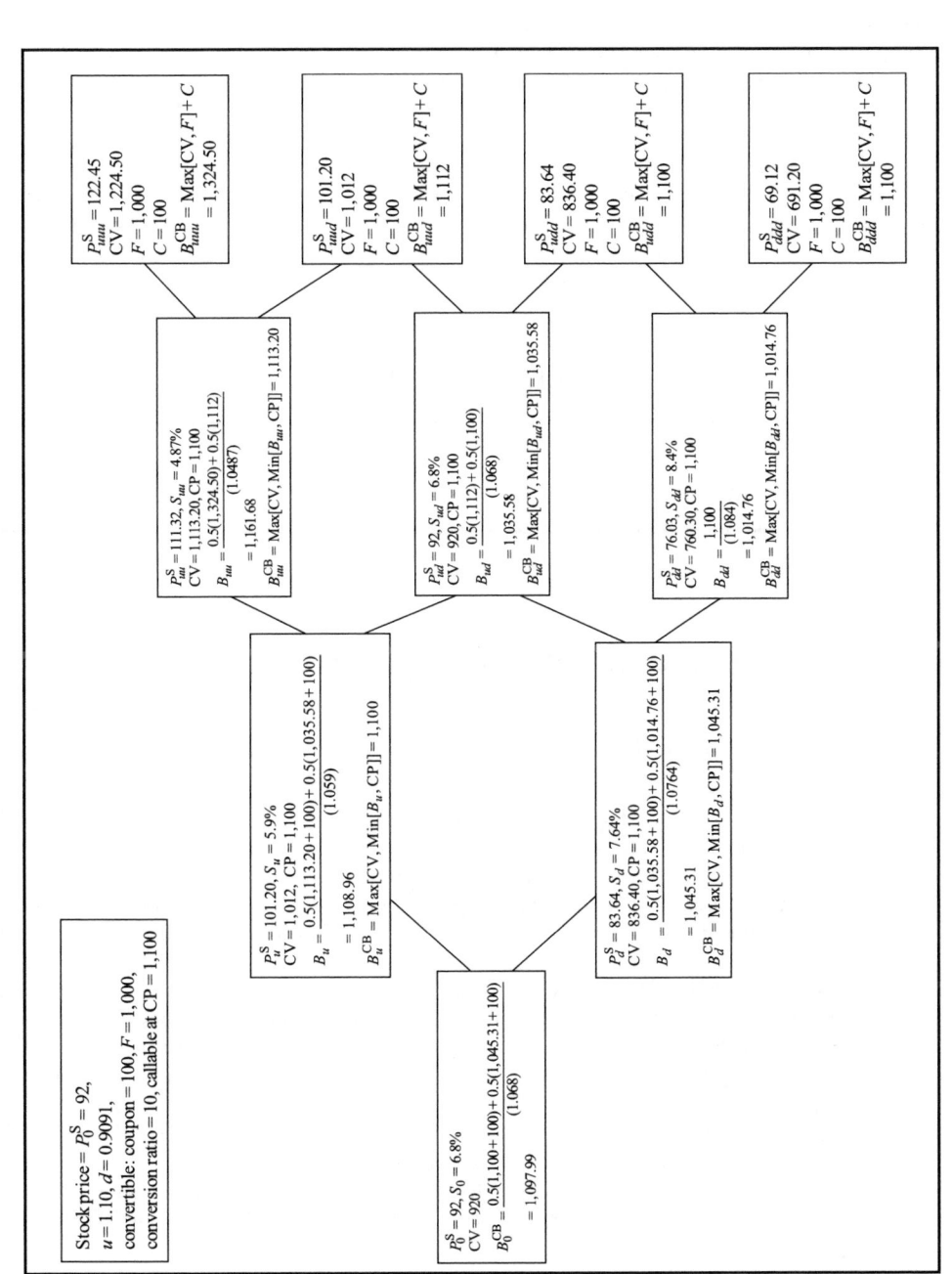

Stock price $= P_0^S = 92$,
$u = 1.10$, $d = 0.9091$,
convertible: coupon $= 100$, $F = 1,000$,
conversion ratio $= 10$, callable at CP $= 1,100$

$P_0^S = 92$, $S_0 = 6.8\%$
CV $= 920$
$B_0^{CB} = \dfrac{0.5(1,100 + 100) + 0.5(1,045.31 + 100)}{(1.068)}$
$\quad = 1,097.99$

$P_u^S = 101.20$, $S_u = 5.9\%$
CV $= 1,012$, CP $= 1,100$
$B_u = \dfrac{0.5(1,113.20 + 100) + 0.5(1,035.58 + 100)}{(1.059)}$
$\quad = 1,108.96$
$B_u^{CB} = \text{Max}[\text{CV}, \text{Min}[B_u, \text{CP}]] = 1,100$

$P_d^S = 83.64$, $S_d = 7.64\%$
CV $= 836.40$, CP $= 1,100$
$B_d = \dfrac{0.5(1,035.58 + 100) + 0.5(1,014.76 + 100)}{(1.0764)}$
$\quad = 1,045.31$
$B_d^{CB} = \text{Max}[\text{CV}, \text{Min}[B_d, \text{CP}]] = 1,045.31$

$P_{uu}^S = 111.32$, $S_{uu} = 4.87\%$
CV $= 1,113.20$, CP $= 1,100$
$B_{uu} = \dfrac{0.5(1,324.50) + 0.5(1,112)}{(1.0487)}$
$\quad = 1,161.68$
$B_{uu}^{CB} = \text{Max}[\text{CV}, \text{Min}[B_{uu}, \text{CP}]] = 1,113.20$

$P_{ud}^S = 92$, $S_{ud} = 6.8\%$
CV $= 920$, CP $= 1,100$
$B_{ud} = \dfrac{0.5(1,112) + 0.5(1,100)}{(1.068)}$
$\quad = 1,035.58$
$B_{ud}^{CB} = \text{Max}[\text{CV}, \text{Min}[B_{ud}, \text{CP}]] = 1,035.58$

$P_{dd}^S = 76.03$, $S_{dd} = 8.4\%$
CV $= 760.30$, CP $= 1,100$
$B_{dd} = \dfrac{1,100}{(1.084)}$
$\quad = 1,014.76$
$B_{dd}^{CB} = \text{Max}[\text{CV}, \text{Min}[B_{dd}, \text{CP}]] = 1,014.76$

$P_{uuu}^S = 122.45$
CV $= 1,224.50$
$F = 1,000$
$C = 100$
$B_{uuu}^{CB} = \text{Max}[\text{CV}, F] + C$
$\quad = 1,324.50$

$P_{uud}^S = 101.20$
CV $= 1,012$
$F = 1,000$
$C = 100$
$B_{uud}^{CB} = \text{Max}[\text{CV}, F] + C$
$\quad = 1,112$

$P_{udd}^S = 83.64$
CV $= 836.40$
$F = 1,000$
$C = 100$
$B_{udd}^{CB} = \text{Max}[\text{CV}, F] + C$
$\quad = 1,100$

$P_{ddd}^S = 69.12$
CV $= 691.20$
$F = 1,000$
$C = 100$
$B_{ddd}^{CB} = \text{Max}[\text{CV}, F] + C$
$\quad = 1,100$

zero-coupon bond, convertible into the issuer's stock, callable, with the call price increasing over time, and putable with the put price increasing over time. The LYON is a good example of how innovative the investment community can be in structuring debt instruments with option clauses. This type of innovation has also been quite extensive in the construction of mortgage-backed securities. Faced with the problem of prepayment risk, various types of mortgage securities were created in the 1980s with different claims that addressed such risk. Mortgage-backed securities, LYONs, and other securities with embedded option features all can be evaluated, though, using a binomial tree. In chapter 11 we will examine mortgage-backed securities and many of their derivative securities that have option features, and in part IV we will examine interest rate options and futures contracts listed on exchanges and offered by financial institutions and dealers. Before examining these securities, though, we first need to address a more fundamental question of how we estimate the binomial tree. This is the subject of the next chapter.

KEY TERMS

| Theoretical Value | Conversion Value (CV) | Straight Debt |
| Conversion Ratio (CR) | Conversion Price | Value (SDV) |

PROBLEMS AND QUESTIONS

1. Given a current one-period spot rate of $S_0 = 10\%$, upward and downward parameters of $u = 1.1$ and $d = 0.9091$, and probability of the spot rate increasing in one period of $q = 0.5$:

   a. Generate a two-period binomial tree of spot rates.
   b. Using the binomial interest rate tree from question 1a, determine the value of a two-period, option-free 9% coupon bond with $F = 100$.
   c. Using the binomial interest rate tree from question 1a, determine the value of the 9% bond assuming it is callable at a call price of $CP = 99$. Use the minimum constraint approach.
   d. Using the binomial interest rate tree, show at each node the call option values of the callable bond ($CP = 99$). Given your call option values, determine the values at each node of the callable bond as the difference between the option-free values found in question 1b and the call option values. Do your callable bond values match the ones you found in question 1c?
   e. Comment on values of your call options being equal to the present value of the interest savings that the issuer realizes from refunding the bond at lower rates.
   f. Using the binomial interest rate tree, determine the value of the bond assuming it is putable in periods 1 and 2 at a put price of $PP = 99$. Use the maximum constraint approach.
   g. Using the binomial interest rate tree, show at each node the put option values of the putable bond ($PP = 99$). Given your put option values, determine the values at each node of the putable bond as the sum of the option-free bond values found in question 1b and the put option values. Do your putable bond values match the ones you found in question 1f?

2. Given a current one-period spot rate of $S_0 = 10\%$, $u = 1.1$, $d = 0.9091$, and $q = 0.5$, determine the value of the two-period, option-free 9% coupon bond in question 1 as the weighted average value of the possible paths defined by the binomial process. Does the value match the value you obtained in question 1b?

3. Suppose a corporation issues a two-period, 9% coupon bond with the face value of the issue worth $9m. Suppose the issue has a sinking-fund obligation requiring the company to sink $3m in period 1, with the company having the option to either buy the bonds in the market or call them at $CP = 99$ per $100 face value. Using the same interest rate tree you generated in question 1, calculate the value of the sinking-fund bond.

4. Given an ABC convertible bond with $F = 1,000$, maturity of two periods, periodic coupon rate of 5%, conversion ratio of $CR = 10$, and an underlying stock with a current price of $100, $u = 1.05$, $d = 0.952381$, and $q = 0.5$, calculate the value of the bond using a binomial tree of stock prices. Assume no call on the bond and a flat yield curve at 5% that is not expected to change.

5. Given a current one-period spot rate of $S_0 = 5\%$, upward and downward parameters of $u = 1.1$, $d = 1/1.1$, and probability of spot rate increasing in one period of $q = 0.5$:

   a. Generate a two-period binomial tree of spot rates.
   b. Using a binomial tree approach, calculate the value of a three-period, option-free bond paying a 5% coupon per period and with face value of 100.
   c. Using the binomial tree, calculate the value of the bond given it is callable with a call price of 100.
   d. Using the tree, calculate the value of the bond given it is putable in periods 1 and 2 with a put price of 100.

6. Given a current one-period spot rate of $S_0 = 5\%$, $u = 1.1$, $d = 1/1.1$, and $q = 0.5$, determine the value of the three-period, option-free 5% coupon bond in question 5 as the weighted average value of the possible paths defined by the binomial process. Does the value match the value you obtained in question 5b?

7. Given a current one-period spot rate of $S_0 = 5\%$, $u = 1.1$, $d = 1/1.1$, and $q = 0.5$, determine the values of three bonds stripped from the three-period, option-free 5% coupon bond in question 5: one-period zero-coupon bond paying $F = 5$ at maturity, two-period zero-coupon bond paying $F = 5$ at maturity, three-period zero-coupon bond paying $F = 105$ at maturity. Does the sum of the values of the three strips equal the value you obtained for the three-period 5% coupon bond in question 5b?

8. Suppose a corporation issues a $9m, three-period, 5% coupon bond with a sinking-fund obligation requiring the company to sink $3m in period 1 and $3m in period 2, with the company having the option to either buy the bonds in the market or call them at $CP = 100$. Using the same interest rate tree you generated in question 5, calculate the value of the sinking-fund bond.

9. The XYZ convertible bond has the following features:

   • Coupon rate (annual) $= 10\%$
   • Face value $= F = \$1,000$
   • Maturity $= 10$ years
   • Callable at $1,100
   • YTM on a comparable, non-convertible bond $= 12\%$
   • Conversion ratio $= 10$ shares
   • Current stock price $= S_0 = \$90$

Calculate the following:

a. XYZ's conversion price
b. XYZ's conversion value
c. XYZ's straight debt value
d. Minimum price of the convertible
e. The arbitrage strategy if the price of the convertible were $880.

10. Given an ABC convertible bond with $F = 1,000$, maturity of three periods, coupon $= 100$, $CR = 10$, current stock price of $100, and $u = 1.1$, $d = 0.95$, and $q = 0.5$ on the stock:

a. Calculate the value of the bond using a binomial tree of stock prices. Assume no call on the bond and a flat yield curve at 10% that is not expected to change.
b. Calculate the value of the bond using a binomial tree of stock prices. Assume the bond is callable at $CP = 1,200$ and a flat yield curve at 10% that is not expected to change.

11. Given a current annual spot rate of $S_0 = 6\%$, upward and downward parameters on the spot rate of $u = 1.2$, $d = 1/1.2$, and $q = 0.5$:

a. Determine the value of a three-year, option-free, 6% annual coupon bond with $F = \$100$.
b. Assuming the bond is callable in periods 1 and 2 at a call price of 98, determine the values at each node of the embedded call option.
c. Determine the value of the callable bond.

12. Excel problems: the following problems should be done using the Excel programs Binbondcall.xls and Binbondput.xls.

Given a binomial interest rate tree with the following features: $S_0 = 6\%$, length of the tree $= 0.5$ year, and upward and downward parameters for 0.5 years of $u = 1.0488$ and $d = 0.9747$, and $q = 0.5$, determine the values of the following bonds:

a. The value of an option-free bond with maturity of 10 years, annual coupon of $C = 6$, semi-annual payments, and $F = 100$.
b. The value of a callable bond with maturity of 10 years, annual coupon of $C = 6$, semiannual payments, $F = 100$, and call price of 100.
c. The value of a putable bond with maturity of 10 years, annual coupon of $C = 6$, semi-annual payments, $F = 100$, and put price of 100.
d. The value of an option-free bond with maturity of 20 years, annual coupon of $C = 6$, semi-annual payments, and $F = 100$.
e. The value of a callable bond with maturity of 20 years, annual coupon of $C = 6$, semi-annual payments, $F = 100$, and call price of 100.
f. The value of a putable bond with maturity of 20 years, annual coupon of $C = 6$, semi-annual payments, $F = 100$, and put price of 100.
g. Using the Excel program Binbondcall.xls, determine the values and generate the price–yield curves for (1) an option-free bond with a maturity of 10 years, annual coupon of $C = 6$, semi-annual payments, and $F = 100$ and (2) a callable bond with the same features and a call price 100. Determine the values for spot rates of 4%, 4.5%, 5%, 5.5%, 6%, 6.5%, 7%, 7.5%, and 8%. Assume the applicable binomial interest rate tree for the bonds has the following features: length of the tree $= 0.5$ year, and upward and downward parameters for 0.5 years of $u = 1.1$ and $d = 0.9091$, and $q = 0.5$. Comment on the differences between the two bonds' price–yield curves.

WEB EXERCISE

1. Go to www.quicken.com/investments/mutualfunds/finder and find the top 25 convertible bond funds. Examine one or more of the funds by clicking on "Quote."

NOTES

1. In this case, the issuer could buy the bond back at 98, financed by issuing a 1-year bond at 9.5% interest. One period later the issuer would owe $98(1.095) = 107.31$; this represents a saving of $108 - 107.31 = 0.69$. Note, the value of that saving in period one is $0.69/1.095 = 0.63$, which is equal to the difference between the bond price and the call price: $98.630 - 98 = 0.63$.

2. Another convertible bond term is its conversion price. The *conversion price* is the bond's par value divided by the conversion ratio: F/CR.

3. Looking historically at stock prices and general interest rates, there have been some periods where a negative correlation between stock prices and interest rates has been observed. In the high interest rate periods of the late 1970s, early 1980s, and the early 1990s, stock prices were relatively low, and in the mid-1980s and mid-1990s interest rates were relatively low while stock prices were comparatively high. This negative correlation, though, is certainly not always the case. For example, the more recent period from 2001 to 2003 has seen both low interest rates and stock prices.

SELECTED REFERENCES

Bhattacharya, Mihir "Convertible Securities and Their Investment Cation Strategy," in Frank J. Fabozzi (ed.) *The Handbook of Fixed Income Securities*, 6th edn (New York: McGraw-Hill, 2001).

Black, F. and J. C. Cox "Valuing Corporate Securities: Some Effects of Bond Indenture Provisions," *Journal of Finance* 31(2) (1976): 351–67.

Black, Fischer, E. Derman, and W. Toy "A One-Factor Model of Interest Rates and Its Application to Treasury Bond Options," *Financial Analysts Journal* (January–February 1990): 33–9.

Boyle, P. P. "Options: A Monte Carlo Approach," *Journal of Financial Economics* 4 (1977): 323–38.

Boyle, Phelim "A Lattice Framework for Option Pricing with Two State Variables," *Journal of Financial and Qualitative Analysis* 23(1) (March 1988): 1–12.

Courtadon, G. "The Pricing of Options on Default-Free Bonds," *Journal of Financial and Quantitative Analysis*, XVII(1) (1982): 75–100.

Cox, J. C. and S. A. Ross "The Valuation of Options for Alternative Stochastic Processes," *Journal of Financial Economics* 3 (1976): 145–66.

Cox, J. C., S. A. Ross, and M. Rubinstein "Option Pricing: A Simplified Approach," *Journal of Financial Economics* 7 (1979): 229–63.

Cox, J. C. and M. Rubinstein *Options Markets* (Englewood Cliffs, NJ: Prentice Hall, 1985).

Dialynas, Chris P., Sandra Durn, and John C. Ritchie, Jr. "Convertible Securities and Their Investment Characteristics," in Frank J. Fabozzi (ed.) *The Handbook of Fixed Income Securities*, 6th edn (New York: McGraw-Hill, 2001).

Dunn, K. and K. Eades "Voluntary Conversion of Convertible Securities and the Optimal Call Strategy," *Journal of Financial Economics* 23 (1989): 273.

Goldman Sachs *Valuing Convertible Bonds as Derivatives* (Quantitative Strategies Research Notes, Goldman Sachs, November 1994).

Heath, D., R. Jarrow, and A. Morton "Bond Pricing and the Term Structure of Interest Rates: A New Methodology for Contingent Claims Valuation," *Econometrics* 60(1) (1992): 77–105.

Ho, Thomas and Sang-Bin Lee "Term Structure Movements and Pricing Interest Rate Contingent Claims," *The Journal of Finance* 41(5) (1986): 1011–29.

Hull, John and Alan White "Pricing Interest Rate Derivative Securities," *Review of Financial Studies* 3(4) (1990): 573–92.

Jamshidian, P. *Pricing of Contingent Claims in the One-Factor Term Structure Model* (Trading Analysis Group, Merrill Lynch Capital Markets, 1987).

Longstaff, F. and E. Schwartz "Interest Rate Volatility and the Term Structure: A Two-Factor General Equilibrium Model," *The Journal of Finance* (September 1992): 1259–82.

Rendleman, R. J., Jr. and B. J. Bartter "The Pricing of Options on Debt Securities," *Journal of Financial and Quantitative Analysis* XV(1) (1980):11–24.

Stein, J. "Convertible Bonds as Backdoor Financing," *Journal of Financial Economics* 32 (1992): 1–21.

Sundaresan, Suresh *Fixed Income Markets and Their Derivatives* (Cincinnati: Southwestern, 1997).

Taggart, R.A. Quantitative Analysis for Investment Management (Upper Saddle River, NJ: Prentice Hall, 1996).

Tsiveriotis, K. and C. Fernandes "Valuing Convertible Bonds with Credit Risk," *Journal of Fixed Income* 8(2) (September 1998): 95–102.

Tuckman, Bruce *Fixed Income Securities* (New York: John Wiley & Sons, 1995).

CHAPTER TEN

ESTIMATING THE BINOMIAL TREE

10.1 INTRODUCTION

In the previous chapter, we examined how the binomial interest rate tree can be used to price bonds with call and put options, sinking-fund agreements, and convertible clauses. We did not address, though, the more fundamental problem of how to estimate the tree. In this chapter, we examine two models that have been used for estimating binomial interest rate trees. Before we describe these models, though, we first need to look at how we can subdivide the tree so that the assumed binomial process is defined in terms of a realistic length of time, with a sufficient number of possible rates at maturity.

10.2 SUBDIVIDING THE BINOMIAL TREE

The binomial model is more realistic when we subdivide the periods to maturity into a number of subperiods. That is, as the number of sub-periods increases, the length of each period becomes smaller, making more plausible the assumption that the spot rate will either increase or decrease, and the number of possible rates at maturity increases, which again adds realism to the model. For example, suppose the three-period bond in our illustrative example in chapter 9 were a 3-year bond. Instead of using

a three-period binomial tree, where the length of each period is a year, suppose we evaluate the bond using a six-period tree with the length of each period being 6 months. If we do this, we need to divide the 1-year spot rates and the annual coupon by two, adjust the u and d parameters to reflect changes over a 6-month period instead of 1 year (this adjustment will be discussed in the next section), and define the binomial tree of spot rates for five periods, each with a length of 6 months. Exhibit 10.1 shows a five-period binomial tree for 1-year spot rates with the length of each period being 6 months, $u = 1.0488$, and $d = 0.9747$. Given the spot rates in the exhibit, the binomial value of a 3-year, 9 % bond would be determined by using a $45 coupon (reflecting the accrued interest) and discounting at a 6-month rate (annual spot rate divided by two) at each node.

If we wanted to value the bond every quarter, then we would need an 11-period tree of spot rates with the length of each period being 3 months and with the annual rates divided by four and u and d adjusted to reflect movements over 3 months. In general, let:

h = length of the period in years;

n = number of periods of length h defining the maturity of the bond,

where $n = $ (maturity in years)$/h$

Exhibit 10.1   Five-period tree of spot rates ($S_0 = 10\%$, $u = 1.0488$, $d = 0.9747$)

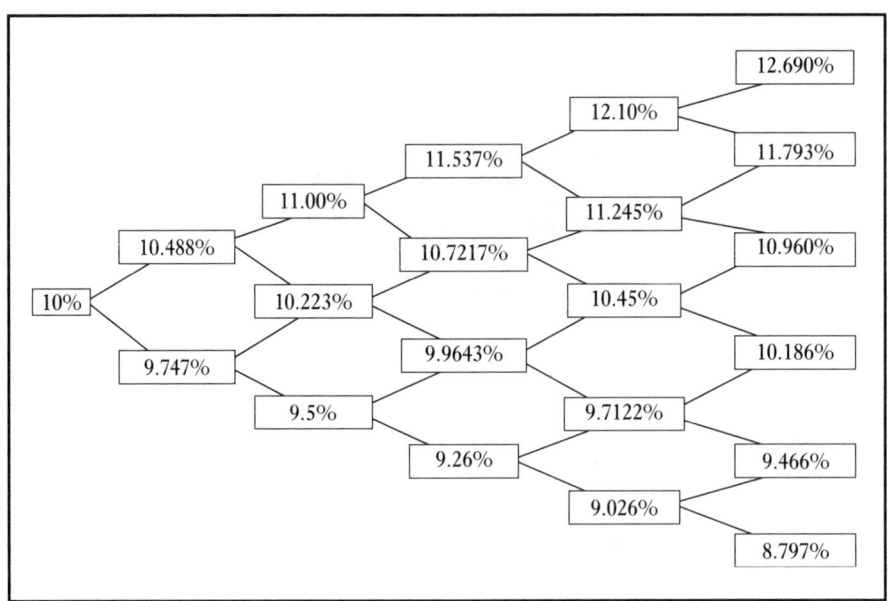

Thus, a 3-year bond evaluated over quarterly periods ($h = \frac{1}{4}$ of a year), would have a maturity of $n = (3 \text{ years})/(\frac{1}{4} \text{ years}) = 12$ periods and would require a binomial interest rate tree with $n - 1 = 12 - 1 = 11$ periods. To evaluate the bond over monthly periods ($h = \frac{1}{12}$ of a year), the bond's maturity would be $n = (3 \text{ years})/(\frac{1}{12} \text{ years}) = 36$ periods and would require a 35-period binomial tree of spot rates; for weekly periods ($h = \frac{1}{52}$), the bond's maturity would be 156 periods of length 1 week, and we would need a 155-period tree of spot rates. Thus, by subdividing we make the length of each period smaller, which makes the assumption of only two possible rates at the end of one period more plausible, and we increase the number of possible rates at maturity.

10.3 ESTIMATING THE TREE

In practice, determining the value of a bond using a binomial tree requires that we be able to estimate the random process that spot rates follow. There are two general approaches to estimating binomial interest rate movements. The first (models derived by Rendleman and Bartter (1979) and Cox, Ingersoll, and Ross (1979)) is to estimate the u and d parameters based on estimates of the spot rate's mean and variability. The estimating formulas for u and d are obtained by solving for the u and d values that make the mean and variance of spot rates resulting from a binomial process equal to their estimated values. Bond values obtained using this approach can then be compared to actual bond prices in order to determine if the bond is mispriced. Binomial interest rate models that generate a process of interest rate movements without a constraint that the model's price matches the market equilibrium price (the price obtained by discounting the bond's cash flows by spot rates) are sometimes referred to as *equilibrium models*. The second approach (models derived by Black, Derman, and Toy (1990), Ho and Lee (1986), and Heath, Jarrow, and Morton (1992)) is to calibrate the binomial tree to the current spot yield curve and to the interest rate's volatility. This approach is analogous to estimating the implied variance used in option pricing. This calibration approach solves for the spot rate that satisfies a variability condition and a price condition that ensures that the binomial tree is consistent with the term structure of current spot rates. Since the binomial tree is calibrated to current spot rates, the *calibration model* yields bond values for option-free bonds that are equal to the equilibrium prices. Given the tree's rates, the model is then used to value bonds with embedded option features.

10.3.1 *u* and *d* Estimation Approach

The formulas for estimating u and d are obtained by solving mathematically for the u and d values that make the statistical characteristics (mean and variance) of the spot rate's logarithmic return equal to the characteristics' estimated values. As background to understanding this approach, let us first examine the probability distribution that characterizes a binomial process.

Probability Distribution Resulting from a Binomial Process

In the previous section, we assumed a simple binomial approach where in each period the one-period spot rate would either increase to equal a proportion u times its initial value or decrease to equal a proportion d times the initial rate, with the probability of the increase in one period being $q = 0.5$. At the end of n periods, this binomial process yields a distribution of $n + 1$ possible spot rates (e.g., for $n = 3$, there are four possible rates: $S_{uuu} = u^3 S_0$, $S_{uud} = u^2 d\ S_0$, $S_{udd} = ud^2 S_0$, and $S_{ddd} = d^3 S_0$). This distribution, though, is not normally distributed since spot rates cannot be negative (i.e., we normally do not have negative interest rates). However, the distribution of spot rates can be converted into a distribution of logarithmic returns, g_n, where:

$$g_n = \ln\left(\frac{S_n}{S_0}\right)$$

This distribution can take on negative values and will be normally distributed if $q = 0.5$. Exhibit 10.2 shows the binomial distributions of spot rates for $n = 1, 2, 3,$ and 4 periods and their corresponding logarithmic returns for the case in which $u = 1.1$, $d = 0.95$, $S_0 = 10\%$, and $q = 0.5$. As shown in the exhibit, when $n = 1$, there are

two possible spot rates of 11% and 9.5%, with respective logarithmic returns of 0.0953 and -0.0513:

$$g_u = \ln\left(\frac{uS_0}{S_0}\right) = \ln(u) = \ln(1.1) = 0.0953$$

$$g_d = \ln\left(\frac{dS_0}{S_0}\right) = \ln(d) = \ln(0.95) = -0.0513$$

When $n = 2$, there are three possible spot rates of 12.1%, 10.45%, and 9.025% with corresponding logarithmic returns of:

$$g_{uu} = \ln\left(\frac{u^2 S_0}{S_0}\right) = \ln(u^2) = \ln(1.1^2) = 0.1906$$

$$g_{ud} = \ln\left(\frac{udS_0}{S_0}\right) = \ln(ud) = \ln[(1.1)(0.95)]$$
$$= 0.044$$

$$g_{dd} = \ln\left(\frac{d^2 S_0}{S_0}\right) = \ln(d^2) = \ln(0.95^2) = -0.1026$$

When $n = 3$, there are four possible spot rates of 13.31%, 11.495%, 9.9275%, and 8.574%, with logarithmic returns of:

$$g_{uuu} = \ln\left(\frac{u^3 S_0}{S_0}\right) = \ln(u^3) = \ln(1.1^3) = 0.2859$$

$$g_{uud} = \ln\left(\frac{u^2 dS_0}{S_0}\right) = \ln(u^2 d) = \ln[(1.1^2)(0.95)]$$
$$= 0.1393$$

$$g_{udd} = \ln\left(\frac{ud^2 S_0}{S_0}\right) = \ln(ud^2) = \ln[(1.1)(0.95^2)]$$
$$= -0.0073$$

$$g_{ddd} = \ln\left(\frac{d^3 S_0}{S_0}\right) = \ln(d^3) = \ln(0.95^3) = -0.1539$$

The probability of attaining any one of these rates is equal to the probability of the spot rate increasing j times in n periods, p_{nj}. That is, the probability of attaining a spot rate of 10.45% in period 2 is equal to the probability of the spot rate increasing once ($j = 1$) in two periods ($n = 2$), p_{21}. In a binomial process this probability can be found using the following formula:[1]

$$p_{nj} = \frac{n!}{(n-j)!j!}q^j(1-q)^{n-j}$$

Thus, after two periods, the probability of the spot rate equaling 12.1% is $p_{22} = 0.25$, 10.45%

Exhibit 10.2 Binomial distribution of logarithmic returns

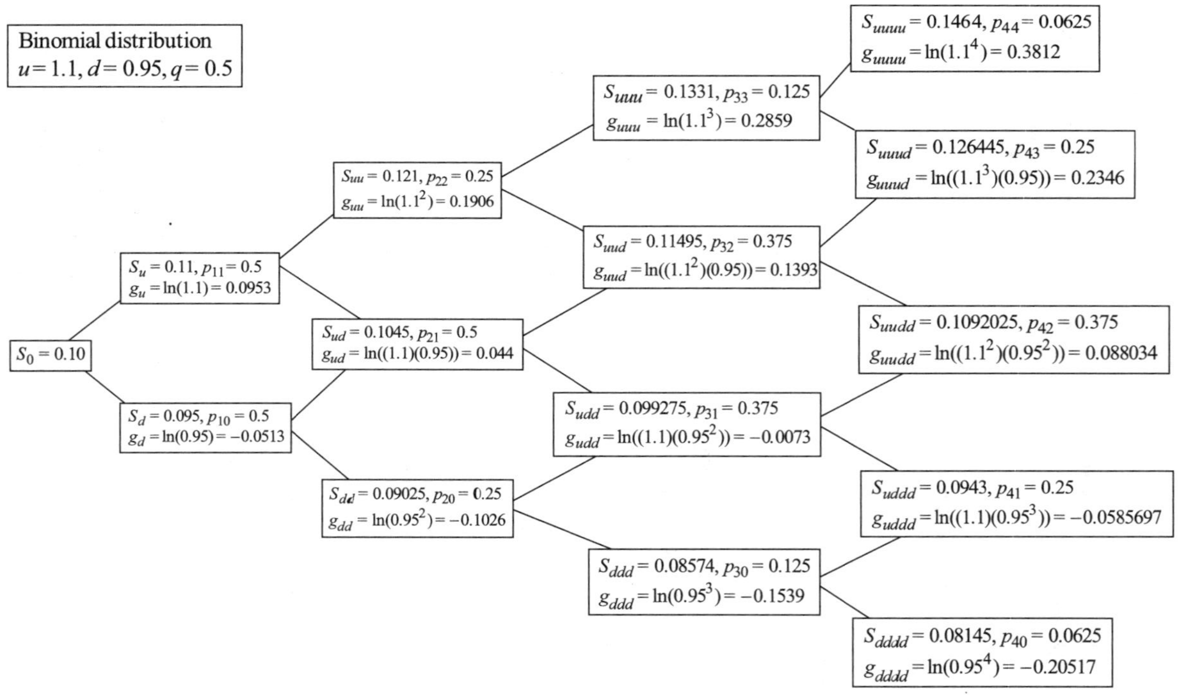

Binomial distribution
$u = 1.1, d = 0.95, q = 0.5$

$S_0 = 0.10$

$S_u = 0.11, p_{11} = 0.5$
$g_u = \ln(1.1) = 0.0953$

$S_d = 0.095, p_{10} = 0.5$
$g_d = \ln(0.95) = -0.0513$

$S_{uu} = 0.121, p_{22} = 0.25$
$g_{uu} = \ln(1.1^2) = 0.1906$

$S_{ud} = 0.1045, p_{21} = 0.5$
$g_{ud} = \ln(1.1)(0.95) = 0.044$

$S_{dd} = 0.09025, p_{20} = 0.25$
$g_{dd} = \ln(0.95^2) = -0.1026$

$S_{uuu} = 0.1331, p_{33} = 0.125$
$g_{uuu} = \ln(1.1^3) = 0.2859$

$S_{uud} = 0.11495, p_{32} = 0.375$
$g_{uud} = \ln((1.1^2)(0.95)) = 0.1393$

$S_{udd} = 0.099275, p_{31} = 0.375$
$g_{udd} = \ln((1.1)(0.95^2)) = -0.0073$

$S_{ddd} = 0.08574, p_{30} = 0.125$
$g_{ddd} = \ln(0.95^3) = -0.1539$

$S_{uuuu} = 0.1464, p_{44} = 0.0625$
$g_{uuuu} = \ln(1.1^4) = 0.3812$

$S_{uuud} = 0.126445, p_{43} = 0.25$
$g_{uuud} = \ln((1.1^3)(0.95)) = 0.2346$

$S_{uudd} = 0.1092025, p_{42} = 0.375$
$g_{uudd} = \ln((1.1^2)(0.95^2)) = 0.088034$

$S_{uddd} = 0.0943, p_{41} = 0.25$
$g_{uddd} = \ln((1.1)(0.95^3)) = -0.0585697$

$S_{dddd} = 0.08145, p_{40} = 0.0625$
$g_{dddd} = \ln(0.95^4) = -0.20517$

| $E(g_n)$ | 0.022 | 0.044 | 0.066 | 0.088 |
| $V(g_n)$ | 0.0054 | 0.0108 | 0.0162 | 0.0216 |

is $p_{21} = 0.5$, and 9.025% is $p_{20} = 0.25$. Using these probabilities, the expected value and the variance of the distribution of logarithmic returns after two periods would be equal to $E(g_2) = 4.4\%$ and $V(g_2) = 0.0108$:

$$E(g_n) = 0.25(0.1906) + 0.5(0.0440)$$
$$+ 0.25(-0.1026) = 0.044$$
$$V(g_n) = 0.25[0.1906 - 0.044]^2$$
$$+ 0.5[0.044 - 0.044]^2$$
$$+ 0.25[-0.1026 - 0.044]^2 = 0.0108$$

The means and variances for the four distributions are shown at the bottom of exhibit 10.2. In examining each distribution's mean and variance, note that as the number of periods increases, the expected value and variance increase by a multiplicative factor such that $E(g_n) = nE(g_1)$ and $V(g_n) = nV(g_1)$. Also, note that the expected value and the variance are also equal to:

$$E(g_n) = nE(g_1) = n[q \ln(u) + (1 - q) \ln(d)]$$
$$V(g_n) = nV(g_1) = nq(1 - q)[\ln(u/d)]^2$$

Solving for u and d

Given the features of a binomial distribution, the formulas for estimating u and d are found by solving for the u and d values that make the expected value and the variance of the binomial distribution of the logarithmic return of spot rates equal to their respective estimated parameter values under the assumption that $q = 0.5$ (or equivalently that the distribution is normal). If we let μ_e and V_e be the estimated mean and variance of the logarithmic return of spot rates for a period equal in length to n periods, then our objective is to solve for the u and d values that simultaneously satisfy the following equations:

$$nE(g_1) = n[q \ln(u) + (1 - q) \ln(d)] = \mu_e$$
$$nV(g_1) = nq(1 - q)[\ln(u/d)]^2 = V_e$$

If $q = 0.5$, then the formula values for u and d that satisfy the two equations are:

$$u = e^{\sqrt{V_e/n} + \mu_e/n}$$
$$d = e^{-\sqrt{V_e/n} + \mu_e/n}$$

In terms of our example, if the *estimated* expected value and variance of the logarithmic return were $\mu_e = 0.044$ and $V_e = 0.0108$ for a period equal in length to $n = 2$, then using the above equations, u would be 1.1 and d would be 0.95:

$$u = e^{\sqrt{0.0108/2} + 0.044/2} = 1.1$$
$$d = e^{-\sqrt{0.0108/2} + 0.044/2} = 0.95$$

Annualized Mean and Variance

In order to facilitate the estimation of u and d for a number of bonds with different maturities, it is helpful to use an annualized mean and variance (μ_e^A and V_e^A). Annualized parameters are obtained by simply multiplying the estimated parameters of a given length by the number of periods of that length that make up a year. For example, if quarterly data are used to estimate the mean and variance (μ_e^q and V_e^q), then we simply multiply those estimates by four to obtain the annualized parameters ($\mu_e^A = 4\mu_e^q$ and $V_e^A = 4V_e^q$). Thus, if the estimated quarterly mean and variance were 0.022 and 0.0054, then the annualized mean and variance would be 0.088 and 0.0216, respectively.[2] Note, when the annualized mean and variance are used, then these parameters must be multiplied by the proportion h, defined earlier as the time of the period being analyzed expressed as a proportion of a year, and n is not needed since h defines the length of the tree's period:

$$u = e^{\sqrt{hV_e^A} + h\mu_e^A}$$
$$d = e^{-\sqrt{hV_e^A} + h\mu_e^A}$$

If the annualized mean and variance of the logarithmic return of 1-year spot rates were 0.044 and 0.0108, and we wanted to evaluate a 3-year bond with 6-month periods ($h = \frac{1}{2}$ of a year), then we would use a six-period tree to value the bond ($n = (3 \text{ years})/(\frac{1}{2}) = 6$ periods) and u and d would be 1.1 and 0.95:

$$u = e^{\sqrt{(1/2)0.0108} + (1/2)0.044} = 1.1$$
$$d = e^{-\sqrt{(1/2)0.0108} + (1/2)0.044} = 0.95$$

If we make the length of the period monthly ($h = 1/12$), then we would value the 3-year

Table 10.1 Estimating mean and variance with historical data

Quarter	Spot rate, S_t (%)	S_t/S_{t-1}	$g_t = \ln(S_t/S_{t-1})$	$(g_t - \mu_e)^2$
Y1.1	10.6	–	–	–
Y1.2	10.0	0.9434	−0.0583	0.003395
Y1.3	9.4	0.9400	−0.0619	0.003829
Y1.4	8.8	0.9362	−0.0659	0.004350
Y2.1	9.4	1.0682	0.0660	0.004350
Y2.2	10.0	1.0638	0.0619	0.003829
Y2.3	10.6	1.0600	0.0583	0.003395
Y2.4	10.0	0.9434	−0.0583	0.003395
Y3.1	9.4	0.9400	−0.0619	0.003829
Y3.2	8.8	0.9362	−0.0660	0.004350
Y3.3	9.4	1.0682	0.0660	0.004350
Y3.4	10.0	1.0638	0.0619	0.003829
Y4.1	10.6	1.0600	0.0583	0.003395
			$\mu_e = 0$	0.046297
				$V_e^q = 0.004209$

$\mu_e^A = 4\mu_e^q = 4(0) = 0;\ V_e^A = 4V_e^q = 4(0.004209) = 0.016836$

Length	h	u	d
Year	1	1.1385	0.8783
Quarter	1/4	1.0670	0.9372
Month	1/12	1.0382	0.9632

bond with 36-period tree and u and d would be equal to 1.03424 and 0.9740:[3]

$$u = e^{\sqrt{(1/12)0.0108} + (1/12)0.044} = 1.03424$$

$$d = e^{-\sqrt{(1/12)0.0108} + (1/12)0.044} = 0.9740$$

Estimating μ_e^A and V_e^A Using Historical Data

To estimate u and d requires estimating the mean and variance: μ_e and V_e. The simplest way to do this is to estimate the parameters using the average mean and variance from an historical sample of spot rates (such as the rates on T-bills). As an example, historical quarterly 1-year spot rates over 13 quarters are shown in table 10.1. The 12 logarithmic returns are calculated by taking the natural log of the ratio of spot rates in one period to the rate in the previous period (S_t/S_{t-1}). From this data, the historical quarterly logarithmic mean return and variance are:

$$\mu_e = \frac{\sum_{t=1}^{12} g_t}{12} = \frac{0}{12} = 0$$

$$V_e = \frac{\sum_{t=1}^{12} [g_t - \mu_e]^2}{11} = \frac{0.046297}{11} = 0.004209$$

Multiplying the historical quarterly mean and variance by four, we obtain an annualized mean and variance, respectively, of 0 and 0.016836. Given the estimated annualized mean and variance, u and d can be estimated once we determine the number of periods to subdivide (see bottom of table 10.1).

Features

The u and d formulas derived here assume an interest rate process in which the variance and mean are stable and where the end-of-the-period distribution is symmetrical. Other models can be used to address cases in which these assumptions do not hold. Merton's mixed diffusion-jump model, for example, accounts for the possibilities of infrequent jumps in the underlying price or interest rate, and Cox and Ross's constant elasticity of variance model is applicable for cases in which the variance is inversely related to the underlying price or rate.

A binomial interest rate tree generated using the u and d estimation approach is constrained to have an end-of-the-period distribution with mean and variance that match the analyst's estimated mean and variance. The tree is not constrained, however, to yield a bond price that matches its equilibrium value. As a result, analysts using such models need to make additional assumptions about the risk premium in order to explain the bond's equilibrium price. In contrast, calibration models are constrained to match the current term structure of spot rates and therefore yield bond prices that are equal to their equilibrium values.

10.3.2 Calibration Model

The calibration model generates a binomial tree by first finding spot rates that satisfy a variability condition between the upper and lower rates. Given the variability relation, the model then solves for the lower spot rate that satisfies a price condition in which the bond value obtained from the tree is consistent with the equilibrium bond price given the current spot yield curve.

Variability Condition

In our derivation of the formulas for u and d, we assumed that the distribution of the logarithmic return of spot rates was normal. This assumption also implies the following relationship between the upper and lower spot rate:

$$S_u = S_d e^{2\sqrt{V_e/n}}$$

That is, from the binomial process we know:

$$S_u = uS_0$$
$$S_d = dS_0$$

Therefore:

$$\frac{S_u}{u} = S_0 = \frac{S_d}{d}$$
$$S_u = S_d \frac{u}{d}$$

Substituting the equations for u and d, we obtain:

$$S_u = S_d \frac{e^{\sqrt{V_e/n}+\mu_e/n}}{e^{-\sqrt{V_e/n}+\mu_e/n}} = S_d e^{2\sqrt{V_e/n}}$$

or in terms of the annualized variance:

$$S_u = S_d e^{2\sqrt{hV_e^A}}$$

Thus, given a lower rate of 9.5% and an annualized variance of 0.0054, the upper rate for a one-period binomial tree of length 1 year ($h = 1$) would be 11%:

$$S_u = 9.5\% e^{2\sqrt{0.0054}} = 0.11$$

If the current 1-year spot rate were 10%, then these upper and lower rates would be consistent with the upward and downward parameters of $u = 1.1$ and $d = 0.95$. This variability condition would therefore result in a binomial tree identical to the one shown in exhibit 10.2.

Price Condition

One of the problems with using just a variability condition (or equivalently just u and d estimates) is that it does not incorporate all of the information. As we discussed in chapter 3, the yield curve reflects not only the supply and demand for bonds of different maturity segments, but also the expectations of investors about future interest rates. Thus, in addition to the variability relation between upper and lower spot rates, the calibration model also tries to generate a binomial tree that is consistent with the current yield curve's spot rates. This is done by solving for a lower spot rate that satisfies the variability relation and also yields a bond price that is equal to the equilibrium bond price. To see this, suppose the current yield curve has 1-, 2-, and 3-year spot rates of $y_1 = 10\%$, $y_2 = 10.12238\%$, and $y_3 = 10.24488\%$, respectively. Furthermore, suppose that we estimate the annualized logarithmic mean and variance to be 0.048167 and 0.0054, respectively. Using the u and d approach, a one-period tree of length 1 year would have up and down parameters of $u = 1.12936$ and $d = 0.975$. Given the current one-period spot rate of 10%, the tree's possible spot rate would be $S_u = 11.2936\%$ and $S_d = 9.75\%$. These rates, though, are not consistent with the existing term structure. That is, if we value a 2-year pure discount bond (PDB) with a face value of $1 using this tree, we obtain a value of 0.82258 that, given the 2-year spot rate of 10.12238%, differs from the equilibrium price on the 2-year zero-discount bond of $B_0^M = 0.8246$:

$$B_0 = \frac{0.5B_u + 0.5B_d}{1 + S_0}$$

$$= \frac{0.5[1/1.112936] + 0.5[1/1.0975]}{1.10}$$

$$= 0.82258$$

$$B_0^M = \frac{1}{(1+y_2)^2} = \frac{1}{(1.1012238)^2} = 0.8246$$

Thus, the tree generated from our estimates of u and d is not consistent with the current interest rate structure, nor with the market's expectation of future rates given that expectations are incorporated into the term structure. To make our tree consistent with the term structure, we need to find the value such that, when

$$S_u = S_d e^{2\sqrt{hV_e^A}} = S_d e^{2\sqrt{0.0054}}$$

the value of the 2-year bond obtained from the tree is equal to the current equilibrium price of a 2-year zero-discount bond. That is, we need to find S_d where:

$$\frac{1}{(1+y_2)^2} = \frac{0.5B_u + 0.5B_d}{1+S_0}$$

$$\frac{1}{(1+y_2)^2} = \frac{0.5[1/(1+S_u)] + 0.5[1/(1+S_d)]}{1+S_0}$$

$$\frac{1}{(1+y_2)^2} = \frac{0.5\left[1/\left(1+S_d e^{2\sqrt{hV_e^A}}\right)\right] + 0.5[1/(1+S_d)]}{1+S_0}$$

Or in terms of the example:

$$\frac{1}{(1.1012238)^2}$$

$$= \frac{0.5[1/(1 + S_d e^{2\sqrt{0.0054}})] + 0.5[1/(1 + S_d)]}{1.10}$$

Solving the above equation for S_d yields a rate of 9.5%. At $S_d = 9.5\%$, we have a binomial tree of 1-year spot rates of $S_u = 11\%$ and $S_d = 9.5\%$ that simultaneously satisfies our variability condition and price condition; that is, the rate is consistent with the estimated volatility of 0.0054 and the current yield curve with 1-year and 2-year spot rates of 10% and 10.12238% (see exhibit 10.3).

It should be noted that the lower rate of 9.5% represents a decline from the current rate of

Exhibit 10.3   Calibration of binomial tree to two-period zero-coupon bond with $F = 1$

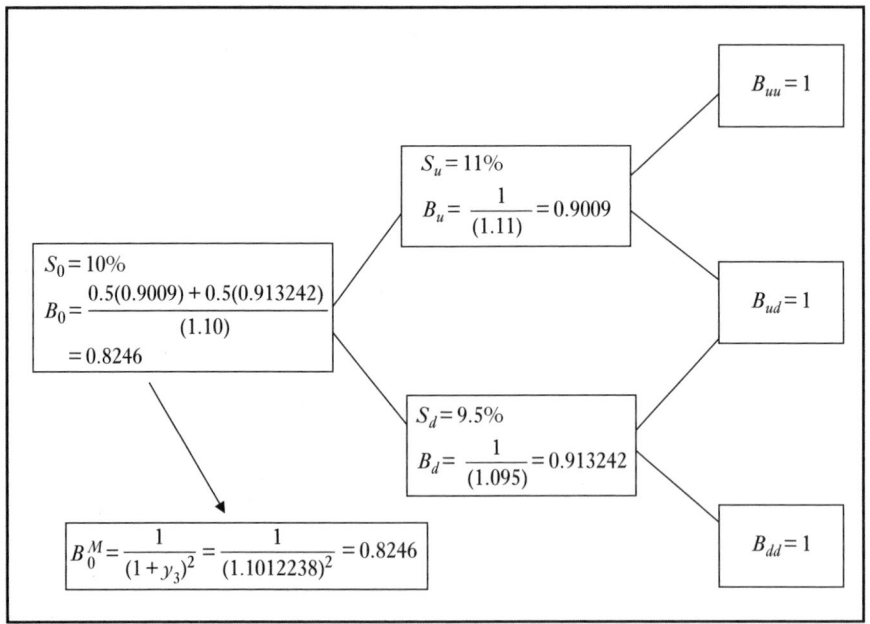

10%, which is what we tend to expect in a binomial process. This is because we have calibrated the binomial tree to a relatively flat yield curve. If we had calibrated the tree to a positively sloped yield curve, then it is possible that both rates next period could be greater than the current rate; although the upper rate will be greater than the lower. For example, if the current 2-year spot rate were 10.5% instead of 10.102238, then the equilibrium price of a 2-year bond would be 0.8189 and the S_d and S_u values that calibrate the tree to this price and variability of 0.0054 would be 10.20066% and 11.8156%. By contrast, if we had calibrated the tree to a negatively sloped curve, then it is possible that both rates next period could be lower than the current one.

Two-Period Binomial Tree

Given our estimated 1-year spot rates after one period of 9.5% and 11%, we can now move to the second period and determine the tree's three possible spot rates using a similar methodology. The variability condition follows the same form as the one period; that is:

$$S_{ud} = S_{dd}e^{2\sqrt{hV_e^A}}$$

$$S_{uu} = S_{ud}e^{2\sqrt{hV_e^A}} = S_{dd}e^{4\sqrt{hV_e^A}}$$

Similarly, the price condition requires that the binomial value of a 3-year zero-coupon bond be equal to the equilibrium price. Analogous to the one-period case, this condition is found by solving for the lower rate S_{dd} that, along with the above variability conditions and the rates for S_u and S_d obtained previously, yields a value for a 3-year zero-coupon bond that is equal to the price on a 3-year zero-coupon bond yielding 10.24488%. This condition can be mathematically stated as one of finding S_{dd} where:

Using an iterative (trial and error) approach, we find that a lower rate of $S_{dd} = 9.025\%$ yields a binomial value that is equal to the equilibrium price of the 3-year bond of 0.7463 (see exhibit 10.4).

The two-period binomial tree is obtained by combining the upper and lower rates found for the first period with the three rates found for the second period (see exhibit 10.5). This yields a tree that is consistent with the estimated variability condition and with the current term structure of spot rates. To grow the tree, we continue with this same process. For example, to obtain the four rates in period 3, we solve for the S_{ddd} that along with the spot rates found previously for periods one and two and the variability relations, yields a value for a 4-year PDB that is equal to the equilibrium price.

Valuation of Coupon Bonds

One of the features of using a calibrated tree to determine bond values is that the tree will yield prices that are equal to the bond's equilibrium price; that is, the price obtained by discounting cash flows by spot rates. For example, the value of a 3-year, 9% option-free bond using the tree we have just derived is 96.9521 (this is the illustrative example from chapter 9; see exhibit 10.6). This value is also equal to the equilibrium bond price obtained by discounting the bond's periodic cash flows at the spot rates of 10%, 10.12238%, and 10.24488%:

$$B_3^M = \frac{9}{1.10} + \frac{9}{(1.1012238)^2}$$
$$+ \frac{109}{(1.1024488)^3} = 96.9521$$

This feature should not be too surprising since we derived the tree by calibrating it to current spot rates. Nevertheless, one of the features of

$$\frac{1}{(1+y_2)^3} = \frac{0.5B_u + 0.5B_d}{1+S_0}$$

$$\frac{1}{(1+y_2)^3} = \frac{0.5\left[\frac{0.5B_{uu}+0.5B_{ud}}{1+S_u}\right] + 0.5\left[\frac{0.5B_{ud}+0.5B_{dd}}{1+S_d}\right]}{1+S_0}$$

$$\frac{1}{(1.1024488)^3} = \frac{0.5\left[\frac{0.5[1/(1+S_{dd}e^{4\sqrt{0.0054}})]+0.5[1/(1+S_{dd}e^{2\sqrt{0.0054}})]}{1.11}\right] + 0.5\left[\frac{0.5[1/(1+S_{dd}e^{2\sqrt{0.0054}})]+0.5[1/(1+S_{dd})]}{1.095}\right]}{1.10}$$

Exhibit 10.4   Calibration of binomial tree to three-period zero-coupon bond with $F = 1$

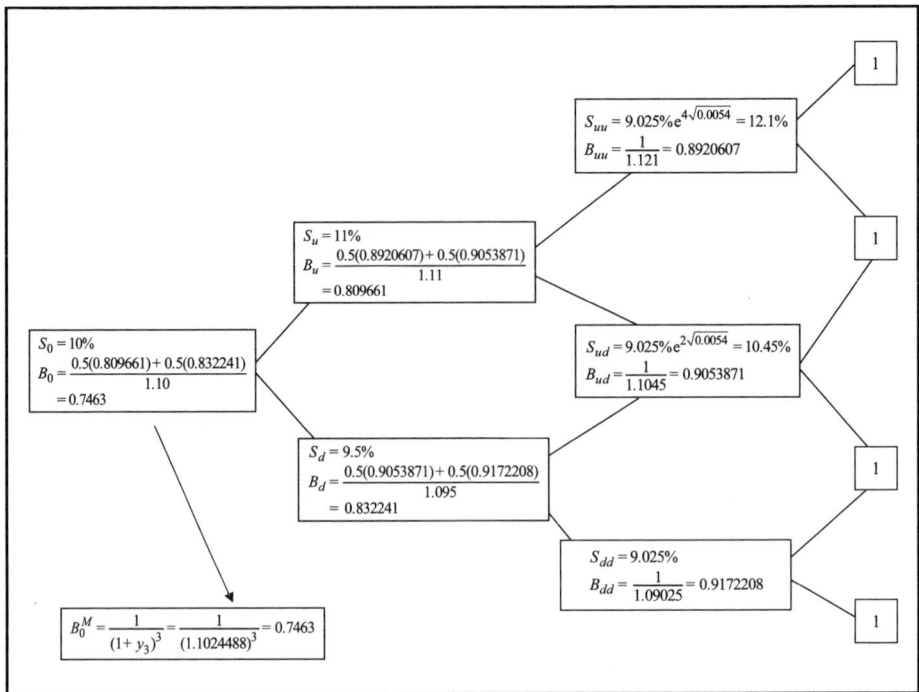

Exhibit 10.5   Calibrated binomial tree

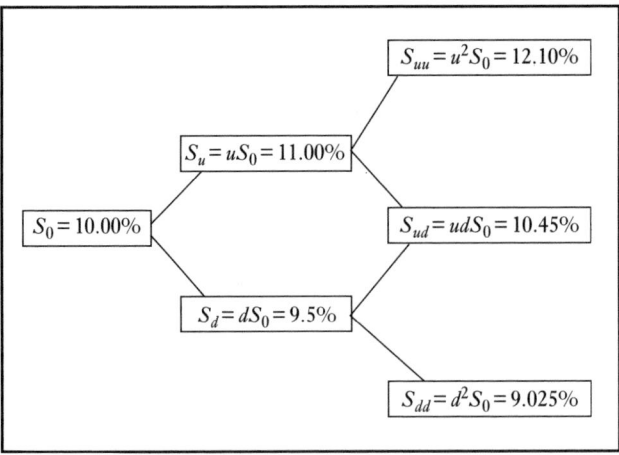

the calibrated tree is that it yields values on option-free bonds that are equal to the bond's equilibrium price. The primary purpose of generating the tree, though, is to value bonds with embedded options. In this example, if the 3-year bond were callable at 98 (our chapter 9 example), then its value would be 96.2584 (see exhibit 10.7).

Exhibit 10.6   Value of three-period option-free 9% bond using the calibrated binomial tree in exhibit 10.5, $C = 9$, $F = 100$

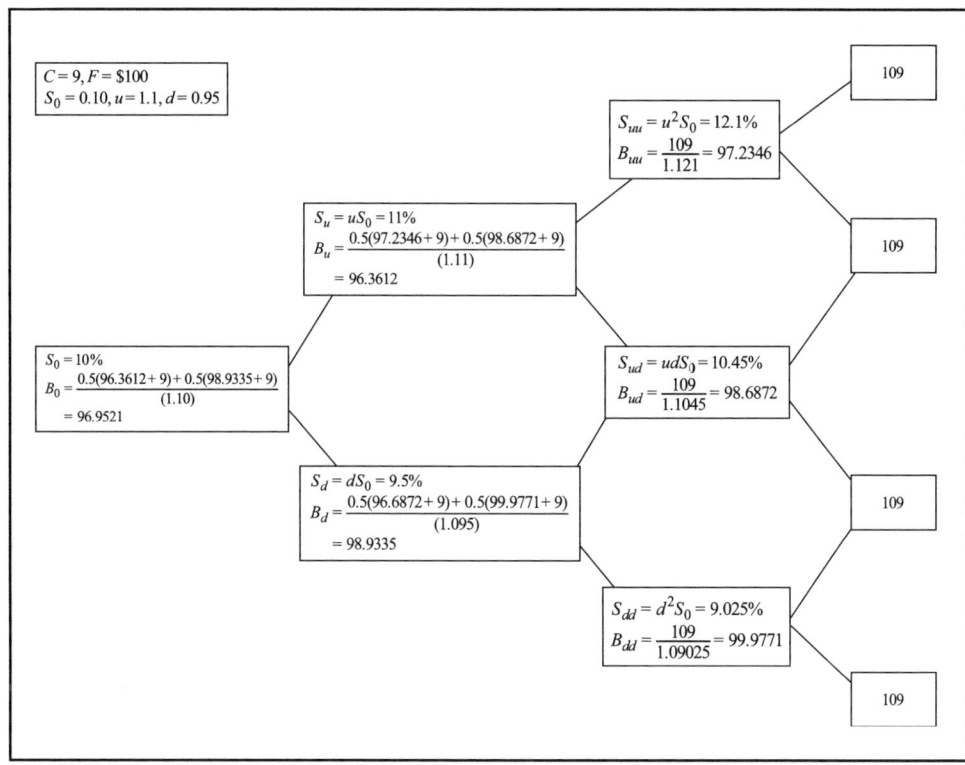

Option-Free Features

One of the features of the calibration model is that it prices a bond equal to its equilibrium price. Recall, a bond's equilibrium price is an arbitrage-free price. That is, if the market does not price the bond at its equilibrium value, then arbitrageurs would be able to realize a riskless return either by buying the bond, stripping it into a number of zero-discount bonds, and selling them, or by buying a portfolio of zero-discount bonds, bundling them into a coupon bond, and selling it. In general, a security can be valued by arbitrage by pricing it to equal the value of its replicating portfolio: a portfolio constructed so that it has the same cash flows. The replicating portfolio of a coupon bond, in turn, is the portfolio of zero-discount bonds. Thus, one of the important features of the calibration model is that it yields prices on option-free bonds that are arbitrage-free.

In addition to satisfying an arbitrage-free condition on option-free bonds, the calibration model also values a bond's embedded options as arbitrage-free prices. To see this, consider a 3-year, 9% callable bond priced in terms of the calibrated binomial tree shown in exhibit 10.5. The values of the bond and its call option are the same as the ones shown in exhibit 10.7. As shown, the value of the call option in period 1 is 0.3095 when the rate is at 11% and 1.2166 when the rate is at 9.5%, and the value of the option in the current period is 0.6937. Each of these values was determined by calculating the present value of each option's expected value. These values are also equal to the values of their replicating portfolios. For example, the current call price of 0.6937 is equal to the value of a portfolio consisting of a 1-year, 9% option-free bond and a 2-year, 9% option-free bond constructed so that next year the portfolio is worth 0.3095 if the spot rate is

Exhibit 10.7   Value of callable bond

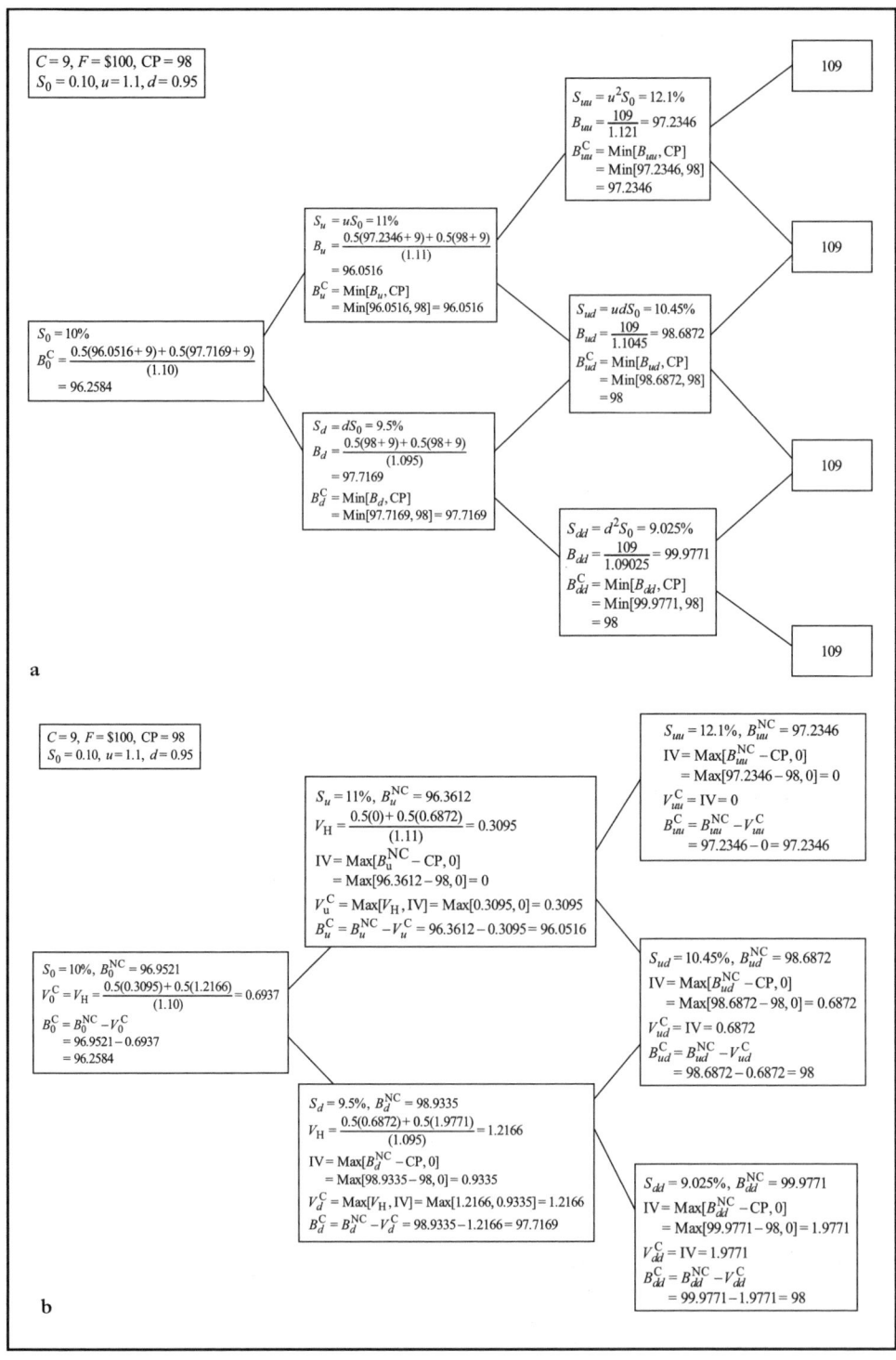

11% and 1.2166 if the rate is at 9.5%. Specifically, given the possible cash flows on the 2-year bond of $B_u + C = (109/1.11) + 9 = 107.198198$ and $B_d + C = (109/1.095) + 9 = 108.543379$, and the cash flow on the 1-year bond of 109, the replicating portfolio is formed by solving for the number of 1-year bonds, n_1, and the number of 2-year bonds, n_2, where:

$$n_1(109) + n_2(107.198198) = 0.3095$$

$$n_1(109) + n_2(108.543379) = 1.2166$$

Solving for n_1 and n_2, we obtain $n_1 = -0.66035$ and $n_2 = 0.674333$. Thus, a portfolio formed by buying 0.674333 issues of a 2-year bond and shorting 0.66035 issues of a 1-year bond will yield possible cash flows next year of 0.3095 if the spot rate is at 11% and 1.2166 if the rate is at 9.5%. Moreover, given the current 1-year and 2-year bond prices of 99.09091 and 98.06435, the value of this replicating portfolio is 0.6937:

$$B_1 = \frac{109}{1.10} = 99.09091$$

$$B_2 = \frac{9}{1.10} + \frac{109}{(1.1012238)^2} = 98.06435$$

$$V_0^{RP} = (-0.66035)(99.09091)$$
$$+ (0.674333)(98.06435) = 0.6937$$

Since the replicating portfolio and the call option have the same cash flows, by the law of one price they must be equally priced. Thus, in the absence of arbitrage, the price of the call is equal to 0.6937, which is the same price that we obtained by discounting the option's expected value using the calibrated binomial interest rate tree.

The two call values in period 1 of 0.3095 and 1.2166 are likewise equal to the values of their replicating portfolios. That is, at the 11% rate a replicating portfolio 0.4730827 of the 2-year, 9% bond (original 3-year bond) and -0.46108027 issues of a 1-year, 9% bond (original 2-year bond) will yield cash flows in period 2 equal to 0 if the spot rate is 12.1% and 0.6872 if the rate is 10.45%. At that node, the price on the 1-year bond

is $109/1.11 = 98.198198$ and the price of the 2-year bond is 96.3612 (see exhibit 10.6). At these prices, the value of the replicating portfolio is $0.30956 = (-0.46108027)(98.198198) + (0.4730827)(96.3612)$, which matches the value of the call. At the lower node, the replicating portfolio consists of -0.98165 1-year, 9% bonds priced at 99.54338 ($=109/1.095$) and one 2-year, 9% bond priced at 98.9335 (see exhibit 10.6). This portfolio's possible cash flows in period 2 match the possible call values of 0.6872 and 1.9771 and its period 1 value is equal to the call value of 1.2166.

With the option values equal to their replicating portfolio values, the calibration model has the feature of pricing embedded options equal to their arbitrage-free prices. Because of this feature and the feature of pricing option-free bonds equal to their equilibrium prices, the calibration model is referred to as an *arbitrage-free model*. Students of option pricing may recall that arbitrage-free models can alternatively be priced using a risk-neutral pricing approach. When applied to bond pricing, this approach requires finding the pseudo probabilities that make a binomial tree of bond prices equal to the equilibrium price. The risk-neutral pricing approach is equivalent to the calibration approach.

The calibration model presented here is the Black–Derman–Toy model. In addition to being arbitrage-free, its major attribute is that it captures the volatility and drift in rates that are dependent on the current level of interest rates. Other calibration models have been developed that differ in terms of the assumptions they make about the evolution of interest rates. The Ho–Lee model, for example, assumes that interest rates in each period are determined by the previous rate plus or minus an additive rather than multiplicative random shock. The Black–Karasinski model, in turn, is characterized by a mean reversion process in which short-term rates revert to a central tendency. Each of these models, though, is characterized by the property that if their assumption about the evolution of rates is correct, the model's bond and embedded option prices are supported by arbitrage. This arbitrage-free feature of the calibration model is one of the main reasons that many practitioners favor this model over the equilibrium model.

10.4 OPTION-ADJUSTED SPREAD

Once we've derived a binomial tree, we can then use it to value any bond with embedded option features. In addition to valuation, the tree also can be used to estimate the option spread (the difference in yields between a bond with option features and an otherwise identical option-free bond), as well as the duration and convexity of bonds with embedded option features.

The simplest way to estimate the option spread is to estimate the YTM for a bond with an option given the bond's values as determined by the binomial model, then subtract that rate from the YTM of an otherwise identical option-free bond. For example, in the previous example the value of the 3-year, 9% callable bond was 96.2584, while the equilibrium price of the non-callable bond was 96.9521. Using these prices, the YTM on the callable bond is 10.51832% and the YTM on the non-callable bond is 10.2306, yielding an option spread of 0.28772%:

Option-free bond:

$$96.9521 = \frac{9}{1+\text{YTM}} + \frac{9}{(1+\text{YTM})^2}$$

$$+ \frac{109}{(1+\text{YTM})^3} \Rightarrow \text{YTM}^{NC}$$

$$= 10.2306\%$$

Callable bond:

$$96.2584 = \frac{9}{1+\text{YTM}} + \frac{9}{(1+\text{YTM})^2}$$

$$+ \frac{109}{(1+\text{YTM})^3} \Rightarrow \text{YTM}^{C}$$

$$= 10.51832\%$$

$$\text{Option spread} = \text{YTM}^{C} - \text{YTM}^{NC}$$

$$= 10.51832\% - 10.2306\%$$

$$= 0.28772\%$$

One of the problems with using this approach to estimate the spread is that not all of the possible cash flows of the callable bond are considered. In three of the four interest rate scenarios, for example, the bond could be called, changing the cash flow pattern from three periods of 9, 9, and 109 to two periods of 9 and 107. An alternative approach that addresses this problem is the *option-adjusted spread (OAS) analysis*.

OAS analysis solves for the option spread, k, that makes the average of the present values of the bond's cash flows from all of the possible interest rate paths equal to the bond's market price. The first step in this approach is to specify the cash flows and spot rates for each path. In the case of the 3-year bond valued with a two-period binomial interest rate tree, there are four possible paths, as shown in following table.

	Path 1		Path 2		Path 3		Path 4	
Time	S_1	CF	S_1	CF	S_1	CF	S_1	CF
0	0.10	–	0.10	–	0.10	–	0.10	–
1	0.0950	9	0.095	9	0.11	9	0.11	9
2	0.09025	107	0.1045	107	0.1045	107	0.121	9
3	–		–		–		–	109

Given the four paths, we next determine the appropriate 2-year spot rates (y_2) and 3-year rates (y_3) to discount the cash flows. These rates can be found using the geometric mean and the 1-year spot rates from the tree; that is:

Path 1
$y_1 = 0.10$
$y_2 = [(1.10)(1.095)]^{1/2} - 1$
$\quad = 0.097497$
$y_3 = [(1.10)(1.095)$
$\quad \times (1.09025)]^{1/3} - 1$
$\quad = 0.095076$

Path 2
$y_1 = 0.10$
$y_2 = [(1.10)(1.095)]^{1/2}$
$\quad - 1 = 0.097497$
$y_3 = [(1.10)(1.095)$
$\quad \times (1.1045)]^{1/3} - 1$
$\quad = 0.099826$

Path 3
$$y_1 = 0.10$$
$$y_2 = [(1.10)(1.11)]^{1/2} - 1$$
$$= 0.104989$$
$$y_3 = [(1.10)(1.11)(1.1045)]^{1/3} - 1$$
$$= 0.104826$$

Path 4
$$y_1 = 0.10$$
$$y_2 = [(1.10)(1.11)]^{1/2} - 1$$
$$= 0.104989$$
$$y_3 = [(1.10)(1.11)(1.121)]^{1/3} - 1$$
$$= 0.110300$$

Given a discount rate equal to the spot rate plus the spread, k, the final step is to solve for a value of k that makes the average present values of the paths equal to the callable bond's market price, B_0^M; that is:

$$B_0^M = (1/4) \left\{ \left[\frac{9}{(1+0.10+k)} + \frac{107}{(1+0.097497+k)^2} \right] \right.$$

$$+ \left[\frac{9}{(1+0.10+k)} + \frac{109}{(1+0.097497+k)^2} \right]$$

$$+ \left[\frac{9}{(1+0.10+k)} + \frac{109}{(1+0.104989+k)^2} \right]$$

$$+ \left[\frac{9}{(1+0.10+k)} + \frac{9}{(1+0.104989+k)^2} \right.$$

$$+ \left. \left. \frac{109}{(1+0.110300+k)^3} \right] \right\}$$

Note, if the market price is equal to the binomial value we obtained using the calibration model, then the option spread, k, is equal to zero. This reflects the fact that we have calibrated the tree to the yield curve and have considered all of the possibilities. In practice, though, we do not expect the market price to equal the binomial value. If the market price is

below the binomial value, then k will be positive. For example, if the market priced the three-period bond at 94.6097, then the OAS (k) would be 2%. Many analysts in trying to identify mispriced bonds use the OAS approach to estimate k instead of comparing the market price with the binomial value.

10.5 DURATION AND CONVEXITY

Like our earlier measure of bond value, we defined a bond's duration (modified and Macaulay's durations) and convexity without factoring in its embedded option features. Bonds with call options are sometimes said to have negative convexity, meaning that the bond's duration moves inversely with rate changes. When a bond has a call option, a rate decrease can lead to an early call, which shortens the life of the bond and lowers its duration, while an interest rate increase tends to lengthen the expected life of the bond, causing its duration to increase. Thus, the option features of a bond can have a significant impact on the bond's duration, as well as its convexity.

The duration and convexity of bonds with embedded option features can be estimated using a binomial tree and the effective duration and convexity measures defined in chapter 4:

$$\text{Effective duration} = \frac{B_- - B_+}{2(B_0)(\Delta y)}$$

$$\text{Effective convexity} = \frac{B_+ + B_- - 2B_0}{(B_0)(\Delta y)^2}$$

where B_- is the price associated with a small decrease in rates and B_+ is the price associated with a small increase in rates.

The binomial tree calibrated to the yield curve can be used to estimate B_0, B_-, and B_+. First, the current yield curve and calibrated tree can be used to determine B_0; next, B_- can be estimated by allowing for a small equal decrease in each of the yield curve rates (e.g., 10 basis points) and then using the tree calibrated to the new rates to find the price; finally, B_+ can be estimated in a similar way by allowing for a small equal increase in the yield curve's rates and then estimating the bond price using the tree calibrated to these higher rates.

10.6 A NOTE ON THE BLACK-SCHOLES OPTION PRICING MODEL

Before finishing our analysis of binomial interest rate models and their use in valuing bonds with embedded options, it should be noted that an approximate value of the embedded option features of a bond can also be estimated using the well-known *Black–Scholes option pricing model (B–S OPM)* – a model commonly used in pricing options. The B–S formula for determining the equilibrium price of an embedded call or put option is:

$$V_0^C = B_0 N(d_1) - XN(d_2)e^{-R_f T}$$
$$V_0^P = X(1 - N(d_2))e^{-R_f T} - B_0(1 - N(d_1))$$
$$d_1 = \frac{\ln(B_0/X) + (R_f + 0.5\sigma^2)T}{\sigma\sqrt{T}}$$
$$d_2 = d_1 - \sigma\sqrt{T}$$

where:

X = call price (CP) or put price (PP)
σ^2 = variance of the logarithmic return of bond prices $= V(\ln(B_n/B_0))$
T = time to expiration expressed as a proportion of a year
R_f = continuously compounded annual risk-free rate (if simple annual rate is R, the continuously compounded rate is $\ln(1+R)$)
$N(d)$ = cumulative normal probability; this probability can be looked up in a standard normal probability table or by using the formula below:

$$N(d) = 1 - n(d), \quad \text{for } d < 0$$
$$N(d) = n(d), \quad \text{for } d > 0$$

where:

$$n(d) = 1 - 0.5[1 + 0.196854\,(|d|) \\ + 0.115194\,(|d|)^2 + 0.0003444\,(|d|)^3 \\ + 0.019527(|d|)^4]^{-4}$$
$|d|$ = absolute value of d

For example, suppose a 3-year, non-callable bond with a 10% annual coupon is selling at par ($F = 100$). A callable bond that is identical in all respects except for its call feature should sell at 100 minus the call price. In this case, suppose

the call feature gives the issuer the right to buy the bond back at any time during the bond's life at an exercise price of 115. Assuming a risk-free rate of 6% and a variability of $\sigma = 0.10$ on the non-callable bond's logarithmic return, the call price using the Black–Scholes model would be 8.95:

$$V_0^C = B_0 N(d_1) - XN(d_2)e^{-R_f T}$$
$$V_0^C = 100(0.62519) - 115(0.55772)e^{-(0.06)(3)}$$
$$= 8.95$$
$$d_1 = \frac{\ln(100/115) + (0.06 + 0.5(0.10^2)3)}{0.10\sqrt{3}}$$
$$= 0.31892$$
$$d_2 = 0.31892 - 0.10\sqrt{3} = 0.14571$$
$$N(d_1) = N(0.31892) = 0.62519$$
$$N(d_2) = N(0.14571) = 0.55772$$

Thus, the price of the callable bond is 91.05:

Price of callable bond = Price of non-

callable bond

− Call premium

Price of callable bond $= 100 - 8.95 = 91.05$

It should be noted that the B–S OPM assumes interest rates are constant. For many bonds, though, the change in their value is due to interest rate changes. Thus, the use of the B–S OPM to value the call option embedded in a bond should be viewed only as an approximation.

10.7 CONCLUSION

In the last two chapters, we've examined how binomial interest rate trees can be constructed and used to value bonds with call and put options, sinking-fund arrangements, and convertibility clauses. Given that many bonds, as well as other debt contracts, have embedded option features, the binomial tree represents both a useful and practical approach to the valuation of debt securities. In this chapter we've focused on introducing how the tree can be estimated. Bonds with multiple option features and ones that are subject to the uncertainties of more than one factor, such as callable convertible bonds or LYONs, are more difficult to evaluate and may require more complex binomial models. Each, though, can be evaluated by extending the basic binomial tree presented here.

> **Web Information**
> For more information on option pricing go to
>   www.derivativesmodels.com
>   www.in-the-money.com and
>   www.optioncentral.com

KEY TERMS

Equilibrium Models
Calibration Model
Arbitrage-Free Model

Option-Adjusted
Spread (OAS)
Analysis

Black–Scholes Option
Pricing Model
(B–S OPM)

PROBLEMS AND QUESTIONS

1. Explain how subdividing the number of periods to expiration makes the binomial interest rate tree more realistic.

2. Assume a one-period spot rate follows a binomial process, is currently at $S_0 = 5\%$, $u = 1.02$, $d = 1/1.02$, and the probability of the spot rate increasing in one period is $q = 0.5$.

   a. Show with a binomial tree the spot rates, logarithmic returns, and probabilities after one period, two periods, and three periods.
   b. What are the spot rate's expected logarithmic return and variance for each period?
   c. Define the properties of a binomial distribution.
   d. Verify that the u and d formulas yield the u and d values of 1.02 and 1/1.02 given the logarithmic return's mean and variance after three periods.

3. Explain the methodology used for deriving the formulas for u and d.

4. Comment on the arbitrage-free features of valuing a bond using the equilibrium model.

5. Suppose a spot rate has the following probability distribution of possible rates after 4 months:

Annualized spot rate (%)	Probability
6.623	0.0625
6.332	0.2500
6.054	0.3750
5.788	0.2500
5.534	0.0625

a. Calculate the spot rate's expected logarithmic return and variance. Assume the current rate is 6%.

b. Calculate the spot rate's annualized variance and mean.

c. What are the spot rate's u and d values for a period of length 1 month (h = length of the period in years = $\frac{1}{12}$), 1 week ($h = \frac{1}{52}$), and 1 day ($h = \frac{1}{360}$)?

d. Suppose the spot rate's mean is equal to zero, what are the rate's u and d values for the periods of lengths 1 month, week, and day? Comment on the importance of the mean in calculating u and d when n is large.

6. Suppose a spot rate has the following prices over the past 13 quarters:

Quarter	Annualized spot rate (%)
Y1.1	5.5
Y1.2	5.0
Y1.3	4.7
Y1.4	4.4
Y2.1	4.7
Y2.2	5.0
Y2.3	5.4
Y2.4	5.0
Y3.1	4.7
Y3.2	4.4
Y3.3	4.7
Y3.4	5.0
Y4.1	5.5

a. Calculate the spot rate's average logarithmic return and variance.

b. What is the rate's annualized mean and variance?

c. Calculate the spot rate's up and down parameters for periods with the following lengths:

   (i) One quarter (h = length in years = $\frac{1}{4}$)
   (ii) One month ($h = \frac{1}{12}$)
   (iii) One week ($h = \frac{1}{52}$)
   (iv) One day ($h = \frac{1}{360}$).

7. Excel problem: The following problem should be done using the Excel program Binbondcall.xls. Suppose the current spot rate in question 6 is currently at 5%. Using the estimated spot rate's mean and variance calculated in question 6c determine the value of a 5-year, 5% option-free bond ($F = 100$) using a binomial tree with monthly steps ($h = \frac{1}{12}$). Determine the value of the bond given that it is callable with a call price of 100.

8. Excel problem: The following problems should be done using the Excel programs Binbondcall.xls and Binbondput.xls.

Given the following:

- Current spot rate = 0.08
- Annualized mean for the spot rate's logarithmic return of 0.022
- Annualized variance for the spot rate's logarithmic return of 0.0054
- Binomial interest rate tree with monthly steps

Determine the values of the following:

a. 5-year, 8% option-free bond, with $F=100$.
b. 5-year, 8% callable bond ($F=100$) with call price $=100$.
c. 5-year, 8% putable bond ($F=100$) with put price $=100$.

9. Explain the methodology for estimating a binomial tree using the calibration model. Comment on the arbitrage-free features of this approach.

10. Given a variability of $\sigma = \sqrt{hV_e^A} = 0.10$ and current one- and two-period spot rates of $y_1 = 0.07$ and $y_2 = 0.0804$:

a. Generate a one-period binomial interest rate tree using the calibration model. (Hint: try $S_d = 0.08148$.)
b. What do the values of upper and lower spot rates relative to the current spot rate of 7% tell you about the structure of interest rates?
c. Using the calibrated tree, determine the equilibrium price of a two-period, option-free, 10.5% coupon bond ($F=100$).
d. Does the binomial tree price the 10.5% option-free bond equal to the bond's equilibrium price? Comment on this feature of the calibration model.
e. Using the tree, calculate the value of a two-period, 10.5% bond ($F=100$) callable in period 1 at $CP=101$. Use the constraint approach.

11. Using the calibrated binomial tree from question 10 ($S_0 = 0.07$, $S_d = 8.148\%$, and $S_u = 9.9952\%$), carry out the following tasks.

a. Show in a binomial tree the following values at each node:

1. The values of an option-free, one-period, 10.5% coupon bond ($F=100$).
2. The values of an option-free, two-period, 10.5% coupon bond ($F=100$).
3. The values of an embedded call option on a two-period, 10.5% callable bond with the call price equal to $CP=101$ and callable in period 1.
4. The values of a two-period, 10.5% coupon bond callable at $CP=101$ in period 1.

b. Construct a portfolio with the one-period and two-period 10.5% option-free bonds that replicates the period 1 up and down values of the embedded call option on the two-period, 10.5% callable bond (hint: try $n_1 = -0.70463$ and $n_2 = 0.701457$). What is the current value of the replicating portfolio? Does the current value of your replicating portfolio match the current value of the callable bond's embedded call option? Comment on the arbitrage-free features of the calibration model.

12. Given a variability of $\sigma = \sqrt{hV_e^A} = 0.10$ and current one-, two-, and three-period spot rates of $y_1 = 0.07$, $y_2 = 0.0804$, and $y_3 = 0.0904952$:

a. Generate a two-period binomial interest rate tree using the calibration model. (Hint: try $S_d = 0.08148$ from problem 11 and $S_{dd} = 0.0906$).
b. Using the calibrated tree, determine the equilibrium price of a three-period, 10.5% option-free bond ($F=100$).
c. Does the binomial tree price the 10.5% option-free bond equal to the bond's equilibrium price?
d. Using the calibrated tree, calculate the value of a three-period, 10.5% bond ($F=100$) callable at $CP=101$ in periods 1 and 2.
e. Based on the option-free and callable bond values you determined in 12b and 12d, estimate the option-adjusted spread.

13. Explain how a spread is estimated using the option-adjusted spread analysis.

14. Using the option-adjusted spread analysis, what is the option-adjusted spread for the three-period, 10.5% callable bond in question 12 if it is priced to equal its equilibrium price of 103.30? What is the spread if the market prices the bond at 102.80?

15. Explain the methodology used to estimate a bond's duration and convexity with the calibration model.

16. The following information relates to a callable bond:

   - Coupon rate = 10% (annual), with payments made annually
   - Face value = $F = \$1,000$
   - Maturity = 5 years
   - Callable at $1,100
   - YTM on a similar non-callable bond = 10%
   - Annualized standard deviation of the non-callable bond's logarithmic return = 0.15
   - Continuously compound annual risk-free rate = 5%.

   Given these details, answer the following questions:

   a. What is the value of the non-callable bond?
   b. Using the B–S OPM, what is the value of the callable bond's call feature to the issuer? Use the B–S Excel program.
   c. What is the value of the callable bond?

17. The following information relates to a putable bond:

   - Coupon rate = 10% (annual), with payments made annually
   - Face value = $F = \$1,000$
   - Maturity = 5 years
   - Putable at $950
   - YTM on a similar non-putable bond = 10%
   - Annualized standard deviation of the non-putable bond's logarithmic return = 0.15
   - Continuously compound annual risk-free rate = 5%.

   Given these details, answer the following questions:

   a. What is the value of the non-putable bond?
   b. Using the B–S OPM, what is the value of the putable bond's put feature to the holder? Use the B–S Excel program.
   c. What is the value of the putable bond?

WEB EXERCISES

1. Calculate the variance of the logarithmic return using historical data on T-bill or CP yields from the Federal Reserve. Go to www.federalreserve.gov/releases and go to "Monthly Releases" and "Interest Rates," and click on "Historical Data." Copy and paste the data to Excel. Given the data, convert the yields to logarithmic returns, and then find the standard deviation.

2. Option pricing models for pricing different options can be found at www.derivativesmodels.com. At the site, click on "Black–Scholes Model."

3. Learn more about option pricing models by going to www.in-the-money.com.

NOTES

1. $n!$ (read as "n factorial") is the product of all numbers from 1 to n; also $0! = 1$.
2. Note that the annualized standard deviation cannot be obtained simply by multiplying the quarterly standard deviation by four. Rather, one must first multiply the quarterly variance by four and then take the square root of the resulting annualized variance.
3. Note, in the equations for u and d, as n increases the mean term in the exponent goes to zero quicker than the square root term. As a result, for large n (e.g., $n = 30$), the mean term's impact on u and d is negligible and u and d can be estimated as:

$$u = e^{\sqrt{V_e/n}} \quad \text{and} \quad d = e^{-\sqrt{V_e/n}} = 1/u.$$

SELECTED REFERENCES

Black, F., E. Derman, and W. Toy "A One-Factor Model of Interest Rates and Its Application to Treasury Bond Options," *Financial Analysts Journal* (January/February 1990): 33–9.

Black, Fisher and Piotr Karasinski "Bond and Option Pricing when Short Rates are Lognormal," *Financial Analysts Journal* 47(4) (1991): 52–9.

Black, Fisher and M. Scholes "The Valuation of Option Contracts and a Test of Market Efficiency," *Journal of Finance* (May 1972).

Black, Fisher and M. Scholes "The Pricing of Options and Corporate Liabilities," *Journal of Political Economy*, 81 (1973): 637–59.

Brennan, M. J. and E. S. Schwartz "A Continuous Time Approach to the Pricing of Bonds," *Journal of Banking and Finance* 3 (1979): 133–55.

Buser, S. A., P. H. Hendershott, and A. B. Sanders "Determinants of the Value of Call Options on Default-free Bonds," *Journal of Business* 63(1) (1990): 533–50.

Cox, J. C., J. Ingersoll, and S. Ross "Duration and the Measurement of Basis Risk," *Journal of Business* 52 (1979): 51–61.

Cox, J. C. and S. A. Ross "The Valuation of Options for Alternative Stochastic Processes," *Journal of Financial Economics* 3 (1976): 145–66.

Cox, J. C., S. A. Ross, and M. Rubenstein "Option Pricing: A Simplified Approach," *Journal of Financial Economics*, 7 (1979): 229–63.

Heath, D., R. Jarrow, and A. Morton "Bond Pricing and the Term Structure of Interest Rates: A Discrete Time Approximation," *Journal of Financial and Quantitative Analysis* 25(4) (December 1990): 419–40.

Heath, D., R. Jarrow, and A. Morton "Bond Pricing and the Term Structure of the Interest Rates: A New Methodology," *Econometrica* 60(1) (1992): 77–105.

Ho, T. S. Y. and S. B. Lee "Term Structure Movements and Pricing Interest Rate Contingent Claims," *Journal of Finance* 41 (December 1986): 1011–29.

Hull, J. and A. White "Bond Option Pricing Based on a Model for the Evolution of Bond Prices," *Advances in Futures and Options Research* 6 (1993): 1–13.

Hull, J. and A. White "Numerical Procedures for Implementing Term Structure Models I: Single-Factor Models," *Journal of Derivatives* 2(1) (Fall 1994): 7–16.

Johnson, R. S. and J. E. Pawlukiewicz "Derivation of the Up and Down Parameters of the Binomial Option Pricing Model," *Journal of Financial Education* 24 (1998): 44–9.

Johnson, R. S., J. E. Pawlukiewicz, and J. M. Mehta "Binomial Option Pricing with Skewed Asset Returns," *Review of Quantitative Finance and Accounting* 9 (1997): 89–101.

Kopprasch, Robert, William Boyce, Mark Koenigsberg, Armand Tatevossian, and Michael Yampol *Effective Duration and the Pricing of Callable Bonds* (Salomon Brothers, 1987).

Li, A., P. Ritchken, and L. Sankarasubramanian "Lattice Models for Pricing American Interest Rate Claims," *Journal of Finance* 50(2) (June 1995): 719–37.

Merton, R. "Option Pricing When Underlying Stock Returns are Discontinuous," *Journal of Financial Economics* 3 (1976): 125–44.

Rendleman, R. J. and B. J. Bartter "Two-State Option Pricing," *Journal of Finance* 34 (1979): 1093–110.

CHAPTER ELEVEN

SECURITIZATION AND MORTGAGE-BACKED SECURITIES

11.1 INTRODUCTION

One of the most innovative developments to occur in the security markets over the last two decades has been the securitization of assets. *Securitization* refers to a process in which the assets of a corporation or financial institution are pooled into a package of securities backed by the assets. The process starts when an *originator*, who owns the assets (e.g., mortgages or accounts receivable), sells them to an issuer. The issuer then creates a security backed by the assets called an *asset-backed security* or *pass-through* that he sells to investors. As shown in figure 11.1, the securitization process often involves a third-party trustee who ensures that the issuer complies with the terms underlying the asset-backed security. Further, many securitized assets are backed by credit enhancements, such as a third-party guarantee against the default on the underlying assets.

The most common types of asset-backed securities are those secured by mortgages, automobile loans, credit card receivables, and home equity loans. By far the largest type and the one in which the process of securitization has been most extensively applied is mortgages. Asset-backed securities formed with mortgages are called *mortgage-backed securities, MBSs*, or *mortgage pass-throughs*. These securities entitle the holder to the cash flow from a pool of mortgages. Typically, the issuer of a MBS buys a portfolio or pool of mortgages of a certain type from a mortgage originator, such as a commercial bank, savings and loans, or mortgage banker. The issuer finances the purchase of the mortgage portfolio through the sale of the mortgage pass-throughs, which have a claim on the portfolio's cash flow. The mortgage originator usually agrees to continue to service the loans, passing the payments on to the MBS holders.

In this chapter we examine the construction and characteristics of asset-backed securities, with particular emphasis on mortgage-backed securities. As we will see, the characteristics and value of such securities ultimately depend on the characteristics of the underlying asset. We begin our analysis with an overview of mortgage loans.

11.2 MORTGAGE LOANS

A mortgage is a loan secured by a specific real estate property, typically the one being acquired by the borrower. Real estate property can be either residential or non-residential. Residential includes houses, condominiums, and apartments; it is classified as either single-family or multiple-family. Non-residential includes commercial and agricultural property.

Most mortgages originate from commercial banks, savings and loans, other thrifts, or

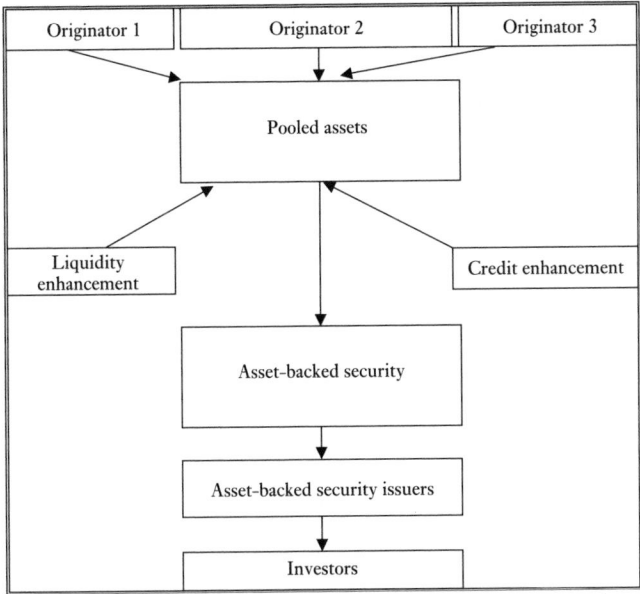

Figure 11.1   Securitization process

mortgage bankers.[1] The mortgage originator underwrites the loan, processes the necessary documents, conducts credit checks, evaluates the property, sets up the loan contracts and terms, and provides the funds.

The typical mortgage has an original maturity of 30 years (360 months), with 15-year mortgages increasing in popularity in recent years. The majority of mortgages are fully amortized, meaning each month the mortgage payment includes both a payment of interest on the mortgage balance and a payment of principal, with the total number of monthly payments being such that the loan is retired at maturity. Most mortgage loans are either fixed rate, FRM, with the rate fixed for the life of the mortgage, or adjustable rate, ARM, in which the rate is reset periodically based on some prespecified rate or index. Since the late 1970s, other types of mortgage loans have been introduced. These include *graduated payment mortgages (GPMs)*, which start with low monthly payments in earlier years and then gradually increase, and *reset mortgages*, which allow the borrower to renegotiate the terms of the mortgage at specified future dates.

The monthly payment on a mortgage, p, is found by solving for the p that makes the present value of all scheduled payments equal to the mortgage balance, F_0. That is:

$$F_0 = \sum_{t=1}^{M} \frac{p}{(1 + (R^A/12))^t}$$

$$F_0 = p \left[\frac{1 - 1/(1 + (R^A/12))^M}{R^A/12} \right]$$

$$p = \frac{F_0}{\left[\dfrac{1 - 1/(1 + (R^A/12))^M}{R^A/12} \right]} \tag{11.1}$$

where:

F_0 = face value of the loan
R^A = annualized interest rate
p = monthly payment
M = maturity in months

Thus, the monthly payment on a $100,000, 30-year, 9% fixed rate home mortgage would be $804.62:

$$p = \frac{\$100,000}{\left[\dfrac{1 - 1/(1 + (0.09/12))^{360}}{0.09/12} \right]} = \$804.62$$

Exhibit 11.1 Cash flow from fixed-rate mortgage (maturity = 30 years (360 months), rate = 9%)

Period	Balance (100,000)	Interest	Principal	Payment
1	100,000.00	750.00	54.62	804.62
2	99,945.38	749.59	55.03	804.62
3	99,890.35	749.18	55.45	804.62
4	99,834.90	748.76	55.86	804.62
5	99,779.04	748.34	56.28	804.62
6	99,722.76	747.92	56.70	804.62
263	55,698.95	417.74	386.88	804.62
264	55,312.07	414.84	389.78	804.62
265	54,922.28	411.92	392.71	804.62
266	54,529.58	408.97	395.65	804.62
267	54,133.93	406.00	398.62	804.62
268	53,735.31	403.01	401.61	804.62
269	53,333.70	400.00	404.62	804.62
270	52,929.08	396.97	407.65	804.62
360	798.63	5.99	798.63	804.62

Month
Monthly interest and principal payments

The $804.62 payment applies towards both the interest and principal. After the monthly payment p has been made, the principal balance at the end of month t is

$$F_t = F_{t-1} + [(R^A/12)F_{t-1}] - p \qquad (11.2)$$

and the interest payment for month t is

$$\text{Interest payment} = (R^A/12)F_{t-1} \qquad (11.3)$$

Exhibit 11.1 shows the schedule of interest and principal payments on a $100,000, 30-year, 9% mortgage for selected months, and the graph shows the pattern of scheduled interest and principal payments over the life of the mortgage. The figure highlights the pattern that in the early life of the mortgage most of the monthly payments go towards paying interest, while in the later life of the mortgage, the payments are applied more towards the payment of the principal.

In addition to the property securing the mortgage, many mortgages are also insured against default by the borrower. If the *loan-to-value ratio* is greater than 80%, the lender often will require the borrower to purchase private mortgage insurance; alternatively, the lender can also acquire the insurance and then pass on the cost to the borrower in the form of a higher borrowing rate. Three federal agencies, the Federal Housing Administration (FHA), the Veteran's Administration (VA), and the Farmer's Home Administration (FMHA), also provide mortgage insurance to qualified borrowers. FHA and VA mortgages typically require smaller down-payments than conventional mortgages.

After creating a number of mortgages, the mortgage originator ends up with a mortgage loan portfolio. Since most mortgages allow the borrower to prepay, a mortgage portfolio is quite sensitive to interest rate changes. That is, since borrowers have the option to refinance their loans and take on new ones when rates fall, the originator is subject to the risk that the loan will be paid off early and he will have to invest or create new loans in a market with a lower rate. This risk is known as *prepayment risk*.

11.2.1 Prepayment

For the holder of a mortgage portfolio, prepayment creates an uncertainty concerning the portfolio's cash flows. For example, if a bank has a pool of mortgages with a weighted average mortgage rate of 9%, and mortgage rates, in turn, decrease in the market to 7%, then the bank's mortgage portfolio is likely to experience significant prepayment as borrowers refinance their loans. The option borrowers have to prepay makes it difficult for the lender to predict future cash flows or determine the value of the portfolio. A number of prepayment models have been developed to try to predict the cash flows from a portfolio of mortgages. Most of these models estimate the prepayment rate, referred to as the *prepayment speed* or simply *speed*, in terms of four factors: refinancing incentive, seasoning (the age of the mortgage), monthly factors, and prepayment burnout.

The refinancing incentive is the most important factor influencing prepayment. If mortgage rates decrease below the mortgage loan rate, borrowers have a strong incentive to refinance. This incentive increases during periods of falling interest rates, with the greatest increases occurring when borrowers determine that rates have bottomed out. The refinancing incentive can be measured by the difference between the mortgage portfolio's weighted average rate, referred to as *the weighted average coupon rate, WAC*, and the refinancing rate, R^{ref}. A study by Goldman, Sachs, and Company found that the annualized prepayment speed, referred to as the *conditional*

prepayment rate, CPR, is greater the larger the positive difference between the WAC and R^{ref}. The study reported that when $\text{WAC} - R^{\text{ref}} = 0$ (known as the current coupon), FHA and VA mortgages prepay at a rate of approximately 6%, and conventionals prepay at approximately 9%. The study also found that prepayment rates decrease slightly when mortgage rates are at a discount, $\text{WAC} < R^{\text{ref}}$, and the refinancing rate is increasing relative to the mortgage rate. In such cases, prepayment is primarily due to new home purchases and defaults. In contrast, Goldman, Sachs, and Company found that prepayment rates increase significantly when mortgage rates are at a premium, $\text{WAC} > R^{\text{ref}}$, and the refinancing rate is decreasing relative to the mortgage rate. For example, when the difference between the WAC and R^{ref} is between 3% and 4%, the prepayment rate for conventional mortgages equals approximately 50% of the outstanding pool, and for FHA/VA mortgages the rate equals 40%.

A second factor determining prepayment is the age of the mortgage, referred to as *seasoning*. Prepayment tends to be greater during the early part of the loan, then stabilizes after about 3 years. Figure 11.2 depicts a commonly referenced seasoning pattern known as the *PSA model (Public Securities Association)*. In the standard PSA model, known as 100 PSA, the CPR starts at 0.2% for the first month and then increases at a constant rate of 0.2% per month to equal 6% at the 30th month; then after the 30th month the CPR stays at a constant 6%. Thus for any month t, the CPR is:

$$\text{CPR} = 0.06\left(\frac{t}{30}\right), \quad \text{if } t \le 30,$$
$$\text{CPR} = 0.06, \quad \text{if } t > 30 \tag{11.4}$$

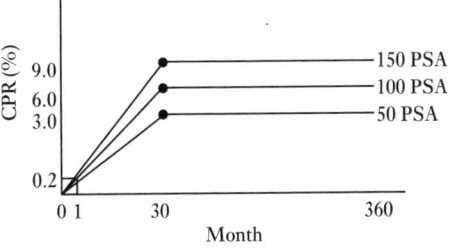

Figure 11.2 PSA prepayment model

Note that the CPR is quoted on an annual basis. The monthly prepayment rate, referred to as the *single monthly mortality rate, SMM*, can be obtained given the annual CPR by using the following formula:

$$\text{SMM} = 1 - [1 - \text{CPR}]^{1/12} \qquad (11.5)$$

The 100 PSA model is often used as a benchmark. The actual aging pattern will differ depending on whether the mortgage pool is current (WAC $= R^{\text{ref}}$), at a discount (WAC $< R^{\text{ref}}$), or at a premium (WAC $> R^{\text{ref}}$). Analysts often refer to the applicable pattern as being a certain percentage of the PSA. For example, if the pattern is described as being 200 PSA, then the prepayment speeds are twice the 100 PSA rates, and if the pattern is described as 50 PSA, then the CPRs are half of the 100 PSA rates (see figure 11.2). Thus, a current mortgage pool described by a 100 PSA would have an annual prepayment rate of 2% after 10 months (or a monthly prepayment rate of SMM $=$ 0.00168), and a premium pool described as 150 PSA would have a 3% CPR (or SMM $=$ 0.002535) after 10 months.

In addition to the effect of seasoning, mortgage prepayment rates are also influenced by the month of the year, with prepayment tending to be higher during the summer months. *Monthly factors* can be taken into account by multiplying the CPR by the estimated monthly multiplier to obtain a monthly adjusted CPR. PSA provides estimates of the monthly multipliers. Finally, many prepayment models also try to capture what is known as the **burnout** *factor*. The burnout factor refers to the tendency for premium mortgages to hit some maximum CPR and then level off. For example, in response to a 2% decrease in refinancing rates, a pool of premium mortgages might peak at a 40% prepayment rate after 1 year, then level off at approximately 25%.

In addition to the refinancing incentives, seasoning, monthly adjustments, and burnout factors, there are other factors that can influence the pool of mortgages: secular variations (variations due to different locations such as California or New York mortgages), types of mortgages (e.g., FRM or ARM, single-family or multiple-family, residential or commercial, etc.), and the original terms of the mortgage

(30 years or 15 years). With these myriad factors influencing prepayment, analysts have found that estimating the cash flows from a pool of mortgages is significantly more difficult than estimating the cash flows of other fixed income securities.

11.2.2 Estimating a Mortgage Pool's Cash Flow with Prepayment

The cash flow from a portfolio of mortgages consists of the interest payments, scheduled principal, and prepaid principal. Consider a bank that has a pool of current fixed rate mortgages that are worth $100m, yield a WAC of 8%, and have a weighted average maturity of 360 months. For the first month, the portfolio would generate an aggregate mortgage payment of $733,765:

$$p = \frac{\$100,000,000}{\left[\dfrac{1 - 1/(1 + (0.08/12))^{360}}{0.08/12}\right]} = \$733,765$$

From the $733,765 payment, $666,667 would go towards interest and $67,098 would go towards the scheduled principal payment:

$$\text{Interest} = \left(\frac{R^A}{12}\right) F_0$$

$$= \left(\frac{0.08}{12}\right) \$100,000,000 = \$666,667$$

$$\text{Scheduled principal payment} = p - \text{Interest}$$
$$= \$733,765 - \$666,667 = \$67,098$$

The projected first month prepaid principal can be estimated with a prepayment model. Using the 100% PSA model, the monthly prepayment rate for the first month ($t = 1$) is equal to SMM $= 0.0001668$:

$$\text{CPR} = \left(\frac{1}{30}\right) 0.06 = 0.002$$

$$\text{SMM} = 1 - [1 - 0.002]^{1/12} = 0.00016682$$

Given the prepayment rate, the projected prepaid principal in the first month is found by multiplying the balance at the beginning of the month minus the scheduled principal by the SMM. Doing this yields a projected prepaid principal of $16,671 in the first month:

Prepaid principal

$= \text{SMM}[F_0 - \text{Scheduled principal}]$

Prepaid principal

$= 0.00016682[\$100,000,000 - \$67,098]$

$= \$16,671.$

Thus, for the first month, the mortgage portfolio would generate an estimated cash flow of $750,435, and a balance at the beginning of the next month of $99,916,231:

$$\text{CF} = \text{Interest} + \text{Scheduled principal}$$
$$+ \text{Prepaid principal}$$
$$= \$666,666 + \$67,098 + \$16,671$$
$$= \$750,435$$

Beginning balance for month 2

$$= F_0 - \text{Scheduled principal}$$
$$- \text{Prepaid principal}$$
$$= \$100,000,000 - \$67,098$$
$$- \$16,671$$
$$= \$99,916,231$$

In the second month ($t = 2$), the projected payment would be $733,642 with $666,108 going to interest and $67,534 to scheduled principal:

$$p = \frac{\$99,916,231}{\left[\dfrac{1 - 1/(1 + (0.08/12))^{359}}{0.08/12}\right]} = \$733,642$$

$$\text{Interest} = \left(\frac{0.08}{12}\right)(\$99,916,231) = \$666,108$$

$$\text{Scheduled principal} = \$733,642 - \$666,108$$
$$= \$67,534$$

Using the 100% PSA model, the estimated monthly prepayment rate is 0.000333946, yielding a projected prepaid principal in month 2 of $33,344:

$$\text{CPR} = \left(\frac{2}{30}\right)0.06 = 0.004$$

$$\text{SMM} = 1 - [1 - 0.004]^{1/12} = 0.000333946$$

Prepaid principal

$$= 0.000333946\,[\$99,916,231 - \$67,534]$$
$$= 33,344.$$

Thus, for the second month, the mortgage portfolio would generate an estimated cash flow of $766,986 and have a balance at the beginning of month 3 of $99,815,353:

$$\text{CF} = \$666,108 + \$67,534 + \$33,344$$
$$= \$766,986$$

Beginning balance for month 3

$$= \$99,916,231 - \$67,534 - \$33,344$$
$$= \$99,815,353$$

Table 11.1 summarizes the mortgage portfolio's cash flow for the first 2 months and other selected months. In examining the table, two points should be noted. First, starting in month 30 the SMM remains constant at 0.005143; this reflects the 100% PSA model's assumption of a constant CPR of 6% starting in month 30. Second, the projected cash flows are based on a static analysis in which rates are assumed fixed over the time period. A more realistic model would incorporate interest rate changes and corresponding different prepayment speeds. Such models are discussed in section 11.6.

Web Information

For more information on the mortgage industry, statistics, trends, and rates go to
www.mbaa.org

Mortgage rates in different geographical areas can be found by going to
www.interest.com

For historical mortgage rates go to
http://research.stlouisfed.org/fred2

and click on "Interest Rates."

11.3 MORTGAGE-BACKED SECURITIES

A mortgage originator with a pool of mortgages has the option of either holding the portfolio, selling it, or using it as collateral on securities to be issued. If the originator decides to sell the portfolio, there are three federal agencies, the Federal National Mortgage Association (FNMA), the Government National Mortgage Association (GNMA), and the Federal Home Loan Mortgage

Table 11.1   Projected cash flows (mortgage portfolio = $100m, WAC = 8%, WAM = 360, prepayment = 100 PSA)

Period	Balance 100,000,000	Interest	p	Scheduled principal	SMM	Prepaid principal	CF
1	100,000,000	666,667	733,765	67,098	0.0001668	16,671	750,435
2	99,916,231	666,108	733,642	67,534	0.0003339	33,344	766,986
3	99,815,353	665,436	733,397	67,961	0.0005014	50,011	783,409
4	99,697,380	664,649	733,029	68,380	0.0006691	66,664	799,694
5	99,562,336	663,749	732,539	68,790	0.0008372	83,294	815,833
6	99,410,252	662,735	731,926	69,191	0.0010055	99,892	831,817
7	99,241,170	661,608	731,190	69,582	0.0011742	116,449	847,639
23	94,291,147	628,608	703,012	74,405	0.0039166	369,010	1,072,023
24	93,847,732	625,652	700,259	74,607	0.0040908	383,607	1,083,866
25	93,389,518	622,597	697,394	74,798	0.0042653	398,017	1,095,411
26	92,916,704	619,445	694,420	74,975	0.0044402	412,234	1,106,653
27	92,429,495	616,197	691,336	75,140	0.0046154	426,250	1,117,586
28	91,928,105	612,854	688,146	75,292	0.0047909	440,059	1,128,204
29	91,412,755	609,418	684,849	75,430	0.0049668	453,653	1,138,502
30	90,883,671	605,891	681,447	75,556	0.005143	467,027	1,148,475
31	90,341,088	602,274	677,943	75,669	0.005143	464,236	1,142,179
32	89,801,183	598,675	674,456	75,781	0.005143	461,459	1,135,915
110	54,900,442	366,003	451,112	85,109	0.005143	281,916	733,028
111	54,533,417	363,556	448,792	85,236	0.005143	280,028	728,820
112	54,168,153	361,121	446,484	85,363	0.005143	278,148	724,632
113	53,804,641	358,698	444,188	85,490	0.005143	276,278	720,466
114	53,442,873	356,286	441,903	85,617	0.005143	274,417	716,320
115	53,082,839	353,886	439,631	85,745	0.005143	272,565	712,195
357	496,620	3,311	126,231	122,920	0.005143	1,922	128,153
358	371,778	2,479	125,582	123,103	0.005143	1,279	126,861
359	247,395	1,649	124,936	123,287	0.005143	638	125,574
360	123,470	823	124,293	123,470	0.005143	0	124,293

$$\text{Monthly payment} = p = \frac{\text{Balance}}{\left[\dfrac{1 - [1/(1 + (0.08/12))]^{\text{Remaining periods}}}{(0.08/12)}\right]}$$

Interest = (0.08/12)(Balance)
Scheduled principal = p − (0.08/12) Balance
Prepaid principal = SMM [Beginning balance − Scheduled principal]

Corporation (FHLMC) (see chapter 6), that buy certain types of mortgage loan portfolios (e.g., FHA- or VA-insured mortgages) and then pool them to create MBSs to sell to investors. Collectively, the MBSs created by these agencies are referred to as *agency pass-throughs*. Agency pass-throughs are guaranteed by the agencies, and the loans they purchase must be conforming loans, meaning they meet certain standards. In addition, there are also private entities that buy mortgages to create their own MBSs. These MBSs are referred to as *conventional pass-throughs*. When the mortgages are sold, the originator typically continues to service the loan for a service fee (that is, collect payments, maintain records, forward tax information, and the like).

11.3.1 Government National Mortgage Association's Mortgage-Backed Securities

The Government National Mortgage Association's (GNMA) mortgage-backed securities or pass-throughs are formed with FHA- or VA-insured mortgages. They are put together by an originator (bank, thrift, or mortgage banker), who presents a block of FHA and VA mortgages to GNMA. If GNMA finds them in order, they will issue a guarantee and assign a pool number that identifies the MBS that is to be issued. The originator will transfer the mortgages to a trustee, and then issue the pass-throughs, often selling them to investment bankers for distribution. The mortgages underlying GNMA's MBSs are very similar (e.g., single-family, 30-year maturity, and fixed rate), with the mortgage rates usually differing by no more than 50 basis point from the WAC. GNMA does offer programs in which the underlying mortgages are more diverse. Finally, since GNMA is a federal agency, its guarantee of timely interest and principal payments is backed by the full faith and credit of the US government – the only MBS with this type of guarantee.

11.3.2 Federal Home Loan Mortgage Corporation's Mortgage-Backed Securities

The Federal Home Loan Mortgage Corporation (FHLMC or Freddie Mac) issues MBSs that it refers to as participation certificates (PCs).[2] The FHLMC has a regular MBS (also called a cash PC), which is backed by a pool of either conventional, FHA, or VA mortgages that the FHLMC has purchased from mortgage originators. They also offer a pass-though formed through their Guarantor/Swap Program. In this program, mortgage originators can swap mortgages for an FHLMC pass-through. Unlike GNMA's MBSs, Freddie Mac's MBSs are formed with more heterogeneous mortgages. Like GNMA, the Federal Home Loan Mortgage Corporation backs the interest and principal payments of its securities, but the FHLMC's guarantee is not backed by the US government.

11.3.3 Federal National Mortgage Association's Mortgage-Backed Securities

The Federal National Mortgage Association (FNMA or Fannie Mae) offers several types of pass-throughs, referred to as FNMA mortgage-backed securities. Like FHLMC's pass-throughs, FNMA's securities are backed by the agency, but not by the government. Like the

FHLMC, FNMA buys conventional, FHA, and VA mortgages, and offers a SWAP program whereby mortgage loans can be swapped for FNMA-issued MBSs. Finally, like the FHLMC, FNMA's mortgages are more heterogeneous than GNMA's mortgages, with mortgage rates in some pools differing by as much as 200 basis points from the portfolio's average mortgage rate.

11.3.4 Conventional Pass-Throughs

Conventional pass-throughs are sold by commercial banks, savings and loans, other thrifts, and mortgage bankers. These non-agency pass-throughs, also called *private labels*, are often formed with non-conforming mortgages; that is, mortgages which fail to meet size limits and other requirements placed on agency pass-throughs. Larger issuers of conventional MBSs include Citicorp Housing, Countrywide, Prudential Home, Ryland/Saxon, and GE Capital Mortgage. These pass-throughs are often guaranteed against default through external credit enhancements, such as the guarantee of a corporation, a bank letter of credit, or private insurance from such insurers as the Financial Guarantee Insurance Corporation (FGIC), the Capital Markets Assurance Corporation (CAPMAC), or the Financial Security Assurance Company (FSA). Some conventionals are guaranteed internally through the creation of senior and subordinate classes of bonds with different priority claims on the pool's cash flows in the case where some of the mortgages in the pool default. For example, a conventional pass-through, known as an *A/B pass-through*, consists of two types of claims on the underlying pool of mortgages – senior and subordinate. The senior claim is backed by the mortgages, while the subordinate claim is not. The more subordinate claims sold relative to senior, the more secured the senior claims. Because of the default risk, conventional MBSs are rated by Moody's and Standard & Poor's, and, unlike agency pass-throughs, they must be registered with the SEC when they are issued. Finally, most financial entities that issue private-labeled MBSs or derivatives of MBSs are legally set up so that they do not have to pay taxes on the interest and principal that pass through them to their MBS investors. The requirements that MBS issuers must meet to ensure tax-exempt status are specified in the Tax Reform Act of 1983 in the section on trusts referred to as *Real Estate Mortgage Investment Conduits, REMICs*. Private-labeled MBS issuers who comply with these provisions are sometimes referred to as REMICs.

Web Information

Agency information:

     www.fanniemae.com

     www.ginniemae.gov

     www.freddiemac.com

For general information on MBSs go to

     www.ficc.com

11.4 FEATURES OF MORTGAGE-BACKED SECURITIES

11.4.1 Cash Flows

Cash flows from MBSs are generated from the cash flows from the underlying pool of mortgages, minus servicing and other fees. Typically, fees for constructing, managing, and servicing the underlying mortgages (also referred to as the mortgage collateral) and the MBSs are equal to the difference between the WAC associated with the mortgage pool and the MBS *pass-through (PT) rate*. Table 11.2 shows the monthly cash flows for an MBS issue constructed from a mortgage pool with a current balance of $100m, a WAC of 8%, and a WAM of 355 months. The PT rate is 7.5%. The monthly fees implied on the MBS issue are equal to $0.04167\% = (8\% - 7.5\%)/12$ of the monthly balance.

The cash flow for the MBS issue shown in table 11.2 differs in several respects from the cash flows for the $100m mortgage pool shown in table 11.1. First, the MBS issue has a WAM of 355 months and an assumed prepayment speed equal to 150% of the standard PSA model, compared to 360 months and an assumption of 100% PSA for the pool. As a result, the first month's CPR for the MBS issue reflects a 5-month seasoning in which $t = 6$, and a speed that is 150% greater than the 100 PSA. For the

MBS issue, this yields a first-month SMM of 0.0015125 and a constant SMM of 0.0078284 starting in month 25. Secondly, for the mortgage pool, a WAC of 8% is used to determine the mortgage payment, scheduled principal, and interest; on the MBS issue, though, the WAC of 8% is only used to determine the mortgage payment and scheduled principal, while the PT rate of 7.5% is used to determine the interest.

11.4.2 Price Quotes

Investors can acquire newly issued mortgage-backed securities from the agencies, originators, or dealers specializing in specific pass-throughs. There is also a secondary market consisting of dealers who operate in the OTC market as part of the *Mortgage-Backed Security Dealers Association*. These dealers form the core of the secondary market for the trading of existing pass-throughs.

Mortgage pass-throughs are normally sold in denominations ranging from $25,000 to $250,000, although some privately-placed issues are sold with denominations as high as $1m. The prices of MBSs are quoted as a percentage of the underlying mortgages' balance. The mortgage balance at time t, F_t, is usually calculated by the servicing institution and is quoted as a proportion of the original balance, F_0. This proportion is referred to as the *pool factor, pf*:

$$\text{pf}_t = \frac{F_t}{F_0} \qquad (11.6)$$

For example, suppose a GNMA MBS, backed by a mortgage pool with an original par value of $100m, is currently priced at 95-16 (the fractions on GNMA's MBSs are quoted like Treasury bonds and notes in terms of 32nds), with a pool factor of 0.92. An institutional investor who purchased $10m of the MBS when it was first issued would now have securities valued at $8.786m that are backed by mortgages that are worth $9.2m:

Par value remaining $= (\$10m)(0.92) = \$9.2m$

Market value $= (\$9.2m)(0.9550) = \$8.786m$

The market value of $8.786m represents a clean or flat price that does not include accrued interest. If the institutional investor were to sell the MBS, the accrued interest (ai) would need to be added to the flat price to determine the invoice price. The normal

Table 11.2 Projected cash flow from MBS issue (WAC = 8%, WAM = 355, PT rate = 7.5%, PSA = 150%)

Period	Balance 100,000,000	Interest	p	Scheduled principal	SMM	Prepaid principal	Principal	CF
1	100,000,000	625,000	736,268	69,601	0.0015125	151,147	220,748	845,748
2	99,779,252	623,620	735,154	69,959	0.0017671	176,194	246,153	869,773
3	99,533,099	622,082	733,855	70,301	0.0020223	201,148	271,449	893,531
4	99,261,650	620,385	732,371	70,627	0.0022783	225,990	296,617	917,002
5	98,965,033	618,531	730,702	70,936	0.002535	250,701	321,637	940,168
6	98,643,396	616,521	728,850	71,227	0.0027925	275,262	346,489	963,011
20	91,641,550	572,760	684,341	73,398	0.0064757	592,971	666,369	1,239,128
21	90,975,181	568,595	679,910	73,408	0.0067447	613,101	686,510	1,255,105
22	90,288,672	564,304	675,324	73,399	0.0070144	632,804	706,204	1,270,508
23	89,582,468	559,890	670,587	73,370	0.0072849	652,066	725,436	1,285,327
24	88,857,032	555,356	665,702	73,321	0.0075563	670,873	744,194	1,299,550
25	88,112,838	550,705	660,671	73,253	0.0078284	689,211	762,463	1,313,169
26	87,350,375	545,940	655,499	73,164	0.0078284	683,243	756,406	1,302,346
27	86,593,968	541,212	650,368	73,075	0.0078284	677,322	750,397	1,291,609
28	85,843,572	536,522	645,277	72,986	0.0078284	671,448	744,434	1,280,957
29	85,099,137	531,870	640,225	72,897	0.0078284	665,621	738,519	1,270,388
30	84,360,619	527,254	635,213	72,809	0.0078284	659,840	732,649	1,259,903
31	83,627,969	522,675	630,240	72,721	0.0078284	654,106	726,826	1,249,501
32	82,901,143	518,132	625,307	72,632	0.0078284	648,416	721,049	1,239,181
33	82,180,094	513,626	620,411	72,544	0.0078284	642,772	715,317	1,228,942
100	44,933,791	280,836	366,433	66,874	0.0078284	351,237	418,111	698,947
101	44,515,680	278,223	363,564	66,793	0.0078284	347,965	414,758	692,981
102	44,100,923	275,631	360,718	66,712	0.0078284	344,718	411,430	687,061
103	43,689,493	273,059	357,894	66,631	0.0078284	341,498	408,129	681,188
200	16,163,713	101,023	166,983	59,225	0.0078284	126,073	185,298	286,321
201	15,978,416	99,865	165,676	59,153	0.0078284	124,623	183,776	283,641
353	148,527	928	50,171	49,181	0.0078284	778	49,958	50,887
354	98,569	616	49,778	49,121	0.0078284	387	49,508	50,124
355	49,061	307	49,388	49,061	0.0078284	0	49,061	49,368

Monthly payment $= p = \dfrac{\text{Balance}}{\left[\dfrac{1-[1/(1+(0.08/12))]^{\text{Remaining periods}}}{(0.08/12)}\right]}$

Interest $= (0.075/12)(\text{Balance})$
Scheduled principal $= p - (0.08/12) \, \text{Balance}$
Prepaid principal $= \text{SMM}[\text{Beginning balance} - \text{Scheduled principal}]$

practice is to determine accrued interest based on the time period between the settlement date (SD) (usually 2 days after the trade date) and the first day of the month, M_0. If the coupon rate on the GNMA MBS held by the institutional investor were 9% and the time period between SD and M_0 were 20 days, then the accrued interest would be $46,000:

$$ai_t = \frac{SD - M_0}{30} \frac{WAC}{12} F_t$$

$$ai_t = \left(\frac{20}{30}\right)\left(\frac{0.09}{12}\right)\$9.2\,\text{m} = \$46,000$$

11.4.3 Extension Risk and Average Life

Like other fixed-income securities, the value of an MBS is determined by the MBS's future cash flow, maturity, default risk, and other features germane to fixed-income securities. In contrast to other bonds, though, MBSs are also subject to prepayment risk. As discussed earlier, the mortgage borrower's option to prepay makes it difficult to estimate the cash flow from the MBS. The prepayment risk associated with MBSs is primarily a function of interest rates. If interest rates decrease, then the prices of MBSs,

Table 11.3 Sequential-pay CMO (collateral: balance = $100m, WAM = 355 months, WAC = 8%, PT rate = 7.5%, PSA = 150; tranches: A = $50m, B = $30m, C = $20m)

	Par = $100m Rate = 7.5% Collateral			A: Par = $50m Rate = 7.5% Tranche A			B: Par = $30m Rate = 7.5% Tranche B			C: Par = $20m Rate = 7.5% Tranche C		
Month	Balance 100,000,000	Interest	Principal	Balance 50,000,000	Interest	Principal	Balance 30,000,000	Principal	Interest	Balance 20,000,000	Principal	Interest
1	100,000,000	625,000	220,748	50,000,000	312,500	220,748	30,000,000	0	187,500	20,000,000	0	125,000
2	99,779,252	623,620	246,153	49,779,252	311,120	246,153	30,000,000	0	187,500	20,000,000	0	125,000
3	99,533,099	622,082	271,449	49,533,099	309,582	271,449	30,000,000	0	187,500	20,000,000	0	125,000
4	99,261,650	620,385	296,617	49,261,650	307,885	296,617	30,000,000	0	187,500	20,000,000	0	125,000
5	98,965,033	618,531	321,637	48,965,033	306,031	321,637	30,000,000	0	187,500	20,000,000	0	125,000
85	51,626,473	322,665	471,724	1,626,473	10,165	471,724	30,000,000	0	187,500	20,000,000	0	125,000
86	51,154,749	319,717	467,949	1,154,749	7,217	467,949	30,000,000	0	187,500	20,000,000	0	125,000
87	50,686,799	316,792	464,204	686,799	4,292	464,204	30,000,000	0	187,500	20,000,000	0	125,000
88	50,222,595	313,891	460,488	222,595	1,391	222,595	30,000,000	237,893	187,500	20,000,000	0	125,000
89	49,762,107	311,013	456,802	0	0	0	29,762,107	456,802	186,013	20,000,000	0	125,000
90	49,305,305	308,158	453,144	0	0	0	29,305,305	453,144	183,158	20,000,000	0	125,000
91	48,852,161	305,326	449,515	0	0	0	28,852,161	449,515	180,326	20,000,000	0	125,000
92	48,402,646	302,517	445,915	0	0	0	28,402,646	445,915	177,517	20,000,000	0	125,000
178	20,650,839	129,068	222,016	0	0	0	650,839	222,016	4,068	20,000,000	0	125,000
181	19,990,210	124,939	216,625	0	0	0	0	0	0	19,990,210	216,625	124,939
182	19,773,585	123,585	214,856	0	0	0	0	0	0	19,773,585	214,856	123,585
183	19,558,729	122,242	213,101	0	0	0	0	0	0	19,558,729	213,101	122,242
184	19,345,627	120,910	211,360	0	0	0	0	0	0	19,345,627	211,360	120,910
353	148,527	928	49,958	0	0	0	0	0	0	148,527	49,958	928
354	98,569	616	49,508	0	0	0	0	0	0	98,569	49,508	616
355	49,061	307	49,061	0	0	0	0	0	0	49,061	49,061	307

Tranche	Maturity	Window	Average life
A	88 months	87 months	3.69 years
B	179 months	92 months	10.71 years
C	355 months	176 months	20.59 years
Collateral	355 months	355 months	9.18 years

PSA	Collateral	Tranche A	Tranche B	Tranche C
50	14.95	7.53	19.4	26.81
100	11.51	4.92	14.18	23.99
150	9.18	3.69	10.71	9.18
200	7.55	3.01	8.51	17.46
300	5.5	2.26	6.03	12.82

like the prices of all bonds, increase as a result of lower discount rates. However, the decrease in rates will also augment prepayment speed, causing the earlier cash flow of the mortgages to be larger, which, depending on the level of rates and the maturity remaining, could also contribute to increasing the MBS's price. In contrast, if interest rates increase, then the prices of MBSs will decrease as a result of higher discount rates and possibly the smaller earlier cash flow resulting from lower prepayment speeds.

The effect of an interest rate increase in lowering the price of the bond by decreasing the value of its cash flow is known as *extension risk*. Extension risk can be described in terms of the relationship between interest rates and the MBS's *average life*. The average life of an MBS is the weighted average of the security's time periods, with the weights being the periodic principal payments (scheduled and prepaid principal) divided by the total principal:

$$\text{Average life} = \frac{1}{12} \sum_{t=1}^{T} t \left(\frac{\text{Principal received at } t}{\text{Total principal}} \right)$$

For example, the average life for the MBS issue described in table 11.2 is 9.18 years:

be absent of prepayment risk. Moreover, one of the more creative developments in the security market industry over the last two decades has been the creation of derivative securities formed from MBSs that have different prepayment risk characteristics, including some that are formed which have average lives that are invariant to changes in prepayment rates. The most popular of these derivatives are collateralized mortgage obligations and stripped MBSs.

11.5 COLLATERALIZED MORTGAGE OBLIGATIONS

To address the problems of prepayment risk, many MBS issuers began to offer *collateralized mortgage obligations (CMOs)*. Introduced in the mid-1980s, these securities are formed by dividing the cash flow of an underlying pool of mortgages or an MBS issue into several classes, with each class having a different claim on the mortgage collateral and with each sold separately to different types of investors. The different classes making up a CMO are called *tranches* or bond classes. There are two general types of CMO tranches – sequential-pay tranches and planned amortization class tranches.

$$\text{Average life} = \frac{1}{12} \left(\frac{1(\$220,748) + 2(\$246,153) + \ldots + 355(\$49,061)}{\$100,000,000} \right) = 9.18 \text{ years}$$

The average life of an MBS depends on prepayment speed. For example, if the PSA speed of the \$100m MBS issue were to increase from 150 to 200, the MBS's average life would decrease from 9.18 to 7.55, reflecting greater principal payments in the earlier years; in contrast, if the PSA speed were to decrease from 150 to 100, then the average life of the MBS would increase to 11.51. For MBSs, prepayment risk can be evaluated in terms of how responsive an MBS's average life is to changes in prepayment speeds:

$$\text{Prepayment risk} = \frac{\Delta \text{Average life}}{\Delta \text{PSA}}$$

Thus, an MBS with an average life that did not change with PSA speeds, in turn, would have stable principal payments over time and would

11.5.1 Sequential-Pay Tranches

A CMO with sequential-pay tranches, called a *sequential-pay CMO*, is divided into classes with different priority claims on the collateral's principal. The tranche with the first priority claim has its principal paid entirely before the next priority class, which has its principal paid before the third class, and so on. Interest payments on most CMO tranches are made until the tranche's principal is retired.

An example of a sequential-pay CMO is shown in table 11.3. This CMO consists of three tranches, A, B, and C, formed from the collateral making up the \$100m MBS described in table 11.2. In terms of the priority disbursement rules, tranche A receives all principal payment from the collateral until its principal of \$50m is

Table 11.4 Cash flows from sequential-pay CMO with Z tranche (collateral: balance = $100m, WAM = 355 months, WAC = 8%, PT rate = 7.5%; tranches: A = $50m, B = $30m, Z = $20m)

Period	Par = $100m Rate = 7.5% Collateral			A: Par = $50m Rate = 7.5%			B: Par = $30m Rate = 7.5%			Z: Par = $20m Rate = 7.5%		
Month	Balance 100,000,000	Interest	Principal	Balance 50,000,000	Interest	Principal	Balance 30,000,000	Principal	Interest	Bal. + Cum Int 20,000,000	Principal 0	Interest
1	100,000,000	625,000	220,748	50,000,000	312,500	345,748	30,000,000	0	187,500	20,000,000	0	0
2	99,779,252	623,620	246,153	49,654,252	310,339	371,153	30,000,000	0	187,500	20,125,000	0	0
3	99,533,099	622,082	271,449	49,283,099	308,019	396,449	30,000,000	0	187,500	20,250,000	0	0
4	99,261,650	620,385	296,617	48,886,650	305,542	421,617	30,000,000	0	187,500	20,375,000	0	0
5	98,965,033	618,531	321,637	48,465,033	302,906	446,637	30,000,000	0	187,500	20,500,000	0	0
68	60,253,239	376,583	540,668	1,878,239	11,739	665,668	30,000,000	0	187,500	28,375,000	0	0
69	59,712,571	373,204	536,352	1,212,571	7,579	661,352	30,000,000	0	187,500	28,500,000	0	0
70	59,176,219	369,851	532,069	551,219	3,445	551,219	30,000,000	105,850	187,500	28,625,000	0	0
71	58,644,150	366,526	527,821	0	0	0	29,894,150	652,821	186,838	28,750,000	0	0
72	58,116,329	363,227	523,605	0	0	0	29,241,329	648,605	182,758	28,875,000	0	0
122	36,470,935	227,943	350,111	0	0	0	1,345,935	475,111	8,412	35,125,000	0	0
123	36,120,824	225,755	347,292	0	0	0	870,824	472,292	5,443	35,250,000	0	0
125	35,429,038	221,431	341,719	0	0	0	0	0	0	35,429,038	341,719	221,431
126	35,087,319	219,296	338,966	0	0	0	0	0	0	35,087,319	338,966	219,296
354	98,569	616	49,508	0	0	0	0	0	0	98,569	49,508	616
355	49,061	307	49,061	0	0	0	0	0	0	49,061	49,061	307

Tranche	Window	Average life
A	69 months	3.06 years
B	54 months	8.23 years

retired. No other tranche's principal payments are disbursed until the principal on A is paid. After tranche A's principal is retired, all principal payments from the collateral are then made to tranche B until its principal of $30m is retired. Finally, tranche C receives the remaining principal that is equal to its par value of $20m. While the principal is paid sequentially, each tranche does receive interest each period equal to its stated coupon rate (7.5%) times its outstanding balance at the beginning of each month.

Given the different possible prepayment speeds, the actual amount of principal paid each month and the time it will take to pay the principal on each tranche is uncertain. Table 11.3 shows the cash flow patterns on the three tranches based on a 150% PSA prepayment assumption. As shown, the first month cash flow for tranche A consists of a principal payment (scheduled and prepaid) of $220,748 and an interest payment of $312,500 [(0.075/12)($50m) = $312,500]. In month 2, tranche A receives an interest payment of $311,120 based on the balance of $49.779252m and a principal payment of $246,153. Based on the assumption of a 150% PSA speed, it takes 88 months before A's principal of $50m is retired. During the first 88 months, the cash flows for tranches B and C consist of just the interest on their balances, with no principal payments made to them. Starting in month 88, tranche B begins to receive the principal payment. Tranche B is paid off in month 180, at which time principal payments begin to be paid to tranche C. Finally, in month 355 tranche C's principal is retired.

Features of Sequential-Pay CMOs

By creating sequential-pay tranches, issuers of CMOs are able to offer investors maturities, principal payment periods, and average lives different from those defined by the underlying mortgage collateral. For example, tranche A in our example has a maturity of 88 months (7.33 years) compared to the collateral's maturity of 355 months; tranche B's maturity is 180 months (15 years); tranche C's maturity is 355 months (29.58 years). Each tranche also has larger cash flows during the periods when

their principal is being retired. The period between the beginning and ending principal payment is referred to as the *principal pay-down window*. Tranche A has a window of 87 months, B's window is 92 months, and C's window is 176 months (see the bottom of table 11.3). CMOs with certain size windows and maturities often are attractive investments for investors who are using cash-flow matching strategies. Moreover, issuers of CMOs are able to offer a number of CMO tranches with different maturities and windows by simply creating more tranches.

Finally, each of the tranches has an average life that is either shorter or longer than the collateral's average life of 9.18 years. With a 150% PSA model, tranche A has an average life of 3.69 years, B has an average life of 10.71 years, and C has a life of 20.59 years. In general, a CMO tranche with a lower average life is less susceptible to prepayment risk. Such risk, though, is not eliminated. As noted earlier, if prepayment speed decreases, an MBS's average life will increase, resulting in lower than projected early cash flow and therefore lower returns. In the table at the bottom of table 11.3, the average lives for the collateral and the three tranches are shown for different PSA models. Note that the average life of each of the tranches still varies as prepayment speed changes.

Accrual Tranche

Most sequential-pay CMOs have an *accrual bond class*. Such a tranche, also referred to as the *Z bond*, does not receive current interest but has it deferred. Instead, the Z bond's current interest is used to pay down the principal on the other tranches, increasing their speed and reducing their average life. For example, suppose in our illustrative sequential-pay CMO example we make tranche C an accrual tranche in which its interest of 7.5% is to be paid to the earlier tranches and its principal of $20m and accrued interest is to be paid after tranche B's principal has been retired (see table 11.4). Since the accrual tranche's current interest of $125,000 is now used to pay down the other classes' principals, the other tranches now have lower maturities and average lives. For example, as shown in table 11.4, the principal payment on tranche A is $345,748 in the first month ($220,748 of scheduled and projected prepaid principal and $125,000 of Z's interest); in contrast, the principal is only $220,748 when there is no Z bond (see table 11.3). As a result of the Z bond, tranche A's window is reduced from 87 months to 69 months and its average life from 3.69 years to 3.06 years (see the bottom of table 11.4).

Floating-Rate Tranches

In order to attract investors who prefer variable-rate securities, CMO issuers often create floating-rate and inverse floating-rate tranches. The monthly coupon rate on the floating-rate tranche is usually set equal to a reference rate such as the London Interbank Offer Rate, LIBOR, while the rate on the inverse floating-rate tranche is determined by a formula that is inversely related to the reference rate. An example of a sequential-pay CMO with floating and inverse floating tranches is shown in table 11.5. The CMO is identical to our preceding CMO, except that tranche B has been replaced with a floating-rate tranche, FR, and an inverse floating-rate tranche, IFR. The par values of the FR and IFR tranches are equal to the par value of tranche B, with the FR tranche's par value of $22.5m representing 75% of B's par value of $30m, and the IFR's par value of $7.5m representing 25% of B's par value. The rate on the FR tranche, R_{FR}, is set to the LIBOR plus 50 basis points, with the maximum rate permitted being 9.5%; the rate on the IFR tranche, R_{IFR}, is determined by the following formula:

$$R_{IFR} = 28.5 - 3\,\text{LIBOR}$$

This formula ensures that the weighted average rate (WAR) of the two tranches will be equal to the PT rate on tranche B of 7.5%, provided the LIBOR is less than 9.5%. For example, if the LIBOR is 8%, then the rate on the FR tranche is 8.5%, the IFR tranche's rate is 4.5%, and the WAC of the two tranches is 7.5%:

LIBOR = 8%

$R_{FR} = \text{LIBOR} + 50\text{BP} = 8.5\%$

$R_{IFR} = 28.5 - 3\,\text{LIBOR} = 4.5\%$

$\text{WAR} = 0.75R_{FR} + 0.25R_{IFR} = 7.5\%$

Table 11.5 Sequential-pay CMO with floaters

Tranche	Par value ($ millions)	PT rate
A	50	7.5%
FR	22.5	LIBOR + 50BP
IFR	7.5	28.3−3 LIBOR
Z	20	7.5%
Total	100	7.5%

Notional Interest-Only Class

Each of the fixed-rate tranches in the previous CMOs have the same coupon rate as the collateral rate of 7.5%. Many CMOs, though, are structured with tranches that have different rates. When CMOs are formed this way, an additional tranche, known as a *notional interest-only (IO) class*, is often created. This tranche receives the excess interest on the other tranches' principals, with the excess rate being equal to the difference in the collateral's PT rate minus the tranches' PT rates. To illustrate, a sequential-pay CMO with a Z bond and notional IO tranche is shown in table 11.6. This CMO is identical to our previous CMO with a Z bond, except that each of the tranches has a coupon rate lower than the collateral rate of 7.5% and there is a notional IO class. The notional IO class receives the excess interest on each tranche's remaining balance, with the excess rate based on the collateral rate of 7.5%. In the first month, for example, the IO class would receive interest of $87,500:

$$\text{Interest} = \left(\frac{0.075 - 0.06}{12}\right)\$50,000,000$$

$$+ \left(\frac{0.075 - 0.065}{12}\right)\$30,000,000$$

$$\text{Interest} = \$62,500 + \$25,000 = \$87,500$$

In the table, the IO class is described as paying 7.5% interest on a notional principal of $15,333,333. This notional principal is determined by summing each tranche's notional principal. A tranche's notional principal is the number of dollars that makes the return on the tranche's principal equal to 7.5%. Thus, the notional principal for tranche A is $10,000,000, for B, $4,000,000, and for Z, $1,333,333, yielding

Table 11.6 Sequential-pay CMO with notional IO tranche (collateral: balance = $100m, WAM = 355, WAC = 8%, PT rate = 7.5%, PSA = 150%; tranches: A = $50m, B = $30m, Z = $20m, notional IO = $15.333m)

Period	Collateral: Par = $100m, Rate = 7.5%			Tranche A: Par = $50m, Rate = 6%			Notional	Tranche B: Par = $30m, Rate = 6.5%			Notional	Tranche Z: Par = $20m, Rate = 7%			Notional	Notional Par = $15.333m
Month	Balance	Interest	Principal	Balance	Interest 0.06	Principal	Interest 0.015	Balance	Principal	Interest 0.065	Interest 0.01	Balance	Principal	Interest 0.07	Interest 0.005	Total CF
1	100,000,000	625,000	220,748	50,000,000	250,000	345,748	62,500	30,000,000	0	162,500	25,000	20,000,000	0	0	0	87,500
2	99,779,252	623,620	246,153	49,654,252	248,271	371,153	62,068	30,000,000	0	162,500	25,000	20,125,000	0	0	0	87,068
3	99,533,099	622,082	271,449	49,283,099	246,415	396,449	61,604	30,000,000	0	162,500	25,000	20,250,000	0	0	0	86,604
4	99,261,650	620,385	296,617	48,886,650	244,433	421,617	61,108	30,000,000	0	162,500	25,000	20,375,000	0	0	0	86,108
5	98,965,033	618,531	321,637	48,465,033	242,325	446,637	60,581	30,000,000	0	162,500	25,000	20,500,000	0	0	0	85,581
70	59,176,219	369,851	532,069	551,219	2,756	551,219	689	30,000,000	105,850	162,500	25,000	28,625,000	0	0	0	25,689
71	58,644,150	366,526	527,821	0	0	0	0	29,894,150	652,821	161,927	24,912	28,750,000	0	0	0	24,912
72	58,116,329	363,227	523,605	0	0	0	0	29,241,329	648,605	158,391	24,368	28,875,000	0	0	0	24,368
122	36,470,935	227,943	350,111	0	0	0	0	1,345,935	475,111	7,290	1,122	35,125,000	0	0	0	1,122
123	36,120,824	225,755	347,292	0	0	0	0	870,824	472,292	4,717	726	35,250,000	0	0	0	726
124	35,773,533	223,585	344,494	0	0	0	0	398,533	398,533	2,159	332	35,375,000	54,038	206,354	14,740	15,072
125	35,429,038	221,431	341,719	0	0	0	0	0	0	0	0	35,429,038	341,719	206,669	14,762	14,762
126	35,087,319	219,296	338,966	0	0	0	0	0	0	0	0	35,087,319	338,966	204,676	14,620	14,620
127	34,748,353	217,177	336,235	0	0	0	0	0	0	0	0	34,748,353	336,235	202,699	14,478	14,478
353	148,527	928	49,958	0	0	0	0	0	0	0	0	148,527	49,958	866	62	62
354	98,569	616	49,508	0	0	0	0	0	0	0	0	98,569	49,508	575	41	41
355	49,061	307	49,061	0	0	0	0	0	0	0	0	49,061	49,061	286	20	20

Table 11.7 PAC and support bonds (collateral: balance = $100m, WAM = 355, WAC = 8%, PT rate = 7.5%, PSA = 150%; PAC: low PSA = 100, high PSA = 300)

Period	PAC					Collateral				Support			
Month	Low PSA pr. 100	High PSA pr. 300	Min. principal	Int. 0.075	CF	Balance 100,000,000	Interest	Principal	CF	Principal Col. pr. – PAC pr.	Balance	Interest 0.075	CF
1	170,085	374,456	170,085	398,606	568,692	100,000,000	625,000	220,748	845,748	50,662	36,222,970	226,394	277,056
2	187,135	425,190	187,135	397,543	584,678	99,779,252	623,620	246,153	869,773	59,018	36,172,308	226,077	285,095
3	204,125	475,588	204,125	396,374	600,499	99,533,099	622,082	271,449	893,531	67,324	36,113,290	225,708	293,032
4	221,048	525,572	221,048	395,098	616,147	99,261,650	620,385	296,617	917,002	75,568	36,045,966	225,287	300,856
5	237,895	575,064	237,895	393,716	631,612	98,965,033	618,531	321,637	940,168	83,742	35,970,398	224,815	308,557
98	381,871	386,139	381,871	135,237	517,108	45,780,181	286,126	424,898	711,025	43,028	24,142,190	150,889	193,916
99	380,032	379,499	379,499	132,851	512,349	45,355,283	283,471	421,491	704,962	41,993	24,099,163	150,620	192,613
100	378,204	372,970	372,970	130,479	503,449	44,933,791	280,836	418,111	698,947	45,141	24,057,170	150,357	195,498
101	376,384	366,552	366,552	128,148	494,700	44,515,680	278,223	414,758	692,981	48,205	24,012,029	150,075	198,281
102	374,575	360,242	360,242	125,857	486,099	44,100,923	275,631	411,430	687,061	51,188	23,963,824	149,774	200,962
201	235,460	61,932	61,932	19,312	81,245	15,978,416	99,865	183,776	283,641	121,844	12,888,435	80,553	202,396
202	234,395	60,806	60,806	18,925	79,731	15,794,640	98,716	182,266	280,982	121,460	12,766,592	79,791	201,251
203	233,336	59,699	59,699	18,545	78,244	15,612,374	97,577	180,768	278,345	121,069	12,645,131	79,032	200,101
204	232,283	58,611	58,611	18,172	76,783	15,431,606	96,448	179,282	275,729	120,671	12,524,062	78,275	198,946
205	231,235	57,542	57,542	17,806	75,348	15,252,325	95,327	177,807	273,134	120,265	12,403,392	77,521	197,786
206	230,193	56,492	56,492	17,446	73,938	15,074,517	94,216	176,344	270,560	119,852	12,283,127	76,770	196,622
354	124,660	2,559	2,559	32	2,591	98,569	616	49,508	50,124	46,948	93,517	584	47,533
355	124,203	2,493	2,493	16	2,509	49,061	307	49,061	49,368	46,568	46,568	291	46,859
			Par = 63,777,030								Par = 36,222,970		

PSA	Collateral	Average life PAC	Support
50	14.95	7.90	21.50
100	11.51	6.98	19.49
150	9.18	6.98	13.05
200	7.55	6.98	8.55
250	6.37	6.98	5.31
300	5.50	6.98	2.91
350	4.84	6.34	2.71

a total notional principal of $15,333,333:

A's notional principal

$$= \frac{(\$50,000,000)(0.075 - 0.06)}{0.075} = \$10,000,000$$

B's notional principal

$$= \frac{(\$30,000,000)(0.075 - 0.065)}{0.075} = \$4,000,000$$

Z's notional principal

$$= \frac{(\$20,000,000)(0.075 - 0.07)}{0.075} = \$1,333,333$$

Total notional principal

$$= \$15,333,333$$

11.5.2 Planned Amortization Class

Sequential-pay-structured CMOs provide investors with different maturities and average lives. As noted earlier, though, they are still subject to prepayment risk. A CMO with a *planned amortization class, PAC*, though, is structured such that there is virtually no prepayment risk. In a PAC-structured CMO, the underlying mortgage or MBS (i.e., the collateral) is divided into two general tranches: the PAC (also called the PAC bond) and the *support class* (also called the *support bond* or the *companion bond*). The two tranches are formed by generating two monthly principal payment schedules from the collateral; one schedule is based on assuming a relatively low PSA speed, while the other is obtained by assuming a relatively high PSA speed. The PAC bond is then set up so that it will receive a monthly principal payment schedule based on the minimum principal from the two principal payments. Thus, the PAC bond is designed to have no prepayment risk provided the actual prepayment falls within the minimum and maximum assumed PSA speeds. The support bond, on the other hand, receives the remaining principal balance and is therefore subject to prepayment risk.

To illustrate, suppose we form PAC and support bonds from the $100m collateral that we used to construct our sequential-pay tranches (underlying MBS = $100m, WAC = 8%, WAM = 355 months, and PT rate = 7.5%). To generate the minimum monthly principal payments for the PAC, assume a minimum speed of 100% PSA, referred to as the *lower collar*, and a maximum speed of 300% PSA, called the *upper collar*. Table 11.7 shows the principal payments (scheduled and prepaid) for selected months at both collars. The fourth column in the table shows the minimum of the two payments. For example, in the first month the principal payment is $170,085 for the 100% PSA and $374,456 for the 300% PSA; thus, the principal payment for the PAC would be $170,085. In examining the table, note that for the first 98 months the minimum principal payments come from the 100% PSA model, and from month 99 onwards the minimum principal payments come from the 300% PSA model. Based on the 100–300 PSA range, a PAC bond can be formed that would promise to pay the principal based on the minimum principal payment schedule shown in table 11.7. The support bond would receive any excess monthly principal payment. The sum of the PAC's principal payments is $63.777m. Thus, the PAC can be described as having a par value of $63.777m, a coupon rate of 7.5%, a lower collar of 100% PSA, and an upper collar of 300% PSA. The support bond, in turn, would have a par value of $36.223m ($100m − $63.777m) and pay a coupon of 7.5% (see table 11.7).

As noted, the objective in creating a PAC bond is to eliminate prepayment risk. In this example, the PAC bond has no risk as long as the actual prepayment speed is between 100 and 300. This can be seen by calculating the PAC's average life given different prepayment rates. The appended section at the bottom of table 11.7 shows the average lives for the collateral, PAC bond, and support bond for various prepayment speeds ranging from 50% PSA to 350% PSA. As shown, the PAC bond has an average life of 6.98 years between 100% PSA and 300% PSA; its average life does change, though, when prepayment speeds are outside the 100–300 PSA range. In contrast, the support bond's average life changes as prepayment speed changes. In fact, changes in the support bond's average life due to changes in speed are greater than the underlying collateral's responsiveness.

Other PAC-Structured CMOs

The PAC and support bond underlying a CMO can be divided into different classes. Often the

Table 11.8 Stripped IO and PO MBSs (collateral: balance = $100m, WAM = 360, WAC = 8%, PT rate = 8%, PSA = 100%)

| Period | Collateral | | | | | | Stripped | |
| | Balance 100,000,000 | Interest | Scheduled principal | Prepaid principal | Total principal | CF | PO | IO |
Month								
1	100,000,000	666,667	67,098	16,671	83,769	750,435	83,769	666,667
2	99,916,231	666,108	67,534	33,344	100,878	766,986	100,878	666,108
3	99,815,353	665,436	67,961	50,011	117,973	783,409	117,973	665,436
4	99,697,380	664,649	68,380	66,664	135,044	799,694	135,044	664,649
5	99,562,336	663,749	68,790	83,294	152,084	815,833	152,084	663,749
100	58,669,646	391,131	83,852	301,307	385,159	776,290	385,159	391,131
101	58,284,486	388,563	83,977	299,326	383,303	771,866	383,303	388,563
200	27,947,479	186,317	97,308	143,234	240,542	426,858	240,542	186,317
201	27,706,937	184,713	97,453	141,996	239,449	424,162	239,449	184,713
358	371,778	2,479	123,103	1,279	124,382	126,861	124,382	2,479
359	247,395	1,649	123,287	638	123,925	125,574	123,925	1,649
360	123,470	823	123,470	0	123,470	124,293	123,470	823

Price sensitivity

Discount rate	PSA	Value of PO	Value of IO	Value of collateral
8%	150	54,228,764	47,426,196	101,654,960
8.50%	125	49,336,738	49,513,363	98,850,101
9.00%	100	44,044,300	51,795,188	95,799,488

PAC bond is divided into several sequential-pay tranches, with each PAC having a different priority in principal payments over the other. Each sequential-pay PAC, in turn, will have a constant average life if the prepayment speed is within the lower and upper collars. In addition, it is possible that some PACs will have ranges of stability that will increase beyond the actual collar range, expanding their effective collars.

In addition to a sequential structure, a PAC-structured CMO can also be formed with PAC classes having different collars; in fact, some PACs are formed with just one PSA rate. These PACs are referred to as *targeted amortization class (TAC) bonds*. Finally, different types of tranches can be formed out of the support bond class. These include sequential-pay, floating and inverse-floating rate, and accrual bond classes.

Given the different ways in which CMO tranches can be formed, as well as the different objectives of investors, perhaps it is not surprising to find PAC-structured CMOs with as many as 50 tranches. In the mid-1990s, the average number of tranches making up a CMO was 23.[3]

11.5.3 STRIPPED MORTGAGE-BACKED SECURITIES

In the mid-1980s, FNMA introduced *stripped mortgage-backed securities*. Similar to Treasury-stripped securities, stripped MBSs consist of two classes: a *principal-only (PO) class* and an *interest-only (IO) class*. As the names imply, the PO class receives only the principal from the underlying mortgages, while the IO class receives just the interest.

In general, the return on a PO MBS is greater with greater prepayment speed. For example, a PO class formed with $100m of mortgages (principal) and priced at $75m would yield an immediate return of $25m if the mortgage borrowers prepaid immediately. Since investors can reinvest the $25m, this early return will have a greater return per period than a $25m return that is spread out over a longer period. Because of prepayment, the price of a PO MBS tends to be more responsive to interest rate changes than an option-free bond. That is, if interest rates are decreasing, then like the price of most bonds, the price of a PO MBS will increase. In addition, the price of a PO

MBS is also likely to increase further because of the expectation of greater earlier principal payments as a result of an increase in prepayment caused by the lower rates. In contrast, if rates are increasing, the price of a PO MBS will decrease as a result of both lower discount rates and lower returns from slower principal payments. Thus, like most bonds, the prices of PO MBSs are inversely related to interest rates, and, like other MBSs with embedded principal prepayment options, their prices tend to be more responsive to interest rate changes.

Cash flows from an IO MBS come from the interest paid on the mortgages portfolio's principal balance. In contrast to a PO MBS, the cash flows and the returns on an IO MBS will be greater, the slower the prepayment rate. For example, if the mortgages underlying a $100m, 7.5% MBS with PO and IO classes were paid off in the first year, then the IO MBS holders would receive a one-time cash flow of $7.5m = (0.075)($100m). If $50m of the mortgages were prepaid in the first year and the remaining $50m in the second year, then the IO MBS investors would receive an annualized cash flow over 2 years totaling $11.25m = (0.075)($100m) + (0.075) × ($100m − $50m); if the mortgage principal is paid down $25m per year, then the cash flow over 4 years would total $18.75m (= (0.075) × ($100m) + (0.075)($100m − $25m) + (0.075) × ($75m − $25m) + (0.075)($50m − $25m)). Thus, IO MBSs are characterized by an inverse relationship between prepayment speed and returns: the slower the prepayment rate, the greater the total cash flow on an IO MBS. Interestingly, if this relationship dominates the price and discount rate relation, then the price of an IO MBS will vary directly with interest rates.

Examples of a PO MBS and an IO MBS are shown in table 11.8. The stripped MBSs are formed from the collateral described in table 11.1 (mortgage = $100m, WAC = 8%, PT rate = 8%, WAM = 360, and PSA = 100). The appended section at the bottom of table 11.1, in turn, shows the values of the collateral, PO MBS, and IO MBS for different discount rate and PSA combinations of 8% and 150, 8.5% and 125, and 9% and 100. As shown in the table, the IO MBS is characterized by a direct relation between its value and rate of return.

Note that issuers can form IO and PO classes not only with MBSs, but also with CMOs. For example, one of the tranches of the PAC-structured CMOs or sequential-structured CMOs discussed in the preceding sections could be divided into an IO class and a PO class. Such tranches are referred to as *CMO strips*. CMOs can also be formed from PO MBSs. These CMOs are called *PO-collateralized CMOs*.

Web Information
For information on the market for mortgage-backed securities go to
  www.bondmarkets.com

and click on "Research Statistics" and "Mortgage-Backed Securities." For information on links to other sites click on "Gateway to Related Links."

11.6 EVALUATING MORTGAGE-BACKED SECURITIES

Like all securities, MBSs can be evaluated in terms of their characteristics. With MBSs, such an evaluation is more complex because of the difficulty in estimating cash flows due to prepayment. Two approaches are used to evaluate MBS and CMO tranches: yield analysis and Monte Carlo simulation.

11.6.1 Yield Analysis

Yield analysis involves calculating the yields on MBSs or CMO tranches given different prices and prepayment speed assumptions or alternatively calculating the values on MBSs or tranches given different rates and speeds. For example, suppose an institutional investor is interested in buying an MBS issue described by the collateral in table 11.2. This MBS issue has a par value of $100m, WAC of 8%, WAM of 355 months, and a PT rate of 7.5%. The value, as well as average life, maturity, duration, and other characteristics of this security would depend on the rate the investor requires on the MBS and the prepayment speed she estimates. If the investor's required return on the MBS is 9% and her estimate of the PSA speed is 150, then she would value the MBS issue at $93,702,142. At that rate and speed, the MBS would have an average life of 9.18 years (see table 11.9). Whether a purchase of the MBS issue at $93,702,142 to yield 9% represents a good investment depends, in part, on rates for other securities with similar maturities, durations, and risk, and in part, on how good the prepayment rate assumption is. For example, if the investor felt that the prepayment rate should be 100% PSA and her required rate with that level of prepayment is 9%, then she would

Table 11.9 Cash flow analysis (mortgage portfolio = $100m, WAC = 8%, WAM = 355 months, PT rate = 7.5%)

Rate/PSA	50	100	150
		Value	
7%	106,039,631	105,043,489	104,309,207
8%	98,251,269	98,526,830	98,732,083
9%	91,442,890	92,732,145	93,702,142
10%	85,457,483	87,554,145	89,146,871
Average life	14.95	11.51	9.18
		Vector	
		Month range: PSA	
	1–50: 200	1–50: 200	1–50: 200
	51–150: 250	51–150: 300	51–150: 150
	151–250: 150	151–250: 350	151–250: 100
	251–355: 200	251–355: 400	251–355: 50
Rate		*Value*	
7%	103,729,227	103,473,139	104,229,758
8%	98,893,974	98,964,637	98,756,370
9%	94,465,328	94,794,856	93,826,053
10%	90,395,704	90,929,474	89,364,229

price the MBS issue at $92,732,145 and the average life would be 11.51 years. In general, for many institutional investors the decision on whether or not to invest in a particular MBS or tranche depends on the price the institution can command. For example, based on an expectation of a 100% PSA, our investor might conclude that a yield of 9% on the MBS would make it a good investment. In this case, the investor would be willing to offer no more than $92,732,145 for the MBS issue.

One common approach used in conducting a yield analysis is to generate a matrix of different yields by varying the prices and prepayment speeds. Table 11.9 shows the different values for our illustrative MBS given different required rates and different prepayment speeds. Using this matrix, an investor could determine, for a given price and assumed speed, the estimated yield, or determine, for a given speed and yield, the price. Using this approach, an investor can also evaluate for each price the average yield and standard deviation over a range of PSA speeds.

One of the limitations of the above yield analysis is the assumption that the PSA speed used to estimate the yield is constant during the life of the MBS; in fact, such an analysis is sometimes referred to as *static yield analysis*. In practice, prepayment speeds change over the life of an MBS as interest rates change in the market. To address this, a more dynamic yield analysis, known as *vector analysis*, can be used. In applying vector analysis, PSA speeds are assumed to change over time. In the above case, a matrix of values for different rates can be obtained for different PSA vectors formed by dividing the total period into a number of periods with different PSA speeds assumed for each period. A vector analysis example is also shown in table 11.9.

11.6.2 Monte Carlo Simulation

Monte Carlo simulation involves generating a set of cash flows for an MBS or CMO tranche based on simulated future interest rates. From the cash flows, the value of the MBS can be determined given the assumed rates and an assumed speed. The simulation involves first generating a number of interest rate paths; next, estimating the cash flow for each path based on a prepayment model that is dependent on the assumed interest rates; third, determining the present values of each path's cash flows; and last, calculating the average value and standard deviation of the distribution of values from the assumed paths. The average value is referred to as the theoretical value; it can be compared to the market price of the MBS or tranche to determine if it is over- or underpriced.

Interest Rate Paths

The first step in the simulation process is to generate interest rate paths. This can be done by using a binomial interest rate tree model. Typically, the trees are generated for monthly spot rates and for mortgage refinancing rates, with the length of each period being one month and with the number of periods equaling the maturity of the MBS or tranche (e.g., 360 months). From these trees, thousands of interest rate paths can be generated. Exhibit 11.2 shows a simpler (and more manageable) three-period interest rate tree defined for a 1-year spot rate, S_t, and a mortgage refinancing rate with a maturity between 7 and 10 years, R_t^{ref}, with the length of each period being 1 year. Both the 1-year spot rates and the refinancing rates shown in the exhibit are derived by assuming that in each period the rates will either increase to equal a proportion $u = 1.1$ of the beginning period's rate or decrease to equal a proportion $d = 0.9091$ of that rate. With this three-period binomial process, there are four possible rates at the end of the third period for the spot and refinancing rates, and as shown at the bottom of the exhibit, there are eight possible interest rate paths. For example, to get to the third-period spot rate of 4.508%, there is one path (rates decreasing three consecutive periods); to get to rate 5.4546% there are three paths (decrease in the first period, decrease in the second period, and increase in the third; decrease in the first, increase in the second, and decrease in the third; increasing in the first and then decreasing in the second and third); to get to rate 6.6%, there are also three paths; to get to rate 7.986, there is one path.

Estimating Cash Flows

The second step is to estimate the cash flow for each interest rate path. The cash flow depends on the prepayment rates assumed. As noted, most

Exhibit 11.2   Binomial tree for spot and refinancing rates

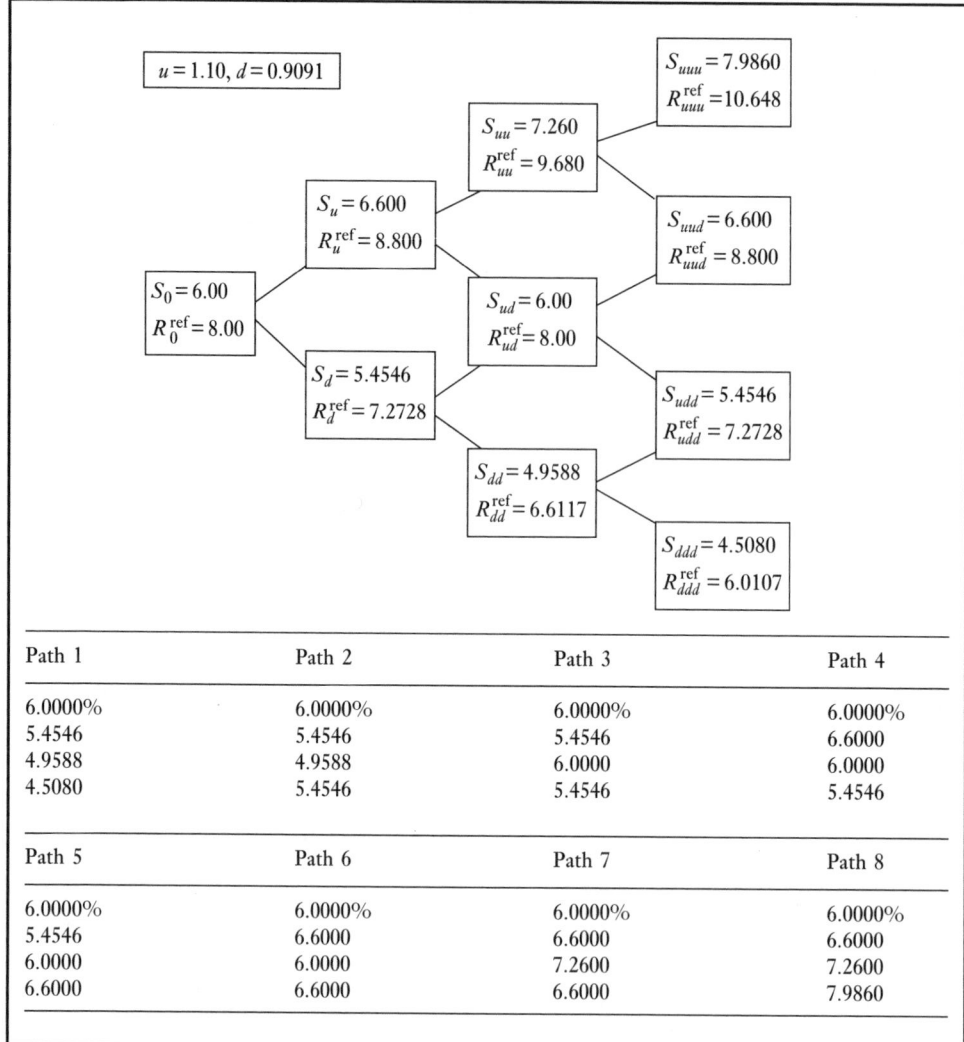

Path 1	Path 2	Path 3	Path 4
6.0000%	6.0000%	6.0000%	6.0000%
5.4546	5.4546	5.4546	6.6000
4.9588	4.9588	6.0000	6.0000
4.5080	5.4546	5.4546	5.4546

Path 5	Path 6	Path 7	Path 8
6.0000%	6.0000%	6.0000%	6.0000%
5.4546	6.6000	6.6000	6.6000
6.0000	6.0000	7.2600	7.2600
6.6000	6.6000	6.6000	7.9860

analysts use a prepayment model in which the conditional prepayment rate (CPR) is determined by the seasonality of the mortgages, and by a refinancing incentive that ties the interest rate paths to the proportion of the mortgage collateral prepaid. To illustrate, consider an MBS formed from a mortgage pool with a par value of $1m, WAC$=8\%$, and WAM$=$ 10 years. To fit this example with the 3-year binomial tree assume that the mortgages in the pool all make annual cash flows (instead of monthly); all have a balloon payment at the end

of year 4; and the pass-through rate on the MBS is equal to the WAC of 8%.[4] Thus, the mortgage pool can be viewed as a 4-year asset with a principal payment made at the end of year 4 that is equal to the original principal less the amount paid down. As shown in table 11.10, if there were no prepayments, then the pool would generate cash flows of $149,029m each year and a balloon payment of $688,946 at the end of year 4.

Such a cash flow is, of course, unlikely given prepayment. A simple prepayment model to apply to this mortgage pool is shown in

Table 11.10 Cash flows from an MBS (par value = $1m, WAC = 8%, WAM = 10 years, PT rate = 8%, balloon at end of 4th year, annual cash flows, and no prepayment)

Year	Balance	p	Interest	Scheduled principal	Cash flow
1	$1,000,000	$149,029	$80,000	$69,029	$149,029
2	$930,971	$149,029	$74,478	$74,552	$149,029
3	$856,419	$149,029	$68,513	$80,516	$149,029
4	$775,903	$149,029	$62,072	$86,957	$837,975

Balloon = Balance(year 4) − Scheduled principal(year 4)
      = $775,903 − $86,957 = $688,946
CF_4 = Balloon + p
      = $688,946 + $149,029 = $837,975
CF_4 = Balance(year 4) + Interest
      = $775,903 + $62,072 = $837,975

Table 11.11 Prepayment model

Range $X = WAC - R^{ref}$	CPR (%)
$X \leq 0$	5
$0.0\% < X \leq 0.5\%$	10
$0.5\% < X \leq 1.0\%$	20
$1.0\% < X \leq 1.5\%$	30
$1.5\% < X \leq 2.0\%$	40
$2.0\% < X \leq 2.5\%$	50
$2.5\% < X \leq 3.0\%$	60
$X > 3.0\%$	70

table 11.11. The model assumes the annual CPR is equal to 5% if the mortgage pool rate is at a par or discount (that is, if the current refinancing rate is equal to the WAC of 8% or greater). If the rate on the mortgage pool is at a premium, though, the model assumes that the CPR will exceed 5% and that it will increase within certain ranges as the premium increases. Finally, for simplicity the model posits that the relationship between the CPRs and the range of rates is the same in each period; that is, there is no seasoning factor.

With this prepayment model, cash flows can be generated for the eight interest rate paths. These cash flows are shown in table 11.12. As shown, the cash flows for path 1 (the path with three consecutive decreases in rates) consist of $335,224 in year 1 (interest = $80,000, scheduled principal = $69,029.49, and prepaid principal = $186,194.10, reflecting a CPR of 0.20), $324,764 in year 2, with $205,540 being prepaid principal (CPR = 0.30), $257,259 in year 3, with $173,802 being prepaid principal

(CPR = 0.40), and $281,560 in year 4. The year 4 cash flow with the balloon payment is equal to the principal balance at the beginning of the year and the 8% interest on that balance. In contrast, the cash flows for path 8 (the path with three consecutive interest rate increases) are smaller in the first 3 years and larger in year 4, reflecting the low CPR of 5% in each period.

Valuing Each Path

Like any bond, an MBS or CMO tranche should be valued by discounting the cash flows by the appropriate risk-adjusted spot rates. For an MBS or CMO tranche, the risk-adjusted spot rate, z_t, is equal to the riskless spot rate, S_t, plus a risk premium. If the underlying mortgages are insured against default, then the risk premium would only reflect the additional return needed to compensate investors for the prepayment risk they are assuming. As noted in chapter 4, this premium is referred to as the option-adjusted spread (OAS). If we assume no default risk, then the risk-adjusted spot rate can be defined as

$$z_t = S_t + k_t$$

where $k = $ OAS, and the value of each path can be defined as:

$$V_i^{Path} = \sum_{M=1}^{T} \frac{CF_M}{(1 + z_M)^M}$$

$$= \frac{CF_1}{1 + z_1} + \frac{CF_2}{(1 + z_2)^2} + \frac{CF_3}{(1 + z_3)^3} + \cdots$$

$$+ \frac{CF_T}{(1 + z_T)^T}$$

Table 11.12   Cash flow analysis of an MBS

Year	1 R^{ret}	2 Balance	WAC	3 Interest	4 Sch. prin.	5 CPR	6 Prepaid prin.	7 CF	8 $z_{1,t-1}$	9 z_{t0}	10 Value	11 Prob.
Path 1												
1	0.072728	1,000,000	0.08	80,000	69,029	0.20	186,194	335,224	0.080000	0.080000	310,392	0.5
2	0.066117	744,776	0.08	59,582	59,641	0.30	205,540	324,764	0.074546	0.077270	279,846	0.5
3	0.060107	479,594	0.08	38,368	45,089	0.40	173,802	257,259	0.069588	0.074703	207,255	0.5
4		260,703	0.08	20,856				281,560	0.065080	0.072289	212,972	
										Value =	1,010,465	0.125
Path 2												
1	0.072728	1,000,000	0.08	80,000	69,029	0.20	186,194	335,224	0.080000	0.080000	310,392	0.5
2	0.066117	744,776	0.08	59,582	59,641	0.30	205,540	324,764	0.074546	0.077270	279,846	0.5
3	0.072728	479,594	0.08	38,368	45,089	0.20	86,901	170,358	0.069588	0.074703	137,245	0.5
4		347,604	0.08	27,808				375,413	0.074546	0.074664	281,461	
										Value =	1,008,945	0.125
Path 3												
1	0.072728	1,000,000	0.08	80,000	69,029	0.20	186,194	335,224	0.080000	0.080000	310,392	0.5
2	0.080000	744,776	0.08	59,582	59,641	0.05	34,257	153,480	0.074546	0.077270	132,253	0.5
3	0.072728	650,878	0.08	52,070	61,192	0.20	117,937	231,200	0.080000	0.078179	184,465	0.5
4		471,749	0.08	37,740				509,489	0.074546	0.077270	378,301	
										Value =	1,005,411	0.125
Path 4												
1	0.088000	1,000,000	0.08	80,000	69,029	0.05	46,549	195,578	0.080000	0.080000	181,091	0.5
2	0.080000	884,422	0.08	70,754	70,824	0.05	40,680	182,258	0.086000	0.082996	155,393	0.5
3	0.072728	772,918	0.08	61,833	72,666	0.20	140,050	274,550	0.080000	0.081996	216,742	0.5
4		560,202	0.08	44,816				605,018	0.074546	0.080129	444,494	
										Value =	997,720	0.125
Path 5												
1	0.072728	1,000,000	0.08	80,000	69,029	0.20	186,194	335,224	0.080000	0.080000	310,392	0.5
2	0.080000	744,776	0.08	59,582	59,641	0.05	34,257	153,480	0.074546	0.077270	132,253	0.5
3	0.088000	650,878	0.08	52,070	61,192	0.05	29,484	142,747	0.080000	0.078179	113,892	0.5
4		560,202	0.08	44,816				605,018	0.086000	0.080129	444,494	
										Value =	1,001,031	0.125
Path 6												
1	0.088000	1,000,000	0.08	80,000	69,029	0.05	46,549	195,578	0.080000	0.080000	181,091	0.5
2	0.080000	884,422	0.08	70,754	70,824	0.05	40,680	182,258	0.086000	0.082996	155,393	0.5
3	0.088000	772,918	0.08	61,833	72,666	0.05	35,013	169,512	0.080000	0.081996	133,820	0.5
4		665,240	0.08	53,219				718,459	0.086000	0.082996	522,269	
										Value =	992,574	0.125
Path 7												
1	0.088000	1,000,000	0.08	80,000	69,029	0.05	46,549	195,578	0.080000	0.080000	181,091	0.5
2	0.096000	884,422	0.08	70,754	70,824	0.05	40,680	182,258	0.086000	0.082996	155,393	0.5
3	0.088000	772,918	0.08	61,833	72,666	0.05	35,013	169,512	0.092600	0.086188	132,277	0.5
4		665,240	0.08	53,219				718,459	0.086000	0.086141	516,247	
										Value =	985,008	0.125
Path 8												
1	0.088000	1,000,000	0.08	80,000	69,029	0.05	46,549	195,578	0.080000	0.080000	181,091	0.5
2	0.096000	884,422	0.08	70,754	70,824	0.05	40,680	182,258	0.086000	0.082996	155,393	0.5
3	0.106480	772,918	0.08	61,833	72,666	0.05	35,013	169,512	0.092600	0.086188	132,277	0.5
4		665,240	0.08	53,219				718,459	0.099860	0.089590	509,741	
										Value =	978,502	0.125
										Wt. value	$997,457	

where:

$i = i$th path

$z_M =$ spot rate on bond with M-year maturity

$T =$ maturity of the MBS

For this example, assume the option-adjusted spread is 2% greater than the 1-year, riskless spot rates shown in table 11.12. From these current and future 1-year spot rates, the current 1-year, 2-year, 3-year, and 4-year equilibrium spot rates can be obtained for each path by using the geometric mean:

$$z_M = \left((1 + z_{10})(1 + z_{11}) \cdots (1 + z_{1, M-1})\right)^{1/M} - 1$$

Thus, the set of spot rates z_1, z_2, z_3, and z_4 needed to discount the cash flows for path 1 would be:

$z_1 = 0.08$

$z_2 = \left((1 + z_{10})(1 + z_{11})\right)^{1/2} - 1$

$\quad = \left((1.08)(1.074546)\right)^{1/2} - 1 = 0.07727$

$z_3 = \left((1 + z_{10})(1 + z_{11})(1 + z_{12})\right)^{1/3} - 1$

$\quad = \left((1.08)(1.074546)(1.069588)\right)^{1/3} - 1$

$\quad = 0.074703$

$z_4 = \left((1 + z_{10})(1 + z_{11})(1 + z_{12})(1 + z_{13})\right)^{1/4} - 1$

$\quad = \left((1.08)(1.074546)(1.069588)(1.06508)\right)^{1/4} - 1$

$\quad = 0.072289$

Using these rates, the value of the MBS following path 1 is $1,010,465:

$$V_1^{\text{Path}} = \frac{\$335,224}{1.08} + \frac{\$324,764}{(1.07727)^2} + \frac{\$257,259}{(1.074703)^3}$$

$$+ \frac{\$281,560}{(1.072289)^4}$$

$$= \$1,010,465$$

The spot rates and values of each of the eight paths are shown in columns 9 and 10 in table 11.12.

Theoretical Value

In a Monte Carlo simulation, the *theoretical value of the MBS* is defined as the average of the values of all the interest rate paths:

$$\bar{V} = \frac{1}{N} \sum_{i=1}^{N} V_i^{\text{path}}$$

In this example, the theoretical value of the MBS issue is $997,457 or 99.7457% of its par value (see bottom of table 11.12).

The theoretical value along with the standard deviation of the path values are useful measures in evaluating an MBS or CMO tranche relative to other securities. An MBS's theoretical value can also be compared to its actual price to determine if the MBS is over- or underpriced. For example, if the theoretical value is 98% of par and the actual price is at 96%, then the mortgage security is underpriced, "$2 cheap," and if it is priced at par, then it is considered overpriced, "$2 rich."

Option-Adjusted Spread and Other Parameters

Instead of determining the theoretical value of the MBS or tranche given a path of spot rates and option-adjusted spreads, analysts can use a Monte Carlo simulation to estimate the mortgage security's rate of return given its market price. Since the security's rate of return is equal to a riskless spot rate plus the OAS (assuming no default risk), most analysts use the simulation to estimate just the OAS. From the simulation, the OAS is determined by finding that OAS which makes the theoretical value of the MBS equal to its market price. This spread can be found by iteratively solving for the k that satisfies the following equation:

Market price

$$= \frac{1}{N} \left(\left[\sum_{M=1}^{T} \frac{CF_{(1)M}}{(1 + S_{(1)M} + k)^M} \right] \right.$$

$$+ \left[\sum_{M=1}^{T} \frac{CF_{(2)M}}{(1 + S_{(2)M} + k)^M} \right] + \cdots$$

$$\left. + \left[\sum_{M=1}^{T} \frac{CF_{(N)M}}{(1 + S_{(N)M} + k)^M} \right] \right)$$

where N is the number of paths.

In addition to estimating the theoretical value, OAS, and standard deviation, a Monte Carlo simulation can be used to estimate the average life of each path, and from that the mean and standard deviation of the average life of all the paths.

11.7 OTHER ASSET-BACKED SECURITIES

MBSs represent the largest and most extensively developed asset-backed security. Since 1985, a number of other asset-backed securities have been developed. The three most common types are those backed by automobile loans, credit card receivables, and home equity loans. These asset-backed securities are structured as pass-throughs and many have tranches.

11.7.1 Automobile Loan-Backed Securities

Automobile loan-backed securities are often referred to as *CARs (certificates for automobile receivables)*. The automobile loans underlying these securities are similar to mortgages in that borrowers make regular monthly payments that include interest and a scheduled principal. Also like mortgages, automobile loans are characterized by prepayment. For such loans, prepayment can occur as a result of car sales, trade-ins, repossessions and subsequent resales, wrecks, and refinancing when rates are low. Finally like MBSs, CARs are . structured as PACs. CARs differ from MBSs in that they have much shorter lives, their prepayment rates are less influenced by interest rates than mortgage prepayment rates, and they are subject to greater default risk.

11.7.2 Credit-Card Receivable-Backed Securities

Credit-card receivable-backed securities are commonly referred to as *CARDs (certificates for amortizing revolving debts)*. In contrast to MBSs and CARs, CARDs' investors do not receive an amortized principal payment as part of their monthly cash flow. Instead, CARDs are often structured with two periods. In one period, known as the *lockout period*, all principal payments made on the receivables are retained and either reinvested in other receivables or invested in other securities. In the other period, known as the *principal-amortization period*, all current and accumulated principal payments are paid.

11.7.3 Home Equity Loan-Backed Securities

Home-equity loan-backed securities are referred to as *HELSs*. They are similar to MBSs in that they pay a monthly cash flow consisting of interest, scheduled principal, and prepaid principal. In contrast to mortgages, the home equity loans securing HELSs tend to have a shorter maturity and different factors influencing their prepayment rates.

> **Web Information**
> For information on the market for asset-backed securities go to
>   www.bondmarkets.com
> and click on "Research Statistics" and "Asset-Backed Securities."

11.8 CONCLUSION

Up until the mid-seventies most mortgages originated when savings and loans, commercial banks, and other thrifts borrowed funds or used their deposits to provide loans, possibly later selling the resulting instruments in the secondary market to FNMA or GNMA. To a large degree, residential real estate until then was financed by individual deposits, with little financing coming from institutional investors. In an effort to attract institutional investors' funds away from corporate bonds and other securities, as well as to minimize their poor hedge, financial institutions began to sell mortgage-backed securities. Over time, these securities were structured in different ways (as PACs, POs, IOs, etc.) to make them more attractive to different types of investors. Today, MBSs are becoming one of the most popular securities held by institutional investors, competing with a number of different types of bonds for inclusion in the portfolio of institutional investors. More significantly, they have revolutionized the way in which real estate is financed.

KEY TERMS

Securitization
Originator
Asset-Backed Security or
  Pass-Through
Mortgage-Backed Securities
  (MBSs) or Mortgage
  Pass-Throughs
Mortgage Bankers
Graduated Payment
  Mortgages (GPMs)
Reset Mortgages
Loan-to-Value Ratio
Prepayment Risk
Prepayment Speed or Speed
Weighted Average Coupon
  Rate (WAC)
Conditional Prepayment Rate
  (CPR)
Seasoning
PSA Model (Public Securities
  Association)
Single Monthly Mortality
  Rate (SMM)
Monthly Factors
Burnout Factor
Agency Pass-Throughs
Conventional Pass-
  Throughs

Fully Modified Pass-
  Through
Modified Pass-Through
Private Labels
A/B Pass-Through
Real Estate Mortgage
  Investment Conduits
  (REMICs)
Pass-Through (PT) Rate
Mortgage-Backed Security
  Dealers Association
Pool Factor (pf)
Extension Risk
Average Life
Collateralized Mortgage
  Obligations (CMOs)
Tranches
Sequential-Pay CMO
Principal Pay-Down
  Window
Accrual Bond Class
Z Bond
Notional Interest-Only (IO)
  Class
Planned Amortization Class
  (PAC)
Support Class or Support
  Bond or Companion Bond

Lower Collar
Upper Collar
Targeted Amortization
  Class (TAC) Bonds
Agency CMOs
Private-Labeled CMOs
Whole-Loan CMOs
Stripped Mortgage-Backed
  Securities
Principal-Only (PO) Class
Interest-Only (IO) Class
CMO Strips
PO-Collateralized CMOs
Static Yield Analysis
Vector Analysis
Theoretical Value of
  the MBS
CARs (Certificates for
  Automobile Receivables)
CARDs (Certificates For
  Amortizing Revolving
  Debts)
Lockout Period
Principal-Amortization
  Period
Home-Equity Loan-
  Backed Securities
  (HELSs)

PROBLEMS AND QUESTIONS

1. Suppose ABC Bank has a fixed-rate mortgage portfolio with the following features:

   - Mortgage portfolio balance = $100,000,000
   - Weighted average coupon rate (WAC) = 8%
   - Weighted average maturity (WAM) = 360 months
   - Estimated prepayment speed = 150 PSA.

   Calculate the figures required to complete the table below.

Item	Month 1	Month 2
Balance	100,000,000	
Interest	666,667	
P	733,765	
Scheduled principal		
CPR		
SMM		
Prepaid principal		
Total principal		
Cash flow		

2. Suppose ABC Bank in question 1 sells mortgage-backed securities backed by its $100m portfolio of fixed-rate mortgages with the MBS having the following features:

   - Mortgage collateral = $100,000,000
   - Weighted average coupon rate (WAC) = 8%
   - Weighted average maturity (WAM) = 360 months
   - Estimated prepayment speed = 150 PSA
   - MBS pass-through rate = PT rate = 7%
   - ABC will service the mortgage portfolio.

   a. Follow the outline table below, and calculate the first 2 months of cash flows going to the MBS investors.

Item	Month 1	Month 2
Balance	100,000,000	
Interest	583,333	
P	733,765	
Scheduled principal		
CPR		
SMM		
Prepaid principal		
Total principal		
Cash flow		

   b. What compensation would ABC receive for servicing the mortgages?

3. Suppose the standard (100) prepayment profile for 10-year (120-month) conventional mortgages is one in which the CPR starts at zero and increases at a constant 0.2% per month rate for 20 months to equal 4% at the 20th month; then after the 20th month the CPR stays at a constant 4%.

   a. Show graphically the 100% prepayment profile.
   b. In the same graph show the prepayment profile for speeds of 200%, 150%, and 50% of the standard.
   c. Using the outline table below, work out the first month cash flow for an MBS portfolio of 10-year mortgages with the following features:

   - Mortgage collateral = $50,000,000
   - Weighted average coupon rate (WAC) = 9%
   - Weighted average maturity (WAM) = 120 months

- Estimated prepayment speed = 200 PSA
- MBS pass-through rate = PT rate = 8.5%.

Item	Month 1
Balance	
Interest	
P	
Scheduled principal	
CPR	
SMM	
Prepaid principal	
Total principal	
Cash flow	

4. Explain some of the factors that determine the prepayment speed on a mortgage portfolio.

5. Define agency pass-throughs and describe some of their features.

6. Define conventional pass-throughs and describe some of their features.

7. What is the market value (clean price) of an 8% MBS issue backed by a mortgage pool with an original par value of $100m, if its price is quoted at 105-16 with a pool factor of 0.95? What would be the invoice price that an institutional investor holding $10m of par value of these bonds would receive if she sold her holdings at 105-16 when there were 10 days on the settlement date on the sale and the first day of the next month?

8. Explain how interest rate changes affect an MBS differently from an option-free bond.

9. Explain the relationship between extension risk, prepayment risk, and average life.

10. What was the primary motivation behind the creation of MBS derivatives in the 1980s?

11. Explain how the following CMOs are constructed and their features:
    a. Sequential-pay tranche
    b. Sequential-pay tranches with an accrual bond tranche
    c. Floating-rate and inverse floating-rate tranches
    d. Notional IO tranche
    e. PAC and support bonds
    f. Sequential-pay PAC.

12. Explain the interest rate and value relation for a principal-only stripped MBS and an interest-only stripped MBS.

13. Suppose an interest-only and principal-only stripped MBS are formed from the following mortgage collateral:
    - Mortgage collateral = $100,000,000
    - Weighted average coupon rate (WAC) = 8%
    - Weighted average maturity (WAM) = 360 months
    - Estimated prepayment speed = 150 PSA
    - MBS pass-through rate = PT rate = 7.5%.

Calculate the figures required to complete the table below.

Period: month	Collateral: balance	Collateral: interest	Collateral: scheduled principal	Collateral: prepaid principal	Collateral: total principal	Stripped PO: cash flow	Stripped IO: cash flow
1	100,000,000						
2							

14. Given the following mortgage collateral and sequential-pay CMO:

  - Mortgage collateral = $100,000,000
  - Weighted average coupon rate (WAC) = 8%
  - Weighted Average Maturity (WAM) = 360 months
  - Estimated prepayment speed = 150 PSA
  - MBS pass-through rate = PT rate = 7.5%.

Sequential-pay CMO:

  - Tranche A receives all principal payment from the collateral until its principal of $50m is retired.
  - Tranche B receives its principal of $50m after A's principal is paid.
  - Tranche B receives interest each period equal to its stated coupon rate of 7.5% times its outstanding balance at the beginning of each month.

a. Calculate the figures required to complete the table below.

Month	Collateral: balance	Collateral: interest	Collateral: principal	A Balance	A Interest	A Principal	B Balance	B Principal	B Interest
1	100,000,000								
92	50,324,347	314,527	460,885	324,347	2,027	324,347	50,000,000	136,538	312,500
93	49,863,462	311,647	457,196						

b. Suppose the CMO has a PT rate of 7% on Tranche A, a rate of 6.5% on Tranche B, and a notional principal. What would Tranche A's and Tranche B's interest receipts be in the first month? What would the notional principal tranche's cash flow be in the first month? What would be the quoted principal on the notional principal tranche?

15. Given the following mortgage collateral and sequential-pay CMO:

  - Mortgage collateral = $100,000,000
  - Weighted average coupon rate (WAC) = 8%
  - Weighted average maturity (WAM) = 360 months
  - Estimated prepayment speed = 150 PSA
  - MBS pass-through rate = PT rate = 7.5%.

Sequential-pay CMO:

  - Tranche A receives all principal payment from the collateral until its principal of $50m is retired.
  - Tranche B receives its principal of $25m after A's principal is paid.
  - Tranche B receives interest each period equal to its stated coupon rate of 7.5% times its outstanding balance at the beginning of each month.
  - Tranche Z is an accrual bond that receives its principal of $25m after B's principal is paid.

a. Calculate the figures required to complete the table below.

Month	Collateral: balance	Collateral: interest	Collateral: principal	A Balance	A Interest	A Principal	B Balance	B Principal	B Interest	Z Balance	Z Principal	Z Interest
1	100,000,000	625,000	92,116									
2	99,907,884	624,424	117,586									
70	61,458,838	384,118	549,863	677,588	4,235	677,588	25,000,000	28,525	156,250	35,781,250	0	0
71	60,908,975	380,681	545,475	0	0	0	24,971,475	701,725	156,071	35,937,500	0	0
111	42,171,175	263,570	395,531	0	0	0	0	0	0	42,171,175	395,531	263,570

b. Suppose the CMO has a PT rate of 7% on Tranche A, a PT rate of 6.5% on Tranche B (Tranche Z's rate stays at 7.5%), and a notional principal tranche. What would Tranche A's and Tranche B's interests receipts be in the first month? What would the notional principal tranche's cash flow be in the first month? What would be the quoted principal on the notional principal tranche?

16. Given the following mortgage collateral and PAC:

- Mortgage collateral $= \$100,000,000$
- Weighted average coupon rate (WAC) $= 8\%$
- Weighted average maturity (WAM) $= 360$ months
- Estimated prepayment speed $= 150$ PSA
- MBS pass-through rate $=$ PT rate $= 7.5\%$
- PAC formed from the collateral with a lower collar of 100 and upper collar of 300
- Support bond receiving the residual principal.

Complete the table:

Month	Collateral: balance	Collateral: interest	Collateral: principal	PAC: low PSA principal	PAC: high PSA principal	PAC: minimum principal	Support: principal
1	100,000,000						

17. What is yield analysis? Explain the difference between static yield analysis and vector analysis.

18. Explain the process involved in applying a Monte Carlo simulation using a binomial interest rate tree to value a mortgage portfolio or the collateral on an MBS.

19. Explain how the following asset-backed securities are constructed and their features:

a. CARs
b. CARDs
c. HELSs.

20. Using a Monte Carlo simulation approach, determine the theoretical value of an MBS issue with a face value of $1,000,000, WAC $= 8\%$, WAM $= 10$ years, PT rate $= 8\%$, *annual* cash flows (instead of the standard monthly), and a balloon at the end of the *second* year.

Assume:

- The current 1-year spot rate is $S_0 = 6\%$ and the current refinancing rate is $R_0^{\text{ref}} = 8\%$.
- The future spot and refinancing rates can both be described by a *two*-period binomial interest rate where $u = 1.1$, $d = 1/1.1$, the length of the period is 1 year, and $q = 0.5$.

- The following prepayment model applies:

  $CPR = 20\%$ if $(WAC - R^{ref}) > 0$

  $CPR = 5\%$ if $(WAC - R^{ref}) \leq 0$.

- A risk-adjusted 1-year spot rate is equal to the spot rate plus an option-adjusted spread of 2%: $S^{RA} = S + 2\%$.

21. Using the MBScollateral Excel program, create an Excel table for the following MBS:
    - Mortgage collateral $= \$50,000,000$
    - WAC $= 7\%$
    - PT rate $= 6.5$
    - WAM $= 350$
    - Seasoning $= 10$
    - PSA $= 75\%$.

    Note: in your table, you may want to hide many of the rows and some of the columns. Do keep columns for period, balance, interest, scheduled principal, prepaid principal, and cash flow.

22. Using the MBScollateral program, determine for the MBS in question 21 the values and average lives for the following yield analysis matrix:

Discount rate/PSA	50	150
	Value	Value
5%		
6%		
7%		
8%		
Average life		

23. Using the MBScollateral Excel program, create an Excel table for a principal-only stripped MBS and interest-only stripped MBS formed from the MBS described in question 21. In your table, hide many of the rows and hide all columns *except* the ones for period, collateral balance, collateral interest, collateral principal, cash flow for PO strip, and cash flow for IO strip.

24. Using the MBScollateral program:

    a. Determine the values for the following yield analysis matrix for the PO and IO strip MBSs in question 23.

PSA/discount rate	50 PO	50 IO	150 PO	150 IO
	Value	Value	Value	Value
5%				
6%				
7%				
8%				

b. Given that PSA speeds increase as rates decrease, determine the values for the IO strip MBS for the following discount rate and PSA pairs.

Discount rate	PSA	Value of IO strip
5%	200	
6%	150	
7%	100	
8%	50	

c. Comment on the interest rate and value relation you observe.

25. Given the following MBS:
    - Mortgage collateral = $100,000,000
    - Weighted average coupon rate (WAC) = 6%
    - Weighted average maturity (WAM) = 180 months
    - Standard (100%) prepayment model
      - Number of periods to fixed CPR = 15
      - Fixed CPR = 0.06
      - Seasoning = 0
    - MBS pass-through rate = PT rate = 5.5%.

    Determine the values and average lives for the following discount rate and prepayment speed pairs:

Discount rate, speed (as % of standard)	Value	Average life
5%,	200	
6%,	150	
7%,	100	
8%,	50	

26. Given the following sequential-pay CMO with a notional IO tranche formed from the MBS in question 25:
    - Tranche A receives all principal payment first from the collateral until its principal of $50m is retired. Its interest is 5.5%.
    - Tranche B receives its principal of $25m after A's principal is paid. Its PT rate is 5%.
    - Tranche C receives its principal of $25m after A's principal is paid. Its PT rate is 5%.
    - Notional IO tranche that receives the residual interest.

    a. Using the MBSseqNIO Excel program, create an Excel table for the CMO. Assume the estimated PSA is 150. In your table, hide many of the rows and hide all columns *except* the ones for the period, the balance, interest, and principal for the collateral and each tranche, and the cash flows for the notional class.
    b. Using the MBSseqNIO Excel program, determine the average lives and windows for the collateral and each tranche:

	Window	Average life
Collateral		
Tranche A		
Tranche B		
Tranche C		

   c. What is the principal for the notional IO tranche?

27. Given the following mortgage collateral and PAC:
   - Mortgage collateral = $100,000,000
   - Weighted average coupon rate (WAC) = 7%
   - Weighted average maturity (WAM) = 350 months
   - Seasoning = 10 months
   - Estimated prepayment speed = 150 PSA
   - MBS pass-through rate = PT rate = 6.5%
   - PAC formed from the collateral with a lower collar of 100 and upper collar of 300
   - Support bond receiving the residual principal.

   a. Using the MBSpac Excel program, create an Excel table for the CMO. In your table, hide many of the rows and hide all columns *except* for the following: period, the balance, interest, and principal for the collateral, the interest, lower collar principal, upper collar principal, PAC principal, and cash flow for the PAC bond, and principal, interest, and cash flow for the support bond.

   b. Using the MBSpac Excel program, determine the average life for the collateral, PAC bond, and support bond given the PSA speeds shown in the table:

PSA	Collateral Average life	PAC Average life	Support Average life
50			
100			
150			
200			
250			
300			
350			

   c. Comment on the PAC's average life given the different PSA speeds.

WEB EXERCISES

1. Learn more about agency MBSs by going to their websites: www.fanniemae.com, www.ginniemae.gov, and www.freddiemac.com.

2. Explain the GNMA I MBS Program and GNMA II MBS Program. For information go to www.ginnniemae.gov.

3. Examine the growth in MBSs by going to www.bondmarkets.com and clicking on "Research Statistics" and "Agency MBS."

4. Find out the functions of the Mortgage-Backed Securities Clearing Corporation by going to www.ficc.com.

5. Learn more about the mortgage industry by going to the home page of the Mortgage Bankers Association of America: www.mbaa.org.

6. Evaluate the quality ratings of MBSs and CMOs by going to www.moodys.com. At the site, click on "Structured Finance" and go to "Commercial MBS," "Residential MBS" or "CDOs/Derivatives" and then to "Watchlist" or "Ratings Action."

NOTES

1. *Mortgage bankers* are dealers, not bankers, who either provide mortgage loans or purchase them, holding them for a short period before selling them to a financial institution.

2. Agencies can guarantee both interest and principal on a pass-through at the time payments are due (called a *fully modified pass-through*) or they will guarantee both interest and principal but not at the time payments are due. For example, principal payments could be guaranteed to be paid 1 year later. This latter is called a *modified pass-through*.

3. PAC-structured CMOs, as well as sequential-pay CMOs, are issued by agencies and financial institutions. By definition, CMOs issued by FNMA, GNMA, and FHLMC are called *agency CMOs*. CMOs issued by non-agencies in which the collateral consists of mortgage-backed securities that are guaranteed by one of the federal agencies are called *private-labeled CMOs*. Finally, CMOs formed with a pool of unsecured mortgages or MBSs are called *whole-loan CMOs*.

4. In a balloon mortgage, the borrower is given a long-term financing deal, but at a specified future date the mortgage rate and terms are renegotiated. The balloon payment is the original amount borrowed minus the principal amortized. Both FNMA and FHLMC have programs for the purchase of these types of mortgage.

SELECTED REFERENCES

Anderson, G. A., J. R. Barber, and C. H. Chang "Prepayment Risk and the Duration of Default-Free Mortgage-Backed Securities," *Journal of Financial Research* 16 (1989): 1–9.

Bartlett, W. W. *Mortgage Backed Securities: Products, Analysis, Trading* (New York: New York Institute of Finance, 1989).

Bhattacharya, A. and H. Chin "Synthetic Mortgage Backed Securities," *Journal of Portfolio Management* 18(3) (1992): 44–55.

Carron, A. S. "Understanding CMOs, REMICs and other Mortgage Derivatives," *Journal of Fixed Income* 2 (1992): 25–43.

Dunn, K. and J. McConnell "Valuation of GNMA Mortgage-Backed Securities," *Journal of Finance* 36(3) (1981): 599–616.

Fabozzi, Frank J. (ed.) *The Handbook of Mortgage-Backed Securities* (Chicago: Probus, 1992).

Fabozzi, Frank J. *Bond Markets, Analysis, and Strategies*, 3rd edn (Upper Saddle River, NJ: Prentice Hall, 1996): 214–321.

Goldman, Sachs, and Company *Understanding Securitized Investments and their Use in Portfolio Management* (Charlottesville, VA: Association of Investment Management and Research, 1990).

Hayre, Lakhbir, Cyrus Mohebbi, and Thomas A. Zimmerman "Mortgage Pass-Throughs," in Frank J. Fabozzi (ed.) *The Handbook of Fixed Income Securities*, 6th edn (New York: McGraw-Hill, 2001).

Hurst, R. Russell "Securities Backed by Closed-End Home Equity Loans," in Frank J. Fabozzi (ed.) *The Handbook of Fixed Income Securities*, 6th edn (New York: McGraw-Hill, 2001).

Lehman Brothers, Inc. "Collateralized Mortgage Obligations," in Frank J. Fabozzi (ed.) *The Handbook of Fixed Income Securities*, 6th edn (New York: McGraw-Hill, 2001).

McElravey, John N. "Securities Backed by Credit Card Receivables," in Frank J. Fabozzi (ed.) *The Handbook of Fixed Income Securities*, 6th edn (New York: McGraw-Hill, 2001).

Morris, D. V. *Asset Securitization: Principles and Practices* (Executive Enterprise Publications, 1990).

Norton, Joseph and Paul Spellman (eds) *Asset Securitization* (Cambridge, MA: Basil Blackwell, Inc., 1991).

Richard, S. F. and R. Roll "Prepayments on Fixed Rate Mortgage Backed Securities," *Journal of Portfolio Management* 15(3) (1989): 73–83.

Roever, W. Alexander, John N. McElravey, and Glenn M. Schultz "Securities Backed by Automobile Loans," in Frank J. Fabozzi (ed.) *The Handbook of Fixed Income Securities*, 6th edn (New York: McGraw-Hill, 2001).

Schwartz, B. and W. Torous "Prepayment and the Valuation of Mortgage Pass-Through Securities," *Journal of Business* 15(2) (1992): 221–40.

PART FOUR

DEBT DERIVATIVES: FUTURES, OPTIONS, AND SWAPS

CHAPTER TWELVE

INTEREST RATE FUTURES: FUNDAMENTALS

12.1 INTRODUCTION

In the 1840s, Chicago emerged as a transportation and distribution center for agriculture products. Midwestern farmers transported and sold their products to wholesalers and merchants in Chicago, who often would store and later transport the products by either rail or the Great Lakes to population centers in the East. Partly because of the seasonal nature of grains and other agriculture products and partly because of the lack of adequate storage facilities, farmers and merchants began to use *forward contracts* as a way of circumventing storage costs and pricing risk. These contracts were agreements in which two parties agreed to exchange commodities for cash at a future date, but with the terms and the price agreed upon in the present. For example, an Ohio farmer in June might agree to sell his expected wheat harvest to a Chicago grain dealer in September at an agreed-upon price. This forward contract enabled both the farmer and the dealer to lock in a September wheat price in June. In 1848, the Chicago Board of Trade (CBOT) was formed by a group of Chicago merchants to facilitate the trading of grain. This organization subsequently introduced the first standardized forward contract, called a "to-arrive" contract. Later, it established rules for trading the contracts and developed a system in which traders

ensured their performance by depositing good-faith money to a third party. These actions made it possible for speculators as well as farmers and dealers who were hedging their positions to trade their forward contracts. By definition, *futures* are marketable forward contracts. Thus, the CBOT evolved from a board offering forward contracts to the first organized exchange listing futures contracts – a futures exchange.

Since the 1840s, as new exchanges were formed in Chicago, New York, London, Singapore, and other large cities throughout the world, the types of futures contracts grew from grains and agricultural products to commodities and metals and finally to financial futures: futures on foreign currency, debt securities, and security indexes. Because of their use as a hedging tool by financial managers and investment bankers, the introduction of financial futures in the early 1970s led to a dramatic growth in futures trading, with the user's list reading as a who's who of major investment houses, banks, and corporations. The financial futures market formally began in 1972 when the Chicago Mercantile Exchange (CME) created the International Monetary Market (IMM) division to trade futures contracts on foreign currency. In 1976, the CME extended its listings to include a futures contract on a Treasury bill. The CBOT introduced its first futures contract in October of 1975 with a contract on the GNMA pass-through, and in 1977 they introduced the Treasury bond futures contract. The first cash-settled futures contract was introduced by the CME in 1981 with its contract on a 3-month Eurodollar deposit. The Kansas City Board of Trade was the first exchange to offer trading on a futures contract on a stock index, when it introduced the Value Line Composite Index contract (VLCI) in 1983. This was followed by the introduction of the SP 500 futures contract by the CME and the NYSE index futures contract by the New York Futures Exchange (NYFE).

While the 1970s marked the advent of financial futures, the 1980s saw the globalization of futures markets with the openings of the London International Financial Futures Exchange, LIFFE (1982), Toronto Futures Exchange (1984), New Zealand Futures Exchange (1985), Tokyo International Financial Futures Exchange (1985), and Singapore International Monetary Market (1986). Exhibit 12.1 lists the major exchanges trading futures and options and their websites. The increase in the number of futures exchanges internationally led to a number of trading innovations: electronic trading systems, 24-hour worldwide trading, and alliances between exchanges. The growth in the futures market also led to the need for more governmental oversight to ensure market efficiency and guard against abuses. In 1974 the Commodity Futures Trading Commission, CFTC, was created by Congress to monitor and regulate futures trading and in 1982 the National Futures Association, NFA, an organization of futures market participants, was established to oversee futures trading.

Formally, a forward contract is simply an agreement between two parties to trade a specific asset at a future date with the terms and price agreed upon today. A futures contract, in turn, is a "marketable" forward contract, with marketability provided through futures exchanges that not only list hundreds of contracts that can be traded but also provide the mechanisms for facilitating trades. In this chapter, we examine the markets and fundamental uses of interest rate futures and in chapter 13 we look at hedging and speculative positions formed with futures and the pricing of futures contracts. In chapters 14–17, we will focus on the markets and uses of the other interest rate derivatives: interest rate options and swap contracts.

Web Information

Chicago Mercantile Exchange:
www.cme.com

Chicago Board of Trade:
www.cbot.com

See exhibit 12.1 for a listing of derivative exchanges and their websites

Commodity Futures Trading Commission:
www.cftc.gov

National Futures Association:
www.nfa.futures.org

12.2 THE MARKET AND CHARACTERISTICS OF INTEREST RATE FUTURES

12.2.1 Microstructure

Like other organized exchanges, futures exchanges are typically structured as membership organizations with a fixed number of seats and with the seat being a precondition for direct trading on the exchange.[1] On most futures exchanges, there are two major types of futures traders/members: commission brokers and locals. Commission brokers buy and sell for their customers. They carry out most of the trading on the exchanges, serving the important role of linking futures traders. *Locals*, on the other hand, trade from their own accounts, acting as speculators or arbitrageurs. They serve to make the market operate more efficiently. Some exchanges also permit members to engage in *dual trading*. Under dual trading rules, a broker is allowed to fill orders for customers as well as trade for their own account as long as the customer's order is given priority.[2]

The mode of trading on futures exchanges in the US, London (LIFFE), Paris (MATIF), Sydney (SFE), Singapore (SIMEX), and other

Exhibit 12.1   Major futures and options exchanges

US exchanges

American Exchange (AMEX)	www.amex.com
Chicago Board of Options Exchange (CBOE)	www.cboe.com
Chicago Board of Trade (CBOT)	www.cbot.com
Chicago Mercantile Exchange (CME)	www.cme.com
Coffee, Sugar, and Coca Exchange (NY)	www.csce.com
Commodity Exchange (COMEX) (NY)	www.nymex.com
Kansas City Board of Trade (KCBT)	www.kcbt.com
Mid-American Commodity Exchange (MidAm)	www.midam.com
Minneapolis Grain Exchange (MGE)	www.mgex.com
New York Cotton Exchange (NYCE)	www.nyce.com
New York Futures Exchange (NYFE)	www.nyfe.com
New York Mercantile Exchange (NYMEX)	www.nymex.com
Pacific Exchange (PXS)	www.pacificex.com
Philadelphia Exchange (PHLX)	www.phlx.com

Non-US exchanges

Amsterdam Exchange (AEX)	www.aex.nl
Australian Stock Exchange (ASX)	www.asx.com
Bolsa de Mercadorias y Futuros, Brazil (BM&F)	www.bmf.com.br
Brussels Exchange (BXS)	www.bxs.be
Copenhagen Stock Exchange (FUTOP)	www.xcse.dk
Deutsche Termin Borse, Germany (DTB)	www.exchange.de
Eurex (EUREX)	www.eurexchange.com
Hong Kong Futures Exchange (HKFE)	www.hkfe.com
International Petroleum Exchange, London (IPE)	www.ipe.uk.com
Kuala Lumpur Options and Financial Futures Exchange (KLOFFE)	www.kloffe.com.my
London International Financial Futures Exchange (LIFFE)	www.liffe.com
Marche a Terme International de France (MATIF)	www.matif.com
Marche des Options Negociables de Paris (MONEP)	www.monep.fr
MEFF Renta Fija and Variable, Spain (MEFF)	www.meff.es
New Zealand Futures and Options Exchange (NZFOE)	www.nzfoe.com
Osaka Securities Exchange (OSA)	www.ose.or.jp
Singapore International Monetary Exchange (SIMEX)	www.simex.com.sg
Stockholm Options Exchange (SOM)	www.omgroup.com
Sydney Futures Exchange (SFE)	www.sfe.com.au
Tokyo International Financial Futures Exchange (TIFFE)	www.tiffe.com
Toronto Stock Exchange (TSE)	www.tse.com
Winnipeg Commodity Exchange (WCE)	www.wce.mba.ca

Alliances

Eurex is an alliance of DTB, CBOT, and exchanges in Switzerland and Finland	www.eurexchange.com
Euronext is an alliance of exchanges in Amsterdam, Brussels, and Paris	
GLOBEX is an alliance of CME, ME, MATIF, SIMEX and exchanges in Brazil and the Paris Bourse	www.globexalliance.com

locations still takes place the same way it did over 100 years ago on the CBOT with brokers and dealers going to a pit and using the *open outcry* method to trade. In this system, orders are relayed to the floor by runners or by hand signals to a specified trading pit. The order is then offered in open outcry to all participants in the pit, with the trade being done with the first person to respond.[3]

While the open outcry system is still extensively used on the major exchanges, electronic trading systems are being used by the physical exchanges in the US, London, Paris, and Sydney for after-hours trading. The CME and CBOT developed with Reuters (the electronic information service company) the *GLOBEX* trading system. This is a computerized order-matching system with an international network linking member traders. Similarly, SFE offers after-hours trading through their SYCOM system and LIFFE offers such trading through their Automated Pit Trading (APT) system. In addition to dual systems, since 1985 all new derivative exchanges have been organized as electronic exchanges. The German exchange (Deutsche Termin Borse (DTB)) and Stockholm Option Market (SOM), for example, were both set up as screen-based trading systems. Most of these electronic trading systems are order-driven systems in which customer orders (bid and ask prices and size) are collected and matched by a computerized matching system. This contrasts with a price-driven system such as the one used on the Swiss Options and Futures Exchange (SOFE) in which dealers provide bid and ask quotes and make markets.

In addition to linking futures traders, the futures exchanges also make contracts more marketable by standardizing contracts, providing continuous trading, establishing delivery procedures, and providing 24-hour trading through exchange alliances.

Standardization

The futures exchanges provide standardization by specifying the grade or type of each asset and the size of the underlying asset. Exchanges also specify how contract prices are quoted. For example, the contract prices on T-bill futures are quoted in terms of an index equal to

100 minus a discount yield, and a T-bond is quoted in terms of dollars and $\frac{1}{32}s$ of a T-bond with a face value of $100.

Continuous Trading

Many security exchanges use market-makers or specialists to ensure a continuous market. On many futures exchanges, continuous trading also is provided, but not with market-makers or specialists assigned by the exchange to deal in a specific contract. Instead, futures exchanges such as the CBOT, CME, and LIFFE provide continuous trading through locals who are willing to take temporary positions in one or more futures. These exchange members fall into one of three categories: *scalpers*, who offer to buy and sell simultaneously, holding their positions for only a few minutes and profiting from a bid-asked spread; *day traders*, who hold positions for less than a day; and *position traders*, who hold positions for as long as a week before they close. Collectively, these exchange members make it possible for the futures markets to provide continuous trading.

Price and Position Limits

Without market-makers and specialists to provide an orderly market, futures exchanges impose price limits as a tool to stopping possible destabilizing price trends from occurring. The exchanges specify the maximum price change that can occur from the previous day's settlement price. The price of a contract must be within its daily price limits, unless the exchange intervenes and changes the limit. When the contract price hits its maximum or minimum limit, it is referred to as being limited up or limited down. In addition to price limits, futures exchanges also set position limits on many of their futures contracts. This is done as a safety measure both to ensure sufficient liquidity and to minimize the chances of a trader trying to corner a particular asset.

Delivery Procedures

Only a small number of contracts that are entered into lead to actual delivery. As we will discuss in section 12.3, most futures contracts are closed prior to expiration. Nevertheless, detailed delivery procedures are important to ensure that the contract prices on futures are determined by the spot price on the underlying asset and that the futures price converges to the spot price at expiration. The exchanges have various rules and procedures governing the deliveries of contracts and delivery dates. The date or period in which delivery can take place is determined by the exchange. When there is a delivery period, the party agreeing to sell has the right to determine when the asset will be delivered during that period. For financial futures, delivery is usually done by wire transfer.

Alliances and 24-Hour Trading

In addition to providing off-hour trading via electronic trading systems, 24-hour trading is also possible by using futures exchanges that offer trading on the same contract. The CME, LIFFE, and SIMEX all offer identical contracts on 90-day Eurodollar deposits. This makes it possible to trade the contract in the US, Europe, and the Far East. Moreover, these exchanges have alliance agreements making it possible for traders to open a position in one market and close it in another. A similar alliance exists between SFE, CBOT, and LIFFE on US T-bond contracts.

12.2.2 Types of Interest Rate Futures

Exhibit 12.2 describes the features of various interest rate futures contracts traded on the CBOT, CME, LIFFE, and other exchanges. Of these contracts, the four most popular are T-bills, Eurodollar deposits, T-bonds, and T-notes.

T-Bill Futures

T-bill futures contracts call for the delivery (short position) or purchase (long position) of a T-bill with a maturity of 91 days and a face value (F) of $1m. Futures prices on T-bill contracts are quoted in terms of an index. This index, I, is equal to 100 minus the annual percentage discount rate, R_D, for a

90-day T-bill:

$$I = 100 - R_D(\%)$$

Given a quoted index value or discount yield, the actual contract price on the T-bill futures contract is:

$$f_0 = \frac{100 - R_D\%(90/360)}{100} \$1,000,000 \quad (12.1)$$

Note, the index is quoted on the basis of a 90-day T-bill with a 360-day year. This implies that a one-point move in the index would equate to a $2,500 change in the futures price. The implied yield to maturity (YTM_f) on a T-bill that is delivered on the contract is often found using 365 days and the actual maturity on the delivered bill of 91 days. For example, a T-bill futures contract quoted at a settlement index value of 95.62 $(R_D = 4.38\%)$ would have a futures contract price (f_0) of $989,050 and an implied YTM_f of 4.515%:

$$f_0 = \frac{100 - 4.38(90/360)}{100} \$1,000,000 = \$989,050$$

and

$$YTM_f = \left[\frac{F}{f_0}\right]^{365/91} - 1$$

$$YTM_f = \left[\frac{\$1,000,000}{\$989,050}\right]^{365/91} - 1 = 0.04515$$

Expiration months on T-bill futures are March, June, September, and December, and extend out about 2 years. The last trading day occurs during the third week of the expiration month, on the business day preceding the issue of spot T-bills. Under the terms of the contract, delivery may occur on one of three successive business days with the delivered T-bill having a maturity of 89, 90, and 91 days.

Eurodollar Futures Contract

As noted in chapter 7, a Eurodollar deposit is a time deposit in a bank located or incorporated outside the United States. A Eurodollar interest rate is the rate that one large international bank is willing to lend to another large international bank. The average rate paid by a sample of

Exhibit 12.2　Select interest rate futures contracts

Contract	Exchange	Contract size	Delivery month	Delivery
Treasury bond	CBOT	T-bond with $100,000 face value (or multiple of that)	Mar/June/ Sept/Dec	T-bonds with an invoice price that is equal to the futures settlement price times a conversion factor plus accrued interest
5-year Treasury note	CBOT	T-note with $100,000 face value (or multiple of that)	Mar/June/ Sept/Dec	T-notes that have maturity of no more than 5 years and 3 months. Invoice price is equal to the futures settlement price times a conversion factor plus accrued interest
Treasury note	CBOT	T-note with $100,000 face value (or multiple of that)	Mar/June/ Sept/Dec	T-notes maturing at least $6\frac{1}{2}$ years, but no more than 10 years. Invoice price is equal to the futures settlement price times a conversion factor plus accrued interest
3-month Treasury bill	CME	$1,000,000	Mar/June/ Sept/Dec	Delivery can be made on three successive business days. The first delivery day is the first day on which a 13-week T-bill is issued
3-month Eurodollar	CME	$1,000,000	Mar/June/ Sept/Dec	Cash settlement
1-month LIBOR	CME	$3,000,000	All calendar months	Cash settlement; settlement price based on a survey of participants in London Interbank Eurodollar market.
Municipal Bond Index	CBOT	$1,000 times the closing value of the *Bond Buyer*™ Municipal Bond Index (a price of 95 means a contract size of $95,000)	Mar/June/ Sept/Dec	Cash settlement; settlement price based on *Bond Buyer*™ Municipal Bond Index value at expiration
3-month Euroyen	SIMEX	100,000,000 yen	Mar/June/ Sept/Dec	Cash settlement
10-year Japanese government bond index	TSE	100,000,000 yen face value	Mar/June/ Sept/Dec	Exchange-listed Japanese government bond having a maturity of 7 years or more, but less than 11 years
Long gilt	LIFFE	50,000 British pounds	Mar/June/ Sept/Dec	Delivery may be any gilt with 15 to 25 years to maturity
3-month sterling interest rate	LIFFE	500,000 British pounds	Mar/June/ Sept/Dec	Cash settlement; settlement price based on the 3-month sterling deposit rate being offered to prime banks

London Eurobanks is known as the London Interbank Offer Rate (LIBOR). The LIBOR is higher than the T-bill rate, and as noted in chapter 7, it is used as a benchmark rate on bank loans and deposits.

The CME's futures contract on the Eurodollar deposit calls for the delivery or purchase of a Eurodollar deposit with a face value of $1m and a maturity of 90 days. The expiration months on Eurodollar futures contracts are March, June, September, and December and extend up to 10 years. Like T-bill futures contracts, Eurodollar futures are quoted in terms of an index equal to 100 minus the annual discount rate, with the actual contract price found by using equation (12.1). For example, given a settlement index value of 95.09 on a Eurodollar contract, the actual futures price would be $987,725:

$$f_0 = \frac{100 - 4.91(90/360)}{100} \$1,000,000 = \$987,725$$

The major difference between the Eurodollar and T-bill contracts is that Eurodollar contracts have cash settlements at delivery, while T-bill contracts call for the actual delivery of the instrument. When a Eurodollar futures contract expires, the cash settlement is determined by the futures price and the settlement price. The settlement price or expiration futures index price is 100 minus the average 3-month LIBOR offered by a sample of designated Eurobanks on the expiration date:

Expiration futures price $= 100 - \text{LIBOR}$

In addition to the CME's Eurodollar futures, there are also a number of other contracts traded on interest rates in other countries. For example, there are Euroyen contracts traded on the CME and the Singapore Exchange, Euroswiss contracts traded on the LIFFE, and Euribor contracts (three-month LIBOR contract for the euro) traded on the LIFFE and Marche a Terme International de France, MATIF.

T-Bond Futures Contracts

The most heavily traded long-term interest rate futures contract is the CBOT's T-bond contract. The contract calls for the delivery or purchase of a T-bond with a maturity of at least 15 years. The CBOT has a conversion factor to determine the actual price received by the seller. The futures contract is based on the delivery of a T-bond with a face value of $100,000. The delivery months on the contracts are March, June, September, and December, going out approximately 2 years; delivery can occur at any time during the delivery month. To ensure liquidity, any T-bond with a maturity of 15 years is eligible for delivery, with a conversion factor used to determine the actual price of the deliverable bond. Since T-bond futures contracts allow for the delivery of a number of T-bonds at any time during the delivery month, the CBOT's delivery procedure on such contracts is more complicated than the procedures on other futures contracts. The T-bond delivery procedure is discussed in chapter 13.

T-bond futures prices are quoted in dollars and 32nds for T-bonds with a face value of $100. Thus, if the quoted price on a T-bond futures was 106-14 (i.e., $106 \frac{14}{32}$ or 106.437), the price would be $106,437 for a face value of $100,000. The actual price paid on the T-bond or revenue received by the seller in delivering the bond on the contract is equal to the quoted futures price times the conversion factor, CFA, on the delivered bond plus any accrued interest:

Seller's revenue $= (\text{Quoted futures price})(\text{CFA})$
$+ \text{Accrued interest}$

Thus, at the time of delivery, if the delivered bond has a CFA of 1.3 and accrued interest of $2 and the quoted futures price is 94-16, then the cash received by the seller of the bond and paid by the futures purchaser would be $124.85 per $100 face value:

Seller's revenue $= (94.5)(1.3) + 2 = 124.85$

T-Note Futures Contracts

T-note contracts are similar to T-bond contracts, except that they call for the delivery of any T-note with maturities between $6\frac{1}{2}$ and

10 years; the 5-year T-note contracts are also similar to T-bond and T-note contracts except that they require delivery of the most recently auctioned 5-year T-note. Both contracts, though, have delivery procedures similar to T-bond contracts.

Forward Contracts – Forward Rate Agreements

Forward contracts for interest rate products are private, customized contracts between two financial institutions or between a financial institution and one of its clients. Interest rate forward contracts predate the establishment of interest rate futures markets. A good example of an interest rate forward product is a *forward rate agreement, FRA*.[4] This contract requires a cash payment or provides a cash receipt based on the difference between a realized spot rate such as the LIBOR and a prespecified rate. For example, the contract could be based on a specified rate of $R_k = 6\%$ (annual) and the 3-month LIBOR (annual) in 5 months and a notional principal, NP (principal used only for calculation purposes) of $10m. In 5 months the payoff would be

$$\text{Payoff} = (\$10\text{m}) \frac{[\text{LIBOR} - 0.06](91/365)}{1 + \text{LIBOR}(91/365)}$$

If the LIBOR at the end of 5 months exceeds the specified rate of 6%, the buyer of the FRA (or long position holder) receives the payoff from the seller; if the LIBOR is less than 6%, the seller (or short position holder) receives the payoff from the buyer. Thus, if the LIBOR were at 6.5%, the buyer would be entitled to a payoff of $12,267 from the seller; if the LIBOR were at 5.5%, the buyer would be required to pay the seller $12,297. Note that the terminology is the opposite of futures. In Eurodollar or T-bill futures, the party with the long position hopes rates will decrease and prices will go up, while the short position holder hopes that rates will increase and prices will go down.

In general, an FRA that matures in T months and is written on an M-month LIBOR rate is referred to as a $T \times (T + M)$ agreement. Thus, in this example the FRA is a 5×8 agreement. At the maturity of the contract (T), the value of the contract, V_T, is

$$V_T = \text{NP} \frac{[\text{LIBOR} - R_k](M/365)}{1 + \text{LIBOR}(M/365)}$$

FRAs originated in 1981 amongst large London Eurodollar banks that used these forward agreements to hedge their interest rate exposure. Today, FRAs are offered by banks and financial institutions in major financial centers and are often written for the bank's corporate customers. They are customized contracts designed to meet the needs of the corporation or financial institution. Most FRAs do follow the guidelines established by the British Banker's Association. Settlement dates do tend to be less than 1 year (e.g., 3, 6, or 9 months), although settlement dates going out as far as 4 years are available. The NP on an FRA can be as high as a billion and can be drawn in dollars, British pounds, and other currencies. FRAs are used by corporations and financial institutions to manage interest rate risk in the same way as financial futures are used. Different from financial futures, FRAs are contracts between two parties and therefore are subject to the credit risk of either party defaulting. This is not the case with futures contracts where the clearinghouse and marked-to-market rules effectively eliminate credit risk. The customized FRAs are also less liquid than standardized futures contracts. The banks that write FRAs often take a position in the futures market to hedge their position or a long and short position in spot money market securities to lock in a forward rate. As a result, in writing the FRA, the specified rate R_k is often set equal to the rate implied on a futures contract or the implied forward rate (discussed in chapter 2). If the forward rate or futures rate were certain to be realized, then the value of the FRAs would be zero.

12.3 THE NATURE OF FUTURES TRADING AND THE ROLE OF THE CLEARINGHOUSE AND MARGINS

12.3.1 Futures Positions

A futures holder can take one of two positions on a futures contract: a long position (or futures purchase) or a short position (futures sale). In a long futures position, the holder agrees to buy the contract's underlying asset at a specified price, with the payment and delivery to occur on the expiration date (also referred to as the delivery date); in a short position, the holder agrees to sell an asset at a specific price, with delivery and payment occurring at expiration.

To illustrate how positions are taken, suppose that in June, speculator A believes that the Federal Reserve will expand its open market purchases over the next 6 months, leading to lower interest rates and higher prices on T-bills. With hopes of profiting from this expectation, suppose speculator A decides to take a long position in a September T-bill futures contract and instructs her broker to buy one September futures contract listed on the CME (one contract calls for the purchase of a T-bill with $1m face value and maturity of 91 days). To fulfill this order, suppose A's broker finds in the CME T-bill pit a broker representing speculator B, who believes that an expanding economy and tighter monetary policy in the ensuing months will push short-term rates up and prices down and as such is wanting to take a short position in the September T-bill contract. After hearing bid and ask quotes, suppose the brokers agree to a price on the September contract for their clients that is equal to the CME index of 95 ($R_D = 5$) or $f_0 = \$987,500$. In terms of futures positions, speculator A would have a long position in which she agrees to buy a 91-day T-bill with a face value of $1m for $987,500 from speculator B at the delivery date in September, and speculator B would have a short position in which he agrees to sell a 91-day T-bill to A at the delivery date in September:

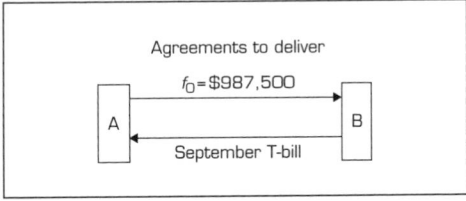

If both parties hold their contracts to delivery, their profits or losses would be determined by the price of the T-bill on the spot market. For example, suppose the Fed does engage in expansionary monetary policy, causing the spot discount yield on T-bills to fall to $R_D = 4\%$ at the time of the expiration date on the September futures contracts. At 4%, the spot price (S) on a T-bill with $1m face value would be $990,000. Accordingly, speculator A would be able to buy a 91-day T-bill on her September futures contract at $987,500 from speculator B, then sell the bill for $990,000 on the spot market to earn a profit of $2,500. On the other hand, to deliver a T-bill on the September contract, speculator B would have to buy the security on the spot market for $990,000, then sell it on the futures contract to speculator A for $987,500, resulting in a $2,500 loss.

12.3.2 The Clearinghouse

To provide contracts with marketability, futures exchanges use clearinghouses. The exchange clearinghouse is an adjunct of the exchange. It consists of clearinghouse members (many of whom are brokerage firms) who guarantee the performance of each party of the transaction and act as intermediaries by breaking up each contract after the trade has taken place. Thus, in the above example, the clearinghouse (CH) would come in after speculators A and B have reached an agreement on the price of a September T-bill, becoming the effective seller on A's long position and the effective buyer on B's short position:

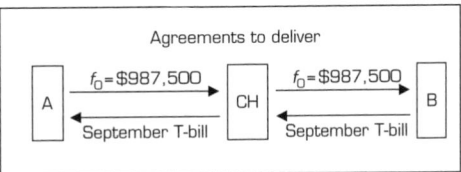

Once the clearinghouse has broken up the contract, then A's and B's contract would be with the clearinghouse. The clearinghouse, in turn, would record the following entries in its computers:

Clearinghouse record:

---

1. Speculator A agrees to buy September T-bill at $987,500 from the clearinghouse.
2. Speculator B agrees to sell September T-bill at $987,500 to the clearinghouse.

---

the following:

Clearinghouse records for speculator A:

---

1. Speculator A agrees to *buy* September T-bill from the clearinghouse for $987,500.
2. Speculator A agrees to *sell* September T-bill to the clearinghouse for $988,750.

Thus

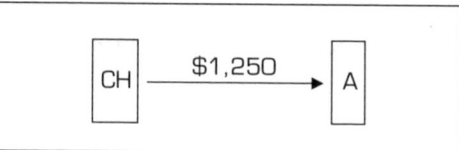

The clearinghouse accordingly would close speculator A's positions by paying her $1,250 at expiration. Since speculator A's short position effectively closes her position, it is variously referred to as a *closing*, *reversing out*, or *off-setting position* or simply as an offset. Thus, the clearinghouse makes it easier for futures contracts to be closed prior to expiration.

The intermediary role of the clearinghouse makes it easier for futures traders to close their positions before expiration. To see this, suppose that in June, short-term interest rates drop, leading speculators such as C to want to take a long position in the September T-bill contract. Seeing a profit potential from the increased demand for long positions in the September contract, suppose speculator A agrees to sell a September T-bill futures contract to speculator C for $988,750 ($R_D = 4.5\%$ and index $= 95.5$). Upon doing this, speculator A now would be short in the new September contract, with speculator C having a long position, and there now would be two contracts on September T-bills. Without the clearinghouse intermediating, the two contracts can be described as follows:

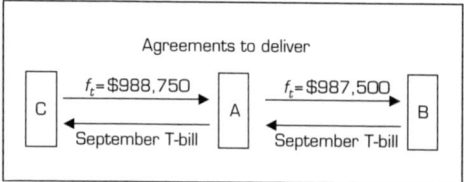

Agreements to deliver

After the new contract between A and C has been established, the clearinghouse would step in and break it up. For speculator A, the clearinghouse's records would now show

The expense and inconvenience of delivery cause most futures traders to close their positions instead of taking delivery. As the delivery date approaches, the number of outstanding contracts, referred to as *open interest*, declines, with only a relatively few contracts still outstanding at delivery. Moreover, at expiration (T), the contract prices on futures contracts established on that date (f_T) should be equal (or approximately equal for some contracts) to the prevailing spot price on the underlying asset (S_T). That is, at expiration: $f_T = S_T$. If f_T does not equal S_T at expiration, an arbitrage opportunity would exist. Arbitrageurs could take a position in the futures contract and an opposite position in the spot market. For example, if the September T-bill futures contracts were trading at $990,000 on the delivery date in September and the spot price on T-bills were trading at $990,500, an arbitrageur could go long in the September contract, take delivery by buying the T-bill at $990,000 on the futures contract, then sell the bill on the spot at $990,500 to earn a risk-free profit of $500. The arbitrageur's efforts to take a long position, though, would drive the contract price up to $990,500. On the other hand, if f_T exceeds $990,500, then an arbitrageur would reverse their strategy, pushing f_T down to $990,500. Thus at delivery, arbitrageurs will ensure that the price on an expiring contract is equal to the spot price. As a result, closing a futures contract with an offsetting position at expiration will yield the same profits or losses as purchasing (selling) the asset on the spot and selling (buying) it on the futures contract.

Returning to our example, suppose near the delivery date on the September contract the spot T-bill price and the price on the expiring September futures contracts are $990,000 ($R_D = 4\%$ or index $= 96$). To close his existing short contract, speculator B would need to take a long position in the September contract, while to offset her existing long contract, speculator C would need to take a short position. Suppose speculators B and C take their offsetting positions with each other on the expiring September T-bill contract priced at $f_T = S_T = \$990,000$. After the clearinghouse breaks up the new contract, speculator B would owe the clearinghouse $2,500 and speculator C would receive $1,250 from the clearinghouse:

Clearinghouse records for speculator B:

---

1. Speculator B agrees to *sell* September T-bill to CH for $987,500.
2. Speculator B agrees to *buy* September T-bill from CH at $990,000.

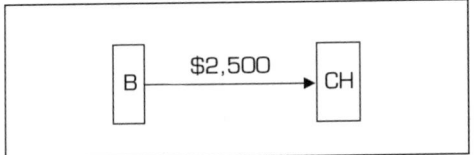

And,

Clearinghouse records for speculator C:

---

1. Speculator C agrees to *buy* September T-bill at $988,750.
2. Speculator C agrees to *sell* September T-bill for $990,000.

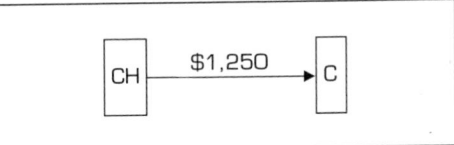

To recapitulate, in this example, the contract prices on September T-bill contracts went from $987,500 on the A and B contract, to $988,750 on the A and C contract, to $990,000 on the B and C contract at expiration. Speculators A and C each received $1,250 from the clearinghouse, while speculator B paid $2,500 to the clearinghouse, the clearinghouse with a perfect hedge on each contract received nothing (other than clearinghouse fees attached to the commission charges), and no T-bill was actually purchased or delivered.

12.3.3 Margin Requirements

Since a futures contract is an agreement, it has no initial value. Futures traders, however, are required to post some security or good faith money with their brokers. Depending on the brokerage firm, the customer's margin requirement can be satisfied either in the form of cash or cash equivalents.

Futures contracts have both initial and maintenance margin requirements. The *initial (or performance) margin* is the amount of cash or cash equivalents that must be deposited by the investor on the day the futures position is established. The futures trader does this by setting up a margin (or commodity) account with the broker and depositing the required cash or cash equivalents. The amount of the margin is determined by the margin requirement, defined as a proportion (m) of the contract value (usually 3% to 5%). For example, if the initial margin requirement is 5%, then speculators A and B in our example would be required to deposit $49,375 in cash or cash equivalents in their commodity accounts as good faith money on their September futures contracts:

$$m[\text{Contract value}] = 0.05[\$987,500] = \$49,375$$

At the end of each trading day, the futures trader's account is adjusted to reflect any gains or losses based on the settlement price on new contracts.[5] In our example, suppose the day after speculators A and B established their respective long and short positions, the settlement index value on the September T-bill was 95.5 ($f_t = 988,750$, $R_D = 4.5$). The value of A's and B's margin accounts would therefore be:

A: Account value

$$= \$49,375 + (\$988,750 - \$987,500)$$
$$= \$50,625$$

B: Account value

$$= \$49,375 + (\$987,500 - \$988,750)$$
$$= \$48,125$$

With a lower rate and higher futures price, A's long position has increased in value by $1,250 and B's short position has decreased by $1,250. When there is a decrease in the account value, the futures trader's broker has to exchange money through the clearing firm equal to the loss on the position to the broker and clearinghouse with the gain. This process is known as *marking to market*. Thus in our case, B's broker and clearing firm would pass on $1,250 to A's broker and clearing firm.

To ensure that the balance in the trader's account does not become negative, the brokerage firm requires a margin to be maintained by the futures traders.[6] The *maintenance (or variation) margin* is the amount of additional cash or cash equivalents that futures traders must deposit to keep the equity in their commodity account equal to a certain percentage (e.g., 75%) of the initial margin value. If the maintenance margin requirements were equal to 100% of the initial margin, then A and B would have to keep the equity values of their accounts equal to $49,375. If speculator B did not deposit

the required margin immediately, then he would receive a *margin call* from the broker instructing him to post the required amount of funds. If speculator B did not comply with the margin call, the broker would close the position.

12.3.4 Points on Margin Requirements

Several points should be noted in describing margin requirements. First, the marking to market of futures contracts effectively settles the futures contract daily. Each day the futures holder's gain or loss is added to or subtracted from the holder's account to bring the value of the position back to zero. Once marking to market has occurred, there are no outstanding balances. On the CME, clearing members' exchange payments in a day can range from $100m to over $2.5b. The purpose of this stringent settlement system is to reduce the chance of default.

Second, the minimum levels of initial and maintenance margins are set by the exchanges, with the brokerage firms allowed to increase the levels. Margins levels are determined by the variability of the underlying asset and can vary by the type of trader. The margins for hedgers are less than those for speculators.

Third, the maintenance margin requirements on futures necessitate constant management of one's account. With daily resettlement, futures traders who are undermargined have to decide each day whether to close their positions and incur losses or post additional collateral; similarly, those who are overmargined must decide each day whether or not they should close. One way for an investor to minimize the management of her futures position is to keep her account overmargined by depositing more cash or cash equivalents than initially required or by investing in one of a number of *futures funds*. A futures fund pools investors' monies and uses them to set up futures positions. Typically, a large percentage of the fund's money is invested in money market securities. Thus, the funds represent overmargined futures positions.

Fourth, maintaining margin accounts can be viewed as part of the cost of trading futures. In addition to margin requirements, transaction costs are also involved in establishing futures positions. Such costs include broker commissions, clearinghouse fees, and the bid–asked spread. On futures contracts, commission fees usually are charged on a per contract basis and for a round lot (i.e., the fee includes both opening and closing the position), and the fees are negotiable. The clearinghouse fee is relatively small and is collected along with the commission fee by the broker. The bid–asked spreads are set by locals and represent an indirect cost of trading futures.

Finally, the margin requirements and clearinghouse mechanism that characterize futures exchanges also serve to differentiate them from customized forward contracts on debt and interest rate positions written by banks and investment companies. Forward contracts are more tailor-made contracts with the underlying security or rate, delivery date, and size negotiated between the parties; they usually do not require margins; forwards often are delivered at maturity instead of closed; they are less marketable than exchange-traded futures.

12.3.5 Note on Taxes

In the US, futures positions are treated as capital gains and losses for tax purposes. For speculators, a marked-to-market rule applies in which the profits on a futures position are taxed in the year the contract is established. That is, at the end of the year, all futures contracts are marked to the market to determine any unrealized gain or loss for tax purposes. For example, suppose in September a futures speculator takes a long position on a March contract at a contract price of $1,000. If the position were still open at the end of the year, the speculator's taxes on the position would be based on the settlement price at year's end. If the contract were marked to market at $1,200 at the end of the year, then a $200 capital gain would need to be added to the speculator's net capital gains to determine her tax liability. If the speculator's position were later closed in March of the following year at a contract price of $1,100, then she would realize an actual capital gain of $100. For tax purposes, though, the speculator would report a loss equal to the difference in the settlement price at the end of the year ($1,200) and the position's closing price ($1,100): that is,

a $100 loss. Both realized and unrealized capital losses, in turn, are deductibles that are subtracted from the investor's capital gains.

Note: the end-of-the-year marked-to-market rule on futures applies only to speculative positions and not to hedging positions. Gains or losses from hedges are treated as ordinary income with the time of the recognition occurring at the time of the gain or loss of income from the hedged item. Also note that when delivery on a futures contract takes place, taxes are applied when the asset actually is sold.[7]

12.4 FUTURES HEDGING

Futures markets provide corporations, financial institutions, and others with a tool for hedging their particular spot positions against adverse price movements, for speculating on expected spot price changes, and for creating synthetic debt and investment positions with better rates than direct positions. Of these uses, the most extensive one is hedging.

Two hedging positions exist: long hedge and short hedge. In a *long hedge* (or hedge purchase), a hedger takes a long position in a futures contract to protect against an increase in the price of the underlying asset or commodity. Long hedge positions on debt securities are used by money market managers, fixed-income managers, and dealers to lock in their costs on future security purchases. In a *short hedge*, a hedger takes a short futures position to protect against a decrease in the price of the underlying asset. In contrast to long hedging, short hedge positions are used by bond and money market managers, investment bankers, and dealers who are planning to sell securities in the future, by banks and other intermediaries to lock in the rates they pay on future deposits, and by corporate treasurers and other borrowers who want to lock in the future rates on their loans or who want to fix the rates on the variable rate loans.

12.4.1 Long Hedge

A long position in an interest rate futures contract can be used by money market and fixed-income managers to lock in the purchase price on a future investment. As illustrated in

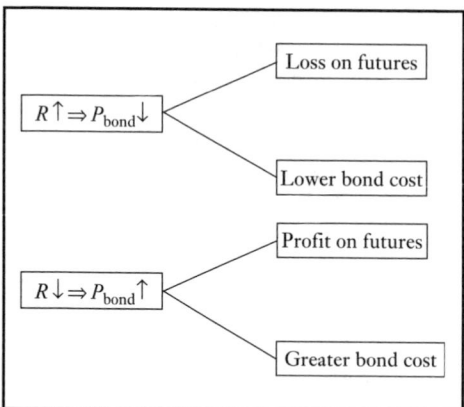

Exhibit 12.3 Long hedge: hedging bond purchase with long position in interest rate futures

exhibit 12.3, if interest rates are lower at the time of the investment, then the price on the fixed-income securities will be higher, and as a result the cost of buying the securities will be higher. With a long futures position, though, the manager will be able to profit when he closes his long futures position. With the profit from the futures, the manager will be able to defray the additional cost of purchasing the higher priced fixed-income securities. In contrast, if rates increase, the cost of securities will be lower, but the manager will have to use part of the investment cash inflow to cover losses on his futures position. In either interest rate scenario, though, the manager will find he can purchase approximately the same number of securities given his hedged position.

Long Hedge Example: Future Eurodollar Investment

To illustrate a long hedge position, consider the case of a money market manager who is expecting a cash flow of $9,875,000 in September that he plans to invest in a 90-day jumbo certificate of deposit, CD, with a face value of $10m. Fearing that short-term rates could decrease (causing CD prices to increase), suppose the manager goes long in ten September Eurodollar futures trading at $R_D = 5\%$ or $f_0 = \$987,500$. Given equal spot and expiring futures prices at expiration, the manager will

find that any additional costs of buying the jumbo CD above the $9,875,000 price on the spot market will be offset by a profit from his futures position; while on the other hand, any benefits from the costs of the CD being less than the $9,875,000 price would be negated by losses on the Eurodollar futures position. As a result, the manager's costs of buying CDs on the spot and closing his futures position would be $9,875,000.

The money market manager's long hedge position is shown in exhibit 12.4. In the exhibit, the third row shows three possible costs of buying the $10m face value CD at the September delivery date of $9,850,000, $9,875,000, and $9,900,000 given settlement LIBORs of 6%, 5%, and 4%. The fourth row shows the profits and losses from the long futures position in which the offset position has a contract or cash settlement price (f_T) equal to the spot price (S_T). The last row shows the net costs of $9,875,000 resulting from purchasing the CDs and closing the futures position. Thus, if the spot Eurodollar discount rate is at 6% at the September delivery date, the manager would pay $9,850,000 for the jumbo CD and $25,000 to the clearinghouse to close his futures positions (i.e., the agreement to buy ten contracts at $987,500 per contract and the offsetting agreement to sell at $985,000 means the manager must pay the clearinghouse $25,000); if the spot Eurodollar rate is 4%, then the manager will have to pay $9,900,000 for the CD, but will be able to finance part of that expenditure with the $25,000 received from the clearinghouse from closing (i.e., agreement to buy ten contracts at $987,500 and the offsetting agreement to sell at $990,000 means the clearinghouse will pay the manager $25,000).

12.4.2 Short Hedge

Short hedges are used when corporations, municipal governments, financial institutions, dealers, and underwriters are planning to sell bonds or borrow funds at some future date and want to lock in the rate. As illustrated in exhibit 12.5, if interest rates are higher at the time the fixed-income securities are sold (or the loan starts), then the price on the fixed-income securities will be lower, and as a result,

Exhibit 12.4   Long hedge example

Initial position: long in 10 September Eurodollar futures contracts at $R_D = 5$ (index $= 95$, $f_0 = \$987,500$) to hedge \$9,875,000 CD investment in September

Positions	6%	5%	4%
(1) September spot R_D	6%	5%	4%
(2) September spot and futures price	\$985,000	\$987,500	\$990,000
(3) Cost of \$10m face value 90-day CD	\$9,850,000	\$9,875,000	\$9,900,000
(4) Profit on futures	(\$25,000)	0	\$25,000
Net costs: row (3)−row (4)	\$9,875,000	\$9,875,000	\$9,875,000

Profit on futures $= 10$ (spot price $- \$987,500$)

Exhibit 12.5   Short hedge: hedging bond sale with short position in interest rate futures

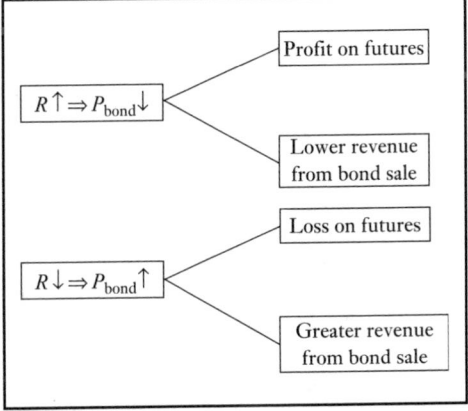

the revenue from selling the fixed-income securities will be less (or the rate on the loan is higher). With a short futures-hedged position, though, the security seller (or borrower) will be able to profit when he closes his short position by going long in lower priced expiring futures. With the profit from the futures, the seller will be able to offset the lower revenue from selling the securities (or defray the additional interest cost of the loan). In contrast, if rates decrease, the revenue from selling the securities at higher prices will be greater (or loan interest cost lower), but the security seller will have to use part of the investment cash inflow (interest savings) to cover losses on his futures position.

In either interest rate scenario, though, the manager will find less revenue variation from selling securities and closing his futures (or effective rate paid on loans) given his hedged position.

Short Hedge Example: Future T-Bond Sale

To illustrate how a short hedge works, consider the case of a fixed-income manager who in July anticipates needing cash in September that she plans to obtain by selling ten 6% T-bonds, each with a face value of \$100,000 and currently trading at par. Suppose that the September T-bond futures contract is trading at 100, and at the time of the anticipated September sale, the T-bonds will be at a coupon date with a maturity of exactly 15 years and no accrued interest at that date. If the manager wants to lock in a September selling price on her T-bonds of \$100,000 per bond, she could go short in ten September T-bond futures contracts. At the September expiration, if the cheapest-to-deliver bond is the 15-year, 6% coupon bond with a conversion factor of 1, then she would receive \$1m in revenue at delivery from selling her T-bonds on the spot market and closing the futures contract by going long in the expiring September contract trading at a price equal to the spot price on the 15-year, 6% T-bond. This can be seen in exhibit 12.6. In the exhibit, the second row shows three revenue

Exhibit 12.6   Short hedge example

Initial position: short in 10 September T-bond futures contracts at $f_0 = 100$ to hedge a September sale of 10 T-bonds

At the delivery date the 10 T-bonds each have a maturity of 15 years, no accrued interest, and can be delivered on the futures contracts with a conversion factor of 1

Positions	95	100	105
(1) September spot and futures price	$95,000	$100,000	$105,000
(2) Revenue from sale of 10 T-bonds	$950,000	$1,000,000	$1,050,000
(3) Profit on futures	$50,000	0	($50,000)
Net revenue: row (2) + row (3)	$1,000,000	$1,000,000	$1,000,000

Profit on futures = 10($100,000 – spot price)

---

amounts from selling the ten T-bonds at three possible spot T-bond prices of 95, 100, 105; the third row shows the profits and losses from the futures position, and the last row shows the hedged revenue from aggregating both positions. For example, at 95, the manager receives only $950,000 from selling her ten bonds. This lower revenue, though, is offset by $50,000 profit from her futures position (the agreement to sell September 10 T-bonds for $100,000 per bond is closed with an agreement to buy ten expiring September T-bond futures for $95,000 per bond, resulting in a $50,000 receipt from the clearinghouse). On the other hand, if the manager is able to sell her ten bonds for $105,000 per bond, she also will have to pay the clearinghouse $50,000 to close the futures position. Thus, regardless of the spot price, the manager receives $1,000,000 from selling the bonds and closing the futures positions.

It should be noted that in determining the futures positions hedgers need to take into account the cheapest-to-deliver bond, accrued interest, and a conversion factor that is likely to be different than the 1 that was used in this example. The pricing of T-bond futures is discussed in chapter 13.

12.4.3 Hedging Risk

The above examples represent perfect hedging cases in which certain revenues or costs can be locked in at a future date. In practice, perfect hedges are the exception and not the rule. There are three types of hedging risk that preclude one from obtaining a zero risk position: *quality risk*, *timing risk*, and *quantity risk*.

Quality risk exists when the commodity or asset being hedged is not identical to the one underlying the futures contract. The manager in our long hedge example, for instance, may be planning to purchase commercial paper instead of a T-bill. In such hedging cases, futures contracts written on a different underlying asset are often used to hedge the spot asset. In this case, the manager could use a T-bill futures contract to hedge the CP purchase. Similarly, a portfolio manager planning to buy corporate bonds in the future might hedge the acquisition by going long in T-bond futures. These types of hedges are known as *cross hedges*. Unlike *direct hedges* in which the future's underlying assets are the same as the assets being hedged, cross-hedging cannot eliminate risk, but can minimize it.[8] Cross-hedging cases are presented in the next chapter.

Timing risk occurs when the delivery date on the futures contract does not coincide with the date the hedged asset needs to be purchased or sold. For example, timing risk would exist in our long hedging example if the manager needed to buy the T-bills on the first of September instead of at the futures' expiration at the end of the September. If the spot asset is purchased or sold at a date that differs from the expiration date on the futures contract, then the price on the futures (f_t) and the spot price (S_t) will not necessarily be equal. The difference between the futures and spot price is called the *basis* (B_t). The basis tends to narrow as expiration nears, converging to zero at expiration ($B_T = 0$). Prior to expiration, the basis can vary, with greater variability usually observed the longer the time is to expiration. Given this *basis risk*, the greater the time difference between buying or selling the hedged asset and the futures' expiration date, the less perfect the hedge. To minimize timing risk or basis risk, hedgers often select futures contracts which mature before the hedged asset is to be bought or sold but as close as possible to that date. For very distant horizon dates, though, hedgers sometimes follow a strategy known as *rolling the hedge forward*. This hedging strategy involves taking a futures position, then at expiration closing the position and taking a new one. Finally, because of the standardization of futures contracts, futures hedging also is subject to quantity risk.

The presence of quality, timing, and quantity risk means that pricing risk cannot be eliminated totally by hedging with futures contracts. As a result, the objective in hedging is to try to minimize risk. Several hedging models try to achieve this objective: naive-hedge, price-sensitivity, minimum variance, and utility-based hedging models. The first two of these models and their applications are examined in the next chapter.

12.5 CONCLUSION

During the 1980s, many countries experienced relatively sharp swings in interest rates. Because of their hedging uses, the market for interest rate futures grew dramatically during this period. Currently, the most popular interest rate futures are the T-bond contracts offered by the CBOT and the Eurodollar and T-bill contracts offered by the CME. In this chapter we've examined the characteristics and hedging uses of these contracts. Given this foundation, in the next chapter we present some additional applications of interest rate futures and show how the prices of interest rate futures contracts are determined using the carrying-cost model.

Web Information
For more information on futures and links to other sites with futures information go to
  www.citylink-uk.com

KEY TERMS

Forward Contracts	Forward-Forward	Futures Funds
Futures	Contracts	Long Hedge
Locals	Closing	Short Hedge
Dual Trading	Reversing Out	Quality Risk
Front Running	Offsetting Position	Timing Risk
Open Outcry	Open Interest	Quantity Risk
GLOBEX	Initial (or Performance)	Cross Hedges
Scalpers	Margin	Direct Hedges
Day Traders	Marking to Market	Basis
Position Traders	Maintenance (or Variation)	Basis Risk
Forward Rate Agreement	Margin	Rolling the Hedge
(FRA)	Margin Call	Forward

PROBLEMS AND QUESTIONS

1. Explain the differences between forward and futures contracts.

2. Define and explain the functions provided by futures exchanges.

3. Explain why the price on an expiring futures contract must be equal or approximately equal to the spot price on the contract's underlying asset.

4. What is the major economic justification of the futures market?

5. Define price limits and explain why they are used by the exchanges.

6. Calculate the actual futures prices and implied futures YTM for the following three T-bill futures contracts:

T-bill futures contract	IMM index
March	93.764
June	93.3092
September	91.8607

7. Suppose you took a short position in a June Eurodollar futures at $R_D = 5.5\%$. Determine the futures settlement prices and your position's profits and losses given the following LIBORs at the June futures' expiration: 4.75%, 5.00%, 5.25%, 5.5%, 5.75%, 6%, and 6.25%. Determine your profits and losses if you had taken a long position in the June contract at $R_D = 5.5\%$.

8. Suppose you took a long position in a September T-bill futures priced at IMM index 95.5. What would be your profit or loss on the position if the price of a spot 91-day T-bill were trading at YTM of 5% (actual/365 day count convention) at the September expiration?

9. Suppose you were long in a June T-bond futures contract at 92-16. What would you have to pay at the futures' expiration for a delivered T-bond if the bond's conversion factor were 1.2 and the accrued interest on the deliverable bond was $1.50 per $100 face value?

10. Suppose you were short in a September T-bond futures contract at 93-16. What would your profit or loss be at the September expiration if the cheapest deliverable bond you could purchase in the market were a 15-year, 7% T-bond trading at 115 (clean price) that had accrued interest of $2 and a conversion factor of 1.25?

11. Define a forward rate agreement (FRA). Provide your own example of an FRA.

12. Given an FRA with the following terms:
   - Notional principal = $20m
   - Reference rate = LIBOR
   - Contract rate = $R_k = 0.05$ (annual)
   - Time period = 90 days
   - Day count convention = actual/365

   Show in a table the payments and receipts for long and short positions on the FRA given possible spot LIBORs at the FRA's expiration of 4%, 4.5%, 5%, 5.5%, and 6%.

13. Explain the similarities and differences between an FRA tied to the LIBOR and a Eurodollar futures contract.

14. Explain how a clearinghouse would record the futures trades in (a)–(d). Include the clearinghouse's payments and receipts needed to close each position.

 a. Mr A buys a September T-bond futures contract from Ms B for $95,000 on June 20.
 b. Mr D buys a September T-bond futures contract from Mr E for $94,500 on June 25.
 c. Ms B buys a September T-bond futures from Mr D for $94,250 on June 28.
 d. Mr E buys a September T-bond futures from Mr A for $96,000 on July 3.

15. Suppose on March 1 you take a long position in a June T-bill futures contract at $R_D = 5\%$.

 a. How much cash or risk-free securities would you have to deposit to satisfy an initial margin requirement of 5%?
 b. Calculate the values of your equity account on the following days, given the following discount yields:

March 2	5.1%
March 3	5.2%
March 4	5.0%
March 5	4.8%
March 8	4.7%
March 9	5.0%

 c. If the maintenance margin requirement specifies keeping the value of the equity account equal to 100% of the initial margin requirement each day, how much cash would you need to deposit in your commodity account each day?

16. Ms Hunter is a money market manager. In July, she anticipates needing cash in September that she plans to obtain by selling ten $1m face value T-bills she currently holds. At the time of the anticipated September sale, the T-bills will have a maturity of 91 days. Suppose there is a September T-bill futures contract trading at a discount yield of $R_D = 6\%$.

 a. If Ms Hunter is fearful that the short-term interest rate could increase, how could she lock in the selling price on her T-bills?
 b. Show in a table Ms Hunter's net revenue at the futures' expiration date from closing the futures position and selling her ten T-bills at possible discount yields of 5%, 6%, and 7%. Assume no quality, quantity, or timing risk.

17. Suppose Ms Hunter anticipates a cash inflow of $9.875m in September that she plans to invest in ten $1m face value T-bills with a maturity of 91 days. Suppose there is a September T-bill futures contract trading at a discount yield of $R_D = 5\%$.

 a. If Ms Hunter is fearful that short-term interest rates could decrease, how could she lock in the purchase price on her T-bills?
 b. Show in a table Ms Hunter's net costs at the futures' expiration date from closing the futures position and buying her ten T-bills at possible discount yields of 4%, 5%, and 6%. Assume no quality, quantity, or timing risk.

18. Cagle Manufacturing forecast a cash inflow of $10m in two months that it is considering investing in a Sun National Bank CD for 90 days. Sun National Bank's jumbo CD pays a rate equal to the LIBOR. Currently such rates are yielding 5.5% (annual rate with an actual/365 day count convention). Cagle is concerned that short-term interest rates could decrease in the next two months and would like to lock in a rate now. As an alternative to hedging its investment with Eurodollar futures, Sun National suggests that Cagle hedge with a forward rate agreement (FRA).

 a. Define the terms of the FRA that would effectively hedge Cagle's futures CD investment.
 b. Show in a table the payoffs that Cagle and Sun National would pay or receive at the maturity of the FRA given the following LIBORs: 5%, 5.25%, 5.5%, 5.75%, and 6%.

c. Show in a table Cagle's cash flows from investing the $10m cash inflow plus or minus the FRA receipts or payments at possible LIBORs of 5%, 5.25%, 5.5%, 5.75%, and 6%. What is the hedged rate of return Cagle would earn from its $10m investment?

19. Suppose there is a Eurodollar futures contracts listed on the IMM that expires at the same time as the FRA in question 18.

a. What would Cagle's FRA equivalent positions be using the Eurodollar futures? What would Cagle's cash flows be from the equivalent Eurodollar futures if the LIBOR were 5% and 6% at expirations?

b. What would Sun National Bank's FRA equivalent positions be using the Eurodollar futures? What would Sun National's cash flows be from the equivalent Eurodollar futures if the LIBOR were 5% and 6% at expirations?

c. Explain how Sun Bank could hedge its FRA in question 18 by taking a position in the Eurodollar futures contract. Using a table, evaluate their hedge position (net position in Eurodollar futures plus FRA) at possible LIBORs at the FRA and Eurodollar futures expiration of 5%, 5.25%, 5.5%, 5.75%, and 6%.

20. Briefly comment on the following:

a. The importance of the delivery procedure on futures contracts, even though most futures contracts are closed by offsetting positions.

b. The advantages and disadvantages of price limits.

c. The marked-to-market tax rule on speculative futures positions.

d. The benefits of futures funds.

e. The role of locals in ensuring continuous futures markets.

f. The basis and its relationship to the time to expiration.

g. Rolling the hedge.

21. Short-answer questions:

(1) What was the primary factor that contributed to the dramatic growth in futures trading over the last 20 years?

(2) What is a hedge called in which the asset underlying the futures contract is not the same as the asset being hedged?

(3) A bond manager who hedged her expected sale of 10-year, AA bonds in early September with a CBOT T-bond futures would be subject to what types of hedging risks?

(4) How much cash or risk-free securities would a speculator have to deposit in a commodity account if he goes long in one September T-bond futures contract at 95 and the initial margin requirement is 5%?

(5) Who ensures that the price on an expiring futures contract is equal or approximately equal to its spot price?

(6) What is the number of futures contracts outstanding at a given point in time called?

(7) How does a futures market provide continuous trading without market-makers or specialists?

(8) What is the trading referred to when exchange members trade for both their clients and themselves?

(9) What is the actual price on a T-bill futures contract, if its quoted IMM index price is 92?

(10) What is the implied YTM on a September T-bill futures contract that is trading at 93 (IMM index price)?

(11) What is the expiration futures price per $100 face value on an expiring Eurodollar futures contract if the 3-month LIBOR is 5% on the expiration day?

(12) What is the major difference between the Eurodollar and the T-bill futures contracts?

(13) How much would the actual Eurodollar futures price change, if the IMM index moves one point?

(14) What is the implied futures YTM on a March T-bill futures contract trading at 93.75 (IMM index)?

WEB EXERCISES

1. Explore some of the information and links available about futures at www.citylink-uk.com. At the site, click on "Exchanges" to find links to derivative exchanges and click on "Quotes" to find links to futures quotes.

2. Determine the recent prices on futures contracts on Eurodollars, T-bills, and other interest rate futures listed on the Chicago Mercantile Exchange by going to www.cme.com and clicking on "Delayed Quotes" in "Market Data."

3. Determine the recent prices on futures contracts on 30-year T-bonds and 10-year T-notes, listed on the Chicago Board of Trade by going to www.cbot.com and clicking on "Interest Rate Futures" in "Quotes and Data."

NOTES

1. On a number of exchanges, partial seats are available at lower prices. These seats allow the member to trade in a limited number of contracts. Also, many exchanges allow seats to be leased.

2. As a matter of security law, dual traders are not allowed to trade on their own accounts when they are about to trade for their clients. With advance knowledge of a client's position, a dual trader could profit by taking a favorable position before executing the client's order. This type of price manipulation is known as *front running*.

3. There are two rules governing an open outcry system. The first is that there can be only one best bid and best ask in the pit at a time. If the market on a particular commodity is at 12 bid and 14 offered, a trader may not start bidding at 11 or offering at 13. Anyone can match the best bid and ask. If someone offers to buy at 13, then all previous bidders must either match the new best bid or stay quiet. The second rule is that traders must trade with the party they recognize who meets their bid or offer. This rule results in different mannerisms (waves, jumps, shouts, and the like) employed by traders to be recognized. On most exchanges, the open outcry system requires that every order be offered for execution. The SFE, SIMEX, and MATIF allow for cross-trading on large block trades in which the trade is prearranged off the exchange.

4. To avoid exchanging principals, the FRA evolved from *forward-forward contracts* in which international banks would enter an agreement for a future loan at a specified rate.

5. On futures contracts, the settlement price is determined by the clearinghouse officials and is based on the average price of the last several trades of the day.

6. Clearinghouse members are also required to maintain a margin account with the clearinghouse. This is known as a clearing margin.

7. The marked-to-market tax rule was established in 1981. One of the reasons for the law was to stop the activities of future spreaders who would take long and short positions in similar futures contracts, then for tax purposes at the end of the year would close the position, thus showing a loss.

8. Cross-hedging can occur when an entire group of assets or liabilities is hedged by one type of futures contract; this is referred to as macro-hedging. Micro-hedging, on the other hand, occurs when each individual asset or liability is hedged separately.

SELECTED REFERENCES

Carlton, D. "Futures Markets: Their Purpose, Their History, Their Growth, Their Successes and Failures," *Journal of Futures Markets* 4 (1984): 237–71.

Chance, D. *An Introduction to Derivatives*, 4th edn (Orlando, FL: Dryden Press, 1997).

Cox, J. C., J. E. Ingersoll, and S. A. Ross "The Relation between Forward Prices and Futures Prices," *Journal of Financial Economics* 9 (1981): 321–46.

Haley, Charles W. "Forward Rate Agreements (FRA)," in Jack Clark Francis and Avner Simon Wolf (eds) *The Handbook of Interest Rate Risk Management* (New York: Irwin Professional Publishing, 1994).

Hull, J. *Options, Futures and Other Derivative Securities* (Englewood Cliffs, NJ: Prentice Hall, 1989).

Jarrow, R. and G. Oldfield "Forward Contracts and Futures Contracts," *Journal of Financial Economics* 9(4) (1981): 373–82.

Johnson, R. Stafford and C. Giaccotto *Options and Futures* (St. Paul, MN: West Publishing, 1995).

Kolb, Robert *Futures, Options, and Swaps*, 4th edn (Blackwell Publishing, 2002).

Livingston, M. "The Cheapest Deliverable Bond for the CBT Treasury Bond Futures Contract," *Journal of Futures Markets* 4 (1984): 161–72.

Park, H. Y. and A. H. Chen "Differences between Futures and Forward Prices: A Further Investigation of Marking to Market Effects," *Journal of Futures Markets* 5 (February 1985): 77–88.

Petzel, Todd E. "Structure of the Financial Futures Markets," in Jack Clark Francis and Avner Simon Wolf (eds) *The Handbook of Interest Rate Risk Management* (New York: Irwin Professional Publishing, 1994).

CHAPTER THIRTEEN

INTEREST RATE FUTURES: APPLICATIONS AND PRICING

13.1 INTRODUCTION

There are many debt positions that can be hedged using futures contracts. The basic hedging principles used for centuries by farmers and businesses to hedge their future revenue or cost positions apply to the hedging of debt positions. A portfolio manager, corporation, municipal government, financial intermediary, dealer, or underwriter who is planning to sell debt securities in the future or borrow funds can hedge against interest rate increases and bond price decreases by going short in a futures contract; a portfolio manager, corporation, municipal government, intermediary, or dealer planning to invest future funds in debt securities can hedge against interest rate decreases and bond price increases by going long in a debt futures contract. In this chapter, we extend our analysis of interest rate futures by examining some additional hedging cases using interest rate futures. In addition, we also look at how futures can be used to create different speculative positions and to form synthetic fixed-rate and floating-rate debt and investment positions, and we examine the pricing of futures contracts using the carrying-cost model. Finally, we conclude the chapter by looking at how foreign currency futures contracts can be used to hedge international investment and debt position against exchange-rate risk and how

such contracts are priced using the interest rate parity model.

13.2 HEDGING DEBT POSITIONS

As we examined in chapter 12, a fixed-income manager planning to invest a future inflow of cash in high-quality bonds could hedge the investment against possible higher bond prices and lower rates by going long in T-bond futures contracts. If long-term rates were to decrease, the higher costs of purchasing the bonds would then be offset by profits from his T-bond futures positions. On the other hand, if rates increased, the manager would benefit from lower bond prices, but he would also have to cover losses on his futures position. Similar long hedging positions using T-bill or Eurodollar futures could also be applied by money managers who were planning to invest future cash inflows in short-term securities and wanted to minimize their risk exposure to short-term interest rate changes.

For cases in which bond or money market managers are planning to sell some of their securities in the future, hedging can be done by going short in a T-bond, T-bill, or Eurodollar futures contracts. If rates were higher at the time of the sale, the resulting lower bond prices and therefore revenue from the bond sale would be offset by profits from the futures positions (just the opposite would occur if rates were lower).

Short hedging positions with futures can be used not only by holders of fixed-income securities planning to sell their instruments before maturity, but also by bond issuers, borrowers, and debt security underwriters. A company planning to issue bonds or borrow funds from a financial institution at some future date, for example, could hedge the debt position against possible interest rate increases by going short in debt futures contracts. Similarly, a bank that finances its short-term loan portfolio of 1-year loans by selling 90-day CDs could manage the resulting maturity gap (maturity of the assets (1-year loans) not equal to the maturity of liabilities (90-day CDs)) by taking short positions in Eurodollar futures. Finally, an underwriter or a dealer who is holding a debt security for a short period of time could hedge the position against interest rate increases by going short in an appropriate futures contract.

13.2.1 Naive Hedging Model

The simplest model to hedge a debt position is a *naive hedging model*. For debt positions, a naive hedge can be formed by hedging each dollar of the face value of the spot position with one market-value dollar in the futures contract. For example, if a T-bond futures' price is at 90, then $100/90 = 1.11$ futures contracts could be used to hedge each dollar of the face value of the bond. A naive hedge also can be formed by hedging each dollar of the market value of the spot position with one market-value dollar of the futures. Thus, if $98 were to be used to buy the above T-bond at some future date, then $98/90 = 1.089$ futures contracts could be purchased to hedge the position.

Example 1: Long Hedge – Future 91-Day T-Bill Investment

Consider the case of a treasurer of a corporation who is expecting a $5m cash inflow in June, which she is planning to invest in T-bills for 91 days. If the treasurer wants to lock in the yield on the T-bill investment, she could do so by going long in June T-bill futures contracts. For example, if the June T-bill contract were

trading at the index price of 95, the treasurer could lock in a yield (YTM_f) of 5.1748% on a 91-day investment made at the futures' expiration date in June:

$$f_0(\text{June}) = \frac{100 - (5)(90/360)}{100}(\$1m)$$

$$= \$987,500$$

$$YTM_f = \left[\frac{\$1m}{\$987,500}\right]^{365/91} - 1 = 0.051748$$

To obtain the 5.1748% yield, the treasurer would need to form a hedge in which she bought $n_f = 5.063291$ June T-bill futures contracts (assume perfect divisibility):

$$n_f = \frac{\text{Investment in June}}{f_0} = \frac{\$5,000,000}{\$987,500}$$

$$= 5.063291 \text{ long contracts}$$

At the June expiration date, the treasurer would close the futures position at the price on the spot 91-day T-bills. If the cash flow from closing is positive, the treasurer would invest the excess cash in T-bills; if it is negative, the treasurer would cover the shortfall with some of the anticipated cash inflow earmarked for purchasing T-bills. For example, suppose at expiration the spot 91-day T-bill were trading at a YTM of 4.5%, or $S_T = \$1m/(1.045^{91/365}) = \$989,086$. In this case, the treasurer would realize a profit of $8,030.38 from closing the futures position:

$$\pi_f = [S_T - f_0]n_f$$

$$= [\$989,086 - \$987,500]5.063291$$

$$= \$8,030.38$$

With the $8,030.38 profit on the futures, the $5m inflow of cash (assumed to occur at expiration), and the spot price on the 91-day T-bill at $989,086, the treasurer would be able to purchase 5.063291 T-bills ($M = 91$ days and face value of $1m):

Number of 91-day T-bills

$$= \frac{\$5,000,000 + \$8,030.38}{\$989,086} = 5.063291$$

Ninety-one days later the treasurer would have $5,063,291, which equates to a rate of return from the $5m inflow of 5.1748% – the rate that is implied on the futures contract:

$$\text{Rate} = \left[\frac{5.063291(\$1m)}{\$5m}\right]^{365/91} - 1$$

$$= 0.051748$$

On the other hand, if the spot T-bill rate were 5.5% at expiration, or $S_T = \$1m/(1.055)^{91/365} = \$986,740$, the treasurer would lose \$3,848 from closing the futures position: [\$986,740 − \$987,500]5.063291 = − \$3,848. With the inflow of \$5m, the treasurer would need to use \$3,848 to settle the futures position, leaving her only \$4,996,152 to invest in T-bills. However, with the price of the T-bill lower in this case, the treasurer would again be able to buy 5.063291 T-bills (\$4,996,152/\$986,740 = 5.063291), and therefore realize a 5.1748% rate of return from the \$5m investment. Note, the hedge rate of 5.1748% occurs for any rate scenario.

Example 2: Long Hedge – Future 182-Day T-Bill Investment

Suppose in the preceding example, the treasurer was planning to invest the expected \$5m June cash inflow in T-bills for a period of 182 days instead of 91 days, and again wanted to lock in the investment rate. Since the underlying T-bill on a futures contract has a maturity of 91 days, not 182, the treasurer would need to take two long futures positions: one position expiring at the end of 91 days (the June contract) and the other expiring at the end of 182 days (the September contract). By purchasing futures contracts with expirations in June and September, the treasurer would have the equivalent of one June T-bill futures contract on a T-bill with 182-day maturity.

The implied futures rate of return earned on a 182-day investment made in June, YTM$_f$(June, 182), is equal to the geometric average of the implied futures rate on the contract expiring in June, YTM$_f$(June, 91), and the implied futures rate on the contract expiring in September, YTM$_f$(Sept, 91):

YTM$_f$(June, 182)

$$= \left[(1 + \text{YTM}_f(\text{June}, 91))^{91/365}\right.$$
$$\left. \times (1 + \text{YTM}_f(\text{Sept}, 91))^{91/365}\right]^{365/182} - 1$$

In this example, if the index on the June T-bill contract is at 95 and the index on a September T-bill contract is at 95.2, then the implied futures rate on each contract's underlying T-bill would be 5.1748% and 5.38865%, respectively, and the implied futures rate on a 182-day investment made in June would be 5.28167%:

$$f_0(\text{June}) = \frac{100 - (5)(90/360)}{100}(\$1m)$$
$$= \$987,500$$

$$\text{YTM}_f(\text{June}) = \left[\frac{\$1m}{\$987,500}\right]^{365/91} - 1$$
$$= 0.051748$$

$$f_0(\text{Sept}) = \frac{100 - (5.2)(90/360)}{100}(\$1m)$$
$$= \$987,000$$

$$\text{YTM}_f(\text{Sept}) = \left[\frac{\$1m}{\$987,000}\right]^{365/91} - 1$$
$$= 0.0538865$$

YTM$_f$(June, 182)

$$= \left[(1.051748)^{91/365}(1.0538865)^{91/365}\right]^{365/182} - 1$$
$$= 0.0528167$$

To actually lock in the 182-day rate for the \$5m investment, the treasurer would need to purchase 5.063291 June contracts and 5.065856 September contracts (again, assume perfect divisibility). That is, using a naive hedging model, the required hedging ratios would be:

$$n_f(\text{June}) = \frac{\$5,000,000}{\$987,500}$$
$$= 5.06329 \text{ long contracts}$$

$$n_f(\text{Sept}) = \frac{\$5,000,000}{\$987,000}$$
$$= 5.065856 \text{ long contracts}$$

At the June expiration date, the treasurer would close both contracts and invest the cash inflows plus (or minus) the futures profit (costs) in 182-day T-bills. By doing this, the treasurer in effect would be creating a June futures contract on a T-bill with a maturity of 182 days. If the equilibrium pricing model governing futures (discussed in section 13.6) holds, then the treasurer will earn a rate of return on the 182-day investment equal to 5.28167%.

Example 3: Short Hedge – Managing the Maturity Gap

An important use of short hedges is in minimizing the market risk that financial institutions are exposed to when the maturity of their assets does not equal the maturity of their liabilities – maturity gap. As an example, consider the case of a small bank with a maturity gap problem in which its short-term loan portfolio has an average maturity greater than the maturity of the CDs that it is using to finance its loans. Specifically, suppose that in June the bank makes loans of $1m, all with maturities of 180 days. To finance the loans, though, suppose the bank's customers prefer 90-day CDs to 180-day CDs, and as a result, the bank sells $1m-worth of 90-day CDs at a rate equal to the current LIBOR of 5%. Ninety days later (in September) the bank would owe $1,012,103 = $1m(1.05)^{90/365}$; to finance this debt, the bank would have to sell $1,012,103-worth of 90-day CDs at the LIBOR at that time. In the absence of a hedge, the bank would be subject to market risk. If short-term rates increase, the bank would have to pay higher interest on its planned September CD sale, lowering the interest spread it earns (the rate earned from $1m 180-day loans minus the interest paid on CDs to finance them); if rates decrease, the bank's spread would increase.

Suppose the bank is fearful of higher rates in September and decides to minimize its exposure to market risk by hedging its $1,012,103 CD sale in September with a September Eurodollar futures contract trading at an index value of 95. To hedge the liability, the bank would need to go short in 1.02491 September Eurodollar futures (assume perfect divisibility):

$$f_0(\text{Sept}) = \frac{100 - (5)(90/360)}{100}(\$1m)$$

$$= \$987,500$$

$$n_f = \frac{\$1,012,103}{\$987,500}$$

$$= 1.02491 \text{ short eurodollar contracts}$$

At a futures price of $987,500, the bank would be able to lock in a rate on its September CDs of 5.23376%. With this rate and the 5% rate it

pays on its first CDs, the bank would pay 5.117% on its CDs over the 180-day period:

$$YTM_f(\text{Sept}) = \left[\frac{\$1m}{\$987,500}\right]^{365/90} - 1$$

$$= 0.0523376$$

$$YTM_{180}$$
$$= \left[(1.05)^{90/365}(1.0523376)^{90/365}\right]^{365/180} - 1$$

$$= 0.05117$$

That is, when the first CDs mature in September, the bank will issue new 90-day CDs at the prevailing LIBOR to finance the $1,012,103 first CD debt plus (minus) any loss (profit) from closing its September Eurodollar futures position. If the LIBOR in September has increased, the bank will have to pay a greater interest on the new CD, but it will realize a profit from its futures contracts that, in turn, will lower the amount of funds it needs to finance at the higher rate. On the other hand, if the LIBOR is lower, the bank will have lower interest payments on its new CDs, but it will also incur a loss on its futures position and therefore will have more funds that need to be financed at the lower rates. The impact that rates have on the amount of funds needed to be financed and the rate paid on them will exactly offset each other, leaving the bank with a fixed debt amount when the September CDs mature in December. This can be seen in exhibit 13.1, where the bank's December liability (the liability at the end of the 180-day period) is shown to be $1,024,914 given September LIBOR scenarios of 4.5% and 5.5% (this will be true at any rate). Note, the debt at the end of 180 days of $1,024,914 equates to a 180-day rate for the period of 5.117%:

$$R = \left[\frac{\$1,024,914}{\$1,000,000}\right]^{365/180} - 1 = 0.05117$$

13.3 CROSS-HEDGING

13.3.1 Price-Sensitivity Model

The above examples represent perfect hedging cases in which certain revenues or costs can be locked in at a future date. As we noted in chapter 12, the presence of quality risk, timing

Exhibit 13.1   Hedging maturity gap

(1) September LIBOR	R	0.045	0.055
(2) September spot and expiring futures price	$S_T = f_T = \$1m/(1 + R)^{90/365}$	\$989,205	\$986,885
(3) Profit on futures	$\pi_f = 1.02491[\$987,500 - f_T]$	-\$1,747	\$630
(4) Debt on June CD	$\$1m(1.05)^{90/365}$	\$1,012,103	\$1,012,103
(5) Total funds to finance	Row (4) − row (3)	\$1,013,850	\$1,011,473
(6) Debt at end of period	$[\text{Row }(5)](1 + R)^{90/365}$	\$1,024,914	\$1,024,914
(7) Rate paid for 180-day period	$[(\text{Row }(6))/\$1,000,000]^{365/180}$	5.117%	5.117%

risk, and quantity risk makes perfect hedges the exception and not the rule. In practice, hedging risk cannot be eliminated totally by hedging with futures contracts. As a result, the objective in hedging is to try to minimize risk. Several hedging models try to achieve this objective: the above naive hedging model, price-sensitivity model, minimum variance model, and utility-based hedging model. These models have as their common objective the determination of a *hedge ratio*: the optimal number of futures contracts needed to hedge a position. If the debt position to be hedged has a futures contract with the same underlying asset, such as in the above hedging cases, then a naive hedge usually will be effective in reducing interest rate risk. Many debt positions, though, involve securities and interest rate positions in which a futures contract on the underlying security does not exist. In such cases, an effective cross-hedge needs to be determined to minimize the price risk in the underlying spot position. Two commonly used models for cross-hedging are the regression model and the price-sensitivity model. In the *regression model*, the estimated slope coefficient of the regression equation is used to determine the hedge ratio. The coefficient, in turn, is found by regressing the spot price on the bond to be hedged against the futures price.

The second hedging approach is to use the *price-sensitivity model* developed by Kolb and Chiang (1981) and Toevs and Jacobs (1986). This model has been shown to be relatively effective in reducing the variability of debt positions. The model determines the number of futures contracts that will make the value of a portfolio consisting of a fixed-income security

and an interest rate futures contract invariant to small changes in interest rates. The optimum number of futures contracts that achieves this objective is:

$$n_f = \frac{\text{Dur}_S}{\text{Dur}_f} \frac{S_0}{f_0} \frac{(1 + \text{YTM}_f)^T}{(1 + \text{YTM}_S)^T}$$

where:

Dur_S = duration of the bond being hedged

Dur_f = duration of the bond underlying the futures contract (for T-bond futures this would be the cheapest-to-deliver bond)

YTM_S = yield to maturity on the bond being hedged

YTM_f = yield to maturity implied on the futures contract

13.3.2 Cross-Hedging Examples

Example 1: Hedging a Commercial Paper Issue

Suppose that in June the treasurer of the ABC Manufacturing Company makes plans to sell CP in September in order to finance a \$9.7m purchase of the company's raw materials needed for its fall production levels. To ensure funds of \$9,713,634, the treasurer would like to issue CP in September with a face value of \$10m, maturity of 182 days, and paying the current CP rate of 6%. Fearing short-term interest rates could increase over the next

Exhibit 13.2   Cross-hedge: hedging CP sale with T-bill futures

(1) Spot T-bill discount yield, R_D	(2) T-bill spot and expiring futures, price $S_T = f_T$	(3) Futures profit, $\pi_f = 20[\$987,500 - f_T]$	(4) Price of CP	(5) Hedged CP revenue Col. (3) + Col. (4)
4%	$990,000	− $50,000	$9,787,500	$9,737,500
5%	$987,500	0	$9,737,500	$9,737,500
6%	$985,000	$50,000	$9,687,500	$9,737,500

- CP is assumed to be sold at a discount yield that is 25 BP greater than the discount yield on T-bill
- Hedged rate on CP is 5.48%

$$S_T = f_T = \frac{100 - R_D(90/360)}{100}(\$1m)$$

$$P_{CP} = \frac{100 - (R_D + 0.25)(180/360)}{100}(\$10m)$$

$$\text{Hedged rate} = \left[\frac{\$10m}{\$9,737,500}\right]^{365/182} - 1 = 0.0548$$

3 months, the treasurer would like to hedge the future CP issue by taking a short position in September T-bill futures contracts trading at an index value of 95. Using the price-sensitivity model, this could be accomplished with 20 September T-bill futures contracts:

$$n_f = \frac{\text{Dur}_S}{\text{Dur}_f} \frac{S_0}{f_0} \frac{(1 + \text{YTM}_f)^T}{(1 + \text{YTM}_S)^T}$$

$$= \frac{182}{91} \frac{\$9,713,634}{\$987,500} \frac{(1.05175)^{91/365}}{(1.06)^{182/365}}$$

$$\cong 20 \text{ short T-bill futures}$$

where:

Dur_S = duration of CP = 182

Dur_f = duration of T-bill = 91

YTM_S = yield to maturity on CP

$\quad = 6\%$

$$f_0(\text{Sept}) = \frac{100 - (5)(90/360)}{100}(\$1m)$$

$$= \$987,500$$

$$\text{YTM}_f(\text{Sept}) = \left[\frac{\$1m}{\$987,500}\right]^{365/91} - 1$$

$$= 0.05175$$

To illustrate the impact of the hedge, suppose the 182-day CP issue is sold at the September futures' expiration at a price that reflects an annual discount yield (R_D) that is 0.25% higher than the spot T-bill discount yield. As shown in exhibit 13.2, with 20 September T-bill futures contracts, the treasurer would be able to lock in $9,737,500 cash proceeds from selling the CP issue and closing the futures contracts. With $9,737,500 cash locked in, his hedged rate on the 182-day hedged CP issue would be 5.48%:

$$\text{Hedged rate} = \left[\frac{\$10,000,000}{\$9,737,500}\right]^{365/182} - 1$$

$$= 0.0548$$

Example 2: Hedging a Bond Portfolio with T-Bond Futures

T-bond futures contracts often are used by fixed-income portfolio managers to protect the future values of their portfolios against interest rate changes. To see this, suppose in January a fixed-income portfolio manager believes that she may be required to liquidate the fund's long-term bond holdings in mid-May. Also, suppose the bond portfolio has an aggregate face value of $1m, average coupon rate of 12%, average maturity of 15 years, and currently is valued at 102 per $100 par value. The average YTM on the bond portfolio is 11.75% and its duration is 7.66 years. Further, suppose the manager is considering hedging the portfolio against interest rate changes by going short in June T-bond futures contracts that currently are trading at $f_0 = 72\frac{16}{32}$. Finally, suppose that after tracking several bonds, a T-bond futures expert advises the manager that an 18-year T-bond trading at a YTM of 9% and with a duration of 7 years is the most likely bond to be delivered on the June futures contract. Using the price-sensitivity model, the portfolio manager could hedge the bond portfolio by selling 14 futures contracts:

$$
n_f = \frac{\text{Dur}_S}{\text{Dur}_f} \frac{S_0}{f_0} \frac{(1 + \text{YTM}_f)^T}{(1 + \text{YTM}_S)^T}
$$

$$
= \frac{7.66}{7} \frac{\$1,020,000}{\$72,500} \frac{(1.09)^{18}}{(1.1175)^{15}}
$$

$$
\cong 14 \text{ short T-bond futures}
$$

If the manager hedges the bond portfolio with 14 June T-bond short contracts, she will be able to offset changes in the bond portfolio's value resulting from interest rate changes. For example, suppose interest rates increased from January to mid-May causing the price of the bond portfolio to decrease from 102 to 95 and the futures price on the June T-bond contract to decrease from $72\frac{16}{32}$ to $68\frac{22}{32}$. In this case, the fixed-income portfolio would lose $70,000 in value (decrease in value from $1,020,000 to $950,000). This loss, though, would be partially offset by a profit of $53,375 on the T-bond futures position: futures profit = 14[$72,500 − $68,687.50] = $53,375. Thus, by using T-bond futures the manager is able to reduce some of the potential losses in her portfolio value that would result if interest rates increase.

13.4 SPECULATING WITH INTEREST RATE FUTURES

While interest rate futures are extensively used for hedging, they are also frequently used to speculate on expected interest rate changes. A long futures position is taken when interest rates are expected to fall and a short position is taken when rates are expected to rise. Speculating on interest rate changes by taking such outright or naked futures positions represents an alternative to buying or short selling a bond on the spot market. Because of the risk inherent in such *outright futures positions*, though, some speculators form spreads instead of taking a naked position. A futures spread is formed by taking long and short positions on different futures contracts simultaneously. Two general types of spread exist: intracommodity and intercommodity. An *intracommodity spread* is formed with futures contracts on the same asset but with different expiration dates; an *intercommodity spread* is formed with two futures contracts with the same expiration but on different assets.

13.4.1 Intracommodity Spread

An intracommodity spread is often used to reduce the risk associated with a pure outright position. As we will see later in examining futures price relations, more distant futures contracts (T_2) are more price sensitive to changes in the spot price, S, than near-term futures (T_1):

$$
\frac{\%\Delta f_{T_2}}{\%\Delta S} > \frac{\%\Delta f_{T_1}}{\%\Delta S}
$$

Thus, a speculator who expects the interest rate on long-term bonds to decrease in the future could form an intracommodity spread by going long in a longer-term T-bond futures contract and short in a shorter-term one. This type of intracommodity spread will be profitable if the expectation of long-term rates decreasing occurs. That is, the increase in the T-bond price resulting from a decrease in long-term rates will cause the price on the longer-term T-bond futures to increase more than the shorter-term one. As a result, a speculator's gains from his long position in the longer-term futures will exceed his losses from his short position. If rates rise, though, losses will occur on the long position; these losses will be offset partially by profits realized from the short position on the shorter-term contract. On the other hand, if a bond speculator believes rates would increase but did not want to assume the risk inherent in an outright short position, he could form a spread with a short position in a longer-term contract and a long position in the shorter-term one. Note that in forming a spread, the speculator does not have to keep the ratio of long-to-short positions one-to-one, but instead could use any ratio (2-to-1, 3-to-2, etc.) to obtain his desired return–risk combination.

13.4.2 Intercommodity Spread

Intercommodity spreads consist of long and short positions on futures contracts with the same expirations, but with different underlying assets. Recall that in chapter 8 we defined two active bond strategies: the rate-anticipation swap and the quality swap. These swap strategies can be set up as intercommodity spreads formed with different debt security futures.

Consider the case of a speculator who is forecasting a general decline in interest rates across all maturities (i.e., a downward parallel shift in the yield curve). Since bonds with greater maturities are more price sensitive to interest rate changes than those with shorter maturities, the speculator could set up a rate-anticipation swap by going long in a longer-term bond with the position partially hedged by going short in a shorter-term one. Instead of using spot securities, the speculator alternatively could form an intercommodity spread by going long in a T-bond futures contract that is partially hedged by a short position in a T-note (or T-bill) futures contract. On the other hand, if an investor were forecasting an increase in rates across all maturities, instead of forming a rate-anticipation swap with spot positions, she could go short in the T-bond futures contract and long in the T-note (or T-bill). Forming spreads with T-note and T-bond futures is sometimes referred to as the *NOB strategy* (Notes over Bonds).

Another type of intercommodity spread is a quality swap formed with different futures contracts on bonds with different default risk characteristics; for example, a spread formed with futures contracts on a T-bond and a Municipal Bond Index (MBI) or contracts on T-bills and Eurodollar deposits. Like the quality swap formed with spot position that was discussed in chapter 8, profits from these futures spreads are based on the ability to forecast a

narrowing or a widening of the spread between the yields on the underlying bonds. For example, in an economic recession the demand for lower default-risk bonds often increases relative to the demand for higher default-risk bonds. If this occurs, then the default risk spread (lower grade bond yields minus higher grade bond yields) would tend to widen. A speculator forecasting an economic recession could, in turn, profit from an anticipated widening in the risk premium by forming an intercommodity spread consisting of a long position in a T-bond futures contract and a short position in an MBI contract. Similarly, since Eurodollar deposits are not completely risk free, while T-bills are, a spreader forecasting riskier times (and therefore a widening of the spread between Eurodollar rates and T-bill rates) could go long in the T-bill futures contract and short in the Eurodollar futures contract. A spread with T-bills and Eurodollars contracts is referred to as a *TED spread*.

13.4.3 Managing Asset and Liability Positions

Interest rate futures can also be used by financial and non-financial corporations to alter the exposure of their balance sheets to interest rate changes. The change can be done for speculative purposes (increasing the firm's exposure to interest rate changes) or for hedging purposes (reducing exposure). Consider the case of an insurance company that as a matter of policy maintains an immunized position in which the duration of its bond portfolio is equal to the duration of its liabilities: $D_A = D_L$. With a duration gap of zero, $D_A - D_L = 0$, the company's economic surplus is invariant to interest rate changes. Suppose, though, that the managers expect rates will fall across all maturities in the future and would like to change the insurance company's interest rate exposure to a moderately speculative one in which the company has a positive duration gap: $D_A - D_L > 0$. As noted in chapter 8, one way for the company to do this would be to increase the duration of its bond portfolio by changing the allocation: sell short-term bonds and buy long-term ones. An alternative to this expensive strategy would be to take a long position in T-bond futures.

If rates decrease as expected, then the value of the company's bond portfolio would increase and it would also profit from its long futures position; on the other hand, if rates were to increase, then the company would see not only a decline in the value of its bond portfolio but also losses on its futures position. Thus, by adding futures the company has effectively increased its balance sheet's interest rate exposure by creating a positive duration gap.

Instead of increasing its balance sheet's exposure to interest rate changes, a company may choose to reduce it. For example, a company with a positive duration gap and a concern over futures interest rate increases could reduce the gap by taking a short position in an interest rate futures contract. This action is similar to the bond portfolio hedging example discussed in section 13.3.2. This method of hedging or speculating in which the original composition of assets and liabilities is not changed is referred to as *off-balance-sheet restructuring*.

It should be noted that companies need to guard against unplanned actions that might change their hedging positions to speculative ones. Many companies have traders hired to manage their risk exposure to interest rates. As time goes by, some traders (often under the illusion they can beat the market) take more speculative positions, often causing a transformation of the company's treasury department into a de facto profit center. Moreover, there are a number of cases in which companies incurred spectacular losses as a result of their traders taking speculative positions with derivatives. One classic case is the one of Orange County California which lost $2b in 1994 when its fund trader Robert Citron lost on speculative interest rate derivative positions.

13.5 SYNTHETIC DEBT AND INVESTMENT POSITIONS

In the maturity-gap example, we assumed the bank's gap problem was created as a result of the bank's borrowers wanting 180-day loans and its depositors wanting 90-day CDs. Suppose the bank, though, does not have a maturity-gap problem; that is, it can easily sell 180-day CDs to finance its 180-day loans and 90-day CDs to finance its 90-day loans. With no gap problem,

the bank still may find that instead of financing with a 180-day spot CD, it would be cheaper if it financed its 180-day June loans with synthetic 180-day CDs formed by (1) selling 90-day June CDs, (2) rolling over the obligation three months later by selling 90-day September CDs, and (3) locking in the September CD rate now by taking a short position in the September Eurodollar futures contract. For example, in the maturity-gap case, the bank was able to create a synthetic 180-day CD paying 5.117% given a September futures price at 95. If the actual 180-day CD exceeded 5.117%, then the bank would gain by financing its 180-day loans with 180-day synthetic CDs instead of by selling direct 180-day CDs.

In practice, exchange-traded interest rate futures contracts are usually priced so that such arbitrage opportunities for banks are rare. As we will discuss in section 13.6, if the equilibrium carrying-cost model governing Eurodollar futures prices holds, then the rate on the synthetic position will be equal to the rate on the spot. Thus, the opportunity for the above bank to gain from a synthetic position is unlikely. There are some cases, though, in which the rate on debt and investment positions can be improved by creating synthetic positions with futures and other derivative securities such as swaps. These cases involve creating a synthetic fixed-rate loan by combining a floating-rate loan with short positions in Eurodollar contracts and creating a synthetic floating-rate loan by combining a fixed-rate loan with long positions in Eurodollar contracts. Similar synthetic fixed-rate and floating-rate investment positions can also be formed.

13.5.1 Synthetic Fixed-Rate Loan

A corporation wanting to finance its operations or capital expenditures with fixed-rate debt has a choice of either a direct fixed-rate loan or a synthetic fixed-rate loan formed with a floating-rate loan and short positions in Eurodollar futures contracts, whichever is cheaper. Consider the case of a corporation that can obtain a 1-year $10m fixed-rate loan from a bank at 9.5% or alternatively can obtain a 1-year, floating-rate loan from a bank. In the floating-rate loan agreement, suppose the loan starts on date

September 20 at a rate of 9.5% and then is reset on December 20, March 20, and June 20 to equal the spot LIBOR (annual) plus 250 basis points divided by four: (LIBOR + 0.025)/4.

To create a synthetic fixed-rate loan from this floating-rate loan, the corporation could go short in a series of Eurodollar futures contracts – Eurodollar strip. For this case, suppose the company goes short in a series of ten contracts expiring at $T = 12/20$, $3/20$, and $6/20$ and trading at the following prices:

	12/20	3/20	6/20
Index	93.5	93.75	94
f_0	$983,750	$984,375	$985,000

The locked-in rates obtained using Eurodollar futures contracts are equal to 100 minus the index plus the basis points on the loan:

Locked-in rate $= [100 - \text{Index}] + BP/100$

$12/20 : R_{12/20} = [100 - 93.5] + 2.5 = 9\%$

$3/20 : R_{3/20} = [100 - 93.75] + 2.5 = 8.75\%$

$6/20 : R_{6/20} = [100 - 94] + 2.5 = 8.5\%$

For example, suppose on date 12/20, the settlement LIBOR is 7%, yielding a settlement index price of 93 and a closing futures price of $982,500. At that rate, the corporation would realize a profit of $12,500 = (10)($1,250) from its ten short positions on the 12/20 futures contract:

$$f_T = \frac{(100 - (100 - 93))(90/360)}{100}(\$1m)$$

$$= \$982,500$$

Profit on 12/20 contract

$$= (10)(\$983,750 - \$982,500) = \$12,500$$

At the 12/20 date, though, the new interest that the corporation would have to pay for the next quarter would be set at $237,500:

$12/20$ interest $= [(\text{LIBOR} + 0.025)/4](\$10m)$

$= [(0.07 + 0.025)/4](\$10m)$

$= \$237,500$

Subtracting the futures profit of $12,500 from the $237,500 interest payment (and ignoring the time value factor), the corporation's hedged

interest payment for the next quarter is $225,000. On an annualized basis, this equates to a 9% interest rate on a $10m loan, the same rate as the locked-in rate:

$$\text{Hedged rate} = \frac{4(\$225,000)}{\$10,000,000} = 0.09$$

On the other hand, if the 12/20 LIBOR were 6%, then the quarterly interest payment would be only $212,500 ((($0.06 + 0.025)/4) × ($10m) = $212,500). This gain to the corporation, though, would be offset by a $12,500 loss on the futures contract (i.e., at 6%, $f_T = \$985,000$, yielding a loss on the 12/20 contract of $10($983,750 − $985,000) = −$12,500). As a result, the total quarterly debt of the company again would be $225,000 ($212,500 + $12,500). Ignoring the time value factor, the annualized hedged rate the company pays would again be 9%. Thus, the corporation's short position in the 12/20 Eurodollar futures contract at 93.5 enables it to lock in a quarterly debt obligation of $225,000 and a 9% annualized borrowing rate.

Given the other locked-in rates, the 1-year fixed rate for the corporation on its variable-rate loan hedged with the Eurodollar futures contracts would be 8.9369%:

Synthetic fixed rate

$$= \left[(1.095)^{0.25}(1.09)^{0.25}(1.0875)^{0.25}(1.085)^{0.25} \right]^{1} - 1$$

$$= 0.089369$$

Thus, the corporation would gain by financing with a synthetic fixed-rate loan at 8.9369% instead of a direct fixed-rate loan at 9.5%.

13.5.2 Synthetic Floating-Rate Loan

A synthetic floating-rate loan is formed by borrowing at a fixed rate and taking a long position in a Eurodollar or T-bill futures contract. For example, suppose the corporation in the preceding example had a floating-rate asset and wanted a floating-rate loan instead of a fixed one. It could take the one offered by the bank of LIBOR plus 250 BP or it could form a synthetic floating-rate loan by borrowing at a fixed rate for 1 year and going long in a series of Eurodollar futures expiring at 12/20, 3/20, and 6/20. The synthetic loan will provide a lower rate than the direct floating-rate loan if the fixed rate is less than 9%. For example, suppose the corporation borrows at a fixed rate of 8.5% for 1 year with interest payments made quarterly at dates 12/20, 3/20, and 6/20 and then goes long in the series of Eurodollar futures to form a synthetic floating-rate loan. On date 12/20, if the settlement LIBOR were 7% (settlement index price of 93 and a closing futures price of $982,500), the corporation would lose $12,500 (= (10)($982,500 − $983,750)) from its ten long positions on the 12/20 futures contracts and would pay $212,550 on its fixed-rate loan ((0.085/4)($10m)= $212,500). The company's effective annualized rate would be 9% ([4($212,500 + $12,500)]/ $10,000,000 = 0.09), which is 0.5% less than the rate paid on the floating-rate loan (LIBOR + 250 BP = 7% + 2.5% = 9.5%). If the settlement LIBOR were 6%, though (settlement index price of 94 and a closing futures price of $985,000), the corporation would realize a profit of $12,500 (=(10)($985,000 − $983,750)) from the ten long positions on the 12/20 futures contracts and would pay $212,550 on its fixed-rate loan. Its effective annualized rate would be 8% ([4($212,500 − $12,500)]/$10,000,000 = 0.08), which again is 0.5% less than the rate on the floating-rate loan (LIBOR + 250 BP= 6% + 2.5% = 8.5%).

13.5.3 Synthetic Investments

Futures can also be used on the asset side to create synthetic fixed- and floating-rate investments. An investment company setting up a 3-year unit investment trust offering a fixed rate could invest funds either in 3-year fixed-rate securities or a synthetic one formed with a 3-year floating-rate note tied to the LIBOR and long positions in a series of Eurodollar futures, whichever yields the higher rate. By contrast, an investor looking for a floating-rate security could alternatively consider a synthetic floating-rate investment consisting of a fixed-rate security and a short Eurodollar strip. Several problems at the end of this chapter deal with constructing these synthetic investments.

13.6 FUTURES PRICING

13.6.1 Basis

The underlying asset price on a futures contract primarily depends on the spot price of the underlying asset. As noted in chapter 12, the difference between the futures (or forward price) and the spot price is called the basis (B_t):

$$\text{Basis} = B_t = f_t - S_t$$

(The basis also can be expressed as $S_t - f_t$.) For most futures (and forward) contracts, the futures price exceeds the spot price before expiration and approaches the spot price as expiration nears. Thus, the basis usually is positive and decreasing over time, equaling zero at expiration ($B_t = 0$). Futures and spot prices also tend to be highly correlated with each other, increasing and decreasing together; their correlation, though, is not perfect. As a result, the basis tends to be relatively stable along its declining trend, even when futures and spot prices vacillate.

Theoretically, the relationship between the spot price and the futures or forward price can be explained by the *carrying-cost model* (or cost of carry model). In this model, arbitrageurs ensure that the equilibrium forward price is equal to the net costs of carrying the underlying asset to expiration. The model is used to explain what determines the equilibrium price on a forward contract. However, if short-term interest rates are constant, the carrying-cost model can be extended to pricing futures contracts.

In terms of the carrying-cost model, the price difference between futures and spot prices can be explained by the costs and benefits of carrying the underlying asset to expiration. For futures on debt securities, the carrying costs include the financing costs of holding the underlying asset to expiration, and the benefits include the coupon interest earned from holding the security.

13.6.2 Pricing a T-Bill Futures Contract

To illustrate the carrying-cost model, consider the pricing of a T-bill futures contract. With no coupon interest, the underlying T-bill does not generate any benefits during the holding period and the financing costs are the only carrying costs. In terms of the model, the equilibrium relationship between the futures and spot price on the T-bill is:

$$f_0 = S_0(1 + R_f)^T \qquad (13.1)$$

where:

f_0 = contract price on the T-bill futures contract

T = time to expiration on the futures contract

S_0 = current spot price on a T-bill identical to the T-bill underlying the futures ($m = 91$ and $F = \$1m$) except it has a maturity of $91 + T$

R_f = risk-free rare or repo rate

$S_0(1 + R_f)^T$ = financing costs of holding a spot T-bill

If equation (13.1) does not hold, an arbitrage opportunity occurs. The arbitrage strategy is referred to as a *cash-and-carry arbitrage* and involves taking opposite positions in the spot and futures contracts. For example, suppose in June the following:

• 161-day T-bill priced at $97.5844 per $100 face value to yield 5.7%
• September T-bill futures contract expiring in 70 days
• 70-day risk-free rate or repo rate of 6.38%.

Using the carrying-cost model, the equilibrium price of a September T-bill futures contract is $f_0 = 987,487$ or 98.74875 per $100 par value:

$$f_0 = S_0(1 + R_f)^T$$
$$= 97.5844(1.0638)^{70/365} = 98.74875$$

where:

$$S_0 = \frac{100}{(1.057)^{161/365}} = 97.5844$$

If the market price on the T-bill futures contract was not equal to 98.74875, then a cash-and-carry arbitrage opportunity would exist. For example, if the T-bill futures price is at $f_0^M = 99$, an arbitrageur could earn a risk-free profit of $2,512.50 per $1m face value or 0.25125 per $100 face value ($99 - 98.74875$) at the expiration date by executing the following strategy.

1. Borrow $97.5844 at the repo (or borrowing) rate of 6.38%, then buy a 161-day spot T-bill for $S_0(161) = 97.5844$.
2. Take a short position in a T-bill futures contract expiring in 70 days at the futures price of $f_0^M = 99$.

At expiration, the arbitrageur would earn $0.25125 per $100 face value ($2,512.50 per $1m par) when he:

1. Sells the T-bill on the spot futures contract at 99; and
2. Repays the principal and interest on the loan of $97.5844(1.0638)^{70/365} = 98.74875$:

$$\pi_T = f_0^M - f_0^*$$
$$= 99 - 97.5844(1.0638)^{70/365}$$
$$= 99 - 98.74875 = 0.25125$$
$$\pi_T = \frac{0.25125}{100}(\$1m) = \$2,512.50$$

In addition to the arbitrage opportunity when the futures is overpriced at 99, a money market manager currently planning to invest for 70 days in a T-bill at 6.38% also could benefit with a greater return by creating a synthetic 70-day investment by buying a 161-day bill and then going short at 99 in the T-bill futures contract expiring in 70 days. For example, using the above numbers, if a money market manager were planning to invest 97.5844 for 70 days, she could buy a 161-day bill for that amount and go short in the futures at 99. Her return would be 7.8%, compared to 6.38% from the 70-day spot T-bill:

$$R = \left[\frac{99}{97.5844}\right]^{365/70} - 1 = 0.078$$

Both the arbitrage and the investment strategies involve taking short positions in the T-bill futures. These actions would therefore serve to move the price on the futures down towards 98.74875.

If the market price on the T-bill futures contract is below the equilibrium value, then the cash-and-carry arbitrage strategy is reversed. In our example, suppose the futures were priced at 98. In this case, an arbitrageur would go long in the futures, agreeing to buy a 91-day T-bill 70 days later, and would go short in the spot T-bill, borrowing the 161-day bill, selling it for 97.5844, and investing the proceeds at 6.38% for 70 days. Seventy days later (expiration), the arbitrageur would buy a 91-day T-bill on the futures for 98 (f_0^M), use the bill to close his short position, and collect 98.74875 (f_0^*) from his investment, realizing a cash flow of $7,487.50 or $0.74875 per $100 par:

$$\pi_T = f_0^* - f_0^M$$
$$= 97.5844(1.0638)^{70/365} - 98$$
$$= 98.74875 - 98 = 0.74875$$
$$\pi_T = \frac{0.74875}{100}(\$1m) = \$7,487.50$$

In addition to this cash-and-carry arbitrage, if the futures price is below 98, a money manager currently holding 161-day T-bills also could obtain an arbitrage by selling the bills for 97.5844 and investing the proceeds at 6.38% for 70 days, then going long in the T-bill futures contract expiring in 70 days. Seventy days later, the manager would receive 98.74875 from the investment and would pay 98 on the futures to reacquire the bills for a cash flow of 0.74875 per $100 par.

13.6.3 Other Equilibrium Conditions Implied by the Carrying-Cost Model

For T-bill futures as well as Eurodollar futures contracts, the equilibrium condition defined by the carrying-cost model in equation (13.1) can be redefined in terms of the following equivalent conditions: (1) the rate on a spot T-bill (or actual repo rate) is equal to the rate on a synthetic T-bill (or implied repo rate); (2) the rate implied on the futures contract is equal to the implied forward rate.

Equivalent Spot and Synthetic T-Bill Rates

As illustrated in the above example, a money market manager planning to invest funds in a T-bill for a given short-term horizon period either can invest in the spot T-bill or construct a synthetic T-bill by purchasing a longer-term T-bill, then locking in its selling price by going short in a T-bill futures contract. In the preceding example, the manager either could buy a 70-day spot T-bill yielding a 6.38% rate of return and trading at $S_0 = 98.821$:

$$S_0 = 100/(1.0638)^{70/365} = 98.821$$

or could create a long position in a synthetic 70-day T-bill by buying the 161-day T-bill trading at $S_0 = 97.5844$, then locking in the selling price by going short in the T-bill futures contract expiring in 70 days. If the futures price in the market exceeds the equilibrium value as determined by the carrying-cost model ($f_0^M > f_0^*$), then the rate of return on the synthetic T-bill (R_{syn}) will exceed the rate on the spot; in this case, the manager should choose the synthetic T-bill. As we saw, at a futures price of 99, the manager earned a rate of return of 7.8% on the synthetic, compared to only 6.38% from the spot. On the other hand, if the futures price is less than its equilibrium value ($f_0^M < f_0^*$), then R_{syn} will be less than the rate on the spot; in this case, the manager should purchase the spot T-bill.

Note that in an efficient market, money managers will drive the futures price to its equilibrium value as determined by the carrying-cost model. When this condition is realized, R_{syn} will be equal to the rate on the spot and the money manager would be indifferent to either investment. In our example, this occurs when the market price on the futures contract is equal to the equilibrium value of 98.74875. At that price, R_{syn} is equal to 6.38%.

$$R_{syn} = \left[\frac{98.74875}{97.5844}\right]^{365/70} - 1 = 0.0638$$

Thus, if the carrying-cost model holds, the rate earned from investing in a spot T-bill and the rate from investing in a synthetic will be equal.

Implied and Actual Repo Rates

The rate earned from the synthetic T-bill is commonly referred to as the *implied repo rate*. Formally, the implied repo rate is defined as the rate in which the arbitrage profit from implementing the cash-and-carry arbitrage strategy is zero:

$$\pi = f_0 - S_0(1 + R_f)^T$$
$$0 = f_0 - S_0(1 + R_f)^T$$
$$R = \left[\frac{f_0}{S_0}\right]^{1/T} - 1$$

The actual repo rate is the one we use in solving for the equilibrium futures price in the carrying-cost model; in our example, this was the rate on the 70-day T-bill (6.38%). Thus, the equilibrium condition that the synthetic and spot T-bill be equal can be stated equivalently as an equality between the actual and the implied repo rates.

Implied Forward and Futures Rates

The other condition implied by the carrying-cost model is the equality between the rate implied by the futures contract, YTM_f, and the implied forward rate, R_I, defined in chapter 2:

Implied futures rate = Implied forward rate
$$YTM_f = R_I$$

$$\left[\frac{F}{f_0}\right]^{365/91} - 1 = \left[\frac{S(T)}{S(T+91)}\right]^{365/91} - 1$$

where F is the face value on the spot T-bill and $T + 91$ is the maturity of the spot T-bill.

The right-hand side of the above equation is the implied forward rate. This rate is determined by the current spot prices on T-bills maturing at T and at $T + 91$. In our illustrative example, the implied forward rate is 5.18%:

$$R_I = \left[\frac{S(70)}{S(161)}\right]^{365/91} - 1$$

$$= \left[\frac{98.821}{97.5844}\right]^{365/91} - 1 = 0.0518$$

The left-hand side of the equation is the rate implied on the futures contract. If an investor purchases a 91-day T-bill on the futures contract at the equilibrium price, then the implied futures rate will be equal to the implied forward rate. In terms of our example, if $f_0 = 98.74875$, then the implied futures rate will be 5.18%. That is:

$$YTM_f = \left[\frac{F}{f_0^*}\right]^{365/91} - 1$$

$$= \left[\frac{100}{98.74875}\right]^{365/91} - 1 = 0.0518$$

Recall from chapter 2 that the implied forward rate is the interest rate attained at a future date that is implied by current rates. This rate can be attained by a locking-in strategy consisting of a short position in a shorter-term bond and a long position in a longer-term one. In terms of our example, the implied forward rate on a 91-day T-bill investment to be made 70 days from the present, $R_I(91,70)$, is obtained by:

1. Selling short the 70-day T-bill at 98.821 (or equivalently borrowing 98.821 at 6.38%);
2. Buying $S_0(T)/S_0(T+91) = S_0(70)/S_0(161) = 98.821/97.5844 = 1.01267$ issues of the 161-day T-bill;
3. Paying 100 at the end of 70 days to cover the short position on the maturing bond (or the loan); and
4. Collecting 1.01267(100) at the end of 161 days from the long position.

This locking-in strategy would earn an investor a return of $101.267, 91 days after the investor expends $100 to cover the short sale; thus, the implied forward rate on a 91-day investment made 70 days from the present is 1.267%, or annualized, 5.18%:

$$R_I(91, 70) = \left[\frac{\$101.267}{\$100}\right]^{365/91} - 1 = 0.0518$$

If the futures price does not equal its equilibrium value, then the implied forward rate will not be equal to the implied futures rate, and an arbitrage opportunity will exist from the cash-and-carry arbitrage strategy.

In summary, we have three equivalent equilibrium conditions governing futures prices on T-bill and Eurodollar futures contracts: (1) the futures price is equal to the costs of carrying the underlying spot security; (2) the rate on the spot is equal to the rate on the synthetic security (or the implied repo rate is equal to the actual repo rate); (3) the implied rate of return on the futures contract is equal to the implied forward rate.

13.6.4 T-Bond Delivery Procedure and Equilibrium Pricing

Cheapest-to-Deliver Bond

The T-bond futures contract gives the party with the short position the right to deliver, at any time during the delivery month, any bond with a maturity of at least 15 years. When a particular bond is delivered, the price received by the seller is equal to the quoted futures price on the futures contract times a conversion factor, CFA, applicable to the delivered bond. The invoice price, in turn, is equal to that price plus any accrued interest on the delivered bond:

Invoice price $= (f_0)(\text{CFA}) + \text{Accrued interest}$

The CBOT uses a conversion factor based on discounting the deliverable bond by a 6% YTM. The CBOT's rules for calculating the CFA on the deliverable bond are as follows:

- The bond's maturity and time to the next coupon date are rounded down to the closest 3 months.
- After rounding, if the bond has an exact number of 6-month periods, then the first coupon is assumed to be paid in 6 months.
- After rounding, if the bond does not have an exact number of 6-month periods, then the first coupon is assumed to be paid in 3 months and the accrued interest is subtracted.

Using these rules, a 5.5% T-bond maturing in 18 years and 1 month would be (1) rounded down to 18 years; (2) the first coupon would be assumed to be paid in 6 months; (3) the CFA would be determined using a discount rate of

6% and face value of $100. The CFA for the bond would be 0.945419:

$$V = \sum_{t=1}^{36} \frac{2.75}{(1.03)^t} + \frac{100}{(1.03)^{36}} = 94.5419$$

$$\text{CFA} = \frac{94.5419}{100} = 0.945419$$

If the bond matured in 18 years and 4 months, the bond would be assumed to have a maturity of 18 years and 3 months. Its CFA would be found by determining the value of the bond 3 months from the present, discounting that value to the current period, and subtracting the accrued interest $((3/6)(2.75) = 1.375)$:

$$V = \frac{94.5419}{(1.03)^{0.5}} = 93.1549$$

$$\text{CFA} = \frac{93.1549 - 1.375}{100} = 0.917799$$

During the delivery month, there are a number of possible bonds that can be delivered. The party with the short position will select that bond that is cheapest to deliver. The CBOT maintains tables with possible deliverable bonds. The tables show the bond's current quoted price and its CFA. For example, suppose three possible bonds are:

Bond	Quoted price	CFA
1	110.5	1.15
2	97.50	1.05
3	125.75	1.35

If the current quoted futures price were 90-16 or 90.5, the costs of buying and delivering each bond would be:

Bond	Cost of bond minus revenue from selling bond on futures
1	$110.5 - (90.5)(1.15) = 6.425$
2	$97.5 - (90.5)(1.05) = 2.475$
3	$125.75 - (90.5)(1.35) = 3.575$

Thus, the cheapest bond to deliver would be number 2. Over time and as rates change, the cheapest-to-deliver bond can change. In general, if rates exceed 6%, the CBOT's conversion system favors bonds with higher maturities and lower coupons; if rates are less than 6%, the system tends to favor higher coupon bonds with shorter maturities.

Wild-Card Play

Under the CBOT's procedures, a T-bond futures trader with a short position who wants to deliver on the contract has the right to determine during the expiration month not only the eligible bond to deliver, but also the day of the delivery. The delivery process encompasses the following 3 business days:

- **Business day 1** (*Position day*): The short position holder notifies the clearinghouse that she will deliver.
- **Business day 2** (*Notice of intention day*): The clearinghouse assigns a long position holder the contract (typically the holder with the longest outstanding contract).
- **Business day 3** (*Delivery day*): The short holder delivers an eligible T-bond to the assigned long position holder who pays the short holder an invoice price determined by the futures price and a conversion factor.

Since a short holder can notify the clearinghouse of her intention to deliver a bond by 8 p.m. (Chicago time) at the end of the position day (not necessarily at the end of the futures' trading day), an arbitrage opportunity has arisen because of the futures exchange's closing time being 2:00 (Chicago time) and the closing time on spot T-bond trading being 4:00. Thus, a short holder knowing the settlement price at 2:00 p.m. could find the price of an eligible T-bond decreasing in the next two hours on the spot market. If this occurred, she could buy the bond at the end of the day at the lower price, then notify the clearinghouse of her intention to deliver that bond on the futures contract; if the bond price does not decline, the short holder can keep her position and wait another day. This feature of the T-bond futures contract is known as the *wild-card option*. This option tends to lower the futures price.

Equilibrium T-Bond Futures Price

The pricing of a T-bond futures contract is more complex than the pricing of T-bill or Eurodollar futures because of the uncertainty over the bond to be delivered and the time of the delivery. Like T-bill futures, the price on a T-bond futures contract depends on the spot price on the underlying T-bond (S_0) and the risk-free rate. If we assume that we know the cheapest-to-deliver bond and the time of delivery, the equilibrium futures price is

$$f_0 = [S_0 - PV(C)](1 + R_f)^T$$

where S_0 is the current spot price of the cheapest-to-deliver T-bond (clean price plus accrued interest) and $PV(C)$ is the present value of coupons paid on the bond during the life of the futures contract.

Example

As an example, suppose the following:

- The cheapest-to-deliver T-bond underlying a futures contract pays a 10% coupon, has a CFA of 1.2, and is currently trading at 110 (clean price).
- The cheapest-to-deliver T-bond's last coupon date was 50 days ago, its next coupon is 132 days from now, and the coupon after that comes 182 days later.
- The yield curve is flat at 6%.
- The T-bond futures' estimated expiration is $T = 270$ days.

The current T-bond spot price is 111.37 and the present value of the $5 coupon received in 132 days is 4.8957:

$$S_0 = 110 + \frac{50}{50 + 132}(5) = 111.37$$

$$PV(C) = \frac{5}{(1.06)^{132/365}} = 4.8957$$

The equilibrium futures price based on a 10% deliverable bond is therefore 111.16 per $100 face value:

$$f_0^* = [S_0 - PV(C)](1 + R_f)^T$$
$$= [111.37 - 4.8957](1.06)^{270/365} = 111.16$$

The quoted price on a futures contract written on the 10% delivered bond would be stated net of accrued interest at the delivery date. The delivery date occurs 138 days after the last coupon payment $(270 - 132)$. Thus, at delivery, there would be 138 days of accrued interest. Given the 182-day period between coupon payments, accrued interest would therefore be 3.791 ($=(138/182)(5)$). The quoted futures price on the delivered bond would be 107.369 ($=111.16 - 3.791$), and with a CFA of 1.2, the equilibrium quoted futures price would be 89.47:

Quoted futures price on bond

$= 111.16 - (138/182)5 = 107.369$

Quoted futures price $= 107.369/1.2 = 89.47$

Arbitrage

Like T-bill futures, cash-and-carry arbitrage opportunities will exist if the T-bond futures were not equal to 111.16 (or its quoted price of 89.47). For example, if futures were priced at $f^M = 113$, an arbitrageur could go short in the futures at 113 and then buy the underlying cheapest-to-deliver bond for 111.37, financed by borrowing 106.4743 ($=S_0 - PV(C) = 111.37 - 4.8957$) at 6% for 270 days and 4.8957 at 6% for 132 days. 132 days later, the arbitrageur would receive a $5 coupon that he would use to pay off the 132-day loan of $5 (= 4.8957(1.06)^{132/365})$. At expiration, the arbitrageur would sell the bond on the futures contract at 113 and pay off his financing cost on the 270-day loan of 111.16 ($=106.4743 (1.06)^{270/365}$). This, in turn, would equate to an arbitrage profit of $f^M - f_0^* = 113 - 111.16 = \$1.84$ per $100 face value. This risk-free return would result in arbitrageurs pursuing this strategy of going short in the futures and long in the T-bond, causing the futures price to decrease to 111.16 where the arbitrage disappears. If the futures price were below 111.16, arbitrageurs would reverse the strategy, shorting the bond, investing the proceeds, and going long in the T-bond futures contract.

13.6.5 Notes on Futures Pricing

Several points should be noted in discussing futures pricing. First, for many assets the costs of carrying the asset for a period of time exceed the benefits. As a result, the futures price on such assets exceeds the spot price prior to expiration and the basis ($f_t - S_t$) on such assets is positive. By definition, a market in which the futures price exceeds the spot price is referred to as a *contango* or *normal market*. In contrast, if the futures price is less then the spot price (a negative basis), the costs of carrying the asset are said to have a *convenience yield* in which the benefits from holding the asset exceed the costs. A market in which the basis is negative is referred to as *backwardation* or an *inverted market*. For futures on debt securities, an inverted market could occur if large coupon payments are to be paid during the period.

Second, the same arbitrage arguments governing the futures and spot price relation also can be extended to establish the equilibrium relationship between futures prices with different expirations.

Finally, the futures price is related to an unknown expected spot price. Several expectation theories have been advanced to explain the relationship between the futures and expected spot prices. One of the first theories was broached by the famous British economists John Maynard Keynes and J. R. Hicks. They argued that if a spot market were dominated by hedgers who, on balance, wanted a short forward position, then for the market to clear (supply to equal demand) the price of the futures contract would have to be less than the expected price on the spot commodity at expiration ($E(S_T)$): $f_0 < E(S_T)$. According to Keynes and Hicks, the difference between $E(S_T)$ and f_0 represents a risk premium that speculators in the market require in order to take a long futures position. Keynes and Hicks called this market situation *normal backwardation*. C. O. Hardy argued for the case of $f_0 > E(S_T)$, even in a market of short hedgers. His argument, though, is based on investors' risk behavior. He maintained that since speculators were akin to gamblers, they were willing to pay for the opportunity to gamble (risk-loving behavior). Thus, a gambler's fee, referred to as a contango or forwardation, would result in a negative risk premium. Finally, there is a risk-neutral pricing argument. In this argument, the futures price represents an unbiased estimator of the expected spot price ($f_0 = E(S_T)$) and, with risk-neutral pricing, investors purchasing an asset (bond) for S_0 and expecting an asset value at T of $E(S_T) = f_0$ require an expected rate of return equal to the risk-free rate. As a result:

$$S_0 = \frac{E(S_T)}{(1 + R_f)^T} = \frac{f_0}{(1 + R_f)^T}$$

$$f_0 = E(S_T)$$

Thus, in a risk-neutral market, the futures price is equal to the expected spot price.

13.7 HEDGING INTERNATIONAL POSITIONS WITH FOREIGN CURRENCY FUTURES CONTRACTS

When investors purchase and hold foreign securities or when corporations and governments sell debt securities in external markets or incur foreign debt positions, they are subject to exchange-rate risk. As noted in chapter 7, major banks provide exchange-rate protection by offering forward contracts to financial and non-financial corporations to hedge their international positions. In addition to contracts offered in this interbank forward market, hedging exchange rate risk can be done using foreign currency futures contracts listed on the Chicago Mercantile Exchange (CME), as well as a number of exchanges outside the US. The standardized contracts listed on these exchanges call for delivery or purchase of a specified amount of foreign currency (FC) on a delivery date at a specified price or exchange rate.[1]

13.7.1 Hedging

Large corporations usually hedge their currency positions in the interbank market, whereas smaller companies, many portfolio managers with foreign security investments, and individuals use the futures market. Either way, the currency position is usually hedged with a naive-hedging model. To illustrate, consider a US fund that has a sizable investment in Eurobonds that will pay a principal in British pounds of £10m next September. Suppose the current spot exchange rate is $1.425/£, making the dollar value of the principal worth $14.25m. Suppose the fund is concerned that the $/£ exchange rate could decrease by September, reducing the amount of dollars they would receive when they convert £10m. To minimize its exchange-rate exposure, the fund could go short in an interbank forward contract in which it agrees to sell £10m at the September principal payment date at a specified forward exchange rate (the prices of forward and futures contracts are determined by a carrying-cost model discussed in the next section). Alternatively, the fund could take a short position in a CME September futures contract. Given the contract size on the CME's British pound contract of £62,500, the fund would need to go short in 160 CME British pound contracts in order to hedge its £10m September receipt: $n_f = £10,000,000/£62,500 = 160$. If the futures price on the September contract were equal to $f_0 = \$1.425/£$, and the September principal payment occurred at the same time as the futures' expiration, then the fund would be able to realize a $14.25m cash inflow when it converted its £10m principal to dollars at the spot $/£ exchange rate at the September principal payment date and closed its 160 British pound futures contracts at an expiring futures price equal to the spot exchange rate. This is illustrated in exhibit 13.3, which show the fund's hedged revenue of $14.25m at expiration from converting the £10m at spot exchange rates of $1.47/£ and $1.39/£ and from closing its 160 short futures contracts by going long at expiring futures prices equal to the different spot exchange rates.

Short foreign currency hedges are used to lock in the currency value of a future receipt or asset denominated in another currency. By contrast, long currency hedges are used to lock in the currency value of a future payment or liability. To illustrate a long hedge, consider the case of a US corporation that has issued a Eurobond denominated in British pounds. Suppose the company has to make a September principal payment in pounds of £5m and that the September CME British pound futures is trading at $f_0 = \$1.425/£$ and expires at the same time the principal payment is due. In this case, the US company could hedge the dollar cost on its principal payment against exchange rate changes by going long in 80 September futures contracts: $n_f = £5,000,000/£62,500 = 80$. At expiration, the company would realize a hedged dollar cost of $7.125m when it purchased £5m at the spot exchange rate and closed its 80 long futures contracts at expiring futures prices

Exhibit 13.3 Hedging dollar revenue from converting £10m

	$1.47/£	$1.39/£
(1) $E_T = f_T$		
(2) Dollar revenue: E_T (£10,000,000)	$14,700,000	$13,900,000
(3) Futures profit $= 160[\$1.425 - f_T]$ (£62,500)	$-\$450,000	$350,000
(4) Hedged revenue $=$ row (2) $+$ row (3)	$14,250,000	$14,250,000

Exhibit 13.4 Hedging dollar cost of buying £5m

	$1.47/£	$1.39/£
(1) $E_T = f_T$		
(2) Dollar cost: E_T (£5,000,000)	$7,350,000	$6,950,000
(3) Futures profit $= 80[f_T - \$1.425]$ (£62,500)	$225,000	$-\$175,000
(4) Hedged cost $=$ row (2) $-$ row (3)	$7,125,000	$7,125,000

equal to the spot exchange. This hedge is illustrated in exhibit 13.4.

13.7.2 Pricing Futures and Forward Exchange Rates

Like all futures and forward contracts, the carrying-cost model can be used to determine the equilibrium price of a currency forward or futures exchange rate. In international finance, the carrying-cost model governing the relationship between spot and forward exchange rates is referred to as the *interest rate parity theorem (IRPT)*. In terms of the IRPT, the forward price of a currency or forward exchange rate (f_0) is equal to the cost of carrying the spot currency (priced at the spot exchange rate of E_0) for the contract's expiration period.

In terms of a US dollar position, carrying a foreign currency for the period (T) would require borrowing $E_0/(1 + R_F)^T$ dollars at the rate R_{US}, where R_F is the foreign risk-free rate, converting the dollars to $1/(1 + R_F)^T$ units of foreign currency at the spot exchange rate of E_0, and investing the currency in the foreign risk-free security yielding R_F. At the end of the period, one would have one unit of FC and a debt obligation of $[E_0/(1 + R_F)^T](1 + R_{US})^T$. Thus, the forward price of purchasing one unit of currency at T should not be different from the debt obligation or net financing cost of

carrying the currency. Thus, the equilibrium forward price or exchange rate is:

$$f_0 = E_0 \frac{(1 + R_{US})^T}{(1 + R_F)^T}$$

The equation defines the IRPT. It shows that the relation between the forward and the spot rates depends on the relative levels of domestic and foreign interest rates. If the interest rate parity condition does not hold, an arbitrage opportunity will exist. The arbitrage strategy to apply in such situations is known as *covered interest arbitrage (CIA)*. Introduced by John Maynard Keynes, CIA involves taking long and short positions in the currency spot and forward markets, as well as positions in the domestic and foreign money markets. To illustrate, suppose the annualized US and foreign interest rates are $R_{US} = 4\%$ and $R_F = 6\%$, respectively, and the spot exchange rate is $E_0 = \$0.40/FC$. By the IRPT, a 1-year forward contract would be equal to $\$0.39245283/FC$:

$$f_0 = [\$0.40/FC]\left(\frac{1.04}{1.06}\right) = \$0.39245283/FC$$

If the actual forward rate, f_0^M, exceeds $\$0.39245283/FC$, an arbitrage profit would exist by: (1) borrowing dollars at R_{US}, (2) converting the dollar to FC at E_0, (3) investing the fund in a foreign risk-free rate at the rate

R_F, and (4) and entering a short forward contract to sell the FC at the end of the period at f_0^M. For example, if $f_0^M = \$0.40/FC$, an arbitrageur could:

- Borrow \$40,000 at $R_{US} = 4\%$ (creating a loan obligation at the end of the period of $\$41,600 = (\$40,000)(1.04))$;
- Convert the dollars at the spot exchange rate of $E_0 = \$0.40/FC$ to 100,000 FC $(= (2.5FC/\$)(\$40,000))$;
- Invest the 100,000 FC in the foreign risk-free security at $R_F = 6\%$ (creating a return of principal and interest of 106,000 FC 1 year later); and
- Enter a forward contract to sell 106,000 FC at the end of the year at $f_0^M = \$0.40/FC$.

One year later, the arbitrageur would receive \$42,400 when she sells the 106,000 FC on the forward contract and would owe \$41,600 on her debt obligation, for an arbitrage return of \$800. Such risk-free profit opportunities, in turn, would lead arbitrageurs to try to implement the CIA strategy. This would cause the price on the forward contract to fall until the riskless opportunity disappears. The zero arbitrage profit would occur when the interest rate parity condition is satisfied.

If the forward rate is below the equilibrium value, then the CIA is reversed. In the example, if $f_0^M = \$0.38/FC$, an arbitrageur could:

- Borrow 100,000 FC at $R_F = 6\%$ (creating a 106,000 FC debt);
- Convert the 100,000 FC at the spot exchange rate to \$40,000;
- Invest the \$40,000 in the US risk-free security at $R_{US} = 4\%$; and
- Enter a forward contract to buy 106,000 FC at the end of the year at $f_0^M = \$0.38/FC$.

At the end of the period, the arbitrageur's profit would be \$1,320:

$$\$40,000(1.04) - (\$0.38/FC)(106,000)$$
$$= \$1,320$$

As arbitrageurs attempt to implement this strategy, they will push up the price on the forward contract until the arbitrage profit is zero; this occurs when the interest rate parity condition is satisfied.

It should be noted that banks that provide forward contracts to their customers typically hedge their contracts by taking a position in the spot markets. For example, given $R_{US} = 4\%$, $R_F = 6\%$, and $E_0 = \$0.40/FC$, a bank could offer a 1-year forward contract at $f_0 = \$0.39245283/FC$, then hedge the contract by using a CIA strategy. For example, if a bank's customer wanted to buy 10,000,000 FC 1 year from the present, then the bank could provide the customer with a forward contract in which the bank agrees to sell forward 10,000,000 FC to the customer at the end of 1 year for \$3,924,528. To hedge this short forward position, the bank, in turn, could:

- Borrow \$3,773,585 $(=(10,000,000 \text{ FC}/ 1.04)(\$0.39245283))$;
- Convert the \$3,773,585 to 9,433,962 FC $(=\$3,773,585(2.5FC/\$))$; and
- Invest the 9,433,962 FC for 1 year at $R_F = 6\%$.

One year later the bank would have 10,000,000 FC $(=9,433,962(1.06))$ and would owe \$3,924,528 $(=\$3,773,585(1.04))$, which would exactly offset the bank's forward position. On the other hand, if a bank's customer wanted to sell 10,000,000 FC one year from the present, then the bank could provide the customer with a forward contract in which it agrees to buy forward 10,000,000 FC to the customer at the end of 1 year for \$3,924,528. To hedge this long forward position, the bank would reverse the previous strategy: borrow 9,433,962 FC at 6\%, convert to \$3,773,585, and invest in US security at 4\%. At the end of 1 year, the bank would have \$3,924,528 and would own 10,000,000 FC, which would offset its long forward position.

In hedging their forward contracts, banks are in a position in which they can take care of any mispricing that occurs if the forward price does not satisfy the interest rate parity condition. By taking advantage of such opportunities, they would push the forward price to its equilibrium level. It should be noted that the interest rate parity condition strictly holds for forward contracts. If rates are stable, then the IRPT can be extended to determine the equilibrium futures price; if not, then the IRPT should be used only as an estimate.[2]

13.7.3 Investment Uses of the Interest Rate Parity Theorem

In addition to determining the equilibrium currency futures or forward price, investors and borrowers can also use the IRPT to define the cutoff expected spot exchange rate for determining whether they should invest or borrow domestically or internationally. To illustrate, consider the preceding example where $R_{US} = 4\%$ and $R_F = 6\%$, $E_0 = \$0.40/$ FC, and $f_0 = \$0.39245283/$FC. If an investor knew with certainty that the exchange rate 1 year later would be $f_0 = \$0.39245283/$FC, then she would be indifferent to an investment in a 1-year US risk-free security yielding 4% and a 1-year foreign risk-free security yielding 6%. If the US investor, though, was certain that the spot exchange 1 year later would exceed $\$0.39245283/$FC, then she would prefer to invest her dollars in the foreign security than the US one. For example, if a US investor knew the spot exchange rate 1 year later would be $E(E_T) = \$0.41/$FC, then she would prefer the foreign investment, in which a rate of 8.65% could be earned, instead of the US security, which earns only 4%. To attain 8.65%, the investor would have to convert each of her investment dollars to $1/E_0 = 1/\$0.40/$FC $=$ 2.5 FC and invest the 2.5 FC at $R_F = 6\%$. One year later, the investor would have 2.65 FC ($=2.5$ FC(1.06)), which she would be able to convert to $\$1.0865$ if the spot exchange rate were $\$0.41/$FC. Thus, the dollar investment in the foreign security would yield a dollar rate of 8.65%.

$$\text{Rate} = \frac{(\$0.41/\text{FC})[(2.5 \text{ FC})(1.06)]}{\$1} - 1$$

$$= 0.0865$$

On the other hand, if a US investor knew with certainty that the exchange rate would be less than $\$0.39245283/$FC, then she would prefer the US risk-free investment to the foreign one. For example, if $E(E_T) = \$0.39/$FC, then the US investor would earn only 3.35% from the foreign investment compared to 4% from the US investment:

$$\text{Rate} = \frac{(\$0.39/\text{FC})[(2.5 \text{ FC})(1.06)]}{\$1} - 1 = 0.0335$$

The example suggests that in a world of certainty, the equilibrium forward rate as specified by the IRPT can be used to define the expected cutoff exchange rate, $E(E_T^c)$, needed to determine if one should invest in a domestic or risk-free security:

$$E(E_T^c) = f_0 = E_0 \frac{(1 + R_{US})^T}{(1 + R_f)^T}$$

In a real world of uncertainty in which futures spot exchange rates are unknown, the required cutoff rate depends on investors' attitudes toward risk. For example, if investors were risk-neutral, then they would require no risk premium and their required expected rate from the risky investment would be equal to the risk-free investment. In this case, the cutoff exchange rate for investors would be the equilibrium forward rate. However, if investors were risk-averse, as we would expect, then the required expected rate from the risky investment would have to exceed the risk-free rate. This would require that investors' cutoff exchange rate exceed the forward rate. For example, if risk-averse US investors required an annualized 2% risk premium (RP) in order to invest in a foreign security, then the expected cutoff exchange rate would be $\$0.40/$FC:

$$E(E_T^c) = E_0 \frac{(1 + R_{US} + RP)^T}{(1 + R_f)^T}$$

$$= (\$0.40/\text{FC}) \frac{(1 + 0.04 + 0.02)^1}{(1.06)^1}$$

$$= \$0.40/\text{FC}$$

Thus, if investors are risk-averse, then $E(E_T)$ would have to be greater than f_0 for them to invest in the foreign security that is subject to exchange rate risk instead of the domestic investment.

Web Information

For information on forward exchange rates go to

www.fxstreet.com

For information on CME currency futures contracts go to

www.cme.com

and click on "Delayed Quotes" in "Market Data," and then "Currency Products."

13.8 CONCLUSION

Introduced during the volatile interest rate periods of the 1970s and 1980s, interest rate futures have become one of the most popular futures contracts. In this chapter and in chapter 12, we've examined the characteristics, applications, and pricing of these futures contracts. As we've seen, they can be used by financial institutions to manage the maturity gap between their assets and liabilities, by financial and non-financial corporations to fix the rates on their floating-rate loans or to create synthetic fixed-rate or floating-rate debt and investment positions, and by fixed-income managers, money market managers, and dealers to lock in the future purchase or selling price of their fixed-income securities. In addition to interest rate futures, we also examined in this chapter how foreign currency futures contracts can be used to hedge international investment and debt positions against exchange rate risk and how such contracts are priced in terms of the interest rate parity condition. In the next chapter, we focus on another important derivative security that is also extensively used for debt and bond management – interest rate options.

KEY TERMS

Naive Hedging Model	TED Spread	Convenience Yield
Hedge Ratio	Off-Balance-Sheet	Backwardation or Inverted
Regression Model	Restructuring	Market
Price-Sensitivity Model	Carrying-Cost Model	Normal Backwardation
Outright Futures Positions	Cash-and-Carry Arbitrage	Interest Rate Parity Theorem
Intracommodity Spread	Implied Repo Rate	(IRPT)
Intercommodity Spread	Wild-Card Option	Covered Interest Arbitrage
NOB Strategy	Contango or Normal Market	(CIA)

PROBLEMS AND QUESTIONS

1. In June, the Prudential Money Market Fund forecast a September cash inflow of $9m that it plans to invest for 91 days in T-bills. The fund is uncertain about future short-term interest rates and would like to lock in the rate on the September investment with T-bill futures contracts. Currently, September T-bill contracts are trading at 93 (IMM index).

   a. What is the implied YTM on the September T-bill futures contract?
   b. How many September contracts does Prudential need to lock in the implied futures YTM (assume perfect divisibility)?
   c. Assuming the fund's $9m cash inflow comes at the same time as the September futures contract's expiration, show how the fund's futures-hedged T-bill purchase yields the same rate from a $9m investment as the implied YTM on the futures. Evaluate at spot T-bill rates at the futures' expiration of 6.5% and 8.5%.

2. First American Bank is planning to make a $20m short-term loan to Midwest Mining Company. In the loan contract, Midwest agrees to pay the principal and an interest of 12% (annual) at the end of 180 days. Since First American sells more 90-day CDs than 180-day CDs, it is planning to finance the loan by selling a 90-day CD now at the prevailing LIBOR of 8.25%, then 90 days later (mid-September) sell another 90-day CD at the prevailing LIBOR. The bank would like to

minimize its exposure to interest rate risk on its future CD sale by taking a position in a September Eurodollar futures contract trading at 92 (IMM index).

    a. How many September Eurodollar futures contracts would First American Bank need in order to effectively hedge its September CD sale against interest rate changes? Assume perfect divisibility.

    b. Determine the total amount of funds the bank would need to raise on its CD sale 90 days later if the LIBOR is 7.5% and if it is 9% (assume futures are closed at the LIBOR). What would the bank's debt obligations be at the end of 180-day period? What is the bank's effective rate for the entire 180-day period? Assume 30/365 day count convention.

3. In January, the Patton Development Company closed a deal with local officials to develop a new office building. The project is expected to begin in June and take 272 days to complete. The cost of the development is expected to be $16m, with the L. B. Insurance Company providing the permanent financing of the development once the construction is completed. Patton Development has obtained a 272-day construction loan from Star Financing Company. Star Financing will disperse funds to Patton at the beginning of the project in June, with the interest rate on the loan being set equal to the prevailing CP rate on that date plus 50 BP. The loan will have a maturity of 272 days with the principal and interest on the loan to be paid at maturity. Fearful that interest rates could increase between January and June, Patton Development would like to lock in its rate on the $16m construction loan by taking a position in June T-bill futures contracts. Any profits from the futures, Patton would use to defray the $16m construction costs, and any losses, it would add to its $16m loan. Currently, 272-day CP is trading at YTM of 10% (annual) and June T-bill futures are trading at 91 (IMM index).

    a. Using the price-sensitivity model, explain how Patton Development could immunize its construction loan against interest rate changes. Assume perfect divisibility.

    b. How much would Patton need to borrow at the June expiration if the CP rate was at 11% and the spot 91-day T-bill was trading at a discount yield of 10% (R_D)? What would Patton's futures-hedge interest rate on the 272-day $16m loan be?

    c. How much would Patton need to borrow at the June expiration if the CP rate was at 9% and the spot 91-day T-bill was trading at a discount yield of 8% (R_D)? What would Patton's futures-hedge interest rate on the 272-day $16m loan be?

4. Mr Slife is a fixed-income portfolio manager for Stacy Investments. Mr Slife forecast a cash inflow of $10m in June and plans to invest the funds in his baseline bond portfolio which currently has an "A" quality rating, duration of 7 years, weighted average maturity of 15 years, annual coupon rate of 10.25%, and YTM of 10.25% (note that the bond portfolio is currently worth its par value). Afraid that long-term interest rates could decline, suppose that Mr Slife decides to hedge his June investment by taking a position in June T-bond futures contracts when the June T-bond contract is trading at 80-16 and the T-bond most likely to be delivered on the contract has a YTM of 9.5%, maturity of 15 years, and a duration of 9 years.

    a. Using the price-sensitivity model, show how Mr Slife could hedge his June bond portfolio purchase against interest rate risk.

    b. Suppose long-term interest rates decrease over the period such that at the June expiration bonds matching Mr Slife's baseline portfolio (A-rated, 10.25% coupon rate, 15-year maturity, and 7-year duration) are trading at 104 of par and the price on the expiring June T-bond contract (f_T) is 85. Determine Mr Slife's costs of purchasing his baseline bond portfolio, his profit on the futures contracts, and his hedged-portfolio costs.

5. Suppose Mr Slife in question 4 forecast a cash outflow of $10m in June and plans to sell his baseline bond portfolio. The fund currently is worth $10m, has an "A" quality rating, duration of 7 years, weighted average maturity of 15 years, annual coupon rate of 10.25%, and YTM of

10.25%. Suppose Mr Slife is afraid that long-term interest rates could increase and decides to hedge his June sale by taking a position in June T-bond futures contracts when the June T-bond contract is trading at 80-16 and the T-bond most likely to be delivered on the contract has a YTM of 9.5%, maturity of 15 years, and a duration of 9 years.

   a. Using the price-sensitivity model, show how Mr Slife could hedge his June bond portfolio sale against interest rate risk.

   b. Suppose long-term interest rates increase over the period such that at the June expiration Mr Slife's baseline portfolio (A-rated, 10.25% coupon rate, 15-year maturity, and 7-year duration) is trading at 96 of par and the price on the expiring June T-bond contract (f_T) is 76. Determine Mr Slife's revenue from selling his baseline bond portfolio, his profit on the futures contracts, and his total revenue.

6. As an alternative to a 9-month, 10.5% fixed-rate loan to finance its $15m inventory, Roberts Department Store is considering a synthetic fixed-rate loan formed with a $15m floating-rate loan from West National Bank and a Eurodollar strip. The floating-rate loan has a maturity of 270 days (0.75 of a year), starts on December 20, and the rate on the loan is set each quarter. The initial quarterly rate is equal to 9.5%/4, the other rates are set on 3/20 and 6/20 equal to one fourth of the annual LIBOR on those dates plus 100 basis points: (LIBOR% + 1%)/4. On December 20, the Eurodollar futures contract expiring on 3/20 is trading at 91 (IMM index) and the contract expiring on 6/20 is trading at 92 and the time separating each contract is 0.25/year.

   a. Explain how Roberts could use the strip to lock in a fixed rate. Calculate the rate the Roberts Department Store could lock in with a floating-rate loan and Eurodollar futures.

   b. Calculate and show in a table the company's quarterly interest payments, futures profits, hedged interest payments (interest minus futures profit), and hedged rate for each period (12/20, 3/20, and 6/20) given the following rates: LIBOR = 10% on 3/20 and LIBOR = 9% on 6/20.

7. ABC Trust is planning to invest $15m for 1 year. As an alternative to a 1-year fixed-rate note paying 8.5%, ABC is considering a synthetic investment formed by investing in a Commerce Bank 1-year floating-rate note (FRN) paying LIBOR plus 100 basis points and a Eurodollar strip. The FRN starts on 12/20 at 9% (LIBOR = 8%) and is then reset the next three quarters on 3/20, 6/20, and 9/20. On December 20, the Eurodollar futures contract expiring on 3/20 is trading at 91 (IMM index), the contract expiring on 6/20 is trading at 92, and the contract expiring on 9/20 is trading at 92.5; the time separating each contract is 0.25/year and the reset dates on the floating-rate note and the expiration dates on the futures expiration are the same.

   a. Explain how ABC Trust could use a strip to lock in a fixed rate. Calculate the rate ABC could lock in with a floating-rate note and Eurodollar futures.

   b. Calculate and show in a table the company's quarterly interest receipts, futures profits, hedged interest return (interest plus futures profit), and hedged rate for each period (12/20, 3/20, 6/20, and 9/20) given the following rates: LIBOR = 9.5% on 3/20, LIBOR = 9% on 6/20, and LIBOR = 7% on 9/20.

8. Explain the types of spreads bond speculators could use given the following cases:

   a. The yield curve is expected to shift down with rates for bonds with differing maturities decreasing by roughly the same percentage.

   b. While the economy is growing, leading economic indicators augur for an economic recession.

   c. While the economy is in recession, leading economic indicators point to an economic expansion.

9. Given (1) 121-day spot T-bill trading at 98.318 to yield 5.25%; (2) 30-day risk-free rate of 5.15%; (3) a T-bill futures contract with an expiration of $T = 30$ days:

a. What is the equilibrium T-bill futures price and its implied futures YTM (annualized)?
b. Explain what a money market manager planning to invest funds for 30 days should do if the price on the T-bill futures were trading at 98.8. What rate would the manager earn?
c. Explain the arbitrage a money market manager could execute if she were holding a 121-day T-bill and the T-bill futures were trading at 98.

10. In the table below the IMM index prices on three T-bill futures contracts with expirations of 91, 182, and 273 days are shown, along with the YTM on a spot 182-day T-bill.

T-bill contract	Days to expiration	IMM index
March	91	93.764
June	182	93.3092
September	273	91.8607

Spot 182-day T-bill: YTM $= 0.0625$

a. Calculate the actual futures prices and the YTMs (annualized) on the futures.
b. Given the spot 182-day T-bill is trading at annualized YTM of 6.25%, what is the implied 91-day repo rate?
c. If the carrying-cost model holds, what would be the price of a 91-day spot T-bill?
d. What would be the equilibrium price on the March contract if the actual 91-day repo rate were 4.75%? What strategy would an arbitrageur pursue if the IMM index price were at 93.764?

11. Suppose the McDonald Money Market fund wanted to invest its expected $3m September cash inflow in 182-day T-bills and wanted to lock in the rate. Assume that September and December T-bill futures are available, with 91 days separating the expiration dates of the contracts, and assume the IMM prices of each are IMM(Sept) $= 92$ and IMM(Dec) $= 93$.

a. Calculate the rate of return on the 182-day investment implied by the September and December contracts.
b. Explain how McDonald could lock in the implied futures rate on the 182-day investment using September and December contracts. Assume perfect divisibility.
c. Show how McDonald could attain the implied 182-day rate on its $3m cash flow in September by investing the $3m and the futures profit (or covering the futures loss). Assume at the September expiration date, 91-day spot T-bills are trading at a YTM of 8% (annual) and 182-day spot T-bills are at 7.5%, the 91-day repo rate is 8%, the carrying-cost model holds, and perfect divisibility.

12. In the table, the YTMs are shown for spot T-bills with maturities of 91, 182, and 273 days.

Days to maturity on spot T-bills	YTM (%)
91	6.00
182	6.25
273	6.50

a. Calculate the implied forward rates and outline the locking-in strategy for the following:

(i) 91-day investment made 91 days from the present
(ii) 91-day investment made 182 days from the present.

b. Assuming the carrying-cost model holds, determine the actual price and IMM index price on futures contracts with expirations of 91 and 182 days.

c. Given the futures prices, check to see if the implied YTM on each futures contract is equal to the implied forward rule.

13. In the table, the prices for T-bill futures contracts with expiration of 91, 182, and 273 days are shown, along with the price for the spot 91-day T-bill.

T-bill contract	Days to expiration	Price $= f_0(\$)$
March	91	984,410
June	182	983,273
September	273	979,652

Price of spot 91-day T-bill $= \$985,578$

a. Calculate the implied YTM on the futures contracts.

b. Explain in general how a money market fund planning to purchase 91-day T-bills every 91 days could use the T-bill futures in the table to offer its fund investors a guaranteed 1-year fixed rate investment. What would be the average annual rate the fund could promise its investors?

c. How many March (expiration $= T = 91$ days), June ($T = 182$ days), and September ($T = 273$ days) futures contracts would the fund need if it had $10m that it planned to invest in a series of 91-day T-bills (assume perfect divisibility)?

d. Given the futures contracts needed for hedging in (c), explain how the fund would be managed under the following scenario (assume perfect divisibility):

   (i) At the March expiration, the spot 91-day T-bill is trading at a YTM of 6%.
   (ii) At the June expiration, the spot 91-day T-bill is trading at a YTM of 7.25%.
   (iii) At the September expiration, the spot 91-day T-bill is trading at a YTM of 8%.

e. Based on your answer in (d), does the fund earn the average rate you determined in question (b)? Given the rates in the above scenario, what would be the fund's rate without the hedge?

14. Using the information from the table in question 13 answer the following:

a. How many March and June futures contracts would a bank need in order to hedge the sale 91 days later of its current holdings of ten 273-day T-bills, currently trading at a YTM of 6.5%. (Assume perfect divisibility and use the implied futures rates determined in question 12: R_I (91,91) $= 0.065$.).

b. Determine the amount of cash the bank would have at the March expiration when it liquidates its spot and futures positions if spot 91-day T-bills were trading at a YTM of 7% and spot 182-day T-bills were trading at 7.25%. Assume the carrying-cost model holds and the 91-day repo rate is 7%. What is the rate of return the bank would earn on its T-bill holdings for the 91-day period?

15. Determine the conversion factors for the following T-bonds:

a. 4.5% (annual) T-bond maturing in 16 years and 2 months
b. 4.5% (annual) T-bond maturing in 16 years and 4 months
c. 8.0% (annual) T-bond maturing in 17 years and 7 months
d. 8.0% (annual) T-bond maturing in 17 years and 10 months.

16. The table below shows the conversion factors and quoted prices for three T-bonds eligible for delivery on a T-bond futures contract. Determine the cheapest-to-deliver bond for a T-bond futures contract with a contract price of 91.

Bond	Quoted price	CFA
1	98.50	1.05
2	115.75	1.15
3	125.50	1.35

Given the following information related to a T-bond futures contract expiring in 6 months:

- The best estimate of the cheapest-to-deliver bond on the T-bond futures contract pays an 8% coupon, is currently priced at 108 (clean price), has a conversion factor of 1.21; the bond's last coupon date was 30 days ago and its next coupon is 152 days with the coupon after that coming in the next 183 days.
- The yield curve is flat at 5%.
- The best estimate for the expiration on a T-bond futures contract is 180 days.

Using the carrying-cost model, determine the equilibrium price on the T-bond futures contract.

18. Explain what a contango market and a backwardation market are in terms of the carrying-cost model.

19. Explain the relationship between the expected spot price on an asset $(E(S_T))$ and the futures prices for the following markets in which there are more short hedgers than long:

a. Risk-averse (Keynes–Hicks normal backwardation market).
b. Risk-loving (Hardy's gambler's market).
c. Risk-neutral.

20. Short-answer questions:

(1) What is the actual price on a T-bill futures contract, if its quoted IMM index price is 92?
(2) Interest rates on Eurodollar deposits are quoted in terms of what?
(3) What is the implied YTM on a September T-bill futures contract that is trading at 93 (IMM index price)?
(4) What is the expiration futures' index price on an expiring Eurodollar futures contract if the 3-month LIBOR is 5% on the expiration day?
(5) The feature of T-bond futures contracts that allows a short position holder the right to notify the clearinghouse of the eligible bond he will deliver at the end of the position day is known as what?
(6) What is the equilibrium futures price on a T-bill expiring in 60 days if a spot T-bill maturing in 151 days is trading at 5% and the 60-day repo rate is 5.25%?

Questions (7)–(11) are based on the following information: the YTM on a 121-day spot T-bill is 6% and the 30-day repo rate is 5.75% (allow for some minor rounding).

(7) What is the equilibrium price of a T-bill futures contract expiring in 30 days?
(8) What would an arbitrageur do if the market price on the T-bill futures exceeded the equilibrium price?
(9) What is the YTM on a synthetic 30-day T-bill if the futures price is at $990,012?
(10) What is the YTM on a synthetic 30-day T-bill if the futures price is equal to its equilibrium value?
(11) What is the implied forward rate on a 91-day T-bill investment to be made 30 days from the present $(R_I(91,30))$?
(12) What is the implied 50-day repo rate if the price on a spot 141-day T-bill is $977,742 and the price on a T-bill futures contract expiring in 50 days is $992,317?
(13) Given a Eurodollar futures contract calling for the delivery of a Eurodollar deposit of $1m, with maturity of 90 days, that expires in $T=90$ days and is trading at

$f_0 = \$980,000$, how many short Eurodollar futures contracts would a bank need in ord
to lock in the rate on a 90-day CD that it plans to sell in 90 days to finance the princi
and interest payment on a $5m, 90-day spot CD it just sold at 5% (annual)?

(14) What is the implied forward rate on a 90-day loan made 90 days from the presen
180-day CDs are selling at $S_0(180) = \$961,000$ and 90-day CDs are selling
$S_0(90) = \$980,750$?

(15) What is the term for a spread formed with T-note and T-bond futures?

Questions (16)–(18) are based on the following case. Suppose the ABC Company obtains
$10m, 1-year variable rate loan. The loan starts on 12/20, with the rate set equal to 1/4
the LIBOR of 0.0775. The loan rate is reset every quarter (90 days or 0.25 per year) to equa
1/4 of the annual LIBOR. Also, suppose March, June, and September Eurodollar contract
(expiring at the dates the loans are reset) are trading at: IMM(March) = 92
IMM(June) = 92.25, and IMM(Sept) = 92.5. Finally, suppose there is 0.25 per year betwee
each contract.

(16) What average annual fixed rate could the ABC Company lock in by going short in ter
March, June, and September Eurodollar contracts?

(17) If ABC were short in ten March contracts, what would its future profits be at the March
expiration if the LIBOR is 7.5%?

(18) If ABC were short in ten March contracts, and if the spot LIBOR was at 7.5% at the
March expiration, what would the total cost of ABC's interest payment and closing cost
of its March futures position be 90 days later at the June expiration?

Questions (19)–(21) are based on the following case: Suppose the Treasury Office of the
State of Ohio plans to sell a $10m, 273-day tax-anticipation note (discount bond) in Sep-
tember. Currently, such notes are trading at 5.57% and September T-bill futures are
trading at $f_0 = \$987,500$.

(19) What is the implied YTM on the September T-bill futures contract?

(20) Using the price-sensitivity model, how many short September T-bill futures contracts
would the Treasury office need in order to hedge its $10m issue against interest
rate risk?

(21) How much cash would the Treasury Office raise if it sold the notes at the September
expiration date at 6% and closed 30 short September T-bill futures when spot 91-day
T-bills were trading at 5.75%?

(22) What is the major difference between the Eurodollar contract and the T-bill futures
contract?

(23) How much would the actual futures price change if the IMM index moves one point?

(24) What is the term for a spread formed with T-bills and Eurodollars?

WEB EXERCISE

1. Find links to other derivative sites by going to www.isda.org and clicking "Educational
Information" "Useful Links."

NOTES

1. The foreign currency futures market grew significantly from the mid-1970s to the early 1990s. Since 1992, the volume has declined such that today trading volume is equal to only half of the 1992 level. This is due primarily to the emergence of the euro, which has reduced the number of international positions.
2. Empirically, several studies comparing currency futures and forward contracts have found no significant difference between them. For a discussion, see Park, H. Y. and A. H. Chen "Differences between Futures and Forward Prices: A Further Investigation of Marking to Market Effects," *Journal of Futures Markets* 5 (February 1985): 77–88.

SELECTED REFERENCES

Agmon, T. and Y. Amihud "The Forward Exchange Rate and the Prediction of the Future Spot Rate," *Journal of Banking and Finance* (September 1981): 425–37.

Anderson, T. and R. Hasan *Interest Rate Risk Management* (London: JFK Publishing, 1989).

Arrow, K. "Futures Markets: Some Theoretical Perspectives," *Journal of Futures Markets* 1 (Summer 1981): 107–16.

Chang, E. C. "Returns to Speculators and the Theory of Normal Backwardation," *Journal of Finance* 40 (March 1985): 193–208.

Cornell, B. and M. Reinganum "Forward and Futures Prices: Evidence from Foreign Exchange Markets," *Journal of Finance* 36 (December 1981): 1035–45.

Cox, J. C., J. E. Ingersoll, and S. A. Ross "The Relation between Forward Prices and Futures Prices," *Journal of Financial Economics* 9 (December 1981): 321–46.

Gartland, William J. and Nicholas C. Letica "The Basics of Interest-Rate Options," in Frank J. Fabozzi (ed.) *The Handbook of Fixed Income Securities*, 6th edn (New York: McGraw-Hill, 2001).

Gay, G. D., R. W. Kolb, and R. Chiang "Interest Rate Hedging: An Empirical Test of Alternative Strategies," *Journal of Financial Research* 6 (Fall 1983): 187–97.

Hardy, C. *Risk and Risk Bearing* (Chicago: University of Chicago Press, 1940): 67–9.

Hardy, C. and L. Lyon "The Theory of Hedging," *Journal of Political Economy* 31 (1923): 271–87.

Hicks, J. *Value and Capital* 2nd edn (Oxford: Clarendon Press, 1939).

Houthakker, H. S. "Can Speculators Forecast Prices?" *Review of Economics and Statistics* 39 (1957): 143–51.

Kane, A. and A. Marcus "Valuation and Optimal Exercise of the Wild Card Option in the Treasury Bond Futures Market," *Journal of Finance* 41 (March 1986): 195–207.

Kane, E. "Market Incompleteness and Divergence Between Forward and Futures Interest Rates," *Journal of Finance* (May 1980): 221–34.

Keynes, J. *A Treatise On Money* (London: Macmillan, 1930).

Kim, David T. "Treasury Bond Futures Mechanics and Basis Valuation," in Frank J. Fabozzi (ed.) *The Handbook of Fixed Income Securities*, 6th edn (New York: McGraw-Hill, 2001).

Klemkosky, R. and D. Lasser "An Efficiency Analysis of the T-Bond Futures Market," *Journal of Futures Markets* 5 (1985): 607–20.

Kolb, R. W. and R. Chiang "Improving Hedging Performance Using Interest Rate Futures," *Financial Management* 10 (Fall 1981): 72–9.

McCable, G. and C. Franckle "The Effectiveness of Rolling the Hedge Forward in the Treasury Bill Futures Market," *Financial Management* 12 (Summer 1983): 21–9.

Rendleman, R. and C. Carabini "The Efficiency of the Treasury Bill Futures Market," *Journal of Finance* 34 (September 1979): 895–914.

Rentzler, J. "Trading Treasury Bond Spreads Against Treasury Bill Futures – A Model and Empirical Test of the Turtle Trade," *Journal of Futures Market* 6 (1986): 41–61.

Resnick, B. "The Relationship Between Futures Prices for U.S. Treasury Bonds," *Review of Research in Futures Markets* 3 (1984): 88–104.

Resnick, B. and E. Hennigar "The Relation Between Futures and Cash Prices for U.S. Treasury Bonds," *Review of Research in Futures Markets* 2 (1983): 282–99.

Senchak, A. and J. Easterwood "Cross Hedging CDs with Treasury Bill Futures," *Journal of Futures Markets* 3 (1983): 429–38.

Siegel, D. and D. Siegel *Futures Markets* (Chicago: Dryden Press, 1990): 203–342, 493–504.

Tamarkin, R. *The New Gatsbys: Fortunes and Misfortunes of Commodity Traders* (New York: William Morrow and Company, Inc., 1985).

Toevs, A. and D. Jacob "Futures and Alternative Hedge Methodologies," *Journal of Portfolio Management* (Spring 1986): 60–70.

Viet, T. and W. Reiff "Commercial Banks and Interest Rate Futures: A Hedging Survey," *Journal of Futures Markets* 3 (1983): 283–93.

Virnola, A. and C. Dale "The Efficiency of the Treasury Bill Futures Market: An Analysis of Alternative Specifications," *Journal of Financial Research* 3 (1980): 169–88.

CHAPTER FOURTEEN

INTEREST RATE OPTIONS: FUNDAMENTALS

14.1 INTRODUCTION

Like the futures market, the option market in the United States can be traced back to the 1840s, when options on corn meal, flour, and other agriculture commodities were traded in New York. These option contracts gave the holders the right, but not the obligation, to purchase or to sell a commodity at a specific price on or possibly before a specified date. Like forward contracts, options made it possible for farmers or agriculture dealers to lock in future prices. In contrast to commodity futures trading, though, the early market for commodity option trading was relatively thin. The market did grow marginally when options on stocks began trading on the over-the-counter (OTC) market in the early 1900s. This market began when a group of investment firms formed the Put and Call Brokers and Dealers Association. Through this association, an investor who wanted to buy an option could do so through a member of the association who either would find a seller through other members or would sell (write) the option himself.

The OTC option market was functional, but suffered because it failed to provide an adequate secondary market. In 1973, the Chicago Board of Trade formed the Chicago Board of Options Exchange (CBOE). The CBOE was the first organized option exchange for the trading of options. Just as the CBOT had served to increase the popularity of futures, the CBOE helped to increase the trading of options by making the contracts more marketable.

Since the creation of the CBOE, organized stock exchanges, such as the New York Stock Exchange (NYSE), the American Stock Exchange (AMEX), the Philadelphia Stock Exchange (PHLX), and the Pacific Stock Exchange (PSE), most of the organized futures exchanges, and many security exchanges outside the US also began offering markets for the trading of options. As the number of exchanges offering options increased, so did the number of securities and instruments with options written on them. Today, option contracts exist not only on stocks but also on foreign currencies, security indexes, futures contracts, and of particular interest here, debt and interest-rate-sensitive securities.

In this chapter and the next, we continue our discussion of derivative debt securities by examining option contracts on interest-sensitive securities. In this chapter, we define some of the common option terms, examine the fundamental option strategies, and identify some of the important factors that determine the price of an option. With this foundation, we extend our analysis of interest rate options in chapter 15 by looking at some of the hedging applications using these derivatives and by examining how the binomial interest rate tree that was examined in chapters 9 and 10 can be used to value options on interest-sensitive securities.

14.2 OPTION TERMINOLOGY

14.2.1 Spot Options

By definition, an option is a security that gives the holder the right to buy or sell a particular asset at a specified price on, or possibly before, a specific date. Depending on the parties and types of assets involved, options can take on many different forms. Certain features, however, are common to all options. First, with every option contract there exists a right, but not the obligation, to either buy or sell. Specifically, by definition a *call* is the right to buy a specific asset or security, whereas a *put* is the right to sell. Every option contract has a buyer who is referred to as the option *holder* (who has a *long position* in the option). The holder buys the right to *exercise* or evoke the terms of the option claim. Every option also has a seller, often referred to as the option *writer* (and having a *short position*), who is responsible for fulfilling the obligations of the option if the holder exercises. For every option there is an option price, exercise price, and exercise date. The price paid by the buyer to the writer when an option is created is referred to as the *option premium* (call premium and put premium). The *exercise price* or *strike price* is the price specified in the option contract at which the asset or security can be purchased (call) or sold (put). Finally, the *exercise date* is the last day the holder can exercise. Associated with the exercise date are the definitions of European and American options. A *European option* is one that can be exercised only on the exercise date, while an *American option* can be exercised at any time on or before the exercise date.

14.2.2 Futures Options

Option contracts on stocks, debt securities, foreign currency, and indexes are sometimes referred to as *spot options* or options on actuals. This reference is to distinguish them from *options on futures* contracts (also called options on futures, futures options, and commodity options). A futures option gives the holder the right to take a position in a futures contract. Specifically, a call option on a futures contract gives the holder the right to take a long position in the underlying futures contract when she exercises, and requires the writer to take the corresponding short position in the futures. Upon exercise, the holder of a futures call option in effect takes a long position in the futures contract at the *current* futures price and the writer takes the short position and pays the holder via the clearinghouse the difference between the current futures price and the exercise price. In contrast, a put option on a futures option entitles the holder to take a short futures position and the writer the long position. Thus, whenever the put holder exercises, he in effect takes a short futures position at the current futures price and the writer takes the long position and pays the holder via the clearinghouse the difference between the exercise price and the current futures price. Like all option positions, the futures option buyer pays an option premium for the right to exercise, and the writer, in turn, receives a premium when he sells the option and is subject to initial and maintenance margin requirements on the option position.

In practice, when the holder of a futures call option exercises, the futures clearinghouse will establish for the exercising option holder a long futures position at the futures price equal to the exercise price and a short futures position for the assigned writer. Once this is done, margins on both positions will be required and the position will be marked to market at the current settlement price on the futures. When the positions are marked to market, the exercising call holder's margin account on his long position will be equal to the difference between the futures price and the exercise price, $f_t - X$, while the assigned writer will have to deposit funds or near monies worth $f_t - X$ to satisfy her maintenance margin on her short futures position. Thus, when a futures call is exercised, the holder takes a long position at f_t with a margin account worth $f_t - X$; if he were to immediately close the futures he would receive cash worth $f_t - X$ from the clearinghouse. The assigned writer, in turn, is assigned a short position at f_t and must deposit $f_t - X$ to meet her margin. If the futures option is a put, the same procedure applies except that the holder takes a short position at f_t (when the exercised position is marked to market), with a margin account worth $X - f_t$, and the writer is assigned a long position at f_t and must deposit $X - f_t$ to meet her margin.

The current US market for futures options began in 1982 when the Commodity Futures Trading Commission (CFTC) initiated a pilot program in which it allowed each futures exchange to offer one option on one of its futures contracts. In 1987, the CFTC gave the exchanges permanent authority to offer futures options. Currently, the most popular futures options are the options on the financial futures: SP 500, T-bond, T-note, T-bill, Eurodollar deposit, and the major foreign currencies. In addition to options on financial futures contracts, futures options also are available on gold, precious metals, agriculture commodities, and energy products.[1]

It should be noted that spot options and futures options are equivalent if the options and the futures contracts expire at the same time, the carrying-cost model holds, and the options are European. (In contrast, spot and futures options will differ to the extent that these conditions do not hold.) There are, though, several factors that serve to differentiate the two contracts. First, since many futures contracts are relatively more liquid than their corresponding spot security, it is usually easier to form hedging or arbitrage strategies with futures options than with spot options. Second, futures options often are easier to exercise than their corresponding spot. For example, to exercise an option on a T-bond futures, one simply assumes the futures position, while exercising a spot T-bond option requires an actual purchase or delivery. Finally, most futures options are traded on the same exchange as their underlying futures contract, while most spot options are traded on

exchanges different from their underlying securities. This, in turn, makes it easier for futures options traders to implement arbitrage and hedging strategies than spot options traders.

Web Information

For market information and prices on futures options go to
  www.cme.com

and click on "Market Data," and go to
  www.cbot.com

and click on "Quotes and Trades."

14.3   MARKETS AND TYPES OF INTEREST RATE OPTIONS

14.3.1   Markets

Many different types of interest rate options are available on both the OTC market and the organized futures and options exchanges in Chicago, London, Singapore, and other major cities. Exchange-traded interest rate options include both futures options and spot options. On the US exchanges, the most heavily traded options are the CME's and CBOT's futures options on T-bonds, T-notes, T-bills, and Eurodollar contracts. The CBOE, AMEX, and PHLX have offered options on actual Treasury securities and Eurodollar deposits. These spot options, however, proved to be less popular than futures options and have been delisted. A number of non-US exchanges, though, do list options on actual debt securities, typically government securities. For example, options listed on the European Options Exchange are all spot options. Exhibit 14.1 shows the listing of interest rate option contracts on the major derivative exchanges and exhibit 12.1 list the futures and options exchanges with their websites.

In addition to exchange-traded options, there is also a large OTC market in debt and interest-sensitive securities and products in the US and a growing OTC market outside the US. Currently, security regulations in the US prohibit off-exchange trading in options on futures. All US OTC options are therefore options on

Exhibit 14.1   Options on non-US exchanges

Exchange	Select contracts (O = option; F = futures)

Sydney Futures Exchange (SFE)	A$500,000 90-day banker's acceptance (O F)
	A$100,000 3-year Commonwealth
	  T-bond (O F)
	A$100,000 10-year Commonwealth
	  T-bond (O F)

Montreal Exchange	C$ 25,000 10-year government of Canada bond (O) C$ 250,000 Canadian T-bill (O)
Toronto Stock Exchange (TSE)	C$ 100,000 10-year government of Canada bond (O)

Copenhagen Stock Exchange & Guaranteed
  Fund for Danish Futures and Options (FUTOP)
	Danish government bonds (various
	  maturities) (O F)
	Mortgage credit bonds (O)

Marche a Terme International de France (MATIF)	10-year government bond (O F) 90-day Paris interbank offer rate (O F)
Deutsche Terminborse (DTB), Germany	10-year government bond (O)
Tokyo International Financial Futures Exchange (TIFFE)	90-day Euroyen deposit (O F)
Tokyo Stock Exchange	JY 100m 10-year government bond (O F)
European Options Exchange (EOE), Netherlands	Dutch government bonds (O) FTA Bullet Bond Index (O)
New Zealand Futures and Options Exchange (NZFOE)	Government bonds (various maturities) (O F) 90-day bank-accepted bill (O F)
Singapore Monetary Exchange (SIMEX)	US $1m 90-day Eurodollar deposit (O F) JY 100m 90-day Euroyen deposit (O F)
Mercada de Opciones Financieras Espanol (MEFF)	3-year notional government bond (O) 3-year notional government bond (O) 90-day Madrid interbank offer rate (O)
OM Stockholm	7-year notional government bond (O) BP 50,000 coupon gilt (15–25 years) (O F)
London International Financial Futures Exchange (LIFFE)	US $1m 90-day Eurodollar deposit (O F) BP 500,000 90-day Eurosterling deposit (O F) US $100,000 T-bond (O F) 10-year German government bond (O F)

actuals. The OTC markets inside and outside the US consist primarily of dealers who make markets in the underlying spot security, investment banking firms, and commercial banks. OTC options are primarily used by financial institutions and non-financial corporations to hedge their interest rate positions. The option contracts offered in the OTC market include spot options on Treasury securities, LIBOR-related securities, and special types of interest rate products, such as interest rate calls and puts, caps, floors, and collars.

14.3.2 Types of Interest Rate Options

As noted, on the organized exchanges the most heavily traded exchange-traded options are futures options on T-bonds, T-notes, T-bills, and Eurodollar contracts. On the OTC market, the most popular interest rate options include options on spot Treasury securities and caps and floors.

CBOT's Futures Options

The CBOT offers trading on interest rate futures options on T-bonds, T-notes with maturities of 10 years, 5 years, and 2 years, the Municipal Bond Index, and the Mortgage-Backed bond contract. Exhibit 14.2 shows the *Wall Street Journal* quotes for March 28, 2003 on the CBOT's options on T-bond and T-note futures contracts, as well as the Eurodollar futures contracts traded on the CME. As shown, the call and put contracts on the T-bonds and T-notes are set with exercise prices that are one point apart (109, 110, 111) and with expiration months on the T-bond and 5-year T-note of May, June, and July. The premiums on the options are quoted as a percentage of the face value of the underlying bond or note. For example, a buyer of the May 109 T-bond futures call trading at 2-60 (or $2\frac{60}{64} = 2.9375$) would pay \$2,937.50 for the option to take a long position in the May T-bond futures at an exercise price of \$109,000. If long-term rates were to subsequently drop, causing the May T-bond futures price to increase to $f_t = 113$, then the holder, upon exercising, would have a long position in the May T-bond futures contract and a margin account worth \$4,000. If she closed her futures contract at 113, she would have a profit of \$1,062.50:

$$\text{Value of margin} = \frac{f_t - X}{100} F$$

$$= \left[\frac{113 - 109}{100}\right] \$100,000 = \$4,000$$

$$\pi = \$4,000 - \$2,937.50 = \$1,062.50$$

By contrast, if long-term rates were to stay the same or increase, then the call would be worthless and the holder would simply allow it to expire, losing the \$2,937.50 premium.

CME's Futures Options

The CME offers trading on short-term interest rate futures options on T-bills, Eurodollar deposits, and 30-day LIBOR contracts. The

Exhibit 14.2   *WSJ* quotes on futures options

STRIKE	CALLS-SETTLE			PUTS-SETTLE		

Interest Rate

T-Bonds (CBT)
$100,000; points and 64ths of 100%

Price	May	Jun	Jul	May	Jun	Jul
109	2-60	3-31	...	0-38	1-10	2-04
110	2-14	2-54	2-34	0-56	1-32	2-34
111	1-39	2-16	...	1-17	1-59	...
112	1-08	1-49	1-42	1-50	2-27	...
113	0-48	1-22	1-20	2-26	3-00	...
114	0-30	1-00	1-01	3-08	3-42	...

Est vol 23,528;
Wd vol 8,312 calls 7,760 puts
Op int Wed 198,541 calls 225,705 puts

T-Notes (CBT)
$100,000; points and 64ths of 100%

Price	May	Jun	Jul	May	Jun	Jul
112	2-18	2-40	2-17	0-23	0-45	1-22
113	1-35	1-61	1-46	0-40	1-02	1-51
114	0-60	1-24	1-16	1-01	1-29	...
115	0-33	0-59	...	1-38	2-00	...
116	0-17	0-38	...	2-22	2-43	...
117	0-07	0-23	...	3-12	3-28	...

Est vol 76,473 Wd 52,504 calls 50,960 puts
Op int Wed 538,270 calls 609,138 puts

5 Yr Treas Notes (CBT)
$100,000; points and 64ths of 100%

Price	May	Jun	Sep	May	Jun	Sep
11200	1-14	1-29	1-33	0-24	0-39	1-41
11250	0-57	1-09	...	0-35	0-51	...
11300	0-39	0-57	...	0-49	1-03	...
11350	0-27	0-42	...	1-05	1-20	...
11400	0-18	0-31	...	1-28	1-41	...
11450	0-11	0-22	...	1-53	2-00	...

Est vol 32,424 Wd 10,426 calls 10,561 puts
Op int Wed 166,038 calls 396,069 puts

Eurodollar (CME)
$ million; pts. of 100%

Price	Apr	May	Jun	Apr	May	Jun
9825	...	...	5.60	0.00	0.02	...
9850	3.07	3.07	3.12	0.02	0.02	0.05
9875	0.82	1.15	1.32	0.27	0.60	0.77
9900	0.15	0.35	0.45	...	2.30	2.40
9925	0.02	0.05	0.10	...	...	4.55
9950	0.00	0.02	0.05	...	...	...

Est vol 286,470;
Wd vol 337,360 calls 35,028 puts
Op int Wed 4,180,414 calls 2,724,494 puts

Source: Wall Street Journal, March 28, 2003, p. B16. Republished by permission of Dow Jones, Inc. via Copyright Clearance Center, Inc. @ 2003 Dow Jones and Company, Inc. All Rights Reserve Worldwide.

maturities of the options correspond to the maturities on the underlying futures contracts, and the exercise quotes are based on the system used for quoting the futures contracts. Thus, the exercise prices on the Eurodollar and T-bill contracts are quoted in terms of an index (I) equal to 100 minus the annual discount yield: $I = 100 - R_D$. The option premiums are quoted in terms of an index point system. For T-bills and Eurodollars, the dollar value of an option quote is based on a $25 value for each basis point underlying a $1m T-bill or Eurodollar. The actual quotes are in percents; thus a 1.25 quote would imply a price of $25 times 12.5 basis points: ($25)(12.5) = $312.50. In addition, for the closest maturing month, the options are quoted to the nearest quarter of a basis point; for other months, they are quoted to the nearest half of a basis point. For example, the actual price on a March Eurodollar call with an exercise price of 94.5 quoted at 5.92 is $1,481.25. The price is obtained by rounding the 5.92 quoted price to 5.925, converting the quote to basis points (multiply by ten), and multiplying by $25: (5.925)(10)($25) = $1,481.25. The 10.30 quote on the 94.5 April call indicates a call price (10.30)(10)($25) = $2,575 (or simply, (10.30)($250) = $2,575).

An investor buying the 94.5 March call would therefore pay $1,481.25 for the right to take a long position in the CME's $1m March Eurodollar futures contract at an exercise price of $986,250:

$$X = \frac{100 - (100 - 94.5)(90/360)}{100} \$1,000,000$$

$$= \$986,250$$

If short-term rates were to subsequently drop, causing the March Eurodollar futures price to increase to an index price of 95.5 ($R_D = 4.5$ and $f_t = [[100 - 4.5(90/360)]/100]($1,000,000) = $988,750$), the holder, upon exercising, would have a long position in the CME March Eurodollar futures contract and a futures margin account worth $2,500. If she closed the position at 95.5, she would realize a profit of $1,018.75:

Margin value $= f_t - X = \$988,750 - \$986,250$

$\qquad = \$2,500$

$\qquad = \$25(\text{Futures index}$

$\qquad\quad - \text{Exercise index})$

$\qquad = \$25[95.5 - 94.5](100)$

$\qquad = \$2,500$

$\pi = \$2,500 - \$1,481.25$

$\qquad = \$1,018.75$

If short-term rates were at $R_D = 5.5\%$ and stayed there or increased, then the call would be worthless and the holder would simply allow the option to expire, losing her $1,481.25 premium.

OTC Options

While OTC options can be structured on almost any interest-sensitive position an investor or borrower may wish to hedge, US Treasuries, LIBOR-related instruments, and mortgage-backed securities are often the underlying security. When spot options are structured on securities, terms such as the specific underlying security, its maturity and size, the option's expiration, and the delivery are all negotiated. For Treasuries, the underlying security is often a recently auctioned Treasury (on-the-run bond), although some selected existing securities (off-the-run securities) are used. While the prices on OTC options tend to conform to the basic option pricing relation (discussed in section 14.6), their bid-asked spreads tend to be larger than exchange-trade ones. The option maturities on OTC contracts can range from one day to several years, with many of the options being European.

OTC T-Bond and T-Note Options

In the case of OTC spot T-bond or T-note options, OTC dealers often offer or will negotiate contracts giving the holder the right to purchase or sell a specific T-bond or T-note. For example, a dealer might offer a T-bond call option to a fixed-income manager giving him the right to buy a specific T-bond maturing in year 2016 and paying a 6% coupon with a face value of $100,000. Because the option contract specifies a particular underlying bond, the maturity of the bond, as well as its value, will be changing during the option's expiration period. For example, a 1-year call option on the 15-year bond, if held to expiration, would be a call option to buy a 14-year bond. Note that in contrast, a spot T-bill option contract offered by a dealer on the OTC market usually calls for the delivery of a T-bill meeting the specified criteria (e.g., principal = $1m, maturity = 91 days). With this clause, a T-bill option is referred to as a *fixed deliverable bond*, and unlike specific-security T-bond options, T-bill options can have expiration dates that exceed the T-bill's maturity.

A second feature of a spot T-bond or T-note option offered or contracted on the OTC market is that the underlying bond or note can pay coupon interest during the option period. As a result, if the option holder exercises on a non-coupon paying date, the accrued interest on the underlying bond must be accounted for. For a T-bond or T-note option, this is done by including the accrued interest as part of the exercise price. Like futures options, the exercise price on a spot T-bond or T-note option is quoted as an index equal to a proportion of a bond with a face value of $100 (e.g., 95). If the underlying bond or note has a face value of $100,000, then the exercise price would be:

$$X = \left[\frac{\text{Index}}{100}\right](\$100,000) + \text{Accrued interest}$$

Finally, the prices of spot T-bond and T-note options are typically quoted like futures T-bond options in terms of points and 32nds of a point. Thus, the price of a call option on a $100,000 T-bond quoted at $1\frac{5}{32}$ is $1,156.25 = (1.15625/100)(\$100,000)$.

Interest rate call

In addition to option contracts on specific securities, the OTC market also offers a number of interest rate option products. These products are usually offered by commercial or investment banks to their clients. Two products of note are the interest rate call and the interest rate put. An *interest rate call*, also called a *caplet*, gives the buyer a payoff on a specified payoff date if a designated interest rate, such as the LIBOR, rises above a certain exercise rate, R_x. On the payoff date, if the rate is less than R_x, the interest rate call expires worthless; if the rate exceeds R_x, the call pays off the difference between the actual rate and R_x, times a notional principal, NP, times the fraction of the year specified in the contract. For example, given an interest rate call with a designated rate of LIBOR, $R_x = 6\%$, NP = $1m, time period of 180 days, and day count convention of $\frac{180}{360}$, the buyer would receive a $5,000 payoff on the payoff date if the LIBOR were 7%: $(0.07 - 0.06)(180/360)(\$1m) = \$5,000$.

Interest rate call options are often written by commercial banks in conjunction with futures loans they plan to provide to their customers.

The exercise rate on the option usually is set near the current spot rate, with that rate often being tied to the LIBOR. For example, a company planning to finance a future $10m inventory 60 days from the present by borrowing from a bank at a rate equal to the LIBOR+ 100 BP at the start of the loan could buy from the bank an interest rate call option with an exercise rate equal to, say, 8%, expiration of 60 days, and notional principal of $10m. At expiration (60 days later) the company would be entitled to a payoff if rates were higher than 8%. Thus, if the rate on the loan were higher than 8%, the company would receive a payoff that would offset the higher interest on the loan.

Interest rate put

An *interest rate put*, also called a *floorlet*, gives the buyer a payoff on a specified payoff date if a designated interest rate is below the exercise rate, R_x. On the payoff date, if the rate is more than R_x, the interest rate put expires worthless; if the rate is less than R_x, the put pays off the difference between R_x and the actual rate times a notional principal, NP, times the fraction of the year specified in the contract. For example, given an interest rate put with a designated rate of LIBOR, $R_x = 6\%$, NP = $1m, time period of 180 days, and day count convention of $\frac{180}{360}$, the buyer would receive a $5,000 payoff on the payoff date if the LIBOR were 5%: $(0.06 - 0.05)(180/360)(\$1m) = \$5,000$.

A financial or non-financial corporation that is planning to make an investment at some future date could hedge that investment against interest rate decreases by purchasing an interest rate put from a commercial bank, investment banking firm, or dealer. For example, suppose that instead of needing to borrow $10m, the previous company was expecting a net cash inflow of $10m in 60 days from its operations and was planning to invest the funds in a 90-day bank CD paying the LIBOR. To hedge against any interest rate decreases, the company could purchase an interest rate put (corresponding to the bank's CD it plans to buy) from the bank with the put having an exercise rate of, say, 7%, expiration of 60 days, and notional principal of $10m. The interest rate put would provide a payoff for the company if the LIBOR were less than 7%, giving the company a hedge against interest rate decreases.

Cap

A popular option offered by financial institutions in the OTC market is the *cap*. A plain vanilla cap is a series of European interest rate call options – a portfolio of caplets. For example, a 7%, 2-year cap on a 3-month LIBOR, with an NP of $100m, provides, for the next 2 years, a payoff every 3 months of (LIBOR– 0.07)(0.25) ($100m) if the LIBOR on the reset date exceeds 7% and nothing if the LIBOR equals or is less than 7%. (Typically, the payment is not on the reset date, but rather on the next reset date 3 months later.) Caps are often written by financial institutions in conjunction with a floating-rate loan and are used by buyers as a hedge against interest rate risk. For example, a company with a floating-rate loan tied to the LIBOR could lock in a maximum rate on the loan by buying a cap corresponding to its loan. At each reset date, the company would receive a payoff from the caplet if the LIBOR exceeded the cap rate, offsetting the higher interest paid on the floating-rate loan; on the other hand, if rates decrease, the company would pay a lower rate on its loan while its losses on the caplet would be limited to the cost of the option. Thus, with a cap, the company would be able to lock in a maximum rate each quarter, while still benefiting with lower interest costs if rates decrease.

Floor

A plain-vanilla *floor* is a series of European interest rate put options – a portfolio of floorlets. For example, a 7%, 2-year floor on a 3-month LIBOR, with an NP of $100m, provides, for the next 2 years, a payoff every 3 months of (0.07 − LIBOR)(0.25)($100m) if the LIBOR on the reset date is less than 7% and nothing if the LIBOR equals or exceeds 7%. Floors are often purchased by investors as a tool to hedge their floating-rate investments against interest rate declines. Thus, with a floor, an investor with a floating-rate security is able to lock in a minimum rate each period, while still benefiting with higher yields if rates increase.

14.4   OPTION POSITIONS

Many types of option strategies with esoteric names such as straddles, strips, spreads, combinations, and so forth, exist. The building blocks for these strategies are four fundamental option strategies: call and put purchases and call and put writes. The features of these fundamental strategies can be seen by examining the relationship between the price of the underlying security and the possible profits or losses that would result if the option either is exercised or expires worthless.[2]

14.4.1   Fundamental Spot Option Positions

Call Purchase

To see the major characteristics of a call purchase, suppose an investor buys a spot call option on a 6% T-bond with a face value of $100,000, a maturity at the option's expiration of 15 years, no accrued interest at the option's expiration date, and currently selling at par. Suppose the T-bond's exercise price (X) is $100,000 (quoted at 100) and the investor buys the options at a call premium of $C_0 = \$1,000$ (quoted at 1). If the bond price reaches $105,000 at expiration, the holder would realize a profit of $4,000 by exercising the call to acquire the bond for $100,000, then selling the bond in the market for $105,000: a $5,000 capital gain minus the $1,000 premium. If the holder exercises at expiration when the bond is trading at $101,000, she will break even: the $1,000 premium will be offset exactly by the $1,000 gain realized by acquiring the bond from the option at $100,000 and selling in the market at $101,000. Finally, if the price of the bond is at the exercise price of $100,000 or below, the holder will not find it profitable to exercise, and as a result, she will let the option expire, realizing a loss equal to the call premium of $1,000. Thus, the maximum loss from the call purchase is $1,000.

The investor's possible profit/loss and bond price combinations can be seen graphically in exhibit 14.3 and the accompanying table. In the graph, the profits/losses are shown on the vertical axis and the market prices of the spot T-bond, S, at expiration or when the option is exercised (signified as T: S_T) are shown along the horizontal axis. This graph is known as a *profit graph*. The line from the coordinate

($100,000, − $1,000) to the ($105,000, $4,000) coordinate and beyond shows all the profit and losses per call associated with each bond price. The horizontal segment shows a loss of $1,000 that is equal to the premium paid when the option was purchased. Finally, the horizontal intercept is the break–even price ($101,000). The break–even price can be found algebraically by solving for the bond price at the exercise date (S_T) in which the profit (π) from the position is zero. The profit from the call purchase position is:

$$\pi = (S_T - X) - C_0$$

where C_0 is the initial ($t = 0$) cost of the call. Setting π equal to zero and solving for S_T yields the break–even price of S_T^*:

$$S_T^* = X + C_0 = \$100,000 + \$1,000 = \$101,000$$

The profit graph in exhibit 14.3 highlights two important features of call purchases. First, the position provides an investor with unlimited profit potential; second, losses are limited to an amount equal to the call premium.

Naked Call Write

The second fundamental strategy involves the sale of a call in which the seller does not own the underlying security. Such a position is known as a *naked call write*. To see the characteristics of this position, assume the same spot T-bond call option with an exercise price of $100,000 and premium of $1,000. The profits or losses associated with each bond price from selling the call are depicted in the graph in exhibit 14.4. As shown, when the price of the bond is at $105,000 at expiration, the seller suffers a $4,000 loss when the holder exercises the right to buy the bond from the writer at $100,000. Since the writer does not own the bond, he would have to buy it in the market at its market price of $105,000, then turn it over to the holder at $100,000. Thus, the call writer would realize a $5,000 capital loss, minus the $1,000 premium received for selling the call, for a net loss of $4,000. When the T-bond is at $101,000, the writer will realize a $1,000 loss if the holder exercises. This loss will offset the $1,000 premium received. Thus, the break–even price for the writer is $101,000 – the same as the holder's. This price also can be found algebraically by solving for the spot price S_T^* in which the profit from the naked call write position is zero. Finally, at a bond price of $100,000 or less the holder will not exercise, and the writer will profit by the amount of the premium, $1,000.

As highlighted in the graph, the payoffs to a call write are just the opposite of the call

Exhibit 14.3 Call purchase

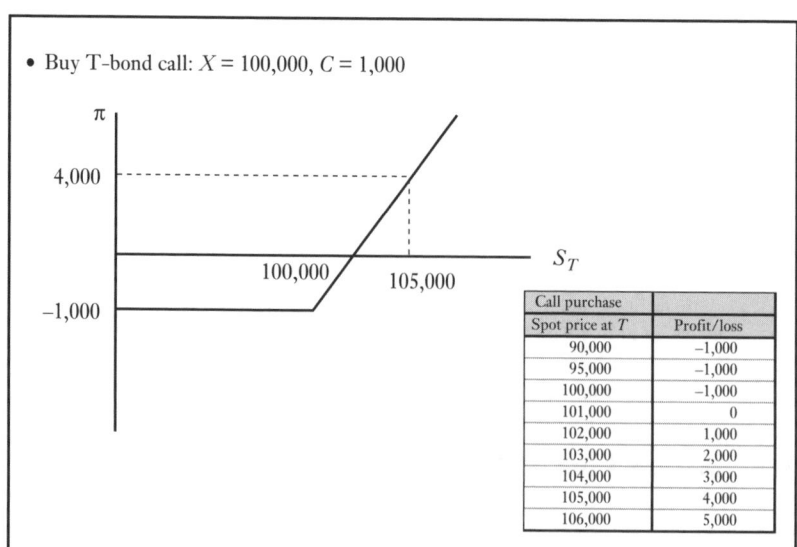

Call purchase	
Spot price at T	Profit/loss
90,000	−1,000
95,000	−1,000
100,000	−1,000
101,000	0
102,000	1,000
103,000	2,000
104,000	3,000
105,000	4,000
106,000	5,000

Exhibit 14.4   Naked call write

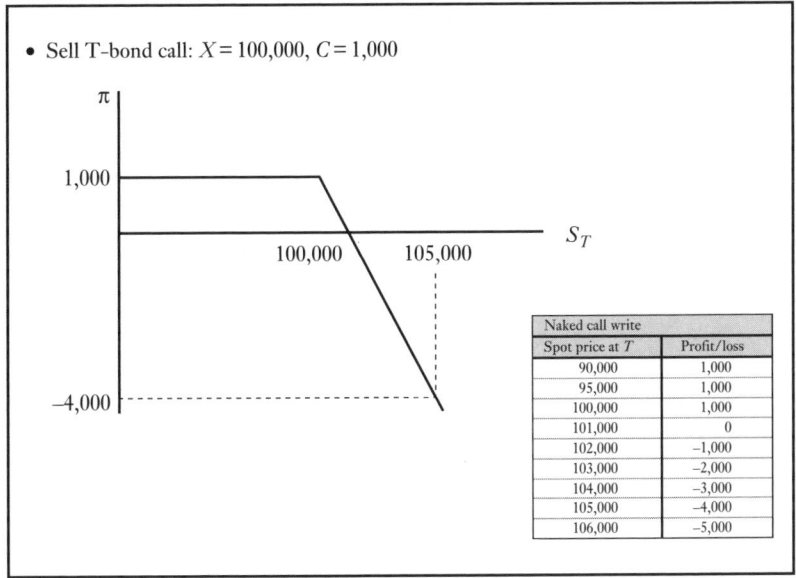

- Sell T-bond call: $X = 100,000$, $C = 1,000$

Naked call write	
Spot price at T	Profit/loss
90,000	1,000
95,000	1,000
100,000	1,000
101,000	0
102,000	–1,000
103,000	–2,000
104,000	–3,000
105,000	–4,000
106,000	–5,000

purchase; that is, gains/losses for the buyer of a call are exactly equal to the losses/gains of the seller. Thus, in contrast to the call purchase, the naked call write position provides the investor with only a limited profit opportunity equal to the value of the premium, with unlimited loss possibilities. While this limited profit and unlimited loss feature of a naked call write may seem unattractive, the motivation for an investor to write a call is the cash or credit received and the expectation that the option will not be exercised. Like futures contracts, though, there are margin requirements on an option write position in which the writer is required to deposit cash or risk-free securities to secure the position.

Put Purchase

Since a put gives the holder the right to sell the underlying security, profit is realized when the security's price declines. With a decline, the put holder can buy the security at a low price in the market, then sell it at the higher exercise price on the contract. To see the features related to the put purchase position, assume the exercise price on a put option on the 6% T-bond is again $100,000 and the put premium

(P) is $1,000. If the T-bond is trading at $95,000 at expiration, the put holder could purchase a 15-year, 6% T-bond at $95,000, then use the put contract to sell the bond at the exercise price of $100,000. Thus, as shown by the profit graph in exhibit 14.5 and its accompanying table, at $95,000 the put holder would realize a $4,000 profit (the $5,000 gain from buying the bond and exercising minus the $1,000 premium). The break-even price in this case would be $99,000:

$$\pi = X - S_T - P_0 = 0$$
$$S_T^* = X - P_0$$
$$= \$100,000 - \$1,000 = \$99,000$$

Finally, if the T-bond is trading at $100,000 or higher at expiration, it will not be rational for the put holder to exercise. As a result, a maximum loss equal to the $1,000 premium will occur when the stock is trading at $100,000 or more (again assuming no accrued interest at expiration).

Thus, similar to a call purchase, a long put position provides the buyer with potentially large profit opportunities (not unlimited since the price of the security cannot be less than zero), while limiting the losses to the amount of the

Exhibit 14.5 Put purchase

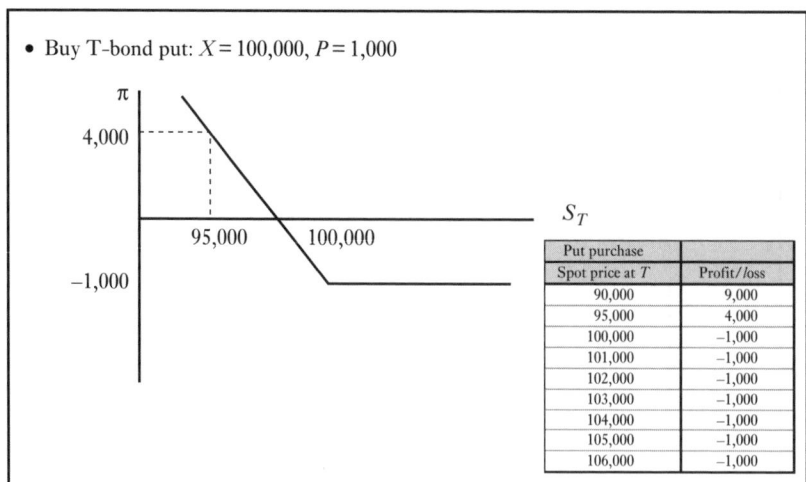

Exhibit 14.6 Naked put write

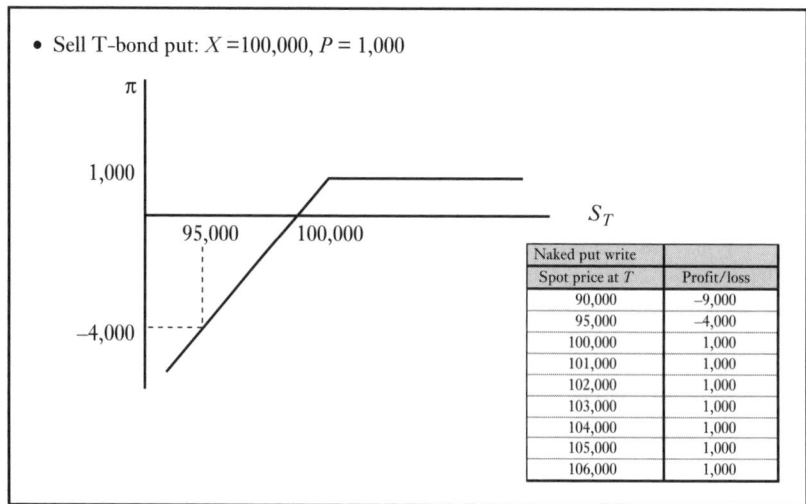

premium. Unlike the call purchase strategy, the put purchase position requires the security price to decline before profit is realized.

Naked Put Write

The exact opposite position to a put purchase (in terms of profit/loss and security price relations) is the sale of a put, defined as the naked put write. This position's profit graph is shown in exhibit 14.6. Here, if the T-bond price is at $100,000 or more at expiration, the holder will not exercise and the writer will profit by the amount of the premium, $1,000. In contrast, if the T-bond decreases, a loss is incurred. For example, if the holder exercises at $95,000, the put writer must buy the bond at $100,000. An actual $5,000 loss will occur if the writer elects to sell the bond and a paper loss if he holds on to it. This loss, minus the $1,000 premium, yields a loss of $4,000 when the market price is $95,000. For this naked put

Exhibit 14.7 Futures options call on Treasury securities

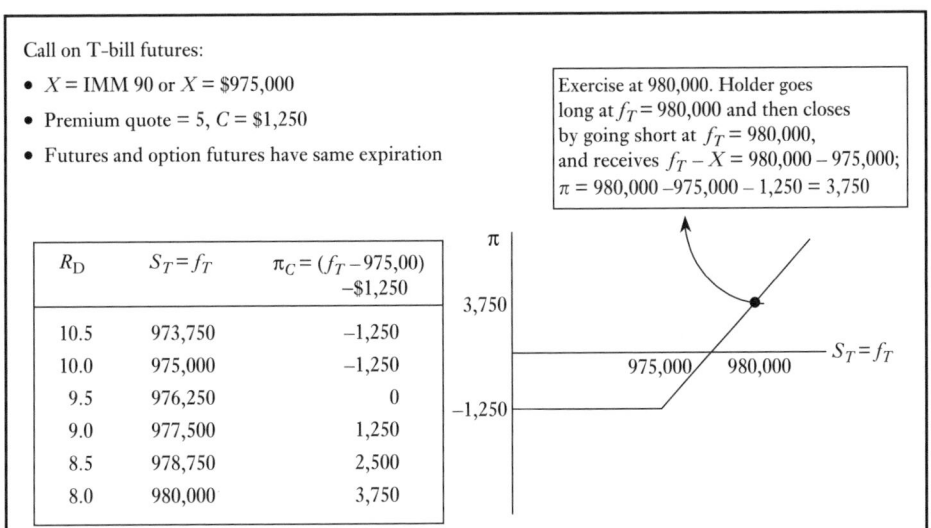

Call on T-bill futures:

- X = IMM 90 or X = $975,000
- Premium quote = 5, C = $1,250
- Futures and option futures have same expiration

Exercise at 980,000. Holder goes long at f_T = 980,000 and then closes by going short at f_T = 980,000, and receives $f_T - X$ = 980,000 – 975,000; π = 980,000 –975,000 – 1,250 = 3,750

R_D	$S_T = f_T$	$\pi_C = (f_T - 975,00)$ $-\$1,250$
10.5	973,750	–1,250
10.0	975,000	–1,250
9.5	976,250	0
9.0	977,500	1,250
8.5	978,750	2,500
8.0	980,000	3,750

write position, the break-even price in which the profit from the position is zero is $S_0^* =$ $99,000$, the same as the put holder's.

14.4.2 Fundamental Futures Options Positions

The important characteristics of futures options can also be seen by examining the profit relationships for the fundamental call and put positions formed with these options. Exhibit 14.7 shows the profit and futures price relationship at expiration for the long call position on a T-bill futures. The call has an exercise price equal to 90 (index) or $X =$ $975,000$, is priced at $1,250 (quote of 5: (5)(10)($25) = $1,250) and it is assumed the T-bill futures option expires at the same time as the underlying T-bill futures contract. The numbers shown in the exhibit reflect a case in which the holder exercises the call at expiration, if profitable, when the spot price is equal to the price on the expiring futures contract. For example, at $S_T = f_T =$ $980,000$, the holder of the 90 T-bill futures call would receive a cash flow of $5,000 for a profit of $3,750 ($=$ $5,000 - $1,250$). That is, upon exercising the holder would assume a long position in the expiring T-bill futures priced at $980,000 and a futures margin account worth

$5,000 (($f_T - X$) = $980,000 - $975,000 =$ $5,000$). Given we are at expiration, the holder would therefore receive $5,000 from the expired futures position, leaving her with a profit of $3,750. The opposite profit and futures price relation is attained for a naked call write position. In this case, if the T-bill futures is at $975,00 or less, the writer of the futures call would earn the premium of $1,250, and if $f_T >$ $975,000$, he, upon the exercise by the holder, would assume a short position at f_T and would have to pay $f_T - X$ to bring the margin on his expiring short position into balance.

Exhibit 14.8 shows a long put position on the 90 T-bill futures purchased at $1,250. In the case of a put purchase, if the holder exercises when f_T is less than X, then he will have a margin account worth $X - f_T$ on an expiring short futures position. For example, if $S_T = f_T =$ $970,000$ at expiration, then the put holder upon exercising would receive $5,000 from the expiring short futures $(X - f_T = $975,000 -$ $970,000$) yielding a profit from her futures option of $3,750. The put writer's position, of course, would be the opposite.

It should be noted that while the technicalities on exercising futures options are cumbersome, the profits from closing a futures option at expiration still are equal to the maximum of either zero or the difference in $f_T - X$ (for calls) or

Exhibit 14.8 Futures options put on Treasury securities

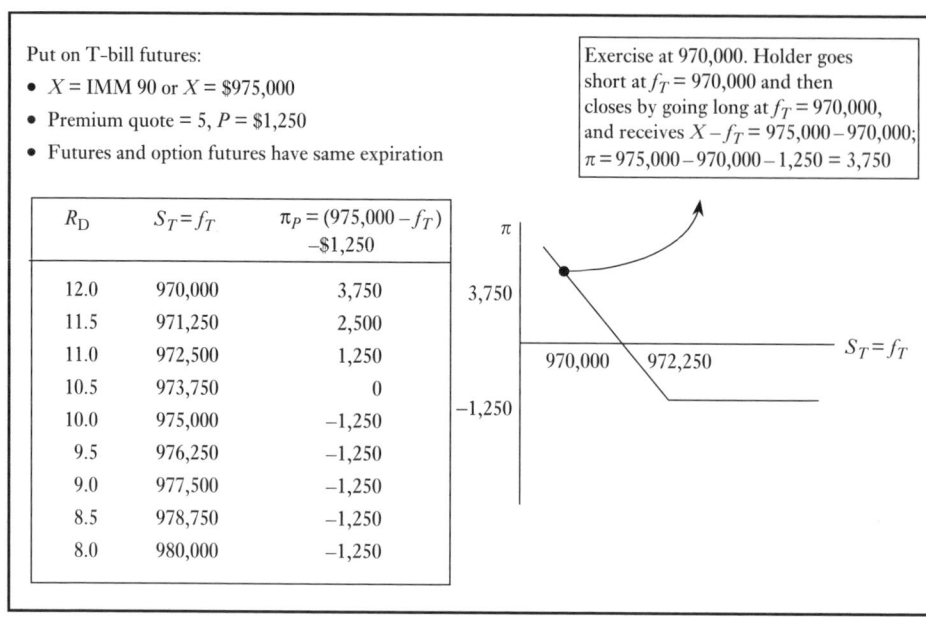

Put on T-bill futures:
- $X =$ IMM 90 or $X = \$975,000$
- Premium quote $= 5$, $P = \$1,250$
- Futures and option futures have same expiration

Exercise at 970,000. Holder goes short at $f_T = 970,000$ and then closes by going long at $f_T = 970,000$, and receives $X - f_T = 975,000 - 970,000$; $\pi = 975,000 - 970,000 - 1,250 = 3,750$

R_D	$S_T = f_T$	$\pi_P = (975,000 - f_T)$ $-\$1,250$
12.0	970,000	3,750
11.5	971,250	2,500
11.0	972,500	1,250
10.5	973,750	0
10.0	975,000	−1,250
9.5	976,250	−1,250
9.0	977,500	−1,250
8.5	978,750	−1,250
8.0	980,000	−1,250

Exhibit 14.9 Interest rate call option (exercise rate $= 6\%$, reference rate $=$ LIBOR, NP $= \$10$m, period $= 0.25$ year, option cost $= \$12,500$)

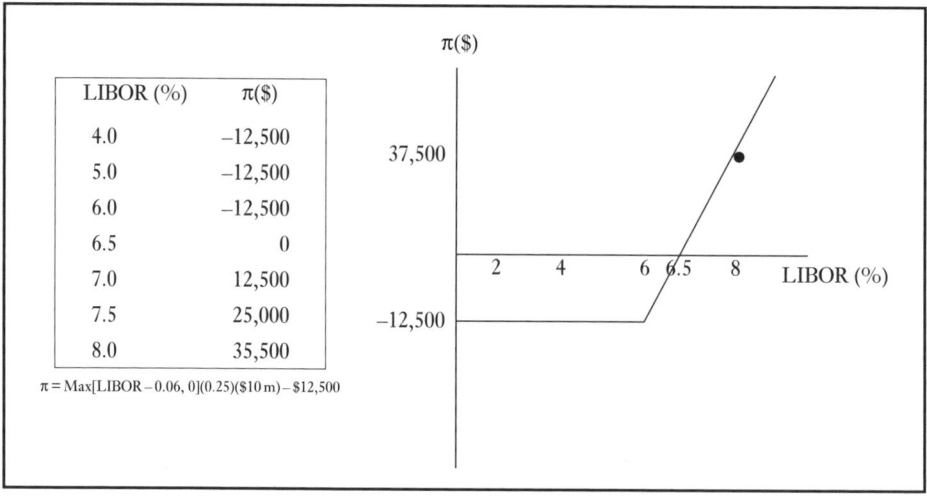

LIBOR (%)	$\pi(\$)$
4.0	−12,500
5.0	−12,500
6.0	−12,500
6.5	0
7.0	12,500
7.5	25,000
8.0	35,500

$\pi = \text{Max}[\text{LIBOR} - 0.06, 0](0.25)(\$10\,\text{m}) - \$12,500$

$X - f_T$ (for puts), minus the option premium. Moreover, if the futures option and the underlying futures contract expire at the same time, as we assumed above, then $f_T = S_T$, and the futures option can be viewed simply as an option on the underlying spot security with the option having a cash settlement clause.

14.4.3 Fundamental Interest Rate Call and Put Positions

The profit graphs for interest rate calls and puts can be defined in terms of the profit and interest rate relations for the option. Exhibit 14.9 shows the profit graph and table for an interest

Exhibit 14.10 Interest rate put option (exercise rate $= 6\%$, reference rate $=$ LIBOR, $NP = \$10m$, period $= 0.25$ year, option cost $= \$12,500$)

LIBOR (%)	$\pi(\$)$
4.0	37,500
4.5	25,000
5.0	12,500
5.5	0
6.0	−12,500
7.0	−12,500
8.0	−12,500

$\pi = \text{Max}[0.06 - \text{LIBOR}, 0]\,(0.25)(\$10\,\text{m}) - \$12,500$

rate call with the following terms: exercise rate $= 6\%$, reference rate $=$ LIBOR, NP=$10m, time period as proportion of a year $= 0.25$, and the cost of the option $= \$12,500$. As shown in the exhibit, if the LIBOR reaches 7.5% at expiration, the holder would realize a payoff of $(0.075 - 0.06)(\$10m)(0.25) = \$37,500$ and a profit of $25,000; if the LIBOR is 6.5%, the holder would break even with the $12,500 payoff equal to the option's cost; if the LIBOR is 6% or less, there would be no payoff and the holder would incur a loss equal to the call premium of $12,500. Just the opposite relationship between profits and rates exists for an interest rate put. Exhibit 14.10 shows the profit graph and table for an interest rate put with terms similar to those of the interest rate call.

14.4.4 Other Option Strategies

One of the important features of an option is that it can be combined with positions in the underlying security and other options to generate a number of different investment strategies. Two well-known strategies formed by combining option positions are *straddles* and *spreads*.

Straddle

A straddle purchase is formed by buying both a call and put with the same terms – the same

underlying security, exercise price, and expiration date. A straddle write, in contrast, is constructed by selling a call and a put with the same terms.

In exhibit 14.11, the profit graphs are shown for spot T-bond call, put, and straddle purchases in which both the call and the put have exercise prices of $100,000 and premiums of $1,000 and there is no accrued interest at expiration.[3] The straddle purchase shown in the figure is geometrically generated by vertically summing the profits on the call purchase position and put purchase position at each bond price. The resulting straddle purchase position is characterized by a V-shaped profit and spot price relation. Thus, the motivation for buying a straddle comes from the expectation of a large price movement in either direction. Losses on the straddle occur if the price of the underlying security remains stable, with the maximum loss being equal to the costs of the straddle ($2,000) and occurring when the bond price is equal to the exercise price. Finally, the straddle is characterized by two break-even prices ($98,000 and $102,000).

In contrast to the straddle purchase, a straddle write yields an inverted V-shaped profit graph. The seller of a straddle is betting against large price movements. A maximum profit equal to the sum of the call and put premiums occurs when the bond price is equal

Exhibit 14.11   Straddle purchase

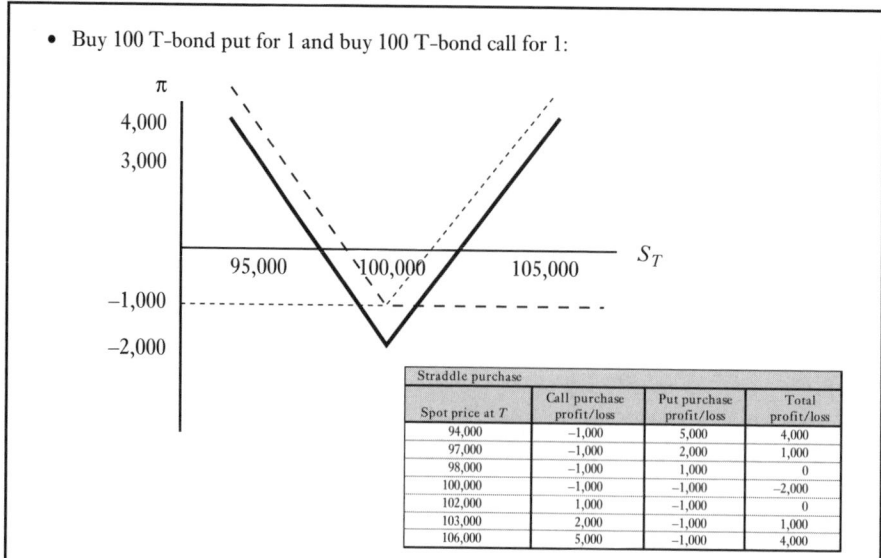

to the exercise price; losses occur if the bond price moves significantly in either direction.

Spread

A spread is the purchase of one option and the sale of another on the same underlying security but with different terms: different exercise prices (*money spread*), different expirations (*time spread*), or both (*diagonal spread*). Two of the most popular time spread positions are the *bull spread* and the *bear spread*. A bull call spread is formed by buying a call with a certain exercise price and selling another call with a higher exercise price, but with the same expiration date. A bear call spread is the reversal of the bull spread; it consists of buying a call with a certain exercise price and selling another with a lower exercise price. (The same spreads also can be formed with puts.)

In exhibit 14.12, the profit graph and table for a bull call spread strategy are shown. The spread is formed with the purchase of a 100 T-bond call ($X = \$100{,}000$) for 1 ($C = \$1{,}000$) and the sale of a 101 T-bond call ($X = \$101{,}000$) for 0.75 ($C = \$750$) (same underlying T-bond and expirations). The bull spread is characterized by losses limited to $250 when the T-bond price is $100,000 or less, limited profits

of $750 starting when the bond price hits $101,000, and a break-even price of $100,250.

A bear call spread results in the opposite profit and security price relation as the bull spread: limited profits occur when the security price is equal to or less than the lower exercise price and limited losses occur when the security price is equal to or greater than the higher exercise price.

14.4.5   Speculation

The above profit graphs illustrate how interest rate options can be used to hedge, as well as speculate, on movements in interest rates. A speculator who believes the Federal Reserve System will lower short-term interest rates in the near future to stimulate the economy could profit (if her expectation is correct) by taking a long position in a T-bill futures call. As a speculative strategy, this long call position can be viewed as an alternative to a long position in a T-bill futures contract. When compared to the futures position, the call position provides a limited loss and unlimited profit, while the futures position provides an unlimited profit and loss profile. In contrast, if a speculator believes that short-term interest rates are going to increase in the near future, then she should

Exhibit 14.12 Bull spread

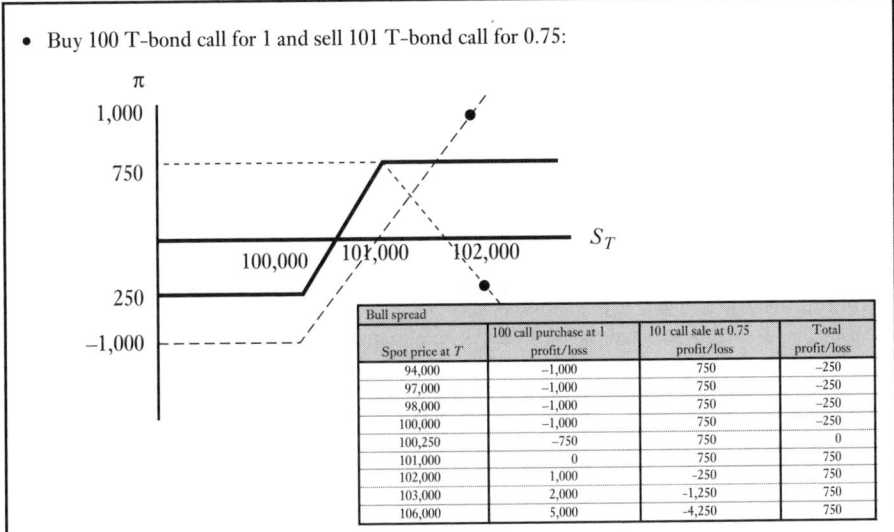

- Buy 100 T-bond call for 1 and sell 101 T-bond call for 0.75:

Bull spread			
Spot price at T	100 call purchase at 1 profit/loss	101 call sale at 0.75 profit/loss	Total profit/loss
94,000	−1,000	750	−250
97,000	−1,000	750	−250
98,000	−1,000	750	−250
100,000	−1,000	750	−250
100,250	−750	750	0
101,000	0	750	750
102,000	1,000	−250	750
103,000	2,000	−1,250	750
106,000	5,000	−4,250	750

take a long position in a T-bill futures put option. Similar positions could be taken in T-bond futures options by speculators who expect long-term rates to change. For example, a speculator convinced that the current economic growth will push long-term interest rates up (and therefore the price on long-term bonds down) over the next 3 months could try to profit from this expectation by buying a T-bond futures put, while a speculator who expected long-term rates to decrease could try to profit by buying a T-bond futures call.

Finally, between outright call and put positions, options can be combined in different ways to obtain various types of profit relations. A speculator who expected rates to increase in the future but didn't want to assume the risk inherent in a put purchase position could form a bear call spread. In contrast, a speculator who expected rates to be stable over the near term could, in turn, try to profit by forming a straddle write. Thus, by combining different option positions, speculators can obtain positions that match their expectation and their desired risk–return preference. Exhibit 14.13 lists some of the other option positions. An exercise of generating profit tables and graphs to illustrate the features of different option positions is included in the end-of-the-chapter problems. In the next

chapter, we will focus on how interest rate options are used for hedging positions.

14.5 OPTION TRADING: MICROSTRUCTURE

The primary objective of derivative exchanges offering options is to provide marketability to option contracts by linking brokers and dealers, standardizing contracts, establishing trading rules and procedures, guaranteeing and intermediating contracts through a clearinghouse, and providing continuous trading through market makers, specialists, and locals.

14.5.1 Standardization

Similar to the futures exchanges, the option exchanges standardize contracts by setting expiration dates, exercise prices, and contract sizes on options. The expiration dates on options are defined in terms of an expiration cycle. Until 1984, the cycles on most exchanges were the January cycle with expiration months of January, April, July, and October, the February cycle with February, May, August, and November expiration months, and the March cycle with expiration months of March, June,

Exhibit 14.13   Different option positions

1. **Bull call spread**: Long in call with low X and short in call with high X.
2. **Bull put spread**: Long in put with low X and short in put with high X.
3. **Bear call spread**: Long in call with high X and short in call with low X.
4. **Bear put spread**: Long in put with high X and short in put with low X.
5. **Long butterfly spread**: Long in call with low X, short in 2 calls with middle X, and long in call with high X (similar position can be formed with puts).
6. **Short butterfly spread**: Short in call with low X, long in 2 calls with middle X, and short in call with high X (similar position can be formed with puts).
7. **Straddle purchase**: Long call and put with similar terms.
8. **Strip purchase**: Straddle with additional puts (e.g., long call and long 2 puts).
9. **Strap purchase**: Straddle with additional calls (e.g., long 2 calls and long put).
10. **Straddle sale**: Short call and put with similar terms (strip and strap sales have additional calls and puts).
11. **Money combination purchase**: Long call and put with different exercise prices.
12. **Money combination sale**: Short call and put with different exercise prices.

September, and December. On many option contracts, the expiration day is the Saturday after the third Friday of the expiration month; the last day on which the expiring option trades, though, is Friday. In a 3-month option cycle, only the options with the three nearest expiration months trade at any time. Thus, as an option expires, the exchange introduces a new option. Because of a high demand for short-term options, the CBOE and other option exchanges introduced new exercise cycles in 1984. These cycles have options with expirations in the current month, the next month, and then the next two months in either of the original January, February, or March cycles.

For futures options, such as the CBOT's mortgage-backed option, the last trading day is the same as the futures delivery date. For these options, exercising at expiration would be essentially a cash settlement. For other futures options, such as the CBOT's T-bond futures option, the expiration date on the option can be 1 to 2 weeks before the futures delivery period. Exercising such options at their expiration date gives the holder a futures position with a 1- or 2-week expiration and a current margin position equal to the difference between the futures and exercise prices.

In addition to setting the expiration, the exchanges also choose the exercise prices for each option. Usually, at least three strike prices (sometimes as many as six) are associated with

each option when an option cycle begins. Once an option with a specific exercise price has been introduced, it will remain listed until its expiration date. The exchange can, however, introduce new options with different exercise prices at any time. The derivative exchanges also impose two limits on option trading: exercise limits and position limits. These limits are intended to prevent an investor or groups of investors from having a dominant impact on a particular option. An *exercise limit* specifies the maximum number of option contracts that can be exercised on a specified number of consecutive business days (e.g., 5 days) by any investor or investor group. A *position limit* sets the maximum number of options an investor can buy and sell on one side of the market; the limit on an option is usually the same as the exercise limit. A side of the market is either a bullish or bearish position. An investor who is bullish could profit by buying calls or selling puts, while an investor with a bearish position could profit by buying puts and selling calls.

14.5.2   Continuous Trading

As noted in chapter 12, on the futures exchanges such as the CBOT, CME, and LIFFE, continuous trading is provided through locals who are willing to take temporary positions to make a market. Many of the option exchanges, though, use market-makers and specialists to ensure a continuous market.

14.5.3 Clearinghouse and Option Clearing Corporation

As we discussed in chapter 12, to make derivative contracts more marketable, derivative exchanges provide a clearinghouse (CH) or option clearing corporation (OCC), as it is referred to on the option exchange. In the case of options, the CH intermediates each transaction that takes place on the exchange and guarantees that all option writers fulfill the terms of their options if they are assigned. In addition, the CH also manages option exercises, receiving notices and assigning corresponding positions to clearing members.

As an intermediary, the CH functions by breaking up each option trade. After a buyer and seller complete an option trade, the CH steps in and becomes the effective buyer to the option seller and the effective seller to the option buyer. At that point, there is no longer any relationship between the original buyer and seller. If the buyer of a futures call option, for example, decides to later exercise, her broker will notify the exchange's CH (the brokerage firm may well be the clearing member). Overnight, the CH will select a writer from its pool of option sellers on the exercised futures call option and assign that writer the obligation of fulfilling the terms of the exercise request. Before trading commences on the following day, the CH will establish a long futures position at a futures price equal to the exercise price for the exercising option holder and a short futures position for the assigned writer. Once this is done, margins on both positions will be required and the positions will be marked to market at the current settlement price on the futures. As noted earlier, when the positions are marked to market, the exercising call holder's margin account on his long position will be equal to the difference between the futures price and the exercise price, $f_t - X$, while the assigned writer will have to deposit funds in a futures margin account equal to $f_t - X$ to satisfy his maintenance margin on his short futures position. At this point, the futures positions are indistinguishable from any other futures. If the futures option is a put, the same procedure

applies except that the holder takes a short position at f_t (when the exercised position is marked to market), with a margin account worth $X - f_t$, and the assigned writer is assigned a long position at f_t and must deposit $X - f_t$ to meet his margin.[4]

By breaking up each option contract, the CH makes it possible for option investors to close their positions before expiration. If a buyer of an option later becomes a seller of the same option, or vice versa, the CH computer will note the offsetting position in the option investor's account and will therefore cancel both entries. For example, suppose in January, investor A buys a March 95 T-bill futures call for 10 ($X = \$987,500$, $C = (10)(\$250) = \$2,500$) from investor B. When the CH breaks up the contract, it records investor A's *right to exercise* with the CH (take a long T-bill futures position at X) and investor B's responsibility to take a short futures position at X if a party long on the contract decides to exercise and the CH subsequently assigns B the responsibility. The transaction between A and B would lead to the following entry in the clearing firms records:

January clearinghouse records for March 95 T-bill futures call

---

1. Investor A has the *right* to exercise
2. Investor B has *responsibility*

Suppose that in late January, 60 days before the expirations on the T-bill futures and futures option, short-term rates have decreased resulting in the following prices:

- The price on the spot 151-day T-bills is at $988,000.
- The price on the March T-bill futures is priced at its carrying-cost value of $995,956 ($f_t = S_0(1 + R_f)^T = f_t = \$988,000(1.05)^{(60/365)} = \$995,956$, where $R_f = 60$-day repo rate $= 0.05$).
- The price on the March 95 T-bill futures call is at $9,000.

Seeing profit potential, suppose instead of exercising, investor A decides to close her call position by selling a March 95 T-bill futures call at $9,000 to investor C. After the CH breaks up this contract, its records would have a new entry showing investor A with the responsibility of taking a short position at $X = \$987,500$ if assigned. This entry, though, would cancel out investor A's original entry giving her the right to take a long position at $X = \$987,500$:

Late January clearinghouse records for March 95 T-bill futures call	
1. ~~Investor A has the~~ *right* ~~to exercise~~	
2. Investor B has *responsibility*	Closed
3. Investor C has the *right* to exercise	
4. ~~Investor A has~~ *~~responsibility~~*	

The CH would accordingly close investor A's position. Thus, investor A bought the call for $2,500 and then closed her position by simply selling the call for $9,000. Her call sale, in turn, represents an offsetting position and is referred to as an *offset* or *closing sale*.

If a writer also wanted to close his position at this date, he could do so by simply buying a March 95 T-bill futures call. For example, suppose investor B feared that rates could go lower and therefore decided to close his short position by buying a March 95 T-bill futures call at $9,000 from investor D. After this transaction, the CH would again step in, break up the contracts, and enter investor B's and D's positions on its records. The CH's records would now show a new entry in which investor B has the right to take a long position in the T-bill futures at $987,500. This entry, in turn, would cancel investor B's previous entry in which he had a responsibility to take a short position at $987,500 if assigned. The offsetting positions (the right to buy and the obligation to sell) cancel each other and the CH computer system simply erases both entries.

Late January clearinghouse records for March 95 T-bill futures call	
1. ~~Investor B has~~ *~~responsibility~~*	
2. Investor C has the *right* to exercise	Closed
3. ~~Investor B has the~~ *right* ~~to exercise~~	
4. Investor D has *responsibility*	

Since investor B's second transaction serves to close his opening position, it is referred to as a

closing purchase. In this case, investor B loses $6,500 by closing: selling the call for $2,500 and buying it back for $9,000.

14.5.4 Margin Requirements

To secure the CH's underlying positions, exchange-traded option contracts have initial and maintenance margin requirements. Different from the margin requirements on futures contracts, the margin requirements on options only apply to the option writer. On most exchanges, the initial margin is the amount of cash or cash equivalents that must be deposited by the writer; some exchanges, such as the German exchange (DTM), do allow a third-party guarantee to be used as a substitute for cash margins to secure the position. For written positions, the amount of margin required is equal to a certain percentage (e.g., 3% to 5%) of the exercise value of the contract. The CH sets the minimum initial margin requirement, with the brokerage firm allowed to increase it. In addition to the initial margin, the writer also has a maintenance margin requirement with the brokerage firm in which he has to keep the value of his account equal to a certain percentage of the initial margin value. Thus, if the value of the option position moves against the writer, he is required to deposit additional cash or cash equivalents to satisfy his maintenance requirement.

In discussing margin requirements for futures options, one should remember that there are two sets of margins: a margin requirement for the option writer and a futures margin requirement that must be met if the futures option is exercised. If the futures option is exercised, both the holder and writer must establish and maintain the futures margin positions, with the writer's margin position on the option now being replaced by his new futures position.

14.5.5 Types of Option Transactions

The CH provides marketability by making it possible for option investors to close their positions instead of exercising. In general, there are four types of trades an investor of an exchange-traded option can make: opening, expiring, exercising, and closing transactions. The *opening transaction* occurs when investors initially buy or sell an option. An *expiring transaction*, in turn, is allowing the option to expire: that is, doing nothing when the expiration date arrives because the option is worthless (out of the money). If it is profitable, a holder can exercise. Finally, holders or writers of options can close their positions with *offsetting* or *closing transactions* or orders.

As a general rule, option holders should close their positions rather than exercise. As we will discuss in section 14.6, if there is some time to expiration, an option holder who sells her option will receive a price that exceeds the exercise value. Because of this, many exchange-traded options are closed.

14.5.6 OTC Options

In the OTC option market, interest rate option contracts are negotiable, with buyers and sellers entering directly into an agreement. Thus, the dealer's market provides option contracts that are tailor-made to meet the holder's or writer's specific needs. The market, though, does not have a clearinghouse to intermediate and guarantee the fulfillment of the terms of the option contract, nor market-makers or specialists to ensure continuous markets; the options, therefore, lack marketability.

Since each OTC option has unique features, the secondary market is limited. Prior to expiration, holders of OTC options who want to close their position may be able to do so by selling their positions back to the original option writers or possibly to an OTC dealer who is making a market in the option. This type of closing is more likely to occur if the option writer is a dealer that can hedge an option position and also if the option is relatively standard (e.g., an OTC option on a T-bond). Because of this inherent lack of marketability, the premiums on OTC options are higher than exchange-trade ones. For example, the bid-asked spread on an OTC T-bond is typically twice that of an exchange-traded T-bond futures option (e.g., $\frac{4}{32}$ compared to $\frac{2}{32}$). Finally, since there is no CH to guarantee the option writer, OTC options also have different credit structures from exchange-traded options. Depending on who the option writer is, the contract may require initial and maintenance margins to be established.

14.6 OPTION PRICE RELATIONSHIPS

In our discussion of the fundamental option strategies, we treated the option premium as a given. The price of an option, though, is determined in the market and is a function of the time to expiration, the strike price, the security price, and the volatility of the underlying security. These factors and how the option price is determined form the basis of the option pricing model. The option pricing model for pricing interest rate options is examined in chapter 15. Here, we identify some of the factors that determine the prices of spot and futures interest rate options.

14.6.1 Call Price Relationships

Boundary Conditions and Time Value Premium

The price of any option is constrained by certain boundary conditions. One of those boundary conditions is the intrinsic value. By definition, the *intrinsic value (IV)* of a call at a time prior to expiration (let t signify any time *prior* to expiration), or at expiration (T again signifies expiration date) is the maximum of the difference between the price of the underlying security or futures (S_t or f_t) and the exercise price or zero: $IV = \text{Max}[f_t - X, 0]$ or $\text{Max}[S_t - X, 0]$. The intrinsic value can be used as a reference to define *in-the-money*, *on-the-money*, and *out-of-the-money* calls. Specifically, an in-the-money call is one in which the price of the underlying security or futures contract exceeds the exercise price; as a result, its IV is positive. When the price of the security or futures is equal to the exercise price, the call's IV is zero and the call is said to be on-the-money. Finally, if the exercise price exceeds the security or futures price, the call would be out-of-the-money and the IV would be zero:

Type	Spot call	Futures call
In-the-money	$S_t > X => IV > 0$	$f_t > X => IV > 0$
On-the-money	$S_t = X => IV = 0$	$f_t = X => IV = 0$
Out-of-the-money	$S_t < X => IV = 0$	$f_t < X => IV = 0$

For an American futures option, the IV defines a boundary condition in which the price of a call has to trade at a value at least equal to its IV:

$$C_t \geq \text{Max}[f_t - X, 0]$$

If this condition does not hold ($C_t < \text{Max}[f_t - X, 0]$), an arbitrageur could buy the call, exercise, and close the futures position. For example, suppose a T-bill futures contract expiring in 182 days were trading at $987,862 (index = 95.1448) and a 95 T-bill futures call expiring in 182 days ($X = \$987,500$) were trading at $100, below its IV of $362. Arbitrageurs could realize risk-free profits by (1) buying the call at $100, (2) exercising the call to obtain a margin account worth $f_t - X = \$987,862 - \$987,500 = \$362$ plus a long position in the T-bill futures contract priced $987,862, and (3) immediately closing the long futures position by taking an offsetting short position at $987,862. Doing this, arbitrageurs would realize a risk-free profit of $262. By pursuing this strategy, though, arbitrageurs would push the call premium up until it is at least equal to its IV of $f_t - X = \$362$ and the arbitrage profit is zero.

The above arbitrage strategy requires that the option be exercised immediately. Thus, the condition applies only to an American futures option. The boundary conditions for European futures, American spot, and European spot interest rate options are explained in exhibit 14.14.

The other component of the value of an option is the *time value premium (TVP)*. By definition, the TVP of a call is the difference between the price of the call and its IV: TVP = C_t − IV. For example, if the 95 T-bill futures call expiring in 182 days ($X = \$987,500$) was trading at $562 when the T-bill futures contract expiring in 182 days was trading at $987,862 (index = 95.1448), the IV would be $362 and the TVP would be $200. It should be noted that the TVP decreases as the time remaining to expiration decreases.

Call Price Curve

Graphically, the relationship between C_t, TVP, and IV is depicted in figure 14.1. In the figure, graphs plotting the call price and the IV (on the vertical axis) against the futures price (on the horizontal axis) are shown for the American 95 T-bill futures call option. The IV line shows the linear relationship between the IV and the futures price. The line emanates from a horizontal intercept equal to the exercise price. When the price of the futures is equal to or less than the exercise price, the IV is equal to zero; when the futures price exceeds the exercise price, the IV is positive and increases as the futures price increases. The IV line, in turn, serves as a reference for the call price curve (CC). The noted arbitrage condition dictates that the price of the call cannot trade (for long) at a value below its IV. Graphically, this means that the call price curve cannot go below the IV line. Furthermore, the IV line would be the call price curve if we are at expiration since the TVP = 0 and thus C_T = IV. The call price curve (CC) in figure 14.1 shows the positive relationship between C_t and f_t. The vertical distance between the CC curve and the IV line, in turn, measures the TVP. The CC curve for a comparable call with a greater time to expiration would be above the CC curve, reflecting the fact that the call premium increases as the time to expiration increases. It should be noted that the slopes of the CC curves approach the slope of the IV line when the security price is relatively high (known as a *deep in-the-money call*), and it approaches zero (flat) when the price of the futures is relatively low (a *deep out-of-the-money call*).

Variability

The call price curve illustrates the positive relation between a call price and the underlying security or futures price and the time to expiration. An option's price also depends on the volatility of the underlying security or futures contract.

Since a long call position is characterized by unlimited profits if the security or futures increases but limited losses if it decreases, a call holder would prefer more volatility rather than less. Specifically, greater variability suggests, on the one hand, a given likelihood that the security will increase substantially in price, causing the call to be more valuable. On the other hand, greater volatility also suggests a given likelihood of the security price decreasing

Exhibit 14.14   Boundary conditions for European futures and European and American spot
interest rate call options

---

1. European futures option: $C_t^E \geq \text{Max}[\text{PV}(f_t - X), 0]$

This condition implies that if a European call is priced less than $\text{PV}(f_t - X)$, an arbitrage exists by going long in the call, short in a futures at f_t, and short in a risk-free zero-discount bond with a face value of $f_t - X$ and maturity equal to the option and futures expiration. This arbitrage strategy would yield a positive initial cash flow of $\text{PV}(f_t - X) - C_t^E$ (note that the initial futures position has no cost), and regardless of the futures prices at expiration, f_T, there would be no liabilities when the position is closed:

Closing position	$f_T < X$	$f_T = X$	$f_T > X$
Short bond	$-(f_t - X)$	$-(f_t - X)$	$-(f_t - X)$
Short futures	$f_t - f_T$	$f_t - f_T$	$f_t - f_T$
Long call	0	0	$(f_T - X)$
Net	$X - f_T > 0$	0	0

Arbitrageurs would therefore push the price of the call up until the initial cash flow is negative or equivalently where $C_t^E \geq \text{Max}[\text{PV}(f_t - X), 0]$.

2. Price of an American spot call is at least equal to its intrinsic value: $C_t^A \geq \text{Max}[S_t - X, 0]$

If an American call option is trading for less than its IV, arbitrageurs could realize risk-free returns by buying the call, exercising it, and selling the security in the market.

Example:

- Call on an actual T-bill with $F = \$1m$, maturity of 91 days.
- Exercise price = $\$987,500$ $(R_D = 5)$.
- Spot T-bill $(F = \$1m$, maturity of 91 days) trading at $\$988,000$.
- Intrinsic value of the call = $\$500$.
- Call trading at $\$450$.

Given these prices, arbitrageurs could obtain the T-bill by buying the call and exercising it immediately at a cost of $\$987,500$ and then selling the bill on the spot market for $\$988,000$ to realize a risk-free profit of $\$50$. In executing this strategy, arbitrageurs would push the call premium up until it is at least equal to its IV of $\$500$ and the arbitrage profit is zero.

Note that in this case, the IV of the call is $S_t - X = \$988,000 - \$987,500 = \$500$. If the option were American and thus could be exercised at any time, this price would be the minimum boundary. However, if the yield curve were negatively sloped such that the 91-day bill was priced at $\$987,800$ to yield 5.046%, then the call's IV would be $\$300$. If the call were trading at IV of $\$300$, then an arbitrageur could earn a riskless profit of $\$191$ by executing the arbitrage strategy governing the price of the European call (discussed below). Thus, the minimum price condition for an American spot interest rate call is $C_t^A \geq \text{Max}[S_{M+T} - \text{PV}(X), \text{IV}, 0]$.

3. European spot interest rate call has to be priced at least equal to $C_t^E \geq \text{Max}[S_{M+T} - \text{PV}(X), 0]$

Example: Suppose that the spot T-bill call option has an exercise price of $X = \$987,500$ and an expiration of 182 days $(T = 182/365)$. Also suppose the yield curve is flat at 4.96% such that:

- A spot $\$1m$, 91-day T-bill is trading at $S_0 = \$988,000 = \$1m/1.0496^{91/365}$;
- A spot $\$1m$, 273-day T-bill (maturity = maturity of underlying T-bill + option's expiration = 91 days + 182) is selling at $\$964,440 = \$1m/1.0496^{273/365}$;
- A riskless bill (T-bill or Treasury strip) with a face value equal to the call's exercise price of $\$987,500$ and maturity of 182 days is trading at $\text{PV}(X) = \$963,949 = \$987,500/1.0496^{182/365}$.

In this case, the price of the European call must be at least equal to $S_{T+91} - \text{PV}(X) = \$964,440 - \$963,949 = \$491$.

If the call were priced below $491, an arbitrageur could profit by shorting the 273-day bill with face value of $1m, going long in the 182-day bill with face value of X, and buying the call. For example, if the call were priced at $400, the arbitrageur would obtain an initial cash inflow $91 by:

- Buying the call at $400,
- Buying the 182-day bill with face value of $987,500 for PV($X$) = $963,949, and
- Shorting the 273-day T-bill at S_{T+91} = $964,440.

At expiration:

- If the price of a spot 91-day T-bill is greater than $987,500 ($S_T > X$), the arbitrageur could use the $987,500 proceeds from the maturing bond (original maturity of 182 days) to exercise the call and buy the 91-day T-bill, then use the T-bill to cover the short position on the original 273-day bill (now with a maturity of 91 days); the net cash flow in this case is zero.
- If the price of a 91-day T-bill is less than or equal to $987,500 at expiration ($S_T \leq X$), then the call would be worthless. In this case, the arbitrageur would receive $987,500 from the maturing bond, while the cost of buying a a of a 91-day bill to close the short T-bill position would be less than or equal to $987,500 ($S_T \leq X$).

Thus, the position has no liabilities at expiration:

Closing position	$S_T < X$	$S_T = X$	$S_T > X$
Long bill with face value of X and original maturity of T (182-day)	X	X	X
Short bill with original maturity of $M + T$ (273-day)	$-S_T$	$-S_T$	$-S_T$
Long call	0	0	$S_T - X$
Net	$X - S_T > 0$	0	0

With the arbitrage position yielding an initial positive cash flow and no liabilities at expiration, arbitrageurs would push the price of the European call to at least S_{T+91} − PV(X) = $964,440 − $963,949 = $491. Thus, in the absence of arbitrage: $C_t^E \geq \text{Max}[S_{M+T} - \text{PV}(X), 0]$.

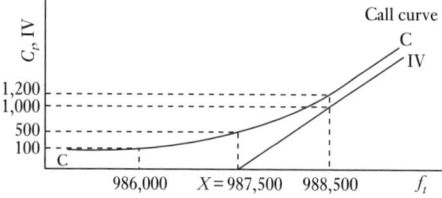

Figure 14.1 Call and futures price relation: 95 T-bill futures call price curve

substantially. However, given that a call's losses are limited to just the premium when the security price is equal to the exercise price or less, the extent of the price decrease would be inconsequential to the call holder. Thus, the market will value a call option on a volatile security or contract more highly than a call on one with lower variability.

The positive relationship between a call's premium and its underlying security's volatility is illustrated in exhibit 14.15. The exhibit shows

two call options: (1) a call option on bond A with an exercise price of $X = 100$ in which the underlying bond is trading at 100 and has a variability characterized by an equal chance of bond A either increasing by 10% or decreasing by 10% by the end of the period (assume these are the only possibilities); (2) a call option on bond B with an exercise price of $X = 100$ in which the underlying bond is trading at 100 but has a greater variability characterized by an equal chance of bond B increasing or decreasing by 20% by the end of the period. As can be seen, given the variability of the underlying bonds, the IV on the call for bond B would be either 20 or 0 at the end of the period, compared to a value of only 10 and 0 for the call on bond A. Since bond B's call cannot perform worse than bond A's call, and can do better, it follows that there would be a higher demand and therefore price for the bond B call than the bond A call. Thus, given the limited loss characteristic of an option, the more volatile

Exhibit 14.15 Call price and variability relation

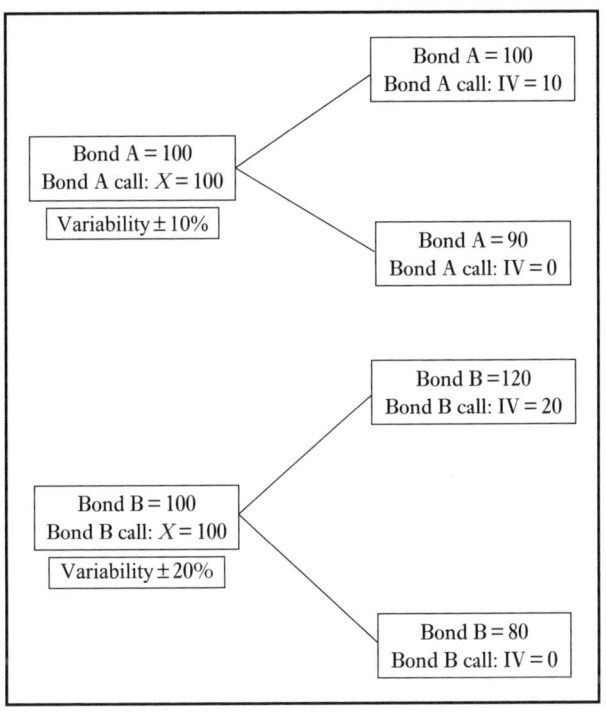

the underlying security, the more valuable the option, all other factors being equal.

14.6.2 Put Price Relationships

Boundary Conditions

Analogous to calls, the price of a put at a given point in time prior to expiration (P_t) also can be explained by reference to its IV, boundary conditions, and TVP. In the case of puts, the IV is defined as the maximum of the difference between the exercise price and the security or futures price or zero: $IV = Max[X - f_t, 0]$ or $Max[X - S_t, 0]$. Similar to calls, in-the-money, on-the-money, and out-of-the-money puts are defined as:

Type	Spot put	Futures put
In-the-money	$X > S_t => IV > 0$	$X > f_t => IV > 0$
On-the-money	$X = S_t => IV = 0$	$X = f_t => IV = 0$
Out-of-the-money	$X < S_t => IV = 0$	$X < f_t => IV = 0$

For an American futures option, the IV defines a boundary condition in which the price of the put has to trade at a price at least equal to its IV: $P_t \geq Max[X - f_t, 0]$. If this condition does not hold, an arbitrageur could buy the put, exercise, and close the futures position. For example, suppose a T-bill futures contract expiring in 182 days were trading at $987,200 and a 95 T-bill futures put expiring in 182 days ($X = $987,500$) were trading at $100, below its IV of $300. Arbitrageurs could realize risk-free profits by (1) buying the put at $100, (2) exercising the put to obtain a margin account worth $X - f_t = $987,500 - $987,200 = 300 plus a short position in the T-bill futures contract priced $987,200, and (3) immediately closing the short futures position by taking an offsetting short position at $987,200. Doing this, the arbitrageur would realize a risk-free profit of $200. By pursuing this strategy, though, arbitrageurs would push the put premium up until it is at least equal to its IV of $X - f_t = 300 and the arbitrage profit is zero. Exhibit 14.16 explains with examples the arbitrage strategies governing

Exhibit 14.16   Boundary conditions for European futures and European and
American spot interest rate put options

---

1. **European put futures option: boundary condition: $P_t^E \geq \text{Max}[\text{PV}(X - f_t), 0]$**
   For a European put futures option, the boundary condition is $P_t^E \geq \text{Max}[\text{PV}(X - f_t), 0]$. This condition
   implies that if a European put is priced less than $\text{PV}(X - f_t)$, an arbitrage exists by going long in the put,
   long in a futures at f_t, and short in a riskless zero discount bond with a face value of $X - f_t$ and maturity
   equal to the futures option's expiration. This arbitrage strategy would yield a positive initial cash flow of
   $\text{PV}(X - f_t) - P_t^E$ (note that the initial futures position has no cost), and regardless of the futures prices
   at expiration, there would be no liabilities when the position is closed:

Closing position	$f_T < X$	$f_T = X$	$f_T > X$
Short bond	$-(X - f_t)$	$-(X - f_t)$	$-(X - f_t)$
Long futures	$f_T - f_t$	$f_T - f_t$	$f_T - f_t$
Long put	$X - f_T$	0	0
Net	0	0	$f_T - X > 0$

   Arbitrageurs would therefore push the price of the put up until the initial cash flow is negative or equivalently where
   $P_t^E \geq \text{Max}[\text{PV}(X - f_t), 0]$.

2. **The minimum price of an American spot option is the option's IV: $P_t^A \geq \text{Max}[S_t - X, 0]$**
   If the put were trading below its IV, arbitrageurs would buy the put, buy the bond, and exercise.
   Example:

   - A spot \$1m, 91-day T-bill is trading at $S_0 = \$987,000$,
   - American spot put on the T-bill with $X = \$987,500$ is trading at \$400.

   Strategy: buy put for \$400, buy spot T-bill for \$987,000, exercise: sell T-bill for $X = \$987,500$. Profit $= \$100$.

3. **The minimum price of European spot interest rate put is $P_t^E \geq \text{Max}[\text{PV}(X) - S_{M+T}, 0]$**
   Example: Suppose that a spot European T-bill put option has exercise price of $X = \$988,500$ and an expiration of 182
   days ($T = 182/365$). Also suppose the yield curve is flat at 4.96% such that:

   - A spot \$1m, 91-day T-bill is trading at $S_0 = \$988,000 = \$1m/1.0496^{91/365}$;
   - A spot \$1m, 273-day T-bill (maturity $=$ maturity of underlying T-bill $+$ option's expiration $= 91$ days$+$ 182) is
     selling at $\$964,440 = \$1m/1.0496^{273/365}$;
   - A riskless bill (T-bill or Treasury strip) with a face value equal to the call's exercise price of \$988,500 and maturity
     of 182 days is trading at $\text{PV}(X) = \$964,925 = \$988,500/1.0496^{182/365}$.

   In this case, the price of the European call must be at least equal to $\text{PV}(X) - S_{T+91} = \$964,925 - \$964,440 = \$485$.

   If the put were priced below \$485, an arbitrageur could profit by shorting the 182-day bill with face value of X, going
   long in the 273-day bill with face value of \$1m, and buying the put. For example, if the put were priced at \$400, then
   the arbitrageur would obtain an initial cash inflow of \$85 by

   - Buying the put at \$400,
   - Shorting the 182-day bill with face value of \$988,500 for $\text{PV}(X) = \$964,925$, and
   - Buying the 273-day T-bill at $S_{T+91} = \$964,440$.

   At expiration, the position has no liabilities:

Closing position	$S_T < X$	$S_T = X$	$S_T > X$
Short bill with face value of X and original maturity of T (182-day)	$-X$	$-X$	$-X$
Long bill with original maturity of $M + T$ (273-day)	S_T	S_T	S_T
Long put	$X - S_T$	0	0
Net	0	0	$S_T - X > 0$

   With the arbitrage position yielding an initial positive cash flow and no liabilities at expiration, arbitrageurs would push
   the price of the European put to at least $\text{PV}(X) - S_{T+91} = \$964,925 - \$964,440 = \$485$. Thus, in the absence of
   arbitrage: $P_t^E \geq \text{Max}[\text{PV}(X) - S_{M+T}, 0]$.

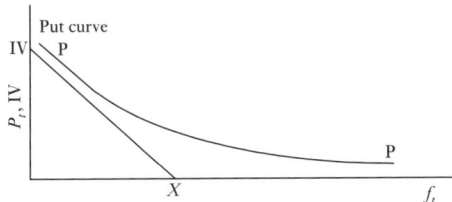

Figure 14.2 Put and futures price relation: put price curve

the boundary conditions for the European futures put options and the American and European spot put options.

Put Price Curve

Similar to calls, the TVP for a put is defined as $TVP = P_t - IV$. Graphically, the IV and TVP can be seen for an American futures option in figure 14.2. The figure shows a negatively sloped put price curve (PP) and a negatively sloped IV line going from the horizontal intercept (where $f_t = X$) to the vertical intercept where the IV is equal to the exercise price when the futures option is trading at zero (i.e., $IV = X$, when $f_t = 0$). The slope of the PP curve approaches the slope of the IV line for relatively low futures prices (*deep in-the-money puts*) and approaches zero for relatively large futures prices (*deep-out-of-the money puts*).

Variability

Like calls, the price of a put option depends not only on the underlying security or futures price and time to expiration, but also on the volatility of the underlying security or futures contract. Since put losses are limited to the premium when the price of the underlying security or futures is greater than or equal to the exercise price, put buyers, like call buyers, will value puts on securities or futures with greater variability more highly than those with lower variability.

14.6.3 Closing

As noted earlier, if there is some time to expiration, an option holder who sells her option will receive a price that exceeds the exercise value; that is, if she sells the option, she will receive a price that is equal to an IV plus a TVP; if she exercises, though, her exercise value is only equal to the IV. Thus, by exercising instead of closing she loses the TVP. For example in our CH case, investor A sold her 95 T-bill futures call ($X = \$987,500$) at \$9,000 when the T-bill futures contract was trading at \$995,956; the \$9,000 price was equal to an $IV = \$8,456$ and a $TVP = \$544$. If investor A had exercised her futures call instead of simply closing it, she would have received a long T-bill futures position at \$995,956 and a margin account worth the IV of \$8,456. Thus, by exercising instead of selling the option, she lost the TVP. Thus, an option holder in most cases should close her position instead of exercising. There are some exceptions to the general rule of closing instead of exercising. For example, if an American option on a security that was to pay a high coupon that exceeded the TVP on the option, then it would be advantageous to exercise.

14.6.4 Put–Call Parity

Since the prices of options on the same security are derived from that security's price, it follows that the put and call prices are related. The relationship governing put and call prices is known as *put–call parity*. The relation can be defined in terms of an arbitrage formed with a position known as a *conversion*. For European spot options on debt securities with no coupons (e.g., T-bills and Eurodollar deposits), the conversion consists of (1) a long position in an underlying security that will have a maturity equal to the maturity of the option's underlying security (e.g., a T-bill that will have maturity of 91 days at the expiration on the spot T-bill option), and (2) a short position in a call and a long position in a put with the same exercise price and time to expiration. As shown below, the conversion yields a certain cash flow at expiration equal to the exercise price.

Closing position	$S_T < X$	$S_T = X$	$S_T > X$
Long bond	S_T	S_T	S_T
Long put	$X - S_T$	0	0
Short call	0	0	$-(S_T - X)$
Net	X	X	X

Exhibit 14.17 Put–call futures parity: arbitrage example

Put–call futures parity:

$$P_0^E - C_0^E = \frac{X - f_0}{(1 + R_f)^T}$$

If the equality defining put–call parity does not hold, then an arbitrage opportunity will exist. Suppose the following:

- T-bill futures contract expiring in 182 days is trading at $987,200;
- 95 T-bill futures put expiring in 182 days ($X = \$987,500$) is trading at $300;
- 95 T-bill futures call expiring in 182 days is trading at $100;
- 182-day risk-free rate (rate on a 182-day T-bill) is 5%.

In this case the put–call parity condition is violated:

$$P_0^E - C_0^E = \frac{X - f_0}{1 + R_f}$$

$$\$300 - \$100 < \frac{\$987,500 - \$987,200}{(1.05)^{182/365}}$$

$$(\$300 - \$100)(1.05)^{182/365} < \$987,500 - \$987,200$$

$$\$204.92 < \$300$$

Arbitrageurs, in turn, could exploit this price imbalance by taking:

- A long position in the futures contract;
- A long position in the futures put; and
- A short position in the futures call.

To implement the strategy will require $200: the cost of buying the put minus sale of the call. Suppose the arbitrageurs finance this cost by borrowing the $200 at $R_f = 5\%$ for 182 days.

- At expiration, closing the futures and option positions would yield a certain cash flow of $300 ($X - f_0 = \$987,500 - \$987,200$). With the arbitrageur's debt only $204.92, this represents a risk-free profit of $95.08.
- As these and other arbitrageurs go after this free lunch, they would drive the price of the futures put up and the price of the futures call down until put–call parity equality is reached.

Note: if $P_0 - C_0 > (X - f)/(1 + R_f)^T$, then the strategy is reversed.

To preclude arbitrage, the risk-free conversion portfolio must be worth the same as a risk-free pure discount bond with a face value of X maturing at the same time as the option's expiration. Thus, in equilibrium:

$$P_0^E - C_0^E + S_0 = \frac{X}{(1 + R_f)^T}$$

The put–call parity condition on options on T-bonds, T-notes, and other debt securities paying interest is similar to options on zero-coupon bonds except that the accrued interest

on the underlying bond is included. That is, at expiration the conversion will yield a risk-free cash flow equal to the exercise price plus the accrued interest. Thus, the equilibrium value of the conversion will equal the value of a risk-free bond with a face value of X plus the accrued interest:

$$P_0^E - C_0^E + S_0 = \frac{X + \text{Accrued interest}}{(1 + R_f)^T}$$

For European futures options, the conversion is formed with a long position in the futures contract and a long position in a put and a short position in a call on the futures contract. As shown below, if the options and the futures contracts expire at the same time, then the conversion would be worth $X - f_0$ at expiration, regardless of the price on the futures contract.

Closing position	$f_T < X$	$f_T = X$	$f_T > X$
Long futures	$f_T - f_0$	$f_T - f_0$	$f_T - f_0$
Long futures put	$X - f_T$	0	0
Short futures call	0	0	$-(f_T - X)$
Net	$X - f_0$	$X - f_0$	$X - f_0$

Since this position yields a risk-free return, in equilibrium its value would be equal to the present value of a risk-free bond with a face value of $X - f_0$ (remember the futures contract has no initial value). Thus:

$$P_0^E - C_0^E = \frac{X - f_0}{(1 + R_f)^T}$$

Note: if the carrying-cost model holds and the futures and options expire at the same time, then the equilibrium relation defining put–call parity for European futures options will be equal to the put–call parity for European spot options. This can be seen algebraically, by substituting the carrying-cost equation $S_0(1 + R_f)^T$ for f_0 in the above equation. Finally, note that

put–call parity is defined in terms of European options, not American. (For an example of the arbitrage governing put–call futures parity, see exhibit 14.17.)

14.7 CONCLUSION

In this chapter, we have provided an overview of interest rate options by defining option terms and markets, examining the fundamental option strategies, and describing the basic option pricing relations. Like interest rate futures, exchange-traded and OTC options can be used as a tool for speculating on interest rates and for managing different types of debt positions. Also like futures, the price of interest rate options is governed by arbitrage forces. In the next chapter, we extend our analysis of these derivatives by examining some of their hedging applications and by showing how the binomial interest rate tree can be used to value interest rate option contracts.

KEY TERMS

Call	Interest Rate Put (Floorlet)	Expiring Transaction
Put	Floor	Offsetting or Closing Trans-
Holder	Cap	actions
Long Position	Naked Call Write	Intrinsic Value (IV)
Exercise	Straddles	In-the-Money
Writer	Spreads	On-the-Money
Short Position	Money Spread	Out-of-the-Money
Option Premium	Time Spread	Time Value Premium (TVP)
Exercise Price or Strike Price	Diagonal Spread	Deep In-the-Money Call
Exercise Date	Bull Spread	Deep Out-of-The-
European Option	Bear Spread	Money-Call
American Option	Exercise Limit	Deep In-the-Money Puts
Spot Options	Position Limit	Deep Out-of-the-Money
Options on Futures	Offset or Closing Sale	Puts
Fixed Deliverable Bond	Closing Purchase	Put–Call Parity
Interest Rate Call (Caplet)	Opening Transaction	Conversion

PROBLEMS AND QUESTIONS

Note on problems: a number of the problems can be done in Excel by writing a program.

1. Show graphically and in a table the profit and T-bond price relationships at expiration for the following positions on OTC T-bond options. In each case, assume that the T-bond spot call and put options each have exercise prices of $100,000 and premiums of $1,000, and that there is no accrued interest at expiration. Evaluate at spot T-bond prices of $90,000, $95,000, $100,000, $105,000, and $110,000.

   a. A straddle purchase formed with long positions in the T-bond call and put options.
   b. A straddle write formed with short positions in T-bond call and put options.
   c. A simulated long T-bond position formed by buying the T-bond call and selling the T-bond put.
   d. A simulated short stock position formed by selling the T-bond call and buying the T-bond put.
   e. A strip purchase formed with long positions in one T-bond call and two puts.
   f. A strap write formed with short positions in two T-bond calls and one put.

2. Assume that there is an OTC T-bond spot call with an exercise price of $100,000 and premium of $1,000 and an OTC T-bond spot call option with an exercise price of $101,000 and premium of $500. Also assume the options expire at the same time and that there is no accrued interest at expiration. Show graphically and in a table the profit and T-bond price relationships at expiration for the following positions on the OTC T-bond options. Evaluate at spot T-bond prices of $95,000, $97,500, $100,000, $102,500, $105,000, and $107,500.

   a. A bull call spread formed by buying the 100 T-bond call and selling the 101 T-bond call.
   b. A bear call spread formed by buying the 101 T-bond call and selling the 100 T-bond call.

3. Assume that there is an OTC T-bond spot call with an exercise price of $100,000 and premium of $1,000, an OTC T-bond spot call option with an exercise price of $101,000 and premium of $500, and an OTC T-bond spot call option with an exercise price of $102,000 and premium of $250. Also assume that the three options expire at the same time and that there is no accrued interest at expiration. Show graphically and in a table the profit and T-bond price relationships at expiration for the following positions on the OTC T-bond options. Evaluate at spot T-bond prices of $99,500, $99,750, $100,000, $100,250, $100,500, $100,750, $101,000, $101,250, $101,500, $101,750, $102,000, $102,250, and $102,500.

   a. A long butterfly spread formed by buying one 100 T-bond call, selling two 101 T-bond calls, and buying one 102 T-bond call.
   b. A short butterfly spread formed by selling one 100 T-bond call, buying two 101 T-bond calls, and selling one 102 T-bond call.

4. Show graphically and in a table the profit and T-bill futures price relationships at expiration for the following positions on T-bill futures options. In each case, assume that the T-bill futures call and put options each have exercise prices of $987,500 (IMM index = 95) and premiums of $1,250. Evaluate at spot discount yields at expiration of 6.5%, 6%, 5.5%, 5%, 4.5%, 4%, and 3.5%.

   a. A straddle purchase formed with T-bill futures call and put options.
   b. A straddle write formed with T-bill futures call and put options.
   c. A simulated long T-bill position formed by buying a T-bill futures call and selling a T-bill futures put.

d. A simulated short T-bill position formed by selling a T-bill futures call and buying a T-bill futures put.

5. Show graphically and in a table the profit and LIBOR relationships at expiration for the following positions on interest rate options. In each case, assume that the interest rate call and put options each have exercise rates of 7%, a LIBOR reference rate, notional principals of $20m, time period of 0.25 per year, and premiums of $25,000. Evaluate at spot discount yields at expiration of 5%, 5.5%, 6.0%, 6.5%, 7%, 7.5%, 8%, 8.5%, and 9.0%.

   a. An interest rate call purchase.
   b. An interest rate put purchase.
   c. An interest rate call sale.
   d. An interest rate put sale.

6. Explain what arbitrageurs would do if the price of an American T-bill futures call with an exercise price of $987,500 were priced at $900 when the underlying futures price was trading at $988,500. What impact would their actions have in the option market on the call's price? Would arbitrageurs follow the same strategy if the call option were European? If not, why?

7. Explain what arbitrageurs would do if the price of an American T-bill futures put with an exercise price of $987,500 were priced at $900 when the underlying futures price was trading at $986,500. What impact would their actions have in the option market on the put's price?

8. If the premium on an option increases, does that mean there is a greater demand for the option? Comment.

9. Explain the role and functions of the Option Clearing Corporation.

10. Suppose that in February Ms X sold a June 95 Eurodollar futures call contract to Mr Z for 5, then later closed her position by buying a June 95 Eurodollar futures call from Mr Y. Explain how the OCC would handle these contracts. Use actual prices and not the index values.

11. Explain the various types of option transactions.

12. Evaluate a long position in an OTC December 97 T-bond call option purchased at 1.6 (1 6/32). Evaluate in terms of the profit at T-bond index values at expiration of 95, 96, 97, 98, 99, 100, and 101. Assume no accrued interest. What is the break-even index price?

13. Evaluate a long position in an OTC December 97 T-bond put option purchased at 0.25 (0 25/32). Evaluate in terms of the profits at T-bond index values at expiration of 94, 95, 96, 97, 98, 99, and 100. Assume no accrued interest. What is the break-even price?

14. Show that the December 97 T-bond call and put options in problems 12 and 13 conform to the put–call parity model. To show this, assume the T-bond underlying the option currently is priced at 96, the December expiration is exactly 0.25 years from the present, and the annual risk-free rate on securities maturing in 90 days is 6.0154%.

15. Prove the following boundary conditions using an arbitrage argument. In your proof, show the initial positive cash flow when the condition is violated and prove there are no liabilities at expiration or when the positions are closed.

   a. European futures call option: $C_t \geq \text{Max}[\text{PV}(f_t - X), 0]$
   b. European futures put option: $P_t \geq \text{Max}[\text{PV}(X - f_t), 0]$
   c. American spot call option: $C_t \geq \text{Max}[(S_t - X), 0]$
   d. American spot put option: $P_t \geq \text{Max}[(X - S_t), 0]$
   e. Put–call futures parity for European options: $P_t - C_t = (X - f_t)/(1 + R_f)^T$.

16. Explain intuitively and with an example why call and put options are more valuable the greater their underlying security's variability.

17. Explain why option holders should, in most cases, close their options instead of exercising. Under what condition would it be beneficial to exercise a call option early?

18. Short-answer questions:

(1) What is the profit–loss characteristic that characterizes a naked call write?

(2) What term is used to describe the number of option contracts outstanding?

(3) What exchange listed then later delisted spot T-bill spot options?

(4) A September 92 Eurodollar futures call option gives the holder the right to do what?

(5) A September 92 Eurodollar futures put option gives the holder the right to do what?

(6) What is the conversion strategy underlying the put–call futures parity model?

(7) What conditions are necessary to make the spot options and futures options equivalent?

(8) True or false: if the futures option contract and the underlying futures contract expire at the same time, then the futures options can be viewed as an option on the underlying spot security with the option having a cash settlement clause.

(9) Define a cap and explain one of its uses.

(10) Define a floor and explain one of its uses.

WEB EXERCISES

1. Determine the recent prices on an exchange option by going to www.cboe.com and clicking on "Market Quotes" and "Delayed Option Quotes."

2. Determine the recent prices on futures option contracts on Eurodollars, T-bills, and other interest rate futures options listed on the Chicago Mercantile Exchange by going to www.cme.com and clicking on "Market Data," "Delayed Quotes, and "Interest Rate Products."

3. Determine the recent prices on futures option contracts on 30-year T-bonds and 10-year T-notes listed on the Chicago Board of Trade by going to www.cbot.com and clicking on "Quotes and Data."

NOTES

1. Before 1936, the US futures exchanges offered futures options for a number of years. In 1936, though, the instruments were banned when US security regulations were tightened following the 1929 stock market crash. Futures options have been available on foreign exchanges for a number of years.

2. While many OTC options are exercised, most exchange-traded options are not exercised, but instead are closed by holders selling contracts and writers buying contracts. As a starting point in developing a fundamental understanding of options, though, it is helpful to first examine what happens if the option is exercised.

3. In many of our examples we assume calls and puts with the same terms are priced the same. We do this for simplicity. In most cases, though, calls and puts with the same terms are not priced equally.

The relation between call and put prices is discussed in section 14.6.

4. On the CBOT, the assignment of exercises is random; on other exchanges it is based on first in and first out (clearing member with the oldest written position will be assigned first).

SELECTED REFERENCES

Gombola, Michael J., Rodney L. Roenfeldt, and Philip L. Cooley "Spreading Strategies in CBOE Options: Evidence on Market Performance," *The Journal of Financial Research* 1 (Winter 1978): 35–44.

Grube, R. Corwin, Don B. Panton, and J. Michael Terrell "Risks and Rewards in Covered Call Positions," *The Journal of Portfolio Management* 5 (Winter 1979): 64–8.

Johnson, R. Stafford and C. Giaccotto *Options and Futures* (St. Paul, MN: West Publishing, 1995).

Junkus, Joan "The Structure of Markets for Interest Rate Options," in Jack Clark Francis and Avner Simon Wolf (eds) *The Handbook of Interest Rate Risk Management*. (New York: Irwin Professional Publishing, 1994).

McMillan, Lawrence G. *Options as a Strategic Investment*, 2nd edn (New York: New York Institute of Finance, 1986).

Merton, R. "Theory of Rational Option Pricing," *Bell Journal of Economics* 4 (Spring 1973): 141–83.

Ritchken, Peter *Options: Theory, Strategy, and Applications* (Glenview, IL: Scott, Foresman, 1987): chapter 4.

CHAPTER FIFTEEN

INTEREST RATE OPTIONS: HEDGING APPLICATIONS AND PRICING

15.1 INTRODUCTION

During the 1970s and 1980s, the US economy experienced relatively sharp swings in interest rates. The resulting volatility in rates, in turn, increased the exposure of many debt positions to market risk. Faced with this risk, many corporate borrowers, money managers, intermediaries, and bond portfolio managers increased their use of derivative contracts on debt securities as a hedge against such risk. In chapter 13, we examined how futures contracts on debt securities could be used by such institutions to hedge their fixed income and debt positions. In this chapter, we continue that analysis by examining how such positions can be hedged with interest rate options. We begin by first looking at how options are used for hedging applications, including revisiting some of the hedging cases examined in chapters 12 and 13; we then look at how OTC caps, floors, and other interest derivatives are used to hedge a series of cash flows; we finish the chapter by re-examining the binomial interest rate tree and showing how it can be used to value interest rate options.

15.2 HEDGING DEBT POSITIONS WITH INTEREST RATE OPTIONS

15.2.1 Hedging with Interest Rate Options

In chapter 13, we presented several cases showing how a fixed-income manager planning to invest a future inflow of cash in bonds could hedge the investment against possible lower rates by going long in an interest rate futures contract. In such hedging cases, if rates were to decrease, the higher costs of purchasing the bonds would be offset by profits from the manager's interest rate futures position. On the other hand, if rates increased, the manager would benefit from lower bond prices, but he would also have to cover losses on his futures position. Thus, hedging future fixed-income investments with futures locks in a future price and return and therefore eliminates not only the costs of unfavorable price movements but also the benefits from favorable movements. However, by hedging with either exchange-traded futures call options on Treasury or Eurodollar contracts or with an OTC spot call option on a debt security or an interest rate put (floorlet), a hedger can obtain protection against adverse price increases while still realizing lower costs if security prices decrease.

For cases in which bond or money market managers are planning to sell some of their securities in the future, hedging can be done by going short in Treasury or Eurodollar futures contracts. If rates turn out to be higher at the time of the security sale, the resulting lower bond prices and therefore revenue from the bond sale would be offset by profits from the futures positions (just the opposite would occur if rates were lower). However, for the costs of buying an interest rate option, a manager can obtain downside protection if bond prices decrease while earning increasing revenues if security prices increase. Similar downside protection from hedging positions using interest rate put options can be obtained by bond issuers, borrowers, and underwriters. For example, a company planning to issue bonds or borrow funds from a financial institution at some future date could hedge the debt position against possible interest rate increases by buying exchange-traded futures put options, a spot put option on a security, or an interest rate call (or caplet). Similarly, a bank that finances its short-term loan portfolio of 1-year loans by selling 90-day CDs could manage the resulting maturity gap by also buying a put on a Eurodollar futures contract.

Like a futures-hedged position, option-hedged positions are subject to quality, quantity, and timing risk. For OTC options, some of the hedging risk can be minimized, if not eliminated, by customizing the contract; for exchange-traded option-hedged positions the objective is to minimize hedging risk by determining the appropriate number of option contracts. For direct hedging cases (cases in which the future value of the asset or liability to be hedged, V_T, is the same as the one underlying the option contract) the number of options can be determined by using the naive hedge where $n = V_T/X$. For cross-hedging cases (cases in which the asset or liability to be hedged is not the same as the one underlying the option contract), the number of options can be determined by using the price-sensitivity model defined in chapter 13. In this section, we examine a number of direct and cross-hedging cases, including some of the hedging cases discussed in chapter 13, and show how they can be hedged with interest rate options.

15.2.2 Long Hedging Cases

Example 1: Future CD Purchase

Consider the case of a money market manager who is expecting a cash inflow of approximately $985,000 in September that he plans to invest in a 90-day jumbo CD with a face value of $1m and yield tied to the LIBOR. Assume that such CDs are currently trading at a spot index of 94.5 ($S_0 = \$98.625$ per $100 face value), implying a YTM of 5.7757% (that is: YTM = $(\$100/\$98.625)^{365/90} - 1 = 0.057757$). Suppose the manager would like to earn a minimum rate on his September investment that is near the current rate, with the possibility of a higher yield if short-term rates increase. To achieve these objectives, the manager could take a long position in a September Eurodollar futures call. For example, suppose the manager buys one September 94 Eurodollar futures call option quoted at 4 ($R_D = 6\%$, $X = \$985,000$, $C_0 = \$1,000$ ($= 4(\$250)$), $n_C = V_T/X = \$985,000/\$985,000 = 1$ call contract), with plans to close the futures call at expiration at its intrinsic value ($f_T - X$) if the option is in-the-money and then buy the $1m, 90-day CD at the spot price. Table 15.1 shows the effective investment expenditures at expiration (costs of the CD minus the profit from the Eurodollar futures call) and the hedged YTM earned from the hedged investment (YTM = $[\$1,000,000/$ Effective investment$]^{365/90} - 1$). As shown, if spot rates (LIBOR) are lower than $R_D = 6\%$ at expiration, the Eurodollar futures call will be in-the-money and the manager will be able to profit from the call position, offsetting the higher costs of buying the 90-day, $1m CD. As a result, the manager will be able to lock in a maximum purchase price $986,000 and a minimum yield on his 90-day CD investment of 5.885% when R_D is 6% or less. On the other hand, if spot discount rates (LIBOR) are 6% or higher, the call will be worthless. In these cases, though, the manager's option losses are limited to just the $1,000 premium he paid, while the prices of buying CDs decrease, the higher the rates. As a result, for rates higher than 6%, the manager is able to obtain lower CD prices and therefore higher yields on his CD investment as rates increase. Thus, by

Table 15.1 Hedging the cost of a September purchase of a 90–day, $1m face value CD with a September Eurodollar futures call

(1) Spot CD discount rates, R_D (%)	(2) Cost of $1m face value CD, spot price = futures price at T ($)	(3) Call profit/ loss ($)	(4) Effective cost, (col. 2–col. 3)	(5) YTM (%)
5.00	987,500	1,500	986,000	5.885
5.25	986,875	875	986,000	5.885
5.50	986,250	250	986,000	5.885
5.75	985,625	– 375	986,000	5.885
6.00	985,000	– 1,000	986,000	5.885
6.25	984,375	– 1,000	985,375	6.157
6.50	983,750	– 1,000	984,750	6.431
6.75	983,125	– 1,000	984,125	6.705
7.00	982,500	– 1,000	983,500	6.980
7.25	981,875	– 1,000	982,875	7.256
7.50	981,250	– 1,000	982,250	7.534

Profit $= [Max(f_T - \$985,000),\ 0] - \$1,000$
YTM $= [\$1m/\text{column } 4]^{365/90} - 1$

hedging with the Eurodollar futures call, the manager is able to obtain at least a 5.885% YTM, with the potential to earn higher returns if rates on CDs increase.

Example 2: Future 91-Day T-Bill Investment

In chapter 13, we examined the case of a corporate treasurer who was expecting a $5m cash inflow in June, which she was planning to invest in T-bills for 91 days. In that example, the treasurer locked in the yield on the T-bill investment by going long in June T-bill futures contracts. Suppose the treasurer expected higher short-term rates in June but was still concerned about the possibility of lower rates. To be able to gain from the higher rates and yet still hedge against lower rates, the treasurer could alternatively buy a June call option on a T-bill futures. For example, suppose there is a June T-bill futures call with an exercise price of $987,500 (index = 95, $R_D = 5$) priced at $1,000 (quote = 4; $C = (4)(\$250) = \$1,000$), with the June expiration (on both the underlying futures and futures option) occurring at the same time as the $5m cash inflow is to be received. To hedge the 91-day investment with this call, the

treasurer would need to buy five calls at a cost of $5,000:

$$n_C = \frac{V_T}{X} = \frac{\$5m}{\$987,500} \cong 5 \text{ calls}$$

$$\text{Cost} = n_C C = (5)(\$1,000) = \$5,000$$

If T-bill rates were lower at the June expiration, then the treasurer would profit from the calls and could use the profit to defray part of the cost of the higher priced T-bills. As shown in table 15.2, if the spot discount rate on T-bills is 5% or less, the treasurer would be able to buy 5.058 spot T-bills (assume perfect divisibility) with the $5m cash inflow and profit from the futures calls, locking in a YTM for the next 91 days of approximately 4.75% on the $5m investment. On the other hand, if T-bill rates are higher, then the treasurer would benefit from lower spot prices while her losses on the call would be limited to just the $5,000 costs of the calls. For spot discount rates above 5%, the treasurer would be able to buy more T-bills, the higher the rates, resulting in higher yields as rates increase. Thus, for the cost of the call options, the treasurer is able to establish a floor by locking in a minimum YTM on the $5m June investment of approximately 4.75%, with

Table 15.2 Hedging a $5m cash flow in June with June T-bill futures calls

(1) Spot discount rates, R_D (%)	(2) Spot price = futures price at T ($)	(3) Call profit/ loss ($)	(4) Hedged investment funds ($5m + col. 3) ($)	(5) Number of bills (col. 4/col. 2)	(6) YTM (%)
3.75	990,625	10,625	5,010,625	5.058044164	4.74
4.00	990,000	7,500	5,007,500	5.058080808	4.74
4.25	989,375	4,375	5,004,375	5.058117498	4.74
4.50	988,750	1,250	5,001,250	5.058154235	4.75
4.75	988,125	− 1,875	4,998,125	5.058191018	4.75
5.00	987,500	− 5,000	4,995,000	5.058227848	4.75
5.25	986,875	− 5,000	4,995,000	5.061431286	5.02
5.50	986,250	− 5,000	4,995,000	5.064638783	5.29
5.75	985,625	− 5,000	4,995,000	5.067850349	5.56
6.00	985,000	− 5,000	4,995,000	5.07106599	5.82
6.25	984,375	− 5,000	4,995,000	5.074285714	6.09

Profit $= 5[\text{Max}(f_T - \$987,500), 0] - \$5,000$
YTM $= [[(\text{Number of bill})(\$1m)]/\$5m]^{365/91} - 1$

the chance to earn a higher rate if short-term rates increase.

Note, if the treasurer wanted to hedge a 182-day investment instead of 91-days with calls, then she would need to buy both June and September T-bill futures calls. At the June expiration, the manager would then close both positions and invest the $5m inflow plus (minus) the call profits (losses) in 182-day spot T-bills.

Example 3: Hedging a CD Rate with an OTC Interest Rate Put

Suppose the ABC manufacturing company was expecting a net cash inflow of $10m in 60 days from its operations and was planning to invest the excess funds in a 90-day CD from Sun Bank paying the LIBOR. To hedge against any interest rate decreases occurring 60 days from now, suppose the company purchases an interest rate put (corresponding to the bank's CD it plans to buy) from Sun Bank for $10,000, with the put having the following terms:

- Exercise rate $= 7\%$
- Reference rate $=$ LIBOR
- Time period applied to the payoff $= 90/360$
- Day count convention $= 30/360$
- Notional principal $= \$10m$

- Payoff made at the maturity date on the CD (90 days from option's expiration)
- Interest rate put's expiration $= T = 60$ days (time of CD purchase)
- Interest rate put premium of $10,000 to be paid at the option's expiration with 7% interest: cost $= \$10,000(1 + (0.07)(60/360)) = \$10,117$.

As shown in table 15.3, the purchase of the interest rate put makes it possible for the ABC company to earn higher rates if the LIBOR is greater than 7% and to lock in a minimum rate of 6.993% if the LIBOR is 7% or less. For example, if 60 days later the LIBOR is at 6.5%, then the company would receive a payoff (90 days later at the maturity of its CD) on the interest rate put of $12,500 = (\$10m)[0.07 - 0.065](90/360)$. The $12,500 payoff would offset the lower (than 7%) interest paid on the company's CD of $162,500 = (\$10m)(0.065)(90/360)$. At the maturity of the CD, the company would therefore receive CD interest and an interest rate put payoff equal to $175,000 = \$162,500 + \$12,500$. With the interest rate put's payoffs increasing the lower the LIBOR, the company would be able to hedge any lower CD interest and lock in a hedged dollar return of $175,000. Based on an investment of $10m plus the $10,117 costs of the put, the hedged return equates to an effective annualized

Table 15.3 Hedging a CD investment with an interest rate put option

(1) LIBOR	(2) Interest rate put, payoff: $10m[Max[0.07 − LIBOR, 0]](0.25)	(3) Cost of the option at T: $10,000(1 + 0.07(60/360))	(4) Interest received on CD at its maturity: (LIBOR)(0.25)($10,000,000)	(5) Revenues at maturity (col. 2 + col. 4)	(6) Annualized hedged rate 4[col. 5/($10m + col. 3)]
0.0550	37,500	10,117	137,500	175,000	0.06993
0.0575	31,250	10,117	143,750	175,000	0.06993
0.0600	25,000	10,117	150,000	175,000	0.06993
0.0625	18,750	10,117	156,250	175,000	0.06993
0.0650	12,500	10,117	162,500	175,000	0.06993
0.0675	6,250	10,117	168,750	175,000	0.06993
0.0700	0	10,117	175,000	175,000	0.06993
0.0725	0	10,117	181,250	181,250	0.07243
0.0750	0	10,117	187,500	187,500	0.07492
0.0775	0	10,117	193,750	193,750	0.07742
0.0800	0	10,117	200,000	200,000	0.07992
0.0825	0	10,117	206,250	206,250	0.08242
0.0850	0	10,117	212,500	212,500	0.08491

Company's investment: $10m at LIBOR for 90 days (0.25 per year)

Interest rate put option: exercise rate = 7%, reference rate = LIBOR, NP = $10m, time period = 0.25, option expiration = T = 60 days

Cost of option = $10,000, payable at T plus 7% interest

yield of 6.993% = [(4)($175,000)]/[$10m + $10,117]. On the other hand, if the LIBOR exceeds 7%, the company benefits from the higher CD rates, while its losses are limited to the $10,117 costs of the puts.

15.2.3 Short Hedging Cases

Example 1: Hedging Future T-Bond Sale with an OTC T-Bond Put

Consider the case of a trust-fund manager who plans to sell ten $100,000 face value T-bonds from her fixed income portfolio in September to meet an anticipated liquidity need. The T-bonds the manager plans to sell pay 6% interest and are currently priced at 94 (per $100 face value), and at their anticipated selling date in September, they will have exactly 15 years to maturity and no accrued interest. Suppose the manager expects long-term rates in September to be lower and therefore expects to benefit from higher T-bond prices when she sells her

bonds, but she is also concerned that rates could increase and does not want to risk selling the bonds at prices lower than 94. As a strategy to lock in minimum revenue from the September bond sale if rates increase, while obtaining higher revenues if rates decrease, the manager decides to buy spot T-bond puts from an OTC Treasury security dealer who is making a market in spot T-bond options. Suppose the manager pays a dealer $10,000 for a put option on ten 15-year, 6% T-bonds with an exercise price of 94 per $100 face value and expiration coinciding with the manager's September sales date. Table 15.4 shows the manager's revenue from either selling the T-bonds on the put if T-bond prices are less than 94 or on the spot market if prices are equal to or greater than 94. As shown in the table, if the price on a 15-year T-bond is less than 94 at expiration (or rates approximately 6.60% or more) the manager would be able to realize a minimum net revenue of $930,000 by selling her T-bonds to the dealer on the put contract at X = $940,000 and paying the $10,000 cost for the put; if T-bond prices are greater than 94 (below approximately

Table 15.4 Hedging a T-bond sale with an OTC T-bond put option

(1) Spot T-bond price per $100 face value	(2) Average rate to maturity	(3) Revenue from selling 10 T-bonds by exercising put	(4) Revenue from selling the 10 T-bonds on spot market if put is not exercised	(5) Cost of the put	(6) Hedged revenue (col. 3 + col. 4 − col. 5)
90.0	0.0702	940,000	0	10,000	930,000
90.5	0.0696	940,000	0	10,000	930,000
91.0	0.0691	940,000	0	10,000	930,000
91.5	0.0686	940,000	0	10,000	930,000
92.0	0.0681	940,000	0	10,000	930,000
93.0	0.0670	940,000	0	10,000	930,000
93.5	0.0665	940,000	0	10,000	930,000
94.0	0.0660	940,000	0	10,000	930,000
94.5	0.0655	0	945,000	10,000	935,000
95.0	0.0650	0	950,000	10,000	940,000
95.5	0.0645	0	955,000	10,000	945,000
96.0	0.0639	0	960,000	10,000	950,000
96.5	0.0634	0	965,000	10,000	955,000
97.0	0.0629	0	970,000	10,000	960,000

T-bond: maturity = 15, coupon = 6%, face value = $100,000, number of T-bonds to sell = 10
OTC T-bond put: right to sell 10 T-bonds at $940,000, cost of the option = $1,000

Table 15.5 Hedging maturity gap with Eurodollar futures puts

(1) LIBOR%	(2) Spot and futures price	(3) Put profit	(4) Debt on June CD	(5) Sept funds needed (col. 4 − col. 3)	(6) December debt obligation ([col. 5](1 + LIBOR)$^{(90/365)}$)	(7) June to Dec hedged rate ([col. 6/$1m]$^{(365/180)}$ − 1)
3.50	991,553.33	− 512.46	1,012,103	1,012,615.46	1,021,242	0.04354
3.75	990,963.66	− 512.46	1,012,103	1,012,615.46	1,021,849	0.04480
4.00	990,375.75	− 512.46	1,012,103	1,012,615.46	1,022,456	0.04606
4.25	989,789.60	− 512.46	1,012,103	1,012,615.46	1,023,061	0.04732
4.50	989,205.21	− 512.46	1,012,103	1,012,615.46	1,023,666	0.04857
4.75	988,622.55	− 512.46	1,012,103	1,012,615.46	1,024,269	0.04983
5.00	988,041.63	− 512.46	1,012,103	1,012,615.46	1,024,871	0.05108
5.25	987,462.42	− 473.94	1,012,103	1,012,576.94	1,025,433	0.05225
5.50	986,884.93	117.93	1,012,103	1,011,985.07	1,025,434	0.05225
5.75	986,309.14	708.06	1,012,103	1,011,394.94	1,025,434	0.05225
6.00	985,735.05	1,296.46	1,012,103	1,010,806.54	1,025,434	0.05225
6.25	985,162.64	1,883.13	1,012,103	1,010,219.87	1,025,435	0.05225
6.50	984,591.91	2,468.08	1,012,103	1,009,634.92	1,025,435	0.05225

Spot and futures price at $T = \$1m/(1 + LIBOR)^{90/365}$
Put profit $= 1.02491(Max(\$987,500 - col. (2), 0)) - \$512.46$
Debt on June CD $= \$1m(1.05)^{90/365}$

6.60%), her put option would be worthless, but her revenue from selling the T-bond would be greater at the higher T-bond prices, while the loss on her put position would be limited to the $10,000 cost of the option. Thus, by buying the put option, the trust-fund manager has attained insurance against decreases in bond prices. Such a strategy represents a bond insurance strategy. In contrast, if the portfolio manager were planning to buy long-term bonds in the future and was worried about higher bond prices (lower rates), she could hedge the future investment by buying T-bond spot or futures calls.

Note that instead of an OTC spot T-bond call, the manager alternatively could have hedged her position with an exchange-traded T-bond futures call. In this case, the hedge position would be subject to some hedging risk, but the option contract would be more liquid and less expensive.

Example 2: Managing the Maturity Gap with a Eurodollar Futures Put

In chapter 13, we examined the case of a small bank with a maturity gap problem resulting from making $1m loans in June with maturities of 180 days, financed by selling $1m-worth of 90-day CDs at the current LIBOR of 5% and then 90 days later selling new 90-day CDs to finance its June CD debt of $1,012,103 ($=$1m(1.05)^{90/365}$). To minimize its exposure to market risk, the bank hedged its $1,012,103 CD sale in September by going short in 1.02491 ($1,012,103/$987,500) September Eurodollar futures contract trading at quoted index of 95 ($987,500). Instead of hedging its future CD sale with Eurodollar futures, the bank could alternatively buy put options on Eurodollar futures. By hedging with puts, the bank would be able to lock in or cap the maximum rate it pays on its September CD. For example, suppose the bank decides to hedge its September CD sale by buying a September Eurodollar futures put with an expiration coinciding with the maturity of its September CD, an exercise price of 95 ($X = $987,500$), and a quoted premium of 2 ($P = 500). With the September debt from the June CD of $1,012,103, the bank would need to buy 1.02491

September Eurodollar futures puts (assume perfect divisibility) at a total cost of $512.46 to cap the rate it pays on its September CD:

$$n_P = \frac{\$1,012,103}{\$987,500} = 1.02491 \text{ contracts}$$
$$\text{Cost} = (1.02491)(\$500) = \$512.46$$

If the LIBOR at the September expiration is greater than 5%, the bank will have to pay a higher rate on its September CD, but it will profit from its Eurodollar futures put position, with the put profits being greater, the higher the rate. The put profit would serve to reduce part of the $1,012,103 funds the bank would need to pay the maturing June CD, in turn, offsetting the higher rate it would have to pay on its September CD. As shown in table 15.5, if the LIBOR is at discount yield of 5% or higher, then the bank would be able to lock in a debt obligation 90 days later of $1,025,435 (allow for slight rounding differences), for an effective 180-day rate of 5.225%. On the other hand, if the rate is less than or equal to 5%, then the bank would be able to finance its $1,012,615.46 debt (June CD of $1,012,103 and put cost of $512.46) at lower rates, while its losses on its futures puts would be limited to the premium of $512.46. As a result, for lower rates the bank would realize a lower debt obligation 90 days later and therefore a lower rate paid over the 180-day period. Thus, for the cost of the puts, hedging the maturity gap with puts allows the bank to lock in a maximum rate on its debt obligation, with the possibility of paying lower rates if interest rates decrease.

Example 3: Hedging a Future Loan Rate with an OTC Interest Rate Call

Suppose a construction company plans to finance one of its projects with a $10m, 90-day loan from Sun Bank, with the loan rate to be set equal to the LIBOR + 100 BP when the project commences 60 day from now. Furthermore, suppose that the company expected rates to decrease in the future, but is concerned that they could increase. To obtain protection against higher rates, suppose the company buys an interest rate call option from Sun Bank for

Table 15.6 Hedging a future $10m, 90-day loan with an OTC interest rate call

(1) LIBOR	(2) Interest rate call, payoff: $10m[Max[LIBOR − 0.07, 0](0.25)	(3) Cost of the option at T: $20,000(1 + 0.07(60/360))	(4) Interest paid on loan at its maturity: (LIBOR + 100 BP) (0.25)($10,000,000)	(5) Cost at maturity (col. 4 − col. 2)	(6) Annualized hedged rate (4)[col. 5/($10m − col. 3)]
0.0550	0	20,233	162,500	162,500	0.06513
0.0575	0	20,233	168,750	168,750	0.06764
0.0600	0	20,233	175,000	175,000	0.07014
0.0625	0	20,233	181,250	181,250	0.07265
0.0650	0	20,233	187,500	187,500	0.07515
0.0675	0	20,233	193,750	193,750	0.07766
0.0700	0	20,233	200,000	200,000	0.08016
0.0725	6,250	20,233	206,250	200,000	0.08016
0.0750	12,500	20,233	212,500	200,000	0.08016
0.0775	18,750	20,233	218,750	200,000	0.08016
0.0800	25,000	20,233	225,000	200,000	0.08016
0.0825	31,250	20,233	231,250	200,000	0.08016
0.0850	37,500	20,233	237,500	200,000	0.08016

Company's loan: $10m at LIBOR + 100 BP for 90 days (0.25 per year)
Interest rate call option: exercise rate = 7%, reference rate = LIBOR, NP = $10m, time period = 0.25, option expiration = T = 60 days
Cost of option = $20,000, payable at T plus 7% interest

$20,000 with the following terms:

- Exercise rate $= 7\%$
- Reference rate $=$ LIBOR
- Time period applied to the payoff $= 90/360$
- Notional principal $= \$10m$
- Payoff made at the maturity date on the loan (90 days after option's expiration)
- Interest rate call's expiration $= T = 60$ days (time of the loan)
- Interest rate call premium of $20,000 to be paid at the option's expiration with 7% interest: cost $= \$20,000(1 + (0.07)(60/360)) = \$20,233$.

Table 15.6 shows the company's cash flows from the call, interest paid on the loan, and effective interest costs that would result given different LIBORs at the starting date on the loan and the expiration date on the option. As shown in column 6 of the table, the company is able to lock in a maximum interest cost of 8.016% if the LIBOR is 7% or greater at expiration, while still benefiting with lower rates if the LIBOR is less than 7%.

Example 4: Hedging a Bond Portfolio with T-Bond Puts – Cross-Hedge

In chapter 13, we defined the price-sensitivity model for hedging debt positions in which the underlying futures contract was not the same as the debt position to be hedged. The model determines the number of futures contracts that will make the value of a portfolio consisting of a fixed-income security and an interest rate futures contract invariant to small changes in interest rates. The model also can be extended to hedging with put or call options. The number of options (calls for hedging long positions and puts for hedging short positions) using the price-sensitivity model is:

$$n_{options} = \frac{Dur_S}{Dur_{option}} \frac{V_0 (1 + YTM_{option})^T}{X (1 + YTM_S)^T}$$

where:

$Dur_S =$ duration of the bond being hedged
$Dur_{option} =$ duration of the bond underlying the option contract

$V_0 =$ current value of bond to be hedged
$YTM_S =$ yield to maturity on the bond being hedged
$YTM_{option} =$ yield to maturity on the option's underlying bond

As an example, suppose a bond portfolio manager is planning to liquidate part of his portfolio in September. The portfolio he plans to sell consists of a mix of A to AAA quality bonds with a weighted average maturity of 15.25 years, face value of $10m, weighted average yield of 8%, portfolio duration of 10, and current value of $10m. Suppose the manager would like to benefit from lower long-term rates that he expects to occur in the future but would also like to protect the portfolio sale against the possibility of a rate increase. To achieve this dual objective, the manager could buy a spot or futures put on a T-bond. Suppose there is a September 95 ($X = \$95,000$) T-bond futures put option trading at $1,156 with the cheapest-to-deliver T-bond on the put's underlying futures being a bond with a current maturity of 15.25 years, duration of 9.818, and currently priced to yield 6.0%. Using the price-sensitivity model, the manager would need to buy 81 puts at a cost of $93,636 to hedge his bond portfolio:

$$n_P = \frac{Dur_S}{Dur_P} \frac{V_0 (1 + YTM_P)^T}{X (1 + YTM_S)^T}$$

$$= \frac{10}{9.818} \frac{\$10m}{\$95,000} \frac{(1.06)^{15.25}}{(1.08)^{15.25}} \cong 81$$

$$Cost = (81)(\$1,156) = \$93,636$$

Suppose that in September, long-term rates were higher, causing the value of the bond portfolio to decrease from $10m to $9.1m and the prices on September T-bond futures contracts to decrease from 95 to 86. In this case, the bond portfolio's $900,000 loss in value would be partially offset by a $635,364 profit on the T-bond futures puts: $\pi = 81(\$95,000 - \$86,000) - \$93,636 = \$635,364$. The manager's hedged portfolio value would therefore be $9,735,364; a loss of 2.6% in value (this loss includes the cost of the puts) compared to a 9% loss in value if the portfolio were not hedged. On the other hand, if rates in September were lower, causing the value of the bond portfolio to increase from $10m to $10.5m and the prices on the September T-bond

Table 15.7   Cross-hedge: bond portfolio hedged with T-bond futures

Pairs of T-bond futures and bond portfolio prices

Prices T-bond futures	T-bond yield ARTM	Bond portfolio values	Bond yield ARTM	Profit on T-bond futures put	Hedged bond portfolio value	% change in value	% change in unhedged value
86	0.0746	9,100,000	0.0901	635,364	9,735,364	− 0.0265	− 0.09
87	0.0734	9,200,000	0.0889	554,364	9,754,364	− 0.0246	− 0.08
88	0.0723	9,300,000	0.0877	473,364	9,773,364	− 0.0227	− 0.07
89	0.0713	9,400,000	0.0866	392,364	9,792,364	− 0.0208	− 0.06
90	0.0702	9,500,000	0.0855	311,364	9,811,364	− 0.0189	− 0.05
91	0.0691	9,600,000	0.0844	230,364	9,830,364	− 0.0170	− 0.04
92	0.0681	9,700,000	0.0832	149,364	9,849,364	− 0.0151	− 0.03
93	0.0670	9,800,000	0.0822	68,364	9,868,364	− 0.0132	− 0.02
94	0.0660	9,900,000	0.0811	− 12,636	9,887,364	− 0.0113	− 0.01
95	0.0650	10,000,000	0.0800	− 93,636	9,906,364	− 0.0094	0
96	0.0639	10,100,000	0.0789	− 93,636	10,006,364	0.0006	0.01
97	0.0629	10,200,000	0.0779	− 93,636	10,106,364	0.0106	0.02
98	0.0620	10,300,000	0.0768	− 93,636	10,206,364	0.0206	0.03
99	0.0610	10,400,000	0.0758	− 93,636	10,306,364	0.0306	0.04
100	0.0600	10,500,000	0.0748	− 93,636	10,406,364	0.0406	0.05

T-bond futures price based on the price of 15-year, 6% T-bond
Bond portfolio has a weighted maturity of 15 years and a weighted coupon of 8%
Hedge: purchase of 81 T-bond futures puts, $X = 95$, $P = \$1,156$; cost $= \$93,636$

futures contracts to increase from 95 to 100, then the puts would be out-of-the-money and the loss of the options would be limited to the $93,636. In this case, the hedged portfolio value would be $10.406365m − a 4.06% gain in value compared to the 5% gain for an unhedged position. Table 15.7 shows the put-hedged bond portfolio values for a number of pairs of T-bond futures and bond portfolio values (and their associated yields). As shown, for increasing interest rates cases in which the pairs of the T-bond and bond portfolio values are less than 95 (the exercise price) and $10,000,000, respectively, the hedge portfolio losses are between 1% and 2.6%, while for increasing interest rate cases in which the pairs of T-bond prices and bond values are greater than 95 and $10,000,000, the portfolio increases as the bond value increases.

15.3 HEDGING A SERIES OF CASH FLOWS: OTC CAPS AND FLOORS

The above cases involved hedging a single cash flow. When there is a series of cash flows, such as a floating-rate loan or an investment in a floating-rate note, a series or strip of interest rate options can be used. For example, a company with a 1-year floating-rate loan starting in September at a specified rate and then reset in December, March, and June to equal the spot LIBOR plus BP, could obtain a maximum rate or cap on the loan by buying a series of Eurodollar futures puts expiring in December, March, and June. At each reset date, if the LIBOR exceeds the discount yield on the put, the higher LIBOR applied to the loan will be offset by a profit on the nearest expiring put, with the profit increasing the greater the LIBOR; if the LIBOR is equal to or less than the discount yield on the put, the lower LIBOR applied to the loan will only be offset by the limited cost of the put. Thus, a strip of Eurodollar futures puts used to hedge a floating-rate loan places a ceiling on the effective rate paid on the loan. In the case of a floating-rate investment, such as a floating-rate note tied to the LIBOR or a bank's floating-rate loan portfolio, a minimum rate or floor can be obtained by buying a series of Eurodollar futures calls, with each call having an expiration near the reset date on the investment. If rates decrease, the lower investment return will be offset by profits on the calls; if rates increase, the only offset will be the limited cost of the calls.

Using exchange-traded options to establish interest rate floors and ceilings on floating-rate assets and liabilities is subject to hedging risk. As a result, many financial and non-financial companies looking for such interest rate insurance prefer to buy OTC caps or floors that can be customized to meet their specific needs. As noted in chapter 14, an OTC cap is a series of interest rate calls (caplets), and an OTC floor is a series of interest rate puts (floorlets). Caps, floors, and other similar interest rate products are offered by commercial and investment banks who often act as dealers, offering to buy and sell the products to their clients and then hedging their exposure with positions in options and futures. These institutions typically provide caps and floors with terms that range from 1 to 5 years, have monthly, quarterly, or semi-annual reset dates or frequencies, and use the LIBOR as the reference rate. The notional principal and the reset dates usually match the specific investment or loan (the better the fit, though, the more expensive the cap or floor), and the settlement dates usually come after the reset date. In cases where a floating-rate loan (or investment) and cap (or floor) come from the same financial institution, the loan and cap (or investment and floor) are usually treated as a single instrument so that when there is a payoff, it occurs at an interest payment (receipt) date, lowering (or increasing) the payment (receipt). The exercise rate is often set so that the cap or floor is initially out-of-the-money, and the payments for these interest rate products are usually made up-front, although some are amortized.

15.3.1 Example: Floating-Rate Loan Hedged with an OTC Cap

As an example, suppose the Diamond Development Company borrows $50m from Commerce Bank to finance a 2-year construction project. Suppose the loan is for 2 years, starting on March 1 at a known rate of 8%, then resets every 3 months – June 1, September 1, December 1, and March 1 – at the prevailing

LIBOR plus 150 BP. In entering this loan agreement, suppose the company is uncertain of future interest rates and therefore would like to lock in a maximum rate, while still benefiting from lower rates if the LIBOR decreases. To achieve this, suppose the company buys a cap corresponding to its loan from Commerce Bank for $150,000, with the following terms:

- The cap consist of seven caplets with the first expiring on June 1, 2003 and the others coinciding with the loan's reset dates
- Exercise rate on each caplet $= 8\%$
- NP on each caplet $= \$50m$
- Reference rate $=$ LIBOR
- Time period to apply to payoff on each caplet $= 90/360$ (typically the day count convention is defined by actual number of days between reset dates)
- Payment date on each caplet is at the loan's interest payment date, 90 days after the reset date
- The cost of the cap is $150,000; it is paid at the beginning of the loan, March 1, 2003.

On each reset date, the payoff on the corresponding caplet would be:

$$\text{Payoff} = (\$50m)(\text{Max}[\text{LIBOR} - 0.08, 0]) \\ \times (90/360)$$

With the 8% exercise rate (sometimes called the cap rate), the Diamond Company would be able to lock-in a maximum rate each quarter equal to the cap rate plus the basis points on the loan, 9.5%, while still benefiting with lower interest costs if rates decrease. This can be seen in table 15.8, where the quarterly interests on the loan, the cap payoffs, and the hedged and unhedged rates are shown for different assumed LIBORs at each reset date on the loan. For the five reset dates from December 1, 2003 to the end of the loan, the LIBOR is at 8% or higher. In each of these cases, the higher interest on the loan is offset by the payoff on the cap, yielding a hedged rate on the loan of 9.5% (the 9.5% rate excludes the $150,000 cost of the cap; the rate is 9.53% with the cost included). For the first two reset dates on the loan, June 1, 2003 and September 1, 2003, the LIBOR is less than the cap rate. At these rates, there is no

Table 15.8 Hedging a floating-rate loan with a cap

(1) Reset date	(2) Assumed LIBOR	(3) Loan interest on payment date: (LIBOR + 150BP)(0.25)($50m)	(4) Cap payoff on payment date: (Max[LIBOR − 0.08, 0])(0.25)($50m)	(5) Hedged interest payment (col. 3 − col. 4)	(6) Hedged rate: 4[col. 5/$50m]	(7) Unhedged rate: (LIBOR + 150BP)
2003: 3/1[n]	0.065					
2003: 6/1	0.070	1,000,000	0	1,000,000	0.080	0.080
2003: 9/1	0.075	1,062,500	0	1,062,500	0.085	0.085
2003: 12/1	0.080	1,125,000	0	1,125,000	0.090	0.090
2004: 3/1	0.085	1,187,500	0	1,187,500	0.095	0.095
2004: 6/1	0.090	1,250,000	62,500	1,187,500	0.095	0.100
2004: 9/1	0.095	1,312,500	125,000	1,187,500	0.095	0.105
2004: 12/1	0.100	1,375,000	187,500	1,187,500	0.095	0.110
2005: 3/1		1,437,500	250,000	1,187,500	0.095	0.115

[n] There is no caplet for this date

Loan: Floating-rate loan; term = 2 years; reset dates: 3/1, 6/1, 9/1, 12/1; time frequency = 0.25; rate = LIBOR + 150BP; payment date = 90 days after reset date

Cap: Cost of cap = $150,000; cap rate = 8%; reference rate = LIBOR; time frequency = 0.25; caplets' expiration: on loan reset dates, starting at 6/1/2003; payoff made 90 days after reset date

payoff on the cap, but the rates on the loan are lower with the lower LIBORs.

15.3.2 Example: Floating-Rate Asset Hedged with an OTC Floor

As noted, floors are purchased to create a minimum rate on a floating-rate asset. As an example, suppose the Commerce Bank in the above example wanted to establish a minimum rate or floor on the rates it was to receive on the 2-year floating-rate loan it made to the Diamond Company. To this end, suppose the bank purchased from another financial institution a floor for $100,000 with the following terms corresponding to its floating-rate asset:

- The floor consists of seven floorlets with the first expiring on June 1, 2003 and the others coinciding with the reset dates on the bank's floating-rate loan to the Diamond Company
- Exercise rate on each floorlet $= 8\%$
- NP on each floorlet $= \$50m$
- Reference rate $=$ LIBOR
- Time period to apply to payoff on each floorlet $= 90/360$ (payment date on each floorlet is at the loan's interest payment date, 90 days after the reset date)
- The cost of the floor $= \$100,000$; it is paid at the beginning of the loan, March 1, 2003.

On each reset date, the payoff on the corresponding floorlet would be

$$\text{Payoff} = (\$50m)(\text{Max}[0.08 - \text{LIBOR}, 0])$$
$$\times (90/360)$$

With the 8% exercise rate, Commerce Bank would be able to lock in a minimum rate each quarter equal to the floor rate plus the basis points on the floating-rate asset, 9.5%, while still benefiting with higher returns if rates increase. In table 15.9, Commerce Bank's quarterly interests received on its loan to Diamond, its floor payoffs, and its hedged and unhedged yields on its loan are shown for different assumed LIBORs at each reset date. For the first two reset dates on the loan, 6/1/2003 and 9/1/2003, the LIBOR is less than the floor rate of 8%. At these rates, there is a payoff on the floor that compensates for the lower interest Commerce receives on the loan; this results in a

hedged rate of return on the bank's loan asset of 9.5% (the rate is 9.52% with the $100,000 cost of the floor included). For the five reset dates from 12/1/2003 to the end of the loan, the LIBOR equals or exceeds the floor rate. At these rates, there is no payoff on the floor, but the rates the bank earns on its loan are greater, given the greater LIBORs.

15.3.3 Financing Caps and Floors: Collars and Corridors

The purchaser of a cap or a floor is, in effect, paying a premium for insurance against adverse interest rate movements. The cost of that insurance can be reduced by forming a collar, corridor, or reverse collar.

A *collar* is combination of a long position in a cap and a short position in a floor with different exercise rates. The sale of the floor is used to defray the cost of the cap. For example, the Diamond Company in our above case could reduce the cost of the cap it purchased to hedge its variable rate loan by selling a floor. By forming a collar to hedge its floating-rate debt, the Diamond Company, for a lower net hedging cost, would still have protection against a rate movement against the cap rate, but it would have to give up potential interest savings from rate decreases below the floor rate. For example, suppose the Diamond Company decided to defray the $150,000 cost of its 8% cap by selling a 7% floor for $70,000, with the floor having similar terms to the cap (effective dates on floorlet $=$ reset date, reference rate $=$ LIBOR, NP on floorlets $= \$50m$, and time period for rates $= 0.25$). By using the collar instead of the cap, the company reduces its hedging cost from $150,000 to $80,000 and, as shown in table 15.10, can still lock in a maximum rate on its loan of 9.5%. However, when the LIBOR is less than 7%, the company has to pay on the 7% floor, offsetting the lower interest costs it would pay on its loan. For example, when the LIBOR is at 6% on 6/1/2003, Diamond has to pay $125,000 ninety days later on its short floor position, and when the LIBOR is at 6.5% on 9/1/2003, the company has to pay $62,500; these payments, in turn, offset the benefits of the respective lower interest of 7.5% and 8% (LIBOR + 150) it pays on its floating-rate loan.

Table 15.9 Hedging a floating-rate asset with a floor

(1) Reset date	(2) Assumed LIBOR	(3) Interest received on payment date: (LIBOR + 150BP) (0.25)($50m)	(4) Floor payoff on payment date: (Max[0.08 − LIBOR, 0])(0.25)($50m)	(5) Hedged interest income (col. 3 + col. 4)	(6) Hedged rate: 4[col. 5/$50m]	(7) Unhedged rate: (LIBOR + 150BP)
2003: 3/1[n]	0.065					
2003: 6/1	0.070	1,000,000	0	1,000,000	0.080	0.080
2003: 9/1	0.075	1,062,500	125,000	1,187,500	0.095	0.085
2003: 12/1	0.080	1,125,000	62,500	1,187,500	0.095	0.090
2004: 3/1	0.085	1,187,500	0	1,187,500	0.095	0.095
2004: 6/1	0.090	1,250,000	0	1,250,000	0.100	0.100
2004: 9/1	0.095	1,312,500	0	1,312,500	0.105	0.105
2004: 12/1	0.100	1,375,000	0	1,375,000	0.110	0.110
2005: 3/1		1,437,500	0	1,437,500	0.115	0.115

[n] There is no caplet for this date

Asset: floating-rate loan made by bank; term = 2 years; reset dates: 3/1, 6/1, 9/1, 12/1; time frequency = 0.25; rate = LIBOR + 150BP; payment date = 90 days after reset date

Floor: cost of floor = $100,000; floor rate = 8%; reference rate = LIBOR; time frequency = 0.25; floorlets' expirations: on loan reset dates, starting at 6/1/2003; payoff made 90 days after reset date

Table 15.10 Hedging a floating-rate loan with a collar

(1) Reset date	(2) Assumed LIBOR	(3) Loan interest: (LIBOR + 150BP) (0.25)($50m)	(4) Cap payoff: Max[LIBOR − 0.08, 0] (0.25)($50m)	(5) Floor payment: Max[0.07 − LIBOR, 0] (0.25)($50m)	(6) Hedged interest payment (col. 3 − col. 4 + col. 5)	(7) Hedged rate: (4[col. 6/$50m])	(8) Unhedged rate: (LIBOR + 150BP)
2003: 3/1	0.050	812,500	0	0	812,500	0.065	0.065
2003: 6/1	0.060	937,500	0	125,000	1,062,500	0.085	0.075
2003: 9/1	0.065	1,000,000	0	62,500	1,062,500	0.085	0.080
2003: 12/1	0.070	1,062,500	0	0	1,062,500	0.085	0.085
2004: 3/1	0.075	1,125,000	0	0	1,125,000	0.090	0.085
2004: 6/1	0.080	1,187,500	0	0	1,187,500	0.095	0.090
2004: 9/1	0.085	1,250,000	62,500	0	1,187,500	0.095	0.095
2004: 12/1	0.090	1,312,500	125,000	0	1,187,500	0.095	0.100
2005: 3/1							0.105

Loan interest, cap payoff, and floor payment made on payment date

Loan: floating-rate loan; term = 2 years; reset dates: 3/1, 6/1, 9/1, 12/1; time frequency = 0.25; rate = LIBOR + 150BP; payment date = 90 days after reset date

Cap purchase: cost of cap = $150,000; cap rate = 8%; reference rate = LIBOR; time frequency = 0.25; caplets' expiration: on loan reset dates, starting at 6/1/2003; payoff made 90 days after reset date

Floor sale: sale of floor = $70,000; floor rate = 7%; reference rate = LIBOR; time frequency = 0.25; floorlets' expiration: on loan reset dates, starting at 6/1/2003; payoff date = 90 days after reset date

Table 15.11 Hedging a floating-rate asset with a reverse collar

(1) Reset date	(2) Assumed LIBOR	(3) Interest received: (LIBOR + 150BP) (0.25)($50m)	(4) Floor payoff: Max[0.08 − LIBOR, 0] (0.25)($50m)	(5) Cap payment: Max[LIBOR − 0.09, 0] (0.25)($50m)	(6) Hedged interest income (col. 3 + col. 4 − col. 5)	(7) Hedged rate (4[col. 5/($50m)])	(8) Unhedged rate: (LIBOR + 150BP)
2003: 3/1	0.065	1,000,000	0		1,000,000	0.080	0.080
2003: 6/1	0.070	1,062,500	125,000	0	1,187,500	0.095	0.085
2003: 9/1	0.075	1,125,000	62,500	0	1,187,500	0.095	0.090
2003: 12/1	0.080	1,187,500	0	0	1,187,500	0.095	0.095
2004: 3/1	0.085	1,250,000	0	0	1,250,000	0.100	0.100
2004: 6/1	0.090	1,312,500	0	0	1,312,500	0.105	0.105
2004: 9/1	0.095	1,375,000	0	62,500	1,312,500	0.105	0.110
2004: 12/1	0.100	1,437,500	0	125,000	1,312,500	0.105	0.115
2005: 3/1							

Interest received, floor payoff, and cap payment made on payment date

Asset: floating-rate loan made by bank; term = 2 years; reset dates: 3/1, 6/1, 9/1, 12/1; time frequency = 0.25; rate = LIBOR + 150BP; payment date = 90 days after reset date

Floor purchase: cost of floor = $100,000; floor rate = 8%; reference rate = LIBOR; time frequency = 0.25; floorlets' expirations: on loan reset dates, starting at 6/1/2003; payoff made 90 days after reset date

Cap sale: revenue from cap = $70,000; cap rate = 9%; reference rate = LIBOR; time frequency = 0.25; caplets' expiration: on loan reset dates, starting at 6/1/2003; payoff made 90 days after reset date

Thus, for LIBORs less than 7%, Diamond has a floor in which it pays an effective rate of 8.5% (losing the benefits of lower interest payments on its loan) and for rates above 8% it has a cap in which it pays an effective 9.5% on its loan.

In forming collars to finance capped floating-rate loans, the borrower needs to determine the exercise rates on the caps and floors that best meet the cost of the hedge and his acceptable floor and cap rates. Specifically, if the exercise rate on the floor and cap are the same (e.g., 8% in our example), then the long cap and short floor will be equivalent to a forward contract. This low-cost (if not zero-cost) collar makes the floating-rate loan combined with a collar a synthetic fixed-rate loan. For floors, the lower the exercise rate, the lower the premium. As a result, by selling a floor with a lower floor rate (e.g., 7% or 6%), the borrower's net costs of forming a collar will increase, but the floor rate at which the borrower gives up interest savings will be lower. On the other hand, for caps, the higher the cap rate, the lower the premium. Thus, by buying a cap with a higher floor rate (e.g., 9% or 10%), the borrower's net costs of forming a collar will decrease, but the effective maximum rate on his loan will be higher.

An alternative financial structure to a collar is a corridor. A *corridor* is a long position in a cap and a short position in a similar cap with a higher exercise rate. The sale of the higher exercise-rate cap is used to partially offset the cost of purchasing the cap with the lower strike rate. For example, the Diamond Company, instead of selling a 7% floor for $70,000 to partially finance the $150,000 cost of its 8% cap, could sell a 9% cap for, say, $70,000. If cap purchasers believed there was a greater chance of rates increasing than decreasing, they would prefer the collar to the corridor as a tool for financing the cap. In practice, collars are more frequently used than corridors, reflecting a market of purchasers with such expectations.

A *reverse collar* is combination of a long position in a floor and a short position in a cap with different exercise rates. The sale of the cap is used to defray the cost of the floor. For example, the Commerce Bank in our above floor example could reduce the $100,000 cost of the 8% floor it purchased to hedge the floating-rate loan it made to the Diamond Company by selling a cap. By forming a reverse collar to hedge its floating-rate asset, the bank would still have protection against rates decreasing against the floor rate, but it would have to give up potential higher interest returns if rates increase above the cap rate. For example, suppose Commerce sold a 9% cap for $70,000, with the cap having similar terms to the floor. By using the reverse collar instead of the floor, the company would reduce its hedging cost from $100,000 to $30,000, and as shown in table 15.11, would lock in an effective minimum rate on its asset of 9.5% and an effective maximum rate of 10.5%.

As with collars, in forming reverse collars to finance a floating-rate asset with a floor, the investor needs to determine the exercise rates on the caps and floors that best meet the cost of the hedge and the investor's acceptable floor and cap rates. Also, instead of financing a floor with a cap, an investor could form a *reverse corridor* by selling another floor with a lower exercise rate.

15.4 OTHER INTEREST RATE PRODUCTS

Caps and floors are two of the more popular interest rate products offered by the OTC derivative market. In addition to these derivatives, a number of other interest rate products have been created over the last decade to meet the many different interest rate hedging needs. Many of these products are variations of the generic OTC caps and floors; two of these to note are barrier options and path-dependent options.

15.4.1 Barrier Options

Barrier options are options in which the payoff depends on whether an underlying security price or reference rate reaches a certain level. They can be classified as either knock-out or knock-in options: a *knock-out option* is one that ceases to exist once the specified barrier rate or price is reached; a *knock-in option* is one that comes into existence when the reference rate or price hits the barrier level. Both types of option can be formed with either a call or put and the barrier level can be either above

Table 15.12 Hedging a floating-rate loan with a Q-cap

(1) Reset date	(2) Assumed LIBOR	(3) Interest to be paid at next reset date: (LIBOR + 150BP) (0.25)($50m)	(4) Cumulative interest	(5) Q-cap payment to be paid at next reset date	(6) Hedged interest payment at payment date (col. 3 − col. 5)	(7) Hedged rate (4[col. 6/$50m])
2003: 3/1	0.070	1,062,500	1,062,500	0	1,062,500	0.085
2003: 6/1	0.075	1,125,000	2,187,500	0	1,125,000	0.090
2003: 9/1	0.080	1,187,500	3,375,000	0	1,187,500	0.095
2003: 12/1	0.085	1,250,000	4,625,000	62,500	1,187,500	0.095
2004: 3/1	0.085	1,250,000	1,250,000	0	1,187,500	0.095
2004: 6/1	0.090	1,312,500	2,562,500	0	1,250,000	0.100
2004: 9/1	0.095	1,375,000	3,937,500	187,500	1,312,500	0.105
2004: 12/1	0.100	1,437,500	5,375,000	250,000	1,187,500	0.095
2005: 3/1					1,187,500	0.095

Comparison of cap and Q-cap

(1) Reset date	(2) Assumed LIBOR	(3) Loan interest	(4) Unhedged loan rate	(5) Q-cap payment	(6) Q-cap hedged rate	(7) cap payments	(8) Cap hedged rate
2003: 3/1	0.070	1,062,500	0.085	0	0.085	0	0.085
2003: 6/1	0.075	1,125,000	0.090	0	0.090	0	0.090
2003: 9/1	0.080	1,187,500	0.095	0	0.095		0.095
2003: 12/1	0.085	1,250,000	0.100	62,500	0.095	62,500	0.095
2004: 3/1	0.085	1,250,000	0.100	0	0.095	62,500	0.095
2004: 6/1	0.090	1,312,500	0.105	0	0.100	125,000	0.095
2004: 9/1	0.095	1,375,000	0.110	187,500	0.105	187,500	0.095
2004: 12/1	0.100	1,437,500	0.115	250,000	0.095	250,000	0.095
2005: 3/1					0.095		0.095

Loan: floating-rate loan; term = 2 years; reset dates: 3/1, 6/1, 9/1, 12/1; time frequency = 0.25; rate = LIBOR + 150BP; payment date = 90 days after reset date

Cap: cost of cap = $150,000; cap rate = 8%; reference rate = LIBOR; time frequency = 0.25; caplets' expiration: on loan reset dates, starting at 6/1/2003; payoff made 90 days after reset date

Q-Cap: cost of Q-cap = $125,000; cap rate = 8%; reference rate = LIBOR; time frequency = 0.25; caplets' expiration: on loan reset dates, starting at 6/1/2003; payoff made 90 days after reset date; cap becomes effective once cumulative interest reaches $3m; protection periods: 2003 and 2004

or below the current reference rate or price when the contract is established (down-and-out or up-and-out knock-outs or up-and-in or down-and-in knock-in options). For example, a down-and-out, knock-out call is a call that ceases to exist once the reference price or rate reaches the barrier level and the barrier level is below the reference rate or price when the option was purchased.

Barrier caps and floors with termination or creation features are offered in the OTC market at a premium above comparable caps and floors without such features. Down-and-out caps and floors are options that cease to exist once rates hit a certain level. For example, a 2-year, 8% cap that ceases when the LIBOR hits 6.5%, or a 2-year, 8% floor that ceases once the LIBOR hits 9%. By contrast, an up-and-in cap is one that becomes effective once rates hit a certain level: a 2-year, 8% cap that becomes effective when the LIBOR hits 9% or a 2-year, 8% floor that becomes effective when rates hit 6.5%.

15.4.2   Path-Dependent Options

In the generic cap or floor, the underlying payoff on the caplet or floorlet depends only on the reference rate on the effective date. The payoff does not depend on previous rates; that is, it is independent of the path the LIBOR has taken. Some caps and floors, though, are structured so that their payoff is dependent on the path of the reference rate. An *average cap*, for example, is one in which the payoff depends on the average reference rate for each caplet. If the average is above the exercise rate, then all the caplets will provide a payoff; if the average is equal or below, the whole cap expires out-of-the-money. Consider a 1-year average cap with an exercise rate of 7% with four caplets. If the LIBOR settings turned out to be 7.5%, 7.75%, 7%, and 7.5%, for an average of 7.4375%, then the average cap would be in-the-money: $(0.074375 - 0.07)(0.25)(NP)$. If the rates, though, turned out to be 7%, 7.5%, 6.5%, and 6%, for an average of 6.75%, then the cap would be out-of-the-money.

Another type of path-dependent interest rate option is a *cumulative cap (Q-cap)*. In a Q-cap, the cap seller pays the holder when the periodic interest on the accompanying floating-rate loan hits or exceeds a specified level. As an example, suppose the Diamond Company in our earlier cap example decided to hedge its 2-year floating-rate loan (paying LIBOR + 150 BP) by buying a Q-cap from Commerce Bank with the following terms:

- The cap consists of seven caplets with the first expiring on 6/1/2003 and the others coinciding with the loan's reset dates
- Exercise rates on each caplet = 8%
- NP on each caplet = $50m
- Reference rate = LIBOR
- Time period to apply to payoff on each caplet = 90/360
- For the period 3/1/2003 to 12/1/2003, the caplet will payoff when the cumulative interest starting from loan date 3/1/2003 on the company's loan hits $3m
- For the period 3/1/2004 to 12/1/2004, the caplet will payoff when the cumulative interest starting from date 3/1/2004 on the company's loan hits $3m
- Payment date on each caplet is at the loan's interest payment date, 90 days after the reset date
- The cost of the cap = $125,000; it is paid at the beginning of the loan, 3/1/2003.

Table 15.12 shows the quarterly interest, cumulative interest, Q-cap payment, and effective interest for assumed LIBORs. In the Q-cap's first protection period, 3/1/2003 to 12/1/2003, Commerce Bank will pay the Diamond Company on its 8% caplet when the cumulative interest hits $3m. The cumulative interest hits the $3m limit on reset date 9/1/2003, but on that date the 9/1/2003 caplet is not in-the-money. On the following reset date, though, the caplet is in-the-money at the LIBOR of 8.5%. Commerce would, in turn, have to pay Diamond $62,500 (90 days later) on the caplet, locking in a hedged rate on Diamond's loan of 9.5%. In the second protection period, 3/1/2004 to 12/1/2004, the assumed LIBOR rates are higher. The cumulative interest hits the $3m limit on reset date 9/1/2004. Both the caplet on that date and the next reset date (12/1/2004) are in-the-money. As a result, with the caplet payoffs, Diamond is

Exhibit 15.1   Exotic options

- **Asian option**: An option in which the payoff depends on the average price of the underlying asset during some part of the option's life; call: $IV = Max[S_{av} - X, 0]$; put: $IV = Max[X - S_{av}, 0]$.
- **Lookback option**: An option in which the payoff depends on the minimum or maximum price reached during the life of the option.
- **Binary option**: An option with a discontinuous payoff such as a payoff or nothing. For example, if the price is equal to or less than X, the option pays nothing; if the price exceeds X, the option pays a fixed amount.
- **Compound option**: An option on an option: call on a call, call on put, put on put, and put on call.
- **Chooser option**: An option which gives the holder the right to choose whether the option is a call or a put after a specified period of time.
- **Bermudan option**: An option in which early exercise is restricted to certain dates.
- **Forward start option**: An option that will start at some time in the future.
- **Trigger option**: An option that depends on another index; that is, whether the option is in-the-money depends on the value of another index.
- **Caption**: An option on a cap.
- **Floortion**: An option on a floor.
- **Yield curve option**: An option between two points on a yield curve. For example, a yield curve with an exercise equal to 200 BP on the difference between the yields on 2-year and 10-year notes: payoff $= Max[(YTM_{10} - YTM_2) - 0.02, 0]NP$.

able to obtained a hedged rate of 9.5% for the last two payment periods on its loan.

When compared to a standard cap, the Q-cap provides protection for the 1-year protection periods, while the standard cap provides protection for each period (quarter). As shown in the lower section of table 15.12, a standard 8% cap provides more protection given the assumed increasing interest rate scenario than the Q-cap, capping the loan at 9.5% from date 12/1/2003 to the end of the loan and providing a payoff on five of the seven caplets for a total of $687,500. In contrast, the Q-cap pays on only three of the seven caplets for a total of only $500,000. Because of its lower protection limits, the Q-cap costs less than the standard cap.

15.4.3   Exotic Options

Q-caps, average caps, knock-in options, and knock-out options are sometimes referred to as exotic options. Exotic-option products are non-generic products that are created by financial engineers to meet specific hedging needs and return–risk profiles. Exhibit 15.1 defines some of the popular exotic options used in interest rate management.

15.4.4   Foreign Currency Options

As we noted in chapter 13, when investors purchase and hold foreign securities or when corporations and governments sell debt securities in external markets or incur foreign debt positions, they are subject to exchange rate risk. In chapter 13, we examined how foreign currency futures contracts could be used by financial and non-financial corporations to hedge their international positions. These positions can also be hedged with currency options.

In 1982, the Philadelphia Stock Exchange (PHLX) became the first organized exchange to offer trading in foreign currency options (it is also the US's first stock exchange). The contract sizes for many of PHLX's options are equal to half the size of the currency's futures listed on the International Monetary Market. For example, the foreign currency call option contract on the British pound requires (upon exercise) the purchase of 31,250 British pounds, while a long BP futures contract requires the purchase of 62,500 BP. The expiration months for PHLX's currency options are the next two months from the present and also the months of March, June, September, and December. The expiration date is the Saturday before the third

Wednesday of the expiration month, with the third Wednesday of the expiration month being the settlement date. If a foreign currency call (put) is exercised, the exercising holder is required to deliver dollars (foreign currency) to a bank designated by the OCC. The assigned writer is required to deliver the foreign currency (dollars) to the bank.

Foreign currency options also are traded on a number of derivative exchanges outside the US (see exhibit 12.1). In addition to offering foreign currency futures, the International Monetary Market and other futures exchanges also offer options on foreign currency futures. Finally, there is a sophisticated dealer's market. This interbank currency options market is part of the interbank foreign exchange market. In this dealer's market, banks provide tailor-made foreign currency option contracts for their customers, primarily multinational corporations. Compared to exchange-traded options, options in the interbank market are larger in contract size, often European, and are available on more currencies. Because these options are tailor-made to fit customer needs, though, there is not a significant secondary market for these options.

Until the introduction of currency options, exchange rate risk usually was hedged with foreign currency forward or futures contracts. Hedging with these instruments allows foreign exchange participants to lock in the local currency values of their international revenues or expenses. However, with exchange-traded currency options and dealers' options, hedgers, for the cost of the options, can obtain not only protection against adverse exchange rate movements, but (unlike forward and futures positions) benefit if the exchange rates move in favorable directions.

To illustrate the use of currency options as a hedging tool for international debt and investment position, consider the case presented in chapter 13 of a US fund with investments in Eurobonds that were to pay a principal in British pounds of £10m next September. For the costs of BP put options, the US fund could protect its dollar revenues from possible exchange rate decreases when it converts, while still benefiting if the exchange rate increases. For example, suppose a September BP put with an exercise price of $X = \$1.425/£$ is available at $P = \$0.02/£$. Given a contract size of 31,250

British pounds, the US fund would need to buy 320 put contracts ($n_P = £10,000,000/£31,250 = 320$) at a cost of $200,000 (cost $= (320)(£31,250)(0.02/£)$) to establish a floor for the dollar value of its £10,000,000 receipt in September. Table 15.13 shows the dollar cash flows the US fund would receive in September from converting its receipts of £10,000,000 to dollars at the spot exchange rate (E_T) and closing its 320 put contracts at a price equal to the put's intrinsic value (assume the September payment date and option expiration date are the same). As shown in table 15.13, if the exchange rate is less than $X = \$1.425/£$, the company would receive less than $14,250,000 when it converts its £10,000,000 to dollars; these lower revenues, however, would be offset by the profits from the put position. For example, at a spot exchange rate of $\$1.325/£$ the company would receive only $13,250,000 from converting its £10,000,000, but would earn a profit of $800,000 from the puts ($800,000 $= 320$ Max[($\$1.425/£$) − ($\$1.325/£$), 0]($£31,250$) − $200,000); this would result in a combined receipt of $14,050,000. As shown in the table, if the exchange rate is $\$1.425/£$ or less, the company would receive $14,050,000. This amount equals the hedged amount ($14,250,000) minus the $200,000 costs of the put options. On the other hand, if the exchange rate at expiration exceeds $\$1.425/£$, the US fund would realize a dollar gain when it converts the £10,000,000 at the higher spot exchange rate, while its losses on the put would be limited to the amount of the premium. Thus, by hedging with currency put options, the company is able to obtain exchange rate risk protection in the event that the exchange rate decreases while still retaining the potential for increased dollar revenues if the exchange rate rises.

Suppose that instead of receiving foreign currency, a US company had a foreign liability requiring a foreign currency payment at some future date. To protect itself against possible increases in the exchange rate while still benefiting if the exchange rate decreases, the company could hedge the position by taking a long position in a currency call option. For example, suppose a US company owed £10,000,000, with the payment to be made in September. To benefit from the lower exchange rates and still limit the dollar costs

Table 15.13 Hedging £10,000,000 cash inflow with a British pound put option
($X=\$1.425/£$, $P=0.02$, contract size $=£31,250$, number of puts $=320$)

(1) Exchange rate ($E_T=\$/BP$)	(2) Dollar revenue (E_T (10,000,000BP))	(3) Put profit	(4) Hedged revenue (col. 2 + col. 3)
1.200	12,000,000	2,050,000	14,050,000
1.250	12,500,000	1,550,000	14,050,000
1.275	12,750,000	1,300,000	14,050,000
1.300	13,000,000	1,050,000	14,050,000
1.325	13,250,000	800,000	14,050,000
1.350	13,500,000	550,000	14,050,000
1.375	13,750,000	300,000	14,050,000
1.400	14,000,000	50,000	14,050,000
1.425	14,250,000	– 200,000	14,050,000
1.450	14,500,000	– 200,000	14,300,000
1.475	14,750,000	– 200,000	14,550,000
1.500	15,000,000	– 200,000	14,800,000
1.525	15,250,000	– 200,000	15,050,000
1.550	15,500,000	– 200,000	15,300,000

Put profit $=(320)(31,250BP)(Max[\$1.425/BP - E_T, 0]) - \$200,000$

Table 15.14 Hedging £10,000,000 cash outflow with a British pound call option
($X=\$1.425/£$, $C=0.02$, contract size $=£31,250$, number of calls $=320$)

(1) Exchange rate ($E_T=\$/BP$)	(2) Dollar cost (E_T (10,000,000BP))	(3) Call profit	(4) Hedged cost (col. 2 – col. 3)
1.200	12,000,000	– 200,000	12,200,000
1.250	12,500,000	– 200,000	12,700,000
1.275	12,750,000	– 200,000	12,950,000
1.300	13,000,000	– 200,000	13,200,000
1.325	13,250,000	– 200,000	13,450,000
1.350	13,500,000	– 200,000	13,700,000
1.375	13,750,000	– 200,000	13,950,000
1.400	14,000,000	– 200,000	14,200,000
1.425	14,250,000	– 200,000	14,450,000
1.450	14,500,000	50,000	14,450,000
1.475	14,750,000	300,000	14,450,000
1.500	15,000,000	550,000	14,450,000
1.525	15,250,000	800,000	14,450,000
1.550	15,500,000	1,050,000	14,450,000

Call profit $=(320)(31,250BP)(Max[E_T - \$1.425/BP, 0]) - \$200,000$

of purchasing £10,000,000 in the event the $/£ exchange rate rises, the company could buy September British pound call options. Table 15.14 shows the costs of purchasing £10,000,000 at different exchange rates and the profits and losses from purchasing 320 September British pound calls with $X=$ $1.425/£ at $0.02/£ (contract size $=£31,250$) and closing them at expiration at a price equal to the call's intrinsic value. As shown in the table, for cases in which the exchange rate is greater than $1.425/£, the company has dollar expenditures exceeding $14,250,000; the expenditures, though, are offset by the profits from the calls. On the other hand, when the exchange rate is less than $1.425/£, the dollar costs of purchasing £10,000,000 decrease as the exchange rate decreases, while the losses on the call options are limited to the option premium.

Web Information

For information on currency options and currency futures options go to

www.phlx.com

and

www.cme.com

15.5 PRICING INTEREST RATE OPTIONS WITH A BINOMIAL INTEREST TREE

The most widely used model for pricing equity options is the Black–Scholes option pricing model (OPM) that was defined in chapter 10. The model explains the price of an option in terms of the price of the underlying security, exercise price, time to expiration, interest rate, and the underlying security's variability. In 1976, Black extended the B–S OPM for spot options to the pricing of futures options. While the B–S OPM and the Black model can be used to estimate the equilibrium price of interest rate options and futures options, there are at least two problems. First, the OPM is based on the assumption that the variance of the underlying asset is constant. In the case of a bond, though, its variability tends to decrease as its maturity becomes shorter. Second, the OPM assumes that the interest rate is constant. This assumption does not hold for options on interest-sensitive securities. In spite of these problems, the B–S OPM and the Black futures model are still used to value interest rate options. Newer models, however, have been developed to estimate the value of options on interest-sensitive securities. Of these newer models, the most extensively used one is the binomial interest rate model. In chapter 9, we examined how the binomial interest rate model can be used to price bonds with embedded call and put options, sinking-fund arrangements, and convertible clauses, and in chapter 10,

we looked at two approaches to estimating the tree. In this section, we show how the binomial interest rate tree can be used to price interest rate options, and in section 15.6, we show how the Black futures model can be used.

15.5.1 Valuing T-Bill Options with a Binomial Tree

Exhibit 15.2 shows a two-period binomial tree for an annualized risk-free spot rate (S) and the corresponding prices on a T-bill (B) with a maturity of 0.25 years and face value of $100 and also a futures contract (f) on the T-bill, with the futures expiring at the end of period 2. The length of each period is 6 months (6-month steps), the upward parameter on the spot rate (u) is 1.1, and the downward parameter (d) is $1/1.1 = 0.9091$, the probability of the spot rate increasing in each period is 0.5, and the yield curve is assumed flat. As shown in the exhibit, given an initial spot rate of 5% (annual), the two possible spot rates after one period (6 months) are 5.5% and 4.54545%, and the three possible rates after two periods (1 year) are 6.05%, 5%, and 4.13223% . At the current spot rate of 5%, the price of the T-bill is $B_0 = 98.79$ $(= 100/(1.05)^{0.25})$; in period 1, the price is 98.67 when the spot rate is 5.5% $(= 100/(1.055)^{0.25})$ and 98.895 when the rate is 4.54545% $(= 100/(1.0454545)^{0.25})$. In period 2, the T-bill prices are 98.54, 98.79, and 99 for spot rates of 6.05%, 5%, and 4.13223%, respectively.

The futures prices shown in exhibit 15.2 are obtained by assuming a risk-neutral market. Recall, in chapter 13 we showed that if the market is risk-neutral, then the futures price is an unbiased estimator of the expected spot price: $f_t = E(S_T)$. The futures prices at each node in the exhibit are therefore equal to their expected price next period. Given the spot T-bill prices in period 2, the futures prices in period 1 are 98.665 $(= E(B) = 0.5(98.54) + 0.5(98.79))$ and 98.895 $(= E(B) = 0.5(98.79) + 0.5(99))$. Given these prices, the current futures price is $f_0 = 98.78$ $(= E(f_1) = 0.5(98.665) + 0.5(98.895))$.[1]

Given the binomial tree of spot rates, prices on the spot T-bill, and prices on the T-bill futures, we can determine the values of call and

Exhibit 15.2   Binomial tree of spot rates, T-bill prices, and T-bill futures prices

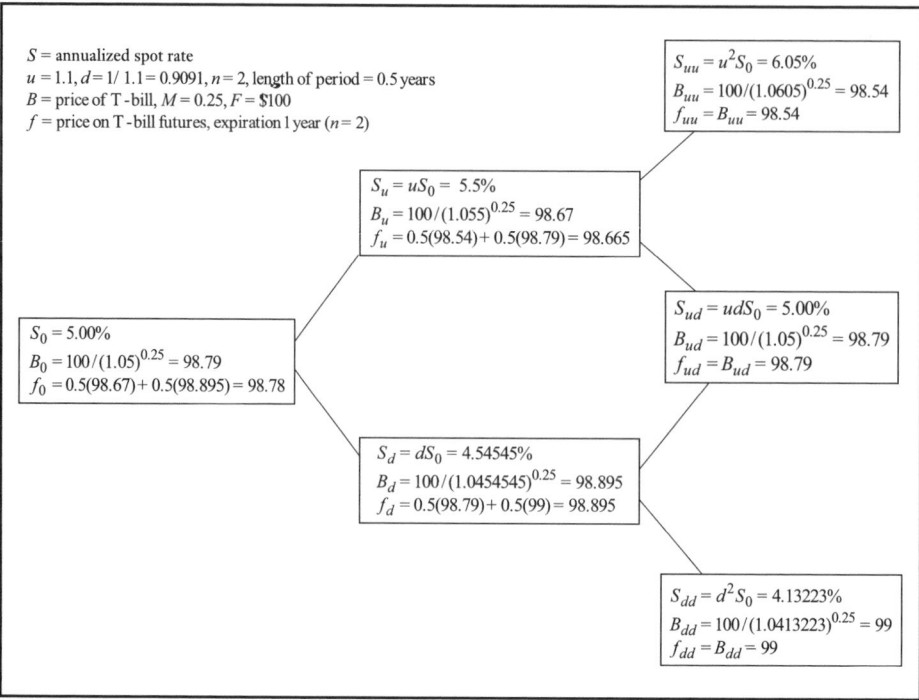

put options on spot and futures T-bills. For European options, the methodology for determining the price is to start at expiration where we know the possible option values are equal to their intrinsic values, IVs. Given the option's IVs at expiration, we then move to the preceding period and price the option to equal the present value of its expected cash flows for the next period. Given these values, we then roll the tree to the next preceding period and again price the option to equal the present value of its expected cash flows. We continue this recursive process to the current period. If the option is American, then its early exercise advantage needs to be taken into account by determining at each node whether or not it is more valuable to hold the option or exercise. This is done by starting one period prior to the option's expiration and constraining the price of the American option to be the maximum of its binomial value (present value of next period's expected cash flows) or the intrinsic value (i.e., the value from exercising). Those values are then rolled to the next preceding period, and

the American option values for that period are obtained by again constraining the option prices to be the maximum of the binomial value or the IV; this process continues to the current period.

Spot T-Bill Call

Suppose we want to value a European call on a spot T-bill with an exercise price of 98.75 per $100 face value and expiration of 1 year. To value the call option on the T-bill, we start at the option's expiration, where we know the possible call values are equal to their intrinsic values, IVs. In this case, at spot rates of 5% and 4.13223%, the call is in-the-money with IVs of 0.04 and 0.25, respectively, and at the spot rate of 6.05% the call is out-of-the-money and thus has an IV of zero (see exhibit 15.3). Given the three possible option values at expiration, we next move to period 1 and price the option at the two possible spot rates of 5.5% and 4.54545% to equal the present values of their expected cash flows next period. Assuming

Exhibit 15.3   Binomial tree of spot rates and T-bill call prices

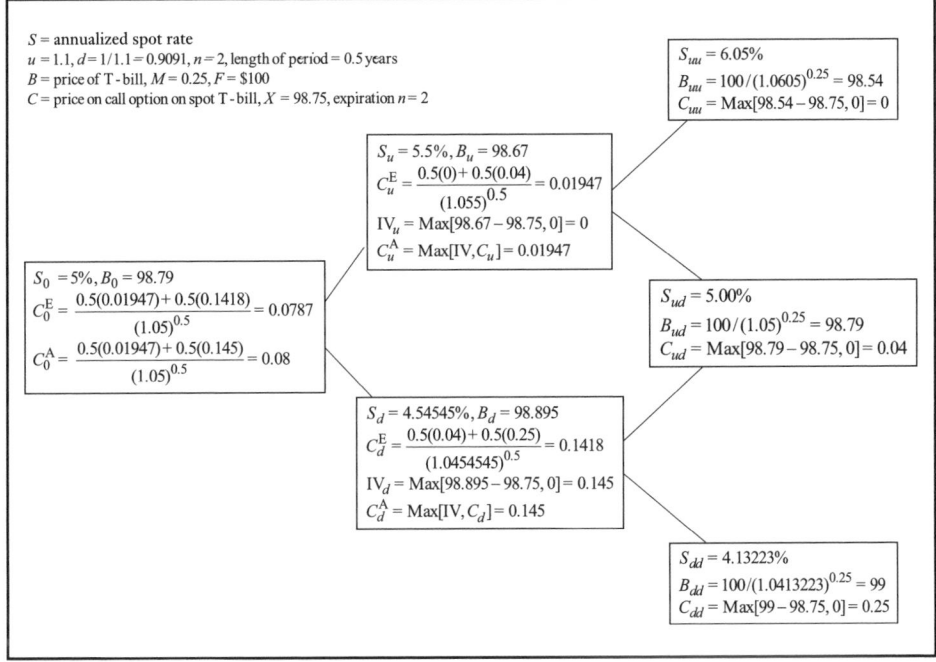

there is an equal probability of the spot rate increasing or decreasing in one period ($q = 0.5$), the two possible call values in period 1 are 0.01947 and 0.1418:

$$C_u = \frac{0.5(0) + 0.5(0.04)}{(1.055)^{0.5}} = 0.01947$$

$$C_d = \frac{0.5(0.04) + 0.5(0.25)}{(1.0454545)^{0.5}} = 0.1418$$

Rolling these call values to the current period and again determining the option's price as the present value of the expected cash flow, we obtain a price on the European T-bill call of 0.0787:

$$C_0^E = \frac{0.5(0.01947) + 0.5(0.1418)}{(1.05)^{0.5}} = 0.0787$$

If the call option were American, its two possible prices in period 1 are constrained to be the maximum of the binomial value (present value of next period's expected cash flows) or the intrinsic value (i.e., the value from exercising):

$$C_t^A = \text{Max}[C_t, \text{IV}]$$

In period 1, the IV slightly exceeds the binomial value when the spot rate is 4.54545%. As a result, the American call price is equal to its IV of 0.145 (see exhibit 15.3). Rolling this price and the upper rate's price of 0.01947 to the current period yields a price for the American T-bill call of 0.08. This price slightly exceeds the European value of 0.0787, reflecting the early exercise advantage of the American option.

Futures T-Bill Call

If the call option were on a European T-bill futures contract, instead of a spot T-bill, with the futures and option having the same expiration, then the value of the futures option will be the same as the spot option. That is, at the expiration spot rates of 6.05%, 5%, and 4.13223%, the futures prices on the expiring contract would be equal to the spot prices (98.54, 98.79, and 99), and the corresponding IVs of the European futures call would be 0, 0.04, and 0.25 – the same as the spot call's IV. Thus, when we roll these call values back to the

Exhibit 15.4   Binomial tree of spot rates and T-bill futures put prices

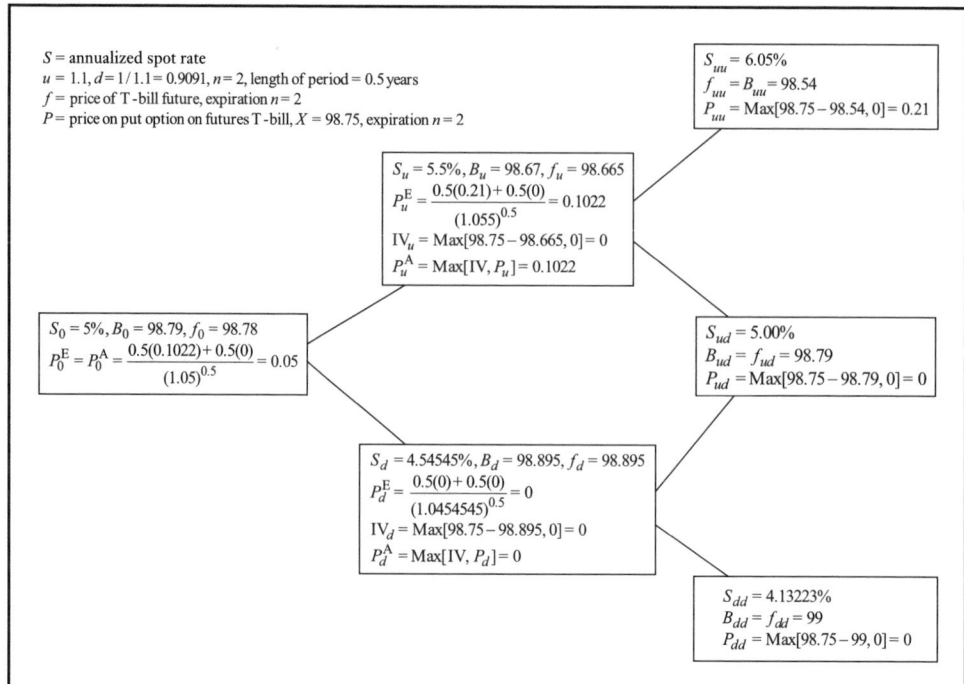

present period, we end up with the price on the European futures call of 0.0787 – the same as the European spot.

If the futures call option were American, then the option prices at each node need to be constrained to be the maximum of the binomial value or the futures option's IV. The IV of the futures call in period 1 is 0 when the spot rate is 5.5% (IV = Max[98.665 – 98.75, 0] = 0) and 0.145 when the rate is 4.54545% (IV = Max[98.895 – 97.75, 0] = 0.145). The corresponding prices of the American futures option would therefore be the same as the spot option: 0.01947 and 0.145. Rolling these prices to the current period yields a price on the American T-bill futures call of 0.08 – the same price as the American spot option.[2]

T-Bill Put

In the case of a spot or futures T-bill put, their prices can be determined given a binomial tree of spot rates and their corresponding spot and futures prices. Exhibit 15.4 shows the binomial

valuation of a European T-bill futures put with an exercise price of 98.75 and expiration of 1 year (2 periods). At the expiration spot rate of 6.05%, the put is in-the-money with an IV of 0.21, and at the spot rates of 5% and 4.13223% the put is out-of-the-money. In period 1, the two possible values for the European put are 0.1022 and 0. Since these values exceed or equal their IV, they would also be the prices of the put if it were American. Rolling these values to the current period, we obtain the price for the futures put of 0.05.

It should be noted that the put price of 0.05 is consistent with the put–call futures parity relation defined in chapter 14. That is:

$$P_0 - C_0 = \frac{X - f_0}{(1 + R_f)^T} = -\frac{f_0 - X}{(1 + R_f)^T}$$

$$P_0 = C_0 - \frac{f_0 - X}{(1 + R_f)^T}$$

$$= 0.0787 - \frac{98.78 - 98.75}{(1.05)^{0.5}} = 0.05$$

Exhibit 15.5   Binomial tree: caplet and floorlet

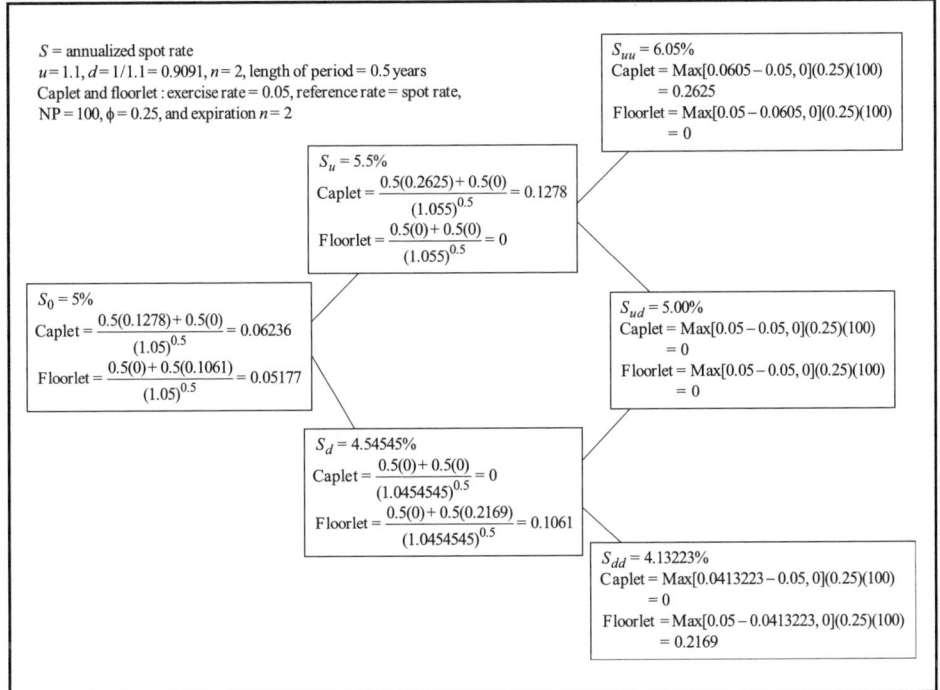

15.5.2 Valuing a Caplet and Floorlet with a Binomial Tree

The price of a caplet or floorlet can also be valued using a binomial tree of the option's reference rate. For example, consider an interest rate call on the spot rate defined by our binomial tree, with an exercise rate of 5%, time period applied to the payoff of $\phi = 0.25$, and notional principal of $NP = 100$. As shown in exhibit 15.5, the interest rate call is in-the-money at expiration only at the spot rate of 6.05%. At this rate, the caplet's payoff is 0.2625 ($= (0.0605 - 0.05)(0.25)(100)$). In period 1, the value of the caplet is 0.1278 ($= [0.5(0.2625) + 0.5(0)]/(1.055)^{0.5}$) at spot rate 5.5% and 0 at spot rate 4.54545%. Rolling these values to the current period, in turn, yields a price on the interest rate call of 0.06236 ($= [0.5(0.1278) + 0.5(0)]/(1.05)^{0.5}$). In contrast, an interest rate put with similar features would be in-the-money at expiration at the spot rate of 4.13223%, with a payoff of 0.2169 ($= (0.05 - 0.0413223)(0.25)(100)$) and out-of-the-money

at spot rates 5% and 6.05%. In period 1, the floorlet's values would be 0.1061 ($= [0.5(0) + 0.5(0.2169)]/(1.0454545)^{0.5}$) at spot rate 4.454545% and 0 at spot rate 6.05%. Rolling these values to the present period, we obtain a price on the floorlet of 0.05177 ($= [0.5(0) + 0.5(0.1061)]/(1.05)^{0.5}$).

Since a cap is a series of caplets, its price is simply equal to the sum of the values of the individual caplets making up the cap. To price a cap, we can use a binomial tree to price each caplet and then aggregate the caplet values to obtain the value of the cap. Similarly, the value of a floor can be found by summing the values of the floorlets comprising the floor.

15.5.3 Valuing T-Bond Options with a Binomial Tree

The T-bill underlying the spot or futures T-bill option is a *fixed-deliverable bill*; that is, the features of the bill (maturity of 91 days and principal of $1m) do not change during the life of the option. In contrast, the T-bond or

Exhibit 15.6   Binomial tree: spot rates, T-bond prices, and T-bond futures prices

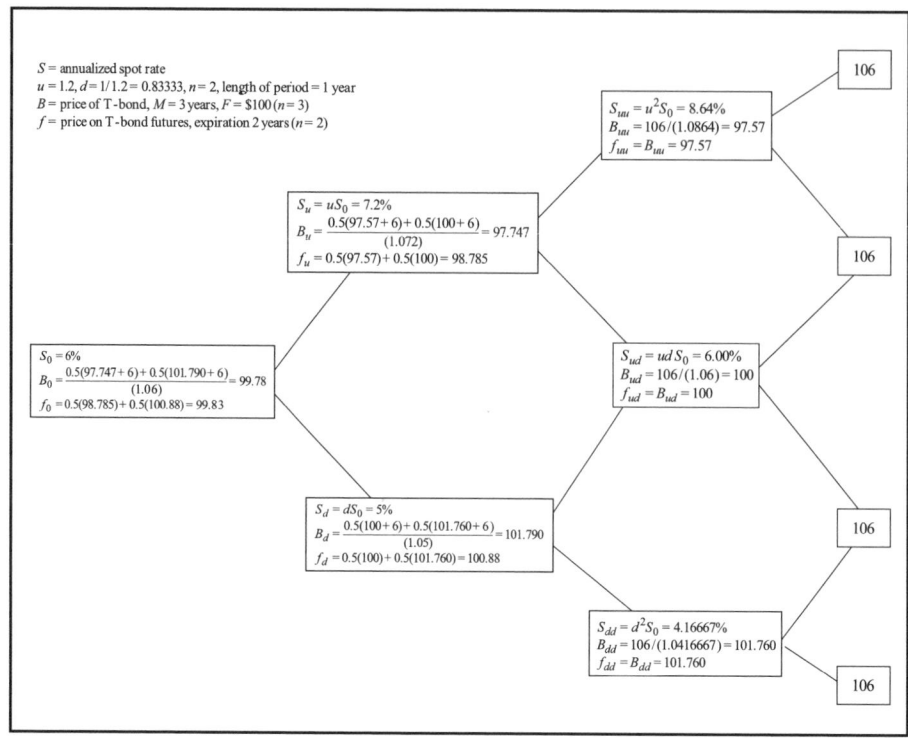

T-note underlying a T-bond or T-note option or futures option is a specified T-bond or note or the bond from an eligible group that is most likely to be delivered. Because of the clause on a T-bond or note option or futures option, the first step in valuing the option is to determine the values of the specified T-bond (or bond most likely to be delivered) at the various nodes on the binomial tree, using the same methodology as we used in chapter 9 to value a coupon bond.

As an example, consider an OTC spot option on a T-bond with a 6% annual coupon, face value of $100, and with 3 years left to maturity. In valuing the bond, suppose we have a 2-period binomial tree of risk-free spot rates, with the length of each period being 1 year, the estimated upward and downward parameters being $u = 1.2$ and $d = 0.8333$, and the current spot rate being 6% (see exhibit 15.6). To value the T-bond, we start at the bond's maturity (end of period 3) where the bond's value is equal to the principal plus the coupon, 106. We next determine the three possible values in

period 2 given the three possible spot rates. As shown in exhibit 15.6, the three possible values of the T-bond in period 2 are 97.57 ($= 106/$ 1.084), 100 ($= 106/1.06$), and 101.760 ($= 106/$ 1.0416667). Given these values, we next roll the tree to the first period and determine the two possible values. The values in that period are equal to the present values of the T-bond's expected cash flows in period 2; that is:

$$B_u = \frac{0.5[97.57 + 6] + 0.5[100 + 6]}{1.072} = 97.747$$

$$B_d = \frac{0.5[100 + 6] + 0.5[101.760 + 6]}{1.05} = 101.79$$

Finally, using the bond values in period 1, we roll the tree to the current period where we determine the value of the T-bond to be 99.78:

$$B_0 = \frac{0.5[97.747 + 6] + 0.5[101.79 + 6]}{1.06} = 99.78$$

Exhibit 15.6 also shows the prices on a 2-year futures contract on the 3-year, 6% T-bond.

Exhibit 15.7 Binomial tree: T-bond call prices

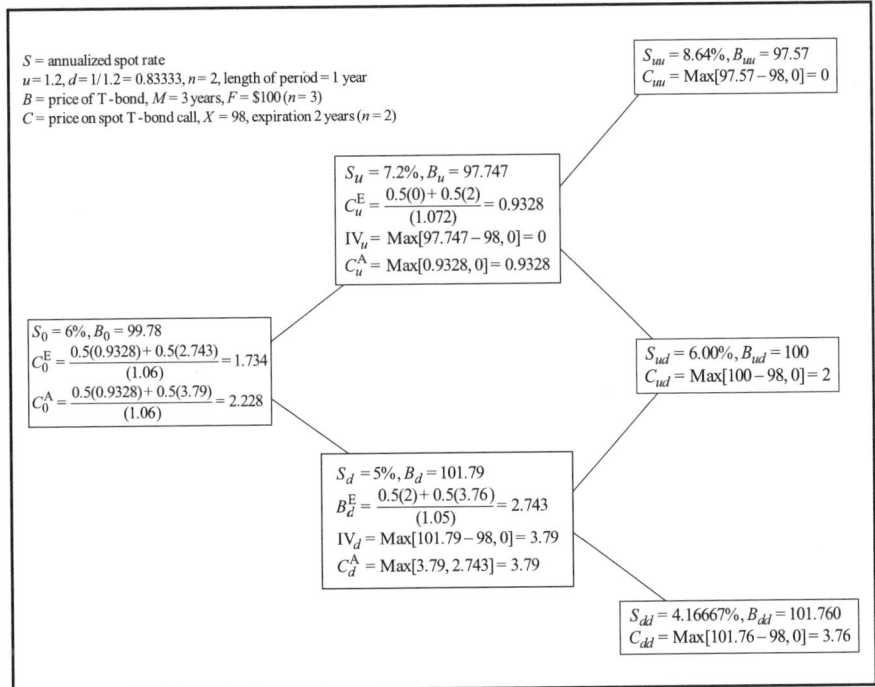

The prices are generated by assuming a risk-neutral market. As shown, at expiration (period 2) the three possible futures prices are equal to their spot prices: 97.57, 100, 101.76; in period 1, the two futures prices are equal to their expected spot prices: $f_u = E(B_T) = 0.5(97.57) + 0.5(100) = 98.785$ and $f_d = E(B_T) = 0.5(100) + 0.5(101.76) = 100.88$; in the current period, the futures price is $f_0 = E(B_T) = 0.5(98.785) + 0.5(100.88) = 99.83$.

Spot T-Bond Call

Suppose we want to value a European call on the T-bond, with the call having an exercise price of 98 and expiration of 2 years. At the option's expiration, the underlying T-bond has three possible values: 97.57, 100, and 101.76. The 98 T-bill call's respective IVs are therefore 0, 2, and 3.76 (see exhibit 15.7). Given these values, the call's possible values in period 1 are 0.9328 $(= (0.5(0) + 0.5(2))/1.072)$ and 2.743 $(= (0.5(2) + 0.5(3.76))/1.05)$. Rolling these values to the current period, we obtain the price

on the European T-bond call of 1.734 $(= (0.5(0.9328) + 0.5(2.743))/1.06)$. If the call option were American, then its value at each node is the greater of the value of holding the call or the value from exercising. As we did in valuing American T-bill options, this valuation requires constraining the American price to be the maximum of the binomial value or the IV. In this example, if the T-bond option were American, then in period 1 the option's price would be equal to its IV of 3.79 at the lower rate. Rolling this price and the upper rate's price of 0.9328 to the current period yields a price of 2.228.

Futures T-Bond Call

If the European call were an option on a futures contract on the 3-year, 6% T-bond (or if that bond were the most likely to-be-delivered bond on the futures contract), with the futures contract expiring at the same time as the option (end of period 2), then the value of the futures option will be the same as the spot. That is, at expiration the futures prices on the expiring contract would be equal to the spot prices, and the corresponding IVs of the European futures call would be the same as the spot call's IV. Thus, when we roll these call values back to the present period, we end up with the price on the European futures call being the same as the European spot: 1.734. If the futures call were American, then at the spot rate of 5% in period 1, its IV would be 2.88 ($= \text{Max}[100.88 - 98, \ 0]$), exceeding the binomial value of 2.743. Rolling the 2.88 value to the current period yields a price on the American futures option of 1.798 ($= 0.5(0.9328) + 0.5(2.88)$) – this price differs from the American spot option price of 2.228.

T-Bond Put

Suppose we want to value a European put on a spot or futures T-bond with the put having similar terms to the call. Given the bond's possible prices at expiration of 97.57, 100, and 101.76, the corresponding IVs of the put are 0.43, 0, and 0. In period 1, the put's two possible values are 0.2006 ($= (0.5(0.43) + 0.5(0))/1.072$) and 0. Rolling these values to the current period yields a price on the European put of 0.0946 ($= (0.5(0.2006) + 0.5(0))/1.06$). Note that if the spot put were American, then its possible prices in period 1 would be 0.253 and 0, and its current price would be 0.119 ($= (0.5(0.253) + 0.5(0))/1.06$); if the futures put were American, there would be no exercise advantage in period 1 and thus the price would be equal to its European value of 0.0946.

15.5.4   Arbitrage-Free Feature of the Binomial Tree

In chapter 10, we explained how the calibration model has the feature that it prices an option-free bond to equal its arbitrage-free equilibrium price (price obtained by discounting cash flows by spot rates) and how it values a bond's embedded options as arbitrage-free prices. The same arbitrage-free feature also applies to the binomial valuation of exchange-traded or OTC options on a bond whose value is determined by a binomial tree of spot rates calibrated to the current spot yield curve. To see this,

suppose the binomial tree of spot rates shown in exhibit 15.6 were calibrated to the current spot yield curve. The binomial price of the 3-year 6% bond would, in turn, be equal to the value of a portfolio of three stripped bonds: 1-year zero-coupon paying $6, a 2-year zero paying $6, and a 3-year zero paying $106. This point was examined in chapter 10 and is illustrated in exhibit 15.8. The exhibit shows the prices on the 1-year, 2-year, and 3-year stripped securities as 5.66, 5.33, and 88.79, respectively. Summing these prices, we obtain a portfolio value of 99.78 – the same value as the 3-year 6% T-bond. Thus, the bond valuation approach yields a bond value equal to the value of a portfolio of stripped zero-coupon bonds.

In addition to satisfying the arbitrage-free condition for the bond, the model also values the option as an arbitrage-free price. In this example, the 1.734 value of the spot European T-bond call is also equal to the value of a replicating portfolio consisting of a 1-year zero and a 2-year zero constructed so that next year the portfolio is worth 0.9328 if the spot rate is 7.2% and 2.743 if the spot rate is 5%. The replicating portfolio is formed by solving for the number of 1-year zero-coupon bonds, n_1, and number of 2-year zeros, n_2, where:

$$n_1(6) + n_2(5.597) = 0.9328$$
$$n_1(6) + n_2(5.71428) = 2.743$$

Solving for n_1 and n_2, we obtain $n_1 = -14.1711$ and $n_2 = 15.35812$. This replicating portfolio yields possible cash flows next period that match the option's cash flows of 0.9328 and 2.743. The value of this portfolio is also equal to 1.734 ($= (-14.1711)(5.66) + (15.35812)(5.3355)$) – the equilibrium price of the option. The two call values in period 1 can also be shown to be equal to the values of their replicating portfolio. Thus, the binomial model yields an arbitrage-free price in which the value of the option is equal to the value of the replicating portfolio.

15.5.5   Realism

In the above examples, the binomial trees' 6-month and 1-year steps were too simplistic. Ideally, binomial trees need to be subdivided

Exhibit 15.8 Binomial tree: 1-year, 2-year, and 3-year stripped securities formed from 3-year, 6% T-bond

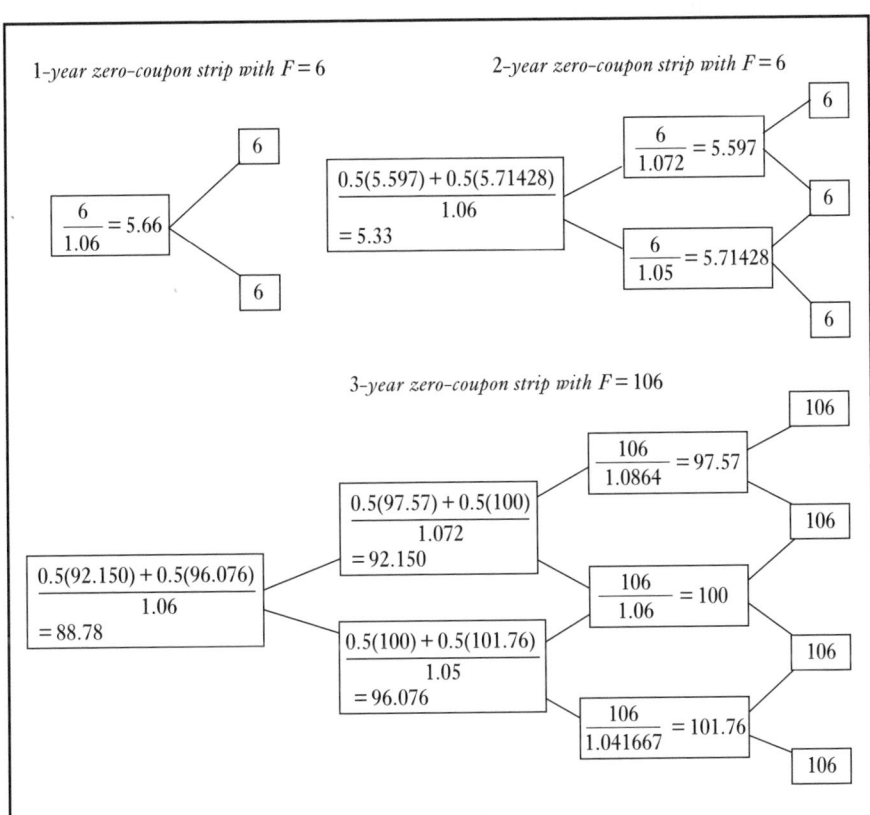

into a number of periods. In pricing a 5-year T-bond, for example, we might use 1-month steps and a 5-year horizon. This would, in turn, translate into a 60-period tree with the length of each period being 1 month. By doing this, we would have a distribution of 60 possible T-note values one period from maturity. A spot option on the 2-year T-note or a T-note futures option in which this 5-year note was the most likely to be delivered would translate into a 24-period tree with a distribution at expiration of 25 possible futures prices. If we use 1-week steps instead of monthly steps, then we would have a 260-period tree for the 5-year T-note and a 104-period tree for the 2-year option. While the question of how much we need to subdivide the tree to obtain a realistic model is unresolved,

we can say that, in general, by subdividing we do make the length of each period smaller, making the binomial assumption that the spot rate will either increase or decrease more plausible, and we do increase the number of possible rates and prices at expiration, which again adds realism.

In addition to subdividing the tree, the practical application of the tree also requires estimating the binomial tree's interest rates. In chapter 10, we examined two general approaches to estimating binomial interest rate movements – estimating the u and d parameters based on the rate's mean and variability, and using a calibration model in which the tree is calibrated to the current spot yield curve. Of the two approaches, the calibration model is the one used by most practitioners.

15.6 PRICING INTEREST RATE OPTIONS WITH THE BLACK FUTURES OPTION MODEL

15.6.1 Black Futures Model

An extension of the B–S OPM that is sometimes used to price interest rate options is the Black futures option model. The model is defined as follows:

$$C_0^* = [f_0 N(d_1) - X N(d_2)]e^{-R_f T}$$
$$P_0^* = [X(1 - N(d_2)) - f_0(1 - N(d_1))]e^{-R_f T}$$
$$d_1 = \frac{\ln(f_0/X) + (\sigma_f^2/2)T}{\sigma_f \sqrt{T}}$$
$$d_2 = d_1 - \sigma_f \sqrt{T}$$

where:

σ_f^2 = variance of the logarithmic return of futures prices = $V(\ln(f_n/f_0))$

T = time to expiration expressed as a proportion of a year

R_f = continuously compounded annual risk-free rate (if simple annual rate is R, the continuously compounded rate is $\ln(1 + R)$)

$N(d)$ = cumulative normal probability (this probability can be looked up in a standard normal probability table or by using the formula below)

$$N(d) = 1 - n(d), \quad \text{for } d < 0$$
$$N(d) = n(d), \quad \text{for } d > 0$$

where:

$$n(d) = 1 - 0.5[1 + 0.196854(|d|)$$
$$+ 0.115194(|d|)^2 + 0.0003444(|d|)^3$$
$$+ 0.019527(|d|)^4]^{-4}$$

$|d|$ = absolute value of d

Example: T-Bill Futures

Consider the European futures T-bill call options we priced earlier in which the futures option had an exercise price of 98.75 and expiration of 1 year and the current futures price was $f_0 = 98.7876$. If the simple risk-free rate is

5%, implying a continuously compound rate of 4.879% ($= \ln(1.05)$), and the annualized standard deviation of the futures logarithmic return, $\sigma(\ln(f_n/f_0))$, is 0.00158, then using the Black futures model the price of the T-bill futures call would be 0.0792.

$$C_0^* = [98.7876(0.595462)$$
$$- 98.75(0.594847)]e^{-(0.04879)(1)}$$
$$= 0.0792$$

where:

$$d_1 = \frac{\ln(98.7876/98.75) + ((0.00158)^2/2)(1)}{0.00158\sqrt{1}}$$
$$= 0.24175$$
$$d_2 = 0.24175 - 0.00158\sqrt{1} = 0.24017$$
$$N(0.24175) = 0.595462$$
$$N(0.24017) = 0.594847$$

Example: T-Bond Futures

As a second example, consider 1-year put and call options on a CBOT T-bond futures contract, with each option having an exercise price of $100,000. Suppose the current futures price is $96,115, the futures volatility is $\sigma(\ln(f_n/f_0)) =$ 0.10, and the continuously compound risk-free rate is 0.065. Using the Black futures option model, the price of the call option would be $2,137 and the price of the put would be $5,777:

$$C_0^* = [\$96,115(0.36447)$$
$$- \$100,000(0.327485)]e^{-(0.065)(1)}$$
$$= \$2,137$$
$$P_0^* = [\$100,000(1 - 0.327485)$$
$$- \$96,115(1 - 0.36447)]e^{-(0.065)(1)}$$
$$= \$5,777$$

where:

$$d_1 = \frac{\ln(96,115/100,000) + (0.01/2)(1)}{0.10\sqrt{1}}$$
$$= -0.34625$$
$$d_2 = -0.34625 - 0.10\sqrt{1} = -0.44625$$
$$N(-0.34625) = 0.36447$$
$$N(-0.44625) = 0.327485$$

It should be noted that the call and futures prices are also consistent with put–call futures parity:

$$P_0^* - C_0^* = \text{PV}(X - f_0)$$
$$P_0^* = (X - f_0)e^{-R_f T} + C_0^*$$
$$= (\$100,000 - \$96,115)e^{-(0.065)(1)}$$
$$+ \$2,137 = \$5,777$$

Also, note that the Black model can be used to price a spot option. In this case, the current futures price, f_0, is set equal to its equilibrium price as determined by the carrying-cost model: $f_0 = S_0(1 + R_f)^T -$ (Accrued interest at T). If the carrying-cost model holds, the price obtained using the Black model will be equal to the price obtained using the B–S OPM.

15.6.2 Pricing Caplets and Floorlets with the Black Futures Option Model

The Black futures option model also can be extended to pricing caplets and floorlets by (1) substituting T^* for T in the equation for C^* (for a caplet) or P^* (for a floorlet), where T^* is the time to expiration on the option plus the time period applied to the interest rate payoff time period, ϕ: $T^* = T + \phi$; (2) using an annual continuous compounded risk-free rate for period T^* instead of T; (3) multiplying the Black adjusted-futures option model by the notional principal times the time period: (NP) ϕ.

$$C_0^* = \phi(\text{NP})[RN(d_1) - R_X N(d_2)]e^{-R_f T^*}$$
$$P_0^* = \phi(\text{NP})[R_X(1 - N(d_2))$$
$$- R(1 - N(d_1))]e^{-R_f T^*}$$
$$d_1 = \frac{\ln(R/R_X) + (\sigma^2/2)T}{\sigma\sqrt{T}}$$
$$d_2 = d_1 - \sigma\sqrt{T}$$

Example: Pricing a Caplet

Consider a caplet with an exercise rate of $X = 7\%$, NP $= \$100,000$, $\phi = 0.25$, expiration $= T = 0.25$ year, and reference rate $=$ LIBOR. If the current LIBOR were $R = 6\%$, the estimated annualized standard deviation of the LIBOR's

logarithmic return were 0.2, and the continuously compounded risk-free rate were 5.8629%, then using the Black model, the price of the caplet would be 4.34.

$$C_0^* = 0.25(\$100,000)[0.06(0.067845)$$
$$- 0.07(0.055596)]e^{-(0.058629)(0.5)}$$
$$= 4.34$$

where:

$$d_1 = \frac{\ln(0.06/0.07) + (0.04/2)(0.25)}{0.2\sqrt{0.25}}$$
$$= -1.49151$$
$$d_2 = d_1 - 0.2\sqrt{0.25} = -1.59151$$
$$N(-1.49151) = 0.067845$$
$$N(-1.59151) = 0.055596$$

Example: Pricing a Cap

Suppose the caplet represented part of a contract that caps a 2-year floating-rate loan of $100,000 at 7% for a 3-month period. The cap consist of seven caplets, with expirations of $T = 0.25$ years, 0.5, 0.75, 1, 1.25, 1.5, and 1.75. The value of the cap is equal to the sum of the values of the caplets comprising the cap. If we assume a flat yield curve such that the continuous rate of 5.8629% applies, and we use the same volatility of 0.2 for each caplet, then the value of the cap would be $254.38:

Expiration	Price of caplet
0.25	4.34
0.50	15.29
0.75	26.74
1.00	37.63
1.25	47.73
1.50	57.04
1.75	65.61
	254.38

In practice, different volatilities for each caplet are used in valuing a cap or floor. The different volatilities are referred to as spot volatilities. They are often estimated by calculating the implied volatility on comparable Eurodollar futures options.

15.7 CONCLUSION

In this chapter, we've examined how interest rate options can be used to manage different types of fixed-income investment and debt management positions, and how the binomial interest rate tree and the Black futures model can be used to price interest rate options. In contrast to interest rate futures that fix the rate on a loan or an investment, options allow investors and borrowers to attain limits on the rates they can earn on their investments or must pay on their loans, while still allowing them to benefit if rates move in a favorable direction. In the final two chapters, we examine another popular derivative used extensively in managing interest rate positions – interest rate swaps.

KEY TERMS

Collar	Barrier Options	Cumulative Cap
Corridor	Knock-Out Option	(Q-Cap)
Reverse Collar	Knock-In Option	Fixed-Deliverable
Reverse Corridor	Average Cap	Bill

PROBLEMS AND QUESTIONS

Note on problems: for problems requiring a number of calculations, the reader may want to use Excel.

1. The Prudential Money Market Fund (question 1 in chapter 13) expects interest rates to be higher in September when it plans to invest its $9m cash flow in 91-day T-bills, but is worried that rates could decrease. Suppose there is a September T-bill futures call contract with an exercise price of 93 (IMM index), trading at 5, and expiring at the same time as the September T-bill futures contract.

   a. How many September T-bill futures calls does Prudential need to lock in a minimum rate on its investments? (Do not assume perfect divisibility.) What is the cost?
   b. Assuming the fund's $9m cash inflow comes at the same time as the September T-bill futures call contract expires, follow the outline table below to determine the fund's option-hedged T-bill yield for possible spot discount rates at the option's expiration date of 6%, 6.25%, 6.5%, 7%, 7.5%, and 8%.

(1) Spot discount rates (%)	(2) Spot price = futures price	(3) Call profit/loss	(4) Hedged investment funds	(5) Number of bills	(6) YTM
6.00					
6.25					
6.50					
7.00					
7.50					
8.00					

2. Suppose the Prudential Money Market Fund in question 1 plans to invest its $9m cash flow in a 90-day CD offered by Sun Bank paying the LIBOR. Suppose the fund decides to hedge the September investment by buying an interest rate put from Sun Bank. The floorlet has the following terms:

- Exercise rate of 7%
- Payoff at the maturity of the CD
- Reference rate of LIBOR
- Time period of 90 days (0.25)
- Notional principal of $9m
- Expiration at the time of the September cash flow investment
- Cost of floorlet is $50,000, payable at expiration.

Following the table outline below, determine the fund's hedged yield for possible spot LIBORs at the option's expiration date of 6%, 6.5%, 7%, 7.5%, and 8%.

(1) LIBOR (%)	(2) Interest rate put	(3) Cost of the option at T	(4) Interest received on CD at its maturity	(5) Total revenue at maturity	(6) Annualized hedged rate
6.00					
6.50					
7.00					
7.50					
8.00					

3. The Patton Development Company (question 3, chapter 13) closed a deal in January with local officials to develop a new office building. The project is expected to begin in June and take 272 days to complete. The cost of the development is expected to be $16m, with the L. B. Insurance Company providing the permanent financing of the development once the construction is completed. Patton Development has obtained a 270-day construction loan from Star Financing Company. Star Financing will disperse funds to Patton at the beginning of the project in June, with the interest rate on the loan being set equal to the LIBOR plus 150 BP. The loan will have a maturity of 270 days with the principal and interest on the loan to be paid at maturity. Star is also willing to sell Patton an interest rate call with the following terms:

- Exercise rate of 10%
- Payoff at the maturity of the loan
- LIBOR reference rate
- Time period of 270 days or 0.75 per year
- Notional principal of $16m
- Expiration at the June start of the loan
- Cost of the caplet is $75,000.

Following the outline table below, determine Patton's hedged loan rate for possible LIBORs at the June date of 8%, 9%, 10%, 11%, 11.5%, and 12%.

(1) LIBOR (%)	(2) Interest rate call	(3) Cost of the option at T	(4) Interest paid on loan at its maturity	(5) Total cost at maturity	(6) Annualized hedged rate (1/0.75) multiple
8.00					
9.00					
10.00					
11.00					
11.50					
12.00					

4. A fixed-income fund manager plans to sell twenty $100,000 face value T-bonds from her government fund in March. The T-bonds she plans to sell pay 7% interest and are currently priced at 105. At the anticipated selling date, the bonds will have 15 years to maturity and no accrued interest. The manager believes that long-term rates could decrease but does not want to risk selling the bond at lower prices if rates increase. For $20,000, the manager can purchase an OTC T-bond option on her bonds from a dealer at an exercise price equal to the current price and expiration coinciding with her March T-bond sales date.

a. Describe the OTC option and its terms.
b. Show in a table the manager's option-hedged revenue (do not include option cost) for possible spot T-bond prices at the March sale of 98, 99, 100, 101, 102, 103, 104, 105, 106, 107, 108, 109, and 110. Assume the manager will exercise her option, if it is feasible (instead of closing), and that she will sell her bond in the market, if it is not feasible.

5. Suppose the fixed-income fund manager in question 4 were expecting a cash flow of $2,100,000 in March and planned to invest the fund in 20 100,000 T-bonds. Suppose the T-bonds she plans to buy pay 7% interest, have 15 years to maturity, and are currently priced at 105. At the anticipated purchase date, assume such bonds will have no accrued interest. The manager believes that long-term rates could increase but does not want to risk buying the bond at higher prices if rates decrease. For $20,000, the manager can purchase an OTC T-bond option on the 20 bonds from a dealer at an exercise price equal to the current price and expiration coinciding with her March T-bond purchase date.

a. Describe the OTC option and its terms.
b. Show in a table the manager's option-hedged cost (do not include option cost) for possible spot T-bond prices at the March purchase date of 98, 99, 100, 101, 102, 103, 104, 105, 106, 107, 108, 109, and 110. Assume the manager will exercise her option, if it is feasible (instead of closing), and that she will buy her bonds in the market, if it is not feasible.

6. First American Bank (from question 2, chapter 13) is planning to make a $20m short-term loan to Midwest Mining Company. In the loan contract, Midwest agrees to pay the principal and an interest of 12% (annual) at the end of 180 days. Since First American sells more 90-day CDs than 180-day CDs, it is planning to finance the loan by selling a 90-day CD now at the prevailing LIBOR of 8.25%, then 90 days later (mid-September) sell another 90-day CD at the prevailing LIBOR. The bank would like to minimize its exposure to interest rate risk on its future CD sale but would also like to benefit if CD rates decrease. Suppose the September Eurodollar futures put with an exercise price of 92 (IMM index) is trading at 2.

a. How many September Eurodollar futures puts would First American Bank need in order to effectively hedge its September CD sale against interest rate changes? Assume perfect divisibility.

b. Assume that the Eurodollar futures are closed at the LIBOR and the Eurodollar futures and futures options expire at the same time as the bank's first CD. Following the outline table below, determine the total amount of funds the bank would need to raise on its September CD, the bank's debt obligations at the end of the 180-day period in December, and the bank's hedged rates for the entire 180-day period (assume a 30/360 day count convention) for the following LIBORs at the options and first CD maturity date of 7%, 7.5%, 8%, 8.5%, 9%, 9.5%, and 10%.

(1) LIBOR	(2) Spot and futures price	(3) Put profit	(4) Debt on Sept-issued CD	(5) Sept funds needed	(6) Dec debt obligation	(7) Hedged rate for 180 days
0.070						
0.075						
0.080						
0.085						
0.090						
0.095						
0.100						

c. Suppose a money-center bank is willing to sell First American an interest rate call option tied to the LIBOR with a reference rate of 8.25% for $12,500, payable at the option's expiration. Define the terms of the caplet such that they will match First American Bank's September debt.

d. Assuming First American Bank buys the caplet, follow the outline table below to show the total amount of funds it would need to raise on its September CD, the bank's debt obligations at the end of the 180-day period in December, and the bank's caplet hedged rates for the entire 180-day period (assume a 30/360 day count convention) for the following LIBORs at the options and first CD maturity date of 7%, 7.5%, 8%, 8.5%, 9%, 9.5%, and 10%.

(1) LIBOR	(2) Interest rate call payoff	(3) Cost of caplet	(4) Sept debt on CD	(5) Sept funds needed	(6) Dec debt obligation	(7) Hedged rate for 180 days
0.070						
0.075						
0.080						
0.085						
0.090						
0.095						
0.100						

7. Mr Slife (questions 4 and 5 in chapter 13) anticipates a liability of $10m in June and plans to sell his baseline bond portfolio. The fund currently is worth $10m, has an "A" quality rating, weighted average maturity of 15 years, duration of 7 years, annual coupon rate of 7.5%, and YTM of 7.5% (note that the bond portfolio is currently worth its par value). Suppose Mr Slife believes that long-term rates will decrease, but is also afraid that they could increase. Suppose that there is a 100 June T-bond futures put trading for 1-16, where the underlying June T-bond futures contract is trading at 100 and the T-bond most likely to

be delivered on the futures contract has a YTM of 5.5%, maturity of 15 years, duration of 9 years, and trading at par.

  a. Using the price-sensitivity model, explain how Mr Slife could hedge his June bond portfolio sale against interest rate risk by buying a 100 June T-bond futures put.

  b. Suppose long-term interest rates increase over the period such that at the June expiration Mr Slife's baseline portfolio is trading at 96 of par, the price on the expiring June T-bond contract (f_T) is 94, and the price on the 100 T-bond futures put is trading at its intrinsic value. Determine Mr Slife's revenue from selling his baseline bond portfolio, his cash flow on the 100 T-bond futures put contracts, and his total revenue.

  c. Suppose long-term interest rates decrease over the period such that at the June expiration Mr Slife's baseline portfolio is trading at 105 of par, the price on the expiring June T-bond contract (f_T) is 106, and the price on the 100 T-bond futures put is trading at its intrinsic value. Determine Mr Slife's revenue from selling his baseline bond portfolio, his cash flow on the 100 T-bond futures put contracts, and his total revenue.

8. Suppose West Bank offers Roberts Department Store a $15m variable rate loan to finance its inventory along with a cap. The variable rate loan has a maturity of 270 days (0.75 of a year), starts on December 20, and is reset the next two quarters. The initial quarterly rate is equal to 9.5%/4, the other rates are set on 3/20 and 6/20 equal to one fourth of the annual LIBOR on those dates plus 100 basis points: (LIBOR% + 1%)/4. The cap West Bank is offering Roberts has the following terms:

- Two caplets with expiration dates of 3/20 and 6/20
- The cap rate on each caplet is 9.5%
- The time period for each caplet is 0.25 per year
- The payoffs for each caplet are at the interest payment dates
- The reference rate is the LIBOR
- Notional principal is $15m
- The cost of the cap is $15,000.

Following the outline table below, determine the company's quarterly interest payments, caplet cash flows, hedged interest payments (interest minus caplet cash flow), and hedged rate as a proportion of a $15m loan (do not include cap cost) for each period (12/20, 3/20, and 6/20) given the following rates: LIBOR = 10% on 3/20 and LIBOR = 9% on 6/20.

(1) Date	(2) LIBOR	(3) Cap payoff on payment date	(4) Loan interest on payment date	(5) Hedged debt	(6) Hedged rate	(7) Unhedged rate
Dec 20						
Mar 20						
Jun 20						
Sep 20						

9. Given the following IMM Eurodollar futures put options:

- March Eurodollar futures put with exercise price of 91 (IMM index) selling at 2.
- June Eurodollar futures put with exercise price of 91 (IMM index) selling at 2.1.

  a. Explain how Roberts Department Store in question 8 could alternatively attain a cap on its variable-rate loan with a Eurodollar futures strip formed with the above options. What is the cost of the strip?

b. Following the outline table below, determine the company's quarterly interest payments, option cash flow, hedged interest payments (interest minus option cash flow), and hedged rate as a proportion of a $15m loan (do not include option cost) for each period (12/20, 3/20, and 6/20) given the following rates: LIBOR = 10% on 3/20 and LIBOR = 9% on 6/20. Assume the interest payment dates and option expiration dates coincide and that the day count convention is 30/360.

(1) Date	(2) LIBOR	(3) Futures and spot price	(4) Put cash flow at option expiration	(5) Value of put CF at payment date	(6) Loan interest on payment date	(7) Hedged debt	(8) Hedged rate	(9) Unhedged rate
Dec 20								
Mar 20								
Jun 20								

10. ABC Trust is planning to invest $15m in a Commerce Bank 1-year floating-rate note paying LIBOR plus 150 basis points. The investment starts on 3/20 at 9% (when the LIBOR = 7.5%) and is then reset the next three quarters on 6/20, 9/20, and 12/20. ABC Trust would like to establish a floor on the rates it obtains on the note. A money center bank is offering ABC a floor for $100,000 with the following terms corresponding to the floating-rate note:

- The floor consists of three floorlets coinciding with the reset dates on the note
- Exercise rate on the floorlets = 7%
- Notional principal = $15m
- Reference rate = LIBOR
- Time period on the payoffs is 0.25
- Payoff is paid on the payment date on the notes
- Cost of the floor is $100,000 and is paid on 3/20.

Calculate and show, following the outline table below, ABC's quarterly interest receipts, floorlet cash flow, hedged interest revenue (interest plus floorlet cash flow), and hedged rate as a proportion of the $15m investment (do not include floor cost) given the LIBORs shown in the table.

(1) Date	(2) LIBOR	(3) Interest on FRN on payment date	(4) Floor payoff on payment date	(5) Hedged interest income	(6) Hedged rate	(7) Unhedged rate
Mar 20	0.075					
Jun 20	0.070					
Sep 20	0.065					
Dec 20	0.060					
Mar 20						

11. Given the following IMM Eurodollar futures call options:

- June Eurodollar futures with exercise price of 93 (IMM index) selling at 2.
- September Eurodollar futures with exercise price of 93 (IMM index) selling at 2.1.
- December Eurodollar futures with exercise price of 93 (IMM index) selling at 2.2.

a. Explain how ABC Trust in question 10 could alternatively attain a floor on its floating-rate loan with a Eurodollar futures strip formed with the above options. What is the cost of the strip?

b. Following the outline table below, determine the company's quarterly interest receipts, option cash flow, hedged interest revenue (interest plus option cash flow), and hedged rate as a proportion of a $15m investment (do not include option cost) for each period given the following rates: LIBOR = 7.5% on 3/20, 7% on 6/20, 6.5% on 9/20, and 6% on 12/20. Assume the interest payment dates and option expiration dates coincide and that the day count convention is 30/360.

(1) Date	(2) LIBOR	(3) Futures and spot price	(4) Call cash flow at option expiration	(5) Value of CF at payment date	(6) Interest receipt on payment date	(7) Hedged income	(8) Hedged rate	(9) Unhedged rate
Mar 20								
Jun 20								
Sep 20								
Dec 20								

12. Suppose the Second National Bank sells XU Trust a 2-year $15m FRN paying the LIBOR plus 150 basis points. The note starts on 3/20 at 9% and is then reset the next seven quarters on dates 6/20, 9/20, and 12/20. Suppose a money center bank offers Second National a cap for $200,000 with the following terms corresponding to its floating-rate liability:

- The cap consists of seven caplets coinciding with the reset dates on the note
- Exercise rate on the caplets = 7%
- Notional principal = $15m
- Reference rate = LIBOR
- Time period on the payoffs is 0.25
- Payoff is paid on the payment date on the notes
- Cost of the cap is $200,000 and is paid on 3/20.

a. Show in a table Second National Bank's quarterly interest payments, caplet cash flows, hedged interest cost (interest minus caplet cash flow), and hedged rate as a proportion of the $15m FRN loan (do not include cap cost) for each period given the following rates: LIBOR = 7.5% on 3/20, 8% on 6/20, 9% on 9/20, 8% on 12/20, 7% on 3/20, 6.5% on 6/20, 6% on 12/20, and 5.5% on 12/20.

b. To help defray part of the cost of the cap, suppose Second National Bank decides to set up a collar by selling a floor to one of its customers with a floor rate of 6.5% for $150,000 with the following terms:

- The floor consists of seven floorlets coinciding with the reset dates on the note
- Exercise rate on the floorlets = 6.5%
- Notional principal = $15m
- Reference rate = LIBOR
- Time period on the payoffs is 0.25
- Payoff is paid on the payment date on the notes
- Cost of the floor is $150,000 and is paid on 3/20.

Evaluate Second National Bank's hedged interest costs using the collar given the interest rate scenario in 12a.

  c. Contrast Second National Bank's cap hedge with its collar hedge.

  d. Define another interest rate option position Second National Bank might use to defray the costs of its cap-hedged floating-rate liability.

13. Suppose the Second National Bank in question 12 decides to hedge its 2-year $15m FRN it sold to XU Trust (FRN terms: pays the LIBOR plus 150 BP; starts on 3/20/2004 at 9%; reset the next seven quarters on dates 6/20, 9/20, and 12/20) by buying a Q-cap (or cumulative cap) from a money center bank for $150,000 with the following terms corresponding to its floating-rate liability:

- The cap consists of seven caplets coinciding with the reset dates on the note
- Exercise rate on the caplets = 7%
- Notional principal = $15m
- Reference rate = LIBOR
- Time period on the payoffs is 0.25
- For the period from 3/20/2004 to 12/20/2004, the caplet will pay when the cumulative interest starting from the loan date 3/20/2004 hits $700,000
- For the period from 3/20/2005 to 12/20/2005, the caplet will pay when the cumulative interest starting from the loan date 3/20/2005 hits $700,000
- Payoff is paid on the payment date on the notes
- Cost of the cap is $150,000 and is paid on 3/20/2004.

  a. Using the table below for guidance, show Second National Bank's quarterly interest payments, caplet cash flows from the Q-cap, hedged interest cost (interest minus caplet cash flow), and hedged rate as a proportion of the $15m FRN loan (do not include Q-cap cost) for each period given the following interest rate scenarios: LIBOR = 7.5% on 3/20, 8% on 6/20, 9% on 9/20, 8% on 12/20, 7% on 3/20, 8% on 6/20, 9% on 12/20, and 10% on 12/20.

(1) Date	(2) LIBOR	(3) Interest paid on FRN on payment date	(4) Cumulative interest	(5) Q-cap payoff on payment date	(6) Hedged interest payment	(7) Hedged rate	(8) Unhedged rate
3/20/2004	0.075		337,500				
6/20/2004	0.08	337,500	693,750				
9/20/2004	0.09	356,250		0			
12/20/2004	0.08			75,000			
3/20/2005	0.07		318,750				
6/20/2005	0.08	318,750	675,000				
9/20/2005	0.09	356,250					
12/20/2005	0.10						
3/20/2006							

  b. Given the interest rate scenario in question 13a, show in a table Second National Bank's quarterly hedged interest costs if it were to hedge with the cap described in question 12.

  c. Compare the bank's Q-cap-hedged rates and the cap-hedged rates. Should the Q-cap be priced higher or lower than the cap?

14. Suppose ABC Trust in question 10 plans to invest $15m in a 2-year FRN paying LIBOR. The FRN starts on 3/20 at 7.5% and is then reset the next seven quarters on 6/20, 9/20,

and 12/20. ABC Trust would like to establish a floor on the rates it obtains on the note. A money center bank is offering ABC a floor for $200,000 with the following terms corresponding to the floating-rate note:

- The floor consists of seven floorlets coinciding with the reset dates on the note
- Exercise rate on the floorlets = 7%
- Notional principal = $15m
- Reference rate = LIBOR
- Time period on the payoffs is 0.25
- Payoff is paid on the payment date on the notes
- Cost of the floor is $100,000 and is paid on 3/20.

ABC would like to finance the $200,000 cost of the floor by forming a reverse collar by selling a cap. The money center bank is willing to buy a cap with an exercise rate of 8% from ABC for $150,000 with similar terms to the floor.

a. Evaluate the reverse collar-hedged FRN investments that ABC could form with the cap and floor offered by the money center bank given the following interest rate scenarios: LIBOR = 7.5% on 3/20, 7% on 6/20, 6.5% on 9/20, 6% on 12/20, 7% on 3/20, 8% on 6/20, 8.5% on 12/20, and 9% on 12/20. In your evaluation, include the quarterly interest receipts, cap and floor cash flows, hedged interest revenue, and hedged rate (do not include cost of the floor or revenue from selling the cap).

b. Define another interest rate option position ABC Trust might use to defray the costs of its floor-hedged floating-rate investment.

15. Binomial tree problem 1.

15.1. Assume: binomial process; current annualized spot rate on risk-free bond with maturity of 0.25 years of $S_0 = 4\%$; up and down parameters for period equal in length to 0.5 years of $u = 1.1$, $d = 1/1.1$; length of binomial period 0.5 years (6-month steps); probability of the spot rate increase in one period of $q = 0.5$.

a. Generate a three-period binomial tree of spot rates.
b. Using the binomial tree, calculate the values at each node of a T-bill with a $100 face value and maturity of 0.25 years.
c. Using the binomial tree and assuming a risk-neutral world, calculate the values at each node of a futures contract on the above T-bill with the expiration on the futures being at the end of the third period (1.5 years).

15.2. Using the binomial tree from question 15.1, determine the values of the following spot options on the T-bill described in question 15.1b.:

a. European call option with an exercise price of 99 and expiration of 1.5 years (the end of three periods).
b. American call option with an exercise price of 99 and expiration of 1.5 years (the end of three periods).
c. European put option with an exercise price of 99 and expiration of 1.5 years (the end of three periods).
d. American put option with an exercise price of 99 and expiration of 1.5 years (the end of three periods).

15.3. Using the binomial tree, determine the values of the following futures options on the T-bill futures described in question 15.1c.:

a. European call option with an exercise price of 99 and expiration of 1.5 years (the end of three periods).

   b. American call option with an exercise price of 99 and expiration of 1.5 years (the end of three periods).
   c. European put option with an exercise price of 99 and expiration of 1.5 years (the end of three periods).
   d. American put option with an exercise price of 99 and expiration of 1.5 years (the end of three periods).

15.4. Using the binomial tree, determine the values of an interest rate call option and interest rate put options, each with exercise rates of 4%, spot rates as reference rates, time periods of 0.25 years, and notional principal of 100.

16. Binomial tree problem 2.

16.1. Assume: binomial process; current annualized spot rate on risk-free bond with maturity of 1 year of $S_0 = 5\%$; up and down parameters for period equal in length to 1 year equal to $u = 1.1$, $d = 1/1.1$; length of binomial period equal to 1 year; probability of the spot rate increasing in one period of $q = 0.5$.

   a. Generate a two-period binomial tree of spot rates.
   b. Using the binomial tree, calculate the values at each node of a risk-free bond with a $100 face value, 5% annual coupon, and maturity of 3 years.
   c. Using the binomial tree and assuming a risk-neutral world, calculate the values at each node of a futures contract on the above bond with the expiration on the futures being at the end of the second period.
   d. Determine the values of three zero stripped bonds: 1-year zero coupon paying 5, 2-year zero paying 5, and a 3-year zero coupon paying 105. Does the value of the portfolio of zero strips equal the value of the 3-year, 5% coupon bond?

16.2. Using the binomial tree from question 16.1, determine the values of the following spot options on the risk-free bond defined in question 16.1b.:

   a. European call option with an exercise price of 100 and expiration of 2 years.
   b. American call option with an exercise price of 100 and expiration of 2 years.
   c. European put option with an exercise price of 100 and expiration of 2 years.
   d. American put option with an exercise price of 100 and expiration of 2 years.

16.3. Using the binomial tree from question 16.1, determine the values of the following futures options on the risk-free bond defined in question 16.1b.:

   a. European call option with an exercise price of 100 and expiration of 2 years.
   b. American call option with an exercise price of 100 and expiration of 2 years.
   c. European put option with an exercise price of 100 and expiration of 2 years.
   d. American put option with an exercise price of 100 and expiration of 2 years.

16.4. Assuming that the binomial tree of spot rates is calibrated to the current spot yield curve, show that the value of the European spot call option on the bond is equal to the value of a replicating portfolio consisting of 1-year zeros and 2-year zeros.

17. Suppose a T-bill futures is priced at $f_0 = 99$ and has an annualized standard deviation of 0.00175, and that the continuously compounded annual risk-free rate is 4%.

   a. Using the Black futures option model, calculate the equilibrium price for a 3-month T-bill futures call option with an exercise price of 98.95.
   b. Using the Black futures option model, calculate the equilibrium price for a 3-month T-bill futures put option with an exercise price of 98.95.
   c. Show that the Black futures model put price is the same price obtained using the put–call futures parity model.

18. Suppose a T-bond futures expiring in 6 months is priced at $f_0 = 95,000$ and has an annualized standard deviation of 0.10, and that the continuously compounded annual risk-free rate is 5%.

   a. Using the Black futures option model, calculate the equilibrium price for a 6-month T-bond futures call option with an exercise price of 100,000.
   b. Using the Black futures option model, calculate the equilibrium price for a 6-month T-bond futures put option with an exercise price of 100,000.
   c. Show that the Black futures model put price is the same price obtained using the put–call futures parity model.

WEB EXERCISE

1. Option pricing models for pricing different options can be found at www.derivativesmodels.com. At the site, examine the Black–Scholes and Trinomial Cap and Floor models.

NOTES

1. The T-bill underlying the IMM's futures has a maturity of 91 days. For simplicity, we are assuming 90 days to maturity and a 360-day year.
2. It should be noted that if the futures option expired in one period while the T-bill futures expire in two, then the value of the futures option would be 0.071:

Fabozzi (ed.) *The Handbook of Fixed Income Securities*, 6th edn (New York: McGraw-Hill, 2001).

Black, Fischer, Emanuel Derman, William Toy, and Jack C. Francis "Using a One-Factor Model to Value Interest Rate-Sensitive Securities: With an Application to Treasury Bond Options," in Jack Clark Francis and Avner Simon Wolf (eds) *The Handbook of Interest Rate Risk Management* (New York: Irwin Professional Publishing, 1994).

$$C_0 = \frac{0.5(IV_u) + 0.5(IV_d)}{(1.05)^{0.5}} = \frac{0.5\text{Max}(98.665 - 98.75, 0) + 0.5\text{Max}(98.895 - 98.75, 0)}{(1.05)^{0.5}} = 0.071$$

SELECTED REFERENCES

Abken, P. "Interest Rate Caps, Collars, and Floors," *Federal Reserve Bank of Atlanta Economic Review* 74(6) (1989): 2–24.

Abken, Peter A. "Chapter 25: Introduction to Over-the-Counter (OTC) Options," in Jack Clark Francis and Avner Simon Wolf (eds) *The Handbook of Interest Rate Risk Management* (New York: Irwin Professional Publishing, 1994).

Andersen, L. "A Simple Approach to the Pricing of Bermudan Swaption in the Multi-Factor LIBOR Market Model," *Applied Mathematical Finance* 7(1) (2000): 1–32.

Bhattacharya, Anand K. "Interest-Rate Caps and Floors and Compound Options," in Frank J.

Black, F. and M. Scholes "The Pricing of Options and Corporate Liabilities," *Journal of Political Economy* 81 (May/June 1973): 637–59.

Boyle, P. P. "Options: A Monte Carlo Approach," *Journal of Financial Economics* 4 (1977): 323–38.

Boyle, P. P. "A Lattice Framework for Option Pricing with Two State Variables," *Journal of Financial and Quantitative Analysis* 23 (March 1988): 1–12.

Cox, J. C. and S. A. Ross "The Valuation of Options for Alternative Stochastic Processes," *Journal of Financial Economics* 3 (1976): 45–66.

Cox, J. C., S. A. Ross, and M. Rubinstein "Option Pricing: A Simplified Approach," *Journal of Financial Economics* 7 (October 1979): 229–64.

Cox, J. C. and M. Rubinstein *Options Markets* (Upper Saddle River, NJ: Prentice Hall, 1985).

Dehnad, Kosrow "Characteristics of OTC Options," in Jack Clark Francis and Avner Simon Wolf (eds) *The Handbook of Interest Rate Risk Management* (New York: Irwin Professional Publishing, 1994).

Geske, R. "The Valuation of Compound Options," *Journal of Financial Economics* 7 (1979): 63–81.

Goldman, B., H. Sosin, and M. A. Gatto "Path Dependent Options: Buy at the Low, Sell at the High," *Journal of Finance* 34 (December 1979): 1111–27.

Ho, T. S., R. S. Stapleton, and M. G. Subrahmanyam "The Valuation of American Options with Stochastic Interest Rates: A Generalization of the Geske–Johnson Technique," *Journal of Finance* 52(2) (June 1997): 827–40.

Hull, J. and A. White "The Pricing of Options on Interest Rate Caps and Floors Using the Hull–White Model," *Journal of Financial Engineering* 2(3) (1993): 287–96.

Hull, J. and A. White "Using Hull–White Interest Rate Trees," *Journal of Derivatives* (Spring 1996): 26–36.

Jamshidian, F. "An Exact Bond Option Pricing Formula," *Journal of Finance* 44 (March 1989): 205–9.

Johnson, H. "Options on the Maximum and Minimum of Several Assets," *Journal of Financial and Quantitative Analysis* 22(3) (September 1987): 277–83.

Klemkosky, R. C. and B. G. Resnick "Put–Call Parity and Market Efficiency," *Journal of Finance* 34 (December 1979): 1141–55.

Merton, R. C. "Theory of Rational Option Pricing," *Bell Journal of Economics and Management Science* 4 (Spring 1973): 141–83.

Rendleman, R. and B. Bartter "Two State Option Pricing," *Journal of Finance* 34 (1979): 1092–110.

Rendleman, R. and B. Bartter "The Pricing of Options on Debt Securities," *Journal of Financia and Quantitative Analysis* 15 (March 1980): 11–24.

Ritchken, P., L. Sankarasubramanian, and A. M. Vijh "The Valuation of Path Dependent Contracts on the Average," *Management Science* 39 (1993): 1202–13.

Ritchken, P. "On Pricing Barrier Options," *Journal of Derivatives* 3(2) (Winter 1995): 19–28.

Rubinstein, M. and E. Reiner "Unscrambling the Binary Code," *RISK* (October 1991): 75–83.

Stulz, R. "Options on the Minimum or Maximum of Two Assets," *Journal of Financial Economics* 10 (1982): 161–85.

CHAPTER SIXTEEN

INTEREST RATE SWAPS

16.1 INTRODUCTION

The Student Loan Marketing Association (Sallie Mae) was established in 1970 to develop a secondary market for student loans. Functioning similar to FNMA's secondary market operations, Sallie Mae issued securities and used the proceeds to buy students' loans held by banks and other institutions. The loans bought by Sallie Mae had intermediate terms and floating rates tied to the 91-day T-bill rate. To maintain its hedge, the securities sold by Sallie Mae to finance the loan purchases tended to be short term, paying rates that were highly correlated with T-bill rates. As a federal agency, Sallie Mae had access to intermediate fixed-rate funds at favorable rates, but preferred the floating-rate funds given the nature of its loan assets. At the same time, there were a number of corporations that had access to favorable floating rates, but preferred fixed-rate funds to finance their assets. In 1982, Sallie Mae issued its first fixed-rate, intermediate-term bond through a private placement and swapped it for a floating-rate note issued by ITT. This exchange of the floating-rate loan for the fixed-rate one represented the first of what is referred to today as an *interest rate swap*. The swap provided ITT with fixed-rate funds that were 17 basis points below the rate it could obtain on a direct fixed-rate loan, and it provided

Sallie Mae with cheaper intermediate-term, floating-rate funds – both parties therefore benefited from the swap.

Today there exists an interest rate swap market consisting of financial and non-financial corporations who annually conduct over $5 trillion dollars (as measured by contract value) in swaps of fixed-rate loans for floating-rate loans. Financial institutions and corporations use the market to hedge their liabilities and assets more efficiently – transforming their variable-rate liabilities and assets into fixed-rate ones or vice versa and creating synthetic fixed- or variable-rate liabilities and assets with better rates than the ones they can directly obtain. The strategy of swapping loans, though, is not new. In the 1970s, corporations began exchanging loans denominated in different currencies, creating a *currency swap* market. This market evolved from corporations who could obtain favorable borrowing terms in one currency but needed a loan in a different currency. To meet such needs, companies would go to swap dealers who would try to match their needs with other parties looking for the opposite positions.

Whether it is an exchange of currency-denominated loans or fixed and floating interest rate payments, a swap, by definition, is a legal arrangement between two parties to exchange specific payments. There are three types of financial swaps:

1. *Interest rate swaps:* the exchange of fixed-rate payments for floating-rate payments;
2. *Currency swaps:* the exchange of liabilities in different currencies;
3. *Cross-currency swaps:* the combination of an interest rate and currency swap.

In this chapter, we examine the features, markets, uses, and valuation of standard interest rate swaps, and in chapter 17 we look at non-standard swaps and currency swaps.

16.2 GENERIC INTEREST RATE SWAPS

16.2.1 Features

The simplest type of interest rate swap is called the *plain vanilla swap* or *generic swap*. In this agreement, one party provides fixed-rate interest payments to another party who provides floating-rate payments. The parties to the agreement are referred to as *counterparties*: the party who pays fixed interest and receives variable is called the *fixed-rate payer*; the other party (who pays floating and receives fixed) is the *floating-rate payer*. The fixed-rate payer is also called the floating-rate receiver and is often referred to as having bought the swap or having a long position; the floating-rate payer is also called the fixed-rate receiver and is referred to as having sold the swap and being short.

On a generic swap, principal payments are not exchanged. As a result, the interest payments are based on a notional principal (NP). The interest rate paid by the fixed payer often is specified in terms of the yield to maturity on a T–note plus basis points (BP); the rate paid by the floating payer on a generic swap is the LIBOR. Swap payments on a generic swap are made semi-annually and the maturities typically range from 3 to 10 years. In the swap contract, a trade date, effective date, settlement date, and maturity date are specified. The *trade date* is the day the parties agree to commit to the swap; the *effective date* is the date when interest begins to accrue; the *settlement* or *payment date* is when interest payments are made

(interest is paid in arrears 6 months after the effective date); and the *maturity date* is the last payment date. On the payment date, only the interest differential between the counterparties is paid. That is, generic swap payments are based on a *net settlement basis*: the counterparty owing the greater amount pays the difference between what is owed and what is received. Thus, if a fixed-rate payer owes $1.2m and a floating-rate payer owes $1m, then only a $0.2m payment by the fixed payer to the floating payer is made. All of the terms of the swap are specified in a legal agreement signed by both parties called the *confirmation*. The drafting of the confirmation often follows document forms suggested by the *International Swap and Derivatives Association (ISDA)* in New York. This organization provides a number of master agreements delineating the terminology used in many swap agreements (e.g., what happens in the case of default, the business day convention, and the like). Exhibit 16.1 summarizes the basic features of a plain vanilla swap.

Web Information:
For information on the International Swap and Derivatives Association and size of the markets go to
 www.isda.org

16.2.2 Interest Rate Swap: Example

Consider an interest rate swap with a maturity of 3 years, first effective date of March 1, 2003, and a maturity date of March 1, 2006. In this swap agreement, assume the fixed-rate payer agrees to pay the current YTM on a 3-year T–note of 5% plus 50 basis points and the floating-rate payer agrees to pay the 6-month LIBOR as determined on the effective dates with no basis points. Also assume the semi-annual interest rates are determined by dividing the annual rates (LIBOR and 5.5%) by two. Finally, assume the notional principal on the swap is $10m. (The calculations will be slightly off because they fail to include the actual day count convention; this is discussed in section 16.3.2.)

Exhibit 16.1   Generic swap terms

- *Rates*:
  - Fixed rate is usually a T-note rate plus BP
  - Floating rate is a benchmark rate: LIBOR.
- *Reset Frequency*: Semi-annual
- *Notional Principal*: Interest is applied to a notional principal; the NP is used for calculating the swap payments.
- *Maturity* ranges between 3 and 10 years.
- *Dates*: Payments are made in arrears on a semi-annual basis:
  - *Effective Date* is the date interest begins to accrue
  - *Payment Date* is the date interest payments are made.
- *Net Settlement Basis*: The counterparty owing the greater amount pays the difference between what is owed and what is received.
- *Documentation*: Most swaps use document forms suggested by the International Swap and Derivatives Association (ISDA) or the British Bankers' Association. The ISDA publishes a book of definitions and terms to help standardize swap contracts.

Table 16.1   Interest rate swap: 5.5%/LIBOR swap with NP = $10m

(1) Effective dates	(2) LIBOR	(3) Floating-rate payer's payment*	(4) Fixed-rate payer's payment**	(5) Net interest received by fixed-rate payer (column 3 − column 4)	(6) Net interest received by floating-rate payer (column 4 − column 3)
3/1/03	0.045				
9/1/03	0.05	225,000	275,000	−50,000	50,000
3/1/04	0.055	250,000	275,000	−25,000	25,000
9/1/04	0.06	275,000	275,000	0	0
3/1/05	0.065	300,000	275,000	25,000	−25,000
9/1/05	0.07	325,000	275,000	50,000	−50,000
3/1/06		350,000	275,000	75,000	−75,000

* (LIBOR/2)($10,000,000)
** (0.055/2)($10,000,000)

Table 16.1 shows the interest payments on each settlement date based on assumed LIBORs on the effective dates. In examining the table, several points should be noted. First, the payments are determined by the LIBOR prevailing 6 months prior to the payment date; thus payers on swaps would know their obligations in advance of the payment date. Second, when the LIBOR is below the fixed 5.5% rate, the fixed-rate payer pays the interest differential to the floating-rate payer; when it is above 5.5%, the fixed-rate payer receives the interest differential from the floating-rate payer. The net interest received by the fixed-rate payer is shown in column 5 of the table, and the net interest received by the floating-rate payer is

shown in column 6. As we will discuss later, the fixed-rate payer's position is very similar to a short position in a series of Eurodollar futures contracts, with the futures price determined by the fixed rate; that is, it is similar to a Eurodollar strip. The fixed payer's cash flows also can be replicated by the fixed payer buying a $10m, 3-year, flexible-rate note (FRN) paying the LIBOR and shorting (issuing) a $10m, 5.5% fixed-rate bond at par. The floating-rate payer's position, on the other hand, is similar to a long position in a Eurodollar strip, and it can be replicated by purchasing a 3-year, $10m FRN paying the LIBOR and shorting (issuing) a 3-year, $10m, 5.5% fixed-rate bond at par.

16.2.3 Synthetic Loans

Like the Sallie Mae and ITT swap in the early 1980s, one of the important uses of swaps is in creating a synthetic fixed- or floating-rate liability that yields a better rate than the conventional one. To illustrate, suppose a corporation with an AAA credit rating wants a 3-year, $10m fixed-rate loan starting on March 1, 2003. Suppose one possibility available to the company is to borrow $10m from a bank at a fixed rate of 6% (assume semi-annual payments) with a loan maturity of 3 years. Suppose, though, that the bank also is willing to provide the company with a 3-year floating-rate loan, with the rate set equal to the LIBOR on March 1 and September 1 each year for 3 years. If a swap agreement identical to the one described above were available, then instead of a direct fixed-rate loan, the company alternatively could attain a fixed-rate loan by borrowing $10m on the floating-rate loan, then fix the interest rate by taking a fixed-rate payer's position on the swap:

Conventional floating-rate loan	Pay floating rate
Swap: fixed-rate payer position	Pay fixed rate
Swap: fixed-rate payer position	Receive floating rate
Synthetic fixed rate	Pay fixed rate

As shown in table 16.2, if the floating-rate loan is hedged with a swap, any change in the LIBOR would be offset by an opposite change in the net receipts on the swap position. In this example, the company (as shown in the table) would end up paying a constant $0.275m every sixth month, which equates to an annualized borrowing rate of 5.5%: $R = 2(\$0.275m)/\$10m = 0.055$. Thus the corporation would be better off combining the swap position as a fixed-rate payer with the floating-rate loan to create a synthetic fixed-rate loan rather than simply taking the straight fixed-rate loan.

In contrast, a synthetic floating-rate loan can be formed by combining a floating-rate payer's position with a fixed-rate loan. This loan then can be used as an alternative to a floating-rate loan:

Conventional fixed-rate loan	Pay fixed rate
Swap: floating-rate payer position	Pay floating rate
Swap: floating-rate payer position	Receive fixed rate
Synthetic floating rate	Pay fixed rate

An example of a synthetic floating-rate loan is shown in table 16.3. The synthetic loan is formed with a 5% fixed-rate loan (semi-annual payments) and the floating-rate payer's position on our illustrated swap. As shown in the table, the synthetic floating-rate loan yields a 0.5% lower interest rate each period (annualized rate) than a floating-rate loan tied to the LIBOR.

Note, in both of the above examples, the borrower is able to attain a better borrowing rate with a synthetic loan using swaps than with a direct loan. When differences between the rates on actual and synthetic loans do exist, then swaps provide an apparent arbitrage use in which borrowers and investors can obtain better rates with synthetic positions formed with swap positions than they can from conventional loans.

16.2.4 Similarities Between Swaps and Bond Positions and Eurodollar Futures Strips

Bond Positions

Swaps can be viewed as a combination of a fixed-rate bond and flexible-rate note (FRN). A fixed-rate payer position is equivalent to buying an FRN paying the LIBOR and shorting (issuing) a fixed-rate bond at the swap's fixed rate. From the previous example, the purchase of $10m-worth of 3-year FRNs with the rate reset every 6 months at the LIBOR and the sale of $10m-worth of 3-year, 5.5% fixed-rate bonds at par would yield the same cash flow as the fixed-rate payer's swap. On the other hand, a floating-rate payer's position is equivalent to

Table 16.2 Synthetic fixed-rate loan: variable-rate loan set at LIBOR and fixed-payer position on 5.5%/LIBOR swap

| (1) Effective dates | (2) LIBOR | Swap | | | | Synthetic loan | |
		(3) Floating-rate payer's payment*	(4) Fixed-rate payer's payment**	(5) Net interest received by fixed-rate payer (column 3 − column 4)	(6) Loan interest paid on floating-rate loan*	(7) Payment on swap and loan (column 6 − column 5)	(8) Effective annualized rate***
3/1/03	0.045						
9/1/03	0.05	225,000	275,000	−50,000	225,000	275,000	0.055
3/1/04	0.055	250,000	275,000	−25,000	250,000	275,000	0.055
9/1/04	0.06	275,000	275,000	0	275,000	275,000	0.055
3/1/05	0.065	300,000	275,000	25,000	300,000	275,000	0.055
9/1/05	0.07	325,000	275,000	50,000	325,000	275,000	0.055
3/1/06		350,000	275,000	75,000	350,000	275,000	0.055

* (LIBOR/2)($10,000,000)
** (0.055/2)*($10,000,000)
*** 2(Payment on swap and loan)/$10,000,000

Table 16.3 Synthetic floating-rate loan: 5% fixed-rate loan and floating-payer position on 5.5%/LIBOR swap

		Swap			Synthetic loan		
(1) Effective dates	(2) LIBOR	(3) Floating-rate payer's payment*	(4) Fixed-rate payer's payment**	(5) Net interest received by floating-rate payer (column 4 – column 3)	(6) Loan interest paid on 5% fixed-rate loan	(7) Payment on swap and loan (column 6 – column 5)	(8) Effective annualized rate***
3/1/03	0.045						0.04
9/1/03	0.05	225,000	275,000	50,000	250,000	200,000	0.045
3/1/04	0.055	250,000	275,000	25,000	250,000	225,000	0.05
9/1/04	0.06	275,000	275,000	0	250,000	250,000	0.055
3/1/05	0.065	300,000	275,000	–25,000	250,000	275,000	0.06
9/1/05	0.07	325,000	275,000	–50,000	250,000	300,000	0.065
3/1/06		350,000	275,000	–75,000	250,000	325,000	

* (LIBOR/2)($10,000,000)
** (0.055/2)*($10,000,000)
*** 2 (Payment on swap and loan)/$10,000,000

shorting (or issuing) an FRN at the LIBOR and buying a fixed-rate bond at the swap's fixed rate. Thus, the purchase of $10m-worth of 3-year 5.5% fixed-rate bonds at par and the sale of $10m-worth of FRNs paying the LIBOR would yield the same cash flow as the floating-rate payer's swap in the above example.

Since the cash flows on swaps can be replicated, a relevant question is what is the economic justification for swaps? The answer is that swaps provide a given set of flows more efficiently and at less credit risk than the equivalent bond position. With swaps there is no underwriting and they can be treated as an off-balance-sheet item for accounting purposes. Also, unlike bond positions that fall under security laws, swaps fall under contract law. Thus, the holder of a portfolio of a short FRN and a long fixed-rate bond would still have to meet his obligations on the FRN if the issuer of the fixed-rate bond defaulted. On a swap, though, if the other party defaults, the party in question no longer has to meet her obligation. Thus, swaps have less credit risk than their equivalent bond positions.

Eurodollar Futures Strip

A plain vanilla swap can also be viewed as a series of Eurodollar futures contracts. To see the similarities, consider a short position in a Eurodollar strip in which the short holder agrees to sell ten Eurodollar deposits, each with face values of $1m and maturities of 6 months, at the IMM index price of 94.5 (or discount yield of $R_D = 5.5\%$), with the expirations on the strip being March 1 and September 1 for a period of 2.5 years.

With the index at 94.5, the contract price on one Eurodollar futures contract is $972,500:

$$f_0 = \left[\frac{100 - (5.5)(180/360)}{100}\right](\$1,000,000)$$

$$= \$972,500$$

Table 16.4 shows the cash flows at the expiration dates from closing the ten short Eurodollar contracts at the same assumed LIBOR used in the above swap example, with the Eurodollar settlement index being $100 - \text{LIBOR}$. For example, with the LIBOR at 5% on 9/1/03, a

Table 16.4 Short positions in Eurodollar futures

(1) Closing dates	(2) LIBOR	(3) f_T	(4) Cash flow $(10[f_0 - f_T])$
9/1/03	5	975,000	−25,000
3/1/04	5.5	972,500	0
9/1/04	6	970,000	25,000
3/1/05	6.5	967,500	50,000
9/1/05	7	965,000	75,000

$f_0 = 972,500$

$f_T = \left[\frac{100 - (\text{LIBOR})(180/360)}{100}\right](\$1,000,000)$

$25,000 loss occurs from settling the ten futures contracts. That is:

$$f_T = \left[\frac{100 - (5)(180/360)}{100}\right](\$1,000,000)$$

$$= \$975,000$$

$$\text{Futures cash flow} = 10[f_0 - f_T]$$

$$= 10[\$972,500 - \$975,000]$$

$$= -\$25,000$$

Comparing the fixed-rate payer's net receipts shown in column 5 of table 16.1 with the cash flows from the short positions on the Eurodollar strip shown in table 16.4, one can see that the two positions yield the same numbers. There are, however, some differences between the Eurodollar strip and the swap. First, a 6-month differential occurs between the swap payment and the futures payments. This time differential is a result of the interest payments on the swap being determined by the LIBOR at the beginning of the period, while the futures position's profit is based on the LIBOR at the end of its period. Second, we've assumed the futures contract is on a Eurodollar deposit with a maturity of 6 months instead of the standard 3 months. For the standard Eurodollar strip and swap to be more similar, we would need to compare the swap to a synthetic contract on a 6-month Eurodollar deposit formed with two short positions on 3-month Eurodollar deposits: one expiring at T and one at $T + 90$ days. In addition to these technical differences, other differences exist: strips are guaranteed by a clearinghouse, while banks can act as guarantors for swaps; strip contracts are standardized, while swap agreements often are tailor-made.

Exhibit 16.2   Comparison between swap and Eurodollar futures strip

- *Credit Risk*: On a futures contract, the parties transfer credit risk to the exchange. The exchange then manages the risk by requiring margin accounts. Swaps, on the other hand, are exposed to credit risk.
- *Marketability*: Swaps are not traded on an exchange like futures and therefore are not as liquid as futures.
- *Standardization*: Swaps are more flexible in design than futures which are standardized.
- *CF Timing*: CFs on swaps are based on the LIBOR 6 months earlier; CFs on futures are based on the current LIBOR.

Exhibit 16.2 summarizes the difference between the two positions.

16.3 SWAP MARKET

16.3.1 Structure

Corporations, financial institutions, and others who use swaps are linked by a group of brokers and dealers who collectively are referred to as *swap banks*. These swap banks consist primarily of commercial banks and investment bankers. As brokers, swap banks try to match parties with opposite needs (see exhibit 16.3). Many of the first interest rate swaps were very customized brokered deals between counterparties, with the parties often negotiating and transacting directly between themselves. As brokers, the swap bank's role in the contract is to bring the parties together and provide information; swap banks often maintain lists of companies and financial institutions that are potential parties to a swap. Once the swap agreement is closed, the swap broker usually has only a minor continuing role. With some *brokered swaps*, the swap bank guarantees one or both sides of the transaction. With many, though, the counterparties assume the credit risk and make their own assessment of the other party's default potential.

One of the problems with a brokered swap is that it requires each party to have knowledge of the other party's risk profile. Historically, this problem led to more swap banks taking positions as dealers instead of as brokers. With *dealer swaps*, the swap dealer often makes commitments to enter a swap as a counterparty before the other end party has been located.

Each of the counterparties – or, in this context, the end parties – contracts separately with the swap bank, who acts as a counterparty to each. The end parties, in turn, assume the credit risk of the financial institution instead of that of the other end party, while the swap dealer assumes the credit risk of both of the end parties.

In acting as dealers, swap banks often match a swap agreement with multiple end parties. For example, as illustrated in exhibit 16.3, a $30m fixed-for-floating swap between a swap dealer and party A might be matched with two $15m floating-for-fixed swaps. Ideally, a swap bank tries to maintain a perfect hedge. In practice, though, swap banks are prepared to enter a swap agreement without another counterparty. This practice is sometimes referred to as *warehousing*. In warehousing, swap banks will try to hedge their swap positions with opposite positions in T-notes and FRNs or using Eurodollar futures contracts. For example, a swap bank might hedge a $10m, 3-year floating-rate position by selling $10m-worth of 3-year T-notes, then use the proceeds to buy either FRNs tied to the LIBOR or 180-day spot Eurodollar CDs, with the investment rolled over each period into new Eurodollar CDs. In general, most of the commitments a swap bank assumes are hedged through a portfolio of alternative positions – opposite swap positions, spot positions in T-notes and FRNs, or futures positions. This type of portfolio management by swap banks is referred to as *running a dynamic book*.

16.3.2 Swap Market Price Quotes

By convention, the floating rate on a swap is quoted flat without basis point adjustments.

Exhibit 16.3   Swap market structure

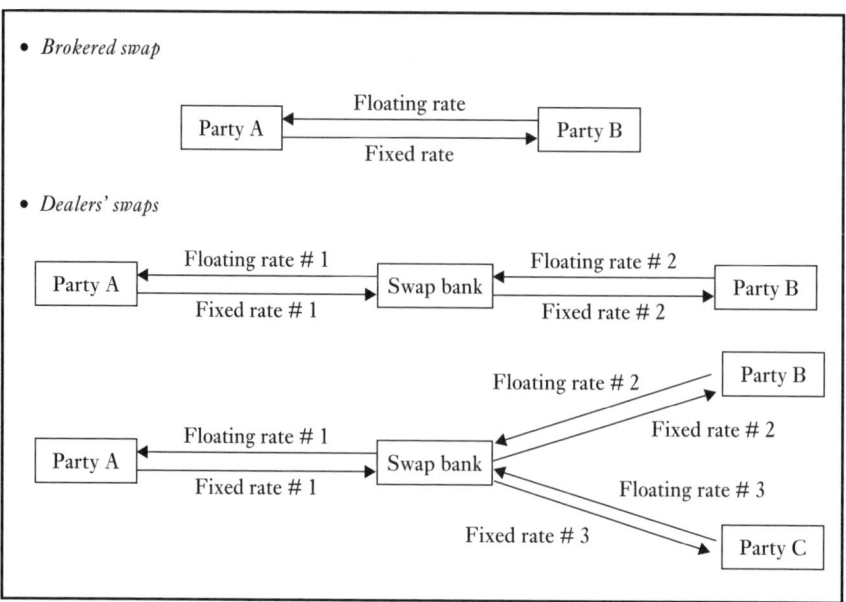

Table 16.5   Swap bank quote

Swap maturity	Treasury yield	Bid swap spread (BP)	Ask swap spread (BP)	Fixed swap rate spread	Swap rate
2 year	4.98%	67	74	5.65%–5.72%	5.69%
3 year	5.17%	72	76	5.89%–5.93%	5.91%
4 year	5.38%	69	74	6.07%–6.12%	6.10%
5 year	5.50%	70	76	6.20%–6.26%	6.23%

The fixed rate on a generic swap, in turn, is quoted in terms of the YTM on an on-the-run T-bond or T-note; that is, the most recent note or bond issued with a maturity matching the swap. In a dealer swap, the swap dealer's compensation comes from a mark-up or bid–asked spread extended to the end parties. The spread is reflected on the fixed-rate side. The swap dealer will provide a bid–asked quote to a potential party, and will in some cases post the bid-and-asked quotes. The quotes are stated in terms of the bid rate the dealer will pay as a fixed payer in return for the LIBOR, and the asked rate they will receive as a floating-rate payer in return for paying the LIBOR. For example, a 70/76 swap spread implies the dealer will buy (take fixed-payer position) at 70 BP over the T-note yield and sell (take

floating-payer position) at 76 BP over the T-note yield. Table 16.5 shows some illustrative quotes being offered by a swap bank on four generic swaps. The quote on the 5-year swap, for example, indicates that the swap bank will take the fixed-rate payer's position at 6.20%/ LIBOR (fixed rate = 5.5% + 70 BP), and the floating-rate payer's position at 6.26%/LIBOR (fixed rate = 5.5% + 76 BP). The average of the bid-and-asked rates is known as the *swap rate*.

It should be noted that the fixed and floating rates quoted on a swap are not directly comparable. That is, the T-note assumes a 365-day basis, while the LIBOR assumes 360 days. In addition, these rates also need to be pro-rated to the actual number of days that have elapsed between settlement dates to determine the actual payments. These adjustments can

Table 16.6 Cash flow for fixed-rate payer on 6.26%/LIBOR, NP = $20m

Settlement date	Number of days	LIBOR	Fixed payment	Floating payment	Fixed net payment
6/10/02		5.50%			
12/10/02	183	5.75%	627,715.07	559,166.67	68,548.40
6/10/03	182	6.00%	624,284.93	581,388.89	42,896.04
12/10/03	183	6.25%	627,715.07	610,000.00	17,715.07
6/10/04	182	6.50%	624,284.93	631,944.44	−7,659.51
12/10/04	183	6.75%	627,715.07	660,833.33	−33,118.26
6/10/05	182		624,284.93	682,500.00	−58,215.07

Fixed payment = (0.0626)(no. of days/365)($20,000,000)
Floating payment = LIBOR(no. of days/360)($20,000,000)

be accounted for by using the following formulas:

Fixed-rate settlement payment

$$= (\text{Fixed rate}) \left[\frac{\text{No. of days}}{365} \right] \text{NP}$$

Floating-rate settlement payment

$$= (\text{LIBOR}) \left[\frac{\text{No. of days}}{360} \right] \text{NP}$$

Table 16.6 shows the cash flows for a fixed-rate payer for the following 6.26%/LIBOR swap. Swap agreement:

- Initiation date = June 10, 2002
- Maturity date = June 10, 2005
- Effective dates: June 10 and December 10
- NP = $20m
- Fixed-rate payer: pay = 6.26% (semi-annual)/receive LIBOR
- Floating-rate payer: pay LIBOR/receive 6.20% (semi-annual)
- LIBOR determined in advance and paid in arrears.

Different from the cash flows shown earlier (tables 16.1, 16.2, and 16.3), these flows, in turn, reflect the number of days between settlement dates and the 360-day and 365-day basis for LIBOR and the T-note yields. For ease of exposition, we will ignore the day count conventions in our other examples of generic swaps and simply divide annual rates by two (i.e., we will use a 180/360 day count convention).

16.3.3 Opening Swap Positions

Suppose a corporate treasurer wants to fix the rate on the company's 5-year, $50m floating-rate liability by taking a fixed-rate payer's position on a 5-year swap with an NP of

$50m. To obtain the swap position, the treasurer would call a swap trader for a quote on a fixed-rate payer's position. After assessing the corporation's credit risk, suppose the swap dealer gives the treasurer a swap quote of 100 BP over the current 5-year T-note yield, and the corporate treasurer, in turn, accepts. Thus, the treasurer would agree to take the fixed payer's position on the swap at 100 BP above the current 5-year T-note. Except for the fixed rate, both parties would mutually agree to the terms of the swap; for example:

- Swap bank will pay 6-month LIBOR
- Corporation will pay 5-year T-note rate + 100 BP
- Settlement dates will be March 23 and June 23
- Maturity date is March 23, 2008
- Interest will be paid in arrears
- NP is $50m
- Net payments will be made
- US laws govern the transaction.

After agreeing to the terms of the swap, the actual rate paid by the fixed payer is often set once the swap trader hedges her swap position by taking a position in an on-the-run T-note. If this is the case, the swap trader will usually call the swap bank's bond trader for an exact quote on the T-note rate. In our example, suppose the swap banker, after receiving quotes from her bond trader, instructs the trader to sell $50m of 5-year T-notes with the proceeds invested in a 5-year FRN paying LIBOR. The yield on the T-note purchased plus the 100 BP would determine the actual rate on the swap. The swap trader would later close the bond positions used to hedge the swaps as other floating-rate swaps are created.

16.3.4 Closing Swap Positions

Prior to maturity, swap positions can be closed by selling the swap to a swap dealer or another party. If the swap is closed in this way, the new counterparty pays or receives an upfront fee to or from the existing counterparty in exchange for receiving the original counterparty's position. Alternatively, the swap holder could also hedge his position by taking an opposite position in a current swap or possibly by hedging the position for the remainder of the maturity period with a futures position. Thus, a fixed-rate payer who unexpectedly sees interest rates decreasing and, as a result, wants to change his position, could do so by selling the swap to a dealer, taking a floating-rate payer's position in a new swap contract, or by going long in an appropriate futures contract; this latter strategy might be advantageous if there is only a short period of time left on the swap.

If the fixed-payer swap holder decides to hedge his position by taking an opposite position on a new swap, the new swap position would require a payment of the LIBOR that would cancel out the receipt of the LIBOR on the first swap. The difference in the positions would therefore be equal to the difference in the higher fixed interest rate that is paid on the first swap and the lower fixed interest rate received on the offsetting swap. For example, suppose in our first illustrative swap example (table 16.1), a decline in interest rates occurs 1 year after the initiation of the swap, causing the fixed-rate payer to want to close his position. To this end, suppose the fixed-rate payer offsets his position by entering a new 2-year swap as a floating-rate payer in which he agrees to pay the LIBOR for a 5% fixed rate. The two positions would result in a fixed payment of $25,000 semi-annually for 2 years ((0.0025)NP). If interest rates decline over the next 2 years, this offsetting position would turn out to be the correct strategy.

Instead of hedging the position, the fixed-rate payer is more likely to close his position by simply selling it to a swap dealer. In acquiring a fixed position at 5.5%, the swap dealer would have to take a floating-payer's position to hedge the acquired fixed position. If the fixed rate on a new 2-year swap were at 5%, the dealer would likewise lose $25,000 semi-annually for 2 years on the two swap positions given an NP of $10m. Thus, the price the swap bank would charge the fixed payer for buying his swap would be at least equal to the present value of $25,000 for the next four semi-annual periods. Given a discount rate of 5%, the swap bank would charge the fixed payer a minimum of $94,049 for buying his swap.

$$B_0 = \sum_{t=1}^{4} \frac{\$25,000}{(1 + (0.05/2))^t} = \$94,049$$

In contrast, if rates had increased, the fixed payer would be able to sell the swap to a dealer at a premium. For example, if the fixed rate on a new swap were 6%, a swap dealer would realize a semi-annual return of $25,000 for the next 2 years by buying the 5.5%/LIBOR swap and hedging it with a floating position on a 2-year 6%/LIBOR swap. Given a 6% discount rate, the dealer would pay the fixed payer a maximum of $92,927 for his 5.5%/LIBOR swap.

$$B_0 = \sum_{t=1}^{4} \frac{\$25,000}{(1 + (0.06/2))^t} = \$92,927$$

In general, the above cases illustrate that the value of an existing swap depends on the rates on current swaps that, in turn, depend on the yields on spot or futures T-notes. Swap valuation is discussed in more detail in section 16.6.

Offsetting swap positions

Original swap: fixed payer's position	Pay 5.5%	− 5.5%
Original swap: fixed payer's position	Receive LIBOR	+ LIBOR
Offsetting swap: floating payer's position	Pay LIBOR	− LIBOR
Offsetting swap: floating payer's position	Receive 5.0%	+ 5%
	Pay 0.5%	− 0.5%

16.4 COMPARATIVE ADVANTAGE AND HIDDEN OPTIONS

16.4.1 Comparative Advantage

Swaps are often used by financial and non-financial corporations to take advantage of apparent arbitrage opportunities resulting from capital market inefficiencies. To see this, consider the case of the BBB Company, a large conglomerate that is working on raising $300m with a 5-year loan to finance the acquisition of a communications company. Based on its moderate credit ratings, suppose BBB can borrow 5-year funds at a 9.5% fixed rate or at a floating rate equal to LIBOR + 75 BP. Given the choice, though, BBB prefers the fixed-rate loan. Suppose the treasurer of the BBB Company contacts his investment banker for suggestions on how to finance the acquisition. The investment banker knows that the AAA Development Company is looking for 5-year funding to finance its proposed $300m shopping mall development. Given its high credit rating, suppose AAA can borrow the funds for 5 years at a fixed rate of 8.5% or at a floating rate equal to the LIBOR + 25 BP. Given the choice, AAA

comparative advantage for BBB in the floating market. That is, AAA has a relative advantage in the fixed market where it gets 100 BP less than BBB; BBB, in turn, has a relative advantage (or relatively less disadvantage) in the floating-rate market where it only pays 50 BP more than AAA. Thus, lenders in the fixed-rate market supposedly assess the difference between the two creditors to be worth 100 BP, while lenders in the floating-rate market assess the difference to be only 50 BP. Whenever comparative advantage exists, arbitrage opportunities can be realized by each firm borrowing in the market where it has a comparative advantage and then swapping loans or having a swap bank set up a swap.

For the swap to work, the two companies cannot just pass on their respective costs: BBB swaps a floating rate at LIBOR + 75 BP for a 9.5% fixed; AAA swaps an 8.5% fixed for floating at LIBOR + 25 BP. Typically, the companies divide the differences in credit spreads, with the most creditworthy company taking the most savings. In this case, suppose the investment banker arranges a 5-year, 8.5%/LIBOR generic swap with an NP of $300m in which BBB takes the fixed-rate position and AAA takes the floating-rate payer position:

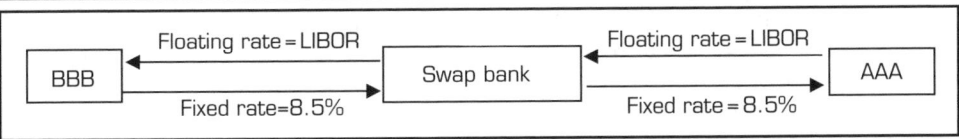

prefers a floating-rate loan. In summary, BBB and AAA have the following fixed- and floating-rate loan opportunities:

Company	Fixed rate	Floating rate
BBB company	9.5%	LIBOR + 75 BP
AAA company	8.5%	LIBOR + 25 BP
Credit spread	100 BP	50 BP

In this case, the AAA Company has an absolute advantage in both the fixed and floating markets because of its higher quality rating. However, looking at the credit spreads of the borrowers in each of the markets, the investment banker realizes that there is a *comparative advantage* for AAA in the fixed market and a

The BBB Company would then issue a $300m FRN paying LIBOR + 75 BP. This loan, combined with the fixed-rate swap, would give BBB a synthetic fixed-rate loan paying 9.25% (0.25% less than its direct fixed-rate loan):

BBB Company's synthetic fixed-rate loan		
Issue FRN	Pay LIBOR +75 BP	−LIBOR −0.75%
Swap: fixed-rate payer's position	Pay 8.5%	− 8.5%
Swap: fixed-rate payer's position	Receive LIBOR	+LIBOR
Synthetic fixed rate	Pay 8.5% + 0.75%	−9.25%
Direct fixed rate	Pay 9.5%	− 9.5%

The AAA Company, on the other hand, would issue a $300m, 8.5% fixed-rate bond that, when combined with the floating-rate swap, would give AAA a synthetic floating-rate loan paying LIBOR, which is 0.25 BP less than the rates paid on the direct floating-rate loan of LIBOR plus 25 BP:

AAA Company's synthetic floating-rate loan		
Issue 8.5% fixed-rate bond	Pay 8.5%	−8.5%
Swap: floating-rate payer's position	Pay LIBOR	−LIBOR
Swap: floating-rate payer's position	Receive 8.5%	+8.5%
Synthetic fixed rate	Pay LIBOR	−LIBOR
Direct fixed rate	Pay LIBOR +25 BP	−LIBOR −0.25%

As a rule, for a swap to provide arbitrage opportunities, at least one of the counterparties must have a comparative advantage in one market. The total arbitrage gain available to each party depends on whether one party has an absolute advantage in both markets or each has an absolute advantage in one market. If one party has an absolute advantage in both markets (as in this case), then the arbitrage gain is the difference in the comparative advantages in each market: 50 BP = 100 BP − 50 BP. In this case, BBB and AAA split the difference in the 50 BP gain. In contrast, if each party has an absolute advantage in one market, then the arbitrage gain is equal to the sum of the comparative advantages.

16.4.2 Hidden Option

The comparative advantage argument has often been cited as the explanation for the growth in the swap market. This argument, though, is often questioned on the grounds that the mere use of swaps should over time reduce the credit interest rate differentials in the fixed and flexible markets, taking away the advantages from forming synthetic positions. With observed credit spreads and continuing use of swaps to create synthetic positions, some scholars (Smith, Smithson, and Wakeman, 1986) have argued that the comparative advantage that is apparently extant is actually a hidden option embedded in the floating-rate debt position that proponents of the comparative advantage argument fail to

include. They argue that the credit spreads that exist are due to the nature of the contracts available to firms in fixed and floating markets. In the floating market, the lender usually has the opportunity to review the floating rate each period and increase the spread over the LIBOR if the borrower's creditworthiness has deteriorated. This option, though, does not exist in the fixed market.

In the preceding example, the lower quality BBB Company is able to get a synthetic fixed rate at 9.25% (0.25% less than the direct loan). However, using the hidden option argument, this 9.25% rate is only realized if BBB can maintain its creditworthiness and continue to borrow at a floating rate that is 75 BP above LIBOR. If its credit ratings were to subsequently decline and it had to pay 150 BP above the LIBOR, then its synthetic fixed rate would increase. Moreover, studies have shown that the likelihood of default increases faster over time for lower quality companies than it does for higher quality. In our example, this would mean that the BBB Company's credit spread is more likely to rise than the AAA Company's spread and that its expected borrowing rate is greater than the 9.25% synthetic rate. As for the higher quality AAA Company, its lower synthetic floating rate of LIBOR does not take into account the additional return necessary to compensate the company for bearing the risk of a default by the BBB Company. If it borrowed floating funds directly, the AAA Company would not be bearing this risk.

16.5 SWAP APPLICATIONS

16.5.1 Arbitrage Applications: Synthetic Positions

In the above case, the differences in credit spreads in the fixed-rate and floating-rate debt markets or the hidden options on the floating debt position made it possible for both corporations to obtain different rates with synthetic positions than with direct. This example represents what is commonly referred to as an arbitrage use of swaps. In general, the presence of comparative advantage or a hidden option makes it possible to create not only synthetic loans with lower rates than direct, but

Table 16.7 Synthetic fixed-rate loan at 9%: FRN issued at LIBOR + 100 BP; fixed-rate position on 8%/ LIBOR swap

Swap: Fixed payer's position on 8%/LIBOR swap; NP = $20m; maturity = 5 years.
$20m, 5-year FRN paying LIBOR + 100 BP. Synthetic fixed: FRN and fixed-payer's position

Effective date	LIBOR	Fixed payment	Floating payment	Fixed net payment	FRN payment	FRN + swap payment	Annualized rate
6/10/02	7.00%						
12/10/02	7.25%	800,000	700,000	100,000	800,000	900,000	0.09
6/10/03	7.50%	800,000	725,000	75,000	825,000	900,000	0.09
12/10/03	7.75%	800,000	750,000	50,000	850,000	900,000	0.09
6/10/04	8.00%	800,000	775,000	25,000	875,000	900,000	0.09
12/10/04	8.25%	800,000	800,000	0	900,000	900,000	0.09
6/10/05	8.50%	800,000	825,000	−25,000	925,000	900,000	0.09
12/10/05	8.75%	800,000	850,000	−50,000	950,000	900,000	0.09
6/10/06	9.00%	800,000	875,000	−75,000	975,000	900,000	0.09
12/10/06	9.25%	800,000	900,000	−100,000	1,000,000	900,000	0.09
6/10/07		800,000	925,000	−125,000	1,025,000	900,000	0.09

Fixed payment = (0.08/2)($20,000,000)
Floating payment = (LIBOR/2)($20,000,000)
FRN payment = ((LIBOR + 100 BP)/2)($20,000,000)
Annualized rate = 2(FRN + swap payment)/$20,000,000

Synthetic fixed-rate loan
FRN   Pay LIBOR + 1% = − LIBOR − 1%
Swap   Pay 8% fixed = − 8%
Swap   Receive LIBOR = + LIBOR
             Pay 8% + 1% = − 9%

Direct loan rate = 10%

also synthetic investments with rates exceeding those from direct investments. To illustrate this, four cases showing how swaps can be used to create synthetic fixed-rate and floating-rate loans and investments are presented below.

Synthetic Fixed-Rate Loan

Suppose a company is planning on borrowing $20m for 5 years at a fixed rate. Given a swap market, suppose its alternatives are to issue a 5-year, 10%, fixed-rate bond paying coupons on a semi-annual basis or create a synthetic fixed-rate bond by issuing a 5-year FRN paying LIBOR plus 100 BP and taking a fixed-rate payer's position on a swap with an NP of $20m. The synthetic fixed loan will be equivalent to the direct fixed-rate loan if it is formed with a swap that has a fixed rate equal to 9%; that is, the swap rate is equal to the fixed rate on

the direct loan (10%) minus the BP (100 BP) on the FRN:

Synthetic fixed-rate loan

Issue FRN	Pay LIBOR + 1%	−LIBOR −1%
Swap: fixed-rate payer's position	Pay 9% fixed rate	−9%
Swap: fixed-rate payer's position	Receive LIBOR	+LIBOR
Synthetic rate	Pay 9% + 1%	−10%
Direct loan rate	Pay 10%	−10%

If the company can obtain a fixed rate on a swap that is less than 9%, then the company would find it cheaper to finance with the synthetic fixed-rate loan than the direct. For example, if the company could obtain an

Table 16.8 Synthetic floating-rate loan: 9% fixed-rate loan; floating-rate position on 9.5%/LIBOR swap

Swap: Floating payer's position on 9.5%/LIBOR swap; NP = $20m; maturity = 5 years.
$20m, 5-year, 9% fixed-rate loan. Synthetic variable: Fixed-rate loan and
floating-payer's position

Effective date	LIBOR	Fixed payment	Floating payment	Floating payer's net payment	Fixed-rate payment	Fixed rate + swap payment	Annualized rate
6/10/02	8.00%						
12/10/02	8.25%	950,000	800,000	−150,000	900,000	750,000	0.075
6/10/03	8.50%	950,000	825,000	−125,000	900,000	775,000	0.0775
12/10/03	8.75%	950,000	850,000	−100,000	900,000	800,000	0.08
6/10/04	9.00%	950,000	875,000	−75,000	900,000	825,000	0.0825
12/10/04	9.25%	950,000	900,000	−50,000	900,000	850,000	0.085
6/10/05	9.50%	950,000	925,000	−250,00	900,000	875,000	0.0875
12/10/05	9.75%	950,000	950,000	0	900,000	900,000	0.09
6/10/06	10.00%	950,000	975,000	25,000	900,000	925,000	0.0925
12/10/06	10.25%	950,000	1,000,000	50,000	900,000	950,000	0.095
6/10/07		950,000	1,025,000	75,000	900,000	975,000	0.0975

Fixed payment = (0.095/2)($20,000,000)
Floating payment = (LIBOR/2)($20,000,000)
Fixed payment = (0.09/2)($20,000,000)
Annualized rate = 2(Fixed rate + swap payment)/$20,000,000

Synthetic floating-rate loan
Loan   Pay 9% fixed = − 9%
Swap   Pay LIBOR = − LIBOR
Swap   Receive 9.5% fixed rate = + 9.5%
        Pay LIBOR − 0.5% = − (LIBOR − 0.5%)

Rate on direct floating-rate loan = LIBOR

8%/LIBOR swap, then as illustrated in table 16.7, the company would be able to create a synthetic 9% fixed-rate loan by issuing the FRN at LIBOR plus 100 BP and taking the fixed payer's position on the swap.

Synthetic Floating-Rate Loan

Suppose a bank with an AA rating has just made a 5-year, $20m floating-rate loan that is reset every 6 months at the LIBOR plus 100 BP. The bank could finance this variable-rate asset by either selling CDs every 6 months at the LIBOR or by creating a synthetic floating-rate loan by selling a 5-year fixed-rate note at 9% and taking a floating-rate payer's position on a 5-year swap with an NP of $20m. The synthetic floating-rate loan will be equivalent to the direct floating-rate loan paying LIBOR if the swap has a fixed rate that is equal to the 9% fixed rate on the note.

Synthetic floating-rate loan

Issue 9% fixed-rate note	Pay 9% fixed rate	−9%
Swap: floating-rate payer's position	Pay LIBOR	−LIBOR
Swap: floating-rate payer's position	Receive 9% fixed rate	+9%
Synthetic rate	Pay LIBOR	−LIBOR
Direct loan rate	Pay LIBOR	−LIBOR

Thus, if the bank can obtain a fixed rate on the swap that is greater than 9%, then it would find it cheaper to finance its floating-rate loan asset by issuing fixed-rate notes at 9% and taking the floating-rate payer's position on the swap. Such a case is illustrated in table 16.8. The table shows that the bank's effective interest payments are 50 BP less than LIBOR with a synthetic floating-rate loan formed by selling the 9% fixed-rate bond and taking a floating-rate payer's position on a 5-year, 9.5%/LIBOR swap with NP of $20m.

Synthetic Fixed-Rate Investment

In the early days of the swap market, swaps were primarily used as a liability management tool. In the late 1980s, investors began to use swaps to try to increase the yield on their investments. A swap used with an asset is sometimes referred to as an *asset-based interest rate swap* or simply an asset swap. In terms of synthetic positions, asset-based swaps can be used to create either fixed-rate or floating-rate investment positions.

Consider the case of an investment company that is setting up a $100m unit investment trust consisting of 5-year, AAA quality, option-free, fixed-rate bonds. If the YTM on such bonds is 6%, then the investment company could form the trust by simply buying $100m-worth of 6% coupon bonds at par. Alternatively, it could try to earn a higher return by creating a synthetic fixed-rate bond by buying 5-year, high-quality FRNs currently paying the LIBOR plus 100 BP and taking a floating-rate payer's position on a 5-year swap with an NP of $100m. If the fixed rate on the swap is equal to 5% (the 6% rate on the bonds minus the 100 BP on the FRN), then the synthetic fixed-rate investment will yield the same return as the 6% fixed-rate bonds:

Synthetic fixed-rate investment		
Purchase FRN	Receive LIBOR + 1%	+LIBOR +1%
Swap: floating-rate payer's position	Pay LIBOR	−LIBOR
Swap: floating-rate payer's position	Receive 5% fixed rate	+5%
Synthetic rate	Receive 5% + 1%	+6%
Direct investment rate	Receive 6%	+6%

If the fixed rate on the swap is greater than 5%, then the synthetic fixed-rate loan will yield a higher return than the 6% T-notes. For example, if the investment company could take a floating-payer's position on a 5.75%/LIBOR swap with maturity of 5 years, NP of 100m, and effective dates coinciding with the FRNs' dates, then as shown in table 16.9, the investment company would earn a fixed rate of 6.75%.

Synthetic Floating-Rate Investment

This time consider an investment fund that is looking to invest $20m for 5 years in an FRN. Suppose the fund can either invest directly in a high-quality, 5-year FRN paying LIBOR plus 50 BP, or it can create a synthetic floating-rate investment by investing in a 5-year, 7% fixed-rate note selling at par and taking a fixed-rate payer's position. If the fixed rate on the swap is equal to 6.5% (the rate on the fixed-rate note minus the BP on the direct FRN investment), then the synthetic floating-rate investment will yield the same return as the FRN:

Synthetic floating-rate investment		
Purchase fixed-rate note	Receive 7%	+7%
Swap: fixed-rate payer's position	Pay 6.5% fixed rate	−6.5%
Swap: fixed-rate payer's position	Receive LIBOR	+LIBOR
Synthetic rate	Receive LIBOR + 0.5%	+LIBOR +0.5%
Floating investment rate	Receive LIBOR + 0.5%	+LIBOR +0.5%

If the fixed rate on the swap is less than 6.5%, then the synthetic floating-rate investment will yield a higher return than the FRN. This case is shown in table 16.10. The table shows the fund could obtain a yield of LIBOR plus 100 BP from a synthetic floating-rate investment formed with an investment in the 5-year, 7% fixed-rate note and fixed-rate payer's position on a 6%/LIBOR swap.

16.5.2 Hedging Applications

Initially, interest rate swaps were used predominantly in arbitrage strategies. Today, there is an increased use of swaps for hedging and speculation. Hedging with swaps is done primarily to minimize the market risk of positions currently exposed to interest rate changes. To see this, consider a company that has financed its capital budget with intermediate-term FRNs tied to the LIBOR. Suppose that while the company's revenues have been closely tied to short-term interest rates in the past, the company has recently

Table 16.9 Synthetic fixed-rate investment: 5-year, $100m, FRN paying LIBOR + 100 BP; floating-rate position on 5-year, 5.75%/LIBOR swap, with NP = $100m

Swap: Floating payer's position on 5.75%/LIBOR swap; NP = $100m; maturity = 5 years.
Investment in $100m, 5-year, FRN paying LIBOR plus 100 BP. Synthetic fixed-rate
investment: FRN investment and floating-payer's position

Effective date	LIBOR	Fixed payment	Floating payment	Floating payer's net payment	FRN return	Fixed rate – swap payment	Annualized rate
6/10/02	4.50%						
12/10/02	4.75%	2,875,000	2,250,000	−625,000	2,750,000	3,375,000	0.0675
6/10/03	5.00%	2,875,000	2,375,000	−500,000	2,875,000	3,375,000	0.0675
12/10/03	5.25%	2,875,000	2,500,000	−375,000	3,000,000	3,375,000	0.0675
6/10/04	5.50%	2,875,000	2,625,000	−250,000	3,125,000	3,375,000	0.0675
12/10/04	5.75%	2,875,000	2,750,000	−125,000	3,250,000	3,375,000	0.0675
6/10/05	6.00%	2,875,000	2,875,000	0	3,375,000	3,375,000	0.0675
12/10/05	6.25%	2,875,000	3,000,000	125,000	3,500,000	3,375,000	0.0675
6/10/06	6.50%	2,875,000	3,125,000	250,000	3,625,000	3,375,000	0.0675
12/10/06	6.75%	2,875,000	3,250,000	375,000	3,750,000	3,375,000	0.0675
6/10/07		2,875,000	3,375,000	500,000	3,875,000	3,375,000	0.0675

Fixed payment = (0.0575/2)($100,000,000)
Floating payment = (LIBOR/2)($100,000,000)
FRN return = ((LIBOR + 1%)/2)($100,000,000)
Annualized rate = 2(FRN − swap payment)/$100,000,000

Synthetic fixed-rate investment

FRN	Receive LIBOR + 1%	= LIBOR + 1%
Swap	Pay LIBOR	= − LIBOR
Swap	Receive 5.75% fixed rate	= + 5.75%
	Receive 6.75% fixed rate	= 6.75%

Rate on fixed-rate bond = 6%

experienced fundamental changes that have altered its earnings patterns. To avoid potential cash flow problems, suppose the company decides it would now like to pay fixed instead of variable rates on its debt. To this end, one alternative would be for the company to refund its floating-rate debt with fixed-rate obligations. This, though, would require the cost of issuing new debt (underwriting, registration, etc.), as well as the cost of calling the current FRNs or buying the notes in the market if they are not callable. Thus, refunding would be a relatively costly alternative. Another possibility would be for the company to hedge its variable-rate debt with a strip of short Eurodollar futures contracts. This alternative is relatively inexpensive, but there may be hedging risk. The third and perhaps obvious alternative would be to combine the company's FRNs with a fixed-rate payer's position on a swap, thereby creating a synthetic fixed-rate debt position. This alternative of hedging FRNs with swaps, in turn, is less

expensive and more efficient than the first alternative of refinancing; it can also effectively minimize hedging risk.

An opposite scenario to the above case would be a company that has intermediate to long-term fixed-rate debt that it wants to make floating either because of a change in its economic structure or because it expects short-term rates will be decreasing. Given the costs of refunding fixed-rate debt with floating-rate and the hedging risk problems with futures, the most efficient way for the company to meet this objective would be to create synthetic floating-rate debt by combining its fixed-rate debt with a floating-rate payer's position on a swap.

16.5.3 Speculation Applications

Since swaps are similar to Eurodollar futures contracts, they can be used like them to speculate on short-term interest rate movements.

Table 16.10 Synthetic floating-rate investment: 5-year, $20m, 7% fixed-rate bond; fixed-rate position on 5-year, 6%/LIBOR swap, with NP = $20m

Swap: Fixed payer's position on 6%/LIBOR swap; NP = $20m; maturity = 5 years.
Investment of $20m in 5-year bond paying 7%. Synthetic fixed-rate investment: Fixed
investment and fixed-payer's position

Effective date	LIBOR	Fixed payment	Floating payment	Fixed payer's net payment	Fixed investment return	Fixed inv. return − swap payment	Annualized rate
6/10/02	4.50%						
12/10/02	4.75%	600,000	450,000	150,000	700,000	550,000	0.055
6/10/03	5.00%	600,000	475,000	125,000	700,000	575,000	0.0575
12/10/03	5.25%	600,000	500,000	100,000	700,000	600,000	0.06
6/10/04	5.50%	600,000	525,000	75,000	700,000	625,000	0.0625
12/10/04	5.75%	600,000	550,000	50,000	700,000	650,000	0.065
6/10/05	6.00%	600,000	575,000	25,000	700,000	675,000	0.0675
12/10/05	6.25%	600,000	600,000	0	700,000	700,000	0.07
6/10/06	6.50%	600,000	625,000	−25,000	700,000	725,000	0.0725
12/10/06	6.75%	600,000	650,000	−50,000	700,000	750,000	0.075
6/10/07		600,000	675,000	−75,000	700,000	775,000	0.0775

Fixed payment = (0.06/2)($20,000,000)
Floating payment = (LIBOR/2)($20,000,000)
Fixed investment return = (0.07/2)($20,000,000)
Annualized rate = 2(Fixed inv. return − swap payment)/$20,000,000

Synthetic FRN

Fixed-rate bond	Receive 7%	= + 7%
Swap	Receive LIBOR	= + LIBOR
Swap	Pay 6% fixed rate	= − 6%
	Receive LIBOR + 1%	= LIBOR + 1%

Rate on direct FRN = LIBOR + 0.5%

Specifically, as an alternative to a Eurodollar futures strip, speculators who expect short-term rates to increase in the future can take a fixed-rate payer's position; in contrast, speculators who expect short-term rates to decrease can take a floating-rate payer's position. Note, though, that there are differences in maturity, size, and marketability between futures and swaps that need to be taken into account when considering which one to use (see exhibit 16.2).

16.5.4 Changing the Balance Sheet's Interest Rate Exposure

In chapter 13, we discussed how a financial or non-financial corporation could alter the exposure of its balance sheet to changes in interest rates. The change can be done for speculative purposes (increasing the firm's exposure to interest rate changes) or for hedging purposes (reducing their exposure). In chapter 13, we looked at the case of an insurance company that expected lower rates in the future and wanted to change its immunized position (in which the duration of its bond portfolio was equal to the duration of its liabilities) to a speculative one in which it had a positive duration gap: $D_A - D_L > 0$. Short of changing the allocation of its bond portfolio, one way that we suggested the company could increase the duration of its assets would be to go long in T-bond futures contracts. With swaps, another possibility would be to decrease the duration of its liabilities by taking a floating-rate payer's position on a swap. If the company did this and rates were to decrease as expected, then not only would the value of the company's bond portfolio increase but the company would also profit from the swap; on the other hand, if rates were to increase, then the company would see decreases in the value of its bond portfolio, as well as

Exhibit 16.4   Procter & Gamble and Banker's Trust swap

In 1993, Procter & Gamble (P&G) and Banker's Trust (BT) entered into a swap agreement referred to as a 5/3 swap. The swap features included:

- Maturity of 5 years
- NP = $200m
- Fixed rate = 5.3%
- Floating rate = Average 30-day CP rate − 75 BP + spread
  - Average 30-day CP rate each day from the preceding period
  - Spread:

$$\text{Spread} = \text{Max}\left[0, \frac{98.5\left(\dfrac{\text{Yield on 5-year T-note}}{5.78\%}\right) - (\text{Bond price of 6.25\% T-bond maturing 2023})}{100}\right]$$

- P&G was the floating payer
- BT was the floating payer.

In this swap agreement, P&G was hoping that CP rates would decrease and that the rather complex spread would be zero. Unfortunately for P&G, rates increased in 1994 and bond prices declined, causing the spread to increase. P&G lost an estimated $90m from this exotic swap. P&G subsequently sued BT and settled out of court.

losses from its swap positions. By adding swaps, though, the company has effectively increased its interest rate exposure by creating a positive duration gap.

Instead of increasing its balance sheet's exposure to interest rate changes, a company may choose to reduce its exposure. For example, a company with a positive duration gap and a concern over future interest rate increases could reduce the gap by lengthening the duration of its liabilities with a fixed-rate payer's position on a swap. If rates were to later increase, then the decline in the value of the company's bond portfolio would be offset by the cash inflows realized from the fixed-payer's position on the swap.

As we noted in chapter 13, companies need to guard against unplanned actions that change their hedging positions to speculative ones. Exhibit 16.4 describes the 1994 case in which Procter & Gamble lost $90m from a speculative swap position.

16.6   SWAP VALUATION

16.6.1   Valuation of Off-Market Swaps

At origination, most plain vanilla swaps have an economic value of zero. This means that neither counterparty is required to pay the other to induce that party into the agreement. An economic value of zero requires that the swap's underlying bond positions trade at par − *par value swap*. If this were not the case, then one of the counterparties would need to compensate the other. In this case, the economic value of the swap is not zero. Such a swap is referred to as an *off-market swap*.

While most plain vanilla swaps are originally par value swaps with economic values of zero, as we previously noted, their economic values change over time as rates change; that is, existing swaps become off-market swaps as rates change. For example, suppose a bond with a maturity of 1.5 years and a coupon of 6.26% were priced at 100.37 of par to yield 6%:

$$B_0 = \sum_{t=1}^{3} \frac{6.26/2}{(1 + (0.06/2))^t} + \frac{100}{(1 + (0.06/2))^3}$$

$$= 100.37$$

At the 6% discount rate, an existing 6.26%/LIBOR swap with 1.5 years to maturity would not have an economic value of zero, and as a result, some compensation or payment (depending on the position) would be required to close the position. For example, suppose the floating payer on the 6.26%/LIBOR swap wanted to close her position by transferring it to a new party who would take the floating payer's position (the new party perhaps being a swap bank). With rates at 6%, the prospective floating payer could hedge the cash flows for the 1.5-year 6.26%/LIBOR swap, by forming a replicating position by selling a 1.5-year 6.26% bond for 100.37 per par and buying a 1.5-year FRN paying LIBOR for 100. The prospective party would pick up $0.37 by taking the floating position on a 6.26%/LIBOR swap and hedging it with the replicating position:

6.26%/LIBOR floating-rate position			
Swap: floating-rate payer's position		Pay LIBOR	−LIBOR
Swap: floating-rate payer's position		Receive 6.26%	+6.26
Replication	Initial cash flow		
Issue 6.26% fixed bond	Receive 100.37	Pay 6.26%	−6.26%
Buy FRN	Pay 100	Receive LIBOR	+LIBOR
Net	Receive 0.37		
Net	0.37	0	0

The prospective party would therefore be willing to pay up to $0.37 for the floating payer's position on the 1.5-year, 6.26%/LIBOR swap.

In contrast, suppose the fixed payer on the 6.26%/LIBOR swap wanted to close his position by transferring it to a new party (again, the new party may be a swap bank). At a 6% yield, the prospective fixed payer could replicate the cash flows for a 1.5-year 6.26%/LIBOR swap, by buying a 1.5-year bond paying an annual coupon of 6.26% at 100.37 of par and selling a 1.5-year FRN paying LIBOR for 100. The prospective party would lose $0.37 by taking the fixed payer's position on a 6.26%/LIBOR swap and hedging it with the replicating position:

6.26%/LIBOR fixed-rate position			
Swap: fixed-rate payer's position		Pay 6.26%	−6.26%
Swap: fixed-rate payer's position		Receive LIBOR	+LIBOR
Replication	Initial cash flow		
Buy 6.26% fixed bond	Pay 100.37	Receive 6.26%	+6.26%
Issue FRN	Receive 100	Pay LIBOR	−LIBOR
Net	Pay −0.37		
Net	−0.37	0	0

The prospective party would therefore require at least $0.37 in compensation from the current holder to take the fixed-payer's position on the 1.5-year, 6.26%/LIBOR swap.

In this example, the value of the 6.26%/LIBOR swap is a positive $0.37 for the floating payer's position (i.e., the floating payer could sell her swap for $0.37 to the new party) and a negative $0.37 for the fixed payer's position (i.e., the fixed payer would have to pay $0.37 to the new party to assume the swap). In general, the value of an existing swap is equal to the value of replacing the swap – *replacement swap*. In this example, the current par value swap would be a 6%/LIBOR. Instead of a replicating portfolio, the fixed payer with the 6.26%/LIBOR swap could offset his position by taking a floating payer's position on a current 1.5-year, 6%/LIBOR par value swap. By doing this, he would be losing $0.13 $(=(0.06 − 0.0626)/2)$ per $100 par value:

6.26%/LIBOR fixed-rate position	Annual	Annual	Semi-annual
Swap: fixed-rate payer's position	Pay 6.26%	−6.26%	Pay $3.13
Swap: fixed-rate payer's position	Receive LIBOR	+LIBOR	Receive LIBOR/2
Replacement: 6%/LIBOR floating-rate position			
Swap: floating-rate payer's position	Pay LIBOR	−LIBOR	Pay LIBOR/2
Swap: floating-rate payer's position	Receive 6%	+6%	Receive $3
Net	Pay 0.26%	−0.26%	Pay $0.13

Thus, the replacement swap represents a loss of $0.13 per $100 par per period for three periods. Using 6% as the discount rate, the present value of this 6.26%/LIBOR fixed position is −$0.37:

$$PV = \sum_{t=1}^{3} \frac{-\$0.13}{(1 + (0.06/2))^t} = -\$0.37$$

In contrast, the floating payer with the 6.26%/LIBOR swap could offset her position by taking a fixed payer's position on a current 1.5-year, 6%/LIBOR par value swap. By doing this, she would be gaining \$0.13 ($=(0.0626-0.06)/2$) per \$100 par value:

6.26%/LIBOR floating-rate position	Annual	Annual	Semi-annual
Swap: floating-rate payer's position	Pay LIBOR	− LIBOR	Pay LIBOR/2
Swap: floating-rate payer's position	Receive 6.26%	+ 6.26	Receive \$3.13
Replacement: 6%/LIBOR fixed-rate position			
Swap: fixed-rate payer's position	Pay 6%	− 6%	Pay \$3
Swap: fixed-rate payer's position	Receive LIBOR	+ LIBOR	Receive LIBOR/2
Net	Receive 0.26%	+ 0.26%	Receive \$0.13

Thus, the replacement swap represents a periodic gain of \$0.13 per \$100 par for three periods. Using 6% as the discount rate, the present value of the 6.26%/LIBOR floating position is \$0.37:

$$PV = \sum_{t=1}^{3} \frac{\$0.13}{(1+(0.06/2))^t} = \$0.37$$

The underlying valuation concept here is that the current swap rate determines the value of an existing swap or any off-market swap.

16.6.2 Equilibrium Value of a Swap: Zero-Coupon Approach

Formally, the values of the fixed and floating swap positions are:

$$SV^{fix} = \left[\sum_{t=1}^{M} \frac{K^P - K^S}{(1+K^P)^t}\right] NP$$

$$= \left[\sum_{t=1}^{3} \frac{(0.06/2) - (0.0626/2)}{(1+(0.06/2))^t}\right](100)$$

$$= -0.37$$

$$SV^{fl} = \left[\sum_{t=1}^{M} \frac{K^S - K^P}{(1+K^P)^t}\right] NP$$

$$= \left[\sum_{t=1}^{3} \frac{(0.0626/2) - (0.06/2)}{(1+(0.06/2))^t}\right](100)$$

$$= 0.37$$

where:

K^S = fixed rate on the existing swap

K^P = fixed rate on current par-value swap

SV^{fix} = swap value of the fixed position on the existing swap

SV^{fl} = swap value of the floating position on the existing swap

Note that these values are obtained by discounting the net cash flows at the current YTM (K^P or 6% on the three-period bond). As a result, this approach to valuing off-market swaps is often referred to as the *YTM approach*. However, recall from our discussion of bond valuation in chapter 2 that the equilibrium price of a bond is obtained not by discounting all of the bond's cash flows by a common discount rate, but rather by discounting each of the bond's cash flows by their appropriate spot rates – the rate on a zero-discount bond. As we discussed in chapter 2, valuing bonds by using spot rates instead of a common YTM ensures that there are no arbitrage opportunities from buying bonds and stripping them or buying zero-discount bonds and bundling them. In addition to the arbitrage argument, the valuation of bonds using a common YTM for all cash flows also leads to under- and overvaluation of the separate cash flows. That is, if the yield curve is positively sloped, early cash flows will be underpriced and later cash flows will be overpriced; the opposite if the yield curve is negatively sloped.

The argument for pricing bonds in terms of spot rates also applies to the valuation of off-market swaps. Similar to bond valuation, the equilibrium value of a swap is obtained by discounting each of the swap's cash flows by their appropriate spot rates. The valuation of swaps using spot rates is referred to as the *zero-coupon approach*. The approach, in turn, requires generating a spot yield curve for swaps.

16.6.3 Zero-Coupon Swap Yield Curve: Bootstrapping

Since there is not an active market for zero-discount swaps, implied zero-coupon swap rates need to be determined. As we discussed in chapter 2, spot rates can be estimated using a bootstrapping technique. For swaps, this

Table 16.11 Generic swap yield curve for zero-coupon rates

(1) Maturity in years	(2) Yield on T-note	(3) Swap spread (BP)	(4) Swap rate	(5) Zero-coupon rate	(6) Implied 1-year forward rates
1	0.04	100	0.05	0.05	0.05671
2	0.045	80	0.053	0.05308	0.06576
3	0.05	70	0.057	0.05729	0.07697
4	0.055	65	0.0615	0.062176	0.08891
5	0.06	62	0.0662	0.0674697	

Zero-coupon rates from bootstrapping

$$Z(2): 1 = \frac{0.053}{1+0.05} + \frac{1.053}{1+Z(2)}$$

$$Z(2) = \left[\frac{1.053}{1 - 0.05047619}\right]^{1/2} - 1 = 0.05308$$

$$Z(3): 1 = \frac{0.057}{1.05} + \frac{0.057}{(1.05308)^2} + \frac{1.057}{(1+Z(3))^3}$$

$$Z(3) = \left[\frac{1.057}{1 - 0.1056844}\right]^{1/3} - 1 = 0.05729$$

$$Z(4): 1 = \frac{0.0615}{1.05} + \frac{0.0615}{(1.05308)^2} + \frac{0.0615}{(1.05729)^3} + \frac{1.0615}{(1+Z(4))^4}$$

$$Z(4) = \left[\frac{1.0615}{1 - 0.1660626}\right]^{1/4} - 1 = 0.062176$$

$$Z(5): 1 = \frac{0.0662}{1.05} + \frac{0.0662}{(1.05308)^2} + \frac{0.0662}{(1.05729)^3} + \frac{0.0662}{(1.062176)^4} + \frac{1.0662}{(1+Z(5))^5}$$

$$Z(5) = \left[\frac{1.0662}{1 - 0.23076177}\right]^{1/5} - 1 = 0.0674697$$

One-year implied forward rates, f_{1M}

$$f_{11}: Z(2) = [(1+Z(1)(1+f_{11})]^{1/2} - 1$$

$$f_{11} = \frac{(1+Z(2))^2}{(1+Z(1))} - 1 = \frac{(1.05308)^2}{1.05} - 1 = 0.05671$$

$$f_{12}: Z(3) = [(1+Z(1)(1+f_{11})(1+f_{12})]^{1/3} - 1$$

$$f_{12} = \frac{(1+Z(3))^3}{(1+Z(1)(1+f_{11}))} - 1 = \frac{(1.05729)^3}{(1.05)(1.05671)} - 1 = 0.06576$$

$$f_{13}: Z(4) = [(1+Z(1)(1+f_{11})(1+f_{12})(1+f_{13})]^{1/4} - 1$$

$$f_{13} = \frac{(1+Z(4))^4}{(1+Z(1)(1+f_{11})(1+f_{13}))} - 1 = \frac{(1.062176)^4}{(1.05)(1.05671)(1.06576)} - 1 = 0.07697$$

$$f_{14}: Z(5) = [(1+Z(1)(1+f_{11})(1+f_{12})(1+f_{13})(1+f_{14})]^{1/5} - 1$$

$$f_{14} = \frac{(1+Z(5))^5}{(1+Z(1)(1+f_{11})(1+f_{13})(1+f_{14}))} - 1 = \frac{(1.0674697)^5}{(1.05)(1.05671)(1.06576)(1.07697)} - 1$$

$$= 0.08891$$

requires applying the technique to a series of current generic swaps. For a yield curve defined by annual periods, the first step is to calculate the 1-year zero-coupon rate, $Z(1)$.

Since current generic swaps are priced at par, the 1-year zero-coupon rate for a swap would be equal to the annual coupon rate on a 1-year generic swap, $C(1)$ (assume annual payment frequency instead of semi-annual). That is, for a par value of $1:

$$1 = \frac{1 + C(1)}{1 + Z(1)}$$

$$Z(1) = C(1)$$

The 2-year swap, with an annual coupon rate of $C(2)$ and the 1-year zero-coupon rate of $Z(1)$ can be used to calculate the 2-year zero discount rate, $Z(2)$:

$$1 = \frac{C(2)}{1 + Z(1)} + \frac{1 + C(2)}{(1 + Z(2))^2}$$

$$Z(2) = \left[\frac{1 + C(2)}{1 - [C(2)/(1 + Z(1))]} \right]^{1/2} - 1$$

The 3-year zero-coupon rate is found using the 3-year swap and the 1-year and 2-year zero-coupon rates. Other rates are determined in a similar manner. Using this recursive method, a zero coupon (or spot) yield curve for swaps can be generated from a series of generic swaps applicable to the counterparty in question. These zero-coupon rates can then be used to discount the cash flows on a swap to determine its value.

Table 16.11 shows a yield curve of zero-coupon rates generated from a series of current generic swap rates. The swap rates shown in column 4 are the annual fixed rates paid on the swaps. Each rate is equal to the yield on a corresponding T-note plus the swap spread. The swap spread reflects the credit risk of the swap party and the maturity of the swap. The zero-coupon swap rates shown in column 5 are generated from these swap rates using the bootstrapping approach. Note that since swaps involve semi-annual cash flows, the annualized zero spot rates at 0.5 intervals are usually interpolated. Thus, the rate at 1.5 years is $(0.05 + 0.053)/2 = 0.0515$; the rate at 2.5 years is $(0.053 + 0.057)/2 = 0.055$; the rate at 3.5 years is 0.05925; the rate at 4.5 years is 0.06385.

16.6.4 Valuation

Given the zero-coupon rates shown in table 16.11 (column 5) and the 5.7% coupon on the current 3-year par value swap (column 4), the value of the fixed-payer position on an original 5-year, 5%/LIBOR swap with an NP of $10m, annual payment frequency, and 3 years

remaining to term would be $189,014 using the zero-coupon approach:

SV^{fix}

$$= \left[\frac{0.057 - 0.05}{1.05} + \frac{0.057 - 0.05}{(1.05308)^2} + \frac{0.057 - 0.05}{(1.05729)^3} \right]$$

$$\times (\$10m) = \$189,014$$

The value of the floating position would be $-$189,014:

SV^{fl}

$$= \left[\frac{0.05 - 0.057}{1.05} + \frac{0.05 - 0.057}{(1.05308)^2} + \frac{0.05 - 0.057}{(1.05729)^3} \right]$$

$$\times (\$10m) = -\$189,014$$

In contrast, the value of the swap to the fixed payer using the YTM approach with a 5.7% YTM would be $188,154:

$$SV^{fix} = \left[\sum_{t=1}^{3} \frac{0.057 - 0.05}{(1.057)^3} \right] (\$10m) = \$188,154$$

Thus, if the fixed position were valued by the YTM approach at $188,154, then a swap dealer could realize an arbitrage by buying the 3-year swap at $188,154, then selling (i.e., taking floating positions) three off-market 5.7%/LIBOR swaps with maturities of 1, 2, and 3 years priced to yield their zero-coupon rates for a total of $189,014. As swap dealers try to exploit this arbitrage, they would drive the price of the swap to the $189,014. Thus, like bonds, the equilibrium price of a swap is obtained by discounting each of the net cash flows from an existing and current swap by their appropriate spot rates.

16.6.5 Break-Even Swap Rate

A corollary to the zero-coupon approach to valuation is that in the absence of arbitrage, the fixed rate on the swap (the swap rate) is that rate, C^*, that makes the present value of the swap's fixed-rate payments equal to the present value of the swap's floating payments, with implied one-period forward rates, f_{M1}, being used to estimate the future floating payments. Recall that implied forward rates are future interest rates implied by today's rates; these rates are also equal to the rates on futures contracts if the carrying-cost model holds. For an N-year swap with an NP of \$1, this condition states that in equilibrium:

$$\frac{C^*}{(1+Z(1))} + \frac{C^*}{(1+Z(2))^2} + \cdots$$
$$+ \frac{C^*}{(1+Z(N))^N} = \frac{Z(1)}{(1+Z(1))} + \frac{f_{11}}{(1+Z(2))^2}$$
$$+ \cdots + \frac{f_{1,N-1}}{(1+Z(N))^N}$$

16.7 CREDIT RISK

When compared to their equivalent fixed- and floating-bond positions, swaps have less credit risk. To see this, consider a party with a short position in an FRN and a long position in a fixed-rate bond that when combined are equivalent to a generic swap. If the issuer of the fixed-rate bond defaults, the party still has to meet its obligations on the FRN. By contrast, on an equivalent swap position, if one party defaults, the other party no longer has an obligation. As

$$C^* = \frac{(Z(1)/(1+Z(1))) + (f_{11}/(1+Z(2))^2) + \cdots + (f_{1,N-1}/(1+Z(N))^N)}{(1/(1+Z(1))) + (1/(1+Z(2))^2) + \cdots + (1/(1+Z(N))^N)}$$

The swap rate C^* that equates the present value of the swap's fixed-rate payments to the present value of the swap's floating payments is sometimes referred to as the **break-even rate** or the **market rate**. Accordingly, if swap dealers were to set swap rates equal to the break-even rates, then there would be no arbitrage from forming opposite positions in fixed-rate and floating-rate bonds priced at their equilibrium values nor any arbitrage from taking opposite positions in a swap and a strip of swaps.

Column 6 in table 16.11 shows the 1-year implied forward rates obtained from the zero-coupon rates (column 5) generated in the above example. Using these rates and the above equation one can obtain the break-even swap rates for the series of swaps in table 16.11. These break-even rates, in turn, are equal to the swap rates shown in column 4. For example, the break-even rate for the 3-year swap is 0.057, which, in turn, matches the 3-year swap rate shown in the table:

we noted earlier, swaps fall under contract law and not security law, and as a result have less credit risk than an equivalent bond position.

The mechanism for default is governed by the swap contract, with many patterned after International Swap and Derivatives Association (ISDA) documents. When a party to a swap defaults, the contract often allows the non-defaulting party the right to give up to a 20-day notice that a particular date will be the termination date. This notice gives the parties time to determine a settlement amount. The settlement amount depends on the value of an existing swap or equivalently on the terms of a replacement swap. For example, suppose the fixed payer on a 9.5%/LIBOR swap with NP of \$10m runs into severe financial problems and defaults on the swap agreement when there are 3 years and six payments remaining and the LIBOR is now relatively low. Suppose the current 3-year swap calls for an exchange of 9% fixed for LIBOR. To replace the defaulted swap, the

$$C^* = \frac{(0.05/(1.05)) + (0.05671/(1.05308)^2) + (0.06576/(1.05729)^3)}{(1/(1.05)) + (1/(1.05308)^2) + (1/(1.05729)^3)}$$
$$C^* = 0.057$$

Break-even rates are used by swap dealers to help them determine the rates on new par value swaps, as well as the compensation to receive or pay on new off-market swaps in which the swap rates are set different than the break-even rates.

non-defaulting floating payer would have to take a new floating position on the 9%/LIBOR swap. As a result, she would be receiving only \$450,000 each period instead of the \$475,000 on the defaulted swap. Thus, the default represents a loss of \$25,000 for 3 years and six periods. Using 9% as the discount rate, the present value of this loss would be $128,947:

$$PV = \sum_{t=1}^{6} \frac{\$25,000}{(1+(0.09/2))^t} = \$128,947$$

Thus, given a replacement fixed swap rate of 9%, the actual credit risk exposure is $128,947. The replacement value of $128,947 is also the economic value of the original 9.5%/LIBOR swap. Note: if the replacement fixed swap rate had been 10% instead of 9%, then the floating payer would have had a positive economic value of $126,892:

$$PV = \sum_{t=1}^{6} \frac{\$25,000}{(1+(0.10/2))^t} = \$126,892$$

Under a higher interest rate scenario, the fixed payer experiencing the financial distress would not have defaulted on the swap, although he may be defaulting on other obligations. The increase in rates in this case has made the swap an asset to the fixed payer instead of a liability.

The example illustrates that two events are necessary for default loss on a swap: an actual default on the agreement and an adverse change in rates. Credit risk on a swap is therefore a function of the joint probability of financial distress and adverse interest rate movements. In practice, credit risk is often managed by adjusting the negotiated fixed rate on a swap to include a credit risk spread between the parties: a less risky firm (which could be the swap bank acting as dealer) will pay a lower fixed rate or receive a higher fixed rate the riskier the counterparty. The credit rate adjustment also takes into account the probability of rates increasing and decreasing and its impact on the future economic value of the couterparty's swap position. In addition to rate adjustments, swap dealers also manage credit risk by requiring collateral and maintenance margins.

It should be noted that historically the default rate on swaps has been very small. This reflects the fact that swap agreements are made by financial institutions and relatively large companies with good credit ratings.

16.8 CONCLUSION

In this chapter, we have examined the market, uses, and valuations of generic interest rate swaps. Like exchange-traded options and futures, swaps provide investors and borrowers with a tool for more effectively managing their asset and liability positions. They have become a basic financial engineering tool to apply to a variety of financial problems. Over the years, the underlying structure of the generic swap has been modified in a number of ways to accommodate different uses. In the next chapter, we look at some of the non-generic swaps that have been introduced over the last decade as well as the standard currency swap.

KEY TERMS

Interest Rate Swap	Maturity Date	Swap Rate
Currency Swap	Net Settlement Basis	Comparative Advantage
Plain Vanilla Swap or	Confirmation	Asset-Based Interest Rate
Generic Swap	International Swap and	Swap
Counterparties	Derivatives Association	Par Value Swap
Fixed-Rate Payer	(ISDA)	Off-Market Swap
Floating-Rate Payer	Swap Banks	Replacement Swap
Trade Date	Brokered Swaps	YTM Approach
Effective Date	Dealer Swaps	Zero-Coupon Approach
Settlement or Payment	Warehousing	Break-Even Rate or Market
Date	Running a Dynamic Book	Rate

PROBLEMS AND QUESTIONS

Note on problems: for problems requiring a number of calculations, the reader may want to use Excel.

1. Given the following interest rate swap:

   - Fixed-rate payer pays half of the YTM on a T-note of 6.5%
   - Floating-rate payer pays the LIBOR
   - Notional principal is $10m
   - Effective dates are March 23 and September 23 for the next 3 years.

   a. Determine the net receipts of the fixed-rate payer given the following LIBORs:
      - 3/23/y1   0.055
      - 9/23/y1   0.060
      - 3/23/y2   0.065
      - 9/23/y2   0.070
      - 3/23/y3   0.075
      - 9/23/y3   0.080

   b. Show in a table how a company with a 3-year, $10m variable-rate loan, with the rate set by the LIBOR on the dates coinciding with the swap, could make the loan a fixed-rate one by taking a position in the swap. What would be the fixed rate?

   c. Show in a table how a company with a 2-year, $10m fixed-rate loan at 6.0% could make the loan a floating-rate one by taking a position in the swap.

2. Explain how the fixed-payer and floating-payer positions in question 1 could be replicated with positions in fixed-rate and floating-rate bonds.

3. Define a Eurodollar futures strip and the positions on the strip that would be similar to the fixed-payer and floating-payer positions in question 1. Following the outline table below, determine the cash flows for each strip position given the LIBOR scenario in question 1. Note: the interest payments on the swap are determined by the LIBOR at the beginning of the period, while the futures position's cash flows are based on the LIBOR at the end of its period.

Eurodollar closing dates	LIBOR	f_T	Cash flow from short position	Cash flow from long position
3/23/y1	0.055			
9/23/y1	0.060			
3/23/y2	0.065			
9/23/y2	0.070			
3/23/y3	0.075			
9/23/y3	0.080			

4. Explain some of the differences between a plain vanilla swap position and a Eurodollar strip.

5. Using a table showing payments and receipts, prove that the following positions are equivalent:

   a. Floating-rate loan plus fixed-rate payer's position is equivalent to a fixed-rate loan.

   b. Fixed-rate loan plus floating-rate payer's position is equivalent to a floating-rate loan.

   c. Floating-rate note investment plus floating-rate payer's position is equivalent to a fixed-rate investment.

   d. Fixed-rate bond investment plus fixed-rate payer's position is equivalent to a floating-rate investment.

6. What are the dealer's bid and asked quotes on a 5-year swap with a quoted 60/70 swap spread over a T-note with a yield of 6.5%?

7. The table below shows a swap bank's quotes on four generic swaps.

Swap	Swap maturity	Treasury yield (%)	Bid swap spread (BP)	Ask swap spread (BP)	Fixed swap rate spread	Swap rate
1	2 years	4.95	54	64		
2	3 years	5.12	72	76		
3	4 years	5.32	69	74		
4	5 years	5.74	70	76		

a. Determine the figures needed to complete the table by calculating the swap bank's fixed swap rate spreads and swap rates for the four swaps.
b. Explain in more detail the positions the swap bank is willing to take on the first swap contract.
c. Describe the swap arrangement for a swap bank customer who took a floating-rate payer's position with a notional principal of $50m on the third contract offered by the bank.
d. Suppose two of the swap bank's customers take fixed-rate payer positions on the third contract offered by the bank, each with notional principals of $25m. Show in a flow diagram (similar to the one in exhibit 16.3) the contracts between the swap bank and these customers and its customer in Question 6c.

8. The table below shows the effective dates on a 6%/LIBOR swap NP = $20m, the number of days between effective dates, and assumed LIBORs on effective dates. Calculate the figures needed to complete the table by determining the swap's fixed payments, floating payments, and net receipts received by the fixed- and floating-rate payers.

Settlement date	Number of days	LIBOR (%)	Fixed payment	Floating payment	Fixed payer's net receipts	Floating payer's net receipts
6/10/y1		6.50				
12/10/y1	183	6.75				
6/10/y2	182	6.25				
12/10/y2	183	6.00				
6/10/y3	182	5.50				
12/10/y3	183	5.25				
6/10/y4	182					

9. Suppose a swap bank can go long and short in 3-year FRNs paying LIBOR and 3-year T-notes yielding 5%.

a. Given these securities, define the 3-year generic par value swap the bank could offer its customers. Exclude the basis point that the swap bank might add to its bid and asked prices.
b. Explain how the swap bank determines basis points to add to the fixed rate on its fixed and floating positions.
c. Suppose the swap bank provided one of its customers with a 5%/LIBOR fixed-rate position. Explain how the bank would hedge its position with the above securities if it did not have a customer taking an opposite swap position.
d. Suppose the swap bank provided one of its customers with a 3-year 5%/LIBOR floating-rate position. Explain how the bank would hedge its position with the above securities if it did not have a customer taking an opposite swap position.

10. Given the 5% yield on 3-year T-notes and LIBOR yields on FRN in question 9, how much would the swap bank pay or charge to buy an *existing* floating-rate payer's position on a 3-year, 6%/LIBOR swap with a notional principal of $50m if it planned to hedge the purchase with positions in the T-note and FRN? How much would it pay or charge for an existing fixed payer's position on a 3-year, 6%/LIBOR with a notional principal of $50m? Exclude the basis point that the swap bank might add to its bid and asked prices.

11. If the swap bank in question 9 were offering 3-year generic 5%/LIBOR par value swaps, how much would it pay or charge to buy a floating-rate payer's position on an *existing* 3-year, 6%/LIBOR swap with a notional principal of $50m if it planned to hedge the purchase with a position on its par value swaps? How much would it pay or charge for an existing fixed payer's position on a 3-year, 6%/LIBOR with a notional principal of $50m? Exclude the basis point that the swap bank might add to its bid and asked prices.

12. Explain the alternative ways a swap holder could close her swap position instead of selling it to a swap bank.

13. If the fixed rate on a new par value 2-year swap were at 5%, how much would a swap dealer pay or charge to assume an existing fixed payer's position on a 5.5%/LIBOR generic swap with 2 years left to maturity and notional principal of $20m? How much would the dealer pay or charge if the fixed rate on a new par value 2-year swap were at 6%?

14. If the fixed rate on a new par value 2-year swap were at 5%, how much would a swap dealer pay or charge for assuming an existing 5.5%/LIBOR floating-rate position on a generic swap with 2 years left to maturity and notional principal of $20m? How much would the dealer pay or charge if the fixed rate on a new par value 2-year swap were at 6%?

15. The Star Chemical Company wants to raise $150m with a 5-year loan to finance an expansion of one of its production plants. Based on its moderate credit ratings, Star can borrow 5-year funds at a 10.5% fixed rate or at a floating rate equal to LIBOR + 75 BP. Given the choice of financing, Star prefers the fixed-rate loan. The Moon Development Company is also looking for 5-year funding to finance its proposed $150m office park development. Given its high credit rating, suppose Moon can borrow the funds for 5 years at a fixed rate of 9.5% or at a floating rate equal to the LIBOR + 25 BP. Given the choice, Moon prefers a variable-rate loan. In summary, Star and Moon have the following fixed- and floating-rate loan alternatives:

Company	Fixed rate	Floating rate
Star Company	10.5%	LIBOR + 75 BP
Moon Company	9.5%	LIBOR + 25 BP

a. Describe Moon's absolute advantage and each company's comparative advantage.
b. What is the total possible interest rate reduction gain for both parties if both parties were to create synthetic positions with a swap?
c. Explain how a swap bank could arrange a 5-year, 9.5%/LIBOR swap that would benefit both the Star and Moon companies. What is the total interest rate reduction gain and how is it split?

16. Suppose the Star and Moon companies in question 15 both have the same quality ratings with the following fixed- and floating-rate loan alternatives:

Company	Fixed rate	Floating rate
Star Company	9.50%	LIBOR + 50 BP
Moon Company	9.25%	LIBOR + 75 BP

    a. Describe each company's absolute and comparative advantages.
    b. What is the total possible interest rate reduction gain for both parties if both parties were to create synthetic positions with a swap?
    c. Explain how a swap bank could arrange a 5-year swap in which Star and Moon split the total interest rate reduction gain.

17. Explain the idea of comparative advantage in terms of questions 15 and 16.

18. Explain the idea of hidden options in terms of question 15.

19. Suppose a company wants to borrow $100m for 5 years at a fixed rate. Suppose the company can issue both a 5-year, 11%, fixed-rate bond paying coupons on a semi-annual basis and a 5-year FRN paying LIBOR plus 100 BP.

    a. Explain how the company could create a synthetic 5-year fixed-rate loan with a swap.
    b. What would the fixed rate on the swap have to be for the synthetic position to be equivalent to the direct loan position? Show the synthetic position in a table.
    c. Define the company's criterion for selecting the synthetic loan.

20. Suppose a financial institution wants to finance its 3-year $100m floating-rate loans by selling 3-year floating-rate notes. Suppose the institution can issue a 3-year, 7%, fixed-rate note paying coupons on a semi-annual basis and also a 3-year FRN paying LIBOR plus 100 BP.

    a. Explain how the institution could create a synthetic 3-year floating-rate note with a swap.
    b. What would the fixed rate on the swap have to be for the synthetic position to be equivalent to the floating-rate note? Show the synthetic position in a table.
    c. Define the institution's criterion for selecting the synthetic loan.

21. Suppose a financial institution wants to invest $100m in a 3-year fixed-rate note. Suppose the institution can invest in a 3-year, 7%, fixed-rate note paying coupons on a semi-annual basis and selling at par and also in a 3-year FRN paying LIBOR plus 100 BP.

    a. Explain how the institution could create a synthetic 3-year fixed-rate note with a swap.
    b. What would the fixed rate on the swap have to be for the synthetic position to be equivalent to the fixed-rate note? Show the synthetic position in a table.
    c. Define the institution's criterion for selecting the synthetic investment.

22. Suppose a financial institution wants to invest $100m in a 3-year floating-rate note. Suppose the institution can invest in a 3-year, 7%, fixed-rate note paying coupons on a semi-annual basis and also in a 3-year FRN paying LIBOR plus 100 BP.

    a. Explain how the institution could create a synthetic 3-year floating-rate note with a swap.
    b. What would the fixed rate on the swap have to be for the synthetic position to be equivalent to the floating-rate note? Show the synthetic position in a table.
    c. Define the institution's criterion for selecting the synthetic investment.

23. Given a generic 5-year par value swap with a fixed rate of 6%, determine the values of the following off-market swap positions using the YTM approach:

    a. Fixed-rate position on a 5-year, 5%/LIBOR generic swap with NP=$50m.
    b. Floating-rate position on a 5-year 5%/LIBOR generic swap with NP=$50m.
    c. Fixed-rate position on a 5-year 7%/LIBOR generic swap with NP=$50m.
    d. Floating-rate position on a 5-year 7%/LIBOR generic swap with NP=$50m.

24. The table shows the swap rates for generic par value swaps with maturities from 1 to 4 years.

    a. Using the bootstrapping approach, determine the zero-coupon swap rates with maturities of 1, 2, and 3 years.
    b. Interpolate the zero-coupon swap rates for semi-annual periods: 0.5, 1, 1.5, 2, 2.5, and 3.
    c. Using the zero-coupon approach, determine the values of fixed and floating positions on a 2-year, 6.5%/LIBOR off-market swap with NP=$10m.

Maturity in years	Swap rate
0.5	0.050
1	0.050
2	0.055
3	0.060
4	0.065

25. Short-answer questions:

    (1) Who generally assumes the credit risk in a brokered swap?
    (2) Who assumes the credit risk in a dealer's swap?
    (3) What is one of the problems with brokered swaps that contributed to the growth in the dealer swap market?
    (4) What does the term warehousing mean?
    (5) What does the term running a dynamic book mean?
    (6) How do dealers typically quote the fixed rate and floating rate on the swap agreements that they offer?
    (7) Describe the comparative advantage argument that is often advanced as the reason for the growth in the swap market.
    (8) If one borrower has a comparative advantage in the fixed-rate market and another borrower has a comparative advantage in the floating-rate market, what is the total possible interest rate reduction gain for both borrowers from creating synthetic debt positions using swaps given that one of the borrowers has an absolute advantage in both the fixed-rate and floating-rate credit markets?
    (9) If one borrower has a comparative advantage in the fixed-rate market and another borrower has a comparative advantage in the floating-rate market, what is the total possible interest rate reduction gain for both borrowers from creating synthetic debt positions using swaps given that each party has an absolute advantage in each market?
    (10) What is the criticism that is often advanced against the comparative advantage argument?
    (11) What is the hidden option and how does it relate to the difference in credit spreads in the fixed and floating credit markets?
    (12) Explain how a company could take a swap position to replace its current floating-rate debt with a fixed-rate debt obligation.
    (13) Explain how a company could take a swap position to replace its current fixed-rate debt with a floating-rate debt obligation.

(14) Explain how a company with investments in intermediate fixed-rate notes could take a swap position to create a floating-rate note. Why might a company want to do this?

(15) Explain how an insurance company that expected lower rates in the future could change its currently immunized position to a more speculative one with a positive duration gap.

(16) Define the YTM approach to valuing off-market swaps.

(17) What is the problem with using the YTM approach to value off-market swaps?

(18) Define the zero-coupon approach to valuing off-market swaps.

(19) What is the most important property of the zero-coupon approach to swap valuation?

(20) What is the break-even swap rate?

WEB EXERCISES

1. Find out who the International Swap and Derivatives Association is by going to their website, www.isda.org, and clicking on "About ISDA." At the site, also click on "Educational Information" to find a bibliography of swaps and derivatives articles and links to other derivative sites.

2. Examine the growth in the interest rate swap market by looking at the International Swap and Derivatives Association's Market Survey. Go to www.isda.org and click on "Survey and Market Statistics" and "Historical Data."

SELECTED REFERENCES

Bhattacharya, Anand K. and Frank J. Fabozzi "Interest-Rate Swaps," in Frank J. Fabozzi (ed.) *The Handbook of Fixed Income Securities*, 6th edn (New York: McGraw-Hill, 2001).

Bicksler, J. and A. H. Chen "An Economic Analysis of Interest Rate Swaps," *Journal of Finance* 41 (1986): 645–55.

Brotherton-Ratcliffe, R. and B. Iben "Yield Curve Applications of Swap Products," in R. Schwartz and C. Smith (eds) *Advanced Strategies in Financial Risk Management* (New York: New York Institute of Finance, 1993).

Brown, Jeffry P. "Variations to Basic Swaps," in Carl R. Beidleman (ed.) *Interest Rate Swaps* (Homewood, IL: Business One Irwin, 1991).

Brown, Keith C. and Donald J. Smith "Plain Vanilla Swaps: Market Structures, Applications, and Credit Risk," in Carl R. Beidleman (ed.) *Interest Rate Swaps* (Homewood, IL: Business One Irwin, 1991).

Cooper, I. and A. S. Mello "The Default Risk of Swaps," *Journal of Finance* 48 (1991): 597–620.

Darby, M. R. "Over-the-Counter Derivatives and Systemic Risk to the Global Financial System,"

National Bureau of Economic Research Working Paper Series, No. 4801, 1994.

Goodman, Laurie S. "Capital Market Applications of Interest Rate Swaps," in Carl R. Beidleman (ed.) *Interest Rate Swaps* (Homewood, IL: Business One Irwin, 1991).

Haubrich, Joseph G. "Swaps and the Swaps Yield Curve," *Economic Commentary* (Federal Reserve Bank of Cleveland, December 2001): 1–4.

Litzenberger, R. H. "Swaps: Plain and Fanciful," *Journal of Finance* 47(3) (1992/1993): 831–50.

Marshall, J. F. and K. R. Kapner *Understanding Swaps* (New York: Wiley, 1993).

Pergam, Albert S. "Chapter 23: Swaps: A Legal Perspective," in Jack Clark Francis and Avner Simon Wolf (eds) *The Handbook of Interest Rate Risk Management* (New York: Irwin Professional Publishing, 1994).

Smith, C. W., C. W. Smithson, and L. M. Wakeman "The Evolving Market for Swaps," *Midland Corporate Finance Journal* 3 (1986): 20–32.

Smith, C. W., C. W. Smithson, and L. M. Wakeman "The Market for Interest Rate Swaps," *Financial Management* 17 (1988): 34–44.

Sun, T., S. Sundaresan, and C. Wang "Interest Rate Swaps: An Empirical Investigation," *Journal of Financial Economics* 36 (1993): 77–99.

Turnbull, S. M. "Swaps: A Zero Sum Game," *Financial Management* 16(1) (Spring 1987): 15–21.

Wall, L. D. and J. J. Pringle "Alternative Explanations of Interest Rate Swaps: A Theoretical and Empirical Analysis," *Financial Management* 18(2) (Summer 1989): 59–73.

CHAPTER SEVENTEEN

NON-GENERIC INTEREST RATE AND CURRENCY SWAPS

17.1 INTRODUCTION

Since the mid-1970s there has been an active currency swap market amongst financial and non-financial corporations. Although there is some debate over the exact swap agreement marking the beginning of this market, many observers point to the World Bank and IBM swap in 1981 as the agreement that propelled the tremendous growth that has occurred in both currency and interest rate swap markets over the last two decades. Concomitant with this growth has been the number of innovations introduced in swaps contracts over the years. Today, there are a number of non-standard or non-generic swaps used by financial and non-financial corporations to manage their varied cash flow and return–risk problems. In this chapter, we extend our analysis of generic interest rate swaps by examining some of the non-generic interest rate swaps and the generic currency swap.

17.2 NON-GENERIC SWAPS

While approximately 80% of all interest rate swaps are generic, the underlying structure of the generic swap has been modified in a number of ways to accommodate different uses.

Non-generic swaps usually differ in terms of their rates, principal, or effective dates. For example, instead of defining swaps in terms of the LIBOR, some swaps use the T-bill rate, prime lending rate, or the Federal Reserve's Commercial Paper Rate Index with different maturities. Similarly, the principals defining a swap can vary. An *amortizing swap*, for example, is a swap in which the NP is reduced over time based on a schedule, while a *set-up swap* (sometimes called an *accreting swap*) has its NP increasing over time. There are also *zero-coupon swaps* in which one or both parties do not exchange payments until the maturity on the swap. Finally, there are *forward swaps* and options on swaps or *swaptions*. A forward swap is an agreement to enter into a swap that starts at a future date at an interest rate agreed upon today. A swap option, in turn, is a right, but not an obligation, to take a position on a swap at a specific swap rate. In addition to non-generic swaps, there are also *non-US dollar interest rate swaps*. These swaps often differ in terms of their floating rate: London rate, Frankfurt (FIBOR), Copenhagen (CIBOR), Madrid (MIBOR), or Vienna (VIBOR). Exhibit 17.1 summarizes some of the common non-generic swaps. Of the non-generic swaps, the two most extensively used ones are the forward swap and the swaption.

Exhibit 17.1   Non-generic swaps

- *Non-LIBOR swaps*: Swaps with floating rates different than LIBOR. Example: T-bill rate, CP rate, or prime lending rate.
- *Forward swap*: Swap with an agreement to take a swap position at specified swap rate at some future date. For example, a party enters into an agreement now to pay the fixed rate on a 3-year, 6%/LIBOR swap 1 year later.
- *Delayed-rate set swap*: Swap that allows the fixed payer to wait before locking in a fixed swap rate – the opposite of a forward swap.
- *Extension swap*: Swap that gives a party an option to lengthen the terms of the original swap. It allows the party to take advantage of current rates and extend the maturity of their swap.
- *Cancelable swap*: Swap that gives one of the parties the right to terminate the swap before maturity.
  - ○ *Callable swap* is an interest rate swap in which the fixed payer has the right to early termination of the swap.
  - ○ *Putable swap* is an interest rate swap in which the floating payer has the right to early termination of the swap.
- *Zero-coupon swap*: Swap in which one or both parties do not exchange payments until maturity on the swap.
- *Prepaid swap*: Swap in which the future payments due are discounted to the present and paid at the start.
- *Delayed-reset swap*: The effective date and payment date are the same. The cash flows at time t are determined by the floating rate at time t rather than the rate at time $t-1$.
- *Amortizing swaps*: Swaps in which the NP decreases over time based on a set schedule.
- *Set-up swap or accreting swap*: Swaps in which the NP increases over time based on a set schedule.
- *Index-amortizing swap*: Swap in which the NP is dependent on interest rates.
- *Equity swap*: Swap in which one party pays the return on a stock index and the other pays a fixed or floating rate.
- *Basis swap*: Swaps in which both rates are floating; each party exchanges different floating payments – one party might exchange payments based on LIBOR and the other based on the Federal Reserve Commercial Paper Index.
- *Swap option or swaption*: An option on a swap. The buyer of the swaption has the right to start an interest rate option with a specific interest rate and maturity at or during a specific period of time in the future.
  - ○ *Call swaption* is the right to receive a specific fixed rate in a swap, the strike rate, and pay the floating rate – right to a floating-rate payer's position.
  - ○ *Put swaption* is the right to pay a specific fixed rate in a swap, the strike rate, and receive the floating rate – right to a fixed-rate payer's position.
- *Credit default swap*: Swap in which one counterparty buys default protection against a company.
- *Total return swap*: Returns from one asset are swapped for the returns on another asset.
- *Non-US dollar interest rate swap*: Interest-rate swap in a currency different than US dollars with a floating rate often different than the LIBOR: Frankfurt rate (FIBOR), Vienna (VIBOR), and the like.

17.3 FORWARD SWAPS

17.3.1 Applications

As just noted, a forward swap is an agreement to enter into a swap that starts at a future date at an interest rate agreed upon today. Like futures contracts on debt securities, forward swaps provide borrowers and investors with a tool for locking in a future interest rate.

Hedging a Future Loan

Financial and non-financial institutions that have future borrowing obligations can lock-in a future rate by obtaining forward contracts on fixed-payer swap positions. For example, a company wishing to lock-in a rate on a 5-year, fixed-rate $100 loan to start 2 years from today, could enter into a 2-year forward swap agreement to pay the fixed rate on a 5-year 9%/LIBOR swap. At the expiration date on the forward swap, the company could issue floating-rate debt at LIBOR that, when combined with the fixed position on the swap, would provide the company with a synthetic fixed-rate loan paying 9% on the floating debt. At the expiration date on the forward swap:

Instrument	Action	
Issue flexible rate note	Pay LIBOR	− LIBOR
Swap: fixed-rate payer's position	Pay fixed rate	− 9%
Swap: fixed-rate payer's position	Receive LIBOR	+ LIBOR
Synthetic fixed rate	Net payment	9%

Alternatively, at the forward swaps' expiration date, the company could sell the 5-year 9%/LIBOR swap underlying the forward swap contract and issue a 5-year fixed-rate debt. If the rate on 5-year fixed-rate bonds were higher than 9%, for example at 10%, then the company would be able to offset the higher interest by selling its fixed position on the 9%/LIBOR swap to a swap dealer for an amount equal to the present value of a 5-year annuity equal to 1% (difference in rates: 10% − 9%) times the NP. For example, at 10% the value of the underlying 9%/LIBOR swap would be $3.8609 per $100 NP using the YTM swap valuation approach:

$$SV^{fix} = \left[\sum_{t=1}^{10} \frac{(0.10/2)-(0.09/2)}{(1+(0.10/2))^t} \right] \$100 = \$3.8609$$

With the proceeds of $3.8609 from closing its swap, the company would only need to raise $96.1391 (= $100 − $3.8609). The company, though, would have to issue $96.1391-worth of 5-year fixed-rate bonds at the higher 10% rate. This would result in semi-annual interest payments of $4.8070 (= (0.10/2)($96.1391)). Using the ARR and assuming a flat yield curve, the company's effective rate based on the $100 funds needed would be 9.2%:

$$ARR = 2 \left(\left[\frac{\sum_{t=1}^{9} \$4.8070(1.05)^t + \$96.1391}{\$100} \right]^{1/10} - 1 \right)$$

$$ARR = 2 \left(\left[\frac{\$96.1391(1.05)^{10}}{\$100} \right]^{1/10} - 1 \right)$$

$$= 2 \left(\left[\frac{\$156.60}{\$100} \right]^{1/10} - 1 \right) = 0.092$$

Thus, the forward swap position in this higher interest rate case has lowered the effective debt rate for the company from 10% to 9.2%.

In contrast, if the rate on 5-year fixed-rate loans were lower than 9%, say 8%, then the company would benefit from the lower fixed-rate loan, but would lose an amount equal to the present value of a 5-year annuity equal to 1% (difference in rates: 8% − 9%) times the NP when it closed the fixed position. Specifically, at 8%, the value of the underlying 9%/LIBOR swap is − $4.055 using the YTM approach:

$$SV^{fix} = \left[\sum_{t=1}^{10} \frac{(0.08/2)-(0.09/2)}{(1+(0.08/2))^t} \right] \$100 = -\$4.055$$

The company would therefore have to pay the swap bank $4.055 for assuming its fixed-payers position. With a payment of $4.055, the company would need to raise a total of $104.055 from its bond issue. The company, though, would be able to issue $104.055-worth of 5-year fixed-rate bonds at the lower rate of 8%. Its semi-annual interest payments would be $4.1622 (= 0.08/2)($104.055), and its ARR based on the $100 funds needed would be 8.8%:

$$ARR = 2 \left(\left[\frac{\sum_{t=1}^{9} \$4.1622(1.04)^t + \$104.055}{\$100} \right]^{1/10} - 1 \right)$$

$$ARR = 2 \left(\left[\frac{\$104.055(1.04)^{10}}{\$100} \right]^{1/10} - 1 \right)$$

$$= 2 \left(\left[\frac{\$154.027}{\$100} \right]^{1/10} - 1 \right) = 0.088$$

Thus, the forward swap position for the lower interest rate scenario results in an increase in the effective debt rate from 8% to 8.8%.

Table 17.1 summarizes the swap values, loanable funds needed, semi-annual interest payments, and ARRs based on the $100 funds

Table 17.1   Hedged rates on a $100, 5-year loan to be made in 2 years

Rates at forward swap expiration	Value of 9%/LIBOR fixed-payer position	Funds borrowed $100 − swap value	Semi-annual interest paid: (Rate/2) × funds borrowed	ARR
0.070	− 8.3166	108.3166	3.7911	0.087
0.075	− 6.1596	106.1596	3.9810	0.087
0.080	− 4.0554	104.0554	4.1622	0.088
0.085	− 2.0027	102.0027	4.3351	0.089
0.090	0.0000	100.0000	4.5000	0.090
0.095	1.9541	98.0459	4.6572	0.091
0.100	3.8609	96.1391	4.8070	0.092
0.105	5.7216	94.2784	4.9496	0.093

Loan hedged with 2-year forward swap on 3-year, 9%/LIBOR fixed-payer position

needed by the company given several interest rate cases. As shown, the forward swap enables the company to lock-in a borrowing rate of approximately 9%. (Valuing the swap using the YTM approach results in hedged ARRs that are close to 9%, but are not equal.)

Hedging a Future Investment

Instead of locking-in the rate on a future liability, forward swaps can also be used on the asset side to fix the rate on a future investment. Consider the case of an institutional investor planning to invest an expected $10m cash inflow 1 year from now in a 3-year, high-quality fixed-rate bond. The investor could lock-in the future rate by entering a 1-year forward swap agreement to receive the fixed rate and pay the floating rate on a 3-year, 9%/LIBOR swap with an NP of $10m. At the expiration date on the forward swap, the investor could invest the $10m cash inflow in a 3-year FRN at LIBOR which, when combined with the floating position on the swap, would provide the investor with a synthetic fixed-rate loan paying 9%. At the expiration date on the forward swap:

Instrument	Action	
Buy flexible-rate note	Receive LIBOR	LIBOR
Swap: floating-rate payer's position	Pay LIBOR	− LIBOR
Swap: floating-rate payer's position	Receive fixed rate	+ 9%
Synthetic fixed-rate investment	Net receipt	9%

Instead of a synthetic fixed-investment position, the investor alternatively could sell the 3-year 9%/LIBOR swap underlying the forward swap contract and invest in a 5-year fixed-rate note. If the rate on the 5-year fixed-rate note were lower than the 9% swap rate, then the investor would be able to sell his floating position at a value equal to the present value of an annuity equal to the $10m NP times the difference between 9% and the rate on 3-year fixed-rate bonds; this gain would offset the lower return on the fixed-rate bond. For example, if at the forward swaps' expiration date, the rate on 3-year, fixed-rate bonds were at 8%, and the fixed rate on a 3-year par value swap were at 8%, then the institution investment firm would be able to sell its floating payer's position on the 3-year 9%/LIBOR swap underlying the forward swap contract to a swap bank for $262,107 (using the YTM approach with a discount rate of 8%):

$$SV^{fl} = \left[\sum_{t=1}^{6} \frac{(0.09/2) - (0.08/2)}{(1 + (0.08/2))^t} \right] \$10,000,000$$
$$= \$262,107$$

The investment firm would therefore invest $10m plus the $262,107 proceeds from closing its swap in a 3-year, fixed-rate bond yielding 8%. Assuming a flat yield curve, the ARR based on a $10m investment is 8.9%:

$$ARR = 2\left(\left[\frac{\$10,262,107(1.04)^6}{\$10,000,000} \right]^{1/6} - 1 \right) = 0.089$$

Table 17.2   Hedged rates on a $10m, 3-year investment to be made in 1 year

Rates at forward swap expiration	Value of 9%/LIBOR Floating-payer position	Funds invested $100 − swap value	ARR
0.075	396,380	10,396,380	0.088
0.080	262,107	10,262,107	0.089
0.085	129,993	10,129,993	0.089
0.090	0	10,000,000	0.090
0.095	−127,913	9,872,087	0.091
0.100	−253,785	9,746,215	0.091
0.105	−377,652	9,622,348	0.092

Investment hedged with 1-year forward swap on 3-year, 9%/LIBOR floating-payer position

On the other hand, if the rate on 3-year fixed-rate securities were higher than 9%, the investment company would benefit from the higher investment rate, but would lose on closing its swap position. For example, if at the forward swaps' expiration date, the rate on 3-year, fixed-rate bonds were at 10%, and the fixed rate on a 3-year par value swap were at 10%, then the institution investment firm would have to pay the swap bank $253,785 for assuming its floating payer's position on the 3-year 9%/LIBOR swap underlying the forward swap contract:

$$SV^{fl} = \left[\sum_{t=1}^{6} \frac{(0.09/2) - (0.10/2)}{(1 + (0.10/2))^t}\right]\$10,000,000$$

$$= -\$253,785$$

The investment firm would therefore invest $9,746,215 ($10m minus the $253,785 costs incurred in closing its swap) in 3-year, fixed-rate bonds yielding 10%. Assuming a flat yield curve, the ARR based on a $10m investment would be 9.1%:

$$ARR = 2\left(\left[\frac{\$9,746,215(1.05)^6}{\$10,000,000}\right]^{1/6} - 1\right) = 0.091$$

Table 17.2 summarizes the swap values, investment funds, and ARRs based on the $10m investment given several interest rate cases. As shown, the forward swap enables the investment fund to lock-in an investment rate of approximately 9%.

Other Uses

The examples illustrate that forward swaps are like futures on debt securities. As such, they are used in many of the same ways as futures: locking-in future interest rates, speculating on future interest rate changes, and altering a balance sheet's exposure to interest rate changes. Different from futures, though, forward swaps can be customized to fit a particular investment or borrowing need and with the starting dates on forward swaps ranging anywhere from 1 month to several years, they can be applied to not only short-run but also long-run positions. Consider for example a company with an existing 10%, fixed-rate debt having 10 years remaining to maturity, but not callable for 3 more years. Suppose that as a result of the currently low interest rates, the company expects rates to increase in the future and would like to call its bonds now. While the company cannot call its debt for 3 years, it can take advantage of the current low rates by using a forward swap. In this case, suppose the company enters into a 3-year forward swap agreement to pay fixed on a 7-year, 8%/LIBOR swap with an NP equal to the par value of its current 10-year, 10% fixed-rate debt (7-year swap, 3 years forward). Three years later, if rates are lower than 10%, the company could issue flexible-rate debt to finance the call of its 10% debt. This action, combined with its fixed payer's position on the 8%/LIBOR swap obtained from its forward swap, would give the company an effective fixed rate of 8%. On the other hand, if rates are higher than 10% on the call date, the company would not call its debt, but it would be able to offset its 10% debt by selling its 8%/LIBOR swap at a premium. Thus, by using a 3-year forward agreement on a 7-year swap, the company is able to take advantage of a period of low interest rates to refinance its long-term debt; this opportunity would not have been possible using more standardized, shorter-term, exchange-traded futures contracts.

17.3.2 Valuation of Forward Swaps

As with many non-generic swaps, there can be an up-front fee for a forward swap. The value of a forward swap depends on whether the rate on the forward contract's underlying swap is different than its break-even forward swap rate. Recall that in chapter 16 we defined the break-even rate on a generic swap as that rate which equates the present values of the fixed and floating cash flows with the floating cash flows estimated as implied forward rates generated from the zero–coupon rates on swaps. For example, using the estimated zero–coupon rates and 1-year implied forward rates from table 16.11, we showed earlier that the break-even rate on the 3-year swap was 5.7% (see section 16.6.5). Like the break-even rate on a generic swap, the break-even rate on a forward swap, C_f^*, is that rate that equates the present value of the fixed-rate flows to the present value of floating-rate flows corresponding to the period of the underlying swap. To illustrate, consider a 2-year 7%/LIBOR swap, 3 years forward, in which the applicable zero swap yield curve and corresponding implied forward rates are the ones shown in table 16.11; that is:

Maturity in years	Swap rate	Zero-coupon rate	Implied 1-year forward rates
1	0.05	0.05	0.05617
2	0.053	0.05308	0.06576
3	0.057	0.05729	0.07697
4	0.0615	0.062176	0.08891
5	0.0662	0.0674697	

The break-even forward rate for this 2-year 7%/LIBOR swap, 3 years forward is found by solving for that coupon rate, C_f^*, which equates the present value of the forward swap's future fixed-rate payments of C_f^* in years 4 and 5 to the present value of the implied 1-year forward rates 3 years and 4 years from the present

($f_{13}=0.07697$ and $f_{14}=0.08891$; assume the first effective date on the underlying swap starts at the expiration of the forward swap) in years 4 and 5. That is, C_f^* where:

$$\frac{C_f^*}{(1+Z(4))^4}+\frac{C_f^*}{(1+Z(5))^5}=\frac{f_{13}}{(1+Z(4))^4}+\frac{f_{14}}{(1+Z(5))^5}$$

$$C_f^*=\frac{\dfrac{f_{13}}{(1+Z(4))^4}+\dfrac{f_{14}}{(1+Z(5))^5}}{\dfrac{1}{(1+Z(4))^4}+\dfrac{1}{(1+Z(5))^5}}$$

Substituting the implied forward rates and zero–coupon rates into the above equation, we obtain an 8% break-even forward rate for the 2-year 7%/LIBOR swap, 3 years forward:

$$C_f^*=\frac{\dfrac{0.07697}{(1.062176)^4}+\dfrac{0.08891}{(1.0674697)^5}}{\dfrac{1}{(1.062176)^4}+\dfrac{1}{(1.0674697)^5}}=0.08$$

Given that the specified fixed rate on the forward swap is at 7% and not at its break-even rate of 8%, the fixed payer's position on the underlying swap would have a value beginning in year 4 equal to the annual 1% rate differential times the swap's NP for 2 years. The present value of this cash flow is equal to 1.5071% times the NP or 151.71 BP. Thus, the current value of the 2-year 7%/LIBOR swap 3 years forward is therefore 150.71 BP times the NP:

Forward swap rate = 7% per year
Break-even swap rate = 8% per year
Value = 100 BP for years 4 and 5

$$\text{Present value}=\frac{100\text{BP}}{(1.062176)^4}$$
$$+\frac{100\text{BP}}{(1.0674697)^5}$$
$$=150.71\text{BP}$$

If the NP on the swap is $10m, then the value of the forward swap would be $150,710. Note, if the forward swap rate had been set equal to the 8% break-even rate, then the economic value of the forward swap would be zero.

17.4 SWAPTIONS

One of the most innovative non-generic swaps is the swap option or simply swaption. As the name suggests, a swaption is an option on a swap. The purchaser of a swaption buys the right to start an interest rate swap with a specific fixed rate or exercise (strike) rate, and with a maturity at or during a specific time period in the future. If the holder exercises, she takes the swap position, with the swap seller obligated to take the opposite counterparty position. For swaptions, the underlying instrument is a forward swap and the option premium is the up-front fee. The swaption can be either a call or a put. A *call swaption* gives the holder the right to receive a specific fixed rate and pay the floating rate (that is, the right to take a floating payer's position), while a *put swaption* gives the holder the right to pay a specific fixed rate and receive the floating rate (that is, the right to take a fixed payer's position). Finally, swaptions can be either European or American: a European swaption can be exercised only at a specific point in time, usually just before the starting date on the swap; an American swaption is exercisable at any point in time during a specified period of time.

Swaptions are similar to interest rate options or options on debt securities. They are, however, more varied: they can range from options to begin a 1-year swap in 3 months to a 10-year option on an 8-year swap (sometimes referred to as a 10×8 swaption); the exercise periods can vary for American swaptions; swaptions can be written on generic swaps or non-generic. Like interest rate and debt options, swaptions can be used for speculating on interest rates, hedging debt and asset positions against market risk, and managing a balance sheet's exposure to interest rate changes. In addition, like swaps they also can be used in combination with other securities to create synthetic positions.

17.4.1 Applications

Speculation

Suppose a speculator expects the rates on high-quality, 5-year fixed-rate bonds to increase from their current 8% level. As an alternative to a short T-note futures position or an interest rate call, the speculator could buy a put swaption. Suppose she elects to buy a 1-year European put swaption on a 5-year, 8%/LIBOR swap with an NP of $10m for 50 BP times the NP; that is:

- 1×5 put swaption
- Exercise date $= 1$ year
- Exercise rate $= 8\%$
- Underlying swap $= 5$-year, 8%/LIBOR with NP $= \$10m$
- Swap position $=$ fixed payer
- Option premium $= 50$ BP times NP.

On the exercise date, if the fixed rate on a 5-year swap were greater than the exercise rate of 8%, then the speculator would exercise her right to pay the fixed rate below the market rate. To realize the gain, she could take her 8% fixed-rate payer's swap position obtained from exercising and sell it to another counterparty. For example, if current 5-year par value swaps were trading at 9% and swaps were valued by the YTM approach (or the yield curve were flat), then she would be able to sell her 8% swap for $395,636:

$$\text{Value of swap} = \left[\sum_{t=1}^{10} \frac{(0.09/2) - (0.08/2)}{(1 + (0.09/2))^t} \right] (\$10m)$$
$$= \$395,636$$

Alternatively, she could exercise and then enter into a reverse swap; for example, at the current swap rate of 9%, she could take the floating payer's position on a 5-year, 9%/LIBOR swap. By doing this she would receive an annuity equal to 1% of the NP for 5 years (or 0.5% semi-annually for 10 periods), which has a current value of $395,636:

From put swaption:		
Swap: fixed-rate payer's position	Pay	8% per year for 5 years
Swap: fixed-rate payer's position	Receive	LIBOR
From replacement swap:		
Swap: floating-rate payer's position	Receive	9% per year for 5 years
Swap: floating-rate payer's position	Pay	LIBOR
Net position	Receive	1% per year for 5 years

Exhibit 17.2 Value and profit at expiration from 8%/LIBOR put swaption

Rates on 5-year par value swaps at expiration R	Put swaption's interest differential $Max((R-0.08)/2, 0)$	Value of 8%/LIBOR put swaption at expiration $\Sigma PV(Max$ $[(R-0.08)/2, 0]$ ($10m)$)	Put swaption cost	Profit from put swaption
0.060	0.0000	0	50,000	− 50,000
0.065	0.0000	0	50,000	− 50,000
0.070	0.0000	0	50,000	− 50,000
0.075	0.0000	0	50,000	− 50,000
0.080	0.0000	0	50,000	− 50,000
0.085	0.0025	200,272	50,000	150,272
0.090	0.0050	395,636	50,000	345,636
0.095	0.0075	586,226	50,000	536,226
0.100	0.0100	772,173	50,000	722,173

$$\text{Value of swap} = \left[\sum_{t=1}^{10} \frac{Max[(R/2) - (0.08/2), 0]}{(1 + (R/2))^t} \right] (\$10m)$$

If the swap rate at the expiration date were less than 8%, then the put swaption would have no value and the speculator would simply let it expire, losing the premium she paid. More formally, the value of the put swaption at expiration is:

$$\text{Value of swap} = \left[\sum_{t=1}^{10} \frac{Max[(R/2) - (0.08/2), 0]}{(1 + (R/2))^t} \right]$$
$$\times (\$10m)$$

For rates, R, on par value 5-year swaps exceeding the exercise rate of 8%, the value of the put swaption will be equal to the present value of the interest differential times the notional principal on the swap and for rates less than 8%, the swap is worthless. Exhibit 17.2 shows graphically and in a table the values and profits at expiration obtained from closing the put swaption on the 5-year 8%/LIBOR swap given different rates at expiration.

Instead of higher rates, suppose the speculator expects rates on 5-year high-quality bonds to be lower 1 year from now. In this case, her strategy would be to buy a call swaption. If she bought a call swaption similar in terms to the above put swaption (1-year call option on a

5-year, 8%/LIBOR swap), and the swap rate on a 5-year swap were less than 8% on the exercise date, then she would realize a gain from exercising and then either selling the floating payer's position or combining it with a fixed payer's position on a replacement swap. For example, if the fixed rate on a 5-year par value swap were 7%, the investor would exercise her call swaption by taking the 8% floating-rate payer's swap and then sell the position to another counterparty. With the current swap rate at 7% she would be able to sell the 8% fixed payer's position for $415,830:

$$\text{Value of swap} = \left[\sum_{t=1}^{10} \frac{(0.08/2) - (0.07/2)}{(1 + (0.07/2))^t}\right]($10\text{m})$$
$$= \$415,830$$

Alternatively, the swaption investor could exercise and then enter into a reverse swap. At the swap rate of 7%, she could take the fixed payer's position on a 5-year, 7%/LIBOR swap. By doing this, the investor would receive an annuity equal to 1% of the NP for 5 years. The value of the annuity would be $415,830:

From call swaption:		
Swap: floating-rate payer's position	Pay	LIBOR
Swap: floating-rate payer's position	Receive	8% per year for 5 years

From replacement swap:		
Swap: fixed-rate payer's position	Receive	LIBOR
Swap: fixed-rate payer's position	Pay	7% per year for 5 years

Net position	Receive	1% per year for 5 years

Thus, if rates were at 7%, then the investor would realize a profit of $365,830 (= $415,830 − $50,000) from the call swaption. If the swap rate were higher than 8% on the exercise date, then the investor would allow the call swaption to expire, losing, in turn, her premium of $50,000.

Formally, the value of the 8%/LIBOR call swaption at expiration is:

$$\text{Value of swap} = \left[\sum_{t=1}^{10} \frac{\text{Max}[(0.08/2) - (R/2), 0]}{(1 + (R/2))^t}\right]$$
$$\times ($10\text{m})$$

For rates, R, on par value 5-year swaps less than the exercise rate of 8%, the value of the call swaption will be equal to the present value of the interest differential times the notional principal on the swap and for rates greater than 8%, the swap is worthless. Exhibit 17.3 shows graphically and in a table the values and profits at expiration obtained from closing the call swaption on the 5-year 8%/LIBOR swap given different rates at expiration.

Hedging

Caps and floors on future debt and investment positions

Like other option hedging tools, swaptions give investors and borrowers protection against adverse interest rate movements, while allowing them to benefit if rates move in their favor. Since call swaptions increase in value as rates decrease below the exercise rate, they can be used to establish floors on the rates of return obtained from future bond investments. In contrast, put swaptions increase in value as rates increase above the exercise rate, making them a useful tool for capping the rates paid on debt positions.

To illustrate how call swaptions are used for establishing a floor, consider the case of a fixed-income investment fund that has a Treasury bond portfolio worth $30m in par value that is scheduled to mature in 2 years. Suppose the fund plans to reinvest the $30m in principal for another 3 years in Treasury notes that are currently trading to yield 6%, but is worried that interest rates could be lower in 2 years. To establish a floor on its investment, suppose the fund purchased a 2-year call swaption on a 3-year 6%/LIBOR generic swap with a notional principal of $30m from First Bank for $100,000. Table 17.3 shows for different rates at the swaption's expiration, the values that the fund would obtain from closing its call swaption, and the hedged ARR (based on $30m investment and the assumption of a flat yield curve) it would obtain from reinvesting for 3 years the $30m plus the proceeds from the swaption. As shown, for rates less than 6% the swaption values increase as rates fall, in turn offsetting the lower investment rates and yielding a fixed ARR on the investment of 6%.

Exhibit 17.3   Value and profit at expiration from 8%/LIBOR call swaption

Rates on 5-year par value swaps at expiration R	Call swaption's interest differential Max$((0.08 - R)/2, 0)$	Value of 8%/LIBOR call swaption at expiration ΣPV(Max$[(0.08 - R)/2, 0]$($\$10$m))	Call swaption cost	Profit from call swaption
0.060	0.0100	853,020	50,000	803,020
0.065	0.0075	631,680	50,000	581,680
0.070	0.0050	415,830	50,000	365,830
0.075	0.0025	205,320	50,000	155,320
0.080	0.0000	0	50,000	− 50,000
0.085	0.0000	0	50,000	− 50,000
0.090	0.0000	0	50,000	− 50,000
0.095	0.0000	0	50,000	− 50,000
0.100	0.0000	0	50,000	− 50,000

$$\text{Value of swap} = \left[\sum_{t=1}^{10} \frac{\text{Max}[(0.08/2) - (R/2), 0]}{(1 + (R/2))^t} \right] (\$10\text{m})$$

On the other hand, for rates higher than 6%, the swaption is worthless while the investment's ARR increases as rates increase. Thus, for the cost of $100,000, the call swaption provides the fund with a floor with a rate of 6%.

In contrast to the use of swaptions to establish a floor on an investment, suppose a firm had a future debt obligation whose rate it wanted to cap. In this case, the firm could purchase a put swaption. To illustrate, suppose a company has a $60m, 9% fixed-rate bond obligation maturing in 3 years that it plans to finance by issuing new 5-year fixed-rate bonds. Suppose the company was worried that interest rates could increase in 3 years and as a result wanted to establish a cap on the rate it would pay on its future 5-year bond issue. To cap the rate, suppose the company purchases a 3-year put swaption on a 5-year 9%/LIBOR generic swap with notional principal of $60m from

First Bank for $200,000. Table 17.4 shows, for different rates at expiration, the values that the company would obtain from closing its put swaption and the hedged ARR (based on $60m debt and the assumption of a flat yield curve) it would obtain from borrowing for 5 years $60m minus the proceeds from the swaption. As shown, for rates greater than 9% the swaption values increase as rates increase, in turn offsetting the higher borrowing rates and yielding a fixed ARR on the bond issue of approximately 9%. On the other hand, for rates less than 9%, the swaption is worthless while the debt's ARR decreases as rates decrease. Thus, for the cost of $200,000, the put swaption provides the fund with a cap on its future debt with a rate of 9%.

Hedging the risk of embedded option positions

The cap and floor hedging examples illustrate that swaptions are a particularly useful tool in hedging future investment and debt positions against adverse interest rate changes. Swaptions can also be used to hedge against the impacts that adverse interest rate changes have on investment and debt positions with embedded options. Consider, for example, a fixed-income manager holding $10m-worth of 10-year, high-quality, 8% fixed-rate bonds that are callable in 2 years at a call price equal to par. Suppose the manager expects a decrease in rates over the next 2 years, increasing the likelihood that his bonds will be called and he will be forced to reinvest in a market with lower rates. To minimize his exposure to this call risk, suppose the manager buys a 2-year call swaption on an 8-year, 8%/LIBOR swap with an NP of $10m. If 2 years later, rates were to increase, then the bonds would not be called and the swaption would have no value. In this case, the fixed-income manager would lose the premium he paid for the call swaption. However, suppose 2 years later, rates on 8-year bonds were lower at, say, 6%, and the bonds were called at a call price equal to par. In this case, the manager would be able to exercise his call swaption, taking the floating payer's position on the $10m, 8-year, 8%/LIBOR swap. He could then combine the swap with an FRN paying the LIBOR financed with the proceeds from the call price to obtain an effective rate of 8% for the next 8 years.

	Action	Receipt
Bond called	Receive call price	+$10m
From call swaption:		
Swap: floating-rate payer's position	Pay LIBOR	− LIBOR per year for 8 years
Swap: floating-rate payer's position	Receive fixed rate	+8% per year for 8 years
Purchase FRN	Pay	− $10m
From FRN	Receive	+ LIBOR per year for 8 years
Net position	Net receipt	+8% per year for 8 years

The manager also could obtain 8% by selling his swap and buying an 8-year, 6% fixed-rate bond. With 6% rates on new swaps, he would be able to sell his floating position on the 8%/LIBOR at a price equal to an 8-year annuity paying an annual amount equal to the 2% interest differential times the $10 NP. In this case, if he were to sell the swap at a 6% YTM, then he would receive $1,256,110:

$$\text{Value of swap} = \left[\sum_{t=1}^{16} \frac{(0.08/2)-(0.06/2)}{(1+(0.06/2))^t} \right](\$10m)$$
$$= \$1,256,110$$

The $1,256,110 proceeds from the swap sale would offset the 2% lower annual return he would receive as a result of having to sell his 8% bonds back to the issuer on the call and invest in new 8-year bonds at 6%. The manager's ARR from reinvesting $10m plus $1,256,110 at 6% for 8 years based on a $10m investment is approximately 7.5% (note the YTM valuation approach may underprice the swap value):

$$\text{ARR}$$
$$= 2\left(\left[\frac{(\$10,000,000+\$1,256,110)(1.03)^{16}}{\$10,000,000} \right]^{1/16} -1 \right)$$
$$= 0.075$$

Finally, the manager could get an effective 8% rate by buying a new 8-year, 6% fixed bond with the call proceeds and then combining his 8%/LIBOR floating payer's position obtained

Table 17.3 Future rate on 3-year investment hedged with 6%/LIBOR call swaption

Rates on 3-year par value swaps and T-notes at expiration R	Call swaption's interest differential $\text{Max}((0.06 - R)/2, 0)$	Value of 6%/LIBOR call swaption at expiration $\Sigma PV(\text{Max}[(0.06 - R)/2, 0](\$30m))$	Call swaption cost	Profit from call swaption	Funds invested $\$30m + \text{swaption value}$	ARR
0.040	0.0100	1,680,429	100,000	1,580,429	31,680,429	0.059
0.045	0.0075	1,249,757	100,000	1,149,757	31,249,757	0.059
0.050	0.0050	826,219	100,000	726,219	30,826,219	0.059
0.055	0.0025	409,678	100,000	309,678	30,409,678	0.060
0.060	0.0000	0	100,000	−100,000	30,000,000	0.060
0.065	0.0000	0	100,000	−100,000	30,000,000	0.065
0.070	0.0000	0	100,000	−100,000	30,000,000	0.070
0.075	0.0000	0	100,000	−100,000	30,000,000	0.075
0.080	0.0000	0	100,000	−100,000	30,000,000	0.080

$$\text{ARR} = 2\left(\left[\frac{(\$30m + \text{swap value})(1 + (R/2))^6}{\$30,000,000}\right]^{1/6} - 1\right)$$

Table 17.4 Future rate paid on 5-year bond hedged with 9%/LIBOR put swaption

Rates on 5-year par value swaps and bond at expiration R	Put swaption's interest differential $\text{Max}((R - 0.09)/2, 0)$	Value of 9%/LIBOR put swaption at expiration $\Sigma PV(\text{Max}[(R - 0.09)/2, 0](\$60m))$	Put swaption cost	Profit from put swaption	Funds borrowed $\$60m - \text{swaption value}$	ARR
0.070	0.0000	0	200,000	−200,000	60,000,000	0.070
0.075	0.0000	0	200,000	−200,000	60,000,000	0.075
0.080	0.0000	0	200,000	−200,000	60,000,000	0.080
0.085	0.0000	0	200,000	−200,000	60,000,000	0.085
0.090	0.0000	0	200,000	−200,000	60,000,000	0.090
0.095	0.0025	1,172,452	200,000	972,452	58,827,548	0.091
0.100	0.0050	2,316,520	200,000	2,116,520	57,683,480	0.092
0.105	0.0075	3,432,978	200,000	3,232,978	56,567,022	0.093
0.110	0.0100	4,522,575	200,000	4,322,575	55,477,425	0.094

$$\text{ARR} = 2\left(\left[\frac{(\$60m - \text{swap value})(1 + (R/2))^{10}}{\$60,000,000}\right]^{1/10} - 1\right)$$

from the swap with a current 6%/LIBOR fixed position on a replacement swap.

The contrasting case of a fixed-income manager hedging callable bonds would be the case of a financial manager who issued putable bonds some time ago and was now concerned that rates might increase in the future. If rates did increase and bondholders exercised their option to sell the bonds back to the issuer at a specified price, the issuer would have to finance the purchase by issuing new bonds paying higher rates. To hedge against this scenario, the financial manager could buy a put swaption with a strike rate equal to the coupon rate on the putable bonds. Later, if the current swap rate exceeded the strike rate and the bonds were put back to the issuer, the manager could exercise his put swaption to take the fixed-payer position at the strike rate and then do one of the following:

1. Sell an FRN to finance the bond purchase; the FRN combined with the fixed payer's position on the swap would create a synthetic fixed-rate bond with a fixed rate equal to the rate on the swap plus any basis points on the FRN.
2. Combine the fixed payer swap with a floating payer's position on a new swap with a higher market rate and then finance the purchase of the bond by issuing new fixed-rate bonds.
3. Sell the swap and use the proceeds to defray part of the higher financing cost of buying the bonds on the put.

On the other hand, if rates were to decrease, then the put option on the bond would not be exercised and the put swaptions would have no value. In this case, the manager would lose the swaption premium.

Arbitrage: Synthetic Positions

Like other swaps, swaptions can be used to create synthetic bond or debt positions with supposedly better rates than conventional ones. Consider for example a company that wants to finance a $10m capital expenditure with 5-year, option-free, fixed-rate debt. As we examined earlier, the company could either issue 5-year straight (option-free), fixed-rate bonds or create a synthetic 5-year bond by issuing 5-year FRNs

and taking a fixed payer's position on a 5-year swap. With swaptions, as well as other non-generic swaps, there are actually several other ways in which this synthetic fixed-rate bond could be created.

One of the other alternatives to a straight fixed-rate bond would be for the company to issue a callable bond and then sell a call swaption with terms similar to the bond. For example, as an alternative to 5-year, option-free, 10% fixed-rate bonds, suppose the company sells a 5-year, 10.2% fixed-rate bond callable after 2 years at par and then sells a 2-year call swaption on a 3-year 10%/LIBOR swap at a price equal to 30 BP per year for 5 years. If, 2 years later, swap rates were the same or higher, then neither the company nor the swaption holders would exercise. With the company having sold the swaption at a premium equivalent to 30 BP per year for 5 years, the effective rate on the debt over the entire 5-year period would therefore be 9.9% under this interest rate scenario:

Rates 2 years later greater than 10%	Company's actions	
10.2% callable bonds not called	Pay 10.2% per year	− 10.2% per year
Call swaption not exercised	No liability	
Premium from selling call swaption	Receive equivalent of 0.3% per year	+ 0.3%
Net position	Pay 9.9% per year	− 9.9%

On the other hand, if 2 years later rates were to decrease and the call swaption holders exercise, the company could call its bonds, financing the purchase by selling FRNs at the LIBOR. For the next 3 years, the company would have a fixed payer's position on the exercised swap at the 10% strike rate and would pay the LIBOR on its FRNs. The company would therefore pay an effective 10% for the next 3 years. On the swap, it would pay 10% for 3 years and receive the LIBOR, with the LIBOR being used to service its floating debt. Subtracting the 30 BP per year premium that the company received from selling the swap from the 10% rate paid on the combined FRN and swap, yields an effective interest rate for the company of only 9.7% per year for the next 3 years.

Rates 2 years later less than 10%	Company's actions	
Call swaption exercised:		
Issuer assumes fixed payer's position	Pay 10% per year for 3 years	−10% per year
	Receives LIBOR for 3 years	+ LIBOR per year
Company sells $10m of 3-year FRNs at LIBOR	Receive $10m Pay LIBOR for 3 years	+$10m −LIBOR per year
Company calls 10.2% bond	Pays $10m	−$10m
Premium from selling call swaption is 30 BP	Receive equivalent of 30 BP for 3 years	+0.3% per year
Net position	Pays 9.7% per year for 3 years	−9.7% per year

In summary, the synthetic 5-year, option-free bond formed with a 5-year callable bond and a short call swaption position engenders a lower payment of 9.9% or less compared to the 10% rate paid on the 5-year, straight bond.

Arbitrages like this often exist because investors underprice the call option on callable debt. It may be the case that the market overprices the underlying put option on a putable bond. If this is the case, borrowers may find a synthetic option-free bond formed by selling putable bonds and buying a put swaption cheaper than a direct option-free bond (see problem 19 at the end of the chapter). With swaptions, generic swaps, and non-generic swaps, there are a number of synthetic asset and liability permutations: callable and putable debt, callable and putable bonds, flexible-rate securities, and flexible-rate debt. Exhibit 17.4 summarizes some of the possible ways synthetic fixed-rate and floating-rate debt positions can be formed using generic swaps, non-generic swaps, and swaptions. The interested reader may want to consider how some of those positions can be changed to create synthetic fixed-rate and floating-rate investment positions.

17.4.2 Swaption Valuation

Intrinsic Value

As with other options, the value of a swaption can be broken down into its intrinsic value, IV, and time value premium, TVP. In determining a swaption's IV, it is important to remember that the asset underlying the option is a forward contract. That is, a 3-year put swaption on a 2-year 7%/LIBOR swap is an option to take a fixed payer's position on a 2-year swap 3 years forward. The asset underlying this put swaption is therefore the fixed payer's position on a 3-year forward contract with a forward swap rate of 7%. Thus, the first step in calculating a swaption's IV is to determine the break-even rate on the underlying forward contract. Recall, the break-even forward swap rate, C_f^*, is that rate that equates the present value of the fixed-rate flows to the present value of floating-rate flows (estimated as implied forward rates) corresponding to the period of the underlying swap. In an earlier example, we used the estimated zero-coupon rates and 1-year implied forward rates from table 16.11 to calculate an 8% break-even forward rate for a 2-year swap, 3 years forward:

$$C_f^* = \frac{\dfrac{0.07697}{(1.062176)^4} + \dfrac{0.08891}{(1.0674697)^5}}{\dfrac{1}{(1.062176)^4} + \dfrac{1}{(1.0674697)^5}}$$

$$= 0.08$$

In the case of a 3-year put swaption on a 2-year 7%/LIBOR swap, the option buyer is purchasing a 3-year option on a 2-year swap to receive the LIBOR and pay 7%. Since the strike rate is 7% and the market forward rate is 8%, the put swaption's intrinsic value is the 1% interest rate differential on the NP for 2 years beginning 3 years from the present. Using the rates from table 16.11, the IV of this put swaption is 150.71 BP times the NP of the swap ($150,710 given NP of $10m):

Put swaption exercise rate $= C^X = 7\%$

Break-even forward swap rate $= C_f^* = 8\%$

Exhibit 17.4   Synthetic debt positions

OPTION-FREE, FIXED-RATE DEBT

1. Issue FRN and take fixed payer's position on generic swap.
2. Issue callable debt and sell call swaption.
3. Issue callable debt, take fixed payer's position on generic swap, and take floating payer's position on a callable swap contract (the couterparty is the fixed payer with the right to terminate the swap at the bond's call date).

  • Prior to the call date, the issuer has a fixed-rate position: fixed-rate callable bond, fixed payer's position on the generic swap, and floating payer's position on the callable swap.
  • If rates are low at the call date: (1) issuer calls the bond and issues FRN to fund the call; (2) the counterparty on the callable swap terminates the swap; (3) the issuer's fixed payer's position on the generic swap remains outstanding. The FRN and fixed payer's position on the swap equate to the fixed-rate loan.
  • If rates are high at the call date: (1) issuer does not call the bond; (2) the counterparty on the callable swaps does not terminate. The issuer, therefore, has a fixed and floating payer's swap outstanding. The issuer pays the fixed rate on the bond plus or minus any difference in the fixed rates on the two swaps.

4. Issue putable debt and buy put swaption.
5. Issue putable debt, take floating-rate position on putable swap (swap gives issuer the right to early termination), and take fixed payer's position on generic swap.

  • Prior to put date, the issuer has a fixed-rate position: fixed-rate callable bond, fixed payer's position on the generic swap, and floating payer's position on the putable swap.
  • If rates are high at the put date: (1) bondholders sell bonds back to the issuer who funds the purchase by selling FRNs; (2) the issuer terminates the putable bond; (3) the issuer's fixed payer's position on the generic swap remains outstanding. The FRN and fixed payer's position on the swap equate to the fixed-rate loan.
  • If rates are low at the put date: (1) bondholders take no action on their put; (2) the issuer does not terminate the putable bond, leaving him with fixed payer's and floating payer's positions. The issuer pays the fixed rate on the bond plus or minus any difference in the fixed rates on the two swaps.

FLOATING-RATE DEBT

1. Issue fixed-rate debt and take floating payer's position on the generic swap.
2. Issue callable debt and take floating payer's position on a callable swap contract.

  • Prior to call date, the issuer has a synthetic FRN: fixed-rate callable bond and floating payer's position on the swap.
  • If rates are low at the call date: (1) issuer calls the bond and issues FRN to fund the call; (2) the counterparty on the callable swaps terminates the swap. Issuer therefore pays flexible rate.
  • If rates are high at the call date: (1) issuer does not call the bond; (2) the counterparty on the callable swaps does not terminate. The issuer, therefore, has a fixed-rate bond and floating payer's position on the swap which is equivalent to a flexible-rate debt position.

3. Issue putable debt and take floating payer's position on a putable swap contract.

  • Prior to put date, the issuer has a synthetic FRN: fixed-rate putable bond and floating payer's position on swap.
  • If rates are low at the put date: (1) bondholders take no action on their put; (2) the issuer does not terminate the putable bond, leaving him with floating payer's positions. The fixed-rate bond and floating payer's position on the swap are equivalent to a floating-rate debt position.
  • If rates are high at the put date: (1) bondholders sell the bond back to the issuer who funds the purchase by selling FRNs; (2) the issuer terminates the putable bond, leaving him with a flexible-rate debt position.

Intrinsic value $= \text{Max}[C_f^* - C^X, 0]$

$$\times \left[\frac{1}{(1+Z(4))^4} + \frac{1}{(1+Z(5))^5}\right] NP$$

$\text{Max}(0.08 - 0.07, 0)(\$10,000,000) = \$100,000$

$$\text{Intrinsic value} = \frac{\$100,000}{(1.062176)^4} + \frac{\$100,000}{(1.0674697)^5}$$

$$= \$151,710$$

Note, the IV of the put swaption is directly related to the underlying break-even rate; that is, for break-even rates above the exercise rate, C^X (7%), the IV increases as the break-even rate increases, and for rates below, it is zero. Also note that if the strike rate were below the break-even rate, then the put swaption would be in-the-money and its IV would be positive, if it were equal, the option would be at-the-money and its IV would be zero, and if the strike rate were above the forward rate, then the put swaption would be out-of-the-money with an IV of zero. In general, the IV of a put swaption is:

$$IV_p = \text{Max}[C_f^* - C^X, 0] \left[\sum_{t=1}^{M} \frac{1}{(1+Z(T+t))^t}\right] NP$$

where T is the expiration on the swaption and M is the maturity on the underlying swap.

Just the opposite relations hold for call swaptions. The call swaption's IV is:

$$IV_c = \text{Max}[C^X - C_f^*, 0] \left[\sum_{t=1}^{M} \frac{1}{(1+Z(T+t))^t}\right] NP$$

Thus, the IV on a 3-year call swaption on a 2-year swap with a strike rate of 9% (the right to receive 9% and pay LIBOR) would be 150.71 BP or $151,710 given NP of $10m:

$$IV_c = \text{Max}[0.09 - 0.08, 0] \left[\frac{1}{(1.062176)^4}\right.$$

$$\left. + \frac{1}{(1.067469)^5}\right] (\$10m) = \$151,710$$

The call swaption, in turn, would be at-the-money with an IV of zero when its strike and forward rates are equal, out-of-the-money with a zero IV when the forward rate is greater than

the strike rate, and in-the-money when the forward rate is below the strike rate, increasing as the forward rate decreases.

Time Value Premium

Given that there is some time to expiration, a swaption will trade at a value above its IVs. The difference between the swaption's value and its IV is the swaption's time value premium, TVP. Like other options, the swaption's TVP depends primarily on the volatility of the underlying forward rate, with the greater the volatility, the greater the swaption's TVP and value. The volatility of forward rates is often estimated using current swap rates or spot Treasury rates as a proxy or the implied futures rates on T-note futures contracts.

Black Futures Option Model

Swaptions can be valued using a binomial interest rate framework similar to the one presented in chapter 9. A simpler model for valuing swaptions, though, is the Black futures option model described in chapter 15. For put swaptions that give the holder the right to pay a fixed rate C^X and receive the LIBOR (a put swaption), the value of the cash flow received at each payment date t_i after the swaption's expiration T is:

$$V = \frac{NP}{m} e^{-R_{fi} t_i} [C_f N(d_1) - C^X N(d_2)]$$

$$d_1 = \frac{\ln(C_f/C^X) + \sigma^2 T/2}{\sigma\sqrt{T}}$$

$$d_2 = d_1 - \sigma\sqrt{T}$$

where:

$C^X =$ swaption exercise rate (annual)
$C_f =$ break-even forward rate underlying the swaption (annual)
$R_{fi} =$ continuously compound annual risk-free rate for period of t_i
$m =$ number of payments on a swap in a year
$\sigma^2 =$ volatility of the forward or swap rate $= \text{Var}(\ln(R_t^{\text{Swap}}/R_0^{\text{Swap}}))$
$t_i =$ payment dates in years on the swap $= T + i/m$
$T =$ swaption's expiration in years

The value of the put swaption, in turn, is the sum of the values of each cash flow. If the underlying swap lasts n years starting at the swaption expiration in T years, then the value of the swaption is:

$$V_p = \sum_{i=1}^{mn} \frac{NP}{m} e^{-R_{fi}t_i} [C_f N(d_1) - C^X N(d_2)]$$

and its intrinsic value is:

$$IV_p = \sum_{i=1}^{mn} \frac{NP}{m} e^{-R_{fi}t_i} [\text{Max}(C_f - C^X, 0)]$$

To illustrate, consider a 3-year put swaption on a 2-year 7%/LIBOR swap: $C^X = 0.07$, the forward rate $= C_f = 0.08$, $T = 3$, $m = 2$, $n = 2$, and $NP = \$10m$. If we assume a flat yield curve for risk-free securities in which the continuously compounded rate is 6.74% and a volatility of the swap rate of $\sigma = 0.2$, then the value of the swaption would be $241,752:[1]

$$V_p = [0.08(0.71202) - 0.07(0.583944)]$$
$$[\$10m/2][e^{-(0.0674)(3.5)} + e^{-(0.0674)(4)}$$
$$+ e^{-(0.0674)(4.5)} + e^{-(0.0674)(5)}]$$
$$= \$241,752$$

where:

$$d_1 = \frac{\ln(0.08/0.07) + 0.2^2(3/2)}{0.2\sqrt{3}} = 0.558677$$
$$d_2 = d_1 - 0.2\sqrt{3} = 0.212267$$
$$N(d_1) = N(0.558677) = 0.71202$$
$$N(d_2) = N(0.212267) = 0.583944$$

The put swaption's intrinsic value using the Black continuous model is $150,292:

$$IV = [\text{Max}(0.08 - 0.07, 0)][\$10m/2] \times$$
$$[e^{-(0.0674)(3.5)} + e^{-(0.0674)(4)} + e^{-(0.0674)(4.5)}$$
$$+ e^{-(0.0674)(5)}]$$
$$= \$150,292$$

As we would expect, the Black futures model yields put swaption values that are directly related to the break-even forward rates. This can be seen in exhibit 17.5, which shows a graph and table of the Black model values

for the 3-year put swaption on a 2-year 7%/LIBOR swap given different break-even forward rates. As shown in the exhibit, for low forward rates where the put is deep out-of-the-money, the Black model yields very low put swaption values. As the forward rates increase by equal increments, the put swaption values increase at an increasing rate, up to a point, with the values never being below the IV. In addition, the Black model yields put swaption values that are directly related to the time to expiration on the swaption, the maturity on the swap, and the underlying swap rate's volatility.

For a call swaption, the swaption gives the holder the right to receive the fixed rate and pay the LIBOR. The value of each cash flow is:

$$V = \frac{NP}{m} e^{-R_{fi}t_i} [-C_f(1 - N(d_1)) + C^X(1 - N(d_2))]$$

and the value and the intrinsic value of the call swaption are:

$$V_c = \sum_{i=1}^{mn} \frac{NP}{m} e^{-R_{fi}t_i} [-C_f(1 - N(d_1)) + C^X(1 - N(d_2))]$$

$$IV_c = \sum_{i=1}^{mn} \frac{NP}{m} e^{-R_{fi}t_i} [\text{Max}(C^X - C_f, 0)]$$

Using the Black futures model, the value of a 3-year call swaption on a 2-year 7%/LIBOR swap would be $91,461 and its intrinsic value would be zero:

$$V_c = [-0.08(1 - N(0.558677)) + 0.07(1 - N(0.212267))] \times$$
$$[\$10m/2][e^{-(0.0674)(3.5)} + e^{-(0.0674)(4)}$$
$$+ e^{-(0.0674)(4.5)} + e^{-(0.0674)(5)}]$$
$$= \$91,461$$

$$IV_c = [\text{Max}(0.07 - 0.08, 0)][\$10m/2] \times$$
$$[e^{-(0.0674)(3.5)} + e^{-(0.0674)(4)}$$
$$+ e^{-(0.0674)(4.5)} + e^{-(0.0674)(5)}] = 0$$

The Black futures model yields call swaption values that are inversely related to the break-even forward rates, and directly related to the time to expiration on the swaption, the maturity on the swap, and the underlying swap rate's volatility. The inverse relation between the call

Exhibit 17.5 Put swaptions values using Black futures model given different forward rates

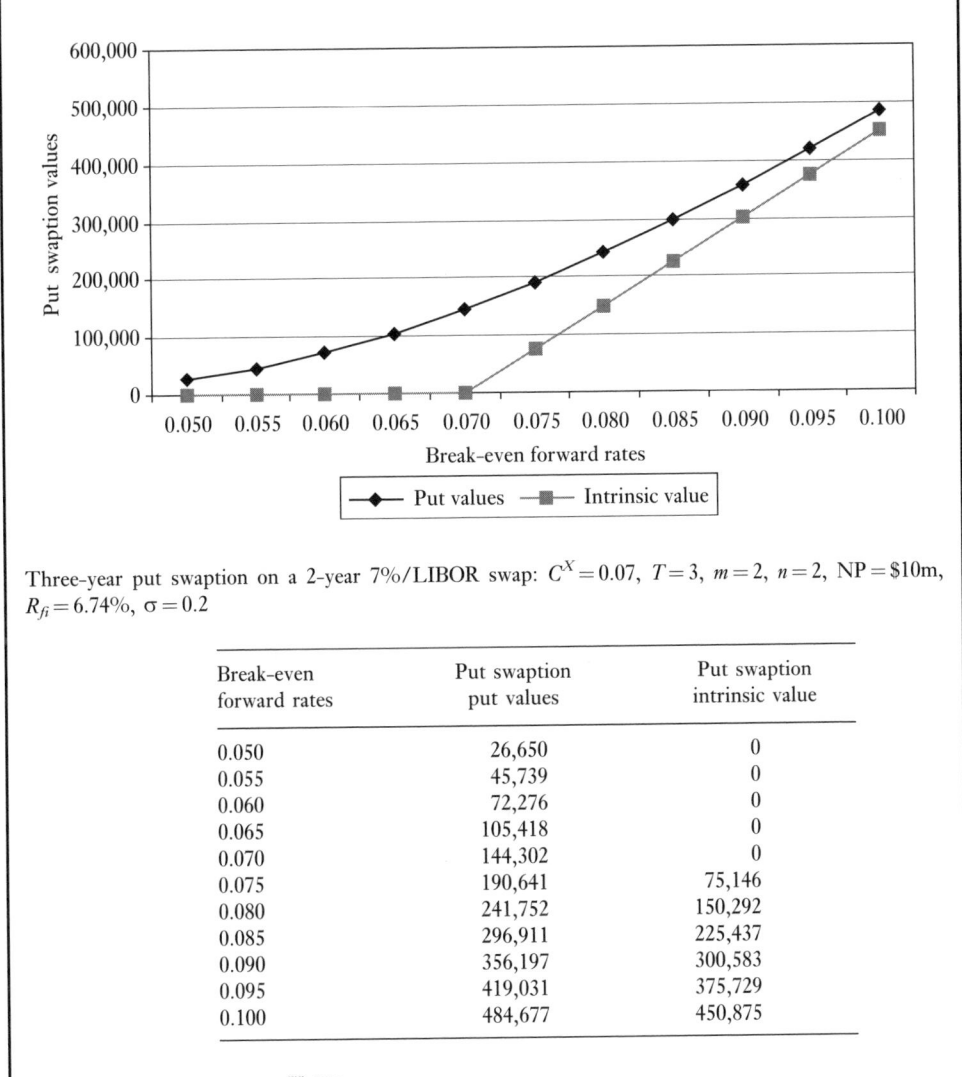

Three-year put swaption on a 2-year 7%/LIBOR swap: $C^X = 0.07$, $T = 3$, $m = 2$, $n = 2$, NP = \$10m, $R_{fi} = 6.74\%$, $\sigma = 0.2$

Break-even forward rates	Put swaption put values	Put swaption intrinsic value
0.050	26,650	0
0.055	45,739	0
0.060	72,276	0
0.065	105,418	0
0.070	144,302	0
0.075	190,641	75,146
0.080	241,752	150,292
0.085	296,911	225,437
0.090	356,197	300,583
0.095	419,031	375,729
0.100	484,677	450,875

$$V_P = \sum_{i=1}^{mn} \frac{NP}{m} e^{-R_{fi}t_i}[C_f N(d_1) - C^X N(d_2)]$$

$$IV_P = \sum_{i=1}^{mn} \frac{NP}{m} e^{-R_{fi}t_i}[Max(C_f - C^X, 0)]$$

swaption value and the forward rate is presented in exhibit 17.6. The exhibit shows a graph and table of the Black model values for the 3-year call swaption on a 2-year 7%/LIBOR swap given different break-even forward rates. As shown in the exhibit, for large forward rates where the call is deep out-of-the-money, the Black model yields very low call swaption values, and as the forward rates decrease by equal increments, the call swaption values increase at an increasing rate, up to a point.

Exhibit 17.6   Call swaptions values using Black futures model given different forward rates

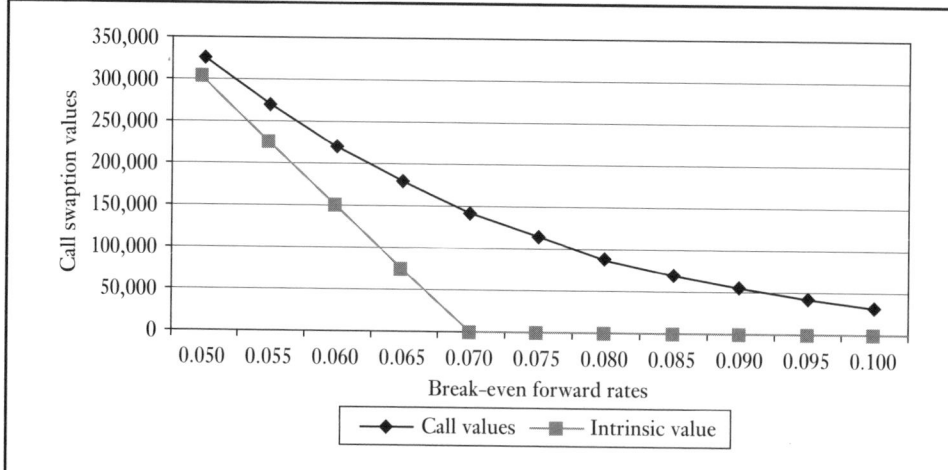

Three-year call swaption on a 2-year 7%/LIBOR swap: $C^X = 0.07$, $T = 3$, $m = 2$, $n = 2$, NP $= \$10m$, $R_{fi} = 6.74\%$, $\sigma = 0.2$

Break-even forward rates	Call swaption call value	Call swaption intrinsic value
0.050	327,233	300,583
0.055	271,176	225,437
0.060	222,568	150,292
0.065	180,563	75,146
0.070	144,302	0
0.075	115,495	0
0.080	91,461	0
0.085	71,473	0
0.090	55,614	0
0.095	43,302	0
0.100	33,802	0

$$V_c = \sum_{i=1}^{mn} \frac{NP}{m} e^{-R_{fi}t_i}[-C_f(1 - N(d_1)) + C^X(1 - N(d_2))]$$

$$IV_c = \sum_{i=1}^{mn} \frac{NP}{m} e^{-R_{fi}t_i}[\text{Max}(C^X - C_f, 0)]$$

Put–Call Futures Parity

Since the values of the forward swap, call swaption, and put swaption ultimately depend on the underlying swap value at expiration, these derivative swaps are necessarily related. A put–call parity relation similar to the put–call futures parity condition governing options and futures governs the relationship between

them. In the case of swaptions, a put swaption can be synthetically created with a similar call swaption and a forward swap contract as a fixed payer. This can be seen by observing that the possible values at expiration of the above 3-year put swaption on a 2-year swap with a strike rate of 7% are identical to the values obtained from (1) a 3-year call swaption on a 2-year swap with an exercise rate of 7% and (2) a fixed position on a 2-year, 7%/LIBOR swap 3 years forward. Values at expiration of a put swaption and a synthetic put swaption consisting of a call swaption and a forward contract are:

Swap rate on 2-year generic swap	6%	7%	8%
Long put swaption: right to pay 7%/receive LIBOR	0	0	PV (8% − 7%)
Long call swaption: right to receive 7%/pay LIBOR	PV (7% − 6%)	0	0
Forward swap: pay 7%/receive LIBOR	PV (6% − 7%)	PV (7% − 7%)	PV (8% − 7%)
Net value	0	0	PV (8% − 7%)

Thus, by the law of one price, the value of a put swaption is equal to the value of a similar call swaption plus the value of a similar long forward swap contract, F: $V_p = V_c + F$ or the value of the forward contract is equal to the difference between the put and call swaption values: $F = V_p - V_c$. In our example, the call and put swaption prices and the forward swaption price are consistent with the put–call futures parity. That is, the value on the 2-year 7%/LIBOR swap 3 years forward contract using continuous compounding and the 6.74% continuous compounded rate is $150,291:

$$F = [0.08 - 0.07][\$10m/2][e^{-(0.0674)(3.5)} +$$
$$e^{-(0.0674)(4)} + e^{-(0.0674)(4.5)} + e^{-(0.0674)(5)}]$$
$$= \$150,291$$

This value is equal to the difference in the Black futures model's put and call swaptions values:

$$F = V_p - V_c = \$241,752 - \$91,461 = \$150,291$$

17.5 OTHER NON-GENERIC SWAPS

Just as forward swaps and swaptions provide investors and borrowers with tools for hedging

future interest rate risk, other non-generic swaps have been introduced to address other asset and liability management problems (see exhibit 17.1). Of particular note are cancelable and extendable swaps, index amortizing swaps, credit default swaps, total return swaps, and equity swaps.

17.5.1 Cancelable Swaps

A *cancelable swap* is a generic swap in which one of the counterparties has the option to terminate one or more payments. Cancelable swaps can be callable or putable. A callable swap is one in which the fixed payer has the right to early termination. Thus, if rates decrease, the fixed-rate payer on the swap with this embedded call option to early termination can exercise her right to cancel the swap. A putable swap, on the other hand, is one in which the floating payer has the right to early cancelation. A floating-rate payer with this option may find it advantageous to exercise his early-termination right when rates increase.

If there is only one termination date, then a cancelable swap is equivalent to a standard swap plus a position in a European swaption. For example, a 5-year putable swap to receive 7% and pay LIBOR that is cancelable after 3 years is equivalent to a floating position in a 5-year 7%/LIBOR generic swap and a long position in a 3-year put swaption on a 2-year 7%/LIBOR swap (the same put swaption used in the example in section 17.4.2); that is, after 3 years, the put swaption gives the holder the right to take a fixed payer's position on a 2-year swap at 7% which offsets the floating position on the 7% generic swap. On the other hand, a 5-year callable swap to pay 7% and receive LIBOR that is cancelable after 3 years would be equivalent to a fixed position in a 5-year 7%/LIBOR generic swap and a long position in a 3-year call swaption on a 2-year 7%/LIBOR swap.

The value of a cancelable swap is equal to the value of the generic swap plus the value of the underlying option (IV + TVP). Thus, if a 5-year 7%/LIBOR generic swap is at par, then the value of a 5-year putable swap cancelable after 3 years would be equal to the value of a 3-year put swaption on a 2-year, 7%/LIBOR swap. If the break-even forward rate on a 2-year swap 3 years forward were 8%, as was the case in our put swaption example, then the value of cancelable swap with an NP of $10m would be equal to the put swaption's value ($241,752 using the Black futures model).

Since cancelable swaps are equivalent to generic swaps with a swaption, they can be used like swaptions to create synthetic positions. For example, the synthetic fixed rate debt position formed by issuing FRNs and taking a fixed payer's position on a generic swap or by issuing callable bonds and selling a call swaption could also be created by: (1) issuing callable bonds, (2) taking a fixed payer's position on a generic swap, and (3) taking a floating payer's position on a callable swap. It also could be formed by: (1) issuing putable bonds, (2) taking a fixed payer's position on a generic swap, and (3) taking a floating position on a putable swap (the details on each of these synthetic positions are presented in exhibit 17.4).

17.5.2 Extendable Swaps

An *extendable swap* is just the opposite of a cancelable swap: it is a swap that has an option to lengthen the terms of the original swap. The swap allows the holder to take advantage of current rates and extend the maturity of the swap. Like cancelable swaps, extendable swaps can be replicated with a generic swap and a swaption. The floating payer with an extendable option has the equivalent of a floating position on a generic swap and a call swaption. That is, a 3-year swap to receive 7% and pay LIBOR that is extendable at maturity to 2 more years would be equivalent to a floating position in a 3-year 7%/LIBOR generic swap and a long position in a 3-year call swaption on a 2-year 7%/LIBOR. In 3 years, the call swaption gives the holder the right to take a floating payer's position on a 2-year swap at 7% which in effect extends the maturity of the expiring floating position on the 7% generic swap. In contrast, the fixed payer with an extendable option has the equivalent of a fixed position on a generic swap and a put swaption. Also like cancelable swaps, the values of extendable swaps can be estimated by determining the values of the underlying options.

17.5.3 Amortizing, Accreting, and Index-Amortizing Swaps

An amortizing swap is one in which the NP decreases over time based on a set schedule, while an accreting swap (also called a set-up swap) is one in which the NP increases over time based on a set schedule. Amortizing swaps can be used by companies that have fixed-rate borrowing obligations with a certain prepayment schedule, but would like to swap them for floating rates. An accreting swap is also useful to companies that plan to borrow increasing amounts at floating rates and want to swap them for fixed-rate funds; accreting swaps are particularly popular in construction financing.

A variation of the amortizing swap is the *index-amortizing swap* (also called index-principal swap). In this swap, the NP is dependent on interest rates; for example, the lower the interest rate the greater the reduction in principal. The fixed side of index amortizing swaps is often structured to replicate the possible cash flow patterns of mortgage-backed securities (MBSs). As such, they are used by MBS investors as a tool for hedging against prepayment risk.

17.5.4 Credit Default Swaps

In a standard *credit default swap (CDS)*, a counterparty, such as a bank, buys protection against default by a particular company from a counterparty (seller). The company is known as the reference entity and a default by that company is known as a credit event. The buyer of the CDS makes periodic payments or a premium to the seller until the end of the life of the CDS or until the credit event occurs. Depending on the contract, if the credit event occurs, the buyer has either the right to sell a particular bond issued by the company for its par value (physical delivery) or receive a cash settlement based on the difference between the par value and the defaulted bond's market price times a notional principal equal to the bond's total par value.

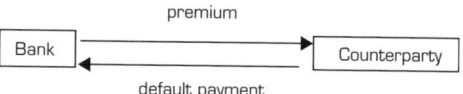

To illustrate, suppose two parties enter into a 5-year CDS with an NP of $100m. The buyer agrees to pay 95 BP annually for protection against default by the reference entity. If the reference entity does not default, the buyer does not receive a payoff and ends up paying $950,000 each year for 5 years. If a credit event does occur, the buyer will receive the default payment and pay a final accrual payment on the unpaid premium; for example, if the event occurs half way through the year, then the buyer pays the seller $475,000. If the swap contract calls for physical delivery, the buyer will sell $100m par value of the defaulted bonds for $100m. If there is a cash settlement, then an agent will poll dealers to determine a mid-market value. If that value were $30 per $100 face value, then the buyer would receive $70m minus the $475,000 accrued interest payment.

There are several variations from this standard CDS. For example, in a *binary CDS*, the payoff in the case of a default is a specified dollar amount. In a *basket credit swap*, there is a group of reference entities instead of one and there is usually a specified payoff whenever one of the reference entities defaults. Thus, in the event of a default by any of the entities, the seller pays a fixed amount to the buyer and the other defaults are terminated. Finally, there is a *contingent CDS*. In this swap, the payoff requires both a credit default of the reference entity and an additional event such as a credit event with another entity or a change in a market variable.

17.5.5 Total Return Swaps

In a *total return swap*, the return from one asset or portfolio of assets is swapped for the return on another asset or portfolio. These swaps can be used to pass credit risk on to another party or to achieve a more diversified portfolio. For example, a California bank with a relatively heavy proportion of loans to technology companies could enter into a swap with a Michigan bank with a relatively large proportion of loans to auto-related companies. The banks could enter into a total return swap in which the California bank swaps some of the return on its technology company loans to the Michigan bank who swaps some of the

returns from its loans to auto-related companies. The purpose of this swap would be to achieve some credit diversification.

17.5.6 Equity Swaps

In an equity swap, one party agrees to pay the return on an equity index, such as the S&P 500, and the other party agrees to pay a floating rate (LIBOR) or fixed rate. For example, on an S&P 500/LIBOR swap, the equity payer would agree to pay the 6-month rate of change on the S&P 500 (e.g., proportional change in the index between effective dates) times an NP in return for LIBOR times NP, and the debt payer would agree to pay the LIBOR in return for the S&P 500 return. Equity swaps are useful to fund managers who want to increase or decrease the equity exposure of their portfolios.

17.6 CURRENCY SWAPS

In its simplest form, a currency swap involves an exchange of principal and interest in one currency for the interest and principal in another. For example, Ford Motor Company swaps a 12% loan in dollars to British Petroleum Company for their 10% loan in sterling. Currency swaps can differ in terms of whether or not principals are exchanged and whether the rates are fixed or floating. In the generic currency swap, though, principals are exchanged at both the beginning and at maturity and both rates are fixed: fixed-for-fixed swap.

The market for currency swaps comes primarily from corporations who can borrow in one currency at relatively favorable terms but need to borrow in another.[2] For example, a US multinational corporation that can obtain favorable borrowing terms for a dollar loan made in the US, but really needs a loan in sterling to finance its operations in London, might use a currency swap. To meet such a need, the company could go to a swap dealer who would try to match its needs with another party wanting the opposite position. For example, the dealer might match the US corporation with a British multinational corporation with operations in the US that it is financing with a sterling-denominated loan, but would prefer instead a dollar-denominated loan. If the loans are approximately equivalent, then the dealer could arrange a swap agreement in which the companies simply exchange their principal and interest payments. If the loans are not equivalent, the swap dealer may have to bring in other parties who are looking to swap, or the dealer could take the opposite position and warehouse the swap.

17.6.1 Example

As an example, suppose there is a Canadian beverage company that can issue a 5-year, C$142.857m bond paying 7.5% interest to finance the construction of its US brewery, but really needs an equivalent dollar loan, which at the current spot exchange rate of $0.70/C$ would be $100m. Suppose also there is an American development company that can issue 5-year, $100m bonds at 10% to finance the development of a hotel complex in Montreal, but really needs a 5-year, C$142.857m loan. To meet each other's needs, suppose that both companies go to a swap bank that sets up the following agreement.

1. The Canadian company will issue a 5-year C$142.857m bond paying 7.5% interest, then will pay the C$142.857m to the swap bank who will pass it on to the American company to finance its Canadian investment project.
2. The American company will issue a 5-year $100m bond paying 10% interest, then will pay the $100m to the swap bank who will pass it on to the Canadian company to finance its US investment project.

The initial cash flows of the agreement are shown in exhibit 17.7a.

For the next 5 years, each company will make annual interest payments. To this end, the swap dealer would make the following arrangements:

1. The Canadian company, with its US asset (brewery), will pay the 10% interest on $100m ($10m) to the swap bank who will pass it on to the American company so it can pay its US bondholders.
2. The American company, with its Canadian asset (hotel), will pay the 7.5% interest on

C$142.857m (C$10.714m) to the swap bank who will pass it on to the Canadian company so it can pay its Canadian bondholders.

The yearly cash flows of interest are summarized in exhibit 17.7b.

Finally, to cover the principal payments at maturity, the swap dealer would set up the following agreement:

1. At maturity, the Canadian company will pay $100m to the swap bank who will pass it on to the American company so it can pay its US bondholders.
2. At maturity, the American company will pay C$142.857m to the swap bank who will pass it on to the Canadian company so it can pay its Canadian bondholders.

The cash flows of principals are shown in exhibit 17.7c.

17.6.2 Valuation

Equivalent Bond Positions

In the above swap agreement, the American company, after the initial exchange, will receive $10m each year for 5 years and a principal of $100m at maturity and will pay C$10.714m each year for 5 years and C$142.857m at maturity. To the American company, this swap agreement is equivalent to a position in two bonds: a long position in a US dollar-denominated, 5-year, 10% annual coupon bond with a principal of $100m and trading at par and a short position in a Canadian dollar-denominated, 5-year, 7.5% annual coupon bond with a principal of C$142,857 and trading at par. The dollar value of this swap position where dollars are received and Canadian dollars are paid is

$$SV = B_\$ - E_0 B_{C\$}$$

where:

$B_\$ =$ Dollar-denominated bond value

$B_{C\$} =$ Canadian dollar-denominated bond value

$E_0 =$ Spot exchange rate $= \$/C\$$

In this example, the initial value of the swap to the American company in terms of equivalent bond positions is zero:

$$SV = \$100m - (\$0.70/C\$)(C\$142.857m) = 0$$

Exhibit 17.7   Currency swap

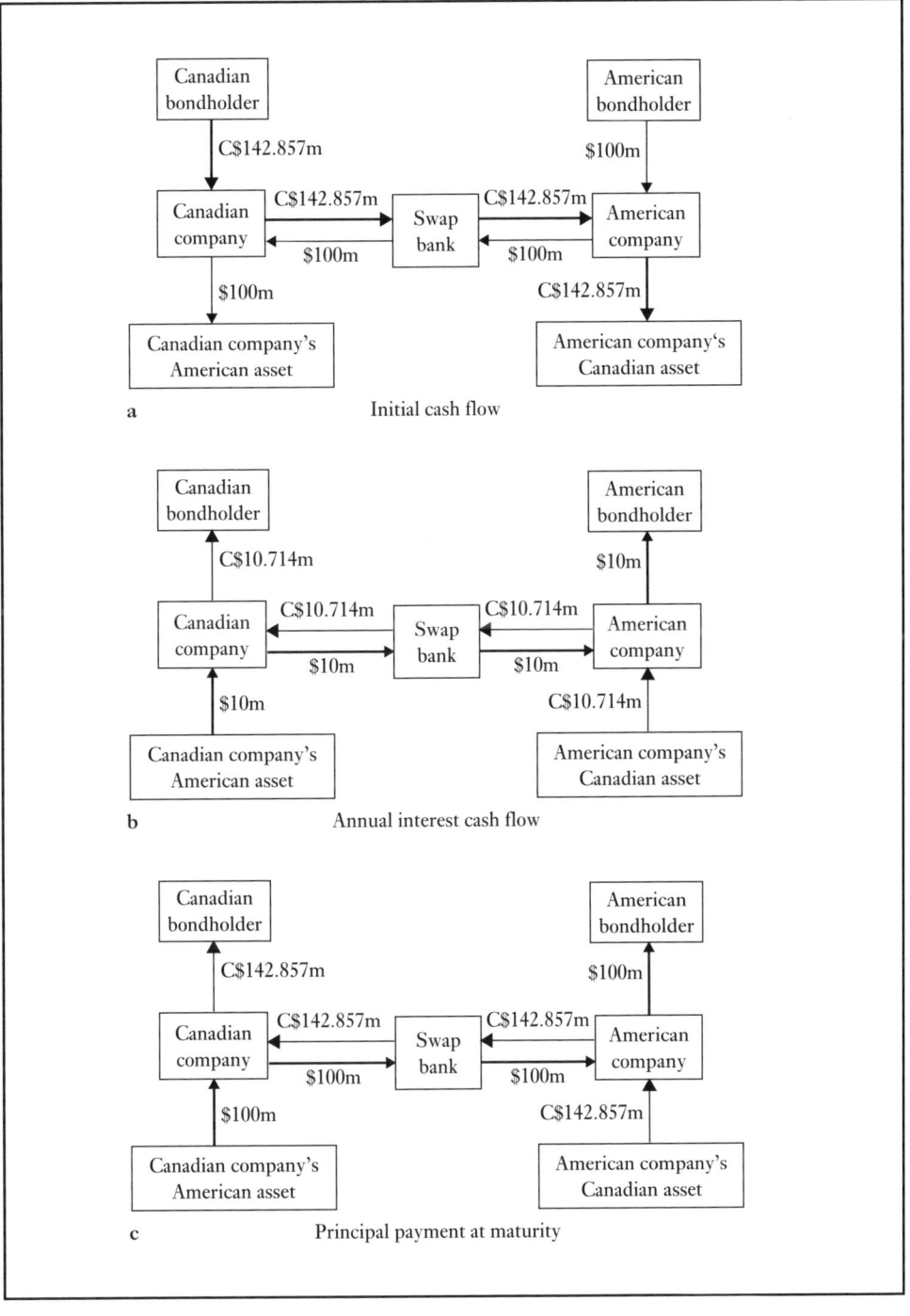

a   Initial cash flow

b   Annual interest cash flow

c   Principal payment at maturity

where:

$$B_\$ = \sum_{t=1}^{5} \frac{\$10m}{(1.10)^t} + \frac{\$100m}{(1.10)^5} = \$100m$$

$$B_{C\$} = \sum_{t=1}^{5} \frac{C\$10.714m}{(1.075)^t} + \frac{C\$142.857m}{(1.075)^5} = C\$142.857m$$

The Canadian company's swap position in which it will receive Canadian dollars and pay US dollars is just the opposite of the American company's position. It is equivalent to a long position in a Canadian dollar-denominated bond and a short position in a US dollar-denominated bond; in this example it likewise has a value of zero:

$$SV = E_0 B_{C\$} - B_\$$$
$$= (\$0.70/C\$)(C\$142.857m) - \$100m = 0$$

Similar to interest rate swaps, the currency swap's economic value of zero means that neither counterparty is required to pay the other. The zero value also implies that the underlying bond positions trade at par. Thus, the currency swap in this example is a par value swap. Note that the swap dealer in this example has a perfect hedge given his two opposite positions. If the dealer, though, had been warehousing swaps and provided a swap to just the American company, then it could have hedged its swap position of paying $10m and receiving C$10.714m by shorting the 7.5% Canadian dollar-denominated bond and buying the 10% US dollar-denominated bond:

4-year, 10% dollar-denominated bond would be $98.43207m and the value of the 4-year $10m received/C$10.714m paid swap would be − $1.56784m:

$$SV = \$98.43207m - (\$0.70/C\$)(C\$142.857m)$$
$$= -\$1.56784m$$

where:

$$B_\$ = \sum_{t=1}^{4} \frac{\$10m}{(1.105)^t} + \frac{\$100m}{(1.105)^4} = \$98.43207m$$

$$B_{C\$} = \sum_{t=1}^{4} \frac{C\$10.714m}{(1.075)^t} + \frac{C\$142.857m}{(1.075)^4} = C\$142.857m$$

If the American company wanted to close its swap position by selling (or transferring) its remaining 4-year $10m received/C$10.714m paid swap to a dealer, that dealer would require compensation of at least $1.56784m. The dealer's fee of $1.56784m would, in turn, defray his net hedging cost of selling a 4-year, 10% dollar-denominated bond trading at 10.5% and buying a 4-year, 7.5% Canadian dollar-denominated bond at par.

In general, the value of a dollar received/ foreign currency paid swap is inversely related to US interest rates and the exchange rate and directly related to the foreign rate, while the value of a foreign currency received/dollar paid swap, valued in dollars, is directly related to US rates and the exchange rate and inversely related to the foreign rate. These relations are shown in table 17.5, which shows the different values of our illustrative swap given different

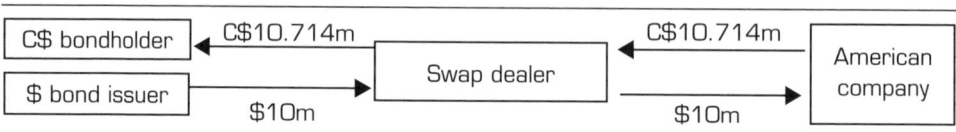

The economic values of the swap positions will change with changes in US rates, R_{US}, Canadian rates, R_C, and the spot exchange rate:

$$SV = f(R_{US}, R_C, E_0)$$

For example, suppose in our example that 1 year later Canadian rates and the exchange rate were the same, but rates in the US were higher with the YTM on the US dollar-denominated bond at 10.5%. In this case, the value of a

US interest rates, Canadian interest rates, and spot exchange rates.

Equivalent Forward Exchange Positions

Instead of viewing its swap as a bond position, the Canadian company could alternatively view its interest agreement to pay $10m for C$10.714m each year for 5 years and its

Table 17.5 Currency swap value for different interest rates and exchange rates

US rate	Canadian rate	$E_0 = \$/C\$$	$ value of swap (millions), $ received/C$ paid	$ value of swap (millions), C$ received/$ paid
0.100	0.075	0.700	0.00000	0.00000
0.095	0.075	0.700	1.91995	−1.91995
0.105	0.075	0.700	−1.87130	1.87130
0.100	0.070	0.700	−2.05000	2.05000
0.100	0.080	0.700	1.99645	−1.99645
0.100	0.075	0.725	−3.571325	3.571325
0.100	0.075	0.690	1.42867	−1.42867

Swap: 5-year 10%, $100m/5-year 7.5%, C$142.857m

principal agreement to pay $100m for C$142.857m at maturity as a series of long currency forward contracts in years 1, 2, 3, 4, and 5. In contrast, the American company could view its swap agreements to sell C$10.714m each year for $10m and sell C$142.857m at maturity for $100m as a series of short currency forward contracts.

Exhibit 17.8 shows the annual cash flow exchanges for the two companies with each of the exchanges representing a forward exchange contract. In the absence of arbitrage, the value of the American company's swap of dollars received/Canadian dollars paid should be equal to (1) the sum of the present values of $10m received each year from the swap minus the dollar cost of buying C$10.714m at the forward exchange rate, and (2) the present value of the $100m received at year 5 minus the dollar cost of buying C$142.857m at the 5-year forward exchange rate. The equilibrium forward exchange rates, E_f, can be determined by using the interest rate parity relation explained in chapter 13:

$$E_f = E_0 \left(\frac{1 + R_{US}}{1 + R_{C\$}} \right)^T$$

Assuming a flat yield curve in the US and Canada and using the 10% and 7.5% rates on the swap, the equilibrium forward rates for years 1, 2, 3, 4, and 5 are:

$$T = 1: E_f = (\$0.70/C\$)\left(\frac{1.10}{1.075}\right)^1 = \$0.716279/C\$$$

$$T = 2: E_f = (\$0.70/C\$)\left(\frac{1.10}{1.075}\right)^2 = \$0.732937/C\$$$

$$T = 3: E_f = (\$0.70/C\$)\left(\frac{1.10}{1.075}\right)^3 = \$0.749982/C\$$$

$$T = 4: E_f = (\$0.70/C\$)\left(\frac{1.10}{1.075}\right)^4 = \$0.767423/C\$$$

$$T = 5: E_f = (\$0.70/C\$)\left(\frac{1.10}{1.075}\right)^5 = \$0.78527/C\$$$

In this example, the value of the American company's swap as a series of forward contracts is zero:

$$SV = \frac{\$10m - (\$0.716279/C\$)(C\$10.714)}{(1.10)^1}$$

$$+ \frac{\$10m - (\$0.732937/C\$)(C\$10.714)}{(1.10)^2}$$

$$+ \frac{\$10m - (\$0.749982/C\$)(C\$10.714)}{(1.10)^3}$$

$$+ \frac{\$10m - (\$0.767423/C\$)(C\$10.714)}{(1.10)^4}$$

$$+ \frac{\$10m - (\$0.78527/C\$)(C\$10.714)}{(1.10)^5}$$

$$+ \frac{\$100m - (\$0.78527/C\$)(C\$142.857)}{(1.10)^5}$$

$$= 0$$

Similarly, in the absence of arbitrage, the dollar value of the Canadian company's swap of Canadian dollars received/US dollars paid should be equal to (1) the sum of present values from receiving C$10.714m each year and converting it to dollars at the forward exchange rate minus the $10m payments, and (2) the present value of the C$142.857m principal received times the 5-year forward exchange minus the

Exhibit 17.8 Swap cash flows to American and Canadian companies

American company

Year	$ CF (million)	C$ CF
0	− 100	+ 142.857
1	+ 10	− 10.714
2	+ 10	− 10.714
3	+ 10	− 10.714
4	+ 10	− 10.714
5	+ (100 + 10)	− (142.857 + 10.714)

Canadian company

Year	$ CF (million)	C$ CF
0	+ 100	− 142.857
1	− 10	+ 10.714
2	− 10	+ 10.714
3	− 10	+ 10.714
4	− 10	+ 10.714
5	− (100 + 10)	+ (142.857 + 10.714)

The values of $ received/C$ paid swap as forward contracts for different interest rates and exchange rates

US rate	Canadian rate	$E_0 = \$/C\$$	$ value of swap (millions), $ received/C$ paid	$ value of swap (millions), C$ received/$ paid
0.100	0.075	0.700	0.00000	0.00000
0.095	0.075	0.700	1.91995	−1.91995
0.105	0.075	0.700	−1.87130	1.87130
0.100	0.070	0.700	−2.05000	2.05000
0.100	0.080	0.700	1.99645	−1.99645
0.100	0.075	0.725	−3.571325	3.571325
0.100	0.075	0.690	1.42867	−1.42867

$$SV = \frac{\$10m - (E_{f1})(C\$10.714)}{(1 + R_{US})^1} + \frac{\$10m - (E_{f2})(C\$10.714)}{(1 + R_{US})^2}$$
$$+ \frac{\$10m - (E_{f3})(C\$10.714)}{(1 + R_{US})^3} + \frac{\$10m - (E_{f4})(C\$10.714)}{(1 + R_{US})^4}$$
$$+ \frac{\$10m - (E_{f5})(C\$10.714)}{(1 + R_{US})^5} + \frac{\$100m - (E_{f5})(C\$142.857)}{(1 + R_{US})^5}$$

$$E_{fT} = E_0 \left[\frac{1 + R_{US}}{1 + R_C} \right]^T$$

$100m paid. Like the American company, given flat yield curves at 10% and 7.5%, the value of the Canadian company's swap is also zero.

In general, the value of a dollar received/ foreign currency paid swap as a series of forward contracts is:

$$SV = \sum_{t=1}^{M} \frac{(\$ \text{ received}) - E_{ft}(\text{FC paid})}{(1 + R_{US})^t}$$

and the dollar value of an FC received/$ paid swap is:

$$SV = \sum_{t=1}^{M} \frac{E_{ft}(\text{FC paid}) - (\$ \text{ received})}{(1 + R_{US})^t}$$

Note that in the absence of arbitrage, the values of the swap positions as forward contracts are equal to their values as bond positions:

$$SV = \sum_{t=1}^{M} \frac{(\$\text{received}) - E_{ft}(\text{FC paid})}{(1 + R_{US})^t} = B_\$ - E_0 B_{FC}$$

For example, if 1 year later rates were at 10.5%, then the value of the US dollar received/Canadian dollar paid position as forward contracts is $-\$1.56784m$, the same value we obtained using the bond valuation approach:

$$T = 1: E_f = (\$0.70/C\$)\left(\frac{1.105}{1.075}\right)^1 = \$0.719535/C\$$$

$$T = 2: E_f = (\$0.70/C\$)\left(\frac{1.105}{1.075}\right)^2 = \$0.739615/C\$$$

$$T = 3: E_f = (\$0.70/C\$)\left(\frac{1.105}{1.075}\right)^3 = \$0.760255/C\$$$

$$T = 4: E_f = (\$0.70/C\$)\left(\frac{1.105}{1.075}\right)^4 = \$0.78142/C\$$$

$$SV = \frac{\$10m - (\$0.719535/C\$)(C\$10.714)}{(1.105)^1}$$
$$+ \frac{\$10m - (\$0.739615/C\$)(C\$10.714)}{(1.105)^2}$$
$$+ \frac{\$10m - (\$0.760255/C\$)(C\$10.714)}{(1.105)^3}$$
$$+ \frac{\$10m - (\$0.781472/C\$)(C\$10.714)}{(1.105)^4}$$
$$+ \frac{\$10m - (\$0.781472/C\$)(C\$142.857)}{(1.105)^4}$$
$$= -\$1.56784m$$

17.6.3 Comparative Advantage

The currency swap in the above example represents an exchange of equivalent loans. Most currency swaps, though, are the result of financial and non-financial corporations exploiting a comparative advantage resulting from different rates in different currencies for different borrowers. Recall, in the case of interest rate swaps, we pointed out that observed differences in credit spreads could be the result of either comparative advantage or hidden options on floating-rate loans. In the case of currency swaps, though, the existence of such differences is more likely to be the result of actual comparative advantages.

To see the implications of comparative advantage with currency swaps, suppose the American and Canadian companies in the preceding example both have access to each country's lending markets and that the American company is more creditworthy, and as such, can obtain lower rates than the Canadian company in both the US and Canadian markets. For example, suppose the American company can obtain 10% US dollar-denominated loans in the US market and 7.25% Canadian dollar-denominated loans in the Canadian market, while the best the Canadian company can obtain is 11% in the US market and 7.5% in the Canadian market:

	US market $ loans	Canadian market C$ loans
American company	10%	7.25%
Canadian company	11%	7.50%

With these rates, the American company has a comparative advantage in the US market: it pays 1% less than the Canadian company in the US market, compared to only 0.25% less in the Canadian market. On the other hand, the Canadian company has a comparative advantage in the Canadian market: it pays 0.25% more than the US company in Canada, compared to 1% more in the US. When such a comparative advantage exists, a swap bank is in a position to arrange a swap to benefit one or both companies.

Exhibit 17.9   Currency swap: comparative advantage

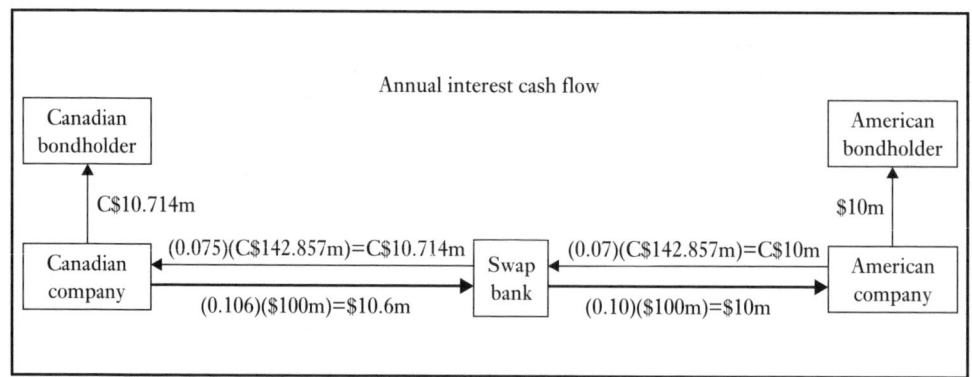

For example, suppose in this case a swap bank sets up the following swap arrangement:

1. The American company borrows $100m at 10%, then agrees to swap it for a C$142.857m loan at 7%.
2. The Canadian company borrows C$142.857m at 7.5%, then agrees to swap it for a $100m loan at 10.6%.

Exhibit 17.9 shows the annual cash flows of interest for the agreement (the cash flow at the outset and at maturity are the same as in the previous example shown in exhibit 17.7). In this swap arrangement, the American company benefits by paying 0.25% less than it could obtain by borrowing Canadian dollars directly in the Canadian market, and the Canadian company gains by paying 0.4% less than it could obtain directly from the US market.

Note that the swap bank in this case will receive $10.6m each year from the Canadian company, while only having to pay $10m to the American company, for a net dollar receipt of $0.6m. On the other hand, the swap bank will receive only C$10m from the American company, while having to pay C$10.714m to the Canadian company, for a net Canadian dollar payment of C$0.714m:

Swap bank's $ position	Swap bank's C$ position
Receives: (0.106) ($100m) = $10.6m	Receives: (0.07) (C$142.857) = C$10m
Pays: (0.10) ($100m) = $10m	Pays: (0.075) (C$142.857) = C$10.714
Net $ receipt: $10.6m − $10m = $0.6m	Net C$ payment: C$10.714m − C$10m = C$0.714m

Thus, the swap bank has a position equivalent to a series of long currency forward contracts in which it agrees to buy C$0.714m for $0.6m each year. The swap bank's implied forward rate on each of these contracts is $0.84/C$:

$$E_f = \frac{\$0.6m}{C\$0.714m} = \frac{\$0.84}{C\$}$$

The swap bank can hedge its position with currency forward contracts. If the forward rate is less than $0.84/C$, then the bank could gain from hedging the swap agreement with forward contracts to buy C$0.714m each year for the next 5 years. For example, suppose the yield curve applicable for the swap bank is flat at 9.5% in the US dollars and flat at 7% in Canadian dollars. Using the interest rate parity relation, the 1-, 2-, 3-, 4-, and 5-year forward exchange rates would be:

$$E_f = E_0 \left(\frac{1+R_{US}}{1+R_{C\$}} \right)^T$$

$$T=1: E_f = (\$0.70/C\$) \left(\frac{1.095}{1.07} \right)^1 = \$0.716355/C\$$$

$$T=2: E_f = (\$0.70/C\$) \left(\frac{1.095}{1.07} \right)^2 = \$0.73309/C\$$$

$$T=3: E_f = (\$0.70/C\$) \left(\frac{1.095}{1.07} \right)^3 = \$0.75022/C\$$$

$$T=4: E_f = (\$0.70/C\$) \left(\frac{1.095}{1.07} \right)^4 = \$0.76775/C\$$$

$$T=5: E_f = (\$0.70/C\$) \left(\frac{1.095}{1.07} \right)^5 = \$0.785687/C\$$$

Table 17.6 Swap bank's hedged position

(1) Year	(2) $ CF (millions)	(3) C$ CF (millions)	(4) Forward exchange: $/C$	(5) $ cost of C$ (millions) (column 4 × column 3)	(6) Net $ revenue (millions) (column 2 − column 5)
1	0.6	0.714	0.716355	0.51147747	0.08852253
2	0.6	0.714	0.73309	0.52342626	0.07657374
3	0.6	0.714	0.75022	0.53565708	0.06434292
4	0.6	0.714	0.76775	0.5481735	0.0518265
5	0.6	0.714	0.785687	0.560980518	0.039019482
					0.320285172

The swap bank could enter into forward contracts to buy C$0.714m each year for the next 5 years at these forward rates. With all of the forward rates less than $0.84/C$, the bank's dollar costs of buying C$0.714m each year would be less than its $0.6m annual inflow from the swap. By combining its swap position with forward contracts, the bank would be able to earn a total profit from the deal of $320,285 (see table 17.6).

Instead of forward contracts, the swap bank also could hedge its swap positions by using a money market position. For example, on its first Canadian dollar liability of C$0.714m due in 1 year, the bank would need to create a Canadian asset worth C$0.714m 1 year later (current value of C$0.66729m = C$0.714m/1.07) and a dollar liability worth $0.6m or less. The bank could do this by borrowing $0.4671m (= C$0.66729m($0.70/BP)) at 9.5%, converting it to C$0.66729m, and investing the Canadian dollars at 7% interest for the next year. One year later, the bank would have C$0.714m (= C$0.66729(1.07)) from the investment to cover its sterling swap liability and would have a US dollar liability of $0.51147m (= $0.4671(1.095)) that is less than the $0.6m dollar inflow from the swap. The bank would thus earn a profit of $0.088m from the hedged cash flow − the same profit it would earn from hedging with the forward exchange contracts if the interest rate parity relation holds. By forming the same types of money market positions for each sterling liability, the bank could obtain the same total profit of $320,285 that it would have received from the forward-hedged positions.

In summary, the presence of comparative advantage creates a currency swap market in which swap banks look at the borrowing rates offered in different currencies to different borrowers and at the forward exchange rates and money market rates that they can obtain for hedging. Based on these different rates, they will arrange swaps that provide each borrower with rates better than the ones they can directly obtain and a profit for them that will compensate them for facilitating the deal and assuming the credit risk of each counterparty.

17.6.4 Non-Generic Currency Swaps

Like interest rate swaps, the currency swaps have been modified to accommodate different uses. Of particular note is the *cross-currency swap* that is a combination of the currency swap and interest rate swap. This swap calls for an exchange of floating-rate payments in one currency for fixed-rate payments in another. There are also currency swaps with amortizing principals, cancelable and extendable currency swaps, forward currency swaps, and options on currency swaps.

17.7 CONCLUSION

In this final chapter, we have examined currency swaps and some of the newer swap contracts that have been introduced over the last decade. Like interest rate options and futures, swaps provide investors and borrowers with a tool for hedging asset and liability positions against interest rate and exchange rate fluctuations, speculating on interest rate and exchange rate movements, and improving the returns received on fixed income investments or paid on debt positions. We, of course, have not exhausted all derivative securities, just as we have not covered all the strategies, uses, markets, and pricing of debt securities. What we hope we have done here and in this last part of the book, though, is develop a foundation for the understanding of derivative products and their important applications in debt management. To this extent we hope we also have established a foundation and methodology for understanding the markets and uses of fixed-income securities.

KEY TERMS

Amortizing Swap	Call Swaption	Binary CDS
Set-Up Swap or Accreting Swap	Put Swaption	Basket Credit Swap
	Cancelable Swap	Contingent CDS
Zero-Coupon Swaps	Extendable Swap	Total Return Swap
Forward Swaps	Index-Amortizing Swap	Cross-Currency Swap
Swaptions		
Non-US Dollar Interest Rate Swaps	Credit Default Swap (CDS)	

PROBLEMS AND QUESTIONS

Note on problems: for problems requiring a number of calculations, the reader may want to use Excel.

1. Explain how a company planning to issue 5-year, fixed-rate bonds in 3 years could use a forward swap to lock in the fixed rate it will pay on the bonds. Explain how the hedge works at the expiration of the forward contract.

2. The ABC Development Company is constructing a $150m shopping mall that it anticipates will be completed in 2 years. At the project's completion, the company plans to refinance its short-term construction and development loans by borrowing $150m through the private placement of 10-year bonds. The ABC Company has an A quality rating and its option-free, fixed-rate bonds trade 200 basis points above comparable Treasury bonds and its floating-rate bonds trade at 150 basis points above the LIBOR. Currently, 10-year T-bonds are trading to yield 6%. With current rates relatively low, ABC is expecting interest rates to increase and would like to lock-in a rate on the 10-year, fixed-rate bond 2 years from now. The company is considering locking-in its rate by entering a forward swap with Commerce Bank. To hedge its future loan, Commerce is willing to provide ABC with a 2-year forward swap agreement on a 10-year 7.25%/LIBOR swap.

   a. Explain the forward swap position that ABC would need to take in order to lock-in the rate on its 10-year, fixed-rate bond to be issued 2 years from now.
   b. Given ABC hedges with a swap position, explain how it would obtain a fixed rate for 10 years at the forward swap's expiration date by issuing its floating-rate notes at LIBOR plus 150 BP. What is the fixed rate ABC would have to pay on its position?

3. Suppose the ABC Development Company in question 2 hedges its planned $150m bond sale in 2 years by taking a position in the forward swap contract offered by Commerce Bank. Also suppose that at the forward swap's expiration date, 10-year T-bonds are trading at 7% and the fixed rate on 10-year par value swaps that Commerce Bank would offer ABC is 150 BP above the T-bond yield.

   a. What would be the value of the swap underlying ABC's forward swap at the expiration date? Use the YTM valuation approach.

   b. What would be the amount of funds ABC would need in order to refinance its $150m short-term loan obligation and close its swap position?

   c. Given that ABC's fixed-rate bonds trade at 200 basis points above T-bond rates, what would be ABC's semi-annual interest payments on the funds that it borrows?

   d. What would be ABC's annualized rate based on the $150m refinancing funds it needs?

4. Suppose the ABC Development Company in question 2 hedges its planned $150m bond sale in 2 years by taking a position in the forward swap contract offered by Commerce Bank. Also suppose that at the forward swap's expiration date, 10-year T-bonds are trading at 5% and the fixed rate on 10-year par value swaps that Commerce Bank would offer ABC is 50 BP above the T-bond yield.

   a. What would be the value of the swap underlying ABC's forward swap at the expiration date? Use the YTM valuation approach.

   b. Given that ABC's fixed-rate bonds trade at 200 basis points above T-bond rates, what would be the amount of funds ABC would need in order to refinance its $150m short-term loan obligation and close its swap position?

   c. What would be ABC's annualized rate based on the $150m funds it needs for refinancing?

5. JEP Investment Trust has bonds worth $20m in par value that are to mature in 1 year. The trust plans to reinvest the principal for another 3 years. At that time, it anticipates it will need the investment to meet some of its intermediate liabilities. The bonds pay a fixed interest, are option-free, have a quality rating of "A," and trade 200 basis points above comparable Treasury notes. JEP Trust plans to reinvest the $20m in principal in similar fixed-income bonds with a maturity of 3 years; it could also invest in 3-year, A-rated, floating-rate bonds that trade at 150 basis points above the LIBOR. Currently, 3-year T-notes are trading to yield 6%. JEP is worried, though, that the Fed will lower interest rates in the next year to stimulate a sluggish economy. As a result, the trust would like to lock-in a rate on its $20m investment. The company is considering locking-in a rate by entering a forward swap agreement with Commerce Bank. To hedge its future loan, Commerce is willing to provide ABC with a 1-year forward swap agreement on a 3-year 6.5%/LIBOR swap.

   a. Explain the forward swap position that JEP would need to take in order to lock-in the rate on a 3-year, fixed-rate bond investment to be made in 1 year.

   b. Given JEP's swap position, explain how it would obtain a fixed rate for 3 years at the forward swap's expiration date by investing in A-rated floating-rate notes at LIBOR plus 150 BP. What is the fixed rate JEP would earn from this hedged investment?

6. Suppose the JEP Investment Trust in question 5 hedges its planned $20m bond investment in 1 year by taking a position in the 1-year, 6.5%/LIBOR forward swap contract offered by Commerce Bank. Also suppose that at the forward swap's expiration date, 3-year T-notes are trading at 5% and the fixed rate on 3-year par value swaps that Commerce Bank would offer JEP is 50 BP above the T-note yield.

   a. What would be the values of the swap underlying ABC's forward swap at the expiration date if 3-year T-notes are trading at 5% and 7%? Use the YTM valuation approach.

b. Determine JEP's investments after its closes its swap position and its ARR based on the $20m investment at T-note yields of 5% and 7%.

7. The table below shows swap rates for current par value swaps along with zero-coupon swap rates obtained using the bootstrapping approach (these are the same rates found in question 24 in chapter 16).

Maturity in years	Swap rate	Zero-coupon rate: Z(maturity)
1	0.050	0.0500000
2	0.055	0.0551380
3	0.060	0.0603950
4	0.065	0.0658547

a. Given the zero-coupon swap rates, determine the implied 1-year forward rates for years 1, 2, and 3: f_{11}, f_{12}, and f_{13}.
b. Using the rates in the table, determine the break-even forward rates for the following.

(i) One-year swap 1 year forward.
(ii) One-year swap 2 years forward.
(iii) Two-year swap 1 year forward.

Assume the underlying swaps each make payments annually and not the standard semi-annual interval. Also assume that the first effective date on the underlying swap starts at expiration of the forward swap.

c. Determine the current values of the following forward swap positions.

(i) Fixed payer's and floating payer's positions on 1-year 6.03%/LIBOR swap 1 year forward with a notional principal of $10m.
(ii) Fixed payer's and floating payer's positions on 1-year 7%/LIBOR swap 2 years forward with a notional principal of $10m.
(iii) Fixed payer and floating payer's positions on 2-year 6.5%/LIBOR swap 1 year forward with a notional principal of $10m.

Assume the underlying swaps each make payments annually and payment dates are 1 year after the effective dates; use the zero-coupon valuation approach.

8. The table below shows zero-coupon swap rates and implied 1-year forward rates. Using the zero-coupon valuation approach, determine the current value of a fixed payer's position on a forward swap position on a 3-year 9%/LIBOR swap 3 years forward with a notional principal of $10m. Assume the underlying swap makes payments annually and not the standard semi-annual length, that the first effective date on the underlying swap starts at the expiration of the forward swap, and that payment dates are 1 year after the effective dates.

Maturity in years	Zero-coupon rates: Z(maturity)	Implied 1-year forward rates: f_{1M}
1	5.0%	6.0%
2	5.5%	7.0%
3	6.0%	8.0%
4	6.5%	9.0%
5	7.0%	10.0%
6	7.5%	11.0%
7	8.0%	

9. Suppose a speculative hedge fund anticipating higher rates in several years purchased a 3-year put swaption on a 3-year 6%/LIBOR generic swap with semi-annual payments and notional principal of $10m for a price equal to 50 BP times the NP. Explain what the fund would do at the swaption's expiration if the fixed rate on a 3-year par value swap were at 7% and at 5%. What would be the fund's profits or losses at those rates? Use the YTM approach in valuing the swap's position.

10. Show graphically and in a table the values and profits/losses at expiration that the hedge fund in question 9 would obtain from closing its put swaption on a 6%/LIBOR swap with a notional principal of $10m purchased at a price equal to 50 BP times the NP. Evaluate at fixed rates on the 3-year par value swap at expiration of 4%, 4.5%, 5%, 5.5%, 6%, 6.5%, 7%, 7.5%, and 8%. Use the YTM approach in valuing the swap's position.

11. Suppose the speculative hedge fund was anticipating lower rates in several years and purchased a 3-year call swaption on a 3-year 6%/LIBOR generic swap with semi-annual payments and notional principal of $10m for a price equal to 60 BP times the NP. Explain what the fund would do at the swaption's expiration if the fixed rate on the 3-year par value swap at expiration were at 7% and at 5%. What would be the fund's profits or losses at those rates? Use the YTM approach in valuing the swap's position.

12. Show graphically and in a table the values and profits/losses at expiration that the hedge fund in question 11 would obtain from closing its call swaption on a 6%/LIBOR swap with a notional principal of $10 m purchased at a price equal to 60 BP times the NP. Evaluate at fixed rates on the 3-year par value swaps at expiration of 4%, 4.5%, 5%, 5.5%, 6%, 6.5%, 7%, 7.5%, and 8%. Use the YTM approach in valuing the swap's position.

13. The Devine Investment Fund has a Treasury bond portfolio worth $50m in par value that is scheduled to mature in 3 years. Devine plans to reinvest the $50m in principal for another 3 years in similar fixed-income bonds. Currently, such bonds are trading to yield 6%. Devine is worried that interest rates could be lower in 3 years and would like to establish a floor on the rate it would obtain for its futures 3-year investment. Devine is considering purchasing a 3-year call swaption on a 3-year 6%/LIBOR generic swap and notional principal of $50m from First Bank for $250,000. Show in a table the values and profits/losses at expiration that Devine would obtain from closing the call swaption (use the YTM approach to determine values) and the hedged ARR (based on $50m investment) they would obtain from reinvesting for 3 years the $50m plus the proceeds from selling the swaption (do not include $250,000 cost). Determine the values, profits, and ARRs at fixed rates on a 3-year par value swap at expiration of 4%, 4.5%, 5%, 5.5%, 6%, 6.5%, 7%, 7.5%, and 8%. Assume the rate on the par value swaps and the 3-year T-note rate are the same and that the yield curve is flat.

14. The Webb Communications Company has a $50m, 8% fixed-rate bond obligation maturing in 2 years. The company plans to finance the $50m principal liability by issuing new 5-year fixed-rate bonds. Currently, 5-year T-notes are trading to yield 6% and Webb's bonds are trading at 200 basis points above the Treasury yields. Webb is worried that interest rates could increase in 2 years and would like to establish a cap on the rate it would pay on its future 5-year bond issue. Webb is considering purchasing a 2-year put swaption on a 5-year 8%/LIBOR generic swap with notional principal of $50m from First Bank for $500,000. Show in a table the values and profits/losses at expiration that Webb would obtain from closing the swaption (use the YTM approach to determine values) and the hedged ARR (based on $50 m debt) they would pay from issuing 5-year bonds to raise $50m minus the proceeds from selling the swaption (do not include $500,000 cost). Determine the values, profits, and ARRs at fixed rates on 5-year par value swaps at expiration of 6%, 6.5%, 7%, 7.5%, 8%, 8.5%, 9%, 9.5%, and 10%. Assume the rate on

the par value swaps and Webb's 5-year bond rate are the same and that the yield curve is flat.

15. The ABC Development Company in questions 2, 3, and 4 was planning to refinance its short-term construction and development loans in 2 years by borrowing $150m through the private placement of 10-year bonds currently trading at 8%. The company was also considering locking-in the rate on that future debt obligation by entering a 2-year forward swap agreement as a fixed payer on a 10-year swap with Commerce Bank. Suppose Commerce Bank also offered ABC a 2-year put swaption on a 10-year 8%/LIBOR generic swap with notional principal of $150m for $1,000,000. Evaluate ABC's potential swaption-hedge position by showing in a table the values at expiration that ABC would obtain from closing the swaption (use the YTM approach) and the hedged ARR (based on $150m debt) they would pay from issuing 10-year bonds to raise $150m minus the proceeds from selling the swaption (do not include $1,000,000 swaption cost). Determine the values and ARRs at fixed rates on 10-year par value swaps at expiration of 6%, 6.5%, 7%, 7.5%, 8%, 8.5%, 9%, 9.5%, and 10%. Assume that the rate on the par value swaps and ABC's 10-year bond rate are the same and that the yield curve is flat. Explain the tradeoffs between swaption hedging and forward swap hedging.

16. Bluegrass Trust manages a portfolio of high-quality corporate bonds with a weighted average maturity of 10 years, weighted average coupon rate of 10%, and par value of $100m. Many of the bonds in the portfolio are callable with the weighted average call price equal to par. Bluegrass Trust expects an economic scenario over the next 2 years of slower economic growth and expansionary monetary policy, leading to yields on its bonds decreasing to 6%. The Trust, in turn, is concerned about some of the bonds in its portfolio being called. The Trust has determined that there is a high likelihood that 2 years from now $25m of its bond portfolio will be called. As a hedging tool, Commonwealth Bank is offering Bluegrass Trust 2-year call or put swaptions on an 8-year 10%/LIBOR generic swap for $100,000.

    a. Explain how Bluegrass Trust could minimize the call risk on $25m of its callable bonds with a swaption position offered by Commonwealth Bank.
    b. Explain what Bluegrass Trust would do 2 years later at the swaption's exercise date if it had hedged $25m of its callable bonds with swaptions and the following low interest rate scenario occurred: (1) $25m of Bluegrass's bonds are called at par; (2) the rate on similar, but option-free, bonds and the rate on 8-year par value generic swaps Commonwealth would offer the trust are both at 6%; (3) 8-year floating notes with similar quality ratings as Bluegrass fixed-rate bonds are available at LIBOR. Use the YTM approach to value swaps. Note, there are several positions that Bluegrass could take.
    c. Explain what Bluegrass Trust would do 2 years later if it had hedged $25m of its callable bonds with swaptions and interest rates had increased and no bonds were called.

17. Buckeye Conglomerate financed one of its acquisitions by issuing $20m of 10-year, 8% bonds through a private placement with a select group of institutional investors. To make the bonds more attractive and to lower the rates at the time of the issue, Buckeye included a deferred put option on the bonds, giving the bond investors the right to sell the bonds back to Conglomerate after 2 years at a put price equal to par. Buckeye expects an economic scenario over the next 2 years of greater economic growth leading to higher interest rates and resulting in the yields on its bonds increasing to 10%. Buckeye, in turn, has determined that there is a high likelihood that 2 years from now the institutional investors holding their bonds will exercise their put option, forcing Buckeye to raise $20m with new debt at a higher interest rate. As a hedging tool, Star Bank is offering Buckeye Conglomerate a 2-year call or put swaptions on an 8-year 8%/LIBOR generic swap for $100,000.

   a. Explain how Buckeye Conglomerate could minimize the put risk on the $20m putable bonds with a swaption position offered by Star Bank.

   b. Explain what Buckeye Conglomerate would do 2 years later at the swaption's exercise date if it had hedged its $20m of putable bonds with swaptions and the following high interest rate scenario occurred: (1) institutional investors exercise their put options; (2) the rate on similar, but option-free, bonds and the rate on 8-year par value generic swaps Star Bank would offer Buckeye are both at 10%; (3) 8-year floating notes that Buckeye could issue pay LIBOR plus 50 BP. Use the YTM approach to value swaps. Note, there are several positions that Buckeye could take.

   c. Explain what Buckeye would do 2 years later if it had hedged its putable bonds with swaptions and interest rates had increased and no put options were exercised.

18. The O'Brien Beverage Company is considering financing the construction of its new $5m brewery by selling 7-year, 9% fixed-rate, option-free bonds at par through a private placement. The company's investment banker has informed them that the company could also sell 7-year, 9.5% fixed-rate bonds at par with a call option giving O'Brien the right to buy back the bonds at par after 2 years. In addition, the company is also informed it can sell FRNs paying the LIBOR plus 25 BP. O'Brien does not believe rates will decrease over the next 2 years and prefers the non-callable bonds. The company, though, can take a long or short position with its investment banker on a 2-year call swaption on a 5-year, 9%/LIBOR swap selling at a price equal to 75 BP per year for 7 years.

   a. Explain how the O'Brien Company could create a synthetic option-free bond with the callable bond and a position on the call swaption.

   b. What would be the effective rate O'Brien would pay on its synthetic option-free bond if rates 2 years later were greater than 9% and the swaption holder does not exercise and O'Brien does not exercise the call option on its bonds?

   c. What actions would O'Brien have to take to fix its rate if rates 2 years later were less than 9% and the swaption holder exercises? What would be O'Brien's effective rate for the remaining 5 years?

   d. Based on your analysis in (b) and (c), what would be your financing recommendation to O'Brien: the synthetic option-free bond or the straight option-free bond?

19. To finance part of the state's capital expenditures, the Secretary of Finance is considering issuing $50m-worth of 7-year, 6% option-free general obligation bonds at par. The bonds would be privately placed with a number of commercial banks in the state. Recently, several states have included a put option in their bonds to make them more attractive to investors and to lower the rate they pay on their debt. The Secretary estimates that their bonds could be issued at par with a 5.5% coupon rate if the issue included a put option giving the investors the right to sell the bond back to the issuer at par after 2 years. The Secretary of Finance, though, believes that interest rates will increase in the future and prefers to issue the option-free general obligations instead of the putable bonds. The state can take a long or short position with one of the state's commercial banks on a 2-year put swaption on a 5-year, 5.5%/LIBOR swap with NP of $50m selling at a price equal to 25 BP per year for 7 years. In addition, the state can also issue FRNs paying the LIBOR.

   a. Explain how the state could create a synthetic option-free bond with the putable bond and a position on the put swaption.

   b. What would be the effective rate the state would pay on its synthetic option-free bond if rates 2 years later were less than 5.5% and the put options and put swaption were not exercised?

   c. What actions would the state have to take to fix its rate if rates 2 years later were greater than 6% and bondholders exercised their put option? What would be the state's effective rate on its debt for the remaining 5 years?

d. Based on your analysis in (b) and (c), what would be your recommendation to the Secretary of Finance: the synthetic option-free bond or the straight option-free bond?

20. The table below shows zero-coupon swap rates and implied 1-year forward rates (the same rates from question 8).

Maturity in years	Zero-coupon rates: Z(maturity)	Implied 1-year forward rates: f_{1M}
1	5.0%	6.0%
2	5.5%	7.0%
3	6.0%	8.0%
4	6.5%	9.0%
5	7.0%	10.0%
6	7.5%	11.0%
7	8.0%	

Using these rates, determine the intrinsic value of the following swaptions:

a. Three-year put swaption on a 3-year 7.94%/LIBOR swap with a notional principal of $10m.

b. Three-year put swaption on a 3-year 11%/LIBOR swap with a notional principal of $10m.

c. Three-year call swaption on a 3-year 9.94%/LIBOR swap with a notional principal of $10m.

d. Three-year call swaption on a 3-year 7%/LIBOR swap with a notional principal of $10m.

Assume that the underlying swaps each make payments annually and not the standard semi-annual length, that the first effective date on the underlying swap starts at the expiration of the forward swap, and that payment dates are 1 year after effective dates.

21. Use the Black futures option model to determine the value of a 3-year put swaption on a 3-year 9%/LIBOR swap with notional principal of $10m, break-even rate on the underlying forward contract of 0.10, semi-annual periods, continuous compounded risk-free rate of 5%, and a volatility of the swap rate of $\sigma = 0.075$. What is the value of a call swaption with similar terms? Do the call and put values conform to the put–call futures parity condition?

22. Given a 2-year put swaption on a 3-year 7%/LIBOR swap with notional principal of $10m, semi-annual periods, continuous compounded risk-free rate of 5%, and a volatility of the swap rate of $\sigma = 0.10$, use the Black futures option model to determine the values and intrinsic values of the swaption given the following break-even rates on the underlying forward contract: 5%, 5.5%, 6%, 6.5%, 7%, 7.5%, 8%, 8.5%, and 9%. Plot the break-even forward rates, put swaption values, and put swaption intrinsic values. Comment on the relation you observe.

23. Given a 2-year call swaption on a 3-year 7%/LIBOR swap with notional principal of $10m, semi-annual periods, continuous compounded risk-free rate of 5%, and a volatility of the swap rate of $\sigma = 0.10$, use the Black futures option model to determine the values and intrinsic values of the swaption given the following break-even rates on the underlying forward contract: 5%, 5.5%, 6%, 6.5%, 7%, 7.5%, 8%, 8.5%, and 9%. Plot the break-even forward rates, and call swaption values, and call swaption intrinsic values. Comment on the relation you observe.

24. Explain how a 10-year 8%/LIBOR putable swap cancelable after 5 years can be created with positions in a 10-year 8%/LIBOR generic swap and a 5-year put swaption on a 5-year 8%/LIBOR swap.

25. Explain how a 10-year 8%/LIBOR callable swap cancelable after 5 years can be created with positions in a 10-year 8%/LIBOR generic swap and a 5-year call swaption on a 5-year 8%/LIBOR swap.

26. Based on your answer to question 21, what is the price of a 6-year, 9%/LIBOR putable swap with notional principal of $10m cancelable after 3 years given (1) a current 6-year 9%/LIBOR generic swap is at par, and (2) a 10% break-even rate on the underlying forward contract on a 3-year put swaption on a 3-year 9%/LIBOR swap. Assume the continuous compounded risk-free rate is 5% and the volatility of the swap rate is $\sigma = 0.075$.

27. Based on your answer to question 21, what is the price of a 6-year, 9%/LIBOR callable swap with notional principal of $10m cancelable after 3 years given (1) a current 6-year 9%/LIBOR generic swap is at par, and (2) a 10% break-even rate on the underlying forward contract on a 3-year call swaption on a 3-year 9%/LIBOR swap. Assume the continuous compounded risk-free rate is 5% and volatility of the swap rate is $\sigma = 0.075$.

28. Given that a borrower can issue floating-rate notes, callable and putable bonds, and can take positions in comparable generic swaps, callable and putable swaps, and call and put swaptions, define five ways in which the borrower could form synthetic fixed-rate positions.

29. Define the following swaps and give an example of their use: amortizing, accreting, index amortizing, total return, and equity swaps.

30. Define a credit default swap and its terms. Explain how the swap works with an example.

31. Suppose the British Auto Company plans to issue a 5-year bond worth £100m at 7.5% interest, but actually needs an equivalent amount in dollars, $142.857m (current $/£ rate is $1.42875/£), to finance its new manufacturing facility in the US. Also, suppose that the Barkley Shoe Company, a US company, plans to issue $142.857m in bonds at 10%, with a maturity of 5 years, but it really needs £100m to set up its distribution center in London.

   a. Explain how a swap bank could arrange a currency swap between the British Auto Company and the Barkley Company after each company issues its bonds. Show the initial cash flow swap arrangements in a diagram.
   b. Explain how the swap bank would arrange for the annual interest payments. Assume the swap bank determines the interest swap exchange based on the rates each company pays on its bonds. Show the annual interest cash flow in a diagram.
   c. Explain how the swap bank would arrange for the exchange principal payments at maturity.

32. The American company in question 31 has a swap position in which it has agreed to swap with the swap bank a 5-year, 10% loan of $142.857m for a 5-year, 7.5% loan of £100m, while the British company has a swap position in which it has agreed to swap with the swap bank a 5-year, 7.5% loan of £100m for a 5-year, 10% loan of $142.857m.

   a. Define the American and British companies' swap positions as equivalent bond positions in dollars and pounds.
   b. Define the American and British companies' swap positions as equivalent forward exchange rate positions.
   c. What are the values of the American and British companies' swap positions?
   d. What would be the values of the American and British swap positions 1 year later if the spot exchange was $1.46/£ and rates available to the American company were 9% on dollar loans and rates to the British company were 8% on British pound loans?

33. The table shows the annual loan rates American and Mexican companies can each obtain on a 5-year, $20m loan in the US, and/or equivalently on a 5-year 114.2857m peso loan in the Mexican market.

Loan rates for American and Mexican companies in the US and Mexico

	American market	Mexican market
Risk-free rate	8%	6%
American company	11%	8.5%
Mexican company	12%	9.0%

Spot: $E_0 = \$/\text{peso} = \$0.175/\text{peso}$

a. Explain the comparative advantages that exist for the American and Mexican companies.
b. Suppose the US company wants to borrow 114.2857m pesos for 5 years to finance its Mexican operations, while the Mexican company wants to borrow $20m for 5 years to finance its US operations. Explain how a swap bank could arrange a currency swap that would benefit the American company by lowering its peso loan by 0.25% and would benefit the Mexican company by lowering its dollar loan by 0.1%. Show the initial cash flow, interest rate, and principal swap arrangements in a diagram.
c. Describe how the swap bank's position is similar to a series of peso forward contracts.
d. What would the bank's dollar position be if it hedged the swap position using the forward market at forward rates determined by the IRPT and at the risk-free rates shown in the table? Assume a flat yield curve. Determine the swap bank's profit from its swap position and forward exchange rate position.

34. The table shows the annual loan rates American and British multinational companies can each obtain on a 5-year, $142.857m loan in dollars and an equivalent 5-year, £100m loan in pounds.

Loan rates for American and British companies in dollars and pounds

	Dollar market (rate on $)	Pound market (rate on £)
American company	10%	7.25%
British company	11%	7.5%

Spot: $E_0 = \$/£ = \$1.42857/£$

a. Suppose the US multinational wants to borrow £100m for 5 years to finance its British operations, while the British company wants to borrow $142.857m for 5 years to finance its US operations. Explain how a swap bank could arrange a currency swap that would benefit the American company by lowering the rate on its British pound loan by 0.25% and would benefit the British company by lowering its dollar loan by 0.4%. Describe the foreign currency market conditions that allow the swap bank to provide such rates.
b. Show the swap arrangement's dollar and pound interest payments and receipts in a diagram.
c. Describe the swap bank's dollar and British pound positions.
d. Explain how the swap bank's position is equivalent to a series of long currency forward contracts at the rates shown in the table. What is the swap bank's implied forward on the contracts?

e. Assume that forward rates are governed by the interest rate parity theorem, that the swap bank can borrow and lend dollars at 9.5% and pounds at 7%, and that the yield curves for rates in both currencies are flat. Explain how the bank could hedge its swap position using currency forward contracts. What would be the swap bank's profit from its swap and forward positions?

f. Explain how the bank could hedge its swap position using a money market position instead of forward contracts.

35. Short-answer questions:

(1) Explain how a company planning to issue 3-year, fixed-rate bonds in 1 year could use a forward swap to lock-in the fixed rate it will pay on the bond.

(2) Suppose a company has hedged the rate on a 3-year fixed-rate bond issue it plans to sell in 2 years with a 2-year forward swap on a fixed payer's position on a 3-year swap. Explain how the rate is locked-in at the forward swap's expiration with a floating-rate bond issue.

(3) Suppose a company has hedged the rate on a 3-year fixed rate bond issue it plans to sell in 2 years with a 2-year forward swap on a fixed payer's position on a 3-year swap. Explain how the rate is locked-in at the forward swap's expiration by closing the underlying swap position.

(4) Define how a synthetic fixed-rate bond can be constructed with callable bonds, putable bonds, call swaptions, and put swaptions.

(5) What is the fundamental reason the rates on synthetic fixed-debt positions formed with callable or putable bonds and call swaption or put swaption are less than straight debt positions?

(6) Define in-the-money, at-the-money, and out-of-the-money put swaptions.

(7) Define in-the-money, at-the-money, and out-of-the-money call swaptions.

(8) Define put–call futures parity in terms of swaptions and forward swaps.

(9) Define a cancelable swap, callable swap, and putable swap.

(10) Why would a fixed payer on an interest rate swap want a callable swap?

(11) Why would a floating payer on an interest rate swap want a putable swap?

(12) How would you determine the price of a 6-year, 9%/LIBOR putable swap cancelable after 3 years given a current 6-year 9%/LIBOR generic swap is at par?

(13) How would you determine the price of a 6-year, 9%/LIBOR callable swap cancelable after 3 years given a current 6-year 9%/LIBOR generic swap is at par?

(14) Define an extendable swap.

(15) Explain how a floating payer's position on a 3-year 8%/LIBOR swap extendable at maturity to 2 more years is equivalent to a floating payer's position in a 3-year 8%/LIBOR generic swap and a 3-year call swaption on a 2-year 8%/LIBOR swap.

(16) Explain how a fixed payer's position on a 3-year 8%/LIBOR swap extendable at maturity by 2 more years is equivalent to a fixed payer's position in a 3-year 8%/LIBOR generic swap and a 3-year put swaption on a 2-year 8%/LIBOR swap.

(17) What is the bond equivalent of a currency swap position in which the counterparty agrees to swap a 3-year, 10% loan of $14.6m for a 3-year, 7% loan of £10m?

(18) What is the bond equivalent of a currency swap position in which the counterparty agrees to swap a 3-year, 7% loan of £10m for a 3-year, 10% loan of $14.6m?

(19) What is the forward exchange rate equivalent of a currency swap position in which the counterparty agrees to swap a 3-year, 10% loan of $14.6m for a 3-year, 7% loan of £10m?

(20) What is the forward exchange rate equivalent of a currency swap position in which the counterparty agrees to swap a 3-year, 7% loan of £10m for a 3-year, 10% loan of $14.6m?

(21) What is the value of an existing currency swap position in which the counterparty agrees to swap a 2-year, 10% loan of $14.6m for a 2-year, 7% loan of £10m if the current dollar rate is 9%, sterling rate is 7.5%, and spot $/£ exchange rate is $1.45/£?

(22) Describe comparative advantage in terms of American and British multinational companies who can each obtain loans in dollars and pounds at the following rates:

	Dollar market (rate on $)	Pound market (rate on £)
American company	11%	8.25%
British company	12%	8.5%

Questions 23–26 are based on the following swap. An American company agrees to exchange a 5-year, $10m, 9% fixed-rate loan to a swap bank for a 6%, 5-year 25m euro loan, and a German company agrees to exchange a 5-year, 25m, 6.5% fixed-rate euro loan to a swap bank for a 5-year, $10m, 9.5% loan.

(23) What would the American company exchange each year?

(24) What would the German company exchange each year?

(25) What would the swap bank position be each year?

(26) How could the swap bank hedge its position?

WEB EXERCISE

1. Examine the growth in currency swaps, credit default swaps, and equity swaps by looking at the International Swap and Derivatives Association's Market Survey. Go to www.isda.org and click on "Survey and Market Statistics" and "Historical Data."

NOTES

1. Some investment companies provide estimates of the implied volatilities for swap options.
2. Currency swaps evolved from back-to-back loans and parallel loans. In a back-to-back loan, companies exchange loans denominated in different currencies; in a parallel loan, one corporation loans to the subsidiary of a foreign multinational and vice versa. For example, a British parent company provides a loan to a British subsidiary of a US-based multinational, while a US parent company provides a dollar loan to an American subsidiary of a British multinational.

SELECTED REFERENCES

Alworth, J. "The Valuation of US Dollar Interest Rate Swaps," *BIS Economic Papers* 35 (Basel, Switzerland: January 1993).

Arak, M., L. Goodman, and A. Rones "Credit Lines for New Instruments: Swaps, Over-the-Counter Options, Forwards and Floor-Ceiling Agreements," in *Proceedings of the Conference on Bank Structure and Competition* (Federal Reserve Bank of Chicago, 1989).

Becker, B., T. Gira, and J. P. Burns *Recent Developments in the Derivative Markets* (New York City: American Bar Association, 1991).

Chance, D. and D. Rich "The Pricing of Equity Swaps and Swaptions," *Journal of Derivatives* 5(4) (Summer 1998): 19–31.

Cooper, I. and A. Mello "The Default Risk of Swap," *Journal of Finance* 46 (1991): 597–620.

Cucchissi, Paul G. and Reto M. Tuffli "Swaptions Applications," in Carl R. Beidleman (ed.) *Interest Rate Swaps* (Homewood, IL: Business One Irwin, 1991).

Dattatreya, R. E. and K. Hotta *Advanced Interest Rate and Currency Swaps: State-of-the Art Products*

Strategies and Risk Management Applications (Chicago: Irwin, 1993).

Hull, J. C. and A. White "Valuing Credit Default Swaps I: No Counterparty Default Risk," *Journal of Derivatives* 8(1) (Fall 2000): 29–40.

Hull, J. C. and A. White "Valuing Credit Default Swaps II: Modeling Default Correlations," *Journal of Derivatives* 8(3) (Spring 2001): 12–22.

Iben, Benjamin "Chapter 12: Interest Rate Swap Evaluation," in Carl R. Beidleman (ed.) *Interest Rate Swaps* (Homewood, IL: Business One Irwin, 1991).

Kawaller, Ira B. "A Swap Alternative: Eurodollar Strips," in Carl R. Beidleman (ed.) *Interest Rate Swaps* (Homewood, IL: Business One Irwin, 1991).

Kijima, M. "A Markov Chain Model for Valuing Credit Derivatives," *Journal of Derivatives* 6(1) (Fall 1998): 97–108.

O'Brien, Thomas "A No-Arbitrage Term Structure Model and the Valuation of Interest Rate Swaps," in Jack Clark Francis and Avner Simon Wolf (eds) *The Handbook of Interest Rate Risk Management* (New York: Irwin Professional Publishing, 1994).

Smith, D. J. "Aggressive Corporate Finance: A Close Look at the Procter and Gamble–Bankers Trust Leveraged Swap," *Journal of Derivatives* 4(4) (Summer 1997): 67–79.

Smith, David R. "Chapter 20: Techniques for Deriving a Zero Coupon Curve for Pricing Interest Rate Swaps: A Simplified Approach," in Jack Clark Francis and Avner Simon Wolf (eds) *The Handbook of Interest Rate Risk Management* (New York: Irwin Professional Publishing, 1994).

Tavakoli, J. M. *Credit Derivatives: A Guide to Instruments and Applications* (New York: Wiley, 1998).

USES OF EXPONENTS AND LOGARITHMS

A.1 EXPONENTIAL FUNCTIONS

An exponential function is one whose independent variable is an exponent. For example:

$$y = b^t$$

where:

$y = $ dependent variable
$t = $ independent variable
$b = $ base $(b > 1)$

In calculus, many exponential functions use as their base the irrational number 2.71828, denoted by the symbol e:

$$e = 2.71828$$

An exponential function that uses e as its base is defined as a natural exponential function. For example:

$$y = e^t$$
$$y = Ae^{Rt}$$

These functions also can be expressed as:

$$y = \exp(t)$$
$$y = A\exp(Rt)$$

In calculus, natural exponential functions have the useful property of being their own derivative. In addition to this mathematical property, e also has a finance meaning. Specifically, e is equal to the future value (FV) of $1 compounded continuously for one period at a nominal interest rate (R) of 100%.

To see e as a future value, consider the future value of an investment of A dollars invested at an annual nominal rate of R for t years, and compounded m times per year. That is:

$$FV = A\left(1 + \frac{R}{m}\right)^{mt} \qquad (A.1)$$

If we let $A = \$1$, $t = 1$ year, and $R = 100\%$, then the FV would be:

$$FV = \$1\left(1 + \frac{1}{m}\right)^{m} \qquad (A.2)$$

If the investment is compounded one time $(m = 1)$, then the value of the $1 at the end of the year will be $2; if it is compounded twice $(m = 2)$, the end-of-year value will be $2.25; if it is compounded 100 times $(m = 100)$, then the value will be 2.7048138.

$$m = 1: \quad FV = \$1\left(1 + \frac{1}{1}\right)^{1} = \$2.00$$

$$m = 2: \quad FV = \$1\left(1 + \frac{1}{2}\right)^{2} = \$2.25$$

$$m = 100: \quad \text{FV} = \$1\left(1 + \frac{1}{100}\right)^{100} = \$2.7048138$$

$$m = 1,000: \quad \text{FV} = \$1\left(1 + \frac{1}{1,000}\right)^{1,000} = \$2.716924$$

As m becomes large, the FV approaches the value of $2.71828. Thus, in the limit:

$$\text{FV} = \lim_{m \to \infty}\left(1 + \frac{1}{m}\right)^m = 2.71828 \qquad \text{(A.3)}$$

If A dollars are invested instead of $1, and the investment is made for t years instead of 1 year, then given a 100% interest rate the future value after t years would be:

$$\text{FV} = Ae^t \qquad \text{(A.4)}$$

Finally, if the nominal interest rate is different than 100%, then the FV is:

$$\text{FV} = Ae^{Rt} \qquad \text{(A.5)}$$

To prove equation (A.5), rewrite equation (A.1) as follows:

$$\text{FV} = A\left(1 + \frac{R}{m}\right)^{mt}$$

$$\text{FV} = A\left[\left(1 + \frac{R}{m}\right)^{m/R}\right]^{Rt} \qquad \text{(A.6)}$$

If we invert R/m in the inner term, we get:

$$\text{FV} = A\left[\left(1 + \frac{1}{m/R}\right)^{m/R}\right]^{Rt} \qquad \text{(A.7)}$$

The inner term takes the same form as equation (A.2). As shown earlier, this term, in turn, approaches e as m approaches infinity. Thus, for continuous compounding the FV is:

$$\text{FV} = Ae^{Rt}$$

Thus, a 2-year investment of $100 at a 10% annual nominal rate with continuous compounding would be worth $122.14 at the end of year 2:

$$\text{FV} = \$100e^{(0.10)(2)} = \$122.14$$

A.2 LOGARITHMS

A logarithm (or log) is the power to which a base must be raised to equal a particular number. For example, given:

$$5^2 = 25,$$

the power (or log) to which the base 5 must be raised to equal 25 is 2. Thus, the log of 25 to the base 5 is 2:

$$\log_5 25 = 2$$

In general:

$$y = b^t \Leftrightarrow \log_b y = t$$

Two numbers that are frequently used as the base are 10 and the number e. If 10 is used as the base, the logarithm is known as the common log. Some of the familiar common logs are:

$$\log_{10} 1,000 = 3 \qquad (10^3 = 1,000)$$
$$\log_{10} 100 = 2 \qquad (10^2 = 100)$$
$$\log_{10} 10 = 1 \qquad (10^1 = 10)$$
$$\log_{10} 1 = 0 \qquad (10^0 = 1)$$
$$\log_{10} 0.1 = -1 \qquad \left(10^{-1} = \frac{1}{10^1} = 0.10\right)$$
$$\log_{10} 0.01 = -2 \qquad \left(10^{-2} = \frac{1}{10^2} = 0.01\right)$$

When e is the base, the log is defined as the natural logarithm (denoted $\log_e$ or ln). For the natural log we have:

$$y = e^t \Leftrightarrow \log_e y = \ln y = t$$
$$\ln e^t = t$$

Thus given an expression such as $y = e^t$, the exponent t is automatically the natural log.

A.3 RULES OF LOGARITHMS

Like exponents, logarithms have a number of useful algebraic properties. The properties are stated below in terms of natural logs, but note that these properties apply to any log, regardless of its base.

Equality: If $X = Y$, then $\ln X = \ln Y$
Product rule: $\ln(XY) = \ln X + \ln Y$
Quotient rule: $\ln(X/Y) = \ln X - \ln Y$
Power rule: $\ln(X^a) = a \ln X$

A.4 USES OF LOGARITHMS

The above properties of logarithms make logarithms useful in solving a number of algebraic problems.

Solving for Interest Rates (R)

In finance, logs can be used to solve for R when there is continuous compounding. That is, from equation (A.5):

$$FV = Ae^{Rt}$$

Using the above log properties, R can be found as follows:

$$Ae^{Rt} = FV$$
$$e^{Rt} = \frac{FV}{A}$$
$$\ln(e^{Rt}) = \ln\left(\frac{FV}{A}\right)$$
$$Rt = \ln\left(\frac{FV}{A}\right)$$
$$R = \frac{\ln(FV/A)}{t}$$

Thus, a \$100 investment that pays \$120 at the end of 2 years would yield a nominal annual rate of 9.12% given continuous compounding: $R = \ln(\$120/\$100)/2 = 0.0912$. Similarly, a pure discount bond selling for \$980 and paying \$1,000 at the end of 91 days would yield a nominal annual rate of 8.10% given continuous compounding:

$$R = \frac{\ln(\$1,000/\$980)}{91/365} = 0.0810$$

Logarithmic Return

The expression for the rate of return on a security currently priced at S_0 and expected to be S_T at the end of one period ($t=1$) can be found using equation (A.5). That is:

$$S_T = S_0 e^{Rt}$$
$$R = \ln\left(\frac{S_T}{S_0}\right)$$

When the rate of return on a security is expressed as the natural log of S_T/S_0, it

is referred to as the security's logarithmic return. Thus, a security currently priced at \$100 and expected to be \$110 at the end of the period would have an expected logarithmic return of 9.53%: $R = \ln(\$110/\$100) = 0.0953$.

Time

Using logarithms, one can solve for t in either the discrete or continuous compounding cases. That is:

$$FV = A(1+R)^t$$
$$A(1+R)^t = FV$$
$$\ln[(1+R)^t] = \ln\left(\frac{FV}{A}\right)$$
$$t\ln[1+R] = \ln\left(\frac{FV}{A}\right)$$
$$t = \frac{\ln(FV/A)}{\ln(1+R)}$$
$$Ae^{Rt} = FV$$
$$e^{Rt} = \frac{FV}{A}$$
$$\ln(e^{Rt}) = \ln\left(\frac{FV}{A}\right)$$
$$Rt = \ln\left(\frac{FV}{A}\right)$$
$$t = \frac{\ln(FV/A)}{R}$$

The equations can be used in problems in which one knows the interest or growth rate and wants to know how long it will take for an investment to grow to equal a certain terminal value. For example, given an annual interest rate of 10% (no annual compounding) an investment of \$800 would take 2.34 years to grow to \$1,000:

$$t = \frac{\ln(\$1,000/\$800)}{\ln(1.10)} = 2.34 \text{ years}$$

SELECTED REFERENCE

Chiang, A. C. *Fundamental Methods of Mathematical Economics* (New York: McGraw-Hill, 1976): 267–302.

MATHEMATICAL STATISTICAL CONCEPTS

In this appendix we define some of the important statistical concepts used in analyzing investment strategies.

Random Variable: A random variable is a variable whose value is uncertain. Signified with a $\sim$ (tilde) over the symbol of the variable, a random variable is sometimes referred to as a stochastic variable. The opposite of a random variable is a deterministic or controlled variable, referred to as a non-stochastic variable.

Probability Distribution: A probability distribution is a function that assigns probabilities to the possible values of a random variable. The function can be objective (such as using past frequencies or assuming the distribution takes a certain form) or subjective. Also, the distribution either can be continuous, where it takes on all possible values over the range of the distribution with the probabilities being defined for a particular range, or discrete, where the distribution takes on only a few possible values with probabilities assigned to each possible value. In table B.1 a probability distribution is shown for the next period's interest rates (random variable r). This discrete distribution is defined by five possible interest rate values (column 1) and their respective probabilities (column 2) and is shown graphically in figure B.1.

The most common way to describe the probability distribution is in terms of its parameters: expected value or mean, variance, and skewness.

Expected Value: The expected value of a random variable is the weighted average of the possible values of the random variable with the weights being the probabilities assigned to each possible value (P_i). The expected value or mean, along with the median and the mode, is a measure of the central tendency of the distribution. The expected value for random variable $\tilde{r}$ is

$$E(\tilde{r}) = \sum_{i=1}^{T} P_i r_i = P_1 r_1 + P_2 r_2 + \ldots + P_T r_T$$

$$E(\tilde{r}) = (0.1)(4\%) + (0.2)(5\%) + (0.4)(6\%) + (0.2)(7\%) + (0.1)(8\%) = 6\%$$

A random variable may be described in terms of an algebraic equation, for example:

$$\tilde{r} = a + b\tilde{Y}$$

where a and b are coefficients and $\tilde{Y}$ is the independent variable. To describe the expected value of $\tilde{r}$ as $E(a + b\tilde{Y})$, one can make use of the following expected value

Table B.1 Probability distribution

(1) r_i	(2) P_i	(3) $P_i r_i$	(4) $[r_i - E(r)]$	(5) $[r_i - E(r)]^2$	(6) $P_i[r_i - E(r)]^2$	(7) $[r_i - E(r)]^3$	(8) $P_i[r_i - E(r)]^3$
4%	0.1	0.4	-2	4	0.4	-8	-0.8
5%	0.2	1.0	-1	1	0.2	-1	-0.2
6%	0.4	2.4	0	0	0.0	0	0.0
7%	0.2	1.4	1	1	0.2	1	0.2
8%	0.1	0.8	2	4	0.4	8	0.8
	1	$E(r)=6\%$			$V(r)=1.2$		$S_k(r)=0$

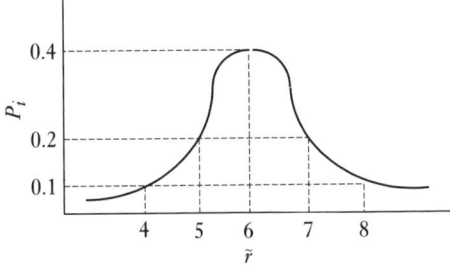

Figure B.1 Probability distribution

operator rules:

1. Expected value of a constant (a) is equal to the constant:

$$\text{EV Rule 1}: E(a) = a.$$

2. Expected value of a constant times a random variable is equal to the constant times the expected value of the random variable:

$$\text{EV Rule 2}: E(b\tilde{X}) = bE(\tilde{X})$$

3. Expected value of a sum is equal to the sum of the expected values:

$$\text{EV Rule 3}: E(\tilde{X} + \tilde{Y}) = E(\tilde{X}) + E(\tilde{Y})$$

Applying the three rules to the equation $\tilde{r} = a + b\tilde{Y}$, $E(\tilde{r})$ can be expressed as:

$$E(\tilde{r}) = a + bE(\tilde{Y})$$

Variance: The variance of a random variable $(V(\tilde{r}))$ is the expected value of the squared deviation from the mean:

$$V(\tilde{r}) = E[\tilde{r} - E(\tilde{r})]^2$$

The variance is defined as the second moment of the distribution. It is a measure of the distribution's dispersion, measuring the squared deviation most likely to occur. As an expected value, the variance is obtained by calculating the weighted average of each squared deviation, with the weights being the relative probabilities:

$$V(\tilde{r}) = \sum_{i=1}^{T} p_i[\tilde{r}_i - E(\tilde{r})]^2$$

$$V(\tilde{r}) = p_1[\tilde{r}_1 - E(\tilde{r})]^2 + p_2[\tilde{r}_i - E(\tilde{r})]^2 + \cdots$$
$$+ p_T[\tilde{r}_T - E(\tilde{r})]^2$$

The random variable described in table B.1 has a variance of 1.2.

$$V(\tilde{r}) = (0.1)[4\% - 6\%]^2 + (0.2)[5\% - 6\%]^2$$
$$+ (0.4)[6\% - 6\%]^2 + (0.2)[7\% - 6\%]^2$$
$$+ (0.1)[8\% - 6\%]^2$$
$$= 1.2$$

Standard Deviation: The standard deviation, $\sigma(\tilde{r})$, is the square root of the variance:

$$\sigma(\tilde{r}) = \sqrt{V(\tilde{r})}$$

The standard deviation provides a measure of dispersion that is on the same scale as the distribution's deviations. The standard deviation of the random variable in table B.1 is 1.0954451; this indicates the distribution has an average deviation of plus or minus 1.0954451.

Note, the risk of a security is defined as the uncertainty that the actual return earned from investing in a security will deviate from the expected. By definition, the variance and standard deviation of a security's rate of return

Table B.2 Correlation between random variables

State	P_i	$\tilde{r}_{1i}$	$\tilde{r}_{2i}$	$P_i\tilde{r}_{1i}$	$P_i\tilde{r}_{2i}$	$P_i[\tilde{r}_{1i} - E(\tilde{r}_1)]^2$	$P_i[\tilde{r}_{2i} - E(\tilde{r}_2)]^2$	$P_i[\tilde{r}_{1i} - E(\tilde{r}_1)][\tilde{r}_{2i} - E(\tilde{r}_2)]$
A	1/8	6%	24%	0.75	3.0	(1/8)(144)	(1/8)(64)	$(1/8)(-12)(8) = -12$
B	6/8	18%	16%	13.5	12.0	(6/8)(0)	(6/8)(0)	$(6/8)(0)(0) = 0$
C	1/8	30%	8%	3.75	1.0	(1/8)(144)	(1/8)(64)	$(1/8)(12)(-8) = -12$
				$E(\tilde{r}_1) = 18$	$E(\tilde{r}_2) = 16$	$V(\tilde{r}_1) = 36$	$V(\tilde{r}_2) = 16$	$\text{Cov}(\tilde{r}_1\tilde{r}_2) = -24$
						$\sigma(\tilde{r}_1) = 6$	$\sigma(\tilde{r}_2) = 4$	$\rho_{12} = -1$

define the security's relative risk. That is, the greater a security's variance relative to another security, the greater that security's actual return can deviate from its expected return and thus the greater the security's risk relative to the other security.

Skewness: Skewness measures the degree of symmetry of the distribution. A distribution that is symmetric about its mean is one in which the probability of $\tilde{r} = E(\tilde{r}) + x$ is equal to the probability of $\tilde{r} = E(\tilde{r}) - x$, for all values of x. Skewness, $S_k(\tilde{r})$, is defined as the third moment of the distribution and can be measured by calculating the expected value of the cubic deviation:

$$S_k(\tilde{r}) = \sum_{i=1}^{T} p_i[\tilde{r}_i - E(\tilde{r})]^3$$

$$S_k(\tilde{r}) = p_1[\tilde{r}_1 - E(\tilde{r})]^3 + p_2[\tilde{r}_i - E(\tilde{r})]^3 + \ldots \\ + p_T[\tilde{r}_T - E(\tilde{r})]^3$$

The skewness of the distribution in table B.1 is zero.

Covariance: The covariance is a measure of the extent to which one random variable is above or below its mean at the same time or state that another random variable is above or below its mean. The covariance measures how two random variables move with each other. If two random variables, on average, are above their means at the same time and, on average, are below at the same time, then the random variables would be positively correlated with each other and would have a positive covariance. In contrast, if one random variable, on average, is above its mean when another is below and vice versa, then the random variables would move inversely or

negatively to each other and would have a negative covariance.

The covariance between two random variables, $\tilde{r}_1$ and $\tilde{r}_2$, is equal to the expected value of the product of the variables' deviations:

$$\text{Cov}(\tilde{r}_1\tilde{r}_2) = E[\tilde{r}_1 - E(\tilde{r}_1)][\tilde{r}_2 - E(\tilde{r}_2)]$$

$$\text{Cov}(\tilde{r}_1\tilde{r}_2) = \sum_{i=1}^{T} p_i[\tilde{r}_{1i} - E(\tilde{r}_1)][\tilde{r}_{2i} - E(\tilde{r}_2)]$$

In table B.2, the possible rates of return for securities 1 and 2 are shown for three possible states (A, B, and C) along with the probabilities of occurrence of each state. As shown in the table, $E(\tilde{r}_1) = 18\%, V(\tilde{r}_1) = 36, E(\tilde{r}_2) = 16\%$, and $V(\tilde{r}_2) = 16$. In addition, the table also shows that in state A security 1 yields a return below its mean while security 2 yields a return above its mean; in state B both yield rates of return equal to their mean; in state C security 1 yields a return above its mean while security 2 yields a return below. Securities 1 and 2 therefore are negatively correlated and, as shown in table B.2, have a negative covariance of -24.

Correlation Coefficient: The correlation coefficient between two random variables $\tilde{r}_1$ and $\tilde{r}_2(\rho_{12})$ is equal to the covariance between the variables divided by the product of each random variable's standard deviation:

$$\rho_{12} = \frac{\text{Cov}(\tilde{r}_1\tilde{r}_2)}{\sigma(\tilde{r}_1)\sigma(\tilde{r}_2)}$$

The correlation coefficient has the mathematical property that its value must be within the range of minus and plus one:

$$-1 \leq \rho_{12} \leq 1$$

If two random variables have a correlation coefficient equal to one, they are said to be perfectly positively correlated; if their coefficient is equal to minus one, they are said to be perfectly negatively correlated; if their correlation coefficient is equal to zero, they are said to be zero correlated and statistically independent. That is:

If $\rho_{12} = -1 \Rightarrow$ Perfect negative correlation

If $\rho_{12} = 0 \Rightarrow$ Uncorrelated

If $\rho_{12} = 1 \Rightarrow$ Perfect positive correlation

Parameter Estimates using Historical Averages: In most cases we do not know the probabilities associated with the possible values of the random variable and must therefore estimate the parameter characteristics. The simplest way to estimate is to calculate the parameter's historical average value from a sample. For the rate of return on a security, this can be done by calculating the average rate of return per period or the holding period yield, HPY_t (stock $\text{HPY} = [(P_t - P_{t-1}) + \text{dividend}]/P_{t-1})$ over n historical periods:

$$\bar{r} = \frac{1}{n}\sum_{t=1}^{n}\text{HPY}_t$$

Similarly, the variance of a security can be estimated by averaging the security's squared deviations, and the covariance between two securities can be estimated by averaging the product of the securities' deviations. Note, in estimating variances and covariances, averages usually are found by dividing by $n-1$ instead of n in order to obtain better unbiased estimates:

$$\hat{V}(r) = \frac{1}{n-1}\sum_{t=1}^{n}(\text{HPY}_t - \bar{r})^2$$

$$\hat{\text{Cov}}(r_1 r_2) = \frac{1}{n-1}\sum_{t=1}^{n}(\text{HPY}_{1t} - \bar{r}_1)(\text{HPY}_{2t} - \bar{r}_2)$$

An example of estimating parameters is shown in table B.3 in which the average HPY, variances, and covariance are computed for a stock and a stock index (S_m).

Linear Regression: Regression involves estimating the coefficients of an assumed algebraic equation. A linear regression model has only one explanatory variable; a multiple regression model has more than one independent variable. As an example, consider a linear regression model relating the rate of return on a security (dependent variable) to the market rate of return (R_m) (independent variable), where R_m is measured by the proportional change in a stock index. That is:

$$\tilde{r}_j = \alpha + \beta\tilde{R}_{mj} + \varepsilon_j$$

where:
$\alpha = $ intercept
$\beta = $ slope $= \Delta r/\Delta R_m$
$j = $ observation
$\varepsilon = $ error

In the above equation, ε_j is referred to as the error term or stochastic disturbance term. Thus, the model assumes that for each observation j, errors in the relationship between r and R_m can exist, causing r to deviate from the algebraic relation defined by α and β. Since, a priori, the errors are not known, the regression model needs to provide assumptions concerning ε. The standard assumptions are:

$$E(\varepsilon_j) = 0$$
$$V(\varepsilon_j) \text{ does not change}$$
$$\text{Cov}(\varepsilon, R_m) = 0$$

Using the above assumptions and the expected value operator rules, the expected value and variance can be defined in terms of the regression model as follows:

$$E(r) = E[\alpha + \beta R_m + \varepsilon]$$
$$E(r) = \alpha + \beta E(R_m) + E(\varepsilon)$$
$$E(r) = \alpha + \beta E(R_m)$$
$$V(r) = E[r - E(r)]^2$$
$$V(r) = \beta^2 V(R_m) + V(\varepsilon)$$

The first term on the right of the equation for $V(r)$ defines systematic risk: the amount of variation in r that can be attributed to the market (factors that affect all securities); the second term defines unsystematic risk: the amount of variation in r that can be attributed to factors unique to that security (industry and firm factors).

Table B.3 Historical averages and regression estimates

Time	S	Dividend	HPY	(HPY − Av.)	(HPY − Av.)^2
1	100	0			
2	105	0	0.050000	0.032324	0.0010448
3	110	1	0.057143	0.039467	0.0015576
4	115	0	0.045455	0.027779	0.0007716
5	110	1	− 0.034783	− 0.052459	0.0027519
6	105	0	− 0.045455	− 0.063131	0.0039855
7	100	1	− 0.038095	− 0.055771	0.0031104
8	105	0	0.050000	0.032324	0.0010448
9	110	1	0.057143	0.039467	0.0015576
			0.141408		0.0158244
			Av. = 0.017676		Var. = 0.0022606
					Stand. dev. = 0.0475457

Time	S_m	R_m = HPY	$(R_m − Av.)$	$(R_m − Av.)^2$	$(R_m − Av.)$(HPY − Av.)
1	300				
2	315	0.050000	0.035583	0.001266	0.0011502
3	333	0.057143	0.042726	0.001825	0.0016863
4	346	0.039039	0.024622	0.000606	0.0006840
5	334	− 0.034682	− 0.049099	0.002411	0.0025757
6	319	− 0.044910	− 0.059327	0.003520	0.0037454
7	306	− 0.040752	− 0.055169	0.003044	0.0030769
8	320	0.045752	0.031335	0.000982	0.0010129
9	334	0.043750	0.029333	0.000860	0.0011577
		0.115339		0.014514	0.0150888
		Av. = 0.014417		Var. = 0.0020735	Cov. = 0.002156

$$\hat{\alpha} = \bar{r} - \hat{\beta}\bar{R}_m$$
$$= 0.017676 - 1.04(0.014417) = 0.00268$$
$$\hat{\beta} = \frac{\widehat{Cov}(rR_m)}{\hat{V}(R_m)} = \frac{0.002156}{0.002073} = 1.04$$
$$V(\varepsilon) = V(R) - \hat{\beta}^2 V(R_m)$$
$$= 0.0022606 - (1.04)^2 0.002073 = 0.0000184$$
$$E(r) = \alpha + \beta E(R_m)$$
$$= 0.00268 + 1.04 E(R_m)$$
$$V(r) = \beta^2 V(R_m) + V(\varepsilon)$$
$$= (1.04)^2 V(R_m) + 0.0000184$$

If two securities (1 and 2) both are related to R_m such that

$$r_1 = \alpha_1 + \beta_1 R_m + \varepsilon_1$$
$$r_2 = \alpha_2 + \beta_2 R_m + \varepsilon_2$$

(the j subscript is deleted) and ε_1 and ε_2 are independent (Cov(ε_1, ε_2) = 0), then the Cov(r_1 r_2) expression simplifies to

$$Cov(r_1 r_2) = \beta_1 \beta_2 V(R_m)$$

The intercept and slope of the regression model can be estimated by the ordinary least squares estimation procedure. This technique uses sample data for the dependent and independent variables (time-series data or cross-sectional data) to find the estimates of α and β that minimize the sum of the squared errors.

The estimates for α and β in which the errors are minimized are:

$$\hat{\alpha} = \bar{r} - \hat{\beta}\bar{R}_m$$

$$\hat{\beta} = \frac{\hat{Cov}(r, R_m)}{\hat{V}(R_m)}$$

where $\hat{Cov}(r, R_m), \hat{V}(R_m), \bar{r}$, and $\bar{R}_m$ are estimates (averages).

An estimate of unsystematic risk, $V(\varepsilon)$, can be found using the equation for $V(r)$. That is:

$$\hat{V}(\varepsilon) = \hat{V}(r) - \hat{\beta}^2 V(\hat{R}_m)$$

where $V(r)$ and $V(R_m)$ can be estimated using the sample averages and β can be estimated using the ordinary least squares estimating equation. In table B.3, a regression model relating the rate of return on the security to the market rate as measured by the rate of change in the index is shown.

It should be noted that the coefficients between any variables can be estimated using a regression model. Whether the relationship is good or not depends on the quality of the regression model. All regression models, therefore, need to be accompanied by information about the quality of the regression results. Regression qualifiers include the coefficient of determination (R^2), t-tests, and F-tests.

1. CFA LEVEL II, 2000

A. **Discuss** how *each* of the following theories for the term structure of interest rates could account for a downward sloping term structure of interest rates:
   i. Pure expectations
   ii. Liquidity preference
   iii. Market segmentation

The spot rates of interest for five US Treasury Securities are shown in the exhibit 1. Assume all securities pay interest annually.

Exhibit 1   Spot rates of interest

Term to maturity (years)	Spot rate of interest
1	13.00%
2	12.00%
3	11.00%
4	10.00%
5	9.00%

B. i. **Compute** the two-year implied forward rate three years from now.
   ii. **Explain** your answer using the Pure Expectations theory.

C. **Compute** the price of a five-year annual-pay Treasury security with a coupon rate of 9 percent, using the information in the exhibit.

2. CFA LEVEL II, 2000

Martin Bowman is preparing a report distinguishing traditional debt securities from structured note securities.

A. **Discuss** how the following structured note securities differ from a traditional debt security with respect to coupon and principal payments:
   i. Equity index-linked notes
   ii. Commodity-linked bear bond

Bowman is also analyzing a dual currency bond (USD/CHF) as a possible addition to his bond portfolio. Bowman is a USO-based investor and believes the CHF will appreciate against the USD over the life of the bond.

B.   i. **Describe** the principal and coupon components of a dual currency bond.
    ii. **State** *one* reason why a dual currency bond might trade at a premium over an otherwise identical single currency bond.
   iii. **Discuss** whether there is an impact on a dual currency bond's interest payments and principal payments if the CHF appreciates against the LJSD over the life of the bond.

3. CFA LEVEL II, 2000

Acree Corporation issued a floating rate note that pays 1-year LIBOR + 1 percent annually. The note has a par value of $100 million and a remaining term of five years.

A. **Describe** the interest rate risk that Acree faces.

John Whalen, Acree's Chief Financial Officer, is considering entering a five-year interest rate swap.

B. **Describe** how *each* of the following strategies would be structured, and explain how each strategy can eliminate Acree's interest rate risk:
   i. A plain vanilla interest rate swap
   ii. A portfolio of Eurodollar futures contracts

Whalen is entering into a five-year swap, and would like the right to cancel the swap after three years if interest rates decline.

C. **Identify** the appropriate instrument that Whalen could purchase and explain how Whalen can use the instrument to achieve his objective.

4. CFA LEVEL II, 2000

Exhibits 1 and 2 contain information on three newly issued AAA-rated bonds.

Exhibit 1   Bond characteristics

	Bond A	Bond B	Bond C
Coupon	7.00%	7.00%	7.00%
Maturity	June 3, 2005	June 3, 2005	June 3, 2005
Modified Duration	4.15	4.17	4.16
Standard Convexity	0.21	0.21	0.21

Exhibit 2   Effective duration and effective convexity for various shifts in the term structure

Term structure shift (basis points)	Bond A		Bond B		Bond C	
	Effective duration	Effective convexity	Effective duration	Effective convexity	Effective duration	Effective convexity
−500	0.49	0.47	4.35	22.65	4.34	22.51
−300	0.49	0.47	4.28	22.04	4.27	21.86
−100	0.48	0.48	4.20	21.56	4.18	21.18
+100	4.11	20.57	0.48	0.47	4.12	20.66
+300	4.04	19.98	0.48	0.44	4.05	20.03
+500	3.97	19.35	0.47	0.44	3.98	19.45

A. State and justify which of the three bonds is:
   i. Putable
   ii. Callable
   iii. Option-free

   The justification for *each* should include discussion of the extent to which price compression and truncation are relevant.

B. Compute the percentage price change for Bond A for an increase in yield of 50 basis points immediately following a 300 basis point downward shift in the term structure.

5.   CFA LEVEL IIi, 2000

Janice Delsing, a US-based portfolio manager, manages an $800 million portfolio ($600 million in stocks and $200 million in bonds). In reaction to anticipated short-term market events, Delsing wishes to adjust the allocation to 50 percent stock and 50 percent bonds through the use of futures. Her position will be held only until "the time is right to restore the original asset allocation." Delsing determines a financial futures-based asset allocation strategy is appropriate. The stock futures index multiplier is 250 and the denomination of the bond futures contract is $100,000. Other information relevant to a futures-based strategy is given in exhibit 1.

Exhibit 1   Information for futures-based strategy

Bond portfolio modified duration	5 years
Bond portfolio yield to maturity	7%
Basis point value (BPV) of bond futures	$97.85
Stock index futures price	$1378
Stock portfolio beta	1.0

A. **Describe** the financial futures-based strategy needed and **explain** how the strategy allows Delsing to implement her allocation adjustment. No calculations are necessary.

B. **Compute** the number of *each* of the following needed to implement Delsing's asset allocation strategy:
  i. Bond futures contracts
  ii. Stock index futures contracts

C. **Discuss** *one* advantage and one disadvantage of using each of the following for asset allocation:
  i. Financial futures
  ii. Index put options

One month later, the yield to maturity on comparable bond portfolios has increased by 10 basis points and the stock index has risen by $28.

D. **Calculate** the percentage return (from price changes only) for the past month, assuming:
  i. Delsing executed the 50/50 asset allocation strategy using futures.
  ii. Delsing did not execute the strategy but instead preserved her original long-term asset allocation.

6. CFA LEVEL III, 2000

James Norwood, a fixed income portfolio manager, was recently hired to manage two US Treasury portfolios for HEY Corporation. These portfolios, shown in exhibit 1, comprise HEY's total investments. Norwood noticed that although the yields to maturity and modified durations of the two portfolios were similar, the portfolios were structured differently.

Exhibit 1   Portfolio characteristics

Characteristics	Portfolio A	Portfolio B
2-year maturity	0%	50%
10-year maturity	100%	0%
30-year maturity	0%	50%
Modified Duration	7.2	7.7
Yield to Maturity	5.9%	5.8%

A. **Select** and **justify** the portfolio in exhibit 1 that will provide the higher return in *each* of the following scenarios (assume an initial yield curve that is upward sloping). No calculations are necessary.
  i. An upward parallel shift of 50 basis points in the yield curve.
  ii. A twist in the slope of the yield curve. Two-year interest rates rise by 10 basis points, while three-year interest rates decline by 10 basis points.

One year has passed. Each investment portfolio now has a total market value of $200 million and a modified duration of 7.2. HEY's liabilities now total $180 million and have a modified duration of 6.

B. **Calculate** the effect on HEY's assets and liabilities if interest rates decline by 100 basis points (ignore convexity). **Show** your calculations.

7. CFA LEVEL III, 2000

Fran Arseneault manages investment assets and liabilities for Allied Corporation. Allied's portfolio currently has the following characteristics:

- $300 million of the assets must be invested short term. These assets currently earn a six-month LIBOR rate of 5 percent.
- $300 million in debt is outstanding; $100 million is seven-year term fixed at a 6.5 percent rate and $200 million is short term at the six-month LIBOR rate.

A. **Describe** Arseneault's asset/liability exposure to declining interest rates.

Allied has been unable to issue additional variable rate debt at reasonable fees. Hogan Stanfield Investment Bank stands ready to swap intermediate term 6.5 percent fixed and six-month LIBOR.

B. **Diagram** an appropriate interest rate swap. Draw and label arrows to specify the rates, the payer and receiver for all fixed and floating rates, and the notional amount(s) involved. Your diagram must identify the fixed-rate bonds and variable-rate assets.

After the swap is executed, LIBOR immediately decreases substantially and remains at the lower level until the swap contract expires.

C. **Determine** the effect of the LIBOR decline on Allied's asset and liability positions. **Explain** why this effect occurs.

8. CFA LEVEL III, 2000

Benjamin Sparks is a consultant to Regal, Incorporated, a large US corporation. Regal's chief financial officer is considering adding bonds from other countries to Regal's fixed income portfolio. In a presentation to the CFO, Sparks makes the following statements:

1. Forward currency exchange rates are poor predictors of future spot exchange rates.
2. The presence of a significant non-government bond market in developed countries provides opportunities to enhance returns through sector selection.
3. Investing in bond markets in countries outside the target international index can enhance returns, but also dramatically increases the risk in the portfolio.
4. Duration management is equally challenging for US bond portfolios and for portfolios containing bonds from several developed markets.

Indicate whether *each* statement is correct or incorrect. If incorrect, **justify** your conclusion by citing *one* reason.

9. CFA LEVEL III, 2000

Carol Harrod is the investment officer for a $100 million US pension fund. The fixed income portion of the portfolio is actively managed, and a substantial portion of the fund's large capitalization US equity portfolio is indexed and managed by Webb Street Advisors.

Harrod has been impressed with the investment results of Webb Street's equity index strategy and is considering asking Webb Street to index a portion of the actively managed fixed income portfolio.

A. **Describe** *two* advantages and *two* disadvantages of bond indexing relative to active bond management.

Webb Street manages indexed bond portfolios that are constructed using two different methods. Webb Street has stated that the source of tracking error is different for each method.

B. **Discuss** how an indexed portfolio is constructed under each of the following methods:
   i. Stratified sampling
   ii. Optimization

C. **Describe** the main source of tracking error for *each* of the following methods:
   i. Stratified sampling
   ii. Optimization

Harrod believes that an indexed bond portfolio should have less tracking error than an indexed equity portfolio.

D. **Indicate** whether Harrod's belief is correct or incorrect. Give *two* reasons to support your position.

10. CFA LEVEL II, 2001

Singh is also analyzing a convertible bond. The characteristics of the bond and the underlying common stock are given in exhibit 1:

Exhibit 1 Convertible bond and underlying stock characteristics

Convertible bond characteristics	
Par value	$1,000
Annual coupon rate (annual pay)	6.5%
Conversion ratio	22
Market price	105% of par value
Straight value	99% of par value
Underlying stock characteristics	
Current market price	$40 per share
Annual cash dividend	$1.20 per share

A. **Compute** the bond's:
   i. Conversion value
   ii. Market conversion price
   iii. Premium payback period

B. **Determine** whether the value of a callable convertible bond will increase, decrease, or remain unchanged in response to *each* of the following changes, and **justify** *each* of your responses with *one* reason:
   i. An increase in stock price volatility
   ii. An increase in interest rate volatility

11. CFA LEVEL II, 2002

Rone Company asks Paula Scott, a treasury analyst, to recommend a flexible way to manage the company's financial risks.

Two years ago, Rone issued a $25 million (US $), five-year floating rate note (FRN). The FRN pays an annual coupon equal to one-year LIBOR plus 75 basis points. The FRN is non-callable and will be repaid at par at maturity.

Scott expects interest rates to increase and she recognizes that Rone could protect itself against the increase by using a pay-fixed swap. However, Rone's Board of Directors prohibits both short sales of securities and swap transactions. Scott decides to replicate a pay-fixed swap using a combination of capital market instruments.

A. **Identify** the instruments needed by Scott to replicate a pay-fixed swap and **describe** the required transactions.

B. **Explain** how the transactions in part A are equivalent to using a pay-fixed swap.

12. CFA LEVEL II, 2002

Alex Siegel is a mortgage-backed securities portfolio manager. Recently he has been given the authority to purchase other asset-backed securities (ABS). He is aware that the credit quality of ABS is a primary consideration in their evaluation but is uncertain about credit enhancement structures.

A. **Identify** and **describe** *one* example of *each* of the following types of credit enhancement structures:
  i. External
  ii. Internal

Siegel is considering two asset-backed securities to purchase for his portfolio, but he is concerned about the performance of each security if interest rates decline. Characteristics of the two securities are given in exhibit 1.

Exhibit 1   Characteristics of two asset-backed securities

Type	Structure	Lockout	Seasoning	Weighted average maturity
Home equity loans	Closed-end	None	10 months	350 months
Automobile receivables	—	18 months	10 months	50 months

B. **Identify** which of the two securities in exhibit 1 is likely to experience the greater effect on its cash flows as the result of a 100 basis point parallel decline in interest rates. **Justify** your response by referring to *one* characteristic of each security.

Siegel is also considering the purchase of collateralized mortgage obligations (CMOs).

C. **Contrast** the effects of a 100 basis point parallel decline in interest rates on the cash flows of the following types of CMOs:
  i. Planned amortization class
  ii. Support class

ANSWERS TO SELECTED END-OF-CHAPTER PROBLEMS

CHAPTER 1

1. In the private sector, real assets consist of both the tangible and intangible capital goods, as well as human capital, which are combined with labor to form the business. The business, in turn, transforms ideas into the production and sale of goods or services that will generate a future stream of earnings. The financial assets, on the other hand, consist of the financial claims on the earnings. These claims are sold to raise the funds necessary to acquire and develop the real assets. In the public sector, the federal government's capital expenditures and state and local governments' capital expenditures represent the development of real assets that these units of government often finance through the sale of financial claims on either the revenue generated from a particular public sector project or from future tax revenues.

2. The financial market can be described as a market for loanable funds; that is, a market where there is a supply and demand for loanable funds. The supply of loanable funds comes from the savings of households, the retained earnings of businesses, and the surpluses of units of government; the demand for loanable funds comes from businesses who need to raise funds to finance their capital purchases of equipment, plants, and inventories, households who need to purchase houses, cars, and other consumer durables, and the Treasury, federal agencies, and municipal governments who need to finance the construction of public facilities, projects, and operations. The exchange of loanable funds from savers to borrowers is done either directly through the selling of financial claims (stock, bonds, commercial paper, etc.) or indirectly through financial institutions.

5. Brokers are agents who bring security buyers and sellers together for a commission. Dealers, in turn, provide markets for investors to buy and sell securities by taking a temporary position in a security; they buy from investors who want to sell and sell to those who want to buy.

6. The New York Stock Exchange is a corporate association consisting of member brokers. Most brokerage firms with membership on the NYSE function as commission brokers, executing buy and sell orders on behalf of their clients.

7. Specialists are dealers who are part of the exchange and who are required by the exchange to take opposite positions in a security if conditions dictate. Under a specialist system, the exchange board assigns a specific security to a specialist to deal. In this role, a specialist acts by buying the security from sellers at bid prices and selling to buyers at asked prices. The NYSE and other exchanges using a specialist system also require that the specialists maintain the limit order book on the securities they are assigned and that they execute these orders. A limit order is an investor's request to his broker to buy or sell a security at a given price or better.

10. Securitized assets are claims on a portfolio of loans. In creating a securitized asset, an intermediary will put together a package of loans of a certain type (mortgages, auto, credit cards, etc.). The institution then sells claims on the package to investors, with the claim being secured by the package of assets – securitized asset. The package of loans, in turn, generates interest and principal that is passed on to the investors who purchased the securitized asset.

14. An efficient market can be defined as one in which all information on which investors base their investment decision are reflected in the security's price. In an efficient market, speculators, on average, would not earn abnormal returns. An inefficient market is one in which the information the market receives is asymmetrical: some investors have information that others don't, or some investors receive information earlier than others. In this market, the market price is not equal to its equilibrium value at all times, and there are opportunities for speculators to earn abnormal returns.

16. For an instrument to be liquid it must be highly marketable and have little, if any, short-run risk. Thus, the difference between marketability and liquidity is the latter's feature of low or zero risk that makes the security cash-like.

CHAPTER 2

1.

$$V_0 = \sum_{t=1}^{5} \frac{80}{(1.08)^t} + \frac{1,000}{(1.08)^5} = 80 \left[\frac{1 - (1/1.08)^5}{0.08} \right] + \frac{1,000}{(1.08)^5} = \$1,000$$

$$V_0 = \sum_{t=1}^{5} \frac{80}{(1.06)^t} + \frac{1,000}{(1.06)^5} = 80 \left[\frac{1 - (1/1.06)^5}{0.06} \right] + \frac{1,000}{(1.06)^5} = \$1,084.25$$

$$V_0 = \sum_{t=1}^{5} \frac{80}{(1.10)^t} + \frac{1,000}{(1.10)^5} = 80 \left[\frac{1 - (1/1.10)^5}{0.10} \right] + \frac{1,000}{(1.10)^5} = \$924.18$$

The problem shows the inverse relationship that exists between the price of a bond and its rate of return. From 8% to 6%, the percentage change in value is 8.425%; from 8% to 10%, the percentage change in value is −7.582%.

2. $1,000, $1,147.20, $877.11.

From 8% to 6%, the percentage change in value is 14.72%; from 8% to 10%, the percentage change in value is −12.289%.

Comment: The percentage changes in value for given changes in yields are greater for the 10-year bond than the 5-year bond. This illustrates the bond price relation that the greater the maturity on a bond the greater its price sensitivity to interest rate changes.

3. $680.58, $747.26, $620.92.

From 8% to 6%, the percentage change in value is 9.7975%; from 8% to 10%, the percentage change in value is −8.766%.

Comment: The percentage changes in value for given changes in yields are greater for the 5-year, zero-coupon bond than the 5-year, 8% coupon bond. This illustrates the bond price relation that the lower the coupon rate on a bond, the greater its price sensitivity to interest rate changes.

4. Values, effective rates: semi-annual: $960.44, 9.2025%; monthly: $959.86, 9.3807%; weekly: $959.76, 9.4089%.

5. Monthly: $81.941; weekly: $81.8889; daily: $81.875; continuously: $81.873.

6.

Yields	0.04	0.0425	0.045	0.0475	0.05	0.0525	...	0.06	...	0.07	...
Values	97.2449	97.0787	96.9132	96.7484	96.5842	96.4208	...	95.9343	...	95.2948	...

7.
a.

Yields	0.050	0.055	0.060	...	0.100
Values	123.384	119.034	114.877	...	87.538

b. The price change when the yield increases from 8% to 8.5% is −3.32.
c. The price change when the yield decreases from 8% to 7.5% is +3.47.
d. The capital gain and capital loss in b and c are not equal in absolute value. This suggests that gains and losses are not symmetrical.

8. Full price = $1,147.45; accrued interest = $50; clean price = $1,097.45.

9. Purchase price = $968.30, selling price (full) = $1,048.85.

10.
a. The dealer would offer to buy the bonds from investors at $951.25: ((95 + (4/32))/100) × ($1,000) = (95.125/100)($1,000) = $951.25.
b. The dealer would be willing to sell the bond for $1,100.625: (110.0625/100)($1,000) = $1,100.625.
c. The dealer would be willing to buy the bond for $975: (97.5/100)($1,000) = $975.
d. The dealer would sell the bond for $947.87: $1,000/(1.055) = $947.87.
e. The dealer is willing to sell the bond for $9,943: $10,000[1−0.04(52/360)] = $9,943.

11. 10%, $924.18; 10.5%, $906.43.

12. $V_0 = $898.94; effective yield = 12.36%.

14. ARTM = 7.8776%, $V_0 = $913.04.

15. ARTC = 9.42634%.

16. Discount yield = 4.8%; YTM = 5.039%; logarithmic return = 4.916%.

17. b. Yield = 8%.

18. c. Bond-equivalent yield $= 9.013\%$.

19. a. \$938.55; c. 1,046.23; d. HD value $= \$1,451.78$, ARR $= 11.52\%$.

20. a. ARR $= 10\%$; b. ARR $= 10.67\%$; c. ARR $= 9.43\%$.

21. a. \$98.75; b. \$96.83.

22. a. $S_1 = 0.06$; $S_2 = 0.08$; b. 100.14.

23.
$$\text{YTM}_4 = \sqrt[4]{(1+y_1)(1+f_{11})(1+f_{12})(1+f_{13})} - 1$$

$$\text{YTM}_4 = \sqrt[4]{(1+y_2)^2(1+f_{12})(1+f_{13})} - 1$$

$$\text{YTM}_4 = \sqrt[4]{(1+y_1)(1+f_{21})^2(1+f_{13})} - 1$$

$$\text{YTM}_4 = \sqrt[4]{(1+y_1)(1+f_{31})^3} - 1$$

24. a. $f_{11} = 8.62\%$; b. (1) Sell X short at \$945; (2) buy $945/870 = 1.0862$ issues of Y; (3) after 1 year, cover short bond: cost $= \$1,000$; (4) at the end of year 2 (1 year after covering the short position) receive $(1.0862)1,000 = 1,086.20$ from original 2-year bond. Rate on 1-year investment made 1 year from the present period: $R_{11} = (1,086.20-1,000)/1,000 = 8.62\%$.

25. Use f_{mt} rule: short in t-bond and long in $m+t$ bond. For example, for f_{11}: short in 1-year bond (t) and long in 2-year $(m+t)$ bond. After 1 year, you would cover your short position using your funds and then 1 year later you would collect on the original 2-year bond investment. Thus, the strategy results in a 1-year investment to be made 1 year from now.

26. $f_{91,91} = 4.25\%$.

Strategy: Prices on the T-bills per \$100 face value are $P(91) = 100/(1.0375)^{91/365} = 99.08637$ and $P(182) = 100/(1.04)^{182/365} = 98.0633$. To lock in an implied forward rate on a 91-day investment to be made 91 days from now one could: (1) short the 91-day bill: borrow the bill and sell it for 99.08637 (or borrow 99.08637 at 3.75% interest); (2) use 99.08637 proceeds from the short sale to buy $99.08637/98.0633 = 1.0104327$ issues of the 182-day bill; (3) at the end of 91 days, cover the short position: cost $= 100$ (equivalent of a 100 investment made 91 days in the future; (4) at the end of 182 days (91 days after covering the short position) collect on the 182-day investment: $1.0104327(100) = 101.04327$. Annualized rate on 91-day investment made 91 days from now would be 4.25%.

CHAPTER 3

4.
  a. Central bank buys bonds, decreasing the bond supply and shifting the bond supply curve to the left. The impact would be an increase in bond prices and a decrease in interest rates. Intuitively, as the central bank buys bonds, they will push the price of the bond up and the interest rate down.
  b. In an economic recession, there is less capital formation and therefore fewer bonds are sold. This leads to a decrease in bond supply and a leftward shift in the bond supply curve. The decrease in supply initially leads to an excess demand for bonds given fewer bonds; this excess demand increases bond prices and lowers interest rates.

c. With a government deficit, the Treasury will have to sell more bonds to finance the shortfall. Their sale of bonds will increase the supply of bonds, shifting the bond supply curve to the right, and initially creating an excess supply of bonds. This excess supply will force bond prices down and interest rates up.

d. In a period of economic expansion, there is an increase in capital formation and therefore more bonds are being sold to finance the capital expansion. This leads to an increase in bond supply and a rightward shift in the bond supply curve. The increase in supply initially leads to an excess supply for bonds, decreasing bond prices and increasing interest rates.

5. The increased riskiness on the one bond would cause its demand to decrease, shifting its bond demand curve to the left. That bond's riskiness would also make the other bond more attractive, increasing its demand and shifting its demand curve to the right. At the new equilibriums, the riskier bond's price is lower and its rate greater than the other. The different risk associated with bonds leads to a market adjustment in which at the new equilibrium there is a positive risk premium.

6. The markets are defined in terms of their risk premium, RP: RP = YTM on risky bond − YTM on risk-free bond. By definition, a risk-neutral market is one in which the RP is zero, a risk-averse market is one with a positive RP, and a risk-loving market is one in which the RP is negative.

7.
a. The expected dollar return on the risky bond is $775 (0.75($1,000) + 0.25($100)). In a risk-neutral market, the risk premium is equal to zero. As a result, the price of the risky bond is found by discounting its $775 by the risk-free rate of 5%. In this problem, the price of the risky bond is $738.0952 (= 775/1.05).

b. In a risk-averse market, investors would not want the risky bond when it is priced to equal the risk-free rate. This would cause the demand for the risky bond to decrease, decreasing its price and increasing its yields, and also cause the demand for the risk-free bond to increase, causing its price to increase and its yield to fall. In this problem, the price of the risky bond would fall below $738.0952, resulting in an expected yield that exceeds the initial risk-free yield of 5%, and the price of the risk-free bond would rise above $952.35, resulting in a risk-free yield lower than 5%. Combining these market adjustments would result in a positive risk premium: RP = E(YTM on risky bond) − YTM on risk-free bond > 0.

c. In a risk-loving market, investors would want the risky bond when it is priced to equal the risk-free rate. This would cause the demand for the risky bond to increase, increasing its price and lowering its yields, and also cause the demand for the risk-free bond to decrease, causing its price to decrease and its yield to rise. In this problem, the price of the risky bond would increase above $738.0952, resulting in an expected yield that is less than the initial risk-free yield of 5%, and the price of the risk-free bond would fall below $952.35, resulting in a risk-free yield greater than 5%. Combining these market adjustments would result in a negative risk premium: RP = E(YTM on risky bond) − YTM on risk-free bond < 0.

8. The decrease in the liquidity on one bond would cause its demand to decrease, shifting its bond demand curve to the left. The decrease in that bond's liquidity would also make the other bond relatively more liquid, increasing its demand and shifting its demand curve to the right. Once the markets adjust to the liquidity difference between the bonds, then the less liquid bond's price would be lower and its rate greater than the relatively more liquid bond. Thus, the difference in liquidity between the bonds leads to a market adjustment in which there is a difference between rates due to their different liquidity features.

9. If investors know with certainty the probabilities and payoffs on the risky bond, then they would know that by buying a number of such bonds they would earn $775 per bond. That is, if they bought 100 risky bonds, 75 of the bonds would pay $1,000 and 25 would pay $100, yielding an average return of $775 [(75)($1,000) + (25)($100)]/100 = $775. Or, if they were to buy risky bonds for the next 100 periods, then in 75 of the periods they would get a payoff of $1,000 and in 25 of the periods, they would get $100, yielding an average payoff of $775. To be assured that they would earn an average of $775 per bond, investors would have to buy a sufficient number of bonds (e.g., 100) or have a sufficient number of time periods (e.g., 100). Buying a sufficient number of bonds now or over time can therefore eliminate the risk of a loss. For there to be a sufficient number of such bonds, in turn, requires a big enough market, which is a liquidity or marketability requirement. Such a requirement is not the case for the risk-free bond. Thus, for liquidity or marketability reasons, investors may price the so-called risky bond at a price to yield a rate above the risk-free bond of 5%.

10. $ATY = 5.2\%$; $P_0 = 1,051.92$.

12.

   a. Outline: Decrease in capital formation (ST and LT) $\Rightarrow$ Fewer bonds sold (ST and LT) $\Rightarrow$ Excess demand for bonds (ST and LT) $\Rightarrow$ Bond prices increase and rates decrease. $\therefore$ Downward shift in YC.

   b. Outline: Increase in capital formation (ST and LT) $\Rightarrow$ More bonds sold (ST and LT) $\Rightarrow$ Excess supply of bonds (ST and LT) $\Rightarrow$ Bond prices decrease and rates increase. $\therefore$ Upward shift in YC.

   c. Outline: Central bank buys ST Treasuries (T-bills) $\Rightarrow$ T-bill prices increase and rates decrease $\Rightarrow$ Substitution effect in which the demand for ST corporate securities increases, causing their prices to increase and their yields to decrease. $\therefore$ Tendency for YC to become positively sloped.

   d. Outline: Treasury sells LT Treasuries (T-bonds) $\Rightarrow$ T-bond prices decrease and yields increase $\Rightarrow$ Substitution effect in which the demand for LT corporate securities decreases, causing their prices to decrease and their rates to increase. $\therefore$ Tendency for YC to become positively sloped.

   e. Outline: Treasury buys LT Treasuries (T-bonds) $\Rightarrow$ T-bond prices increase and yields decrease $\Rightarrow$ Substitution effect in which the demand for LT corporate securities increases, causing their prices to increase and their rates to decrease. $\therefore$ Tendency for YC to become negatively sloped.

13.

   a. The combination of investors preferring short-term bonds investments, while corporations prefer to sell long-term bonds, would lead to an excess demand for short-term bonds and an excess supply for long-term claims. An equilibrium adjustment would have to occur in both markets. Specifically, the excess supply in the long-term market would force issuers to lower their bond prices, thus increasing bond yields and inducing some investors to change their short-term investment demands. In the short-term market, the excess demand would cause bond prices to increase and rates to fall, inducing some corporations to finance their long-term assets by selling short-term claims. Ultimately, equilibriums in both markets would be reached with long-term rates higher than short-term rates, a premium necessary to compensate investors and borrowers/issuers for the risk they've assumed.

   b. In this case the combination of investors preferring long-term bonds investments, while corporations prefer to sell short-term bonds, would lead to an excess supply for short-term bonds and an excess demand for long-term claims. The excess supply in the short-term market would force issuers to lower their bond prices, thus increasing bond yields and inducing some investors to change their long-term investment demands. In the long-term market, the excess demand would cause bond prices to increase and rates to fall, inducing some corporations to finance their long-term assets by selling long-term claims. Equilibriums in both markets would be reached with long-term rates lower than short-term rates.

14. Investors with horizon dates of 2 years can buy the 2-year bond with an annual rate of 6%, or they can buy the 1-year bond yielding 6%, then reinvest the principal and interest 1 year later in another 1-year bond expected to yield 8%. In a risk-neutral market, such investors would prefer the latter investment since it yields a higher expected average annual rate for the 2 years of 7% ($[[(1.06)(1.08)]^{1/2}-1$). Similarly, investors with 1-year horizon dates would also find it more advantageous to buy a 1-year bond yielding 6% than a 2-year bond (priced at $890 = \$1,000/1.06^2$) that they would sell 1 year later to earn an expected rate of only 4.037% ($E(P_{11}) = 1000/1.08 = 925.93$; $E(R) = (925.93/890)-1 = 0.0437$). Thus, in a risk-neutral market with an expectation of higher rates next year, both investors with 1-year horizon dates and investors with 2-year horizon dates would purchase 1-year instead of 2-year bonds. If enough investors do this, an increase in the demand for 1-year bonds and a decrease in the demand for 2-year bonds would occur until the average annual rate on the 2-year bond is equal to the equivalent annual rate from the series of 1-year investments (or the 1-year bond's rate is equal to the rate expected on the 2-year bond held 1 year).

15.

   a. Outline: (1) Given HD = 2 years, investors would prefer a series of 1-year bonds at 10% = $[(1.08)(1.12)]^{1/2}-1$ to a 2-year bond at 8% (also holds for investors with HD = 1 year). (2) Market response: demand for 2-year bonds would decrease, causing their price to decrease and their yield to increase, and the demand for 1-year bonds would increase, causing their price to increase and their yield to decrease. Impact: tendency for the yield curve to become positively sloped.
   b. Outline: (1) Given HD = 2 years, investors would prefer a 2-year bond at 10% to a series of 1-year bonds at 9% = $[(1.10)(1.08)]^{1/2}-1$ (also holds for investors with HD = 1 year). (2) Market response: demand for 2-year bonds would increase, causing their price to increase and their yield to decrease, and the demand for 1-year bonds would decrease, causing their price to decrease and their yield to increase. Impact: tendency for the yield curve to become negatively sloped.
   c. Outline: (1) Given HD = 2 years, investors would be indifferent to a 2-year bond at 7% and a series of 1-year bonds at 7% = $[(1.06)(1.08)]^{1/2}-1$ (also holds for investors with HD = 1 year). (2) Market response: no change in the yield curve.

16.

   a. Outline: (1) Given the expectation of higher rates in the future, borrowers wishing to finance 2-year assets would prefer to issue 2-year bonds at 8% rather than sell a series of 1-year bonds at 10% = $[(1.08)(1.12)]^{1/2}-1$. (2) Market response: the supply of 2-year bonds would increase, causing their price to decrease and their yield to increase, and the supply of 1-year bonds would decrease, causing their price to increase and their yield to decrease. Impact: tendency for the yield curve to become positively sloped, complementing the impact of investors' response to the expectation.
   b. Outline: (1) Given the expectation of lower rates in the future, borrowers wishing to finance 2-year assets would prefer to issue a series of 1-year bonds at 9% = $[(1.10)(1.08)]^{1/2}-1$ to

2-year bonds at 10%. (2) Market response: the supply of 2-year bonds would decrease, causing their price to increase and their yield to decrease, and the supply of 1-year bonds would increase, causing their price to decrease and their yield to increase. Impact: tendency for the yield curve to become negatively sloped, complementing the impact of investors' response to the expectation.

c. Outline: (1) Given $HD = 2$ years, borrowers would be indifferent to issuing a 2-year bond at 7% and a series of 1-year bonds at 7% $= [(1.06)(1.08)]^{1/2} - 1$. (2) Market response: no change in the yield curve.

17.

a. $f_{11} = 9\%, f_{21} = 8.5\%, f_{31} = 7\%, f_{41} = 5.751\%$.

b. $f_{12} = 8\%, f_{22} = 6.01\%, f_{32} = 4.69\%$.

c. The expected rate of return from buying a 3-year bond and selling it 1 year later is equal to the yield on the 1-year bond of 7% if the implied forward rate, f_{21}, is used as the expected rate on a 2-year bond 1 year later: $P_3 = 100/(1.08)^3 = 79.383$; $E(P_{21}) = 100/(1.085)^2 = 84.9455$; $E(R) = (84.9455/79.383) - 1 = 0.07$.

d. The expected rate of return from buying a bond of any maturity and selling it 1 year later is equal to the yield on the 1-year bond of 7% if the implied forward rate is used as the expected rate on the bond 1 year later.

e. The expected rate of return from buying a 4-year bond and selling it 2 years later is equal to the yield on the 2-year bond of 8% if the implied forward rate, f_{22}, is used as the expected rate on a 2-year bond 2 years later: $P_4 = 100/(1.07)^4 = 76.2895$; $E(P_{22}) = 100/(1.0601)^2 = 88.98285$; $E(R) = (88.9825/76.2895)^{1/2} - 1 = 0.08$.

f. The expected rate of return from buying a bond of any maturity and selling it 2 years later is equal to the yield on the 2-year bond of 8% if the implied forward rate is used as the expected rate on the bond 2 years later.

18.

a. $P_0 = 98.61113$.

b. $f_{11} = 7.002\%, f_{21} = 7.5035\%, f_{31} = 8.0047\%$.

c. $E(P_{31}) = 97.5278$.

d. If bonds are equal to their equilibrium prices and the implied forward rates are used as estimates of futures rates, then the 1-year expected rates will be equal to the current 1-year rate. The 1-year expected rate on the 4-year, 7% bond held 1 year is 6% – the same as the 1-year rate:

$$E(R) = \frac{7 + 97.5278}{98.61113} - 1 = 0.06$$

e. $f_{12} = 8.0071\%; f_{22} = 8.5094\%$.

f. The expected price on the 4-year, 7% coupon bond 2 years later is 97.357 ($= (7/(1.080071) + (107/(1.085094)^2) = 97.357$). Assuming that the $7 coupon is reinvested to year 2 at f_{11} of 7%, the expected rate of return for holding the 4-year, 7% bond 2 years is 6.5% – the same as the 2-year spot rate:

$$E(R_{22}) = \left[\frac{7(1.07) + 7 + 97.357}{98.61113} \right]^{1/2} - 1 = 0.065$$

19. (1) A contractionary open market operation in which the central bank sells short-term government securities. (2) A Treasury purchase of long-term Treasury securities. (3) A

poorly hedged economy in which investors prefer long-term investments and borrowers prefer short-term. (4) A market expectation of lower interest rates.

20. The liquidity premium theory (LPT) posits that there is a liquidity premium for long-term bonds over short-term bonds because the prices of long-term securities tend to be more volatile and therefore more risky than short-term securities. According to LPT, if investors were risk averse, then they would require some additional return (liquidity premium) in order to hold long-term bonds instead of short-term ones. The yield curve in questions 17 and 18 had no risk premium factored in to compensate investors for the additional volatility they assumed from buying long-term bonds. Thus a liquidity premium would need to be added to longer-term yields to reflect the additional risk associated with the longer-term bonds.

21. Short-answer questions: (1) The market expects higher interest rates in the future. (2) The market expects lower interest rates in the future. (3) The risk premium should narrow since investors would be more confident and therefore would increase their proportional investment in lower quality bonds. (4) In a risk-neutral market the risk premium is zero; that is, the rates on risky investments are equal to the risk-free rate. Thus, the risk-free rate would be used to discount future cash flows on a risky bond. (5) Expected rates for holding bonds for a specified period (e.g., 1 year, 2 years) will be equal to the applicable current rate if expected rates are equal to implied forward. If investors expect the future rate to be less than the applicable implied forward rate, then they would have expected holding period yields that exceed the current rates. Thus, the implied forward rates can be used as a cutoff rate in evaluating and selecting bonds. (6) Municipals are tax-exempt. As a result, they trade at lower before-tax YTM than many other bonds that are taxable. (7) The preferred habitat theory posits that investors and borrowers will move away from their preferred maturity segment if rates are attractive enough to compensate them for foregoing their preferences.

CHAPTER 4

1. During recessions investors are more concerned with safety than during expansionary times. As a result, a relatively low demand for lower grade bonds and a high demand for higher grades occurs, leading to lower prices for the lower grade bonds and thus a higher interest premium. On the other hand, during periods of economic expansion there is usually less concern about default. This tends to increase the demand for lower grade bonds relative to higher grades, causing a smaller premium.

2. The negatively sloped yield curve for low-grade bonds suggests that investors have more concern over the repayment of principal (or the issuer's ability to refinance at favorable rates) than they do about the issuer meeting interest payments. This concern would explain the low demand and higher yields for short-term bonds, in which principal payment is due relatively soon compared to long-term bonds.

7. $ARR_4 = 12.78448\%$; $ARR_{10} = 9.889\%$.

9. a. 9.806%; b. 8.232%.

10. a. 10%; b. 10%. Comment: Since the ARR stays at 10% at the different rates, there is no market risk.

11. The 8-year, 8.5% coupon bond given a flat yield curve at 10% has Macaulay's duration of 6.03. The bond's modified duration is −5.482. Comment: The problem illustrates how an

investor with an HD of 6 years can eliminate, or at least minimize, market risk by buying a bond that has a duration equal to the HD of 6.

12. a. For zero-coupon bonds, Macaulay's duration is equal to the bond's maturity. b. $w_1 = \frac{1}{3}$ and $w_2 = \frac{2}{3}$.

13.

Bond	Period coupon, C	P	F	Period yield, y	Periods to maturity, M	Payments per year, n	Modified duration	Macaulay's duration	Convexity
a	90	1,000.00	1,000	0.0900	4	1	−3.2397	3.5313	14.2221
b	0	708.42	1,000	0.0900	4	1	−3.6698	4.0000	16.8337
c	90	1,000.00	1,000	0.0900	5	1	−3.8897	4.2397	20.1848
d	35	1,000.00	1,000	0.0350	20	2	−7.1062	7.3549	64.2998
e	35	1,000.00	1,000	0.0350	6	2	−2.6643	2.7575	8.7515
f	0	816.30	1,000	0.0700	3	1	−2.8037	3.0000	10.4812

15. Short-answer questions: (5) Price compression refers to limitations on a bond's price. For callable bonds, the percentage increases in their prices may be limited when interest rates decrease to a level where the bond is likely to be called, given that the market expects the bonds to be redeemed at the call price. (6) There is a direct relation when the direct interest-on-interest effect dominates the inverse price effect. (7) There is an inverse relation when the inverse price effect dominates the direct interest-on-interest effect. (8) The ARR would be invariant to interest rate changes when the inverse price effect and the direct interest-on-interest effect exactly offset each other; this occurs when the bond's duration is equal to the investor's horizon date.

CHAPTER 5

4. While it is true that a sinking fund provision benefits bondholders by allaying their concern over the ability of the issuer to pay the principal, many sinking funds have a provision that allows the issuer to buy up the requisite amount of bonds either at a stipulated call price or in the secondary market at its market price. This sinking fund call option provision benefits the issuer and is a disadvantage to the bondholder.

5. The average life is 8.5 years.

7. YTM = 14.64%.

8. Call protection means that the bond cannot be called. Refunding protection means that the bond cannot be called from the proceeds of certain types of refunding debt. Bonds that have refunding protection may still be called.

9. The initial year's call price is equal to the offering price of $950 plus the $100 coupon: $1,050. The call price will then decrease by $2.50 each year (= $1,050−$1,000)/20) to equal $1,000 at the end of year 20. The call price will be equal to $1,000 for years 21–25.

11. A release and substitution provision allows the issuer of a mortgage bond to sell the collateral in order to retire the bond; that is, the proceeds from the asset sale are used to retire the bonds.

13. (1) Provision requiring the issuer to deliver to the trustee the pledged securities. (2) Provision allowing the company to retain its voting right if the collateral is the stock of one of its subsidiaries. (3) Provision requiring that the company maintain the value of its securities, positing additional collateral if the collateral decreases in value. (4) Provision allowing the company to withdraw the collateral provided there is an acceptable substitute.

15. The creditworthiness of debentures can be improved with protective covenants, subordination, and credit enhancements.

16. The guarantee does not eliminate the risk but shifts it from the corporation to the insurer.

19. The Board of Directors hires the managers and officers of a corporation. Since the Board represents the stockholders, this arrangement can create a moral hazard problem in which the managers may engage in activities that could be detrimental to the bondholders. Since bondholders cannot necessarily seek redress from managers after they've made decisions that could harm them, they need to include protective covenants that place restrictions on the company in the bond indenture.

20. Some of the standard covenants specify the financial criteria that must be met before borrowers can incur additional debt (debt limitation) or pay dividends (dividend limitations). Other possible covenants include limitations on liens, borrowing from subsidiaries, asset sales, mergers and acquisitions, and leasing.

22. a. A company is considered insolvent if the value of its liabilities exceeds the value of its assets; it is considered in default if it cannot meet its obligations. Technically, default and insolvency are dependent: a company with liabilities exceeding assets will inevitably be in default when the future income from its assets is insufficient to cover future obligations on its liabilities. b. A company can be illiquid and not insolvent. A company with assets that are not expected to generate a return for some time in the future, may very well be a solvent company, but with current cash flow problems.

25. The investment banker underwriting a bond issue bears the risk that the price of the issue could decrease during the time the bonds are being sold. A classic example discussed in the chapter was the $1 billion bond issue of IBM in 1979.

30. (1) Commercial paper is usually sold as a zero-coupon bond; (2) many have maturities less than 270 days to avoid registration; (3) CP is sold either directly (direct paper) or through dealers (dealer paper); (4) many CP issues include credit enhancements such as lines of credit.

32. Reverse inquiry is when institutional investors indicate to agents of an MTN program the type of maturity they want. The agent will inform the corporation of the investor's request; the corporation could then agree to sell the notes with that maturity from its MTN program, even if they are not posted.

33. As a source of financing, MTNs provide corporations with *flexibility* in their financing choices. Corporations selling an MTN through a shelf registration are able to enter the market constantly or intermittently, with the flexibility to finance a number of different short-, intermediate-, and long-term projects over a 2-year period.

CHAPTER 6

2.

Year	Inflation	Inflation-adjusted principal	TIP cash flow
1	2%	$1,020.00	$30.60
2	2%	$1,040.40	$31.21
3	2%	$1,061.21	$31.84
4	2%	$1,082.43	$37.47 + $1,082.43

4.

  a. $S_{0.5} = 5\%$, $S_1 = 5.25\%$, $S_{1.5} = 6.03\%$, $S_2 = 6.55\%$, $S_{2.5} = 7.08\%$, $S_3 = 7.62\%$.

  b. $P_{0.5} = 3.658537$, $P_1 = 3.560614$, $P_{1.5} = 3.431781$, $P_2 = 3.299674$, $P_{2.5} = 3.157399$, $P_3 = 83.18777$; total value of the strips $= 100.2958$.

  c. An arbitrage exists by buying the 3-year note for 100, stripping it into six zero coupons, and selling the strips for 100.2958.

  d. If the actual yield curve matches the theoretical spot yield curve, then the proceeds from the sale of the strips would be equal to the cost of the 3-year note of 100. Thus, no arbitrage exists: $P_{0.5} = 3.658537$, $P_1 = 3.560614$, $P_{1.5} = 3.430510$, $P_2 = 3.296742$, $P_{2.5} = 3.151571$, $P_3 = 82.902026$; total value of the strips $= 100$.

  e. When the yield curve had yields equal to the YTMs on the Treasury securities, arbitrageurs could buy a T-note, strip it, and sell the strips for a risk-free profit. In contrast, if the yields on the yield curve were equal to the spot rates estimated from bootstrapping, then the arbitrage profit would be zero. Thus, the process of stripping will change the supply and demand for bonds causing their yields to move to their theoretical spot yield curve levels.

6. a. 2.84% or 99.2821; b. 11.9 billion; c. 68.75%; d. 2.798%; e. 0.042%.

8. Income comes from two sources: carry income and position profit. *Carry income* is the difference between the interest that dealers earn from holding the securities and the interest they pay on the funds they borrow to purchase the securities. The *position profit* of dealers comes from long positions, as well as short positions. In a long position, a dealer purchases the securities and then holds them until a customer comes along. The dealer will realize a position profit if rates decrease and prices increase during the time she holds the securities. In contrast, in a short position, the dealer borrows securities and sells them hoping that rates will subsequently increase and prices will fall by the time he purchases the securities.

9. *On-the-run issues* are recently issued Treasury securities; they are the most liquid securities with a very narrow bid–asked spread. *Off-the-run issues* are Treasury securities issued earlier; they are not quite as liquid and can have slightly wider spreads.

10. The interdealer market is a market in which dealers trade amongst themselves. The market functions through government security brokers.

11. Under a repurchase agreement, RP, the holder of a security, such as a dealer, sells securities to another party, often a financial institution, with an agreement to buy the securities back at a later date and price. To the seller/repurchaser, the RP represents a collateralized loan, with the underlying securities serving as the collateral. To the buyer/reseller the RP represents a secured investment. Their position is referred to as a reverse repo.

12.
a. The dealer would buy the notes and then per the repurchase agreement sell the acquired notes on the repurchase agreement with an agreement to buy them back the next day.
b. Interest $= (\$100,000,000)(0.03)(1/360) = \$8,333$; selling price $= \$99,991,667$; repurchase price $= \$100,000,000$.
c. The dealer could use an open repo.

CHAPTER 7

2. Today, approximately 25 dealers and brokers form the core of the primary and secondary markets for CDs, selling new CDs and trading and maintaining inventories in existing ones. Major investors: money market funds, banks, bank trust departments, state and local governments, foreign governments and central banks, and corporations.

3. In 1961, First Bank of New York (now Citicorp) issued a negotiable CD that was accompanied by an announcement by First Boston Corporation and Salomon Brothers that they would stand ready to buy and sell the CDs, thus creating a secondary market for CDs. The secondary market provided a way for banks to circumvent Regulation Q and offer investors rates competitive with other money market securities. Specifically, with Federal Reserve Regulation Q setting the maximum rates on longer-term CDs (e.g., 6 months), and with those rates set relatively higher than shorter-term CDs (e.g., 3 months), the existence of a secondary market meant that an investor could earn a rate higher than either a short- or longer-term CD, by buying a longer-term CD and selling it later in the secondary market at a higher price associated with the short-term maturity.

4. Bank notes are similar to medium-term notes. They are sold as a program consisting of a number of notes with different maturities typically ranging from 1 to 5 years and offered either continuously or intermittently. They differ from corporate MTNs in that they are not registered with the SEC, unless it is the bank's holding company, and not the individual bank, issuing the MTN.

5. Banker's acceptances (BAs) are time drafts (postdated checks) guaranteed by a bank – guaranteed postdated checks. The guarantee of the bank improves the credit quality of the draft, making it marketable. BAs are used to finance the purchase of goods that have to be transferred from a seller to a buyer. They are often created in international business transactions where finished goods or commodities have to be shipped. The use of BAs to finance transactions is known as *acceptance financing* and banks that create BAs are referred to as *accepting banks*.

6. The US company would obtain a letter of credit (LOC) from its bank. The LOC would say that the bank would pay the German company $20m if the US company failed to do so. The LOC would then be sent by the US bank to the German company's bank. Upon receipt of the LOC, the German bank would notify the German manufacturing company who would then ship the drilling equipment. The German company would then present the shipping documents to the German bank and receive the present value of $20m in local currency from the bank. The German bank would then present a time draft to the US bank who would stamp "accepted" on it, thus creating the BA. The US company would sign the note and receive the shipping documents. At this point, the German bank is the holder of the BA. The bank can hold the BA as an investment or sell it to the American bank at a price equal to the present value of $20m. If the German bank opts for the latter, then the US bank holds the BA and can either retain it or sell it to an investor such as a money

market fund or a BA dealer. If all goes well, at maturity the US company will present the shipping documents to the shipping company to obtain the drilling equipment, as well as deposit the $20m funds in his bank; whoever is holding the BA on the due date will present it to the US bank to be paid.

10. A unit investment trust has a specified number of fixed-income securities that are rarely changed, and the fund usually has a fixed life. A unit investment trust is formed by a sponsor who buys a specified number of securities, deposits them with a trustee and then sells claims on the security, known as redeemable trust certificates, at their net asset value plus a commission fee. The financial institution would purchase $100 million worth of 10-year Treasury bonds, place them in a trust, and then issue 100,000 redeemable trust certificates at a net asset value of $1,000 plus commission: NAV = ($100 million/ 100,000) = $1,000. The financial institution's sale of trust certificates provides the proceeds to purchase the $100 million of T-bonds.

11. Hedged funds are structured so that they can be largely unregulated. To achieve this, they are often set up as limited partnerships. By federal law, as limited partnerships, hedged funds are limited to no more than 99 limited partners each with annual incomes of at least $200,000 or a net worth of at least $1m (excluding home), or to no more than 499 limited partners each with a net worth of at least $5m. Many funds or partners are also domiciled offshore to circumvent regulations. Hedged funds acquire funds from many different individual and institutional sources; the minimum investments range from $100,000 to $20m, with the average investment being $1m.

16. $1,425,761.

19. A separate account contract (SAC) is a GIC in which the underlying securities are separated from other liabilities of the insurer and managed separately in a SAC. They are considered legally protected against the liabilities arising from other businesses of the insurance company.

20. a. *Bank investment contracts* (BICs) are deposit obligations with a guaranteed rate and fixed maturity; they are similar to a GIC. b. *Stable value investment* is the term used to describe investments in bank investment contracts and guaranteed investment contracts. c. *Bullet contract* is the term used to describe a generic GIC. d. *Window GIC* refers to a GIC that allows for premium deposits to be made over a specified period, such as a year; they are designed to attract the annual cash flow from a pension or 401(k) plan. e. *Floating-rate GIC* is a GIC in which the rate is tied to a benchmark rate.

CHAPTER 8

1. a.

	Current bond: 5 yr, 10% coupon bond	Substitute bond: 10 yr, 10% coupon bond
Current value	100	100
Current Macaulay's duration	4.17	6.76
Coupons	10	10
Bond price 1 year later	103.24	106.00
Dollar return 1 year later	13.24	16.00
One-year ARR	13.24%	16%

b.

	Current bond: 5 yr, 10% coupon bond	Substitute bond: 10 yr, 10% coupon bond
Current value	100	100
Current Macaulay's duration	4.17	6.76
Coupons	10	10
Bond price 1 year later	96.90	94.46
Dollar return 1 year later	6.90	4.46
One-year ARR	6.90%	4.46%

c. If interest rates are expected to decrease across all maturities, then a rate-anticipation swap in which the investor sells her lower duration bonds and buys higher duration ones would provide greater upside gains in value if rates decrease but also greater losses in value if rates increase.

2.

a.

	Current bond: 15 yr, 7% coupon bond	Substitute bond: 3 yr, 10% coupon bond
Current value per 100 face value	109.80	110
Coupons	7	10
Interest on interest	0.105	0.15
Bond price 1 year later	100	105.51
Dollar return 1 year later	−2.695	5.66
One-year ARR	−2.454%	5.145%

$+3.5(1.03)+3.5-7=0.105;\ 5(1.03)+5-10=0.15.$

4.
   a. The price on the AAA, 2-year zero-coupon bond is 89 and the price on the BBB, 2-year zero-coupon bond is 86.533. The strategy is go short in the AAA bond and long in the BBB bond: short AAA bond at 89; use 89 proceeds to buy $n = 89/86.533 = 1.0285$ issues of the 2-year BBB bond.
   b. Cash flow if the yield on the AAA bond were 7% and the spread were 100 BP a year later would be 1.774.
   c. Cash flow if the yield on the AAA bond were 5% and the spread were 100 BP a year later would be 1.791.
   d. If the spread widens, profit on the position decreases with losses occurring when the spread is above 300 points.

5. Bond A is trading at par, 100, and Bond B is trading at 98.48. To take advantage of the mispricing, a yield pick-up swap could be formed by going long in Bond B at 98.48 (the underpriced bond) and shorting Bond A at 100 (the overpriced bond) to realize an initial cash flow of 1.52. Since the bonds are identical, their prices will eventually converge. When this occurs, the arbitrageur can sell Bond B, and then use the proceeds to buy Bond A and return the borrowed bond to the bond lender to close her short position. The risk in a yield pick-up swap is that the bonds are not identical.

6. The fundamental objective of many credit analysis strategies is to determine expected changes in default risk. If changes in quality ratings of a bond can be projected prior to an

upgrade or downgrade announcement, bond investors can realize significant gains by buying bonds they project will be upgraded, and they can avoid significant losses by selling or not buying bonds they project will be downgraded.

12. Suppose a bond investor realized a capital gain and also a capital gains tax liability. One way for the investor to negate the tax liability would be to offset the capital gain with a capital loss. If the investor were holding bonds with current capital losses, he could sell those to incur a capital loss to offset his gain. Except for the offset feature, though, the investor may not otherwise want to sell the bond. If this were the case, then the investor could execute a bond swap in which he sells the bond needed for creating a capital loss and then uses the proceeds to purchase a similar, though not identical, bond.

14. Using three durations ranges ($D < 4$; $4 \leq D \leq 7$; $D > 7$), two quality ratings (investment grade, IG, and speculative grade, SG), and the two sectors (municipal and corporate), the following 12 cells can be created:

$C_1 = D < 4$, IG, Corp $C_7 = D < 4$, SG, Corp
$C_2 = 4 \leq D \leq 7$, IG, Corp $C_8 = 4 \leq D \leq 7$, SG, Corp
$C_3 = D > 7$, IG, Corp $C_9 = D > 7$, SG, Corp
$C_4 = D < 4$, IG, Mun $C_{10} = D < 4$, SG, Mun
$C_5 = 4 \leq D \leq 7$, IG, Mun $C_{11} = 4 \leq D \leq 7$, SG, Mun
$C_6 = D > 7$, IG, Mun $C_{12} = D > 7$, SG, Mun

To form a bond index portfolio with these cells one would purchase bonds matching each of the cells with the funds allocated to each bond based on the cell's proportion to the index.

17.

a. Match strategy (1) The $10m liability at the end of year 4 is matched by buying $9,433,962 worth of 4-year bonds: $9,433,962 = $10,000,000/1.06. (2) The $7m liability at the end of year 3 is matched by buying $6,069,776 of 3-year bonds: $6,069,776 = ($7,000,000−(0.06)($9,433,962))/1.06. (3) The $12m liability at the end of year 2 is matched by buying $10,443,185 of 2-year bonds: $10,443,185 = ($12,000,000−(0.06)($9,433,962)−(0.06)($6,069,776))/1.06. (4) The $2m liability at the end of year 1 is matched by buying $418,099 of 1-year bonds: $418,099 = ($2,000,000−(0.06)($9,433,962)−(0.06)($6,069,776)−(0.06)($10,443,185))/1.06.

b. Total investment: $9,433,962 + $6,069,776 + $10,443,185 + $418,099 = $26,365,021.

(1) Year	(2) Total bond value outstanding	(3) Coupon income	(4) Maturing principal	(5) Liability	(6) Ending balance (3)+(4)−(5)
1	$26,365,021	$1,581,901	$418,099	$2,000,000	0
2	$25,946,923	$1,556,815	$10,443,185	$12,000,000	0
3	$15,503,738	$930,224	$6,069,776	$7,000,000	0
4	$9,433,962	$566,038	$9,433,962	$10,000,000	0

19.

Cash flow at year 8 4%	Cash flow at year 8 4%
Price $= 92.64$ $5(1.04)^7 = 6.58$ $5(1.04)^6 = 6.33$ $5(1.04)^5 = 6.08$ $5(1.04)^4 = 5.85$ $5(1.04)^3 = 5.62$ $5(1.04)^2 = 5.41$ $5(1.04)^1 = 5.20$ $\quad\quad 5 = 5.00$ $P_8 = (5/1.04) + (105/(1.04)^2)$ $\quad = 101.89$	Price $= 92.64$ $5(1.08)^7 = 8.57$ $5(1.08)^6 = 7.93$ $5(1.08)^5 = 7.35$ $5(1.08)^4 = 6.80$ $5(1.08)^3 = 6.30$ $5(1.08)^2 = 5.83$ $5(1.08)^1 = 5.40$ $\quad\quad 5 = 5.00$ $P_8 = (5/1.08) + (105/(1.08)^2)$ $\quad = 94.65$
Target value $= 147.96$ ARR $= 0.0603$	Target value $= 147.83$ ARR $= 0.0602$

20. a. *Duration-matching strategy*: At 4%: target value $= 134.12$, ARR $= 0.0602$; at 6%: target value $= 133.94$, ARR $= 0.06$; at 8%: target value $= 133.90$, ARR $= 0.06$. *Maturity-matching strategy*: At 4%: target value $= 139.80$, ARR $= 0.0574$; at 6%: target value $= 141.85$, ARR $= 0.06$; at 8%: target value $= 144.02$, ARR $= 0.0627$.

b. The duration-matching strategy yields the same target value and ARR, while a maturity-matching strategy does not. A duration-matching strategy works by having offsetting price and reinvestment effects. In contrast, a maturity-matching strategy has no price effect and therefore no way to offset the reinvestment effect.

c.

Cash flow at year 6 after yield curve shifts to 4% at the end of year 2	Cash flow at year 6 after yield curve shifts to 8% at the end of year 2
Price $= 94.42$ $5(1.06)^2(1.04)^3 = 6.32$ $5(1.06)^2(1.04)^2 = 6.08$ $5(1.04)^3 = 5.62$ $5(1.04)^2 = 5.41$ $5(1.04) = 5.20$ $5 = 5.00$ $105/(1.04)^1 = \underline{100.96}$	Price $= 94.42$ $5(1.06)^2(1.08)^3 = 7.08$ $5(1.06)^2(1.08)^2 = 6.55$ $5(1.08)^3 = 6.30$ $5(1.08)^2 = 5.83$ $5(1.08) = 5.40$ $5 = 5.00$ $105/(1.08)^1 = \underline{97.22}$
Target value $= 134.59$ ARR $= 0.06086$	Target value $= 133.38$ ARR $= 0.0593$

After 2 years, the bond would have a maturity of 5 years and would be priced at 104.45 if rates were at 4% and 88.02 if rates were at 8%. At the 4% yield, the bond's duration would be 4.56 and at 8%, the duration would be 4.52; neither duration matches the remaining horizon period of 5 years. Comment: The ARRs now differ given different rates, indicating market risk. In addition, the duration no longer matches the horizon period. The implication is that for a position to be immunized the duration of the asset and the liability need to be matched at all times.

26.
  a. MTV = \$68,024,448; safety margin = \$3,538,387.
  b. Value of the fund = \$63,245,000; safety margin = \$9,245,000; ARR = 12.35.
  c. Value of the fund = \$48,461,200; safety margin = \$3,813; ARR = 8%.

CHAPTER 9

1.
  a. $S_{uu} = 12.10\%$, $S_{ud} = 10\%$, $S_{dd} = 8.2646\%$, $S_u = 11\%$, $S_d = 9.091\%$, $S_0 = 10\%$.
  b. 98.234.
  c. 97.81736.
  d. Call option values: $V_u^C = 0$, $V_d^C = 0.9166$, and $V_0^C = 0.416636$; callable bond values: $B_u^C = 98.1982$, $B_d^C = 99$, and $B_0^C = 97.81736$.
  e. At spot rate 9.091% in period 1, the issuer could buy the bond back at 99 on the call option, financing the refunding by issuing a 1-year bond at 9.091% interest. One period later the issuer would owe $99(1.09091) = 108$; this represents a saving of $109 - 108 = 1$. The value of that saving in period one is $1/1.09091 = 0.9166$, which is equal to the value of the call option: $99.9166 - 99 = 0.9166$.
  f. 98.59845.
  g. Put option values: $V_u^P = 0.8018$, $V_d^P = 0$, and $V_0^P = 0.364454$; putable bond values: $B_u^P = 99$, $B_d^P = 99.9166$, and $B_0^P = 98.59845$.

2.

Period	Path 1	Geometric mean	CF	PV
1	0.10000	0.100000	9	8.181818
2	0.09091	0.095446	109	90.833258
				99.015076

Period	Path 2	Geometric mean	CF	PV
1	0.10000	0.10000	9	8.181818
2	0.11000	0.10499	109	89.271089
				97.452907

Weighted average value = $(99.015076 + 97.452907)/2 = 98.234$

3. The value of the sinking-fund call option per \$100 face value is 0.416636. Since the option represents $\frac{1}{3}$ of the issue, the value of the bond's sinking-fund option is 0.13888, and the value of the sinking-fund bond per \$100 face value is 98.09512. Thus, the total value of the \$9m face value issue is \$8.8285608m.

4. The value of the convertible bond is 1,023.81:

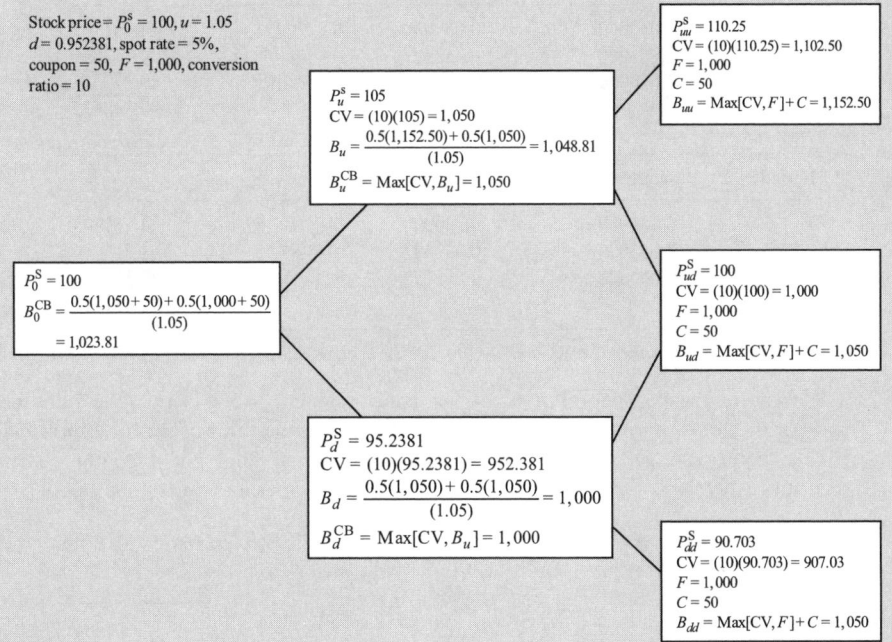

Stock price $= P_0^S = 100$, $u = 1.05$
$d = 0.952381$, spot rate $= 5\%$,
coupon $= 50$, $F = 1,000$, conversion
ratio $= 10$

$P_u^S = 105$
$CV = (10)(105) = 1,050$
$B_u = \dfrac{0.5(1,152.50) + 0.5(1,050)}{(1.05)} = 1,048.81$
$B_u^{CB} = \text{Max}[CV, B_u] = 1,050$

$P_{uu}^S = 110.25$
$CV = (10)(110.25) = 1,102.50$
$F = 1,000$
$C = 50$
$B_{uu} = \text{Max}[CV, F] + C = 1,152.50$

$P_0^S = 100$
$B_0^{CB} = \dfrac{0.5(1,050 + 50) + 0.5(1,000 + 50)}{(1.05)}$
$\quad = 1,023.81$

$P_{ud}^S = 100$
$CV = (10)(100) = 1,000$
$F = 1,000$
$C = 50$
$B_{ud} = \text{Max}[CV, F] + C = 1,050$

$P_d^S = 95.2381$
$CV = (10)(95.2381) = 952.381$
$B_d = \dfrac{0.5(1,050) + 0.5(1,050)}{(1.05)} = 1,000$
$B_d^{CB} = \text{Max}[CV, B_u] = 1,000$

$P_{dd}^S = 90.703$
$CV = (10)(90.703) = 907.03$
$F = 1,000$
$C = 50$
$B_{dd} = \text{Max}[CV, F] + C = 1,050$

5.
a. Binomial tree of spot rates: $S_{uu} = 6.05\%$, $S_{ud} = 5\%$, $S_{dd} = 4.13223\%$, $S_u = 5.5\%$, $S_d = 4.5454\%$, and $S_0 = 5\%$.

b. Binomial tree of bond values: $B_{uu} = 99.009901$, $B_{ud} = 100$, $B_{dd} = 100.83333$, $B_u = 99.056825$, $B_d = 100.833339$, and $B_0 = 99.94772$.

c. The value of a three-period, option-free bond paying a 5% coupon per period and callable with a call price of 100 is 99.550869. Binomial tree values: $B_{uu} = 99.009901$, $B_{ud} = 100$, $B_{dd} = 100$, $B_u = 99.056825$, $B_d = 100$, and $B_0 = 99.550869$.

d. The value of a three-period, option-free bond paying a 5% coupon per period and putable with put price of 100 is 100.39684. Binomial tree values: $B_{uu} = 100$, $B_{ud} = 100$, $B_{dd} = 100.8333$, $B_u = 100$, $B_d = 100.833339$, and $B_0 = 100.39684$.

6.

Period	Path 1	Geometric mean	CF	PV
1	0.050000	0.050000	5	4.761905
2	0.045454	0.047725	5	4.554868
3	0.041322	0.045586	105	91.856502
				101.173274

Period	Path 2	Geometric mean	CF	PV
1	0.050000	0.050000	5	4.761905
2	0.045454	0.047725	5	4.554868
3	0.050000	0.048482	105	91.097356
				100.414129

Period	Path 3	Geometric mean	CF	PV
1	0.050000	0.050000	5	4.761905
2	0.055000	0.052497	5	4.513654
3	0.050000	0.051664	105	90.273076
				99.548635

Period	Path 4	Geometric mean	CF	PV
1	0.050000	0.050000	5	4.761905
2	0.055000	0.052497	5	4.513654
3	0.060500	0.055158	105	89.379283
				98.654842

Weighted average value $= (101.173274 + 100.414129 + 99.548635 + 98.654842)/4 = 99.94772$

7. The value of the one-period zero-coupon bond paying $F = 5$ is 4.762, the value of the two-period zero-coupon bond paying $F = 5$ is 4.534, and the value of the three-period zero-coupon bond paying $F = 105$ is 90.649. The sum of the values of these three stripped securities is 99.94 – the same value found for the three-period 5% coupon bond.

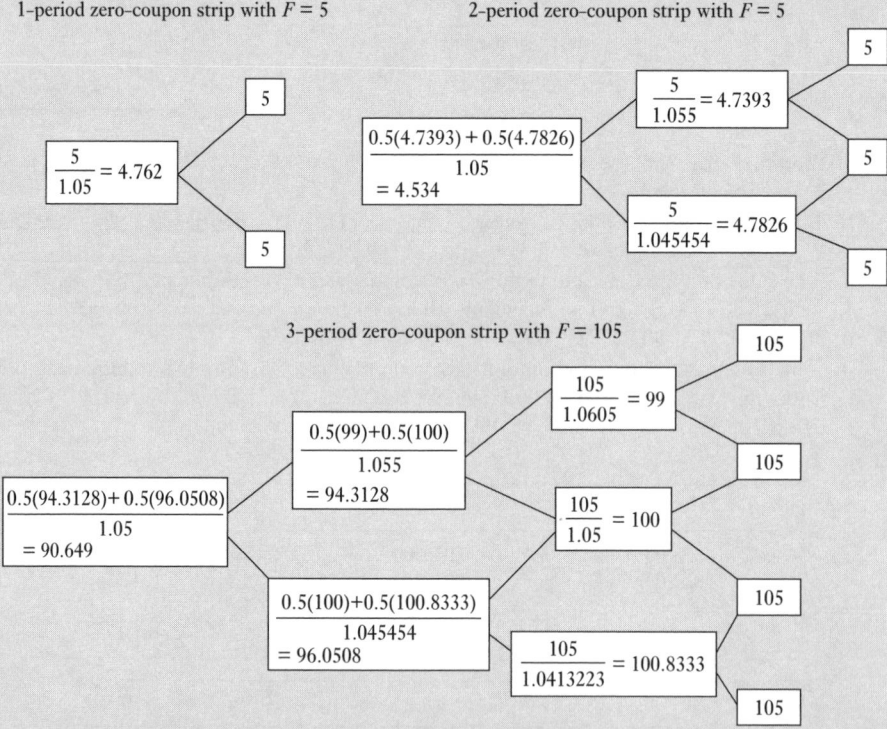

8. The value of the first sinking-fund call option per $100 face value is 0.396828 and the value of the second is 0.189785. Since each option represents $\frac{1}{3}$ of the issue, the value of the bond's sinking-fund option is 0.19554, and the value of the sinking fund bond per $100 face value is 99.75218. Thus, the total value of the $9m face value issue is $8.9776962m.

9. a. Conversion price = 100; b. Conversion value = 900; c. Straight debt value = 887; d. Minimum price of the convertible = 900; e. Arbitrage strategy: buy convertible for $880, convert to 10 shares of XYZ stock, then sell the stock at $S_0 = \$90$ per share for a profit of $20: Profit = (10)($90) − $880 = $20.

10. a. 1073.20; b. 1071.47.

11. a. $B_{uu} = 97.57$, $B_{ud} = 100$, $B_{dd} = 101.760$, $B_u = 97.747$, $B_d = 101.790$, and $B_0 = 99.78$.

b.

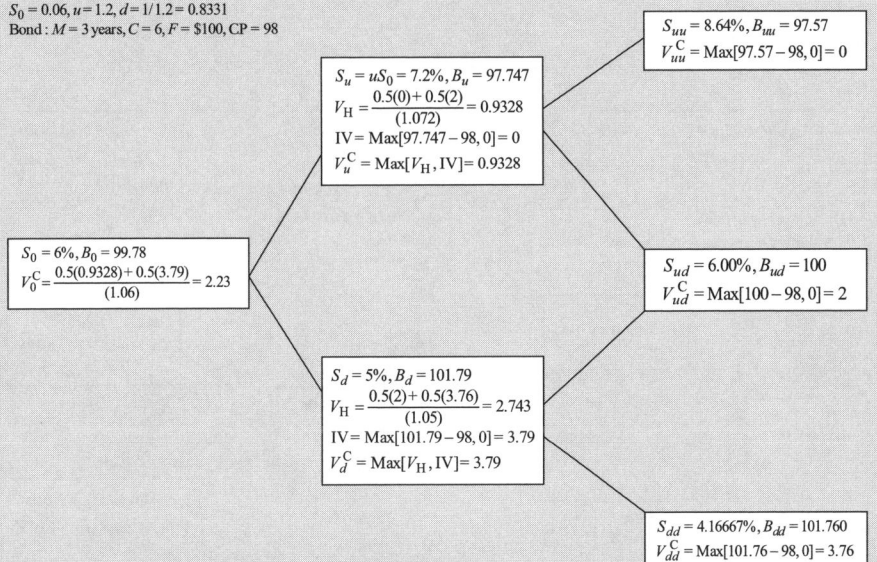

$S_0 = 0.06, u = 1.2, d = 1/1.2 = 0.8331$
Bond : $M = 3$ years, $C = 6, F = \$100$, CP = 98

$S_{uu} = 8.64\%, B_{uu} = 97.57$
$V_{uu}^C = \text{Max}[97.57 − 98, 0] = 0$

$S_u = uS_0 = 7.2\%, B_u = 97.747$
$V_H = \dfrac{0.5(0) + 0.5(2)}{(1.072)} = 0.9328$
$IV = \text{Max}[97.747 − 98, 0] = 0$
$V_u^C = \text{Max}[V_H, IV] = 0.9328$

$S_0 = 6\%, B_0 = 99.78$
$V_0^C = \dfrac{0.5(0.9328) + 0.5(3.79)}{(1.06)} = 2.23$

$S_{ud} = 6.00\%, B_{ud} = 100$
$V_{ud}^C = \text{Max}[100 − 98, 0] = 2$

$S_d = 5\%, B_d = 101.79$
$V_H = \dfrac{0.5(2) + 0.5(3.76)}{(1.05)} = 2.743$
$IV = \text{Max}[101.79 − 98, 0] = 3.79$
$V_d^C = \text{Max}[V_H, IV] = 3.79$

$S_{dd} = 4.16667\%, B_{dd} = 101.760$
$V_{dd}^C = \text{Max}[101.76 − 98, 0] = 3.76$

c. $B_{uu} = 97.57$, $B_{ud} = 98$, $B_{dd} = 98$, $B_u = 96.8142$, $B_d = 98$, and $B_0 = 97.55$.

12.
a. 95.50
b. 95.36
c. 100.31
d. 87.84
e. 87.76
f. 100.35.

Spot rates	Bond values option-free	Bond values callable
0.040	115.33	100.00
0.045	110.93	100.00
0.050	106.75	99.63
0.055	102.76	98.08
0.060	98.97	95.85
0.065	95.36	95.83
0.070	91.92	90.48
0.075	88.65	87.60
0.080	85.52	84.84

Comment: Note that for low spot rates the price–yield curve for the callable bond becomes relatively flat. This reflects the negative convexity or price compression discussed in chapter 4.

CHAPTER 10

2.

a.

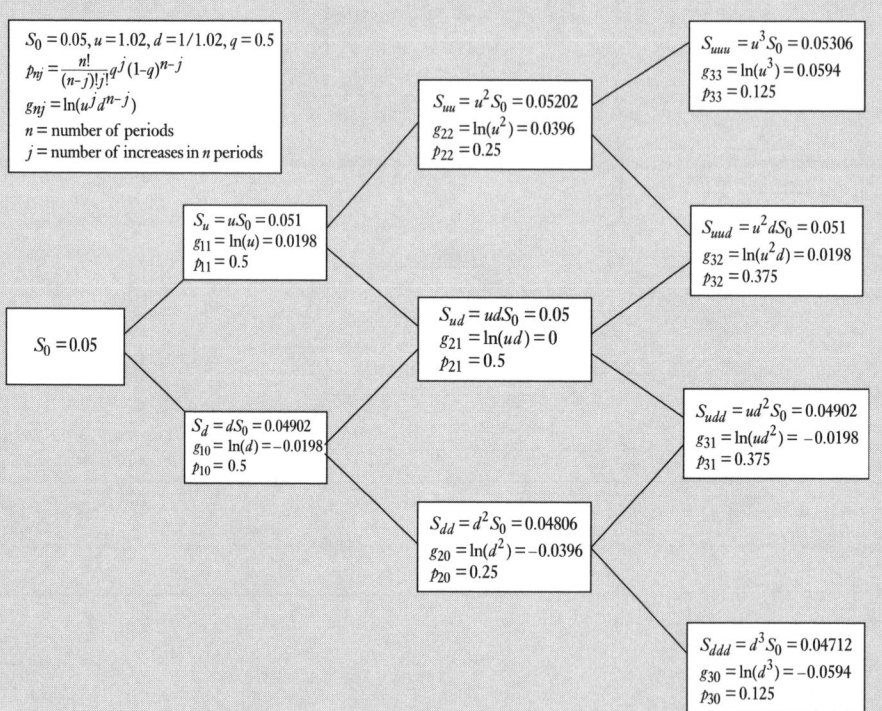

$S_0 = 0.05, u = 1.02, d = 1/1.02, q = 0.5$
$p_{nj} = \dfrac{n!}{(n-j)!j!} q^j (1-q)^{n-j}$
$g_{nj} = \ln(u^j d^{n-j})$
n = number of periods
j = number of increases in n periods

$S_{uuu} = u^3 S_0 = 0.05306$
$g_{33} = \ln(u^3) = 0.0594$
$p_{33} = 0.125$

$S_{uu} = u^2 S_0 = 0.05202$
$g_{22} = \ln(u^2) = 0.0396$
$p_{22} = 0.25$

$S_u = uS_0 = 0.051$
$g_{11} = \ln(u) = 0.0198$
$p_{11} = 0.5$

$S_{uud} = u^2 d S_0 = 0.051$
$g_{32} = \ln(u^2 d) = 0.0198$
$p_{32} = 0.375$

$S_0 = 0.05$

$S_{ud} = udS_0 = 0.05$
$g_{21} = \ln(ud) = 0$
$p_{21} = 0.5$

$S_d = dS_0 = 0.04902$
$g_{10} = \ln(d) = -0.0198$
$p_{10} = 0.5$

$S_{udd} = ud^2 S_0 = 0.04902$
$g_{31} = \ln(ud^2) = -0.0198$
$p_{31} = 0.375$

$S_{dd} = d^2 S_0 = 0.04806$
$g_{20} = \ln(d^2) = -0.0396$
$p_{20} = 0.25$

$S_{ddd} = d^3 S_0 = 0.04712$
$g_{30} = \ln(d^3) = -0.0594$
$p_{30} = 0.125$

b. $n = 1$: $E(r_1) = 0$, $V(r_1) = 0.000392$; $n = 2$: $E(r_2) = 0$, $V(r_2) = 0.000784$; $n = 3$: $E(r_3) = 0$, $V(r_3) = 0.001176$.

d. Suppose the estimated mean and variance for a period equal in length to $n = 3$ periods were $\mu_e = 0$ and $V_e = 0.001176$. Substituting these values into the formulas for u and d, we obtain $u = 1.02$ and $d = 1/1.02$.

5.

a. The logarithmic return is $g_n = \ln(S_T/S_0)$. Given the distribution of spot rates, the parameter values are $\mu_e = E(g_n) = 0.008952$ and $V_e = 0.002017$.

b. Since the distribution is for future spot rates after four months, the parameter values in (a) reflect average logarithmic returns for a 4-month period. To annualize the parameters, one needs to multiply each by 3. Doing this yields: $\mu_e^A = 3(0.008952) = 0.026856$ and $V_e^A = 3(0.002017) = 0.006051$.

c.

Length	h	u	d
One month	1/12	1.025001	0.97999
One week	1/52	1.011368	0.98978
One day	1/360	1.004183	0.99598

d.

Length	n	u	d
One month	1/12	1.02271	0.97780
One week	1/52	1.01084	0.98927
One day	1/360	1.00411	0.99591

There is very little difference between the u and d values with the mean of 0.026856 and with a mean of zero when $n = 360$. This is consistent with the equations for u and d that show that as n gets large the impact of the mean on u and d is small. Thus for large n the mean is not important in estimating u and d.

6.

a. The average logarithmic return is zero and the variance is 0.0057027.
b. The annualized mean and variance are $\mu_e^A = 4$ $\mu_e^q = 4(0) = 0$ and $V_e^A = 4$ $V_e^q = 4(0.0057027) = 0.0228108$.
c.

Length of period	u	d
Quarter: $h = 1/4$	1.078441	0.927265
Month: $h = 1/12$	1.044564	0.957337
Week: $h = 1/52$	1.021165	0.979273
Day: $h = 1/360$	1.007992	0.992071

7. Option-free bond: $B = 99.50$; callable bond: $B^C = 98.21$.

8. a. 98.15. b. 97.75. c. 100.47.

10. a. Given $\sigma = 0.10$, the variability condition governing the upper and lower rates is

$$S_u = S_d e^{2\sqrt{hV_e}}$$

$$S_u = S_d e^{2\sigma} = S_d e^{2(0.10)}$$

Given the variability condition, the tree is generated by solving for the S_d value that makes the value of a two-period zero-discount bond obtained from the tree equal to its current equilibrium price. Given the spot rate on a two-period bond of $y_2 = 0.0804$, this requires solving for the S_d value where:

$$\frac{1}{(1.0804)^2} = \frac{0.5[1/(1+S_d e^{2(0.10)})] + 0.5[1/(1+S_d)]}{1.07}$$

Solving the above equation for S_d yields a rate of 8.148%. At $S_d = 8.148\%$, S_u is equal to 9.952%. A one-period binomial tree with upper and lower spot rate in period 1 of $S_d = 8.148\%$ and $S_u = 9.9952\%$ yields a price for a two-period zero-coupon bond with a face value of \$1 of 0.857 – the same value as the equilibrium price.

b. Both S_u and S_d are greater than the current rate of 7%. This implies that we have calibrated the tree to a positively sloped yield curve.

c. Using the tree, the price of a two-period, 10.5% coupon bond is 104.5.

d. The equilibrium price on a two-period, 10.5% coupon bond is 104.5 – the same as the price obtained using the calibrated binomial tree:

$$B_2^M = \frac{10.50}{1.07} + \frac{110.50}{(1.0804)^2} = 104.5$$

This illustrates that one of the features of a calibrated binomial tree is that it yields a value on an option-free bond that is equal to the bond's equilibrium price.

e. Using the tree, the price of a two-period, 10.5% coupon bond callable at CP = 101 is 103.97.

12. a. Given $\sigma = 0.10$, the variability condition governing the upper and lower rates is

$$S_u = S_d e^{2\sqrt{hV_e}}$$
$$S_u = S_d e^{2\sigma} = S_d e^{2(0.10)}$$

Given the variability condition, the tree is generated by first solving for the S_d value that makes the value of a 2-year zero-discount bond obtained from the tree equal to its current equilibrium price of 0.857 $(= 1/(1.0804)^2)$:

$$\frac{1}{(1.0804)^2} = \frac{0.5[1/(1+S_d e^{2(0.10)})] + 0.5[1/(1+S_d)]}{1.07}$$

Solving the above equation for S_d yields a rate of 8.148%. Thus, at $S_d = 8.148\%$, S_u is equal to 9.952% and the binomial tree yields a bond price of 0.857 for the two-period zero-coupon bond with $F = 1$.

Given the variability condition, $S_d = 8.148\%$, and $S_u = 9.952\%$, the spot rates for period 2 are next found by solving for the S_{dd} value that makes the value of a 3-year zero-discount bond obtained from the tree equal to its current equilibrium price of 0.77113 $(= 1/(1.0904952)^3)$. The S_{dd} value that satisfies the above equation can be found iteratively (or take the hint); in this case, S_{dd} is 9.06%. Given $S_{dd} = 9.06\%$, by the variability condition S_{ud} is 11.066% and S_{uu} is 13.516%. This tree yields a price for a three-period zero-coupon bond with a face value of \$1 of 0.77113 – the same value as the equilibrium price.

b. Using the tree, the price of a three-period, 10.5% coupon bond is 104.02.

c. The equilibrium price on a three-period, 10.5% coupon bond is 104.02 – the same as the price obtained using the calibrated binomial tree.

d. Using the tree, the price of a three-period, 10.5% coupon bond callable at $CP = 101$ is 103.30.

e. Option-adjusted spread is 0.2772%.

14. If the market price is equal to 103.30 (the binomial value using the calibration model), then the option spread, k, is equal to zero. This reflects the fact that we have calibrated the tree to the yield curve and have considered all of the possibilities. If the market price is 102.80, the option-adjusted spread is 1%.

16. a. 1,000. b. The value of the bond's call feature is $208.19. c. The price callable bond is worth $791.81.

17. a. 1,000. b. The value of the bond's put feature is $28.56. c. The value of a putable bond is 1,028.56.

CHAPTER 11

1.

Item	Month 1	Month 2
Balance	100,000,000	99,907,884
Interest	666,667	666,053
P	733,765	733,581
Scheduled principal	67,098	67,528
CPR	0.003	0.006
SMM	0.0002503	0.0005014
Prepaid principal	25,018	50,058
Total principal	92,116	117,586
Cash flow	758,782	783,639

2. a.

Item	Month 1	Month 2
Balance	100,000,000	99,907,884
Interest	583,333	582,796
P	733,765	733,581
Scheduled principal	67,098	67,528
CPR	0.003	0.006
SMM	0.0002503	0.0005014
Prepaid principal	25,018	50,058
Total principal	92,116	117,586
Cash flow	675,449	700,382

b. The monthly fees on the MBS issue are equal to $0.08333\% = (8\% - 7\%)/12$ of the monthly balance. In the first month this is $83,333 and in the second month it is $83,257.

3. c.

Item	Month 1
Balance	50,000,000
Interest	354,167
P	633,379
Scheduled principal	258,379
CPR	0.004
SMM	0.000333946
Prepaid principal	16,611
Total principal	274,990
Cash flow	629,157

13.

Period: month	Collateral: balance	Collateral: interest	Collateral: scheduled principal	Collateral: prepaid principal	Collateral: total principal	Stripped PO: cash flow	Stripped IO: cash flow
1	100,000,000	625,000	67,098	25,018	92,116	92,116	625,000
2	99,907,884	624,424	67,528	50,058	117,586	117,586	624,424

14.

a.

Month	Collateral: balance	Collateral: interest	Collateral: principal	A Balance	A Interest	A Principal	B Balance	B Principal	B Interest
1	100,000,000	625,000	92,116	50,000,000	312,500	92,116	50,000,000	0	312,500
92	50,324,347	314,527	460,885	324,347	2,027	324,347	50,000,000	136,538	312,500
93	49,863,462	311,647	457,196	0	0	0	49,863,462	457,196	311,647

b.

- The first month interest for Tranche A = $(0.07/12)(\$50,000,000) = \$291,667$.
- The first month interest for Tranche B = $(0.065/12)(\$50,000,000) = \$270,833$.
- The first month cash flow on the notional principal is $62,500$: $((0.075-0.07)/12) \times (\$50,000,000) + ((0.075-0.065)/12)(\$50,000,000) = \$62,500$.
- The quoted principal on the notional principal tranche is $10,000,000$: $[(0.075-0.07) \times (\$50,000,000) + (0.075-0.065)(\$50,000,000)]/0.075 = \$10,000,000$.

16.

Month	Collateral: balance	Collateral: interest	Collateral: principal	PAC: low PSA principal	PAC: high PSA principal	PAC: minimum principal	Support: principal
1	100,000,000	625,000	92,116	83,769	117,202	83,769	8,347

20.

Paths:

Period	Path 1	Path 2	Path 3	Path 4
0	6.0000%	6.0000%	6.0000%	6.0000%
1	5.4545%	5.4545%	6.6000%	6.6000%
2	4.9587% balloon	6.0000% balloon	6.0000% balloon	7.2600% balloon

Note: With the balloon payment in period 2, path 1 and path 2 have the same cash flow, and path 3 and path 4 have the same cash flow.

Cash flows: paths 1 and 2: $CF_1 = \$335,223$, $CF_2 = \$804,359$; paths 3 and 4: $CF_1 = \$195,578$, $CF_2 = \$955,176$.

Discount rates: paths 1 and 2: $z_{10} = 0.08$, $z_{20} = 0.0773$; paths 3 and 4: $z_{10} = 0.08$, $z_{20} = 0.083$.

Path values and theoretical value: path $1 = 1,003,461$; path $2 = 1,003,461$; path $3 = 995,470$; path $4 = 995,470$; theoretical value $= 999,466$.

22.

Discount rate/PSA	50	150
	Value	Value
5%	$57,565,779	$55,167,657
6%	$52,884,127	$52,005,608
7%	$48,833,080	$49,174,840
8%	$45,306,641	$46,629,042
Average life	14.28	8.74

27. b.

	Collateral	PAC	Support
PSA	Average life	Average life	Average life
50	14.28	7.48	20.86
100	10.98	6.60	18.89
150	8.74	6.60	12.59
200	7.16	6.60	8.17
250	6.01	6.60	4.96
300	5.16	6.60	2.58
350	4.51	5.97	2.39

CHAPTER 12

6.

(1) Contract	(2) IMM index	(3) f_0	(4) Implied YTM
March	93.764	$984,410	0.065
June	93.3092	$983,273	0.07
September	91.8607	$979,652	0.086

7.

LIBOR at expiration (%)	Settlement price $f_t = [(100 - \text{LIBOR} (0.025))/100](\$1\text{m})$	Short futures profit $[\$986,250 - f_t]$	Long futures profit $[f_T - \$986,250]$
4.75	988,125	−1,875	1,875
5.00	987,500	−1,250	1,250
5.25	986,875	−625	625
5.50	986,250	0	0
5.75	985,625	625	−625
6.00	985,000	1,250	−1,250
6.25	984,375	1,875	−1,875

8. Loss of $840.

9. 112.50 per $100 face value.

10. 1.875 per $100 face value.

12.

LIBOR	Long FRA agreement	Short FRA agreement
0.04	−48,833	48,833
0.045	−24,387	24,387
0.05	0	0
0.055	24,328	−24,328
0.06	48,596	−48,596

15. a. $49,375.
    b. and c.

Date	R_D	Futures price	Initial margin	Value of equity account $M_0 +$ (futures price − 987,500)	Deposit required on maintenance margin	Value of equity account with deposits
Mar 1	5.0	987,500	49,375	49,375	0	49,375
Mar 2	5.1	987,250	49,375	49,125	250	49,375
Mar 3	5.2	987,000	49,375	48,875	250	49,375
Mar 4	5.0	987,500	49,375	49,375	0	49,875
Mar 5	4.8	988,000	49,375	49,875	0	50,375
Mar 8	4.7	988,250	49,375	50,125	0	50,625
Mar 9	5.0	987,500	49,375	49,375	0	49,875

16. a. Ms Hunter needs to go short in ten September T-bill futures contracts at $f_0 = \$985,000$.
    b. At delivery, Ms Hunter closes the futures contracts at $f_T = S_T$ and sells the ten T-bills on the spot market at S_T. Her hedged revenue is $9.85m regardless of rates.

17. a. Ms Hunter needs to go long in ten September T-bill futures contracts at $f_0 = \$987,500$.
    b. At delivery, Ms Hunter closes the futures contracts at $f_T = S_T$ and buys ten T-bills on the spot market at S_T. Her hedged cost is $9.875m.

18. a. FRA terms: (1) FRA would mature in two months (T) and would be written on a 90-day (three-month) LIBOR $T \times (T + M) = 2 \times 5$ agreement; (2) NP = $10m; (3) Contract rate = $R_k = 5.5\%$; (4) Day-count convention = 90/365; (5) Cagle would take the short

position on the FRA, receiving the payoff from Sun National if the LIBOR were less than $R_k = 5.5\%$; (6) Sun National would take the long position on the FRA, receiving the payoff from Cagle if the LIBOR were greater than $R_k = 5.5\%$.

b. Cagle's and Sun National's payoffs:

LIBOR	Sun National payoff	Cagle payoff
0.0500	−12,179	12,179
0.0525	−6,086	6,086
0.0550	0	0
0.0575	6,078	−6,078
0.0600	12,149	−12,149

c. Cash flows = $10,135,616; Hedged rate = 5.5%.

19.
a. Cagle's position would be equivalent to a long position in ten Eurodollar futures at a futures price of $100 - (5.5\% (0.25)) = 98.625$ per $100 face value. If the LIBOR were 5% at expiration, then the settlement price would be $S_T = 98.75$ and Cagle's cash flow would be $12,500:

$$10 \left[\frac{f_0 - S_T}{100} \right] (\$1m) = 10 \left[\frac{98.75 - 98.625}{100} \right] (\$1m) = \$12,500$$

At 5%, the present value of $12,500 is $12,500/(1 + (0.05(90/365))) = \$12,348$, which is approximately equal to the value of the short FRA position. In contrast, if the LIBOR were 6%, then the settlement price would be $S_T = 98.5$ and Cagle's cash flow would be −$12,500. At 6%, the present value of −$12,500 is −$12,500/(1 + (0.06(90/ 365))) = −$12,318$, which is approximately equal to the value of the short FRA position.

b. Sun National's position would be equivalent to a short position in ten Eurodollar futures at a futures price of $100 - (5.5\%(0.25)) = 98.625$ per $100 face value. If the LIBOR were 5% at expiration, then the settlement price would be $S_T = 98.75$ and Sun National's cash flow would be −$12,500. At 5%, the present value of −$12,500 is −$12,500/ (1 + (0.05(90/365))) = −$12,348$, which is approximately equal to the value of the long FRA position. In contrast, if LIBOR were 6%, then the settlement price would be $S_T = 98.5$ and Sun's cash flow would be $12,500. At 6%, the present value of $12,500 is $12,500/(1 + (0.06(90/365))) = \$12,318$, which is approximately equal to the value of the long FRA position.

c. To hedge, Sun National would need to go long in ten Eurodollar futures. With the hedge, Sun National's net position (Eurodollar + FRA) would be no more than $351 at the possible rates at expiration of 5%, 5.25%, 5.5%, 5.75%, and 6%.

LIBOR	Sun National FRA payoff	Eurodollar settlement price: $S_T = 100 - LIBOR(0.25)$	Cash flow from Eurodollar futures $(10)([S_T-98.625]/100)(\$1m)$	Net position Eurodollar + FRA
0.0500	−12,179	98.7500	12,500.0000	321
0.0525	−6,086	98.6875	6,250.0000	164
0.0550	0	98.6250	0.0000	0
0.0575	6,078	98.5625	−6,250.0000	−172
0.0600	12,149	98.5000	−12,500.0000	−351

21. Short-answer questions: (1) The introduction of financial futures. (2) Cross-hedge. (3) Quality and quantity risk. (4) $4,750. (5) Arbitrageurs. (6) Open interest. (7) Through locals: scalpers, day traders, and position traders. (8) Dual trading. (9) $980,000. (10) 7.34%. (11) 98.75. (12) The Eurodollar contracts have cash settlement at delivery while T-bill contracts call for actual delivery. (13) $2,500. (14) 6.52%.

CHAPTER 13

1. a. 7.338%; b. 9.1603 long contracts; c. At 6.5%: $S_T = f_T = 984,422$, futures profit $= 17,606$, number of T-bills purchased $= 9.1603$, and rate from investment of $9m $= 7.338%$. At 8.5%: $S_T = f_T = 979,866$, futures profit $= -24,128$, number of T-bills purchased $= 9.1603$, and rate from investment of $9m $= 7.338%$.

2. a. $f_0 = 980,000$, CD debt in September $= 20,394,782$, $n_f = 20.811$ short contracts.

   b.

LIBOR (R)	0.075	0.09
(1) Spot 90-day CD price and closing Eurodollar futures price: $S_T = f_T = \$1m/(1+R)^{90/365}$	$982,326 −$48,406	$978,975 $21,331
(2) Futures profit: $\pi_f = n_f[f_0 - f_T] = 20.811[\$980,000 - f_T]$		
(3) Debt on 1st CD: $\$20m(1.0825)^{90/365}$	$20,394,782	$20,394,782
(4) Total funds to finance for next 90 days: Row 3−Row 2	$20,443,188	$20,373,451
(5) Debt at end of the next 90 days: [Row 4]$(1+R)^{90/365}$	$20,811,000	$20,811,000
(6) Rate paid for 180-day period: [Row (5)/$20,000,000]$^{365/180}-1$	8.394%	8.394%

3.

   a. Go short in 46.46 T-bill futures contracts.
   b. $f_T = \$975,000, \pi_f = \$116,150$, Patton loan $= \$15,883,850$, debt at maturity $= \$17,226,033$, and hedged rate $= 0.10415$.
   c. $f_T = \$980,000, \pi_f = -\$116,150$, Patton loan $= \$16,116,150$, debt at maturity $= \$17,243,798$, hedged rate $= 0.10568$.

4. a. To hedge his June bond portfolio purchase, Mr Slife would go long in 87 T-bond contracts.
   b. Portfolio cost $= \$10,000,000(1.04) = \$10,400,000$; futures profit $= 87[\$85,000 - \$80,500] = \$391,500$; net cost $= \$10,400,000 - \$391,500 = \$10,008,500$.

5. a. To hedge his June bond portfolio purchase, Mr Slife would go short in 87 T-bond contracts.

   b. Portfolio value $= \$10,000,000(0.96) = \$9,600,000$; futures profit $= 87[\$80,500-\$76,000] = \$391,500$; revenue $= \$9,600,000 + \$391,500 = \$9,991,500$.

6. a. To obtain a synthetic fixed-rate loan, Roberts would obtain the floating-rate loan and go short in a Eurodollar strip: short in 15 3/20 Eurodollar futures contracts and short in 15 6/20 contracts. The locked-in rates are 10% for the 3/20 period and 9% for the 6/20 period; the synthetic fixed rate $= 9.5\%$.

   b.

(1) Date	(2) LIBOR	(3) Futures settlement price: $f_T = 100 -$ LIBOR(0.25)	(4) Futures profit[***] profit $= [(f_0 - f_T)/100](\$1m)(15)$	(5) Quarterly interest $0.25[(LIBOR\% + 1)/100](\$15m)$	(6) Hedged debt Col. 5 − Col. 4	(7) Hedged rate: [(4)(Col. 6)]/ $\$15m$
Dec 20	0.085			356,250	356,250	0.095
Mar 20	0.1	97.5	37,500	412,500	375,000	0.1
Jun 20	0.09	97.75	37,500	375,000	337,500	0.09

[***] $f_0(3/20) = 100 - 9(0.25) = 97.75$, $f_0(6/20) = 100 - 8(0.25) = 98$

7. a. To obtain a synthetic fixed-rate investment, ABC could invest in the floating-rate loan and go long in 15 Eurodollar strips: long 3/20, 6/20, and 9/20 Eurodollar futures contract. Locked-in rates: 3/20 rate $= 10\%$, 6/20 rate $= 9\%$, and 9/20 rate $= 8.5\%$; synthetic fixed rate $= 9.12364\%$.

   b.

(1) Date	(2) LIBOR	(3) Futures settlement price: $f_T = 100 -$ LIBOR(0.25)	(4) Futures profit[***] profit $= [(f_T - f_0)/100](\$1m)(15)$	(5) Quarterly interest $0.25[(LIBOR + 0.01)]$ $(\$15m)$	(6) Hedged return Col. 5 + Col. 4	(7) Hedged rate [(4)(Col. 6)]/ $\$15m$
Dec 20	0.080			337,500	337,500	0.09
Mar 20	0.095	97.625	−18,750	393,750	375,000	0.1
Jun 20	0.090	97.75	−37,500	375,000	337,500	0.09
Sep 20	0.070	98.25	18,750	300,000	318,750	0.085

[***] $f_0(3/20) = 100 - 9(0.25) = 97.75$, $f_0(6/20) = 100 - 8(0.25) = 98$, $f_0(9/20) = 100 - 7.5(0.25) = 98.125$

9. a. $f_0 = 98.7246$ per 100 face value; $YTM_f = 5.283\%$.

   b. Create a synthetic 30-day investment by buying a 121-day bill and then going short at 98.8 in the T-bill futures contract expiring in 30 days. Her return would be 6.13%, compared to 5.15% from the 30-day spot T-bill.

   c. A money manager currently holding 121-day T-bills could obtain an arbitrage by selling the bills for 98.318 and investing the proceeds at 5.15% for 30 days, then going long in the T-bill futures contract expiring in 30 days. Thirty days later the manager would receive 98.7246 from the investment and would pay 98 on the futures to reacquire the bills for a cash flow of 0.7246 per $100 par.

10. a.

(1) Contract	(2) Days to expiration	(3) IMM index	(4) f_0	(5) Implied YTM
March	91	93.764	$984,410	0.065
June	182	93.3092	$983,273	0.070
September	273	91.8607	$979,652	0.086

   b. The implied 91-day repo rate is 6%.

   c. Given a 91-day repo rate of 6%, the price on a 91-day spot T-bill with a face value of $1m would be $985,578 = $1,000,000/(1.06)^{91/365}$.

   d. Given the price of $970,223 on the spot 182 T-bill, the equilibrium price on the March contract would be $981,513 given a repo rate of 4.75%. If the IMM index price were 93.764, then the March futures would be trading at $984,410. In this case, the T-bill futures would be overpriced. To exploit this, an arbitrageur would short the March futures contract and borrow $970,223 at 4.75% for 91 days to finance the purchase of a 182-day T-bill. At expiration (91 days later), the arbitrageur would sell the T-bill on the futures contract for $f_0^m = \$984,410$, and repay the debt of $981,513 = $970,223 \times (1.0475)^{91/365}$, for a positive cash flow of $2,897(= \$984,410 - \$981,513)$.

11. a. The YTM implied on the September contract is 8.44% and the YTM implied on the December contract is 7.34%. The YTM implied on a 182-day T-bill investment is, therefore, 7.89%.

   b. To lock in a 7.89% rate on a 182-day investment to be made at the September expiration date, McDonald would need to go long in 3.0612 September contracts and 3.0534 December contracts.

   c. At the September expiration, spot 91-day T-bills would be trading at $S(91) = \$980,995$, spot 182-day bills would be priced at $S(182) = \$964,581$, and the futures price on the December contract would be $f(\text{Dec}) = \$983,268$. Closing the September and December contracts at $S(91) = f_T$ and $f(\text{Dec})$, respectively, would result in a profit of $5,391. This profit and $3m cash inflow would allow McDonald to buy 3.11575 182-day T-bills, which for a $3 investment would yield a rate of 7.89%.

12. a. (i) The implied forward rate on a 91-day investment made 91 days from now ($R_I(91, 91)$) is 6.5%. To attain $R_I(91, 91) = 0.065$, you would short the 91-day T-bill at $S_0(91) = 98.55777$, then buy $S_0(182)/S_0(91) = 1.015826$ 182-day T-bills at $S(182) = 97.02231$. Ninety-one days later you would pay $100 to cover the short position, then 91 days after that you would receive $(1.015826)(\$100) = \$101.5826$ from your initial 182-day T-bill, yielding an annualized rate of return for the 91-day period of 6.5%. (ii) The implied forward rate on a 91-day investment made 182 days from the present ($R_I(91, 182)$) is 7%. To attain $R_I(91, 182) = 0.07$, you would short the 182-day T-bill at $S_0(182) = \$97.0223$, then buy $S_0(182)/S_0(273) = \$97.0223/95.3990 = 1.017016$ 273-day T-bills. One hundred and eighty-two days later you would pay $100 to cover the short position, then 91 days after that you would receive $1.017016(\$100) = \$101.7016$ from your initial 273-day T-bill, yielding an annualized return for the 91-day period of 7%.

   b. The futures price on a 91-day T-bill futures contract is $984,422 and the IMM index quote on the futures contract is 93.769; the futures price on the 182-day contract is $983,273 and the IMM index price is 93.309.

13. a. The implied YTMs on the March, June, and September contracts are 6.5%, 7%, and 8.6%, respectively.
   b. To lock in a 1-year rate from a series of investments in 91-day T-bills the fund would have to go long in March, June, and September T-bill futures contracts. Given a spot rate of 6% and the implied futures rates, the 1-year locked-in rate is 7%.
   c. The number of long contracts: March $n_f = 10.307$, June $n_f = 10.48223$, and September $n_f = 10.7$.
   d. (i) At a spot T-bill rate of 6% at the March expiration day, the spot T-bill and expiring March futures contract price would be trading at $985,578. At this price, the 10.307 March futures contracts would generate a profit of $12,039, and the fund would be able to buy 10.307 91-day T-bills:

   $$\text{Futures profit} = 10.307(\$985,578 - \$984,410) = \$12,039.$$
   $$\text{Number of T-bills} = \frac{\$10,146,333 + \$12,039}{\$985,578} = 10.307.$$

   (ii) At a spot rate of 7.25% at the June expiration, the spot T-bill price and expiring June futures price would be $982,701. At this price, closing the 10.48223 June contracts would result in a loss of $5,996 and the fund would be able to buy only 10.4823 91-day T-bills:

   $$\text{Futures profit} = 10.48223(\$982,701 - \$983,273) = -\$5,996.$$
   $$\text{Number of T-bills} = \frac{\$10,307,000 - \$5,996}{\$982,701} = 10.4823.$$

   (iii) At a spot rate of 8% at the September expiration, the spot T-bill price and expiring September futures price would be $980,995. At this price, the 10.7 September futures contracts would generate a profit of $14,370, and the fund would be able to buy 10.7 T-bills:

   $$\text{Futures profit} = 10.7(\$980,995 - \$979,652) = \$14,370.$$
   $$\text{Number of T-bills} = \frac{\$10,482,300 + \$14,370}{\$980,995} = 10.7.$$

   e. Yes, with the hedge, the fund yields an average annual rate of 7%; without the hedge the rate would be 6.79%.

15. a. 0.847084; b. 0.8234067; c. 1.214872; d. 1.177049.

16. Bond 3 has the lowest net costs (cost of bond minus revenue from selling on the futures contract) of 2.65 per 100 face value.

17. The full price of the cheapest-to-deliver bond is $108 + (30/182)(4) = 108.66$ per $100 face value and the present value of the next coupon is $4/(1.05)^{152/365} = 3.92$. The equilibrium T-bond futures is 107.42:

$$f_0 = [S_0 - \text{PV}(C)](1 + R)^T$$
$$f_0 = [108.66 - 3.92](1.05)^{180/365} = 107.29$$

The quoted price is stated net of accrued interest. If it were written on the 8% bond, then at delivery on the futures contract (180 days), there would be 28 days of accrued interest on the T-bond (180-152). Given the 183-day coupon period, the accrued interest would be $(28/183)(4) = 0.61$. The quoted futures price on the deliverable bond would therefore be $107.29 - 0.61 = 106.68$. With a conversion factor of 1.21, the quoted equilibrium price would be $106.68/1.21 = 88.16$.

20. Short-answer questions: (1) $980,000. (2) LIBOR. (3) 7.34%. (4) 95. (5) Wild-card option clause. (6) $988,296. (7) $985,386. (8) Borrow $980,896 at 5.75% for 30 days, buy 161-day T-bill, and go short in the T-bill futures contract. (9) 11.9%. (10) 5.75%. (11) 6.08%. (12) 11.41%. (13) 5.16. (14) 8.6%. (15) NOB strategy. (16) 7.75%. (17) −$12,500. (18) $200,000. (19) 5.175%. (20) 30. (21) $9,613,799. (22) Eurodollar contracts have cash settlement at delivery while T-bill contracts call for actual delivery. (23) 2,500. (24) TED spread.

CHAPTER 14

1.
   a. 8,000, 3,000, −2,000, 3,000, 8,000
   b. −8,000, −3,000, 2,000, −3,000, −8,000
   c. −10,000, −5,000, 0, 5,000, 10,000
   d. 10,000, 5,000, 0, −5,000, −10,000
   e. 17,000, 7,000, −3,000, 2,000, 7,000
   f. −7,000, −2,000, 3,000, −7,000, −17,000

2.
   a. −500, −500, −500, 500, 500, 500
   b. 500, 500, 500, −500, −500, −500

3.
   a. −250, −250, −250, 0, 250, 500, 750, 500, 250, 0, −250, −250, −250
   b. 250, 250, 250, 0, −250, −500, −750, −500, −250, 0, 250, 250, 250

4.
   a. 1,250, 0, −1,250, −2,500, −1,250, 0, 1,250
   b. −1,250, 0, 1,250, 2,500, 1,250, 0, −1,250
   c. −3,750, −2,500, −1,250, 0, 1,250, 2,500, 3,750
   d. 3,750, 2,500, 1,250, 0, −1,250, −2,500, −3,750

5.
   a. −25,000, −25,000, −25,000, −25,000, −25,000, 0, 25,000, 50,000, 75,000
   b. 75,000, 50,000, 25,000, 0, −25,000, −25,000, −25,000, −25,000, −25,000
   c. 25,000, 25,000, 25,000, 25,000, 25,000, 0, −25,000, −50,000, −75,000
   d. −75,000, −50,000, −25,000, 0, 25,000, 25,000, 25,000, 25,000, 25,000

6. In this case the American call option is selling below its intrinsic value $(C_t < \text{Max}[f_T - X, 0] = \text{Max}[\$988,500 - \$987,500, \ 0] = \$1,000)$. An arbitrage opportunity exists by buying the call for $900, exercising the futures call to obtain a long futures position at $988,500 and a margin account of $1,000, and then closing the futures position at $988,500. By implementing this strategy, an arbitrageur would receive a positive cash flow of $100. However, as arbitrageurs try to exploit this situation they will increase the price of the call as they try to go long in the option. The call price will increase until it is at least equal to the intrinsic value of $1,000; at that price the arbitrage opportunity disappears. Note that this

strategy requires an immediate exercising of the call. Thus, the strategy and condition applies only to an American call option and not European in which exercise can only occur at expiration.

7. In this case the American put option is selling below its intrinsic value ($P_t <$ Max[$X - f_T$, 0] = Max[\$987,500 − \$986,500, 0] = \$1,000). An arbitrage opportunity exists by buying the put for \$900, exercising the futures put to obtain a short futures position at \$986,500 and a margin account of \$1,000, and then closing the futures position at \$986,500. By implementing this strategy, an arbitrageur would receive a positive cash flow of \$100. However, as arbitrageurs try to exploit this situation they will increase the price of the put as they try to go long in the option. The put price will increase until it is at least equal to the intrinsic value of \$1,000; at that price the arbitrage opportunity disappears.

8. Options are derivative securities. They derive their values from the underlying asset. Thus, regardless of demand, the price of a call would increase if the price of the call's underlying security increased, and the price of a put would decrease if the price of the put's underlying security decreased.

12. Profit: −1,187.50, −1,187.50, −1,187.50, −187.50, 812.50, 1,812.50, and 2,812.50. Break-even price = 98.1875.

13. Profit: 2,218.75, 1,218.75, 218.75, −781.25, −781.25, −781.25, and −781.25. Break-even price = 96.21875.

14. Given a risk-free rate of 6.0154%, expiration of 0.25 per year, spot T-bond priced at 96, and a T-bond call priced at 1.1875, the price on the 97 T-bond put should be 0.78125 using put−call parity:

$$P_0 = PV(X) + C_0 - S_0$$
$$P_0 = \frac{97}{(1.060154)^{0.25}} + 1.1875 - 96 = 0.78125$$

15. a. Condition: $C_t \geq$ Max[PV($f_t - X$), 0]. This condition is violated if $C_t <$ Max[PV($f_t - X$), 0]. To exploit this, you would go long in the call, short in the futures at f_t, and short in a risk-free bond with a face value of $f_t - X$ and maturity equal to the option's expiration. This would result in an initial positive cash flow (CF$_0$), with no liabilities at expiration:

$$CF_0 = PV(f_t - X) - C_0 > 0$$

Closing position	$f_T < X$	$f_T = X$	$f_T > X$
Long call	0	0	$f_T - X$
Short bond	$-(f_t - X)$	$-(f_t - X)$	$-(f_t - X)$
Short futures	$f_t - f_T$	$f_t - f_T$	$f_t - f_T$
Net	$X - f_T > 0$	0	0

b. Condition: $P_t \geq$ Max[PV($X - f_t$), 0]. This condition is violated if $P_t <$ Max[PV($X - f_t$), 0]. To exploit this, you would go long in the futures put, long in the futures at f_t, and short in a risk-free bond with a face value of $X - f_t$ and maturity equal to the option's expiration. This would result in an initial positive cash flow (CF$_0$), with no liabilities at expiration:

$$CF_0 = PV(X - f_t) - P_0 > 0$$

Closing position	$f_T < X$	$f_T = X$	$f_T > X$
Long put	$X - f_T$	0	0
Short bond	$-(X - f_t)$	$-(X - f_t)$	$-(X - f_t)$
Long futures	$f_T - f_t$	$f_T - f_t$	$f_T - f_t$
Net	0	0	$f_T - X > 0$

c. Condition for American spot call option: $C_t \geq \text{Max}[(S_t - X), 0]$. This condition is violated if $C_t < \text{Max}[S_t - X, 0]$. To exploit this, an arbitrageur would buy the call, exercise the call to acquire the bond at X, then sell the bond in the market at S_t. This would result in a positive cash flow (CF_0) with no risk: $\text{CF}_0 = S_t - X - C_t > 0$.

d. Condition for American spot put option: $P_t \geq \text{Max}[(X - S_t), 0]$. This condition is violated if $P_t < \text{Max}[X - S_t, 0]$. To exploit this, an arbitrageur would buy the put, buy the bond in the market at S_t, and then exercise the put, selling the bond at X. This would result in a positive cash flow (CF_0) with no risk: $\text{CF}_0 = X - S_t - P_t > 0$.

e. Condition: Put–call futures parity for European option: $P_t - C_t = (X - f_t)/(1 + R_f)^T$. This condition is violated if $P_t - C_t < (X - f_t)/(1 + R_f)^T$. To exploit this, you would go long in the put, short in the call, long in the futures at f_t, and short in a risk-free bond with a face value of $X - f_t$ and maturity equal to the option's expiration. This would result in an initial positive cash flow (CF_0), with no liabilities at expiration:

$$\text{CF}_0 = \text{PV}(X - f_t) - P_t + C_t > 0$$

Closing position	$f_T < X$	$f_T = X$	$f_T > X$
Short futures call	0	0	$-(f_T - X)$
Long futures put	$X - f_T$	0	0
Short bond	$-(X - f_t)$	$-(X - f_t)$	$-(X - f_t)$
Long futures	$f_T - f_t$	$f_T - f_t$	$f_T - f_t$
Net	0	0	0

This condition is also violated if $P_t - C_t > (X - f_t)/(1 + R_f)^T$. To exploit this, you would go short in the put, long in the call, short in the futures at f_t, and long in a risk-free bond with a face value of $X - f_t$ and maturity equal to the option's expiration. This would result in an initial positive cash flow (CF_0), with no liabilities at expiration:

$$\text{CF}_0 = P_t - C_t - \text{PV}(X - f_t) > 0$$

Closing position	$f_T < X$	$f_T = X$	$f_T > X$
Long futures call	0	0	$f_T - X$
Short futures put	$-(X - f_T)$	0	0
Long bond	$X - f_t$	$X - f_t$	$X - f_t$
Short futures	$f_t - f_T$	$f_t - f_T$	$f_t - f_T$
Net	0	0	0

17. If a holder sells the option, she will receive a price that is equal to the intrinsic value plus the time value premium; if she exercises, though, her exercise value is only equal to the intrinsic value. Thus, by exercising instead of closing she loses the time value premium. Thus, an option holder in most cases should close instead of exercise. An exception

to the rule of closing instead of exercising would be a case in which the underlying security pays a coupon (or in the case of a stock, a dividend) that exceeds the time value premium.

18. Short-answer questions: (1) Limited profit and unlimited loss. (2) Open interest. (3) AMEX. (4) Upon exercise, the right to go long in a September T-bill futures contract at the current futures price, with the assigned writer paying the holder the difference between the current futures price and the exercise price: $f_t - X = f_t - \$980,000$. (5) Upon exercise, the right to go short in a September T-bill futures contract at the current futures price, with the assigned writer paying the holder the difference between the exercise price and the current futures price: $X - f_t = \$980,000 - f_t$. (6) Long position in a futures, long position in a put, and short position in a call. (7) The options are equivalent if the futures contract expires at the same time as the option contracts, if the carrying-cost model holds, and the options are European. (8) True. (9) A cap is a series of interest rate call options. They can be purchased by borrowers in order to place a cap on a floating-rate loan. (10) A floor is a series of interest rate put options. It can be purchased by an investor in order to place a floor on a floating-rate investment.

CHAPTER 15

1. a. $n_c = 9$, cost $= 11,250$.

   b.

(1) Spot discount rates R_D (%)	(2) Spot price = futures price at T ($)	(3) Call profit/loss ($)	(4) Hedged investment funds $9m + $ col. 3 ($)	(5) Number of bills Col. 4/col. 2	(6) YTM (%)
6.00	985,000	11,250	9,011,250	9.14848	6.78
6.25	984,375	5,625	9,005,625	9.14857	6.79
6.50	983,750	0	9,000,000	9.14867	6.79
7.00	982,500	−11,250	8,988,750	9.14885	6.80
7.50	981,250	−11,250	8,988,750	9.16051	7.35
8.00	980,000	−11,250	8,988,750	9.17219	7.90

Call profit $= 9[\text{Max}(f_T - \$982,500, 0)] - \$11,250$
YTM $= [(\text{Number of bills})(\$1m)/\$9m]^{365/91} - 1$

2.

(1) LIBOR	(2) Interest rate put payoff: $9m[\text{Max}[0.07 − LIBOR, 0](0.25)$	(3) Cost of the option at T $50,000	(4) Interest received on CD at its maturity (LIBOR)(0.25)($9,000,000)	(5) Total revenue at maturity Col. 2 + col. 4	(6) Annualized hedged rate 4[Col. 5/($9m + col. 3)]
0.060	22,500	50,000	135,000	157,500	0.06961326
0.065	11,250	50,000	146,250	157,500	0.06961326
0.070	0	50,000	157,500	157,500	0.06961326
0.075	0	50,000	168,750	168,750	0.074585635
0.080	0	50,000	180,000	180,000	0.079558011

Company's investment: $9m at LIBOR for 90 days (0.25 per year)
Interest rate put option: exercise rate $= 7\%$, reference rate $=$ LIBOR, NP $= \$9m$, time period $= 0.25$, cost of option $= \$50,000$, payable at T

3.

(1) LIBOR	(2) Interest rate call payoff: $16m[Max[LIBOR− 0.10, 0](0.75)	(3) Cost of the option at T	(4) Interest paid on loan at its maturity: (LIBOR + 150 BP)(0.75)($16m)	(5) Total cost at maturity Col. 4−col. 2	(6) Annualized hedged rate: (1/0.75)[col. 5/ ($16m−col. 3)]
0.080	0	75,000	1,140,000	1,140,000	0.0954
0.090	0	75,000	1,260,000	1,260,000	0.1055
0.100	0	75,000	1,380,000	1,380,000	0.1155
0.110	120,000	75,000	1,500,000	1,380,000	0.1155
0.115	180,000	75,000	1,560,000	1,380,000	0.1155
0.120	240,000	75,000	1,620,000	1,380,000	0.1155

Company's loan: $16m at LIBOR + 150 BP for 270 days (0.75 per year)
Interest rate call option: exercise rate = 10%, reference rate = LIBOR, NP = $16m, time period = 0.75
Cost of option = $75,000, payable at T.

4.

  a. The manager would pay $20,000 to a dealer for a T-bond put option giving her the right to sell twenty 15-year, 7% T-bonds at an exercise price of $105 per $100 face value (exercise value of $2,100,000) and expiration coinciding with the March T-bond sales date.

  b. The manager will exercise her option if T-bond prices are less than $X = 105$ and will sell her bonds in the market if prices are 105 or higher.

(1) Spot T-bond price per $100 face value	(2) YTM	(3) Revenue from selling 20 T-bonds by exercising put	(4) Revenue from selling the 20 T-bonds on spot market if put is not exercised	(5) Cost of the put	(6) Hedged revenue Col. 3 + col. 4
98	0.0721	2,100,000	0	20,000	2,100,000
99	0.0711	2,100,000	0	20,000	2,100,000
100	0.0700	2,100,000	0	20,000	2,100,000
101	0.0684	2,100,000	0	20,000	2,100,000
102	0.0679	2,100,000	0	20,000	2,100,000
103	0.0668	2,100,000	0	20,000	2,100,000
104	0.0658	2,100,000	0	20,000	2,100,000
105	0.0647	0	2,100,000	20,000	2,100,000
106	0.0637	0	2,120,000	20,000	2,120,000
107	0.0627	0	2,140,000	20,000	2,140,000
108	0.0617	0	2,160,000	20,000	2,160,000
109	0.0608	0	2,180,000	20,000	2,180,000
110	0.0598	0	2,200,000	20,000	2,200,000

T-bond: maturity = 15, coupon = 7%, face value = $100,000, number of T-bonds to sell = 20
OTC T-bond put: right to sell 20 T-bonds at $2,100,000 = (20)($105,000), cost of the option = $20,000

6.

a. Number of puts $= 20.811$, cost $= (2)(250)(20.811) = 10,405.50$.

b.

(1) LIBOR	(2) Spot and futures price	(3) Put profit	(4) Debt on Sept-issued CD	(5) Sept funds needed Col. 4−col. 3	(6) Dec debt obligation [Col. 5]$(1+$ LIBOR$)^{(90/360)}$	(7) Hedged rate for 180 days: [Col. 6/ $20m]$^{(360/180)}-1$
0.070	983,227.59	−10,405.50	20,400,319.63	20,410,725.13	20,758,901.99	0.0773
0.075	982,082.30	−10,405.50	20,400,319.63	20,410,725.13	20,783,110.67	0.0798
0.080	980,943.65	−10,405.50	20,400,319.63	20,410,725.13	20,807,235.04	0.0824
0.085	979,811.57	−6,484.18	20,400,319.63	20,406,803.80	20,827,273.67	0.0844
0.090	978,686.00	16,940.17	20,400,319.63	20,383,379.46	20,827,292.38	0.0844
0.095	977,566.86	40,230.58	20,400,319.63	20,360,089.04	20,827,311.04	0.0844
0.100	976,454.09	63,388.44	20,400,319.63	20,336,931.19	20,827,329.62	0.0844

Spot and futures price at $T = \$1m/(1 + \text{LIBOR})^{(90/360)}$
Put profit $= 20.811(\text{Max}(\$980,000 - \text{col. } 2, 0) - \$10,405.50$
Debt on June CD $= \$20m(1.0825)^{(90/360)}$

c. Terms of First American Bank's interest rate call:

- Exercise rate of 8.25%
- LIBOR reference rate
- Payoff at the maturity of the loan
- Payoff date is 90 days or 0.25 per year
- Notional principal of $\$20m(1.0825)^{(90/360)} = \$20,400,319.63$
- Expiration in 90 days at the maturity of the bank's September CD
- Cost of the caplet is $12,500 to be paid at payoff date.

d.

(1) LIBOR	(2) Interest rate call payoff	(3) Cost of caplet	(4) Sept debt on CD	(5) Sept funds needed Col. 4 + col. 3− col. 2	(6) Dec debt obligation [Col. 5]$(1+$ LIBOR$)^{(90/360)}$	(7) Hedged rate for 180 days: [Col. 6/ $20m]$^{(360/180)}-1$
0.070	0.00	12,500.00	20,400,319.63	20,412,819.63	20,761,032.22	0.078
0.075	0.00	12,500.00	20,400,319.63	20,412,819.63	20,785,243.38	0.080
0.080	0.00	12,500.00	20,400,319.63	20,412,819.63	20,809,370.23	0.083
0.085	12,750.20	12,500.00	20,400,319.63	20,400,069.43	20,820,400.53	0.084
0.090	38,250.60	12,500.00	20,400,319.63	20,374,569.03	20,818,290.08	0.084
0.095	63,751.00	12,500.00	20,400,319.63	20,349,068.63	20,816,037.72	0.083
0.100	89,251.40	12,500.00	20,400,319.63	20,323,568.23	20,813,644.44	0.083

Caplet payoff $= \$20,400,319.63(\text{Max}(\text{LIBOR} - 0.0825), 0)(0.25)$
Sept CD debt $=$ debt on June-issued CD $= \$20m(1.0825)^{(90/360)}$

7. a. To hedge his June bond portfolio purchase, Mr Slife would buy 59 T-bond futures put
   options for \$88,500.

$$n_p = \frac{\text{Dur}_S}{\text{Dur}_f} \frac{S_0}{X} \frac{(1 + \text{YTM}_f)^T}{(1 + \text{YTM}_S)^T}$$

$$= \frac{7}{9} \frac{\$10,000,000}{\$100,000} \frac{(1.055)^{15}}{(1.075)^{15}} = 59 \text{ puts}$$

$$\text{Cost} = (\$1,500)(59) = \$88,500$$

   b. With the bond portfolio selling at 96 of par, Mr Slife would sell the portfolio for
   \$9.6m: $(0.96)(\$10,000,000) = \$9,600,000$. Mr Slife, though, would realize a cash flow
   of \$236,000 from the T-bond futures position, leaving him with a revenue of
   \$9.836m.
   c. With the bond portfolio selling at 105 of par, Mr Slife would sell the portfolio for
   $(1.05)(\$10,000,000) = \$10,500,000$. Mr Slife's puts would be worthless, leaving him with
   a revenue of \$10.5m.

8.

(1) Date	(2) LIBOR	(3) Cap payoff on payment date: Max [LIBOR−0.095, 0] (\$15m)(0.25)	(4) Loan interest on payment date 0.25(LIBOR + 0.01)/ (\$15m)	(5) Hedged debt Col. 4−col. 3	(6) Hedged rate: [(4) (col. 5)]/ \$15m	(7) Unhedged rate: [(4) (col. 4)]/ \$15m
Dec 20	0.085					
Mar 20	0.100	0	356,250	356,250	0.095	0.095
Jun 20	0.090	18,750	412,500	393,750	0.105	0.110
Sep 20	0.090	0	375,000	375,000	0.100	0.100

10.

(1) Date	(2) LIBOR	(3) Interest on FRN on payment date (LIBOR + 150 BP) (0.25)(\$15m)	(4) Floor payoff on payment date: Max[0.07− LIBOR, 0](0.25) (\$15m)	(5) Hedged interest income: Col. 3 + col. 4	(6) Hedged rate: 4[Col. 5/ \$15m]	(7) Unhedged rate: LIBOR + 150 BP
Mar 20	0.075					
Jun 20	0.070	337,500	0	337,500	0.090	0.090
Sep 20	0.065	318,750	0	318,750	0.085	0.085
Dec 20	0.060	300,000	18,750	318,750	0.085	0.080
Mar 20		281,250	37,500	318,750	0.085	0.075

12.

a.

(1) Reset date	(2) Assumed LIBOR	(3) Interest paid on payment date (LIBOR + 150 BP) (0.25)($15m)	(4) Cap payoff on payment date Max[LIBOR−0.07, 0] (0.25)($15m)	(5) Hedged interest payment Col. 3− col. 4	(6) Hedged rate 4[col. 5/ $15m]	(7) Unhedged rate LIBOR + 150 BP
Mar 20	0.075					
Jun 20	0.080	337,500	0	337,500	0.090	0.090
Sep 20	0.090	356,250	37,500	318,750	0.085	0.095
Dec 20	0.080	393,750	75,000	318,750	0.085	0.105
Mar 20	0.070	356,250	37,500	318,750	0.085	0.095
Jun 20	0.065	318,750	0	318,750	0.085	0.085
Sep 20	0.060	300,000	0	300,000	0.080	0.080
Dec 20	0.055	281,250	0	281,250	0.075	0.075
Mar 20		262,500	0	262,500	0.070	0.070

b.

(1) Reset date	(2) Assumed LIBOR	(3) Interest paid on payment date (LIBOR + 150 BP) (0.25)($15m)	(4) Cap payoff on payment date Max[LIBOR−0.07, 0] (0.25)($15m)	(5) Floor payment on payment date Max[0.065−LIBOR, 0] (0.25)($15m)	(6) Collar-hedged interest payment Col. 3−col. 4+ col. 5	(7) Hedged rate 4[col. 6/ $15m]	(8) Unhedged rate LIBOR + 150 BP
Mar 20	0.075						
Jun 20	0.080	337,500			337,500	0.090	0.090
Sep 20	0.090	356,250	37,500	0	318,750	0.085	0.095
Dec 20	0.080	393,750	75,000	0	318,750	0.085	0.105
Mar 20	0.070	356,250	37,500	0	318,750	0.085	0.095
Jun 20	0.065	318,750	0	0	318,750	0.085	0.085
Sep 20	0.060	300,000	0	0	300,000	0.080	0.080
Dec 20	0.055	281,250	0	18,750	300,000	0.080	0.075
Mar 20		262,500	0	37,500	300,000	0.080	0.070

13.

a.

(1) Date	(2) LIBOR	(3) Interest paid on FRN on payment date (LIBOR + 150 BP)(0.25) ($15m)	(4) Cumulative interest	(5) Q-cap payoff on payment date If cum. int. > $700,000: Max [LIBOR−0.07, 0] (0.25)($15m)	(6) Hedged interest payment Col. 3−col. 5	(7) Hedged rate 4[col. 6/$15m]	(8) Unhedged rate: LIBOR + 150 BP
3/20/2004	0.075		337,500				
6/20/2004	0.080	337,500	693,750		337,500	0.090	0.090
9/20/2004	0.090	356,250	1,087,500	0	356,250	0.095	0.095
12/20/2004	0.080	393,750	1,443,750	75,000	318,750	0.085	0.105
3/20/2005	0.070	356,250	318,750	37,500	318,750	0.085	0.095
6/20/2005	0.080	318,750	675,000	0	318,750	0.085	0.085
9/20/2005	0.090	356,250	1,068,750	0	356,250	0.095	0.095
12/20/2005	0.100	393,750	1,500,000	75,000	318,750	0.085	0.105
3/20/2005		431,250		112,500	318,750	0.085	0.115

b.

(1) Date	(2) LIBOR	(3) Interest paid on FRN on payment date (LIBOR + 150 BP) (0.25)($15m)	(4) Cap payoff on payment date Max[LIBOR − 0.07, 0](0.25)($15m)	(5) Cap-hedged interest payment col. 3−col. 4	(6) Hedged rate 4[col. 6/ $15m]	(7) Unhedged rate LIBOR + 150 BP
3/20/2004	0.075					
6/20/2004	0.080	337,500		337,500	0.090	0.090
9/20/2004	0.090	356,250	37,500	318,750	0.085	0.095
12/20/2004	0.080	393,750	75,000	318,750	0.085	0.105
3/20/2005	0.070	356,250	37,500	318,750	0.085	0.095
6/20/2005	0.080	318,750	0	318,750	0.085	0.085
9/20/2005	0.090	356,250	37,500	318,750	0.085	0.095
12/20/2005	0.100	393,750	75,000	318,750	0.085	0.105
3/20/2005		431,250	112,500	318,750	0.085	0.115

c. In comparing hedging with the Q–cap and the cap, note that on date 6/20/2004, LIBOR exceeds the cap rate of 7%. The caplet on the cap pays $37,500, but the caplet on the Q–cap does not since the cumulative interest on the loan has not yet reached $700,000. On the next date, though, the Q–cap does pay off since the cumulative interest exceeds $700,000 and the LIBOR again exceeds 7%. A similar situation occurs at date 6/20/05. Since the Q–cap places a constraint on when the caplet can pay, it should be priced less than a comparable standard cap.

15.1a., b., and c.

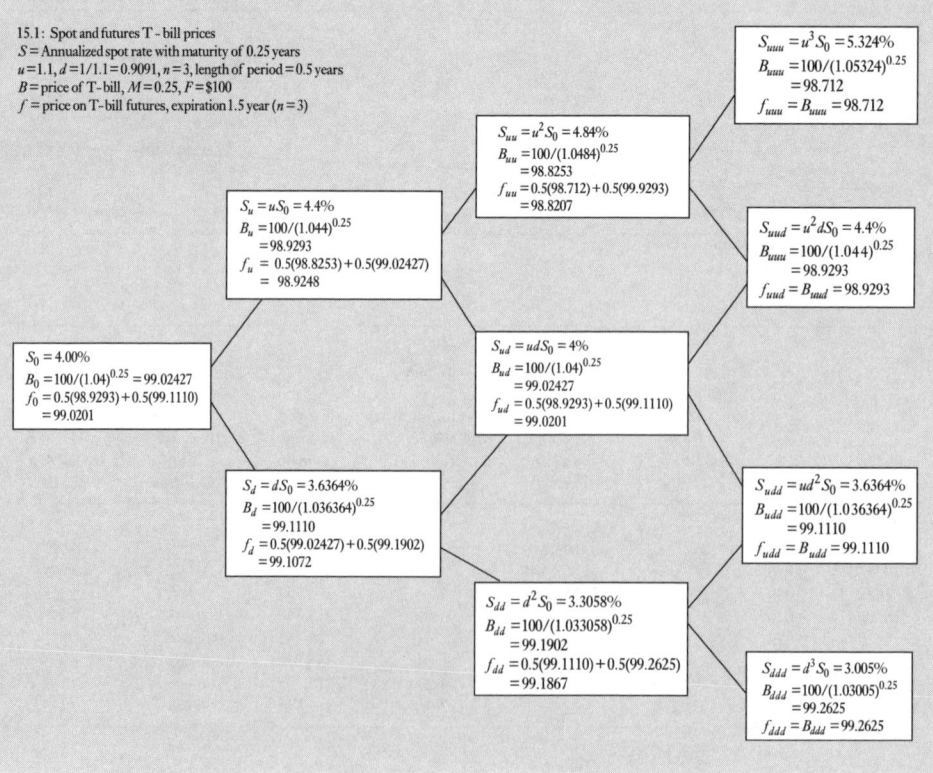

15.1: Spot and futures T - bill prices
S = Annualized spot rate with maturity of 0.25 years
$u = 1.1$, $d = 1/1.1 = 0.9091$, $n = 3$, length of period = 0.5 years
B = price of T-bill, $M = 0.25$, $F = \$100$
f = price on T-bill futures, expiration 1.5 year ($n = 3$)

$S_{uuu} = u^3 S_0 = 5.324\%$
$B_{uuu} = 100/(1.05324)^{0.25}$
$= 98.712$
$f_{uuu} = B_{uuu} = 98.712$

$S_{uu} = u^2 S_0 = 4.84\%$
$B_{uu} = 100/(1.0484)^{0.25}$
$= 98.8253$
$f_{uu} = 0.5(98.712) + 0.5(99.9293)$
$= 98.8207$

$S_u = u S_0 = 4.4\%$
$B_u = 100/(1.044)^{0.25}$
$= 98.9293$
$f_u = 0.5(98.8253) + 0.5(99.02427)$
$= 98.9248$

$S_{uud} = u^2 d S_0 = 4.4\%$
$B_{uud} = 100/(1.044)^{0.25}$
$= 98.9293$
$f_{uud} = B_{uud} = 98.9293$

$S_0 = 4.00\%$
$B_0 = 100/(1.04)^{0.25} = 99.02427$
$f_0 = 0.5(98.9293) + 0.5(99.1110)$
$= 99.0201$

$S_{ud} = u d S_0 = 4\%$
$B_{ud} = 100/(1.04)^{0.25}$
$= 99.02427$
$f_{ud} = 0.5(98.9293) + 0.5(99.1110)$
$= 99.0201$

$S_d = d S_0 = 3.6364\%$
$B_d = 100/(1.036364)^{0.25}$
$= 99.1110$
$f_d = 0.5(99.02427) + 0.5(99.1902)$
$= 99.1072$

$S_{udd} = u d^2 S_0 = 3.6364\%$
$B_{udd} = 100/(1.036364)^{0.25}$
$= 99.1110$
$f_{udd} = B_{udd} = 99.1110$

$S_{dd} = d^2 S_0 = 3.3058\%$
$B_{dd} = 100/(1.033058)^{0.25}$
$= 99.1902$
$f_{dd} = 0.5(99.1110) + 0.5(99.2625)$
$= 99.1867$

$S_{ddd} = d^3 S_0 = 3.005\%$
$B_{ddd} = 100/(1.03005)^{0.25}$
$= 99.2625$
$f_{ddd} = B_{ddd} = 99.2625$

15.2a. $C_{uuu} = 0$, $C_{uud} = 0$, $C_{udd} = 0.1110$, $C_{ddd} = 0.2625$, $C_{uu} = 0$, $C_{ud} = 0.05496$, $C_{dd} = 0.1852$, $C_u = 0.02718$, $C_d = 0.1190$, $C_0 = 0.0724$.

15.2b. $C_{uuu} = 0$, $C_{uud} = 0$, $C_{udd} = 0.1110$, $C_{ddd} = 0.2625$, $C_{uu} = 0$, $C_{ud} = 0.05496$, $C_{dd} = 0.1902$, $C_u = 0.02718$, $C_d = 0.1215$, $C_0 = 0.0736$.

15.2c. $P_{uuu} = 0.288$, $P_{uud} = 0.0707$, $P_{udd} = 0$, $P_{ddd} = 0$, $P_{uu} = 0.177$, $P_{ud} = 0.035$, $P_{dd} = 0$, $P_u = 0.1049$, $P_d = 0.0173$, $P_0 = 0.0605$.

15.2d. Same as 15.2c. The binomial value exceeds the IV at each node, implying no exercise advantage.

15.3a. $C_{uuu} = 0$, $C_{uud} = 0$, $C_{udd} = 0.1110$, $C_{ddd} = 0.2625$, $C_{uu} = 0$, $C_{ud} = 0.05496$, $C_{dd} = 0.1852$, $C_u = 0.02718$, $C_d = 0.1190$, $C_0 = 0.0724$.

15.3b. $C_{uuu} = 0$, $C_{uud} = 0$, $C_{udd} = 0.1110$, $C_{ddd} = 0.2625$, $C_{uu} = 0$, $C_{ud} = 0.05496$, $C_{dd} = 0.1867$, $C_u = 0.02718$, $C_d = 0.1197$, $C_0 = 0.0727$.

15.3c. Since the futures and option expire at the same time, the values of the European futures option and European spot option are the same. See 15.2c.

15.3d. $P_{uuu} = 0.288$, $P_{uud} = 0.0707$, $P_{udd} = 0$, $P_{ddd} = 0$, $P_{uu} = 0.1793$, $P_{ud} = 0.035$, $P_{dd} = 0$, $P_u = 0.1060$, $P_d = 0.0173$, $P_0 = 0.0610$.

15.4 Caplet: $C_{uuu} = 0.331$, $C_{uud} = 0.100$, $C_{udd} = 0$, $C_{ddd} = 0$, $C_{uu} = 0.21297$, $C_{ud} = 0.0495$, $C_{dd} = 0$, $C_u = 0.1298$, $C_d = 0.0245$, $C_0 = 0.0764$.
Floorlet: $P_{uuu} = 0$, $P_{uud} = 0$, $P_{udd} = 0.0909$, $P_{ddd} = 0.24875$, $P_{uu} = 0$, $P_{ud} = 0.045$, $P_{dd} = 0.1685$, $P_u = 0.02226$, $P_d = 0.1058$, $P_0 = 0.0634$

16.1a., b., and c.

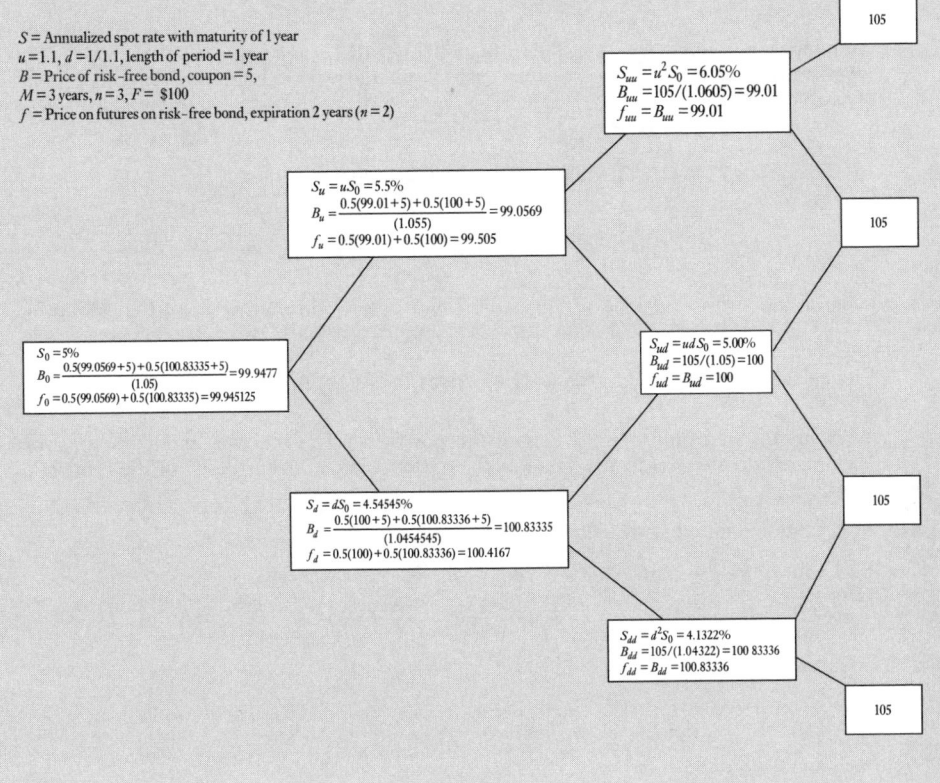

S = Annualized spot rate with maturity of 1 year
$u = 1.1$, $d = 1/1.1$, length of period = 1 year
B = Price of risk-free bond, coupon = 5,
M = 3 years, n = 3, F = \$100
f = Price on futures on risk-free bond, expiration 2 years ($n = 2$)

$S_{uu} = u^2 S_0 = 6.05\%$
$B_{uu} = 105/(1.0605) = 99.01$
$f_{uu} = B_{uu} = 99.01$

$S_u = u S_0 = 5.5\%$
$B_u = \dfrac{0.5(99.01+5)+0.5(100+5)}{(1.055)} = 99.0569$
$f_u = 0.5(99.01)+0.5(100) = 99.505$

$S_0 = 5\%$
$B_0 = \dfrac{0.5(99.0569+5)+0.5(100.83335+5)}{(1.05)} = 99.9477$
$f_0 = 0.5(99.0569)+0.5(100.83335) = 99.945125$

$S_{ud} = ud S_0 = 5.00\%$
$B_{ud} = 105/(1.05) = 100$
$f_{ud} = B_{ud} = 100$

$S_d = d S_0 = 4.54545\%$
$B_d = \dfrac{0.5(100+5)+0.5(100.83336+5)}{(1.0454545)} = 100.83335$
$f_d = 0.5(100)+0.5(100.83336) = 100.4167$

$S_{dd} = d^2 S_0 = 4.1322\%$
$B_{dd} = 105/(1.04322) = 100\ 83336$
$f_{dd} = B_{dd} = 100.83336$

105

105

105

105

16.1d. The value of the stripped securities: 1-year strip = 4.7619, 2-year strip = 4.5342, 3-year strip = 90.6516; aggregate value = 99.9477.

16.2a. European call value = 0.18979.

16.2b. American call value = 0.3968.

16.2c. European put value = 0.2234.

16.2d. American put value = 0.4478.

16.3a. European futures call = 0.18979.

16.3b. American futures call = 0.1984.

16.3c. European futures put = 0.2234.

16.3d. American futures put = 0.2357.

16.4   The value of the replicating portfolio for the European spot call option consists of 1-year zero and 2-year zero bonds constructed so that next year's portfolio matches the two possible call values 0 and 0.39856. Using the 1-year and 2-year zero-coupon bonds with face value of 5 from question 16.1d., the portfolio is found by solving for n_1 and n_2 where:

$$n_1(5) + n_2(4.7393) = 0$$

$$n_1(5) + n_2(4.7826) = 0.39856$$

Solving for n_1 and n_2, we obtain $n_1 = 8.724690107$ and $n_2 = -9.204618938$. This replicating portfolio yields possible cash flows next period that match the option's possible values:

$$(8.724690107)(5) + (-9.204618938)(4.7393) = 0$$

$$(8.724690107)(5) + (-9.204618938)(4.7826) = -0.39856$$

The value of this portfolio is equal to 0.189 – the equilibrium price of the call option:

$$(8.724690107)(4.7619) + (-9.204618938)(4.5342) = -0.189$$

(The minus sign indicates the cost of the portfolio.) The binomial model yields arbitrage-free prices in which the value of the option is equal to the value of the replicating portfolio.

17. a. Call value = 0.065; b. put value = 0.0154.

18. a. Call value = 911; b. put value = 5,788.

CHAPTER 16

1. a.

(1) Effective dates	(2) LIBOR	(3) Floating-rate payer's payment*	(4) Fixed-rate payer's payment**	(5) Net interest received by fixed-rate payer Col. 3−col. 4	(6) Net interest received by floating-rate payer Col. 4−col. 3
3/23/y1					
9/23/y1	0.055				
3/23/y2	0.060	275,000	325,000	−50,000	50,000
9/23/y2	0.065	300,000	325,000	−25,000	25,000
3/23/y3	0.070	325,000	325,000	0	0
9/23/y3	0.075	350,000	325,000	25,000	−25,000
	0.080	375,000	325,000	50,000	−50,000
		400,000	325,000	75,000	−75,000

* (LIBOR/2)($10,000,000)
** (0.065/2)($10,000,000)

b.

(1) Effective dates	(2) LIBOR	(3) Floating-rate interest payment*	(4) Net interest received by fixed-rate payer	(5) Net interest paid Col. 3−col. 4	(6) Rate 2(col. 5)/10m
3/23/y1					
9/23/y1	0.055				
3/23/y2	0.060	275,000	−50,000	325,000	0.065
9/23/y2	0.065	300,000	−25,000	325,000	0.065
3/23/y3	0.070	325,000	0	325,000	0.065
9/23/y3	0.075	350,000	25,000	325,000	0.065
	0.080	375,000	50,000	325,000	0.065
		400,000	75,000	325,000	0.065

* (LIBOR/2)($10,000,000)

c.

(1) Effective dates	(2) LIBOR	(3) Net interest received by floating-rate payer	(4) Interest paid on fixed-rate loan*	(5) Net interest paid	(6) Rate 2(col. 5)/$10m
3/23/y1					
9/23/y1	0.055				
3/23/y2	0.060	50,000	300,000	250,000	0.050
9/23/y2	0.065	25,000	300,000	275,000	0.055
3/23/y3	0.070	0	300,000	300,000	0.060
9/23/y3	0.075	−25,000	300,000	325,000	0.065
	0.080	−50,000	300,000	350,000	0.070
		−75,000	300,000	375,000	0.075

* (0.06/2)($10,000,000)

5. a. Synthetic fixed-rate loan

Conventional floating-rate loan	Pay floating rate
Swap: fixed-rate payer position	Pay fixed rate
Swap: fixed-rate payer position	Receive floating rate
Synthetic fixed rate	Pay fixed rate

c. Synthetic fixed-rate investment

Floating-rate note investment	Receive floating rate
Swap: floating-rate payer position	Pay floating rate
Swap: floating-rate payer position	Receive fixed rate
Synthetic fixed rate	Receive fixed rate

6. The swap bank will take the fixed-rate payer's position at 7.10%/LIBOR and the floating-rate payer's position at 7.2%/LIBOR.

7. a. Swap rate spreads: 5.49%–5.59%, 5.84%–5.88%, 6.01%–6.06%, and 6.44%–6.50%. Swap rates: 5.54%, 5.86%, 6.035%, and 6.47%.

8. Floating payer's net receipts: −59,189.50, −84,143.84, −33,772.83, −8,310.50, 42,477.17, and 67,522.83.

9.
   a. With 3-year T-notes trading at 5%, the swap bank could offer a 5%/LIBOR par value swap.
   b. The bank would add basis points to the fixed rate, with the basis points on its fixed payer's position being less than the points on its floating payer's position.
   c. The swap bank would have a floating payer's position on a 5%/LIBOR. To hedge its swap's 5% fixed-rate receipt and payment of LIBOR, the bank would short the 3-year T-note and use funds to buy a 3-year FRN paying LIBOR.
   d. The swap bank would have a fixed payer's position on a 5%/LIBOR. To hedge its swap's 5% fixed-rate payment and LIBOR receipt, the bank would short or issue a 3-year FRN and use the funds to buy a 3-year T-note yielding 5%.

10. To hedge the acquired 6%/LIBOR floating payer position, the swap dealer would have to go short in $50m-worth of 3-year T-notes yielding 5% and long in $50m-worth of 3-year FRNs paying LIBOR. The combined swap and bonds positions would provide the dealer with $250,000 cash inflow per semi-annual period for 3 years.

Purchased floating-rate payer's position on 6%/LIBOR swap	
Swap: floating-rate payer position swap: floating-rate payer position Hedge	Receive 6% fixed rate Pay LIBOR
Short: 5% T-note Long: FRN paying LIBOR	Pay 5% Receive LIBOR
	Receive 1% Semi-annual receipts: $50,000,000(0.01)/2 = $250,000

Thus, the maximum price the swap bank *would pay* the fixed payer for buying her swap would be equal to the present value of $250,000 cash inflows received for the next six semi-annual periods. Given a discount rate of 5%, the swap bank would be willing to pay the fixed payer up to $1,377,031 for her swap.

$$B_0 = \sum_{t=1}^{6} \frac{\$250,000}{(1 + (0.05/2))^t} = \$1,377,031$$

To hedge the acquired 6%/LIBOR fixed payer position, the swap dealer would have to go short in $50m-worth of 3-year FRNs paying LIBOR and long in $50m-worth of 3-year T-notes yielding 5%. The combined swap and bonds positions would cost the dealer $250,000 per semi-annual period for 3 years.

Purchased fixed-rate payer's position on 6%/LIBOR swap	
Swap: fixed-rate payer position Swap: fixed-rate payer position Hedge	Pay 6% fixed rate Receive LIBOR
Long: 5% T-note Short: FRN paying LIBOR	Receive 5% Pay LIBOR
	Pay 1% Semi-annual receipts: $50,000,000(0.01)/2 = $250,000

Thus, the minimum price the swap bank *would charge* the fixed payer for buying her swap would be equal to the present value of the $250,000 loss each semi-annual period for the next six periods. Given a discount rate of 5%, the swap bank would charge the fixed payer at least $1,377,031 for assuming her swap.

$$B_0 = \sum_{t=1}^{6} \frac{\$250,000}{(1 + (0.05/2))^t} = \$1,377,031$$

11. In the first case, the maximum price the swap bank would pay the fixed payer for buying her swap is $1,377,031. In the second case, the swap bank would charge the fixed payer at least $1,377,031.

13. To hedge the assumed 5.5%/LIBOR fixed payer's position, the swap dealer would have to take a floating payer's position on a new par value swap with a notional principal of $20m. If the fixed rate on a new 2-year swap were at 5%, the dealer would lose $50,000 per period for 2 years on the two swap positions given an NP of $20m.

Purchased fixed-rate payer's position on 5.5%/LIBOR swap
    Swap: fixed-rate payer position
    Swap: fixed-rate payer position
Hedge
Floating-payer position on new
5%/LIBOR par value swap
    Swap: floating-rate payer position
    Swap: floating-rate payer position
	
	Pay 5.5% fixed rate
	Receive LIBOR
	
	Pay LIBOR
	Receive 5%

	Pay 0.5% Semi-annual payments: $20,000,000(0.005)/2 = $50,000

Thus, the price the swap bank *would charge* the fixed payer for assuming (buying) his swap would be at least equal to the present value of $50,000 paid semi-annually for the next four semi-annual periods. Given a discount rate of 5%, the swap bank would charge the fixed payer at least $188,099 for assuming his swap.

$$B_0 = \sum_{t=1}^{4} \frac{\$50,000}{\left(1 + (0.05/2)\right)^t} = \$188,099$$

If the fixed rate on a new 2-year swap were at 6%, the dealer would receive $50,000 per semi-annual period for 2 years on the two swap positions given an NP of $20m. Thus, the maximum price the swap bank *would pay* the fixed payer for buying his swap would be equal to the present value of $50,000 for the next four semi-annual periods. Given a discount rate of 6%, the swap bank would be willing to pay the fixed payer up to $185,855 for his swap.

14. The swap dealer would have to take a fixed payer's position (NP = $20m) to hedge the acquired floating position. If the fixed rate on a new 2-year swap were at 5%, the dealer would gain $50,000 per period for 2 years on the two swap positions given an NP of $20m. Thus, the maximum price the swap bank would pay the fixed payer for buying his swap would be $188,099. If the fixed rate on a new 2-year swap were at 6%, the dealer would lose $50,000 per period for 2 years on the two swap positions given an NP of $20m. Thus, the amount the swap bank would charge the fixed payer for assuming his swap would be equal to the present value of $50,000 for the next four semi-annual periods. Given a discount rate of 6%, the swap bank would charge the fixed payer $185,855 for assuming his swap.

15.

    a. The Moon Company has an absolute advantage in both the fixed and floating markets because of its higher quality rating. Moon, though, has a relative advantage in the fixed market where it gets 100 BP less than Star, while Star has a relative advantage (or relatively less disadvantage) in the floating-rate market where it only pays 50 BP more than Moon. Thus, lenders in the fixed-rate market supposedly assess the difference between the two creditors to be worth 100 BP, while lenders in the floating-rate market assess the difference to be only 50 BP.

    b. 50 BP.

    c. With this swap, the Star Company could issue a $150m FRN paying LIBOR + 75 BP. This loan, combined with the fixed payer swap position, would give Star a synthetic fixed-rate loan paying 10.25%−0.25% less than its direct fixed-rate loan. The Moon Company, on the other hand, could issue a $150m, 9.5% fixed-rate bond which, when combined with the floating payer swap position, would give Moon a synthetic floating-rate loan paying LIBOR−0.25 BP less than the direct floating rate of LIBOR plus 25 BP.

17. In question 15, lenders in the fixed-rate market supposedly assess the differences between the two creditors to be worth 100 BP, while lenders in the floating-rate market assess the differences to be only 50 BP. In question 16, lenders in the fixed-rate market supposedly assess the Moon Company to be more creditworthy, offering the company a loan 25 BP less than Star, while lenders in the floating-rate market assess Star to be more creditworthy, offering it a floating loan 25 BP less than they offer Moon. According to the comparative advantage argument, whenever comparative advantage exists, arbitrage opportunities can be realized by each firm borrowing in the market where it has a comparative advantage and then swapping loans or having a swap bank set up a swap. The total arbitrage gain available to each party depends on whether one party has an absolute advantage in both markets or each has an absolute advantage in one market.

19.

    a. The company needs to issue a 5-year FRN paying LIBOR plus 100 BP and take a fixed-rate payer's position on a swap with an NP of $100m.

    b. 10%.

    c. For the synthetic loan to be preferred over the direct, the fixed rate on the swap must be less than 10%.

20.

    a. To form a synthetic floating-rate note, the financial institution needs to issue $100m-worth of 3-year fixed-rate notes at 7% and take a floating-rate payer's position on a 3-year swap with an NP of $100m.

    b. 6%.

    c. For the synthetic floating-rate loan to be preferred over the direct, the fixed rate on the swap must be greater than 6%.

21.

    b. 6%.

    c. For the synthetic fixed-rate investment to exceed 7%, the swap rate must be greater than 6%.

22.

    b. 6%.

    c. For the synthetic FRN to yield a rate greater than the $LIBOR + 1\%$, the rate on the swap has to be less than 6%.

23. a. 2,132,551, b. $-2,132,551$, c. $-2,132,551$, and d. 2,132,551

24.

    a. 1-year, 2-year, and 3-year zero rates are $Z(1) = 5\%$, $Z(2) = 5.5138\%$, and $Z(3) = 6.0395\%$.

    b. $Z_{0.5} = 5\%$, $Z_1 = 5\%$, $Z_{1.5} = 5.2569\%$, $Z_2 = 5.5138\%$, $Z_{2.5} = 5.77665\%$, and $Z_3 = 6.0395\%$.

    c. Given the 2-year par value swap has a rate of 5.5%, the value of the fixed payer's position on the 6.5% off-market swap is $-\$187,473$; the value of the floating position is $\$187,473$.

25. Short-answer questions: (1) While some brokered swaps have the swap bank guarantee one or both sides of the transaction, in most cases the counterparties assume the credit risk and make their own assessments of the other party's default potential. (2) With dealer swaps, each of the end parties contract separately with the swap bank, who acts as a counterparty to each. The end parties, in turn, assume the credit risk of the financial institution instead of that of the other end party, while the swap dealer assumes the credit risk of both of the end parties. (3) One of the problems with brokered swaps is that they require each party to have knowledge of the other party's risk profile. This problem led to more swap banks taking positions as dealers instead of as brokers. (4) Warehousing refers to the practice of swap dealers matching a swap agreement with multiple end parties. For example, a $100m fixed-for-floating swap between a swap dealer and one end party might be matched with 5 $20m floating-for-fixed swaps. The swap dealer may also try to hedge its swap positions with opposite positions in T-notes and FRNs or using Eurodollar futures contracts. (5) Running a dynamic book refers to the swap bank hedging their swap commitments through a portfolio of alternative positions – opposite swap positions, spot positions in T-notes and FRNs, or futures positions. (6) The swap dealer will provide a bid–asked quote to a potential party, and will in some cases post the bid-and-asked quotes. The quotes are stated in terms of the bid rate the dealer will pay as a fixed payer in return for the LIBOR, and the asked rate they will receive as a floating-rate payer in return for paying the LIBOR. The floating rate on a swap is quoted flat without basis point adjustments, and the fixed rate on a generic swap, in turn, is quoted in terms of the YTM for an on-the-run T-bond or T-note; that is, the most recent note or bond issued with a maturity matching the swap. (7) The comparative argument argues that gains can be made from creating synthetic positions when there is a comparative advantage. For example, if one borrower has a relative advantage in the fixed market but prefers to borrow at a floating rate, while another party has an advantage in the floating market but prefers to borrow at a fixed rate, then a swap contract can be formed to benefit one or both of the borrowers. In this example, the first borrower can create a synthetic floating-rate loan that has a rate less than its direct floating-rate loan, and the other borrower can create a synthetic fixed-rate loan with a rate that is less than its direct fixed-rate loan rate. See the answer to question 15. (8) When one party has an absolute advantage in both markets, then the arbitrage gain is the difference in the comparative advantages in BP in each market. For example, if the most creditworthy borrower could borrow 100 BP less in the fixed market, while the least creditworthy borrower could borrow 50 BP more in the floating market, then a swap could be formed that would allow each party to create synthetic fixed and floating positions with the maximum interest rate reduction benefit for both totaling $50 \text{ BP} = 100 \text{ BP} - 50 \text{ BP}$. Usually, the most creditworthy creditor is given the

greater amount of the interest reduction. (9) When each party has an absolute advantage in one market, then the arbitrage gain is equal to the sum of the comparative advantages. (10) The comparative advantage argument has often been cited as the explanation for the growth in the swap market. This argument, though, is often questioned on the grounds that the mere use of swaps should over time reduce the credit interest rate differentials in the fixed and flexible markets, taking away the advantages from forming synthetic positions. (11) The hidden option refers to the option the lender usually has on a floating-rate loan to review the floating rate each period and increase the spread over the LIBOR if the borrower's creditworthiness has deteriorated. As noted in section 16.4.2, studies have shown that the likelihood of default increases faster over time for lower quality companies than it does for higher quality. As a result, the lender's hidden option is more valuable on a floating-rate loan to a lower quality borrower than a higher quality one. The differences in credit spreads between fixed and floating credit markets that are extant may, in turn, be due to the hidden options that underlie floating loans but not fixed ones. (12) To create a fixed-rate obligation the company could combine its floating-rate debt with a fixed-rate payer's position on a swap, thereby creating a synthetic fixed-rate debt position. (13) To create a floating-rate obligation the company could combine its fixed-rate debt with a floating rate payer's position on a swap, thereby creating a synthetic floating-rate debt position. (14) To create an investment in a floating-rate note, the company could combine its fixed-rate investment with a fixed-rate payer's position on a swap, thereby creating a synthetic floating-rate investment. The company might do this if it expected rates to increase in the future and the rates on its existing notes were relatively low. (15) The insurance company could create a positive duration gap by decreasing the duration of its liabilities. With swaps it could decrease the duration of its liabilities by taking a floating rate payer's position on a swap. If the company did this and rates were to decrease as expected, then not only would the value of the company's bond portfolio increase but the company would also profit from the swap; on the other hand, if rates were to increase, then the company would see decreases in the value of its bond portfolio, as well as losses from its swap positions. By adding swaps, though, the company has effectively increased its interest rate exposure by creating a positive duration gap. (16) The YTM approach values a swap as the present value of the differences between the cash flow from the fixed rate on the existing swap and the cash flow from the fixed rate on the current par-value swap, with the net cash flows discounted at the current YTM. (17) The valuation of off-market swaps using a common YTM does not ensures that there are no arbitrage opportunities from buying swaps and stripping them. The valuation of off-market swaps using a common YTM for all cash flows also can lead to under- and overvaluation of the separate cash flows. (18) The zero-coupon approach values a swap as the present value of the differences between the cash flow from the fixed rate on the existing swap and the cash flow from the fixed rate on the current par-value swap, with each net cash flow discounted at its zero-coupon rate. The approach, in turn, requires generating a spot yield curve for swaps. (19) The zero-coupon approach has the property of being arbitrage-free. That is, no arbitrage opportunities exist from buying and stripping swaps that are priced to equal their zero-coupon values. (20) The break-even rate or the market rate is that fixed rate on a swap that equates the present value of the swap's fixed-rate payments to the present value of the swap's floating payments, with implied one-period forward rates being used to estimate the future floating payments.

CHAPTER 17

2.

a. To lock-in the rate on its 10-year fixed-rate bonds 2 years from now, ABC would need to enter a 2-year forward contract to take a fixed payer's position on a 10-year, 7.25%/LIBOR swap.

b. At the forward swap's expiration, ABC would issue a 10-year floating-rate note at 150 basis points above the LIBOR and assume its fixed payer's position on the swap underlying the forward contract. Combined, the floating-rate note and fixed payer's position on the swap represents the equivalent of a 10-year fixed-rate loan at 8.75.

At the expiration date on the forward swap:

Instrument	Action	
Issue flexible rate note	Pay	−LIBOR−150 BP
Swap: fixed-rate payer's position	Pay fixed rate	−7.25%
Swap: fixed-rate payer's position	Receive LIBOR	+LIBOR
Synthetic fixed rate	Net payment	8.75%

3.

a. With 10-year T-bonds trading at 7% and the fixed rate on 10-year par value swaps that Commerce Bank offers ABC set at 150 BP above that yield, the current par value swap available to ABC would have a fixed rate of 8.5%. At the forward swaps' expiration date, ABC would therefore be able to sell its fixed payer's position on its 10-year 7.25%/LIBOR swap underlying the forward swap contract to Commerce at $12,463,468 given the swap is valued using the YTM approach with a discount rate of 8.5%:

$$SV^{fix} = \left[\sum_{t=1}^{20} \frac{(0.085/2) - (0.0725/2)}{(1 + (0.085/2))^t} \right] \$150,000,000 = \$12,463,468$$

b. With the $12,463,468 proceeds from closing its swap, ABC would only need to raise $137,536,532 (= $150,000,000−$12,463,468). Given that ABC bonds sell at 200 BP above T-bonds, ABC would therefore issue $137,536,532-worth of 10-year fixed-rate bonds at 9% given that T-bond rates are at 7%.

c. Its semi-annual interest payments would be $6,189,144 (=(0.09/2)($137,536,532)).

d. ABC's interest payments equate to an annualized rate of 8.25% based on a $150m debt.

Funds needed	$150,000,000
−Proceeds from swap	−$12,463,468
= Amount borrowed	= $137,536,532
Semi-annual interest	(0.09/2)($137,536,532) = $6,189,144
Annualized rate based on funds needed	(2)($6,189,144)/$150,000,000 = 0.0825

The forward swap position has therefore lowered the effective debt rate from 9% to 8.25%.

4. a. −19,985,768, b. 169,985,768, c. 8%.

5.

  a. JEP would need to enter a 1-year forward contract to take a floating payer's position on a 3-year, 6.5%/LIBOR swap.

  b. 8%.

6.

  a. At 5%, $SV^{fl} = 546{,}237$; at 7%, $SV^{fl} = -528{,}507$.

  b. At 5%, investment $= 20{,}546{,}237$, ARR $= 8\%$; at 7%, investment $= 19{,}471{,}493$, ARR $= 8\%$.

7.

  a. $f_{11} = 6.03\%$, $f_{12} = 7.099\%$, $f_{13} = 8.2402\%$.

  b. One-year swap 1 year forward $= 6.03\%$; 1-year swap 2 years forward $= 7.099\%$; 2-year swap 1 year forward $= 6.546$:

$$\frac{C_f^*}{(1+Z(2))^2} + \frac{C_f^*}{(1+Z(3))^3} = \frac{f_{12}}{(1+Z(2))^2} + \frac{f_{13}}{(1+Z(3))^3}$$

$$C_f^* = \frac{\dfrac{f_{12}}{(1+Z(2))^2} + \dfrac{f_{13}}{(1+Z(3))^3}}{\dfrac{1}{(1+Z(2))^2} + \dfrac{1}{(1+Z(3))^3}} = \frac{\dfrac{0.0603}{(1.055138)^2} + \dfrac{0.07099}{(1.060395)^3}}{\dfrac{1}{(1.055138)^2} + \dfrac{1}{(1.060395)^3}} = 0.06546$$

  c.

    (i) The fixed payer's and floating payer's positions on the underlying swap would have a value of zero.

    (ii) The current value of the fixed payer's position on the 1-year 7%/LIBOR swap 2 years forward is $8,303:

$$\text{Value} = \frac{(0.07099 - 0.07)(\$10\,\text{m})}{(1.060395)^3} = \$8{,}303$$

    The floating payer's position would be $-\$8{,}303$.

    (iii) The value of the fixed payer's position on the 2-year 6.5%/LIBOR swap 1 year forward is $7,990:

$$\text{Value} = \frac{(0.06546 - 0.065)(\$10\text{m})}{(1.055138)^2} + \frac{(0.06546 - 0.065)(\$10\text{m})}{(1.060395)^3} = \$7{,}990$$

    The floating payer's position would be $-\$7{,}990$, implying the forward position holder would require compensation.

8. The break-even forward rate on a 3-year swap 3 years forward is 8.94%. Given that the specified fixed rate on the forward swap is at 9% (greater than the break-even rate of 8.94%), the fixed payer's position on the underlying swap would have an annual value equal to $-\$6{,}000$ for years 3, 4, and 5: $(-0.0006)(\$10\text{m}) = -\$6{,}000$. The present value of this cash flow is equal to $-\$12,830$:

$$\text{Value} = \frac{-\$6{,}000}{(1.065)^4} + \frac{-\$6{,}000}{(1.07)^5} + \frac{-\$6{,}000}{(1.075)^6} = -\$12{,}830$$

9. On the exercise date, if current 3-year par value swaps were trading at 7% and swaps were valued by the YTM approach, then the fund would be able to sell the 6%

swap for $266,428:

$$\text{Value of swap} = \left[\sum_{t=1}^{6} \frac{(0.07/2) - (0.06/2)}{(1 + (0.07/2))^t} \right] (\$10\,\text{m}) = \$266{,}428$$

The fund would realize a profit of $216,428 (= $266,428–$50,000). If the 3-year par value swap rate at the expiration date were at 5%, then the put swaption would have no value and the fund would simply let its put swaption expire, losing its premium of $50,000.

10. Profit from put swaption: −50,000, −50,000, −50,000, −50,000, −50,000, 84,315, 216,428, 346,380, and 474,214.

11. If the rate were at 5%, then the fund would realize a profit of $215,406 (= $275,406–$60,000). If the rate were at 7%, then the swaption would have no value and the fund would simply let its call swaption expire, losing its premium of $60,000.

12. Profit from call swaption: 500,143, 356,586, 215,406, 76,559, −60,000, −60,000, −60,000, −60,000, and −60,000.

13.

Rates on 3-year par value swaps at expiration R	Call swaption's interest differential Max((0.06− R)/2, 0)	Value of 6%/ LIBOR call swaption at expiration ΣPV(max[(0.06− R)/2, 0]($50m))	Call swaption cost	Profit from call swaption	Funds invested $50m + swaption value	ARR
0.040	0.0100	2,800,715	250,000	2,550,715	52,800,715	0.0586
0.045	0.0075	2,082,929	250,000	1,832,929	52,082,929	0.0590
0.050	0.0050	1,377,031	250,000	1,127,031	51,377,031	0.0593
0.055	0.0025	682,796	250,000	432,796	50,682,796	0.0597
0.060	0.0000	0	250,000	−250,000	50,000,000	0.0600
0.065	0.0000	0	250,000	−250,000	50,000,000	0.0650
0.070	0.0000	0	250,000	−250,000	50,000,000	0.0700
0.075	0.0000	0	250,000	−250,000	50,000,000	0.0750
0.080	0.0000	0	250,000	−250,000	50,000,000	0.0800

14. Swaption values: 0, 0, 0, 0, 0, 1,001,361, 1,978,180, 2,931,130, and 3,860,867; ARRs: 6%, 6.5%, 7%, 7.5%, 8%, 8.08%, 8.16%, 8.24%, and 8.32%.

15. ARRs: 6%, 6.5%, 7%, 7.5%, 8%, 8.15%, 8.3%, 8.45%, and 8.61%.

16.

   a. To hedge against call risk, Bluegrass would buy a 2-year call swaption on an 8-year, 10%/ LIBOR swap with an NP of $25m from Commonwealth Bank for $100,000.
   b. Bluegrass Trust could obtain a 10% yield by selling its swap and buying an 8-year, 6% option-free, fixed-rate bond. With 6% rates on 8-year par value swaps, the Trust would be able to sell its floating position on the 10%/LIBOR at $6,280,551:

$$\text{Value of swap} = \left[\sum_{t=1}^{16} \frac{(0.10/2) - (0.06/2)}{(1 + (0.06/2))^t} \right] (\$25\text{m}) = \$6{,}280{,}551$$

The $6,280,551 proceeds from the swap sale would offset the 4% lower annual return the Trust would receive as a result of having to sell its 10% bonds back to the issuer on the call and invest in new 8-year option-free bonds at 6%. Its ARR from reinvesting $25m plus $6,280,551 at 6% for 8 years based on a $25m investment is approximately 9%.

c. If 2 years later, rates were to increase, then the bonds would not be called and the swaption would have no value. In this case, Bluegrass Trust would lose the premium of $100,000 it paid for the call swaption.

18.

a. As an alternative to 7-year, straight 9% fixed-rate bonds, the O'Brien Company could sell the 7-year, 9.5% fixed-rate bond callable after 2 years at par and then sell the 2-year call swaption on a 5-year 9%/LIBOR swap at a price equal to 75 BP per year for 7 years.

b. With the company having sold the swaption at a premium equivalent to 75 BP per year, the effective rate on the debt would be 8.75% under this interest rate scenario:

Rates two years later greater than 9%	Action	
9.5% callable bonds not called	Pay 9.5% per year	−9.5% per year
Call swaption not exercised	No liability	
Premium from selling call swaption	Receive equivalent of 0.75% per year	+0.75% per year
Net position	Pay 8.75% per year	−8.75%

c. If 2 years later rates were below 9% and the call swaption holder exercised, the O'Brien Company could call its bonds, financing the purchase by selling FRNs at the LIBOR + 25 BP. For the next 5 years, the company would have a fixed payer's position on the exercised swap at the 9% strike rate and would pay the LIBOR plus 25 BP on its FRNs. The company's effective rate would be 8.5%:

Rates two years later less than 9%	O'Brien's actions	
Call swaption exercised: O'Brien assumes fixed payer's position	Pay 9% per year for 5 years	−9% per year
	Receives LIBOR for 5 years	+LIBOR per year
O'Brien sells $5m of 5-year FRNs at LIBOR plus 25 BP	Receive $5m Pay LIBOR + 25 BP for 5 years	+$5m −LIBOR −0.25% per year
O'Brien calls 9.5% bond	Pays $5m	−$5m
Premium from selling call swaption is 75 BP	Receive equivalent of 75 BP for 5 years	+0.75% per year
Net position	Pays 8.5% per year for 5 years	8.5% per year

19.

    a. As an alternative to a 7-year, option-free 6% general obligation bond, the state could sell the 7-year, 5.5% fixed-rate bond putable after 2 years at par and then buy the 2-year put swaption on a 5-year 5.5%/LIBOR swap with an NP of $50m at a price equal to 25 BP per year for 7 years.

    b. 5.75%.

20.

    a. The break-even forward rate on a 3-year swap 3 years forward is 8.94% (the same rate as found in question 8). The intrinsic value of the 3-year put swaption on the 3-year 9%/LIBOR swap is $213,827:

$$\text{Put swaption exercise rate} = C^X = 7.94\%$$

$$\text{Break-even forward swap rate} = C_f^* = 8.94\%$$

$$\text{Intrinsic value} = \text{Max}[C_f^* - C^X, 0]\left[\frac{1}{(1+Z(4))^4} + \frac{1}{(1+Z(5))^5} + \frac{1}{(1+Z(6))^6}\right]\text{NP}$$

$$\text{Max}(0.0894 - 0.0794,\ 0)(\$10,000,000) = \$100,000$$

$$\text{Intrinsic value} = \frac{\$100,000}{(1.065)^4} + \frac{\$100,000}{(1.07)^5} + \frac{\$100,000}{(1.075)^6} = \$213,827$$

    b. Given the exercise rate of 11% on a 3-year put swaption on a 3-year swap is greater than the break-even rate of 8.94%, the intrinsic value of the put swaption would be zero.

    c. The intrinsic value of the 3-year call swaption on the 3-year 9.94%/LIBOR swap is $213,827.

    d. The intrinsic value of the call swaption would be zero.

21. $V_P = \$270,799$; $V_C = \$34,004$.

27. 34,004.

32.

    a. To the American company, this swap agreement is the equivalent to a position in two bonds: a long position in a dollar-denominated, 5-year, 10% annual coupon bond with a principal of $142.857m and trading at par and a short position in a sterling-denominated, 5-year, 7.5% annual coupon bond with a principal of £100m and trading at par. The British company's swap position in which it will receive sterling and pay dollars is just the opposite of the American company's position. It is equivalent to a long position in a sterling-denominated bond and short position in a dollar-denominated bond.

    b. The American company could view its swap agreements to sell £7.5m each year for $14.2857m and to sell £100m at maturity for $142.857m as a series of short currency forward contracts. The British company, in turn, could view its interest agreement to pay $14.2857m for £7.5m each year for 5 years and its principal agreement to pay $142.857m for £100m at maturity as a series of long currency forward contracts in years 1, 2, 3, 4, and 5.

    c. The value of the swap is zero.

d. The value of the American company's swap of $14.2857m received/£7.5m paid as a series of forward contracts is $3,903,019:

(1) Year	(2) $ CF (millions)	(3) £ CF (millions)	(4) Forward exchange: $/£$E_f=$ ($1.46/£)(1.09/1.08)^t	(5) $ cost of sterling (millions) (col. 4 × col. 3)	(6) Net $ revenue (millions) (col. 2−col. 5)	(7) PV at 9% PV(col. 6)
1	14.2857	−7.5	1.47351852	11.051389	3.23431	2.967258
2	14.2857	−7.5	1.48716221	11.153717	3.13198	2.636128
3	14.2857	−7.5	1.50093223	11.256992	3.02871	2.338719
4	14.2857	−7.5	1.51482975	11.361223	2.92448	2.071773
5	142.857	−100	1.51482975	151.482975	−8.62597	−6.110858
						3.903019

The dollar value of the British company's swap of £7.5m recevied/$14.2857m paid as a series of forward contracts is −$3,903,019.

34.

a. Swap arrangement:

(1) The American company borrows $142.857m at 10% and then agrees to swap it for a £100m loan at 7%.

(2) The British company borrows £100m at 7.5% and then agrees to swap it for a $142.857m loan at 10.6%.

The swap arrangement is made possible by the existence of a comparative advantage. The American company has a comparative advantage in the US market: it pays 1% less than the British company in the US market, compared to only 0.25% less in the British market. On the other hand, the British company has a comparative advantage in the British market: it pays 0.25% more than the US company in Britain, compared to 1% more in the US. When such a comparative advantage exists, a swap bank is in a position to arrange a swap to benefit one or both companies.

c.

Swap bank's dollar position
Receives: (0.106) ×
  ($142.857m) = $15.142842m
Pays: (0.10)($142.857m) =
  $14.2857m
Net $ receipt: $15.142842m−
  $14.2857m = $0.857142m

Swap bank's £ position
Receives: (0.07)(£100m) =
  £7m
Pays: (0.075)(£100m) = £7.5m

Net £ payment: £7.5m−£7m =
  £0.5m

---

d. The swap bank has a position equivalent to a series of long currency forward contracts in which it agrees to buy £0.5m for $0.857142m each year. The swap bank's implied forward rate on each of these contracts is $1.714284/£:

$$E_f = \frac{\$0.857142m}{£0.5m} = \frac{\$1.714284}{£}$$

e. The swap bank could enter into forward contracts to buy £0.5m each year for the next 5 years at forward rates. By combining its swap position with forward contracts, the bank would be able to earn a total profit from the deal of $456,020:

(1) Year	(2) $ CF (millions)	(3) £ CF (millions)	(4) Forward exchange: £/BP	(5) $ cost of sterling (millions) (col. 4 × col. 3)	(6) Net $ revenue (millions) (col. 2−col. 5)
1	0.857142	−0.5	1.4619478	0.7309739	0.12617
2	0.857142	−0.5	1.4961055	0.74805275	0.10909
3	0.857142	−0.5	1.5310612	0.7655306	0.09161
4	0.857142	−0.5	1.5668336	0.7834168	0.07373
5	0.857142	−0.5	1.6034419	0.80172095	0.05542
					0.45602

35. Short-answer questions: (2) At the expiration date on the forward swap, the company could issue a 3-year floating-rate debt at LIBOR that, when combined with the fixed position on the 3-year swap underlying the forward swap contract, would provide the company with a synthetic fixed-rate loan. (10) A callable swap is one in which the fixed payer has the right to early termination. Thus, if rates decrease, the fixed-rate payer on the swap with this embedded call option to early termination can exercise her right to cancel the swap. The cancelable clause provides the counterparty with protection against interest rate decreases. (11) A putable swap is one in which the floating payer has the right to early cancellation. A floating-rate payer with this option may find it advantageous to exercise his early-termination right when rates increase. The cancelable clause provides the counterparty with protection against interest rate decreases. (15) In 3 years, the call swaption gives the holder the right to take a floating payer's position on a 2-year swap at 8% that in effect extends the maturity of the expiring floating payer's position on the 8% generic swap. (19) The value of the swap of dollars received/sterling paid is equal to (i) the sum of the present values of the $1.46m received each year from the swap minus the dollar cost of buying £0.7m at the forward exchange rate, and (ii) the present value of the $14.6m received at year 3 minus the dollar cost of buying £10m at the 3-year forward exchange rate. (21) Using the forward exchange rate equivalence approach the value is $487,009.

GLOSSARY OF TERMS

accreting swap Swap in which the notional principal increases over time based on a set schedule.

accrual bond class A sequential-pay tranche whose interest is not paid but accrues until its principal payments are made.

accrued interest The interest on a bond or fixed-income security that has accumulated since the last coupon date.

active strategies Bond strategies that involve taking speculative positions.

adjustable-rate note *See* Variable-rate note.

after-acquired property clause Provision in a mortgage bond that dictates that all property or assets acquired after the issue be added to the property already pledged.

agency pass-throughs Mortgage-backed securities created by agencies: Federal National Mortgage Association, Government National Mortgage Association, and Federal Home Loan Mortgage Corporation.

American option An option which can be exercised at any time on or before the exercise date.

amortizing swap Swap in which the notional principal is reduced over time based on a schedule.

annual realized return, ARR The annual rate earned on a bond for the period from when the bond is bought to when it is converted to cash (which could be either maturity or a date prior to maturity if the bond is sold), with the assumption that all coupons paid on the bond are reinvested to that date.

annualized discount yield Annualized return specified as a proportion of the bill's principal.

annualized mean The mean obtained by multiplying a mean defined for a certain length of period (e.g., one week) by the number of periods of that length in a year (e.g., 52).

annualized variance The variance obtained by multiplying a variance defined for a certain length of period (e.g., one week) by the number of periods of that length in a year (e.g., 52).

annuity An insurance product that pays the holder a periodic fixed income for as long as the policyholder lives in return for an initial lump-sum investment.

anticipation notes Municipal securities sold to obtain funds in lieu of anticipated revenues. They include tax-anticipation notes, revenue-anticipation notes, grant-anticipation notes, bond-anticipation notes, and municipal tax-exempt commercial paper.

arbitrage Transaction that provides a positive cash flow with no liabilities – a free lunch.

An arbitrage opportunity exists when positions generating identical cash flows are not equally priced. In such cases the arbitrage is formed by buying the lower-priced position and selling the higher-priced one.

arbitrageur   An individual who engages in arbitrage.

asked price   The price at which a dealer offers to sell a security.

asset-based interest rate swap   A swap used with an asset. In terms of synthetic positions, asset-based swaps can be used to create either fixed-rate or floating-rate investment positions.

assignment   Procedure in which a brokerage firm or clearing firm selects one of its customers who is short in an option to fulfill the terms of the option after a holder has exercised.

assumed bond   Bond whose obligations are taken over or assumed by another company or economic entity. In many cases such bonds are the result of a merger.

average cap   Cap in which the payoff depends on the average reference rate for each caplet. For example, if the average is above the exercise rate, then all the caplets will provide a payoff; if the average is equal or below the exercise rate, the whole cap expires out-of-the-money.

average life   The average amount of time the debt will be outstanding. It is equal to the weighted average of the time periods, with the weights being relative principal payments.

average rate to maturity   The average return per year as a proportion of the average price of the bond per year. It is used as an estimate of the YTM.

average realized return   *See* Annual realized return.

backwardation   A market in which the futures price is less than the spot price.

bank investment contract (BIC)   Bank deposit obligation with a guaranteed rate and fixed maturity.

banker's acceptances   Time drafts (postdated checks) guaranteed by a bank.

banker's discount yield   *See* Annualized discount yield.

barbell strategy   Bond strategy in which investments are in both short-term and long-term bonds.

barrier options   Options in which the payoff depends on whether an underlying security price or reference rate reaches a certain level.

basis   The difference between futures and spot prices.

basis point (BP) $\frac{1}{100}$ of a percentage point. Fractions on bond yields are often quoted in terms of basis points.

basis risk   *See* Timing risk.

bearer bond   Bond that pays coupons and principal to whoever has physical possession of the bond.

best effort   Investment bankers who sell a security for the issuer for a commission.

beta   A measure of the responsiveness of a change in a security's rate of return to a change in the rate of return of the market.

bid–asked spread   The difference between the bid and asked prices.

bid price   The price at which a dealer offers to buy a security.

binomial interest rate tree model   Model that assumes that a spot rate follows a binomial process.

binomial option pricing model (BOPM)   A model for determining the equilibrium value of an option by finding the option price that equals the value of a replicating portfolio. The model assumes a binomial world in which the option's underlying security price can either increase or decrease in a given period.

Black model   A model for pricing a futures option contract.

Black–Scholes model   A model for valuing European options.

bond-equivalent yield   The yield obtained by multiplying the semi-annual periodic rate by two. Bonds with different payment frequencies often have their rates expressed in terms of their bond-equivalent yield so that their rates can be compared to each other on a common basis.

bond immunization   Bond strategy aimed at minimizing market risk.

bond portfolio yield The yield for a portfolio of bonds that will make the present value of the portfolio's cash flow equal to the market value of the portfolio.

bond swap Active bond strategy involves liquidating one bond group and simultaneously purchasing another.

bootstrapping A sequential process of estimating spot rates. The approach requires having at least one pure discount bond; it solves for the implied spot rates on coupon bonds.

Brady bond Bond issued by a number of emerging countries in exchange for rescheduled bank loans. The bonds were part of a US government program started in 1989 to address the Latin American debt crisis of the 1980s.

break-even swap rate The swap rate that equates the present value of the swap's fixed-rate payments to the present value of the swap's floating payments estimated using implied forward swap rates.

bull call money spread A vertical spread formed by purchasing a call at a certain exercise price and selling another call on the same security at a higher exercise price.

bull put money spread A vertical spread formed by purchasing a put at a certain exercise price and selling another put on the same security at a higher exercise price.

Bulldog bonds Foreign bonds sold in the United Kingdom.

bullet strategy Strategy of constructing a bond portfolio that concentrates on one maturity area.

burnout factor The tendency for mortgages to hit some maximum prepayment rate and then level off.

calendar spread An alternative term for horizontal spread.

calibration model Binomial model that generates a binomial interest rate tree by solving for the spot rate that satisfies a variability condition and a price condition that ensures that the binomial tree is consistent with the term structure of current spot rates.

call An option that gives the holder the right to buy an asset or security at a specified price on or possibly before a specific date.

call market Market set up so that those wishing to trade in a particular security can do so only at that time when the exchange "calls" the security for trading.

call provision Provision in an indenture that gives the issuer the right to redeem some or all of the issue for a specific amount before maturity.

call risk The risk that the issuer/borrower will buy back a bond, forcing the investor to reinvest in a market with lower interest rates.

call spread A strategy in which one simultaneously buys a call and sells another call on the same stock but with different terms.

call swaption Swaption that gives the holder the right to receive a specific fixed rate and pay the floating rate; that is, the right to take a floating payer's position.

callable bond A bond that gives the issuer the right to buy back the bond from the bond-holders at a specified price before maturity.

cancelable swap Swap in which one of the counterparties has the option to terminate one or more payments. Cancelable swaps can be callable or putable: a callable cancelable swap is one in which the fixed payer has the right to early termination; a putable swap is one in which the floating payer has the right to early cancelation.

cap A series of European interest rate calls that expire at or near the interest payment dates on a loan.

capital market Market where long-term securities (original maturities over 1 year) are traded.

caplet *See* Interest rate option.

carry income Difference between the interest dealers earn from holding securities and the interest they pay on the funds they borrow to purchase the securities.

carrying-cost model A model for determining the equilibrium price on a futures contract. In this model the forward price equals the net costs of carrying the underlying asset to expiration.

cash-and-carry arbitrage A riskless strategy formed by taking opposite positions in spot and forward contracts on a security. The strategy underlies the carrying-cost model.

cash-flow matching strategy Strategy of constructing a bond portfolio with cash flows that match the outlays of the liabilities.

cash market *See* Spot market.

cash settlement A feature on some futures and option contracts in which the contract is settled in cash at delivery instead of an exchange of cash for the underlying asset.

cell matching A methodology for constructing a bond index fund based on decomposing the index into cells with each cell defining a different mix of features of the index (duration, credit rating, sector, etc.).

certificates of deposit Short-term bank notes usually sold at their face value, with the principal and interest paid at maturity if the CD is less than 1 year.

Chapter 11 fund A fund consisting of the bonds of bankrupt or distressed companies.

cheapest-to-deliver bond The least expensive bond (or note) among the Chicago Board of Trade's eligible bonds (or notes) that a short holder of a Treasury bond (or note) futures contract can deliver.

classical immunization Bond immunization strategy of equating the duration of the bond to the duration of the liability.

clearinghouse A corporation associated with a futures or options exchange that guarantees the performance of each contract and acts as intermediary by breaking up each contract after the trade has taken place.

closed-end bond Bond that prohibits the company from incurring any additional debt secured by a first lien on the assets already being used as security.

closed-end fund Fund that has a fixed number of non-redeemable shares sold at its initial offering. Unlike an open-end fund, the closed-end fund does not stand ready to buy existing shares or sell new shares.

closing transactions Closing an option or futures position. It requires taking an opposite position: selling an option or futures contract to close an initial long position; buying an option or futures contract to close an initial short position.

collar Combination of a long position in a cap and a short position in a floor with different exercise rates. The sale of the floor is used to defray the cost of the cap.

collateral-trust bond Bond secured by a lien on equity shares of a company's subsidiary, holdings of other companies' stocks and bonds, government securities, and other financial claims.

collateralized mortgage obligations (CMOs) Derivative securities formed by dividing the cash flow of an underlying pool of mortgages or a mortgage-backed security issue into several classes, with each class having a different claim on the mortgage collateral and with each sold separately to different types of investors.

combination matching A bond strategy that combines cash-flow matching and immunization strategies.

commercial paper Short-term debt obligation usually issued by large, well-known corporations.

Commodity Futures Trading Commission (CFTC) The federal agency that oversees and regulates futures trading.

commodity-linked bond Bond that has its coupons and possibly principal tied to the price of a particular commodity.

commodity options *See* Futures options.

companion bond *See* Support class.

conditional prepayment rate The annualized prepayment speed on a mortgage portfolio or mortgage-backed security.

confirmation The legal agreement governing a swap.

consul *See* Perpetuity.

contango Describes a market where the futures price exceeds the spot price.

contingent immunization An enhanced immunization strategy that combines active management to achieve higher returns and immunization strategies to ensure a floor.

continuous market A market that provides constant trading in a security. Such markets operate through specialists or market-makers who are required by the exchange to take temporary positions in a security whenever there is a demand.

continuously compounded return The rate of return in which the value of the asset grows continuously. The rate is equal to the natural logarithm of one plus the simple (non-compounded) rate.

contractual institutions Institutions such as life-insurance companies, property and casualty insurance companies, and pension funds that obtain their funds from legal contracts to protect businesses and households from risk (premature death, accident, etc.), and from savings plans.

convenience yield Describes when the benefits from holding an asset exceed the costs of holding the asset.

conventional pass-throughs Mortgage-backed securities created by private entities.

conversion A risk-free portfolio formed by going long in an underlying security, short in a European call, and long in a European put. The portfolio yields a certain cash flow equal to the exercise price at expiration regardless of the price of the underlying security.

conversion price A convertible bond's par value divided by its conversion ratio.

conversion ratio The number of shares of stock that can be acquired when a convertible bond is tendered for conversion.

conversion value A convertible bond's value as a stock. It is equal to the convertible bond's conversion ratio times the market price of the stock.

convertible bond A bond in which the holder can convert the bond to a specified number of shares of stock.

convexity A measure of the change in the slope of the price–yield curve for a small change in yield; it is the second-order derivative.

corpus Describes a principal-only security.

corridor Long position in a cap and a short position in a similar cap with a higher exercise rate.

cost-of-carry model *See* Carrying-cost model.

counterparties The parties to a swap agreement.

coupon rate The contractual rate the issuer agrees to pay each period. It is expressed as a proportion of the annual coupon payment to the bond's face value.

covered interest arbitrage An arbitrage strategy consisting of long and short positions in currency spot and futures contracts, and positions in domestic and foreign risk-free securities. The strategy is used by arbitrageurs when the interest rate parity condition does not hold.

credit analysis strategy A strategy involving credit analysis of corporate, municipal, or foreign bonds in order to identify potential changes in default risk. This information is then used to identify bonds to include or exclude in a bond portfolio or bond investment strategy.

credit default swap Swap in which one counterparty buys protection against default by a particular company from another counterparty. The company is known as the reference entity and a default by that company is known as a credit event. The buyer of the swap makes periodic payments to the seller until the end of the life of the swap or until the credit event occurs.

credit risk *See* Default risk.

credit-sensitive bond Bond with coupons that are tied to the issuer's credit ratings.

cross-border risk Foreign investment risk resulting from concerns over changes in political, social, and economic conditions.

cross-currency swap Combination of a currency swap and interest rate swap.

cross hedge A futures hedge in which the futures' underlying asset is not the same as the asset being hedged.

cumulative cap A cap in which the seller pays the holder when the periodic interest on an accompanying floating-rate loan hits a certain level.

currency swap A contract in which one party agrees to exchange a liability denominated in one currency to another party who agrees to exchange a liability denominated in a different currency.

cushion bond   A callable bond with a coupon that is significantly above the current market rate.

day count convention   The time measurement used in valuing bonds; it describes the convention used to define the time to maturity (actual days or 30-day months) and days in the year (360 days or 365 days).

day trader   A trader who holds a position for a day.

dealer   A trader who provides a market for investors to buy and sell a security by taking a temporary position in the security.

dealer paper   Commercial paper sold through dealers.

debenture   Corporate bond backed by a general creditor's claim but not by a specified asset.

dedicated portfolio strategy   *See* Cash-flow matching strategy.

deep-discount bonds   Bonds that pay low coupon interest.

default risk   The risk that the issuer/borrower will fail to meet the bond's contractual obligations to pay interest and principal, as well as other obligations specified in the indenture.

deferred call   Provision in a bond that prohibits the issuer from calling the bond before a certain period of time has expired.

deferred coupon bond   Bond with a deferred coupon structure that allows the issuer to defer coupon interest for a specified period.

deficit unit   An economic entity whose current expenditures exceed its income.

demand loans   Short-term loans to dealers, secured by the dealer's securities.

depository institutions   Financial institutions such as commercial banks, credit unions, savings and loans, and savings banks that obtain large amounts of their funds from deposits, which they use primarily to fund commercial and residential loans and to purchase Treasury, federal agency, and municipal securities.

derivative security   A security whose value depends on another security or asset.

direct financial market   Market where surplus units purchase claims issued by the ultimate deficit unit. This market includes the trading of stocks, corporate bonds, Treasury securities, federal agency securities, and municipal bonds.

direct hedge   A futures hedge in which the futures' underlying assets is the same as the asset being hedged.

direct paper   Commercial paper sold by the issuing company directly to investors, instead of through dealers. The issuing companies include the subsidiaries of large companies (captive finance companies), bank holding companies, independent finance companies, and non-financial corporations.

divisibility   The smallest denomination in which an asset is traded.

dollar repo   Repurchase agreement that permits the borrower to repurchase with securities similar, but not identical, to the securities initially sold.

domestic bond   Bond of a foreign government or foreign corporation that is issued in the foreign country or traded on that country's exchange.

double barreled   Describes revenue bonds that are issued with some general obligation backing and thus have characteristics of both general obligations and revenue bonds.

dual-currency Eurobonds   Eurobonds that pay coupon interest in one currency and principal in another.

dual trading   A security trading practice in which an exchange member trades for both her client and herself.

duration   The average date that cash is received on a bond. It can be measured by calculating the weighted average of the bond's time periods, with the weights being the present value of each year's cash flows expressed as a proportion of the bond's price. It is also a measure of a bond's price sensitivity to interest rate changes.

duration gap   The difference in the duration of assets and the duration of the liabilities.

early exercise   The exercise of an American option before its expiration.

economic surplus   The difference between the market value of the assets and the present value of the liabilities.

effective date   The date when interest begins to accrue.

efficient market   A market in which the actual price of a security is equal to its intrinsic (true economic) value.

embedded option   An option characteristic that is part of the features of a debt security. Features include call and put features on debt securities, the call provisions in a sinking fund, and the conversion clauses on convertible bonds.

enhanced bond indexing   A bond indexing approach that allows for minor deviations of certain features and some active management in order to attain a return better than the index.

equilibrium price of a bond   Price obtained by discounting the bond's cash flows by their appropriate spot rates.

equipment-trust bond   Bond secured by a lien on specific equipment, such as airplanes, trucks, or computers.

equity swap   Swap in which one party agrees to pay the return on an equity index, such as the S&P 500, and the other party agrees to pay a floating rate or fixed rate.

Eurobonds   Bonds issued in a number of countries through an international syndicate.

Eurocurrency market   Market in which funds are intermediated (deposited or loaned) outside the currency's country.

event risk   Bond risk resulting from specific actions such as a merger or capital structure change.

exercise price   The price specified in the option contract at which the underlying asset or security can be purchased (call) or sold (put).

extendable bond   Bond that has an option to extend the maturity of the bond.

extendable swap   Swap that has an option to lengthen the terms of the original swap.

external bond market   A market where Eurobonds and Eurodeposits are bought and sold.

federal credit agencies   Federally sponsored agencies and federal agencies. Collectively, the claims sold by federal agencies and federal-sponsored companies are referred to as federal agency securities.

federal funds   Deposits of banks and deposit institutions with the Federal Reserve that are used to maintain the bank's reserve position required to support their deposits.

federal funds market   Market in which depository institutions with excess reserves lend to institutions that are deficient.

federally sponsored agencies   Privately owned companies with a federal charter.

financial engineering   Strategies of buying and selling derivatives and their underlying securities in order to create portfolios with certain desired features.

financial swap   An agreement between two parties to exchange the cash flows from each party's liabilities.

fixed-rate payer   The party in a financial swap that agrees to pay fixed interest and receive variable interest.

floater   *See* Floating-rate notes.

floating-rate notes   Notes that pay a coupon rate that can vary in relation to another bond, benchmark rate, or formula. Typically the rate is based on a short-term index and reset more than once a year.

floating-rate payer   The payer in a financial swap that agrees to pay variable interest in return for fixed interest.

floating-rate tranches   A sequential-pay tranche that pays a floating rate.

floor   A series of interest rate puts that expire at or near the effective dates on a loan. They are often used as a hedging tool by financial institutions.

floorlet   *See* Interest rate option.

foreign bonds   Bonds of a foreign government or corporation being issued or traded in a local country.

foreign currency futures   A futures contract on a foreign currency.

foreign currency option   An option on a foreign currency.

forward contract   An agreement between two parties to trade a specific asset or security at a future date with the terms and price agreed upon today.

forward rate agreement A contract that requires a cash payment or provides a cash receipt based on the difference between a realized spot rate such as the LIBOR and a prespecified rate.

forward swaps An agreement to enter into a swap that starts at a future date at an interest rate agreed upon today.

full faith and credit obligations General obligations bonds issued by states and large municipal governments that have a number of tax revenue sources.

fungible The feature of an asset in which it can be converted into cash or other assets.

futures contract A marketable forward contract.

futures fund A mutual fund that pools investors' monies and uses them to set up futures positions.

futures hedge ratio The optimal number of futures contracts needed to hedge a position.

futures options An option contract that gives the holder the right to take a position in a futures contract on or before a specific date. A call option on a futures contract gives the holder the right to take a long position in the underlying futures contract when she exercises, and requires the writer to take the short position in the futures if he is assigned. A put option on a futures option entitles the holder to take a short futures position and the assigned writer the long position.

futures spread Futures position formed by simultaneously taking long and short positions in different futures contracts.

general obligations bonds (GOs) Intermediate- and long-term municipal debt obligations that are secured by the issuing government's general taxing power and can pay interest and principal from any revenue source.

generic swap An interest rate swap in which fixed-interest payments are exchanged for floating-interest payments.

geometric mean The yield to maturity expressed as the geometric average of the current spot rate and implied forward rates.

gilt Bond that does not mature although it can be redeemed after a specified date.

global bond Bond that is issued and traded as a foreign bond and also sold through a syndicate as a Eurobond.

global funds Funds with stocks and bonds from different countries.

GLOBEX A computer trading system in which bids and asks are entered into a computer which matches them.

government-sponsored agencies *See* Federally sponsored agencies.

graduated payment mortgages (GPMs) Mortgages that start with low monthly payments in earlier years and then gradually increase.

guaranteed bonds Bonds issued by one company and guaranteed by another economic entity.

guaranteed investment contract An obligation of an insurance company to pay a guaranteed principal and rate on an invested premium. For a lump-sum payment, the insurance company guarantees that a specified dollar amount will be paid to the policyholder at a specified future date.

hedgable rate *See* Implied forward rate.

hedge A strategy in which an investor protects the future value of a position by taking a position in a futures contract, option, or other security.

hedged funds Special types of investment funds often structured so that they are largely unregulated. Minimum investment in such funds ranges from $100,000 to $20m, with the average investment being $1m. Many of the funds invest or set up investment strategies reflecting pricing aberrations.

horizon matching *See* Combination matching.

humpedness A non-parallel yield curve shift in which short-term and long-term rates change by greater magnitudes than intermediate rates. An increase in both short- and long-term rates relative to intermediate rates is referred to as a *positive butterfly*, and a decrease is known as a *negative butterfly*.

IMM index The quoted index price for futures on Treasury bill contracts and Eurodollar contracts traded on the International

Monetary Market. The index is equal to 100 minus the annual percentage discount yield.

implied forward rate The rate in the future that is implied by current rates. The implied forward rate can be attained by a locking-in strategy consisting of a position in a short-term bond and an opposite position in a long-term one.

implied futures rate The rate implied on an interest rate futures contract.

implied repo rate The rate where the arbitrage profit from implementing a cash-and-carry arbitrage strategy with futures contracts is zero. This rate is also the one earned from an investment in a synthetic Treasury bill.

implied variance Variance that equates the OPM's price to the market price. Conceptually, it can be thought of as the market's consensus of the stock's volatility.

implied volatility *See* Implied variance.

income bond Corporate bond that pays interest only if the earnings of the firm are sufficient to meet the interest obligations.

indenture Contract between the borrower and the lender (all the bondholders).

index-amortizing swap Swap in which the notional principal is dependent on interest rates.

index funds Investment funds constructed so that returns are highly correlated with the market.

index-principal swap *See* Index-amortizing swap.

indexing The construction of bond portfolios whose returns over time replicate those of some specified bond index.

industrial paper *See* Dealer paper.

initial margin The amount of cash or cash equivalents that must be deposited by the investor on the day a futures or options position is established.

interbank market A spot and forward currency exchange market consisting primarily of major banks who act as currency dealers.

intercommodity spread A spread formed with futures contracts with the same expiration dates but on different underlying assets.

interdealer market Market in which dealers trade amongst themselves.

interest equalization tax (IET) Tax on income from foreign securities purchased by local investors.

interest on interest The interest earned from reinvesting coupons.

interest-only security Zero-discount bond that pays a principal received from the coupon interest from another security.

interest rate option An option which gives the holder the right to a payoff if a specific interest rate is greater (call) or less (put) than the option's exercise rate.

interest rate parity theorem (IRPT) The carrying-cost model that governs the relationship between spot and forward exchange rates.

interest rate swap An agreement between parties to exchange interest payments on loans.

intermediary financial market Market where financial institutions, such as commercial banks, savings and loans, credit unions, insurance companies, pension funds, trust funds, and mutual funds, sell securities and then use the proceeds to provide loans or buy securities.

intermediary securities Securities such as certificates of deposit and mutual fund shares that are created in the intermediary financial markets.

internal bond market A market where there are domestic bonds and foreign bonds.

intracommodity spread A spread formed with futures contracts on the same underlying asset but with different expiration dates.

intrinsic value of a call The maximum of zero or the difference between the call's underlying security price and its exercise price.

intrinsic value of a put The maximum of zero or the difference between a put's exercise price and its underlying security's price.

inverted market Market where the futures price is less then the spot price.

investment banker Middleman who for a fee or share in the trading profit finds surplus units who want to buy securities being offered by a deficit unit.

investment-grade bonds Bonds with a relatively low chance of default; they have a quality rating of BAA (or BBB) or higher.

junk bonds *See* Speculative-grade bonds.

Knock-in option Option that comes into existence when the reference rate or price hits the barrier level.

knock-out option Option that ceases to exist once the specified barrier rate or price is reached.

Kolb–Chiang price-sensitivity model A price-sensitivity model for hedging interest rate positions. The model determines the number of futures contracts that will make the value of a portfolio consisting of fixed-income security and an interest rate futures contract invariant to small changes in interest rates.

ladder strategy Strategy of constructing a bond portfolio with equal allocations in each maturity group.

law of one price An economic principle that two assets with the same future payouts will be priced the same.

legal opinion Document accompanying a municipal issue that interprets legal issues related to the bond's collateral, priority of claims, and the like.

limited-tax general obligations bonds General obligations bonds issued by smaller municipalities or authorities whose revenues are limited to only one or two sources.

liquidity The cash-like property of a security.

liquidity premium The difference in the yield of a less liquid bond and the yield of a more liquid one.

liquidity premium theory Term structure theory that posits that there is a liquidity premium for long-term bonds over short-term bonds.

locals Members of an exchange who trade from their own accounts, acting as speculators or arbitrageurs.

logarithmic return The continuously compounded return. It is equal to the natural logarithm of the security price relatives.

London interbank bid rate (LIBID) The rate paid on funds purchased by large London Eurobanks in the interbank market.

London interbank offer rate (LIBOR) The rate on funds offered for sale by London Eurobanks. The average LIBOR among London Eurobanks is a rate commonly used to set the rate on bank loans, deposits, and floating-rate notes and loans. There are also similar rates for other currencies (e.g., sterling LIBOR) and areas (e.g., Paris interbank offer rate, PIBOR, or the Singapore interbank offer rate, SIBOR).

long futures hedge A long position in a futures contract taken in order to protect against an increase in the price of the underlying asset or commodity.

long futures position A position in which one agrees to buy the futures' underlying asset at a specified price, with the payment and delivery to occur on the expiration date.

LYON Zero-coupon bond that has the features of being convertible into the issuer's stock, callable, with the call price increasing over time, and putable with the put price increasing over time.

Macaulay's duration Duration as measured as the weighted average of the time periods.

maintenance margin The value of the commodity equity account that must be maintained.

mark (or marking) to market Process of adjusting the equity in a commodity or margin account to reflect the daily changes in the market value of the account.

mark-to-market tax rule Tax requirement in which the profits on a futures position are taxed in the year the contract is established. The rule requires that at the end of the year, all futures contracts be marked to the market to determine any unrealized gain or loss for tax purposes.

market-maker A dealer on an exchange who specializes in the trading of a specific security.

market rate *See* Break-even swap rate.

market risk The risk that interest rates will change, changing the price of the bond and the return earned from reinvesting coupons.

market segmentation theory (MST) Term structure theory which posits that financial markets are segmented into a number of smaller markets by maturity, with supply and demand forces unique to each segment determining the equilibrium yields for each segment.

marketability The speed with which an asset can be bought and sold.

marketability An asset characteristic that defines the ease or speed with which the asset can be traded.

Matador bonds Foreign bonds sold in Spain.

maturity The length of time from the present until the last contractual payment is made.

medium-term note Debt instrument sold on a continuing basis to investors who are allowed to choose from a group of bonds from the same corporation, but with different maturities.

Mello–Roos bonds Municipal securities issued by local governments in California that are not backed by the full faith and credit of the government.

modified convexity Convexity estimated by determining the price of the bond when the yield increases by a small number of basis points (e.g., 2–10 basis points) and when the yield decreases by the same number of basis points.

modified duration Duration measured as the percentage change in a bond's price given a small change in yield.

money market Market where short-term instruments (by convention defined as securities with original maturities of 1 year or less) are traded.

money spread Spread with different exercise prices.

moral-obligation bonds Bonds issued without the legislature approving appropriation. The bonds are considered backed by the permissive authority of the legislature to raise funds, but not the mandatory authority.

mortgage-backed securities Asset-backed securities formed with mortgages.

Mortgage-Backed Security Dealers Association Association of mortgage-backed securities dealers who operate in the over-the-counter market. These dealers form the core of the

secondary market for the trading of existing pass-throughs.

mortgage bond Bond secured by a lien on real property or buildings.

mortgage pass-throughs *See* Mortgage-backed securities.

multiple discriminant analysis A statistical technique that can be used to forecast default or changes in credit ratings.

multiple listings The listing of a security on more than one exchange.

municipal bond index futures contract A futures contract on the municipal bond index; an index based on the average value of 40 municipal bonds.

Municipal Securities Rule Board (MSRB) Self-regulatory board responsible for establishing rules for brokers, dealers, and banks operating in the municipal bond market.

mutual fund *See* Open-end fund.

naive hedging ratio A hedge ratio in which one unit of a futures position hedges one unit of a spot position. The ratio is found by dividing the value of the spot position to be hedged by the price of the futures contract.

naked call write An option position in which an option trader sells a call but does not own the underlying stock.

naked position A long or short speculative futures position.

naked put write An option position in which an option trader sells a put but does not cover the put obligation by selling the underlying stock short.

National Association of Security Dealers Automatic Quotation System, NASDAQ An information system in which current bid–asked quotes of dealers are offered; the system also sends brokers' quotes to dealers, enabling them to close trades.

National Futures Association (NFA) An organization of firms that oversees futures trading.

national market *See* Internal bond market.

negotiated market Market in which securities are privately placed.

net settlement basis Feature of a swap in which the counterparty owing the greater amount pays the difference between what is owed and what is received.

net worth maintenance clause Provision in the indenture requiring that the issuer redeem all or part of the debt or to give bondholders the right to sell (offer-to-redeem clause) their bonds back to the issuer if the company's net worth falls below a stipulated level.

NOB spread A futures spread formed with Treasury note and Treasury bond futures contracts.

non-prime certificates of deposit Certificates of deposit of smaller banks.

normal market Market where the futures price exceeds the spot price.

notional interest-only class A tranche that receives the excess rate from other tranches' principals, with the excess rate being equal to the difference in the collateral rate minus the tranches' coupon rates.

notional principal The principal used to determine the amount of interest paid on a swap agreement. This principal is not exchanged.

off-balance-sheet restructuring A method of changing a balance sheet's return–risk exposure by using derivatives such that the original composition of assets and liabilities is not changed.

off-market swap Swap that has a value. Many existing swaps are off-market swaps.

official statement Document similar to the prospectus for a stock or corporate bond, which details the return, risk, and other characteristics of a municipal issue and provides information on the issuer.

offsetting order *See* Closing transactions.

offshore market *See* External bond market.

on-the-run issues Recently issued Treasury securities trading on the secondary market.

open-end bond Bond that allows for more debt to be secured by the same collateral.

open-end fund Fund that stands ready to buy back shares of the fund at any time the fund's shareholders want to sell and sell new shares any time an investor wants to buy into the fund.

Technically, a mutual fund is an open-end fund.

open interest The number of option or futures contracts that are outstanding at a given point in time.

open market Securities that are issued to the public at large.

open outcry The process of shouting bids and offers in an exchange trading area.

open repo An overnight repo that is automatically rolled over into another overnight repo until one party closes.

opening transaction The transaction in which an investor initially buys or sells an option or futures contract.

option A security that gives the holder the right to buy (call) or sell (put) an asset at a specified price on or possibly before a specific date.

option-adjusted spread (OAS) analysis An analysis that solves for the option spread that makes the average of the present values of the bond's cash flows from the possible interest rate paths equal to the bond's market price.

option clearing corporation (OCC) A firm whose primary function is to facilitate the marketability of option contracts. It does this by intermediating each option transaction which takes place on the exchange and by guaranteeing that all option writers fulfill the terms of their option contracts.

option-currency Eurobonds Eurobonds that offer investors a choice of currency.

option holder The buyer of an option. The holder buys the right to exercise or evoke the terms of the option claim. An option buyer is said to have a long position in the option.

option premium The price of the option (call premium and put premium).

option writer The seller of an option. The writer is responsible for fulfilling the obligations of the option if the holder exercises. The option writer is said to have short position in the option.

options on actuals *See* Spot option.

options on futures *See* Futures options.

order book official An employee of an exchange who keeps the limit order book.

original-issue discount The difference between the bond's face value and the offering price when the bond is issued.

out-of-the-money A call (put) option in which the price of the underlying security is below (above) the exercise price.

outright position *See* Naked position.

over-the-counter market An informal exchange for the trading of stocks, corporate and municipal bonds, investment fund shares, mortgage-backed securities, shares in limited partnerships, and Treasury and federal agency securities. There are no membership or listing requirements for trading on the OTC; any security can be traded.

over-the-counter options Options provided by dealers in the over-the-counter market. The option contracts are negotiable, with buyers and sellers entering directly into an agreement.

par value swap Swap that has a value of zero. An economic value of zero requires that the swap's underlying bond positions trade at par. Many plain vanilla swaps are originally par value swaps.

parallel shift Yield-curve shift in which the yields on all maturities change by the same magnitude.

participating bond Corporate bond that pays minimum rate plus an additional interest up to a certain point if the company achieves a certain earnings level.

participation certificates *See* Pass-through securities.

pass-through rate Rate paid to mortgage-backed security holders.

pass-through securities Securities formed by pooling a group of mortgages and other financial assets and then selling a security representing interest in the pool and entitling the holder to the income generated from the pool of assets.

passive strategy Bond strategy in which there is no change in the investment strategy once it is set up.

payment-in-kind bond Bond that gives the issuer the option on the interest-payment date to pay the coupon interest either in cash or in kind, usually by issuing the bondholder with a new bond.

perfect market A market in which the price of the security is equal to its equilibrium value at all times.

perpetuity A coupon bond with no maturity.

plain vanilla swap *See* Generic swap.

planned amortization class, PAC A tranche formed by generating two monthly principal payment schedules from the collateral; one schedule is based on assuming a relatively low PSA speed, while the other is obtained by assuming a relatively high PSA speed. The PAC bond is then set up so that it will receive a monthly principal payment schedule based on the minimum principal from the two principal payments. The PAC bond is designed to have no prepayment risk provided the actual prepayment falls within the minimum and maximum assumed PSA speeds.

poison put Clause in the indenture giving the bondholders the right to sell the bonds back to the issuer at a specified price under certain conditions arising from a specific event such as a takeover, change in control, or an investment ratings downgrade.

position limit The maximum number of option or futures contracts an investor can buy and sell on one side of the market. A side of the market is either a bullish or bearish position.

position profit The profit dealers realize from taking long and short positions in securities in which they deal.

position trader A futures dealer who holds a position for a period longer than a day.

preferred habitat theory (PHT) Term structure theory that posits that investors and borrowers may stray away from desired maturity segments if there are relatively better rates to compensate them.

prepayment risk The risk that a loan will be paid off early and the lender or bondholder will have to invest or create new loans in a market with a lower rate.

prepayment speed The estimated prepayment rate on a portfolio of mortgages or a mortgage-backed security.

price compression Refers to limitations on a bond's price. For example, the percentage increases in the prices of a callable bond may be limited when interest rates decrease given that the market expects the bonds to be redeemed at the call price.

price limits The maximum and minimum prices that a futures contract can trade.

primary market Market where financial claims are created.

primary securities Claims traded in the direct financial market.

prime certificates of deposit Certificates of deposit of larger banks.

principal-only security Zero-discount bond that pays a principal received from another security.

principal pay-down window The period between the beginning and ending principal payment.

private labels *See* Conventional pass-throughs.

private placement Securities that are issued by economic entities under a private contract.

prospectus Document that summarizes the main provisions included in the indenture.

PSA models The prepayment models of the Public Securities Association prepayment model. In the standard PSA model for 30-year mortgages, known as 100 PSA, the CPR starts at 0.2% for the first month and then increases at a constant rate of 0.2% per month to equal 6% at the 30th month; then after the 30th month the CPR stays at a constant 6%.

pure discount bond A bond which pays no coupon interest. The bond sells at a price below its face value. It is also called a zero–coupon bond.

pure expectations theory Term structure theory in which the term structure of interest rates is based on the impact of investors' and borrowers' expectations about future interest rates.

put An option that gives the holder the right to sell an asset or security at a specified price on or possibly before a specific date.

put–call futures parity The equilibrium relationship between the prices on put, call, and futures contracts on the same asset. If the equilibrium condition for put–call futures parity does not hold, then an arbitrage opportunity will exist by taking a position in the put and futures contract and an opposite position in the call and a riskless bond with a face value equal to the difference in the exercise price and futures price.

put–call parity The equilibrium relationship governing the prices on put and call contracts. If the equilibrium condition for put–call parity does not hold, then an arbitrage opportunity will exist by taking a position in the put and the underlying security and an opposite position in the call and a riskless bond with face value equal to the exercise price.

put swaption Swap that gives the holder the right to pay a specific fixed rate and receive the floating rate; that is, the right to take a fixed payer's position.

putable bond A bond that gives the bondholder the right to sell the bond back to the issuer at a specified price.

q-cap *See* Cumulative cap.

quality risk A hedging risk that precludes one from obtaining zero risk because the commodity or asset being hedged is not identical to the one underlying the futures contract.

quality swap A strategy of moving from one quality group to another in anticipation of a change in economic conditions.

quantity risk A hedging risk that precludes one from obtaining zero risk because the size of the standard futures contract differs from the number of units of the underlying asset to be hedged.

rate-anticipation strategies Active strategies of selecting bonds or a bond portfolio with specific durations based on interest rate expectations.

rate-anticipation swap Active strategies involving simultaneously selling and buying bonds with different durations based on interest rate expectations.

rate of return The total dollar return received from the asset per period of time expressed as a proportion of the price paid for the asset.

real estate investment trust (REIT) Fund that specializes in investing in real estate and real estate mortgages.

rebalancing Resetting the bond position when a bond's duration is no longer equal to the duration of the liability.

rebundling The buying of zero-coupon bonds and stripped securities and then forming coupon bonds to sell. This process is also known as *reconstruction*.

red herring A preliminary prospectus that details all the pertinent information the official prospectus will have, except the price.

refunded bonds Municipal bonds secured by an escrow fund consisting of high-quality securities such as Treasuries and federal agencies.

registered bond Bond in which the bondholders are registered with the issuer or the trustee; the issuer pays coupons and principal to those registered.

regression hedging model A hedging model where the estimated slope coefficient from a regression equation is used to determine the hedge ratio. The coefficient, in turn, is found by regressing the spot price on the security to be hedged against its futures price.

release and substitution provision Provision in a mortgage bond that allows the mortgaged asset to be sold provided it is replaced with a suitable substitute or allows for the asset to be sold with the proceeds used to retire the bonds.

repo rate The rate on a repurchase agreement.

repurchase agreement, repo A transaction in which one party sells a security to another party with the obligation of repurchasing it at a later date. To the seller, the repurchase agreement represents a secured loan in which he receives funds from the sale of the security, with the responsibility of purchasing the security later at a higher price that reflects the shorter time remaining to maturity.

reset mortgages Mortgages that allow the borrower to renegotiate the terms of the mortgage at specified future dates.

revenue bonds Municipal securities paid by the revenues generated from specific public or quasi-public projects, by the proceeds from a specific tax, or by a special assessment on an existing tax.

reverse collar Combination of a long position in a floor and a short position in a cap with different exercise rates. The sale of the cap is used to defray the cost of the floor.

reverse corridor Long position in a floor and a short position in a similar floor with a lower exercise rate.

reverse inquiry Cases in which institutional investors indicate to the agents of a medium-term note the type of maturity they want.

risk The uncertainty that the rate of return an investor will obtain from holding an asset will be less than expected.

risk-averse market Market in which investors require compensation in the form of a positive risk premium over a risk-free investment to pay them for the risk they are assuming.

risk-loving market Market in which investors enjoy the excitement of the gamble and are willing to pay for it by accepting an expected return from a risky investment that is less than the risk-free rate. The market has a negative risk premium.

risk-neutral market A market in which investors accept the same expected rate of return from a risky investment as a risk-free one.

risk-neutral pricing An approach for pricing securities in which it is assumed that the value of a security is determined as though it and other securities are trading in a risk-neutral market. This approach can be used to price options and other derivative securities.

risk premium The difference between the yield on a risky bond and the yield on a less risky or risk-free bond. The risk premium indicates how much additional return investors must earn in order to induce them to buy the riskier bond.

risk premium theory *See* Liquidity premium theory.

risk spread *See* Risk premium.

rolling the hedge forward A hedging strategy that involves taking a futures position, then at expiration closing the position and taking a new one.

running a dynamic book Describes how swap banks hedge their positions through a portfolio of alternative positions – opposite swap positions, spot positions in T-notes and FRNs, or futures positions.

Samurai bonds Foreign bonds sold in Japan.

scalper A floor trader who buys and sells securities on her own account, holding them for a short period.

seasoning Defines the age of a mortgage.

seat Membership on an exchange.

SEC Rule 144 SEC rule that allows the issuer to sell unregistered securities to one or more investment bankers who could resell the securities to "qualified investment buyers."

SEC Rule 415 SEC rule that allows a firm to register an inventory of securities of a particular type for up to 2 years.

secondary market Market for the buying and selling of existing assets and financial claims.

secondary securities *See* Intermediary securities.

sector rotation The reallocations of funds to a specific quality sector in anticipation of a price change.

secured bond Bond that has a lien giving the bondholder the right to sell the pledged asset in order to pay the bondholders if the company defaults.

securitization Process in which the assets of a corporation or financial institution are pooled into a package of securities backed by the assets. The most common types of asset-backed securities are those secured by mortgages, automobile loans, credit card receivables, and home equity loans.

securitized assets Claim on cash flows from a portfolio of loans or assets.

selling group agreement The agreement between the investment banker and the selling group on a security issue. The agreement can define the period of time the members of the group have to sell their portion of the issue, commissions that can be charged, and restrictions such as prohibiting members from selling below a certain price.

sequential-pay collateralized mortgage obligation A collateralized mortgage obligation that is divided into classes with different priority claims on the collateral's principal. The tranche with the first priority claim has its principal paid entirely before the next priority class, which has its principal paid before the third class, and so on.

serial bond issue Bond issue consisting of a series of bonds with different maturities.

shelf registration rule *See* SEC Rule 415.

short futures hedge A short position in a futures contract that is taken in order to protect against a decrease in the price of the underlying asset.

short futures position A position in which an investor agrees to sell the underlying asset on a futures contract.

short sale The sale of a security now, then purchasing it later. To implement this strategy the investor must borrow the security, sell it in the market, then repay his debt obligation by later buying the security and returning it to the share lender.

single monthly mortality rate Defines the monthly prepayment rate.

sinking fund Provision in the indenture requiring that the issuer make scheduled payments into a fund. Many sinking-fund agreements require an orderly retirement of the issue, commonly handled by the issuer being required to buy up a certain portion of bonds each year either at a stipulated call price or in the secondary market at its market price.

sovereign risk Foreign investment risk on sovereign securities resulting from concern that the government is unable, or in some cases unwilling, to service its debt.

specialist A dealer on the exchange who specializes in the trading of a specific security and who is responsible for maintaining the order book.

speculative-grade bonds Bonds with a relatively high chance of default; they have quality rating below BAA.

speed *See* Prepayment speed.

spot market A market in which there is an immediate sale and delivery of the asset or commodity.

spot option Option contracts on stocks, debt securities, foreign currency, and indexes. The term is used to distinguish them from options on futures contracts.

spot price The price an asset or commodity trades for in the spot market.

spot rates The rate on a zero-coupon bond.

spread An option or futures position consisting of a long position in one contract and a short position in a similar, but not identical, contract.

stable value investment Guaranteed investments contracts and bank investment contracts.

standby underwriting agreement An agreement in which the investment banker sells an issue on a commission, but agrees to buy all unsold securities at a specified price.

stop price or stop-out price The lowest price at a Treasury security auction at which at least some securities are awarded to bidders. Those bidding above the stop price are awarded the quantity they requested, while those with bids below the stop price do not receive any bills.

straddle purchase A strategy formed by buying a put and a call with the same underlying security, exercise price, and expiration date.

straddle write A strategy formed by selling a put and a call with the same underlying security, exercise price, and expiration date.

straight debt value A convertible bond's value as a non-convertible bond. It is found by discounting the convertible bond's cash flows by the yield to maturity on an identical, but non-convertible, bond.

strap purchase A strategy formed by purchasing more calls than puts, with the calls and puts having the same terms.

strap write A strategy formed by selling more calls than puts, with the calls and puts having the same terms.

strike price *See* Exercise price.

strip A series of futures contracts with different maturities. Also, a term used to describe a combination of long or short call and put positions in which the number of puts exceeds the number of calls.

strip bills A package of T-bills with different maturities in which the buyer agrees to buy bills at their bid price for several weeks.

strip purchase A strategy formed by purchasing more puts than calls, with the calls and puts having the same terms.

strip write A strategy formed by selling more puts than calls, with the calls and puts having the same terms.

stripped mortgage-backed securities Stripped mortgage-backed securities consisting of a principal-only class and an interest-only class.

STRIPS, Separate Trading of Registered Interest and Principal of Securities Treasury strip securities that are the direct obligations of the government, and, for clearing and payment purposes, the names of the buyers of these securities are included in the book entries of the Treasury.

Student Loan Marketing Association (Sallie Mae) Association that provides funds and guarantees for lenders who provide college students' loans through the Federal Guaranteed Student Loan Program, and college loans to parents of undergraduates through the PLUS (Parents' Loans of Undergraduate Students) program.

support class (or support bond) Tranche formed with a PAC bond that receives principal equal to the collateral's principal minus the PAC's principal.

surplus economic unit An economic entity whose income from its current production exceeds its current expenditures; it is a saver or net lender.

surplus management The management of the surplus value of assets over liabilities.

swap *See* Financial swap.

swap banks Group of brokers and dealers who intermediate swap agreements between swap users. As brokers, swap banks try to match parties with opposite needs; as dealers, swap banks take positions as counterparties.

swap rate The average of the bid and asked rates offered by a swap bank on an interest rate swap.

swaptions   Option on a swap. The purchaser of a swaption buys the right to start an interest rate swap with a specific fixed rate or exercise rate, and with a maturity at or during a specific time period in the future. If the holder exercises, she takes the swap position, with the swap seller obligated to take the opposite counterparty position.

systematic risk   The risk of a security that is attributed to market factors (i.e., factors which affect all securities).

targeted amortization class (TAC) bond   A PAC-structured collateralized mortgage obligation with PACs with just one PSA rate.

tax-exempt corporate bond   Corporate bond issued to finance projects such as the construction of solid and hazardous waste disposal facilities that qualify for tax exemption; the holders of the bond do not have to pay federal income tax on the interest they receive.

tax swap   Strategy in which an investor sells one bond and purchases another in order to take advantage of the tax laws.

taxability   The claims that the federal, state, and local governments have on the cash flows of an asset.

TED spread   A spread formed with Treasury bill and Eurodollar contracts.

term certificates of deposit   Certificates of deposit issued with maturities greater than 1 year.

term repo   A repurchase agreement that is not overnight.

term structure of interest rates   The relationship between the yields on financial assets and their maturities.

time value premium (TVP)   The difference between the price of an option and its intrinsic value.

timing risk   A hedging risk that precludes one from obtaining zero risk because the delivery date on the futures contract does not coincide with the date on which the hedged assets or liabilities need to be purchased or sold.

TIPS (Treasury Inflation Protection Securities)   Inflation-adjusted securities issued by the US Treasury.

total return   *See* Annual realized return.

total return analysis   A method for identifying an active bond position based on possible yield-curve shifts. In this approach, potential returns from several yield-curve strategies are evaluated for a number of possible interest rate changes over different horizon periods to identify the best strategy.

total return swap   Swap in which the return from one asset or portfolio of assets is swapped for the return on another asset or portfolio.

tracking errors   The difference between the returns on the index and the index fund.

trade date   Day on which counterparties agree to commit to the swap.

trademark   Various types of strip securities offered by investment firms.

tranches   The different classes making up a collateralized mortgage obligation. There are two general types of tranches – sequential-pay tranches and planned amortization class tranches.

Treasury-bill futures   A futures contract that calls for the delivery or purchase of a Treasury bill.

Treasury-bill option   An option that gives the holder the right to buy (call) or sell (put) a Treasury bill.

Treasury bills   Short-term Treasury instruments sold on a pure discount basis.

Treasury-bond futures contract   A futures contract which calls for the delivery or purchase of a Treasury bond.

Treasury-bond option   An option on a Treasury bond.

Treasury bonds and notes   The Treasury's coupon issues. Both are identical except for maturity: T-notes have original maturities up to 10 years (currently, original notes are offered with maturities of 2, 5, and 10 years), while T-bonds have maturities ranging between 10 and 30 years.

Treasury-note futures contract   A futures contract which calls for the delivery or purchase of a Treasury note.

Treasury strip   Zero-discount bond that pays a principal received from the interest or principal from a T-bond or T-note.

trustee Third party to a bond contract. The party represents the bondholders and is responsible for ensuring that the bond issue has been drawn up in accordance with all legal requirements and that the issuer meets all of the prescribed functions specified in the indenture. The trustee can take legal action against the corporation if it fails to meet its interest and principal payments or satisfy other terms specified in the indenture.

twist A non-parallel yield-curve shift in which there is either a flattening or steepening of the yield curve.

unbiased expectations theory *See* Pure expectations theory.

underwrite Action of investment bankers of buying securities from the issuer and then selling them.

underwriting syndicate Group of investment bankers who underwrite an issue.

unit investment trust An investment fund that has a specified number of fixed-income securities and a fixed life.

unsystematic risk The risk of a security that is attributed to factors other than market factors.

variable-rate note Debt security with its coupon based on a long-term rate, with the rate often reset no more than once a year.

voting bond Bond that gives voting privileges to the holders. The vote is usually limited to specific corporate decisions under certain conditions.

vulture funds Funds consisting of debt securities of companies that are in financial trouble or in bankruptcy.

warehousing Practice of swap banks in which they enter a swap agreement without another counterparty. Swap banks often will hedge their swap positions with opposite positions in T-notes and FRNs or using Eurodollar futures contracts.

warrant A security or a provision in a security that gives the holder the right to buy a specified number of shares of stock or another designated security at a specified price.

wash sale The sale of a security at a loss and its subsequent repurchase. Tax laws disallow claiming such losses for tax purposes.

wild-card option The right on a Chicago Board of Trade's Treasury bond futures contract to deliver the bond after the close of trading on the exchange.

Yankee bonds Foreign bonds sold in the US.

yield approximation formula *See* Average rate to maturity.

yield curve A graph showing the relationship between the yields to maturity on comparable bonds and their maturities.

yield pick-up swap Bond strategy in which investors or arbitrageurs try to find bonds that are identical, but are mispriced and trading at different yields.

yield to call The yield obtained by assuming that the bond is called on the first call date.

yield to maturity (YTM) The discount rate on a bond. It is the rate that equates the price of the bond to the present value of its coupons and principal.

yield to worst The lowest of the yield to maturity and yield to call.

YTM approach The valuation of off-market swaps by discounting the net cash flows at the current YTM.

zero-coupon approach The valuation of off-market swaps by discounting the net cash flows using spot rates.

zero-coupon bond *See* Pure discount bond.

zero-coupon swaps Swap in which one or both parties do not exchange payments until the maturity on the swap.

INDEX

Note: "n." after a page reference indicates the number of a note on that page.